WHO'S WHO
in
SPACE

WHO'S WHO in SPACE

The International Space Station Edition

MICHAEL CASSUTT

Macmillan Library Reference USA
New York

Cover photos (from left, back cover): Cosmonauts G. Strekalov and V. Dezhurov aboard the Russian Space Station, December 1995; Soviet Air Force Major Yuri Gagarin, first space traveler in history, April 12, 1961; American astronaut aboard the Russian Space Station, 1995; Astronaut Mary Ellen Weber; Astronaut Alan B. Shepard standing with American flag on lunar surface, January 31, 1971; Astronauts Jan Davis and Mae Jemison undergoing training at Spacelab-J Crew Training facility, April 1992; the first crew of the International Space Station aboard a Black Sea freighter following water survival training, October 1997; untethered astronaut on Discovery flight in space walk with new EVA unit, 1994. Photo of Earth taken from the Apollo 11 spacecraft during its translunar coast to the Moon, July 17, 1969. All photos courtesy of NASA except Yuri Gagarin, © AP/Wide World Photos.

Copyright © 1999, 1993, 1987 by Michael Cassutt

Macmillan Library Reference USA
1633 Broadway
New York, New York 10019

Library of Congress Catalog Card Number: 98-35587

Printed in the United States of America

Printing number
1   2   3   4   5   6   7   8   9   10

Library of Congress Cataloging-in-Publication Data

Cassutt, Michael.
  Who's who in space / Michael Cassutt. International space station ed.
  cm.
  Includes bibliographical references and index.
  ISBN 0-02-864965-6
    Manned spaceflight—History—Encyclopedias. 2. Astronauts—Biography—
      Encyclopedias. I. Title.
  TL788.5.C37 1999
  629.45'0092'2—dc21   98-35587
                                                                 CIP

This paper meets the requirements of ANSI/NISO Z.39.48-1992 (Permanence of Paper).

CONTENTS

CREDITS AND PERMISSIONS

Credits

"Aboard Friendship Seven," excerpted from *We Seven* by The Astronauts Themselves (M. Scott Carpenter, L. Gordon Cooper, Jr., John H. Glenn, Jr., Virgil I. Grissom, Walter M. Schirra, Jr., Alan B. Shepard, Jr., Donald K. Slayton). New York: Simon & Schuster, 1962. Copyright © 1962 by Simon & Schuster. By permission of the publisher.

Gemini 4 EVA transcript courtesy of NASA.

"Live, from the Moon," adapted from *Countdown* by Frank Borman with Robert J. Serling. New York: Silver Arrow Books, a division of William Morrow, 1988. Copyright © 1988 by Frank Borman and Robert J. Serling. By permission of the authors.

"Selecting the Apollo 11 Crew," adapted from *Deke! From Mercury to the Shuttle*, by Donald K. "Deke" Slayton with Michael Cassutt. New York: Forge, 1994. Copyright © 1994 by the Estate of Deke Slayton and by St. Croix Productions. By permission of the authors.

"Landing at Tranquility" by Buzz Aldrin, adapted from *Men from Earth* by Buzz Aldrin and Malcolm McConnell. New York: Bantam, 1989. Copyright © by Research Engineering Consultants, Inc., and Malcolm McConnell. By permission of the authors.

"Making Adjustments" by Bill Pogue, adapted from *How Do You Go to the Bathroom in Space?* New York: Tom

Doherty & Assoc., 1991. Copyright © 1991 by William R. Pogue. By permission of the author.

"Launching Aboard the Shuttle," adapted from *Do Your Ears Pop in Space? And 500 Other Surprising Questions about Space Travel*, by R. Mike Mullane. (New York: John Wiley & Sons, Inc., 1997). Copyright © 1997 by R. Mike Mullane.

Shuttle Challenger transcript courtesy of NASA.

"Letters to My Son from Mir" by Jerry M. Linenger, courtesy of NASA.

"The View from Mir" by Andrew S. W. Thomas, courtesy of NASA.

"Gagarin's Report," translated by Vadim Molchanov and Michael Cassutt. Courtesy of Vadim Molchanov.

"Soyuz 1," excerpted from *Secret Space, the Diaries of Nikolai Kamanin*, vol. 2. (Moscow: 1996). Copyright © 1997 by Lev N. Kamanin and TOO Infotext. Translated by Bart Hendrickx. By permission of the publisher.

"A Year Above Earth" by Valery Ryumin. First published in *Orbits of Peace and Progress* (Moscow: Mir, 1988). Used by permission.

"Life Aboard Salyut" by Valentin Lebedev, adapted from *211 Days in Space*, Houston: G.L.O.S.S. 1988. By permission of the author.

"Fire in Space" by Valery Korzun, based on an interview with Bert Vis. Used by permission.

"Emergency!" by Abdul Ahad Mohmand, based on an interview with Bert Vis. Used by permission.

"Research in Space" by Helen Sharman, from *Seize the Moment* by Helen Sharman & Christopher Priest. London: Gollancz, 1993. Copyright © 1993 by Helen Sharman & Christopher Priest. By permission of the publisher.

"Canada from Space" by Roberta Bondar, from *Touching the Earth*. Toronto: Key Porter Books Ltd., 1994. Copyright © 1994 by Roberta Bondar. By permission of the publisher.

PHOTOS

NASA: NASA astronaut, astronaut candidates, and civilian Shuttle payload specialists, crew patches and group portraits. In addition, international astronauts Bondar, Chretien, Clervoy, Cheli, Doi, Duque, Favier, Fuglesang, Garneau, Guidoni, Hadfield, Kadenyuk, Kondakova, MacLean, Mohri, Money, Noguchi, Payette, Perrin, Pustovyi, Thiele, Tognini, Tryggvason, Urbani, Wakata, Williams.

USAF: Military Shuttle payload specialists, X-15 pilots, MOL astronauts. Portrait of Bechis copyright Bert Vis. Used by permission. Portrait of Boesen copyright 1989 by Lee Weaver. Used by permission.

EASTFOTO: Farkas, Jaehn, Magyari, Remek; Gubarev and Remek.

Library of Congress: Alexandrov, Ivanov, Jankowski, Kohllner, Bui Thanh Liem, Lopez-Falcon, Pelczak, Prunariu.

National Research Council of Canada: Thirsk.

Canadian Space Agency: McKay.

SOVFOTO: Andreyev, Artyukhin, Belyayev, Beregovoy, Bykovsky, Chretien, Dobrovolsky, Faris, Filipchenko, Ganzorig, Grechko, Gubarev, Gurragcha, Habib, Hermaszewski, Khrunov, Klimuk, Leonov, Makarov, Malhotra, Malyshev, Pham Tuan, Popov, Popovich, Rozhdestvensky, Ryumin, Savinykh, Serebrov, Sevastyanov, Sharma, Tamayo-Mendez, G. Titov, Volk, Zholobov, Zudov. All photos in the Soviet Space Travelers photo essay with the exception of Gubarev-Remek.

CNES: Deshays, Haignere, Patat, Viso.

U.K. Ministry of Defense: Boyle.

VAAP: Aksenov, Alexandrov, Anikeyev, Anokhin, Atkov, Berezovoy, Bondarenko, Demin, Dzhanibekov, Feoktistov, Filatyev, Gagarin, Glazkov, Gorbatko, Ivanchenkov, Kizim, Kovalenok, Kubasov, Lazarev, Lebedev, Lyakhov, Mace, Mohmand, Nelyubov, Nikolayev, Patsayev, Ponomareva, Romanenko, Rukavishnikov, Sarafanov, Savitskaya, Sharman, Shatalov, Shonin, V. Solovyov, Strekalov, Sultanov, Tereshkova, V. Titov, Tresvyatsky, Vasyutin, A. Volkov, V. Volkov, Volynov, Yegorov, Yeliseyev, Zabolotsky, Zaikin.

Portraits of Viktorenko, Viehbock and Lothaller copyright 1991 by AustroMir. Used by permission.

Portraits of Avdeyev, Fefelov, and Poleshchuk copyright 1992 by Bert Vis. Used by permission. Portrait of Shargin courtesy of Bert Vis, 1998.

Videocosmos: Kozeyev, Revin, Severin, Kolomitsev, O.D. Kononenko, Kramarenko, Preobrazhensky, Stankyavichus, Zabolotsky, Zaitsev.

Sergei Shamsutdinov: Kartashov, Kondratyev, Lonchakov, Moshkin, Ponomarev, Skvortsov Jr., Valkov, Volkov Jr., Romanenko Jr., Surayev, Sologub, Skvortsov Sr.

Neil Da Costa: Wu Ji Li, Li Quinlong, Bella, Fulier

These portraits were either in the public domain or obtained from the subjects themselves:

Russian cosmonauts Afanasyev, Alexeyev, Andryushkov, Artsebarsky, Arzamazov, Aubakirov, Baberdin, Bachurin, Beloborodov, Belousov, Borodai, Budarin, Buinovsky, Burdayev, Dedkov, Dezhurov, Dobrokvashina, Fedorov, Gaidukov, Gizdenko, Grishchenko, Illarionov, Isakov, Isaulov, Ivanov, Ivanova, Kaleri, Katys, Khludeyev, Kolesnikov, Kolodin, O. G. Kononenko, Korzun, Kozelsky, Kramarenko, Krichevsky, Krikalev, Kugno, Kuklin, Laveikin, Lazutkin, Lisun, Lukyanyuk, Machinsky, Malenchenko, Manakov, Manarov, Matinchenko, Moskalenko, Mossolov, Mukhortov, Musabayev, Omelchenko, Onufriyenko, Padalka, Petrushenko, Polyakov, Porvatkin, Potapov, Pozharskaya, Prikhodko, Pronina, Protchenko, Rafikov, Salei, Sharafutdinov, Sharipov, Sheffer, E. Stepanov, Yu. Stepanov, Tolboyev, Treshchev, Tsibliyev, Usachev, Varlamov, Voloshin, Vorobyov, Voronov, Vozovikov, Yakovlev, Yazdovsky, Zakharova, Zaletin.

ACKNOWLEDGMENTS

Life in Space represents the work of many people in addition to the author and bylined contributors. Special thanks are due to the following:

Dr. Neil Da Costa, London, for several unique portraits.

Bart Hendrickx, Antwerp, Belgium, who provided superb translation.

Igor Lissov of *Novosti Kosmonavtiki*, who answered questions and provided photographs. Published by AOZT VideoCosmos (icosmos@dol.ru), *Novosti Kosmonavtiki* is the world's foremost space publication, an authoritative source for data on Russian, American, and international programs.

The late Vadim Molchanov of Tula, Russia, who in addition to being a tireless and pioneering researcher, provided notes and corrections on earlier editions.

Dennis Newkirk, whose on-line *Russian Aerospace Guide* (http://www.mcs.net/~rusaerog) proved helpful.

Sergei Shamstudinov of the Russian Center for the Documentation of Space History, who provided photographs, biographical material, and the first two volumes of Nikolai Kamanin's diaries, *Secret Space*.

Kathy Strawn, audiovisual manager, external affairs division, NASA Johnson Space Center, who provided astronaut photographs.

The late Anne van den Berg of Hardinxveld-Giessendam, Netherlands, kept me updated on European astronaut matters.

Charles P. Vick of the Federation of American Scientists (http://www.fas.org), who provided valuable historical material.

Sergei Voevodin of Kostroma, Russia, who offered his insights.

Mark Wade, author of the online *Encyclopedia of Space Flight* (http://solar.rtd.utk.edu/~mwade.spaceflt.htm), a valuable resource.

The many astronauts and cosmonauts who took the time to answer queries, as well as the NASA Spacelink internet site (http://spacelink.msfc.nasa.gov/home.index.html).

I must make special mention of Gordon R. Hooper's pioneering *Soviet Cosmonaut Team* (Suffolk, England: GRH Publications, 1990) and Douglas Hawthorne's valuable *Men and Women of Space* (San Diego: Univelt, 1993).

Finally thanks to my agent, Richard Curtis, my production supervisor, Jane Andrassi, and my editor, Catherine Carter.

M.C.

INTRODUCTION

In July 1997, during the flight of the Materials Science Laboratory aboard the Shuttle orbiter Columbia, astronaut Janice Voss was asked by a reporter if she was disappointed that the mission was being ignored by the public. On the contrary, Voss responded. "This is what we always dreamed of when we were little kids. We would have a space station in orbit, a planetary mission going on, and Shuttles going up and down." At the time Voss spoke, cosmonauts Vasily Tsibliyev and Alexandr Lazutkin were in their fifth month aboard the Mir space station, along with NASA astronaut Michael Foale. The unmanned Mars Pathfinder had just touched down on the red planet, deploying the Sojourner rover and igniting an unprecedented wave of interest. (NASA's Pathfinder web site took ten million hits in less than two days.) Voss's Shuttle mission, STS-94, devoted to the unspectacular but necessary study of space manufacturing, was halfway through its sixteen-day duration.

The International Space Station program was aiming at launch of its first elements within a year.

There were, of course, darker sides to these same triumphs: the Mir space station was still reeling from a series of system failures caused by age (launched in February 1986, Mir had doubled its expected five-year lifespan by the summer of 1997) and a horrifying collision with an errant Progress supply vehicle on June 25, 1997. Pathfinder and Sojourner were "faster, better, cheaper" replacements for the disappointing loss of NASA's Mars Observer and Russia's Mars-96 space probes. STS-94 was a re-flight, with the same payload and crew, of STS-83, launched April 3, 1997, and forced to a premature end because of a fuel cell problem aboard the orbiter Columbia.

The ISS program was beginning to suffer cost overruns and schedule delays that would push back first element launches by six months or more.

Nevertheless, it is clear that manned spaceflight has come a long way from the relatively brief, daring orbit of Yuri Gagarin (April 1961) and the even briefer ballistic rides of Alan Shepard and Gus Grissom (May and July 1961). Through May 1998 over 380 different human beings have voyaged beyond the atmosphere, some of them as many as six times. A race to be first on the Moon has been run, and won. Former rivals have become partners. Dreams have been fulfilled; others have died a-borning. But space has become a home and a workplace, not just a frontier to be explored.

Who's Who in Space: The International Space Station Edition, tells the individual stories of this unique generation of humans, from the explorers to the settlers, from those who through ill-health, tragedy, or bad luck never flew beyond the atmosphere, and those whose turn is yet to come.

Who's Who in Space is not a comprehensive history of manned spaceflight; no such history exists. You will find history here, of course, along with essays, biographical profiles, portraits, acronyms, and abbreviations as well as sidebars about what it is like to live in space, and several appendices.

The essays that precede the three main sections give an overview of the evolution of the American, Russian, and International astronaut groups. The profiles give each subject's personal facts in the following sequence: name (and nickname, if any), notable achievement in spaceflight, birthdate and place, education, and career. The list of acronyms and abbreviations explains unfamiliar terms and names found in the text.

The appendices include a log of all manned and manned-related space launches, lists of all space travelers, all American and Russian (and now international) space crews, highlights of all EVAs, and the assembly sequence for the upcoming International Space Station.

In spite of challenges and setbacks, the human race is in space to stay. Whether we realize it or not, an evolutionary leap has been made: we are no longer confined to the surface and lower atmosphere of a single world. We have taken the first important steps toward making our home in the rest of the universe. *Who's Who in Space* allows you to share in that voyage.

MICHAEL CASSUTT
LOS ANGELES, MAY 1998

ACRONYMS AND ABBREVIATIONS

AAC   United States Army Air Corps, forerunner of the U.S. Air Force

AAP   Apollo Applications Program, the original name for proposed manned Apollo missions to follow the first lunar landing

AFB   air force base

ALT   Space Shuttle Approach and Landing Tests, a series of unpowered test flights conducted with the orbiter Enterprise at Edwards AFB in 1977

AMU   Astronaut Maneuvering Unit, a rocket-powered backpack designed for Gemini and Apollo astronauts

ARPS   Aerospace Research Pilot School, an advanced course at the USAF Test Pilot School at Edwards AFB designed to train pilots for space-flight

ASTP   Apollo-Soyuz Test Project, the American name for the joint U.S.-USSR manned space program (1973–75)

ATDA   Augmented Target Docking Adaptor, a one-time replacement for failed Agena upper stages intended for use in manned Gemini missions

ATLAS   Atmospheric Life and Sciences Spacelab

AWACS   Airborne Warning and Control System, specially equipped U.S. Air Force planes carrying sophisticated electronic detection gear

B.A.   bachelor of arts degree

BMDO   Ballistic Missile Defense Organization, successor to the Strategic Defense Initiative Organization

B.S.   bachelor of science degree

capcom   originally a contraction for "capsule communicator," now refers to astronauts or cosmonauts serving in mission control as voice contacts with colleagues in space

CERN   *Centre Europeen de Recherches Nucleaire,* the European Nuclear Research Center near Geneva

CFES   Continuous Flow Electrophoresis System, a space manufacturing project of McDonnell Douglas and the Johnson & Johnson company

CM   command module, the portion of a manned spacecraft that contains crew couches and controls, and that must return to Earth

CNES   *Centre National d'Etudes Spatiales,* the French national space agency

DDM   drop dynamics module, an experiment flown aboard Spacelab 3 in 1985

DFVLR   *Deutsche Forschungs- und* Versuchsanstalt *fur Luft- und Rumfahrt,* or the Federal German Aerospace Research Establishment, the German national space agency, since replaced by the DLR

DLR   *Deutsche Furschungsanstalt fur Luft-und Raumfahrt*—the unified German Space Agency

DOD   U.S. Department of Defense

DOSAAF   Russian abb. for the Voluntary Society for Assistance to the Army, Air Force and Navy, a civil defense organization in the USSR that trained young people to be pilots and parachutists

DOS   Russian for long-term orbital station, another name for the civilian Salyut stations developed by the Korolev-Mishin TsKBEM beginning in 1970

DOSO   the Bulgarian equivalent of the USSR DOSAAF (see)

DSCS   Defense Satellite Communication System, a series of American military communications satellites deployed in geosynchronous orbit

Dyna-Soar   contraction of "dynamic soaring," a phrase originally intended to describe the flight characteristics of delta-winged space vehicles

E   east

EDT   U.S. Eastern Daylight Time

EnergoMash   Russian rocket-building organization originally founded by Valentin Glushko as OKB-GDL, then OKB-456, later merged with the TsKBEM (former OKB-1) to form NPO Energiya in 1974

EOM   Spacelab Earth Observation Mission, a series of proposed follow-ups to Spacelab 1, using the same experiment package. See ATLAS

EOS   designation for the advanced model of the McDonell Douglas CFES, originally scheduled to fly on the Shuttle in 1986

ESA   the European Space Agency

EST   U.S. Eastern Standard Time

ET   Space Shuttle External Tank

EVA   extravehicular activity or "space walk"

FAA   U.S. Federal Aviation Administration

FAI   French *Federation Aeronautique Internationale*, the world aviation record-keeping body

FGB   the Russian-built control module for the International Space Station, based on earlier Chelomei bureau cargo module

FSL   flight simulation laboratory, an installation located in Downey, California, home of Rockwell (now Boeing) builders of the Space Shuttle, and used for astronaut training in the early 1980s

G   G-force, intended to refer to one Earth gravity (acceleration of 32 feet per second squared) and in this context used to measure the amount of stress placed on space travelers during launch and reentry. For example, during a 3G launch, a person weighing 150 pounds on Earth will feel as though he weighed 450 pounds

GIRD   Russian contraction for Gas Dynamics Laboratory, the famed group of Russian rocket pioneers of the 1930s

Glavkosmos   Russian organization of the 1980s formed for the commercial exploitation of space technology

GMVK   Russian for Joint State Commission, a multiministry board that reviews cosmonaut applications and makes final approvals for training

GUKOS   Russian for the Main Directorate for Space, the military space branch of GURVO (1970–1982)

GURVO   Russian for the Main Directorate for Missile Systems, the unit of the Strategic Rocket Forces that developed and operated ICBMs

HEAO   High Energy Astrophysical Observatory, a U.S. scientific satellite program

HMCS   Her Majesty's Canadian Ship

HOTOL   Horizontal Takeoff and Landing project, a proposed British aerospace plane

ICBM   intercontinenal ballistic missile

IMBP   Russian Institute for Medical and Biological Problems, a civilian research institute for space medicine founded in 1963, based in Moscow

IML   International Microgravity Laboratory, a series of Shuttle Spacelab missions (STS-42, 1992, and STS-65, 1994)

IPS   instrument pointing system, part of the Spacelab 2 experiments

ISRO   Indian Space Research Organization, guiding force for the Indian space program

ISS   International Space Station, a 16-member program formed in 1993 with launch of first elements planned in late 1998, completion expected in 2003

IUS   inertial upper stage, a Boeing rocket built for the U.S. Air Force and designed to boost heavy satellites into geosynchronous orbit following deployment from the Shuttle

JSC   NASA Johnson Space Center, in Houston, Texas. Until 1973 known as the Manned Spacecraft Center

KSC   NASA Kennedy Space Center on Merritt Island, Florida

LDEF   long duration exposure facility, an experiment package deployed from the Shuttle in 1984 and retrieved in 1990

LGU   Leningrad University, now Baltic State University in St. Petersburg

LM   Apollo lunar module

LMS   Life and Microgravity Spacelab, flown aboard STS-78 in 1996

LTA   Apollo lunar test article, a mockup of the lunar module

LTV Aerospace   Ling-Temco-Vought, U.S. company

M.A.   master of arts degree

MAI   Sergo Ordzhonikidze Moscow Aviation School, one of the foremost Russian aerospace universities

MAKS   Russian for multiuse aerospace system, a proposed spaceplane to be launched by a jet-powered mother ship

MAP   Russian for Ministry of Aviation Production, which controled aircraft design and manufacture, including the Buran space shuttle

M.B.A   master of business administration degree

McDAC   McDonnell Douglas Aerospace Corporation, now a division of Boeing

MECO   main engine cutoff, the point in a Shuttle launch where the three main engines cease firing, ideally about eight minutes into the flight

M.I.T.   Massachusetts Institute of Technology, Cambridge

MMU   manned maneuvering unit, the rocket backpack used on Shuttle mission in 1984 and 1985

MOL   Manned Orbiting Laboratory, a U.S. Air Force manned space project from 1965 to 1969

MOM   Russian acronym for the Ministry of General Machine-Building, which controled the Soviet space industry from 1965 to 1992

M.S.   master of science degree

MSE   manned spaceflight engineer, U.S. Air Force Shuttle payload specialists

MSL   Materials Science Lab, a Spacelab mission flown twice in 1997 (STS-83 and STS-94)

MT   Moscow Time

MVK   Russian for State Medical Commission, the board that reviews and certifies cosmonaut health

N   north

NACA   the National Advisory Committee on Aeronautics, a U.S. government agency devoted to aviation research. Founded in 1915, its facilities and personnel were absorbed by NASA in 1958.

NASA   the National Aeronautics and Space Administration, the U.S. government's civilian space and aviation agency

NASDA   National Space Development Agency, the Japanese national space agency

NBC   National Broadcasting Company

NE   northeast

NII   Russian for Scientific Research Institute

NOAA   National Oceans and Atmospheric Administration, the U.S. government's environmental research organization

NPO   Russian for Scientific Production Association

NRL   the Naval Research Laboratory, a U.S. Navy scientific installation in Washington, D.C.

NRO   National Reconaissance Office, since 1961 the joint USAF-CIA-Navy organization that develops and operates surveillance satellites. Its existence was secret until 1992.

NSAU   National Space Agency of Ukraine

NW   northwest

OFT   orbital flight tests, an early NASA designation for the first manned Shuttle flights

OKB   Russian for Experimental Design Bureau

OPS   Russian for Piloted Space Station, another name for the Chelomei bureau's Almaz

OSS   Office of Space Sciences, a NASA department which developed scientific experiments carried on early Shuttle missions

OSTA   Office of Space and Terrestrial Applications, a NASA department which developed Earth-sensing experiments carried on early Shuttle missions

PDT   U.S. Pacific Daylight Time

Ph.D.   doctor of philosophy degree

PST   U.S. Pacific Standard Time

RAF   British Royal Air Force

RMS   the Shuttle remote manipulator system, the Canadian-built robot arm

S   south

SAIL   Shuttle Avionics Integration Laboratory, a facility at the NASA Johnson Space Center where Shuttle computer software is created and tested

SAFER   Simplified Aid for EVA Rescue, a smaller maneuvering unit developed for use on Shuttle missions and tested on STS-64 (1994)

SAS   space adaptation syndrome, formal name for the "space sickness" that afflicts about half of all space travelers

SDI, SDIO   U.S. Strategic Defense Initiative Organization, the so-called "Star Wars" missile defense program, now known as the BMDO

SE   southeast

SEAL   contraction of Sea/Land, refers to U.S. Navy elite fighting force

SHEAL   Shuttle High-Energy Astrophysics Laboratory, a series of once-planned Spacelab missions

SL   originally an abbreviation for Skylab, later used for Spacelab

SLS   Spacelab Life Sciences missions, dedicated to medical studies

SM   service module

SMD-III Spacelab Mission Demonstration III

SMEAT   Skylab Medical Experiments Altitude Test, a 56-day simulation of a Skylab mission performed by astronauts Bobko, Crippen and Thornton in 1970

SPO   systems project office, U.S. military unit which supervises the development of a space system

SRB   the Shuttle solid rocket booster

STA   the Shuttle training aircraft, a Gulfstream II executive jet modified to give it landing characteristics similar to a Shuttle orbiter

STS   Space Transportation System, formal name for the Shuttle program

SVS   Space Vision System, a Canadian medical experiment designed to fly aboard the Shuttle

SW   southwest

TDRS   Tracking and Data Relay Satellite, a series of communications satellites designed to permit constant contact between orbiting Shuttles and mission control

TKS   manned spacecraft system consisting of a VA and FGB developed by Chelomei's OKB-52 for use with the Almaz space station

T-minus T refers to scheduled launch time; T minus is any time prior to that

T-pad   a jaw-like device used by astronaut George Nelson during his attempted capture of the Solar Maximum Mission satellite in 1984

TsKBEM Russian for the Central Construction Bureau for Experimental Machine- Building, name of the former OKB-1 (Korolev) under the Ministry of General Machine-Building, 1966-74

TsKBM   Russian for the Central Construction Bureau for Machine-Building, name of the former OKB-52 (Chelomei) under the Ministry of General Machine-Building, 1966–74

TsPK   Russian acronym for the Center for Cosmonaut Training (named for Yuri Gagarin) near Moscow, usually called the Gagarin Center

TsUKOS   Russian for the Central Directorate for Space, forerunner of the VKS (Military Space Forces), formed 1964

TsUP   Russian acronym for the Center for Flight Control, the flight control center based in Korolev, northeast of Moscow

TWA   U.S. airline

UFO   unidentified flying object

UNKS   Russian for Office of the Commander for Space Units, name for the former GUKOS when it separated from GURVO in 1982.

USAF   United States Air Force

USCG   United States Coast Guard

USGS   United States Geological Survey

USML   U.S. Microgravity Laboratory, a series of Shuttle Spacelab missions flown as STS-50 (1992) and STS-73 (1995)

USN   United States Navy

USS   United States ship

VA   Russian for Return Vehicle, a Chelomei-built spacecraft

VKS   Russian acronym for the Military Space Forces, successor to UNKS

VVS   Russian acronym for Military Air Forces

W   west

Wright-Pat   shorthand for Wright-Patterson Air Force Base, Dayton, Ohio

NOTES ON CONTRIBUTORS

David J. Shayler is the author of several books on the American space program including *NASA Space Shuttle* (1987), *Shuttle Challenger* (1987), *Apollo 11 Moon Landing* (1989) and *Exploring Space* (1994). The founder of Astro Info Service, he lives in West Midlands, England.

Rex Hall is the world's foremost private authority on the Russian cosmonaut team and a frequent contributor to *Spaceflight* and *The Journal of the British Interplanetary Society*. He lives in London.

Lida Shkorking is a teacher and translator in Zhukovsky, Moscow Region, Russia, home of the Gromov Flight Research Institute and the Buran test pilots.

Bert Vis has interviewed astronauts and cosmonauts all over the world. A resident of The Hague, Netherlands, he has published articles in *Spaceflight*.

NASA ASTRONAUTS

David J. Shayler

Between April 1959 and May 1996 the National Aeronautics and Space Administration selected 268 men and women to train for America's civilian space program. Selected in sixteen different groups, they included 232 men and 36 women, of whom 211 (186 men and 25 women) made at least one spaceflight through December 1997.

The majority were selected as pilot astronauts (138, three of them women), with another 17 classed as scientist-astronauts, with 121 mission specialists (33 of them women).

Of the whole group, only 24 ventured to the Moon, and of these 12 walked on its surface between 1969 and 1972. A total of 66 NASA astronauts (63 men and three women) have logged time in extravehicular activity (EVA).

In December 1997 100 astronauts (77 men and 17 women), including members of Group 16, then completing their training and evaluation period, remained eligible for assignment to future missions. In addition, 12 astronauts (11 men and one woman) had lost their lives during training for or flying a mission. A further 11 men had died either in off-duty accidents, or from natural causes after leaving NASA.

The change in selection criteria with the NASA program is reflected in the demise of the "Right Stuff" hero test pilot and its replacement by the scientist-engineer ethic.

The Original Seven

When the National Aeronautics and Space Administration began its activites in October 1958, one of its first tasks was to select a group of suitably qualified persons who, after a period of training, would complete the first manned orbits of the Earth in the small spacecraft then in initial stages of development.

At that time there was international interest in the exploration of space by unmanned automated space satellites and growing interest in America for manned exploration of space. A large number of scientific journals and books had been written on what could be expected by travelers in space, but no human had yet ventured beyond the atmosphere.

A great deal of experience in high-altitude flying had been gathered by many years of manned balloon flights and by NASA (and its forerunner NACA) high-speed and high-altitude aeronautical research flights in rocket aircraft of the X series.

Initial requirements for the selection of astronaut applications for what eventually became Project Mercury had been worked out by NASA's Space Task Group at Langley Research Center, Virginia, during November 1958. It was decided to arrange a meeting between the NASA group and representatives from industry and the military services. The result would be a joint selection of a pool of some 150 men from which 36 candidates would be selected for physical and psychological testing. A group of 12 would be selected from this group to undergo a training and qualification program that would last nine months, on the completion of which a final group of six would be selected to make the Mercury spaceflights.

It was decided that only males between the ages of 25 and 40 would be selected for the program, due to the expected high physical stress a human body might endure in flight. Candidates were limited to a height of less than 5 feet, 11 inches, so that they could fit into the one-man Mercury capsule, whose size in turn was governed by the available booster rockets, the Redstone and Atlas ballistic missiles. All candidates were also required to hold at least a bachelor's degree to be considered.

In addition, candidates with three years' work in the physical or biological sciences could apply, as could those with similar experience in engineering or technical research. This meant that people such as pilots of aircraft or balloons, commanders of submarines, navigators and communications engineers, medical doctors, mountaineers, deep-sea divers, race car drivers, parachutists, Arctic explorers would all technically qualify as candidates for spaceflight.

But in December 1958 President Dwight Eisenhower declared that the first American astronauts would be selected from the ranks of military test pilots, men who were used to risking their lives in the high-speed testing of modern performance jet aircraft, who already possessed security clearances, and who were used to the disciplines of military life. (This decision had a long-lasting effect on the nature of future NASA astronauts over the next thirty years.)

On January 5, 1959, NASA finalized its selection criteria. A candidate had to

- be under the age of 40
- be less than 5'11"
- be in excellent physical condition
- be a graduate of a test pilot school
- hold a bachelor's degree or its equivalent
- have 1500 hours of flight time (10 years of experience)
- be a qualified jet pilot

A screening of military personnel records produced 110 men who met these criteria, 58 from the Air Force, 47 from the Navy, and 5 from the Marine Corps. Thirty-five of these men were invited to a meeting in Washington on February 2, 1959, and following a briefing about Project Mercury and the man in space project, 24 of them volunteered. When an even higher percentage of the second group of candidates also volunteered, NASA realized it had more than enough qualified men and canceled the invitation to the rest of the original 110. At the same time, the number of men to be selected, originally set at 12 because of an anticipated high dropout rate, was reduced to six.

A series of written tests, technical interviews, psychiatric examinations, and medical history reviews followed, and by March 32 men had been invited to the Lovelace Clinic in Albuquerque, New Mexico, for an extraordinarily detailed set of physical tests. They were subjected to seventeen different eye examinations; they had their brain waves measured; they were dunked in water to determine their bodies' specific gravity; they pedaled stationary bicycles against increasing loads; they had water dripped in their ears to study reactions to motion sickness; they were shocked, spun, prodded, and punctured; their hearts and lungs were measured; and they were placed in chambers exposing them to extreme heat and extreme cold.

Only one candidate dropped out during this phase of testing. Another round of tests, this time psychological, was conducted at Wright-Patterson Air Force Base in Ohio, and a fourth round at Lovelace again. By the end of March the selection board reviewed the results of the exhaustive testing and evaluated each man's career and achievements and, failing to reduce them to six, on April 2 selected seven pilots as America's Mercury astronauts.

At 2 P.M. on April 9, 1959, they were introduced to the press:

Lieut. Malcolm Scott Carpenter, USN

Capt. Leroy Gordon Cooper Jr., USAF

Lieut. Col. John H. Glenn Jr., USMC

Capt. Virgil I. "Gus" Grissom, USAF

Lieut. Cmdr. Walter M. Schirra Jr., USN

Lieut. Cmdr. Alan B. Shepard Jr., USN

Capt. Donald K. "Deke" Slayton, USAF

Of the seven Mercury atronauts, six would make flights in the Mercury program. The seventh, Slayton, finally went into space on the Apollo-Soyuz Test Project in 1975. Grissom, Cooper, and Schirra flew Gemini missions, while Schirra and Shepard flew in Apollo, with Shepard the only Mercury astronaut to walk on the

Moon. Their story was immortalized in the book *The Right Stuff* by Tom Wolfe (1979).

In early 1998, thirty-six years after he became the first American to orbit the Earth, Mercury astronaut John Glenn was assigned to a Shuttle mission, scheduled to be flown when he is 77 years old.

Women in Space?

At the time the Mercury astronauts were being trained for their first flights, a group of women pilots were making the first of many attempts to see the selection of a woman astronaut. The greatest obstacle—other than institutional resistance to the whole idea—was the test pilot requirement. It was not until 1970 that American women were allowed to undergo military test pilot training.

In February 1960 a woman pilot named Jerri Cobb successfully underwent the same physical examinations completed by the Mercury astronauts a year before. Aviatrix Jacqueline Cochran, the first woman to break the sound barrier and who had a lifelong interest in spaceflight, provided financial backing for Cobb, who recruited 20 women as potential astronauts, though there was little chance they would ever join the space program.

In early 1961 these 20 went to the Lovelace Clinic for medical screening with the cooperation of Dr. Randolph Lovelace—though not of NASA. A total of 13 women passed the examinations:

Rhea Hurrle Allison, 32, a schoolteacher and pilot

Myrtle Cagle, 38, a flight instructor since the age of 14

Geraldyn (Jerri) Cobb, 30, a pilot since the age of 12, holder of four world aviation records and an airline executive

Jan and Marion Dietrich, 36-year-old twins. Jan had logged over 8000 hours of flying time and held a transport pilot's rating. Marion flew charter planes and held degrees in mathematics and psychology

Mary Wallace Funk, at 24 the youngest of the group, chief pilot for a California flying service. She had also volunteered for the USMC high-altitude chamber and centrifuge test program (which involved Marine pilot John Glenn)

Sarah Lee Gorelick, 29, holder of degrees in mathematics, physics and chemistry in addition to aeronautics

Jane Briggs Hart, 40, the oldest of the group. She was the wife of Michigan Senator Philip Hart (D, 1958-76) and often flew his campaign plane

Jean Hixson, 39, a school teacher who was also a captain in the Air Force Reserve in addition to being a WASP test pilot and instructor

Irene Leverton, 36, who completed pre-spaceflight tests at Edwards AFB. She was also a parachutist and skier and supervisor of a flight school

Geraldine Sloan, 33, a pilot with a Texas aviation company

Bernice Trimble Steadman, 37, who ran an air charter service

Gene Nora Stumough, 26, a flying instructor for an aircraft

Cochran agreed to fund a second series of tests at the Naval Air Station in Pensacola, Florida, but the tests never took place. It would be 17 years before any American woman would be selected as an astronaut.

Gemini and Apollo

On April 18, 1962, three years after the selection of the Mercury Seven and following successful manned flights by Soviet cosmonauts Gagarin and Titov and Americans Shepard, Grissom, and Glenn, NASA announced that it would accept applications for a second group of astronaut trainees. The agency planned to select between five and ten who, after an initial training period, would join the Mercury astronauts in flying the two-man Gemini spacecraft in 1964 and who would probably crew early Apollo missions beginning in 1967.

The list of qualifications, which was modified to allow applications by civilians, demanded that candidates

- be experienced jet test pilots and preferably presently engaged in flying high-performance jet aircraft

- have attained experimental test pilot status through military service, the aircraft industry or NASA, or have graduated from a military test pilot school

- hold a degree in physical or biological sciences or in engineering

- be a citizen of the United States, under 35 years of age at the time of selection, and no taller than six feet in height. [The increase in allowable height was due to the slightly larger size of the Gemini spacecraft.]

• be recommended by his parent organization

By June 1962 NASA had screened a total of 253 suitable candidates from those who applied. On September 17, 1962, following several weeks of medical tests and other examinations, nine men were selected:

Neil A. Armstrong

Maj. Frank Borman, USAF

Lieut. Charles "Pete" Conrad Jr., USN

Lieut. Cmdr. James Lovell Jr., USN

Capt. James McDivitt, USAF

Elliott M. See Jr.

Capt. Thomas P. Stafford, USAF

Capt. Edward H. White II, USAF

Lieut. John W. Young, USN.

They reported to the new Manned Spacecraft Center in Houston, Texas, where their training was directed by Mercury astronaut Donald Slayton, who had been named "coordinator of astronaut activities" or chief astronaut following his disqualification for flight assignment early in 1962.

The "Original Nine," as they jokingly dubbed themselves, were the most experienced group of astronauts ever selected. Eight of its members would fly in space; two would die during training, one of them just prior to his first flight. Armstrong, a former X-15 pilot, became the first person to walk on the Moon. Borman and Lovell not only set a space endurance record, they were also two of the first humans to orbit the Moon. White became the first American to walk in space. McDivitt commanded the first manned flight of the Apollo lunar module. Conrad commanded the first Skylab mission. Stafford commanded the joint U.S.-Soviet mission. Young went on to fly six missions over 18 years, including command of the first Space Shuttle mission.

Even before the astronauts in the second group reported to NASA it was clear that a third selection would be needed. Several of the Mercury astronauts (Glenn, Carpenter, Slayton) were grounded or otherwise unavailable for future flights, and with ten manned Gemini mis-

sions scheduled to begin in late 1964, followed by an unknown number of Apollo missions, it was clear that NASA needed more than thirteen active astronauts.

In June 1963 NASA issued a call for its third astronaut group. The selection criteria this time required a candidate to

• be a citizen of the United States

• hold a bachelor's degree in engineering or the physical or biological sciences

• have logged 1,000 hours of flying time with the armed services, NASA or the aircraft industry

• be 34 years of age or younger at the time of selection

For the first time pilots without test flying experience were allowed to apply. It was hoped that the lower number of flying hours required might tempt applications from persons with scientific backgrounds as well. The age limit of 34 reflected NASA's belief that members of this group should plan on having long careers as astronauts.

By July 1, 1963, NASA had received 271 applications, 200 from civilians and 71 from military personnel, including two African-American pilots. Two women also applied. By the end of August, 32 finalists had been selected, all of them white males, and these were invited to Brooks AFB, Texas, for medical examinations.

On October 17 the fourteen new astronauts were announced

Maj. Edwin E. "Buzz" Aldrin Jr., USAF

Capt. William A. Anders, USAF

Capt. Charles E. Bassett II, USAF

Lieut. Alan L. Bean, USN

Lieut. Eugene A. Cernan, USN

Lieut. Roger B. Chaffee, USN

Capt. Michael Collins, USAF

R. Walter Cunningham

Capt. Donn F. Eisele, USAF

Capt. Theodore C. Freeman, USAF

Lieut. Cmdr. Richard F. Gordon Jr., USN

Russell L. Schweickart

Capt. David R. Scott, USAF

Capt. Clifton C. Williams Jr., USMC

They reported in January 1964, raising the number of active astronauts to 28. Only half of the selectees (Bassett, Bean, Collins, Eisele, Freeman, Gordon, Scott, and Williams) had test pilot backgrounds. Aldrin held a doctorate in science from the Massachusetts Institute of Technology and civilians Cunningham and Schweickart were performing scientific research at the time of selection. Navy pilot Chaffee had flown reconnaissance aircraft over Cuba during the October 1962 missile crisis.

Four of the new astronauts—Freeman, Bassett, Chaffee and Williams—would die in training or space-related accidents before they could fly in space. Anders was a member of the first crew to orbit the Moon. Two members of the class of 1963, Aldrin and Collins, would take part in the first lunar landing. Bean, Scott, and Cernan would walk on the Moon.

An African-American Astronaut?

U.S. president John F. Kennedy believed that NASA should select an African-American astronaut and, through Attorney General Robert Kennedy, the president's brother, the Air Force and Navy were encouraged to find a suitable candidate. The search resulted in the enrollment of 28-year-old Air Force captain Edward Dwight in the Aerospace Research Pilot's School in 1962.

Dwight had entered the Air Force in 1953, eventually logging over 2,000 hours of flying time in jet fighters while also doing a two-year tour as a B-57 pilot. He held a degree in aeronautical engineering.

Though his qualifications for ARPS were minimal, Dwight managed to graduate. When submitted to NASA as a candidate, for the 1963 group, however, Dwight was not selected.

Following the death of President Kennedy in November 1963 the political pressure on NASA to select an African American disappeared; none was chosen until 1978.

Dwight remained in the Air Force until 1966, then resigned. He went on to become a noted sculptor.

Expanding the Team

Even as military pilots were being recruited and trained as astronauts, NASA officials were concluding that professional scientists should also be selected for the manned space program. Trained geologists could explore the Moon, oceanographers could study the Earth from space, astronomers could operate orbiting telescopes, and physician-astronauts could examine firsthand human adaptation to weightlessness.

Following a recommendation by the NASA Space Science Board in July 1962 that "scientist-astronauts" should be included in the astronaut group and assigned to the first lunar landing, and after months of internal debate over selection criteria, NASA and the National Academy of Sciences issued a call for astronaut candidates who were

- born on or after August 1, 1930
- citizens of the United States
- no taller than 6'
- holders of a Ph.D. or the equivalent in natural science, medicine or engineering.

Pilot experience was not required, though preference was given to applicants who had it. All selectees would be required to attend a yearlong course at a U.S. Air Force flight school to qualify as jet pilots.

Coincidentally, the call was issued on October 19, 1964, just one week after the Soviet Union launched the first Voskhod spacecraft carrying a physician and an aerospace engineer, neither of whom were pilots.

By December 31, 1964, NASA had received a total of 1,351 applications or letters of interest and by February 10, 1965, had forwarded the names of 400 applicants (including four women) to the National Academy of Sciences, which would judge their scientific credentials. The Academy was to select 10 to 15 candidates for final judging by NASA's astronaut selection board. Sixteen candidates were sent to NASA for medical and psychological testing, and six—only half the number NASA had originally intended to recruit—were announced on June 28, 1965:

Owen K. Garriott

Edward G. Gibson

Duane E. Graveline

Lieut. Cmdr. Joseph P. Kerwin, USN-Medical Corps

Frank Curtis Michel

Harrison H. Schmitt

The first group of scientist-astronauts consisted of an electrical engineer (Garriott), two physicists (Gibson and Michel), two physicians (Kerwin and Graveline), and a geologist (Schmitt). Kerwin and Michel were qualified jet pilots and reported for astronaut training on July 1, 1965. The others were sent to Williams Air Force Base in Arizona on July 29, 1965, to enter flight school. (Graveline resigned from the space program shortly thereafter, for personal reasons.)

The scientist-astronauts were never really welcomed by the test-pilot-dominated astronaut office and their selection was later seen to be premature. Nevertheless, geologist Schmitt did walk on the Moon while physician Kerwin was included in the crew of America's first month-long spaceflight. Garriott and Gibson also flew Skylab missions, and Garriott later took part in the first Shuttle-Spacelab mission.

Organizing the Astronaut Office

The Mercury astronauts reported directly to Robert Gilruth, head of Space Task Group at NASA Langley. As NASA expanded to meet the challenges of the Apollo program, so did Gilruth's responsibilities. Space Task Group became the nucleus of the new Manned Spacecraft Center based in Houston, Texas, in the summer of 1962.

Responsibility for selection of the second and third groups of astronauts was given to Donald K. Slayton, coordinator of astronaut activities. In the fall of 1963 Slayton was made director of flight crew operations and given authority over the Manned Spacecraft Center's aircraft operations division and crew systems as well as the astronaut office. Captain Alan Shepard, recently grounded for medical reasons, was named the chief of the astronaut office.

The astronaut office itself—Code CB in NASA's organization chart—was divided into branches for Gemini and Apollo, and for operations and training.

In August 1964, for example, the Gemini branch was headed by Grissom (commander of the first planned Gemini mission), with Young, Schirra, Stafford, McDivitt, White, Borman, and Lovell—the prime and backup crews for GT-3 and GT-4.

The Apollo branch, headed by Cooper, included Conrad (working with Cooper on the CSM and lunar module),

Anders (environmental control system), Cernan (propulsion and Agena), Chaffee (communications and tracking), Cunningham (electrical systems and experiments), Eisele (attitude controls), Freeman (boosters), Gordon (cockpit integration), and Schweickart (future programs and experiments).

The operations and training branch was headed by Armstrong, with See and Aldrin (mission planning), Bassett (simulators and handbooks), Bean (recovery systems), Collins (pressure suits and EVA), Scott (guidance and navigation), and Williams (range operations and crew safety).

Carpenter was assigned to special projects as liaison with the U.S. Navy.

Expansion

By September 1965 NASA had 30 active astronauts (including three scientist-astronauts attending flight school), a sufficient number to provide prime, backup, and support crews for the remaining Gemini missions and the early Apollo mission, including the first lunar landing.

But the space agency also had plans for later manned flights, known successively as Apollo X, Apollo Extension System, and Apollo Applications Program. The AAP schedule called for as many as ten more lunar landings and three orbiting research laboratories, totalling over 40 manned Apollo flights beginning in late 1968. A team of 30 astronauts flying two or three missions each could not meet this schedule, and with attrition would be totally inadequate. So plans were made for a dramatic two-phase expansion in the astronaut team.

Phase one began on September 10, 1965, when NASA began to recruit a fifth group to consist of 15 astronauts. The selection criteria were similar to those of the 1963 group, though the age limit was raised to 36. By December 1, 1965, 351 applications had been received, including six from women pilots and one from a young U.S. Navy officer, Lieutenant Frank E. Ellis, who had lost both his legs in a jet crash in July 1962. (Ellis maintained that in spite of his handicap his flying ability was unimpaired, and that the ability to run and jump was irrelevant to an astronaut. Ellis was not one of the 159 finalists, but NASA did nominate him for special work in the space program.)

On April 4, 1966, NASA announced the selection of 19 new astronauts who would report to the Manned Spacecraft Center in May:

Vance D. Brand

Lieut. John S. Bull, USN

Maj. Gerald P. Carr, USMC

Capt. Charles M. Duke Jr., USAF

Capt. Joe H. Engle, USAF

Lieut. Cmdr. Ronald E. Evans Jr., USN

Maj. Edward G. Givens Jr., USAF

Fred W. Haise Jr.

Maj. James B. Irwin, USAF

Don L. Lind

Capt. Jack R. Lousma, USMC

Lieut. Thomas K. Mattingly II, USN

Lieut. Bruce McCandless II, USN

Lieut. Commander Edgar D. Mitchell, USN

Maj. William R. Pogue, USAF

Capt. Stuart A. Roosa, USAF

John L. Swigert Jr.

Lieut. Cmdr. Paul J. Weitz, USN

Capt. Alfred M. Worden, USAF

All were experienced jet pilots. Engle already held astronaut wings for his work on the X-15 rocket plane. Lind, a NASA physicist, had a background that ultimately caused him to be grouped with the scientist-astronauts in spite of the fact that he had been a Navy jet pilot. He was one of 4 civilians selected (the others were NASA's Haise, Brand of Lockheed, and Swigert of Pratt-Whitney). The rest were from the Air Force, Navy, and Marines. Most had graduated from test pilot schools. Two Navy pilots, Evans and Weitz, had flown combat missions in Southeast Asia.

The fifth group was selected and reported to the MSC just as the fourth group of scientist-astronauts was ready to commence their academic and survival training. (Three members of the group had undergone a yearlong course to qualify as T-38 pilots.) The fourth and fifth groups were combined for that phase of training.

With the complexity of the Apollo program and the planned Apollo Applications, the fifth group of pilots was then split into two groups to specialize in the systems, hardware, and procedures of the North American-built Apollo command-service modules or the Grumman-built lunar module.

CSM specialists	Brand, Evans, Givens, Mattingly, McCandless, Pogue, Roosa, Swigert, Weitz, Worden
LM specialists	Bull, Carr, Duke, Engle, Haise, Irwin, Lind, Lousma, Mitchell, Schmitt

Phase two of the expansion was a second group of scientist-astronauts who would, it was hoped, represent the scientific community in the development of experiments for the Apollo Applications missions in addition to serving as potential crewmembers. On September 26, 1966, NASA and the National Academy of Sciences issued a joint news release announcing that a "limited number" of scientist-astronauts were being sought. Applicants must be

- U.S. citizens as of March 15, 1967
- no taller than 6'
- born on or after August 1, 1930
- holders of a Ph.D. in the natural sciences, medicine, or engineering

By January 8, 1967, 923 applications had been received for the 20 to 30 openings. Two months later the science academy forwarded 69 names to NASA for final screening and selection, and on August 4, 1967, 11 new astronauts were announced:

Joseph P. Allen IV

Philip K. Chapman

Anthony W. England

Karl G. Henize

Donald L. Holmquest

William B. Lenoir

John A. Llewellyn

Franklin S. Musgrave

Brian T. O'Leary

Robert A. R. Parker

William E. Thornton

The August 1967 group included the first naturalized citizens to be chosen for the astronaut group, Welsh-born Llewellyn and Australian Chapman. (Neither would fly in space.) Two of the new astronauts, Henize of Northwestern University and Thornton of the Air Force were technically too old to qualify—Henize was 40 and Thornton was 38—but both had been granted waivers by Manned Spaceflight Center director Robert Gilruth because of their experience and qualifications.

At the other extreme, England of M.I.T. was just 25; he is still the youngest astronaut ever selected.

None of the new astronauts were jet pilots and all were scheduled to attend undergraduate pilot training at either Williams Air Force Base or Vance Air Force Base in early 1968. The delay was caused by the Air Force's need to train more pilots for the Vietnam War. Llewellyn and O'Leary dropped out of the group during flight school. Cuts in the budget of Apollo Applications (finally renamed Skylab) made it apparent to the remaining scientist-astronauts that their chances of flying in space were slim. Holmquest left the space program in 1971 and Chapman and England followed in 1972. Others took leave while awaiting the development of the Space Shuttle.

The first members of this group to fly in space, Allen and Lenoir, waited until November 1982, fifteen years after joining NASA. Henize and England (who returned to NASA in 1979), the last to make initial flights, did so in July 1985.

There was a third, unanticipated addition to the astronaut team in this period. On August 14, 1969, NASA accepted seven more pilots into the program, though by then it was clear that these men would not be making flights in Apollo or Skylab, but would have to wait until the Space Shuttle was ready:

Maj. Karol J. Bobko, USAF

Lieut. Cmdr. Robert L. Crippen, USN

Maj. Charles G. Fullerton, USAF

Maj. Henry W. Hartsfield Jr., USAF

Maj. Robert F. Overmyer, USMC

Maj. Donald H. Peterson, USAF

Lieut. Cmdr. Richard H. Truly, USN

All seven had transferred from the Air Force Manned Orbiting Laboratory program, which had suddenly been canceled in June 1969. (See the entry on MOL for details.) Fourteen pilots were still training with MOL at the time of cancellation and all but one (Lieut. Col. Robert Herres) expressed interest in transferring to NASA, where associate administrator for manned spaceflight George Mueller encouraged flight crew operations director Deke Slayton to take them all. Suspecting that he already had more astronauts than he needed, Slayton chose to take only the seven MOL pilots who were under 36 years of age.

An eighth MOL pilot, Lieut. Col. Albert H. Crews Jr., joined the flight crew directorate at the NASA Manned Spacecraft Center, supporting Shuttle missions through 1997.

The addition of the MOL pilots increased the number of active astronauts to more than 50 at a time when a maximum of 11 Apollo and Skylab flights were planned.

In May 1969 chief astronaut Alan Shepard returned to flight status and turned the chief astronaut job over to Thomas Stafford. At that time CB included branches for Apollo (headed by Armstrong) and for Skylab (headed by Cunningham). Shepard would return to the chief astronaut job in May 1971, following the Apollo 14 mission, at which time Stafford became assistant to Deke Slayton, the director of flight crew operations.

The Shuttle Era

The transfer of the seven former MOL pilots in 1969 was the last addition to the astronaut team for nearly nine years. By 1971 many of the scientist-astronauts selected in 1965 and 1967 had expressed disappointment at not receiving flight assignments. From the 1965 group only one (Schmitt) would get to the Moon while three others (Garriott, Gibson, and Kerwin) would fly on Skylab. The 1967 group had it even worse, having been warned by director of flight crew operations Slayton on their first day at NASA that their chances of flying were slim. Out of the "Excess Eleven," seven would eventually fly on the Shuttle beginning *fifteen years* after selection.

A further sign of the diminished power of the astronaut office came in February 1974, with the splashdown of the last manned Skylab mission. Christopher C. Kraft, the director (since Gilruth's retirement in 1972) of the Johnson Space Center (formerly the Manned Spacecraft

Center), instituted a reorganization which moved the flight crew operations directorate—that included the astronaut office—under the flight operations directorate, headed by Kenneth Kleinknecht.

At that time, the only scheduled manned American mission was Apollo-Soyuz. Donald K. Slayton had resigned as director of flight crew operations to train as an ASTP crewmember. Under Kleinknecht, Rear Admiral Alan Shepard became director of flight control with John Young as chief of the astronaut office. Of 37 active astronauts, 26 were pilots assigned to Space Shuttle development (16) or ASTP (10). Of the pilots, Haise became technical assistant to the Shuttle Orbiter Project Manager, Duke became technical assistant to the Acting Manager of Shuttle Systems Integration, and Cernan became special assistant to the manager for ASTP.

Scientist-astronaut Harrison Schmitt became chief of science and applications within CB, with Owen Garriott as his deputy. Six other scientist-astronauts were assigned here (Parker, Lenoir, Allen, Gibson, England, Henize). Joseph Kerwin became chief of life sciences within CB, with two other scientist-astronauts (Musgrave and Thornton).

Within a year Kleinknecht had been succeeded by George W. S. Abbey, who remained head of the flight, then flight crew operations, directorates until 1987.

By late 1977, with the Space Shuttle still in development and initial flights still two or more years in the future, the number of active NASA astronauts had dropped to 27, and most of them were well into their forties. John Young was then chief astronaut, with Alan Bean as his deputy. Branches within the astronaut office were ASTP, Shuttle development, and Shuttle Approach and Landing Tests.

During the Seventies it became clear to NASA that selection criteria for Shuttle astronauts could be substantially different from those applied to Mercury, Gemini, and Apollo astronauts. Experienced pilots would still be needed to fly the vehicle, but scientists and engineers with no pilot training could perform such duties as satellite deployment, space walks, and operation of scientific experiments. And since the Shuttle would not subject its crew to loads greater than 3 Gs (compared to 8G loads some Apollo crews endured), the physical requirements could also be eased.

Two types of astronauts were needed then, with two sets of selection criteria: pilots would

- have a B.S. in engineering, the physical sciences or mathematics
- have at least 1,000 hours of command pilot time with 2,000 hours desirable; experience with high-performance jet aircraft and in testing was also desirable
- be able to pass a Class I physical examination and be between 5'4" and 6'4"

These were not much different from the requirements for the 1963 and 1966 pilot selections, except for the absence of an upper age limit.

The other type of astronauts sought, called mission specialists, was required to

- have a B.S. in engineering, biological, or physical science or mathematics with an advanced degree or equivalent experience desirable
- be able to pass a Class II physical examination (which has greater latitude for nonstandard vision and hearing) and be between 5'0" and 6'4".

There was no age limit for mission specialists, either, and the size requirements were dictated by the design of Shuttle EVA space suits, not by the size of the spacecraft itself.

The initial announcement, on July 8, 1976, urged women and members of minority groups to apply.

By the end of June 1977, 659 pilots (147 military, 512 civilian) had applied as had 5,680 hopeful mission specialists, including 1,251 women and 338 minorities. The selection board reviewed all 8,079 applications and found that only about half actually met the stated criteria. (Most military applicants had been screened and nominated by their parent service.) The surviving half were reviewed again and 208 were ultimately invited to the NASA Johnson Space Center for a week of interviews and medical tests in August and September of 1977. Of the 208, 149 were found to be medically qualified for the astronaut group and were still interested in participating.

On January 16, 1978, NASA announced the selection of 35 new astronauts, 15 pilots, and 20 mission specialists:

Maj. Guion S. Bluford Jr., USAF   MS
Lieut. Cmdr. Daniel C. Brandenstein, USN   P

Capt. James F. Buchli, USMC	MS
Lieut. Cmdr. John O. Creighton, USN	P
Lieut. Cmdr. Michael L. Coats, USN	P
Capt. Richard O. Covey, USAF	P
Maj. John M. Fabian, USAF	MS
Anna L. Fisher	MS
Lieut. Dale A. Gardner, USN	MS
Lieut. Robert L. Gibson, USN	P
Maj. Frederick D. Gregory, USAF	P
Stanley D. Griggs	P
Terry J. Hart	MS
Lieut. Cmdr. Frederick H. Hauck, USN	P
Steven A. Hawley	MS
Jeffrey A. Hoffman	MS
Shannon W. Lucid	MS
Lieut. Cmdr. Jon A. McBride, USN	P
Ronald E. McNair	MS
Capt. Richard M. Mullane, USAF	MS
Capt. Steven R. Nagel, USAF	P
George D. Nelson	MS
Capt. Ellison S. Onizuka, USAF	MS
Judith A. Resnik	MS
Sally K. Ride	MS
Maj. Francis R. Scobee, USAF	P
Margaret R. Seddon	MS
Capt. Brewster H. Shaw Jr., USAF	P
Capt. Loren J. Shriver, USAF	P
Maj. Robert L. Stewart, USA	MS
Kathryn D. Sullivan	MS
Norman E. Thagard	MS
James D. A. van Hoften	MS
Lieut. Cmdr. David M. Walker, USN	P
Lieut. Cmdr. Donald E. Williams, USN	P

Technically known as astronaut candidates or ASCANS (and unofficially known as the "Thirty-Five New Guys"), they were to report to the NASA Johnson Space Center in July 1978 to commence a two-year training and evaluation course. Dropouts, if any, would be offered jobs elsewhere in NASA. (It was soon discovered that the two-year training course could be completed in one year; there were no dropouts in the 1978 group or in later groups.)

Training for the TFNG was directed by Alan Bean, then acting chief of the astronaut office. (Chief astronaut John Young was then training to command the first Shuttle mission.)

The civilian astronauts, who would be paid according to civil service scale, were expected to remain with NASA for at least five years. Military officers were considered to be on a seven-year (with possible extension) tour of duty governed by an understanding between NASA and the Department of Defense.

The 1978 group was, understandably, the largest and most diverse ever selected by NASA. There were six women, two physicians (Fisher and Seddon), a biochemist (Lucid), a physicist (Ride), a geophysicist (Sullivan), and an engineer (Resnik). There were three African Americans, Bluford, Gregory, and McNair, and an Asian American, Onizuka. Also selected was the first Army officer (Stewart).

What was also significant was the number of Vietnam veterans: twenty of the new ASCANS had combat experience.

The 1980 Selection

Even though by the summer of 1979 the Shuttle program was encountering technical and financial difficulties that postponed the first flight until late 1980, and eventually to April 1981, NASA realized that following the initial series of two-man test flights Shuttle crew size could increase to six or seven astronauts per mission. With an expected launch rate of 10–12 missions per year, and with veteran astronauts selected in the 1960s expected to leave the program after completing one or two early Shuttle flights, combined with the need to place astronauts in various support roles such as Kennedy Space Center launch support (called Cape Crusaders or C-Squares), assisting flight crews during pre-launch and landing activities; capcom, providing the voice link between the orbiter and mission control; payload support; and Shuttle Avionics Integration Laboratory, where "crews" of astronauts worked three 8-hour shifts debugging vital Shuttle computer software), 60 astronauts would simply not be enough.

Therefore, on August 1, 1979, NASA announced that it would begin accepting applications for the astronaut group on a regular basis (ideally every year, though this proved too optimistic). Between October 1 and December 1, hopeful pilots and mission specialists could apply for a group to begin training in the summer of 1980.

Criteria for this ninth group of astronauts were generally the same as for the eighth group, except that pilot applicants could now have a degree in biology and the minimum flight time had to have been logged in jets. Mission specialists would be allowed to substitute an advanced degree for experience, although degrees in technology, aviation, and psychology no longer qualified.

By December 1979 3,465 people had applied for the 10 to 20 openings. Many had also applied in 1978, including all the military personnel, whose names were simply resubmitted by their parent services. During March and April 1980 121 candidates were interviewed at the Johnson Space Center, on on May 19, 1980, 19 new astronaut-candidates were announced, to report to JSC on July 7:

James P. Bagian	MS
Lieut. Col. John E. Blaha, USAF	P
Maj. Charles F. Bolden Jr., USMC	P
Maj. Roy D. Bridges, USAF	P
Franklin R. Chang-Diaz	MS
Mary L. Cleave	MS
Bonnie J. Dunbar	MS
William F. Fisher	MS
Maj. Guy S. Gardner Jr., USAF	P
Maj. Ronald J. Grabe, USAF	P
Capt. David C. Hilmers, USMC	MS
Lieut. Cmdr. David C. Leestma, USN	MS
John M. Lounge	MS
Maj. Bryan D. O'Connor, USMC	P
Lieut. Cmdr. Richard N. Ricards, USN	P
Capt. Jerry L. Ross, USAF	MS
Lieut. Cmdr. Michael J. Smith, USN	P
Maj. Sherwood C. Spring, USA	MS
Maj. Robert C. Springer, USMC	MS

Two of the new ASCANS were women (Cleave and Dunbar), one (Bolden) was African-American, and one (Chang-Diaz) was Hispanic. Also among those selected was William Fisher, husband of 1978 astronaut Anna Fisher.

Five of the pilots (Blaha, Bridges, Grabe, O'Connor, and Richards) had actually been finalists for the 1978 group. Their selection was postponed when NASA managers changed the mix of the 1978 group from 20 pilots and 15 mission specialists to 15 pilots and 20 mission specialists, ostensibly to increase the number of potential women astronauts.

Smith would be killed in the Challenger accident.

Under an agreement with the European Space Agency, ESA payload specialists Claude Nicollier and Wubbo Ockels joined the members of Group Nine for the yearlong training and evaluation course.

John Young was the chief of the astronaut office as the 1980 ASCANS completed training, with Richard Truly as deputy. The mission support branch was headed by Creighton, the mission development branch by Kerwin, and the operations development branch by Crippen.

"Annual Selections"

It wasn't until May 16, 1983, that NASA was able to intiate its annual selection of astronauts. Criteria were now standardized at those used for the 1980 group. Between October 1 and December 1, 1983, 4,934 applications were received for six pilot and six mission specialist openings. In February and March 1984, 128 finalists were interviewed, and on May 23, 1984, 17 new candidates were announced:

Maj. James C. Adamson, USA	MS
Capt. Mark N. Brown, USAF	MS
Capt. Kenneth L. Cameron, USMC	P
Lieut. Cmdr. Manley L. Carter Jr., USN	MS
Lieut. Col. John H. Casper, USAF	P
Lieut. Cmdr. Frank L. Culbertson Jr., USN	P
Capt. Sidney M. Gutierrez, USAF	P
Capt. Lloyd B. Hammond Jr., USAF	P
Marsha S. Ivins	MS
Capt. Mark C. Lee, USAF	MS
George D. Low	MS

Cmdr. Michael J. McCulley, USN	P
Lieut. Cmdr. William M. Shepherd, USN	MS
Ellen L. Shulman	MS
Kathryn C. Thornton	MS
Lieut. Cmdr. James D. Wetherbee, USN	P
Charles L. Veach	MS

Three were women and one (man) was Hispanic. Navy pilot and flight surgeon Carter, a former forward for the Atlanta Chiefs soccer team, became the first professional athlete to join the astronaut team.

It is interesting to note that of the five civilians chosen, four were current NASA employees (Ivins, Veach, and Shulman at JSC and Low at the Jet Propulsion Laboratory) and one (Thornton) worked at the Army Foreign Science and Technology Center, meaning that all new astronauts were already employed by the U.S. government. Low was also the first son of a NASA official to become an astronaut.

The 1984 class adoped the unofficial nickname "Maggots," because of their self-professed love of food.

The training was directed by astronaut Ronald Grabe. John Young was chief of the astronaut office at this time, with P. J. Weitz as his deputy. Branches included mission support (headed by Allen), operations development (headed by Engle), and mission development (headed by Lenoir).

All 17 members of Group 10 flew in space between 1988 and 1991. Carter died in a plane crash in 1991 and Veach died of cancer in 1995.

Group 11

The apparent bias against "outside" applicants was even more notable in that no applications were solicited for the 1985 group. NASA simply reexamined 126 qualified civilian applicants from the 1984 pool, inviting 59 to JSC for interviews. Approximately 120 military candidates were also considered. Thirteen were announced on June 4, 1985, and again, all were either serving military officers or NASA employees. There were no new astronauts from industry or academia:

Jerome Apt	S
Lieut. Cmdr. Michael A. Baker, USN	P

Maj. Robert D. Cabana, USMC	P
Maj. Bryan Duffy, USAF	P
Capt. Charles D. Gemar, USA	MS
Linda M. Godwin	MS
Maj. Terence T. Henricks, USAF	P
Richard J. Hieb	MS
Tamara E. Jernigan	MS
Capt. Carl J. Meade, USAF	MS
Stephen S. Oswald	P
Lieut. Cmdr. Stephen D. Thorne, USN	P
Lieut. Pierre J. Thuot, USN	MS

There were two women (Godwin and Jernigan) and no minority candidates in this selection. Thorne was killed in an off-duty airplane crash just after completing his candidate training in June 1986. The other ten made their first flights in space between 1990 and 1992.

Group 12

In 1985, anticipating the long-awaited full-scale operations of the Shuttle system and with 14 or more flights planned for 1986 alone, NASA announced that beginning on August 1 of that year it would accept applications for the astronaut group from civilians on a continuing basis. Military astronaut applicants would be nominated by their parent services once a year. Selections would take place each spring with successful applicants reporting to JSC that summer. The exact number of candidates to be accepted would be determined by mission requirements and attrition rate in the current astronaut group.

Minimum qualifications for pilot were

- a B.S. from an accredited institution in engineering, physical science, biological science or mathematics;
- 1,000 hours pilot-in-command time in jet aircraft, with test pilot experience highly desirable
- ability to pass a NASA Class I flight physical
- height between 5'4" and 6'4"

Minimum qualifications for mission specialist were:

- a B.S. from an accredited institution in engineering, physical science, biological science or mathematics

- three years of related professional experience; advanced degrees desirable and may be substituted for experience
- Ability to pass a NASA Class II flight physical
- Height between 5'0" and 6'4"

The shuttle Challenger disaster and the subsequent grounding of the fleet forced a cancellation of the first group (Group 12, June 1986) to have been selected under this program.

The selection of Group 12 finally took place in June 1987. A total of 2,061 applications were received, from which 151 were interviewed. On June 5, 1987, the names of 15 new ASCANS were announced by NASA:

Maj. Thomas D. Akers, USAF	MS
Capt. Andrew M. Allen, USMC	P
Lieut. Kenneth J. Bowersox, USN	P
Capt. Curtis L. Brown, USAF	P
Capt. Kevin P. Chilton, USAF	P
N. Jan Davis	MS
C. Michael Foale	MS
Gregory J. Harbaugh	MS
Mae C. Jemison	MS
Maj. Donald R. McMonagle, USAF	P
Lieut. Cmdr. Bruce Melnick, USN	MS
William F. Readdy	P
Lieut. Cmdr. Kenneth Reightler, USN	P
Cmdr. Mario Runco, USCG	MS
Maj. James S. Voss, USA	MS

There were two women (Davis and Jemison), including the first African-American woman selected by NASA (Jemison). Foale was the first Anglo American to become an astronaut, having parents born in both the United States and England. Group 11 also saw the selection of the first representative from the U.S. Coast Guard, Lieut. Cmdr. Bruce Melnick.

The aftermath of the Challenger accident also saw changes in the management of the astronaut office and its parent flight crew operations directorate. Director George Abbey was transferred to a job at NASA Headquarters in Washington, D.C., and replaced by former Apollo flight controller Don Puddy.

At the same time, chief astronaut John Young was pro-

moted to a job in the Johnson Space Center hierarchy and replaced by Daniel Brandenstein. Steven Hawley became Brandenstein's deputy, establishing another tradition within the Shuttle-era astronaut office: the deputy chief of CB is a mission specialist.

Return to Flight (Group 13)

On May 11, 1988, NASA announced plans to select future astronaut groups in two-year cycles, a system that would moderate demands on resources for selection and training. This would allow the agency to adjust the size of selection groups to meet mission requirements.

The cutoff date for applications was June 30, 1989. Applications received after that date would be held for the next selection group. Nominees could be submitted by the military services at the same time.

The selection criteria were now standardized as the same as that for Group 12.

Following a six-month screening period, medical examinations, and personal interviews, the selection of Group 13 would be announced in January 1990, with new ASCANS reporting to JSC in July 1991 for year of training and evaluation.

By the deadline approximately 2,500 applications had been received. Between September and November 1989 106 candidates were interviewed at JSC. On January 17, 1990, NASA announced 23 new ASCANS in Group 13, the second largest ever selected, and the first of the Nineties:

Lieut. Daniel W. Bursch, USN	MS
Leroy Chiao	MS
Maj. Michael U. R. Clifford, USA	MS
Kenneth D. Cockrell	P
Maj. Eileen M. Collins, USAF	P
Maj. William D. Gregory, USAF	P
Maj. James Halsell, USAF	P
Capt. Susan Helms, USAF	MS
Bernard A. Harris	MS
Thomas D. Jones	MS
Maj. William S. McArthur, USA	MS
James H. Newman	MS
Ellen Ochoa	MS
Maj. Charles J. Precourt, USAF	P

Maj. Richard A. Searfoss, USAF	P
Ronald M. Sega	MS
Capt. Nancy J. Sherlock, USA	MS
Donald A. Thomas	MS
Janice E. Voss	MS
Capt. Carl Walz, USAF	MS
Maj. Terence W. Wilcutt, USMC	P
Peter J. K. Wisoff	MS
David A. Wolf	MS

Two-thirds of the new ASCANS were mission specialists, a significant increase over previous groups, emphasizing the continuing change in the makeup of the astronaut team. There were five women selected, including the first woman pilot candidate, Eileen Collins, and the first Hispanic woman, Ellen Ochoa. One candidate was African American (Harris) and one was Japanese American (Chiao).

Their training was directed by astronaut James Voss.

Group 14

The new emphasis on educational backgrounds as opposed to test flying reflected NASA's need to train qualified space station crews in addition to Shuttle flight deck personnel. The selection for Group 14 gave special emphasis to individuals with experience in life sciences and space manufacturing.

While all applicants for NASA astronaut positions had to be U.S. citizens, the space agency announced that it would train candidates from other agencies and foreign countries as Shuttle mission specialists or space station operators, much as ESA astronauts Nicollier and Ockels were trained in 1980-81.

The selection of NASA astronaut Group 14 began on July 1, 1991, and in the following months 2,054 applicants were considered. In December 1991 and January 1992, 87 of the applicants were interviewed at the Johnson Space Center in four weekly groups. The selection of 19 new ASCANS was announced on March 31, 1992:

Daniel T. Barry	MS
Cmdr. Charles E. Brady Jr., USN	MS
Capt. Catherine G. "Cady" Coleman, USAF	MS
Michael L. Gernhardt	MS
John M. Grunsfeld	MS
Capt. Scott J. "Doc" Horowitz, USAF	P
Lieut. Cmdr. Brent W. Jett Jr., USN	P
Kevin R. Kregel	P
Lieut. Cmdr. Wendy B. Lawrence, USN	MS
Cmdr. Jerry M. Linenger, USN	MS
Capt. Richard A. Linnehan, USA	MS
Lieut. Cmdr. Michael Lopez-Alegria, USN	MS
Scott E. Parazynski	MS
Lieut. Cmdr. Kent V. Rominger, USN	P
Cmdr. Winston E. Scott, USN	MS
Steven L. Smith	MS
Joseph R. Tanner	MS
Andrew S. W. Thomas	MS
Mary Ellen Weber	MS

The Group 14 ASCANS were joined in their training by five international astronauts:

Jean-Francois Clervoy (ESA)

Lieut. Col. Maurizio Cheli, Italian Air Force (ESA)

Marc Garneau (CSA)

Maj. Chris Hadfield, Canadian Air Force (CSA)

Koichi Wakata (NASDA)

Garneau had already made a spaceflight, as the Canadian payload specialist in the crew of STS Mission 41-G (October 1984), but he had not been given the full course of training required to qualify as a Shuttle mission specialist.

As the new ASCAN group went through its classroom and simulator training, its ranks also included Russian cosmonauts Sergei Krikalev and Vladimir Titov, who were selected in November 1992 to fly aboard the Shuttle as mission specialists.

Shortly after the 1992 ASCANs reported, Don Puddy left the job of director, flight crew operations, and was succeeded by former astronaut David Leestma. His deputy was former astronaut Steve Hawley. Dan Brandenstein resigned from NASA and was replaced as chief astronaut by Robert "Hoot" Gibson.

Group 15

Selection of a fifteenth group of NASA astronauts began in 1993, and in the next year 2,962 applications were received. Approximately 120 of the applicants were interviewed in Houston between June 26 and August 29, 1994. Following some delays caused by a U.S. government-wide hiring freeze, 19 new ASCANS were announced on December 8, 1994.

Lieut. Cmdr. Scott D. Altman, USN	P
Maj. Michael P. Anderson, USAF	MS
Cmdr. Jeffrey S. Ashby, USN	P
Maj. Michael J. Bloomfield, USAF	P
Kalpana Chawla	MS
Lieut. Cmdr. Robert L. Curbeam Jr., USN	MS
Cmdr. Joe F. Edwards, USN	P
Lieut. Cmdr. Dominic L. Gorie, USN	P
Kathryn P. Hire	MS
Maj. Rick D. Husband, USAF	P
Janet L. Kavandi	MS
Capt. Steven W. Lindsey, USAF	P
Edward T. Lu	MS
Maj. Pamela E. Melroy, USAF	P
Capt. Carlos I. Noriega, USMC	MS
James F. Reilly II	MS
Stephen K. Robinson	MS
Lieut. Cmdr. Susan L. Still, USN	P
Capt. Frederick W. Sturckow, USMC	P

The new group had a higher percentage of pilots than the more recent selections because of unanticipated resignations and retirements. In fact, in 1994 the lack of new pilots forced flight crew operations chief David Leestma to use one veteran astronaut as a pilot for the third time.

The Group 15 ASCANS were joined by two international candidates:

Takao Doi (NASDA)

David R. Williams (CSA)

In addition, CNES astronauts Jean-Loup Chretien and Michel Tognini joined the group in March 1995. As experienced test pilots and veteran space travelers, Chretien and Tognini were not considered "candidates," and underwent a slightly different training schedule to qualify as Shuttle mission specialists.

Their training was supervised by astronaut Jay Apt, chief of the mission support branch. During this time Col. Robert Cabana was chief astronaut, with Linda Godwin as his deputy.

Group 16

Throughout the late 1980s and 1990s, as NASA accepted regular groups of ASCANS and flew an average of seven Shuttle missions per year, a model for an astronaut career emerged. The "typical" astronaut made a first flight between two and three years after selection, followed by a second flight in year four, a third in year six or seven, and a fourth in year eight, though about half of the astronauts chose to move to administrative jobs or to leave NASA after three flights or about ten years of service.

Seven Shuttle missions per year required six crewmembers per mission (some had crews of five, some as many as seven) or about 42 "seats" per year, with each assignment requiring 1.5 years of an astronaut's career, meaning that 60 astronauts were in mission-specific training at any given time. Another 20 would be in either ASCAN training or in their first technical assignments, bringing the number to 80, while another 20 would be in administrative or senior astronaut office jobs. The astronaut office averaged 100 pilots and mission specialists throughout the 1990s.

As the launch of the first elements of the International Space Station approached, it became clear that ISS assembly and habitation crews required much longer training commitments—originally thought to be 2.5 years per mission, but eventually judged to be four years, including Russian language training and visits to facilities in other countries. Four ISS habitation crews per year (12 seats), half of them NASA astronauts (6) committed for four years meant that at least 24 additional astronauts were needed.

The "optimum" headcount of the astronaut office, then, jumped from 100 to 130. With attrition running at 10 astronauts per year, NASA felt it necessary, in 1996, to select its largest ASCAN group since 1978. Over 2,400 applications were received and between October 1995 and January 1996 120 of the applicants were interviewed in Houston. On May 1, 1996, 35 new ASCANS were announced:

Cmdr. David M. Brown, USN	MS
Lieut. Cmdr. Daniel C. Burbank, USCG	MS
Yvonne D. Cagle	MS
Francisco (Frank) Caldeiro	MS
Charles J. Camarda	MS
Maj. Duane G. Carey, USAF	P
Lieut. Cmdr. Laurel B. Clark, USN	MS
Capt. Edward M. Fincke, USAF	MS
Lieut. Col. Patrick G. Forrester, USA	MS
Lieut. Cmdr. Stephen N. Frick, USN	P
Cmdr. John B. Herrington, USN	MS
Joan E. Higginbotham	MS
Capt. Charles O. Hobaugh, USMC	P
Capt. James M. Kelly, USAF	P
Lieut. Scott Kelly, USN	P
Lieut. Mark Kelly, USN	P
Maj. Paul S. Lockhart, USAF	P
Maj. Christopher Loria, USMC	P
Sandra H. Magnus	MS
Michael J. Massimino	MS
Richard A. Mastracchio	MS
Lieut. Cmdr. William C. McCool, USN	P
Cmdr. Lee Morin, USN	MS
Lt. Cmdr. Lisa H. Nowak, USN	MS
Donald R. Petit	MS
John L. Phillips	MS
Mark L. Polansky	P
Paul W. Richards	MS
Piers J. Sellers	MS
Lt. Cmdr. Heidiemarie Stefanyshyn-Piper, USN	MS
Daniel M. Tani	MS
Maj. Rex J. Walheim, USAF	MS
Peggy Whitson	MS
Maj. Jeffrey N. Williams, USA	MS
Stephanie D. Wilson	MS

The group of 35 was joined upon reporting to JSC August 12, 1996, by an unprecedented nine international candidates:

Pedro Duque (ESA)

A. Christer Fuglesang (ESA)

Umberto Guidoni (ISA)

Steven G. MacLean (CSA)

Mamoru M. Mohri (NASDA)

Soichi Noguchi (NASDA)

Julie Payette (CSA)

Lt. Col. Phillipe Perrin, French Air Force (CNES)

Gerhard P. J. Theile (DARA)

Three of the international ASCANS—Guidoni of Italy, MacLean of Canada, and Mohri of Japan—had already flown as payload specialists aboard the Shuttle.

Group 16 had the distinction of selecting the first "twin" astronauts, lieutenants Scott Kelly and Mark Kelly. Ten of the astronauts were civilian NASA employees or military officers detailed to NASA.

The sheer size of Group 16 (whose members dubbed themselves, appropriately, "The Sardines") placed a strain on available training facilities, so the ASCAN qualification period was doubled in length to two years, meaning that the 44 new ASCANS will probably not be assigned to flight crews until the fall of 1998.

Kenneth Cockrell succeeded Cabana as chief of the astronaut office in October 1997. Godwin remained his deputy, with McArthur (flight support), Grunsfeld (computer support), Lee (EVA/robotics), Chang-Diaz (operations planning), Searfoss (vehicle systems and operations), Hammond (safety), and Wisoff (payload and habitation) as branch chiefs.

Group 17: June 1998

Interviews for NASA's seventeenth group of astronaut candidates, expected to number around 20, commenced in October 1997, with six groups of finalists being examined through January 1998 from over 2,500 applicants.

As the new ASCAN group was still being formed, one member of the group was announced: former Teacher-in-Space alternate payload specialist Barbara M. Morgan was selected to become an educator-mission specialist with the June 1998 group.

When finally announced on June 3, 1998, the group numbered 25, 8 pilots, and 17 mission specialists:

Clayton C. Anderson	MS
Maj. Lee J. Archambeault, USAF	P
Tracy E. Caldwell	MS
Gregory E. Chamitoff	MS
Maj. Timothy J. Creamer, USA	MS
Lieut. Christopher J. Ferguson, USN	P
Cmdr. Michael J. Foreman, USN	MS
Michael E. Fossum	MS
Lieut. Cmdr. Kenneth T. Ham, USN	P
Patricia C. Hilliard	MS
Gregory C. Johnson	P
Maj. Gregory H. Johnson, USAF	P
Stanley G. Love	MS
Leland D. Melvin	MS
Barbara R. Morgan	MS
Lieut. William A. Osfelein, USN	P
John D. Olivas	MS
Nicholas J. M. Patrick	MS
Lieut. Cmdr. Alan G. Poindexter, USN	P
Garrett E. Reisman	MS
Steven R. Swanson	MS
Maj. Douglas H. Wheelock, USA	MS
Lieut. Cmdr. Sunita L. Williams, USN	MS
Lieut. Neil W. Woodward III, USN	MS
Maj. George D. Zamka, USMC	P

Six international candidates joined the 1998 ASCANs when they reported to the NASA Johnson Space Center in August 1998:

Lt. Col. Leopold Eyharts, French Air Force (ESA)

Paolo Nespoli (ESA)

Capt. Marcos C. Pontes, Brazilian Air Force (Brazilian Space Agency)

Hans W. Schlegel (ESA)

Bjarni V. Tryggvasion (CSA)

Maj. Roberto Vittori, Italian Air Force (ESA)

Their training was directed by Captain James Wetherbee, USN, who became JSC's director of flight crew operations in the fall of 1998, and the new chief astronaut, Colonel Charles J. Precourt, USAF.

SHUTTLE PAYLOAD SPECIALISTS

From the beginning of the Space Shuttle program in 1972 NASA proclaimed that the size of Shuttle crews (from two to seven) and the relatively comfortable environment (space travelers would not be subjected to physical stresses comparable to those inflicted on Mercury, Gemini, and Apollo astronauts) made it possible for non-astronauts to go into space to perform specific scientific experiments or other work, or to simply be passengers.

In fact, NASA's physical criteria for the selection of Shuttle payload specialists required only that candidates

- have vision correctable to 20/40 in one eye
- hearing that can detect a whisper at three feet
- blood pressure lower than 160/100
- pulse rates of 176 to 190 after 12 to 15 minutes on a treadmill
- absence of tuberculosis, glaucoma, pacemaker, anemia, ulcers; no kidney stones for at least two years

There was no age limit; pilot experience was irrelevant. It was even suggested that a handicapped person could qualify.

The most important step in the selection of all payload specialists was approval by the Shuttle customer, whether the European Space Agency, the McDonnell Douglas Corporation, the USAF or NASA itself. Foreign countries were allowed to select their own payload specialists, as long as those chosen could meet these minimal requirements.

Spacelab Scientists

The first Shuttle payload specialists to be selected were professional scientists for the European Space Agency's Spacelab 1 scientific module, then scheduled to be carried aboard a Shuttle in 1981. ESA selections are discussed in the International section. NASA coordinated the selection of American payload specialists through its Marshall Spaceflight Center.

The scientists who had designed the principal experiments for Spacelab 1 were allowed to nominate two candidates each. Forty people were nominated, interviewed, and tested (the physical requirements were originally somewhat stricter), resulting in these semifinalists:

Craig Fischer

Michael L. Lampton

Robert Menzies

Byron K. Lichtenberg

Ann Whitaker

Richard Terrile

In May 1978, two scientists, Lampton and Lichtenberg, were selected. Lichtenberg went into space aboard STS-9/Spacelab 1 in November 1983.

It became obvious that given the years of training the scientific payload specialists ultimately received, it was best to recycle the backups on follow-up missions. In the summer of 1984, Spacelab 1's Lichtenberg and Lampton were named to fly aboard the Earth Observation Mission, a Spacelab 1 follow-up to be launched in the fall of 1986. In December 1985 another American scientist, Rick Chappell (who had headed the original Spacelab 1 selection committee at NASA Marshall) and ESA's Dirk Frimout were chosen to support on EOM as well.

Frimout ultimately replaced Lampton as one of the prime payload specialists for the mission, later named Spacelab ATLAS and launched as STS-45 in the spring of 1992.

Later ATLAS missions were flown in March 1992 (STS-45) and November 1995 (STS-66), but the crews consisted entirely of career NASA astronauts.

Unlike Spacelab 1, which was open to a variety of scientific experiments, Spacelab 2 was dedicated to solar physics, which cut the number of experiments from over 70 (Spacelab 1) to 13 (Spacelab 2), and lowered the number of potential payload specialists as well. Eight candidates were nominated in April 1978:

> Loren J. Acton
>
> John-David F. Bartoe
>
> John W. Harvey
>
> Bruce E. Patchett
>
> Diane K. Prinz
>
> N. Paul Peterson
>
> George Simon
>
> Keith T. Strong

Acton, Bartoe, Prinz, and Simon were selected as prime and backup payload specialists in September of that year. Acton and Bartoe flew aboard Spacelab 2 mission (51-F) in July 1985.

The four Spacelab 2 payload specialists were also candidates for a proposed follow-on mission called SunLab, which was canceled.

For Spacelab 3, a dedicated materials processing mission, only seven semifinalists were interviewed. Four scientists were selected in June 1983:

> Mary Helen Johnston
>
> Lodewijk van den Berg
>
> Taylor G. Wang
>
> Eugene H. Trinh

Van den Berg and Wang flew aboard Shuttle Mission 51-B in April 1985.

The continuing series of materials processing Spacelab missions was renamed the U.S. Microgravity Laboratory following the Challenger disaster. Selections resumed in August 1990, and three new candidates were named in addition to Spacelab 3 backup Eugene Trinh:

> Lawrence J. DeLucas
>
> Joseph M. Prahl
>
> Albert Sacco Jr.

Trinh and DeLucas flew aboard USML-01/STS-50 in July 1990.

Candidates for the second USML were named in November 1992:

> Albert Sacco Jr.
>
> Fred W. Leslie
>
> R. Glynn Holt
>
> David H. Matthiesen

Sacco and Leslie were selected as prime payload specialists in June 1994, and flew aboard USML-02/STS-73 in the fall of 1995.

Materials science studies were continued aboard the Materials Science Laboratory, MSL-01, with three candidates selected in December 1995:

> Roger K. Crouch
>
> Gregory T. Linteris
>
> Paul D. Ronney

Crouch and Linteris were named the flight payload specialists in January 1996. MSL-01 was launched aboard STS-83 in May 1997. Cut to fewer than four days because of a fuel cell problem aboard the orbiter Columbia, the entire MSL payload and crew were successfully re-flown on the next opportunity, as STS-94 in July 1997.

Four medical specialists were selected for Spacelab 4 and its follow-up (later known as the Spacelab Life Sciences series) in January 1984:

> F. Andrew Gaffney
>
> Millie Hughes-Fulford

Robert W. Phillips

Bill Alvin Williams

Williams withdrew from the program in 1985, which was delayed for five years by the Challenger disaster. Phillips and Gaffney were designated as prime payload specialists, but in 1989 Phillips suffered a medical disqualification. Gaffney and Hughes-Fulford flew aboard SLS-1 (STS-40) in June 1991.

In December of that year, payload specialist candidates for the second Spacelab Life Sciences mission (STS-58) were announced:

Jay C. Buckey

Martin J. Fettman

Laurence R. Young

Fettman was named prime payload specialist in October 1992, and STS-58 was flown in November 1993.

Another series of Spacelab missions dedicated to medical experiments was called International Microgravity Labs, and was open to candidates from the international community. Those flights are covered in the International Space Travelers section.

Three astronomers were chosen in June 1984 to fly on three different Spacelab ASTRO (astronomy) missions:

Samuel T. Durrance

Kenneth H. Nordsieck

Ronald A. Parise

Durrance and Parise flew on ASTRO 1 (STS-35) in December 1990. The number of ASTRO missions, which had been cut from three to one following the Challenger disaster, was raised to two following STS-35. Durrance and Parise were re-selected as the payload specialists for ASTRO-02, STS-67, with former Spacelab 2 payload specialist John-David Bartoe, and a new candidate, Scott Vangen, as alternates. ASTRO-02 was launched in March 1995.

Neurolab, scheduled for launch as STS-90 in the spring of 1998, is the last scheduled Spacelab mission on the Shuttle manifest, where most future missions are devoted to assembling and operating the International Space Station. Some members of the scientific community, including Spacelab payload specialists, are hoping for a "visiting scientist" program for ISS, but NASA has yet to announce any specific plans.

Four Neurolab payload specialist candidates were proposed in April 1996, including Chiaki Mukai of the Japanese National Space Development Agency, and veteran of the STS-65/International Microgravity Laboratory-01 mission, and Jay Buckey, an alternate payload specialist from STS-58/Spacelab Life Sciences-02. Two new candidates were James A. Pawelczyk and Alexander W. Dunlap.

In May 1997 Buckey and Pawelczyk were named the flight payload specialists for Neurolab.

Military Payload Specialists

Long before the first manned Shuttle mission in April 1981 the Air Force announced that it would train payload specialists to accompany Department of Defense satellites on missions dedicated to military activities.

Most DOD payload specialists were to have come from the Manned Spaceflight Engineer program, which was begun by Air Force undersecretary Hans Mark in February 1979. Beginning that August, applications were solicited from Air Force, Navy, and Army officers with the following qualifications:

minimum of a B.A. in science or engineering

four years of experience in flying or space-related work (such as engineering or launch operations)

ability to pass a NASA Class II physical

From 222 candidates, 14 officers—12 Air Force, two Navy—were selected in August 1979. One Air Force officer, Major Carl Hatlelid, declined the appointment and was replaced by a candidate from the list of alternates (Capt. Gary Payton). One of the Navy selectees, Lieutenant Commander Paul B. Schlein, also declined, in order to take a position at the Naval Academy. The first thirteen MSEs were

First Lieut. Frank J. Casserino, USAF

First Lieut. Jeff E. Detroye, USAF

Capt. Michael A. Hamel, USAF

Capt. Terry A. Higbee, USAF

Capt. Darryl A. Joseph, USAF

Maj. Malcolm W. Lydon, USAF

Capt. Gary E. Payton, USAF

Capt. Jerry J. Rij, USAF

Maj. Paul A. Sefchek, USAF

Maj. Eric E. Sundberg, USAF

Lieut. Cmdr. David M. Vidrine, USN

Capt. John B. Watterson, USAF

Capt. Keith C. Wright, USAF

They officially began their training at Los Angeles Air Force Station in February 1980, though several men still had duties elsewhere and were forced to commute for several months. The MSE program was originally managed under the Secretary of the Air Force's Special Projects Office, the Air Force segment of the National Reconnaissance Office headed by Mark, and to which most of the MSE candidates were already assigned. Since the NRO is the agency that controls national security satellite programs, the MSE program was classified for its first two years of existence. In fact, it wasn't until October 1985 that the names of MSEs were officially released.

Second Cadre

In the summer of 1982 announcements were circulated at Air Force bases and placed in official publications soliciting applications for a second MSE group, this one limited to Air Force personnel. From a pool of 63 candidates, 14 were selected in September 1982:

Capt. James B. Armor Jr.

First Lieut. Michael W. Booen

Capt. Livingston L. Holder Jr.

Capt. Larry D. James

Capt. Charles M. Jones

First Lieut. Maureen C. Lacomb

Capt. Michael R. Mantz

Capt. Randy T. Odle

Capt. William A. Pailes

Capt. Craig A. Puz

Capt. Katherine E. Roberts

Capt. Jess M. Sponable

Capt. William D. Thompson

Capt. Glenn S. Yeakel

This new MSE cadre included two women officers (Lacomb and Roberts) and an African American (Holder). Training began in January 1983.

The Air Force originally asked NASA to develop a training schedule for its payload specialists, only to have NASA decline. Consequently, the members of the first cadre developed their own training program, which gave them much more extensive involvement with the Shuttle than other payload specialists. For example, MSEs donned pressure suits and performed simulated space walks.

Most MSE time, however, was devoted to the management and acquisition of Department of Defense satellites and scientific payloads to be launched aboard the Shuttle. Several MSEs were assigned to each system program office (SPO), some to more than one, thus providing a small pool of candidates for assignment to each flight.

Air Force selection boards met at regular intervals beginning in June 1982, assigning payload specialist candidates to several missions at a time.

STS-10 Maj. Gary Payton and Maj. Keith Wright

STS-15 Maj. Eric Sundberg, Maj. Brett Watterson and Capt. Jeff Detroye

STS-16 Capt. Frank Casserino and Maj. Daryl Joseph

Scheduling and hardware problems caused all three missions to be delayed, though Payton's mission ultimately flew as Mission 51-C in January 1985. The Casserino/Joseph payload was delayed until 1989 (STS-28), and flew without a military payload specialist.

The Teal Ruby satellite and CIRRIS experiment package for which Sundberg, Watterson and Detroye were selected was delayed for three years, and shifted from an East Coast to West Coast launch aboard Mission 62-A. By the time the payloads were officially manifested, in the fall of 1984, Sundberg and Detroye were leaving the MSE program, though Watterson remained a candidate. Three MSEs were nominated as payload specialists by the selection board:

62-A Maj. Brett Watterson, Capt. Randy Odle and Capt. Michael Mantz

Watterson and Odle trained as prime PS from October 1984 to the summer of 1985. When the Mission 62-A payload specialists were announced, however, Odle had been replaced as prime PS by Air Force undersecretary Edward C. "Pete" Aldridge, Jr. (At the time, Aldridge was also serving as director of the National Reconnaissance Office, which developed Teal Ruby and CIRRIS.)

The October 1984 selection board also selected PS for an entirely different mission, a so-called "launch ready standby" deployment of two Defense Satellite Communications System comsats aboard Shuttle Mission 51-J: Two candidates were nominated:

DOD Standby   Capt. Michael Booen and Capt. William Pailes

In the spring of 1985 Pailes was selected as the prime PS, and became the second MSE to make a flight aboard Atlantis that October.

Eight Shuttle missions were flown in calendar year 1985, the most yet, and NASA was projecting as many as a dozen for 1986, several dedicated to military payloads. For its part, the Air Force and NRO had a number of critical payloads ready for launch, including the oft-delayed Teal Ruby/CIRRIS (Mission 62-A) and the advanced data relay satellite (Mission 61-N), which could only operate in tandem with the first KH-11A, a new series of imaging reconnaissance satellites. Other payloads included a new Defense Support Program early warning satellite, four Navstar satellites that would initate operations of the Global Positioning System, and a military Spacelab called StarLab, dedicated to experiments from the Strategic Defense Initiative Organization.

The third MSE payload specialist selection board met in November 1985, assigning five PS to six different Shuttle missions:

61-N	Capt. Frank Casserino
DSP	Maj. Charles Jones
Navstar 1/2	Capt. Larry James
KH-11A	Maj. Katherine Roberts
StarLab	Maj. Craiz Puz

Backup payload specialists were also in training at this time, for future flights in the program: Major Daryl Joseph

for 61-N, Captain Randy Odle and Captain David Thompson for Navstar, and Captain Maureen LaComb for StarLab.

Third Cadre

The delays had forced a postponement of the selection of a third MSE cadre from October 1984 to September 1985, and a reduction in the number of new MSEs sought from nine to five. From 160 applicants, these officers were selected:

Capt. Joseph A. Carretto

Capt. Frank M. DeArmond

Capt. Robert B. Crombie

Capt. David P. Staib Jr.

First Lieut. Theresa M. Stevens

They arrived at Space Division to begin training in April 1986.

At the time of the Challenger disaster, five MSEs were assigned to future Shuttle missions. During the 33- month hiatus the Department of Defense shifted some of its critical national security payloads to expendable launch vehicles while senior Air Force officials decided that military payload specialists were an unnecessary luxury on "routine" Shuttle missions. The MSE office was closed in July 1988. By that time, most officers had left the service or been reassigned to other stations.

The policy giving MSEs "priority" on military payload specialist assignments never had full force. In July 1987, two civilian scientists, Dennis L. Boesen and Kenneth P. Bechis were assigned as payload specialist candidates for the Strategic Defense Intiative's Starlab mission. They joined MSEs Craig Puz and Maureen LaComb, who had been training for the mission since 1985.

Ultimately Boesen replaced Puz, so as Shuttle flights resumed, Lacomb was the only MSE with a pending assignment. She, too, lost her chance to fly when StarLab was canceled in September 1990.

Military Observers and Scientists

In addition to MSEs, the Department of Defense had other sources for possible Shuttle payload specialists, including senior Air Force and National Reconnaissance space officials, general officers, geologists, meteorologists, oceanographers, and scientists from the Strategic Defense Initiative.

Air Force Undersecretary Edward "Pete" Aldridge, Hans Mark's successor, was assigned to Shuttle Mission 62-A, the first planned Vandenberg flight, in August 1985. General Lawrence Skantze, head of the Air Force Systems Command, was manifested for a scheduled 1986 Shuttle mission. Both flights were canceled following the Challenger disaster.

Just months prior to Challenger the Department of Defense had finalized plans for a series of Military Man-in-Space missions, flights by special observers that would take advantage of the Shuttle's unique ability to view weather, seas, and geological formations from space.

The MMIS program resulted in large part because of the successful flight of oceanographer Paul D. Scully-Power, a civilian employe of the U.S. Navy. In June 1984 Scully-Power was assigned to the crew of Mission 41-G, spending seven days in orbit in October of that year. Results of his observations drew public praise from Admiral James D. Watkins, the Chief of Naval Operations.

The Air Weather Service of the USAF selected three meteorologists as candidate payload specialists in November 1985:

Maj. Fred P. Lewis

Maj. Grant C. Aufderhaar

Maj. Ronald D. Townsend

Lewis was to have flown aboard Mission 61-M in the summer of 1986. During the post–Challenger hiatus, these three meteorologists were reassigned. In March 1988, two new officers were selected:

Maj. Lloyd L. Anderson Jr.

Maj. Carol L. Belt

Belt (who later married, taking the name Weaver) was assigned as the prime payload specialist and commenced training with Anderson at NASA JSC in May 1988, hoping for a Shuttle mission in 1989. But the weather observer mission remained unscheduled and unflown.

A second oceanographer, Robert E. Stevenson, was to have flown aboard Mission 61-K in late 1986, but that flight was postponed for several years because of the Challenger accident, and Stevenson was removed from the crew.

The Navy had hoped to fly a command, control, and communications specialist in 1986. That mission, too, was canceled.

The Army fared better with two proposed observer missions: Terra Geode, a flight by an Army geologist, and Terra Scout, a flight by an Army intelligence officer.

Terra Scout, managed by the Army Intelligence Center at Fort Huachuca, Arizona, was begun in the summer of 1997, with twenty qualified applicants submitted to an Army Intel board, which selected three payload specialist candidates in September 1988:

Sergeant Third Class Michael E. Belt

Chief Warrant Officer John Hawker

Chief Warrant Officer Thomas J. Hennen

Hennen and Belt were chosen as prime and backup payload specialist in August 1990, and Hennen spent seven days in space aboard STS-44 in November 1991.

In 1992 and 1993 the Army and NASA considered a second Terra Scout flight, especially as the first one had been shortened from its planned ten-day duration by problems aboard the orbiter Atlantis. Hawker and Hennen were the candidates, but the mission was ultimately never approved.

Terra Geode was managed by the Army Engineer School (AES) at Fort Leonard Wood, Missouri. Eight candidates for payload specialist candidates were announced in March 1990. Seven of them were:

Col. Robert H. Clegg

Lieut. Col. Palmer K. Bailey

Lieut. Col. Gary Kratochvil

Capt. Michael E. Hoffpauir

CWO3 Robert L. Pickett

Sgt. 1C Thomas Schroder

Merrill Stevens

An AES board met in June 1990, and selected Bailey as the prime payload specialist with Clegg as his backup. Hoffpauir and Picket were the alternates.

Terra Geode observations were made by NASA astronaut James Adamson (an Army officer) on STS-29 in

August 1989, and by Kathryn Sullivan (a geologist) on STS-30 in April 1990. Based on their experiences, in January 1991 the AES requested a specific mission for Terra Geode. However, the buildup of American armed forces for Operations Desert Shield and Desert Storm at this time drew AES resources away from the program. It also lacked high-ranking support within the Army Space Command, and by 1992 it was effectively dead.

Since the early 1990s, military man-in-space experiments have been conducted by career NASA astronauts.

Commercial Payload Specialists

At the time Shuttle flights were suspended in January 1986, two commercial payload specialists had gone into space. Charles Walker, an engineer employed by McDonnell-Douglas Astronautics, actually made three Shuttle flights, one in 1984 and two in 1985, operating his company's pharmaceutical manufacturing unit. Robert Cenker, a satellite systems engineer from RCA, went into space aboard Mission 61-C in January 1986 for the deployment of the RCA Satcom Ku-1.

A third commercial payload specialist, Gregory Jarvis of Hughes Aircraft, was killed in the Challenger explosion.

Commercial payload specialists were given approximately 160 hours of Shuttle training, much of it in workbooks rather than the familiar simulations. It was assumed that their companies would train them to operate their payloads. During a Shuttle flight they were primarily expected to keep out of the way, something Walker of McDonnell-Douglas managed quite well.

Jarvis was one of four Hughes employees who were selected in July 1984 to accompany Syncom (or Leasat) satellites into space. The others were

L. William Butterworth

Steven L. Cunningham.

John H. Konrad

A second McDonnell Douglas engineer, Robert Wood, was chosen in March 1985 for a future Shuttle flight. In November 1985, American Satellite Communications selected Otto Hoernig for a 1986 Shuttle mission. Wood and Hoernig had not even begun training when launches were suspended. Their flights were ultimately canceled.

Civilians in Space

Throughout the late 1970s and early 1980s a NASA advisory panel, which included the novelist James Michener, considered the criteria for flying a civilian passenger on the Shuttle. Journalists were the first group to be considered, and in 1984, with the encouragement of NASA Administrator James H. Beggs, a selection program was begun.

In August 1984, however, President Ronald Reagan announced that the first "ordinary citizen" observer would be a primary or secondary school teacher. That choice was largely greeted with approval, except by some journalists who had expected that the first ordinary citizen would be one of them.

While the Teacher-in-Space was being selected, however, NASA created a real controversy. In November 1984, then NASA administrator James Beggs invited Utah Senator Jake Garn, chairman of the Senate Committee which oversees NASA's budget, to fly on the Shuttle. Garn, a former Navy pilot, underwent approximately 100 hours of training over the next five months, and went into space aboard Mission 51-D, months ahead of the scheduled flight of the teacher.

Some critics charged that NASA was trying to curry favor with politicans. NASA responded that it had always planned to offer opportunities for passengers, either VIPs or ordinary citizens, to fly. Stung by the criticism, some NASA officials declared that no more politicans would fly in space. But in September 1985, Congressman Bill Nelson (D-Florida), Garn's counterpart in the House of Representatives, received an invitation. He, too, flew before the teacher, in January 1986.

The destruction of the Shuttle Challenger, which killed teacher-observer Christa McAuliffe, forced NASA to reevaluate the selection of all kinds of payload specialists. Although President Reagan, acting NASA administrator Graham, and new NASA administrator Fletcher all stated in the spring of 1986 that flights by observers would continue, on January 12, 1989, NASA administrator Richard Truly announced that crew assignments to Shuttle missions would be limited to NASA astronauts and scientists considered to be essential for mission success. The Teacher and Journalist programs were essentially ended at that point.

Five years later, however, a new NASA administrator, Daniel Goldin, formed another advisory committee to revisit the civilian-in-space issue. The panel was chaired by Alan Ladwig, who had headed the earlier Teacher and Journalist selections. The panel concluded that while all Shuttle crew members need not be qualified as mission specialists, they needed more than the hundred hours of training alloted for some of the pre-Challenger payload specialists.

On January 16, 1998, Goldin announced that former astronaut and retiring U.S. senator John Glenn (D-Ohio) was being assigned as a payload specialist in the crew of STS-95, scheduled for launch in October 1998. This move, widely criticized as a political payoff, was actually a response to a two-year-old proposal by Glenn to study the effects of spaceflight on a fit but elderly subject. (Glenn was 77 years old at the time of launch.)

At the same time Goldin announced that Teacher-in-Space backup Barbara Morgan was to be selected as a NASA astronaut candidate with the March 1998 group. She would become a full-fledged member of the astronaut office with the title of "educator-mission specialist", and would have educational duties in addition to a role on International Space Station missions.

X-15 PILOTS

The X-15 was a rocket-powered aircraft built by North American Aviation for joint NASA, Air Force, and Navy research into flight at high speeds and altitudes. On 199 flights between June 1959 and October 1968 the X-15 ultimate achieved a top speed of 4,520 miles per hour (Mach 6.7) and an altitude of 354,200 (66.8 miles).

Fourteen pilots were directly involved with the X-15, although only 12 actually flew the vehicles (there were three). There was no formal selection process, since everyone chosen was already a qualified test pilot.

For example, Scott Crossfield and Alvin White were the prime and backup North American Aviation test pilots and became involved with project first. Air Force captains Iven Kincheloe (prime pilot) and Robert White (backup) were assigned to the X-15 in 1957. When Kincheloe was killed in an accident before flying the rocket plane, White became the prime Air Force pilot and Captain Robert Rushworth become his backup. The first NASA pilots were Joseph Walker and Neil Armstrong. Lieutenant Commander Forrest Peterson represented the Navy.

Walker and Armstrong were eventually replaced by NASA pilots Jack McKay (1960), Milton Thompson (1963), and Bill Dana (1965). White and Rushworth were succeeded by Captain Joe Engle (1963), Captain Pete Knight (1964), and Major Michael Adams (1966). The Navy selected Lieutenant Lloyd Hoover as Peterson's replacement, but Hoover never trained or flew.

The X-15 was not considered a spacecraft by its designers, though it operated at an altitude where conditions were little different from those encountered by orbiting vehicles. By the early 1960s, however, the Air Force had decided that flights of over 50 miles were spaceflights and created a special Astronaut Rating to honor those who did. And the Federation Astronautique Internationale (FAI), the international record-keeping body, recognizes flights of over 100 kilometers or 62 miles as spaceflights.

Thirteen different X-15 flights, by Walker, White, Rushworth, Engle, McKay, Dana, Knight, and Adams, qualified, according to the Air Force, though only White, Rushworth, Engle, Knight, and Adams received astronaut wings. Civilians Walker, McKay, and Dana were not eligible. Two X-15 flights by Joe Walker qualified by FAI rules.

X-15 SPACEFLIGHTS

DATE	PILOT	ALTITUDE	VEHICLE
July 17, 1962	R.White	59.16 miles	#3
Jan. 17, 1963	Walker	51 miles	#3
June 27, 1963	Rushworth	55 miles	#3
July 19, 1963	Walker	65.3 miles	#3
Aug. 22, 1963	Walker	66.75 miles	#3
June 29, 1965	Engle	53.14 miles	#3
Aug. 10, 1965	Engle	51.7 miles	#3
Sept. 28, 1965	McKay	56 miles	#3
Oct. 14, 1965	Engle	50.17 miles	#1
Nov. 1, 1966	Dana	58 miles	#3
Oct. 17, 1967	Knight	53.4 miles	#3
Nov. 15, 1967	Adams	50.4 miles	#3*
Aug. 21, 1968	Dana	50.7 miles	#1

*Pilot killed

X-20 DYNA-SOAR PILOTS

In November 1959, following three years of feasibility studies, the Air Force selected Boeing Aircraft as the prime contractor for a manned glider that would be launched into orbit by a Titan rocket, returning to Earth at Edwards AFB, California. Known informally as Dyna-Soar (a contraction of "dynamic soaring), the spaceplane was officially known as the X-20.

Three months earlier, ten test pilots at Edwards AFB—three NASA civilians and seven Air Force officers—had been given medical examinations to qualify them as possible X-20 pilots. Seven men were selected in secret in April 1960, to train for suborbital flights then scheduled to begin within four years:

NASA test pilot Neil A. Armstrong

NASA test pilot William H. Dana

Air Force Capt. Henry C. Gordon

Air Force Capt. William J "Pete" Knight

Air Force Capt. Russell L. Rogers

NASA test pilot Milton O. Thompson

Air Force Maj. James W. Wood

Dana and Armstrong left the X-20 program in the summer of 1962; only one pilot, Air Force captain Albert H. Crews Jr., was named to replace them. Crews, Gordon, Knight, Rogers, Thompson, and Wood were the six X-20 pilots publicly announced by the Air Force on September 19, 1962.

The pilots trained at Edwards AFB, California, at Boeing in Seattle, Washington, and at Wright-Patterson AFB, Ohio, until December 1963, when the X-20 was canceled in favor of a new Air Force space program, the Manned Orbiting Laboratory.

A winged spacecraft would not fly in space until the launch of the Shuttle Columbia in April 1981.

MANNED ORBITING
LABORATORY PILOTS

The Air Force's second venture into manned spaceflight was the Manned Orbiting Laboratory, better known as MOL. Developed beginning in 1963, and announced in August 1965, MOL was a proposed series of five or more two-man flights in polar orbit, to begin in late 1968. Air Force astronauts would use surplus Gemini spacecraft (called Gemini-B or Blue Gemini) attached to a new, cylindrical laboratory, with the whole complex launched aboard a Titan III rocket from Vandenberg Air Force Base in California. The missions, which were to last up to 30 days, were to involve military reconnaissance with the KH-10 imaging system.

The Air Force announced that it would select and train 20 astronauts, designated "aerospace research pilots." Qualifications for MOL required that each man had to be

a qualified military pilot

a graduate of the Aerospace Research Pilot School

a serving military officer recommended by a commanding officer

a U.S. citizen by birth

Eight men were announced on November 12, 1965

Air Force Maj. Michael J. Adams

Air Force Maj. Albert H. Crews Jr.

Navy Lieut. John L. Finley

Air Force Capt. Richard E. Lawyer

Air Force Capt. Lachlan Macleay

Air Force Capt. Francis Gregory Neubeck

Air Force Maj. James M. Taylor

Navy Lieut. Richard H. Truly

None would go into space aboard MOL-Gemini, but Adams would qualify as an astronaut on the X-15 rocket plane while Truly would make two flights aboard the NASA Space Shuttle.

Another MOL pilot from this group, Albert Crews, joined NASA as a research pilot in 1969.

A second group of five followed on June 30, 1966

Air Force Capt. Karol J. Bobko

Navy Lieut. Robert L. Crippen

Air Force Capt. Charles G. Fullerton

Air Force Capt. Henry W. Hartsfield Jr.

Marine Capt. Robert F. Overmyer.

The members of this group would all eventually fly in space—as NASA astronauts.

A third and final group of four was announced on June 30, 1967

Air Force Maj. James A. Abrahamson

Air Force Lieut. Col. Robert T. Herres

Air Force Maj. Robert H. Lawrence Jr.

Air Force Maj. Donald H. Peterson

Peterson would fly in space as a NASA astronaut. Lawrence would be killed in a training accident.

Lawrence was the only African American chosen for any kind of astronaut training until 1978.

Budgetary problems (made worse by the costs of the Vietnam War) eventually cut the number of planned flights to four and postponed the first manned mission until 1972. (One unmanned test of a MOL/Gemini-B took place in November 1966.) When it became apparent to the Air Force that MOL would essentially be duplicating the effort of the NASA Skylab program, and that unmanned reconnaissance satellites had developed to the point where manned presence in space was unnecessary, MOL was canceled in June 1969.

The selection of a fourth group of MOL pilots, then in progress, was also canceled.

SELECTING THE APOLLO 11 CREW

From Deke!, The Autobiography of Deke Slayton

The guys who were the Apollo program managers—first Joe Shea, then George Low—had always felt that crews should be handpicked for specific missions. I had disagreed with this on the principle that the specifics of the mission kept changing frequently, and so far I had won the argument. My operating rule was to have a pool of guys trained so that anyone could handle anything, and then make selections based on that.

With the success of Apollo Eight, it was time to name the Apollo Eleven crew. On the planning charts this might very well turn out to be the first manned lunar landing. But no one knew for sure. The LM was still a couple of months away from a test flight. There was the Apollo Ten lunar orbit mission, too. Some people were thinking that if Nine went well, we should skip the F mission [rendezvous and docking tests of the lunar module in lunar orbit] and have the Ten crew make the landing.

So it wasn't just a cut and dried decision as to who should make the first steps on the Moon. If I had had to select on that basis, my first choice would have been Gus Grissom, which both Chris Kraft and Bob Gilruth seconded. With Gus dead, the most likely candidates were Frank Borman and Jim McDivitt. I had full confidence in Tom Stafford, Neil Armstrong and Pete Conrad, too. The system had put them in the right place at the right time. Any one of them might very well make the first landing.

Jim McDivitt was still tied up with the LM flight, but here I had Frank and his whole crew available, and given that they had already made a lunar orbit flight, of all the astronauts they were clearly in the best position to train up on the landing procedures.

There were two other things to keep in mind. Frank had been away from home pretty steadily for almost two years. He was tired of the grind and not happy about what it had done to his family life. He had already told me he was ready to move on.

Finally, there was no guarantee that Eleven would turn out to be the landing. So I figured my best choice was to stick to the rotation and assign Neil Armstrong's [Apollo Eight backup] crew. I made one change, however: Mike Collins was available and had lost out on the lunar orbit mission. He deserved the first available mission, which happened to be Eleven.

The crew had Fred Haise, from the 1966 group, assigned as lunar module pilot. Fred was very capable—one of the best people in his group—but he hadn't been in my plans from the beginning and wasn't part of the eighteen guys I promised the landing to.

Further, Buzz Aldrin had already trained as a lunar module pilot for several months prior to the Apollo Eight-Apollo Nine swap. So the crew became Neil Armstrong, commander, Mike Collins, CMP, and Buzz Aldrin, LMP. The backup crew would be Jim Lovell, Bill Anders and Fred Haise.

Later on people would talk about this process as if it were some kind of science. Or as if politics had controlled it—the fact that Neil was a civilian. All I can say is that a lot of factors, most of them beyond anybody's control, put these three guys in the right place at the right time. The first person to walk on the Moon might just as easily have been Tom Stafford, an Air Force officer, or Pete Conrad from the Navy.

I called Neil, Mike and Buzz into my office on Monday, January 6, 1969, and told them, "You're it."

THE END OF SOYUZ-1

From *The Diaries of Nikolai Kamanin*, April 25, 1967

(Lieutenant General Nikolai Kamanin was the deputy commander of the Soviet air forces
in charge of cosmonaut training from 1960 to 1971.)

As we were coming in for landing in Orsk, I thought that I would meet Komarov at the airfield. More than two hours had elapsed between the landing of Soyuz-1 (6:24 A.M.) and our Il-18 (8:25 A.M.). I carefully looked for signs of life at the airfield, but saw none. Anxiety crept into my heart. When the plane had turned off its engines, a bus came into our direction with several officers and the district's Deputy Air Force Commander, General Avtonomov. Avtonomov reported: "The Soyuz-1 spaceship landed at 6:24 sixty-five kilometers east of Orsk. The ship is on fire, the cosmonaut has not been found."

Hopes of seeing Komarov alive faded. To me it was clear that the cosmonaut had perished, but somewhere deep in my soul there was still a glimmer of hope. Then the district's Air Force Commander, Lieutenant-General of Aviation Tserdik,

came to us. He reported that a telephone message had just been received from a unit of the [Strategic] Rocket Forces, situated 20 kilometers from the Soyuz-1 landing spot, in which it was claimed that the cosmonaut had been wounded and hospitalized in the settlement of Karabutak 3 kilometers from the landing site. General Tserdik added that he had personally forwarded this information to Moscow.

We had to fly to the place of the accident as soon as possible. As I boarded the helicopter (I took with me General Voitenko and KGB representative Lieutenant-Colonel Obelchak), I was told that [Minister Dmitri] Ustinov had ordered me to urgently call to Moscow. However, I had nothing to report to the leadership, because we had to find out for ourselves what the situation at the landing site was like. I gave the order to take off. Ten minutes later the navigator passed on a radio telegram: "Marshal Vershinin has ordered you to immediately return to the airfield and call Ustinov." I ordered the pilots to continue the flight to the landing spot of Soyuz-1. I was well aware that the State Commission and the high leadership in Moscow were concerned and very nervous, not having clear information about the fate of the cosmonaut, but I could only be useful to them after having been at the landing site, which is why I continued our flight.

We were supposed to be at the landing site after 25 to 30 minutes, but after 35 minutes we were still flying. I called the navigator and asked him : "How much further is it?".

"Another forty minutes", he answered.

I took the navigator's map and saw that we were not flying to the landing spot of Soyuz-1, but to a point 165 kilomters from Orsk. "Who gave you this spot?" I asked the navigator.

"The command post of the Orsk airfield," he replied. I ordered the commander of the helicopter to gain altitude and get in touch with the command post to clarify where Soyuz-1 had landed and fly there. At that moment I felt burning shame for the search and rescue service of the Air Force. I knew that General Kutasin has been doing a bad job commanding this service, but it hadn't even occurred to me that helicopter pilots and the search and rescue command posts are so badly prepared that they are capable of getting lost in clear weather 100 kilometers from Orsk. Somewhat later, in the evening, we made the same helicopter flight with Marshal Rudenko. In short, every single minute was valuable to me, but still it took not 25 minutes, but one hour and 25 minutes to take me to the landing spot.

When we landed the ship was still burning. Present at the landing site were a search team headed by Lieutenant-Colonel Lapochkin, a group from Academician G.I. Petrov and many local inhabitants. No trace of the cosmonaut had been found amidst the ship's wreckage. The local inhabitants said that the ship had come down at high speed, the parachute was turning around and had not inflated. At the moment of the landing there had been several explosions and a fire had begun. Nobody had seen the cosmonaut. The local inhabitants had tried to quench the fire by throwing a thick layer of dirt onto the ship.

A quick inspection of the ship convinced me that Komarov had died and was somewhere in the wreckage of the ship, which was still burning. I gave an order to remove the dirt from the ship and look for the body of the cosmonaut. At the same time I sent General Tserdik (by helicopter) and Lieutenant-Colonel Obelchak (by car) to the hospital of the nearest settlement to check out the story about the cosmonaut having been wounded. After digging for an hour we discovered Komarov's remains amidst the ship's wreckage. At first it was difficult to tell where the head, the arms and the legs were. Apparently, Komarov had died at the moment of impact and the fire had turned his body into a small burnt and blackened lump measuring 30 by 80 centimeters.

I immediately flew back to Orsk and called Ustinov and then Vershinin. My report was short: "I was at the landing site, cosmonaut Komarov has died, the ship has burnt down. The ship's main parachute did not deploy and the back-up parachute did not fill with air. The ship hit the ground with a speed of 35 to 40 meters per second, after the impact there was an explosion of the braking engines and a fire began. We could not report about the cosmonaut's fate earlier because no one had seen him and the ship was covered with dirt to quench the fire. Only after digging the body of Komarov was discovered."

After talking to Moscow I once again flew to the place of the accident. I ordered General Karpov and a group of doctors to remove Komarov's body from the ship's wreckage and send it to Orsk. I took all necessary measures to leave the bits and pieces of the ship undisturbed and categorically forbade anyone to change their position.

Three hours later Keldysh, Tyulin, Rudenko and other members of the State Commission arrived at the place of the accident. Somewhat later Gagarin arrived from Yevpatoria.

At 21:45 Moscow time a battalion of academy students was formed up at the airfield of Orsk to bid farewell to V.M. Komarov. We walked by the stunned students carrying the coffin with Komarov's body and loaded it into the Il-18 airplane.

PRIVATE
ASTRONAUTS

For almost forty years all humans who traveled in space, no matter what their country of origin, did so on vehicles originally designed, built, and operated by government agencies—NASA in the United States, the Ministry of General Machine-Building in the Soviet Union and Russia.

Sometime in the early years of the twenty-first century a new force will enter the business of human spaceflight—commercial or private enterprises that will construct and launch their own vehicles to carry the first truly "civilian" or private astronauts.

The idea has its roots in much of the classic science fiction published in the 1940s, perhaps best displayed in the feature film *Destination Moon* (1950).

In the 1980s, Robert H. Truax, a former missile designer for the U.S. Navy and early head of the SAMOS spy satellite program, proposed to build what he called the X-3 "Volksrocket" capable of lofting a private astronaut on a suborbital trajectory. (Truax had previously built the X-2 Skycyle for professional daredevil Evel Knievel's attempt to leap the Grand Canyon on September 8, 1974.)

Based in Saratoga, California, Truax built his X-rockets out of spare parts, which required thousands of dollars, if not the millions a military or NASA rocket would have cost. So the passenger's seat in the X-3 was for sale, price $100,000. Early candidates included Martin Yahn, Jenna Yeager (who later joined Burt Rutan on the nonstop round-the-world flight of Voyager in 1987), and Dan Correa. Ultimately Truax settled on Fell Peters, an artist

from San Francisco, as his first astronaut. However, Truax was never able to get the funding to build a Volksrocket.

Private companies did enter the space launch business, from giants like McDonnell Douglas, Martin-Marietta, and General Dynamics marketing their classic ballistic missile-derived launchers Delta, Titan, and Atlas, to smaller operations like Orbital Services, which found a niche market with its Pegasus and Taurus vehicles. Other companies, such as Space Services (once headed by former astronaut Deke Slayton) failed, while some, such as Kistler (whose principals include George Mueller, former head of manned space flight for NASA during Gemini and Apollo, and former astronaut Dan Brandenstein), seem poised for success.

But neither the giants nor the niche companies pursued a manned capability. That only came with the creation of creation of the X-Prize.

The X-Prize

From the early 1900s through the 1930s, progress in aviation was stimulated by dozens of prizes, including the Orteig Prize for the first nonstop flight from New York to Paris, won by Charles Lindbergh in 1927.

Inspired by this history—especially Lindbergh's flight—a young aerospace engineer and manager named Peter H. Diamondis announced the creation of the X-Prize in May 1996. The goal of the X-Prize is to advance private access to space. Ten million dollars, to be raised from private contributors, entrance fees, and user fees from an X-Prize credit card, would be awarded to the first team successfully to loft a crew of 3 to an altitude of 62 miles (100 kilometers), return them to Earth, and then repeat the process within two weeks.

Members of the X-Prize team included former Shuttle payload specialist Byron K. Lichtenberg, movie producer (*The Blues Brothers* and others) Robert K. Weiss, and Erik Lindbergh, grandson of Charles Lindbergh. Contributors to the prize included novelist Tom Clancy.

By May 1998, fourteen teams had entered the competition:

Scaled Composites of Mojave, California. Headed by aircraft designer Burt Rutan, whose Voyager aircraft won the Collier Trophy for its nonstop round-the-world flight in 1987, Scaled Composites proposed the Proteus air-launched vehicle.

Pioneer Rocketplane of Lakewood, Colorado. Headed by Robert Zubrin, a former Martin-Marietta engineer and author of *Mars Direct*, Pioneer proposed the air-refueled Pathfinder spaceplane.

AeroAstro LLC of Herndon, Virginia, headed by Dr. Rick Fleeter, proposed a more conventional rocket launcher called the PA-X2.

Advent Launch Services of Houston, Texas, under James Akkerman, not only proposed a large rocket called Advent, it sold seats to members of its "Civilian Astronaut Corps." See the entry on Space Tourism, below.

The Discraft Company of Portland, Oregon, headed by John Bloomer, proposed a radical saucerlike vehicle called the Space Tourist.

Mickey L. Badgero, an active duty officer with the USAF, proposed to win the prize by using his Lucky Seven rocket.

Another entry came from William Good of Earth Space Transport Systems.

David Ashford of Bristol (England) Spaceplanes proposed the Ascender air-space plane.

The Gauchito rocket was proposed by Pablo De Leon & Associates of Buenos Aires, Argentina.

Dynamica Research of Houston, Texas, under Dr. Norman LaFave, planned to win the prize with its Cosmos Mariner air-space plane.

Len Cormier of the Washington, D.C.-based Pan Aero, proposed the X-Van, a vehicle that takes off like a rocket but lands like an airplane.

The Star-Chaser Foundation, based in Britain and headed by Steven M. Bennett, proposed the Thunderbird, a jet-powered vertical takeoff craft.

A third British entrant, Dr. Graham Dorrington, hoped to win with his Green Arrow rocket concept.

Michael Kelly of Kelly Space and Technology, San Bernardino, California, proposed a unique system in which its Eclipse Astroliner is towed to a high altitude by another aircraft, firing rocket engines at that point.

In addition to the formal entrants for the X-Prize, Rotary Rocket, a company based in Redwood City, California, and headed by Gary Hudson, is reported to be considering a manned version of its Roton space vehicle.

Space Tourism

For years the Hayden Planetarium in New York City jokingly allowed visitors—most of them school children—to register as passengers for future commercial flights to the Moon. In 1968, following the success of the movie *2001: A Space Odyssey*, which featured a space shuttle operated by Pan American, that company offered to take deposits for future trips to orbit. These gestures were public relations gimmicks, however, not serious steps toward space tourism.

But in 1986 Society Expeditions, a company based in Seattle, Washington, actually began taking reservations for suborbital tourist flights. Headed by T. C. Swartz, Society Expeditions originally approached NASA about the construction of a module for the Space Shuttle that, carried in the orbiter's payload bay, would allow as many as 74 passengers to ride into space. NASA declined to consider such a venture, and in September 1984 Swartz made a deal with Gary Hudson and his Pacific American Launch Systems for the development of a passenger-carrying suborbital vehicle called the Phoenix.

While Swartz and Hudson searched for funding, Society Expeditions accepted $5,000 deposits (against an expected ticket price of $50,000 or more), ultimately receiving 500 deposits.

Project Space Voyage was scheduled for launch on the 500th anniversary of Columbus's arrival in America, October 12, 1992. Like so many NASA, military and commercial space ventures, the Society Expeditions plan was shelved because of the Challenger disaster in January of that year. All of the deposits were returned.

But in September 1997, Zegrahm Space Voyages of Seattle started a similar space tourist program. Zegrahm envisons a suborbital launch system consisting of a Sky Lifter mother ship, which takes off from a runway like an aircraft, releasing a six-passenger Space Cruiser at an altitude of 50,000 feet. The Space Cruiser will then use a combination of jet and rocket engines to soar to 62 miles before falling back and landing at a runway.

Priced at $98,000, the Zegrahm Space Voyage is a seven-day package of training and lectures, with meals and hotel included, culminating in a 2.5 hour flight.

The Sky Lifter, whose development is managed by Vela Technologies of Washington State, is to be built by AeroAstro LLC, one of the entrants in the X Prize, beginning in 1999. The first commercial launch is set for December 1, 2001.

A more economical space tour is offered by the Civilian Astronaut Corps, founded in Houston, Texas, by businessman Harry Dace and former NASA propulsion engineer Jim Akkerman. Priced at less than a tenth of Zegrahm's—the CAC started at $3,500 per passenger, but raised prices in July 1998—the CAC's mission uses an Advent rocket plane (here named Mayflower), designed to be launched from and land in the Gulf of Mexico off Galveston. The 70-foot vehicle will be launched twice a day, at sunrise and sunset, on 15-minute flights. (CAC requires two thousand members in order to proceed with its schedule of 340 flights.)

The CAC has announced plans to launch its first flight on July 4, 1999, with former airline captain Vaughn Cordle as pilot. Through May 1998, CAC had booked five flights and had a waiting list:

Flight Members of the Civilian Astronaut Corps Mayflower Expedition

All flights piloted by Captain Vaughn Cordle

Flight #1

1. Donald G. Jones, Fond du Lac, Wisconsin
2. Mark D. Young, Montrose, California
3. Tony Hermes, Houston, Texas
4. Arthur W. Thomas, Bellingham, Washington
5. NAME WITHHELD, Brentwood, Tennessee
6. Vic Economy, Atlanta, Georgia

Flight #2

1. Erin R. Medlicott, Fort Lee, New Jersey
2. Ronald Tumoszwisz, Okechobee, Florida
3. John Kowal, Livonia, Michigan
4. Shirley Ulrich, Minneapolis, Minnesota
5. David E. Peterson, Montrose, Pennsylvania
6. David Lister, Ontario, Canada

Flight #3

1. Karen L. Roberts, Sacramento, California
2. Richard D. Lieb, Uniontown, Pennsylvania
3. Jim Yednock, Deforest, Wisconsin
4. Sarwar Alam Khan, Houston, Texas
5. Reed J. Robinson, Skiatook, Oklahoma
6. NAME WITHHELD, New Jersey

Flight #4

1. Joseph L. Warnock, Independence, Kansas
2. Peter John Newman, Grimsby, England
3. Ronald K. Weir, Gray, Tennessee
4. Race Cargile, Singapore
5. David Kiah, Newton, Massachusetts
6. Dr. John Rozario, Singapore

Flight #5

1. Robert C. Barta, Hobart, Indiana
2. Tam Agosti-Gisler, Anchorage, Alaska
3. David Bliss, Riverside, California
4. Gwen Hendrickson, Anchorage, Alaska
5. open
6. open

Flight #50

1. Michael Martin Smith, Hull, England
2. WINNER OF 1998 INTERNATIONAL SPACE DEVELOPMENT CONFERENCE DRAWING
3. WINNER OF BAYWAY LINCOLN MERCURY DRAWING
4. Tony Hodgson, Houston, Texas
5. Dale Brown, San Leon, Texas
6. open

To be assigned

1. Dennis L. Pearson, Allentown, Pennsylvania
2. Rev. K. D. Baldridge, Newark, Delaware
3. Douglas Duncan, Santa Barbara, California
4. Bill M. Ambrisco, Mountain View, California
5. Phillip T. Krajecki, Alexandria, Virginia
6. Vernon P. Wagner, Seal Beach, California

Interglobal Space Lines of Jackson, Wyoming, has offered one-hour zero-G flights over the Mojave Desert since 1992, price $2,000. Company president Rand Simberg stated in December 1997 that Interglobal would move into space tourism once vehicles had proved themselves.

Which points up one of the major problems of all space tourism proposals: construction and certification of a launch vehicle. United States law gives the Federal Aviation Administration authority over the design and certification for all vehicles operating in U.S. airspace—from zero to 60,000 feet above mean sea level. Authority over vehicles operating above 60,000 feet is not clear. (In 1995 the Office of Commercial Space Transportation was moved from the Department of Transporation to the F.A.A., resulting in a wealth of contradictory policies that have yet to be conformed.)

Until the certification issue is resolved, another potential show-stopper waits in limbo—insurance for the vehicle and its passengers, and liability for the operator, should an errant space tourist craft cause property damage.

What is certain is that at some point in the next few years the commercial need for faster transportation to any point on the globe will help drive the development of cheaper manned access to space. In response to critics who claimed, "As railroad people said about airplanes in 1910," that "Grandma will never fly that way," Pioneer rocketplane designer Robert Zubrin noted, "If a spaceship can get Grandma from New York to Sydney in one hour, she'll go."

ASTRONAUT BIOGRAPHIES

Abrahamson, James Alan

1933–

James Abrahamson trained for two years as a potential military astronaut in the Air Force's Manned Orbiting Laboratory only to see that program canceled in May 1969 before any flights could be made.

Nevertheless, Abrahamson went on to become one of the most important figures in both civilian and military space programs, serving from 1981 to 1984 as NASA associate administrator for Space Transportation Systems—in effect, the man in charge of the Space Shuttle during its difficult orbital flight tests and first operational flights.

He later served as head of the Strategic Defense Initiative Organization (SDIO), also known as the "Star Wars" program.

Abrahamson was born May 19, 1933, in Williston, North Dakota, and grew up in Inglewood, California. He attended the Masschusetts Institute of Technology, receiving a B.S. in aeronautical engineering in 1955, and the University of Oklahoma, where he earned an M.S. in aerospace engineering (1961).

Entering active duty with the Air Force in 1955, Abrahamson underwent pilot training, then served as an instructor at Bryan AFB, Texas, until 1959. After completing graduate work at Oklahoma, he spent three years at the Air Force Space Systems Division in Los Angeles as a systems project officer on the Vela nuclear detection satellite. He did a tour as a combat pilot in Vietnam, then attended the Air Force Aerospace Research Pilot School at Edwards AFB, graduating in 1967.

Abrahamson was one of the 4 pilots assigned to MOL in June 1967. When that program was canceled in May 1969, Abrahamson, who was five months too old to transfer to NASA as an astronaut, was assigned to be a staff member of the National Aeronautics and Space Council. When the Council was dissolved in 1971, he became director of the Maverick missile program, commander of the 495th Test Wing at Wright-Patterson AFB, Ohio, and, from 1974 to 1976, inspector general for the Air Force Systems Command. He later supervised the development of the F-16 fighter.

Abrahamson retired from the Air Force in February 1989 with the rank of lieutenant general, becoming executive vice president for corporate development for Hughes Aircraft, El Segundo, California, a job he held until 1992. He then became chairman of the Oracle Corporation in Redwood Shores, California. Since 1995 he has served as commissioner of the White House Commission on Aviation Safety and Security.

Acton, Loren Wilbur
1936–

Physicist Loren Acton spent nine days in space aboard Spacelab 2 in July and August 1985. The flight, Shuttle Mission 51-F, overcame a launchpad abort and several equipment failures before producing a record amount of data on the sun.

Acton was one of 4 astronomers aboard Mission 51-F who conducted 13 different experiments, including operation of a solar optical telescope, which in just three days of operation returned more images of the sun than did telescopes aboard Skylab in 171 days of operation in 1973–4.

Acton was born March 7, 1936, in Lewistown, Montana. He received a B.S. in engineering physics from Montana State University in 1959 and a Ph.D. in astrophysics from the University of Colorado in 1965. He was a senior staff scientist with Lockheed's Space Sciences Laboratory in Palo Alto, California, when selected as a Spacelab 2 payload specialist in April 1978.

Following his Shuttle flight Acton remained with Lockheed, serving as one of the principal investigators for the Soft X-Ray Telescope experiment launched aboard the Japanese Solar-A spacecraft in August 1991. In 1993 he left Lockheed to become a research professor in the physics department of Montana State University.

Adams, Michael James
1930–1967

Air Force test pilot Mike Adams left the Manned Orbiting Laboratory program to fly the X-15 rocket plane. On November 15, 1967, on his seventh X-15 flight, Adams pushed the aircraft to an altitude of 266,000 feet, 50.4 statute miles, where it went off course and ultimately broke apart. Adams was killed, the only direct fatality of the X-15 program.

Adams was born May 5, 1930, in Sacramento, California. He graduated from Sacramento Junior College in 1950 and joined the Air Force. Following flight training he

flew 49 combat missions in Korea as an F-86 pilot. He later served at bases in Louisiana and France before returning to school to complete his education, earning a bachelor of science degree in aeronautical engineering from the University of Oklahoma at Norman (1958). He later did eighteen months of graduate work at the Massachusetts Institute of Technology.

Adams attended the Air Force Test Pilot School at Edwards AFB in 1962 (earning the Honts Trophy as outstanding student) and the Aerospace Research Pilot School in 1963. His commander at ARPS, Colonel Chuck Yeager, described him as a pilot "good enough to name his own assignment, NASA or Air Force." He chose to remain with the Air Force and was selected as one of the first 8 pilots for the Manned Orbiting Laboratory program in November 1965. He left MOL for the X-15 program on July 20, 1966.

On his fatal flight Adams qualified for the USAF Astronaut Rating, given to pilots who reach altitudes greater than 50 statute miles.

Adamson, James Craig
1946–

Army pilot Jim Adamson was a mission specialist aboard STS-28 in August 1989. During this 5-day flight of the orbiter Columbia, Adamson and four fellow astronauts deployed an advanced communications satellite designed to relay data from the Crystal imaging reconnaissance platforms to stations on Earth. The crew also deployed a small Strategic Defense Initiative satellite.

Adamson later served as a mission specialist aboard STS-43 in August 1991. A Tracking and Data Relay Satellite was deployed from the orbit Atlantis during this 9-day mission.

Adamson was born March 3, 1946, in Warsaw, New York, and grew up in Monarch, Montana. He graduated from high school in Geneseo, New York, in 1964, then attended the United States Military Academy at West Point, becoming a two-time All-American in pistol shooting and receiving a B.S. in engineering (1969). He later earned an M.S. in aerospace engineering from Princeton University in 1977.

As an Army officer Adamson served in a Nike Hercules missile battery based in West Germany from 1969 to 1971, then became an Army aviator flying in the Air Cavalry in Vietnam. Returning to the United States, he studied at Princeton, and after completing his degree he became an assistant professor of aerodynamics at West Point. In 1980 he graduated from the U.S. Naval Test Pilot School at Patuxent River, Maryland, and was then detailed to the NASA Johnson Space Center.

At JSC Adamson worked in mission control as an aerodynamics officer and as a guidance navigation and control officer supporting Shuttle missions from STS-1 (1981) through 41-C (1984). He also served as a research pilot for the JSC aircraft operations division.

Adamson was selected as an astronaut candidate by NASA in May 1984 and qualified as a Shuttle mission specialist the following June. In December 1985 he was assigned to Shuttle Mission 61-N, a Department of Defense mission then scheduled for the fall of 1986. That flight was delayed for three years, eventually becoming STS-28. During the hiatus caused by the Challenger disaster, Adamson worked in the National STS Program Office.

In 1990 and 1991 he also served as director of Shuttle processing operations at the NASA Kennedy Space Center.

He resigned from NASA and retired from the Army in August 1992 to become a consultant. In September 1994 he joined the Lockheed Engineering and Sciences Corporation in Houston, Texas, as executive vice president. He is currently chief operating officer for United Space Alliance, the joint Lockheed-Martin and Boeing company that operates the Shuttle.

Akers, Thomas Dale

1950–

Air Force flight test engineer Tom Akers made four Shuttle missions including two in which he performed EVAs repairing or retrieving spacecraft.

His first EVAs occurred during STS-49, the maiden voyage of the orbiter Endeavour in May 1992. Akers had been scheduled to test space station construction techniques in an EVA with astronaut Kathy Thornton. But when fellow space walkers Pierre Thuot and Rick Hieb failed in two attempts to capture the errant Intelsat VI satellite, Akers joined them in an unrehearsed and unprecedented three-man EVA, in which the astronauts literally grabbed and held the spinning two-ton spacecraft until the Shuttle's robot arm could be locked to it.

The risky maneuver succeeded, and Intelsat was eventually redeployed in its proper orbit. Akers later teamed with Kathy Thornton for their planned EVA.

In December 1993 Akers was one of 4 EVA astronauts who successfully repaired the Hubble Space Telescope during STS-61. Teamed again with Thornton, Akers brought his total EVA time to almost thirty hours.

Akers had previously served as mission specialist in the crew of STS-41, a flight of the orbiter Atlantis in October 1990. During this mission the Ulysses space probe was successfuly sent on its four-year journey toward Jupiter, then into orbit around the poles of the sun. Akers and four fellow astronauts went on to conduct a number of materials processing experiments and tests with the Shuttle remote manipulator arm during the 4-day mission.

His fourth mission was STS-79 in September 1996. This flight of the orbiter Atlantis made the fourth Shuttle visit to the Mir space station, returning NASA-Mir crew member Shannon Lucid to Earth and leaving John Blaha aboard Mir in her place.

Akers was born May 20, 1951, in St. Louis, Missouri, and grew up in nearby Eminence, where he graduated from high school in 1969. He attended the University of Missouri at Rolla, receiving a B.S. (1973) and an M.S. (1975) in applied mathematics in 1973.

While he was a college student Akers spent his summers working as a national park ranger at Alley Springs, Missouri. After graduation from Rolla, he became the principal of his hometown high school in Eminence.

He joined the Air Force in 1979 and upon completion of officer training school, was assigned to the 4484th Fighter Weapons Squadron at Eglin AFB, Florida, as a data analyst working with air-to-air missiles. In 1982 he was selected to attend the Air Force Test Pilot School at Edwards AFB, California, where he completed the flight test engineer course. He returned to Eglin in 1983 and was assigned to the Armaments Division, where he worked on weapons development and also flew F-4 and T-38 aircraft with the 3247th Test Squadron. At the time of his selection by NASA he was executive officer to the Armament Division's Deputy Commander for Research, Development and Acquisition.

Akers was one of the 13 astronauts selected by NASA in June 1987. In August 1988 he qualified as a mission specialist. In his first technical assignment Akers worked on the development of computer software and hardware for the Space Shuttle. In September 1989 he was assigned as mission specialist for STS-41. In early 1991 he served with the astronaut support group at the NASA Kennedy Space Center and following STS-49 (1992) was the astronaut office lead for EVA.

In 1994–95 Akers was deputy director of the JSC's mission operations directorate, overseeing the work of training teams and flight directors, and following STS-79 he returned to management as assistant director (technical) for JSC.

Akers left NASA in July 1997 to become commandant of the Air Force ROTC unit at his alma mater, the University of Missouri at Rolla.

Aldridge, Edward Cleveland "Pete," Jr.

1938–

Air Force Undersecretary Pete Aldridge was assigned as a payload specialist for Shuttle Mission 62-A, the first intended to be launched into polar orbit from Vandenberg Air Force Base, California. The scheduled July 1986 launch, already postponed several times, was finally canceled because of the Challenger disaster on January 28, 1986.

As undersecretary Aldridge was head of all Air Force space programs and served as the director of the then-secret National Reconnaissance Office, the organization that oversees the design, development, and operation of CIA, NSA, and other space systems. In 1984, fearful of DOD and NRO reliance on the often unreliable Shuttle, Aldridge won approval for the purchase of ten new Titan expendable launch vehicles. This decision, unpopular at NASA, made it possible for military launches to continue during the long hiatus following the Challenger accident

and led to the removal of most DOD and NRO payloads from the Shuttle by 1991.

Aldridge was born August 18, 1938, in Houston, Texas, and grew up in Shreveport, Louisiana. He attended Texas A&M University, receiving a B.S. in aeronautical engineering in 1960, and earned an M.S. in aeronautical engineering (1962) from the Georgia Institute of Technology.

From 1962 to 1967 Aldridge worked for Douglas Aircraft in St. Louis, Missouri, as manager of their missile and space divison, then for LTV Aerospace in Dallas. From 1977 to 1981 he was vice-president of the Strategic Systems Corporation.

He was named Undersecretary of the Air Force for the U.S. Department of Defense in August 1981, and announced as a Shuttle payload specialist in September 1985.

Aldridge served as Secretary of the Air Force from 1986 to December 1988, when he left government service to become president of the McDonnell Douglas Corporation's Electronic Systems Division. At McDonnell he served as special advisor to the C-17 transport program. He also served on the Augustine Panel evaluating the future of American manned spaceflight.

He resigned from McDonnell Douglas effective March 1992 to become president and chief executive officer of The Aerospace Corporation, the federally funded research and development center that supports DOD and NRO space programs.

Aldrin, Buzz

1930–

Buzz Aldrin, lunar module pilot of Apollo 11, was the second man to walk on the Moon.

It was just after three in the afternoon, Central Daylight Time, on Sunday, July 20, 1969, when the lunar module Eagle closed to within 50,000 feet of the surface of the Moon. Its descent rocket fired and burned for twelve minutes, slowing the Eagle to a safe landing on the Sea of Tranquility. "Contact light?" Aldrin asked aloud, meaning that wire probes extending from the Eagle's landing pads had touched the lunar surface. "Okay," he went on, as the craft settled to the ground, "engine stop, ACA out of detent." Armstrong broke in to say, "Got it." Aldrin continued, "Mode controls both auto, descent engine command override off. Engine arm off. 413 is in." They were safely on the surface, engine shut down. Astronaut Charles Duke, the capcom in Houston, radioed, "We copy you down, Eagle." Armstrong answered, "Houston, Tranquility Base here. The Eagle has landed."

Seven hours later the two astronauts had donned pressure suits and backpacks and had depressurized the Eagle to allow them to exit. Armstrong was the first down the ladder to the lunar surface. Aldrin followed, uttering his first words, "Beautiful view." For the next two hours the astronauts collected samples of rock and soil and set up a scientific experiment package. They also erected an American flag, read a plaque mounted on the Eagle, and had a conversation with the president of the United States.

The two moonwalkers, together with Michael Collins, who had remained in lunar orbit aboard the command module Columbia, returned to Earth on July 24, 1969, to a three-week quarantine (because of fears that some unknown lunar microorganism could cause contamination), followed by a worldwide tour.

Apollo 11 was Aldrin's second spaceflight. In November 1966 he had served as pilot of Gemini 12, the last manned Gemini mission. During four days in space Aldrin performed the first effective space walks, spending a total of 5.5 hours in EVA. When the Gemini 12 rendezvous radar failed, Aldrin also had the opportunity to use hand-held charts he had developed to perform the very complex rendezvous calculations that usually required a computer.

Aldrin was born Edwin Eugene Aldrin Jr. on January 30, 1930, in Montclair, New Jersey. His father, Gene Sr., was an executive with Standard Oil who was also a pilot and who had served as a colonel in the Army Air Corps. (Buzz was a name given to Aldrin by his sister. In 1988 he made it his legal name.) He graduated from Montclair High School at the age of 17 and entered the United States Military Academy at West Point, receiving a bachelor of science in 1951. He later performed graduate work at the Massachusetts Institute of Technology, earning a doctor of science degree in aeronautics and astronautics in 1963. His thesis dealt with rendezvous between manned orbiting vehicles.

After graduating from West Point in 1951, Aldrin underwent pilot training at bases in Florida, Texas, and Nevada. In December 1951 he was assigned to the 51st Fighter Wing in Seoul, Korea, and eventually flew 66 combat missions in the F-86, destroying two enemy MiGs. He returned to the United States in December 1953 and became aide to the dean of faculty at the new Air Force Academy, where he remained until June 1956. For the next three years he was an F-100 pilot with the 36th Fighter Day Wing at Bitburg, Germany.

As a pilot Aldrin eventually logged over 3,500 hours of flying time, including 2,900 hours in jets and 140 hours in helicopters. He also flew the NASA lunar landing training vehicle.

At the time he was selected as a NASA astronaut in October 1963, Aldrin was already working on Air Force experiments for the Gemini program at the Manned Spacecraft Center. (He had applied for the September 1962 group, asking that the requirement for test pilot experience be waived, but was turned down.) He underwent basic classroom and survival training and also became a member of the panel developing Gemini rendezvous techniques.

He served as capcom for Gemini 5 in August 1965 and for Gemini 10 in July 1966. In January 1966 he was named backup pilot for Gemini 10. Aldrin was disappointed by the assignment, since it would not lead to a later flight (he could expect to rotate to Gemini 13, except that the Gemini program ended with flight 12) and would keep him from joining an early Apollo crew.

But on February 28, 1966, astronauts Elliott See and Charles Bassett, the prime crew for Gemini 9, were killed in a plane crash at St. Louis. Their backups, Thomas Stafford and Eugene Cernan, became prime crewmen for the flight, while Aldrin and Lovell went from backing up Gemini 10 to backing up Gemini 9, thus freeing them to fly on the last Gemini. Without that Gemini flight experience Aldrin would not have been eligible for Apollo 11.

In fact, the composition of the first crew to land on the Moon was the result of a series of accidents and schedule changes, not some deliberate plan. Both Armstrong and Aldrin were assigned to "dead end" Gemini backup jobs when the first Apollo crews began training. The Apollo 1 fire on January 27, 1967, which caused an 18-month hiatus in flights, allowed both men to form, with

LANDING AT TRANQUILITY

by Buzz Aldrin

(On Sunday, July 20, 1969, American astronauts Neil Armstrong and Buzz Aldrin began the first descent to the surface of the Moon, their target the Sea of Tranquility. It was a harrowing experience, marked by persistent warnings—program alarms—from the lunar module's computer.)

We were just 700 feet above the surface when [capcom] Charlie [Duke] gave us the final "go," just as another 12 02 program alarm flashed. Neil and I confirmed with each other that the landing radar was giving us good data, and he punched PROCEED into the keyboard. All these alarms kept us from studying our landing zone. If this had been a simulation back at the Cape, we probably would have aborted. Neil finally looked away from the DSKY screen and out his triangular window. He was definitely not satisfied with the ground beneath us. We were too low to identify the landmark craters we'd studied from the Apollo 10 photographs. We just had to find a smooth place to land. The computer, however, was taking us to a boulder field surrounding a 40-foot crater.

Neil rocked his hand controller in his fist, changing over to manual command. He slowed our descent from 20 feet per second to only nine. Then, at 300 feet, we were descending at only three and a half feet per second. As Eagle slowly dropped, we continued skimming forward.

Neil still wasn't satisfied with the terrain. All I could do was give him the altimeter callouts and our horizontal speed. He stroked the hand-controller and descent-rate switch like a motorist fine-tuning his cruise control. We scooted across the boulders. At two hundred feet our hover slid toward a faster descent rate.

"Eleven forward, coming down nicely," I called, my eyes scanning the instruments. "Two hundred feet, four and a half down. Five and a half down. One sixty. . . . " The low-fuel light blinked on the caution-and-warning panel, ". . . quantity light."

At 200 feet, Neil slowed the descent again. The horizon of the Moon was at eye level. We were almost out of fuel.

"Sixty seconds," Charlie warned.

The ascent engine fuel tanks were full, but completely separate from the descent engine. We had 60 seconds of fuel remaining in the descent stage before we had to land or abort. Neil searched the ground below.

"Down two and a half," I called. The LM moved forward like a helicopter flaring out for landing. We were in the so-called dead man's zone, and couldn't remain there long. If we ran out of fuel at this altitude, we would crash into the surface before the ascent engine could lift us back toward orbit. "Forward. Forward. Good. Forty feet. Down two and a half. Picking up some dust. Thirty feet. . . . "

Thirty feet below the LM's gangly legs, dust that had lain undisturbed for a billion years blasted sideways in the plume of our engine.

"Thirty seconds," Charlie announced solemnly, but still Neil slowed our rate.

The descent engine roared silently, sucking up the last of its fuel supply. I turned my eye to the ABORT STAGE button. "Drifting right," I called, watching the shadow of the footpad probe lightly touching the surface. "Contact light." The horizon seemed to rock gently and then steadied. Our altimeter stopped blinking. We were on the Moon. We had about 20 seconds of fuel remaining in the descent stage.

Immediately I prepared for a sudden abort, in case the landing had damaged the Eagle or the surface was not strong enough to support our weight.

"Okay, engine stop," I told Neil, reciting from the checklist. "ACA out of detent."

"Got it," Neil answered, disengaging the hand control system. Both of us were still tingling with the excitement of the final moments before touchdown.

"Mode controls, both auto," I continued, aware that I was chanting off the readouts. "Descent engine command override, off. Engine arm, off. . . . "

"We copy you down, Eagle," Charlie Duke interrupted from Houston.

I stared out at the rocks and shadows of the Moon. It was as stark as I'd ever imagined it. A mile away, the horizon curved into blackness.

"Houston," Neil called, "Tranquility Base here. The Eagle has landed."

It was strange to be suddenly stationary. Spaceflight had always meant movement to me, but here we were rock-solid still, as if the LM had been standing there since the beginning of time. We'd been told to expect the remaining fuel in the descent stage to slosh back and forth after we touched down, but there simply wasn't enough reserve fuel remaining to do this. Neil had flown the landing to the very edge.

"Roger, Tranquility," Charlie said, "we copy you on the ground. You've got a bunch of guys about to turn blue. We're breathing again. Thanks a lot."

I reached across and shook Neil's hand, hard. We had pulled it off. Five months and 10 days before the end of the decade, two Americans had landed on the Moon.

James Lovell, the backup crew for what was then scheduled to be Apollo 9, the third manned Apollo.

But Apollo 9 and Apollo 8 switched places in the schedule, and the crews switched as well, putting Armstrong and Aldrin in line for the fifth Apollo rather than the sixth. By this time Lovell had replaced Michael Collins on the Apollo 8 prime crew. Collins would become eligible for flights again by late December 1968, so the "magic" decision made by NASA planners was simply assigning the next two astronauts in line, Armstrong and Aldrin, to the next available mission, and replacing Fred Haise (who had not flown in space) with Gemini veteran Collins, who had by then spent two years training as an Apollo command module pilot.

It should also be noted that when the assignment was made in January 1969, there was no guarantee that Apollo 11 would be the first lunar landing. First there were two other missions (Apollo 9 and Apollo 10) that had to go perfectly.

When Aldrin was finally able to return to work after the publicity tour following his mission, he worked on early designs for the Space Shuttle. He also served as host for visiting Soviet cosmonauts Andrian Nikolayev and Vitaly Sevastyanov in October 1970.

He resigned from NASA in July 1971 to return to the Air Force as commander of the Test Pilot School at Edwards AFB, California, becoming the first astronaut to return to military service. But personal problems, culminating in a nervous breakdown, caused him to retire from the Air Force on March 1, 1972.

Aldrin wrote candidly about his personal crisis in an autobiography, *Return to Earth*, published in 1973. The book was filmed in 1976 as a movie-for-television starring Cliff Robertson.

In 1972 Aldrin founded Research & Engineering Consultants. He also served as a consultant to Mutual of Omaha Insurance, the Inforex Computer Company, the Laser Video Corporation, and the Beverly Hills Oil Company. From 1985 to 1988 he was a professor at the Center for Science, University of North Dakota in Grand Forks. He was also involved in a proposed book and television project called *Encounter*.

More recently he coauthored, with Malcolm McConnell, *Men from Earth* (1989), a history of the space race between the United States and USSR, a game (*Buzz Aldrin's Race into Space*, 1994) and a science fiction novel, coauthored with John Barnes, *Encounter with Tiber* (1996).

Allen, Andrew Michael

1955–

Former Marine Corps test pilot Andy Allen commanded the troubled STS-75 Shuttle mission in February 1996. STS-75 was intended to deploy the Italian Space Agency's Tethered Satellite System, a $404 million experiment to test the ability of a long tether to create electrical energy for future space vehicles. (A first attempt in 1992 had failed during STS-46.)

The TSS was being unreeled to its planned length of 12.8 miles from its tower in the orbiter Columbia's payload bay when it suddenly broke. The TSS returned some useful data, generating 3,000 of a planned 5,000 volts for five of the planned 36 hours of testing. The remainder of the STS-75 mission, which ultimately lasted 16 days, concentrated on experiments in the U.S. Microgravity Payload.

Allen had flown two previous missions as a Shuttle pilot, including STS-46, a seven-day flight of the orbiter Discovery launched July 31, 1992. The crew of STS-46 deployed and retrieved the EURECA free-flying science platform and also attempted to deploy the Italian Tethered Satellite System.

In March 1994 Allen was pilot of STS-62, a two-week flight of the orbiter Columbia which carried the U.S. Microgravity Payload.

Allen was born August 4, 1955, in Philadelphia, Pennsylvania, and graduated from high school in the suburb of Warminster. He receved a B.S. in mechanical engineering from Villanova in 1977.

A Navy ROTC student at Villanova, Allen was commissioned upon graduation from college. He underwent Marine flight school, then served as an F-4 Phantom pilot at Beaufort Marine Corps Air Station, South Carolina, from 1980 to 1983. In the four years that followed he served as squadron operations officer for Marine Fighter Squadron 531 at El Toro, California, and also attended the Naval Fighter Weapons (Top Gun) School. He graduated from the Naval Test Pilot School at Patuxent River, Maryland, in 1987, and was working as a test pilot when selected by NASA.

He logged over 6,000 hours of flying time in 30 different types of aircraft.

Allen was selected by NASA in June 1987 and qualified as a Shuttle pilot in August 1988. His first technical assignment was working on Shuttle landing and rollout hardware and procedures. He later worked in the Shuttle Avionics Integration Laboratory (SAIL), as technical assistant to the director of flight crew operations, and leader of the astronaut support team at the Kennedy Space Center.

In April 1996 Allen was named director of space station requirements at NASA Headquarters. He resigned from that post and in March 1997, and retired from NASA and the USMC in October 1997 to become president of FIRST (For Inspiration and Recognition of Science and Technology) Foundation, Manchester, New Hampshire.

Allen, Joseph Percival IV

1937–

Joe Allen took part in the first salvage mission in space history. As a mission specialist aboard Shuttle flight 51-A in November 1984, Allen and fellow astronaut Dale Gardner performed two space walks during which the errant satellites Palapa B-2 and Westar VI were retrieved and loaded aboard the orbiter Discovery for return to Earth. Allen used the Manned Maneuvering Unit backpack in his capture of the Palapa, and found himself literally holding the weightless (but not inertialess) Palapa over his head for an entire orbit of the Earth while Gardner improvised a way to lock the satellite into the Shuttle's cargo bay.

Allen was also a mission specialist aboard the first operational Shuttle mission, STS-5 in November 1982 and supervised the first launching of a satellite, SBS-C, from the Shuttle. A planned space walk by Allen and William Lenoir during that mission had to be canceled.

Allen was born June 27, 1937, in Crawfordsville, Indiana, where he graduated from high school. He attended DePauw University, receiving a B.A. in math/physics in 1959, then earned an M.S. and a Ph.D. in physics from Yale University in 1961 and 1965 respectively.

Allen was a Fulbright Scholar in Germany in 1959 and 1960 and after earning his doctorate from Yale he became a staff physicist at the Nuclear Structure Laboratory there. When selected by NASA he was working as a research associate at the Nuclear Physics Laboratory at the University of Washington.

One of the 11 scientist-astronauts selected by NASA on August 11, 1967, Allen underwent jet pilot training at Vance Air Force Base in Oklahoma, where he earned the "outstanding flying" award. He served as mission scientist, support crewman, and capcom for the Apollo 15 lunar landing in 1971. Between 1972 and 1978 he held several administrative positions while retaining his astronaut status: he was a consultant on science and technology to the President's Council on International Economic Policy in 1974, and from 1975 to 1978 he was assistant administrator for legislative affairs at NASA Headquarters in Washington, D.C.

After returning to the Johnson Space Center, Allen was a member of the support crew and capcom for the first Shuttle mission, STS-1.

In July 1985 Allen resigned from NASA to become vice-president of Space Industries, Inc. (S.I.I.), a Houston-based firm that once hoped to launch a free-flying space manufacturing platform called the Industrial Space Facility from the Shuttle. In March 1989 S.I.I. became support contractor for the Wake Shield Facility, a research vehicle deployed and retrieved on Shuttle missions STS-60 (1994), STS-69 (1995) and STS-80 (1996). Now based in Washington, D.C., Allen is currently president of S.I.I.

Allen also served on the Augustine Panel, which examined current and future American efforts in space in its 1991 report.

Allen is the coauthor of a book, *Entering Space* (1984).

Altman, Scott Douglas
1959–

Navy test pilot Scott Altman was pilot in the crew of STS-90. The April 1998 mission of the orbiter Columbia carried the Neurolab Spacelab on a 16-day mission. Neurolab performed research into the medical effects of space travel on people and carried a crew of 7.

Altman was born August 15, 1959, in Lincoln, Illinois, and grew up in Pekin, where he graduated from Pekin Community High School in 1977. He attended the University of Illinois, receiving a B.S. in aeronautical/astronautical engineering in 1981. He later received an M.S. in aeronautical engineering from the Naval Postgraduate School (1990).

A Navy ROTC student at Illinois, Altman underwent aviator training in Florida and Texas, qualifying as an F-14 pilot in February 1983. Over the next four years he completed two deployments to the Pacific with Fighter Squadron 51. In August 1987 he was selected for a U.S. Naval Postgraduate School-U.S. Naval Test Pilot School cooperative program, earning his master's degree, then attending the test pilot school at Patuxent River, Maryland. Following graduation from the school in June 1990 he served for two years as an F-14 and F-15 test pilot at Pax River.

In 1992 Altman was assigned as maintenance officer and operations officer for Fighter Squadron 31 based at Miramar, California. During this time he flew missions over southern Iraq in support of Operation Southern Watch.

Lieutenant Commander Altman was one of the 19 astronaut candidates selected by NASA on December 8, 1994. He qualified as a Shuttle pilot in May 1996 and worked in the vehicle systems branch of the astronaut office prior to his flight assignment.

Anders, William Alison
1933–

Bill Anders was a member of the first crew of space travelers to leave the Earth and orbit the Moon. The time was December 1968 and the flight was Apollo 8. Anders, Frank Borman, and James Lovell thundered into Earth orbit on the Saturn 5 rocket, the most powerful ever used for a manned spaceflight, then fired one of the Saturn's upper stages to send them into a translunar trajectory. Three days later, on Christmas Eve 1968, they used the engine on their Apollo service module to slow them into lunar orbit. In the next twenty hours the astronauts circled the Moon ten times, becoming the first human beings to see the farside of the Moon with their own eyes. On Christmas morning, just prior to leaving the Moon, the astronauts read a passage from the Book of Genesis to a worldwide audience on television.

The triumph of Apollo 8 was the result of a daring and risky decision by NASA officials, notably George Low, to keep the Apollo program on target for a manned lunar landing in 1969. The essential first flight of the lunar module had been delayed until March 1969 and NASA was facing a five-month gap between missions. Sending Apollo 8, without a lunar module, to the Moon in late December, when lighting conditions were the same as those of the planned landing, would serve to qualify the Saturn 5 for manned flight while gathering data for later lunar missions, and might just beat the Russians, who were suspected (correctly) of planning a manned circumlunar flight of their own. It did all three. The three astronauts were chosen *Time* magazine's men of the year.

Anders was born October 17, 1933, in Kong Kong, where his father, a naval officer, was stationed. Like his father, Anders entered the Naval Academy at Annapolis, graduating with a bachelor of science degree in 1955. He later earned an M.S. in nuclear engineering from the Air Force Institute of Technology in 1962. He also completed the advanced management program at Harvard Business School (1979).

Anders elected to serve in the Air Force and underwent pilot training in Texas and Georgia, receiving his wings in December 1956. For the next three years he was a fighter pilot in all-weather interceptor squadrons of the Air Defense Command in California and Iceland, then attended the Air Force Institute of Technology at Wright-Patterson Air Force Base, Ohio. Upon completing his degree, he became a nuclear engineer and instructor pilot at the USAF Weapons Laboratory at Kirtland AFB, New Mexico.

As a pilot Anders eventually logged over 5,000 hours of flying time.

Anders was one of the 14 astronauts selected by NASA in October 1963. Because of his scientific background he was assigned to work on spacecraft environmental systems and in particular to study the amount and type of radiation exposure astronauts might endure on a trip to the Moon. He served as capcom for Gemini 4 and Gemini 12, and was backup pilot for Gemini 11 prior to joining the Apollo crew commanded by Frank Borman in November 1966.

The Borman crew was originally scheduled to fly the third manned Apollo mission in 1969, riding a Saturn 5 to an altitude of 4,000 miles in a rehearsal for a lunar landing mission. Borman and Anders would have tested a lunar module, and Anders spent months working on LM systems and learning to pilot helicopters and the lunar landing training vehicle in preparation. But when NASA officials developed the Apollo 8 lunar orbit project, they offered Borman and James McDivitt, commander of the second manned Apollo, a choice. Borman elected to take Apollo 8, and lunar module pilot Anders went into space without a lunar module.

Following Apollo 8 Anders served as backup command module pilot for Michael Collins on Apollo 11, the first lunar landing mission. Astronaut chief Donald Slayton told Anders he could serve as command module pilot of a later Apollo mission, and then command a Skylab flight, but Anders had already elected to leave the astronaut group.

In September 1969 he became executive secretary of the National Aeronautics and Space Council, which reported to the president and vice-president concerning space research. He remained with the council until August 1973, when he was appointed to the Atomic Energy Commission. He later served as first chairman of the Nuclear Regulatory Commission (1975) and U.S. Ambassador to Norway (1976–77). During this time he remained a NASA astronaut, though he was classified as "unavailable for flight assignment."

Anders left the federal government in 1977 and, after a brief term as a fellow of the American Enterprise Institute, joined the General Electric Company in San Jose, California, as vice president and general manager of their nuclear products division. In 1980 he became general manager of GE's aircraft equipment division in Dewitt, New York, and later joined Textron, Inc., as senior executive vice president for operations.

During this time he also served as a consultant, and until 1988, as a major general in the U.S. Air Force Reserve.

In September 1989 Anders was named chairman and CEO-designate of the General Dynamics Corporation in St. Louis, Missouri, and took over those jobs in 1990. General Dynamics manufactured the F-16 fighter in addition to the Atlas commercial launch vehicle. Anders guided the company through a major restructuring, turning what was described as "one of the U.S. aerospace industry's biggest money-losers" into a smaller, more profitable organization. He retired from General Dynamics in 1994.

Anderson, Clayton Conrad

1959–

NASA engineer Clayton Anderson is one of the 25 astronaut candidates selected by the space agency in June 1998. In August 1998 he began a training and evaluation course which should qualify him as a Shuttle mission specialist and International Space Station crew member.

Anderson was born February 23, 1959, in Omaha, Nebraska. He graduated from high school in Ashland, Nebraska, in 1977, then attended Hastings College, where he received a B.S. in physics (1981). He later received an M.S. in aerospace engineering from Iowa State (1983).

At the time of his selection, Anderson was manager of the emergency operations center at the NASA Johnson Space Center.

Anderson, Lloyd Lynn, Jr.

1952–

For four years Lloyd Anderson was alternate weather officer/payload specialist for a Department of Defense Shuttle flight. The flight was canceled in 1992 before it could be launched.

Anderson was born February 28, 1952, in Humansville, Missouri, and graduated from Ruskin High School in Kansas City. He earned a B.S. in basic science from the Air Force Academy in 1974, an M.A. in education at Phillips University in Oklahoma (1978) and a Ph.D. in meteorology from Texas A&M through the Air Force Institute of Technology program (1986).

Commissioned in the Air Force in June 1974, Anderson was trained as a weather officer at San Jose State University. From 1975 to 1978 he was a forecaster at Vance AFB, Oklahoma, then served as an Air Force exchange officer with the Canadian Forces Forecast Centre at North Bay, Onatrio, until entering Texas A&M in 1980.

In September 1984 Anderson was assigned to the Space and Electromagnetic Systems Division of Air Force Global Weather Central, Offutt AFB, Nebraska. At the time of his selection as backup weather officer in space in March 1988 he was commander of Detachment 9, 4th Weather Wing, at Learmouth, Australia.

Lieutenant Colonel Anderson is currently assigned to the 1st Weather Group at Fort Hood, Texas.

Anderson, Michael, Phillip

1959–

Physicist and tanker pilot Michael Anderson was a mission specialist in the crew of STS-89. This 11-day flight of the orbiter Endeavour, launched in January 1998, carried two tons of water, food, and other supplies to the Mir space station. STS-89 also picked up NASA-Mir crewman David Wolf and delivered the last NASA-Mir crewman, Andy Thomas.

Anderson was born December 25, 1959, in Plattsburgh, New York. He grew up in Washington state, attending high school in Cheney and receiving a B.S. in physics/astronomy from the University of Washington in 1981. He later received an M.S. in physics from Creighton University (1990).

Upon graduation from Washington in 1981 Anderson entered the Air Force, where he was trained in communications maintenance. From 1982 to 1986 he served with the 2015th Communications Squadron and the 1920th Information Systems Groups at Randolph AFB, Texas.

Anderson was then selected for pilot training, and qualified on the EC-135, ultimately flying the so-called Looking Glass Strategic Air Command airborne command post out of Offutt AFB, Nebraska.

Following graduate school at Creighton, he became an aircraft commander and instructor pilot on the KC-135 tanker with the 920th Air Refueling Squadron based at Wurtsmith AFB, Michigan. At the time of his selection as an astronaut, Major Anderson was tactics officer with the 380th Air Refueling Wing at Plattsburgh AFB, New York.

He has logged over 3,000 hours of flying time in the KC-135 and the T-38A.

Anderson was one of the 19 astronaut candidates selected by NASA on December 8, 1994, and qualified as a Shuttle mission specialist in May 1996. His technical assignment, prior to being named to the STS-89 crew, was with the astronaut support team at the Kennedy Space Center.

Apt, Jay (Jerome)

1949–

Physicist Jay Apt made four Shuttle flights as a mission specialist. On his first, STS-37 in April 1991, he made two EVAs, including an unscheduled contingency EVA necessitated by an antenna failure on the Gamma Ray Observatory satellite. Apt and fellow space walker Jerry Ross succeeded in freeing the stuck antenna, allowing the $617 million GRO to be deployed in Earth orbit. The next day the two astronauts made their scheduled EVA, a 6-hour test of space station construction techniques.

In September 1992 Apt flew as mission specialist aboard STS-47, which carried Spacelab-J. During the 8-day mission he took part in conducting over 40 experiments in space manufacturing and life sciences.

Apt's third mission was STS-59, an April 1994 flight of the orbiter Endeavour that carried the first Shuttle Radar Laboratory. During the 11-day mission the SRL took images of 70 million square kilometer of the Earth's surface.

He made his fourth flight aboard STS-79, the fourth Shuttle-Mir docking mission, which docked with the Russian space station in September 1996.

Apt was born April 28, 1949, in Springfield, Massachusetts. He graduated from Shady Side Academy in Pittsburgh in 1967, then attended Harvard University, where he received a B.A. in physics (magna cum laude) in 1971. He received his Ph.D. in physics from the Massachusetts Institute of Technology in 1976.

From 1976 to 1980 Apt was a member of the Center for Earth & Planetary Physics at Harvard, involved in the Pioneer Venus space probe project. He also made temperature maps of the planet Venus from Mt. Hopkins Observatory. In 1980 Apt joined NASA's Jet Propulsion Laboratory and continued his studies of the solar system. From 1981 to 1985 he was a flight controller for the Space Shuttle at the Johnson Space Center.

He is a private pilot with over 2,700 hours of flying time in 25 different types of aircraft, including sailplanes and man-powered craft.

Apt was selected by NASA as an astronaut candidate in June 1985 and in July 1986 qualified as a Shuttle mission specialist. His technical assignments have included working with the Shuttle orbiter modification team at the Kennedy Space Center, helping to develop EVA servicing techniques for the Hubble Space Telescope and the GRO, and developing EVA construction and servicing methods for the Freedom space station. In 1993 he served as a capcom in mission control.

In 1996 Apt published *Orbit*, a collection of Earth photographs taken by astronauts, coauthored with Michael Helfert and Justin Williamson of the National Geographic Society. He also won first and second place in the 1996 "Space Photo" category by *Aviation Week* Magazine.

Apt resigned from NASA in May 1997 to become director of the Carnegie Museum of Natural History in Pittsburgh, Pennsylvania.

Archambault, Lee Joseph

1960–

Air Force test pilot Lee Archambault is one of the astronaut candidates selected by NASA in June 1998. In August 1988 he reported to the Johnson Space Center to begin a training and evaluation course that should qualify him as a Shuttle pilot.

Archambault was born August 25, 1960, in Oak Park, Illinois. He graduated from Proviso High School in Hillside, Illinois, in 1978, then attended the University of Illinois at Urbana, receiving a B.S. (1982) and M.S. (1983) in aerospace/astronautical engineering.

At the time of his selection by NASA, Archambault was an F-16 test pilot with the 39th flight test squadron at Eglin AFB, Florida.

Armor, James Burton, Jr.
1950–

Air Force engineer Jim Armor was a member of the second cadre of Department of Defense manned spaceflight engineers chosen in January 1983. In late 1985, just weeks before the Shuttle Challenger disaster, he was chosen as payload specialist for a Department of Defense Shuttle mission scheduled for launch in late 1987. The mission was canceled before it could be flown.

Armor was born September 25, 1950, in Oklahoma City, Oklahoma, and attended Lehigh University in Bethlehem, Pennsylvania, where he received a B.S. in electrical engineering and a B.S. in psychology in 1973. He later earned an M.S. in electro-optics from the Air Force Institute of Technology in 1977.

Entering active duty, Armor served for three years as a Strategic Air Command missile crew commander and instructor at McConnell AFB, Kansas. In 1976 he transferred to Wright-Patterson AFB, Ohio, to attend AFIT, then became a laser signal analysis group leader. He was assigned to Los Angeles Air Force Station as a project officer for the Space Transportation System when he was selected for the MSE program.

Highly regarded by his colleagues (one of them described him in print as the "most impressive" MSE), Armor had been selected for promotion to major three years "below the zone," a rare honor. At Space Division he served as deputy to Col. Mart Bushnell, the MSE program director, in 1985, in addition to his duties as a payload specialist candidate and systems project officer.

In October 1986 he transferred to the Pentagon, where he worked for four years in the Office of Space Systems. Following a tour with the U.S. Space Command at Peterson AFB, Colorado, he returned to Los Angeles Air

Force Base, becoming head of the Defense Information Dissemination program office. Since July 1996 he has been director of the Navstar Global Positioning System Joint Program Office.

Armstrong, Neil Alden
1930–

Neil Armstrong will always be remembered as the first man to walk on the Moon. At 9:56 P.M., Houston time, Sunday, July 20, 1969, he stepped off the footpad of the lunar module Eagle, saying, "That's one small step for a man, one giant leap for mankind."

With every one of his early steps a theory about the lunar surface evaporated. The worry that an astronaut would sink in a deep coating of dust? Armstrong reported that his boots sank "maybe an eighth of an inch." Would an astronaut trying to walk in the unwieldy space suit and backpack simply fall over? "There seems to be no difficulty," he said. "It's even perhaps easier than the simulations at one-sixth G."

As millions watched on television, Armstrong dug a small "contingency" sample of lunar soil, in case the Moon walk had to be cut short. Then, joined by Buzz Aldrin, he began to set up scientific experiments and searched for more comprehensive rock samples. He and Aldrin also set up an American flag and took a phone call from President Richard Nixon. They also read the words printed on a plaque mounted on the descent stage of the Eagle, which would remain forever on the Sea of Tranquility: "Here men from the planet Earth first set foot upon the Moon, July 1969 A.D. We came in peace for all mankind."

Just over two and a half hours later Armstrong, Aldrin, and the precious box containing the first Moon rocks were safely back inside the Eagle. At 12:55 P.M. the next day the Eagle lifted off from the Moon to rejoin the orbiting Columbia and its pilot, Michael Collins.

Apollo 11 ended with a successful splashdown in the Pacific and recovery by the carrier USS *Hornet*. Armstrong, Collins and Aldrin faced three weeks of quarantine, and months of public appearances.

Armstrong had commanded one previous spaceflight, Gemini 8 in March 1966. Gemini 8 accomplished the first docking between two spacecraft when it linked up with an unmanned Agena 6.5 hours after liftoff. It also became the first American spaceflight to be aborted. A thruster on the Gemini began to fire uncontrollably, sending the combined Gemini-Agena vehicle into a spin. Suspecting at first that the Agena was causing the problem, Armstrong and pilot David Scott separated from the unmanned craft, which only made matters worse. Forced to use reentry thrusters to stabilize the Gemini, Armstrong and Scott then had to return to Earth. They splashed down 600 miles south of Yokosuka, Japan, and waited in the floating spacecraft for 45 minutes until divers could reach them from a C-54 rescue plane. It wasn't until three hours after splashdown that the weary, seasick astronauts were safe aboard the destroyer *Leonard F. Mason*. They had completed fewer than eleven hours of a planned three-day mission.

Armstrong was born August 5, 1930, at a farm six miles outside of Wapakoneta, Ohio. His father was an auditor for the state of Ohio and so the family moved every year, though Neil graduated from high school in Wapakoneta. He built model airplanes and got his student pilot's license on his sixteenth birthday.

Armstrong wanted to go to college and study aeronautical engineering, but couldn't afford it without some sort of aid. He applied for a U.S. Navy scholarship, got it, and enrolled at Purdue University in 1947. A year and a half later the Navy called him to active duty. He entered flight school at Pensacola, Florida, and became a fighter pilot. Before he could return to Purdue, however, the Korean War broke out. Armstrong was assigned to Fighter Squadron 51 and served in Korea until the spring of 1952. He described his combat experience as "bridge breaking, train stopping, tank shooting and that sort of thing." In September 1951 he had to bail out of his F9F-2 jet when a wire stretched across a Korean valley tore the wing off his plane.

Out of the Navy, he returned to Purdue in the fall of 1952 and graduated with a B.S. in aeronautical engineering in January 1955. He received an M.S. from the University of Southern California in 1970.

Armstrong went to work for the National Advisory Committee on Aeronautics (NACA), the forerunner of NASA, at its Lewis Flight Propulsion Laboratory in Cleveland. He soon transferred to the NACA station at Edwards

AFB, California, where he became an aeronautical research pilot. Among other vehicles, he flew the X-5, F-102A, F5D-1 Skylancer (making simulated X-20 Dyna-Soar launchings and landings in these two), the Paresev, and the X-15 rocket plane.

He was one of the first pilots assigned to the X-20 program in the summer of 1960. At the same time he was involved in the X-15 program, making six flights in the rocket plane between December 1960 and July 1962, ultimately reaching an altitude of 207,000 feet.

Considered a shoo-in for the second group of NASA astronauts selected in 1962, Armstrong was one of the first 2 civilians chosen for the manned space program. He underwent survival training, then became involved in Gemini development. One of his jobs, beginning in 1964, was to supervise the work of the 14 new astronauts, including Aldrin and Collins. Armstrong was assigned as backup commander for Gemini 5, the third manned Gemini mission, in early 1965. He served as capcom for Gemini 5 and for Gemini 9 as well, and also served as backup commander for Gemini 11.

Following Apollo 11 Armstrong served at NASA headquarters in Washington, D.C., as deputy associate administrator for aeronautics, and became known as an advocate of research into computer control of high-performance aircraft.

He resigned from NASA in August 1971 to become professor of engineering at the University of Cincinnati. He remained there through 1979, joining the Cardwell International Corporation of Lebanon, Ohio, as chairman of the board. In 1984 he became chairman of the board of CTA, Inc., in Lebanon.

An intensely private person, Armstrong refrained from making public appearances for many years. However, in early 1984 he accepted an appointment to the National Commission on Space, a presidential panel whose members included, in addition to Armstrong, astronaut Kathryn Sullivan, former test pilot Chuck Yeager, and former NASA administrator Thomas Paine. The NCOS was to develop goals for a national space program extending into the twenty-first century. Before its report could be delivered, however, the shuttle Challenger exploded during launch on January 28, 1986. Armstrong was immediately named vice-chairman of the committee investigating the disaster.

He also served as host for the television series *First Flights* on the Arts & Entertainment Network (1991).

Ashby, Jeffrey Shears
1954–

Navy test pilot Jeff Ashby was assigned in September 1996 as pilot of STS-85. This July 1997 flight of the orbiter Discovery eventually carried the CHRISTA-SPAS payload. But in February 1997 Ashby withdrew from the flight for personal reasons and was replaced by Kent Rominger. Ashby was then assigned as assistant to David Leestma, the director of flight crew operations.

In March 1998 he was assigned as pilot of STS-93. This five-day flight of the orbiter Columbia is scheduled to deploy the AXAF X-ray observatory in April 1999.

Ashby was born June 16, 1954, in Dallas, Texas, and grew up in Colorado, where he graduated from Evergreen High School in 1972. He attended the University of Idaho, where he received a B.S. in mechanical engineering in 1976. He later received an M.S. in aviation systems from the University of Tennessee at Knoxville (1993).

He entered the Navy in 1976 and underwent flight training, ultimately serving as an A-7E and FA-18 pilot on five different carrier deployments. He graduated from the Naval Fighter Weapons School ("Top Gun") in 1986, then attended the Naval Test Pilot School at Patuxent River, Maryland, in 1988. As a test pilot he took part in the early development of the F/A-18's weapons and electronic warfare systems.

He flew missions in support of Operation Desert Shield and Southern Watch (Iraq), and Continue Hope (Somalia). In 1991 he flew 33 combat missions in Operation Desert Storm. At the time of his selection by NASA Captain Ashby was commanding officer of Strike Fighter Squadron 94 at the Lemoore, California, Naval Air Station.

He has logged over 5,000 hours of flying time, including 1,000 carrier landings.

Ashby was one of the 19 astronaut candidates selected on December 8, 1994. In May 1996 he qualified as a Shuttle pilot, and was assigned to the vehicle systems and operations branch of the astronaut office.

Aufderhaar, Grant Clifford
1948–

Air Force meteorologist Grant Aufderhaar was selected as a backup payload specialist for the proposed USAF Weather Office in Space Experiment, originally manifested for Shuttle mission 61-M in the summer of 1986. Following the Challenger disaster the WOSE flight was postponed indefinitely. Aufderhaar and his two colleagues, Major Fred Lewis and Major Ronald Townsend, were reassigned to other programs.

Aufderhaar was born August 20, 1948, in Celina, Ohio, and graduated from Memorial High School in nearby St. Mary's in 1966. He attended the U.S. Air Force Academy, receiving a B.S. in 1970. He later earned an M.S. in meteorology from Texas A&M (1972) and a Ph.D. from the University of Utah (1980).

From 1972 to 1976 he served as a weather officer at Global Weather Central, Offutt AFB; Kwajelein Island; and Shemya AFB, Alaska. After completing his Ph.D. in 1980, he was assigned to Scott AFB, Illinois, as chief of the Air Weather Service's Special Projects Division, in charge of supporting military satellite programs. At the time of his involvement with WOSE in 1985, he was Chief of Politico-Military affairs for the Assistant Director for Special Operations at Air Force Headquarters, the Pentagon.

Aufderhaar was later reassigned to Wright-Patterson AFB, Ohio, and then to the Pentagon. He retired from the Air Force in 1995.

Bagian, James Phillip
1952–

Dr. Jim Bagian was a mission specialist in the crew of STS-29, a 5-day flight of the orbiter Discovery in March 1989. During STS-29 a Tracking and Data Relay Satellite (TDRS) was sent into geosynchronous orbit. The crew of 5 astronauts also performed several scientific experiments and took over 3,000 photographs of the Earth's surface.

In June 1991 Bagian made a second spaceflight, this time as mission specialist in the crew of STS-40. This 9-day Spacelab Life Sciences mission was dedicated to research in space medicine.

Bagian was born February 22, 1952, in Philadelphia, Pennsylvania. He graduated from Central High School there in 1969, then attended Drexel University, receiving his B.S. in mechanical engineering in 1973. He earned his M.D. from Thomas Jefferson University in 1977.

While studying to be a doctor, Bagian worked as a process engineer for the 3M Company and as a mechanical engineer at the Naval Test Center at Patuxent River, Maryland. In 1978 he completed a residency in surgery at Geisinger Medical Center in Danville, Pennsylvania, then went to work at the NASA Johnson Space Center as a flight surgeon and medical officer. He later qualified as an Air Force flight surgeon and was completing a residency in anesthesiology at the University of Pennsylvania when selected as an astronaut by NASA.

In addition to his medical activities, Bagian qualified as a snow and ice rescue instructor, having served on the Denali Medical Research Project on Mt. McKinley in the 1980s; as a freefall parachutist and pilot (with over 1,200 hours of flying time); and as a pararescue flight surgeon for the 939th Air Rescue Wing.

Bagian was one of the 19 astronauts selected by NASA in May 1980. While still an ASCAN he provided medical support for the first six Shuttle missions. After completing his training and evaluation course in August 1981 he also served as the astronaut office coordinator for Shuttle payload software and crew equipment.

Between 1984 and 1986 he trained as a mission specialist on two different Shuttle crews, for Spacelab 4 (originally scheduled for launch in January 1986) and for Mission 61-I. Following the Challenger disaster Bagian was assigned to the board investigating the accident, and was part of the team that discovered the wreckage of the Challenger crew cabin. He was assigned to STS-29 in March 1988.

Bagian took a leave from NASA in July 1994 to perform biomedical research and practice clinical medicine at William Beaumont Hospital in Royal Oak, Michigan. In July 1995 he resigned from NASA and the astronaut office to join the Environmental Protection Agency's National Vehicle and Field Emissions Lab at Ann Arbor.

Bailey, Palmer Kent
1947–

Army geologist Palmer Bailey was selected in June 1990 as the prime payload specialist for Terra Geode, a U.S. Army geological experiment package originally scheduled for a Shuttle flight in 1992. Unlike the Army's Terra Scout program, which flew in 1991, Terra Geode ran into budget problems and was eventually canceled.

Bailey was born October 27, 1947, in Bismarck, North Dakota, and grew up in nearby Washburn, graduating from high school there in 1965. He attended the University of North Dakota at Fargo, receiving a B.S. in geology in 1970. He receieved an M.S. in geology and a B.S. in geological engineering from the same school (1980).

An ROTC graduate at North Dakota, Bailey entered the Army Corps of Engineers in 1970 and served for the next four years in Europe, including two stints as a company commander. From 1975 to 1978 he served with the 172nd Arctic Light Infantry in Alaska.

After two years in graduate school, Bailey became an instructor in geology at the US Military Academy at West Point. In 1986 he was detailed to the NASA Johnson Space Center as a geologic science advisor, where he took part in the initial development of the Terra Geode experiments. From 1987 to 1989 Bailey commanded the 4th Engineering Battalion at Fort Carson, Colorado. At the time of his involvement in Terra Geode, Bailey was an associate professor of geography and environmental engineering at West Point.

In 1992 he became commander of the Cold Regions Research and Engineering Laboratory, Army Corps of Engineers, at Hanover, New Hampshire. He spent the "summer" of 1993-94 at the South Pole.

Bailey retired from the Army in 1995 and currently lives on a farm in Alaska.

Baker, Ellen Louise (Shulman)

1953–

NASA physician Ellen Baker was flight engineer in the crew of STS-50, the longest Shuttle mission flown to that time. This two-week flight of the orbiter Columbia, launched June 26, 1992, carried the U.S. Microgravity Laboratory. Its crew of 7 performed experiments in space manufacturing.

Baker previously served as mission specialist in the crew of STS-34, an October 1989 Shuttle flight that successfully deployed the nuclear-powered Jupiter probe Galileo. During the 6-day mission aboard the Atlantis, Baker performed weather photography and medical tests.

In June 1995 Baker was a member of STS-71, the first Shuttle-Mir docking mission. The flight of the orbiter Atlantis launched with a crew of 7, including Russian cosmonauts Anatoly Solovyov and Nikolai Budarin, who became the new Mir resident crew, and returned with eight, including cosmonauts Yuri Dezhurov and Gennady Strekalov, and the first NASA-Mir crewmember, Norman Thagard. Atlantis also carried a Spacelab module devoted to medical and other life sciences studies.

Baker was born April 27, 1953, at Ft. Bragg in Fayetteville, North Carolina, and grew up in Queens, New York. She attended Bayside High School in Queens, graduating in 1970, then went on to the State University of New York at Buffalo, where she received a B.A. in geology (1974). She earned her M.D. from Cornell University in 1978.

After completing medical school, Baker spent three years training in internal medicine at the University of Texas Health Science Center in San Antonio. In 1981 she joined NASA as a medical officer at the Johnson Space Center. She also graduated with honors from the Air Force Aerospace Medicine Course at Brooks Air Force Base in San Antonio. When selected as an astronaut, Baker was a physician in the Johnson Space Center flight medicine clinic.

Baker was one of the 17 astronauts selected by NASA in May 1984 and in June 1985 qualified as a Shuttle mission specialist. She has had technical assignments involving flight software, engineering, and operations support, and has also worked on space station operations. Since January 1996 she has been detailed to the Life Sciences Directorate at the Johnson Space Center.

Baker, Michael Allen

1953–

Navy aviator Mike Baker commanded two Shuttle missions and served as pilot of two others.

He first served as pilot of STS-43, a 9-day flight of the orbiter Atlantis in August 1991 that deployed a Tracking and Data Relay Satellite into geosynchronous orbit. In November 1992 Baker was pilot of STS-52. This 1992 flight of the orbiter Columbia deployed the LAGEOS satellite.

Baker commanded STS-64, launched in September 1994 after suffering a launchpad abort on August 19, 1994. This flight of the orbiter Endeavour carried a crew of 6 and the second Space Radar Laboratory. The SRL returned over 14,000 photographs of the Earth's surface.

Most recently Baker commanded STS-81, the fifth Shuttle-Mir docking mission, in January 1997. STS-81 delivered three tons of food, water, and experimental equipment to Mir, along with NASA-Mir crewmember Jerry Linenger, returning astronaut John Blaha to Earth.

Captain Baker currently serves as deputy director, Johnson Space Center, for human spaceflight, based at the headquarters of the Russian Space Agency in Moscow.

Baker was born October 27, 1953, in Memphis, Tennessee, and grew up Lemoore, California, graduating from high school there in 1971. He attended the University of Texas at Austin, earning his B.S. in aerospace engineering in 1975.

Baker entered the Navy following graduation from Texas and earned his wings in 1977. From 1978 to 1980 he served as an A-7 pilot with Attack Squadron 56 aboard the carrier U.S.S. *Midway*. He spent the next two years with Carrier Air Wing 30, then attended the Naval Test Pilot School at Patuxent River, Maryland. Following graduation he was a test pilot with the carrier suitability branch. In 1983 he became instructor at the school. At the time he was selected by NASA Baker was an exchange instructor at the Empire Test Pliots School in Boscombe Down, England.

He has logged over 5,400 hours of flying time in 50 different types of aircraft, including vertical takeoff craft, multiengine planes, and helicopters. He has over 300 carrier landings.

Baker was one of the 13 astronaut candidates selected by NASA in June 1985, qualifying as Shuttle pilot the following July. From January 1986 to December 1987 Baker was part of the team that redesigned and modified the Shuttle's landing and braking systems, a move necessitated by results of the investigation into the Challenger accident. Following a year testing software at the Shuttle Avionics Integration Lab (SAIL) Baker served as a mission control capcom from December 1988 to December 1990.

He served as director, operations-Russia, at the Gagarin Center, in 1995–96, and was named to his current post in Russia in October 1997.

Barry Daniel Thomas
1953–

Physician and engineer Dan Barry was a mission specialist in the crew of STS-72. This 9-day January 1996 flight of the orbiter Endeavour retrieved Japan's Space Flyer Unit while deploying and retrieving a Spartan scientific pallet. Barry also took a 6-hour space walk to test space station construction techniques.

Barry was born December 30, 1953, in Norwalk, Connecticut. He graduated from Bolton High School in Alexandria, Louisiana, then attended Cornell University, receiving a B.S. in electrical engineering in 1975. He earned an M.S.E. and an M.A. in electrical engineering/ computer science from Princeton in 1977, and a Ph.D. in those fields from Princeton in 1980. He received his M.D. from the University of Miami in 1982.

At the time of his selection by NASA, Barry was assistant professor at the University of Michigan Medical Center in Ann Arbor.

Barry was one of the 19 astronaut candidates selected by NASA in March 1992 and in August 1993 qualified as a Shuttle mission specialist and International Space Station crewmember. He worked in the mission development branch of the astronaut office, and also served as chief of astronaut appearances.

Bartoe, John-David Francis
1944–

Physicist John-David Bartoe spent almost eight days in space as payload specialist aboard the orbiter Challenger during Mission 51-F/Spacelab 2. Bartoe operated a number of astronomical experiments, including the solar ultraviolet telescope, which he designed.

In December 1990 Bartoe served as alternate payload specialist for the STS-35 flight of the ASTRO-01 observatory, supporting the mission from the NASA Marshall Space Flight Center. He filled the same role for the STS-67 flight of ASTRO-02 in March 1995.

Bartoe was born November 17, 1944, in Abington, Pennsylvania. He received a B.S. in engineering physics from Lehigh University (1966), and an M.S. (1973) and Ph.D. (1976) in physics from Georgetown University.

In 1966 Bartoe became a researcher at the US Naval Research Laboratory in Washington, D.C. His specialty was the study of the sun, and his experiments were carried on sounding rockets, satellites, and on Apollo and Skylab missions in addition to Shuttle flights. He was selected as a Spacelab 2 payload specialist in April 1978.

Following his flight Bartoe returned to the NRL, though from June 1987 to June 1989 he served a term as chief scientist for NASA's Space Station Freedom program. Following another term at NRL as head of the solar spectroscopy section of its space sciences division, he became director of the User/Integration Division of the Spacelab/Space Station Utilization Program at NASA Headquarters. He currently serves as manager for ISS utlization at the NASA Johnson Space Center.

Bassett, Charles Arthur II

1931–1966

Air Force test pilot Charlie Bassett was killed in the crash of a NASA T-38 in St. Louis, Missouri, on February 28, 1966. At the time of his death Bassett was assigned as pilot of the Gemini 9 mission scheduled for launch in June of that year. Killed with him in the crash, which occurred at the McDonnell Aircraft Corporation plant near Lambert Field in St. Louis, was Gemini 9 commander Elliott See.

Bassett was born December 30, 1931, in Dayton, Ohio. He graduated from Berea High School there in 1949, then attended Ohio University at Athens. He left college in 1952 without receiving a degree to join the Air Force. He subsequently earned a B.S. in electrical engineering through the Air Force Institute of Technology at Texas Technological College, Lubbock (1960).

Between October 1952 and April 1954 Bassett underwent pilot training in North Carolina, Texas, and Nevada. His first assignment was with the 8th Fighter Bomber Group in the Pacific. From 1955 until entering AFIT in 1958 he was stationed at Suffolk County AFB, New York.

Bassett was assigned to Edwards AFB, California, as an engineer in 1960. He attended the test pilot school, graduating in April 1962, and later that year was enrolled in the Aerospace Research Pilot School at Edwards. His class at ARPS included Michael Collins, Ed Givens, and Joe Engle. At the time of Bassett's selection by NASA in October 1963 he was a test pilot.

As an astronaut Bassett served as capcom for Gemini 7 and Gemini 6 in December 1965. He had been named as pilot for Gemini 9 that November and was training to perform a spacewalk on that mission.

Bean Alan Laverne

1932–

During the flight of Apollo 12, Al Bean became the fourth person to walk on the Moon. On November 18, 1969, he and commander Charles Conrad landed the lunar module Intrepid in the Oceanus Procellarum just 200 yards from the unmanned Surveyor 3 probe, which had landed there three years earlier. During the next 31.5 hours the astronauts conducted two walks on the Moon, setting up an experiment package and visiting the Surveyor. They and command module pilot Richard Gordon returned to Earth on November 24.

Bean's second spaceflight was as commander of Skylab 3, the second manned visit to the Skylab orbiting space station. For over 59 days, from July 28 to September 25, 1973, Bean and fellow astronauts Owen Garriott and Jack Lousma conducted medical experiments, observations of the sun, and Earth resources photography while also performing necessary maintenance on Skylab, which had been badly damaged during its launch on May 14. The Skylab 3 mission came close to becoming the first manned flight to end with a rescue: problems with thrusters aboard the Apollo service module used to ferry the astronauts to Skylab forced NASA to prepare another Apollo, this one specially modified to carry five astronauts, as a standby. But the Skylab Rescue wasn't needed.

Bean was born March 15, 1932, in Wheeler, Texas, and grew up in Fort Worth, where he graduated from Paschal High School in 1950. He spent a year as an electronics technician with the Naval Reserve in Dallas, then entered the University of Texas at Austin, graduating with a B.S. in aeronautical engineering in 1955.

A Navy ROTC student at Texas, Bean was comissioned upon graduation and received pilot training in Florida and Texas. From 1956 to 1960 he was assigned to Attack Squadron 44 at the Jacksonville, Florida, Naval Air Station. He then attended the Naval Test Pilot School at Patuxent River, Maryland, remaining at Pax River as a test pilot through 1962. When chosen by NASA he was stationed with Attack Squadron 172 at Cecil Field, Florida.

As a pilot Bean eventually logged approximately 5,500 hours of flying time, 4,900 in jets, in 27 different types of aircraft.

Bean was one of the 14 astronauts chosen by NASA in October 1963. His area of specialization was spacecraft recovery systems. He was a capcom for Gemini 7/6 and Gemini 11 and backup command pilot for Gemini 10. In September 1966 he was assigned as chief of the Apollo Applications (later Skylab) branch of the astronaut office, which effectively eliminated his chance of making a flight to the Moon, but when astronaut C. C. Williams was killed in October 1967, Pax River classmate Charles Conrad asked Bean to replace Williams on his Apollo crew. Conrad, Gordon, and Bean were backups for Apollo 9.

After his Skylab flight Bean served as backup commander for the Apollo-Soyuz Test Project. In August 1975 he was assigned to the Space Shuttle program. He retired from the Navy as a captain in October of that year, but remained a NASA astronaut. From May 1978 to June 1981 Bean was acting chief astronaut, replacing John Young, and supervised the training of the 1978 and 1980 astronaut candidates, including NASA's first women astronauts.

Although he was expected to be chosen to command the first Shuttle/Spacelab mission, Bean resigned from NASA on June 26, 1981, to pursue a career as an painter working in the style of famed space artist Robert McCall. (Bean had begun to study painting in 1962, and after an interruption caused by his activities in the Apollo program, resumed study in 1974.) His work has been displayed at the National Air and Space Museum, at the Meredith Long and Company Gallery in Houston, and is published in the book *The Planets* (1985).

Bean is the author of a children's book, *My Life as an Astronaut*, with Beverly Fraknoi (1988). He is also the subject of a film, *Art Off This World* (1990).

Bechis, Kenneth Paul
1949–

Ken Bechis trained for three years as backup payload specialist for the flight of StarLab. StarLab was a Shuttle-Spacelab flight dedicated to the Strategic Defense Initiative Organization and was sched-

uled for launch aboard the STS-50 mission in 1992. In August 1990, however, StarLab was canceled.

Bechis was born July 22, 1949, in Boston, where he grew up. He graduated from Boston Latin School, then attended Harvard, where he received a B.A. in astronomy in 1970. He earned his M.S. in physics from the Massachusetts Institute of Technology in 1973 and a Ph.D. in astronomy from the University of Massachusetts, Amherst, in 1976.

Between 1974 and 1975 Bechis served as a research associate and lecturer at the University of Massachusetts. He was also site manager for the Five College Radio Astronomy Center in New Salem, Massachusetts. In 1979 he joined the technical staff of the Analytical Sciences Corporation (TASC) in Reading, Massachusetts. Bechis and Dennis Boesen were selected as backup payload specialists for StarLab in 1987.

Bechis is currently a department head at TASC.

Belt, Michael Eugene
1957–

Mike Belt is the Army intelligence specialist who served as backup payload specialist for Terra Scout, a military surveillance experiment flown on STS-44 in November 1991.

During the Terra Scout mission, intelligence specialist Tom Hennen observed a series of targets on Earth. Belt supported the mission, which was shortened from 10 to 7 days by equipment problems, from the NASA Johnson Space Center.

Belt was born September 9, 1957, in Syracuse, New York, where he graduated from Paul V. Moore High School in 1975. From 1979 to 1982 he attended the St. Louis B. Chaminade University in Honolulu, Hawaii.

Belt entered the U.S. Army in 1976 and was initially assigned to the 1st Military Intelligence Battalion at Fort Bragg, North Carolina. From 1979 to 1983 he was assigned to the 548th Reconnaissance Technical Group at Hickam AFB, Hawaii, serving not only as an intelligence analyst but also as an instructor. In 1983 he was transferred to Fort Huachuca, Arizona, where he also served as imagery analyst instructor. He was at Fort Huachuca when he was selected as a Terra Scout candidate in September 1988. He was named backup payload specialist in August 1990.

He also operated an aerial photo business specializing in environmental and geological studies.

Sergeant Belt retired from the army in 1996 to work in business in southern Arizona.

Blaha, John Elmer
1942–

Air Force test pilot John Blaha made five spaceflights, including a 128-day flight aboard the Russian space station Mir.

Blaha was delivered to Mir on September 18, 1996, by the orbiter Atlantis on mission STS-79. He replaced fellow astronaut Shannon Lucid in the Mir-22 team, joining cosmonauts Valery Korzun and Alexandr Kaleri. During his four months aboard the station, Blaha took part in a number of experiments in space medicine, plant growth, and biotechnology. Although he got along well with his Russian colleagues (Blaha was considered the most fluent Russian language speaker among the NASA-Mir astronauts), Blaha found himself feeling quite isolated at times. This was partly due to the fact that Korzun and Kaleri were originally assigned as the backup crew for Blaha's mission; he had done most of his training with Gennady Manakov and Pavel Vinogradrov, who were replaced a month prior to the launch of Mir-22 in August 1996.

On returning to Earth aboard STS-81 on January 22, 1997, Blaha allowed himself to be carried off the orbiter Atlantis to give medical researchers a more accurate picture of his condition after his time in orbit.

Previously Blaha had commanded STS-58, the longest Shuttle flight flown to that time. Launched on October 18, 1993, STS-58 carried the second Spacelab Life Sciences and a crew of 7, which performed the most extensive series of experiments ever into human adaptation to space.

Blaha also commanded STS-43, a 9-day flight of the orbiter Atlantis in August 1991, during which a Tracking and Data Relay Satellite was successfully deployed.

In 1989 he served as pilot for two Shuttle missions launched within nine months of each other: STS-29, a 4-day flight of the orbiter Discovery during which another TDRS was successfully deployed, launched March 13, and STS-33, launched November 22.

Blaha's assignment to STS-33 occurred because of the tragic death of astronaut David Griggs, who was killed in a plane crash on June 17, 1989, while training as pilot of STS-33. Blaha, then assigned to STS-40, the Spacelab Life Sciences mission, was called on to replace Griggs. STS-33 successfully deployed a National Security Agency electronic intelligence satellite called Mentor into a geosynchronous orbit.

Blaha was born August 26, 1942, in San Antonio Texas. His father was an Air Force officer and Blaha grew up at bases all over the world. He graduated from Granby High School in Norfolk, Virginia, in 1960, then attended the Air Force Academy in Colorado Springs, graduating with a B.S. in engineering science in 1965. He earned an M.S. in astronautical engineering from Purdue University in 1966.

Blaha won his pilot's wings in 1967, then was assigned as a pilot in Vietnam, where he flew 361 combat missions. Returning to the United States in 1971, he attended the Aerospace Research Pilot School at Edwards Air Force Base, California, piloting an NF-104 research jet to an altitude of 104,000 feet. He was an instructor at the school, then in 1973 was assigned as an exchange test pilot with the Royal Air Force, based at Boscombe Down, England. He returned to the United States in 1976 to attend the Air Command and Staff College and was stationed at USAF Headquarters in the Pentagon when selected by NASA.

Blaha logged over 7,000 hours of flying time in 34 different types of aircraft.

He was one of the 19 astronaut candidates selected by NASA on May 19, 1980, and qualified as a Shuttle pilot the following August. His first technical assignment, in the spring of 1981, was in the development of Shuttle computer software and hardware. From April 1983 to October 1984 he served as a Shuttle capcom. In January 1985 he was assigned as pilot of Mission 61-H, then scheduled for launch in the summer of 1986. That flight was canceled because of the Challenger accident. During the two-year launch hiatus that followed Blaha worked in the Shuttle orbiter project office.

Blaha retired from the USAF with the rank of colonel in August 1993, but continued to serve with NASA as a civilian astronaut. He began Russian language training at the Defense Language Institute, Monterey, California, in August 1994, and moved to the Gagarin Center to begin Mir training in January 1995.

He resigned from NASA on September 26, 1997, to become vice-president for engineering integration of USAA Corporation, San Antonio, Texas.

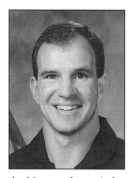

Bloomfield, Michael John
1959–

Air Force test pilot and Air Force Academy football captain Mike Bloomfield was pilot of STS-86. This 11-day flight of the orbiter Endeavour, launched in September 1997, was the seventh Shuttle-Mir docking and carried out a crew exchange, delivering NASA-Mir crewmember Dave Wolf to the station and returning Michael Foale to Earth. STS-96 also transferred five tons of food, water, and experimental and repair gear to Mir.

Bloomfield was born March 16, 1959, in Flint, Michigan, and graduated from high school in Lake Fenton in 1977. He attended the Air Force Academy (where he was voted to the 1980 Western Athletic Conference All-Academic football team), graduating with a B.S. in engineering mechanics in 1981. He later received an M.S. in engineering management from Old Dominion University in 1993.

After graduating from the Air Force Academy Bloomfield underwent pilot training at Vance AFB, Oklahoma. He served as an F-15 combat-ready pilot and instructor pilot at Holloman AFB, New Mexico, from 1983 to 1986, then transferred to Bitburg Air Base, Germany. While at Bitburg he attended the Fighter Weapons Instructor Course.

Bloomfield returned to the United States in 1989, becoming F-15 squadron weapons officer with the 48th Fighter Interceptor Squadron at Langley AFB, Virginia. In 1992 he attended the Air Force Test Pilot School at Edwards AFB, California, becoming an F-16 test pilot with the 416th Flight Test Squadron.

Major Bloomfield was one of the 19 astronaut candidates selected by NASA on December 8, 1994. In May 1996 he qualified as a Shuttle pilot, working in the astronaut office operations planning branch until his flight assignment.

Bluford, Guion Stewart, Jr.
1943–

Air Force pilot Guy Bluford became the first African American to go into space when he served as a mission specialist aboard STS-8, launched August 30, 1983. In addition to deploying an Indian communications satellite and experiments with the Canadian-built remote manipulator arm, STS-8 also made the first night-time launch and landing in the Shuttle program.

Bluford made a second spaceflight aboard Mission 61-A/Spacelab D1 in October and November 1985, one of 8 astronauts aboard this scientific mission controlled by the Federal German Aerospace Research Establishment (DFVLR).

He later flew as a mission specialist on STS-39, a Department of Defense flight launched in April 1991. During this 8-day mission Bluford supervised the operation of a series of military scientific experiments and deployed a small DOD satellite.

In November–December 1992 he made a fourth flight aboard STS-53, which deployed an advanced Satellite Data Systems platform, designed to relay imagery from the Crystal reconnaissance satellite to ground stations.

Bluford was born on November 22, 1942, in Philadelphia, Pennsylvania. His father was a mechanical engineer and Bluford became interested in aviation as a result. He graduated from Overbrook Senior High School in Philadelphia in 1960 and attended Pennsylvania State University, where he received a B.S. in aerospace engineering in 1964. He later received an M.S. with distinction from the Air Force Institute of Technology in 1974, and a Ph.D. in aerospace engineering with a minor in laser physics from that insitute in 1978. After becoming an astronaut he received an M.B.A. from the University of Houston-Clear Lake (1987).

An ROTC student at Penn State, Bluford entered active duty with USAF upon graduation in 1964. He earned his pilot's wings in January 1965, then flew F-4Cs in 144 combat missions—65 of them over North Vietnam—in the next two years. Returning to the United States, he served as a T-38A instructor pilot at Sheppard Air Force Base in Texas and attended Squadron Officers School. In August 1972 he entered the Air Force Institute of Technology at Wright-Patterson AFB, Ohio, and after completing his studies, remained there as a staff engineer. He logged over 4,800 hours of flying time in jets, including 1,300 hours as an instructor. He also published several scientific papers.

Bluford was selected as an astronaut candidate by NASA in January 1968. In August 1979 he qualified as a mission specialist, then worked on the remote manipulator system, Spacelab 3 experiments, Shuttle systems, Shuttle Avionics Integration Laboratory, and other assignments until being chosen for the STS-8 crew in April 1982.

Bluford left the astronaut office and retired from the Air Force in July 1993. He is currently vice-president and general manager of the Engineering Services Division of NYMA, Inc., in Greenbelt, Maryland.

Bobko, Karol Joseph
1936–

Air Force test pilot Karol "Bo" Bobko made three flights aboard the Space Shuttle, each one aboard a different orbiter.

He was pilot of STS-6, the maiden voyage of the orbiter Challenger, in April 1983, during which the first Tracking and Data Relay Satellite was deployed. In April 1985 he was commander of Mission 51-D on the orbiter Discovery. That mission saw the deployment of two communications satellites. When one satellite failed to boost itself into a higher orbit, two astronauts made an unscheduled space walk in an unsuccessful attempt to repair it.

In October 1985 Bobko commanded the maiden voyage of the orbiter Atlantis. Two DSCS III military communications satellites were sent into geosynchronous orbit during that mission, 51-J.

Bobko was born in New York City on December 23, 1937, and graduated from Brooklyn Technical High School in 1955. He was a member of the first graduating class of the Air Force Academy, where he received his bachelor of science in 1959. In 1970 he received an M.S. in aerospace engineering from the University of Southern California.

Following pilot training in 1960, Bobko flew F-100 and F-105 aircraft with the 523rd Tactical Fighter Squadron at Cannon AFB, New Mexico, and the 336th TFS at Seymore Johnson AFB, North Carolina. He attended the Aerospace Research Pilots School at Edwards AFB, California, in 1965 and in June 1966 was assigned to the Manned Orbiting Laboratory program. When that program was canceled in May 1969, Bobko transferred to NASA as an astronaut.

Bobko was a crewmember for the Skylab Medical Experiments Altitude Test in 1970, a 56-day ground simulation of a Skylab mission, then a support crewmember for Apollo-Soyuz Test Project from 1973-5. In 1976–77 he was a support crewmember for the Space Shuttle Approach and Landing Test flights, working as capcom and chase pilot.

On January 1, 1989, Bobko resigned from NASA and retired from the Air Force to join the space systems division of Booz, Allen and Hamilton, directing that company's consulting work in the Houston area for the Freedom Space Station program. Most recently Bobko has worked on the space station for the Grumman Corporation.

Boesen, Dennis Lee
1942–

Dennis Boesen was assigned as a prime payload specialist for the Strategic Defense Initiative's Starlab Shuttle mission, a weeklong Spacelab flight scheduled for launch as STS-50 in 1992. StarLab was canceled in August 1990, however. By then Boesen had been in training for three years. (He was also acting chief scientist for the Air Force Space Systems Division's participation in Starlab.)

Boesen was born August 9, 1942, in rural Howard County, Nebraska, near the town of Boelus, and grew up near Notus, Idaho, graduating from high school there in 1960. He attended the U.S. Air Force Academy, graduating with a B.S. in engineering science in 1964. In 1974 he earned an M.S. (with distinction) in engineering physics (laser optics) from the Air Force Institute of Technology.

Entering active duty with the Air Force in 1964, Boesen underwent flight training, then served as an instructor pilot in the T-37 aircraft. He did a combat tour in Vietnam as pilot of a UH-1H "Huey" helicopter gunship. He would later fly CT-39 aircraft, and also serve as a civilian instructor pilot.

As a laser scientist with the Air Force, Boesen served as technical director of the Airborne Laser Laboratory program, which successfully demonstrated that an air-to-air missile can be "killed" by a laser. For this work Boesen received the Air Force Scientific Achievement Award.

Boesen retired from the Air Force as a lieutenant colonel. He is currently employed by Research and Development Associates as a senior research specialist in RDA's Optical Engineering Laboratory in Albuquerque, New Mexico.

Bolden, Charles Frank, Jr.
1946–

Marine test pilot Charlie Bolden commanded STS-45, the March 1992 flight of the orbiter Atlantis that carried the Spacelab ATLAS. This 8-day mission was devoted to scientific studies of the Earth's atmosphere. The crew of 7 included Belgian scientist Dirk Frimout.

In February 1994 Bolden commanded a second shuttle flight, STS-60. The crew—which included Russian cosmonaut Sergei Krikalev—operated the second Space-Hab experiment module, and also attempted deployment of the Wake Shield Facility.

Bolden had made two prior Shuttle flights. In April 1990 he was a pilot of STS-31, a 5-day mission from which the Hubble Space Telescope was deployed from the orbiter Discovery. STS-31 also reached an altitude of 380 miles, a record for the Shuttle program.

Earlier, Bolden was pilot of shuttle Mission 61-C, which suffered seven different launch delays before finally lifting off on January 12, 1986. Included in the crew were Florida congressman Bill Nelson and RCA engineer Robert Cenker. During a 6-day flight the astro-

nauts deployed the RCA Satcom Ku-1 satellite and conducted experiments in astrophysics and materials processing.

Bolden was born August 19, 1946, in Columbia, South Carolina, where he graduated from C. A. Johnson High School in 1964. He attended the Naval Academy at Annapolis, earning a B.S. in electrical science in 1968. He later received an M.S. in systems management from the University of Southern California in 1978.

Bolden elected to serve in the Marine Corps and was commissioned in 1968. He underwent pilot training in Florida, Mississippi and Texas before earning his wings in May 1970. From 1970 to 1972 he was an A-6A pilot at Cherry Point, North Carolina, then was assigned to Nam Phong, Thailand, where he flew 100 combat missions over North and South Vietnam, Laos, and Cambodia. Returning to the United States in June 1973, he spent two years as a Marine Corps recruiting officer in Los Angeles, then, from 1975 to 1978, was stationed at the Marine Corps Air Station in El Toro, California.

In 1978 Bolden entered the Naval Test Pilot School at Patuxent River, Maryland, and following graduation served as a test pilot there until his selection by NASA.

As a pilot he has accumulated over 6,000 hours of flying time.

Bolden was one of the 19 astronauts selected by NASA in May 1980 and in August 1981 qualified as a Shuttle pilot. He worked in the systems development group (which was involved with tile repair, the solid rocket boosters, and launch debris), on orbiter cockpit displays and controls, and on computer systems at the Shuttle Avionics Integration Laboratory. He has also been technical assistant to the director of flight crew operations and leader of the astronaut support team at the NASA Kennedy Space Center.

In May 1992 Bolden was temporarily assigned as assistant deputy administrator at NASA headquarters in Washington. In this job he assisted the new administrator, Daniel Goldin, in planning and budgeting for future NASA programs.

Bolden left the astronaut office in 1994, following STS-60, to become commandant of cadets at the U.S. Naval Academy. In 1995 he was selected for promotion to brigadier general, and now serves with Marine Air Wing 3 at Miramar, California.

Booen, Michael Warren
1957–

Air Force engineer Michael Booen served as backup payload specialist for William Pailes aboard Shuttle Mission 51-J in October 1985. Two Department of Defense communications satellites were place in geosynchronous orbit during that flight, which Booen supported from mission control at the NASA Johnson Space Center in Houston.

Booen was born May 30, 1957, at Malmstrom AFB, Montana, and attended the U.S. Air Force Academy, graduating with a B.S. in engineering mechanics in 1979. In 1982 he earned an M.S. in systems engineering from Stanford University.

Following graduation from the Air Force Academy Booen served for two years as an engineer at the Air Force Weapons Laboratory at Kirtland AFB, New Mexico. He went from Kirtland to Stanford, and in January 1983 arrived in Los Angeles with the second cadre of manned spaceflight engineers. He worked on the DSCS-III program at Space Division, and was assigned as a Shuttle payload specialist in October 1984.

Booen left the MSE program in 1987 and returned to the Weapons Laboratory, where he worked on the neutral particle beam project for the Strategic Defense Initiative. In 1989 he was selected to serve as executive officer to Gen. Bernard Randolph, commander of the Air Force Systems Command. Upon Randolph's retirement in April 1990, Booen enrolled at the Defense Systems Management School, then returned to Headquarters Space Systems Division in Los Angeles, working on the Defense Support Program, the system of early warning satellites. From 1993 to 1995 he worked at the Pentagon.

Colonel Booen is currently program director for the YBL-1A Airborne Laser system at Kirtland AFB, New Mexico.

Borman, Frank Frederick II
1928–

Frank Borman commanded Apollo 8, which became the first manned spacecraft to orbit the Moon. In a memorable broadcast to the world from Apollo 8 on Christmas Eve 1968, Borman and fellow astronauts James Lovell and William Anders read passages from the book of Genesis. Their safe return to Earth after ten orbits of the Moon made the Apollo 11 lunar landing possible.

Borman's crew was originally scheduled to test the lunar module in a 4,000-mile-high Earth orbit in the third manned Apollo flight, but delays in the preparation of the LM and the fear that the Soviets would launch a manned circumlunar mission in December 1968 forced Apollo officials to consider a risky option: to send three astronauts around the Moon on the second Apollo flight, which would be the first launched aboard the huge Saturn 5 rocket. Given the choice of missions, Borman opted for the lunar flight while astronaut James McDivitt kept his crew on the LM flight.

It was a typically daring move by Borman, who had served on the review board that studied the tragic Apollo 1 fire that killed astronauts Grissom, White, and Chaffee. Borman later headed the team which reengineered the Apollo spacecraft. Astronaut Michael Collins would later write that Borman "made decisions faster than anyone I have ever known, with a high percentage of correct ones which would have been even higher if he'd slowed down."

Apollo 8 was Borman's second spaceflight. In December 1965 he was commander of Gemini 7, during which Borman and Lovell set an endurance record by spending 14 days in space.

Borman was born March 14, 1928, in Gary, Indiana, and grew up in Tucson, Arizona. He earned an appointment to the U.S. Military Academy at West Point, graduating in 1950 with a bachelor of science degree. He later earned an M.S. in aeronautical engineering from the California Institute of Technology in Pasadena in 1957, and graduated from the Advanced Management Training Program at the Harvard Business School in 1970.

Borman entered the Air Force after graduation from West Point and following flight school served as a fighter

LIVE, FROM THE MOON

by Frank Borman

(On Christmas Eve 1968, the Apollo 8 crew of Frank Borman, James Lovell, and William Anders became the first human beings to reach lunar orbit. Aside from the technical challenge of accomplishing the first manned deep space mission, the crew was also required to survey the lunar surface for upcoming Apollo landing sites. They were also the first space crew to fully use television to give earthbound viewers a sense of the experience of being in space.)

During the second orbit, we transmitted Earth's first televised pictures of the Moon from 70 miles above the lunar surface, each of us providing his own commentary based on what he was seeing at a particular time.

Anders: "The color of the Moon looks like a very whitish gray, like dirty beach sand with lots of footprints on it. Some of these craters look like pickaxes striking concrete, creating a lot of fine haze dust."

Lovell: "As a matter of interest, there's a lot of what appear to be small new craters that have these little white rays radiating from them. There's no trouble picking out features that we learned on the map."

Borman: "The Moon is very bright and not too distinct in this area."

On the third pass, we fired the service propulsion engine for just under ten seconds, changing the elliptical orbit to a circular one, as planned. By now I could see that Jim was really fatigued and I told him to get some rest while I took over navigation. Anders was looking increasingly tired, too, as well he might. He kept switching from one side of the spacecraft to the other, alternating between a movie camera and a number of different still cameras.

I happened to glance out one of the still-clear windows just at the moment the Earth appeared over the lunar horizon. It was the most beautiful, heart-catching sight of my life, one that sent a torrent of nostalgia, of sheer homesickness, surging through me. It was the only thing in space that had any color to it. Everything else was either black or white, but not the Earth. It was mostly a soft, peaceful blue, the continents outlined in a pinkish brown. And always the white clouds, like long streaks of cotton suspended above that immense globe.

[...]

On the ninth and next-to-last orbit, after Jim and Bill had gotten about five hours of sleep, we provided the final telecast from the Moon, first summing up our individual impressions of what we had seen, as Anders panned the TV camera across the wasteland beneath us.

Borman: "The Moon is a different thing to each of us. I know my own impression is that it's a vast, lonely, forbidding type of existence . . . a great expanse of nothing, that looks rather like clouds and clouds of pumice stone. It certainly would not be a very inviting place to live and work."

Lovell: "Frank, my thoughts are very similar. The vast loneliness of the Moon up here is awe-inspiring, and it makes you realize just what you have back there on Earth. The Earth from here is a grand oasis in the big vastness of space."

Anders: "I think the thing has impressed me most is the lunar sunrises and sunsets. The long shadows really bring out the relief."

Borman: "The sky is pitch-black and the Moon is quite light. And the contrast between the sky and the Moon is a vivid dark line."

Lovell: "Actually, I think the best way to describe this area is a vastness of black and white, absolutely no color."

I think the absence of color in space was etched more sharply in our minds than anything else, especially the colorless Moon itself. That, plus the bleak mottled lunar landscape. One out of our earlier passed over the so-called dark side of the Moon, Anders had remarked, "The backside looks like a sand pile my kids have been playing in for a long time. It's all beat up, no definition. Just a lot of bumps and holes. The area we're over right now gives some hint of possible volcanic action."

There was one more impression we wanted to transmit: our feelings of closeness to the Creator of all things. This was Christmas Eve, December 24, 1968, and I handed Jim and Bill their lines from the Holy Scriptures.

Anders spoke first. "For all the people back on Earth, the crew of Apollo 8 has a message that we would like to send to you."

He cleared his throat, then began reading the opening words of the book of Genesis.

"'In the beginning, God created the heaven and the Earth. And the Earth was without form, and void; and darkness was upon the face of the deep. And the spirit of God moved upon the face of the waters. And God said, Let there be light: and there was light. And God saw the light, that it was good: and God divided the light from the darkness.'"

Lovell was next, as the camera continued to pan the tortured lunar surface.

"'And God called the light Day, and the darkness he called Night. And the evening and the morning were the first day. And God said, Let there be a firmament in the midst of the waters, and let it divide the waters from the waters. And God made the firmament, and divided the waters which were under the firmament from the waters which were above the firmament: and it was so. And God called the firmament Heaven. And the evening and the morning were the second day.'"

I was last.

"'And God said, Let the waters under the heaven be gathered together in one place, and let the dry land appear: and it was so. And God called the dry land Earth, and the gathering place of the waters he called Seas: and God saw that it was good.'"

I added a postcript just before Apollo 8 disappeared again behind the Moon.

"And from the crew of Apollo 8, we close with a good night, good luck, a merry Christmas and God bless all of you—all of you on the good Earth."

pilot with the 44th Fighter Bomber Squadron in the Philippines from 1951 to 1953. For the next three years he was a pilot and instructor with various fighter squadrons in the United States. From 1957 to 1960 he taught thermodynamics and fluid mechanics at West Point, then became a member of the founding class of the Aerospace Research Pilot School at Edwards AFB, California. He was an instructor there when chosen by NASA.

As a pilot Borman logged over 6,000 hours of flying time.

One of the 9 astronauts selected by NASA in September 1962, Borman quickly established himself as one of the senior members of the group. He was astronaut chief Deke Slayton's first choice to join Gus Grissom on the crew of the first manned Gemini mission, but Grissom vetoed the choice of Borman (who was replaced by John Young). Given his own command, Borman served as backup to James McDivitt on Gemini 4 in 1965. After his flight on Gemini 7 he was named backup commander for the planned Apollo 2 mission with astronauts Stafford and Collins. In a major shuffling of crews and missions in November 1966, just three months prior to the Apollo fire, Borman was named to command the third manned Apollo.

The Apollo 1 fire on January 27, 1967, which killed astronauts Grissom, White, and Chaffee, suspended all manned Apollo flights. Borman was named the astronaut representative on the panel investigating the accident.

After Apollo 8 Borman was the field director of the NASA Space Station Task Force. He retired from the Air Force and NASA in July 1970 to join Eastern Airlines, eventually becoming chairman of the board, president and chief executive officer of that company. Borman was frequently seen in television commercials for Eastern, reminding viewers that "We earn our wings every day."

In addition to these activities, in 1966 and 1968 Borman served as a special presidential ambassador on trips to the Far East and Europe, and in 1970 made a worldwide tour to seek support for the release of American prisoners of war held in North Vietnam.

During his sixteen-year tenure at Eastern, Borman was credited with revitalizing an airline that was widely considered to be failing, leading it to record profits in 1979. But industry deregulation soon caused losses, and sparked wars between Borman and Eastern's labor unions. The airline was sold to Frank Lorenzo's Texas Air in June 1986, and Borman resigned, stating that he planned to help his son Edwin run his Las Cruces, New Mexico, auto dealership.

In June 1988 Borman was named chairman and CEO of Patlex Corporation of Chatsworth, California, a company involved in the production of electronic components and laser systems.

His autobiography, *Countdown*, written with Robert Serling, was published in 1989.

Bowersox, Kenneth Duane
1956–
Navy aviator Ken "Sox" Bowersox has made four Shuttle missions, two of them involving repairs to the Hubble Space Telescope and two more involving Spacelabs.

In December 1993 Bowersox and Shuttle commander Dick Covey piloted the orbiter Endeavour to a rendezvous with the Hubble; over the next week teams of EVA astronauts made five space walks to repair the ailing instrument. Three years later, in February 1997, Bowersox himself commanded STS-82, which made the second rendezvous with Hubble. Two more astronaut teams made EVAs, upgrading Hubble's systems even further.

Bowersox was also pilot of STS-50, the longest shuttle flight flown to that time. This two-week mission of the orbiter Columbia, launched June 25, 1992, carried the U.S. Microgravity Laboratory. The crew of 7 conducted experiments in space manufacturing.

In October 1995 Bowersox commanded USML-2, launched as STS-73 aboard the Columbia. STS-73 carried a crew of 7 who performed experiments in materials science and fluid dynamics on a 16-day-long mission.

Bowersox is currently assigned as commander of the third incremental crew to occupy the International Space Station. Bowersox and Russian cosmonauts Yuri Dezhurov and Mikhail Tyurin will be launched in late 2000 aboard a Soyuz spacecraft for a planned two-month mission aboard the ISS. Bowersox, Dezhurov, and Tyurin are also backups for the first ISS crew, William Shepherd, Yuri Gidzenko, and Sergei Krikalev.

Bowersox was born November 14, 1956, in Portsmouth, Virginia, but considers Bedford, Indiana, to be his hometown. He attended the Naval Academy, receiving a B.S. in aerospace engineering in 1978. In 1979 he earned an M.S. in mechanical engineering from Columbia University.

Commissioned an ensign in the Navy upon graduation from Annapolis, Bowersox entered flight school in 1980. From 1981 to 1984 he was an A-7E pilot with Attack Squadron 22 aboard the carrier *U.S.S. Enterprise*. He then attended the Air Force Test Pilot School at Edwards

AFB, California, and after graduation in 1985, was stationed at the Naval Weapon Center at China Lake, California, flying A-7E and F/A-18 aircraft.

He has logged over 3,500 hours of flying time and 300 carrier landings.

Commander Bowersox was one of the 17 astronauts selected by NASA in June 1987. In August 1988 he qualified as a Shuttle pilot. His technical assignments have included work in the Shuttle Avionics Integration Laboratory (SAIL), capcom for six Shuttle missions flown in 1990, and serving as technical assistant to the director of flight crew operations.

Brady, Charles Eldon, Jr.
1951–

Navy flight surgeon Charles Brady flew on STS-78, the longest Space Shuttle flight to that time. The 17-day flight of the orbiter Columbia carried the Life and Microgravity Spacelab (LMS). The crew of 7, including payload specialists from Canada and Europe, documented 41 different experiments in a mission that was seen as a forerunner of International Space Station operations.

Brady was born August 12, 1951, in Pinehurst, North Carolina. He graduated from North Moore High School in Robbins, North Carolina, then attended Duke University, receiving an M.D. in 1975.

He did his medical internship at the University of Tennessee in Knoxville, then, in 1978, worked as a team physician in sports medicine at Iowa State University in Ames. From 1979 to 1986 he had a family and sports medicine practice at the University of North Carolina, Chapel Hill, and East Carolina University, Greenville.

Brady joined the Navy in 1986, and after training as a Navy flight surgeon served with Carrier Air Wing Two aboard the U.S.S Ranger. He later served with Attack Squadron 45 and Aviation Electronic Countermeasures Squadron 131. From 1988 to 1990 he was the flight surgeon for the Blue Angels flight demonstration team.

At the time of his selection by NASA in March 1991 Commander Brady was at the Naval Air Station on Whidbey Island, Washington. In August 1993 he qualified as a Shuttle mission specialist. His technical assignments have been in the astronaut office mission development branch, at the Shuttle Avionics Integration Laboratory, and most recently as deputy chief for Space Shuttle astronaut training and chief for space station astronaut training in the mission operations division.

Brand, Vance DeVoe
1931–

Vance Brand made four spaceflights between 1975 and 1990, including the first international mission, Apollo-Soyuz, and the first operational flight of the Space Shuttle.

Brand was command module pilot for the Apollo-Soyuz Test Project, launched July 15, 1975, for a docking with the Soviet Soyuz 19. Brand and fellow astronauts Thomas Stafford and Donald Slayton spent two days docked with the Soviet vehicle crewed by cosmonauts Alexei Leonov and Valery Kubasov. During the Apollo splashdown on July 24, poisonous nitrogen tetroxide gas from a leaking thruster flooded the Apollo cabin. Brand was knocked unconscious, but revived when an oxygen mask was placed on his face. The astronauts suffered no lasting injury, but the incident was an embarrassment.

Brand's second trip into space was as commander of STS-5, the first operational flight of the Space Shuttle.

During the November 1982 flight of Columbia and its crew of 4 astronauts, the largest crew sent into space at that time, two communications satellites were successfully deployed. STS-5 ended after five days with a landing at Edwards AFB, California.

In February 1984 Brand commanded Mission 41-B, during which astronaut Bruce McCandless became the first human to fly freely in space with the manned maneuvering unit backpack. Other elements of the mission didn't go as well: two communications satellites, though deployed safely from the Challenger, suffered engine problems and failed to reach their proper orbits. (Both were retrieved and returned to Earth later in 1984.)

Brand's fourth flight was STS-35, a 9-day Spacelab ASTRO mission flown in December 1990. During this oft-delayed science mission a crew of 7, including four astronomers, operated a number of telescopes, which returned over 300 images of 135 deep space objects.

Brand was born May 9, 1931, in Longmont, Colorado, where he grew up, graduating from high school in 1949. He attended the University of Colorado, receiving a B.S. in business in 1953. He later earned a B.S. in aeronautical engineering from Colorado in 1960, and an M.B.A. from the University of California at Los Angeles in 1964.

He joined the Marine Corps in 1953, serving as a jet pilot until 1957. (He would fly for the Marine Corps Reserve and Air National Guard until 1964.) After further schooling at Colorado, he went to work for the Lockheed Aircraft Corporation in 1960, first as a flight test engineer, later, after attending the Naval Test Pilot School, as an experimental test pilot. He applied for the 1963 NASA astronaut group, but was not selected. When finally chosen in 1966 he was working for Lockheed at the flight test center at Istres, France.

As a pilot he logged over 8,700 hours of flying time, including 7,900 hours in jets, in 30 different types of aircraft.

Brand was one of 19 astronauts chosen by NASA in April 1966. In 1968 he and astronauts Joseph Kerwin and Joe Engle conducted vacuum chamber tests of the redesigned Apollo command and service modules. Brand later served on the support crews for Apollo 8 and Apollo 13. He was assigned as backup command module pilot for Apollo 15 and would have flown around the Moon on Apollo 18, but the mission was canceled.

He served as backup commander for the last two Skylab missions, and when an opening occurred on the Apollo-Soyuz crew in late 1972, began training simultaneously for that mission. Following Apollo-Soyuz he worked on Space Shuttle development.

In 1984 Brand was assigned as commander of two Shuttle/Spacelab missions, including the Spacelab Earth Observation Mission, which were canceled before they could be flown. He replaced Jon McBride, who resigned, as STS-35 commander in May 1989.

Brand left the astronaut office in 1991 to work in the program office of the National Aerospace Plane Program at Wright-Patterson AFB, Ohio. When that program was canceled, he transferred to the NASA Dryden Research Center at Edwards AFB, California.

Brandenstein, Daniel Charles

1943–

Former Navy test pilot Dan Brandenstein commanded STS-49, the maiden flight of the orbiter Endeavour in May 1992. During STS-49 astronauts made a record four space walks, including three devoted to retrieving and redeploying an Intelsat VI communications satellite.

Brandenstein and pilot Kevin Chilton also performed some of the most demanding flying of the Space Shuttle era, making three different rendezvous with Intelsat, including a risky maneuver that saw the Endeavour close to within a few feet of the rotating satellite, allowing astronauts Pierre Thuot, Rick Hieb, and Tom Akers literally to grab it.

STS-49 was Brandenstein's fourth shuttle mission, his third as commander. In January 1990 he commanded STS-32, a flight of the orbiter Columbia that retrieved the Long Duration Exposure Facility during a complex 10-day mission, the longest to that time by a Shuttle crew.

Brandenstein also served as pilot of the STS-8 Challenger mission in 1983, which performed the first night launch and landing in the Shuttle program. In 1985 he commanded the 7-astronaut crew of Mission 51-G, which included Saudi prince Sultan al-Saud and French pilot Patrick Baudry. Three communications satellites were launched from the Shuttle Discovery during 51-G.

Brandenstein was born January 17, 1943, in Watertown, Wisconsin, where he graduated from high school in 1961. He received a B.S. in mathematics and physics from the University of Wisconsin at River Falls in 1965.

After completing Navy pilot training in 1967, Brandenstein served two combat tours in Vietnam onboard the carriers *U.S.S. Constellation* and *U.S.S. Ranger*, flying 192 missions. Returning to the United States, he tested weapons and tactics for A-6 aircraft and also attended the Naval Test Pilot School at Patuxent River, Maryland. He was assigned to carrier duty aboard the *U.S.S. Ranger* again from 1975 to 1977, and was an A-6 instructor pilot when selected by NASA.

He logged over 6,400 hours of flying time in 24 different types of aircraft, and made 400 carrier landings.

Brandenstein was one of the 35 astronaut candidates chosen by NASA in January 1978. In August 1979 he qualified as a Shuttle pilot, serving as capcom and support crew member for the first two Shuttle missions in 1981.

Following his second spaceflight in June 1985 Brandenstein served as deputy director of flight crew operations. From May 1987 to August 1992 he served as chief of the astronaut office. He resigned from NASA and retired from the Navy in October 1992 and the next year joined I.B.M. Federal Systems in Houston. From 1994 to 1996 Brandenstein worked for Loral Space Information Systems, first as director of program development, then director of quality assurance.

Brandenstein is currently executive vice-president of Kistler Aerospace, a private company based in Washington state that hopes to launch communication satellites and other commercial payloads into orbit with its reusable K-1 launch vehicle beginning in 1999. Kistler's president is George Mueller, head of manned spaceflight for NASA during Apollo and Gemini.

Bridges, Roy Dunbard, Jr.

1943–

Air Force test pilot Roy Bridges was pilot of Space Shuttle Mission 51-F in July and August 1985. This 8-day Spacelab 2 mission was devoted to astronomy and was completed successfully, but not without several problems. For example, failures in the scientific Instrument Pointing System (IPS), a device intended to aim delicate sensors at distant objects, forced Bridges and commander Gordon Fullerton to perform dozens of extra maneuvers to ensure that Spacelab's telescopes were aimed properly.

In addition, Bridges and six other astronauts had to suffer through the second launchpad abort on the Shuttle program on July 12, and an unusual "abort-to-orbit" during launch on July 29, when one of the 3 Shuttle main engines quit. Because of the problem, the orbiter Challenger and its Spacelab 2 pallet were placed in a lower than desired orbit, which was eventually raised later in the flight. Mission specialist Anthony England, riding on the flight deck with Bridges and Fullerton, later recalled

that Bridges, seeing the light warning of an engine failure, pointed to it and said, "You're a simulation. I don't believe you."

Bridges was born July 19, 1943, in Atlanta, Georgia, and grew up in Gainesville, where he graduated from high school in 1961. He attended the Air Force Academy, receiving a B.S. in engineering science in 1965, and Purdue, where he earned an M.S. in astronautics in 1966.

Following pilot training at Williams AFB, Arizona, in 1967, Bridges became an F-100 tactical fighter pilot. He flew 226 combat missions in Vietnam in 1968, then returned to the United States, where he was an instructor and, in 1970, a student at the Air Force Test Pilot School at Edwards AFB, California. After graduation in 1971 he spent four years there as a test pilot.

He attended the Air Command and Staff College in 1975, then was assigned to Headquarters USAF in the Pentagon, where he took part in the development of the F-15 and A-10 aircraft. He was stationed at Nellis AFB, Nevada, when chosen by NASA.

As a pilot Bridges logged over 4,460 hours of flying time in 20 different types of aircraft.

Bridges was one of the 19 astronauts selected by NASA in May 1980, qualifying as a Shuttle pilot in August 1981. From June 1982 to June 1983 he was a Shuttle capcom, then was named to replace David Griggs on the Spacelab 2 crew in September 1984. He was assigned as pilot of Mission 61-F, the launch of the Galileo space probe scheduled for May 1986, but that mission was canceled following the Challenger disaster.

In May 1986 Bridges left NASA to return to the Air Force, becoming commander of the 6510th Test Wing at Edwards AFB, California. Three years later he became commander of the Eastern Space and Missile Test Center—the Air Force's Cape Canaveral launch site—at Patrick AFB, Florida. Following his promotion to brigadier general in 1990 he was assigned as deputy chief of staff for test and resources, Air Force Systems Command, Andrews AFB, Maryland, then, in August 1991, became commander of the Air Force Flight Test Center at Edwards AFB.

Bridges completed his military career as director of requirements at Headquarters Air Force Materiel Command at Wright-Patterson AFB, Ohio. He retired with the rank of major general on July 1, 1996.

Since March 1997 Bridges has been director of the NASA Kennedy Space Center.

Brown, Curtis Lee, Jr.
1956–

Air Force test pilot Curt Brown commanded STS-85, the August 1997 flight of the orbiter Discovery, which carried a crew of 6 and the CHRISTA-SPAS payload, designed to study the Earth's atmosphere, and a test version of the Japanese Experiment Module for the International Space Station.

Brown had already flown as pilot aboard three different Shuttle missions, including STS-77. This May 1996 flight of the orbiter Endeavour carried the fourth Space-Hab experiment module and accomplished four different rendezvous with satellites deployed by the Shuttle.

In November 1994 Brown was pilot of STS-66, an 11-day flight of the orbiter Atlantis, which carried the third ATLAS Spacelab in addition to the CHRISTA-SPAS platform. ATLAS-03 studied the effects of the sun on Earth's upper atmosphere.

His first mission was STS-47, an 8-day flight of the orbiter Endeavour launched in September 1992. STS-47 carried the Spacelab-Japan mission and a crew of 7, including Japanese payload specialist Mamoru Mohri. Brown served as leader of the red shift, with payload commander Mark Lee and PS Mohri.

Brown was born March 11, 1956, in Elizabethtown, North Carolina, where he graduated from East Bladen High School in 1974. He attended the Air Force Academy, receiving a B.S. in electrical engineering in 1978.

Brown underwent pilot training at Laughlin AFB, Texas, earning his wings in June 1979. He served as an A-10 pilot at Myrtle Beach AFB, South Carolina, from 1980 to March 1982, when he was reassigned to Davis-Monthan AFB, Arizona, as an A-10 instructor. During his tour at Davis-Monthan he attended the Air Force Fighter Weapons School at Nellis AFB, Nevada. In June 1985 he entered the Air Force Test Pilot School at Edwards AFB, California. At the time of his selection by NASA he was an A-10 and F-16 test pilot at Eglin AFB, Florida. He has logged over 4,300 hours of flying time.

Brown was one of the 17 astronauts selected by NASA in June 1987, qualifying as a Shuttle pilot in August 1988. His technical assignments have included work on improvements to the Shuttle mission simulator, and with the astronaut support personnel (ASP) or Cape Crusader team at Cape Canaveral. Following STS-47 Brown served as an ascent/entry capcom in mission control. More recently he has served as weather pilot for Shuttle launches at KSC.

Brown, David McDowell
1956–

Navy flight surgeon David Brown is one of the 35 astronaut candidates selected by NASA on May 1, 1996. In August 1996 he reported to the Johnson Space Center to begin a yearlong training and evaluation course that should qualify him as a Shuttle mission specialist. Since February 1997 he has worked in the payloads and habitation branch of the astronaut office.

Brown was born April 16, 1956, in Arlington, Virginia, where he graduated from Yorktown High School in 1974. He receved a B.S. in biology from the College of William and Mary (1978) and his M.D. from Eastern Virginia Medical School (1982).

Brown entered the Navy after completing his medical internship at the University of South Carolina, qualifying as a flight surgeon in 1984. He spent two years at the Navy Branch Hospital at Adak, Alaska, then moved to Carrier Air Wing Fifteen aboard the carrier *U.S.S. Carl Vinson.*

In 1988 Brown was selected for pilot training, the only flight surgeon in ten years to be so honored. He graduated first in his class at Beeville in 1990, becoming an A-6E Intruder pilot. He did a tour as an instructor and planning officer at the Naval Air Warfare Center, Fallon, Nevada, then deployed to Japan aboard the carrier *U.S.S. Independence* with Naval Air Squadron 115. At the time of his selection by NASA Commander Brown was a flight surgeon at the Naval Test Pilot School, Patuxent River, Maryland.

He has logged over 1,700 hours of flying time.

Brown, Mark Neil

1951–

Air Force pilot Mark Brown was a mission specialist aboard two Shuttle missions.

On STS-28 in August 1989 he took part in a 5-day Department of Defense mission which deployed a satellite designed to relay reconnaissance images into low Earth orbit. In September 1991 Brown was a mission specialist in the crew of STS-48, which deployed the Upper Atmosphere Research Satellite.

Brown was born November 18, 1951, in Valparaiso, Indiana, and graduated from high school there in 1969. He attended Purdue University, receiving his B.S. in aeronautical and astronautical engineering in 1973. He later earned an M.S. in astronautical engineering from the Air Force Institute of Technology in 1980.

An Air Force ROTC student, Brown entered the active duty upon graduation from Purdue and completed pilot training the next year. He flew T-38 and F-106 aircraft at Sawyer Air Force Base, Michigan, before being assigned to the Air Force Institute of Technology. From 1980 to 1984 he was an engineer in the flight activity branch at the NASA Johnson Space Center, supporting STS-2, 3, 4, 6, 8 and 41-C.

Brown was one of the 17 astronaut candidates selected by NASA in May 1984 and in June 1985 qualified as a Shuttle mission specialist. In November 1985 he was assigned to a Department of Defense mission scheduled for launch in 1986. That flight was delayed three years by the Challenger accident.

During the post-Challenger hiatus Brown served as a member of the team redesigning the Shuttle solid rocket motor.

Following STS-48 Brown served as deputy chief of the flight crew operations directorate for the Space Station/Exploration Office. In 1993 he was a member of the team that redesigned Space Station Freedom.

Brown retired from the Air Force with the rank of colonel and resigned from NASA in July 1993. He is currently head of the space division office for General Research Corporation, Dayton, Ohio.

Buchli, James Frederick

1945–

Former Marine platoon commander and flight officer Jim Buchli was a mission specialist aboard four Shuttle flights.

The first was Mission 51-C, a Department of Defense mission launched January 24, 1985, after a delay of more than a year. That 3-day mission (shortened one day because of weather) reportedly deployed a National Security Agency electronic intelligence satellite called Magnum into geosynchronous orbit.

In October 1985 Buchli was aboard Mission 61-A, a German Spacelab mission carrying a record crew of 8 astronauts and scientists. Buchli served as flight engineer and leader of the "blue team" of astronauts manning the lab during one of its 12-hour shifts.

Buchli flew a third time aboard STS-29, a 5-day mission during which a Tracking and Data Relay Satellite was deployed.

His fourth mission was STS-48, which deployed the Upper Atmosphere Research Satellite (UARS) in September 1991.

Buchli was born June 20, 1945, in New Rockford, North Dakota, and grew up in Fargo. He graduated from Fargo Central High School in 1963, then earned an appointment to the Naval Academy in Annapolis, graduating with a B.S. in aeronautical engineering in 1967. He later earned his M.S. in aeronautical engineering systems from the University of West Florida in 1975.

Buchli was commissioned in the Marine Corps following his graduation from Annapolis, and served as a platoon commander with the 9th Marine Regiment and company commander with the 3rd Reconnaissance Battalion in Vietnam. Returning to the United States in 1969, he underwent naval flight officer training and from 1970 to 1974 served with Marine fighter/attack squadrons in Hawaii, Japan, and Thailand. He was at the Naval Test Pilot School at Patuxent River, Maryland, when selected by NASA. He logged over 4,200 hours of flying time, 4,000 hours in jets.

A member of the January 1978 astronaut selection, Buchli qualified as a Shuttle mission specialist in August 1979. He was a member of the support crew for STS-1 and

STS-2 and capcom for STS-2. He was assigned to STS-10, a scheduled Department of Defense mission later flown as Mission 51-C, in November 1982. While training for 51-C he was assigned to the STS-19 crew (commanded by Joe Engle and eventually flown as Mission 51-I in August 1985) but had to be replaced when the first mission was delayed. From March 1989 to May 1992 Buchli was deputy chief of the astronaut office.

He resigned from NASA and retired from the Marine Corps in August 1992 to join the Boeing Defense and Space Group, Huntsville, Alabama, as manager for station systems operations and requirements.

Buckey, Jay Clark

1956–

Jay Buckey flew as payload specialist in the crew of STS-90. The spring 1998 mission of the orbiter Columbia carried Neurolab, a medical Spacelab mission, and a crew of seven on a 16-day mission in Earth orbit.

In 1993 Buckey served as alternate payload specialist for the second Spacelab Life Sciences mission, STS-58. SLS-2 was a 7-day mission devoted to studies in human adaptation to spaceflight.

Buckey was born June 6, 1956, in New York City. He attended Cornell University, receiving a B.S. in electrical engineering in 1977. He received his M.D. from Cornell's Medical College in 1981.

Buckey did his residency at New York Hospital, Cornell, then, in 1982, joined the University of Texas Southwestern Medical Center, Dallas, where he worked on a NASA Space Biology Research Fellowship. He then became research instructor in internal medicine at UTSMC. He is currently an assistant professor there while also serving as a clinical-medical doctor for the Ambulatory Care Clinic at Parkland Memorial Hospital, Dallas.

Bull John Sumter

1934–

Navy test pilot John Bull was a NASA astronaut for two years until discovery of a rare pulmonary illness forced him to leave the space program and the Navy in July 1968. A specialist in the Apollo lunar module, he would have had a chance to be assigned to a lunar landing mission.

Bull was born September 25, 1934, in Memphis, Tennessee. He received a B.S. in mechanical engineering from Rice in 1957. He later earned an M.S. in 1971 and a Ph.D. in 1973 in aeronautics and astronautics from Stanford.

From 1959 to 1963 Bull was a naval aviator flying F-3 Demons and F-4 Phantom IIs in Texas and California, and on three tours aboard the carriers *U.S.S. Ranger*, *U.S.S. Hancock* and *U.S.S. Kitty Hawk* in the Pacific. In February 1964 he graduated from the Naval Test Pilot School at Patuxent River, Maryland, (where he was named "outstanding student") and when selected as an astronaut in April 1966 was a project test pilot in the carrier suitability branch there.

As an astronaut Bull was assigned to the support crew for what was then the third manned Apollo flight (later flown as Apollo 8 by astronauts Borman, Lovell, and Anders) when stricken.

Since leaving the astronaut corps Bull joined the NASA Ames Research Center at Moffet Field, California, where he worked as chief of the aircraft systems branch, then as a research scientist in the aircraft guidance and navigation branch. He is now a private consultant.

Burbank, Daniel Christopher

1961–

Coast Guard aviator Dan Burbank is one of the 35 astronaut candidates selected by NASA on May 1, 1996. In August 1996 he reported to the Johnson Space Center to begin a yearlong training and evaluation course that should qualify him as a Shuttle mission specialist and International Space Station crewmember. Since March 1987 he has had a technical assignment in the operations planning branch of the astronaut office.

Burbank was born July 27, 1961, in Manchester, Connecticut. He graduated from high school in Tolland, Connecticut, in 1979, then entered the U.S. Coast Guard Academy, where he received a B.S. in electrical engineering in 1985. He later earned an M.S. in aeronautical engineering from Embry-Riddle Aeronautical University in 1990.

Following graduation from the Coast Guard Academy, Burank served as deck watch officer and law enforcement/boarding officer aboard the Coast Guard cutter *Gallatin* (WHEC 721). He commenced naval flight training at Pensacola, Florida, in January 1987, and graduated as a helicopter pilot the following February.

His first assignment as a pilot was at the Coast Guard Air Station at Elizabeth City, North Carolina, flying the HH3-F Pelican and the HH-60J Jayhawk. He also earned his master's at this time. In July 1992 Burbank transferred to the Coast Guard Air Station at Cape Cod, Massachusetts.

At the time of his selection by NASA Lieutenant Commander Burbank was aeronautical engineering officer at the Coast Guard Air Station in Sitka, Alaska.

He has logged over 3,000 hours of flying time, including 300 search and rescue missions.

Bursch, Daniel Wheeler

1957–

Navy flight officer Dan Bursch has been a mission specialist on three Shuttle missions, including STS-77. This May 1996 flight of the orbiter Endeavour carried the fourth SpaceHab experiment module, and also accomplished four different rendezvous with satellites released during the mission.

Bursch's first flight was STS-51, a September 1993 flight of the orbiter Discovery that deployed the Advanced Communications Technology Satellite. As the remote manipulator specialist in the crew, Bursch also deployed and retrieved the Spartan/Orfeus free-flying observatory.

Bursch made a second flight aboard STS-68 in October 1994. STS-68 carried the Shuttle Radar Laboratory, which imaged the Earth's surface (including the unexpected eruption of the volcano Klyuchevskoy in Kamchatka) for over ten days, amassing over 60 terrabits of data.

In November 1997 Bursch was assigned to the fourth incremental crew scheduled to occupy the International Space Station during its assembly phase. Bursch, astronaut Carl Walz, and Russian cosmonaut Yuri Onufriyenko will launch to the ISS aboard STS-104 in early 2001 for a planned four-month visit. This crew also serves as back-ups for the second ISS crew, James Voss, Susan Helms, and Yuri Usachev.

Bursch was born July 25, 1957, in Bristol, Pennsylvania, but considers Vestal, New York, to be his hometown. He attended the U.S. Naval Academy, receiving a B.S. in physics in 1979.

Following graduation from Annapolis Bursch underwent training as a flight officer at Pensacola, Florida, earning his wings in April 1980. From 1981 to 1983 he was an A-6E bombardier/navigator with Attack Squadron 34, serving in the Mediterranean aboard the carrier *U.S.S. John F. Kennedy*, and in the North Atlantic and Indian aboard the *U.S.S. America*. In January 1984 he enrolled at the Naval Test Pilot School at Patuxent River, Maryland. In 1985 he served as an A-6 test flight officer at the Flight Test Center at Pax River, then returned to the school as an instructor.

From April 1987 to the summer of 1989 Bursch served as strike operations officer for the commander, Cruise-Destroyer Group 1, aboard the *U.S.S. Long Beach* and *U.S.S. Midway*. At the time of his selection by NASA he was attending the Naval Postgraduate School at Monterey, California.

Bursch has logged over 2,500 hours of flying time in 35 different aircraft, including over 200 carrier landings.

He was one of the 23 astronaut candidates selected by NASA in January 1990, qualifying as a Shuttle mission specialist in July 1991. His technical assignments have included working on orbiter controls and displays in the astronaut office operations development branch, as chief of astronaut appearances, and as spacecraft communicator in mission control.

From August 1996 to November 1997 he was crew representative for the International Space Station.

Butterworth, Louis William
1948–

Hughes Aircraft engineer Bill Butterworth was the backup payload specialist for Gregory Jarvis at the time of the ill-fated Challenger launch on January 28, 1986.

Butterworth was born July 17, 1948, in Casper, Wyoming, and graduated from high school in Hinsdale, Illinois, in 1966. He attended the California Institute of Technology in Pasadena, California, receiving a B.S. in engineering in 1970 and an M.S. in mechanical engineering in 1971.

While a student at Cal Tech Butterworth got a job at the nearby NASA Jet Propulsion Laboratory performing structural analyses on satellite solar power arrays. He joined the staff of Hughes Aircraft in Culver City, California, in 1972, to work on advanced communications satellites, but in 1974 transferred to the Pioneer Venus program, working as a system engineer on the propulsion, pressurization, and environmental test systems. Following the successful launch and operation of Pioneer Venus (1980), Butterworth joined the Hughes team building the Galileo Jupiter probe. He became spacecraft manager for Galileo in 1982, then assistant program manager in 1984, as Galileo suffered through a staggering variety of redesigns forced on it by changes in its Shuttle launch system. (Galileo was ultimately deployed from the Shuttle in October 1989, beginning its 9-year voyage to Jupiter.)

Butterworth was one of 4 Hughes Aircraft engineers selected as Shuttle payload specialists in July 1984. He was originally assigned, with Jarvis, to Mission 51-D, scheduled to deploy a Hughes-built communication satellite, then to Mission 51-L.

Butterworth moved to Hughes DirecTV satellite system unit in 1990, first in development and implementation, and then in 1992 as senior vice president for Direct Broadcast Satellite network systems. He is currently a consultant to Hughes Space and Communications.

Cabana, Robert Donald
1949–

Marine test pilot Bob Cabana is the veteran astronaut assigned to command the first Space station assembly mission, STS-88, scheduled for launch in December 1998, having been delayed for fourteen months by problems with the Russian-built service module. This flight of the orbiter Atlantis will deploy Node 1, the Boeing-built habitation module, docking it to the Russian-built Zarya control module.

Cabana is a veteran of three previous Shuttle missions. He was pilot of STS-41, a flight of the orbiter Discovery in October 1990 that sent the space probe Ulysses on a four-year journey, via the planet Jupiter, to the polar regions of the sun.

He also flew as pilot of STS-53, a Department of Defense Shuttle mission that deployed an advanced Satellite Data Systems payload in November 1992.

In July 1994 he was commander of STS-65, the second International Microgravity Spacelab. IML-02 carried a crew of 7 that conducted 82 different experiments.

Cabana was born January 23, 1949, in Minneapolis, Minnesota, and graduated from Washburn High School there in 1967. He attended the Naval Academy at Annapolis, receiving a B.S. in mathematics in 1971.

After graduation Cabana became a Marine bombardier and navigator for A-6 aircraft and was based in North Carolina and Japan. Returning to the U.S. in 1975, he became a pilot, then was assigned to the 2nd Marine Aircraft Wing at Cherry Point, North Carolina, for four years. He attended the Naval Test Pilot School at Patuxent River, Maryland, in 1981, and served as a test pilot there on a number of aircraft, including the X-29. When selected by NASA Cabana was serving with Marine Aircraft Group 12 in Iwakuni, Japan.

He has logged over 5,000 hours of flying time in 32 different types of aircraft.

Cabana was one of the 13 astronaut candidates selected by NASA in June 1985, qualifying as a Shuttle pilot in July 1986. His technical assignments have included serving as the astronaut office coordinator for flight software (1986), a stint as deputy chief of aircraft operations (1986-89), and a tour in the Shuttle Avionics Integration Lab (SAIL). He has also been a capcom.

From September 1994 to October 1997 Colonel Cabana was chief of the astronaut office.

Cagle, Yvonne Darlene
1959–

Dr. Yvonne Cagle is one of the 35 astronaut candidates selected by NASA on May 1, 1996. In August 1996 she reported to the NASA Johnson Space Center to begin a yearlong training and evaluation course to qualify her as a Shuttle mission specialist and International Space Station crewmember.

Cagle was born April 24, 1959, at West Point, New York. She graduated from high school in Novato, California, in 1977, then attended San Francisco State University, where she received a B.A. in biochemistry in 1981. She received her M.D. from the University of Washington in 1985.

Cagle's medical education was sponsored by the Health Professions Scholarship Program, which commissioned her as a reserve officer in the Air Force. Following an internship at the Transitional Highland General Hospital in Oakland, Cagle entered active duty, serving with Air Force units at RAF Lakenheath, England. While at Lakenheath she was selected for the School of Aerospace Medicine at Brooks AFB, Texas, where in April 1988 she qualified as a flight surgeon.

She returned to England, where she was assigned to the 48th Tactical Hospital. In May 1989 she volunteered as an Air Force medical liaison officer for the STS-30 mission, serving at the contingency Shuttle landing site at Banjul, West Africa.

Cagle left active duty to work in family practice at Eastern Virginia Medical School (1992). At the time of her selection by NASA Cagle was an occupational medicine physician and deputy project manager for the Kelsey-Seybold Clinic at the NASA Johnson Space Center. Among her duties there was the health screening of the Russian support staff for the Mir-18 cosmonaut crew launched aboard STS-71.

Cagle is a certified FAA senior aviation medical examiner, and is currently assigned to the Pentagon Flight Medicine/Special Mission Clinic, as a member of the Air Force Reserve.

Caldeiro, Fernando (Frank)
1958–

Shuttle engineer Frank Caldeiro is one of the 35 astronaut candidates selected by NASA on May 1, 1996. In August 1996 he reported to the Johnson Space Center to begin a training and evaluation course that should qualify him as a Shuttle mission specialist and International Space Station crewmember.

Caldeiro was born June 12, 1958, in Buenos Aires, Argentina. He graduated from W. C. Bryant High School in Long Island City, New York, in 1976, then attended the University of Arizona, where he received a B.S. in mechanical engineering in 1984. In 1995 he received an M.S. in engineering management from the University of Central Florida.

Beginning in 1985 Caldeiro worked for the Rockwell Corporation, Downey, California, as a test director for the B-1B bomber program. When that program ended with the delivery of the one hundredth B-1B, Caldeiro was transferred to the Kennedy Space Center in 1988 to serve as a specialist on the Shuttle's main engine system.

He joined NASA in 1991 as a cryogenic and propulsion systems expert in the safety and mission assurance office, based at the NASA Kennedy Space Center.

Caldwell, Tracy Ellen
1969–

Chemist Tracy Caldwell is one of the astronaut candidates selected by NASA in June 1998. In August of that year she reported to the Johnson Space Center to begin a training and evaluation course which should qualify her as a Shuttle mission specialist and International Space Station crewmember.

Caldwell was born August 14, 1969, in Arcadia, California, and graduated from high school in Beaumont in 1987. She attended the California State University, Fullerton, receiving a B.S. in chemistry in 1993, and received her Ph.D. in chemistry from the University of California, Davis, in 1997.

At the time of her selection by NASA, Caldwell was a postdoctoral fellow at the University of California, Irvine.

Camarda, Charles Joseph
1952–

Aerospace engineer Charles Camarda is one of the 35 astronaut candidates selected by NASA on May 1, 1996. In August of that year he reported to the Johnson Space Center to begin a training and evaluation course that should qualify him as a Shuttle mission specialist and International Space Station crewmember. He is currently assigned to the vehicle systems/operations branch of the astronaut office.

Camarda was born May 8, 1952, in New York City. He graduated from Archbishop Molloy High School in Jamaica, New York, then attended the Polytechnic Institute of Brooklyn, New York, receiving a B.S. in aerospace engineering (1974). He later received an M.S. in engineering science from George Washington University (1980) and a Ph.D. in aerospace engineering from Virginia Polytechnic Institute (1990).

Following graduation from Brooklyn Polytech, Camarda joined the NASA Langley Research Center in Hampton, Virginia, becoming a research scientist in the thermal structures branch of the structures and materials division. This work dealt with the cooling, heat transfer and construction of spacecraft, aircraft and launch vehicles.

In 1989 Camarda was named to lead the structures and materials technology maturation team for the National Aerospace Plane project, a program designing a hypersonic vehicle capable of taking off from a runway and reaching orbit.

At the time of his selection as an astronaut candidate Camarda was head of the thermal structures branch at NASA Langley. He has received 18 NASA awards for technical innovations and accomplishments, holds two patents, and has two more patents pending.

Camerson, Kenneth Donald
1949–

Marine aviator Ken Cameron made three Shuttle flights between 1991 and 1995, two as commander.

His first flight was as pilot of STS-37, the April 1991 mission of the orbiter Atlantis during which the Gamma Ray Observatory was deployed in Earth orbit. Astronauts Jerry Ross and Jay Apt made two space walks during the mission, one of them to ensure the deployment of the GRO. Cameron—an amateur radio enthusiast—also took part in several ham radio conversations with earthbound students.

In April 1993 Cameron commanded STS-56, the second Spacelab ATLAS mission. This 9-day mission carried a crew of 7 and conducted studies of solar effects on the Earth's atmosphere.

Cameron's final mission was STS-74, the second Shuttle-Mir docking mission, flown in November 1995. STS-74 attached a Russian-built docking module to Mir to allow easier Shuttle dockings with the station.

From February to October 1994 Cameron served as the NASA director of operations-Russia, coordinating training for astronauts at the Gagarin Center as well as activities at the Korolev (formerly Kaliningrad) flight control center in preparation for Shuttle visits to the Mir space station.

Cameron was born November 29, 1949, in Cleveland Ohio, and graduated from Rocky River High School in Rocky River, Ohio, in 1967. He earned a B.S. and M.S. in aeronautics and astronautics from the Massachusetts Institute of Technology in 1978 and 1979.

Cameron joined the Marine Corps at the age of 20 and served as an infantry platoon commander with the 1st Battalion, 5th Marine Regiment in Vietnam in 1970. He also served with the Marine Security Guards at the American Embassy in Saigon. After returning to the United States he attended flight school, becoming an A-4A Skyhawk pilot in 1973. As a pilot his duties took him to bases in Yuma, Arizona, and Iwakuni, Japan. Following two years at M.I.T. getting his college degrees, Cameron was assigned to the Pacific Missile Test Center in Hawaii. In 1982 he attended the Naval Test Pilot School at Patuxent

River, Maryland, and was a test pilot there when selected by NASA.

He logged over 4,000 hours of flying time in 48 different types of aircraft.

Cameron was one of the 17 astronauts selected by NASA in May 1984. In June 1985 he qualified as a Shuttle pilot. He worked on the Tethered Satellite project, in the Shuttle Avionics Integration Laboratory (SAIL), and as a capcom for STS-29, 30, 29, 34 and 33. He was assigned to STS-37 in April 1989. Prior to his assignment as STS-56 commander he worked in the Space Station Support Office. From November 1995 to August 1996 Cameron was chief of the vehicle systems/operations branch of the astronaut office.

Cameron retired from the Marine Corps with the rank of colonel and resigned from NASA August 5, 1996, to join the Hughes Training Division, Houston, Texas. Since 1997 he has worked for General Motors, Sweden.

Carey, Duane Gene
1957–

Air Force test pilot Duane "Digger" Carey was one of the 35 astronaut candidates selected by NASA on May 1, 1996. In August of that year he reported to the Johnson Space Center to begin a yearlong training and evaluation course that should qualify him as a Shuttle pilot. Since March 1997 he has also served as astronaut office T-38 safety officer.

Carey was born April 3, 1957, in St. Paul, Minnesota, where he graduated from Highland Park High School in 1975. He attended the University of Minnesota, receiving a B.S. (1981) and M.S. (1982) in aerospace engineering.

He entered the Air Force through ROTC in 1981, and completed undergraduate pilot training in 1983. He served tours at England AFB, Louisiana, and Suwon Air Base, Republic of Korea, as an A-10A pilot. In 1988 he qualified on the F-16, and spent two years at Torrejon Air Base, Spain.

Carey graduated from the Air Force Test Pilot School at Edwards AFB, California, in 1992, then served as an F-16 test pilot and system safety officer at the Flight Test Center there.

Major Carey has logged over 3,000 hours of flying time in 35 different types of aircraft.

Carpenter, Malcolm Scott
1925–

One of the original Mercury astronauts, Scott Carpenter made the second American orbital flight and also pioneered the exploration of the oceans, becoming the world's first astronaut/aquanaut.

Carpenter's only spaceflight, Mercury-Atlas 7 on May 24, 1962, lasted 4 hours and 56 minutes, during which the astronaut made three orbits of the Earth. John Glenn's flight three months earlier had proved that an astronaut could survive in space, so Carpenter's task was to see whether an astronaut could work in space. His flight plan was crowded with scientific experiments that included observations of flares fired on Earth and the deployment of a tethered balloon.

Carpenter found John Glenn's mysterious "fireflies" when he rapped on the side of the spacecraft, raising a cloud of luminous particles. He tried to reproduce the disorientation reportedly suffered by Soviet cosmonaut Gherman Titov (later revealed to be the first case of space adaptation syndrome) and failed. And he radioed greetings—in Spanish—to ground controllers at Guaymas, Mexico.

Seemingly distracted and behind schedule throughout the flight, Carpenter used too much attitude control fuel and was forced to fire his retrorockets manually. He was successful, but late, and Aurora 7 splashed down over 200 miles off course, far from the waiting recovery carrier. Carpenter climbed out of the floating spacecraft and into a life raft to wait for rescue swimmers and ships, which began arriving forty minutes later. The minutes of uncertainty about Carpenter's survival created a tense moment for the American space program. CBS newscaster Walter Cronkite stated on the air that he was afraid America "had lost an astronaut."

Carpenter's performance precluded future space missions. (It was rumored that flight director Christopher Kraft informed him that he would never fly again.) He was assigned to the development of the lunar module and also worked as executive assistant to the director of the Manned Spacecraft Center.

In the spring of 1965 Carpenter took a leave of absence from NASA to participate in the Navy's Man-in-the-Sea program and that summer spent 30 days living and working on the ocean floor in Sealab II. Carpenter was leader of two of the three teams that spent a total of 45 days at a depth of over 200 feet.

Returning to the space program, Carpenter was responsible for liaison with the Navy for underwater zero-G training when he suffered an elbow injury in a motorcycle accident in Bermuda. With his flight status even more questionable, Carpenter left the astronaut team for good on August 10, 1967.

Carpenter was born May 1, 1925, in Boulder, Colorado, and graduated from high school there. His parents separated when he was 3 years old and when his mother was institutionalized for treatment for tuberculosis, Carpenter was raised by a family friend. He would later describe himself as a "hell raising" teenager.

After graduating from high school in 1943 Carpenter entered the Navy's V-5 flight training program, which was intended to give potential pilots advanced academic training at the same time they were given basic experience in aircraft. World War II ended before Carpenter could complete the program and after stays in Iowa and California he wound up as a student at the University of Colorado, majoring in aerospace engineering. He received a bachelor of science degree in 1962.

He returned to the Navy in 1949 and finally earned his wings, following training in Florida and Texas. Assigned to Patrol Squadron 6, he flew antisubmarine, ship surveillance, and aerial mining missions in the Yellow Sea, the South China Sea and the Formosa Straits during the Korean War. Returning to the United States in 1954, he attended the Naval Test Pilot School at Patuxent River, Maryland, and remained at the Naval Test Center there until 1957. He attended the Navy General Line School and the Navy Air Intelligence School in 1957 and 1958 and was assigned as an intelligence officer aboard the carrier *U.S.S. Hornet* when chosen by NASA in April 1959.

As an astronaut Carpenter served as John Glenn's backup for Mercury-Atlas 6, and was named to MA-7, America's second manned orbital flight when Donald Slayton, the original pilot, was grounded.

As a pilot Carpenter logged over 3,500 hours of flying time, including 700 hours in jets.

After leaving NASA he served as assistant for Aquanaut Operations for Sealab III until retiring from the U.S. Navy with the rank of commander on July 1, 1969. Since then he has been an engineering, aeronautical, and environmental consultant in addition to being involved in wasp breeding.

In 1989 he served with his son Marc as a commercial spokesman for Buick automobiles. His novel *The Steel Albatross* was published in January 1991 to generally good reviews.

Carr, Gerald Paul
1932–

Marine aviator Jerry Carr commanded America's longest manned spaceflight, Skylab 4, from November 1973 to February 1974.

Carr, science pilot Edward Gibson, and pilot William Pogue spent 84 days in orbit aboard the Skylab orbiting workshop, the third crew to occupy the station. They carried out experiments in studies of the Earth and the effects of weightlessness on human beings, and made extensive observations of the sun while operating the Apollo Telescope Mount attached to Skylab for 338 hours. Carr also logged almost 16 hours in space walks outside Skylab.

The mission also became notorious when the astronauts staged the first "strike" in space history, complaining of overwork and poor planning by ground controllers.

Carr was born August 22, 1932, in Denver, Colorado, and grew up in Santa Ana, California, graduating from high school there. He attended the University of Southern California, receiving a B.S. in mechanical engineering in 1954, and later earned a second B.S. in aeronautical engineering from the Naval Postgraduate School in 1961. He also earned an M.S. in aeronautical engineering from Princeton University in 1962.

Carr joined the Navy immediately after high school and attended U.S.C. as a Naval ROTC student. Upon graduation in 1954 he was commissioned in the Marine Corps and became a pilot. He was assigned to Marine All-

Weather Fighter Squadron 114 flying F-9 and F-6A aircraft until entering graduate school, then flew with All-Weather Squadron 122 in the United States and the Far East until 1965. His last assignment prior to becoming an astronaut was as a test director with Marine Air Control Squadron 3.

As a pilot Carr logged over 6,100 hours of flying time, 5,400 in jets.

He was one of 19 astronauts selected by NASA in April 1966. After basic astronaut training he specialized in Apollo lunar module systems and, later, the lunar roving vehicle. He served as capcom and support crewmember for Apollo 8 and Apollo 12. In early 1970 he was tentatively assigned to be lunar module pilot for the planned Apollo 19 flight when NASA budget cuts forced its cancellation. He transferred to the Skylab program and was named commander of the third mission in January 1972.

After his Skylab flight Carr was named head of the astronaut office Shuttle design support group. He retired from the Marine Corps as a colonel in September 1975, and from NASA in June 1977 to become vice-president of Bovay Engineers, Inc., Houston, Texas.

Since 1983 Carr has been a senior consultant to the president of Applied Research, Inc., a company based in Los Angeles and Houston. He has also served on the Citizen's Advisory Council on National Space Policy. He is currently partnered with former Skylab astronauts William Pogue and Jack Lousma in an aerospace consulting company based in northwest Arkansas.

Carretto, Joseph Anthony, Jr.

1957–

Joe Carretto was a member of the third cadre of Air Force Manned Spaceflight Engineers who began to train in April 1986 as potential Shuttle payload specialists. The group was disbanded in 1988 before any of its members could fly in space.

Carretto was born January 30, 1957, in West Hempstead, New York, where he grew up. His interest in spaceflight began with John Glenn's Mercury mission in 1962. He attended the Massachusetts Institute of Technology,

graduating with a B.S. in electrical engineering in 1978, and later earned an M.S. in electrical engineering (guidance and control) from the Air Force Institute of Technology (1982).

Entering active duty with the Air Force following graduation from M.I.T., Carretto served at Wright-Patterson AFB, Dayton, Ohio, for four years, first as a project engineer working on navigation systems and hardware, then as a project manager for several research and development efforts, including radio navigation systems for the Global Positioning System of satellites. From 1982 to 1986 he was a Space Shuttle flight controller at the NASA Johnson Space Center responsible for Shuttle electrical, environment, and thermal systems. In 1984 he was a semifinalist for selection to the NASA astronaut group.

As a member of the Manned Spaceflight Engineer cadre from 1986 to 1988, Carretto worked on Starlab, the Strategic Defense Initiative's Spacelab once scheduled for launch on a 1992 Shuttle mission. With the termination of the MSE program he became executive officer to Major General Robert Rankine, deputy director for launch operations at Space Division.

Lieutenant Colonel Carretto has since attended the Air Command and Staff College (1990) followed by duty with the National Reconnaissance Office. He is currently head of integration and launch support at the launch program division, Space and Missile Systems Center, Los Angeles AFB.

Carter, Manley Lanier "Sonny," Jr.

1947–1991

Former Navy pilot and flight surgeon Sonny Carter was a mission specialist aboard STS-33. This November 1989 Department of Defense Shuttle mission deployed an electronic intelligence satellite called Mentor into geosynchronous orbit. The crew of 5 landed after 120 hours in space.

Carter was then assigned as mission specialist and payload commander for STS-42, the flight of the International Microgravity Spacelab scheduled for launch in 1992.

Tragically, on April 5, 1991, Carter was killed in the crash of a commuter aircraft at Brunswick, Georgia. The Atlantic Southeast Airlines Embraer 120 was approaching Glynco Airport in Brunswick when it crashed two miles short of the runway, killing all 23 passengers and crew, including Carter and former Texas senator John Tower.

Carter had been scheduled to make a public appearance. Ironically the weather in the Southeast that day had been so bad that the space agency had forbidden him to fly a NASA T-38 to the engagement.

Carter was born August 15, 1947, in Macon, Georgia, though he considered nearby Warner Robins to be his hometown. He graduated from Sidney Lanier High School in Macon in 1965, then went on to attend Emory University in Atlanta, receiving a B.A. in chemistry (1969) and an M.D. (1973).

While he was a student at medical school Carter played soccer for the Atlanta Chiefs of the North American Soccer League, making him the first ex-professional athlete to go into space. *Sports Illustrated* magazine (Sept. 25, 1989) recalled Carter's athletic career, and recounted a visit by Carter to a Los Angeles Dodgers fantasy baseball camp in 1989.

After completing an internship in internal medicine at Grady Memorial Hospital in Atlanta, Carter entered the Navy in July 1974. He qualified as a Navy flight surgeon and served in that job with the 1st and 3rd Marine Air Wings. In 1978 he graduated from flight school at Beeville, Texas, then was assigned as senior medical officer on the carrier *U.S.S. Forrestal* while qualifying as an F-4 Phantom pilot. He flew F-4s with Marine Fighter Attack Squadrons 333 (Beaufort, South Carolina) and 115 (*U.S.S. Forrestal*) until September 1982, when he attended the Navy Fighter Weapons School ("Top Gun"). Carter had just graduated from the Naval Test Pilot School at Patuxent River, Maryland, when selected by NASA.

He logged 3,000 hours of flying time and 160 carrier landings.

Carter was one of the 17 astronaut candidates selected in May 1984 and in June 1985 qualified as a Shuttle mission specialist. He was immediately assigned to the crew of Mission 61-I, then scheduled for launch in the summer of 1986. While training for that mission he served with the astronaut support team at the Kennedy Space Center, setting up cockpit switches and assisting astronauts in boarding the Shuttle orbiter prior to launch. He was the last person to see the crew of the Challenger alive. For much of 1986 he was involved in the search for Challenger debris, including recovery of the crew cabin.

He later worked on the development of a crew escape system, and as the astronaut office's EVA representative.

The Neutral Buoyancy Training Facility at the NASA Johnson Space Center is named for Carter.

Casper, John Howard
1943–

Air Force test pilot John Casper commanded STS-77, the May 1996 flight of the orbiter Endeavour that set a record by accomplishing four different rendezvous with satellites previously deployed by the orbiter. STS-77 also carried the fourth SpaceHab experiment module.

Casper also commanded STS-62, a 14-day flight of the orbiter Columbia in March 1994. STS-62 carried the U.S. Microgravity Payload in addition to other experiments. The mission was a forerunner of future American space station operations.

In January 1993 Casper commanded STS-54, which deployed the sixth Tracking and Data Relay Satellite. Previously he had been pilot of STS-36, a dedicated Department of Defense Shuttle mission launched on February 28, 1990, after five attempts. During this flight of the orbiter Atlantis, which was flown at a record inclination of 62-degrees and brought the spacecraft as far north as the Arctic Circle, the crew deployed a massive CIA imaging reconnaissance satellite called AFP-731.

Casper was born July 9, 1943, in Greenville, South Carolina, and graduated from Chamblee High School in Chamblee, Georgia, in 1961. He attended the Air Force Academy in Colorado Springs, earning a B.S. in engineering science in 1966. In 1967 he earned an M.S. in astronautics from Purdue. He graduated from the Air War College in 1986.

After completing pilot training, Casper served in Vietnam flying F-100s on 229 combat missions. From

1970 to 1974 he was based in Lakenheath, England, with the 48th Tactical Fighter Wing, then attended the U.S. Air Force Test Pilot School at Edwards AFB, where he remained as a test pilot and, later, commander of the 6513th Test Squadron, until 1980. At the time of his selection by NASA he was at Headquarters USAF in the Pentagon, where he served as action officer for the deputy chief of staff for plans and operations (1980–82) and deputy chief of the Special Projects Office (1982–84).

He has logged over 7,000 hours of flying time in 51 different types of aircraft.

Casper was one of the 17 astronaut candidates selected by NASA in May 1984 and in June 1985 qualified as a Shuttle pilot. His subsequent technical assignments included acting as astronaut office representative for improved Shuttle landing equipment and sites, work in the Shuttle Avionics Integration Laboratory and service as a capcom in mission control. In December 1990 he was assigned as pilot for STS-50; nine months later he was transferred to the command of STS-54. Casper served as chief of the operations development branch in 1994–95.

He retired from the Air Force with the rank of colonel in June 1996, and currently serves as head of the safety, reliability and quality assurance office at NASA JSC.

Casserino, Frank James
1955–

Air Force engineer Frank Casserino was one of the first 13 Department of Defense Manned Spaceflight Engineers selected for training as possible Shuttle payload specialists in February 1980.

In 1983 Casserino was designated as prime payload specialist for STS-16, a dedicated DoD Shuttle mission then scheduled for launch in 1984 but postponed first to October 1985, then to September 1986, and finally, following the Shuttle Challenger disaster, launched as ST-28 in 1988. By then the Air Force had elected not to include a payload specialist in the crew.

Casserino was born July 21, 1955 in the Bronx, New York. He attended the Air Force Academy at Colorado Springs, Colorado, graduating with a B.S. in astronautical engineering in 1977. He later earned an M.B.A. from the University of Santa Clara.

From 1977 to 1980 he was an operations director at the Satellite Control Facility in Sunnyvale, California. When he joined the MSE program in February 1980 he was just 24 years old, the youngest American ever chosen as a candidate for a spaceflight.

Casserino left the MSE group in May 1985 though he continued to be associated with his classified payload and remained at Los Angeles Air Force Station. In late 1987 he resigned from the Air Force to join Wile Applied Research in El Segundo, California. He later returned to reserve duty with the Air Force at Falcon AFS, Colorado, becoming the first commander of the 7th Space Operations Squadron (1993) and, in September 1997, commander of the 310th Space Operations Group.

Casserino is currently employed by the Aerospace Corporation in Colorado Springs, Colorado.

Cenker, Robert Joseph
1948–

RCA satellite engineer Bob Cenker was a payload specialist in the crew of Shuttle Mission 61-C in January 1986. This 6-day flight of the orbiter Columbia, whose launch was delayed a record seven times, deployed RCA's Satcom Ku-1.

Cenker was born November 5, 1948, in Uniontown, Pennsylvania, where he graduated from high school in 1965. He attended St. Fidelis College and Seminary in Herman, Pennsylvania, then transferred to Penn State, where he received a B.S. (1970) and M.S. (1973) in aerospace engineering. He later received an M.S. in electrical engineering from Rutgers University (1977).

While still in grad school Cenker worked as a research assistant at Penn State, and at the Westinghouse Bettis Atomic Power Laboratory in West Mifflin, Pennsylvania. In 1972 he joined the RCA Astro-Electronics Division in East Windsor, New Jersey, working on stabilization and control systems for RCA communications satellites such as Satcoms 1 and 2 and GTE Spacenet in addition to the Navy's Nova navigation satellite.

He was selected as an RCA commercial payload specialist in June 1985. Following his flight aboard Mission 61-C he applied to become a NASA astronaut candidate, but was not selected.

Cenker is currently an aerospace systems consultant with GO-RCA, East Windsor, New Jersey.

Cernan, Eugene Andrew
1934–

Navy pilot Gene Cernan made three spaceflights, including Apollo 17 in December 1972, during which he became the last person to walk on the Moon.

Cernan's crewmates on Apollo 17 were command module pilot Ronald Evans and lunar module pilot Dr. Harrison Schmitt, who is the only scientist to have visited the Moon. Following a spectacular nighttime launch from the Kennedy Space Center, the astronauts arrived in lunar orbit on December 10, 1972. While Evans remained in the command module America, Cernan and Schmitt landed the lunar module Challenger at Taurus-Littrow, on the edge of the Sea of Serenity. For the next three days they explored the rugged terrain there, collecting soil and rock samples and ranging far from their landing site in a lunar rover. Cernan and Schmitt spent more than 24 hours walking on the Moon. After Schmitt preceded him into Challenger at the end of their last excursion, Cernan said, "As we leave the Moon at Taurus-Littrow, we leave as we came and, God willing, as we shall return, with peace and hope for all mankind. God speed the crew of Apollo 17."

Cernan had previously served as pilot of Gemini 9 in June 1966. He and commander Thomas Stafford had intended to dock their Gemini with an orbiting Augmented Target Docking Adaptor (ATDA), a replacement for a target Agena upper stage that had failed. When they made rendezvous with the ATDA, however, they noticed that the shroud covering the adaptor had failed to separate, leaving the vehicle looking, Cernan said, "like an angry alligator." The docking was called off, but later in the mission Cernan made a record 2-hour-and-10-minute space walk. The space walk, unfortunately, only showed how little space officials knew about the rigors of extravehicular activity.

Cernan was supposed to test an astronaut maneuvering unit (AMU) backpack, but found that because Gemini wasn't equipped with the proper restraints he couldn't even don the AMU. His suit also overheated, preventing him from completing most of his tasks.

His second flight came in May 1969, when he was lunar module pilot of Apollo 10. Cernan and commander Stafford flew the lunar module Snoopy to within ten miles of the surface of the Moon in a full-scale dress rehearsal for Apollo 11. (Snoopy couldn't land on the Moon because it was too heavy to take off again. This particular lunar module had been designed only for orbital tests.)

Cernan was born March 14, 1934, in Chicago, Illinois, and graduated from Proviso Township High School in suburban Maywood in 1952. He attended Purdue University, receiving a B.S. in electrical engineering in 1956. In 1963 he received an M.S. in aeronautical engineering from the Naval Postgraduate School. He later attended a petroleum economics and managment seminar at Northwestern University (1978).

A Navy ROTC student at Purdue, Cernan went on active duty in 1956 and served aboard the *U.S.S. Saipan* prior to entering flight school in October of that year. Following training in Florida and Tennessee, he was designated a naval aviator in December 1957, then served as a fighter pilot with Attack Squadrons 26 and 113 at the Naval Air Station at Miramar, California. He entered the Postgraduate School in 1961 and was a student there when chosen by NASA.

As a pilot Cernan eventually logged over 5,000 hours of flying time, 4,800 hours in jets, including over 200 carrier landings.

Cernan was one of 14 astronauts selected by NASA in October 1963. He underwent basic academic and survival training, then worked on spacecraft propulsion systems, including booster rockets such as the Titan and Saturn. He served as a capcom for Gemini 7/6 and was training as backup pilot for Gemini 9 with Stafford when the prime crew, Elliott See and Charles Bassett, were killed in a plane crash on February 28, 1966. Stafford and Cernan took their places. Cernan later served as backup pilot for Gemini 12, backup lunar module pilot for Apollo 7, and backup commander for Apollo 14.

On January 23, 1971, Cernan crashed a helicopter into the Banana River near the Kennedy Space Center.

Fellow astronauts assumed that the accidents had eliminated Cernan and his crew of Ronald Evans and Joe Engle from the Apollo 17 assignment, which was pending. Fueling this speculation was the knowledge that Apollo 17 was to be the last lunar landing, and that NASA was under pressure to fly astronaut-geologist Harrison Schmitt, a member of another crew, to the Moon. When the Apollo 17 crew was finally announced months later, however, it consisted of Cernan, Evans, and Schmitt. It was Joe Engle who lost out.

Following Apollo 17 Cernan became involved with the Apollo-Soyuz Test Project. He met Soviet cosmonauts Leonov, Kubasov, Filipchenko, and Yeliseyev at the Paris Air Show in June 1973, and was soon appointed special assistant to the ASTP manager at the Johnson Space Center. During the next two years Cernan accompanied the astronaut crews on training visits to the Soviet Union.

He resigned from NASA and retired from the Navy (with the rank of captain) on July 1, 1976, to join Coral Petroleum, Inc., of Houston, as vice president. He left Coral in September 1981 to start his own company, the Cernan Corporation, an aerospace and energy management and consulting firm. He has also served as commentator and coanchor on ABC-Television broadcasts of Shuttle missions.

Chaffee, Roger Bruce

1935–1967

Navy pilot Roger Chaffee was one of the 3 astronauts killed in a flash fire aboard the Apollo 1 spacecraft on January 27, 1967.

Chaffee, Virgil "Gus" Grissom and Edward White were training for a planned 14-day Apollo mission scheduled for launch on February 21, 1967, the first manned flight of an Apollo spacecraft. The investigation into the fatal fire delayed the whole Moon program by 18 months. NASA and Apollo builder North American Aviation were criticized for lapses in safety in the design of the spacecraft.

Chaffee was born February 15, 1935, in Grand Rapids, Michigan, where he grew up, graduating from Central High in 1953. He attended Purdue University and received a B.S. in aeronautical engineering in 1957. He

later did graduate work at the Air Force Institute of Technology.

A Navy ROTC student, Chaffee went on active duty upon graduation from Purdue in 1957, and after training in Florida and Texas became a pilot. In March 1960 he was assigned to Heavy Photographic Squadron 62 at Jacksonville, Florida, flying 82 classified photographic missions through October 1962, including several over Cuba during the missile crisis. He then entered A.F.I.T. at Wright-Patterson AFB, Ohio, to work on an M.S. in engineering.

Chaffee was one of the 14 astronauts selected by NASA in October 1963. After completing basic astronaut training he worked on deep space communications and Apollo spacecraft development. He was named to the Apollo 1 crew in March 1966—a replacement for Donn Eisele, who had been slightly injured in a training accident.

At the time of his death Chaffee had logged approximately 2,300 hours of flying time, including 2,000 hours in jets.

. . . *On Course to the Stars*, a biography of Chaffee coauthored by his father, Donald, was published in 1968.

Astronauts Chaffee, Grissom, and White were posthumously awarded the Congressional Space Medal of Honor in 1997.

Chamitoff, Gregory Errol

1962–

Shuttle flight controller Gregory Chamitoff is one of the 25 astronaut candidates selected by NASA in June 1998. He reported to the Johnson Space Center in August of that year to begin a training and evaluation course that should qualify him as a Shuttle mission specialist and International Space Station crewmember.

Chamitoff was born August 6, 1962, in Montreal, Canada, but graduated from Blackford High School in San Jose, California. He attended California Polytechnic State University, graduating with a B.S. in electrical engineering in 1984, then attended the California Institute of Technology, where he received an M.S. in aerospace engineering in 1985. He completed his Ph.D. in aeronautics/astronautics at the Massachusetts Institute of Technology in 1992.

At the time of his selection by NASA, Chamitoff was working for the United Space Alliance, Houston, on the Shuttle program.

Chang-Diaz, Franklin Raymond de Los Angeles
1950–

Plasma physicist Franklin Chang-Diaz became the first Hispanic American astronaut when he served as mission specialist in the crew of Shuttle Mission 61-C, launched January 12, 1986, with a crew of 7, including Florida Congressman Bill Nelson. Mission 61-C successfully deployed an RCA communications satellite, but found that a special photographic unit designed to observe Halley's Comet failed to operate. The return to Earth of 61-C also had to be delayed because of weather problems at Cape Canaveral, and was ultimately switched to Edwards Air Force Base in California.

It was the last Shuttle flight prior to the fatal Mission 51-L Challenger launch on January 28, 1986.

In October 1989 Chang-Diaz made his second spaceflight, as a mission specialist in the crew of STS-34, which successfully deployed the Jupiter probe Galileo from the Shuttle Atlantis.

He was then assigned to the crew of STS-46, launched in August 1992. The 7-day STS-42 flight deployed the European Space Agency's EURECA carrier while failing to deploy the Italian Space Agency's Tethered Satellite System.

Chang-Diaz made a fourth flight aboard STS-60 in February 1994. STS-60 carried the first SpaceHab manufacturing module, and included Sergei Krikalev, the first Russian cosmonaut to fly a Shuttle mission, in its crew.

When the Tethered Satellite System was reflown, aboard STS-75 in January 1996, Chang-Diaz (along with fellow TSS-1 crewmembers Andy Allen, Jeff Hoffman, and Claude Nicollier) was aboard. This time the TSS was actually deployed to a distance of 13 miles, demonstrating the ability to generate power by passing a tether through the Earth's electromagnetic field.

Chang-Diaz was assigned to his sixth Shuttle crew, STS-91, the ninth and last Shuttle-Mir docking mission, launched in June 1998. He operated an experiment in plasma physics during the flight.

Chang-Diaz was born April 5, 1950, in San Jose, Costa Rica, and graduated from Colegio De La Salle there in November 1967. As a grade schooler inspired by the launch of Sputnik, he wrote to Dr. Werner von Braun asking how to become an astronaut. To Franklin's surprise, von Braun wrote back, advising him to come to the United States to study science. In 1967 Chang-Diaz, who spoke very little English, arrived in the United States, staying with relatives in Hartford, Connecticut. He graduated from high school there in 1969, then attended the University of Connecticut, receiving a B.S. in mechanical engineering in 1973. He entered the Massachusetts Institute of Technology, earning a Ph.D. in applied plasma physics in 1977.

As an undergraduate at Connecticut, Chang-Diaz did research in high energy atomic physics, and at MIT became heavily involved in the development of fusion reactors. After earning his doctorate he continued to work on fusion projects at the Charles Stark Draper Laboratory in Cambridge, Massachusetts. Since joining NASA he has studied new concepts in rocket propulsion and remains a visiting professor at the MIT Plasma Fusion Center.

In addition to his research, Chang-Diaz worked as manager of a rehabilitation center for chronic mental patients and drug abusers in Massachusetts.

Chang-Diaz was one of the 19 astronauts selected by NASA in May 1980 and qualified as a Shuttle mission specialist in August 1981. He has worked at the Shuttle Avionics Integration Laboratory (SAIL) and as capcom and support crewman for STS-9/Spacelab-1. From October 1984 to August 1985 he was leader of the astronaut support team—the "Cape Crusaders"—at the NASA Kennedy Space Center, and in 1988 he also helped form the Astronaut Science Support Group, which he headed until January 1989. From April 1996 to October 1997 he headed the operations planning branch of the astronaut office.

Chapman, Phillip Kenyon
1935–

Physicist Phil Chapman was one of the 11 scientist-astronauts selected by NASA in August 1967. He resigned from the space program in July 1972 without making a flight.

Chapman was one of the first 2 naturalized U.S. citizens chosen for the space program. He was born March 5, 1935, in Melbourne, Australia, and became a citizen in May 1967. He received a B.S. in physics from Sydney University in Australia in 1956 and an M.S. in aeronautics and astronautics from the Massachusetts Institute of Technology in 1964. He earned his Ph.D. in physics from M.I.T. in 1967.

From 1957 through 1959 Chapman was a physicist studying the Earth's aurora with the Antarctic Division of the External Affairs Department, Commonwealth of Australia. In 1958 he participated in the International Geophysical Year as a member of the Australia National Antarctic Research Expedition. In 1960 and 1961 he was a staff engineer with Canadian Aviation Electronics in Dorval, Quebec, and prior to joining NASA was a physicist at M.I.T.'s Experimental Astronomy Laboratory.

Chapman also served in the Royal Australian Air Force Reserve from 1953 to 1955.

As an astronaut Chapman underwent USAF pilot training at Randolph AFB, Texas, earning his wings in March 1969. He would ultimately log over 1,000 hours of flying time in jets. He served on the support crew for Apollo 14 from 1969 to 1971 and for Apollo 16 in 1971 and 1972.

After leaving NASA Chapman joined the AVCO Everett Research Laboratories in Everett, Massachusetts, and in September 1977 became a supervisory staff associate with Arthur D. Little in Cambridge, Massachusetts.

More recently he served as president of Echelon Development Corporation, a software company. He is currently president of the Center for Enterprise in Space, based on Scottsdale, Arizona.

Chappell, Charles Richard
1943–

Space scientist Rick Chappell was backup payload specialist for STS-45, the Spacelab ATLAS mission, in March 1992. During this 8-day mission a crew of 7 carried out experiments in Earth resources, solar physics, and life sciences. Chappell supported STS-45 from the NASA Marshall Spaceflight Center.

Chappell was born June 2, 1943, in Greenville, South Carolina, and grew up in Montgomery, Alabama, where he graduated from Sidney Lanier High School in 1961. He

attended Vanderbilt University, receiving a B.A. in physics (magna cum laude) in 1965, and earned his Ph.D. in space science from Rice University in 1968.

From 1968 to 1974 Chappell worked for Lockheed at its Palo Alto, California, Research Laboratory, as a staff scientist. His research involved investigations of the Earth's plasmasphere and magnetosphere. In 1974 he joined the staff of the NASA Marshall Space Flight Center in Huntsville, Alabama, where he soon became mission scientist for Spacelab 1, work that culminated in a 10-day multidisciplinary scientific spaceflight in November and December 1983. During Spacelab 1 Chappell coordinated the efforts of more than 70 scientific investigators at Marshall's Payload Operations Center. He was also the "voice" of Spacelab-1, appearing on television.

When NASA and the European Space Agency decided to refly some Spacelab 1 experiments on the Atlas mission Chappell was chosen as one of the payload specialists.

Chappell later served as associate director of NASA Marshall and chief of the solar terrestrial division of the space science laboratory there. He is the author of over 100 scientific papers and has been principal investigator on instruments flown on several American spacecraft.

In June 1994 Chappell commenced a yearlong assignment as deputy director of the Global Learning and Observations to Benefit the Environment (GLOBE) Program, serving at the White House. GLOBE is an education program involving students and teachers from around the world who will make environmental observations.

Chappell returned to NASA Marshall in 1995 and is associated director for science there.

Chawla, Kalpana
1961–

Aerospace engineer Kalpana Chawla was a mission specialist in the crew of STS-87. This November 1997 flight of the orbiter Columbia carried the fourth U.S. Microgravity Laboratory and the Christa-SPAS retrievable payload. During the Christa-SPAS deployment Chawla, the Columbia's remote manipulator operator, apparently failed to enter a command, preventing the payload from responding to flight control. It had to be retrieved on an unplanned EVA by STS-87 crewmembers Winston Scott and Takao Doi. The remainder of the 16-day mission went as planned.

Chawla was born July 1, 1961, in Karnal, India, where she graduated from the Tagore secondary school in 1976. She received a B.S. in aeronautical engineering from the Punjab Engineering College in 1982, then did graduate work at the University of Texas, where she received an M.S. in aerospace engineering in 1984. She received her Ph.D. from the University of Colorado in 1988.

In 1988 Chawla joined MCAT Institute, San Jose, California, as a researcher supporting studies at the nearby NASA Ames Research Center in simulations of airflows for exotic aircraft such as vertical takeoff-landing vehicles and hovercraft. She joined Overset Methods, Inc., Palo Alto, California, in 1993, as vice president and research scientist. Her work there included simulation of multiple body problems in aerodynamics.

Chawla is a privately licensed pilot who holds single and multi-engine land and seaplane ratings. She is also qualified as a glider pilot and instructor.

She was one of the 19 astronaut candidates selected by NASA on December 8, 1994. In May 1996 she qualified as a Shuttle mission specialist. Her first technical assignment was with the EVA/robotics branch of the astronaut office.

Chiao, Leroy

1960–

Materials engineer Leroy Chiao has been a mission specialist in two Shuttle crews.

The first was STS-65, the July 1994 flight of the orbiter Columbia, which carried the second International Micro-gravity Spacelab. The IML crew of 7 conducted 80 experiments in life sciences and space manufacturing during a 15-day mission stay.

Chiao made a second Shuttle flight aboard STS-72 in January 1996. This 9-day flight of the orbiter Endeavour retrieved the Japanese Space Flyer Unit. Chiao made two EVAs during the mission, one with Winston Scott and the other with Dan Barry.

He is currently assigned to the crew of STS-92, International Space Station assembly mission 3A, scheduled for launch in late 1999.

Chiao was born August 28, 1960, in Milwaukee, Wisconsin, and grew up in Danville, California, where, at the age of 7, he first became interested in spaceflight. He attended the University of California at Berkeley, receiving a B.S. in chemical engineering in 1983, then went on to earn his M.S. (1985) and Ph.D. (1987) in that field from the University of California at Santa Barbara.

After graduation from UC-Santa Barbara Chiao joined the Hexcel Corporation in Dublin, California, working on such projects as the manufacture of a reflector for future space telescopes. In January 1989 he joined the staff of the Lawrence Livermore National Laboratory in Livermore, California.

He has given technical seminars on materials technology in the People's Republic of China and is also a contributor to the International Encyclopedia of Composite Materials.

Chiao was one of the 23 astronaut candidates selected by NASA in January 1990. In July 1991 he qualified as a Shuttle mission specialist while working in SAIL. He later served in the mission development branch of the astronaut office on Spacelab and SpaceHab issues.

In July 1997 Chiao traveled to the Gagarin Cosmonaut Training Center to test procedures for the EVA repair of the damaged Mir space station.

Chilton, Kevin Patick

1954–

Air Force colonel Kevin "Chili" Chilton commanded STS-76, the third Shuttle-Mir docking mission. This March 1996 flight of the orbiter Atlantis delivered NASA-Mir crewmember Shannon Lucid to the Russian space station along with 4,800 pounds of food, water, air, and mission hardware. STS-76 crewmembers Linda Godwin and Rich Clifford also performed the first American EVA at the Russian station.

Chilton previously served as pilot of two Shuttle missions, including STS-59. This April 1994 flight of the orbiter Endeavour carried the first Shuttle Radar Laboratory, an advanced imagining system that surveyed over 70 million square kilometers of the Earth's surface.

In May 1992 Chilton was pilot of STS-49, the maiden voyage of the orbiter Endeavour. During that 10-day mission astronauts made a record four EVAs, including three devoted to rescuing the stranded Intelsat VI satellite. Chilton and commander Dan Brandenstein flew three different rendezvous with Intelsat, another Shuttle record.

Chilton was born November 3, 1954, in Los Angeles, California, graduating from St. Bernard High School in Playa del Rey in 1972. He attended the Air Force Academy, receiving a B.S. in engineering sciences in 1976, and the following year earned an M.S. in mechanical engineering as a Guggenheim Fellow at Columbia University.

Chilton underwent pilot training at Williams AFB, Arizona, in 1978, then for the next four years flew RF-4 and F-15 aircraft at Kadena AFB on the island of Okinawa. In 1982 and 1983 he was stationed at Holloman AFB, New Mexico, prior to entering the Air Force Test Pilot School at Edwards AFB, California. After graduating in 1985 he was assigned as an F-4 and F-15 test pilot at Eglin AFB, Florida.

Chilton has logged over 3,000 hours of flying time.

He was one of the 15 astronauts selected by NASA in June 1987, qualifying as a Shuttle pilot in August 1988 while working in the mission development branch of the astronaut office on the Infrared Background Signature Survey (IBSS) vehicle flown on STS-39, and on the Orbital Maneuvering Vehicle. He later served as a mission control capcom and as leader of the astronaut support team at the NASA Kennedy Space Center. Chilton also played lead guitar in the astronaut rock band Max Q.

Following his flight aboard STS-76 Chilton became deputy manager for operations in the International Space Station Program Office and was promoted to the rank of brigadier general, USAF.

Clark, Laurel Blair Salton
1961–

Navy medical officer Laurel Clark is one of the 35 astronaut candidates selected by NASA on May 1, 1996. In August of that year she reported to the Johnson Space Center to begin a training and evaluation course that should qualify her as a Shuttle mission specialist and Space station crewmember.

Clark was born Laurel Blair Salton on March 10, 1961, in Ames, Iowa, and grew up in Racine, Wisconsin, where she graduated from William Horlick High School in 1977. She attended the University of Wisconsin, Madison, where she received a B.S. in zoology in 1983, and an M.D. in 1987.

Following medical school, Clark did an internship in pediatrics at Bethesda Naval Hospital in Washington, D.C. In 1989 she completed Navy undersea medical officer training and served for two years at Holy Loch, Scotland, as a submarine medical officer and diving medical officer.

Qualified as a Navy flight surgeon in 1992, Clark served with Marine Night Attack Squadron 211 at Yuma, Arizona, for two years. At the time she was selected by NASA she was flight surgeon for the naval flight surgeon training squadron (VT-86) at NAS Pensacola, Florida.

Cleave, Mary Louise
1947–

Mary Cleave used the Shuttle Atlantis's remote manipulator arm to test space construction techniques during Mission 61-B in November and December 1985. Cleave, the mission specialist and flight engineer of a crew of 7, worked with space walkers Jerry Ross and Woody Spring, who assembled a truss-like tower and pyramid during two EVA. At one point Cleave moved the astronauts by remote control from one place to another.

The crew of Mission 61-B, including Mexican engineer Rudolfo Neri Vela, also deployed three communications satellites during their 7-day flight.

In May 1989 Cleave was a mission specialist aboard STS-30, a 4-day flight of the orbiter Atlantis during which the Magellan Venus space probe was deployed.

Cleave was born February 5, 1947, in Southampton, New York, and grew up on Long Island, graduating from Great Neck North High School in 1965. She attended Colorado State University, receiving a B.S. in microbial ecology in 1969, and later earned an M.S. in that subject (1975) and a Ph.D. in civil and environment engineering (1979) from Utah State University.

From September 1971 to June 1980 Cleave was a researcher at the Ecology Center and the Utah Water Research Laboratory at Utah State working on environmental projects. She has published several scientific papers.

Cleave was one of the 19 astronauts selected by NASA in May 1980. In August 1981 she qualified her as a Shuttle mission specialist while working at the Shuttle Avionics Integration Laboratory (SAIL). She then served as capcom for five Shuttle missions, STS-5 (November 1982) through 41-B (February 1984).

Immediately following her STS-30 mission in 1989 she was assigned as a mission specialist for the International Microgravity Laboratory, a Shuttle-Spacelab mission then scheduled for launch in December 1990. However, in January 1990 she withdrew from the assignment because of conflicts with Spacelab program managers at the NASA Marshall Spaceflight Center.

She was then detailed to the engineering branch of the NASA Johnson Space Center, where she served as special assistant for advanced programs in the crew systems and thermal division until transferring to the NASA Goddard Space Center in Greenbelt, Maryland, in April 1991, as deputy project manager for Sea Viewing Wide Field Sensors (SeaWiFS) at Goddard. SeaWiFS was launched aboard the OrbView-2 satellite in August 1997 to provide, among other things, data on global warming and El Nino.

Clegg, Robert Henry

1946–

Army geographer and intelligence officer Robert Clegg was the alternate payload specialist for the flight of Terra Scout, a set of geological experiments scheduled for flight aboard the Shuttle in 1993. Terra Geode lost its funding, however, and was canceled.

Clegg was born August 23, 1946, in Boston, Massachusetts. An Army brat, he lived in several different cities growing up, graduating from Acton-Boxboro Regional High School in 1965. He attended the University of Rhode Island and earned a B.A. in geography in 1969. In 1975 he received an M.S. in civil and environment engineering and

a second M.S. in geography from the University of Wisconsin at Madison. He received his Ph.D. in geography from the University of Maryland at College Park in 1982.

He entered the U.S. Army through ROTC and first served as a tank platoon commander in Germany. From 1971 to 1972 he was an air intelligence officer at Hue in Vietnam. Returning to the United States, he did graduate work at Wisconsin, then served a tour at the Army Imagery Intelligence Center in Washington (1975–1978).

Clegg attended the Army War College (1979), then served at Army Headquarters and with the Joint Chiefs of Staff. In 1983 he became commander of the Special Security Command, U.S. Army-Europe. Three years later he was reassigned as intelligence officer for the 56th Field Artillery Command, a Pershing II missile unit. From 1987 to 1990 he was a professor of geography at West Point.

Clegg was interested in spaceflight and applied several times for selection as a NASA astronaut in the 1980s without success. When he heard about the Terra Geode project in 1989, he applied and in June 1990 was designated the alternate payload specialist.

Until Terra Geode was manifested, however, payload specialists Bailey and Clegg would not undergo active Shuttle training and remained at their posts. In 1991 Clegg served in Operation Desert Storm as director of the Joint Image Complex, U.S. Central Command, Saudi Arabia. Following two years as commander of the U.S. Army Central Secure Facility at Fort Meade, Maryland, he retired with the rank of colonel.

Clegg is currently a professor of military geography at the Armed Forces Staff College. He lives in Virgina.

Clifford, Michael Richard Uram

1952–

Army test pilot Rich Clifford was a mission specialist on three Shuttle flights, including STS-76, the third Shuttle-Mir docking. During that April 1996 flight of the orbiter Atlantis, Clifford and fellow mission specialist Linda Godwin made the first American EVA at the Mir station, installing several experiments on its exterior. The Atlantis crew also unloaded 4,800 pounds of supplies for the Mir team, while returning 1,100 pounds of scientific materials and hardware to Earth.

Earlier Clifford was a mission specialist aboard STS-53, a Department of Defense shuttle mission flown aboard the orbiter Discovery in November-December 1992. STS-53 deployed an advanced Satellite Data Systems platform designed to relay intelligence data from Crystal imaging satellites to ground stations.

His second flight was STS-59. This April 1994 flight of the orbiter Endeavour carried the first shuttle radar laboratory, an advanced sensor system which covered over 70 million square kilometers of the Earth's surface.

Clifford was born October 13, 1952, in San Bernardino, California, and grew up in Ogden, Utah, where he graduated from Ben Lomond High School in 1970. Inspired by the Apollo 11 Moon landing, he was already determined to become an astronaut. He attended the U.S. Military Academy at West Point, earning a B.S. in 1974. In 1982 he received an M.S. in aerospace engineering from the Georgia Institute of Technology.

Clifford was commissioned a second lieutenant in the Army in June 1974. For the next two years he served with the 10th Cavalry at Fort Carson, Colorado, until entering the Army Aviation School. He graduated at the top of his class at flight school in October 1976, then spent the next three years as a platoon commander with the Attack Troop, 2nd Armored Cavalry Regiment in Nuremburg, Germany. Following graduate school at Georgia Tech he was assigned to West Point as an instructor and assistant professor in the department of mechanics.

In 1986 Clifford graduated from the Naval Test Pilot School at Patuxent River, Maryland. The following July he was assigned to the NASA Johnson Space Center as a Shuttle vehicle integration engineer, where he worked on the Shuttle crew escape system and as a member of the board that reviewed the redesigned solid rocket booster.

He was selected for the astronaut group on his fourth try, becoming one of the 23 astronaut candidates announced by NASA in January 1990. In July 1991 he qualifed as a Shuttle mission specialist. His technical assignments included work on the design and development of EVA equipment in the astronaut office mission development branch (April–August 1991) and serving as lead for space station vehicle/assembly issues (May 1994–September 1995).

Clifford logged over 3,400 hours of flying time in several different types of airplanes and helicopters.

He retired from the Army with the rank of lieutenant colonel in December 1995, and resigned from the astronaut office in January 1997. He is currently employed by the Boeing Company as flight operations manager for its space station flight operations group.

Coats, Michael Loyd

1946–

Navy test pilot Mike Coats commanded STS-39, the first unclassified Department of Defense Shuttle mission, in April and May 1991. STS-39 was one of the most complex Shuttle missions flown, requiring extensive maneuvers of the orbiter Discovery in tandem with a free-flying pallet carrying Strategic Defense experiments, in addition to the launch of three DOD subsatellites.

STS-39 also carried AFP-675, a payload bay-mounted experiment package, and a crew of 7, who overcame coolant leaks (in the 675 package) and faulty data recorders in completing the 7-day mission. It ended with a landing at the NASA Kennedy Space Center in Florida.

Coats had made two previous Shuttle flights: in March 1989 he served as commander of STS-29, a 5-day flight of the orbiter Discovery during which a Tracking and Data Relay satellite was deployed. And in August and September 1984 he was pilot of the maiden voyage of Discovery, Shuttle Mission 41-D. During that weeklong flight Coats and five other astronauts deployed three satellites and conducted tests of a huge solar power wing. They also survived the first launchpad abort in Shuttle history on June 26, 1984.

Coats was born January 16, 1946, in Sacramento, California, and grew up in Riverside, where he graduated from Ramona High School in 1964. He was appointed to the Naval Academy, graduating in 1968 with a bachelor of science. He later earned and M.S. in the administration of science and technology from George Washington University (1977) and an M.S. in aeronautical engineering from the Naval Postgraduate School (1979).

Following graduation from Annapolis Coats underwent pilot training, becoming a naval aviator in September 1969. He served as an A-7E pilot with Attack Squadron 192 aboard the carrier *U.S.S. Kitty Hawk* from 1970 to 1972, flying 315 combat missions over Vietnam.

Returning to the United States, he served as a flight instructor at Lemoore, California, until entering the Naval Test Pilot School in 1974. From 1974 to 1976 he was an A-4 and A-7 test pilot, then spent a year as an instructor at the test pilot school. At the time of his selection by NASA he was a student at the Postgraduate School.

He logged over 5,000 hours of flying time, including 400 carrier landings, in 28 different types of aircraft.

Coats was one of the 35 astronaut candidates selected in January 1978. In August 1979 he qualified as a Shuttle pilot. He was a support crewmember for STS-4 and STS-5, and, following his assignment to Mission 41-D, served a tour as a capcom in mission control (May to November 1985).

At the time of the Challenger disaster in January 1986 Coats was assigned as commander of Mission 61-H, then scheduled for launch in the summer of 1986. Mission 61-H was postponed and renamed STS-29.

From May 1989 to March 1990 Coats served as acting chief of the astronaut office, while chief astronaut Dan Brandenstein was training to command STS-32.

Coats resigned from NASA and retired from the Navy with the rank of captain on August 1, 1991. He became director of advanced programs and technical planning for the Loral Corporation in Houston, Texas. Loral's space operations were later sold to Lockheed-Martin, and since July 1996 Coats has been vice-president for the Civil Division of that corporation.

Cockrell, Kenneth Dale

1950–

Former Navy test pilot Ken Cockrell commanded STS-80, the longest Shuttle mission yet flown. This 18-day flight of the orbiter Columbia saw the successful deployment and retrieval of the Wake Shield Facility, and of the SPAS-Orfeus observatory. A major disappointment was the cancellation of two EVAs by crewmembers Tammy Jernigan and Thomas Jones because of a faulty hatch.

Cockrell was aboard two prior Shuttle missions. He was flight engineer/mission specialist aboard STS-56, an April 1993 Shuttle mission that carried the second Spacelab ATLAS. In September 1995 he was pilot of STS-69, which made the second attempt to deploy the Wake Shield Facility.

Cockrell was born April 9, 1950, in Austin, Texas. He attended the University of Texas, receiving a B.S. in mechanical engineering in 1972. In 1974 he earned an M.S. in aeronautical systems from the University of West Florida.

Having wanted to be a pilot from the age of 5, Cockrell joined the Navy after graduation from Texas. He won his wings in August 1974 at Pensacola, Florida, then served as a Corsair II pilot aboard the carrier *U.S.S. Midway* for three years. In 1978–79 he attended the Naval Test Pilot School at Patuxent River, Maryland, and remained at the Test Center as a test pilot through 1982. From 1982 to 1985 he was staff officer to the commander of the *U.S.S. Ranger* and later the *U.S.S. Kitty Hawk* battle groups at San Diego. His last Navy assignment was as an F-18 pilot aboard the carrier *U.S.S. Constellation*.

Cockrell first applied for the astronaut program in 1980, and again in 1984 and 1985. In 1987, feeling that his chances for selection would be improved by more test piloting experience, he resigned from the Navy in the hope of landing a job with Northrop or Lockheed while applying a fourth time for admission to the astronaut group. Again, he was not selected, but this time NASA offered him a job as a research pilot in the aircraft operations division. For the next three years he worked as a T-38 instructor and check pilot, in addition to flying the NASA WB-57 and Gulfstream I.

He has logged over 4,900 hours of flying time and made 650 carrier landings.

As one of the 23 astronaut candidates selected by NASA in January 1990, Cockrell qualified as a Shuttle pilot in August 1991 while working in the operations development branch of the astronaut office. He later served as an ascent/entry capcom and as astronaut office representative for the flight data file. From 1995 to 1996 he was head of the operations development branch.

In October 1997 Cockrell was named chief of the astronaut office.

Coleman, Catherine Grace

1960–

Chemist Catherine "Cady" Coleman was a mission specialist in the crew of STS-73. This 16-day flight of the orbiter Columbia in October–November 1995 carried the second U.S. Microgravity Laboratory and a crew of 7, who conducted experiments in fluid mechanics, biotechnology, and combustion science in the Spacelab module.

In February 1997 Coleman was assigned as a backup crewmember for STS-83, the Materials and Science Spacelab mission then scheduled for launch in April 1997. She was prepared to step in for STS-83 crewmember Don Thomas, who had broken his ankle during training. Thomas recovered in time to fly the mission.

Coleman is currently assigned as a mission specialist for STS-93. This April 1999 flight of the orbiter Columbia will deploy the Advanced X-ray Astrophysics Facility observatory into Earth orbit.

Coleman was born December 14, 1960, in Charleston, South Carolina, and graduated from W. T. Woodson High School in Fairfax, Virginia. She attended the Massachusetts Institute of Technology, receiving a B.S. in chemistry in 1983. She received a Ph.D. in polymer science and engineering from the University of Massachusetts in 1991.

Major Coleman was a research chemist at Wright-Patterson Air Force Base in Dayton, Ohio, when selected by NASA as one of 19 astronaut candidates on March 31, 1992. In August 1993 she qualified as a Shuttle mission specialist, working first in the mission support branch in the Shuttle Avionics Integration Laboratory, then as special assistant to the director, Johnson Space Center. Since returning from STS-73 she has worked in the payloads/habitation branch of the astronaut office.

Collins, Eileen Marie

1956–

Air Force test pilot Eileen Collins has been the pilot for two Shuttle missions that visited the Russian Mir space station.

The first was STS-63, the February 1995 flight of the orbiter Atlantis that carried a crew of 6, including Russian cosmonaut Sergei Krikalev, and made rendezvous with Mir, coming to within 30 feet. (Dockings had to wait until a special docking module could be added to Mir.)

In May 1997 Collins returned to Mir as pilot of STS-84. This flight of the orbiter Atlantis carried a crew of 7, including Yelena Kondakova, another Russian cosmonaut. Atlantis remained docked with Mir for five days, transferring NASA long-duration crewmember Michael Foale and returning Jerry Linenger to Earth.

In February 1998 Collins was named to command STS-93, becoming the first woman Shuttle commander. This flight of the orbiter Columbia, scheduled for launch in April 1999, will deploy the Advanced X-ray Astrophysics Facility, one of NASA's "great telescopes," into Earth orbit.

Collins was born November 19, 1956, in Elmira, New York, where she graduated from Elmira Free Academy in 1974. She received an associate in science degree in mathematics/science from Corning Community College in 1976 and a B.A. in mathematics and economics from Syracuse University in 1978. She earned an M.S. in operations research from Stanford University in 1986 and an M.A. in space systems management from Webster University in 1989.

Collins joined the Air Force in 1978 and underwent pilot training at Vance AFB, Oklahoma, remaining there as a T-38 instructor pilot in until 1982. From 1983 to 1985 she was a C-141 pilot and instructor at Travis AFB, Texas, then entered the Air Force Institute of Technology to work on her graduate degree. She was an assistant professor in mathematics and T-41 instructor pilot at the Air Force Academy from 1986 to 1989. At the time of her selection by NASA she was enrolled at the Air Force Test Pilot School at Edwards AFB, California.

Collins has logged over 4,000 hours of flying time in 30 different types of aircraft. She flew combat missions in the invasion of Grenada in October 1983.

She was one of the 23 astronaut candidates selected by NASA in January 1990 and in July 1991 qualified as a Shuttle pilot. Her first technical assignment was in the mission support branch of the astronaut office in orbiter engineering support, and with the astronaut support team at the Kennedy Space Center. She has also been a Shuttle capcom, and chief of the vehicle systems/operations branch (August 1997–March 1998).

Collins, Michael

1930–

Michael Collins, a self-described underachiever, circled the Moon while astronauts Neil Armstrong and Edwin Aldrin made the first lunar landing. As pilot of the command module Columbia for the flight of Apollo 11, Collins spent 24 hours alone in lunar orbit while Armstrong and Aldrin landed the lunar module Eagle on the Sea of Tranquility. It was the culmination of the entire Apollo program, fulfilling a goal set by President John F. Kennedy in 1961, to "land a man on the Moon and return him safely to Earth in this decade."

Apollo 11 was Collins's second spaceflight. He had previously served as pilot of Gemini 10 in July 1966. During that 3-day rendezvous and docking mission he made two space walks.

Collins was born October 31, 1930, in Rome, Italy. His was an Army family: his father, James, became a major general, another uncle was a brigadier general, his brother was a colonel, and his uncle J. Lawton Collins became Army chief of staff. It was no surprise then, that Collins, after graduating from St. Albans School in Washington, D.C., attended the U.S. Military Academy at West Point, receiving a bachelor of science degree in 1952. He later attended the advanced managment program at the Harvard Business School in 1974.

In spite of his Army heritage, Collins elected to serve in the Air Force. He underwent pilot training in Mississippi and Texas and won his wings in 1953. For the next four years he served with the 21st Fighter Bomber Wing at Nellis Air Force Base, Nevada, and at bases in Europe. From 1957 to 1960 he was assigned to Chanute AFB, Illinois, as a maintenance officer and, later, training officer. He finally entered the Air Force Test Pilot School at Edwards Air Force Base in 1960, and remained there as a test pilot and student (he attended the Aerospace Research Pilot School in 1963) until being chosen by NASA.

As a pilot Collins eventually logged over 5,000 hours of flying time.

He was one of 14 astronauts selected by NASA in October 1963. Reporting in January 1964, he underwent basic academic and survival training, then was assigned to assist in the development of space suits and techniques for walking in space. He became the first member of his class to join a flight crew when he was chosen as backup pilot for Gemini-7 in June 1965.

Following Gemini 10 Collins served as lunar module pilot for a crew commanded by Frank Borman with Thomas Stafford as command module pilot. In a shuffling of flights and astronaut assignments in November 1966, Collins found himself "promoted" to command module pilot for the Borman crew (Stafford was given his own crew) and as he later said, lost his chance to land on the Moon at that point.

It still took a series of accidents to place Collins on the first lunar landing. In July 1968 he was diagnosed as having a bone spur on his neck and underwent surgery. Temporarily removed from flight status, he was replaced on Borman's crew by his backup, James Lovell. A change in the flight schedule at the same time (swapping the Apollo 8 and Apollo 9 crews) made Collins available for assignment to Apollo 11 at the same time as Armstrong and Aldrin, who were backups to Apollo 8. Collins served as capcom for Apollo 8.

Just prior to Apollo 11, astronaut boss Deke Slayton offered Collins a chance to be backup commander for Apollo 14, and almost certainly commander of Apollo 17. Collins told Slayton that if Apollo 11 went well he would prefer to spend more time with his family and planned to leave the space program.

Collins resigned from NASA in January 1970 to become Assistant Secretary of State for Public Affairs. Beginning in 1971 he worked at the Smithsonian Institution, first as director of the National Air and Space Museum and later as under secretary for the Smithsonian, remaining there until 1980. For the next five years he was vice-president of the Vought Corporation in Arlington, Virginia, then president of Michael Collins Associates, an aviation and space consulting firm, in Washington, D.C., and North Carolina.

He is the author of a popular and vivid memoir, *Carrying the Fire: An Astronaut's Journeys* (1973) and of a children's book, *Flying to the Moon and Other Strange Places* (1976). More recently he has published *Liftoff: The Story of America's Adventure in Space* (1988) and *Mission to Mars: An Astronaut's Vision of Our Future in Space* (1990).

Conrad, Charles "Pete," Jr.
1930–

Navy test pilot Pete Conrad had one of the most remarkable careers of any space traveler, making four spaceflights between 1965 and 1973, during which he twice set endurance records, commanded the first successful space station mission, and became the third man to walk on the Moon.

His first flight was as pilot of Gemini 5 in August 1965. With commander Gordon Cooper, Conrad spent almost 191 hours in space, shattering the endurance record held by Soviet cosmonaut Valery Bykovsky. Just over a year later Conrad commanded Gemini 11, a 3-day rendezvous and docking mission that also established a world altitude record of 850 miles.

In November 1969 Conrad became the third person to walk on the Moon when he commanded Apollo 12. He and Alan Bean landed the lunar module Intrepid on the Ocean of Storms while Richard Gordon orbited overhead in the command module Yankee Clipper. As he stepped onto the lunar surface, the five-foot, six-inch tall Conrad's first words were "Whoopie! That may have been a small one for Neil, but it's a long one for me!" During two Moon walks Conrad and Bean set up a package of scientific experiments and walked over to the Surveyor III unmanned probe, which had been on the lunar surface for three years. (In an amazing demonstration of Apollo guidance and navigation capabilities, Intrepid had landed within 200 yards of the Surveyor.)

Conrad's fourth flight was Skylab 2, the first manned visit to the Skylab space station, in May 1973. Skylab suffered a major malfunction during its launch on May 14, 1973, when a micrometeoroid shield tore loose, taking with it one of the station's solar power panels and damaging the other panel. Flight controllers delayed the Skylab 2 launch for ten days while repair procedures could be developed and rehearsed. In a series of space walks, Conrad, Joseph Kerwin, and Paul Weitz were able to activate Skylab, eventually completing 46 of their original 55 scientific experiments and remaining in space for 28 days as planned.

On the way to accomplishing four spaceflights, Conrad also survived a lightning strike (lightning hit Apollo-12 moments after its launch on November 14, 1969) and an emergency bailout from a T-38 jet in 1971.

From 1993 to 1996, long after leaving the NASA manned space program, Conrad served as remote pilot for flight tests of the McDonnell Douglas Delta Clipper vehicle at White Sands Test Range.

Conrad was born June 2, 1930, in Philadelphia, Pennsylvania, and grew up in the suburb of Haverford where his father, a former World War I balloonist, was a stockbroker. He graduated from the Darrow School in New Lebanon, New York, then attended Princeton University, receiving a B.S. in aeronautical engineering in 1953.

Entering active duty with the Navy following college, Conrad underwent pilot training at Pensacola, Florida, and then served at the Jacksonville Naval Air Station. There is a vivid description of his life there in the early chapters of Tom Wolfe's *The Right Stuff* (1979). In 1957 Conrad entered the Naval Test Pilot School at Patuxent River, Maryland, remaining there for several years as a test pilot in the armaments test division, a flight instructor, and a performance engineer. At the time he was selected by NASA he was safety officer for Fighter Squadron 96 at Miramar, California.

As a pilot he eventually logged over 6,500 hours of flying time, including more than 5,000 hours in jets.

Conrad was one of the 9 astronauts chosen by NASA in September 1962. He had been a candidate for the Mercury astronaut group, but rebelled at the endless medical testing, earning a rejection. It's ironic that on his first Gemini flight and on Skylab Conrad found himself at the mercy of NASA doctors.

During early astronaut training Conrad took part in the development of the Apollo lunar module (until December 1968 he was considered the astronaut most likely to be the first man on the Moon). He also served as backup commander for Gemini 8 and Apollo 9. In the summer of 1970 he became chief of the Skylab branch of the astronaut office and was officially named commander of the first mission in January 1972.

In December 1973 Conrad resigned from NASA and retired from the Navy with the rank of captain. He accepted a position as vice-president, operations, and chief operating officer of American Television and Communications Corporation, a Denver-based cable TV company. In March 1976 he left ATC to become a vice president for the McDonnell Douglas Corporation, later serving as senior vice president for marketing for its Douglas Aircraft division in Long Beach, California, then as been staff vice president for international business development at McDonnell's St. Louis, Missouri, office until joining the DC-X program.

He has served as a consultant for a number of space-related projects, including the Hubble Space Telescope, and in September 1985 donned a space suit again to perform underwater simulations of space station assembly techniques for Space Structures International and McDonnell Douglas.

In 1989 he played a supporting role in the ABC movie-for-television *Plymouth*, a story about the first lunar colonists. He has also been featured in print advertisements for Revo sunglasses.

Conrad retired from McDonnell Douglas on March 31, 1996, and is currently heading a private space launch firm called Universal Space Lines based in Irvine, California.

Cooper, Leroy Gordon, Jr.

1927–

One of the original seven Mercury astronauts, Gordon Cooper set American endurance records on both of his two flights into space.

Cooper was pilot of Mercury-Atlas 9, the last Mercury mission, launched on May 15, 1963. For the next 34 hours and 20 minutes, he orbited the Earth in the spacecraft he had named Faith 7, logging more time in space than all five previous Mercury astronauts combined. Cooper's primary job was to manage his "consumable" supplies—oxygen, water, and electricity—and to report on his physical condition. He was the first American astronaut to go to sleep in orbit, for example.

He also saw objects on the Earth's surface in such detail (he reported seeing the wake of a boat on a river in India and actual houses on the plains of Tibet) that, at first, most experts refused to believe him.

Cooper's second spaceflight came two years later, as command pilot of Gemini 5. Charles Conrad accompanied him on a mission designed specifically to prove that astronauts could survive in space for eight days—the time it took for a spacecraft to go from the Earth to the Moon and back again.

To honor Gemini 5's major goal, Cooper designed the first mission patch in what has since become a NASA tradition. The Gemini 5 patch depicted a Conestoga wagon with the slogan "Eight Days or Bust." In what has also become a NASA tradition, NASA officials deleted the slogan, just in case Gemini 5 failed to reach its planned duration.

But Cooper and Conrad did spend eight days in space, thought not without some anxious moments. Gemini 5 was the first manned spacecraft equipped with fuel cells, portable generators of electrical power that made it possible for flights to last longer than a few days (the lifetime of most battery systems.) The fuel cells behaved erratically, requiring flight controllers and the astronauts to nurse them through the whole mission. In fact, Cooper and Conrad spent the last days of their flight in a "powered-down" drift, to conserve electricity.

On August 29, 1965, their final day in space, the astronauts talked by radio with Scott Carpenter, who was in Sealab II at the time, 200 underwater off the coast of California. Gemini 5 set a world space record that unfortunately lasted for less than four months.

The youngest of the original astronauts, Cooper once said, "I'm *planning* on getting to the Moon. I *think* I'll get to Mars." In July 1969 he was in line to be named commander of Apollo 13, a lunar landing mission scheduled for April 1970. But in a shuffle of assignments Cooper was replaced by fellow Mercury astronaut Alan Shepard, who had recently returned to flight status after a 5-year hiatus. By then Cooper's involvement with auto and speedboat racing had caused him problems with NASA officials, who saw him as a maverick and a daredevil. Cooper found himself assigned as assistant to flight crew operations boss Deke Slayton for the Apollo Applications Program (later known as Skylab). He left NASA and the Air Force on July 1, 1970, without getting to the Moon or Mars.

Cooper was born March 6, 1927, in Shawnee, Oklahoma. His father, a World War I pilot, was a district judge, and young Gordon learned to fly before he was 16 years old.

After graduating from high school in Murray, Kentucky, in 1945, Cooper joined the Marines, and wound up a member of the Presidential Honor Guard in Washington, D.C. He also managed to attend the Naval Academy Prep School.

Discharged in August 1946, he entered the University of Hawaii in Honolulu, but left after three years to become an officer in the Army. He quickly transferred that commission to the Air Force and completed flight training in 1949. For the next four years Cooper flew with the 86th Fighter Bomber Group in Munich, Germany. Returning to the United States in 1954, he attended the Air Force Institute of Technology, earning a B.S. in aeronautical engineering in 1956. He was then assigned to the Air Force Experimental Flight Test School at Edwards AFB, California, and was an engineering test pilot there when selected by NASA in April 1959.

Cooper was a capcom for the orbital flights of John Glenn and Scott Carpenter, and was backup for Walter Schirra. In addition to his two flight assignments, he also served as backup commander for Gemini 12 in 1966 and Apollo 10 in 1969.

Upon leaving NASA Cooper formed Gordon Cooper & Associates, Inc., a consulting firm specializing in aviation and aerospace projects, and in hotel and land developments. He has been a member of the board for and a consultant to a number of companies in the aerospace, electronics, and energy fields. In 1975 he was vice-president for research and development for Walt Disney Enterprises.

He is currently president of the Galaxy Group, a company that upgrades the engines of small aircraft, based in Lancaster, California.

Covey, Richard Oswalt

1946–

Air Force test pilot Dick Covey made four Shuttle flights, commanding two of them, including the famous Hubble Space Telescope rescue and repair mission in December 1993. The Hubble mission, STS-61, involved a crew of 7, including four EVA astronauts, who made rendezvous with the orbiting telescope. During a week of EVA repairs, the Hubble was fitting with improved optics, guidance systems, and solar panels.

Prior to this Covey commanded STS-38, a November 1990 flight of the orbiter Atlantis that was the seventh and last classified Department of Defense Shuttle mission. (Its secret payload was later reported to be an advanced data relay satellite for use with the Crystal imaging reconnaissance platform.) STS-38 ended after five days with a landing at the Kennedy Space Center, the first KSC landing by a Shuttle in five years.

In September 1988 Covey was pilot of STS-26, the first post-Challenger Shuttle mission. The crew of STS-26 deployed a Tracking and Data Relay Satellite into geosynchronous orbit during their 4-day mission.

Earlier Covey served as pilot of Shuttle Mission 51-I in August and September 1985, during which the ailing Leasat 3 satellite was retrieved, repaired, and redeployed. The astronauts of Mission 51-I also launched three new communications satellites during a weeklong flight.

Covey was born August 1, 1946, in Fayetteville, Arkansas, and grew up in Fort Walton Beach, Florida. He graduated from Choctawhatchee High School in nearby Shalimar in 1964. He attended the Air Force Academy, receiving a B.S. in engineering sciences in 1968, and earned an M.S. in aeronautics and astronautics from Purdue University in 1969.

Covey became an Air Force pilot in 1970 and in the next four years flew 339 combat missions in Southeast Asia. He then attended the Air Force Test Pilot School at Edwards AFB, California, where he was named outstanding graduate of his class, 74B, and spent the next three years at Eglin AFB, Florida, testing F-4 and A-7D weapons systems and serving as joint test force director for electronic warfare testing of the F-15 Eagle.

He logged over 5,700 hours of flying time in 30 different types of aircraft.

Covey was one of the 35 astronauts selected by NASA in January 1978 and in August 1979 qualified as a Shuttle pilot. He served as a T-38 chase pilot for STS-2 and STS-3 and as support crewman for STS-5. He was also a capcom for STS-5 and STS-6, and in December 1985 began another tour as Shuttle launch capcom. He was in direct contact with the Challenger during its fateful launch on January 28, 1986.

Between assignments to STS-26 and STS-38 Covey served as chairman of the NASA Space Flight Safety Panel. In 1991 he served as acting deputy chief of the astronaut office and also acting director of flight crew operations.

Covey resigned from NASA on July 11, 1994, and retired from the USAF (with the rank of colonel) on August 1 of that year, to join the Houston office of Calspan Services Contracts Division, an operating unit of Space Industries, as director of business development. He moved to McDonnell Douglas Aerospace in 1996 as division director for space programs at its Houston office.

In January 1998 he was appointed deputy program director for operations for Boeing's consolidated space operations contract, a 10-year, multibillion-dollar program designed to improve data collection and transmission between ground and space element of one hundred present and future NASA spacecraft.

Creamer, Timothy John
1959–

Army pilot Tim Creamer is one of the 25 astronaut candidates selected by NASA in June 1998. In August of that year he began a training and evaluation course that should qualify him as a Shuttle mission speciaalist and International Space Station crewmember.

Creamer was born November 15, 1959, at Fort Huachuca, Arizona. He graduated from Bishop McNamara High School in Forestville, Maryland, in 1978, then attended Loyola College, where he received a B.S. in chemistry in 1982. He later earned an M.S. in physics from the Massachusetts Institute of Technology (1992).

At the time of his selection by NASA, Major Creamer was a space operations officer with the Army Space Command, assigned to the Johnson Space Center.

Creighton, John Oliver
1943–

Former Navy test pilot John "J.O." Creighton commanded STS-36, a Department of Defense Shuttle mission launched after several delays on February 28, 1990. Poor weather, computer problems, and Creighton's health—he was suffering from a cold—caused five postponements.

(It was not possible to replace Creighton with a backup astronaut. NASA stopped assigning backup crews to Shuttle missions in 1982, since it was impractical to expect an astronaut to step in and command a mission with only a day's notice, while the pool of experienced Shuttle crewmembers made earlier substitutions relatively painless.)

Eventually the orbiter Atlantis roared into orbit during a nighttime launch. Later that day the crew deployed a massive CIA imaging reconnaissance satellite called Crystal (the advanced KH-11) into low Earth orbit. STS-36 ended after five days.

Earlier Creighton had served as pilot of Mission 51-G, flown in June 1985. The seven astronauts of the crew of 51-G, including a Saudi prince and a French test pilot, deployed three communications satellites and a scientific satellite, and conducted a laser-tracking experiment for the Strategic Defense Initiative Organization.

In September 1991 Creighton commanded STS-48, a 7-day flight of the orbiter Atlantis that deployed the Upper Atmosphere Research Satellite.

Creighton was born April 28, 1943, in Orange, Texas, and grew up Seattle, Washington, where he graduated from Ballard High School in 1961. He attended the Naval Academy, receiving a bachelor of science in 1966, and later earned an M.S. in administration of science and technology from George Washington University (1978).

Creighton completed pilot training in October 1967, then spent two years flying F-4Js from the carrier *U.S.S. Ranger* on combat missions over Vietnam. Returning to the United States in June 1970, he attended the Naval Test Pilot School at Patuxent River, Maryland, and remained at the Test Center as an F-14 pilot until July 1973. From 1973 to 1977 he was a member of the first operational F-14 squadron, making two deployments aboard the carrier *U.S.S. Enterprise*. At the time of his selection by NASA Creighton was again at the Naval Air Test Center, as operations officer and F-14 program manager.

He has logged over 6,000 hours of flying time, including 500 carrier landings and 175 combat missions.

Creighton was one of the 35 astronaut candidates selected by NASA in January 1978. In August 1979 he qualified as a Shuttle pilot. His technical assignments included a tour in the Shuttle Avionics Integration Lab (SAIL) and serving as deputy manager for operations integration in the Shuttle Program Office.

During the launch hiatus caused by the Challenger accident Creighton served as astronaut office representative to the Shuttle Program Manager. He also served as capcom for STS-26, 27, 39 and 30. From 1989 to 1990 he was head of the mission support branch of the astronaut office.

He retired from the Navy and resigned from NASA in August 1992 to join the Boeing Corporation in Seattle, Washington, as a test pilot and flight instructor.

Crews, Albert Hanlin, Jr.
1929–

Air Force test pilot Al Crews had the bad luck to be selected for two military manned space programs that were canceled before he could fly in space.

In September 1962 he was announced as one of the 6 pilots chosen for the X-20 Dyna-Soar spaceplane project, then scheduled for launch in early 1966. When the Manned Orbiting Laboratory project began in 1963, the X-20 was canceled. Crews was one of the first 8 pilots assigned to MOL in November 1965, but that project, too, was canceled, in May 1969.

Most of the 14 pilots still assigned to MOL requested transfers to the NASA astronaut group, but only 7, those who were still 36 years old or younger, were accepted. Crews, who was 40, did transfer to the NASA Johnson Space Center, where he joined the Flight Crew Operations directorate as a pilot. He is currently technical assistant for operations there, still flying NASA aircraft such as

the special KC-135 "vomit comet," which puts astronauts through a rollercoaster series of zero-G rides.

Crews was born March 23, 1929, in El Dorado, Arkansas. He received a B.S. in chemical engineering from the University of Southwestern Louisiana in 1950, and later earned an M.S. in aeronautical engineering from the Air Force Institute of Technology (1959).

Crews joined the Air Force in 1950 and became a jet pilot two years later. For the next five years he served with the Air Defense Command, including one posting to Wheelus AFB, Tripoli, Libya. Following further academic work at the Air Force Institute of Technology Crews was enrolled at the Test Pilot School at Edwards AFB, graduating in 1960. He remained at Edwards as a test pilot and was also a member of the second group of pilots to attend the new Aerospace Research Pilot School (1962). Between his assignments to X-20 and MOL he taught lifting body landing and zoom maneuvering at the Test Pilot School, and also served as a crewman for a series of simulated lunar landing missions conducted at Martin Marietta in Baltimore, Maryland.

Crippen, Robert Laurel
1937–

Former Navy aviator Bob Crippen was one of the most experienced astronauts of the early Space Shuttle era, making four flights between April 1981 and October 1984, including the first Shuttle ever launched. He was chosen to command the first Shuttle launched from Vandenberg Air Force Base, California, but that flight, Mission 62-A, had to be canceled following the Shuttle Challenger disaster.

On April 12, 1981, the twentieth anniversary of the flight of Yuri Gagarin, and after years of frustrating delay, Crippen and commander John Young rocketed into space aboard the Shuttle Columbia, landing two days later at Edwards Air Force Base in California, the first astronauts to pilot their spacecraft to a runway landing.

Crippen's second mission, STS-7 in June 1983, saw the flight of America's first woman in space, Sally Ride. (As commander Crippen had a voice in selecting his crew and asked for Ride.) Crippen's third flight, Mission 41-C in

April 1984, was marked by the rescue of the troubled Solar Max satellite by astronauts George Nelson and James Van Hoften. Crippen's fourth mission, 41-G in October 1984, was notable for being the first manned spaceflight to carry seven astronauts, and for first space walk by an American woman astronaut, Kathryn Sullivan.

Crippen was born September 11, 1937, in Beaumont, Texas, graduating from high school in Caney, Texas. He got interested in airplanes as a teenager and attended the University of Texas at Austin with the idea of becoming a pilot. He received a B.S. in aeronautical engineering in 1960 and entered the Navy via ROTC.

After completing basic flight training in 1962, Crippen served as a carrier pilot in the Pacific aboard the *U.S.S. Independence* until being selected for the Aerospace Research Pilot School (commanded by Colonel Chuck Yeager) in 1964. Crippen was talented enough to remain at the school as an instructor following graduation. In 1966 he was selected for the USAF Manned Orbiting Laboratory Program and trained for military spaceflights in that program until its cancellation in May 1969.

As a pilot Crippen logged over 6,500 hours of flying time, including 5,500 hours in jets.

Crippen was one of 7 ex-MOL pilots who transferred to NASA in August 1969, knowing that any possibility of a flight into space was at least eight or more years away. Nevertheless, Crippen got involved in the Skylab program, serving as team leader for the Skylab Medical Evaluation Altitude Test, a 56-day simulation of a Skylab mission, with astronauts Karol Bobko and William Thornton. He was a member of the astronaut support crew for all three Skylab missions and for the Apollo-Soyuz Test Project, after which he transferred to Space Shuttle development. In March 1978 he was named pilot of the first manned STS flight. His commander, John Young, said of Crippen, "He knows more about the computers that make this thing [the Shuttle] fly than anyone has a right to."

In October 1984 Crippen was named associate director of flight crew operations for the NASA astronaut group, an administrative job parallel to that of chief astronaut John Young. He gave up that position a year later to concentrate on training for Mission 62-A. When the Challenger accident occurred he served as an adviser to the presidential commission investigating the disas-ter. As a result, in 1987 he became deputy director for Shuttle operations at the Kennedy Space Center, a job that made him directly responsible for final go–no go launch decisions.

In October 1989 he turned that job over to fellow astronaut Brewster Shaw and transferred to NASA Headquarters, where for the next two years he served as associate administrator for Shuttle operations. From 1991 to January 1995 he was director of the NASA Kennedy Space Center.

After leaving NASA Crippen worked for a year as vice president of automation systems for Lockheed Martin Corporation, Orlando, Florida. Since December 1996 Crippen has been president of the Aerospace Group of the Thiokol Corporation, heading its space operations, defense and launch vehicles, and science and engineering divisions.

Crombie, Robert Buck
1954–

Air Force test engineer Rob Crombie was one of the 5 members of the third cadre of Manned Spaceflight Engineers chosen to train as Shuttle payload specialists in April 1986. He served as backup PS to NASA astronauts Guy Bluford, Rick Hieb, and Lacy Veach for STS-39, launched April 28, 1991. The 8-day mission was devoted to Department of Defense experiments in sensor technology.

Combie was born February 27, 1954, in Joliet, Illinois, where he grew up. He attended the Air Force Academy in Colorado Springs, Colorado, where he earned a B.S. in engineering science in 1976, followed by the California Institute of Technology in Pasadena, where he received an M.S. in aeronautics (1977).

Crombie's first assignment was as an aircraft stability and control engineer at the Flight Dynamics Laboratory at Wright-Patterson AFB, Ohio. In 1981 he transferred to the NASA Dryden Flight Research Center at Edwards AFB, California, where he served as liaison engineer for Advanced Fighter Technology Tests for two years. He remained at Edwards for an additional year to attend the USAF Test Pilot School, graduating from its flight test engineer course in 1984. He was an F-4/F-16 flight test engineer at Ogden Air Logistics Center, Hill AFB, Utah, when selected for the MSE program.

As an MSE his work also involved the Space Test Program, notably the Gamma Ray Advanced Detector (GRAD), a high-altitude balloon launched from Antarctica to observe Supernova 1987A.

Lieutenant Colonel Crombie is currently assigned to the National Imagery Agency.

Crossfield, Albert Scott

1921–

Scott Crossfield was the first pilot of the X-15 rocket research plane and made 14 flights in it between June 1959 and December 1960. More significantly, perhaps, Crossfield played an important role in the development of the X-15, first as a consultant to North American Aviation, the builders of the rocket plane, then as its prime test pilot.

Crossfield was born October 2, 1921, in Berkeley, California, and grew up in Wilmington, south of Los Angeles, where his father was in the oil business. Childhood bouts with pneumonia and rheumatic fever left young Scott bedridden for long periods of time during which he began to read about pilots and airplanes. When he recovered he took up a paper route that serviced the Wilmington Airport, where 13-year-old Scott made a deal with a pilot there: flying lessons in exchange for free delivery.

Shortly thereafter Crossfield's family moved to a farm in Washington state, where he graduated from Boistfort High School in 1939. He managed to continue his flying lessons at nearby Chehalis Airport.

Crossfield entered the University of Washington in September 1940, intending to study aeronautical engineering, and also found a job at the Boeing aircraft plant, which lasted until he joined the Navy following Pearl Harbor. He completed military pilot training, then served as a flying and gunnery instructor. He was assigned to the aircraft carrier *U.S.S. Langley*, headed for combat over Japan, when the war ended.

After the war Crossfield returned to the University of Washington, receiving a B.S. in aeronautical engineering

in 1949 and an M.S. the following year. He joined NACA in 1950 as a pilot at Edwards Air Force Base, California.

For the next five years Crossfield flew high-speed jets and rocket planes for NACA, including the X-1, D-558 II Skyrocket, X-4, X-5, XF-92A, and the F-100. In 1953 he became the first pilot to fly twice the speed of sound.

Crossfield left NACA in December 1955 to join North American Aviation. He remained with the company as director of test and quality assurance until 1967. He was later employed by Eastern Airlines (1967–74) and by Hawker-Siddeley Corporation (1974–77). From 1977 to 1993 was a member of the staff of the Committee on Science and Technology, U.S. House of Representatives.

He is the author of an autobiography, *Always Another Dawn* (1960).

Crouch, Roger Keith

1940–

NASA physicist Roger Crouch was a payload specialist for both flights of the Materials Science Laboratory, flown aboard STS-83 and STS-94 in 1997, a mission described as a "bridge" between Shuttle-Spacelab science missions, and future International Space Station operations.

The MSL payload was originally launched aboard the orbiter Columbia on April 3, 1997, for a planned 16-day mission. But a problem with Columbia's fuel cells shortened the mission to four days. NASA program managers decided to refly the MSL and its crew at the next opportunity, launching Columbia eight weeks later as STS-94.

The crew of 7 performed 33 different sets of experiments designed by researchers in 23 nations, notably studies of how fires burn in microgravity, a subject of great importance to future International Space Station missions, given the nearly disastrous March 1997 fire aboard the Russian Mir station.

Crouch previously served as backup payload specialist for STS-42, the International Microgravity Laboratory Shuttle mission launched in January 1992. During this 8-day Spacelab flight a crew of 7—which included German physicist Ulf Merbold and Canadian physician Roberta Bondar—performed experiments in space medicine and manufacturing. Crouch supported the flight from the NASA Marshall Spaceflight Center.

Crouch was born September 12, 1940, in Jamestown, Tennessee, and graduated from Polk County High School in Clarksville, Tennessee, in 1958. He attended Tennessee Tech in Cookeville, receiving a B.S. in physics in 1962. He earned his M.S. (1968) and Ph.D. (1971) in physics from Virginia Polytechnic Institute in Blacksburg.

Crouch joined NASA's Langley Research Center in Langley, Virginia, upon graduation from Tennessee Tech in 1962, where he worked on spacecraft heat shields, among other projects. In addition to his NASA work, from 1974 to 1978 Crouch was a college instructor in algebra and mathematics at Christopher Newport College and Thomas Nelson Community College. He was also a visiting scientist at the Massachusetts Institute of Technology from 1979–80. He returned to Langley in 1980 as a group leader and principal investigator for an experiment designed to test the growth of crystals in space.

Since 1985 Crouch has been chief scientist of the Microgravity Space and Applications Division, Office of Space Science and Applications, at NASA Headquarters in Washington, D.C. He has authored over 30 technical papers and holds four patents.

He was a candidate for assignment to the IML-2 mission, STS-65, launched in July 1994.

Culbertson, Frank Lee, Jr.
1949–

Former Navy test pilot Frank Culbertson commanded STS-51, the September 1993 flight of the orbiter Discovery that successfully deployed the Advanced Communications Technology Satellite while deploying and retrieving the Orfeus/Spas scientific satellite.

Previously, Culbertson served as pilot of STS-38, the seventh and last classified Department of Defense Shuttle mission. STS-38 was launched at night from Kennedy Space Center on November 15, 1990, and later that day deployed a data relay satellite for use with the Crystal imaging reconnaissance satellite. The mission ended five days later with the first Shuttle landing at the Kennedy Space Center in five years.

Culbertson was born May 15, 1949, in Charleston, South Carolina. He graduated from high school in Holly Hill, South Carolina, in 1967, then attended the Naval Academy at Annapolis, receiving a B.S. in aerospace engineering in 1971.

After graduation Culbertson served as an ensign aboard the U.S.S. Fox in the Gulf of Tonkin before reporting for pilot training at Beeville, Texas. He won his wings in May 1973 and following F-4 Phantom training served with Fighter Squadron 151 aboard the carrier U.S.S. Midway. From 1976 to 1978 he was an exchange pilot with the Air Force at Luke AFB, Arizona, where he served as an F-4 weapons and tactics instructor. He then served aboard the carrier U.S.S. America until May 1981, when he entered the Naval Test Pilot School at Patuxent River, Maryland.

Following graduation from the school Culbertson was assigned to the Air Test Center as program manager for all F-4 testing, where he served until January 1984. At the time of his selection by NASA he was training as an F-14 pilot at Oceana, Virgina.

He has logged over 4,000 hours of flying time in 36 different types of aircraft, including 350 carrier landings.

Culbertson was one of the 17 astronauts selected by NASA in May 1984 and in June 1985 qualified as a Shuttle pilot. His first technical assignment was to the team redesigning Shuttle landing and braking systems. He was a member of the astronaut support team at the Kennedy Space Center for missions 61-A, 61-B, 61-C and 51-L. Following the Challenger accident in January 1986 he assisted with the investigation at NASA Headquarters in Washington, D.C.

He has since served as lead astronaut in the Shuttle Avionics Integration Lab (SAIL) and as capcom for STS-27, 29, 30, 28, 34, 33 and 32. In 1991–92 he was lead astronaut in the Space station Support Office.

While training for STS-51 in 1992-93 Culbertson took part in planning for proposed Shuttle-Mir docking missions. Following STS-51, he served as head of the astronaut office mission support branch and as chief of the JSC Russian Projects Office before being named manager for Phase 1 of the Shuttle-Mir program in the summer of 1995. In this position he oversaw the complex training and operational matters allowing seven NASA astronauts to work aboard the Russian station, in addition to resupplying the station with the Shuttle.

Culbertson retired from the Navy in 1996 with the rank of captain.

Cunningham, Ronnie Walter

1932–

Marine aviator and RAND researcher Walt Cunningham was a member of the crew of Apollo 7, the first manned Apollo flight. In eleven days following launch on October 11, 1968, Cunningham and fellow astronauts Walter Schirra and Donn Eisele performed rendezvous exercises, propulsion tests, and general spacecraft systems tests in qualifying the Apollo for later flights to the Moon.

The Apollo 7 astronauts also had the unfortunate distinction of being the first space travelers to catch colds, and were generally physically miserable for much of the flight. They were able to make the first effective TV transmissions from an American spacecraft, the "Wally, Walt and Donn Show," which won a special Emmy award from the Academy of Television Arts and Sciences.

Cunningham was born March 16, 1932, in Creston, Iowa, but grew up in Venice, California. He decided at the age of 10 that he wanted to be a Navy pilot. At the age of 19 he dropped out of Santa Monica Community College and joined the Navy. He didn't have the required two years of college necessary for flight school, but was able to pass an equivalency test, and earned his wings in 1953. For the next three years he served as Marine aviator at bases in the United States and in Japan. In August 1956 he was detached from active duty. He would remain a Marine reservist until retiring with the rank of colonel in 1975.

As a pilot Cunningham logged over 4,500 hours of flying time, including 3,400 hours in jets.

On the G.I. Bill, Cunningham studied at the University of California at Los Angeles, earning a B.A. (1960) and an M.A. (1961) in physics. He worked on his doctorate while employed by the RAND Corporation as a scientist. His projects at RAND included studies of defense against submarine-launched ballistic missiles and the problems of the Earth's magnetosphere. His research in the latter lead to an experiment that went into space aboard the first Orbiting Geophysical Satellite.

Cunningham was one of the 14 astronauts selected by NASA in October 1963. After a yearlong general training course Cunningham was assigned to Apollo program development. He also served as a capcom for Gemini 4 and Gemini 8.

In September 1966 Cunningham was officially named to the crew for Apollo 2, then planned for the summer of 1967. (Cunningham, Schirra and Eisele had been training as a team since early 1966.) When that flight was canceled two months after the announcement, the Schirra crew became backups to the Apollo 1 astronauts, Grissom, White, and Chaffee.

The deaths of Grissom, White, and Chaffee in a fire on January 27, 1967, forced a reevaluation of the entire Apollo program. It was five months before NASA was ready to proceed, and the Schirra crew was assigned to make the first flight.

After Apollo 7 Cunningham was assigned to the Apollo Applications Program (later Skylab) branch of the astronaut office, a job he held until succeeded by Charles Conrad in August 1970. Cunningham had been chosen to be backup commander for the first Skylab mission and might have commanded the third and last, but he resigned from NASA on August 1, 1971.

From 1971 to 1976 he was president of the Hydro-Tech Development Company in Houston, and vice-president for operations of Century Development. From December 1976 to October 1979 he was vice-president and director of engineering for the 3D International Corporation in Houston. More recently he has been founder and sole principal in the Capital Group, a private banking investment firm based in Houston (1979 to 1986). He is currently founder/partner of Acorn Ventures, a venture capital company associated with the Genesis Fund.

Cunningham is the author of the most candid book written by an astronaut, *The All-American Boys*, published in 1977.

Cunningham, Steven Lee
1945–

Steven Cunningham, a physicist employed by the Hughes Aircraft Company, was assigned as a backup payload specialist for John Konrad on Shuttle Mission 61-L, scheduled to deploy a Hughes-built Leasat communications satellite in the summer of 1986. The Challenger disaster on January 28, 1986, killed seven astronauts, including Hughes payload specialist Gregory Jarvis, and ended the commercial payload specialist program.

Cunningham was born September 10, 1945, in Renton, Washington, and grew up in Englewood, Colorado, where he graduated from Cherry Creek High School in 1963. He attended the University of Denver, receiving a B.S. in physics in 1967. He went on to graduate school at the University of Nebraska, receiving his M.S. (1969) and Ph.D. (1971) in physics.

From 1971 to 1974 Cunningham was a research assistant at the University of California, Irvine, followed by a year as a visiting associate at the California Institute of Technology. He joined the staff of Cal Tech in 1975 and worked as a research chemist there until 1977, when he joined Hughes Aircraft as a senior staff physicist. With the exception of a year on the Landsat 3 satellite program, Cunningham largely worked on military programs for Hughes, including Leasat.

He was one of 4 Hughes engineers selected as payload specialists in July 1984.

Cunningham is currently deputy business unit leader for the command, control, and operations business unit of Hughes Space and Communications, El Segundo, California.

Curbeam, Robert Lee, Jr.
1962–

Navy intercept officer Robert Curbeam was a mission specialist aboard STS-85. This July 1997 flight of the orbiter Discovery carried the CHRISTA-SPAS payload, designed to study the Earth's atmosphere.

In May 1997 Curbeam was also assigned to International Space Station assembly mission 6A, to be launched as STS-100 in the summer of 2000. Curbeam and astronaut Chris Hadfield will perform a series of EVAs during that mission.

Curbeam was born March 5, 1962, in Baltimore, Maryland, where he graduated from Woodlawn High School in 1980. He attended the Naval Academy, where he received a B.S. in aerospace engineering in 1984. He later earned an M.S. in aeronautical engineering from the Naval Postgraduate School (1990) and the degree of aeronautical and astronautical engineer from that school in 1991.

Curbeam was designated a naval flight officer in 1986, and first served as an F-14 radar intercept officer with Fighter Squadron 11 aboard the carrier *U.S.S. Forrestal* in the Mediterranean and Caribbean Seas, and in the Artic and Indian Oceans. In 1991 he attended the Naval Test Pilot School at NAS Patuxent River, Maryland, then spent two years as project officer for the F-14A/B air-to-ground weapons separation program. At the time of his selection by NASA Curbeam was an instructor at the Naval Academy.

Curbeam was one of the 19 astronaut candidates selected by NASA on December 8, 1994. In May 1996 he qualified as a Shuttle mission specialist. His first technical assignment was with the computer support branch of the astronaut office.

Currie, Nancy Jane (Sherlock)
1958–

Army helicopter pilot Nancy Currie was a mission specialist in the crew of STS-57. Launched in June 1993, STS-57 carried the first SpaceHab cargo carrier. In the summer of 1995 Currie made a second flight, aboard STS-70, which deployed the sixth and last Tracking and Data Relay Satellite.

Currie is currently assigned as the RMS operator for STS-88, scheduled to deploy Node 1, the first element of the International Space Station, in orbit during the winter of 1998–99.

Currie was born Nancy Jane Decker on December 29, 1958, in Wilmington, Delaware, but considers Troy, Ohio, to be her hometown. She attended Ohio State University, receiving a B.A. in biological science in 1980. In 1985 she earned an M.S. in safety engineering from the University of Southern California.

Before going on active duty with the Army in July 1981 Currie was a neuropathology research assistant at the Ohio State University College of Medicine. Commissioned as a second lieutenant in the Air Defense Artillery, Currie went on to attend the Army Aviation School. Assigned to Fort Rucker, Alabama, as a UH-1H instructor pilot, she became a section leader, platoon leader, and brigade flight standardization officer.

She is rated as a Senior Army Aviator and has logged 2,700 hours of flying time in both helicopters and multiengine fixed-wing aircraft.

Currie was assigned to the NASA Johnson Space Center in September 1987 as a flight simulation engineer on the Shuttle Training Aircraft, and become one of the 23 astronaut candidates selected in January 1990. In July 1991 she qualified as a Shuttle mission specialist. (At the time of her selection and her first flight, Currie was known as Nancy Sherlock.) Her technical assignments have included work on crew equipment and the RMS, and as a Shuttle capcom.

Dana, William Harvey
1930–

NASA test pilot Bill Dana made 16 flights in the X-15 rocket plane, including two that exceeded fifty miles in altitude, qualifying him as a space traveler. On November 1, 1966, Dana piloted X-15 #3 to an altitude of 306,900 feet, 58 miles above the surface of the Earth. A second flight on August 21, 1968, in X-15 #1 reached 267,500 feet, or almost 51 miles in altitude.

Dana was born November 3, 1930, in Pasadena, California. He attended the U.S. Military Academy at West Point, graduating with a bachelor of science degree in 1952, and elected to serve in the Air Force. He later earned an M.S. in aeronautical engineering from the University of Southern California (1958).

Dana served in the Air Force as a fighter pilot from 1952 to 1956. After completing graduate work at USC he

went to work for NASA as a research and test pilot at the Dryden Flight Center at Edwards Air Force Base, California. In addition to work on the X-15 program, which he began in 1965, Dana flew all of the lifting body aircraft NASA and the Air Force developed as precursors to the Space Shuttle, including the M2-F1, M2-F2, M2-F3, HL-10, X-24A, and X-24B. He was also involved in the X-20 Dyna-Soar program.

On September 23, 1975. Dana was the pilot for the last rocket-powered flight of the X-24B flight, ending the series of rocket flights that had begun with the X-1 in 1947.

More recently Dana has been a project pilot on the Advanced Fighter Technology Program at Dryden.

Davis, (Nancy) Jan
1953–

Engineer Jan Davis has been a mission specialist aboard three Shuttle missions. The first was STS-47, the 8-day Spacelab J (Japan) mission, flown in September 1992. The crew of 7 included a Japanese astronaut and Davis's husband, STS-47 payload commander Mark Lee, and conducted 40 experiments in space medicine and manufacturing.

In February 1994 Davis made her second flight, aboard STS-60, which carried the second SpaceHab module. The crew of STS-60, which also included Russian cosmonaut Sergei Krikalev, was to have deployed the Wake Shield Facility satellite, but technical problems prevented it.

Davis flew again on STS-85, the July 1997 flight of the orbiter Discovery that carried the CHRISTA-SPAS payload, designed to study the Earth's atmosphere, as well as a new Japanese robot manipulator system designed for use on the International Space Station.

Davis was born November 1, 1953, in Cocoa Beach, Florida, though she considers Huntsville, Alabama, to be her hometown. She attended the Georgia Institute of Technology, graduating with a B.S. in applied biology in 1975, and went on to attend Auburn University, where she received a second B.S., this one in mechanical engineering, in 1977. She later received an M.S. (1983) and a Ph.D. (1985) in mechanical engineering from the University of Alabama at Huntsville.

After graduating from Auburn in 1977 Davis went to work for Texaco in Bellaire, Texas, as a petroleum engineer. Two years later she joined the NASA Marshall Space Flight Center in her hometown of Huntsville, Alabama, as an aerospace engineer. She went on to work on the Hubble Space Telescope and Advanced X-Ray Astrophysics Facility (AXAF) projects. In 1987, following the Challenger disaster, she was part of the team redesigning the Shuttle solid rocket booster.

Davis holds one patent and has authored several technical papers. She is also a pilot.

As an astronaut Davis has worked in the mission development branch on the Tethered Satellite System, Tracking and Data Relay Satellite, and other programs. She is also qualified as a remote manipulator system operator, and as an EVA crewmember. She was a capcom for seven Shuttle missions (April 1991–January 1992).

In 1994–95 Davis served as chair of the NASA Education Working Group, then did a tour as chief of the payloads branch of the astronaut office (1995–96).

DeArmond, Frank Maxton
1954–

Air Force engineer Frank DeArmond was one of the 5 Manned Spaceflight Engineers selected for training as military Shuttle payload specialists in April 1986. The selection process had begun prior to the Challenger accident; by the time DeArmond and his colleagues commenced their training there was increasingly little chance they would fly in space. The MSE program was canceled in 1988.

DeArmond was born November 27, 1954, at Fort Jackson in Columbia, South Carolina, and grew up in Charlotte, North Carolina. He became interested in spaceflight with the first Mercury missions in the early 1960s, and went on to study aerospace engineering at North Carolina State University in Raleigh, receiving his B.S. in 1978. He later earned an M.S. in aeronautical engineering from the Air Force Institute of Technology (1982).

DeArmond's first assignment with the Air Force was with the 6595th Shuttle Test Group at Vandenberg AFB,

California, from 1978 to 1981. Following graduate school he was assigned to the Satellite Control Facility (later Onizuka AFB) in Sunnyvale, California, as chief of the spacecraft engineering branch for a classified program there.

He worked with the Space Test Program at Space Systems Division, Los Angeles, until 1990, when he was reassigned to Falcon AFB. He was commander of the 4th Space Operations Squadron from 1992 to 1994, then, following a tour at Kirtland AFB, New Mexico, he returned to Los Angeles AFB, where he is assigned to the Space and Missile Systems Center.

DeLucas, Lawrence James
1950–

Biochemist Larry DeLucas was a payload specialist in the crew of STS-50, the flight of the U.S. Microgravity Laboratory in June and July 1992. The 2-week mission—the longest in the Shuttle program—was devoted to experiments in crystal growth, space processing, and the effects of long-term flight on human beings.

DeLucas was born July 11, 1950, in Syracuse, New York. In 1968 he enrolled at the University of Alabama at Birmingham, where he went on to receive the following degrees: B.S. (1972) and M.S. (1974) in chemistry, a B.S. in physiological optics (1979), a doctorate in optometry (1981), and a Ph.D. in biochemistry (1982).

DeLucas has spent his academic career at Alabama, originally as a research associate in the Institute of Dental Research there (1975–76), then as a graduate student (1977–82). Since 1982 he has been a member of the Vision Science Research Center and a scientist at the Institute of Dental Research in addition to a member of the graduate faculty and a scientist at the Comprehensive Cancer Center. His current title is professor in the department of optometry. DeLucas has also been an adjunct professor of materials science, medical genetics and biochemistry.

He is the author of over 60 scientific articles, coauthor of two books, and the holder of three patents.

DeLucas began working with NASA in 1987 as a member of the space agency's committee on advanced protein crystal growth. He was selected as a candidate payload specialist for USML-1 in August 1990 and chosen as prime PS the following May.

From December 1994 to the summer of 1995 DeLucas served as acting senior scientist for the space station program.

Detroye, Jeff Eliot
1955–

Air Force engineer Jeff Detroye was one of 13 members of the first cadre of Department of Defense manned spaceflight engineers. In June 1982 he was selected as a payload specialist candidate for a Shuttle mission that was to have carried the Teal Ruby satellite into orbit in 1984. That flight was canceled before launch.

Detroye was born January 14, 1955, in Alexandria, Virginia, and grew up in Darien, Connecticut, where he graduated from high school. As a teenager he grew fascinated with spaceflight and planned to be either an astronaut or a flight director. With those goals in mind, he enrolled at the Air Force Academy, earning a B.S. in astronautical engineering in 1977. He has done graduate work.

Detroye and classmate Frank Casserino were among the first Air Force Academy graduates to study military space operations under professors with actual experience, and to embark on careers in that field. From 1977 to 1979 Detroye was a software engineer at the Satellite Control Facility in Sunnyvale, California, then was assigned to Los Angeles AFS as a project engineer.

As an MSE from 1979 to 1985 Detroye worked as paycom for the STS-4 mission (1982) and also in support of Mission 51-C, the first dedicated DOD flight (1985). He left the program in August 1985 to join the Air Force Shuttle support group at the NASA Johnson Space Center. When he resigned from the USAF a year later he became a NASA employe. He currently works as a Shuttle flight controller.

Duffy, Brian
1953–

Air Force test pilot Brian Duffy commanded STS-72, the January 1996 flight of the orbiter Discovery that retrieved Japan's Space Flyer Unit. Two astronauts also completed a pair of EVAs.

Duffy was also on two previous Shuttle crews: STS-45, the March 1992 Spacelab ATLAS mission that carried a crew of 7 to conduct research in atmospheric science, and STS-57, the first flight of the SpaceHab commercial carrier, in June 1993.

In February 1998 Duffy was named commander of STS-92, International Space Station assembly mission 3A, scheduled for launch in the fall of 1999.

Duffy was born June 20, 1953, in Boston, Massachusetts, and graduated from high school in nearby Rockland in 1971. He attended the Air Force Academy in Colorado Springs, graduating with a B.S. in mathematics in 1975, and later earned an M.S. in systems management from the University of Southern California in 1981.

Duffy completed pilot training in 1976 and flew F-15s at Langley AFB, Virginia, and at Kadena AFB, Okinawa, until 1982, when he attended the Air Force Test Pilot School at Edwards Air Force Base, California. When selected by NASA he was directing F-15 tests at Eglin Air Force Base, Florida. He has logged over 4,500 hours of flying time in 25 different types of aircraft.

He was one of the 13 astronauts selected by NASA in June 1985. In July 1986 he qualified as a Shuttle pilot while working in the Shuttle Avionics Integration Laboratory (SAIL). He has also been technical assistant to the director of flight crew operations. He was selected for the STS-45 crew in May 1990.

Following STS-76 Duffy served as assistant director (technical) of the Johnson Space Center. From December 1996 to January 1998 he was acting deputy director of JSC.

Duke, Charles Moss, Jr.

1935–

Air Force test pilot Charlie Duke became the tenth person to walk on the Moon when he was lunar module pilot of the Apollo 16 mission in April 1972. Duke and commander John Young landed the lunar module Orion on the Cayley Plains near the crater Descartes six hours later than scheduled because of problems with the main rocket engine of their command module, Casper. Concern over the engine would force them to shorten their flight by a day, but Duke and Young nevertheless spent almost three days on the Moon, including almost 21 hours outside Orion. They used a lunar roving vehicle to reach distant geological sites and to drive up nearby Stone Mountain.

Duke was born October 3, 1935, in Charlotte, North Carolina. He attended the Naval Academy, graduating in 1957 with a bachelor of science. In 1964 he earned an M.S. in aeronautics and astronautics from the Massachusetts Institute of Technology.

After pilot training Duke spent three years with the 526th Interceptor Squadron at Ramstein, Germany. He attended the Air Force Aerospace Research Pilot School at Edwards AFB, California, in 1965, and was an instructor there when selected by NASA.

As a pilot Duke logged 4,200 hours of flying time, including 3,600 hours in jets.

Duke was one of the 19 astronauts selected by NASA in April 1966. He served as support crewman for Apollo 10, and was capcom during the first lunar landing by astronauts Neil Armstrong and Edwin Aldrin in July 1969. He later served as backup lunar module pilot for Apollo 13, and backup lunar module pilot for Apollo 17. For several years he worked on Space Shuttle development.

He resigned from NASA in December 1975 and from Air Force active duty on January 1, 1976, to become distributor for Coors Beer in San Antonio, Texas. He left that business in March 1978 to work elsewhere in San Antonio, and has since been a Christian lay minister. Most recently he has headed his own investment company and is president of Southwest Wilderness Art in New Braunfels, Texas.

His autobiography, *Moonwalk*, written with his wife, Dotty, was published in 1990.

Dunbar, Bonnie Jean

1949–

Bonnie Dunbar has made five Shuttle flights, including the first Shuttle-Mir docking mission, STS-71.

That June 1995 flight of the orbiter Atlantis carried two Russian cosmonauts—Anatoly Solovyov and Nikolai Budarin—in addition to its crew of 5 NASA astronauts. Solovyov and Budarin replaced the Mir crew of Yuri Dezhurov, Gennady Strekalov, and NASA astronaut Norman Thagard, who had been aboard Mir since that March. Atlantis returned to Earth with a crew of 8.

Dunbar trained for a year as Thagard's backup, undergoing Russian language schooling and learning to serve as a Soyuz-Mir crewmember.

She returned to Mir as a mission specialist in the crew of STS-89. This flight of the orbiter Endeavour delivered Andy Thomas, the seventh and last NASA-Mir crewmember, to the Russian station, while returning David Wolf to Earth. STS-89 also delivered four tons of water, food and other supplies to Mir.

Dunbar had previously flown as mission specialist aboard Shuttle Mission 61-A/Spacelab D1 in October and November 1985. During the weeklong flight Dunbar and seven other astronauts performed scientific experiments designed and controlled by the Federal German Aerospace Research Establishment (DFVLR) and the European Space Agency (ESA).

Dunbar was also a mission specialist aboard STS-32 in January 1990. On that flight she used the Shuttle Columbia's remote manipulator arm to grapple the massive Long Duration Exposure Facility (LDEF), a scientific satellite that had been in orbit for nearly six years. LDEF was then photographed and latched into Columbia's payload bay for return to Earth. Data from LDEF is expected to assist scientists and engineers in the design of future space stations.

Dunbar's third flight was STS-50, launched June 25, 1992. This 2-week mission carried the U.S. Microgravity

Laboratory and a crew of 7, who performed experiments in space manufacturing.

Dunbar was born March 3, 1949, in Sunnyside, Washington. She graduated from Sunnyside High School in 1967 and attended the University of Washington, where she received a B.S. and M.S. in ceramic engineering in 1971 and 1975. She later earned her Ph.D. in biomedical engineering from the University of Houston in 1983.

After graduating from college in 1971 Dunbar worked for two years at Boeing as a computer systems analyst, then began researching her master's thesis. In 1975 she was invited to be a visiting scientist at Harwell Laboratories in Oxford, England, then became a senior research engineer at Rockwell International Space Divison in Downey, California, where she worked on the development of the Space Shuttle thermal protection system. She became a payload officer and flight controller at NASA's Johnson Space Center in 1978, working as one of the guidance and navigation officers during the Skylab reentry in 1979.

Dunbar was selected as an astronaut candidate in May 1980 and in August 1981 qualified as a Shuttle mission specialist. She worked in the Shuttle Avionics Integration Laboratory before being assigned to Spacelab D1 in 1983. In the hiatus caused by the Challenger accident she participated in the astronaut office Science Support Group.

She is a private pilot with over 200 hours flying time and has also logged 700 hours as a T-38 jet co-pilot. In addition to her astronaut duties, she is an adjunct assistant professor of mechanical engineering at the University of Houston.

Following STS-50 Dunbar spent a year (1993) at NASA Headquarters in Washington as deputy associate administrator for materials science. She was assigned as Thagard's backup in February 1994, and named to the STS-71 crew that June. From October 1995 to November 1996 she was detailed to the Johnson Space Center's mission operations directorate as assistant director for International Space Station readiness and Russian-American cooperation.

Dunlap, Alexander William

1960–

Physician Alexander Dunlap was an alternate payload specialist for STS-90, the April 1998 flight of the Neurolab Spacelab. This 16-day flight of the orbiter Columbia—the last Spacelab mission in a program stretching back to 1983—carried a crew of 7, including four physicians, and conducted thirty-one different experiments in space medicine. Dunlap backed up payload specialist Jim Pawelczyk, supporting Neurolab from the NASA Marshall Spaceflight Center.

Dunlap was born July 15, 1960, in Honolulu, Hawaii, and graduated from high school in West Memphis, Tennessee, in 1978. He entered the University of Arkansas at Fayetteville, where he received B.S. degrees (cum laude) in zoology (1982) and animal science (1984). He went on to earn an doctorate in veterinary medicine from Louisiana State University, Baton Rouge (1989), and an M.D. from the University of Tennessee College of Medicine in Memphis (1996).

After graduation from Arkansas, Dunlap worked as an electron microscopy technician at the University of Tennessee's Center for the Health Sciences. He then became a student resident at Lousiana State in 1986. After receiving his veterinary degree, he worked at Bowling Animal Clinic in Collierville, Tennessee, until 1992.

While attending medical school at Tennessee beginning in 1991 Dunlap supported five NASA missions, with experiments flown on STS-40 (1991), STS-52 (1992), STS-56 and STS-58 (both 1993), and STS-70 (1995). Since 1996 he has been on staff at the University of Tennessee's Department of Family Medicine.

He was announced as an STS-90 payload specialist candidate in April 1996.

Durrance, Samuel Thornton

1943–

Astronomer Sam Durrance spent nine days in space aboard the orbiter Columbia during the STS-35/Spacelab ASTRO mission in December 1990. The $150-million ASTRO observatory carried four different telescopes, with which the astronaut astronomers were able to obtain nearly 400 images of 135 deep space targets.

The mission was threatened by computer failures that made it difficult to point the telescopes with the required precision. The ASTRO crew managed to work around the problem by manually pointing the sensitive instruments with help from ground controllers.

Durrance also assisted astronaut Jeff Hoffman in delivering a televised science lesson from space to two different middle schools on Earth.

Durrance made a second flight in March 1995 with ASTRO-02's ultraviolet telescopes aboard Shuttle mission STS-67. This flight of the orbiter Endeavour carried a crew of 7 and lasted for over sixteen days. One investigator reported that ASTRO-02 had collected three times as much data as the first ASTRO mission.

Durrance was born September 17, 1943, in Tallahassee, Florida. He attended California State University in Los Angeles, receiving a B.S. (1972) and M.S. (1974) in physics. He earned a Ph.D. in astrogeophysics from the University of Colorado in 1980.

A scientist in the physics and astronomy department at Johns Hopkins University in Baltimore, Durrance was assistant project scientist for the Hopkins Ultraviolet Telescope, one of the primary instruments flown on ASTRO-1 and ASTRO-2. He has also used instruments aboard Explorer and Pioneer space probes to study Venus, Mars, Jupiter, Io, Saturn, and Uranus. His main field of interest is the origin and evolution of the solar system and of other planetary systems, and the origin and evolution of life in the universe.

Durrance was selected as an ASTRO payload specialist in June 1984. ASTRO-1 was originally scheduled for launch as Shuttle Mission 61-E in March 1986 and timed to observe Halley's Comet, but the Challenger disaster six weeks prior to that date caused the mission to be postponed for four years.

In addition to serving as principal research scientist at the Johns Hopkins University Department of Physics and Astronomy, Durrance is also president of Earth Systems Technology, an Earth resources company.

Edwards, Joe Frank, Jr.

1958–

Navy test pilot Joe Edwards was pilot in the crew of STS-89. This January 1998 flight of the orbiter Atlantis accomplished the eighth Shuttle-Mir docking, carrying astronaut Andrew Thomas to Mir and returning David Wolf to Earth.

Edwards was born February 3, 1958, in Richmond, Virginia. He graduated from high school in Lineville, Alabama, in 1976, then attended the Naval Academy, where he received a B.S. in aerospace engineering in 1980. He later received an M.S. in aviation systems from the University of Tennessee at Knoxville (1994).

After graduation from Annapolis Edwards qualified as a naval aviator. With Fighter Squadron 143 he flew F-14 Tomcats on fighter escort and reconnaissance missions over Lebanon in 1983. He attended the Navy's Fighter Weapons School ("Top Gun") in 1984, and the Naval Test Pilot School, NAS Patuxent River, Maryland. From 1986 to 1989 he was a test pilot at the Naval Air Test Center on the F-14A (PLUS) and F-14D programs.

Edwards then spent three years as operations and maintenance officer for Fighter Squadron 142 aboard the carrier *U.S.S. America*. He was a candidate for the 1992 astronaut selection, but had to drop out when he was injured in a crash aboard the *America*. In 1992 he became operations officer in the operations directorate of the Joint Chiefs of Staff, Washington D.C.

Commander Edwards has logged 2,500 hours of flying time in 25 different aircraft, including 650 carrier landings.

He was one of the 19 astronaut candidates selected by NASA on December 8, 1994, and in May 1996 qualified as a Shuttle pilot while working in the safety branch of the astronaut office.

Eisele, Donn Fulton
1938–1987

Air Force test pilot Donn Eisele was the command module pilot of Apollo 7, the first manned Apollo flight, in October 1968. The 11-day mission by Eisele and astronauts Walter Schirra and Walter Cunningham qualified the Apollo spacecraft, which had been completely redesigned following the tragic fire that killed three astronauts, clearing the way for future flights to the Moon.

The Apollo 7 astronauts were the first American astronauts to beam live television pictures to the ground. The "Wally, Walt and Don Show" won a special "Emmy" award from the Academy of Television Arts and Sciences. They also had the back luck to be the first astronauts to catch cold in space.

Eisele was born June 30, 1930, in Columbus, Ohio, where he graduated from West High School in 1948. His father was a printer. Eisele earned a competitive appointment to the Naval Academy at Annapolis, graduating with a bachelor of science degree in 1952. He later earned an M.S. in astronautics from the Air Force Institute of Technology (1960).

Because of a lifelong interest in flying, Eisele elected to serve in the Air Force after graduation from Annapolis. He underwent pilot training in Texas, Arizona, and Florida, winning his wings in 1954. Until 1958 he was an interceptor pilot stationed at Ellsworth AFB, South Dakota. In 1958 he became a student at the Air Force Institute of Technology, and remained there as a rocket propulsion and weapons engineer after graduation. In 1961 he attended the Air Force Aerospace Research Pilot School at Edwards AFB, California, later serving as an instructor there as well. When chosen by NASA, Eisele was a test pilot at the Air Force Special Weapons Center at Kirtland AFB, New Mexico.

As a pilot Eisele logged over 4,200 hours of flying time, including over 3,600 hours in jets.

Eisele was one of the 14 astronauts selected by NASA in October 1963. He was assigned to Apollo projects early in training and helped test the pressure suit later used for walks on the Moon. In late 1965 he was assigned as pilot of the first manned Apollo crew commanded by Virgil Grissom, but suffered a shoulder injury during a weightless training flight and was replaced by Roger Chaffee. After recovering, Eisele joined the Schirra crew, then assigned to the second manned Apollo flight.

After Apollo 7 Eisele served as backup command module pilot for Apollo 10. When he was not assigned to a second Apollo flight he left the astronaut office to become technical assistant for manned spaceflight at the NASA Langley Research Center in Hampton, Virginia. He resigned from NASA and and retired from the USAF in July 1972.

He then served as Director of the Peace Corps in Thailand and, after returning to the United States, became sales manager for the Marion Power Shovel Company. He was also an executive with the investment firm of Oppenheimer & Company in Fort Lauderdale, Florida, and later founded his own consulting firm, Space Age America.

He died of a heart attack in Tokyo on December 1, 1987. He had gone there to announce the opening of a space camp for Japanese children.

England, Anthony Wayne
1942–

Geophysicist Tony England was a mission specialist aboard Spacelab 2, Shuttle Mission 51-F in July 1985. For seven days England and six other astronauts aboard the orbiter Challenger conducted experiments in solar physics, astronomy, and studies of the Earth. The flight was only partly successful because an engine failure during launch initially placed Challenger in a lower orbit than planned. And the Instrument Pointing System (IPS), a sophisticated aiming device for astronomical sensors, didn't become fully operational until the last days of the mission.

England was born May 15, 1942, in Indianapolis, Indiana, and grew up in West Fargo, North Dakota. After graduation from high school he attended the Massachusetts Institute of Technology, where he earned B.S. and M.S. degrees in geology in 1965, and a Ph.D. in geophysics in 1970.

From 1965 to 1967 England was a graduate fellow at M.I.T., peforming geophysical studies of the Earth's magnetic field and the structure of glaciers in the western United States.

He was one of 11 scientist-astronauts selected by NASA in August 1967. At 25, England was and remains the youngest person ever selected for astronaut training by NASA. He completed six months of training and familiarization with the Apollo spacecraft, then reported to Laughlin AFB, Texas, for 53 weeks of training, which qualified him as a jet pilot. (As a pilot, he eventually logged over 2,700 hours of flying time.) From 1969 to 1972 he was involved in preparations for Apollo manned lunar landings, and served as a support crewman for Apollo 13 and Apollo 16.

Because NASA budget cuts eliminated future Apollo manned lunar landings, England left the astronaut group in August 1972 to join the U.S. Geological Survey. In the next seven years England led two expeditions to Antarctica, studied glaciers in Alaska (where he served as a bush pilot), was associate editor for *The Journal of Geophysical Research*, and served on several national committees concerned with Antarctic policy, nuclear waste containment, and Earth sciences.

In June 1979 England returned to the Johnson Space Center as a senior scientist-astronaut (mission specialist) and helped develop computer software for the Space Shuttle. In February 1983, more than 15 years after his original selection as an astronaut, England was assigned to Spacelab 2.

The Challenger disaster in January 1986 forced a two-year delay in Shuttle launches. When flights resumed, England was not assigned to a new crew and he elected to resign from NASA. Since October 1988 he has been professor of electrical engineering and head of remote sensing research for the Electrical Engineering and Computer Sciences Department, University of Michigan at Ann Arbor.

Engle, Joe Henry
1932–

Joe Engle, one of the most experienced aviators ever to become an astronaut, commanded Space Shuttle missions in 1981 and 1985. Prior to that he had earned an official astronaut rating from the Air Force for a flight in the X-15 rocket plane, and had also flown approach and landing tests with the orbiter Enterprise.

STS-2 in November 1981 was the first reflight of the orbiter Columbia. Despite the fact that the flight was shortened from five days to two by a fuel cell problem, STS-2 successfully demonstrated that a Shuttle could be reflown and that the Canadian-built Remote Manipulator System (RMS) arm would function.

In August and September 1985 Engle was commander of Shuttle Mission 51-I, during which his crew of 5 astronauts deployed two communications satellites and repaired a third in orbit.

Engle was born in Abilene, Kansas, on August 26, 1932, and grew up on a farm in Dickinson County. He attended the University of Kansas, earning a B.S. in aeronautical engineering in 1955.

An Air Force ROTC student, Engle went on active duty after graduation from college and completed pilot training in 1957. He served with the 474th Fighter Day Squadron and the 309th Tactical Fighter Squadron at George AFB, California, then was assigned to bases in Spain, Italy and Denmark. In 1961 he attended the Air Force Experimental Flight Test Pilot School at Edwards AFB, California, and the following year graduated from the Aerospace Research Pilot School.

In June 1963 Engle was chosen to be an X-15 pilot, and in the next three years made 16 flights in the rocket-powered research craft. Three of those flights in 1965 reached altitudes greater than 50 miles, qualifying Engle for Air Force Astronaut wings.

Engle was one of the 19 astronauts selected by NASA in April 1966. In 1968 he was one of 3 astronauts who tested the redesigned Apollo command module in a vacuum chamber. He served as support crewman for Apollo 10 and was backup lunar module pilot for Apollo 14.

By early 1971 he had informally been assigned as prime lunar module pilot for Apollo 17 when NASA budget cuts made it clear that Apollo 17 would be the last manned lunar landing. Scientist-astronaut Harrison Schmitt, a trained geologist who was informally assigned to Apollo 18, was named to Apollo 17 in Engle's place and became one of the last pair of American astronauts to walk on the Moon. In 1972 Engle was offered the chance to join the crew of the Apollo-Soyuz Test Project, but declined in order to devote his time to Space Shuttle development.

Having worked with the Shuttle from the beginning and given his experience as an X-15 pilot, Engle was a natural choice to pilot the Enterprise on a series of approach and landing tests at Edwards AFB in 1977. Engle and pilot Richard Truly flew one of 3 "captive" flights (with the Enterprise attached to a specially-modified Boeing 747) and two of the five "free" flights, during which the Shuttle was released from the 747 at an altitude of 25,000 feet, gliding to a landing two minutes later.

From March 1978 to April 1981 Engle and Truly served as backups for STS-1, the first manned Shuttle orbital test flight.

Following STS-2, from March to December 1982, Engle served as deputy associate administrator for manned spaceflight at NASA headquarters in Washington, D.C. He returned to the Johnson Space Center in January 1983 and was assigned to his second Shuttle command later that year.

Described as a "natural stick-and-rudder" pilot, Engle has logged over 11,600 hours of flying time, over 8,000 in jets, in 140 different types of aircraft.

Engle retired from the Air Force and resigned from NASA on November 30, 1986. He was appointed by the governor of Kansas and the Secretary of the Air Force as an adviser to the Kansas Air National Guard, where he holds the rank of major general. He was also a consultant to Rockwell International on the National Aerospace Plane and through his company, Engle Technologies, provides technical support to the Stafford Task Force reviewing Shuttle-Mir operations and International Space Station training.

Evans, Ronald Ellwin
1933–1990

Navy aviator Ron Evans was command module pilot on the last manned flight to the Moon, Apollo 17, in December 1972. Evans orbited the Moon for three days while astronauts Eugene Cernan and Jack Schmitt explored the Taurus-Littrow area. On the return to Earth, Evans performed an EVA lasting 1 hour and 6 minutes.

Evans was born November 10, 1933, in St. Francis, Kansas. He received a B.S. in electrical engineering from the University of Kansas in 1956, and earned an M.S. in aeronautical engineering from the Naval Postgraduate School in 1964.

Evans entered the Navy through ROTC and completed flight training in 1957. In the next four years he served as a carrier pilot on two Pacific cruises. From January 1961 to June 1962 he was an F8 flight instructor. Beginning in 1964 he was assigned to Fighter Squadron 51 aboard the carrier *U.S.S. Ticonderoga*, and flew over 100 combat missions over Vietnam. (The *Ticonderoga* was the vessel that later recovered the Apollo 17 crew and spacecraft.)

He was one of the 19 astronauts selected in April 1966 and served as a member of the support crew for the first manned Apollo mission, Apollo 7, and for Apollo 11 as well. He was backup command module pilot for Apollo 14 and for the Apollo-Soyuz Test Project. He resigned from the Navy with the rank of captain in April 1976, and from NASA in March 1977.

After leaving NASA Evans was employed by the Western American Energy Corporation in Scottsdale, Arizona, until 1978. He joined Sperry Flight Systems in Phoenix at that time and eventually became director of space systems marketing. He later formed his own consulting firm.

Evans died of heart attack on April 6, 1990, at his home in Scottsdale.

Fabian, John McCreary
1939–

John Fabian was mission specialist aboard two Shuttle flights, STS-7 in June 1983 and Mission 51-G in June 1985. On both flights Fabian took part in the launching of communications satellites owned by countries such as Canada, Mexico, Indonesia, and those of the Arab League, and in the deployment and retrieval of the scientific satellites SPAS-01 and Spartan.

Fabian was born January 28, 1939, in Goosecreek, Texas, and grew up in Pullman, Washington, where he graduated from high school in 1957. He attended Washington State University, receiving a B.S. in mechanical engineering in 1962. He later earned an M.S. in aerospace engineering from the Air Force Institute of Technology in 1964, and a Ph.D. in aeronautics and astronautics from the University of Washington in 1974.

Fabian joined the Air Force through ROTC in 1962 and after completing basic training and further schooling was assigned as an engineer at Kelly Air Force Base, Texas. He attended flight training at Williams Air Force Base, Arizona, and spent five years as a KC-135 pilot based at Wurtsmith AFB, Michigan. During this time he flew 90 combat missions in Vietnam. When selected by NASA in 1978 he was an instructor at the Air Force Academy.

He logged 4,000 hours flying time, 3,400 hours in jets.

Fabian became an astronaut in August 1979 and for several years assisted in the development of satellite deployment and retrieval systems, and in the Canadian-built Remote Manipulator System (RMS). In April 1982 he was assigned to the STS-7 crew. In addition to his two flights, he trained for many months as a crewman for the Spacelab 4 mission (61-D), which was canceled in June 1985, and was assigned to Mission 61-G when he resigned from the space program in September 1985.

In January 1986 Colonel Fabian became director of space programs at Headquarters USAF in the Pentagon. In this job he was responsible for the operations of Department of Defense communications, early warning, weather, and navigational satellite systems. He also assisted in the investigation of the Challenger accident.

He resigned from the Air Force in 1987 to join the ANSER, a nonprofit aerospace research corporation headquartered in Crystal City, Virginia. He is currently ANSER's president.

In 1989 and 1990 he also served as president of the Association of Space Explorers, and served as guide for U.S. astronauts on their 1990 visit to Russia's Baikonur Cosmodrome.

Ferguson, Christopher John
1961–

Navy test pilot Christopher Ferguson is one of the 25 astronaut candidates selected by NASA in June 1998. In August of that year he reported to the Johnson Space Center to begin a training and evaluation course that should qualify him as a Shuttle pilot.

Ferguson was born September 1, 1961, in Philadelphia, Pennsylvania, where he graduated from Archbishop Ryan School for Boys in 1979. He attended Drexel University, receiving a B.S. in mechanical engineering in 1984, and earned an M.S. in aeronautical engineering from the Naval Postgraduate School in 1991.

At the time of his selection by NASA, Lieutenant Commander Ferguson was an F-14 class desk officer for the commander of naval air forces, Norfolk, Virginia.

Fettman, Martin Joseph
1956–

Veterinarian Martin Fettman was a payload specialist in the crew of STS-58. This October 1993 flight of the orbiter Columbia carried the second Spacelab Life Sciences (SLS-02) payload and a crew of 7 astronauts in addition to 48 experimental rats. The astronauts operated a dozen different major experiments in space medicine while also serving as test subjects: for example, Fettman and SLS-02 mission specialist Shannon Lucid were catheterized to provide measurement of cardiac data during Columbia's ascent. The SLS-02 mission ended after fourteen days.

Fettman was born December 31, 1956, in Brooklyn, New York. He attended Cornell University at the same time as STS-58 alternate payload specialist Jay Buckey, graduating with a doctor of veterinary medicine and M.S. in clinical nutrition in 1980. He later earned a Ph.D. in physiology from Colorado State University, Fort Collins (1982).

Following graduation from Colorado State Fettman joined the university as an assistant professor of veterinary pathology. A year later he received a joint appointment with the department of physiology. Since 1986 he has been an associate professor. He took a yearlong sabbatical leave in 1989 to do research at the Queen Elizabeth Hospital, University of Adelaide, Australia.

Fincke, Edward Michael
1967–

Air Force flight test engineer Mike Fincke is one of the 35 astronaut candidates selected by NASA on May 1, 1996. In August of that year he reported to the Johnson Space Center to begin a training and evaluation course that should qualify him as a Shuttle mission specialist and International Space Station crewmember.

Fincke was born March 14, 1967, in Pittsburgh, Pennsylvania, though he considers Emsworth to be his hometown. He attended Sewickley Academy, graduating in 1985, then attended the Massachusetts Institute of Technology, where he received a B.S. in aeronautics and astronautics in addition to a B.S. in Earth, atmospheric, and planetary sciences. He attended a summer exchange program in astronautics at the Moscow Aviation Institute in 1989, then earned an M.S. in aeronautics and astronautics from Stanford University in 1990.

An ROTC student at M.I.T. and Stanford, Fincke went on active duty with the Air Force in 1990, serving for three years with the Air Force Space and Missile Systems Center at Los Angeles AFB as a space systems and space test engineer. He then attended the Air Force Test Pilot School at Edwards AFB, California, winning the Colonel Ray Jones Award as the top Flight Test Engineer/Navigator in class 93B.

From 1994 to January 1996 Fincke was an F-16 Falcon flight test engineer with the 39th Flight Test Squadron at Eglin AFB, Florida. At the time of his selec-

tion by NASA he was the U.S. flight test liaison to the Japanese/U.S. XF-2 fighter program at the Gifu Test Center, Japan.

Finley, John Lawrence
1935–

Navy test pilot Jack Finley was one of the first 8 pilots selected for the USAF Manned Orbiting Laboratory Program in November 1965. He remained with MOL until April 1968, when he was reassigned to the Navy at his own request.

Finley was born December 22, 1935, in Winchester, Massachusetts. He attended the Naval Academy at Annapolis, graduating with a bachelor of science degree in 1957.

After completing pilot training Finley served for four years aboard the carrier *U.S.S. Ticonderoga* flying F-8 aircraft. In 1964 he entered the Air Force Aerospace Research Pilot School at Edwards AFB, California, and was an instructor there when selected for the MOL program.

After returning to the Navy Finley served in the Department's Bureau of Personnel as commander of attack carrier Air Wing 5 in San Francisco, as commander of the Naval Schools Command, and aboard the *U.S.S. Kawishiwi*. He retired from the Navy as a captain in May 1980.

He worked for several years as an executive with Federal Express in Memphis, Tennessee, and is currently vice-president of Tech/Ops International in San Mateo, California.

Fisher, Anna Lee
1949–

Anna Fisher operated the Shuttle Discovery's remote manipulator arm in assisting astronauts Joseph Allen and Dale Gardner in the retrieval of two errant satellites during Mission 51-A in November 1984. The retrieval of the Palapa B-2 and Westar VI was the first salvage mission in space history. Fisher also took part in the deployment of two new satellites.

Fisher was born Anna Lee Tingle on August 24, 1949, in St. Albans, New York, and grew up in San Pedro, California, where she graduated from high school in 1967. She attended the University of California at Los Angeles, receiving a B.S. in chemistry in 1971 and an M.D. in 1976. In 1987 she received an M.S. in chemistry from UCLA.

After receiving her bachelor's in chemistry, Fisher spent a year study doing research in X-ray crystallography, publishing three papers in the *Journal of Inorganic Chemistry*. She entered UCLA medical school in 1972. She completed her internship at Harbor General Hospital in Torrance, California, in 1977 and was working as an emergency room physician in Los Angeles when selected by NASA.

As a child, Fisher decided she wanted to be an astronaut and became a doctor because she knew that physicians would be needed on future space station missions. In 1977, while going through the astronaut selection process, she married a fellow emergency room physician, William Fisher, who had also applied for the space program. Anna was selected in January 1978; William was not chosen until May 1980.

Fisher completed the training and evaluation course in August 1979, qualifying her as a Shuttle mission specialist. Her technical assignments have included working on the development of the remote manipulator arm, testing emergency EVA procedures (including repair kits for the Shuttle's thermal tiles), verifying Shuttle computer software at the Shuttle Avionics Integration Lab, and integrating payloads. She also served as a standby rescue physician for STS-1 through STS-4, and was a capcom for STS-9/Spacelab-1.

At the time of the Challenger accident in January 1986 Fisher was assigned to the crew of Mission 61-H, then scheduled for launch the following summer. When Shuttle launches and crew assignments resumed, she was temporarily unavailable, due to the birth of her second daughter. She later worked as deputy chief of the mission development branch of the astronaut office, and also in the Freedom space station operations branch prior to taking several years' leave to raise her family. She returned to active training in February 1996 to work in the space station branch of the astronaut office. Since fall 1997 she has been head of the payloads/habitation branch.

Fisher is married to former astronaut William Fisher. They have two daughters, Kristin Anne (whose birth in 1983 meant that Anna Fisher was the first mother in space) and Kara Lynne.

Fisher, William Frederick
1946–

Dr. Bill Fisher made a "house call" on an ailing satellite, the Hughes Syncom IV-3 (Leasat 3), during Shuttle Mission 51-I in August 1985. Leasat 3 had been deployed from the Shuttle in April 1985, but had failed to activate. Fisher, a medical doctor by profession, and astronaut James van Hoften performed two long EVAs during which they retrieved, repaired, and relaunched the satellite, which reached its intended orbit and full operations in October 1985. The astronauts also launched three new communications satellites during their flight.

Fisher was born April 1, 1946, in Dallas, Texas. His father was an Air Force colonel and Fisher moved frequently, graduating from North Syracuse Central High School in North Syracuse, New York, in 1964. He received an A.B. in psychology from Stanford in 1968 and an M.D. from the University of Florida in 1975. He later worked toward an M.S. in engineering from the University of Houston.

After completing medical school Fisher was a surgical resident at Harbor General Hospital in Torrance, California, and later specialized in emergency medicine, practicing at Humana Hospital-Clear Lake in Webster, Texas. He also became a private pilot with over 2,000 hours of flying time.

While at Harbor General Hospital Fisher met another emergency room physician, Anna Tingle, whom he married. Both doctors applied for the 1978 astronaut group but only Anna Fisher was selected. Her husband added an engineering degree to his credentials and was selected by NASA in May 1980, completing his training and evaluation course in August 1991.

Fisher's technical assignments included acting as support crewmember for STS-8, capcom for STS-8 and STS-9, and B-57 scientific equipment operator for high altitude research. He also became a specialist in EVA.

In June 1985 Fisher was assigned to a second Shuttle mission, 61-M, scheduled for launch in the summer of 1986. That mission was canceled because of the Challenger disaster. When flights and crew assignments were resumed, Fisher was passed over for selection for almost four years. His chances for a second flight were not improved by his participation in a widely publicized study critical of NASA's plans for the space station Freedom.

The study, from the External Maintenance Task Team for space station Freedom, concluded in March 1990 that the station was so fragile it would require as many as 3,700 hours of EVA maintenance annually—far more than the 130 annual hours originally envisioned by NASA. Fisher and NASA robotics expert Charles Price were called to testify before congress.

Fisher resigned from NASA effective January 31, 1991, to resume the full-time practice of emergency medicine at Humana Hospital in Clear Lake, Texas.

He is married to Anna Fisher, who remains an active astronaut.

Foale, Colin Michael
1957–

British-born physicist Mike Foale was the fifth NASA-Mir crewmember, arriving at the Russian space station with the crew of STS-84 in May 1997. His 132-day tour aboard the Russian station was marked by a collision between Mir and a Progress supply vehicle and a subsequent series of system failures that came close to destroying the station.

On June 25, 1997, Foale was beginning his second month aboard Mir with Mir-24 crewmembers Vasily Tsibliyev and Alexandr Lazutkin when the crew tried to move Progress M-35 from one Mir docking port to another. This procedure, normally routine, was complicated by the fact that Russian program managers were trying to switch from the Ukraine-built Kurs docking system to a Russian-made one. Tsibliyev, who had very little training on the new system, watched in horror as the Progress failed to respond to commands, and bore down on Mir, ultimately colliding with the Spektr module before sailing off into space. Foale would write later that he floated in one of the modules for a few moments after the collision, waiting in dread to feel his ears pop. It would have signaled a catastrophic loss of pressure in the station.

Fortunately the holes in Spektr were small, and Foale was able to assist Latuzkin in cutting power cables and sealing off the module—which happened to be his living quarters, containing his personal belongings.

By cutting the power cables, the crew also eliminated over half of Mir's power supply, which led to many system failures and shutdowns over the next days and weeks. The station drifted out of control on six different occasions. Nevertheless, conditions aboard Mir eventually stablized, and were improved by repair EVAs, one of them conducted by Foale and Mir-25 commander Anatoly Solovyov in September 1997. Foale returned to Earth in early October aboard STS-86 after four months in space.

He would write later that he was able to keep the troubles aboard Mir in perspective because of a serious traffic accident he had suffered in 1978, in which his brother and his fiancée died. "A personal loss is tougher than anything I went through on Mir."

Foale had made three previous spaceflights, first as a mission specialist in the crew of STS-45, an 8-day flight of the orbiter Atlantis launched in March 1992. The crew of 5 astronauts and two payload specialists conducted studies of the Earth's atmosphere with Spacelab ATLAS. Foale later made a second flight aboard STS-56, the second ATLAS flight, in April 1993.

Foale's third flight — and first visit to the vicinity of Mir — was STS-63. This February 1995 flight of the orbiter Discovery closed to within 30 feet of the Russian station. (It was not intended to dock with Mir.) The crew of STS-63 included Russian cosmonaut Vladimir Titov. Foale and Bernard Harris later conducted an EVA.

Foale was born January 6, 1957, in Louth, England, though he considers Cambridge to be his hometown. He graduated from Kings School at Canterbury in 1975, then attended Queens College, Cambridge, receiving a B.A. in physics with first class honors (1978). He completed his doctorate in laboratory astrophysics at Queens College in 1982.

While working on his doctorate at Cambridge Foale took part in several scientific scuba projects, including two surveys of underwater antiquities with the cooperation of the government of Greece, and one dive on the sunken galleon *Mary Rose* in the fall of 1981.

Foale moved to the United States the next year and joined the McDonnell Douglas Corporation in Houston, Texas, working on Shuttle navigation systems. In June 1983 he joined the staff of the NASA Johnson Space Center as a payload officer, working on the payloads of Shuttle missions 51-G, 51-I, 61-B and 61-C.

He has also worked as a community associate at Rice University, tutoring in freshman physics.

Foale was selected as an astronaut in June 1987 and qualified as a Shuttle mission specialist in August 1988. His technical assignments have included a shift in the Shuttle Avionics Integration Laboratory, and the development of crew rescue techniques for space station Freedom. He has also been deputy chief of the mission development branch of the astronaut office, and head of the science support group. He began training for Shuttle-Mir at the Gagarin Center in early 1996.

From January to July 1998 Foale was assistant for technical matters to George Abbey, the director of the NASA Johnson Space Center.

Foreman, Michael James

1957–

Navy engineer Michael Foreman is one of the 25 astronaut candidates selected by NASA in June 1998. In August of that year he reported to the Johnson Space Center to begin a training and evaluation course that should qualify him as a Shuttle mission specialist and International Space Station crewmember.

Foreman was born March 29, 1957, in Columbus, Ohio. He graduated from high school in Wadsworth, Ohio, in 1975, then attended the Naval Academy at Annapolis, where he received a B.S. in aerospace engineering in 1979. He later earned an M.S. in aeronautical engineering from the Naval Postgraduate School (1986).

At the time of his selection by NASA, Commander Foreman was technical lead for the advanced orbiter cockpit project with the Naval Air Warfare Center aircraft division, Patuxent River, Maryland.

Forrester, Patrick Graham

1957–

Army test pilot Patrick Forrester is one of the 35 astronaut candidates selected by NASA on May 1, 1996. In August of that year he began a training and evaluation course at the Johnson Space Center that should qualify him as a Shuttle mission specialist and International Space Station crewmember.

Forrester was born March 31, 1957, in El Paso, Texas. He graduated from West Springfield High School in Springfield, Virginia, in 1975, then entered the U.S. Military Academy at West Point, where he received a B.S. in applied sciences and engineering (1979). He later earned an M.S. in mechanical and aerospace engineering from the University of Virginia (1989).

Following graduation from West Point in June 1979 Forrester was commissioned in the Army. He qualified as an Army aviator in September 1980, then served as an instructor helicopter pilot at the Army Aviation School and aide-de-camp to its deputy commander. In 1984 he transferred to Schofield Barracks, Hawaii, as platoon leader, aviation company operations office, and assault helicopter battalion officer with the 25th Infantry Division (Light).

In 1990, following a year in graduate school, Forrester was assigned as a flight test engineer with the Army Aviation Engineering Flight Activity at Edwards AFB, California. He entered the Naval Test Pilot School at Patuxent River, Maryland, in 1991, and following graduation the following year was stationed at the Army Aviation Technical Test Center, Fort Rucker, Alabama, as an engineering test pilot.

Lieutenant Colonel Forrester has logged over 3,000 hours of flying time in 49 different aircraft.

At the time of his selection as an ASCAN, Forrester had been aerospace engineer at the NASA Johnson Space Center for three years, working on technical assignments within the astronaut office's operations development branch. He also served as the crew representative for robotics development in the International Space Station office.

Fossum, Michael Edward

1957–

NASA test engineer Michael Fossum is one of the 25 astronaut candidates selected by NASA in June 1998. In August of that year he began a training and evaluation course that should qualify him as a Shuttle mission specialist and International Space Station crewmember.

Fossum was born December 19, 1957, in Sioux Falls, South Dakota, and graduated from high school in McAllen, Texas, in 1976. He attended Texas A&M University, receiving a B.S. in mechanical engineering (1980). He later earned and M.S. in systems engineering from the Air Force Institute of Technology (1981) and an M.S. in physical science from the University of Houston, Clear Lake (1997).

After serving with the U.S. Air Force for twelve years as a flight test engineer, Fossum joined NASA, and at the time of his seleciton as an ASCAN (on his fifth application) was working on the X-38 program.

Freeman, Theodore Cordy

1930–1964

Air Force test pilot Ted Freeman was the first American astronaut to die in a training accident. He was killed in the crash of a T-38 jet while attempting to land at Ellington Air Force Base, near the NASA Manned Spacecraft Center in Houston, on October 31, 1964. Freeman's jet suffered a loss of power when a goose was sucked into its engine. Freeman ejected too low for his parachute to open.

Had he lived he would have been one of the astronauts assigned to the Gemini program.

Freeman was born February 18, 1930, in Haverford, Pennsylvania, and graduated from high school in Lewes, Delaware, in 1948. He attended the University of Delaware for one year, then earned an appointment to the Naval Academy at Annapolis, graduating in 1953 with a bachelor of science. In 1960 he earned an M.S. in aeronautical engineering from the University of Michigan

After pilot training in Texas and Nevada, Freeman served as an Air Force pilot in the Pacific and at George AFB, California. In 1960 he was assigned to Edwards Air Force Base, California, as an aerospace engineer. He later attended the Aerospace Research Pilot School at Edwards, where his classmates were future fellow astronauts David Scott and James Irwin. He was an instructor at ARPS when he was chosen by NASA.

He was one of the 14 astronauts selected by NASA in October 1963 and was on the verge of completing a year of basic training and evaluation at the time of his death. Fellow astronaut Walter Cunningham wrote later that "Freeman was one of the better pilots I have known" and would have rated "near the top" of the 1963 astronaut group.

Frick, Stephen Nathaniel

1964–

Navy test pilot Stephen Frick is one of the 35 astronaut candidates selected by NASA on May 1, 1996. In August of that year he reported to the Johnson Space Center to begin a yearlong training and evaluation course that should qualify him as a Shuttle pilot.

Frick was born September 30, 1964, in Pittsburgh, Pennsylvania. He graduated from Richland High School in Gibsonia, Pennsylvania, in 1982, then entered the Naval Academy at Annapolis, where he received a B.S. in aerospace engineering in 1986. He later earned an M.S. in aeronautical engineering from the Naval Postgraduate School (1994).

Commissioned in the Navy in May 1986, Frick underwent pilot training and was designated a naval aviator in February 1988. After further training as an F/A-18 pilot at Cecil Field, Florida, he joined Strike Fighter Squadron 83, which deployed to the Mediterranean and Red seas aboard the carrier USS Saratoga. During this 8-month deployment Frick took part in Operation Desert Shield and Desert Storm, flying 26 combat missions.

Beginning in December 1991 Frick took part in a cooperative program of academic study at the Naval Postgraduate School followed by a year at the Naval Test Pilot School, Patuxent River, Maryland. In June 1994 Frick joined the Strike Aircraft Test Squadron at Pax Rivert as an F/A-18 project officer and test pilot in the carrier suitability department.

At the time of his selection as an ASCAN, Frick had just transferred from Pax River to Strike Fighter Squadron 125 at Lemoore, California.

Lieutenant Commander Frick has logged over 1,800 hours of flying time in 27 different aircraft, including 370 carrier landings.

Fullerton, Charles Gordon
1936–

Air Force test pilot Charles Gordon Fullerton not only made two flights aboard the Space Shuttle, but after leaving the manned space program was pilot of an airplane that actually launched a satellite into orbit.

Shortly after noon on April 5, 1990, Fullerton was command pilot of a specially modified NASA B-52 that released a Pegasus booster at an altitude of 43,000 feet. Pegasus, which carried a small Navy communications satellite and a NASA science payload, dropped 1,200 feet, then fired its motor. Nine minutes and three stages later, the satellites were in a 315 nautical mile orbit.

Fullerton went on to pilot five more Pegasus launches.

As an astronaut Fullerton served as pilot of STS-3 in March 1982, an 8-day orbital flight test of the orbiter Columbia, during which he and commander Jack Lousma operated the remote manipulator arm and the OSS-1 scientific pallet. STS-3 was extended one day because of weather problems at Edwards Air Force Base, California, its primary landing site, and is the only Shuttle mission to land at Northrup Strip at White Sands, New Mexico.

In July 1985 Fullerton was commander of Mission 51-F, the flight of Spacelab 2. The seven-man crew overcome one launchpad abort, a second abort-to-orbit (one of the Shuttle Challenger's main engines shut down during launch), and numerous equipment problems during an 8-day scientific mission.

Fullerton was born October 11, 1936, in Rochester, New York, and grew up in Oregon, graduating from U.S. Grant High School in Portland. He attended the California Institute of Technology, receiving a B.S. (1957) and M.S. (1958) in mechanical engineering.

While working on his master's degree at Cal Tech, Fullerton was employed by Hughes Aircraft in Culver City, California, as a mechanical design engineer. Upon completion of the degree in July 1958 he joined the Air Force, undergoing pilot training in Georgia, Texas, and Kansas. From 1961 to 1964 he was a B-47 jet bomber pilot with the Strategic Air Command's 303rd Bomb Wing based at Davis-Monthan AFB, Arizona.

Fullerton attended the Aerospace Research Pilot School at Edwards AFB, California, in 1965, then reported to Wright-Patterson AFB, Ohio, as a bomber test pilot. He was at Wright-Pat in June 1966 when he was selected for the Air Force's Manned Orbiting Laboratory program. Three years later, following the cancellation of MOL, he transferred to NASA as an astronaut.

As a pilot Fullerton has logged over 14,000 hours of flying time in 115 different types of aircraft, including gliders.

With NASA Fullerton served on the astronaut support crew for Apollo 14 and Apollo 17, and as capcom for Apollos 14 through 17. He was one of the first astronauts assigned to the Shuttle program, and in 1976 was named to one of the 2 two-man crews for the Shuttle Approach and Landing Tests (ALT). The following year Fullerton and commander Fred Haise flew two captive and three free flights of the Shuttle Enterprise, including the first. In March 1978 he joined the group of astronauts training for the Shuttle's orbital flight tests.

Following his second spaceflight Fullerton wrote a NASA report that criticized some of the agency's plans for the Freedom space station. Fullerton left the astronaut office in October 1986 to become an aerospace test pilot at the NASA Ames-Dryden Research Facility at Edwards AFB, California. He was project pilot for the B-52 launch aircraft, for the Landing Systems Research Aircraft (a specially-modified NASA Convair 990) and the F-18 Systems Research Aircraft. More recently he has served as project pilot for the Propulsion Controlled Aircraft program.

He retired from the Air Force with the rank of colonel after thirty years' service in July 1988.

Gaffney, Francis Andrew

1946–

Cardiologist Drew Gaffney was a payload specialist aboard STS-40, the first life sciences Spacelab, flown in June 1991. The crew of 7 included three medical doctors and a biochemist who performed a series of twenty experiments into how humans adapt to space.

Gaffney served as a human subject: prior to launch a catheter was inserted through a vein his right arm to a position near his heart. The catheter was designed to measure blood pressure in the large vessels near the heart, which indicate how quickly fluid shifts in the body. These fluid shifts were believed to show how the body reacts to microgravity.

The results showed that the first fluid shifts occurred while Gaffney was still on the launchpad, and that his blood pressure was back to normal almost immediately upon reaching orbit.

The catheter was removed four hours into the mission, but the medical crewmen continued to use themselves as experimental subjects throughout the 10-day mission, and after: they also remained at the Edwards AFB landing site for a week following landing to continue their tests.

Gaffney was born June 9, 1946, in Carlsbad, New Mexico, where he graduated from high school in 1964. While a high school student he worked as an orderly and operating room technician at St. Francis Hospital. He attended the University of California at Berkeley, receiving a B.A. in 1968. He received his M.D. from the University of New Mexico in 1972 and did a fellowship in cardiology at the University of Texas in 1975.

Gaffney interned at Cleveland Metropolitan General Hospital in Cleveland, Ohio, from 1972 to 1975, then began his association with the University of Texas Southwestern Medical School in Dallas, where he became associate professor of medicine. He has also been director of echocardiography at Parkland Memorial Hospital in Dallas (1979 to 1987).

Gaffney is the author of 50 medical papers. He is also a pilot with ratings for single and multiengine planes and at one time flew with an air charter service in Dallas.

As a coinvestigator on one of the Spacelab Life Sciences experiments, Gaffney was selected as one of the 4 original SLS payload specialists in January 1984. A year later he and Dr. Robert Phillips were named prime payload specialists for what was then known as Shuttle Mission 61-D/Spacelab-4, scheduled for launch in January 1986. When that mission was later canceled, Gaffney continued to train for a second Spacelab Life Sciences flight. That mission was delayed for several years by the Shuttle Challenger disaster.

In the hiatus following Challenger Gaffney graduated from the Air Force School of Aerospace Medicine. He has also been a lieutenant colonel in the Texas Air National Guard serving as flight surgeon for the 147th Fighter Interceptor Group. (In early 1991 Gaffney was called to active duty for Operation Desert Storm. The early end to hostilities made it possible for him to be assigned to temporary duty at the NASA Johnson Space Center in order to continue training for STS-40.)

Gaffney was visiting senior scientist with the life sciences division at NASA Headquarters in Washington, D.C., from January 1987 through June 1989, working on the Spacelab D-2 project, Space Station Freedom, and a group studying the flight of humans to Mars.

He is currently chief of clinic cardiology at the School of Medicine at Vanderbilt University, Nashville, Tennessee.

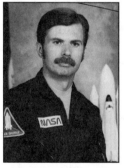

Gardner, Dale Allan

1948–

Dale Gardner was a mission specialist aboard two Shuttle flights. On STS-8 in 1983 he took part in the first nighttime launch and landing in the Shuttle program, and assisted in the deployment of and Indian communications satellite.

During Mission 51-A in November 1984 Gardner and Joseph Allen performed space walks using the manned maneuvering unit (MMU) backpack to retrieve two errant satellites for return to Earth. It was the first salvage operation in space history.

Gardner was born November 8, 1948, in Fairmont, Minnesota, and grew up in Sherburn, Minnesota, and

Savanna, Illinois. He graduated from high school in Savanna in 1966, then attended the University of Illinois, receiving a B.S. in engineering physics in 1970.

In July 1970, just after graduation from Illinois, Gardner joined the Navy and underwent flight officer training in Florida and Georgia. He was immediately assigned to the Naval Air Test Center at Patuxent River, Maryland, to work on navigation systems for the F-14A. Beginning in July 1973 he served as an F-14A flight officer aboard the carrier *U.S.S. Enterprise* during two tours in the Pacific. From December 1976 until his selection by NASA he was with the Air Test and Evaluation Squadron at Pt. Mugu, California.

Gardner was one of the 35 astronauts selected by NASA in January 1978. In August 1979 he qualified as a mission specialist on Shuttle crews. He served as support crewman for STS-4, and in April 1982 was assigned to the crew of STS-8.

In November 1984 he was named to the crew of Mission 62-A, the first Shuttle launch from Vandenberg Air Force Base, originally scheduled for July 1986 and postponed because of the explosion of the Shuttle Challenger in January 1986.

Gardner resigned from NASA in October 1986 to return to the Navy. He was assigned to U.S. Space Command in Colorado Springs, Colorado, as deputy director for space control. In 1989 he was selected for promotion to captain, but in October 1990 he retired from the Navy to join TRW Inc. as a senior systems engineer.

Gardner, Guy Spence, Jr.
1948–

Air Force test pilot Guy Gardner was pilot on the STS-35 mission in December 1990. This 9-day flight of the orbiter Columbia carried a crew of 7, including four scientists, and the Spacelab ASTRO-01 observatory.

Two years earlier, in December 1988 Gardner served as pilot of STS-27, a 4-day flight of the orbiter Atlantis during which an imaging radar satellite called Lacrosse was deployed in low Earth orbit.

Gardner was born January 6, 1948, in Alta Vista, Virginia, and grew up in Alexandria, where he graduated from George Washington High School in 1965. He attended the Air Force Academy, receiving a B.S. in engineering sciences, astronautics and mathematics in 1969, and Purdue University, receiving an M.S. in astronautics in 1970.

Gardner underwent pilot training at Craig AFB, Alabama, and MacDill AFB, Florida, before being sent to Thailand, where he flew F-4s on 177 combat missions. Returning to the United States, he attended the Air Force Test Pilot School at Edwards AFB, California, graduating in 1975, then served with the 6512th Test Squadron at Edwards. He was also an instructor at the test pilot school. When selected by NASA in 1980 he was operations officer with the 1st Test Squadron at Clark AFB, the Philippines.

As a pilot he logged over 4,000 hours of flying time.

Gardner was one of the 19 astronauts selected by NASA in May 1980. In August 1981 he qualified as a Shuttle pilot. He also flew the lead chase plane for STS-4 in 1982, and between June 1983 and April 1984 served as a Shuttle capcom.

In October 1984 he was named as pilot of Mission 62-A, the first planned launch from Vandenberg Air Force Base, California. Following the Challenger disaster 62-A was canceled and in September 1987 Gardner was reassigned to STS-27.

In June 1991 Colonel Gardner left NASA to return to the US Air Force as commandant of the Test Pilot School at Edwards AFB, California. He retired from the Air Force in August 1992 to become director for the U.S.-Russian Shuttle-Mir program at NASA HQ in Washington. He later graduated from the Defense Systems Management College (1994), then became director of the quality assurance division in the office of safety and mission assurance at NASA HQ.

Gardner left NASA in September 1995 to join the Federal Aviation Administration as director of the William J. Hughes Technical Center at the Atlantic City Airport, New Jersey. In October 1996 he was named F.A.A associate administrator for regulation and certification, succeeding Anthony J. Broderick, who lost the position because of the ValuJet accident.

Garn, Edwin Jacob "Jake"
1932–

Utah senator Jake Garn, the Republican chairman of the U.S. Senate Appropriations subcommittee that oversaw NASA's budget, became the first lawmaker in space when he was a payload specialist in the crew of Shuttle Mission 51-D in April 1985.

Garn was invited to fly by NASA Administrator James Beggs in November 1984, who wrote, "Given your NASA oversight responsibilities, we think it appropriate that you consider making an inspection tour and flight aboard the Shuttle." Critics charged that NASA was trying to curry favor with with a powerful senator, who had opposed NASA's commercial launch pricing policies as well as plans for a space station. NASA responded that the offer was in keeping with the common practice of inviting elected officials to fly on military aircraft.

NASA later flew Democratic congressman Bill Nelson, Garn's counterpart in the House, on a 1986 Shuttle mission.

During his seven days aboard Discovery, Garn served as a test subject for space sickness experiments, becoming famous in the comic strip Doonesbury as "Barfin' Jake Garn." He also observed an unscheduled rescue attempt of the failed Leasat 3 satellite, including an EVA by astronauts Dave Griggs and Jeff Hoffman.

Garn was born October 12, 1932, in Richfield, Utah. He attended the University of Utah, receiving a B.S. in business and finance, and worked as an insurance executive for many years.

He was a pilot in the Navy from 1956 to 1960 and also served in the Utah Air National Guard, retiring with the rank of colonel in 1969. At the time of his selection to fly aboard the Shuttle he had more flying time than any active astronaut except Joe Engle—over 10,000 hours in military and civilian aircraft.

As a businessman in Salt Lake City, Garn served on the city council for four years, then in 1971 he was elected mayor. In November 1974 he was elected to the United States Senate, and was reelected in 1980 with 70 percent of the vote. In addition to duties on the Senate Appropriations Committee, Garn was chairman of the Committee on Banking, Housing and Urban Affairs and a member of three other subcommittees.

In November 1986, following his flight, Garn was reelected to the Senate for a third term. He also coauthored a novel, *Night Launch* (1992). He retired from the Senate in 1992 and is currently vice-chairman of the Huntsman Chemical Corporation in Salt Lake City.

Garriott, Owen Kay
1930–

Physicist Owen Garriott has done scientific research in space aboard Skylab and Spacelab.

Garriott was science pilot of Skylab 3, the second manned Skylab mission, launched July 28, 1973. Garriott, Alan Bean, and Jack Lousma occupied the orbiting laboratory for almost sixty days, returning to Earth on September 25. It was the longest manned flight to that time, and the most scientifically productive, as the astronauts were able to devote over 300 manhours to observations of the sun and completed 333 medical experiments. They also continued to repair Skylab itself, which had been damaged during its launch in May 1973. NASA officials judged that the Skylab 3 crew accomplished 150 percent of its goals.

On his second spaceflight, Garriott served as mission specialist of STS-9/Spacelab 1, launched November 28, 1983. The crew of 6 included four scientists who worked 12-hour shifts in Spacelab operating over 70 different experiments in a variety of fields, from life sciences to materials processing to Earth observations. Garriott also managed to find time, during his off-hours, to talk with amateur radio hams around the world (including Jordan's King Hussein) as operator of "station" W5LFL.

Garriott was born November 22, 1930, in Enid, Oklahoma, where he grew up. He attended the University of Oklahoma, graduating in 1953 with a B.S. in electrical engineering. Following a tour of duty with the Navy, he attended Stanford University, receiving an M.S. (1957) and a Ph.D. (1960) in electrical engineering.

He served as an electronics officer in the Navy from 1953 to 1956, aboard the destroyers *U.S.S. Cowell* and *U.S.S. Allen M. Sumner*. When he completed work on his doctorate he became an associate professor in the department of electrical engineering at Stanford and taught there until his selection by NASA.

Garriott was one of 6 scientist-astronauts selected by NASA in June 1965. Although he was already a licensed pilot, he underwent a 53-week jet pilot course at Williams Air Force Base, Arizona, and ultimately logged over 5,000 hours of flying time, 2,900 of it in jets and the rest in light aircraft and helicopters.

His first assignment as an astronaut was working on the design and development of the Apollo Applications Program (AAP), later known as Skylab. In 1968 he served, briefly, as the chief astronaut representative to AAP. He was also a capcom for Apollo 11, the first lunar landing. He was officially named as a Skylab crewmember in January 1972.

Between the conclusion of the Skylab program in 1974 and the first Shuttle assignments in 1978, Garriott served as deputy director, later acting director, for science and applications at the Johnson Space Center. He took a year's sabbatical leave in 1976 to teach at Stanford, and remained a consulting professor with the school for many years.

Garriott and Robert Parker were named mission specialists for Spacelab 1 in August 1978, more than two years before its scheduled launch, and five years before the actual flight. Their training program took them all over the world, especially to Europe, where Spacelab was being built.

After STS-9 Garrriott served as program scientist in the Space Station Freedom Office at the Johnson Space Center, and trained for two Spacelab Earth Observation Missions that were intended to refly experiments from that first flight. Both EOM-1 (originally scheduled for May 1985) and EOM-2 (September 1986) were canceled before launch because of scheduling problems, and, ultimately, the Challenger accident. In June 1986 Garriott resigned from NASA, becoming vice-president of space programs for Teledyne Brown Engineering in Huntsville, Alabama. In 1995 he resigned to become cofounder and president of Immunotherapeutics, based in Huntsville.

Garriott is the author or coauthor of more than 40 scientific papers and a textbook, *Introduction to Ionospheric Physics* (1969).

Gemar, Charles Donald "Sam"

1955–

Army pilot Sam Gemar was a mission specialist in three Shuttle crews between 1990 and 1994. The first was STS-38, a 5-day flight of the orbiter Atlantis in November 1990 during which an advanced data relay satellite was deployed in Earth orbit. STS-38 was the last secret Department of Defense Shuttle mission.

In September 1991 Gemar made a second flight, as mission specialist in the crew of STS-48, which deployed the Upper Atmosphere Research Satellite. His third mission was STS-62, a two-week flight of the orbiter Columbia that carried the U.S. Microgravity Payload.

Gemar got unwanted publicity a week prior to the STS-62 launch when a Houston newspaper reported that he and his wife, Charlotte, were the object of a lawsuit alleging stalking. The suit was filed by a woman who claimed Gemar had fathered her child in an extramarital relationship. The report effectively ended Gemar's astronaut career after STS-62.

Gemar was born August 4, 1955, in Yankton, South Dakota, and graduated from high school in Scotland, South Dakota, in 1973. He earned a B.S. in engineering from the U.S. Military Academy at West Point in 1979.

He enlisted in the Army and was training in the 18th Airborne Corps when he earned an appointment to West Point. After graduation from the academy he became a helicopter and transport pilot. From 1980 to 1985 he was stationed at Hunter Army Airfield, Ft. Stewart, Georgia, where in addition to being a flight operations officer and flight platoon leader he also completed the Army Parachutist Course and Ranger School.

Gemar was one of the 13 astronauts selected by NASA in June 1985. In July 1986 he qualified as a Shuttle mission specialist while working in the Shuttle Avionics Integration Laboratory. He later served with the astronaut support team at the Kennedy Space Center. He was named to the STS-38 crew in May 1989.

Lieutenant Colonel Gemar left the astronaut office in early 1996 to join the Space Master Plan Task Group in the office of the undersecretary of defense for space, the

Pentagon. He has since returned to Houston and works in the Army Space Element Office there.

Gernhardt, Michael Landen
1956–

Deep-sea diver Mike Gernhardt was a mission specialist in the crew of STS-69. This July 1995 Shuttle mission deployed the Wake Shield Facility, and included an EVA by Gernhardt and Jim Voss.

In 1997 Gernhardt made two flights with the Materials Science Laboratory, STS-83—which had to be cut to four days of a planned sixteen day duration because of fuel cell problems aboard the orbiter Columbia—and a reflight of the same mission, with the same crew, as STS-94.

Gernhardt is assigned as an EVA crewmember for International Space Station assembly mission 6A, scheduled for launch in spring 2000.

Gernhardt was born May 4, 1956, in Mansfield, Ohio, where he graduated from Malabar High School. He attended Vanderbilt University, where he received a B.S. in physics in 1978. He went on to the University of Pennsylvania, where he received an M.S. in 1983 and a Ph.D. in 1991 in bioengineering.

Since 1976 Gernhardt has worked as a commercial deep-sea diver and project engineer for undersea oil field project, logging over 700 dives. He has also worked on the development of a new model for decompression.

In 1984 Gernhardt became manager, then later vice-president of special projects, for Oceaneering International, developing new undersea telerobotic systems and diver tools. At the time of his selection as an astronaut candidate, Gernhardt was head of Oceaneering's Space Systems Division, working on EVA tools and equipment for future use on NASA space stations.

Gernhardt was one of the 19 astronaut candidates selected by NASA in March 1992. In July 1993 he qualified as a Shuttle mission specialist and space station crewmember. His first technical assignment was mission support in the Shuttle Avionics Integration Lab (SAIL). He was assigned to STS-69 in July 1994.

Gibson, Edward George
1936–

Physicist Ed Gibson was the science pilot of Skylab 4, the longest American manned spaceflight, spending 84 days aboard the Skylab space station. During Skylab 4 Gibson and fellow astronauts Gerald Carr and William Pogue conducted extensive observations of the sun and of Comet Kahoutek. Gibson also took part in three space walks lasting a total of almost 16 hours.

Gibson was born November 8, 1936, in Buffalo, New York, and graduated from Kenmore High School. He attended the University of Rochester, New York, earning a B.S. in 1959, and the California Institute of Technology, where he received an M.S. in engineering in 1960. He earned his Ph.D. in engineering from Cal Tech in 1964.

While working on his doctorate at Cal Tech Gibson was a research assistant in jet propulsion and atmospheric physics, publishing technical papers on lasers. He then joined the Philco Corporation's Applied Research Laboratory in Newport Beach, California, and was there when selected by NASA.

Gibson was one of the first 6 scientist-astronauts chosen by NASA in June 1965. He underwent jet pilot training at Williams Air Force Base, Arizona, until July 1966, then became involved in the Apollo program, working on plans for the Orbital Workshop (later known as Skylab) and learning to fly helicopters for a possible lunar landing. (In 1969 a helicopter piloted by Gibson crashed, but he walked away unscathed.) He served as capcom and support crewmember for the Apollo 12 lunar landing in November 1969, then, following budget cuts that eliminated any chance of a flight to the Moon, he worked exclusively on Skylab.

As a pilot Gibson eventually logged over 4,300 hours of flying time, including 2,300 hours in jets.

Gibson resigned from NASA in November 1974 to join the Los Angeles-based Aerospace Corporation, where he did research in solar physics. From March 1976 to March 1977 he served as a consultant to ERNO Raumfahrttechnik GmbH, West Germany, a company working on the European Spacelab, then returned to NASA as an astronaut, becoming chief of the selection and training of new mission specialist astronauts.

In October 1980, Gibson, who had been assigned as launch capcom for STS-1, resigned from NASA a second time, joining TRW, Inc., in Redondo Beach, California, where he worked as advanced systems manager for the energy development group. He later joined Booz, Allen and Hamilton, a Bethesda, Maryland-based aerospace consulting and management firm. Gibson is currently president of his own aerospace consulting firm based in Carlsbad, California. Among his projects is a proposed series of commercial weightless aircraft flights.

He is the author of a textbook on solar physics, *The Quiet Sun* (1973), and of a pair of science fiction novels, *Reach* (1989) and *In the Wrong Hands* (1992).

Gibson, Robert Lee

1946–

Navy test pilot Robert "Hoot" Gibson commanded the first Shuttle mission to dock with the orbiting Mir space station. This June 1995 flight of the orbiter Atlantis launched with a crew of 7, including Mir-18 crew of Anatoly Solovyov and Nikolai Budarin. They replaced the Mir-17 team of Yuri Dezhurov, Gennady Strekelov, and American astronaut Norman Thagard, who had been aboard Mir since March of 1995. Atlantis returned to Earth with eight astronauts.

The complex docking mission, for which Gibson, pilot, Charles Precourt, and mission specialists Gregory Harbaugh, Ellen Baker, and Bonnie Dunbar had trained for over a year, was the first international docking mission since the Apollo-Soyuz Test Project twenty years before. It opened a new phase in international spaceflight in which six American astronauts spent 26 months aboard Mir, with the Shuttle providing needed resupply and cargo return.

Gibson made four other Shuttle flights. His first, as pilot of the orbiter Challenger on STS 41-B in February deployed two different satellites whose rocket motors failed, sending them into useless orbits. (The satellites were later retrieved by another Shuttle crew and returned to Earth.) A balloon intended to serve as a ren-

dezvous target exploded, and the Challenger's remote manipulator arm malfunctioned. Nevertheless, during 41-B two astronauts made the first tests of the manned maneuvering unit backpack, and Gibson and commander Vance Brand made the first Shuttle landing at Kennedy Space Center.

In January 1986 Gibson commanded Shuttle Mission 61-C, which set an unwanted record for delays when its launch was postponed seven times. When the orbiter Columbia finally lifted off, an experiment package deigned to observe Halley's Comet wouldn't work. Nevertheless, the crew of 7, including congressman Bill Nelson, was able successfully to deploy an RCA communications satellite.

Ultimately Mission 61-C ended when the Shuttle Columbia landed at Edwards Air Force Base in California. The switch from Kennedy to Edwards added six days to the turnaround time needed to prepare Columbia for its next mission, scheduled for early March. When the very next Shuttle flight, 51-L, exploded on January 28, some NASA officials, including chief astronaut John Young, questioned whether 61-C should have been flown at all, since one of its primary payloads had been removed prior to launch and the RCA satellite could have easily been postponed.

Gibson's third mission, STS-27, was a dedicated Department of Defense flight that received so much press scrutiny that the deployment of its "secret" payload was observed. On December 1, 1988, Gibson and four other astronauts were launched aboard the orbiter Atlantis, which carried in its payload bay a massive Martin Marietta-built imaging radar satellite code-named Lacrosse. Seven hours after launch Lacrosse was deployed via the Atlantis remote manipulator system while the two spacecraft were tracked across the sky by observers in Canada. STS-27 ended after four days.

Gibson also commanded STS-47, the 8-day Spacelab J (Japan) mission, in September 1992. The crew of 7, including Japanese payload specialist Mamoru Mohri, conducted experiments in space manufacturing and life sciences.

Gibson was born October 30, 1946, in Cooperstown, New York, and graduated from high school in Huntington, New York, in 1964. Nevertheless, he considers Lakewood, California, to be his hometown. He attended California

Polytechnic University, receiving a B.S. in aeronautical engineering in 1969. He joined the Navy in 1969 and underwent pilot training in Florida, Mississippi, and Texas. From April 1972 to September 1975 he was assigned to the carriers *U.S.S. Coral Sea* and *U.S.S. Enterprise*, and flew 56 combat missions in Southeast Asia. Returning to the United States, Gibson served as an F-14A instructor pilot, then attended the Naval Test Pilot School at Patuxent River, Maryland. He was a test pilot there when chosen by NASA.

As a pilot Gibson has logged over 6,000 hours of flying time in 45 different types of aircraft. He has held a pilot's license since he was 17.

Gibson was one of the 35 astronauts selected by NASA in January 1978 and in August 1979 qualified as a Shuttle pilot. He worked in the Shuttle Avionics Integration Laboratory and as a chase pilot, and in February 1983 was assigned as pilot of STS-11, later known as Mission 41-B.

During the hiatus caused by the Challenger accident he served on the investigation team, then assisted in the redesign of the faulty solid rocket motors.

In September 1989 Gibson was assigned as commander of STS-46, the scheduled flight of the Italian Space Agency's EURECA platform. But on July 7, 1990, he was involved in a midair collision during a race at n air show in New Braunfels, Texas. Gibson, flying a homebuilt Cassutt racer, landed safely, but the other pilot was killed.

Two days later flight crew operations chief Donald Puddy grounded Gibson for one year for violating written guidelines prohibiting astronauts assigned to missions from engaging in dangerous off-duty activities such as sport flying. The prohibition was a response to the 1989 death of STS-33 pilot David Griggs just months prior to the launch of the mission. Puddy also removed Gibson from command of STS-46.

In August 1991 Gibson was returned to flight status and named commander of STS-47.

From October 1992 to September 1994 Gibson was chief of the astronaut office. Following STS-71 he served as deputy director for flight crew operations until resigning from NASA and retiring from the Navy in November 1996.

He is currently a first officer for Southwest Airlines.

Gibson is married to former astronaut Rhea Seddon.

Givens, Edward Galen, Jr.
1930–1967
Air Force test pilot Ed Givens was one of the 19 astronauts selected by NASA in April 1966. A member of the support team for the first manned Apollo mission, he was killed in an off-duty automobile accident in Pearland, Texas, south of Houston, on June 6, 1967.

Givens was born January 5, 1930, in Quanah, Texas. He attended the Naval Academy at Annapolis, graduating with a B.S. degree in naval science (1952).

He elected to serve in the Air Force and became a pilot in 1953, spending two years with the 35th Fighter Interceptor Group, based in Japan. From January 1956 to March 1958 he was an instructor at the Air Force Interceptor Weapons School. He entered the Air Force Test Pilot School at Edwards AFB, California, in 1958, and upon graduation was named outstanding student of his class. He was then assigned to the Naval Air Station at Point Mugu, California, where he served as a project pilot.

Givens returned to Edwards in November 1961 to become assistant to the commandant of the test pilot school. A year later he entered the Aerospace Research Pilot course, graduating in 1963. His classmates in ARPS included future astronauts Michael Collins, Charles Bassett, and Joe Engle.

As a pilot Givens logged over 3,500 hours of flying time, including 2,800 hours in jets.

At the time of his selection by NASA Givens was a project officer with the USAF Space Systems Division, Detachment 2, at the NASA Manned Spacecraft Center, where he worked on designs for the Astronaut Maneuvering Unit (AMU), the so-called Buck Rogers backpack.

Glenn, John Herschel, Jr.
1921–

The first American to orbit the Earth, John Glenn became the most famous astronaut and a United States senator and presidential hopeful as well. Almost 36 years after that pioneering flight, NASA Administrator Daniel Goldin announced that Glenn was being assigned as a payload specialist in the crew of STS-95, returning to space at the age of 77.

On February 20, 1962, after weeks of frustrating delays caused by technical and weather problems, Glenn, then a 40-year-old Marine lieutenant colonel, was rocketed into space in a Mercury capsule named Friendship 7. In the next five hours he circled the Earth three times, becoming the first American to experience more than a few minutes of weightlessness.

Soviet cosmonauts Yuri Gagarin and Gherman Titov had already orbited the Earth, and Alan Shepard and Gus Grissom, two of Glenn's fellow Mercury astronauts, had made suborbital flights, but Glenn's was the first spaceflight to capture the attention and imagination of an entire world, which followed it on radio and television. The citizens of Perth and several other coastal cities in Australia, for example, turned on their lights as a greeting to the orbiting American.

The flight of Friendship 7 was not without drama. At the beginning of Glenn's second orbit, flight controllers picked up warning signals from the spacecraft telling them that the heat shield was loose. If true, Glenn was doomed to a fiery death on his return to Earth. Controllers suspected that the signal was wrong, but nevertheless instructed Glenn not to jettison the capsule's retrorocket pack, which was strapped atop the shield. It was a nervewracking reentry for Glenn, who could see chunks of burning metal flying past his window, not knowing if that was the retro pack or his heat shield. But Friendship 7 survived, splashing down approximately 800 miles southeast of Cape Canaveral near Grand Turk Island in the Bahamas.

Glenn became the most celebrated national hero since Charles Lindbergh, and soon found a friend in President John F. Kennedy, who, along with his brother Robert, saw the handsome, charismatic Glenn as a possible political ally. They encouraged him to explore a run for the U.S. Senate seat from Ohio.

The assassination of President Kennedy on November 22, 1963, robbed Glenn of his sponsorship, but Glenn went ahead with plans to leave NASA. (In January 1963 Glenn was assigned to Project Apollo, but unknown to him, President Kennedy had instructed NASA not to send Glenn into space a second time.) Saying that he didn't want to be "the world's oldest, permanently training astronaut," Glenn left the astronaut group on January 16, 1964, to campaign for the Senate.

But just weeks later, on February 26, 1964, Glenn suffered a head injury during a fall in a hotel bathroom. Constantly dizzy and nauseous, facing months of recuperation, he withdrew from the race. He had already announced his retirement from the Marines and, after promotion to colonel in October 1964, retired on January 1, 1965.

Though he was named a consultant to the NASA Administrator in February 1965 and remained based in Houston, for the next five years Glenn worked primarily as an executive for Royal Crown, a soft drink company based in Atlanta, Georgia. He also served on the board of several other corporations, and made investments in hotel developments. Successful investments made Glenn a millionaire, but he never gave up his political ambitions. He remained close to the Kennedy family (it was Glenn who broke the news of their father's death to Robert Kennedy's children).

Glenn's 1970 Senate campaign in Ohio was badly organized and underfunded, and he was defeated in the primary by businessman Howard Metzenbaum. Glenn learned from this defeat; his 1974 campaign against Senator Metzenbaum was more efficient, though Metzenbaum defeated himself when he criticized Glenn for "never having held a job." An outraged Glenn blasted Metzenbaum in a debate, pointing out that had indeed held jobs, in the Marines and in the space program, "where it wasn't my checkbook that was on the line, it was my life." Glenn handily defeated Republican Ralph J. Perk in the general election in November 1974 and entered the United States Senate eleven years after announcing his original intention to run.

Freshman senator Glenn earned high marks for his ability to win votes on his amendments in spite of the fact that he had few of the traditional political skills. He became friends with Republican senator Jake Garn of Utah, also elected in 1974. (Garn would later become the first U.S. senator to make a spaceflight as a Congressional observer.) He was also considered briefly as a vice-presidential candidate by then-governor Jimmy Carter.

President Carter and Senator Glenn had a public clash over the SALT II treaty and were never close allies. That became clear when in 1980 Glenn won reelection to the Senate overwhelmingly while Carter failed to carry Ohio.

In 1983 Glenn announced his intention to gain the Democratic presidential nomination in 1984. But his campaign, like his 1970 Senate campaign, struck observers as inefficient and unfocused. Glenn dropped out of the race prior to the convention.

Glenn's Senate career was threatened in 1990 when he was publicly charged with improperly interfering in the federal investigation of Lincoln Savings & Loan owner Charles Keating. Glenn was ultimately cleared by a Senate panel in 1991, but his reputation suffered enormously. In February 1998 he announced his intention to retire from the Senate at the conclusion of his term.

Two years prior to that Glenn had approached NASA chief Goldin with a plan to perform geriatric studies on orbit with himself as a test subject. (Glenn had been interested in returning to space aboard the Shuttle since the late 1970s.) Goldin was intrigued by the possibility, but required Glenn to create a worthwhile series of experiments, complete with medical backing, and to pass a stringent series of tests. Glenn was able to satisfy Goldin and was then assigned to STS-95. He was scheduled to spend ten days in space in October 1998.

Glenn was born July 18, 1921, in Cambridge, Ohio, and grew up in New Concord. His father was a plumber. Glenn graduated from high school in New Concord, and was attending Muskingum College there when World War II broke out. Glenn, who had already earned a private pilot's license, dropped out to enter the Naval Aviation Cadet Program and was eventually commissioned in the Marine Corps. (Based on later study at the Naval Test Pilot School and the University of Maryland, Glenn eventually received a B.S. in mathematics from Muskingum.)

Following pilot training he was assigned to Marine Fighter Squadron 155 and spent the final year of World War II flying F4U fighters on 59 combat missions in the Marshall Islands.

After the war, Glenn was assigned to Fighter Squadron 218 in North China and on Guam. He returned to the United States in June 1948 as an instructor at Corpus Christi, Texas.

In the Korean conflict Glenn flew 63 combat missions with Marine Fighter Squadron 311, where his fellow pilots included Boston Red Sox star Ted Williams. He also flew 27 missions as an exchange pilot with the Air Force. During the last nine days of fighting in Korea, Glenn shot down three enemy MiGs near the Yalu River.

In 1954 Glenn attended the Naval Test Pilot School at Patuxent River, Maryland, and remained there as a project officer for two years. Assigned to the Navy Bureau of Aeronautics in Washington, D.C., he conceived, planned and piloted a record-setting transcontinental jet flight, flying an F8U from Los Angeles to New York in just 3 hours, 23 minutes on July 16, 1957. This earned him a guest spots on television's *I've Got a Secret* and on *Name That Tune*, where he and his partner won $25,000.

When the National Advisory Committee on Aeronautics (NACA, NASA's predecessor) and the Navy began studies on manned spaceflight after the launch of Sputnik in October 1957, Glenn volunteered as a test subject and found himself riding the high-speed centrifuge that would later simulate launch and reentry stress for future astronauts.

Glenn was one of the original 7 Mercury astronauts chosen in April 1959. Widely expected, by journalists covering the space program, to be the first American in space, Glenn was disappointed to see that honor go to Alan Shepard. Glenn served as backup to both Shepard and Gus Grissom on their 1961 Mercury suborbital flights before being named to Mercury-Atlas 6, the first American manned orbital flight, in November 1961.

As a pilot Glenn logged over 5,500 hours of flying time, including 1,900 hours in jets.

Glenn contributed to the book *We Seven, by the Astronauts Themselves* (1962), which described their selection, early training, and first flights. A more enlightening version is told in Tom Wolfe's *The Right Stuff*

(1979). The film version of this book, released in November 1984, was widely expected to act as a "campaign" film for presidential candidate Glenn. Though it received general good reviews, *The Right Stuff* was not a commercially successful film.

Glenn also published a collection of letters written to him, *P.S., We Listened to Your Heartbeat* (1964).

A biography, *Glenn: The Astronaut Who Would Be President*, was published in 1983.

ABOARD FRIENDSHIP 7

by John Glenn

(On February 20, 1962, astronaut John Glenn became the first American to reach Earth orbit aboard the Mercury spacecraft "Friendship 7," launched by an Atlas rocket. Here is what he found during those first few moments on orbit.)

I loosened my chest strap now and went to work. Until this moment, every sequence and event had been extremely time-critical. That is, the successful jumping of each hurdle had depended on split-second timing. Now that I was in orbit and at zero G, however, we did not have to be quite so conscious of each fleeting second until it was time for firing the retro-rockets at the start of re-entry. I had a lot of work to do, and in order to get it all done I would have to adhere to the schedule as closely as possible. But at least I did not have to sit on pins and needles every second. [Astronaut office secretary] Nancy Lowe had typed the flight plan for me on a long piece of paper which we rolled up into a tiny scroll, which I would unroll a bit at a time. I did not discover until later that Nancy had typed a private message at the end of it to give me something pleasant to think about when I saw it at the end of the mission. "Don't get too much sun on GTI," she wrote. This referred to Grand Turk Island, where I would proceed for the debriefing and medical examinations after the mission—assuming it was a success. It was nice to know that Nancy was so sure of the outcome.

The plan called for me to spend most of the first orbit getting used to the new environment and helping the ground stations establishing an accurate pattern of radar tracking so they could pin down an exact orbital path early in the mission. I was also scheduled to test out the various systems on the capsule before we got too far along, so that we would know if we had any problems before we committed ourselves to a second orbit. Eight minutes after launch, as soon as Gus Grissom finished relaying to me the correct times for retro-firing from his capcom desk at the Bermuda tracking station, I started checking out the attitude control systems—automatic, manual and fly-by-wire. I tried each system on all three axes—yaw, pitch and roll—and in all directions—up, down, left and right. This took about two minutes and by the time I was finished with it I was almost across the Atlantic and was in communication with the tracking station in the Canary Islands. All of the controls had responded perfectly, just like clockwork. The stick handled very well. I was happy to see this, for there is always some doubt whether such complicated controls will work as well under actual conditions as they do on the procedure trainers—and whether I would be able to work as well, also. I could see no difference—at least not yet.

Inside the spacecraft I could hear a number of muffled sounds. There was some noise from the gyros which gave us our attitude references, another noise caused by the inverters which were converting D.C. power into A.C., the hiss of the oxygen flow as it ran through the hose in my helmet, and sounds from the nozzles which were spitting out hydrogen peroxide to correct the attitude of the capsule.

In addition to closely monitoring all the systems, I started making a few observations out the window. Since I was facing backwards, everything came out from underneath me, similar to the way things look when you ride backwards in a car, and it seemed to move more rapidly than I thought it would. The sense of speed was similar to what you normally experience in a jet airliner at about 30,000 feet when you are looking down at a cloud bank at low altitude. I think our training devices have been a little inadequate on this score; they had given us less sensation of motion and speed than I could feel in actual flight. Just before I finished crossing the Atlantic, I had my last glimpses of the Atlas. It was still in orbit, about two miles behind me and a mile beneath me. It was bright enough so that I could see it even against the bright background of the Earth.

. . .

Zanzibar was the next tracking station, and here the flight surgeon who was on duty came on the air to discuss how I was doing physically. I gave him a blood-pressure reading, but before I pushed the button and pumped up the bulb I pulled thirty times at the bungee cord which permitted me to exercise with a known workload that could be compared with the same exercise taken on the ground. The cord was attached under the instrument panel, and I gave it one full pull per second for thirty seconds to see what effect exercise would have on my system under a condition of weightlessness. The only real effect it had on me was the same effect it had on me on the ground: it made me tired. My pulse went up from 80 beats per minute to 124 beats in 30 seconds, but returned to 84 beats per minute within a couple of minutes. My blood pressure read 120 over 76 before the exercise period and 129 over 74 afterwards. This was the sort of mild reaction we had expected from doing similar tests on the procedures trainer. The doctor also asked me what physical reactions, if any, I had experienced so far from weightlessness. I was able to tell him that there had been none at all; I assured him that I felt fine. I had had no trouble reaching accurately for the controls and switches. There had been no tendency to get awkward and overreach them, as some people had thought there might be. I could hit directly any spot that I wanted do hit. I had an eye chart on board, a small version of the kind you find in doctor's offices, and I had no trouble reading the same line of type each time. After making a few slow movements with my head to see if this brought on a feeling of disorientation, I even tried to induce a little dizziness by nodding my head up and down and moving it from side to side. I experienced no disturbances, however. I felt no sense of vertigo, astigmatism or nausea whatever.

In fact, I found weightlessness to be extremely pleasant.

Godwin, Linda Maxine

1952–

Physicist Linda Godwin took part in the first American EVA aboard the Russian Mir space station. Godwin and fellow STS-76 mission specialist Rich Clifford exited the airlock of the orbiter Atlantis, which was docked to Mir, and installed several experiments on the exterior of the station.

STS-76 was Godwin's third spaceflight. Previously she was payload commander for STS-59, the April 1994 flight of the orbiter Endeavour that carried the first Shuttle Radar Laboratory. This $366 million imaging system was the most advanced ever devoted to Earth studies. During the 11-day flight the SRL imaged over 70 million square kilometers of the Earth's surface and returned enough data to fill 20,000 encyclopedia volumes.

Godwin also served as a mission specialist aboard STS-37, the April 1991 flight of the orbiter Atlantis that deployed the Gamma Ray Observatory in low Earth orbit. The GRO, a $617 million element in NASA's "great observatory" program, was, at 17.5 tons, the most massive object yet carried by the Shuttle. During deployment an antenna failed to unfold. Using the Atlantis's remote manipulator arm, Godwin positioned the GRO so that astronauts Jerry Ross and Jay Apt could perform a contingency EVA, freeing the stuck antenna. A day later Godwin assisted Ross and Apt in a second EVA, testing space station construction techniques.

Godwin was born July 2, 1952, in Cape Girardeau, Missouri. She graduated from high school in nearby Jackson in 1970, then attended Southeast Missouri State University, receiving a B.S. in mathematics and physics in 1974. She later earned an M.S. (1976) and Ph.D. (1980) in physics from the University of Missouri at Columbia.

While working on her doctorate at Missouri Godwin taught physics and conducted research in low temperature solid state physics, publishing several papers. In 1980 she joined NASA as a flight controller and payload operations officer, working on several Shuttle missions.

She is also a private pilot holding an instrument rating.

Godwin was one of the 13 astronaut candidates selected by NASA in June 1985. In July 1986 she qualified as a Shuttle mission specialist, and has since done a tour in the Shuttle Avionics Integration Lab (SAIL) and worked on the development of inertial upper stage (IUS) and Spacelab missions. Between missions she served as chief of astronaut appearances and head of the astronaut office mission development branch. Since April 1993 she has been deputy chief of the astronaut office, with time off for STS-76 crew training and for a brief tour as acting deputy director of flight crew operations.

Gordon, Henry Charles

1925–

Hank Gordon was one of the test pilots assigned to the X-20 Dyna-Soar program in April 1960. He trained for the series of manned spaceplane missions until December 1963, when Dyna-Soar was canceled, two years before scheduled flights were to begin.

Gordon was born December 23, 1925, in Valparaiso, Indiana, and grew up in Gary, where he graduated from Emerson High School in 1943. He immediately joined the Army Air Corps, hoping to become a pilot, but finished out his World War II service as a military policeman. He then returned to Indiana to attend Purdue University, where he received a B.S. in aeronautical engineering in 1950. (Classmates of Gordon's at Purdue at the time were Gus Grissom and Iven Kincheloe.)

Gordon received an M.B.A. from the University of Southern California in 1966.

He had rejoined the Air Force via ROTC while at Purdue, and was commissioned as a second lieutenant in 1949. Following graduation he finally underwent flight training, then was assigned, with Grissom, to the 334th Fighter Squadron in Korea. He flew 100 combat missions.

Returning to the United States in 1952, Gordon served with the Air Defense Command at bases in New York State. He was enrolled at the Air Force Test Pilot School at Edwards AFB in June 1957, and upon graduation worked on various projects, including the F-106 and the F-104G until his assignment to Dyna-Soar.

Following the cancellation of Dyna-Soar Gordon remained at Edwards AFB working for James Wood on the F-5 test force. He did graduate work at the University of Southern California from January 1965 to July 1966, then joined the Air Staff at the Pentagon, where he worked on the AX (later the A-10) close air support aircraft program. He attended the National War College from 1969 to 1970.

Retrained as an F-100 pilot in 1970, Gordon became vice commander of the 35th Fighter Wing at Fan Ranh, Vietnam, flying 55 combat missions. He later served as commander of the 405th Fighter Wing at Clark AFB, the Philippines, where he managed to fly several more combat missions. He returned to the United States in 1974 to become director of maintenance at the Air Logistics Center, Hill AFB, Utah, and retired with the rank of colonel in 1975.

He logged over 5,500 hours of flying time.

Gordon has since been involved in several business ventures in the Phoenix area, including a self-service auto lube business and video rentals. He is now retired.

For a brief time in the late 1970s Gordon flew medical supplies and doctors into and out of Indian reservations with the Monument Valley Air Service, logging an additional 900 hours of time in Cessna light aircraft. He would call this the most dangerous flying of his entire career.

Gordon, Richard Francis, Jr.
1929–

Navy test pilot Dick Gordon made spaceflights aboard Gemini and Apollo. As pilot of Gemini 11 in September 1966, Gordon and command pilot Charles Conrad set a world record, soaring to an altitude of 850 miles. Gordon also conducted two space walks.

As command module pilot of Apollo 12 in November 1969, Gordon orbited the Moon for a day and a half while Conrad and Alan Bean explored the Ocean of Storms.

Gordon was born October 5, 1929, in Seattle, Washington, and graduated from North Kitsap High School in nearby Poulsbo in 1947. He attended the University of Washington, receiving a B.S. in chemistry in 1951. He later did graduate work in operations analysis at the Naval Postgraduate School.

Entering active duty with the Navy following college, Gordon underwent pilot training, earning his wings in

1953. For the next four years he was an all-weather fighter pilot based in Jacksonville, Florida, then attended the Naval Test Pilot School at Patuxent River, Maryland. From 1957 to 1960 he was a test pilot at Pax River, serving as project pilot for the F4H Phantom II. He also became friends with fellow Navy test pilots Charles Conrad and Alan Bean. Following his tour as a test pilot, Gordon became a flight instructor at Miramar, California, taking part in the introduction of the F4H to the Atlantic and Pacific fleets. In May 1961 he won the Bendix Trophy for setting a new Los Angeles to New York speed record of 870 miles per hour, flying across the United States in 2 hours and 47 minutes.

As a pilot Gordon logged over 4,500 hours of flying time, including 3,500 hours in jets.

Gordon was a student at the Naval Postgraduate School in October 1963 when he became one of the 14 astronauts selected by NASA. (He had been a semifinalist for the 1962 group.) One of his early assignments was to help design the cockpits for Gemini and Apollo spacecraft, and he ultimately became head of the astronaut office Apollo branch. In September 1965 he was named backup pilot for Gemini 8 and also served as a capcom for Gemini 9. Following his Gemini 11 flight he was backup command module pilot for Apollo 9.

In March 1970 Gordon, Vance Brand and scientist-astronaut Harrison Schmitt were named as backups for Apollo 15, then scheduled for October of that year, expecting to be chosen as the prime crew for the Apollo 18 lunar landing. But cuts in the NASA budget that spring eliminated Apollos 18 through 20, and Gordon lost his chance to become the thirteenth person to walk on the Moon. With the completion of his assignment on Apollo 15 in August 1971 Gordon served as chief of advanced programs for the astronaut office, working on the new Space Shuttle, resigning from NASA and retiring from the Navy as a captain on January 1, 1972.

Gordon was hired away from NASA by John W. Mecom Jr. to become executive vice-president of the Mecom-owned New Orleans Saints team in the National Football League. In April 1977 Gordon became general manager of Energy Developers Ltd., a chemical research company owned by Mecom. He left the Mecom organization in May 1978 to become president of Resolution Engineering and Development Company (REDCO), a firm specializing in oil well control and firefighting, remaining with that company through August 1981.

From September 1981 to February 1983 Gordon was director for Scott Science and Technology, Inc., in Los Angeles, an aerospace firm founded by former Apollo 15 commander David Scott. He later served as president of Astro Sciences Corporation in Los Angeles and also worked for J&L Information Systems in Chatsworth, California.

In the summer of 1984 Gordon served as technical consultant to the producers of the CBS television miniseries *Space*, playing the role of Capcom onscreen as well.

Gordon is now retired and lives in Sedona, Arizona.

Gorie, Dominic Lee
1957–

Navy test pilot Dom Gorie was assigned as pilot of STS-91. This June 1998 flight of the orbiter Atlantis made the ninth and last Shuttle-Mir docking mission, returning astronaut Andy Thomas to Earth.

Gorie was born Dominic Pudwill on May 2, 1957, in Lake Charles, Louisiana. He graduated from Miami Palmetto High School in Miami, Florida, in 1975, then attended the U.S. Naval Academy, where he received a B.S. in ocean engineering in 1979. He later earned an M.S. in aviation systems from the University of Tennessee at Knoxville in 1990.

After graduation from Annapolis, Gorie underwent pilot training, then flew A-7E Corsairs with Attack Squadron 46 aboard the carrier *U.S.S. America* from 1981 to 1983. His next tour was flying the F/A-18 with Strike Fighter Squadron 132 aboard the carrier *U.S.S. Coral Sea.*

Gorie attended the Naval Test Pilot School at Patuxent River, Maryland, in 1987, then served as a test pilot at Pax River for two years. He flew 38 combat missions in the F/A-18 with Strike Fighter Squadron 87 aboard the carrier *U.S.S. Roosevelt* in Operation Desert Storm, followed by a two-year tour with the U.S. Space Command at Peterson AFB, Colorado. He was en route to command of Strike Fighter Squadron 37 when selected as a NASA astronaut candidate on December 8, 1994.

Commander Gorie has logged 3,300 hours of flying time in 30 different aircraft, and has over 600 carrier landings.

Gorie qualified as a Shuttle pilot in May 1996. Prior to his STS-91 assignment in October 1997 he served as astronaut office safety officer, and also flew chase planes at Shuttle contingency landing sites during missions.

Grabe, Ronald John
1945–

Air Force test pilot Ron Grabe was commander of STS-42, the first International Microgravity Laboratory, launched in January 1992. This 8-day flight of the orbiter Discovery was devoted to 55 experiments in space manufacturing and medicine developed by an international team of scientists.

In June 1993 Grabe commanded a second Shuttle mission, STS-57, which carried the first SpaceHab commercial facility.

Grabe previously served as pilot of two Shuttle missions. His first, in October 1985, was Mission 51-J, a Department of Defense flight that deployed a pair of DSCS III communications satellites into geosynchronous orbit. It was also the first flight of the orbiter Atlantis.

In May 1989, as pilot of STS-30, Grabe took part in the launch of the Magellan space probe on its 8-month journey to the planet Venus.

Grabe was born June 13, 1945, in New York City. He graduated from Stuyvesant High School there in 1962 and entered the Air Force Academy, where he received his B.S. in engineering science in 1966. In 1967 he studied aeronautics as a Fulbright Scholar at the Technische Hochschule in Darmstadt, West Germany.

After completing pilot training, Grabe flew F-100 aircraft with the 27th Tactical Fighter Wing at Cannon Air Force Base, New Mexico. In 1969 he was assigned to the 3rd Tactical Fighter Wing at Bien Hoa Air Base, Vietnam, where he took part in 200 combat missions. Upon his return to the United States he attended the Air Force Test Pilot School, graduating in 1975, and from 1976 to 1979 served as an exchange test pilot with the Royal Air Force at Boscombe Down, United Kingdom. Prior to becoming an astronaut he was an instructor at the test pilot school at Edwards.

As a pilot Grabe logged over 5,500 hours of flying time.

Grabe was selected as an astronaut candidate in May 1980, qualifying as a Shuttle pilot in August 1981. He fulfilled several technical assignments in the astronaut office prior to being named to the Department of Defense standby flight crew—which later became Mission 51-J—in October 1983. He also served as chief of training.

Grabe resigned from NASA and retired from the USAF (with the rank of colonel) on April 11, 1994. He is currently vice-president of business development for Orbital Science Corporation launch systems group in Virginia.

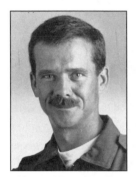

Graveline, Duane Edgar
1931–

Duane Graveline was one of the first 6 scientist-astronauts chosen by NASA in June 1965. Graveline resigned from the program two months later for personal reasons.

Graveline was born March 2, 1931, in Newport, Vermont. He received a B.S. from the University of Vermont in 1952 and an M.D. from the University of Vermont Medical School in 1955. He later earned an M.S. in public health from Johns Hopkins University in 1958. He also served in the Air Force.

While serving as an air force flight surgeon, Graveline conducted a key experiment into testing man's reactions to weightless. Wearing a scuba suit, he floated submerged in a tank of water for a week. Doctors discovered that upon emerging that Graveline had begun to suffer bone softening and other symptoms.

After leaving NASA Dr. Graveline took a position with the State of Vermont Department of Health, and has since set up his own medical practice in Colchester, Vermont. He attended the launch of STS-1 in April 1981.

Gregory, Frederick Drew
1941–

Air Force test pilot Fred Gregory was the first African-American Shuttle commander, leading a crew of 5 astronauts on STS-33, a 5-day flight of the orbiter Discovery in November 1989. STS-33 deployed Mentor, a secret electronic intelligence satellite, into geosynchronous orbit.

Two years later Gregory commanded his second Shuttle mission, STS-44, which successfully deployed the sixteenth Defense Support Program early warning satellite into geosynchronous orbit. STS-44 was shortened to seven days from a planned 10-day duration by the failure of a navigation unit aboard the orbiter Atlantis.

Gregory's first spaceflight was as pilot of Shuttle Mission 51-B, which carried Spacelab 3. The 7-man crew performed medical and materials processing experiments during the mission, which lasted from April 29 to May 6, 1985.

In March 1992 Gregory was appointed NASA associate administrator for safety at NASA headquarters in Washington, D.C.

Gregory was born January 7, 1941, in Washington, D.C. and graduated from Anacostia High School there in 1958. He attended the Air Force Academy, where he received a bachelor of science degree in 1964. He later earned an M.S. in information systems from George Washington University in 1977.

Upon graduation from the Air Force Academy Gregory underwent training as a helicopter pilot at Stead AFB, Nevada. He then spent three years as a rescue crew commander, including a tour in Vietnam. In 1969 he cross-trained to T-38 and F-4 Phantom jets, then entered the Naval Test Pilot School at Patuxent River, Maryland. From 1971 to 1974 Gregory was a test pilot at Wright-Patterson AFB, Ohio, and from 1974 to 1978 for NASA at Langley Research Center, Virginia.

In April 1975, while stationed at Langley, Gregory was briefly recalled to duty in Vietnam, serving as a helicopter rescue pilot flying refugees out of the beseiged American embassy in Saigon to carriers offshore.

As a pilot he has logged over 6,500 hours of flying time in more than 50 different types of aircraft, including helicopters, jet fighters, transports, and gliders. He flew 550 combat missions in Vietnam.

As a teenager Gregory always wanted to be an astronaut but since his military flying was primarily in helicopters rather than high-performance jets, the Air Force was reluctant to submit him to NASA as a candidate in 1977. Gregory offered to resign from the service, submitted his own application, and was chosen as one of 35 astronaut candidates by NASA in January 1978. In August 1979 he qualified as a Shuttle pilot. He then worked in the Shuttle Avionics Integration Laboratory until being assigned to the Spacelab 3 mission in February 1983.

In October 1985, following his first flight, Gregory served as mission control capcom for Shuttle flights. He has also been chief of the operational safety branch at NASA Headquarters and chief of astronaut training.

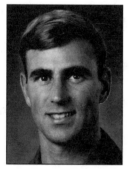

Gregory, William George
1957–

Air Force test pilot Bill Gregory was pilot aboard STS-67, the March 1995 flight of the orbiter Endeavour that carried the second Spacelab ASTRO. The STS-67 mission set s Shuttle duration record of over 16 days, 15 hours.

Although not disclosed publicly, NASA managers at the Johnson Space Center were reportedly unhappy with Gregory's performance as STS-67 pilot. Though he remains assigned to the astronaut office, he has never been assigned to another flight crew.

Gregory was born May 14, 1957, in Lockport, New York. His father was a Navy pilot. Gregory attended the USAF Academy, receiving a B.S. in engineering from Columbia University in 1980, and an M.S. in management from Troy Sate in 1984.

Following flight training in 1981, Gregory flew F-111D and F-111F aircraft at RAF Lakenheath, England, and at Cannon AFB, New Mexico, also serving as an F-111 instructor. He attended the USAF Test Pilot School at Edwards AFB, California, in 1987, then served as a test pilot there until his selection by NASA.

He has logged over 4,000 hours of flying time in 40 different types of aircraft.

Gregory was one of 23 astronaut candidates selected by NASA on January 17, 1990. In July 1991 he qualified as a Shuttle pilot and was given his first technical assignment, working in the Shuttle Avionics Integration Laboratory. He later served as astronaut office representative for landing and rollout issues, T-38 safety officer and with the astronaut support team at the Kennedy Space Center. Following STS-67 Lieutenant Colonel Gregory served as a capcom in mission control.

In 1997 Gregory took part in the Iron Man triathelete competition.

Griggs, Stanley David
1938–1989

Former Navy test pilot Dave Griggs took the first unscheduled and unrehearsed space walk in the American space program on April 16, 1985. Griggs was one of 7 astronauts aboard Shuttle Mission 51-D, which deployed two communications satellites. One of the satellites, the Hughes Syncom IV-3 (also known as Leasat 3), failed to activate because an arming lever was not automatically closed during deployment, leaving Leasat 3 floating useless in orbit.

NASA and Hughes controllers, working with the astronauts, devised a makeshift cardboard-and-electrical tape "flyswatter," which, it was hoped, could be attached to the robot arm of the Shuttle Discovery and used to snag the switch on the satellite. Mission specialists Griggs and Jeffrey Hoffman performed the unique EVA, attaching the "flyswatter," but the attempt by astronaut Rhea Seddon to activate the satellite failed. (Leasat 3 was repaired on a later Shuttle mission, and finally reached its intended orbit in October 1985.)

These events overshadowed the successful deployment of the Canadian Anik 3C communications satellite, and the flight on 51-D of United States senator Jake Garn as a payload specialist and observer.

Griggs was assigned as pilot of STS-33, a dedicated Department of Defense Shuttle mission scheduled for launch in November 1989, when he was killed in an off-duty airplane crash on June 17, 1989. He had been rehearsing aerobatics for an appearance in an airshow when his vintage North American T-6 slammed into a field in Earle, Arkansas.

Griggs was born September 7, 1939, in Portland, Oregon, where he grew up, graduating from Lincoln High School in 1957. He attended the Naval Academy at Annapolis, where he earned a bachelor of science degree in 1962. He later earned an M.S. in administration from George Washington University in 1970.

After completing pilot training in 1964 Griggs was attached to Attack Squadron 74 and flew A-4 aircraft from the carriers *U.S.S. Independence* and *U.S.S. Roosevelt* in Southeast Asia and the Mediterranean. In 1967 he attended the Naval Test Pilot School at Patuxent River, Maryland, and remained there as a test pilot until 1970, when he resigned from the Navy.

He continued to fly with the Naval Reserve for many years, and at the time of his death was a rear admiral commanding the Office of Naval Research/Naval Research Laboratory 410, in Houston.

He logged over 9,500 hours of flying time, including more than 7,500 hours in jets, in 45 different types of aircraft.

Griggs joined NASA in July 1970 as a research pilot based at the Johnson Space Center. In 1974 he was assigned to the development of the Shuttle Training Aircraft (STA), a specially modified jet that would eventually train astronauts to make Shuttle landings. He was chief of STA Operations when he was selected as an astronaut in January 1978. In August 1979 he qualified as a pilot on Shuttle crews. He worked on the manned maneuvering unit and served as a capcom for STS-4.

While training as the pilot for the long-delayed Spacelab 2 mission, Griggs was also assigned to be mission specialist and flight engineer for Mission 41-F, commanded by Karol Bobko and scheduled for launch in August 1984. Problems with the Shuttle manifest forced the Bobko crew eventually to transfer to Mission 51-D. Griggs lost his pilot assignment on Spacelab 2, then was assigned as pilot on Spacelab 4, which was also canceled. He was later chosen to pilot the Spacelab Earth Observation Mission planned for 1986. That mission, too, was canceled.

Grisson, Virgil Ivan "Gus"
1927–1967

Gus Grissom, one of the original 7 Mercury astronauts, died in the Apollo 1 fire at Cape Canaveral on January 27, 1967. Killed with him were Edward White, the first American to walk in space, and Roger Chaffee.

The three astronauts were training for the first manned Apollo flight, a 14-day mission scheduled for launch on February 21, 1967. On Friday, January 27, they were rehearsing launch procedures while strapped in their seats inside their Apollo command module atop its Saturn 1B booster. At 6:31 in the evening, at T-10 minutes and holding (a communications problem had developed), a wire inside the Apollo gave off a spark that flared easily in the 16-pounds-per-square-inch, 100-percent oxygen atmosphere, turning the cabin into an inferno. As Grissom, White, and Chaffee struggled out of their couches and fought to open the hatch, they were overcome by heat and flame.

The subsequent board of inquiry criticized NASA and North American Aviation, builders of Apollo, for failing to correct potential fire hazards in the spacecraft. (The Apollo cabin contained flammable materials and had a hatch that could not be opened quickly in an emergency.) Apollo flights were suspended for 18 months while the spacecraft was re-designed.

Grissom and Chaffee were buried at Arlington National Cemetery. White was buried at West Point.

Grissom was born April 3, 1926, in Mitchell, Indiana, where he grew up, graduating from high school in 1944. He attended Purdue University from 1946 to 1950, receiving a B.S. in mechanical engineering, and later attended the Air Force Institute of Technology.

Grissom enlisted in the Army Air Corps as an aviation cadet in 1944 and was undergoing pilot training at Sheppard Field in Texas when World War II ended. He left the AAC to attend college, then reenlisted upon graduation in February 1950, earning his wings at Randolph AFB, Texas, thirteen months later.

Assigned to the 75th Fighter Interceptor Squadron, Grissom flew 100 combat missions in Korea. He returned to the United States in 1952 and served as an instructor pilot. Then, in August 1955, he entered the Air Force Institute of Technology at Wright-Patterson AFB, Ohio. A year later he was sent to the Air Force Experimental Test Pilot School at Edwards AFB, California, and in May 1957 returned to Wright-Pat as a fighter test pilot.

Grissom logged 4,600 hours as a pilot, including 3,500 hours in jets.

He was selected by NASA as one of its first astronauts in April 1959 and helped develop spacecraft simulators. With John Glenn and Alan Shepard, Grissom was one of 3 candidates for the Mercury-Redstone series of suborbital flights.

On July 21, 1961, Grissom was launched to an altitude of 126 miles aboard Liberty Bell 7. Mercury-Redstone 4, as it was officially known, repeated Alan Shepard's pioneering Mercury flight of May 5. After splashdown in the Atlantic, however, the hatch flew off Liberty Bell 7 and the spacecraft began to take on water. Grissom dived into the ocean, where he was rescued by a recovery helicopter, but Liberty Bell 7 sank.

It was the loss of Liberty Bell 7 that inspired Grissom to name his next spacecraft the Molly Brown, after the stage play *The Unsinkable Molly Brown*. Following his Mercury flight Grissom had begun to work on the development of the Mercury Mark II spacecraft, later known as Gemini, and in April 1964 was named commander of the first mission. Grissom and John Young orbited the Earth three times on March 23, 1965, becoming the first astronauts to maneuver their spacecraft in orbit. (Previous American and Soviet space travelers had been able to change the attitude of their spacecraft, but not its actual orbit.)

Grissom and Young served as backups for Gemini 6 in December 1965, and then Grissom was chosen to command the first Apollo. He would have been the first person to go into space three times, and the first to fly in three different spacecraft.

Grissom contributed to the book *We Seven* (1962) and completed work on *Gemini* (1968) just before his death. He is the subject of *Starfall* (1974) by Betty Grissom and Henry Still.

Grunsfeld, John Mace

1958–

Physicist John Mace Grunsfeld was a mission specialist in the crew of STS-67, the second Spacelab ASTRO mission, that carried a set of three telescopes designed to study the far ultraviolet spectra. This 16-day research mission aboard the orbiter Columbia had a crew of 7 and was launched on March 2, 1995.

Grunsfeld went into space a second time aboard STS-81. This January 1997 flight of the orbiter Atlantis accomplished the fifth Shuttle-Mir docking, transferring five tons of food, water and other supplies between the two spacecraft. STS-81 also delivered NASA-Mir crewmember Jerry Linenger to the station while returning John Blaha to Earth.

Grunsfeld was born October 10, 1958, in Chicago, Illinois. He graduated from high school in Highland Park, Illinois, then attended the Massachusetts Institute of Technology, receiving a B.S. in physics in 1980. He received an M.S. and Ph.D. in physics from the University of Chicago in 1984 and 1988.

Grunsfeld's speciality is X-ray and gamma ray astronomy, and in pursuit of his studies he has served as a visiting scientist at the University of Tokyo's Institute of Space and Astronomical Science (1980–81), as a research assistant, NASA graduate student fellow and postdoctoral fellow at the University of Chicago (1981–89). At the time of his selection as an astronaut candidate, he was a senior research fellow at the California Institute of Technology in Pasadena.

Grunsfeld was one of the 19 astronaut candidates selected by NASA in March 1992. In July 1993 he qualified as a Shuttle mission specialist while assigned to the mission development branch of the astronaut office. Since April 1997 he has been head of the computer support branch.

Guttierrez, Sidney McNeill

1951–

Air Force test pilot Sid Gutierrez commanded STS-59, the April 1994 flight of the orbiter Endeavour that carried the first Shuttle Radar Laboratory. This $366-million sensor package was the most advanced instrument ever used to study the Earth from space. Operated by a crew of 6, the SRL collected radar images of more than 70 million square kilometers of the Earth's surface, compiling enough data to fill 20,000 encyclopedia volumes. STS-59 ended successfully after a flight of 11 days.

Gutierrez also served as pilot of STS-40, the 9-day Spacelab Life Sciences mission flown in June 1991. During STS-40 a crew of 7, including four physicians, conducted experiments into the effects of spaceflight on human beings.

Gutierrez was born June 27, 1951, in Albuquerque, New Mexico, and graduated from Valley High School there in 1969. He attended the Air Force Academy at Colorado Springs, receiving a B.S. in aeronautical engineering in 1973, and later earned an M.S. in management from Webster College in 1977.

At the Air Force Academy Gutierrez became a master parachutist, making over 550 jumps as a member of the team which won a national championship. He earned his pilot's wings at Laughlin Air Force Base, Texas, in 1975 and remained there as an instructor through 1977. After an assignment as an F-15 pilot at Hollomon AFB, New Mexico, Gutierrez attended the Air Force Test Pilot School at Edwards AFB, California, in 1981. He was testing F-16 aircraft there when selected by NASA.

As a pilot Gutierrez logged over 4,500 hours of flying time in 30 different types of aircraft.

Gutierrez was one of the 17 astronauts selected by NASA in May 1984. In June 1985 he qualified as a Shuttle pilot while working in the Shuttle Avionics Integration Laboratory (SAIL), where the highly complex and constantly changing computer software needed to fly the Shuttle is verified. He then worked at the Kennedy Space Center, supporting launch activities. Following the Challenger accident he served as action officer for the associ-

ate administrator for spaceflight at NASA Headquarters, coordinating reports from the Presidential Commission investigating the disaster.

Between his flights Gutierrez served as a capcom for several 1992 Shuttle missions, and headed the astronaut office operations development branch from 1991 to 1993.

He resigned from NASA on August 8, 1994, and retired from the Air Force on October 1 of that year, to join Sandia National Laboratories in Albuquerque, New Mexico, as manager of strategic planning and development.

Haise, Fred Wallace, Jr.

1933–

Fred Haise was one of 3 astronauts aboard the unlucky flight of Apollo 13 in April 1970. Haise and commander James Lovell were to have landed on the Moon in the lunar module Aquarius, but on April 13, 1970, two days after launch from the Kennedy Space Center, an explosion aboard the command module Odyssey forced the two would-be lunar explorers and fellow crewman Jack Swigert to use the Aquarius as a lifeboat. With limited power, limited oxygen, and no possibility of a quick return to Earth, the astronauts struggled for 86 hours—three and a half days—to survive the first deep-space abort in history. They returned safely on April 16, 1970.

The story of this flight was told in *13: The Flight That Failed*, by Henry S. F. Cooper Jr. (New York: Dial Press, 1972). Apollo 13 was also dramatized in a television movie, *Houston, We've Got a Problem*, and the acclaimed Ron Howard-Tom Hanks film *Apollo 13* (1994).

Haise was born November 13, 1933, in Biloxi, Mississippi. He received an associate of arts degree from Perkinston Junior College in 1952 and went on to the University of Oklahoma, intending to become a newspaper reporter. Instead he dropped out to join the Navy. He later earned a B.S. in aeronautical engineering in 1959.

From October 1952 to March 1954 Haise was a Navy aviation cadet. After qualifying as a pilot he became a flight instructor at Kingsville, Texas, then served with

Marine Corps Squadrons 533 and 114 at Cherry Point, North Carolina. He left the Marines in September 1956 to return to school at the University of Oklahoma.

While Haise was a student he flew with the 185th Fighter Interceptor Squadron of Oklahoma Air National Guard. Upon graduation in September 1959 he joined the NASA Lewis Research Center in Cleveland, Ohio, as a research pilot. He also spent 10 months (October 1961 to August 1962) as a pilot with the Air Force. He attended the Air Force Aerospace Research Pilot School at Edwards AFB, California, where he was awarded the A. B. Honts Trophy as outstanding graduate of the class of 1964. At the time he was chosen by NASA to be an astronaut he was a civilian pilot at the NASA Flight Research Center at Edwards AFB.

As a pilot Haise eventually logged over 8,700 hours of flying time, including 5,700 hours in jets.

Haise was one of the 19 astronauts selected by NASA in April 1966. He served as a support crewman for the first flight of the lunar module—eventually flown as Apollo 9—until promoted to the backup crew for the Apollo 8 flight. He was backup lunar module pilot for Buzz Aldrin on Apollo 11, man's first landing on the Moon. After his flight on Apollo 13, Haise was backup commander for Apollo 16 and would have commanded the Apollo 19 lunar landing, had it not been canceled.

In 1973, while piloting a replica of a Japanese World War II aircraft for the Confederate Air Force, a flying air museum, Haise crashed and was badly burned.

When he returned to work, Haise became deeply involved in the Space Shuttle program, primarily as commander of the first Shuttle Approach and Landing Test flight in August 1977. Haise and Gordon Fullerton piloted the Shuttle Enterprise to a dead-stick landing on the dry lakebed at Edwards AFB after the Shuttle was carried aloft by a specially modified Boeing 747. Haise and Fullerton later conducted two more such tests.

The following year Haise was designated as commander of the third planned Shuttle orbital flight test, scheduled to rendezvous with the Skylab space station, then in orbit. A special rocket system was to be attached to Skylab, boosting it into a higher, safer orbit by remote control.

But in June 1979, as technical problems continued to delay the first Shuttle flight, Skylab reentered the atmosphere and was destroyed.

In that same month Haise resigned from NASA to join the Grumman Aerospace Corporation in Bethpage, New York. He later served as president of Grumman space station in Reston, Virginia, and is currently president of the Grumman technical services division, Northrop-Grumman Corporation, in Titusville, Florida.

Halsell, James Donald, Jr.
1956–

Air Force test pilot Jim Halsell commanded two flights of the Materials Science Laboratory, a Spacelab mission originally launched as STS-83 in April 1997, then reflown with the same payload and crew three months later (STS-94, July 1997). The reflight was made necessary by a fuel cell problem aboard Columbia on STS-83 that cut the planned 16-day mission to fewer than four days' duration.

Halsell previously served as pilot of two Shuttle missions, STS-65 (July 1994), which carried the second International Microgravity Lab, and STS-74 (November 1995), which made the second Shuttle-Mir docking.

Halsell was born September 29, 1956, in Monroe, Louisiana. He attended the Air Force Academy, receiving a B.S. in engineering in 1978, and later earned an M.S. in management from Troy State in 1983. In 1985 he received an M.S. in space operations from the Air Force Institute of Technology; his thesis, sponsored by NASA JSC, proposed a space rescue transfer vehicle using off-the-shelf hardware.

Following pilot training at Columbus AFB, Mississippi, in 1979, Halsell was assigned first to Nellis AFB, Nevada, as an F-4D commander, then, from 1981 to 1984, to Moody AFB, Georgia, as an F-4D squadron flight lead and instructor. Following a year doing graduate work at Wright-Patterson AFB, Ohio, Halsell attended the Air Force Test Pilot School at Edwards AFB, California, where he earned the Liethen/Tittle Trophy for best flying and academic record. Upon graduation he was assigned to the Flight Test Center there as an F-16 and SR-71 test pilot.

Halsell was one of the 23 astronaut candidates selected by NASA in January 1990, qualifying as a Shuttle pilot in July 1991 while assigned as a capcom in mission control. He has also served with the astronaut support team at the Kennedy Space Center.

Ham, Kenneth Todd
1964–

Navy test pilot Kenneth Ham is one of the 25 astronaut candidates selected by NASA in June 1998. In August of that year he reported to the Johnson Space Center to begin a training and evaluation course that should qualify him as a Shuttle pilot.

Ham was born December 12, 1964, in Plainfield, New Jersey. He graduated from Arthur L. Johnson Regional High School in nearby Clark in 1983, then attended the Naval Academy, where he received a B.S. in aerospace engineering in 1987. In 1996 he earned an M.S. in aeronautical engineering from the Naval Postgraduate School.

At the time of his selection by NASA, Lieutenant Commander Ham was an F/A-18 test pilot with the strike aircraft test squadron, Patuxent River, Maryland.

Hamel, Michael Anthony
1950–

Air Force engineer Michael Hamel was one of the first 13 DOD manned spaceflight engineers chosen in February 1980 to train as Shuttle payload specialist. He left the program without flying in space.

Hamel was born December 24, 1950, in Minneapolis, Minnesota, and attended the Air Force Academy in Colorado Springs, Colorado, graduating in 1972 with a B.S. in aeronautical engineering.

From 1972 to 1975 he was a project engineer at the Space and Missile Systems Organization in Los Angeles. In August 1975 he transferred to Lowry AFB, Colorado, to become an analyst for the Foreign Technology Division there; he also served as mission director for Lowry's SAMSO detachment. At the time of his selection for the MSE program in August 1979 he was stationed at Air Force Headquarters at the Pentagon.

As an MSE Hamel worked in systems project offices and also served as payload support for Shuttle Mission 51-C from 1983 to 1985. He left the MSE group in May of that

year and was assigned as a program element monitor in the Office of Space Systems, HQ USAF. In 1988 he was assigned as executive officer to Major General Thomas Moorman, director of Space Systems and Command, Control and Communications. Hamel later attended the Defense Systems Management School (1990), then was stationed at Falcon AFB, Colorado Springs.

From July 1994 to 1995 he was commander of the 750th Space Group at Onizuka Air Station, Sunnyvale, California. More recently Hamel, now a brigadier general, has served as military adviser to Vice President Al Gore.

Hammond, Lloyd Blaine, Jr.
1952–

Air Force test pilot Blaine Hammond was pilot on two Shuttle missions, most recently STS-64, the September 1994 flight of the orbiter Columbia that carried the Lidar In-Space Technology Experiment.

Previously Hammond was pilot of STS-39, a 9-day unclassified Department of Defense Shuttle mission flown in April and May 1991. STS-39 called for some of the most complex set of Shuttle maneuvers ever attempted, as the orbiter Discovery flew in tandem with the Infrared Background Signature Survey pallet satellite, which imaged rocket plumes from Discovery as part of a Strategic Defense Initiative sensor experiment.

During the mission Hammond also served as leader of the "red shift" team of three astronauts who deployed IBSS and operated a number of military scientific experiments. Hammond and mission specialist Donald McMonagle became orbital repairmen, rewiring a data recorder for one of the experiments.

Hammond was born January 16, 1952, in Savannah, Georgia, and grew up near St. Louis, Missouri, where he graduated from Kirkwood High School in 1969. He attended the Air Force Academy, where he received a B.S. in engineering mechanics in 1973. He later earned an M.S. in engineering mechanics from the Georgia Institute of Technology in 1974.

After becoming a pilot in 1975 Hammond was assigned to posts in Germany, then Arizona, where he trained pilots from foreign countries. He attended the

Empire Test Pilot School at Boscombe Down, England, in 1981, then was assigned to Edwards AFB, California, as a test pilot and instructor. He has logged over 4,500 hours in 15 American and 10 Royal Air Force aircraft.

Hammond was one of the 17 astronaut candidates selected by NASA in May 1984. In June 1985 he qualified as a Shuttle pilot. His first technical assignment was in mission support, serving as a Shuttle capcom beginning with Mission 61-A in October 1985. Between his two missions he worked on engineering projects.

In late 1994 Hammond underwent Russian language training to prepare him for a detached assignment as director—operations, Russia, but instead became NASA liaison to Air Force Space Command, Peterson AFB, Colorado Springs, Colorado. He returned to JSC as chief of the flight support branch of the astronaut office, serving as capcom from STS-73 (November 1995) through STS-78 (July 1996). He then served as chief of the safety branch before resigning from NASA and retiring from the USAF in January 1998. He is currently a test pilot with Gulfstream.

Harbaugh, Gregory Jordan
1956–

Greg Harbaugh was a mission specialist on four different Shuttle flights between 1991 and 1997. The first was STS-39, an unclassified Department of Defense Shuttle mission flown in April and May 1991. During the 8-day flight of the orbiter Discovery a crew of 7 astronauts performed a number of military scientific experiments and deploy several satellites. Harbaugh was responsible for the free-flying Infrared Background Survey Signature payload and for operation of the Shuttle remote manipulator arm during his shift.

In January 1993 he served as a mission specialist for STS-54, which deployed the sixth Tracking and Data Relay Satellite. He also made a five-hour EVA with astronaut Mario Runco to test future space station construction techniques.

As an EVA-qualified crewmember, Harbaugh served from February 1993 to January 1994 as the backup for STS-61, the first Hubble Space Telescope servicing mission.

He then flew aboard STS-71, the first Shuttle-Mir docking mission, in June 1995. His fourth mission was the second Hubble servicing mission, STS-82, in February 1997. During STS-82 Harbaugh made two EVAs, installing system upgrades and even taking part in an unrehearsed patching of the Hubble's thermal protection system.

Harbaugh was born April 15, 1956, in Cleveland, Ohio, though he considers nearby Willoughby to be his hometown. He graduated from high school in Willoughby in 1974, then attended Purdue University, receiving a B.S. in aeronautical and astronautical engineering in 1978. He later received an M.S. in physical science from the University of Houston-Clear Lake in 1986.

Harbaugh went to work at the NASA Johnson Space Center upon graduation from Purdue, specializing in Shuttle flight operations. He was involved in most STS flights between April 1981 and January 1986, notably as Shuttle Planning and Analysis Manager for flights 51-A through 51-L, acting as the senior flight controller responsible for communication between engineering support groups and the flight controllers themselves.

Following the Challenger accident in 1986 he led a team of engineers analyzing workloads and other factors at the Johnson Space Center that may or may not have contributed to the tragedy. A portion of this work was included in the final report of the Rogers Commission.

He is also a private pilot holding a commercial license and has logged over 1,000 hours of flying time.

Harbaugh was one of the 17 astronaut candidates selected by NASA in June 1987. He completed his preliminary training in August 1988, then was assigned to the Shuttle Avionics Integration Laboratory. He later qualified as a remote manipulator system operator and EVA crewman, and also helped develop telerobotic systems for space station Freedom.

In June 1997 Harbaugh was assigned as manager of the EVA Projects Office at the Johnson Space Center, where he is responsible for supervising the development of EVA techniques for International Space Station assembly missions.

Harris, Bernard Anthony
1955–

Flight surgeon and engineer Bernard Harris made two Shuttle flights. His first was as mission specialist in the crew of STS-55, which carried the second German Spacelab. This 10-day flight of the orbiter Columbia was launched in April 1993, six weeks after its crew of 7 endured a launchpad abort. Once on orbit, the crew of D-2 conducted over 90 experiments in materials science, space physics and biology, astronomy and Earth observations, in addition to testing a German-built robot arm.

In January 1995 Harris returned to space aboard the orbiter Discovery on mission STS-63. Discovery and its crew, which included Russian cosmonaut Vladimir Titov, made the first rendezvous with the Russian Mir space station. Harris and fellow STS-63 crewmember Mike Foale also made an EVA.

Harris was born June 26, 1956, in Temple, Texas. He received a B.S. in biology from the University of Houston in 1978, and his M.D. from the Texas Tech University School of Medicine in 1982. He performed his residency at the Mayo Clinic (1985).

Following completion of his residency Harris was a National Research Council Fellow at the NASA Ames Research Center, Moffet Field, California, studying musculoskeletal physiology. In 1987 he joined the NASA Johnson Space Center as a clinical scientist and flight surgeon. A year later he completed the USAF flight surgeon course at Brooks AFB, Texas.

In addition to his work with NASA, Dr. Harris was assistant professor at the Baylor College of Medicine, a clinical professor at the University of Texas School of Medicine, and an adjunct professor at the University of Texas School of Public Health. He has also been in group medical practice in Texas and California, and is the author of or coauthor of several scientific publications.

Harris was one of the 23 astronaut candidates selected by the space agency in January 1990, qualifying as a Shuttle mission specialist in July 1991. He was assigned to STS-55 in February 1992. Following his second mission, from April 1995 to April 1996, Harris served

as chief of the operations planning branch of the astronaut office.

When his height ruled him out of consideration for a Shuttle-Mir or International Space Station mission, Harris resigned from NASA in April 1996 to join SpaceHab, Inc., builders of the Shuttle's commercial cargo carrier, as vice-president for operations.

He also became associate professor in internal medicine at the University of Texas Medical Branch's Galveston Center for Aerospace Medicine and Physiology.

Hart, Terry Jonathan
1946–

T. J. Hart used the remote manipulator arm of the Shuttle Challenger to latch on to the ailing Solar Max satellite during Shuttle Mission 41-C in April 1984. Hart's "catch" allowed astronauts George Nelson and James van Hoften to make the first satellite repair in space history. Hart redeployed Solar Max in orbit following the repair. The crew of 41-C also deployed the Long Duration Exposure Facility (LDEF), the first satellite designed to be retrieved and returned to Earth at a later date. LDEF was recovered in January 1990.

Hart was born October 27, 1946, in Pittsburgh, Pennsylvania, graduating from Mt. Lebanon High School there in 1964. He attended Lehigh University, receiving a B.S. in mechanical engineering in 1968, and the Massachusetts Institute of Technology, receiving an M.S. in 1969. He later earned an M.S. in electrical engineering from Rutgers University (1978).

From 1968 to 1978 Hart worked for Bell Telephone Laboratories, designing electronic power equipment for the Bell System and receiving two patents.

He joined the Air Force Reserve in June 1969 and completed pilot training at Moody AFB, Georgia, in December 1970. For the next three years he was an F-106 interceptor pilot with the Air Defense Command at Tyndall AFB, Florida, Loring AFB, Maine, and Dover AFB, Delaware. He continues to fly with the Air National Guard and has logged over 3,000 hours of flying time.

Hart was one of 35 astronauts selected by NASA in January 1978. In August 1979 he qualified as a Shuttle mission specialist, serving on the support crews and as capcom for STS-1, STS-2, STS-3 and STS-7. He was named to the crew for Mission 41-C, then known as STS-13, in February 1983. The crew for the challenging Solar Max rescue was widely regarded as a model team, as it included the most experienced Shuttle commander (Crippen), one of the best pilots of the 1978 group (Scobee), the two best EVA specialists (Nelson and van Hoften), and Hart, who was judged to be highly skilled at using the Shuttle's remote manipulator arm.

On May 15, 1984, shortly after the conclusion of Mission 41-C, Hart resigned from NASA to return to Bell Labs in Whippany, New Jersey, becoming supervisor of the military and space applications group. More recently he has been director for satellite operations and engineering for the Skynet program for AT&T.

Hartsfield, Henry Warren, Jr.
1933–

Former Air Force test pilot Hank Hartsfield made three Shuttle flights between 1982 and 1985, two of them as mission commander.

He was pilot of the fourth and last Shuttle orbital test flight, STS-4, in June and July 1982, a mission that carried a Department of Defense payload. He commanded Mission 41-D, the first flight of the orbiter Discovery in August 1984. An attempted launch on June 26, 1984, had to be aborted on the pad, the first abort in the Shuttle program. Hartsfield also commanded the Mission 61-A, Spacelab D1 flight in October and November 1985.

Hartsfield was born November 21, 1933, in Birmingham, Alabama, and graduated from West End High School there in 1950. He attended Auburn University, where he received a B.S. in physics in 1954, and later performed graduate work in physics at Duke University and in astronautics at the Air Force Institute of Technology. He received an M.S. in engineering science from the University of Tennessee in 1971.

An ROTC student at Auburn, Hartsfield began serving with the Air Force in 1955. He became a pilot and was stationed in Bitburg, Germany, and later at the Air Force Test Pilot School at Edwards AFB, California. He was an instructor at the school when assigned in 1966 to the Manned Orbiting Laboratory program. He logged over 7,300 hours of flying time, 6,200 in jets.

When the MOL program was canceled in June 1969 Hartsfield transferred to NASA. He was a member of the astronaut support crew for Apollo 16, and for all three Skylab missions. He worked for many years on Space Shuttle development, serving as backup pilot for STS-2 and STS-3. He resigned from the Air Force in August 1977 with the rank of colonel.

In 1987 Hartsfield was named deputy director for flight crew operations at the NASA Johnson Space Center, supervising the activities of the astronaut office and the aircraft operations division at JSC. In June 1989 he was temporarily assigned to NASA Headquarters in Washington as director of Space Flight/Space Station in the Office of Space Flight, where he was responsible for representing astronaut and Shuttle concerns in the design of the Freedom space station.

In September 1990 he became deputy director of operations in the Space Station Office at the NASA Marshall Space Center. Two years later he returned to JSC, first as man-tended capability manager for the space station Freedom program, later as assistant director for independent assessment within the office safety, reliability and quality assurance.

Hartsfield currently works as a manager for the Raytheon Training Division, supporting crew training at the NASA Johnson Space Center.

Hauck, Frederick Hamilton
1941–

Navy captain Rick Hauck commanded STS-26, the Space Shuttle program's "return to flight" following the Challenger disaster, in September 1988. This 5-day mission of the orbiter Discovery deployed a Tracking and Data Relay Satellite into geosynchronous orbit and ended with a landing at Edwards AFB, California. More important, this mission helped restore confidence in America's manned space program, confidence that had been shattered by the Challenger accident two and a half years before.

In November 1984 Hauck commanded Shuttle Mission 51-A, the first salvage operation in space history, during which astronauts Joseph Allen and Dale Gardner retrieved two errant communications satellites and stowed them in the payload bay of the Shuttle Discovery for return to Earth. Hauck's crew of 5 also deployed two new satellites and operated a materials processing experiment. Their 8-day mission ended November 16, 1984, at the Kennedy Space Center.

On Hauck's first flight, in June 1983, he served as pilot of STS-7 aboard the Shuttle Challenger. STS-7 had the first crew of 5 in space history, including Sally Ride, America's first woman in space.

Hauck was born April 11, 1941, in Long Beach, California, and grew up in Winchester, Massachusetts, and Washington, D.C., where his father was a Navy officer. He graduated from St. Albans School in Washington, D.C., in 1958, then attended Tufts University, receiving a B.S. in physics in 1962. He later earned an M.S. in nuclear engineering from the Massachusetts Institute of Technology (1966).

Hauck was a Navy ROTC student at Tufts, and was commissioned after graduation, serving for twenty months aboard the destroyer *U.S.S. Warrington* as a communications officer. From 1964 to 1966 he attended the Naval Postgraduate School, the Defense Language Institute, and M.I.T., then entered flight school. He received his wings in 1968 and served aboard the carrier *U.S.S. Coral Sea* in Southeast Asia, flying 114 combat and support missions in the A-6.

Returning to the United States in 1970, Hauck became an instructor, then attended the Naval Test Pilot School at Patuxent River, Maryland. He graduated in 1971 and spent three years at Pax River testing, among other things, automatic carrier landing systems for many Navy jets. From 1974 until his selection by NASA he was an operations officer and executive officer for several naval squadrons.

As a pilot Hauck logged over 5,500 hours of flying time.

He was one of the 35 astronauts chosen by NASA in January 1978, and in August 1979 qualified as a Shuttle pilot. He served on the support crew and as capcom for STS-1 and STS-2, and in April 1982 became the first pilot of the 1978 class to be assigned to a flight crew.

At the time of the Challenger accident in January 1986 Hauck was assigned as commander of Mission 61-F, the first of a pair of May 1986 Shuttle missions intended to carry the powerful Centaur upper stage. That mission was canceled, and in August 1986 Hauck was appointed associate administrator for external relations at NASA Headquarters in Washington, D.C. He returned to Houston in February 1987 when named commander of STS-26.

Hauck resigned from NASA in April 1989 to become director of Navy Space Systems Division on the staff of the Chief of Naval Operations at the Pentagon. In this job he supervised the operation of Navy navigation and surveillance satellites.

He retired from the Navy in November 1990 to become president of International Technology Underwriters, Bethesda, Maryland. In 1993 he added the title of chief executive officer.

Hauck also consults with NASA, serving most recently as chairman of a National Research Council study on the threat posed to the International Space Station by orbiting debris.

Hawley, Steven Alan
1951–

Astronomer Steve Hawley was a mission specialist aboard four Shuttle flights, including STS-31. This April 1990 flight of the orbiter Discovery deployed the Hubble Space Telescope into a record 381-mile high orbit. Hawley's responsibility was operation of the Shuttle's remote manipulator arm. The 5-day mission was a success, but technical flaws prevented the Hubble from reaching its full capability until augmented by better optics on STS-61 in late 1993.

Hawley revisited the Hubble with the crew of STS-82 in February 1997. This flight of the orbiter Discovery carried a crew of 7, including four EVA crewmembers, on the second Hubble servicing and repair mission. Hawley operated the remote manipulator system, capturing the billion-dollar observatory he had helped deploy seven years earlier.

During Hawley's first two Shuttle flights he had set an unwanted record for enduring launch delays. During the first attempt to launch Mission 41-D on June 26, 1984, the orbiter Discovery's main engines shut down three seconds after ignition. Flight engineer Hawley reportedly quipped to veteran commander Henry Hartsfield, "Gee, I thought we'd be higher than this at MECO [main engine cutoff]." Discovery finally lifted off on August 30 with a crew of 6, including the first industrial payload specialist, Charles Walker of McDonnell-Douglas. During the 7-day flight the crew deployed three communications satellites and tested an experimental solar power wing. They also used the Shuttle's remote manipulator arm to chip ice off the side of the Discovery, earning themselves the title "icebusters."

The Mission 61-C launch of the orbiter Columbia was delayed six times by weather and technical problems. For the seventh attempt on January 12, 1986, Hawley wore a Groucho Marx mask to the launchpad, hoping, he said, to fool Columbia into thinking a different crew was coming aboard. The trick worked; Columbia finally got off the ground, and the astronauts were able to deploy an RCA communications satellite. A free-flying Spartan satellite, designed to observe Halley's Comet, failed to work, however.

Hawley is currently assigned to make his fifth flight on STS-93. This April 1999 Shuttle mission will deploy the Advanced X-ray Astrophysics Facility, another of NASA's "great telescopes," into Earth orbit.

Hawley was born December 12, 1951, in Ottawa, Kansas, and grew up in Salina, where his father was a minister. He graduated from Salina (Central) High School in 1969, then attended the University of Kansas, where he received a B.S. in physics and astronomy, with the highest distinction (1973). He received a Ph.D. in astronomy and astrophysics from the University of California at Santa Cruz in 1977.

While completing his schooling Hawley worked summers as a research assistant at the Naval Observatory in Washington, D.C. (1972), and the National Radio Observatory in Green Bank, Virginia (1973–4). When selected by NASA Hawley was a research associate at the Cerro Tololo Inter-American Observatory in La Serena, Chile.

Hawley is the author of several scientific papers published in astronomical journals.

He was one of the 35 astronauts chosen by NASA in January 1978. In August 1979 he qualified as a Shuttle mission specialist while serving as a simulator pilot for

flight software in the Shuttle Avionics Integration Laboratory. He was also support crewmember for STS-2, STS-3 and STS-4.

He was assigned to the Hubble Space Telescope mission in September 1985 while concurrently training for Mission 61-C and also working as technical assistant to George Abbey, the director of flight crew operations. The Hubble assignment was made again in March 1988 while Hawley was also serving as deputy chief of the astronaut office.

In June 1990 Hawley left the astronaut office to become associate director of the NASA Ames Research Center in Palo Alto, California. He returned to JSC in 1992 as deputy director for flight crew operations, taking a year's leave from that job in February 1996 to resume active astronaut training in the STS-82 crew.

Helms, Susan Jane
1958–

Air Force test engineer Susan Helms has flown three Shuttle missions, beginning with STS-54, launched in January 1993. This 6-day flight of the orbiter Endeavour deployed the fifth NASA Tracking and Data Relay Satellite.

Helms then served as flight engineer and RMS operator for STS-64 in September 1994. This 10-day flight of the orbiter Discovery tested Lidar-In-Space technology, and also deployed and retrieved the Spartan 201 satellite.

Most recently Helms was payload commander for STS-78. This flight of the orbiter Columbia carried the Life and Microgravity Spacelab (LMS) and an international crew of 7. The STS-78 mission lasted 17 days, a Shuttle record, and conducted 41 different scientific experiments.

In November 1997 Helms was named a member of the second incremental International Space Station crew. Scheduled to launch to the I.S.S. aboard the STS-99 in the summer of 2000, Helms, fellow astronaut James Voss and Russian cosmonaut Yuri Usachev are to spend four months aboard the station.

Helms was born February 26, 1958, in Charlotte, North Carolina, though she considers Portland, Oregon, to be her hometown. She received a B.S. in aeronautical engineering from the Air Force Academy in 1980, and an M.S. in aeronautics/astronautics from Stanford University in 1985.

Commissioned upon graduation from the Air Force Academy, Helms was assigned to Eglin AFB, Florida, as an F-16 and F-15 weapons engineer with the Armaments Laboratory. Following a year of graduate work at Stanford, she became an assistant professor of aeronautics at the Air Force Academy. Two years later, in 1987, she attended the Air Force Test Pilot School at Edwards AFB, California, completing the flight test engineer course. At the time of her selection by NASA she was USAF Exchange Officer at Canada's Engineering Test Establishment at CFB Cold Lake, Alberta, Canada, managing a CF-18 flight control system simulation.

She has flown in 30 different types of U.S. and Canadian aircraft.

Helms was selected by NASA in January 1990 and in July 1991 qualified as a Shuttle mission specialist. Her first technical assignment was in the mission development branch of the astronaut office, on RMS and robotics. From June 1993 to February 1994 she was a capcom in mission control. In 1996 and 1997 she was head of the payloads/habitation branch of the astronaut office.

Helms also plays keyboards in the astronaut band, Max Q.

Henize, Karl Gordon
1926–1993

Astronomer Karl Henize was a mission specialist aboard Shuttle Mission 51-F in July 1985. At the time of launch he was 58 years, 8 months old—the oldest person to fly in space. (His record was broken five years later by Vance Brand.)

During 51-F, the long-delayed Spacelab 2 mission, Henize and six other astronauts operated 13 different scientific experiments, most of them in the field of astronomy, Henize's own specialty. Though plagued by a number of problems, including a launchpad abort, the Spacelab 2 got results from twelve of the experiments. NASA doctors reported no unusual medical problems for Henize during the 7-day mission, confirming that calendar age had no relevance to travelers on the Shuttle.

Henize was born October 17, 1926, in Cincinnati, Ohio, graduating from high school in nearby Mariemont. He attended the University of Virginia, receiving a B.A. in mathematics (1947) and an M.A. in astronomy (1948). He earned his Ph.D. in astronomy in 1954 from the University of Michigan.

His career as a professional astronomer began in 1948, when he worked as an observer for the University of Michigan at the Lamong-Hussey Observatory in Bleomfontein, Union of South Africa. He returned to the United States in 1951, and in 1954 became a Carnegie postdoctoral fellow at Mount Wilson Observatory in Pasadena, California. Two years later he joined the Smithsonian Astrophysical Observatory and began his long involvement with space exploration, establishing a global network of twelve stations for the photographic tracking of artificial Earth satellites.

In 1959 Henize joined the faculty of Northwestern University, where he taught and conducted research on stars and planetary nebulae. He was a guest observer at Mt. Stromlo Observatory in Canberra, Australia, in 1961 and 1962, and developed an ultraviolet stellar spectra experiment that was flown on three manned Gemini flights.

Henize was one of the 11 scientist-astronauts selected by NASA in August 1967. He completed initial academic training, then, at the age of 41, underwent a 53-week jet pilot training program at Vance Air Force Base, Oklahoma. Eventually Henize would log over 2,300 hours of flying time in jets.

By 1968 it was apparent to the 1967 class of astronauts that their chances of making spaceflights in the foreseeable future were slim. Five of them left the program by 1972, and during the long hiatus between the end of Apollo in 1975 and the start of Shuttle missions in 1981, several others took leaves of absence. Henize remained at the Johnson Space Center, however, serving on the astronaut support crew and as capcom for the Apollo 15 lunar landing, and for all three Skylab missions. Another of his scentific experiments was flown on Skylab.

Henize later headed groups developing ultraviolet telescopes for proposed Spacelab missions and, in 1977, served as a mission specialist for the ASSESS II Spacelab simulation. In February 1983 he was officially assigned to the Spacelab 2 crew.

In April 1986 he left the astronaut group to become a senior scientist in the Space Sciences branch at the NASA Johnson Space Center. He was the author or coauthor of over 70 scientific papers and remained active in the International Astronomical Union.

Henize took up mountaineering at the age of 65, climbing Mount Rainier in Washington in 1991. It was during an ascent of Mount Everest in October 1993 that he was stricken with respiratory failure. He died October 5 at a base camp in China, and was buried there.

Hennen, Thomas John

1952–

Warrant Officer Third Class Tom Hennen is the Army intelligence officer who spent seven days in aboard the orbiter Atlantis, the STS-44 mission flown in November 1991.

Hennen was the payload specialist for a military experiment called Terra Scout, designed to determine how effective a human observer would be in battlefield reconnaissance. Using a series of cameras and other optical systems, Hennen and mission specialist Mario Runco took aim at a series of 30 planned targets around the world. Some of the experiments had to be abandoned when STS-44 was called back to Earth three days early, and the Terra Scout results were judged to be mixed.

Hennen was born August 17, 1952, in Albany, Georgia, but grew up all over the world, including the Philippines and Europe. (His father was an Air Force sergeant.) He graduated from Groveport-Madison High School in Groveport, Ohio, in 1970, then spent two years at Urbana College, Urbana, Ohio.

He joined the Army in 1973 and was first assigned to the 163rd Military Intelligence Battalion at Fort Hood, Texas, where he was involved in testing of the Army's Remotely Piloted Vehicle and of new camouflage systems. From 1976 to 1978 he was assigned to the 203rd Military Intelligence Detachment, providing imagery and intelligence support to the 1st Cavalry Division, the 6th Armored Cavalry Regiment, and Headquarters III Corps.

He then spent three years with Detachment A, Combat Intelligence Company, 2nd Military Intelligence Battalion, as noncommissioned officer in charge of analysis for Hungary, Czechoslovakia, Yugoslavia, Albania and Austria.

He was appointed a warrant officer in April 1981.

From 1981 to 1986 Hennen was stationed at Fort Huachuca, Arizona, the home of military intelligence, serving as project officer for imagery intelligence. More recently he was selected by the commanding general of the U.S. Army Intelligence Center to represent him in the Army Space Program Office at the Pentagon. Following his selection as a Terra Scout payload specialist in September 1988, Hennen divided his time between Ft. Huachuca and the Army's space office in Houston.

Chief Hennen retired from the Army in 1995 to found the Atlantis Foundation, devoted to children with special needs.

Henricks, Terence Thomas

1952–

Air Force colonel Tom Henricks made four Shuttle flights between 1991 and 1996, two as pilot and two as commander, including the longest Shuttle mission flown so far.

His first flight was a pilot of STS-44, a Department of Defense Shuttle mission that deployed a Defense Support Program (DSP) early warning satellite into geosynchronous orbit. Crew members also engaged in military observations from orbit. The mission had to be cut short from 10 to 7 days because of the failure of a navigation unit aboard the orbiter Atlantis.

Henricks' second mission was the 10-day Spacelab D-2, which suffered through a launchpad abort prior to its launch on April 16, 1993. The seven-member crew conducted 89 different experiments in life sciences, materials processing, Earth mapping, astronomy, and robotics.

His first command was STS-70, launched in July 1995 following a delay caused by woodpecker attacks on the Shuttle's external tank. STS-70 deployed the sixth Tracking and Data Relay Satellite.

Henricks also commanded STS-78, which carried the Life and Microgravity Spacelab (LMS). This 17-day flight of the orbiter Columbia carried a crew of 7, including payload specialists from France and Canada, and conducted 41 different experiments. It was considered to be a fore-runner of future space station missions.

Henricks was born July 5, 1952, in Bryan, Ohio, and grew up in Woodville. He graduated from Woodmore High School in Elmore, Ohio, in 1970, then attended the Air Force Academy, where he received a B.S. in civil engineering in 1974. He later earned an M.S. in public administration from Golden Gate University in 1982.

At the Air Force Academy Henricks became a master parachutist, making over 740 jumps as a member of the team which won a national championship. He earned his wings at Craig AFB, Alabama, in 1975 and served at bases in England, Iceland and Nevada as an F-4 pilot. In 1983 he attended the Air Force Test Pilot School at Edwards AFB, California. He was an F-16C test pilot there when selected by NASA.

Henricks logged over 5,000 hours of flying time in 30 different types of aircraft. He also holds an F.A.A. commercial pilot rating.

Henricks was one of the 13 astronaut candidates selected by NASA in June 1985. In July 1986 he qualified as a Shuttle pilot while working on the reevaluation of Shuttle landing sites around the world following the Challenger accident. Beginning in August 1987 he was assistant manager for engineering integration in the Shuttle program office. He was lead astronaut in the Shuttle Avionics Integration Laboratory (SAIL) when assigned to STS-44 in May 1990. He has also served with the vehicle test and checkout team and as chief of the astronaut office operations development branch.

Henricks resigned from NASA and retired from the Air Force in October 1997 to join the Timken Company, Canton, Ohio.

Herres, Robert Tralles
1932–

Air Force test pilot Robert Herres was one of the 4 pilots chosen for the Manned Orbiting Laboratory in June 1967. He trained for orbital flights for two years until MOL was canceled in May 1969. Like fellow MOL pilot James Abrahamson, Herres later became a high-ranking official in military space programs.

He was the first commander of the USAF Space Command, based at Peterson AFB, Colorado, and later served as the first vice chairman of the Joint Chiefs of Staff—the number two military officer in the United States.

Herres was born December 1, 1932, in Denver, Colorado. He attended the Naval Academy, graduating in 1954 with a bachelor of science degree. He later earned an M.S. in electrical engineering from the Air Force Institute of Technology (1960) and an M.S. in public administration from George Washington University (1965).

After graduation from Annapolis Herres elected to serve in the Air Force. He underwent flight training at Webb AFB, Texas, and became an interceptor pilot. From 1955 to 1958 he was a pilot and electronics maintenance officer with the 93rd Fighter Interceptor Squadron at Kirtland AFB, Albuquerque, New Mexico.

After a year doing graduate work in at the Air Force Institute of Technology (1959–60) Herres became an intelligence officer with the U.S. European Command Electronic Intelligence Center, Lindsey Air Base, West Germany.

He returned to the United States in 1964 to attend the Air Command and Staff School at Maxwell AFB, Alabama. He was an instructor at the Air War College at Maxwell when selected for test pilot school in 1966.

Following the cancellation of the Manned Orbiting Laboratory in 1969, Herres declined the chance to transfer to NASA as an astronaut, and returned to Edwards AFB as deputy chief of staff for plans and requirements. In 1970 he attended the Industrial College of the Armed Forces at Fort McNair, Washington, D.C.

Herres served as vice commander of the 449th Bombardment Wing at Kincheloe AFB, Michigan, from 1971 to 1973, including a six-month combat tour in Thailand. His later assignments include serving as director of command control for the Strategic Air Command (1974–75); deputy commander for security assistance programs, Electronic Security Command (1975–77); assistant Air Force chief of staff for communications and computer resources (1977–69); and commander of the Air Force Communications Command (1979–81).

In June 1981 Herres assumed command of the 8th Air Force, headquartered at Barksdale AFB, Louisiana. He then served as director of command, control and communications systems for the Joint Chiefs of Staff (1982–84).

He was also commander of the North American Aerospace Defense Command (NORAD) from 1984 to 1986.

Appointed vice chairman of the Joint Chiefs of Staff on February 7, 1987, Herres retired with the rank of general on February 1, 1990. He is currently chairman of USAA Capital Corporation, San Antonio, Texas.

Herrington, John Bennett
1958–

Navy test pilot John Herrington is one of the 35 astronaut candidates selected by NASA on May 1, 1996. In August of that year he reported to the Johnson Space Center to begin a yearlong training and evaluation course that should qualify him as a Shuttle mission specialist and International Space Station crewmember.

Herrington was born September 14, 1958, in Wetumka, Oklahoma, and grew up in Colorado Springs, Colorado, in Riverton, Wyoming, and in Plano, Texas, where he graduated from high school in 1976. He attended the University of Colorado, Colorado Springs, receiving a B.S. in applied mathematics in 1983, and later received an M.S. in aeronautical engineering from the Naval Postgraduate School (1995).

Commissioned as a naval aviation officer candidate in March 1984, Herrington became a naval aviator in March 1985. His was trained as a P-3C Orion pilot with Patrol Squadron 31 (VP-31) at Moffet Field NAS, California, then made deployments to Adak, Alaska, and to Cibi Point, Republic of the Philippines.

He returned to VP-31 in 1988 as a fleet replacement instructor pilot for the P-3C, and in January 1990 was selected for the Naval Test Pilot School at Patuxent River, Maryland. Following graduating in December 1990 he served as a project test pilot for the Joint Primary Aircraft Training System with the Force Warfare Aircraft Test Directorate at Pax River. He did additional test flying on different variants of the P-3 as well as the T-34C and the DeHavilland Dash-7 aircraft before entering graduate school in 1994.

Lieutenant Commander Herrington has logged over 2,300 hours of flying time in 30 different types of aircraft. At the time of his selection by NASA Herrington was a special projects officer with the Bureau of Naval Personnel Sea Duty Component, Arlington, Virginia.

Hieb, Richard James
1955–

Rick Hieb took part in the first 3-man space walk in history, the unplanned but successful rescue of the Intelsat VI satellite during STS-49 in May 1992.

Hieb and fellow spacewalker Pierre Thuot had tried and failed to capture Intelsat during two prior EVAs when ground controllers approved the astronauts' own plan to grab the spinning two-ton satellite. Hieb, Thuot, and Tom Akers arranged themselves in the orbiter Endeavour's payload bay as pilots Dan Brandenstein and Kevin Chilton brought the Shuttle and satellite together. Then the spacewalkers literally reached out and grabbed Intelsat, holding it still for over an hour while Thuot attached a special capture bar. Intelsat was later deployed in its proper orbit.

Hieb previously served as a mission specialist aboard STS-39, a Department of Defense Shuttle flight conducted in April and May 1991. During the 9-day STS-39 mission the free-flying Infrared Background Signature Survey satellite was deployed and a number of military-scientific experiments were performed.

In July 1994 Hieb was payload commander for STS-65, the second International Microgravity Spacelab mission. This 15-day flight of the orbiter Columbia carried a crew of 7 that conducted over 80 experiments for 200 scientists around the world in the fields of space manufacturing and life sciences.

Hieb was born September 21, 1955, in Jamestown, North Dakota, and graduated from high school there in 1973. He attended Northwest Nazarene College in Nampa, Idaho, earning a B.A. in math and physics in 1977, and the University of Colorado, earning an M.S. in aerospace engineering in 1979.

In 1979 Hieb joined NASA at the Johnson Space Center, working as a member of the mission control team for the first Shuttle flight, STS-1. He was also involved in satellite deployments on STS-5 and STS-6, and on rendezvous procedures for STS-7, 41-B, 41-C, 51-A, and other flights.

He was one of the 13 astronauts selected by NASA in June 1985 and in July 1986 qualified as a Shuttle mission specialist. His technical assignments have included a tour in the Shuttle Avionics Integration Lab (SAIL), serving with the launch support team at the Kennedy Space Center, and monitoring the development of the IBSS payload for STS-39.

Hieb resigned from NASA and the astronaut office on March 31, 1995, to join AlliedSignal Technical Services Corporation, Greenbelt, Maryland, as a senior engineering adviser in their civilian space business unit.

Higbee, Terry Alan
1949–

Air Force Captain Terry Higbee was a member of the first group of Department of Defense manned spaceflight engineers from 1980 to 1985. He left the group without having been assigned as a Shuttle payload specialist.

Higbee was born December 3, 1949, in Cedar City, Utah, and attended Utah State University in Logan, where he received a B.S. in electrical engineering in 1972. He later earned an M.S. (1974) and Ph.D. (1980) from Stanford University in the same field.

Higbee entered the Air Force through ROTC in June 1972 and was commissioned as a second lieutenant, though his graduate studies delayed his entry onto active duty until January 1977. During that time he was employed at Lockheed Missiles and Space Company in Sunnyvale, California, as a graduate student engineer.

Assigned to Los Angeles Air Force Station in 1977, Higbee worked in Special Projects for three years until commencing MSE training in February 1980. His eligibility for assignment as a Shuttle payload specialist was always questionable: a medical examination following his selection as an MSE turned up a minor, but disqualifying ailment. Nevertheless, he remained an active member of the program until reassignment to the Pentagon in March 1985, where he worked as the chief of the prediction branch for the Research Projects Office.

He resigned from the Air Force in February 1987 to join Ball Aerospace Systems in Boulder, Colorado, where he is currently staff consultant for program development, working on the development of small military and civilian satellites.

Higginbotham, Joan Elizabeth
1964–

NASA engineer and competition bodybuilder Joan Higginbotham is one of the 35 astronaut candidates selected by the space agency on May 1, 1996. In August of that year she reported to the Johnson Space Center to begin a training and evaluation course that should qualify her as a Shuttle mission specialist and an International Space Station crewmember. She is currently assigned to the computer support branch of the astronaut office, working in SAIL.

Higginbotham was born August 3, 1964, in Chicago, Illinois, where she graduated from Whitney M. Young Magnet High School in 1982. She attended Southern Illinois University, where she received a B.S. in electrical engineering in 1987. She has also earned master's degrees in management (1992) and space systems (1996) from the Florida Institute of Technology.

In 1987 Higginbotham joined NASA as a payload electrical engineer in the electrical and telecommunications systems division of the Kennedy Space Center. Within six months she became the lead engineer for orbiter experiments on the Shuttle Columbia. Later positions included work on payload bay reconfiguration for all orbiters, and serving as executive staff assistant to the director of Shuttle operations and management analyzing and improving the flow of orbiter ground processing between flights. She spent two years as an orbiter project engineer for Atlantis (OV-104), supporting launches from the firing room at KSC.

At the time of her selection as an ASCAN Higginbotham was lead orbiter project engineer for Columbia (OV-102).

Hilliard, Patricia Consolatrix
1963–

NASA physician Patricia Hilliard is one of the 25 astronaut candidates selected in June 1998. In August of that year she began a training and evaluation course that should qualify her as a Shuttle mission specialist and International Space Station crewmember.

Hilliard was born March 12, 1963, in Indiana, Pennsylvania, graduating from Homer-Center High School in Homer City in 1980. She attended the University of Pennsylvania at Indiana, receiving a B.S. in biology in 1985, and earned her M.D. from the Medical College of Pennsylvania in 1989.

At the time of her selection as an ASCAN, Hilliard was a medical officer at the NASA Johnson Space Center.

Hilmers, David Carl
1950–

Marine flight officer Dave Hilmers was a mission specialist on four Shuttle crews, including STS-26, the first Shuttle mission following the Challenger disaster. That September 1988 mission saw the deployment of a Tracking and Data Relay satellite into geosynchronous orbit.

Hilmers also flew on two Department of Defense missions, including Mission 51-J in October 1985. During this flight, the maiden voyage of the orbiter Atlantis, Hilmers was part of a 5-man crew that deployed two DSCS III military communications satellites into geosynchronous orbit.

In February and March 1990 he was aboard the Atlantis again for STS-36. A CIA imaging reconnaissance satellite known as Crystal was deployed into low Earth orbit on that mission.

His fourth mission was STS-42, the flight of the International Microgravity Spacelab, launched in January 1992. (He replaced astronaut Sonny Carter, who was killed in a plane crash in April 1991.) This 8-day flight of the orbiter Discovery was dedicated to studies in space manufacturing and medicine.

Hilmers was born January 28, 1950, in Clinton, Iowa, and grew up in DeWitt, Iowa. He graduated from Central Community High in DeWitt in 1968, then attended Cornell College, where he received a B.S. in mathematics in 1972, graduating summa cum laude. He later studied at the Naval Postgraduate School, where he received an M.S. in

electrical engineering (with distinction) and the degree of electrical engineer in 1978.

Hilmers joined the Marine Corps in 1972 and after completing basic training and flight school, was assigned to the Marine Corps Air Station at Cherry Point, South Carolina, then to the 6th Fleet in the Mediterranean, as an A-6 crewman. After graduating first in his class from the Postgraduate School he was stationed in Iwakuni, Japan, where he also taught mathematics for the University of Maryland's overseas branch. Hilmers has coauthored several technical papers, and has logged over 1,000 hours flight time in 15 different types of aircraft.

Hilmers was selected as an astronaut candidate by NASA in May 1980 and qualified as a Shuttle mission specialist in August 1981. He worked on Shuttle upper stages such as the Centaur, the Payload Assist Module, and the Interial Upper Stage, and as astronaut office coordinator for Department of Defense payloads. He served as capcom for Shuttle missions between October 1984 and April 1985, and was also assigned to Shuttle Mission 61-F, scheduled for launch in the summer of 1986 but canceled following the Shuttle Challenger disaster.

Hilmers resigned from NASA and retired from the Marine Corps in the summer of 1992. He is a medical student at Baylor University.

Hire, Kathryn Patricia
1959–

Navy flight officer and space engineer Kay Hire was assigned to the crew of STS-90. The spring 1998 mission of the orbiter Columbia carried the Neurolab Spacelab and a crew of 7 on a 2-week mission devoted to studies in space medicine. Neurolab was the last Spacelab mission.

Hire was born August 26, 1959, in Mobile, Alabama, where she graduated from Murphy High School in 1977. She attended the U.S. Naval Academy, where she received a B.S. in engineering management in 1981. She later received an M.S. in space technology from the Florida Insitute of Technology (1991).

Following graduation from Annapolis Hire qualified as a naval flight officer in October 1982. She was asigned to

Oceanographic Development Squadron 8 at Patuxent River, Maryland, where she took part in airborne oceanographic missions as a project coordinator, mission commander and detachment officer-in-charge a specially configured P-3 aircraft.

She transferred to Mather AFB, California, where she served as a navigation instructor and course manager for the Naval Air Training Unit there. Hire left active duty in January 1989, joining the Naval Air Reserve at Jacksonville, Florida. She became the first American woman assigned to a combat aircrew when she reported to Patrol Squadron 62 on May 13, 1993, as a patrol plane navigator and communicator for deployments to Iceland, Puerto Rico and Panama. Hire is currently a lieutenant commander in the Naval Reserve attached to the *U.S.S. Kitty Hawk*.

Hire joined the EG&G Company at the NASA Kennedy Space Center in May 1989 as an orbiter processing engineer, later moving to the Lockheed Space Operations Company as a Space Shuttle Test Project Engineer. In this job she worked on Space Shuttle maintenance, checkout of Extravehicular Mobility Suits and the Russian-built Orbiter Docking System, and in 1994 became supervisor for orbit mechanisms and swing arms.

Hire was one of the 19 astronaut candidates selected by NASA on December 8, 1994. In May 1996 she qualified as a Shuttle mission specialist, then worked in the astronaut office flight support branch as a Shuttle capcom prior to her assignment to STS-90.

Hobaugh, Charles Owen
1961–

Marine test pilot Charles Hobaugh is one of the 35 astronaut candidates selected by NASA on May 1, 1996. In August of that year he reported to the Johnson Space Center to begin a yearlong training and evaluation course that should qualify him as a Shuttle pilot.

Hobaugh was born November 5, 1961, in Bar Harbor, Maine. He graduated from high school in North Ridgeville, Ohio, in 1980, then entered the Naval Academy at Annapolis, where he received a B.S. in aerospace engineering (1984).

Commissioned in the Marine Corps upon graduation from Annapolis, Hobaugh completed basic training in December 1984. He spent the next six months in a temporary assignment at the Naval Air Systems Command, then reported to flight school, where he was designated a naval aviator in February 1987.

Hobaugh qualified as an AV-8B Harrier pilot with Marine V/STOL Attack Squadron 203, then served with Marine Attack Squadron 331, making a deployment to Iwakuni, Japan, and flying combat missions during Operation Desert Shield and Desert Storm.

He entered the Naval Test Pilot School at Patuxent River, Maryland, in June 1991, and following graduation a year later was assigned as AV-8 project officer and ASTOVL/JAST/JSF program officer with the test center's strike aircraft test directorate.

Major Hobaugh has logged over 3,000 hours of flying time in over 40 different aircraft, including 200 vertical/short takeoff shipboard landings.

At the time of his selection by NASA Hobaugh was an instructor at the Naval Test Pilot School.

Hoernig, Otto William, Jr.
1938–

Satellite engineer Otto Hoernig had just been assigned as a payload specialist for Shuttle Mission 71-C, scheduled for launch in February 1987, when the Challenger accident occurred, grounding the Shuttle fleet for two and a half years.

Hoernig was to have overseen the deployment of the American Satellite Corporation's ASC-2 communications satellite during that mission. When Shuttle launches resumed, all nonscientific payload specialist assignments had been canceled, and ASC-2 satellite was shifted to the Delta II expendable launch vehicle.

Hoernig was born July 21, 1938, in Kansas City, Missouri. He attended Texas A&M University, graduating with a B.S. in mechanical engineering in 1960. He later earned an M.S. in aerospace systems management from the University of Southern California.

He worked for many years as an independent consultant for satellite communications systems in government and industry prior to joining ASC in June 1984. Since February 1987 he has been vice-president for business development for Contel ASC.

Hoffman, Jeffrey Alan

1944–

Astronomer Jeff Hoffman was a member of five different Shuttle crews between 1985 and 1996, including the acclaimed first Hubble Servicing Mission (STS-61). On that mission Hoffman and fellow repair crewmember Story Musgrave made three different EVAs totalling almost 22 hours installing upgraded optics that allowed the Hubble, crippled since its original deployment in 1990, finally to become a unique astronomical tool.

In 1992 and 1996 he made flights with the Tethered Satellite System, STS-46 (August 1992) and STS-75 (January 1996).

He was also a member of the Spacelab ASTRO crew that made 400 observations of 135 deep space targets during the 9-day STS-35 mission in December 1990. One of four astronomers in the 7-man crew, Hoffman operated four telescopes and other instruments during a troubled mission fraught with launch delays (STS-35 had originally been intended for launch in May 1990), computer failures and plumbing problems. The mission even had to be shortened by a day because of bad weather at the Edwards AFB landing site.

Nevertheless, as the first Spacelab mission flown by NASA in five years, STS-35 proved again that manned missions could produce useful scientific results.

As a bonus, Hoffman and payload specialist Sam Durrance conducted a science class from space for 41 middle school students in Huntsville, Alabama, and Greenbelt, Maryland. The TV class was a tribute to teacher-astronaut Christa McAuliffe, who was killed in the Challenger disaster six weeks prior to ASTRO 1's original launch date of March 1986. Hoffman has the distinction of being the first person to wear a necktie in space.

On his earlier flight, Mission 51-D in April 1985, Hoffman took part in the first unscheduled and unrehearsed space walk in the American space program. Hoffman and fellow astronaut David Griggs donned space suits and left the cabin of the orbiter Discovery in order to attach a makeshift "flyswatter" to the end of the remote manipulator arm. The flyswatter was later used in an unsuccessful attempt to activate the ailing Syncom IV-3 satellite, which had earlier been deployed from Discovery.

Hoffman was born November 2, 1944, in Brooklyn, New York, and grew up in Scarsdale, where he graduated from high school in 1962. He attended Amherst College, where he received a B.S. in astronomy (graduating summa cum laude) in 1966. He received his Ph.D. in astrophysics from Harvard University in 1971. He has since received an M.S. in materials science from Rice University (1988).

As a postdoctoral fellow at Leicester University in England from 1972-75, Hoffman worked on scientific packages for three rocket payloads, all of them relating to X-ray astronomy, his field of study. He was also project scientist for an X-ray experiment flown on the European Space Agency's Exosat satellite.

Returning to the United States in 1975, he joined the Center for Space Research at the Massachusetts Institute of Technology as project scientist for X-ray and gamma ray experiments for the first High Energy Astronomical Observatory (HEAO-1) satellite launched in August 1977. He was at MIT when chosen by NASA.

Hoffman was one of 35 astronauts selected by NASA in January 1978. In August 1979 he qualified as a Shuttle mission specialist, then worked for the next two years on Shuttle guidance, navigation and control systems at the Flight Simulation Laboratory in Downey, California. He later served as support crewman for STS-5 and capcom for STS-8.

He was assigned as a mission specialist for Spacelab Astro's original flight, designed to observe Halley's Comet. When that mission was canceled following the Challenger accident Hoffman worked on development of a pressure suit for the Freedom space station, and on the Tethered Satellite System, until being reassigned to ASTRO 1 in March 1988.

Hoffman is the author or coauthor of more than 20 papers on X-ray astronomy.

Hoffman retired from the astronaut office in July 1997 to become NASA's representative in Europe, based in Paris, France.

Holder, Livingston Lionel, Jr.

1956–

Air Force engineer and launch controller Livingston Holder was a member of the second group of Department of Defense manned spaceflight engineers selected in January 1983. He left the MSE program and the Air Force in 1988 without making a spaceflight.

Holder, the only African American in the MSE group, was born September 29, 1956, in Detroit, Michigan, and graduated from the U.S. Air Force Academy with a bachelor of science in astronautical engineering in 1978. He later earned an M.S. in systems management (1981).

From 1978 to 1982 Holder served at Vandenberg Air Force Base, California, as an engineer and launch controller for the Titan 3 rocket. After joining the MSE program he worked on classified satellite programs in the Special Projects office. He resigned from the Air Force in 1988 to join the Boeing company's space station effort in Huntsville, Alabama, and in 1995 became manager for reusable launch vehicles for Boeing's entry in the X-33 design competition.

Holmquest, Donald Lee

1939–

Physician Don Holmquest was one of 11 scientist-astronauts selected by NASA in August 1967. These astronauts arrived in Houston just as a series of congressional budget cuts wiped out most of the planned Apollo Applications (Skylab) missions for which they were to train. They dubbed themselves the "XS-11" ("excess eleven"). Only seven of them ever flew in space, and then after no less than fifteen years as astronauts.

Holmquest was born April 7, 1939, in Dallas, Texas, where he graduated from W. H. Anderson High School. He attended Southern Methodist University, receiving a B.S. in electrical engineering in 1962. In 1967 he received an M.D. and in 1968 a Ph.D. in physiology, both from the Baylor College of Medicine. He has since earned a J.D. (law) degree from the University of Houston (1980).

Holmquest worked as a research associate at the Massachusetts Institute of Technology from 1962 to 1966 while continuing his studies. At the time of his selection by NASA in 1967 he was serving an internship at Methodist Hospital in Houston.

As an astronaut he underwent Air Force flight training at Williams AFB, Arizona, eventually logging 750 hours as a jet pilot. He was then assigned to the Skylab program, where he worked on medical experiments and habitability systems.

Holmquest took a leave from NASA in May 1971 to become associate professor of radiology and physiology at Baylor. He also underwent training in nuclear medicine. Following a second year of leave at the Eisenhower Medical Center in California, Holmquest resigned from NASA in September 1973 to become associate dean for academic affairs of the College of Medicine at Texas A&M University.

Three years later he left Texas A&M to become director of nuclear medicine at the Navasota, Texas, Medical Center. He was also in practice at Medical Arts Hospital in Houston and studying for a law degree.

In one of the more unusual career changes made by former astronauts, Holmquest joined the Houston law firm of Wood, Lucksinger and Epstein. He is currently partner in his own firm.

Holt, Ray Glynn

1959–

Physicist Glynn Holt was an alternate payload specialist for STS-73, the second U.S. Microgravity Spacelab (USML-02), flown in October 1995. This 16-day long mission completed 24 different scientific experiments. Holt supported USML-02 from the NASA Marshall Spaceflight Center.

Holt was born November 28, 1959, in Plainview, Texas. He graduated from high school in Greenwood, Mississippi, and attended the University of Mississippi, where he received a B.S. in physics in 1982. He received his Ph.D. in physics there in 1989.

Beginning in 1989 Holt was a visiting scientist at the Institute of Applied Physics at the Technical University of Darmstadt, Germany, then a member of the mechanical engineering faculty at Yale University. His specialty involves liquid drop dynamics in microgravity, and he worked on the Drop Physics Module flown on USML-1 (STS-50) in 1992.

Since 1993 Holt has been a member of the microgravity research group at the NASA Jet Propulsion Laboratory.

Horowitz, Scott Jay "Doc"
1957–
Air Force test pilot and aerospace Ph.D. Doc Horowitz was pilot of STS-75. This February 1996 flight of the orbiter Columbia carried the third U.S. Microgravity Payload, and also deployed the Italian Tethered Satellite System. The T.S.S. was deployed to a distance of 13 miles, just short of its maximum, and successfully demonstrated its ability to generate electricity by simply passing through the Earth's magnetic field, when it broke, causing Horowitz and commander Andy Allen quickly to maneuver the Columbia away.

Horowitz also served as pilot for STS-82, the second servicing and repair mission for the Hubble Space Telescope, on which two teams made five different EVAs to upgrade the instrument.

Horowitz was born March 24, 1957, in Philadelphia, Pennsylvania. He graduated from high school in Newbury Park, California, then attended the California State University at Northridge, receiving a B.S. in engineering in 1978. He received an M.S. and Ph.D. in aerospace engineering from the Georgia Institute of Technology in Atlanta in 1979 and 1982.

After a year as a senior scientist for Lockheed, Horowitz went on active duty with the Air Force, qualifying as a pilot in 1983. From 1984 to 1987 he was a T-38 instructor pilot at Williams AFB, Arizona, while also serving as a researcher in the Human Resources Laboratory there. He was transferred to Bitburg Air Base, Germany, to fly F-15s with the 22nd Tactical Fighter Squadron for the next two years, then entered the Air Force Test Pilot School at Edwards AFB, California. At the time of his selection by NASA, Horowitz was an experimental test pilot with the 6512th Test Squadron at Edwards.

From 1985 to 1989 Horowitz was an adjunct professor of aerospace engineering at Embry-Riddle University, teaching graduate courses in aircraft design and propulsion. In 1991 he also taught at California State University, Fresno.

He was one of the 19 astronaut candidates selected by NASA in March 1992. In August 1993 he qualified as a Shuttle pilot while working in the operations development branch of the astronaut office. He later served with the astronaut support team at the Kennedy Space Center.

Since returning from STS-82 Horowitz has been a capcom in mission control.

Hughes-Fulford, Millie Elizabeth
1945–
Biochemist Millie Hughes-Fulford was a payload specialist aboard STS-40, the first Spacelab Life Sciences, in June 1991. This 10-day flight of the orbiter Columbia carried a crew of 7, including four science crewmen, to study the the effects of weightlessness on human beings.

Hughes-Fulford, like the other members of the science crew, not only used herself as an experimental subject, but also monitored the effects of spaceflight on the additional STS-40 passengers—29 rats and 2,478 jellyfish.

Hughes-Fulford was born December 21, 1945, in Mineral Wells, Texas. She attended Tarleton State University in Stephenville, Texas, receiving a B.S. in chemistry in 1968. She earned her Ph.D. in chemistry from Texas Women's University in Denton in 1972.

In 1973 Hughes-Fulford joined the faculty of the University of California at Berkeley and also became a biochemist at the Veteran's Administration Hospital in San Francisco. She has published seventy scientific papers in such fields as cell growth and DNA replication. She is also a private pilot and, until 1995, was a major in the U.S. Army Reserve.

Inspired by science fiction, especially *Star Trek*, Hughes-Fulford applied for the January 1978 NASA astronaut group, but was not selected. She was named as a payload specialist for the long-delayed Spacelab Life

Sciences mission in January 1984. Originally designated as prime for SLS-2, she became prime PS for SLS-01 in 1989 when Dr. Robert Phillips was medically disqualified.

Since her flight Hughes-Fulford has been scientific advisor to the Under Secretary of the Department of Veterans Affairs as well as principal investigator for OSTEO, a series of experiments designed to study bone growth that was flown on STS-76, STS-82 and STS-84.

She is currently deputy associate chief of staff at the Veterans Affairs Medical Center in San Francisco.

Husband, Rick Douglas
1957–

Air Force test pilot Rick Husband is a Shuttle pilot currently assigned as astronaut office representative to Advanced Projects while awaiting a flight assignment.

Husband was born July 12, 1957, in Amarillo, Texas, where he graduated from Amarilla High School in 1975. He then attended Texas Tech, where he received a B.S. in mechanical engineering in 1981. In 1990 he received an M.S. in mechanical engineering from California State University.

An Air Force ROTC student at Texas Tech, Husband went on active duty in 1981 and underwent pilot training at Vance AFB, Oklahoma, and Homestead AFB, Florida. Qualified as an F-4 Phantom pilot, he served at Moody AFB, Georgia, from September 1982 to September 1985. His next tour was as an F-4E instructor pilot at George AFB, California.

Husband attended the Air Force Test Pilot School at Edwards AFB, California, in 1988. Following graduation he remained at Edwards as a test pilot with the F-15 Combined Test Force. In June 1992 he was assigned to the Aircraft and Armament Evaluation Establishment at Boscombe Down, England, as an exchange test pilot on the Tornado GR1, Hawk, Hunter, Buccaneer, Jet Provost, Tucano, and Harvard programs.

Major Husband has logged 3,000 hours of flying time in over 40 different types of aircraft.

Husband was one of the 19 astronaut candidates selected by NASA on December 8, 1994. In May 1996 he qualified as a Shuttle pilot.

Irwin, James Benson
1930–1991

Air Force test pilot Jim Irwin spent almost three days on the Moon in 1971 as lunar module pilot of Apollo 15. While Alfred Worden orbited overhead in the command module Endeavour, Irwin and commander David Scott landed the LM Falcon at Hadley Rille near the lunar Apennines, becoming the seventh and eighth persons to walk on the Moon. They were the first astronauts to use the lunar rover, a specially designed electric car, which carried them a total of 18 miles during three excursions.

Irwin was born March 17, 1930, in Pittsburgh, Pennsylvania, and grew up in New Port Richy and Orlando, Florida; Roseburg, Oregon; and Salt Lake City, Utah. He graduated from East High School in Salt Lake City, then attended the Naval Academy at Annapolis, where he received a bachelor of science in 1951. In 1957 he earned an M.S. in aeronautical engineering and instrumentation engineering from the University of Michigan.

He elected to serve in the Air Force and received flight training at Hondo AFB and Reese AFB in Texas. He served as a fighter pilot, and following graduate school at Michigan, attended the Air Force Experimental Flight Test School (1961) and the Aerospace Research Pilots School (1963) at Edwards AFB, California. He went on to test the F-12 aircraft, forerunner of the SR-71 Blackbird spy plane, at Edwards. At the time of his selection by NASA he was chief of the advanced requirements branch at Headquarters Air Defense Command in Colorado Springs.

Irwin applied to be an astronaut in 1963 and was not selected because he was still recovering from injuries received in a 1961 plane crash. He was one of 19 astronauts selected by NASA in April 1966. Following basic training, he specialized in Apollo lunar module systems, commanding the 2-man Lunar Test Article (LTA)-8 team that tested the lunar module in June 1968. He served on the support crew for Apollo 10 and was backup lunar module pilot for Apollo 12.

In August 1971 Irwin, along with Worden and Scott, was assigned to backup Apollo 17, the last lunar landing mission. But an investigation into the sale of stamps and envelopes carried to the Moon by the Apollo 15 crew led to a NASA reprimand, and to their removal from active astronaut training in May 1972. Now an Air Force colonel, Irwin retired from the USAF and resigned from NASA on July 1, 1972, to found the High Flight Foundation, a Colorado-based nonprofit organization which allowed the former astronaut to share his faith in God through speaking engagements, retreats, and other activities.

Irwin published an autobiography, *To Rule the Night*, (1973), which discussed his astronaut career and the spiritual revelation he experienced while walking on the Moon.

Among his activities with High Flight, Irwin led five expeditions to Mount Ararat in Turkey, searching for the remains of Noah's Ark.

After two heart attacks and triple bypass heart surgery, Irwin also served as spokesman for the Pritikin Longevity Centers.

He died of a heart attack in Glenwood City, Colorado, on August 8, 1991.

Ivins, Marsha Sue
1951–

NASA flight engineer Marsha Ivins has been a mission specialist in four Shuttle crews, beginning with STS-32 in January 1990. This flight of the Shuttle Columbia deployed the Leasat/Syncom IV-5 communications satellite and also retrieved the Long Duration Exposure Facility, a 13-ton satellite that had been in orbit for almost six years. Ivins' job during retrieval was to photograph the 60 experiments in case they were damaged during return to Earth.

In August 1992 she served as a mission specialist in the crew of STS-46, which carried the EURECA recoverable satellite and the Tethered Satellite System.

Her third mission was STS-62, a 2-week flight of the orbiter Columbia that carried the U.S. Microgravity Payload.

Most recently, Ivins flew on STS-81, the sixth Shuttle-Mir docking mission, in January 1997. During five days of docked operations, STS-81 delivered more than three tons of food, water, and technical supplies to Mir, in addition to NASA-Mir crewmember Jerry Linenger, returning astronaut John Blaha to Earth.

Ivins was born April 15, 1951, in Baltimore, Maryland, and graduated from Nether Providence High School in Wallingford, Pennsylvania, in 1969. She attended the University of Colorado, receiving a B.S. in aerospace engineering in 1973.

Ivins went to work for NASA at the Johnson Space Center in 1974, first as an engineer working on Space Shuttle orbiter cockpit displays, later as a flight simulation and test engineer aboard the specially-modified Gulfstream I known as the Shuttle Training Aircraft. She holds a transport pilot license, single engine airplane, and glider ratings, and has logged 5,600 hours of flying time in NASA and other aircraft.

One of the 17 astronauts selected by NASA in May 1984, Ivins qualified as a Shuttle mission specialist in June 1985. She was assigned to the support crew for Shuttle orbiter checkout and later worked in the Shuttle Avionics Integration Laboratory (SAIL) and as a capcom in mission control. In 1997–98 she again led the astronaut support team at the Kennedy Space Center.

James, Larry Dean
1956–

Air Force satellite engineer Larry James was a member of the second cadre of Department of Defense manned spaceflight engineers chosen in January 1983. From 1984 until 1986 he trained as a payload specialist for the first and fourth planned launches of the Navstar Global Positioning System. Following the Challenger disaster GPS satellites were shifted to the unmanned Delta II vehicle for launch, and James never flew in space.

James was born August 8, 1956, in Bristol, Virginia, where he grew up, graduating from John Battle High School. He became interested in manned spaceflight with the Gemini and Apollo missions and entered the Air Force Academy, graduating in 1978 with a B.S. in astronautical engineering. He later attended the Massachusetts Institute of Technology, receiving an M.S. in astronautical engineering in 1982.

From 1978 to 1981 he served as a a project officer in advanced space guidance systems at USAF Space Division in Los Angeles. He was at M.I.T. when selected for the MSE program.

While an MSE James served as deputy director for the Navstar program, earning several awards for this work. He left Space Division in December 1987 to attend the Defense Systems Management School and the Air Command and Staff College. From 1988 to 1992 he was assigned to HQ USAF, the Pentagon, in the office of Space Systems.

James served for two years as commander of the 5th Space Launch Squadron of the 45th Space Wing at Patrick AFB, Florida, overseeing all Titan IV launches from Cape Canaveral. Since 1995 Colonel James has been been director of operations for the 45th Space Wing.

Jarvis, Gregory Bruce
1944–1986

Gregory Jarvis was the Hughes Aircraft satellite engineer who died in the explosion of the Shuttle Challenger on January 28, 1986. He was serving as payload specialist of Mission 51-L, a planned 5-day flight, during which he was to supervise the operation of a fluid dynamics experiment.

Jarvis's presence on 51-L was especially tragic because he had no real task to perform. He had been bumped off two previous Shuttle missions that actually carried the Leasat satellites he had helped design. He had only begun training for 51-L that month.

Jarvis was born August 24, 1944, in Detroit, Michigan, but grew up in Mohawk, New York, where he graduated from high school in 1962. He attended the State University of New York at Buffalo, where he received a B.S. in electrical engineering in 1967. He earned an M.S. in electrical engineering from Northeastern University in Boston in 1969, and completed work on a master's in management science at West Coast University in Los Angeles. That degree was to have been awarded during the flight of Mission 51-L.

An ROTC student at SUNY-Buffalo, Jarvis entered active duty with the Air Force in July 1969. He was assigned to Space Division in El Segundo, California, and

worked there for four years on military communications satellites such as FLTSATCOM. Discharged as a captain in 1973, he joined Hughes Aircraft, and for the next 12 years worked on a variety of satellite programs, including Marisat and Leasat (also known as Syncom). In June 1984, when he was selected to accompany a Leasat into space, Jarvis was the test and integration manager for the program. At the time of his death he was working on advanced communcations satellites.

Jemison, Mae Carol
1956–

Mae Jemison, a computer engineer and physician, was a mission specialist aboard STS-47, the 8-day Spacelab J (Japan) flown in September 1992, becoming the first African-American woman in space. The STS-47 crew conducted over 40 experiments in space manufacturing and life sciences. In order to test human responses to the stress of spaceflight, Jemison served as a test subject.

Jemison was born October 17, 1956, in Decatur, Alabama, and grew up in Chicago, where she graduated from Morgan Park High School in 1973. She attended Stanford University, receiving a B.S. in chemical engineering in 1977 while also fulfilling requirements for a B.A. in African and Afro-American Studies. She received her M.D. from Cornell University in 1981.

Following completion of her internship at Los Angeles County/USC Medical Center in July 1982 Jemison worked as a general practitioner with the Ross Loos Medical Group in Los Angeles until December of that year. In January 1983 she became a Peace Corps area medical officer in Sierra Leone, and later Liberia, in West Africa. (As a graduate student Jemison had visited Cuba, Kenya and Thailand doing medical studies or relief work.) While in Africa she managed health care for the Peace Corps and U.S. Embassy personnel in those areas. She also took part in hepatitis research projects for the National Institutes of Health and the Center for Disease Control.

Returning to the United States in October 1985, Jemison joined the CIGNA Health Plan of California, and was working as a CIGNA general practitioner in Los Angeles when she became one of the the 17 astronaut candidates selected by NASA in June 1987.

After qualifying as a Shuttle mission specialist in August 1988 Jemison worked with the astronaut support group at the Kennedy Space Center, and in the Shuttle Avionics Integration Laboratory. She was assigned to Spacelab J in January 1990.

Reportedly frustrated by her experiences with NASA, Jemison declined a second flight assignment and resigned from the astronaut office in March 1993 to pursue other interests, hosting the television series *World of Wonder* for The Discovery Channel in 1995 and making a guest appearance on *Star Trek: The Next Generation*.

In addition to serving as a lecturer in environmental law at Dartmouth, Jemison heads the Jemison Group, a consulting firm, based in Houston.

Jernigan, Tamara Elizabeth
1959–

Tammy Jernigan served as flight engineer and mission specialist for four Shuttle missions—all of them aboard the orbiter Columbia.

The first was STS-40, the Spacelab Life Sciences mission flown in June 1991. During this 9-day flight of Columbia a crew of 7, including four doctors, performed two dozen experiments in space medicine.

She later served as mission specialist for STS-52, an October 1992 flight which deployed the LAGEOS II geophysical research satellite.

In March 1995 she was payload commander for STS-67, a 16-day flight that carried the ASTRO 2 Spacelab, a set of three telescopes designed to study ultraviolet radiation from distant stars and galaxies.

Most recently she was a mission specialist in the crew of STS-80. This 16-day flight deployed and retrieved the Wake Shield Facility and the Orfeus-SPAS astronomical satellite. A planned EVA by Jernigan and fellow crewmember Thomas Jones had to be canceled because of a faulty hatch.

Jernigan was born May 7, 1959, in Chattanooga, Tennessee, and grew up in southern California, graduating from high school in Santa Fe Springs in 1977. She attended Stanford University, receiving a B.S. in physics (with honors) in 1981 and an M.S. in engineering science in 1983. She earned an M.S. in astronomy from the University of California at Berkeley in 1985. In 1988, after joining the astronaut group, she received a Ph.D. in space physics and astronomy from Rice University.

Beginning in June 1981 Jernigan worked for the NASA Ames Research Center at Moffet Field, California. She was one of the 13 astronauts selected by NASA in June 1985, and in August 1986 qualified as a Shuttle mission specialist. Her first technical assignment was to the Shuttle Avionics Integration Laboratory. She later worked on the development of secondary Shuttle payloads, and from May 1989 to January 1990 served as a capcom for five STS missions. She was assigned to STS-40 in April 1989. Since early 1997 she has been astronaut office deputy for the International Space Station.

Jett, Brent Ward, Jr.
1958–

Navy test pilot Brent Jett has been pilot in two Shuttle crews, beginning with STS-72 in January 1996. This 9-day flight of the orbiter Endeavour retrieved the Japanese Space Flyer Unit, launched ten months earlier, and the OAST Flyer. Two teams also made EVAs testing future International Space Station construction techniques.

Jett made his second flight aboard STS-81. This January 1997 flight of the orbiter Atlantis accomplished the fifth Shuttle-Mir docking, delivering three tons of water, food, and other supplies to the Russian station along with NASA-Mir crewmember Jerry Linenger.

Jett was born October 5, 1958, in Pontiac, Michigan. He graduated from Northeast High School in Oakland Park, Florida, then attended the Naval Academy at Annapolis, where he received a B.S. in aerospace engineering in 1981. He earned an M.S. in aeronautical engineering from the U.S. Naval Postgraduate School, Monterey, California, in 1989.

Jett won his Naval Aviator wings in March 1983 and was assigned to Fighter Squadron 101 at Oceana, Virginia, for F-14 training. He was then assigned to Fighter

Squadron 74 aboard the carrier *U.S.S. Saratoga* and deployed to the Mediterranean Sea and Indian Ocean. He attended the Naval Fighter Weapons School ("Top Gun"), then entered the Naval Postgraduate School Cooperative Education Program in July 1986.

After completing his graduate work, he attended the Naval Test Pilot School at Patuxent River, Maryland, through June 1990, then spent a year with the strike aircraft test directorate at the Naval Air Test Center before returning to Fighter Squadron 74 aboard the carrier *U.S.S. Saratoga.*

He has logged over 3,000 hours of flying time in 30 different types of aircraft, with over 450 carrier landings.

Jett was one of the 19 astronaut candidates selected by NASA in March 1992. In August 1993 he qualified as a Shuttle pilot while assigned to the operations development branch of the astronaut office.

From June 1997 to the spring of 1998 Jett was NASA director of operations, Russia, based at the Gagarin Cosmonaut Training Center near Moscow.

Johnson, Gregory Carl

1954–

NASA pilot Gregory Johnson is one of the 25 astronaut candidates selected in June 1998. In August of that year he began a training and evaluation course that should qualify him as a Shuttle pilot.

Johnson was born July 30, 1954, in Seattle, Washington. He graduated from West Seattle High School in 1972, then attended the University of Washington, where he received a B.S. in aerospace engineering (1977).

At the time of his selection, Johnson was chief of the maintenance and engineering branch and also a research pilot with the aircraft operations directorate, NASA Johnson Space Center.

Johnson, Gregory Harold

1962–

Air Force test pilot Gregory Johnson is one of the 25 astronaut candidates selected by NASA in June 1998. In August of that year he reported to the Johnson Space Center to begin a training and evaluation course that should qualify him as a Shuttle pilot.

Johnson was born May 12, 1962, in Upper Ruislip, Middlesex, England. He graduated from high school in

Fairborn, Ohio, in 1980, then attended the U.S. Air Force Academy, receiving a B.S. in aeronautical engineering in 1984. He later earned an M.S. in civil engineering from Columbia University (1985).

At the time of his selection by NASA, Major Johnson was a student at the Air Command and Staff College, Maxwell AFB, Alabama.

Johnston (McKay), Mary Helen

1943–

Metallurgist Mary Helen Johnston served as the backup payload specialist to Lodewijk van den Berg on the Spacelab 3 mission flown in April and May 1985. She acted as communicator and science support crewman from the Payload Operations Center at NASA Marshall Spaceflight Center during the 7-day flight.

Johnston was born September 17, 1945, in West Palm Beach, Florida, and graduated from Dan McCarty High School in Fort Pierce, Florida, in 1962. She entered Florida State University in Tallahassee and earned a B.S. (1966) and M.S. (1969) in engineering science while working part-time at the NASA Marshall Space Flight Center in Huntsville, Alabama. She earned her Ph.D. in metallurgical engineering from the University of Florida at Gainesville in 1973. One of her professors was former scientist-astronaut J. Anthony Llewellyn, who gave her some guidance about a possible career in space research.

Johnston became a full-time scientist at the Marshall Space Flight Center in 1973 working on experiments and hardware for manned spaceflights. In 1974 she was a member of an all-woman crew that made a 5-day simulated Spacelab flight. She applied in 1977 for the astronaut program but was not selected. Nevertheless, her work on Spacelab 3 materials processing experiments qualified her for selection as a Spacelab payload specialist in June 1983.

Johnston currently works for the Tennessee Space Institute, Tullahoma, Tennessee.

Jones, Charles Edward

1952–

Air Force engineer Chuck Jones was training as the payload specialist for Shuttle Mission 71-L at the time of the Challenger accident. He had been selected in October 1984 for the mission, which would have deployed the fifteenth Defense Support Program early warning satellite into geosynchronous orbit. Following the accident DSP 15 was launched by a Titan 4 booster, and Jones lost his chance to fly in space.

Jones was born November 8, 1952, in Clinton, Indiana. He attended the Air Force Academy, graduating in 1974 with a B.S. in astronautical engineering. He later earned an M.B.A. from California State University (1977) and an M.S. in astronautics from the Massachusetts Institute of Technology (1980). He is also a graduate of the National Security Management College, the Defense Systems Management College and the Air War College.

From November 1974 to May 1978 Jones was a project officer with the Air Force Space and Missile Systems Organization at Los Angeles AFS, California, working on missile reentry systems. Following graduate work at M.I.T. he returned to Los Angeles in 1980, to become chief of the Space Shuttle exploitation branch in the Special Projects Office. He was one of the 14 officers selected for the second cadre of Manned Spaceflight Engineers in January 1983.

In January 1987 Jones left the MSE program to become chief of the STS Flight Operations Division at Space Division, Los Angeles. He later worked as deputy director for ground systems at Los Angeles.

Jones transferred to the Defense Intelligence Agency in April 1988, and spent three years as director, space systems intelligence. From 1992 to 1994 he was director of the office of technology survey for Office of the Secretary of the Air Force.

Colonel Jones is currently systems program director for Intelligence and Information Systems at Hansom AFB, Massachusetts.

Jones, Thomas David

1955–

Tom Jones, a planetary scientist and former CIA researcher, has been a mission specialist in three Shuttle crews, beginning with STS-59 in April 1994. This flight of the orbiter Endeavour carried the Shuttle Radar Laboratory, the most advanced imaging system ever devoted to Earth studies. On its first flight the SRL covered over 70 million square kilometers, 12 percent of the Earth's land surface.

Jones made a second flight aboard Endeavour with the Shuttle Radar Laboratory, SRL-02, in September-October 1994, following an aborted launch on August 18. Thanks to the 6-week delay, SRL-02 was in orbit in time to observe the eruption of the Klyuchevskaya volcano on the Kamchatka peninsula as well as a major earthquake near the Japanese island of Hokkaido.

As a mission specialist in the crew of STS-80, Jones and fellow crewmember Tammy Jernigan were to have made a pair of EVAs to test space construction techniques, but saw them canceled when a faulty hatch prevented their exit from the orbiter Columbia. This 18-day November 1996 mission deployed and retrieved the Wake Shield Facility and the Orfeus-SPAS astronomy payload.

In June 1997 Jones was assigned as an EVA crewmember for International Space Station assembly mission 5A, scheduled for launch as STS-98 in the spring of 2000.

Jones was born January 22, 1955, in Baltimore, Maryland. He attended the Air Force Academy, receiving a B.S. in basic sciences in 1977. He later earned a Ph.D. in planetary science from the University of Arizona in Tucson in 1988.

Originally trained as an Air Force B-52 commander, Jones was stationed at Vance AFB, Oklahoma, from 1977 to 1978, and at Carswell AFB, Texas, from 1978 to 1983, when he resigned his commission. He logged over 2,000 hours of flying time.

For the next five years he was a graduate research assistant at the University of Arizona while completing his doctorate. In 1989 he became a program management engineer in the Office of Development and Engineering with the CIA. He had just joined the Science Applications Corporation in Washington D.C. when he was selected by NASA.

He was one of the 23 astronaut candidates selected by NASA in January 1990. In July 1991 he qualified as a Shuttle mission specialist while working on payloads for the mission development branch of the astronaut office. His next technical assignment, prior to being named to the STS-59 crew, was orbiter systems and safety matters in the operations development branch. In 1997–98 he was astronaut office deputy for the International Space Station.

Joseph Daryl James
1949–

Air Force engineer Daryl Joseph was one of the first 13 Air Force manned spaceflight engineers. He served for six years as a backup payload specialist for a Shuttle mission that was eventually flown as STS-28 in July 1989, but without its prime payload specialist, Frank Casserino.

Joseph was born December 17, 1949 in Albuquerque, New Mexico, where his father, a military policeman, was stationed. He grew up in Los Angeles and attended the Air Force Academy at Colorado Springs, graduating in 1971 with a bachelor of science degree. He went on to attend Purdue University, where he earned a M.S. in aeronautical engineering in 1972. At Purdue his roommate was future MSE and Shuttle payload specialist Gary Payton.

Joseph's first Air Force assignment was as a project officer with the F-16 fighter program at Wright-Patterson AFB, Ohio, where he remained until 1976. He transferred to Edwards AFB, California, to work on the B-1 bomber. When that program was canceled in 1977, he joined the Special Projects Office at Los Angeles AFS. He was a program manager there when selected for the MSE program in August 1979.

In June 1982 Joseph was designated as a payload specialist candidate for a Department of Defense Shuttle mission then scheduled for the summer of 1984. Shuttle manifest changes, upper stage problems and finally the Challenger disaster delayed the mission until 1989.

He left the MSE program in 1985 to become Shuttle flight director at the Satellite Control Facility (later Onizuka Air Force Base) at Sunnyvale, California. In this capacity he served as director for the mission to which he had once been assigned as a PS. In 1992 he became commander of Detachment 2, Space and Missile Systems Center, based at Onizuka. He retired from the Air Force in July 1997.

Kavandi, Janet Lynn
1959–

Chemist Janet Kavandi is assigned as a mission specialist in the crew of STS-91. The June 1998 flight of the orbiter Atlantis carried out the ninth and last Shuttle-Mir docking and resupply mission.

Kavandi was born Janet Lynn Sellers on July 17, 1959, in Springfield, Missouri. She graduated from Carthage Senior High School in Carthage, Missouri, in 1977, then attended Missouri Southern State College, Joplin, where she received a B.S. in chemistry in 1980. She earned an M.S. in chemistry from the University of Missouri, Rolla, (1982) and her Ph.D. in chemistry from the University of Washington (1990).

Upon graduation from Missouri in 1982 Kavandi went to work for Eagle-Picher Industries in Joplin, Missouri, as an engineer. Two years later she moved to the Boeing Company in Seattle, Washington, where she worked as an engineer specializing in power systems for such programs as the Short Range Attack Missile II, the Seal Lance and Lightweight Exo-Atmospheric Projectile, as well as the space station, the Intertial Upper Stage, the Advanced Orbital Transfer Vehicle, the Air-Launched Cruise Missile, Minuteman and Peacekeeper. She holds two patents.

Kavandi was one of the 19 astronaut candidates selected by NASA on December 8, 1994, qualifying as a Shuttle mission specialist in May 1996. Prior to her STS-91 assignment in October 1997 she worked in the payloads and habitation branch of the astronaut office doing payload integration for the International Space Station.

Kelly, James McNeal

1964–

Air Force test pilot James "Vegas" Kelly is one of the 35 astronaut candidates selected by NASA on May 1, 1996. In August of that year he reported to the Johnson Space Center to begin the training and evaluation course that should qualify him as a Shuttle pilot.

Kelly was born May 14, 1964, in Burlington, Iowa, where he graduated from Burlington Community High School in 1982. He attended the Air Force Academy in Colorado Springs, receiving a B.S. in astronautical engineering in 1986. He later earned an M.S. in aerospace engineering from the University of Alabama (1996).

Commissioned in the Air Force upon graduation from the academy, Kelly qualified as a pilot in October 1987. Trained on the F-15, he was assigned to the 67th Fighter Squadron, Kadena Air Base, Okinawa, serving as instructor pilot, evaluator pilot and mission commander. In April 1992 he was reassigned to Otis Air National Guard Base, Cape Cod, Massachusetts, as part of Project TOTAL FORCE.

Kelly entered the Air Force Test Pilot School at Edwards AFB, California, in 1993, and following graduation was assigned to the Flight Test Center's detachment at Nellis AFB, Nevada, as a test pilot and assistant operations officer.

Captain Kelly has logged 1,500 hours of flying time in 35 different aircraft.

Kelly, Mark Edward

1964–

Navy test pilot Mark Kelly is one of the 35 astronaut candidates selected by NASA on December 1, 1996. In August of that year he reported to the Johnson Space Center to begin the training and evaluation course that should qualify him as a Shuttle pilot.

Reporting with Lieutenant Kelly is his twin brother, Lieutenant Scott Kelly, another Navy test pilot selected as an ASCAN at the same time.

Kelly was born February 21, 1964, in Orange, New Jersey, but grew up in West Orange, where he graduated from Mountain High School in 1982. He attended the U.S. Merchant Marine Academy, graduating in 1986 with a B S. in marine engineering and nautical science. He later earned an M.S. in aeronautical engineering at the Naval Postgraduate School(1994).

Commissioned in the Navy in June 1986, Kelly qualified as a naval aviator in December 1987. Following additional training on the A-6E, he was assigned to Attack Squadron 115, Atsugi, Japan, where he made two deployments to the Persian Gulf aboard the carrier *U.S.S. Midway*. It was during his second deployment that he flew 39 combat missions in Operation Desert Storm.

In July 1991 Kelly was selected for a Postgraduate School-Naval Test Pilot School Cooperative Education Program, spending 15 months of graduate work at Monterey, California, then a year at the test pilot school at Patuxent River, Maryland. Following graduation in June 1994 Kelly was a project test pilot in the carrier suitability branch of the strike aircraft test squadron, Naval Air Warfare Center. He was an instructor at the test pilot school when selected by NASA.

Lieutenant Kelly has logged over 2,000 hours of flying time and 375 carrier landings in 40 different aircraft.

Kelly, Scott Joseph

1964–

Navy test pilot Scott Kelly is one of the 35 astronaut candidates selected by NASA on May 1, 1996. In August of that year he reported to the Johnson Space Center to begin the training and evaluation course that should qualify him as a Shuttle pilot.

Lieutenant Kelly is the twin brother of another Navy test pilot, Lieutenant Mark Kelly, selected as an ASCAN at the same time.

Kelly was born February 21, 1964, in Orange, New Jersey, but grew up in West Orange, where he graduated from Mountain High School in 1982. He attended the State University of New York Maritime College, where he receieved a B.S. in electrical engineering in 1987. He later earned an M.S. in aviation systems from the University of Tennessee, Knoxville (1996).

Commissioned in the Navy in May 1987, Kelly underwent pilot training at Beeville, Texas, and Oceana, Virginia. His first assignment was with Fighter Squadron 143, where he made overseas deployments to the North Atlantic, Mediterranean Sea, Red Sea and Persian Gulf aboard the carrier *U.S.S. Dwight D. Eisenhower*, flying F-14 Tomcats.

Kelly attended the Naval Test Pilot School at Patuxent River, Maryland, from January 1993 to June 1994, and following graduation served as a test pilot with the Strike Aircraft Test Squadron of the Naval Air Warfare Center there.

Lieutenant Kelly has logged 1,700 hours of flying time, including 275 carrier landings, in over 30 different types of aircraft.

Kerwin, Joseph Peter
1932–

Dr. Joe Kerwin was the first American physician to make a spaceflight, and the first doctor to perform in-orbit medical research during a long-duration mission.

As science pilot of Skylab 2 (SL-2), Kerwin spent 28 days aboard the 5-story-tall station in 1973. Kerwin and fellow astronauts Charles Conrad and Paul Weitz had to repair Skylab, which had been badly damaged during its launch on May 14, 1973, before they could begin their scientific work. In spite of the delay, the crew completed 80 percent of their original program. Dr. Kerwin, monitoring his physical condition and that of Conrad and Weitz, found no medical reason to prevent longer Skylab missions.

Kerwin was born February 19, 1932, in Oak Park, Illinois, and graduated from Fenwick High School there in 1949. He attended the College of the Holy Cross in Worcester, Massachusetts, receiving a B.A. in philosophy, then entered Northwestern University Medical School in Chicago. He received his M.D. in 1957 and the following year completed his internship at the District of Columbia General Hospital in Washington, D.C. In December 1958

he graduated from the Naval School of Aviation Medicine at Pensacola, Florida, and was designated a naval flight surgeon.

He served as a medical officer at the Marine Corps Air Station at Cherry Point, North Carolina, from 1959 to 1961, then underwent pilot training in Florida and Texas, winning his wings in 1962. At the time of his selection by NASA Kerwin was on the medical staff of Attack Carrier Wing 4 at Jacksonville, Florida.

As a pilot he logged over 4,200 hours of flying time, including 3,000 hours in jets.

Kerwin was one of the first 6 scientist-astronauts selected by NASA in June 1965. Following preliminary academic and survival training he began working on the Apollo and Apollo Applications (later Skylab) programs. He was involved in the design and development of biological insulation garments to be worn by astronauts returning from flights to the Moon, and also worked on the lunar receiving laboratory at the space center. In June 1968 Kerwin commanded an 8-day simulated Apollo mission intended to qualify the redesigned command module for manned flights. He also served as capcom for Apollo 13 prior to being named to a Skylab crew in January 1972.

In January 1974, as Skylab was drawing to a close, Kerwin was named director of life sciences for the astronaut office, a position he held for three years. At the same time he became involved in the development of the Space Shuttle, concentrating on the design of the crew station, controls, and medical monitoring. He also participated in the study group that produced the *Outlook for Space: 1980–2000* report (1975).

Beginning in 1978, when new scientist-astronauts, now known as mission specialists, were accepted into the astronaut program, Kerwin took part in their selection and served as their first boss. He was also in charge of planning operational Shuttle missions, and of astronaut duties in rendezvous, satellite deployment and retrieval, and operation of the remote manipulator arm. He was an early candidate to serve as mission specialist for the Solar Max rescue (Mission 41-C), but in April 1982, before the crew could be chosen, he was named NASA's senior science representative in Australia.

He returned to the Johnson Space Center in January 1984 and became director of space and life sciences, remaining in that job until April 1987, when he retired from the Navy and resigned from NASA to join the Lockheed Missile and Space Company as chief scientist for space station programs at their Houston office. He currently works for the United Space Alliance.

Kincheloe, Ivan Carl, Jr.
1928–1958

Air Force test pilot Iven Kincheloe was the original military project pilot for the X-15, chosen in September 1957. On July 26, 1958, he took off from Edwards Air Force Base to act as chase pilot during the test flight of an F-104. The engine on Kincheloe's F-104 flamed out during takeoff. He tried to eject at low altitude but was killed.

On September 7, 1956, Kincheloe had piloted the X-2 rocket plane to a record altitude of 126,200 feet, becoming famous as the "first man in space." In the next two years, while undergoing strenuous medical tests to prepare him for X-15 flights, Kincheloe placed well ahead of his contemporaries, who included Neil Armstrong. Tom Wolfe, in *The Right Stuff*, described Kincheloe as "a test pilot from out of a dream, blond, handsome, powerful, bright, supremely ambitious and yet popular with all who worked with him, including other pilots. There was absolutely no ceiling on his future in the Air Force." Many space officials considered him a shoo-in to be the first man on the Moon, though his height of 6'1" might have kept him out of the Apollo program had he lived.

Kincheloe was born July 2, 1928, in Detroit, Michigan, and grew up on a farm in Cassopolis. He got interested in aviation as a teenager and took flying lessons, soloing at the age of 14. Following graudation from high school in Dowagiac, Michigan, he entered Purdue University, where he received a B.S. in aeronautical engineering in 1949.

An Air Force ROTC student, Kincheloe underwent pilot training in Texas, Arizona and Illinois. He flew almost 100 combat missions in Korea in F-86s, shooting down 10 enemy aircraft to become a double ace. Returning to the United Street, he was a gunnery instructor at Nellis AFB, Nevada, then attended the British Empire Test Pilot School at Farnborough, England. Following graduation in December 1954, he was assigned to Edwards AFB as a test pilot.

A biography, *First of the Spacemen* by James J. Haggerty Jr. was published in 1960. The Society of Experimental Test Pilots named its yearly trophy after Kincheloe.

Knight, William J "Pete"
1929–

Air Force test pilot Pete Knight set a world speed record by piloting an X-15 rocket plane to Mach 6.7, 4,520 miles per hour, on October 3, 1967. That record for winged aircraft stood until the flight of STS-1, the first Space Shuttle mission, in April 1981. Two weeks after setting the speed record, on October 17, Knight flew an X-15 to an altitude of 280,500 feet, over 53 miles above the Earth, earning U.S. Air Force astronaut wings.

In all, Knight made 16 of the 199 X-15 flights. He was scheduled to pilot number 200 but the flight was postponed five different times, the last time, on December 20, 1968, because of snow. NASA's Paul Bickle, director of the X-15 program, knowing that NASA would not fund further flights past December, and noting that only one of the 3 X-15 aircraft still functioned, concluded that "someone up there is trying to tell us something," and canceled the flight altogether.

Knight had previously trained as a pilot for the Air Force's X-20 Dyna-Soar program.

Knight was born November 18, 1929, in Noblesville, Indiana. He attended Butler and Purdue Universities, then joined the Air Force in 1952. He completed his B.S. in aeronautical engineering at the Air Force Institute of Technology in 1958.

Following flight training Knight served as a fighter pilot, becoming briefly famous in 1954 when he won the Allison Jet Trophy race at the National Air Show in Dayton, Ohio. He entered the Air Force Test Pilot School at Edwards Air Force Base in 1958 and remained at the center as a test pilot. Ultimately he would log over 6,000 hours of flying time in more than 100 different types of aircraft.

In 1969 Knight began a tour of duty in Vietnam, flying 253 combat missions in the F-100. When he returned to the United States he served at Wright-Patterson AFB, Ohio, as test director for the new F-15 fighter and later directed weapons development for ten different fighters. He later became vice commander of the Air Force Flight Test Center at Edwards, and retired as a colonel in October 1982.

Knight had remained active as an F-15 test pilot until his retirement, and continues to fly. In June 1983 he was injured in the crash of an ultralight vehicle near Lancaster, California, but recovered.

He had intended to return to his native Indiana to pursue a political career, but remained in California, and in April 1984 was elected to the city council of Palmdale, then later mayor of that city. Since 1994 he has been a Republican member of the California State Assembly, representing the 43rd District, which includes Palmdale and Lancaster.

Konrad, John Harrison
1949–

Hughes Aircraft satellite engineer John Konrad was assigned as a payload specialist in the crew of Shuttle Mission 61-L, scheduled for launch in the summer of 1986. He was to have observed the deployment of a Hughes-built Leasat communications satellite. The Challenger disaster on January 28, 1986, which killed the crew of 7 astronauts, including Hughes engineer Gregory Jarvis, forced the cancellation of Konrad's assignment.

Konrad was born March 12, 1949, in Pontiac, Illinois, and graduated from high school in Burns Flat, Oklahoma, in 1967. He attended Oklahoma State University, receiving a B.S. in aeronautical engineering (1971). He later received a Ph.D. in fluid mechanics from the California Institute of Technology (1976).

Konrad joined the Space and Communications Division of Hughes Aircraft in 1976, working on the Anik and SBS communications satellites that were deployed from the orbiter Columbia on STS-5, the first operational Shuttle mission, in November 1982. He later served as assis-

tant engineering manager for the Telstar III and Intelsat VI satellites.

He was selected as a Hughes payload specialist for the Shuttle in July 1984.

Koszelak, Stanley Norbert, Jr.
1953–

Biochemist Stan Koszelak was the backup American payload specialist for the flight of Spacelab-Japan in August 1992. During this weeklong mission a crew of 7, including Japanese payload specialist Mamoru Mohri, performed 42 different experiments, notably in the field of materials processing.

Koszelak was born October 20, 1953, in Oklahoma City, Oklahoma, graduating from suburban Midwest City High School in 1971. He attended the University of Oklahoma at Norman, receiving a B.S. in microbiology in 1976, and an M.S. (1981) and Ph.D. (1984) from the Oklahoma Health Sciences Center.

While doing his postgraduate work Koszelak was employed at the Oklahoma Medical Research Foundation studying the structure of macromolecules. After receiving his doctorate he became a research biochemist at the University of California at Riverside. Among his projects was the protein crystal growth experiment flown on previous Shuttle missions and scheduled for Spacelab-J.

In November 1989 Koszelak was selected as backup to NASA astronaut Dr. Mae Jemison, who filled the U.S. payload specialist position for Spacelab-J. Koszelak was also a finalist for the 1996 astronaut candidate group, but was not selected.

Kregel, Kevin Richard
1956–

Former Air Force and NASA test pilot Kevin Kregel commanded STS-87. This November 1997 flight of the orbiter Columbia carried a crew of 6, including Ukrainian astronaut Leonid Kadenyuk, and the fourth U.S. Microgravity Payload, which operated successfully for more than two weeks. Unfortunately, the flight of STS-87 was also marred by problems with the deployment of the Spartan astronomical satellite, which necessitated a retrieval EVA by crewmembers Winston Scott and Takao Doi.

Kregel served as pilot of two previous Shuttle missions, beginning with STS-70, the July 1995 flight of the orbiter Discovery, which deployed the sixth and last Tracking and Data Relay Satellite.

In June–July 1996 Kregel was pilot of STS-78, which carried the Life and Microgravity Spacelab (LMS). This 17-day flight of the orbiter Columbia is the longest in the Shuttle program, and with its international crew of 7 served as a forerunner of future space station missions.

Kregel was born September 16, 1956, in New York City, but grew up in Amityville, on Long Island, where he graduated from high school in 1974. He entered the U.S. Air Force Academy, receiving a B.S. in astronautical engineering in 1978. In 1988 he earned a master's degree in public administration from Troy State University.

Following flight training at Williams AFB, Arizona, in 1978 and 1979, Kregel served as an F-111 pilot at RAF Lakenheath, England. He then became an exchange pilot with the U.S. Navy based at Whidbey Island Naval Air Station, Washington, and aboard the carrier *U.S.S. Kitty Hawk*, where he flew the A-6E and made 66 carrier landings. He attended the Naval Test Pilot School at Patuxent River, Maryland, then was assigned to Eglin AFB, Florida, to test weapons and electronic systems on the F-111, the F-15 and the F-15E. He has logged over 5,000 hours of flying time in 30 different aircraft.

Kregel left active duty in 1990 in order to join NASA, becoming a Shuttle Training Aircraft instructor pilot at Ellington Field, Texas. He was one of the 19 astronaut candidates selected by NASA in March 1992, and in July 1993 qualified as a Shuttle pilot. His first technical assignment was in mission support, working as an astronaut support person (ASP) at the Kennedy Space Center.

LaComb, Maureen Cecil
1956–

Air Force engineer Maureen LaComb was assigned as a payload specialist for Shuttle Spacelab mission dedicated to the Strategic Defense Initiative Organization. The SDIO flight, called Starlab, intended to test tracking and pointing technology during a 9-day mission, was canceled in August 1990 after six years of preparation.

LaComb was born November 16, 1956, in Poughkeepsie, New York. She attended the University of Lowell (Massachusetts), graduating in 1978 with a B.S. in radiation health physics. In 1979 she earned an M.S. in computer science from Trinity University in San Antonio, Texas.

LaComb was a distinguished graduate of ROTC and entered active duty with the Air Force in January 1980. Her first assignment was as a program manager at the Rome Air Development Center, Griffiss AFB, New York. In 1982 she was selected for the Manned Spaceflight Engineer program and reported to Los Angeles Space Division in January 1983.

In 1990 LaComb transferred to the Consolidated Space Test Center at Onizuka AFB, Sunnyvale, California. She later resigned from the Air Force and now works in northern Virginia.

Lampton, Michael Logan
1941–

Physicist Mike Lampton was backup payload specialist for STS-45, the Spacelab ATLAS mission launched in March 1992. ATLAS, the ATmospheric Laboratory for Applications and Science, was an 8-day flight of the orbiter Columbia devoted to studies in several different fields, including Earth sciences, the atmosphere and space medicine.

Lampton was originally selected for ATLAS, then known as the Spacelab Earth Observation Mission (EOM) in May 1984. He trained for almost seven years as the prime payload specialist, but a medical exam in 1991 disqualified him.

Previously Lampton served as a backup to the first American Shuttle payload specialist, Byron Lichtenberg, on the Spacelab 1/STS-9 mission in October and November 1983. During that flight Lampton worked as communicator at the payload operations center at NASA Marshall, Huntsville, Alabama.

Lampton was born March 1, 1941, in Williamsport, Pennsylvania, and graduated from Verde Valley High School in Sedona, Arizona. He attended the California Institute of Technology in Pasadena, graduating with a B.S. in physics in 1962. He earned his Ph.D. in physics from the University of California at Berkeley in 1967.

In 1978 Lampton was a research physicist at the Space Science Laboratory at the University of California when he was selected to train for Spacelab 1. He continued his association with the Laboratory while training for Spacelab missions at the Johnson Space Center and the Marshall Space Flight Center.

Lawrence, Robert Henry, Jr.
1935–1967

Air Force major Robert Lawrence became the first African American chosen for spaceflight training when he was one of 4 pilots assigned to the Manned Orbiting Laboratory Program in June 1967.

Lawrence was killed in the crash of an F-104 jet at Edwards AFB, California, on December 8, 1967. Had he lived he would have been eligible for transfer to NASA as an astronaut in August 1969, and would probably have gone into space aboard the Shuttle.

Lawrence was born October 2, 1935, in Chicago, Illinois. He graduated from Englewood High School there, then went on to Bradley University, where he received a B.S. degree in chemistry in 1956. In 1965 he received a Ph.D. in nuclear chemistry from Ohio State University.

An ROTC student, Lawrence joined the Air Force in 1956. Following pilot training in Missouri he was stationed in West Germany as a fighter pilot and instructor, returning to the U.S. in 1961. He entered the Air Force Institute of Technology at Wright-Patterson AFB, Ohio,

which led to his Ph.D., and became a nuclear research officer at Kirtland AFB, New Mexico. When selected for the MOL program he had just graduated from the Air Force Aerospace Research Pilot School.

All MOL pilots, even those who had attended the Aerospace Research Pilot School, were enrolled in a six-month course at Edwards that included "booming and zooming," flying zero-G arcs or simulating very high-speed spacecraft landings in a modified F-104. It was while "zooming" that Lawrence crashed, ejecting too low for his parachute to open. Another pilot with him, Major Harvey Royer, ejected and lived.

In 1996 Lawrence's name was finally included—due to the efforts of space writer James Oberg and others—on the Astronaut Memorial at the Kennedy Space Center.

Lawrence, Wendy Barrien
1959–

Navy helicopter pilot Wendy Lawrence was a mission specialist in the crew of STS-86, the controversial September 1997 flight of the orbiter Atlantis that docked with the Russian space station Mir. STS-86 returned astronaut Michael Foale, the fifth NASA-Mir crewmember, to Earth after a crisis-filled 132-day mission marked by a collision between Mir and a Progress resupply vehicle and numerous control and life-support system breakdowns. Critics of the Shuttle-Mir program complained that Mir was unsafe for habitation, and tried to stop the replacement of Foale with astronaut David Wolf. After two independent reviews certified that Mir was safe, STS-86 launched and successfully delivered Wolf to Mir.

It was a bittersweet flight for Lawrence, since she had begun training in January 1996 to be the NASA 6 crewmember. She was replaced by Wolf on July 30, 1997, six weeks before launch, because the crises aboard Mir required the NASA crewmember to be capable of performing an EVA in a Russian Orlan space suit. Though Lawrence met all the requirements for the Mir mission, she was not tall enough to fit the Orlan; Wolf was.

During the STS-86 mission the crew of seven, including Russian cosmonaut Vladimir Titov and French astronaut Jean-Loup Chretien, delivered over 4,000 pounds of water and supplies to the beleaguered station.

Because of her familiarity with Mir, Lawrence was immediately reassigned as a mission specialist in the crew of STS-91, scheduled to make the ninth and last Shuttle-Mir docking in June 1998.

Lawrence had made a previous flight aboard the Shuttle, serving as flight engineer and blue shift pilot aboard STS-67. This 16-day flight of the orbiter Discovery carried the second ASTRO Spacelab observatory, a package of three ultraviolet telescopes.

Lawrence was born July 2, 1959, in Jacksonville, Florida. (Her father is Vice Admiral William P. Lawrence, USN-Retired, a winner of the Congressional Medal of Honor during the Vietnam War.) She graduated from Fort Hunt High School in Alexandria, Virginia, in 1977, then entered the Naval Academy, where she received a B.S. in ocean engineering (1981). She earned an M.S. in ocean engineering from the Massachusetts Institute of Technology and the Woods Hole Oceanographic Institution in 1988.

After graduation from Annapolis, Lawrence underwent flight training as a helicopter pilot. In 1982 she became one of the first 2 female helicopter pilots to make a carrier deployment with Helicopter Support Squadron 6. Following graduate work at M.I.T. and Woods Hole, Lawrence spent two years as officer-in-charge of Detachment Alfa, Helicopter Anti-Submarine Squadron Light 30 (HSL-30). At the time of her selection as a NASA astronaut candidate in March 1992, Lawrence was a physics instructor at Annapolis.

Lawrence has logged over 1,500 hours of flight time in six different types of helicopters, with 800 shipboard landings.

She qualified as a Shuttle mission specialist in August 1993, and served in the Shuttle Avionics Integration Laboratory (SAIL) and as assistant training officer until being assigned to STS-67 in January 1994.

Following STS-67 she underwent Russian language training and reported to the Gagarin Cosmonaut Training Center near Moscow in January 1996. She was backup to John Blaha, who was the fourth NASA-Mir crewmember (September 1996 to January 1997).

Lawyer, Richard Earl
1932–

Air Force test pilot Dick Lawyer was one of the 8 pilots chosen for the Manned Orbiting Laboratory Program in November 1965. He specialized in space suits and EVA, remaining with MOL until its cancellation in May 1969.

Lawyer was born November 8, 1932, in Los Angeles, growing up in Inglewood. He attended the University of California at Berkeley, receiving a B.S. in aeronautical engineering in 1955.

An ROTC student at the University of California, Lawyer entered the Air Force in 1955 and underwent pilot training. From 1956 to 1963 he served with the Tactical Air Command, including 30 months stationed on Okinawa, and also served a brief tour in Vietnam as an airborne forward air controller in an L-19 aircraft. He attended the Air Force Test Pilot School at Edwards AFB in 1963, and the Aerospace Research Pilot School in 1964. He was an instructor at ARPS when selected for MOL.

After the cancellation of MOL, Lawyer returned to active duty in the Air Force, eventually becoming deputy commander of operations at the Tactical Air War Center, Eglin AFB, Florida. He retired as a colonel in 1983.

He is currently an instructor at the National Test Pilot School in Lancaster, California.

Lee, Mark Charles
1951–

Air Force pilot Mark Lee has made four Shuttle flights as a mission specialist.

The first was aboard STS-30, a flight of the orbiter Atlantis in May 1989. The crew of STS-30 sent the Magellan space probe on its journey to the planet Venus.

In September 1992 Lee served as payload commander for STS-47, which carried Spacelab J (Japan). The crew of this 8-day flight of the orbiter Endeavour conducted 44 experiments in space manufacturing and life sciences.

Lee's wife, astronaut Jan Davis, was also a member of the crew, making them the first married couple to fly in space together.

Lee's third flight, in September 1994, was STS-64, which carried the Lidar Inspace Technology Experiment. During the mission Lee and fellow mission specialist Carl Meade made a 7-hour untethered EVA to test the SAFER rescue jetpack.

In February 1997 Lee was payload commander for STS-82, the second Hubble Telescope repair mission.

Lee was born August 14, 1952, in Viroqua, Wisconsin, graduating from high school there in 1970. He attended the US Air Force Academy at Colorado Springs, earning a BS in civil engineering in 1974. He earned an MS in mechanical engineering from the Massachusetts Institute of Technology in 1980.

Lee underwent pilot training in Texas and Arizona, then spent two and a half years flying F-4s with the 25th Tactical Fighter Squadron on Okinawa. After further schooling at MIT in 1979 and 1980, he was assigned to the Airborne Warning and Control System (AWACS) program office at Hanscom AFB, Massachusetts. In 1982 he became an F-16 pilot and flight commander at Hill AFB, Utah, where he was stationed when selected by NASA.

He has logged over 3000 hours of flying time.

Lee was one of the 17 astronauts selected by NASA in May 1984. In June 1985 he qualified as a Shuttle mission specialist. Lee has also served as an EVA support crewman, capcom, and leader of the astronaut support team at the Kennedy Space Center.

He is currently assigned to ISS assembly mission 5A.

Leestma, David Cornell

1949–

Navy aviator Dave Leestma has been a mission specialist on three Shuttle flights.

His first was Mission 41-G in October 1984. During that flight Leestma, together with Kathryn Sullivan, America's first woman space walker, made a 3.5-hour EVA demonstrating refueling techniques for satellites. The seven-person crew of 41-G (the largest sent into space at that time) also deployed a scientific satellite and conducted Earth observations during the 8-day mission.

In August 1989 Leestma was a mission specialist aboard STS-28, a Department of Defense Shuttle flight that deployed an advanced satellite Data System vehicle in Earth orbit.

Most recently he served in the crew of STS-45, the Spacelab ATLAS mission devoted to studies of the Earth's atmosphere. This 8-day flight of the orbiter Atlantis took place in late March 1992.

Leestma was born May 6, 1949, in Muskegon, Michigan, but graduated from high school in Tustin, California, in 1967. He attended the US Naval Academy, earning a BS in aeronautical engineering in 1971 and standing first in his class. He later received an MS in aeronautical engineering from the US Naval Postgraduate School (1972).

After a brief tour as an ensign aboard the *USS Hepburn* and further school at the Naval Posgraduate School, Leestma underwent pilot training, receiving his wings in October 1973. For the next three years he served with Squadron 32 in Virginia Beach, Virginia, making three deployments overseas aboard the carrier *USS John F. Kennedy*. In 1977 he was assigned to Air Test and Evaluation Squadron 4 at Point Mugu, California, where he tested new computer software for the F-14A.

As a pilot he has logged approximately 3500 hours of flying time.

Leestma was one of the 19 astronauts selected by NASA in May 1980. In August 1981 he completed a training and evaluation course qualifying him as a mission specialist on Shuttle crews. In August 1983 he became the first member of his astronaut group to be assigned to a flight crew. He was also assigned as mission specialist for Spacelab Astro 1, which was designed to observe Halley's Comet in March 1986. That mission, 61-E, was canceled following the explosion of the Shuttle Challenger. Leestma's third crew assignment, to a Department of Defense mission scheduled for September 1986, eventually became STS-28.

From 1988 to 1992 Leestma served as deputy director for flight crew operations, then as deputy chief astronaut. In November 1992 he became director of flight crew operations overseeing the astronaut office and aircraft operations directorates at the Johnson Space Center.

Lenoir, William Benjamin

1939–

Physicist Bill Lenoir was a mission specialist aboard STS-5, the first operational Shuttle flight, in November 1982. Lenoir and fellow mission specialist Joseph Allen deployed two communications satellites from the orbiter Columbia in the first demonstration of the Shuttle's value as a "space truck." A planned space walk by Lenoir and Allen had to be scrubbed because of mechanical failures in their EVA pressure suits.

Lenoir left NASA in September 1984 when he failed to be assigned to a second Shuttle flight. Ironically, less than five years later he returned to NASA at the request of administrator-designate—and former astronaut—Richard Truly to become associate administrator for the space station program. In 1989 Lenoir was promoted to associate administrator for spaceflight, spending the next three years as the civilian official in charge of all NASA manned missions. He resigned from NASA in May 1992, following Truly's firing as administrator.

Lenoir was born March 14, 1939, in Miami, Florida, and grew up in Coral Gables. He attended the Massachusetts Institute of Technology, where he received his B.S. in electrical engineering in 1961, followed by his M.S. (1962) and Ph.D. (1965).

While working on his doctorate, Lenoir was an instructor at MIT. In 1965 he became assistant professor of electrical engineering at the school, and also worked on the development of scientific experiments for space satellites.

Lenoir was one of the 11 scientist-astronauts selected by NASA in August 1967. After several months of initial ground and systems training, Lenoir entered USAF flight school at Laughlin AFB, Texas. Eventually he would log over 3,200 hours of flying time in jet aircraft.

As an astronaut Lenoir worked on the design and development of Skylab. He served as backup science pilot for the Skylab 3 and Skylab 4 missions in 1973-74, and was capcom for Skylab 4, primarily for solar science observations. From September 1974 to July 1976 Lenoir devoted much of his time to the NASA Satellite Power Team, which was investigating the possibility of adapting space power systems for use on Earth. From 1976 on Lenoir was heavily involved in Shuttle development, especially in the area of payload deployment and retrieval, and in EVA.

From 1984 to 1989 Lenoir worked for Booz, Allen and Hamilton, an aerospace management and consulting firm based in Bethesda, Maryland. Among his projects was consulting on the Freedom space station. He returned to Booz, Allen in June 1992 as manager of its Applied Systems Division.

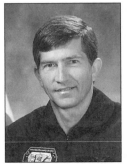

Leslie, Fred Weldon

1951–

Fred Leslie, a specialist in fluid dynamics, was a payload specialist in the crew of STS-73, which carried the second U.S. Microgravity Spacelab (USML-2) into space in October 1995. The crew of seven aboard this 16-day flight of the orbiter Columbia conducted over 40 different experiments, including studies into crystal growth and fluid physics, key steps in such future space manufacturing as the creation of better computer microchips. The crew also pioneered several techniques for handling and monitoring payloads that will be essential for future operations aboard the International Space Station.

Leslie was born December 19, 1951, in Ancon, Panama. He graduated from high school in Irving, Texas, in 1970, then attended the University of Texas, where he received a B.S. in engineering science in 1974. He did his graduate work at the University of Oklahoma, receiving an M.S. (1977) and Ph.D. (1979) in meteorology.

After receiving his doctorate Leslie served as a research associate at Purdue University. He joined the staff of the NASA Marshall Space Flight Center as a research scientist in 1980. His field of research is fluid dynamics, and since 1983 he has been coinvestigator for the Geophysical Fluid Flow Cell Experiment, which went into space on STS 51-B/Spacelab-3 in 1985, and will be aboard STS-73/USML-02. Since 1987 Leslie has been chief of the fluid dynamics branch at NASA Marshall, directing the work of a dozen scientists. He served as mission scientist for Spacelab J (STS-47) in 1992.

Leslie is an avid skydiver, holding a world record as a participant in a 200-person freefall performed in October 1992; a commercial pilot with 900 hours of flying time; and a scuba diver.

He was selected for STS-73 in June 1994.

Lewis, Fred Parker, Jr.
1949–

Air Force meteorologist Fred Lewis was assigned in December 1985 as the first weather officer in space. He would have been a payload specialist aboard Shuttle Mission 61-M in the summer of 1986, but the Challenger disaster in January of that year postponed the mission indefinitely. Lewis transferred to another assignment without flying in space.

The Weather Officer in Space Experiment (WOSE) was intended to allow a trained weather officer to make visual and photographic observations of the atmosphere and ionosphere from orbit. Eighty Air Weather Service officers volunteered for the program when it was announced by Brigadier General George Chapman, commander of the AWS, in early 1985. Twelve semifinalists were selected and reduced to five before final selection was made in October 1985.

Lewis was born March 2, 1949 in Cottonwood, Arizona. He received a B.S. in physics from the University of Arizona at Tucson in 1972, then enrolled in the basic meteorology program at the University of Utah, receiving his Ph.D. in 1979.

Entering active Air Force duty in 1973, Lewis first served at Air Force Global Weather Central, Offutt AFB, Nebraska, for three years, and served again at that station from 1979 to December 1982 after receiving his doctorate. He then served with Detachment 15, 30th Weather Squadron at Suwon Air Base, South Korea, from 1983 to 1984.

At the time of his selection for the WOSE program Lewis was stationed at Headquarters, Military Airlift Command, Scott AFB, Illinois. In July 1987 he transferred to Barksdale AFB, Louisiana, as commander of the 26th Weather Squadron. In 1990 he attended the Air War College, Montgomery, Alabama, then returned to Scott AFB

in a series of assignments, ultimately becoming director, Joint Transportation Corporate Information Management Center, U.S. Transportation Command.

Lewis was promoted to brigadier general in 1996 and currently serves as director of weather for the deputy chief of staff, plans and operations, HQ USAF, the Pentagon.

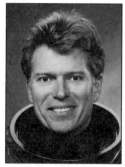

Lichtenberg, Byron Kurt
1948–

Engineer Byron Lichtenberg has made two flights as a Shuttle payload specialist. He was the first American space traveler who was not a career NASA astronaut.

In November and December 1983 Lichtebnerg served in the crew of STS-9, which carried the first reusable Spacelab module built by the European Space Agency. Lichtenberg and fellow payload specialist Ulf Merbold joined four NASA astronauts in carrying out 70 different experiments in a variety of fields, from space medicine to astronomy.

In May 1984 he was selected as one of 2 prime payload specialists for the Spacelab Earth Observation Mission originally scheduled for the summer of 1986, but postponed for several years following the Shuttle Challenger disaster. Spacelab EOM was later renamed Spacelab ATLAS (ATmospheric Laboratory for Applications and Science) and launched in March 1992. The 8-day mission carried a crew of 7 who performed experiments in atmospheric and Earth science.

Lichtenberg was born February 19, 1948, in Stroudsburg, Pennsylvania, and graduated from high school there in 1965. When he was a teenager he decided to become an astronaut and with that in mind studied aerospace engineering at Brown University in Providence, Rhode Island, earning his B.S. in 1969

He joined the Air Force via ROTC upon graduation from Brown and underwent pilot training at Williams AFB, Arizona, earning his wings in 1970. For the next three years he was an F-4 pilot, flying 138 combat missions with the 25th Tactical Fighter Squadron based at Ubon, Thailand. He left active duty in 1973 and returned to college, earning an M.S. in mechanical engineering from the Massachusetts Institute of Technology in 1975 and a doctorate in biomedical engineering in 1979.

In 1977 Lichtenberg applied for the NASA astronaut group but was not chosen. In 1978, however, he was selected as a Spacelab payload specialist—a professional scientist who would be trained to work in space aboard the Shuttle, but whose primary profession was the operation of scientific experiments.

Following his flight on Spacelab Lichtenberg cofounded Payload Systems, Inc., a company devoted to the commercial uses of space. PSI experiments flew aboard the Mir space station.

Lichtenberg also flew A-10 aircraft with the Massachusetts Air National Guard, logging over 2,500 hours of flying time. In 1983 *Esquire* magazine named him as one of its notable Americans under the age of 40.

Since 1995 Lichtenberg has been a pilot with Southwest Airlines.

He continues to be actively involved in the development of spaceflight, helping to found the Assocation of Space Explorers and, more recently, serving as a partner in Space Adventures, a company that hopes to provide adventure tours and guides to space launch and training centers. He is also involved in the X-Prize, a $10 million contest to the first organization to build a private, suborbital, reusable space vehicle capable of carrying three people to an altitude of 100 miles.

Lind, Don Leslie

1930–

Physicist Don Lind holds the unwanted record for the longest wait between commencing astronaut training and making a flight into space. Chosen by NASA as one of 19 astronauts in April 1966, Lind did not fly in space until April 1985, 19 years later.

During his first flight, Mission 51-B/Spacelab 3, Lind was part of a 7-man crew that performed experiments in materials processing and space medicine. Lind himself had developed one of the experiments aboard, a means of making 3-dimensional recordings of the Earth's aurora. The Spacelab 3 mission was notable for problems with several monkeys that were carried aboard, and for the fact that three of its astronauts (Lind, Thornton, and van den Berg) were over 50 years old.

Lind was born May 18, 1930, in Midvale, Utah, where he grew up. He graduated from Jordan High School in Sandy, Utah, then attended the University of Utah, receiving a B.S. (with high honors) in physics in 1953. He earned his Ph.D. in high energy nuclear physics in 1964 from the University of California at Berkeley. He later performed postdoctoral work at the University of Alaska's Geophysical Institute in 1975–76.

Lind served with the U.S. Navy from 1954 to 1957, earning his pilot's wings in 1955 and becoming a carrier pilot flying from the *U.S.S. Hancock*. From 1957 to 1964, while working on his doctorate, he was employed at the Lawrence Radiation Laboratory in Berkeley, and in the two years prior to his selection as an astronaut was employed by NASA's Goddard Space Flight Center in Maryland as a space physicist.

As an astronaut Lind trained initially as an Apollo lunar module pilot and might have made a landing on the Moon, but budget cuts canceled the later Apollo missions. In 1969 he was transferred to the Apollo Applications group, later known as Skylab. He served as backup pilot for Skylab 3 and Skylab 4, the second and third manned Skylab visits, and in 1973 trained briefly as pilot of a Skylab "rescue" crew. Following his leave of absence at the University of Alaska in 1975 and 1976, Lind returned to the astronaut office and assisted in the development of payloads for the first four Shuttle flights. He was assigned to Spacelab 3 in February 1983.

In April 1986 Lind announced his retirement from NASA. He joined the faculty of Utah State University in Logan, where he is currently professor of physics.

An inspirational biography of Lind, *Don Lind: Mormon Astronaut*, written by his wife, Kathleen, was published in 1985.

Lindsey, Steven Wayne

1960–

Air Force test pilot Steven Lindsey was pilot of STS-87. This 18-day flight of the orbiter Columbia carried the fourth U.S. Microgravity Laboratory Shuttle and a crew of 5.

Lindsey was born August 24, 1960, in Arcadia, California, and graduated from Temple City High School in 1978. He attended the U.S. Air Force Academy, graduating with a B.S. in engineering sciences in 1982. He earned an M.S. in aeronautical engineering from the Air Force Institute of Technology in 1990.

Following graduation from the Air Force Academy, Lindsey underwent pilot training at Reese AFB, Texas, qualifying on the RF-4C Phantom II. From 1984 to 1987 he was a combat-ready pilot, instructor pilot and academic instructor with the 12th Tactical Reconaissance Squadron at Bergstrom AFB, Texas.

Lindsey spent a year in graduate school, then, in June 1989, he entered the USAF Test Pilot School at Edwards AFB, California, where he graduated first in his class, winning the school's Liethen-Tittle Award. He was then assigned to the 3247th Test Squadron, Eglin AFB, Florida, as a weapons and systems test pilot for the F-16 and F-4 aircraft. From 1993 to 1994 he was at Maxwell AFB, Alabama, attending the Air Command and Staff College, then he returned to Eglin as an integrated product team leader in the SEEK EAGLE office, conducting weapons certification tests for the F-16, A-10, F-111 and F-117 aircraft.

Major Lindsey has logged over 2,500 hours of flying time in 49 different types of aircraft.

Lindsey was one of the 19 astronaut candidates selected by NASA on December 8, 1994. In May 1996 he qualified as a Shuttle pilot, working the Shuttle Avionics Integration Laboratory (SAIL) and as astronaut office representative to MEDS, the Multifunction Electronic Display System, an improved Shuttle cockpit program, while awaiting a flight assignment.

Linenger, Jerry Michael

1955–

Navy physician J. M. Linenger spent 130 days aboard the Russian station from January to May 1997. His flight was marked by the most serious onboard fire ever experienced by a space crew.

Linenger and his crewmates also suffered through a loss of station electrical power, environmental system shutdowns, and a near-collision with a Progress supply vehicle. Nevertheless, Linenger was able fully to complete his program of scientific and medical experiments, also becoming the first American to make an EVA in a Russian Orlan-M spacesuit.

Linenger's first flight was aboard STS-64 in September 1994.

Linenger was born January 16, 1955, in Mt. Clemens, Michigan. He attended the Naval Academy, where he received a B.S. in bioscience in 1977. He received his M.D. from Wayne State University (1981), an M.S. in systems management from the University of Southern California (1988), a master's in public health (1988), and a Ph.D. in epidemiology from the University of North Carolina (1989).

Following medical school, Linenger served as a naval flight surgeon in the Philippines, and as medical advisor to the commander of naval air forces, U.S. Pacific Fleet, San Diego.

Selected by NASA in March 1992, Lininger qualified as a Shuttle mission specialist in July 1993. He was named a Shuttle-Mir crewmember on March 30, 1995, and served as backup to John Blaha.

Linenger resigned from NASA and retired from the Navy in February 1998.

LETTERS TO MY SON FROM MIR

by Jerry Linenger

(Jerry Linenger was the fourth NASA astronaut to serve a shift aboard the Russian space station Mir, arriving with the STS-81 crew on January 14, 1997. Linenger's wife, Kathryn, was pregnant at the time. During his 130 days on the station Linenger composed over 60 letters to his young son, John—"Johnchek" in Russian—who was 14 months old at the time his father went to Mir.)

January 29, 1997

"Don't spit your toothpaste into your towel"

Dear John:

An old friend just wrote. Said he heard the floor creaking when he walked down his hallway, and wonders if I miss things like that.

Although most fathers want their sons to be like them, I'd rather you not try to follow too closely in your Dad's footsteps. Along the lines of the famous "Do as I say, not as I do" phrase parents always use.

Don't try to fly from point A to point B just because you saw Dad do it.

Don't sleep on the wall.

Don't eat your food upside down above the table.

Don't spit your toothpaste into your towel.

Don't change clothes once every four days.

Don't eat your food directly from a can.

Don't go 5 months without a bath.

Mom is definitely a better role model.

Life is challenging, interesting, and productive every day up here. One fantastic collection of science projects all located in fantastic complex of space station. The constant hum of generators, ventilators, and machinery are good substitute for creaking floors.

Good night, son. Sleep tight. I'll be watching over you as usual. Give Mommy a smile for me.

Dad.

January 30, 1997

"You would enjoy playing hide and seek up here"

Dear John:

Let me tell you about my house.

Spectacular View. Unobstructed, overlooking the oceans, the lakes, the rivers; the mountains, plains, and valleys; the city lights, the stars, the other planets.

Six modules. One toilet. Dining area with two private sleep stations.

Three vessel garage: Soyuz, Shuttle, and supply/garbage truck. Each module a 13 meter tube.

Lots of extras. Two modules are new additions. State of the art freezers, computers, gas analyzers. Built-in treadmills and bicycles for the recreational enthusiast. Utilities: completely solar-powered. Water from tanks, urine and condensate. Oxygen included. Radio, ham radio, and telemetry.

Maybe someday you'll have a house like this, John. It's the frontier now, but perhaps the norm by the time you grow up.

I often try to picture you up here. At first, a bit timid. Looking at me for some reassurance. Then a little smile. Then a big laugh. Skip the crawling and stumbling stage of life and just start flying! For sure, you'd enjoy playing hide and seek up here—it's a maze with all kinds of nooks and crannies and places behind panels. And you could hide on the floor, the walls, or the ceiling. And if you can hide like some of the cables "hide" around here, we may never find you!

You might not think so, but in space you still feel like there is an up and down. Although physically you feel just fine standing on your head or doing somersaults, you still prefer feet toward the floor, head toward the ceiling when working. Flying out of the intersection (the node), more often than not you end up in the next module not right-side up; but you instinctively twist and turn until you see the lights above you and then come in for a landing. To enhance this feeling of earthly normalcy, in each module the ceilings are white, the walls pale blue, and the floors an ugly orange-brown and similarly ugly green. I'm right now floating right-side up, computer attached to an all-Velcro table, typing. And if I don't think about it, I can lose myself and forget I'm in space completely.

Heard you are heading back to Russia on Sunday. Try to be good on that long airplane ride. Crying once or twice is okay, since even we adults feel like crying after sitting still for 11 hours on a plane.

I'll be looking for the contrail of your jet as you head across the ocean (usually, easily seen from space . . .). And I'll be watching over you.

Love you, Johnchek, Hooliganchek.

Dad.

March 3, 1997

"Human beings can adapt to space"

Dear John:

It was great talking to Kathryn today. You lucky dog—you get Mommy all to yourself. But pretty soon you will have to share again. Daddy can't wait!

Mommy said you were the entertainment at Alla's birthday party. Stood in the middle of the room and danced and smiled and laughed and danced some more. You never were shy. And you obviously inherited the rhythm from Mommy.

But you'd be impressed with the gracefulness of your Dad now. I can do triple spins with double turns—no problem. I fly with the greatest of ease. My leaps from module to module are a thing of beauty. I sometimes strike the surfer pose—hands out and crouched down low—and slide (fly) sideways through the air. Hang ten.

I was brushing my teeth this morning and started laughing to myself (actually, out loud; but don't tell the psychologists who are keeping an eye on me to make sure I don't go crazy up here . . .). I realized that I now feel absolutely normal up here—and half the time I forget that I'm in space. I do things, like just letting my tube of toothpaste float in front of me, as if I had operated in that manner my whole life. I fly from experiment to experiment without thinking about it—as naturally as walking on Earth. I just do it. No thinking involved. As if I were born up here.

The adaptability of the human being is remarkable.

Oh, there are some hiccups. For example, on Earth I can usually eat and go for a run within an hour. I used to love coaxing cousin Tommy for a quick run after dinner, then bury him at the finish with him suffering with a sideache. You will someday be subjected to a stupid rule that makes you sit around and wait for a hour, a whole hour, before going for a dip in the lake after lunch. I realize now that that rule had no applicability to me whatsoever; and nearly cost me a happy childhood.

But up here, it's a bit different. If I have something to drink before running on the treadmill I can feel it "floating up" when I run. Need to re-swallow. Nothing terrible, but annoying. Actually, I take that back—if I just drank orange-mango drink, it is terrible.

Taste changes a bit also. Unlike Mommy who can eat five-star hot Thai food and survive—I never liked spicy-hot food. But the shrimp cocktail that burns you all the way to the back of the nose with horseradish—or something resembling horseradish—I like up here.

Anyway, you get the idea. Subtle differences. In general, human beings can adapt to space just as we have adapted to land. And feel comfortable, feel 'at home.'

Heard that you welcomed back my crewmates last night in Star City. Mommy said it made her cry. I understand.

Okay, John. I recommend that you do that spit up trick of yours if Mommy tries to make you drink orange-mango drink.

Love you and miss you. Goodnight. I'll be saying a prayer for you, and watching over you.

Dad.

April 2, 1997

"Up here, you either make it, bring it, or do without it"

Dear John:

The knee bone is connected to the leg bone, and the leg bone connected to the ankle bone, and the ankle bone connected to the foot bone.

The urine is converted into water. The water is hydrolyzed into hydrogen (dumped over into the vacuum of space—don't want hydrogen gas around—it's explosive) and oxygen. The oxygen we breath. We exhale carbon dioxide. Carbon dioxide is scrubbed by an absorbent filter, and the filter flushed periodically by exposing it to the vacuum of space.

When running on the treadmill, we sweat. From our skin, the moisture evaporates in order to cool our bodies. (By the way—those doggies you are so fascinated with use their tongues, panting, to 'sweat' and regulate their temperature). The sweat evaporates into the air. This water, along with all the other humidity in the air, is condensed on cold coils (just like the outside of your cold bottle getting wet on a hot, humid day) and collected. Biocide is added, the condensate boiled, and we use it to drink or rehydrate our freeze-dried foods. Delicious.

Of course, if any link breaks down, you need to work around it. Both oxygen generating systems are stubbornly not working—so we activate three solid-fueled oxygen canisters a day in order to supply us with the oxygen we need to breathe. Water produced by the Shuttle and "donated" to us before they departed is being used to supplement the condensate water. (On the Shuttle, we combine oxygen and hydrogen [stored in tanks] to produce electricity in fuel cells—a byproduct of that reaction being water. Instead of dumping overboard the excess produced [in a rather spectacular blizzard of white "snow" when the dump valve is opened]—we collect it in large rubberized sacks and transfer it to the Mir space station for future drinking.)

Up here, you either make it or bring it; or do without it.

Someday I'll show you my Crazy Clock game (if I can find it down in Grandma Linenger's basement). Drop in a marble which rolls down the slide which opens a gate which bumps a different marble onto a platform that springs a dummy into a wooden bucket. Good fun. Good future astronaut training.

Goodnight. Daddy's into round two of sleeping with

wires connected to my eyelashes, electrodes in my scalp and on my face, already depleted of blood and facing another blood collection first thing in the morning; and all the while trying to keep track of my dreams so that I can record them first thing in the morning. Most of my dreams, in this garb, center around me being electrocuted for a crime I didn't commit.

Wishing you pleasanter dreams, John. Pass along a kiss to Mommy for me, please.

Love, Dad.

(Linenger returned to Earth aboard STS-84 on May 24, 1997, just in time to be with Kathryn and John for the birth of their second son.)

Linnehan, Richard Michael

1957–

Veterinarian Richard Linnehan was a member of the STS-78 crew, which flew the longest Shuttle mission so far. This 17-day flight of the orbiter Columbia in June and July 1996 carried the Life and Microgravity Spacelab (LMS). The LMS crew of 7 conducted over 41 different experiments.

Linnehan later served as payload commander for STS-90, which carried the Neurolab Spacelab, in April 1998.

Linnehan was born September 19, 1957, in Lowell, Massachusetts. He graduated from high school in Pelham, New Hampshire, then attended the University of New Hampshire, receiving a B.S. in zoology in 1980. He earned his doctorate in veterinary medicine from Ohio State University in 1985.

Following graduation Dr. Linnehan entered private veterinary practice, then won a two-year fellowship in zoo animal medicine and comparative pathology at the Baltimore Zoo and Johns Hopkins University. He was commissioned a captain in the U. S. Army in 1989, reporting to the Naval Ocean Systems Center, San Diego, California, where he worked on the Marine Mammal Project as chief clinical veterinarian.

Linnehan was one of the 19 astronaut candidates selected by NASA in March 1992. In August 1993 he completed a yearlong training and evaluation course which qualified him as a Shuttle mission specialist. His first technical assignment was to the Shuttle Avionics Integration Lab. When selected for the STS-78 crew he was working in the astronaut office mission development branch.

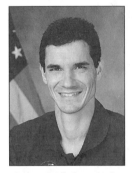

Linteris, Gregory Thomas

1957–

Chemical engineer Greg Linteris was a payload specialist for both 1997 flights of the Materials Science Laboratory.

The first MSL mission, launched as STS-83 on April 4, 1997, had to be cut from a planned 16 days to less than four because of a fuel cell problem aboard the orbiter Columbia. NASA reflew MSL three months later, with the same crew and payload, as STS-94. The crew performed 33 different experiments from scientists in 23 different countries, many of them tests of manufacturing techniques that could be of commercial use in the near future, such as the physics of combustion in microgravity, which happened to be one of Linteris's specialties. Mission scientists had hoped to set 145 fires during the flight, and were pleased when the crew actually set 206.

Linteris was born October 4, 1957—the day the first Sputnik was launched—in Demarest, New Jersey, where he graduated from Northern Valley Regional High School in 1975. He attended Princeton University, earning a B.S.

in chemical engineering (1979), then went on to Stanford University for his M.S. in mechanical engineering (1984). He received his Ph.D. in mechanical and aerospace engineering from Princeton in 1990.

From 1985 to 1990, while completing his doctorate, Linteris did research into the combustion reactions using lasers. He then joined the faculty of the University of California at San Diego, where he specialized in droplet dynamics and modeled the chemistry of solid rocket propellants. In 1992 Linteris transferred to the National Institute of Standards and Technology, Gaithersburg, Maryland, where he developed a program on advanced fire suppressants.

He was principal investigator for one of the MSL-01 experiments, and became a payload specialist for the planned mission in 1995. He was named primary payload specialist for STS-83/MSL-01 on January 29, 1996.

Llewellyn, John

1933–

Welsh-born chemist Tony Llewellyn became one of the first naturalized American citizens to join the astronaut group when he was selected in August 1967. Unfortunately, neither Llewellyn nor fellow immigrant Phillip Chapman flew in space. Llewellyn resigned from the space program in August 1968 because he was unable to become a qualified jet pilot.

Llewellyn was born April 22, 1933, in Cardiff, Wales, and received a B.S. in chemistry from University College there in 1955, and a doctorate in chemistry from the same university in 1958. He became a United States citizen on February 17, 1966.

Llewellyn was a chemist at the National Research Council of Canada from 1958 to 1960, then an associate professor at Florida State University until joining NASA. Since leaving the space program Llewellyn has taught at Florida State (where one of his students was future Spacelab 3 payload specialist Mary Helen Johnston) and at the University of Florida in Tallahassee. He is currently a professor and Director of Engineering Computing at the University of South Florida in Tampa.

Lockhart, Paul Scott

1956–

Air Force test pilot Paul Lockhart was one of the 35 astronaut candidates selected by NASA on May 1, 1996. In September of that year he reported to the Johnson Space Center to begin a training and evaluation course that should qualify him as a Shuttle pilot. He is currently assigned to the vehicle systems/operations branch of the astronaut office working redesigned solid rocket motor issues.

Lockhart was born April 28, 1956, in Amarillo, Texas, where he graduated from Tascosa High School in 1974. He attended Texas Tech University, receiving a B.A. in mathematics in 1978, then went on to study at the University of Innsbruck and the University of Vienna Summer School on a Rotarian Fellowship (1978–79). He earned his M.S. in aerospace engineering from the University of Texas in 1981, and has done additional study at Syracuse University and the University of Florida.

Lockhart was commissioned in the Air Force in 1981. Trained as a T-33 pilot, in 1983 he joined the 49th Fighter Interceptor Squadron. Three years later he transitioned to the F-4, and flew with U.S. Air Force in Germany as an F-4 and F-16 instructor pilot.

In 1991 Lockhart attended the Air Force Test Pilot School at Edwards AFB, California, and upon graduation was assigned to the Developmental Test Center at Eglin AFB, Florida, doing weapons test on the F-16. He also served as operations officer for the 39th Flight Test Squadron at Eglin.

Major Lockhart has logged 3,000 hours of flying time in 30 different aircraft.

Lopez-Algeria, Michael Eladio

1958–

Navy engineer Michael Lopez-Alegria was a mission specialist in the crew of STS-73. This 16-day flight of the orbiter Columbia carried the second U.S. Microgravity Laboratory in November 1995.

He is currently assigned to ISS assembly mission 3A.

Lopez-Alegria was born May 30, 1958, in Madrid, Spain. He graduated from high school in Mission Viejo, California, then attended the U.S. Naval Academy, receiving a B.S. in systems engineering in 1980. He earned an M.S. in aeronautical engineering at the U.S. Naval Postgraduate School, Monterey, California, in 1988.

Lopez-Alegria became a P-3 pilot in September 1981. He served as an instructor at the Pensacola Naval Air Station from 1981 to 1983, then flew the EP-3A electronic warfare craft with Fleet Air Reconnaissance Squadron TWO out of Rota, Spain, until 1986. He attended the Naval Postgraduate School in 1987 and the U.S. Naval Test Pilot School in 1988. At the time of his selection by NASA Lieutenant Commander Lopez-Alegria was program manager for the E-3A aircraft at the Naval Air Test Center, Patuxent River, Maryland.

Lopez-Alegria was one of the 19 astronaut candidates selected by NASA in March 1992. In August 1993 he completed the training and evaluation course and qualifed as a Shuttle mission specialist.

Loria, Christopher Joseph "Gus"

1960–

Marine test pilot Gus Loria is one of the 35 astronaut candidates selected by NASA on May 1, 1996. In August of that year he reported to the Johnson Space Center to begin a training and evaluation course that should qualify him as a Shuttle pilot. He is currently assigned to the vehicle systems/operations branch of the astronaut office working on landing and rollout matters.

Loria was born July 9, 1960, in Newton, Massachusetts, and grew up in Belmont, where he graduated from high school in 1978. Following a year at the Naval Academy Prep School, Loria attended the Naval Academy at Annapolis, receiving a B.S. in general engineering in 1983. He is completing his thesis for an M.S. in aeronautical engineering from the Florida Institute of Technology.

Commissioned in the U.S.M.C. upon graduation from Annapolis, Loria served as a Marine officer for three years before entering pilot training. He was designated a naval aviator in July 1988 and flew F/A-18s with Strike Fighter Squadron 125 at Lemoore, California, until August 1989. His next tour was with Marine Fighter Attack Squadron 314 at El Toro, California, the so-called Black Knights, where Loria flew 42 combat missions in Operation Desert Shield and Desert Storm.

Loria attended the Air Force Test Pilot School at Edwards AFB, California, in 1993. From January 1994 to July 1996, he was assigned to the Strike Aircraft Test Squadron at the Naval Air Warfare Center, Patuxent River, Maryland. In addition to his work at Pax River on the F/A-18 Hornet, he served as the Navy project officer on the X-31 program at the NASA Dryden Research Facility at Edwards AFB. Loria also took part in the testing of a prototype high-altitude G-system suit (HAGS), a combined G-suit and partial pressure suit for the F-16XL program.

Major Loria has logged over 2,000 hours of flying time in 35 different types of aircraft.

Lounge, John Michael

1946–

Mike Lounge was a mission specialist in three Shuttle crews, including STS-26. That flight of the orbiter Discovery in September 1988 returned the Shuttle to flight status following the Challenger disaster. During STS-26 the crew of 5 astronauts deployed a Tracking and Data Relay Satellite into geosynchronous orbit.

In December 1990 Lounge was leader of the Blue Shift team of three astronauts operating the four telescopes of the Spacelab ASTRO mission. This 9-day flight of the orbiter Columbia was the first dedicated science mission flown by NASA in five years, and overcame numerous launch delays and technical problems while returning hundreds of observations of targets in deep space.

Earlier Lounge was mission specialist and flight engineer for Mission 51-I in August and September 1985, deploying the Australian Aussat communications satellite and operating the Shuttle Discovery's remote manipulator arm to assist astronauts William Fisher and James van Hoften in the retrieval and repair of the Syncom IV-3 satellite.

Lounge was born June 28, 1946, in Denver, Colorado, and grew up in Burlington, where he graduated from high school in 1964. He attended the U.S. Naval Academy, receiving a B.S. in physics and mathematics in 1969, and later earned an M.S. in astrogeophysics from the University of Colorado (1970).

Following graduation from Annapolis, Lounge underwent flight officer training at Pensacola, Florida, becoming an F-4J Phantom radar intercept officer. Assigned to the carrier *U.S.S. Enterprise*, he took part in 99 combat missions in Southeast Asia. He later did a tour of duty aboard the *U.S.S. America* in the Mediterranean.

Lounge returned to the United States in 1974 and became an instructor in physics at the Naval Academy. Two years later he transferred to the Navy Space Project Office in Washington, D.C. He resigned from the Navy in 1978 to become a NASA engineer at the Johnson Space Center, working on payload integration and participating in the Skylab Reentry. He continued to fly F-4N aircraft with the U.S. Naval Reserve, and becoming a lieutenant colonel in the Texas Air National Guard.

Lounge was selected as an astronaut in May 1980 and completed a training and evaluation course in August 1981. While an astronaut he served as a member of the launch support team at the Kennedy Space Center for STS-1, STS-2 and STS-3. His main technical assignment has been the Shuttle's computer system. He was named to his first Shuttle crew in August 1983 and following that flight was assigned to Mission 61-F, the launch of the Galileo Jupiter probe, which was was canceled because of the Challenger accident.

Following STS-35 Lounge worked as chief of the Space Station Support Office at the NASA Johnson Space Center. In June 1991 he resigned from NASA to become vice-president of the Spacehab company in Houston, Texas, which provides cargo carriers for a number of Shuttle missions, including the Shuttle-Mir docking flights.

Lousma, Jack
1936–

Marine aviator Jack Lousma commanded the third orbital test flight of the Space Shuttle Columbia, STS-3, in March 1982. He and pilot Gordon Fullerton spent 8 days in space testing Shuttle systems and the remote manipulator arm. They were the first Shuttle astronauts to land at White Sands Missile Range, thanks to a storm that soaked the so-called dry lakebed at their primary landing site, Edwards Air Force Base in California.

Lousma was also pilot of Skylab 3, the second manned Skylab mission, in July, August and September 1973, spending over 59 days aboard the orbiting laboratory performing medical experiments, Earth resources studies, and astronomical observations. He also made two space walks.

Lousma was born February 29, 1936, in Grand Rapids, Michigan, and grew up in Ann Arbor. He attended the University of Michigan, receiving a B.S. in aeronautical engineering in 1959. He later earned the degree of aeronautical engineer from the U.S. Naval Postgraduate School in 1965.

He joined the Marine Corps in 1959 and completed pilot training the following year. He served with the 22nd Marine Air Wing as an attack pilot, and with the 1st Marine Air Wing at Iwakuni, Japan. At the time of his selection by NASA he was a reconnaissance pilot with the 2nd Marine Air Wing at Cherry Point, North Carolina.

As a pilot he logged almost 5,000 hours of flying time, 4,500 hours in jets and 240 hours in helicopters.

Lousma was one of the 19 astronauts selected by NASA in April 1966. During his early training he specialized in the Apollo lunar module and served on support crews for Apollo 9, Apollo 10 and Apollo 13. In early 1970 he was informally assigned as lunar module pilot for

Apollo 20 when that mission was canceled because of NASA budget cuts. Lousma transferred to the Skylab program and was named pilot of the second mission in January 1972. He also served as backup pilot for the Apollo-Soyuz Test Project.

Assigned to Space Shuttle development in 1976, Lousma was first named pilot of STS-3 in March 1978, only to be promoted to commander the following August after the resignation of Fred Haise.

Lousma resigned from NASA on October 1, 1983, and retired from the Marine Corps on November 1 that same year. He was an unsuccessful candidate for the U.S. Senate from Michigan in 1984, and is currently president of his own high technology consulting firm based in Ann Arbor, Michigan. He is also partnered with former Skylab astronauts Gerald Carr and William Pogue in another firm.

Love, Stanley Glen
1965–

NASA astronomer Stanley Love is one of the 25 astronaut candidates selected in June 1998. In August of that year he reported to the Johnson Space Center to begin a training and evaluation course that should qualify him as a Shuttle mission specialist and International Space Station crewmember.

Love was born June 8, 1965, in San Diego, California. He graduated from Winston Churchill High School in Eugene, Oregon, in 1983, then attended Harvey Mudd College, where he received a B.S. in physics (1987). He earned his M.S. (1989) and Ph.D. (1993) in astronomy from the University of Washington.

At the time of his selection as an ASCAN, Dr. Love was working on image processing for the Hubble Space Telescope at the NASA Jet Propulsion Laboratory, Pasadena, California.

Lovell, James Arthur, Jr.
1928–

Navy test pilot Jim Lovell was the first astronaut to make four spaceflights. In December 1965 he was pilot of Gemini 7, spending 14 days in space, a record at the time, and the following November commanded Gemini 12, the last Gemini mission.

In December 1968 he was command module pilot of Apollo 8, man's first flight around the Moon, and in April 1970 commanded Apollo 13, a planned lunar landing that had to be aborted because of an explosion aboard the Apollo service module. Lovell and astronauts Swigert and Haise turned their lunar module into a lifeboat and returned safely to Earth.

Thanks to the 1994 feature film *Apollo 13* Lovell has almost become one f the most famous astronauts of the Apollo era. This film, which starred Tom Hanks as Lovell, was based on Lovell's memoir, *Lost Moon*, written in collaboration with Jeffrey Kluger and published in 1993.

Lovell was born March 25, 1928, in Cleveland, Ohio, and grew up in Milwaukee, Wisconsin. He hoped to attend the Naval Academy at Annapolis beginning in 1946, but wound up listed as an alternate. At the same time he learned about Holloway Plan, which allowed high school graduates to enter the Navy, receive two years of college education in engineering followed by flight school commission as naval ensigns. Only then would the ensigns finish college. Lovell joined the Navy under Holloway and entered the University of Wisconsin. He also resubmitted his application to Annapolis, and in 1948 was informed that he had been selected for the academy while at flight training in Pensacola. He chose to enroll at Annapolis and graduated in 1952 with a B.S. degree. He later attended Harvard Business School (1971).

Lovell resumed his interrupted flight training following graduation from Annapolis and was then assigned to Composite Squadron 3, at Moffet Field in Palo Alto, California. He deployed to the Pacific on the carrier *U.S.S. Shangri-La*, flying the F2H Banshee. He also served as a flight instructor.

He entered the Naval Test Pilot School at Patuxent River, Maryland, in 1958. During a 4-year tour of duty at

Pax River Lovell was program manager for the F4H Phantom. He was safety engineer for Fighter Squadron 101 at the Naval Air Station in Oceana, Virginia, when selected by NASA.

As a pilot Lovell logged over 5,000 hours of flying time, 3,500 hours in jet aircraft, with over 100 carrier landings.

One of the nine NASA astronauts chosen in September 1962, Lovell was first assigned as backup pilot for Gemini 4. In January 1966, after returning from Gemini 7, he was named backup commander for Gemini 10. But on February 28, 1966, Gemini 9 astronauts Elliott See and Charles Bassett were killed in a plane crash at St. Louis. In the subsequent shuffle of crew assignments, Lovell and pilot Buzz Aldrin moved from the Gemini 10 backup job to Gemini 9, and were later assigned to Gemini 12. A year after Gemini 12, in the wake of the tragic Apollo fire, Lovell was assigned with Neil Armstrong and Aldrin to the backup crew for what eventually became Apollo 8. In July 1968 Lovell was promoted to the prime crew, replacing Michael Collins. This sequence of events made it possible for Lovell to become one of the first humans to fly around the Moon, but cost him his participation in the first lunar landing.

A similar mix of good and back luck placed Lovell on Apollo 13. As backup commander of Apollo 11 he was in line to command Apollo 14. But an attempt by flight crew chief Deke Slayton to name Mercury astronaut Alan Shepard, recently returned to flight status, to Apollo 13, was blocked by NASA managment, who thought Shepard needed more training. In August 1969 Lovell was asked if he and his crew could be ready in time to fly Apollo 13 8 months later. Lovell said they could and got the job.

Following Apollo 13 and a leave to attend Harvard, Lovell was named deputy director for science and applications at the Johnson Space Center in May 1971. On March 1, 1973, he retired from the Navy as a captain and resigned from NASA to join the Bay-Houston Towing Company, eventually becoming president and chief executive officer of the company.

In January 1977 Lovell left Bay-Houston to become president of Fisk Telephone Systems in Houston, and since January 1981 he has been group vice-president of the Centel Corporation's business communications group in Chicago, Ill.

Lovell has since retired from Central and works as a public speaker and advocate for spaceflight.

Low, David George

1956–

Space engineer Dave Low made three Shuttle flights as a mission specialist.

The first was aboard STS-32, a January 1990 flight of the Shuttle Columbia during which the Long Duration Exposure Facility satellite was retrieved and returned to Earth. Low was responsible for the successful deployment of the Syncom IV-5 (Leasat 5) communications satellite during the mission.

In August 1991 he made his second flight aboard STS-43, which deployed the fifth Tracking and Data Relay satellite (TDRS).

Low's third mission was STS-57, a June 1994 flight which carried the SpaceHab module in addition to the EURECA science pallet. Low and astronaut Jeff Wisoff conducted a six-hour EVA.

Low was born February 19, 1956, in Cleveland, Ohio, and graduated from high school in Langley, Virginia, in 1974. His father, George Low, was a high-ranking NASA administrator. David attended Washington & Lee University, receiving a B.S. in physics-engineering in 1978. He later earned a second B.S., this one in mechanical engineering from Cornell University, in 1980, and an M.S. in aeronautics and astronautics from Stanford University in 1983.

From March 1980 until being chosen as an astronaut in 1984, Low worked at the NASA Jet Propulsion Laboratory in Pasadena, California, as a spacecraft systems engineer involved in the Galileo space probe and the Mars Geoscience/Climatology Observer project.

Low was one of the 13 astronaut candidates selected by NASA in May 1984. In June 1985 he completed a training and evaluation course which qualified him as a mission specialist on future Shuttle crews. He specialized in EVA and in the use of the remote manipulator system, and served as a capcom for STS-26, STS-27, STS-29 and STS-30. In 1992 he was lead astronaut in the Man Systems Group of the Space Station Support Office. Following his final mission he headed an EVA task group at JSC, and in 1995 served with the legislative affairs office at NASA HQ in Washington.

He resigned from NASA on February 1, 1996, to join the Orbital Sciences Corporation in Dulles, Virginia.

Lu, Edward Tsang
1963–

Physicist Edward Lu was a mission specialist in the crew of STS-84. This May 1997 flight of the orbiter Atlantis carried a SpaceHab module on the sixth Shuttle-Mir docking mission.

Lu was born July 1, 1963, in Springfield, Massachusetts, and grew up in Honolulu, Hawaii, and Webster, New York. He graduated from R. L. Thomas High School in Webster, then attended Cornell University, where he received a B.S. in electrical engineering in 1984. He received a Ph.D. in applied physics from Stanford in 1989.

From 1989 to 1992 Lu was a visiting scientist at the High Altitude Observatory in Boulder, Colorado, doing research in solar physics and astrophysics. During his last year at HAO he was also with the Joint Institute for Applied Physics at the University of Colorado. He then became a postdoctoral fellow at the Institute for Astronomy, University of Hawaii at Manoa.

Lu was one of the 19 astronaut candidates selected by NASA on December 8, 1994. In May 1996 he qualified as a Shuttle mission specialist. His first technical assignment, prior to being assigned to STS-84, was with the computer support branch of the astronaut office.

Lucid, Shannon Wells
1943–

Chemist Shannon Lucid is the American space endurance record holder, including a 188-day tour aboard the Russian Mir space station in 1996.

Delivered to the Russian space station by the orbiter Atlantis and the crew of STS-76 in March 1996, Lucid joined the Mir-20 crew of Yuri Onufriyenko and Yuri Usachev for what was supposed to have been a 140-day mission. Problems with the Shuttle's solid rocket boosters, and a hurricane at the Kennedy Space Center,

delayed the launch of STS-79, her return mission, from July to September.

The 52-year-old mother of three, Lucid operated her own set of scientific experiments while also meeting the day-to-day challenges of living on orbit for weeks at a time: cooking meals and getting exercise, loading and unloading Progress supply vehicles, providing communications support while Onufriyenko and Usachev made EVAs.

In August 1996 Onufriyenko and Usachev were replaced by the Mir-21 crew of Valery Korzun and Alexandr Kaleri, who arrived at the station with French physician Claudie Andre-Deshays. Lucid herself returned to Earth with the crew of STS-79 in September 1996.

Her record-setting stay aboard Mir is chronicled in the 1997 IMAX film *Mission to Mir*.

Lucid has made four Shuttle flights, all of them as a mission specialist, beginning with Shuttle Mission 51-G in June 1985. On this flight of the Discovery the 7-astronaut crew, which included Prince Sultan Salman al-Saud of Saudi Arabia and Patrick Baudry of France, deployed three communications satellites and the Spartan scientific satellite, which was later retrieved.

In October 1989 Lucid flew on board STS-34, during which the Galileo space probe was successfully launched on its way to the planet Jupiter. She later served in the crew of STS-43, an August 1991 flight of the orbiter Atlantis. During this 9-day mission the crew of 5 astronauts successfully deployed a Tracking and Data Relay Satellite (TDRS) while conducting numerous experiments for proposed space station missions.

Her most recent Shuttle flight was STS-58, the second flight of the Life Sciences Spacelab, in October 1993. At sixteen days, STS-58 was the longest medical mission flown to that time. Its crew of 7, including 4 physicians, also served as medical test subjects.

Lucid was born Matilda Shannon Wells on January 14, 1943, in Shanghai, China, where her parents were missionaries. The Lucid family was interned in a Japanese prison camp for a year, but were released in 1944, and eventually settled in Bethany, Oklahoma, where Lucid graduated from high school in 1960. She received a B.S. in chemistry from the University of Oklahoma in 1963, and an M.S. and Ph.D. in biochemistry from the same school in 1970 and 1973.

While working for her doctorate Lucid held a variety of jobs: teaching assistant at the University of Oklahoma Department of Chemistry (1963–64), senior lab technician at the Oklahoma Medical Research Foundation (1964–66), chemist at Kerr-McGee (1966–68), and graduate assistant at the University of Oklahoma Health Science Center's Department of Biochemistry and Molecular Biology (1969–73). When chosen by NASA she was a research associate with the Oklahoma Medical Research Foundation, a position she had held since 1974.

She is also a pilot with ratings in commercial, instrument and multiengine flying.

Lucid was one of the 35 astronauts selected by NASA in January 1978. In August 1979 she completed a training and evaluation course which qualified her as a Shuttle mission specialist. As an astronaut she worked in the Shuttle Avionics Integration Laboratory (SAIL), the flight software laboratory, and in the testing of payloads. From August 1985 to January 1986 she was a mission control capcom for Shuttle flights. She has also served as chief of the mission support branch.

Lucid is currently astronaut office deputy for Shuttle-Mir.

Lydon, Malcolm Webb

1946–

Air Force engineer Mac Lydon was one of the 13 members of the first cadre of Department of Defense manned spaceflight engineers selected in February 1980. He trained as a potential DOD Shuttle payload specialist for five years without going into space.

Lydon was born June 3, 1946, in Hartford, Connecticut. He attended Kent State University in Ohio, graduating with a B.S. in mathematics in 1968. He later earned a B.S. (1973) and an M.S. (1975) in electrical engineering from Texas Tech University.

Lydon entered active duty with the Air Force in 1968. He served as chief of maintenance at King Salmon AFB, Alaska (September 1974 to 1978) and as a project engineer at the Satellite Control Facility in Sunnyvale, California (1978-80) before joining the MSE program.

He left the MSE group in 1986, transferring to HQ USAF, the Pentagon, where he worked in the office of Space Systems. He returned to Los Angeles AFB in 1990 as a director of SP-16, the spacecraft integration program office, but retired from the service (1993) and now lives and works in Florida.

Macleay, Lachlan

1931–

Air Force test pilot Mac Macleay was one of the first 8 pilots chosen for the Manned Orbiting Laboratory Program in November 1965. He remained with MOL until its cancellation in May 1969, when he transferred to other Air Force duties.

Macleay was born June 13, 1931, in St. Louis, Missouri, and grew up in Kirkwood, Missouri, and Redlands, California, where he graduated from high school in 1949. He attended the Naval Academy at Annapolis, graduating with a bachelor of science degree in 1954. He later earned an M.B.A. from the University of Southern California (1971).

Even though he graduated from the Naval Academy, Macleay elected to serve in the Air Force. After pilot training (1955–57) he became an F-86D flight instructor at Moody AFB in Valdosta, Georgia. In August 1960 he entered the Air Force Test Pilot School at Edwards AFB, and remained at Edwards for a year as a Special Projects (U-2) test pilot. In 1961 and 1962 he served as an adviser to the Republic of Korea's 10th Air Force, then returned to Edwards to attend the new Aerospace Research Pilot School. He was a project pilot for the F-4C and F-5 aircraft prior to joining MOL.

Following MOL's cancellation in June 1969 he entered the M.B.A. program at the University of Southern California. After receiving his degree in 1971, he was assigned as commander of the 23rd Tactical Air Surveillance Squadron at Nakon Phanom, Thailand.

He returned to the United States in 1972 to become reconaissance/strike project officer at Wright-Patterson AFB, Ohio. From 1973 to 1974 he attended the Air War College, then went back to Wright-Pat, this time as director of the Maverick cruise missile system program office. When he retired from the Air Force (with the rank of colonel) in June 1978 he was assistant deputy chief of staff for requirements, Tactical Air Command, Langley AFB, Virginia.

As a pilot Macleay logged over 6,000 hours of flying time.

He is currently a manager for the AMRAAM missile program with Hughes Aircraft in Tucson, Arizona.

Magilton, Gerard Edward
1942–

RCA satellite engineer Jerry Magilton was backup for fellow RCA payload specialist Bob Cenker on Shuttle Mission 61-C. This January 1986 flight of the orbiter Columbia deployed the RCA-built Satcom Ku-1 satellite.

Magilton was born May 7, 1942, in Philadelphia, Pennsylvania, where he graduated from Father Judge High School in 1960. He joined the Army and served a tour on active duty as a Nike missile crewmember at Fort Bliss, Texas, then attended Drexel University, receiving a B.S. in electrical engineering in 1965.

His first job after graduation was working for Philco Ford Defense Electronics in Willow Grove, Pennsylvania. Two years later he joined RCA in East Windsor, New Jersey, on the TIROS weather satellite program. At the time of his selection as a Shuttle payload specialist he was manager of integration and test for the astro-electronics division of RCA, responsible for the final assembly of the company's Series 3000 spacecraft, including the Spacenet, G Star and Satcom Ku satellites. He later became manager for on-orbit performance for Martin-Marietta Astro Space. (Martin-Marietta absorbed GE Astro Space, which had in turn acquired RCA. Martin-Marietta itself became part of the Lockheed-Martin conglomerate.)

Magilton was selected as an RCA payload specialist candidate in June 1985.

Magnus, Sandra Hall
1964–

Materials scientist Sandra Magnus is one of the 35 astronaut candidates selected by NASA on May 1, 1996. In August of that year she reported to the Johnson Space Center to begin a yearlong training and evaluation course that should qualify her as a Shuttle mission specialist and International Space Station crewmember.

Magnus was born October 30, 1964, in Belleville, Illinois, where she graduated from Belleville West High School in 1982. She attended the University of Missouri, Rolla, where she received a B.S. in physics (1986) and an M.S. in electrical engineering (1990). She earned her Ph.D. in materials science and engineering from the Georgia Institute of Technology in 1996.

From 1986 to 1991 Magnus worked for the McDonnell Douglas Aircraft Corporation, as a propulsion engineer on the A-12 Attack Aircraft program, and as a researcher studying the effectiveness of stealth radar techniques. In She spent the next five years doing her doctoral research on a graduate student fellowship sponsored by the NASA Lewis Research Center in Cleveland, Ohio.

Mamtz, Michael Ray
1953–

Air Force engineer Mike Mantz was one of 14 officers in the second cadre of Manned Spaceflight Engineers chosen in January 1983 to train as possible military Shuttle payload specialists.

In October 1984, Mantz was selected as backup payload specialist to fellow MSEs Brett Watterson and Randy Odle for Mission 62-A, the planned first Vandenberg Shuttle orbital flight test. By September 1985, however, Air Force undersecretary Pete Aldridge had become one of the prime payload specialists, relegating Odle to the backup position. Mantz served as Aldridge's training officer until the cancellation of Mission 62-A following the Challenger disaster.

Mantz was born February 16, 1953, in Pensacola, Florida. He attended the Air Force Academy, graduating in 1976 with a B.S. in electrical engineering. In 1981 he earned an M.S. in astronautical engineering from the Massachusetts Institute of Technology.

From 1976 to 1979 Mantz was an electronics research engineer with the Electronic Security Command in San Antonio, Texas. After completing his master's degree in 1981 he was assigned as computer development manager at the Ballistic Missile Office, Norton AFB, California.

As an MSE he worked on the Navstar GPS program and in support of the planned first Vandenberg Shuttle mission. He left Space Division in 1987 and was assigned to the Air Logistics Command at Wright-Patterson AFB, Ohio. In 1990 he returned to Los Angeles AFS as project manager for GWEN.

From January 1995 to the spring of 1997 he commanded the 5th Space Operations Squadron, 50th Space Wing, at USAF Space Command, Peterson AFB, Colorado. The 5th SOPS operated the MILSTAR satellite constellation. Following a tour in acquisitions in the Office of Space Systems in the Pentagon, Mantz was named commander of the 821st Space Group, Buckley Air National Guard Base, Colorado.

From 1980 to 1986 Massimino was a systems engineer with the IBM Corporation. While in graduate school at M.I.T beginning in 1986 he helped develop human operator controls for space robotics systems. He was awarded a patent for this work, with a second patent pending. He also spent a summer (1987) at NASA Headquarters in Washington, D.C., as a general engineer in human factors research, and two summers (1988 and 1989) at the NASA Marshall Spaceflight Center, Huntsville, Alabama, working in the man-systems integration branch.

In 1990 Massimino worked for the German Aerospace Research Establishment on the development of the robot technology experiment (ROTEX), which was flown on the second German Spacelab Shuttle mission (STS-55, March 1993).

After leaving M.I.T. in 1992 Massimino joined McDonnell Douglas Aerospace in Houston, Texas, as a research engineer working on displays for the Shuttle's remote manipulator systrem. He also served as an adjunct assistant professor of mechanical engineering and materials science at Rice University. He joined the faculty of the Georgia Institute of Technology in September 1995 as an assistant professor in the School of Industrial and Systems Engineering.

Massimino, Michael James
1962–

Space engineer Mike Massimino is one of the 35 astronaut candidates selected by NASA on May 1, 1996. In August of that year he reported to the Johnson Space Center to begin a training and evaluation course that should qualify him as a Shuttle mission specialist and International Space Station crewmember.

Massimino was born August 19, 1962, in Oceanside, New York, and grew up in Franklin Square, where he graduated from H. Frank Carey High School in 1980. He attended Columbia University, receiving a B.S. in industrial engineering. He later attended the Masschusetts Institute of Technology, where he earned an M.S. in mechanical engineering (1988), the degree of mechanical engineer (1990) and a Ph.D. in mechanical engineering (1992).

Mastracchio, Richard Alan
1960–

NASA flight controller Rick Mastracchio is one of the 35 astronaut candidates selected by the space agency on May 1, 1996. In August of that year he began a training and evaluation course that should qualify him as a Shuttle mission specialist and International Space Station crewmember. He is currently assigned to the computer support branch of the astronaut office.

Mastracchio was born February 11, 1960, in Waterbury, Connecticut, where he graduated from Crosby High School in 1978. He attended the University of Connecticut, receiving a B.S. in electrical engineering/computer science in 1982. He later earned an M.S. in electrical engineering from Rensselaer Polytechnical University (1987) and an M.S. in physical science from the University of Houston, Clear Lake (1991).

After graduation from Connecticut in 1982, Mastracchio worked for the Hamilton Standard Corporation as an engineer in system design for intertial measurement units and flight control computers. He joined the Rockwell Shuttle Operations Company in Houston, Texas, in 1987, and three years later became an engineer with NASA in the flight crew operations directorate, where he first worked on software in the Shuttle Avionics Integration Laboratory. From 1993 to 1996 he served as an ascent/entry guidance and procedures officer (GPO) in mission control, providing support for 17 different Shuttle missions.

Mathiessen, David Henry
1958–

Materials scientist David Mathiessen was an alternate payload specialist for STS-73, the second U.S. Microgravity Spacelab (USML-2). This 16-day flight of the orbiter Columbia carrying a crew of 7 was launched October 5, 1996. The crew conducted over 40 experiments in fluid physics, materials science, and biotechnology. Mathiessen supported USML-2 from the payload operations center at the Marshall Spaceflight Center.

Mathiessen was born August 31, 1958, in Blue Island, Illinois. He graduated from Harold L. Richards High School in Oak Lawn, Illinois, in 1976, then attended the University of Illinois at Urbana, where he received a B.S. in ceramic engineering in 1980. He did graduate work at Illinois, receiving an M.S. in ceramic engineering in 1982, and at the Massachusetts Institute of Technology, where he earned a Ph.D. in materials engineering in 1988.

After completing his doctorate Mathiessen joined GTE Laboratories' Electronic Materials Department, serving as a principal investigator for a joint USAF/GTE/NASA experiment to investigate the growth of gallium arsenide in microgravity. This experiment flew aboard Spacelab Life Sciences 1 (STS-40) in 1991, and ATLAS-1 (STS-45) in 1992.

In 1993 Dr. Mathiessen joined the faculty at Case Western Reserve University in Cleveland, Ohio, as an assistant professor of materials science and engineering.

He was principal investigator on the Crystal Growth Furnace, which flew on USML-1 (STS-50) in 1992 and on USML-2. He was principal investigator for the Diffusion Processes in Molten Semiconductor (DPIMS) experiment flown on the Materials Science Lab, STS-83, in April 1997.

Mattingly, Thomas Kenneth II
1936–

Navy pilot Ken Mattingly lost his first chance at a spaceflight when he was replaced on the Apollo 13 crew just days before launch in April 1970. The temporary grounding occurred because Mattingly, who had trained for months as command module pilot for the lunar landing mission, had been exposed to German measles. NASA officials feared he would become ill during the flight, and might be unable to operate the Apollo command module in lunar orbit. Mattingly watched from mission control as the Apollo 13 service module suffered an explosion that canceled the lunar landing and forced astronauts Lovell, Swigert, and Haise to make an emergency return to Earth.

Mattingly never did come down with the measles. He went on to make three spaceflights.

The first was Apollo 16, in April 1972, for which Mattingly served as pilot of the command module Casper while astronauts John Young and Charles Duke explored the Moon in the lunar module Orion. During the return flight to Earth Mattingly performed an EVA of 1 hour and 13 minutes.

In June and July 1982 Mattingly commanded STS-4, the fourth orbital flight test of the Space Shuttle Columbia, that carried a Department of Defense sensor package called CIRRIS. STS-4 was the first of many scheduled DOD-dedicated Shuttle flights. Some conversations between astronauts Mattingly and Henry Hartsfield and ground controllers at the Johnson Space Center in Houston and the USAF Satellite Control Facility in Sunnyvale, California, were conducted in code.

Mattingly's third flight, Shuttle Mission 51-C, was another DOD mission and was conducted with even greater secrecy. The launch time was not disclosed until T-minus 9 minutes and once the Shuttle Discovery reached orbit, none of the astronauts' transmissions could be heard. There was a total blackout on the payload itself, though it was reported in the press as a National Security Agency electronic intelligence satellite called Magnum. (The USAF did acknowledge that the classified payload was mounted on an intertial upper stage, and that the IUS performed as designed.) Even the mission duration was not disclosed in advance. Mattingly and his 4-man crew, which included the first Air Force Manned Spaceflight Engineer, Major Gary Patyon, returned to Earth on January 28, 1985. Weather problems apparently forced the crew to return a day early; cold weather had also postponed the launch by a day. In fact, 51-C was the coldest Shuttle launch until the tragic Challenger in January 1986.

Mattingly was born March 17, 1936, in Chicago, Illinois. His parents moved to Florida when he was very young and Mattingly graduated from Miami Edison High School in Miami. He attended Auburn University from 1954 to 1958, earning a B.S. in aeronautical engineering.

Mattingly entered the US Navy in 1958 and completed pilot training in 1960. From 1960 to 1963 he flew A1H attack aircraft aboard the carrier *U.S.S. Saratoga*, and for the next two years flew A3Bs from the carrier *U.S.S. Franklin D. Roosevelt*. In 1965 he was enrolled in the USAF Aerospace Research Pilot School at Edwards AFB, California, and was a student there when selected by NASA.

One of the 19 astronauts selected by NASA in April 1966, Mattingly specialized in the systems of the development of the Apollo command module and took part in the development of the Apollo spacesuit and backpack. He served on the support crews for Apollo 8 and Apollo 11 and was named to the prime crew of Apollo 13 in August 1969.

Between January 1973 and April 1981 Mattingly held several administrative jobs in the astronaut office and Shuttle program: head of the Shuttle support group (January 1973 to March 1978), technical assistant to Donald K. Slayton, who was managing the Shuttle orbital flight test program (March 1978 to December 1979), and, finally, head of the ascent/entry group (December 1979 to April 1981). Mattingly and Hartsfield served as backups for STS-2 and STS-3, the last backup or standby crew designated by NASA.

In October 1982 Mattingly was named to command STS-10, the first Department of Defense Shuttle mission, but upper stage problems aboard STS-6 in April 1983 forced several postponements, until January 1985, by which time the flight had received a new designation.

Mattingly resigned from NASA in June 1985 to become commander of the US Navy Electronics Systems Command. He later served as director of space systems for the Space and Naval Warfare Systems Command.

He retired from the Navy as a rear admiral in 1990 to join former crewmate Fred Haise at the Grumman Space Station Integration Division in Reston, Virginia, where he was director of utilization and operations for that program.

In 1993 he joined the General Dynamics Space Systems Division in San Diego as deputy program director for the Atlas launch vehicle. More recently he has been program director for the X-33 reusable launch system for Lockheed-Martin.

McArthur, William Surles, Jr.

1951–

Army pilot Bill McArthur was a mission specialist in the crew of STS-58. This November 1993 flight of the orbiter Columbia carried the second Life Sciences Spacelab. Its crew of 7 conducted 19 different medical experiments during a 16-day flight, also serving as subjects for some experiments.

McArthur's second flight was STS-74, the second Shuttle-Mir docking mission, launched in November 1995. This flight of the orbiter Atlantis attached a permanent docking module to Mir and also delivered 3,000 pounds of supplies to the station.

He is currently assigned as an EVA crewmember for International Space Station assembly mission 3A, scheduled for launch as STS-92 in late 1999.

McArthur was born July 26, 1951, in Laurinburg, North Carolina, though he considers Wakulla to be his hometown. He attended the U.S. Military Academy at West Point, graduating with a B.S. in applied science and engineering in 1973. He later earned an M.S. in aerospace engineering from the Georgia Institute of Technology (1983).

McArthur's first assignment in the U.S. Army was with the 82nd Airborne Division at Fort Bragg, North Carolina. In 1975 he entered the US Army Aviation School, graduating at the top of his class in June 1976. For the next two years he served as an aeroscout team leader with the 2nd Infantry Division in the Republic of Korea. In 1978 he became a company commander, platoon leader and assistant operations office with the 24th Army Combat Aviation Battalion in Savannah, Georgia. Following a year at Georgia Tech, he was assigned to West Point as an assistant professor in the department of mechanics. In 1987 he attended the U.S. Naval Test Pilot School at Patuxent River, Maryland.

After being designated an experimental test pilot McArthur was assigned as a Shuttle vehicle integration test engineer at the NASA Johnson Space Center, working on launch and landing operations.

He has logged 3,700 hours of flying time in 37 different types of aircraft.

McArthur was one of the 23 astronaut candidates selected by NASA in January 1990. In July 1991 he qualified as a Shuttle mission specialist while assigned to the operations development branch of the atrsonaut office. He later served as a capcom in mission control, and in 1996 and 1997 headed the flight support branch.

McAuliffe, Sharon Christa
1948–1986

High school social studies teacher Christa McAuliffe was chosen from over ten thousand applicants to be the first private citizen to go into space. Tragically, she was killed with six other space travelers during the launch of the Shuttle Challenger on January 28, 1986.

McAuliffe had been scheduled to deliver two live TV lessons to schoolchildren all over America during her 5-day trip. In the time between being chosen as the first teacher-in-space in July 1985 and the launch she had become famous—the first space traveler who was not a test pilot, scientist, or an engineer—and her sudden death in a vehicle most Americans viewed as being as safe as an airliner came as a tremendous shock.

McAuliffe was born Sharon Christa Corrigan on September 2, 1948, in Boston, Massachusetts. She grew up in nearby Framingham and graduated from Marian High School there in 1966. She received a B.A. from Framingham State College in 1970 and an M.A. in education from Bowie State College in Maryland in 1978.

McAuliffe began her teaching career at Benjamin Foulois Junior High School in Morningside, Maryland, in 1970. She taught civics, American history, and English at several schools in Maryland and New Hampshire before arriving at Concord Senior High in 1982. There she taught economics, law, American history, and a course she developed called "The American Woman" to 10th, 11th, and 12th graders. She was considered a creative and dynamic teacher who was particularly fond of taking her classes on field trips to court rooms, prisons, and police stations.

When President Reagan announced on August 27, 1984, that a schoolteacher would be the first private citizen in space (rather than the journalist most observers expected), McAuliffe was eager to apply. She wrote in her application essay, "I cannot join the space program and restart my life as an astronaut, but this opportunity to connect my abilities as an educator with my interests in history and space is a unique opportunity to fulfill my early fantasies. I watched the space program being born and would like to participate."

She proposed to keep a 3-part journal of her experiences, the first part dealing with training, the second with the flight itself, and the third with the aftermath. She also planned to keep a video record of her activities on this "ultimate field trip."

Out of the thousands of applicants, 118 were invited to Washington, D.C., in late June for interviews with a panel that included four former astronauts, several university presidents, actress Pam Dawber, artificial heart inventor Robert Jarvik, and former pro basketball star Wes Unseld. Ten finalists were chosen and these were brought to the NASA Johnson Space Center in Houston for more interviews and tests beginning July 1. After a stop at the NASA Marshall Space Flight Center in Huntsville, Alabama, the finalists ended up in Washington, where Vice President George Bush announced in a White House ceremony that McAuliffe was the choice.

Bob Hohler, a reporter from McAuliffe's hometown newspaper, *The Concord Monitor*, wrote a series of articles describing the teacher's adaptation to payload specialist training and to being a celebrity. These articles were the basis of a book, *I Touch the Future* (1986).

McAuliffe's life was dramatized in the television movie *Challenger* (1990). McAuliffe's mother, Grace George Corrigan, published her own account of the tragedy in *A Journal for Christa* (1993).

THE FINAL MOMENTS OF CHALLENGER

(These are the last recorded words of the crew of Challenger, Shuttle Mission 51-L, as they awaited launch on the morning of Tuesday, January 28, 1986. Data was taped by an operational cockpit recorder, activated 2 minutes and 5 minutes prior to launch. The operational recorder normally runs for the entire mission. Flight deck crewmembers heard on the tape are CDR Richard Scobee, PLT Michael Smith, MS1 Ellison Onizuka, and MS2 Judy Resnik. Middeck crewmembers MS3 Ronald McNair, PS1 Christa McAuliffe, and PS2 Gregory Jarvis, could hear the flight deck crew, but made no recorded comments.)

T minus 2:00

SCOBEE: Two minutes downstairs. You got a watch running down there?

SMITH: Okay, there goes the lox arm.

(Smith refers to the liquid oxygen supply arm to the Shuttle's external tank.)

SCOBEE: There goes the beanie cap.

(Scobee means the liquid oxygen vent cap, which moves away from the Shuttle during these final moments.)

ONIZUKA: Doesn't it go the other way? [laughter]

SMITH: God, I hope not, Ellison.

ONIZUKA: Now I see it, I see it. I couldn't see it moving — it was behind the center screen.

T minus 1:33

RESNIK: Got your harnesses locked?

SMITH: What for?

SCOBEE: I won't lock mine. I might have to reach something.

SMITH: Okay.

ONIZUKA: Dick's thinking of somebody there.

SCOBEE: Uh-huh. One minute downstairs.

T-minus :52

RESNIK: Cabin pressure's probably going to give us an alarm.

(Resnik refers to a routine caution alarm, which sounds.)

SCOBEE: Okay. Okay there.

SMITH: Cabin pressure is acceptable.

SCOBEE: Okay.

SMITH: Ullage pressures are up.

(Smith refers to the ullage pressure in the external tank.)

SMITH: Right helium tank is just a little bit low.

(The helium pressure in the Shuttle main engines.)

SCOBEE: It was yesterday, too.

SMITH: Okay.

SCOBEE: Thirty seconds down there!

SMITH: Remember the red button when you make a roll call.

(Smith cautions Scobee about a communications configuration.)

SCOBEE: I won't do that. Thanks a lot.

T minus 15 seconds

SCOBEE: Fifteen.

SSMEs start

SCOBEE: There they go, guys!

RESNIK: All right!

SCOBEE: Three at a hundred.

SRBs ignite. Liftoff. The orbiter clears the tower and begins to roll.

SCOBEE: Houston, Challenger, roll program.

SMITH: Go, you mother!

RESNIK: LV, LH.

(Resnik reminds Scobee and Smith to change configuration of their cockpit switches to local vertical/local horizontal.)

RESNIK: S*** hot!

SCOBEE: Ooo-kay.

SMITH: Looks like we've got a lot of wind here today.

SCOBEE: Yeah. It's a little hard to see out my window here.

SMITH: There's ten thousand feet and Mach point five.

(Smith makes the routine altitude and velocity report at T plus 30 seconds.)

SCOBEE: Point nine.

(Mach 0.9 velocity report.)

SMITH: There's Mach one.

SCOBEE: Going through nineteen thousand.

(Altitude report, 19,000 feet at T plus 42 seconds.)

SCOBEE: Okay, we're throttling down.

(Routine reduction of Shuttle main engine thrust as the vehicle passes through maximum dynamic pressure region, max-Q.)

T plus :57

SCOBEE: Throttling up.

SMITH: Throttle up.

SCOBEE: Roger.

SMITH: Feel that mother go.

UNKNOWN: Woo-ooo!

SMITH: Thirty-five thousand going through one-point-five.

(Altitude and velocity, Mach 1.5 at 35,000 feet.)

SCOBEE: Reading 486 on mine.

(Airspeed indicator check.)

SMITH: Yep, that's what I've got, too.

CAPCOM (Covey): Challenger, go at throttle up.

SCOBEE: Roger, go at throttle up.

(Shuttle main engines now running at 104 percent thrust.)

SMITH: Uh-oh.

T plus 1:13 — loss of all data

McBride, Jon Andrew

1943–

Navy test pilot Jon McBride served as pilot for Shuttle Mission 41-G in October 1984, the first seven-person crew in space. During 41-G the Earth Radiation Budget Satellite was deployed, Earth observations were conducted with the Shuttle Imaging Radar, and spacewalking astronauts conducted a satellite refueling experiment.

McBride was scheduled to command a Spacelab flight intended to observe Halley's Comet in March 1986, but that mission, 61-E, was canceled because of the explosion of the Shuttle Challenger on January 28, 1986.

McBride was born August 14, 1943, in Charleston, West Virginia, and grew up in Beckley, where he graduated from high school in 1960. For the next four years he alternated between work and the study of engineering at West Virginia University in Morgantown, where a Navy recruiter gave him his first ride in an airplane. McBride received a B.S. in aeronautical engineering from the US Naval Postgraduate School in 1971. He also performed graduate work in human resources management at Pepperdine University.

McBride entered the Navy through the Naval Aviation Cadet (NAVCAD) program in January 1965 and underwent pilot training at Pensacola, Florida, winning his wings in 1966. He served with Fighter Squadron 101 in Oceana, Virginia, then with Fighter Squadron 41. He also flew 64 combat missions in Vietnam.

Following attendance at the Naval Postgraduate School and another tour as a fighter pilot, McBride entered the Air Force Test Pilot School at Edwards AFB, California, graduating with future astronauts Guy Gardner, Loren Shriver and Steven Nagel in class 75-A. He was a test pilot with Air Test and Development Squadron 4 at Pt. Mugu, California, when selected by NASA.

As a pilot McBride logged over 4,800 hours of flying time, including 4,300 hours in jets, in over 40 types of military and civilian aircraft. Between 1976 and 1978 he also flew the Navy "Spirit of '76" Bicentennial-painted F-4J Phantom at various air shows.

McBride was one of the 35 astronauts chosen by NASA in January 1978. In August 1979 he completed a training and evaluation course which qualified him as a Shuttle pilot. He was lead chase pilot for the first landing of Columbia (STS-1), worked in the Shuttle Avionics Integration Laboratory (SAIL), and served as capcom for STS-5, STS-6 and STS-7.

In January 1985, following his flight as pilot on Mission 41-G, McBride was named commander of the Spacelab ASTRO mission, then scheduled for launch in March 1986. During the hiatus in Shuttle flights caused by the Challenger disaster McBride served at NASA Headquarters in Washington, D.C., as acting assistant administrator for congressional relations. He was reassigned to the command of ASTRO 1, then known as STS-35, in November 1988. But in May 1989, following additional delays in the scheduled STS-35 launch, McBride chose to resign from NASA and retire from the Navy.

He is currently president of Flying Eagle Corp., a venture capital group, in Lewisburg, West Virginia.

McCandless, Bruce, II
1937–

Navy pilot Bruce McCandless was the first person to make an untethered space walk. On February 8, 1984, he donned a manned maneuvering unit (MMU), the so-called Buck Rogers backpack he had helped develop, and, disconnecting his safety line, flew 320 feet away from the Shuttle Challenger. As he fired the MMU's thrusters and backed away from the Challenger, McCandless said, "That may have been one small step for Neil [Armstrong], but it's a heck of a big leap for me." (In July 1969 McCandless had been the astronaut capcom on duty during the first walk on the Moon.) For almost six hours McCandless and fellow astronaut Robert Stewart tested the MMU. Two days later they performed a second EVA, rehearsing techniques for retrieving and repairing satellites with the MMU.

The tests of the MMU by McCandless and Stewart were highlights of a Shuttle mission plagued by the failure of two satellite rocket motors (which left the Palapa B2 and Westar VI satellites in useless orbits), and the explosion of a balloon deployed from the Challenger to serve as a rendezvous target. Mission 41-B was the first Shuttle to land at the Kennedy Space Center, becoming the first manned spacecraft to end a mission at its launch site.

In April 1990 McCandless made a second spaceflight, as mission specialist in the crew of STS-31. This 5-day flight of the orbiter Discovery deployed the Hubble Space Telescope at a record Shuttle altitude of 381 miles. McCandless and astronaut Kathryn Sullivan stood by throughout the deployment in case an emergency EVA was needed.

The son and grandson of Navy officers, Bruce McCandless II was born June 8, 1937, in Boston, Massachusetts. After graduating from Woodrow Wilson Senior High School in Long Beach, California, he entered the US Naval Academy at Annapolis, receiving a B.S. in science in 1958 and standing second in a class of 899. He later earned an M.S. in electrical engineering from Stanford University in 1965 and performed work toward a Ph.D. in that subject. In 1987 he received an M.B.A. from the University of Houston at Clear Lake.

McCandless underwent pilot training at Pensacola, Florida, and Kingsville, Texas, earning his wings in March 1960. For the next four years he served as a F-6A Skyray and F-4B Phantom II pilot aboard the carriers *U.S.S. Forrestal* and *U.S.S. Enterprise*, taking part in the Cuban blockade of October 1962. He later did a tour as a flight instructor at the naval air station in Oceana, Virginia, then reported to Stanford University for graduate school.

As a pilot McCandless logged over 5,200 hours of flying time, including almost 5,000 hours in jets. In addition to Navy jets and the T-38A used by NASA, he has also flown helicopters.

McCandless was one of the 19 astronauts selected by NASA in April 1966. He served as capcom for Apollo 10, Apollo 11, and Apollo 14 and was also a member of the support crew for the latter. In 1971 he began to work on the Skylab program, becoming coinvestigator for the M-509 astronaut maneuvering unit (AMU), an earlier version of the Shuttle MMU. He was backup pilot for Skylab 2 and capcom for Skylab 3.

Between 1974 and 1983 McCandless worked on projects relating to the Space Shuttle, including the inertial upper stage (IUS), the Space Telescope, and the Solar Maximum Repair mission, in addition to his involvement with the MMU. In February 1983, following a wait of almost 17 years, he was assigned to his first flight crew, STS-11, later known as Mission 41-B. Following 41-B he was named as a mission specialist for the launch of the Hubble Space Telescope, originally scheduled for September 1985, but postponed in the aftermath of the Challenger explosion. During the hiatus McCandless worked on EVA procedures for the Freedom space station program.

He resigned from NASA and retired from the Navy (with the rank of captain) on August 31, 1990 becoming as aerospace consultant in Houston, working on, among other projects, the Hubble repair mission scheduled (STS-61, flown in December 1993). He is now on the staff of Lockheed-Martin in Dnever, Colorado.

McCool, William Cameron
1961–

Navy test pilot Willie McCool is one of the 35 astronaut candidates selected by NASA on May 1, 1996. In August of that year he reported to the Johnson Space Center to begin the training and evaluation course that should qualify him as a Shuttle pilot. He is currently assigned to the vehicle systems/operations branch of the astronaut office.

McCool was born September 23, 1961, in San Diego, California. He graduated from Coronado High School in Lubbock, Texas, in 1979, then attended the Naval Academy at Annapolis, where he received a B.S. in applied science (1983). He later earned an M.S. in computer science from the University of Maryland (1985) and an M.S. in aeronautical engineering from the Naval Postgraduate School (1992).

Commissioned in the Navy following graduation from Annapolis, and following a year at Maryland, McCool qualified as a naval aviator in August 1986. He first served with Tactical Electronic Warfare Squadron 133, making two deployments to the Mediterranean aboard the carrier *U.S.S. Coral Sea*, where he flew EA-6B Prowlers.

In November 1989 McCool was selected for the Naval Postgraduate School/Test Pilot School Cooperative Education Program, and spent 15 months getting his master's degree in engineering, followed by a year at the test pilot school at Patuxent River, Maryland. From 1992 to 1994 he was a TA-4J and EA-6B test pilot with the flight systems department of the strike aircraft test directorate at Pax River.

He was serving as administrative and operations officer for Tactical Electronic Warfare Squadron 132 aboard the carrier *U.S.S. Enterprise* when selected by NASA.

Lieutenant Commander McCool has logged 2,100 hours of flying time with over 400 carrer landings in 24 different types of aircraft.

McCulley, Michael James
1943–

Former Navy test pilot and submariner Mike McCulley served as pilot of STS-34, a flight of the orbiter Discovery that successfully sent the Galileo space probe on its way to Jupiter in October 1989. The 5-day mission had to overcome a legal challenge by antinuclear activists who were concerned that a Challenger-type accident involving Galileo and Discovery could scatter radioactive plutonium (from Galileo's onboard power system) over Florida.

McCulley was born August 4, 1943, in San Diego, California, and grew up in Livingston, Tennessee, graduating from Livingston Academy in 1961. He later earned a B.S. and M.S. in metallurgical engineering from Purdue University in 1970.

He joined the Navy right out of high school and served as an enlisted man aboard submarines. In 1965 he entered Purdue, earning his officer's commission in 1970, the same year he earned both college degrees. He became a pilot and flew A-4 and A-6 aircraft from carriers until being assigned to the Empire Test Pilot School at Farnborough, England. He was a test pilot at the Naval Air Test Center at Patuxent River, Maryland, for several years. When chosen by NASA he was operations officer for Attack Squadron 35 aboard the carrier *U.S.S. Nimitz.*

McCulley logged over 5,000 hours of flying time, including 400 carrier landings on six different carriers, in 50 different types of aircraft.

He was one of the 17 astronauts selected by NASA in May 1984 and in June 1985 qualified him as a Shuttle pilot. His first technical assignment was serving as astronaut weather coordinator at the Kennedy Space Center. In November 1985 he was assigned as pilot for Mission 61-N, a Department of Defense Shuttle mission then scheduled for 1986. During the hiatus caused by the Challenger disaster McCulley served as the technical assistant to Don Puddy, the Director of Flight Crew Operations, and as his representative to the STS program requirements control board. He was assigned as pilot of STS-34 in September 1988.

Following STS-34 McCulley led the astronaut support team at KSC. In October 1990 McCulley retired from the Navy with the rank of captain and resigned from NASA to join the Lockheed Space Operations Company as vice president and deputy director at the Kennedy Space Center launch site. In this position he oversaw 6,000 employees processing Shuttle vehicles for flight. In October 1995 he became director of launch site operations for Lockheed-Martin Space Operations at KSC, now part of the United Space Alliance.

McDivitt, James
1929–

Air Force test pilot Jim McDivitt was command pilot of Gemini 4, the second manned Gemini mission, during which pilot Edward White became the first American to walk in space. McDivitt kidded White during the 20-minute EVA ("You smeared up my windshield, you dirty dog!") and took the now-famous photographs of his fellow astronaut floating at the end of his gold tether. Gemini 4 also set an American space endurance record by remaining in orbit slightly over four days.

In March 1969 McDivitt commanded Apollo 9, the first manned test of the Apollo lunar module, whose development and construction he had helped oversee. It was a vital step toward the first manned lunar landing, accomplished four months later.

McDivitt was born June 10, 1929, in Chicago, Illinois, and grew up in Kalamazoo, Michigan, where he graduated from high school. Following high school he worked for a year as a water boiler repairman and took classes at Jackson Junior College in Jackson, Michigan. He later attended the University of Michigan, earning a B.S. in aeronautical engineering in 1959 and graduating first in his class.

McDivitt joined the U.S. Air Force in 1951 and, after pilot training, flew F-80s and F-86s on 145 combat missions in Korea. Returning to the United States, he remained in the Air Force attending the University of Michigan, the USAF Experimental Test Pilot School, and the USAF Aerospace Research Pilot School. When selected by NASA he was a test pilot at Edwards AFB.

As a pilot McDivitt eventually logged over 5,000 hours of flying time.

He was one of 9 astronauts selected by NASA in September 1962 and quickly established himself as a first-class pilot and a thorough engineer. NASA managers obviously agreed: just two years after joining the space program, McDivitt was chosen to command the complex Gemini 4 mission. He is the only American astronaut to command a mission without ever having served an "apprenticeship" on a backup or support crew. In fact, except for several months in 1966, when he worked as backup to Gus Grissom for the first manned Apollo mission, McDivitt spent his astronaut career training only as a commander of a prime crew.

In May 1969 McDivitt became NASA manager of lunar landing operations, directing the final months of the effort to land a man on the Moon. Following the triumph of Apollo 11, in August 1969, McDivitt was named manager of the entire Apollo spacecraft program, a job he held until June 1972. He was also promoted to the rank of brigadier general.

McDivitt retired from the Air Force and resigned from NASA in August 1972 to join Consumers Power Company as vice-president for corporate affairs. In March 1975 he joined Pullman, Inc., of Chicago, America's largest builder of railroad cars, as president.

Since January 1981 he has worked for Rockwell International Corporation, builders of the Space Shuttle, where he is currently senior vice-president for government operations at their Arlington, Virginia, office.

McKay, John Barron
1922–1975

Jack McKay was a NASA test pilot who flew the X-15 rocket research plane on 29 flights between September 1960 and October 1966. During one of his early X-15 flights, on November 9, 1962, McKay was forced to crash land at Mud Lake near Edwards Air Force Base. The rocket plane flipped over, seriously injuring McKay, and though he recovered and flew the X-15 again, complications from this accident eventually caused his death at Lancaster, California, on April 27, 1975.

He made one flight, on September 28, 1965, in which he reached an altitude of 295,600 feet, qualifying him for the title of astronaut. As a civilian NASA employee, however, he was not eligible for Air Force astronaut wings.

McKay was born December 8, 1922, in Portsmouth, Virginia, where his father, a Navy officer, was based. He grew up in the West Indies and had no formal schooling between third and seventh grades. Returning to Virginia, he completed high school and also learned to fly, soloing at the age of 18. While continuing his education at Virginia Polytechnic Institute, he also went to work for the National Advisory Committee on Aeronautics (NACA), NASA's forerunner, in 1940, as a model builder at Langley Field, Virginia.

When World War II broke out McKay joined the Navy and eventually qualified as a fighter pilot. He flew combat missions against Japan from the carrier *U.S.S. Hornet*. After the war he returned to Virginia Polytechnic Institute, graduating with a B.S. in aeronautical engineering in 1950.

McKay went to work for NACA in 1951 as a test pilot at Edwards Air Force Base in California. For the next 20 years he flew the newest jets and rocket planes in existence: the X-1B, the X-1E, the D-558 Skyrocket, the X-4 and the X-5, in addition to the X-15.

McMonagle, Donald Ray
1952–

Air Force test pilot Don McMonagle made three Shuttle flights between 1991 and 1995.

His first was as mission specialist for STS-39, an unclassified Department of Defense Shuttle mission flown in April and May 1991. A Shuttle pilot by training, McMonagle led Blue Shift operations during the complex 8-day mission. The crew of 7 astronauts conducted a number of military experiments while also deploying and retrieving the Infrared Background Signature Survey satellite. McMonagle and pilot Blaine Hammond also served as in-orbit Shuttle repairmen during the mission.

In January 1993 McMonagle was pilot of STS-54, a 5-day Shuttle mission that deployed a Tracking and Data Relay satellite. He commander of STS-66, the third Spacelab ATLAS mission, flown in November 1994. This flight of the orbiter Atlantis carried a crew of 5 who operated the ATLAS set of experiments to study Earth's atmosphere, and also deployed and retrieved the Christa-SPAS payload, verifying a new rendezvous technique (approaching the target from below) that would be used on future Shuttle-Mir docking missions.

McMonagle was born May 14, 1952, in Flint, Michigan, where he graduated from Hamady High School in 1970. He attended the Air Force Academy, where he received a B.S. in astronautical engineering in 1974. He later earned an M.S. in mechanical engineering from California State University at Fresno in 1985.

McMonagle was trained as a pilot at Columbus AFB, Mississippi, in 1975, and served a 1-year tour as an F-4 pilot at Kunsan Air Base, South Korea, in 1976 and 1977. Returning to the United States, he was an F-4 and F-15 pilot at Holloman AFB, New Mexico. In 1979 he was assigned to Luke AFB, Arizona, as an F-15 instructor pilot. He entered the USAF Test Pilot School at Edwards AFB, California, in 1981, winning the Liethen-Tittle Award as outstanding student in his class.

From 1982 to 1985 McMonagle was operations officer and project test pilot for the Advanced Fighter Technology Integration (AFTI) F-16, a joint Air Force-Navy-NASA program at the Dryden Research Facility at Edwards. He then attended the Air Command and Staff College, returning to Edwards in 1986 as operations officer of the 6513th Test Squadron until his selection by NASA in June 1987.

He has logged over 4,000 hours of flying time.

McMonagle was one of the 15 astronauts selected by NASA in June 1987. He qualified as a Shuttle pilot in August 1988, and his first technical assignment was working on Shuttle main engines, external tank and propulsion system. In 1989 he was reassigned as a capcom in mission control.

Following his command of STS-66 McMonagle headed the EVA Office at the NASA Johnson Space Center. In June 1997 McMonagle was named manager for Space Shuttle Launch Integration at the NASA Kennedy Space Center.

McNair, Ronald
1950–1986

Physicist Ron McNair was one of the 7 space travelers killed in the explosion of the Shuttle Challenger on January 28, 1986. During the planned 6-day flight, mission specialist McNair was to have operated the Spartan scientific package during observations of Halley's Comet. The flight, known as Mission 51-L, would have been McNair's second.

Two years prior to Challenger, in February 1984, McNair was mission specialist aboard Mission 41-B. During that 8-day flight he took part in the deployment of two communications satellites, and also operated the Shuttle Challenger's remote manipulator arm during the first space walks to use the manned maneuvering unit.

McNair was born October 21, 1950, in Lake City, South Carolina, where he graduated from Carver High School in 1967. He attended North Carolina A&T University, receiving a B.S. in physics in 1971, then studied at the Massachusetts Institute of Technology, where he earned his Ph.D. in physics in 1976.

McNair did research in laser physics while at MIT and at the Ecole D'ete Theorique de Physique at Les Houches, France. In 1976 he joined the Hughes Research Laboratories in Malibu, California, and was a scientist there when chosen by NASA.

He was one of the 35 astronauts selected by NASA in January 1978. In August 1979 he completed a training and evaluation course which qualified him as a Shuttle mission specialist. He worked at the Shuttle Avionics Integration Laboratory, and was assigned to STS-11 (later Mission 41-B) in February 1983. He also served as a capcom for flights 41-G and 51-A in October and November 1984.

McNair was the author or coauthor of several technical papers. He also held a black belt in karate and is probably the first person to have played a saxophone in orbit.

Meade, Carl Joseph

1950–

Air Force pilot Carl Meade was a mission specialist on three Shuttle flights. In November 1990 he was one of 5 astronauts in the crew of STS-38, the seventh and last classified Shuttle mission. This flight of the orbiter Atlantis deployed a data relay satellite into Earth orbit.

In June 1992 Meade was aboard STS-50, the longest Shuttle mission flown to that time. The 14-day flight flight of the orbiter Columbia carried the U.S. Microgravity Laboratory. Its crew of 7 performed a series of experiments in space manufacturing.

His third mission was STS-64, which carried the Lidar-Inspace Technology Experiment. Meade and astronaut Mark Lee tested a prototype astronaut rescue pack during an EVA.

An Air Force brat, Meade was born November 16, 1950, at Chanute AFB, Illinois, and graduated from high school at Randolph AFB, Texas, in 1968. He attended the University of Texas, receiving a B.S.(with honors) in electronics engineering in 1973, and in 1975 earned an M.S. in electronics engineering from the California Institute of Technology.

Prior to joining the Air Force, Meade worked as an electronics design engineer with the Hughes Aircraft Company in Culver City, California. (While a graduate student at Cal Tech he had been a Hughes Fellow.) After becoming an Air Force pilot, Meade flew RF-4C reconnaissance aircraft at Shaw AFB, South Carolina, then attended the USAF Test Pilot School at Edwards AFB, California, where he was the outstanding graduate of Class 80B. He remained at Edwards as a test pilot on the F-20 and F-16 aircraft. At the time of his selection by NASA he was an instructor at the test pilot school.

Meade has logged over 3,500 hours of flying time in 27 different types of aircraft.

He was one of the 13 astronauts selected by NASA in June 1985 and in July 1986 qualified as a Shuttle mission specialist. He has tested software in the Shuttle Avionics Integration Lab (SAIL), served with the astronaut support team at the Kennedy Space Center, and represented the astronaut office to the Solid Rocket Booster and Space Shuttle Main Engine programs at the Marshall Spaceflight Center. Following his third mission he worked with the Thermal Systems Division of the Johnson Space Center, and as head of the flight support branch of the astronaut office.

He resigned from NASA and retired from the USAF on March 1, 1996, to join the Lockheed Corporation in Palmdale, California, as deputy program manager for the X-33 reusable spacecraft.

Melnick, Bruce Edward

1949–

Coast Guard pilot Bruce Melnick served as a mission specialist in the crew of STS-49. This maiden flight of the orbiter Endeavour in May 1992 retrieved and redeployed the Intelsat VI communications satellite, which had been stranded in a useless orbit by a rocket failure.

Melnick's job was to operate the Endeavour's remote manipulator arm during EVAs by astronauts Pierre Thuot and Rick Hieb. The first two attempts to capture the satellite failed. A third EVA by Thuot, Hieb, and Tom Akers allowed the astronauts to literally grab the satellite. Once that had been accomplished, Melnick positioned Intelsat atop a new rocket stage. The satellite was later redeployed and fired into its proper orbit.

Melnick previously served as mission specialist aboard STS-41 in October 1990. This 5-day flight of the orbiter Discovery deployed the Ulysses space probe. The crew of 5 astronauts then performed several space manufacturing experiments and tested space construction techniques with the Shuttle's remote manipulator arm.

Melnick was born December 5, 1949, in New York City, and grew up in Clearwater, Florida, graduating from high school there in 1967. He attended the Georgia Institute of Technology in 1967 and 1968, then went on to the US Coast Guard Academy (where in 1971 he was named to the NCAA Academic All-America football team), receiving a B.S. in engineering in 1972. He later earned an M.S. in aeronautical systems from the University of West Florida (1975).

Following graduation from the Coast Guard Academy Melnick spent sixteen months as a deck watch officer aboard the cutter *Steadfast*, homeport St. Petersburg, Florida. Sent to Navy flight training at Pensacola, he won his wings in 1974 and also worked on his master's degree. For the next seven years he was a Coast Guard rescue pilot based at Cape Cod, Massachusetts, and Sitka, Alaska. In 1982 he was assigned to the Aircraft Program Office in Grand Prairie, Texas, to conduct acceptance and development tests of the Coast Guard's new HH-65A Dolphin helicopter. At the time of his selection as an astronaut candidate in June 1987 he was operations officer at the Coast Guard Air Station in Traverse City, Michigan.

Qualified as a Shuttle mission specialist in August 1988, Melnick's first technical assignment was to the astronaut support team at the Kennedy Space Center. He was also the astronaut office representative for the construction of the orbiter Endeavour. He was assigned to the Ulysses mission in October 1989, and following that flight worked in the Shuttle Avionics Integration Lab (SAIL).

Melnick retired from the Coast Guard and resigned from the astronaut group in July 1992 to join the Lockheed Space Operations Company at the Kennedy Space Center. He is currently vice-president and director of Shuttle engineering for Lockheed-Martin, now part of the United Space Alliance.

Melroy, Pamela Ann
1961–

Air Force test pilot Pamela Melroy is assigned as pilot for STS-92. This flight of the orbiter Endeavour will be International Space Station Assembly mission 3A. Scheduled for launch in late 1999, mission 3A will carry a crew of 7, including two 2-man EVA teams, who will attach a 15-foot truss and a pressurized adaptor to the Russian-built control module and American built Node One.

One of three women astronauts qualified as Shuttle pilots, Melroy was born September 17, 1961, in Palo Alto, California, but considers Pittsford, New York, her hometown. She graduated from Bishop Kearney High School in Rockford, New York, then attended Wellesley College, where she received a B.S. in physics and astronomy in

1983. She earned an M.S. in Earth and planetary sciences from the Massachusetts Institute of Technology in 1984.

An Air Force ROTC student at MIT, Melroy went on active duty in 1984, undergoing pilot training at Reese AFB, Texas, qualifying on the KC-10. From 1985 to 1991 she was stationed at Barksdale AFB, Louisiana, as copilot, aircraft commander, and instructor pilot. She also flew over 200 combat and combat support hours in Operation Just Cause and Operation Desert Shield and Desert Storm.

Melroy attended the USAF Test Pilot School beginning in June 1991, and after graduating was assigned as a test pilot with the C-17 Combined Test Force.

She has logged over 3,500 hours of flying time in over 45 different types of aircraft.

Major Melroy was one of the 19 astronaut candidates selected by NASA on December 8, 1994. In May 1996 she qualified as a Shuttle pilot while assigned to the flight support branch of the astronaut office.

Melvin, Leland Devon
1964–

NASA research scientist Leland Melvin was one of the 25 astronaut candidates selected in June 1998. In August of that year he reported to the Johnson Space Center to begin a training and evaluation course that should qualify him as a Shuttle mission specialist and International Space Station crewmember.

Melvin was born February 15, 1964, in Lynchburg, Virginia, where he graduated from Heritage High School in 1982. He attended the University of Richmond, where he received a B.S. in chemistry (1986), then earned an M.S. in materials science from the University of Virginia (1991).

At the time of his selection as an ASCAN, Melvin was on the staff of the NASA Langley Research Center, Hampton, Virginia.

Michel, Frank Curtis

1934–

In June 1965 physicist and pilot Curt Michel became one of the first scientist-astronauts chosen by NASA. He also became the first publicly to criticize the space agency's emphasis on engineering at the expense of pure science, ultimately resigning from the space program without going into space in September 1969.

Michel was born June 5, 1934, in LaCrosse, Wisconsin, and graduated from the California Institute of Technology in Pasadena with a B.S. in physics in 1955. He received his PhD in physics from Cal Tech in 1962.

Michel worked as a junior engineer in the Corporal missile program for the Guided Missile Division of Firestone Tire and Rubber, Southgate, California, while attending CalTech in the USAF reserve officer's training program. He received pilot training in Arizona and Texas from 1955 to 1957, then spent three years as an F-86D fighter pilot in the United States and Europe. When selected as a NASA astronaut he was teaching at Rice University in Houston.

Upon leaving the space program Michel returned to Rice University, where he has been a professor of physics, chairman of the space physics and astronomy program, and most recently Andrew Hays Buchanan professor of astrophysics.

He is the author of a textbook on high-energy astrophysics.

Mitchell, Edgar Dean

1930–

Navy test pilot Ed Mitchell was the sixth person to walk on the Moon. As lunar module pilot of the Apollo 14 mission in February 1971 he and commander Alan Shepard spent over 33 hours on the surface of the Moon near the crater Fra Mauro. They set up an experiment package and pulled a two-wheel trolley to a crater over a mile from their landing site during two walks on the lunar surface.

Mitchell also became famous for his interest in ESP and psychic phenomena and conducted several informal ESP experiments during free moments of the flight.

Mitchell was born September 17, 1930, in Hereford, Texas, and grew up in Artesia, New Mexico. He attended the Carnegie Institute of Technology, receiving a B.S.in industrial management in 1952. He later earned a B.S. in aeronautical engineering from the Naval Postgraduate School in 1961, and a Ph.D. in aeronautics/astronautics from the Massachusetts Institute of Technology in 1964.

Mitchell joined the Navy in 1952 and after completion of basic training, entered officer candidate school. He was commissioned as an ensign in May 1953; he completed pilot training a year later.

For the next four years he flew patrol aircraft from bases in Okinawa and from carriers until 1958, when he became a research project officer with Air Development Squadron 5. Following schooling at MIT, he worked as U.S. Navy representative for the Manned Orbiting Laboratory from 1964 to 1965. He had just graduated first in his class from the USAF Aerospace Research Pilot School at Edwards AFB, California, when chosen by NASA.

As a pilot Mitchell eventually logged over 5,000 hours of flying time, 2,000 hours in jets.

Mitchell was one of 19 astronauts selected by NASA in April 1966. A specialist in the Apollo lunar module, he was a support crewman for the first flight of the LM on Apollo 9. He was backup lunar module pilot for Apollo 10 before being named to the Apollo 14 crew in August 1969. After Apollo 14 he served as backup lunar module pilot for Apollo 16. He retired from the Navy and resigned from NASA on October 1, 1972.

Since then Mitchell has founded the Institute for Noetic Sciences in Palo Alto, California. The Institute conducts research into the powers of the mind and Mitchell remains its chairman. He was president of the Edgar Mitchell Corporation in Palm Beach, Florida, from 1974 to 1978, and has also been chairman of the board of Forecast Systems, Inc., a company based in Provo, Utah and West Palm Beach. More recently he has been president of his own company, Edgar Mitchell Communications.

He is the coauthor of *Psychic Exploration: A Challenge for Science* (1974) and also *The Way of the Explorer* (1996).

Morgan, Barbara Radding

1951–

Idaho elementary schoolteacher Barbara Morgan is the first educator-mission specialist selected by NASA. In the summer of 1998 she began a training and evaluation course to qualify her as a crewmember on the International Space Station.

Earlier Morgan was the alternate payload specialist for the ill-fated Teacher-in-Space program. Following the death of teacher Christa McAuliffe in the Challenger disaster on January 28, 1986, the Teacher-in-Space program was suspended. Morgan continued her association with NASA over the next eleven years, often devoting one week a month to public appearances for the agency, and undergoing annual physical checks to stay eligible for a crew assignment that many felt was never going to be made. In the spring of 1992, outgoing NASA Administrator Richard Truly urged the agency to give Morgan a flight, and in June 1994 an advisory panel chaired by Alan Ladwig, former director of the spaceflight participant program and later a senior advisor to NASA Administrator Dan Goldin, convened to study the matter.

It was only on January 16, 1998, that NASA announced Morgan's selection as a mission specialist astronaut.

Morgan was born November 28, 1951, in Fresno, California, where she graduated from Hoover High School in 1969. She attended Stanford University, receiving a B. A. (with distinction) in human biology in 1973, and earned her teaching credential from the College of Notre Dame in Belmont, California, the following year.

Her first job was as a remedial reading and math teacher at Arlee Elementary School on the Flathead Indian Reservation in Montana. Since 1975 Morgan has been an elementary school teacher at McCall-Donnell School, McCall, Idaho, except for one year spent at the Colegio Americano in Quito, Ecuador.

Morgan was announced as the alternate Teacher-in-Space at a White House ceremony on July 19, 1985.

Morin Lee Miller Emile

1952–

Navy flight surgeon Lee Morin is one of the 35 astronaut candidates selected by NASA on May 1, 1996. In August of that year he reported to the Johnson Space Center to begin a training and evaluation course that should qualify him as a Shuttle mission specialist and International Space Station crewmember. He is currently assigned to the computer support branch of the astronaut office working on ISS software.

Morin was born September 9, 1952, in Manchester, New Hampshire. He graduated from the Western Reserve Academy in Hudson, Ohio, in 1970, then attended the University of New Hampshire, where he received a B.S. in mathematical/electrical science in 1974. He did graduate study in medicine at New York University, receiving an M.D. (1981) and a Ph.D. in microbiology (1982). He also received a master of public health degree from the University of Alabama, Birmingham (1988).

After receiving his M.D. and his doctorate, Morin was commissioned in the U.S. Naval Reserve, and in 1983 he went on active duty, attending the Naval Medical Institute in Groton, Connecticut. From 1983 to 1985 he served aboard the submarine *U.S.S. Henry M. Jackson* as medical officer.

Morin underwent flight surgeon training at the Naval Aerospace Medical Institute (NAMI), Pensacola, Florida, in 1986, remaining on staff there as a flight surgeon and diving medical officer until 1989. He left active duty at that time to practice occupational medicine in Jacksonville, Florida, though he remained in the Reserve, attached to the 3rd Force Reconaissance Company of the U.S. Marine Corps, Mobile, Alabama.

Recalled to active duty in August 1990, he became a flight surgeon and diving medical officer with the Administrative Support Unit, Bahrain, during Operation Desert Storm. Morin returned to the NAMI in Pensacola in 1992, ultimately becoming director of warfare special programs there. He completed a residency in aerospace medicine at NAMI prior to being selected by NASA.

Mullane, Richard Michael

1945–

Air Force flight test engineer Mike Mullane was mission specialist aboard three different Shuttle flights between 1984 and 1990, including the first flight of the Shuttle Discovery, and two secret Department of Defense missions.

On STS-36, a flight of the Shuttle Atlantis in February and March 1990, Mullane took part in the deployment of a massive imaging reconaissance satellite designated AFP-731 over the Soviet Union. Fourteen months earlier he had deployed another large spy satellite, the imaging radar spacecraft called Lacrosse, from the Shuttle Atlantis, during the STS-27 mission.

Mullane's first flight was as mission specialist aboard the maiden voyage of the Shuttle Discovery in August and September 1984. The 6-person crew Discovery crew deployed three communications satellites, erected an experimental solar power wing, and operated a number of scientific and technical experiments during Mission 41-D.

Mullane was born September 10, 1945, in Wichita Falls, Texas, and grew up in Albuquerque, New Mexico, where he graduated from St. Pius X Catholic School in 1963. He went on to attend the U.S. Military Academy at West Point, earning a B.S. in military engineering in 1967. He later received an M.S. in aeronautical engineering from the Air Force Institute of Technology (1975).

After graduation from West Point Mullane served in the U.S. Air Force, including a 1969 tour at Ton Son Nhut Air Base, Viet Nam, where he flew 150 combat missions as an RF-4C weapon system operator. He then spent four years in England at Royal Air Force Base Alconbury. In 1976 he completed the flight test engineer course at the USAF Test Pilot School at Edwards Air Force Base, California, and was assigned to test weapon systems at Eglin AFB, Florida.

LAUNCHING ABOARD THE SHUTTLE

by R. Mike Mullane (STS 41-D, STS-27, STS-36

From *Do Your Ears Pop in Space?*

Crews begin strapping into their seats about 2.5 hours before the scheduled liftoff. Because the seats are miserably uncomfortable (they're just pieces of flat steel with a thin cushion) and NASA worries that the extreme fatigue of lying on them will affect crew performance, limits for "on the back time" have been established. Theoretically, a crew will never be kept on their backs for more than 5 hours (meaning a launch window will never exceed 2.5 hours). I say "theoretically" because most crews would probably consent to wait longer if it appears there's a chance for launch rather than have to try again another day.

. . .

When the liquid engines start, there's a loud roar and heavy vibrations in the cockpit. I can't think of any normal Earth activity to use as an analogy for these sensations. Some astronauts have compared it with driving a car down a railroad track at 60 mph. Others have likened it to sitting too close to the speakers at a rock concert. Perhaps the best way to appreciate the feeling is to visualize what's happening at engine start. The engines produce a million pounds of thrust, but the rocket is being held to the launchpad by an explosive nut/bolt arrangement. Holding this much power to the Earth is obviously going to be loud and teeth-rattling.

When the SRBs ignite, the noise and vibration increase significantly. Nothing I have ever experienced in my aviation career comes close to equaling this noise and shaking. At no time, however, are the vibrations so bad that you can't read instruments, and the noise doesn't prevent you from hearing your fellow astronauts on the intercom. Of course, the helmet and Snoopy cap headphone arrangement insulate astronauts from some of the noise.

. . .

Besides the increase in noise at liftoff, the crew also gets an instantaneous 1.6-G shove into their seats. For comparison, a typical jet airliner gives you about a 0.33-G shove into your seat during acceleration down the runaway for takeoff. In other words, the Shuttle's liftoff Gs are about five times greater than an airline passenger experiences during takeoff roll. The affect of the Shuttle's acceleration is mind-boggling. The launch may look slow and stately on TV but in only four seconds, the Shuttle (weight 4.5 million pounds) has already reached 100 mph and in forty seconds, it's supersonic. It's not your father's Oldsmobile.

The G-forces vary throughout ascent, increasing from 1.6 at lift-off to 2.5 just prior to booster burnout. At SRB burnout (6 million pounds of thrust ends), the Gs drop dramatically—to about 0.9 G. From this point on, the ride is glass-smooth and essentially silent. (One astronaut once described this portion of the ascent as "an electric ride." I think that's a good analogy. The nearly 1.5 million pounds of thrust from the continued operation of the liquid engines is almost an imperceptible hum.)

As fuel is burned and the vehicle lightens, the Gs slowly rise until they reach 3.0 (or about ten times what an airline passenger feels while accelerating down a runway on take-off) about 7.5 minutes into flight. At this point, the computers begin to reduce the throttle settings to keep the Shuttle from exceeding 3 G. For all the shaking and vibrations that a Shuttle has to endure, it's really a very fragile vehicle and would tear itself part if the G's got too much above three. In fact, there's an emergency procedure for the crew to shut off one of the engines if they don't automatically throttle downward.

Main engine cutoff (MECO) occurs about 8.5 minutes after liftoff. In an eye-blink you go from 3 G to weightlessness—and most astronauts let out a little cheer.

Mullane was one of the 35 astronauts selected by NASA in January 1978. In August 1979 he completed a training and evaluation course which qualified him as a Shuttle mission specialist. He served on the support crew for STS-4 prior to being assigned to STS-12 (later known as Mission 41-D) in February 1983.

From November 1983 to October 1984 Mullane trained as mission specialist for a Shuttle crew assigned to a Department of Defense "standby" payload consisting of the Teal Ruby satellite and the AFP-675 CIRRUS experiment package. When AFP-675 was shifted to another DOD mission, Mission 62-A, the first Vandenberg launch, Mullane went with it. He also served as capcom for Shuttle missions from January to July 1985. Mission 62-A was cancelled following the Challenger disaster, and in September 1987 most of the crewmembers, including Mullane, were reassigned to STS-27.

Just prior to the launch of STS-36 on February 28, 1990, Mullane announced his plans to retire from NASA and the USAF on July 1, 1990. He currently serves as a consultant to the U.S. Space Camp in Huntsville, Alabama, and as a lecturer on space, and lives in Albuquerque. He is the author of a novel, *Red Sky* (1994), a children's book, *Liftoff* (1995), and a nonfiction book, *Do*

Your Ears Pop in Space? And 500 Other Surprising Questions about Space Travel (1996).

Musgrave, Franklin Story
1935–

Story Musgrave made six Shuttle flights in a remarkable 30-year astronaut career that began with the Apollo program and climaxed with the daring orbital repair of the Hubble Space Telescope.

Musgrave was one of 11 scientists recruited for astronaut training in the summer of 1967, at a time when NASA was planning an ambitious series of Apollo lunar landings and scientific missions in Earth orbit. Within months budget cuts forced on NASA because of the Vietnam War eliminated most of the scientist-astronauts' flight opportunities. Some of them left space agency in frustration, but Musgrave persevered, supporting the Skylab missions and working on the development of the Space Shuttle, finally going into space in April 1983, sixteen years after selection. That first flight—STS-6, the maiden voyage of the Challenger, in which Musgrave and Don Peterson made the first Shuttle EVA—was the start of a 13-year career as an active space traveler.

In July 1985 he was a member of the 7-man crew of Mission 51-F, the Spacelab-2 flight dedicated to astronomical research. The crew of 51-F suffered through a launch-pad abort and an abort-to-orbit before commencing 24-hour operations. Musgrave served as flight engineer and leader of one of the 2 shifts needed to operate Spacelab's thirteen experiments—the Red Shift consisting of astronaut Karl Henize and payload specialist Loren Acton.

Musgrave's third flight came in November 1989, when he served as a mission specialist aboard STS-33, deploying the Mentor signals intelligence satellite into geosynchronous orbit.

Two years later he flew a fourth time aboard STS-44, which deployed a Defense Support Program early warning satellite into geosynchronous orbit.

Musgrave's fifth flight was STS-61, the first mission to service the orbiting Hubble Space Telescope. Deployed by the Shuttle in April 1990, the HST had not lived up to its billing as a wondrous observing tool because of defects in the manufacture of its main mirror. For two years engineers worked to develop corrective systems, and the tricky EVA techniques which allowed their installation. Assigned as payload commander for STS-61 in January 1992, eighteen months before the scheduled launch, Musgrave took an active role in rehearsing and even choreographing the EVAs, which were carried out flawlessly in orbit in December 1993 by two EVA teams: Musgrave and Jeff Hoffman, and Tom Akers and Kathryn Thornton. Repaired, the Hubble went on to make numerous astronomical discoveries over the next few years, finally reaching its potential as a unique observatory.

Musgrave made a sixth flight into space in November 1996 aboard STS-80. This 18-day flight of the orbiter Columbia carried the fourth U.S. Microgravity Payload and deployed the Wake Shiel Facility and the orfeus-SPAS satellites.

Musgrave was born August 19, 1935, in Boston, Massachusetts, but considers Lexington, Kentucky, his hometown. He attended St. Mark's School in Southborough, Massachusetts, graduating in 1953, then joined the Marine Corps. When he returned to school some years later he accumulated a staggering number of degrees: B.S. in mathematics and statistics from Syracuse University (1958); an M.B.A. in operations analysis and computer programming from the University of California at Los Angeles (1959); a B.A. in chemistry from Marietta College (1960); an MD from Columbia University (1964); and an M.S. in physiology and biophysics from the University of Kentucky (1966). He has also worked toward a Ph.D. in physiology, and in 1987 received an M.A. in literature from the University of Houston.

As a marine, Musgrave served as an aviation electrician and aircraft crew chief aboard the carrier *U.S.S. Wasp* on duty in the Far East. After returning to the United States he also worked for the Eastman Kodak Company, Rochester, New York, as a mathematician. When selected by NASA in August 1967 he was a researcher in cardiovascular and exercise physiology at the University of Kentucky, where he had previously interned as a surgeon and worked as a U.S. Air Force postdoctoral fellow.

He has logged over 16,800 hours of flying time, including 7,100 in jets, in 160 different types of aircraft, and holds instructor, instrument instructor, glider instructor and transport ratings. He has logged more flying time in the Northrop T-38, the plane used by NASA astronauts, than any other pilot. He is also a parachutist with more than 460 free falls to his credit, including 100 experimental descents.

Musgrave was one of the 11 scientist-astronauts chosen by NASA in August 1967. He underwent military jet pilot training, then worked on the design and development of the Skylab space station, serving as backup science pilot for the first Skylab mission, Skylab 2. He was also capcom for Skylab 3 and Skylab 4. From 1974 on he helped design EVA equipment, including space suits, for the Shuttle program, and served as mission specialist for two simulated Spacelab flights. From 1979 to 1982 he was assigned to the Shuttle Avionics Integration Laboratory (SAIL), testing Shuttle computer software.

He also continued to be a part-time surgeon at Denver General Hospital and a part-time professor of physiology and biophysics at the University of Kentucky Medical Center. He has published 44 scientific papers concerning aerospace medicine, exercise physiology, and clinical surgery.

Between his third and fourth flights Musgrave served as head of the mission support branch of the astronaut office, acting as lead capcom in mission control for STS-32 through STS-35.

Informed by NASA that he would no longer be assigned to flight crews because of his age—62—Musgrave retired in September 1997 to work in public speaking and consulting. He serves as a commentator for Shuttle missions on Cable News Networks.

Nagel, Steven Ray

1946–

Air Force test pilot Steve Nagel flew four Shuttle missions, two as commander. He first commanded STS-37, an April 1991 flight of the orbiter Atlantis during which the $617 million Gamma Ray Observatory was deployed. At 17.5 tons, the GRO was the heaviest object

carried into space by a Shuttle. The deployment was successful, though a stuck antenna required attention from astronauts Jerry Ross and Jay Apt during a special EVA. STS-37 ended after five days with a landing at Edwards AFB.

Nagel also commanded STS-55, an April 1993 mission which carried the second German Spacelab. During this 10-day flight the 7-man crew conducted ninety different experiments in a variety of fields, including medicine and materials science, astronomy, Earth observations, and robotics.

In 1985 Nagel made two Space Shuttle flights within five months of each other, one of them as a mission specialist, the other as pilot. His assignment as a mission specialist and flight engineer was aboard Mission 51-G in June 1985. This crew, commanded by Daniel Brandenstein, had originally been scheduled to fly in August 1984, but launcher and payload problems and changes in the Shuttle manifest caused the delay. During the flight of 51-G Nagel took part in the launch of three communications satellites and in the deployment and retrieval of the Spartan scientific satellite.

As pilot of Mission 61-A/Spacelab D1 in October and November 1985, Nagel led one of the two three-astronaut teams that worked 12-hour shifts aboard the European-built laboratory.

He also has flown with citizens of more different countries than any other astronaut: Saudi prince Sultan al-Saud and French test pilot Patrick Baudry were with Nagel on 51-G, while scientists Ernst Messerschmid, Rheinhard Furrer, Ulrich Walter, and Hans Schlegel of Germany were aboard the Spacelab missions. Wubbo Ockels of The Netherlands also flew on Spacelab D1.

Nagel was born October 27, 1946, in Canton, Illinois, and graduated from Canton Senior High School in 1964. He received a B.S. in aeronautical and astronautical engineering (with high honors) from the University of Illinois in 1969, and later earned an M.S. in mechanical engineering from California State University at Fresno in 1978.

An Air Force ROTC student at Illinois, Nagel was commissioned in 1969 and earned his wings in 1970. He was based in Louisiana and Thailand prior to attending the USAF Test Pilot School at Edwards AFB, California, in 1975. When selected by NASA he was a test pilot there. He has logged 6,700 hours of flying time, 4,400 hours in jets.

Nagel was chosen to be an astronaut candidate in January 1978 and completed a yearlong training and evaluation course in August 1979. He has been a chase pilot for STS-1 and support crewman and capcom for STS-2 and STS-3. He has also been assigned to the Shuttle Avionics Integration Laboratory (SAIL) and the Flight Simulation Laboratory (FSL).

During the flight hiatus caused by the Challenger disaster in January 1986, Nagel took part in the development of a crew escape system for the Shuttle, and in 1991 and 1992 Nagel served as acting chief of the astronaut office.

Nagel retired from the Air Force on February 28, 1995, and left the astronaut office the following day to become deputy director of operations development in the Office of Safety, Reliability and Quality Assurance at JSC. In September 1996 he became an instructor pilot with JSC's Aircraft Operations Directorate at Ellington Field.

He is married to astronaut Linda Godwin.

Nelson, Clarence William "Bill," Jr.

1942–

Florida Congressman Bill Nelson, the Democratic chairman of the House Space Science and Applications Subcommittee, became the second politician to make a spaceflight when he served as a payload specialist aboard Shuttle Mission 61-C in January 1986. During the 6-day flight of the orbiter Columbia Nelson served as a subject for space sickness experiments devised by NASA doctors. He also operated a protein growth experiment sponsored by the University of Alabama at Birmingham.

Mission 61-C became best known for having its liftoff delayed seven times by weather problems or technical glitches. Nelson, who also became the first lawyer in space, recounted his experiences as a Shuttle payload specialist in a book, *Mission* (1986).

Nelson was born September 29, 1942, in Miami, Florida, a fifth-generation Floridian whose family homesteaded the area that is now the Kennedy Space Center in 1917. Nelson grew up in Brevard Country and graduated from high school in Melbourne, Florida, in 1960. He attended Yale University, earning a B.A. in 1965, and received a law degree from the University of Virginia in 1968. He was admitted to the Florida bar that same year.

Nelson joined the Army Reserve after graduation from Yale in 1965 and served until 1971, including two years on active duty following completion of law school. Returning to Florida in 1970, he practiced law, and in 1972 won election to the Florida House of Representatives. He was elected to the U.S. House in 1978 from the congressional disctrict that included the NASA Kennedy Space Center.

In 1990 Nelson lost his bid to become the Democratic nominee for governor of Florida, losing to Lawton Chiles. Nelson is currently a partner in the law firm of McGuire, Voorhis, & Wells in Melbourne, Florida.

Nelson, George Driver

1950–

Astronomer George "Pinky" Nelson served as a mission specialist on three Shuttle crews, including the first satellite retrieval and repair, and the first Shuttle mission to be launched following the Challenger disaster.

He was one of 5 astronauts in the crew of Mission 41-C, launched April 6, 1984, for a rendezvous with the malfunctioning Solar Maximum Mission satellite. Using the manned maneuvering unit (MMU) backpack, Nelson left the Shuttle Challenger and flew over to the Solar Max, attempting to lock on to the satellite using a special unit known as the T-pad. The T-pad failed, however, and Nelson was called back to Challenger by commander Robert Crippen. It appeared that the Solar Max rescue hadn't worked, but the next morning mission specialist T. J. Hart was able to grab the satellite with the Shuttle's remote manipulator arm. Nelson and James van Hoften were then able to make a second space walk, repairing the satellite, which was then released into space.

Nelson next served as mission specialist for the seven-times postponed flight 61-C in January 1986. His primary job on that mission was to use a special camera to take pictures of Halley's Comet. Nelson saw the comet, but the camera didn't work.

In February 1987 Nelson was assigned as mission specialist for STS-26, the first Shuttle to be launched after the Challenger disaster. STS-26 was the first Shuttle mission to carry a crew escape system allowing astronauts to bail out of a troubled orbiter during some launch emergencies. Nelson was responsible for the system from his launch position in the Shuttle mid-deck. STS-26 succeeded in its stated goal of deploying a Tracking and Data Relay Satellite into geosynchronous orbit, and also in its larger goal of restoring some faith in the Shuttle program.

Nelson, dubbed "Pinky" because of his complexion, was born July 13, 1950, in Charles City, Iowa, and grew up in Willmar, Minnesota, and Clinton, Iowa. He graduated from Willmar Senior High School in 1968, attracting the attention of baseball scouts, then attended Harvey Mudd College, receiving a B.S. in physics in 1972. He earned an M.S. (1974) and a Ph.D. (1978) in astronomy from the University of Washington.

Nelson performed astronomical research at the Sacramento Peak Solar Observatory in Sunspot, New Mexico; the Astronomical Institute at Utrecht, the Netherlands; and the University of Gottingen Observatory, West Germany. When selected by NASA he was a post-doctoral researcher at the Joint Institute of Laboratory Astrophysics in Boulder, Colorado.

One of the 35 astronauts chosen in January 1978, Nelson completed a training and evaluation course in August 1979. He later flew as a scientific equipment operator on the NASA WB-57F Earth resources aircraft, worked on the Shuttle EVA space suit, and was the photographer in the lead chase plane during the STS-1 landing. He also served as capcom and support crewman for STS-3 and STS-4.

During the post-Challenger hiatus Nelson took a leave of absence to teach at the University of Washington in Seattle. On June 30, 1989, Nelson resigned from NASA to become assistant provost and associate professor of astronomy at the university.

Neubeck, Francis Gregory
1932–

Air Force test pilot Greg Neubeck was one of the first eight pilots chosen for the Manned Orbiting Laboratory Program in November 1965. He trained for 30-day Earth orbital flights in MOL until the program was canceled in May 1969.

Neubeck was born April 11, 1932, in Washington, D.C. He attended the Naval Academy at Annapolis, graduating with a bachelor of science degree in 1955. He later earned an M.B.A. from Auburn University (1971)

He elected to serve in the Air Force and became a pilot, serving as a flight instructor and later working on the development of weapons systems for jet fighters at Eglin AFB, Florida. He attended the Air Force Test Pilot School at Edwards AFB, California, in 1960 and the Aerospace Research Pilot School in 1962. His classmates at ARPS included future NASA astronauts Michael Collins and Joe Engle. From 1962 until his selection for the MOL program he was based at Eglin AFB.

After the cancellation of MOL Neubeck returned to USAF duty, first attending the Air War College (1970), then doing graduate work at Auburn.

In 1972 he was assigned as an F-4 fighter pilot at Ubon Royal Thai AFB, Thailand, and served a combat tour. He returned to the United States in 1973 to work at Tyndall AFB, Georgia, as director of the test and evaluation center. At the time of his retirement from the Air Force as a colonel in 1982 he was vice commander of the Tactical Air War Center at Eglin AFB.

As a pilot he logged over 7,000 hours of flying time.

Since retiring Neubeck has worked in aerospace research and development, authoring a textbook on missile design and writing a book about the American economy. He is the designer of a tactical missile system and holds a patent on one of the most widely used stability devices for fighter aircraft.

In 1986 he was the Republican nominee for the U.S. House from Florida's 1st Congressional District. He is currently an engineering consultant in Lynn Haven, Florida.

Newman, James Hansen
1956–

Physicist Jim Newman, a former NASA training officer, is scheduled to perform the first assembly EVAs for the International Space Station. In December 1998 Newman and fellow STS-88 crewmember Jerry Ross will erect solar power panels on Node One, the first element of the $40 billion space platform.

Newman made two earlier Shuttle flights, first as a mission specialist in the crew of STS-51, which deployed the Advanced Communications Technology Satellite in September 1993. Newman and his fellow STS-51 crewmember Carl Walz also made an EVA to test tools and procedures for the upcoming Hubble Space Telescope repair mission.

In September 1995 Newman made his second flight aboard the orbiter Endeavour on mission STS-69, which was devoted to materials science and astronomical experiments using the Wake Shield Facility and the Spartan 201-03. The WSF suffered control problems, however, and failed to operate as planned.

Newman was born October 16, 1956, in the Trust Territory of the Pacific, though he grew up in San Diego, California. He attended Dartmouth College, where he received a B.S. in physics in 1978, and went on to Rice University, where he received his M.S. (1982) and his Ph.D. (1984).

In 1985, following an additional year of post-graduate work at Rice, Newman became adjunct assistant professor in Rice's department of space physics and astronomy. At the same time he joined the NASA Johnson Space Center, where he first worked as a training officer for mission control teams. He later became a simulation supervisor leading a team of such instructors.

Newman was one of the 23 astronaut candidates selected by the space agency in January 1990. In July 1991 he qualified as a Shuttle mission specialist, and was assigned to the astronaut support team at the Kennedy Space Center. Following the STS-51 flight he worked on payload issues in the mission development branch, and in 1996–97 served as head of the computer support branch.

Nordsieck, Kenneth Hugh
1946–

Astronomer Ken Nordsieck served as backup payload specialist to fellow scientists Samuel Durrance and Ronald Parise for the STS-35/Spacelab ASTRO mission in December 1990. During the 9-day mission the crew of 7 performed dozens of experiments, including infrared observations of distant galaxies, while struggling with a balky telescope control system. Nordsieck supported the flight from Spacelab Mission Control at the NASA Marshall Spaceflight Center in Huntsville, Alabama.

Nordsieck had come close to going on the mission himself. In May 1990, just prior to an earlier attempt to launch STS-35, prime payload specialist Sam Durrance was temporarily disqualified for physical reasons. By the time STS-35 got off the ground five months later, however, Durrance was back on the crew.

Nordsieck was born February 19, 1946, in New York City. He received a B.S. in astronomy from the California Institute of Technology in 1967, an M.S. (1970) and a Ph.D. (1972) in physics from the University of California at San Diego.

Nordsieck is an associate professor at Washburn Observatory at the University of Wisconsin in Madison. It was his work as coinvestigator for the Wisconsin Ultraviolet Photopolarimetry experiment that made him eligible for selection as an ASTRO payload specialist. His field of research includes the structure of spiral galaxies and extragalactic objects.

Nordsieck was selected as an Astro payload specialist in June 1984. ASTRO 1 was originally to have been launched as Shuttle Mission 61-E in March 1986, but the destruction of the Shuttle Challenger six weeks prior to that forced a long delay.

Noriega, Carlos Ismael

1959–

Marine helicopter pilot Carlos Noriega was a mission specialist in the crew of STS-84. This May 1997 flight of the orbiter Atlantis carried a SpaceHab module on the sixth Shuttle-Mir docking mission, transferring three tons of food, water, and other supplies to the Mir crew along with NASA-Mir crewmember Michael Foale, returning Jerry Linenger to Earth.

Noriega is assigned as an EVA crewmember for International Space Station assembly mission 4A, scheduled for launch as STS-97 in the fall of 1999.

Noriega was born October 8, 1959, in Lima, Peru, and grew up in California, where he graduated from Wilcox High School in Santa Clara. He attended the University of Southern California, where he received a B.S. in computer science in 1981. He later received an M.S. in computer science and another in space systems operations at the U.S. Naval Postgraduate School in 1990.

Commissioned in the Marines through Navy ROTC, Noriega attended helicopter flight school from 1981 to 1983, then served as a CH-46 Sea Knight pilot at the Marine Corps Air Station at Kaneohe Bay, Hawaii. During this time he was twice deployed aboard ships in the West Pacific and Indian Ocean, and served with the Multinational Peacekeeping Force in Beirut, Lebanon.

From 1986 to 1988 Noriega was an aviation safety officer and instructor pilot for Marine Air Base Squadron 24 at Tustin, California.

Following two years of graduate school, Noriega did a tour with the U.S. Space Command in Colorado Springs, Colorado, as a space surveillance commander. At the time of his selection by NASA Noriega was operations officer for the 1st Marine Aircraft Wing at Camp Butler, Okinawa, Japan.

Noriega was one of the 19 astronaut candidates selected by NASA on December 8, 1994. In May 1996 he qualified as a Shuttle mission specialist. Prior to his crew assignment he worked in the EVA/Robotics branch of the astronaut office.

Nowak, Lisa Marie

1963–

Navy flight officer Lisa Nowak is one of the 35 astronaut candidates selected by NASA on May 1, 1996. In August of that year she reported to the Johnson Space Center to begin the training and evaluation course that should qualify her as a Shuttle mission specialist and International Space Station crewmember. She is currently assigned to International Space Station issues while completing training.

Nowak was born Lisa Marie Caputo on May 10, 1963, in Washington, D.C., and graduated from C. W. Woodward High School in nearby Rockville, Maryland, in 1981. She attended the Naval Academy at Annapolis, receiving a B.S. in aerospace science in 1985. She later attended the Naval Postgraduate School at Monterey, California, earning an M.S. in aeronautical engineering and the degree of astronautical engineer in 1992.

Nowak was commissioned in the Navy following graduation from Annapolis, then spent six months detailed to the NASA Johnson Space Center, where she provided engineering support for the Shuttle Training Aircraft. She then underwent flight officer training, and was assigned to Electronic Warfare Aggressor Squadron 34 at Point Mugu, California, where she flew missions aboard the EA-7L and ERA-3B aircraft.

In 1992, following two years of graduate work, Nowak joined the system engineering test directorate at Patuxent River, Maryland. A year later she attended the Naval Test Pilot School there, and following graduation became an aircraft systems project officer with the Strike Aircraft Test Squadron, flying aboard the F/A-18 and EA-6B. She was an acquisitions engineer with the Naval Air Systems Command, Arlington, Virginia, when selected by NASA.

She has logged 1,100 hours of flying time in 30 different types of aircraft.

Ochoa, Ellen Lauri

1958–

Physicist Ellen Ochoa became the first Hispanic woman space traveler when she flew aboard STS-56 in April 1993. This 10-day flight of the orbiter Discovery carried the second ATLAS Spacelab and its experiment package designed to study the Earth's atmosphere, especially the ozone layer. Ochoa also served as operator of Discovery's remote manipulator system, deploying and retrieving the Spartan 201 satellite.

Ochoa flew a second time as payload commander for ATLAS-03 aboard STS-66 in November 1994. On this 11-day flight of Atlantis the crew of 5 recorded enough data on the atmosphere to fill 110,000 floppy computer disks. They also deployed and retrieved the Crista-SPAS satellite.

Ochoa was born May 10, 1958, in Los Angeles, California, though she considers La Mesa her hometown. She graduated from Grosemount High School in La Mesa in 1975, then attended San Diego State University, where she received a B.S. in physics in 1980. She later earned an M.S. (1980) and a Ph.D. (1985) in electrical engineering from Stanford University.

After receiving her doctorate Ochoa became a researcher at Sandia National Laboratories in Livermore, California, where she worked on optical systems. In 1988 she joined the staff of the NASA Ames Research Center at Moffett Field, California, working on optical recognition systems for space automation. She later became chief of intelligent systems technology branch, leading a team of 35 scientists and engineers in the development of improved aerospace computer systems.

Ochoa was one of 23 astronaut candidates selected by NASA in January 1990, qualifying as a Shuttle mission specialist in July 1991 while assigned to the Shuttle Avionics Integration Laboratory. In 1993, following her first flight, she served as crew representative for robotics.

Since January 1997 she has been the astronaut office assistant for International Space Station.

O'Connor, Bryan Daniel

1946–

Marine test pilot Bryan O'Connor commanded STS-40, the 9-day Spacelab Life Sciences mission flown in June 1991. The crew of 7, which included three medical doctors and a biologist, conducted the most extensive series of tests into human adaptability to space-flight ever attempted. The mission was marred only by an apparent problem with the orbiter Columbia's payload bay door, which prompted a brief dispute between O'Connor and flight controllers about the need for an EVA to fix the problem. The EVA was proved to be unnecessary.

O'Connor also became the first Irish astronaut, having taken a special Irish citizenship on May 17, 1991.

Five years earlier O'Connor served as pilot of Shuttle Mission 61-B in November and December 1985. The seven astronauts on this second flight of the orbiter Atlantis deployed three communications satellites and tested space construction techniques during their 7-day mission.

O'Connor was born September 6, 1946, in Orange, California, though he considers Twenty-nine Palms, California, where his father served as an officer in the Marine Corps, to be his hometown. O'Connor graduated from high school in Twenty-nine Palms in 1964, then attended the Naval Academy, receiving a B.S. in engineering in 1968. He earned an M.S. in aeronautical systems from the University of West Florida in 1970.

He elected to serve in the Marine Corps and, following basic officer training at Quantico, Virginia, entered flight school at Pensacola, Florida, winning his wings in June 1970. For the next five years he served as an A-4E and A-4F pilot and instructor in California, Texas, North Carolina, Korea and Japan, and also did a Mediterranean tour aboard the carrier *U.S.S. Guam.*

In 1976 he attended the Naval Test Pilot School at Patuxent River, Maryland, and remained as a test pilot at the center there for over three years. He was involved in testing short-takeoff-and-landing aircraft such as the X-22 and the British AV-8 Harrier, and when chosen by NASA was a Harrier officer at the Naval Air Systems Command.

As a pilot O'Connor logged over 4,600 hours of flying time, including 4,100 hours in jets.

He was one of the 19 astronaut candidates selected by NASA in May 1980, and in June 1981 qualified as a Shuttle pilot. He served as T-38 chase plane pilot for STS-3, and as capcom for STS-6 through STS-9. In 1985 he was assigned as pilot of Shuttle Mission 61-M, scheduled for the summer of 1986, but saw it canceled following the Challenger explosion.

During the post-Challenger hiatus he served as assistant to the Shuttle Program Manager (March 1986 to February 1988) and as chairman of the NASA Space Flight Safety Panel (September 1986 to February 1989). From August 1989 to April 1990 he was deputy director of flight crew operations. He was assigned to STS-40 in April 1989.

On July 29, 1991, Colonel O'Connor left NASA to become commander of the Marine Air Detachment at the Naval Air Test Center, Patuxent River, Maryland. He returned to the space agency in 1993 to help with the transformation of the troubled space station Freedom program into the International Space Station, and was widely credited with having helped save the station from cancellation. In April 1994 he was named deputy associate administrator for the Space Shuttle, becoming the second-ranking official at NASA HQ in charge of the program. He resigned in February 1996 following a reorganization of the Shuttle program which shifted more management responsibility to the Johnson Space Center.

Since July 1996 he has been president of Airship Operations, a company based in Washington, D.C.

Odle, Randy Thomas
1951–

Air Force engineer Randy Odle was one of the military payload specialists originally assigned to Mission 62-A, the first planned Vandenberg Shuttle launch. That flight was to have carried the Teal Ruby satellite and the CIRRIS experiment package. In August 1985, after he had been in training for over a year, Odle was bumped from the crew in favor of Air Force undersecretary Pete Aldridge.

Five months later the Challenger disaster occurred, ultimately canceling all manned launches from the Vandenberg site.

Odle was born September 8, 1951, in Port Arthur, Texas. He attended Port Neches-Grove High School, then entered Lamar University in Beaumont, where he received a B.S. in mechanical engineering in 1973. He went on to work for the Proctor & Gamble Company, then did graduate study at Louisiana Tech University in Ruston, receiving an M.S. in biomedical engineering (1976). He attended the Air War College in 1996–97.

He went on active duty with the Air Force in October 1976, spending four years as a bioenvironmental engineer at Brooks AFB, Texas. In January 1980 he was transferred to the Air Force Clinic at Alconbury, England, where he served as chief, bioenvironmental engineering.

Odle was one of the 14 officers selected in the second cadre of manned spaceflight engineers. Following his assignment on Mission 62-A (1984-86) he worked in the Strategic Defense Initiative program office.

From 1988 to 1992 he was stationed at Kirtland AFB, New Mexico, working on the Boeing Argus SDIO aircraft program. He also worked at the AF Office of Technology there until 1995, when he was assigned to the Pentagon as chief of the assessments branch, U.S. Nuclear Command and Control System Support Staff in the Office of the Secretary of Defense.

Since July 1997 Odle has been commander of Detachment 2, Space and Missile Systems Center, at Onizuka AB, Sunnyvale, California.

Oefelein, Wiliam Anthony
1965–

Navy test pilot William Oefelein is one of the 25 astronaut candidates selected by NASA in June 1998. In August of that year he reported to the Johnson Space Center to begin a training and evaluation course that should qualify him as a Shuttle pilot.

Oefelein was born March 29, 1965, at Fort Belvoir, Virginia, graduating from West Anchorage High School in Anchorage, Alaska. He attended Oregon State University, receiving a B.S. in electrical/electronics engineering in 1988.

At the time of his selection by NASA, Lieutenant Oefelein was an aviator with Carrier Wing 8, Oceana, Virginia.

O'Leary, Brian Todd

1940–

Astronomer Brian O'Leary trained as a NASA scientist-astronaut for six months before resigning. His book *The Making of an Ex-Astronaut* (1970) discussed his dislike of jet pilot training and his disillusionment with NASA's treatment of scientist-astronauts at the time.

O'Leary was born January 27, 1940, in Boston, Massachusetts. He received a B.A. in physics from Williams College in 1961, an M.A. in astronomy from Georgetown University in 1964, and his Ph.D. in astronomy from the University of California at Berkeley in 1967. Prior to becoming an astronaut O'Leary was a NASA predoctoral trainee in the Space Sciences Laboratory, Department of Astronomy, at Berkeley.

Selected by NASA in August 1967 as one of eleven scientist-astronauts, O'Leary underwent six months of ground training concentrated on Apollo and Apollo Applications (later Skylab) systems. He reported to Williams Air Force Base in Arizona to begin pilot training in February 1968, but soon resigned.

After leaving NASA O'Leary held teaching and research positions at Cornell University, Hampshire College in Amherst, Massachusetts, the University of Pennsylvania, the California Institute of Technology, and at Princeton University. He was also a consultant for energy matters for the Committee on the Interior, U.S. House of Representatives and served as an adviser to Arizona Congressman Morris Udall's 1976 presidential campaign. More recently O'Leary was employed by Science Applications, Inc., Redondo Beach, California, as a senior scientist.

O'Leary has published many popular articles and scientific papers. In addition to *The Making of an Ex-Astronaut*, he is also the author of *The Fertile Stars* (1981), *The New Solar System* (1981), *Project Space Station* (1983) and *Mars 1999* (1988). He coauthored a novel, *Spaceship Titanic* (1982).

Beginning in the late 1970s, O'Leary began to experiment with the "newer paradigms" of science—New Age phenomena such as telepathy, out-of-body travel, and the Gaia hypothesis. He left Science Applications in early 1987 to devote himself to full-time study, writing and lecturing in these fields, and has published a book recounting this personal journey, *Exploring Inner and Outer Space* (1989).

He currently lives in Oregon.

Olivas, John Daniel

1966–

NASA engineer John Olivas is one of the 25 astronaut candidates selected in June 1998. In August of that year he reported to the Johnson Space Center to begin a training and evaluation course that should qualify him as a Shuttle mission specialist and International Space Station crewmember.

Olivas was born May 25, 1966, in North Hollywood, California. He graduated from Burges High School in El Paso, Texas, in 1985, then attended the University of Texas in that city, receiving a B.S. in mechanical engineering in 1989. He earned an M.S. in mechanical engineering from the University of Houston (1993) and his Ph.D. in mechanical engineering and materials from Rice University (1996).

At the time of his selection as an astronaut candidate, Olivas was a project manager at the NASA Jet Propulsion Laboratory, Pasadena, California.

Onizuka, Ellison Shoji

1946–1986

Air Force flight test engineer El Onizuka was killed in the explosion of the Space Shuttle Challenger on January 28, 1986. He had been scheduled to serve as mission specialist during the planned 5-day flight 51-L, supervising the deployment of a Tracking and Data Relay Satellite.

Onizuka had made a previous spaceflight, aboard Mission 51-C, the first "secret" Shuttle flight, in January 1985. During 51-C Onizuka took part in the deployment of what was later reported to be a National Reconnaissance Office signals intelligence satellite called Magnum. The flight lasted three days.

He was the first Asian American in space.

Onizuka was born June 24, 1946, in Kealakekua, Hawaii, where he graduated from Konawaena High School in 1964. He grew up, however, in nearby Kona. He became interested in spaceflight at the time of Walter Schirra's Mercury mission in 1962, and entered the University of Colorado at Boulder to study aerospace engineering. He received his B.S. and M.S. in 1969.

An ROTC student at Colorado, Onizuka entered active duty in January 1970. For the next four years he served as an aerospace flight test engineer at McClellan Air Force Base, California. In August 1974 he was enrolled in the Air Force Test Pilot School at Edwards AFB, and remained at the school as an instructor and engineer after graduation. He eventually logged over 1,700 hours of flying time as an engineer on 43 different types of aircraft.

Onizuka was one of 35 astronauts selected by NASA in January 1978 and in August 1979 qualified as a Shuttle mission specialist. His technical assignments included working at the Shuttle Avionics Integration Laboratory and serving on the launch support crew for STS-1 and STS-2. In November 1982 he was assigned to the crew of STS-10, scheduled to be the first Department of Defense Shuttle mission, but it was canceled. Ultimately the 5-man crew was assigned to Mission 51-C.

An asteroid and the former Air Force Satellite Control Facility at Sunnyvale, California, have been named for Onizuka.

Oswald, Stephen Scott

1951–

Former Navy test pilot Steve Oswald has made three Shuttle flights.

His first was as pilot of STS-42. Launched in January 1992, STS-42 carried the first International Microgravity Laboratory and a crew of 7, which included Canadian physician Roberta Bondar and German physicist Ulf Merbold. The IML-01 mission concentrated on research in space manufacturing and the effects of spaceflight on humans.

In April 1993 Oswald was pilot of STS-56, the second Spacelab ATLAS mission, which carried a crew of 7 on a mission to study the Earth's atmosphere.

He commanded STS-67, the second Spacelab ASTRO mission, launched in March 1995 aboard the orbiter Columbia. The ASTRO-02 crew operated a suite of three ultraviolet telescopes around the clock for sixteen days.

Oswald was born June 30, 1951, in Seattle, Washington, and graduated from Bellingham High School in 1969. He attended the Naval Academy, receiving a B.S. in aerospace engineering in 1973.

After graduation from Annapolis, Oswald underwent pilot training in Texas, earning his wings in 1974. He flew the A-7 Corsair II aboard the carrier *U.S.S. Midway* in the Pacific and Indian Oceans until 1977. In 1978 he attended the Naval Test Pilot School at Patuxent River, Maryland, and remained at the Naval Air Test Center as an A-7 and F/A-18 test pilot until 1981. Oswald resigned from the Navy in 1982 to join Westinghouse Electric Corporation as a civilian test pilot, working on the radar systems for the F-16C and B-1B. In November 1984 he went to work for NASA as an aerospace engineer and instructor pilot at Ellington AFB, near the Johnson Space Center.

Oswald has logged over 4,700 flying hours in 38 different types of aircraft. He is currently a captain in the Naval Reserve heading the Naval Space Command's reserve unit in Dahlgren, Virginia.

He was one of the 13 astronaut candidates selected by NASA in June 1985, and in July 1986 qualified as a Shuttle pilot. His technical assignments have included serving as flight crew representative to the Kennedy Space Center, verifying software in the Shuttle Avionics Integration Laboratory, working with the solid rocket booster redesign team, and serving as capcom in mission control. He was assigned to STS-42 in January 1990.

Since the spring of 1996 Oswald has been deputy associate administrator for spaceflight at NASA headquarters in Washington.

Overmyer, Robert Franklyn

1936–1996

Marine test pilot Bob Overmyer made Shuttle flights in 1982 and 1985, first as pilot of STS-5, the first operational Shuttle mission, and then as commander of Mission 51-B/Spacelab 3.

Spacelab 3 carried a crew of 7, including two scientific payload specialists, as well as 24 rats and a pair of squirrel monkeys, and was intended to permit research in space manufacturing and medicine. Though plagued by equipment problems and the challenge of caring for animals in weightlessness, the crew completed most of its tasks, returning to Earth after seven days.

Overmyer was born July 14, 1936, in Lorain, Ohio, and grew up in Westlake, where he graduated from high school in 1954. He attended Baldwin Wallace College, receiving a B.S. in physics in 1958, and later earned an M.S. in aeronautics from the Naval Postgraduate School (1964).

Overmyer joined the Marine Corps in January 1958 and underwent pilot training in Texas. Between 1959 and 1965 he served as a fighter pilot at bases in the United States and Japan and was a student at the Naval Postgraduate School. In 1965 he attended the Air Force Test Pilot School at Edwards Air Force Base, California, then was chosen as an astronaut for the Manned Orbiting Laboratory (MOL) program. When MOL was canceled in 1969, Overmyer transferred to NASA.

Overmyer logged over 7,500 hours of flying time, including over 6,000 hours in jets.

As an astronaut Overmyer worked on the design and development of the Skylab orbiting space station, then served as support crewman and capcom for Apollo 17, the last manned lunar landing. From January 1973 to July 1975 he was a member of the support crew for the Apollo-Soyuz Test Project and was American capcom at Soviet mission control near Moscow during the flight. He later served as chase plane pilot for the Shuttle Approach and Landing Tests, and as deputy vehicle manager for the Shuttle Columbia, supervising the final stages of manufacturing and tiling. He was assigned to be a Shuttle pilot as early as March 1978, and named to the STS-5 crew in March 1982.

Overmyer took part in the investigation of the Shuttle Challenger disaster in 1986, then resigned from NASA and retired from the Marine Corps (with the rank of colonel) in June of that year to form Mach 25, his own aerospace consulting firm. He later joined the McDonnell Douglas Corporation as deputy director for flight crew systems in its space station office. (Some of these space station EVA systems were tested by astronauts Jerry Ross

and Jay Apt during STS-37 in April 1991.) Overmyer was also a columnist for the British magazine *Spaceflight News*.

He left McDonnell Douglas in 1995 to join Cirris, a small aircraft builder based in Dayton, Ohio. On March 22, 1996, Overmyer was killed while flight testing the Cirris VK30 prototype at the Duluth, Minnesota, airport.

Pailes, William Arthur
1952–

Air Force rescue pilot Bill Pailes served as the military payload specialist for Shuttle Mission 51-J in October 1985. Pailes supervised the operations of several DoD experiments in addition to the deployment of two Defense Satellite Communications Systems (DSCS) satellites. The 4-day Mission 51-J was the first flight of the orbiter Atlantis.

Pailes was born June 26, 1952, in Hackensack, New Jersey, and grew up in Kinnelon, graduating from high school there in 1970. As a teenager he never thought for a moment he would fly in space. He wanted to be a civil engineer, but when he earned an appointment to the Air Force Academy he wound up studying computer science, receiving a B.S. in 1974. In 1981 he earned an M.S. in that field from Texas A&M University.

With his computer background and "nonstandard" vision (he has color blindness), Pailes thought he would become anything but an Air Force pilot, but he was assigned to flight school at Williams AFB, Arizona, and qualified as an HC-130 pilot. From December 1975 to August 1977 he served with the 41st Aerospace Rescue and Recovery Squadron at McClellan AFB, California, then served with the 67th ARRS at Royal AFB, Woodbridge, England, until July 1980.

Following a year in graduate school Pailes managed the development of minicomputer software at Scott AFB, Illinois, where he read about the manned spaceflight engineer program in the *Air Force Times*. He applied and, in January 1983, was selected.

Pailes and the other thirteen members of the second MSE cadre were told they had a 50 percent chance of flying in space (a promise that became impossible to fulfill after the Challenger disaster). Like the members of the first MSE cadre, the new payload specialists underwent extensive training on Shuttle systems, but spent most of their time acting as payload integration engineers—taking part in the design, purchase, development, and construction of military satellites and space experiments. In October 1984 Pailes was assigned to the crew for Mission 51-J, though no public announcement was made until the following August.

After his flight Pailes was named director of manned spaceflight, becoming the head of the MSE group. He was a candidate for the 1986/7 NASA astronaut group, but was not selected. In July 1987 he left Space Division to return to the Aerospace Rescue and Recovery Service at Eglin AFB, Florida, then served with the Air Force Special Operations Command at Hurlburt Field, Florida, during Operation Desert Storm.

From 1992 to 1995 Pailes was director of the Defense Information Systems Agency at the Pentagon. He retired from active duty with the rank of colonel in October 1995.

Parazynski, Scott Edward
1961–

Physician Scott Parazynski was assigned as a Shuttle-Mir researcher and had spent five months training at the Gagarin Center near Moscow when, in September 1995, he was discovered to be too tall to fit in the emergency Soyuz return vehicle. It wasn't Parazynski's height—at 6'2" he had already met the Soyuz qualifications, though barely—it was his sitting height after several weeks on orbit, during which astronauts and cosmonauts gain one or two inches. Parazynski was replaced as a NASA-Mir crewmember by astronaut Wendy Lawrence, who was later replaced herself for being too short to perform an EVA!

Nevertheless, Parazynski reached the Mir station as a member of the STS-86 crew. This 11-day flight of the orbiter Atlantis made the seventh and most controversial Shuttle-Mir docking, following, as it did, the nearly disastrous June 1997 collision between Mir and a Progress supply vehicle that led to a number of system failures aboard the Russian station. The STS-86 crew delivered David Wolf, the sixth NASA-Mir crewmember, to Mir and returned Michael Foale to Earth. Parazynski and Russian cosmonaut Vladimir Titov performed a 5-hour EVA on the Mir exterior.

Previously Parazynski was a mission specialist in the crew of STS-66, which carried the third Spacelab ATLAS in November 1994. ATLAS-03 was part of a series of studies of the Earth's atmosphere, particularly the ozone layer.

In February 1998 Parazynski was assigned to the crew of STS-95, scheduled to carry SpaceHab and Spartan payloads, as well as payload specialist John Glenn, into space in October 1998.

Parazynski was born July 28, 1961, in Little Rock, Arkansas, and graduated from American Commmunity High School in Athens, Greece. (He also lived in Dakar, Senegal, and Beirut, Lebanon, as a teenager.) He attended Stanford University, receiving a B.S. in biology in 1983, and his M.D. in 1989.

While still at Stanford Parazynski won a NASA Graduate Student Fellowship to study fluid shifts that occur during manned spaceflight. A mountaineer, he has also published papers on high altitude acclimatization.

Parazynski served his internship at the Brigham and Women's Hospital of Harvard Medical School in 1990, and was completing a 22-month emergency medical residence in Denver, Colorado, when selected as one of 19 NASA astronaut candidates in March 1992.

In July 1993 Parazynski qualified as a Shuttle mission specialist while assigned to the mission development branch, working on EVA procedures. He was assigned to STS-66 in August 1993. Following his removal from the Shuttle-Mir assignment in October 1995 he worked in the operations planning branch of the astronaut office on Shuttle-Mir training and EVA matters.

Parise, Ronald Anthony
1951–

Astronomer Ron Parise was a payload specialist aboard both flights of the Spacelab ASTRO, beginning with STS-35, a 9-day flight of the orbiter Columbia flown in December 1990.

Spacelab ASTRO was an astronomical experiment package of four telescopes designed to make simultaneous multispectral observations of deep-space objects such as binary dwarf stars and exploding galaxies. In the STS-35 crew Parise was a member of the red or night shift with astronauts Bob Parker and Guy Gardner, and worked with them to overcome serious computer and data display problems that at one time threatened the mission's success.

Parise made his second flight aboard STS-67 in the spring of 1995. The ASTRO-02 payload centered on three ultraviolet telescopes that imaged faint galactic objects during a 16-day mission.

Parise was born May 24, 1951, in Warren, Ohio, where he grew up. He attended Youngstown State University in Ohio, earning a B.S. in physics in 1973. He received an M.S. (1977) and Ph.D. (1979) in astronomy from the University of Florida.

Parise is manager of the advanced astronomy programs section of the Computer Sciences Corporation in Silver Spring, Maryland. One of his projects was the design of the ultraviolet imaging telescope flown on Spacelab Astro. He also did research with the International Ultraviolet Explorer satellite.

He was announced as an Astro payload specialist in June 1984, when the experiment package was scheduled for launch on Shuttle Mission 61-E in March 1986. The explosion of the Challenger just six weeks earlier forced a 5-year delay.

Parker, Robert Alan Ridley
1936–

Astronomer Bob Parker was a mission specialist aboard STS-9, the first flight of the European research module Spacelab. For 10 days the crew of 6 astronauts, the largest sent into space aboard a single vehicle at that time, carried out scientific experiments in a variety of disciplines. For example, Parker participated in an experiment intended to prove or disprove a 1914 Nobel Prize-winning theory that hot or cold air blown into a person's ears would cause the subject to believe he was turning. Contrary to the theory, it did not. Parker also became famous for a testy public exchange with controllers at the Marshall Space Center when he felt he and payload specialist Ulf Merbold were being rushed to start one experiment before they could finish another.

In December 1990 Parker made a second Spacelab flight aboard STS-35. This long-delayed flight of the ASTRO 1 observatory carried three ultraviolet telescopes and one X-ray band instrument designed to provide astronomers with their best views yet of distant objects in space such as supernovae. Problems developed early in the flight when display units allowing the astronauts to point the instruments overheated, limiting their use. Ultimately the crew was able to coordinate with ground controllers to aim the instruments properly, resulting in 400 observations of 135 deep space objects.

Parker was born December 14, 1936, in New York City, and grew up in Shrewsbury, Massachusetts, where he graduated from high school. He attended Amherst College, receiving a B.A. in astronomy and physics in 1958, and earned a Ph.D. in astronomy at the California Institute of Technology in 1962.

After receiving his doctorate, and until his selection by NASA, Parker was an associate professor of astronomy at the University of Wisconsin.

Parker was one of the 11 scientist-astronauts selected by NASA in August 1967. In March 1968 he reported to Williams Air Force Base, Arizona, for jet pilot training, which he completed a year later. He went on to log over 3,500 hours of flying time in jets.

Immediately upon reporting to NASA in September 1967 the eleven new scientist-astronauts were told that budget cuts had made it likely they would face a long wait to fly in space, if they got the chance at all. Though several members of the XS-11 ("excess eleven," as they dubbed themselves), left the space program, Parker remained, serving on the astronaut support crew for Apollo 15 and Apollo 17, and as program scientist for all three Skylab flights. From 1974 to 1978 he worked on Space Shuttle development, and in August 1978 was named to be mission specialist aboard the first Spacelab. Ultimately he waited over sixteen years for his chance to fly in space.

Parker was assigned as mission specialist for the original flight of ASTRO 1 in June 1984. That mission was delayed for five years because of the Challenger disaster, and a series of technical problems with the orbiter Columbia.

In addition to his flight crew assignments, from March 1988 to March 1989 Parker served as director of the spaceflight/space station integration office at NASA Headquarters in Washington, D.C. He returned to NASA HQ in January 1991, as director of the division of policy and plans in the office of spaceflight, later becoming deputy assciate administrator for operations and director of Spacelab operations.

Since June 1997 Parker has been director of program requirements at the NASA Jet Propulsion Laboratory, Pasadena, California.

Patrick, Nicholas James MacDonald
1964–

Boeing aeronautical engineer Nicholas Patrick is one of the 25 astronaut candidates selected by NASA in June 1998. In August of that year he reported to the Johnson Space Center to begin a training and evaluation course that should qualify him as a Shuttle mission specialist and International Space Station crewmember.

Patrick was born March 22, 1964, in Saltburn, North Yorkshire, United Kingdom, and graduated from Harrow in London in 1982. He attended Cambridge University, receiving a B.A. in engineering (1986) followed by an M.A. (1990). He did further graduate work at the Massachusetts Institute of Technology, earning his M.S. (1990) and Ph.D. (1996) in mechanical engineering.

At the time of his selection by NASA, Patrick was a senior systems and human factors engineer with Boeing's commercial airplane group, Seattle, Washington.

Pawelczyk, James Anthony
1960–

Neurophysiologist Jim Pawelczyk was assigned as a payload specialist in the crew of STS-90, which was scheduled for launch in April 1998. STS-90 will carry the Neurolab Spacelab, the longest (planned 17-day duration), most complex, and last Spacelab mission, dedicated to 26 different experiments of the effects of microgravity on human beings, especially sleep rhythms and blood pressure.

Pawelczyk was born September 20, 1960, in Buffalo, New York, and considers Elmira, New York, where he graduated from Iroquois Central High School in 1978, to be his hometown. He attended the University of Rochester, New York, where he received B.A.s in biology and in psychology (1982). He went on to graduate school at Penn State, earning an M.S. physiology in 1985, then to the University of North Texas, for his Ph.D. in biology (physiology) in 1989.

While completing his postdoctoral fellowship at the University of Texas Southwestern Medical Center in Dallas from 1989 to 1992, Pawelczyk was a visiting scientist in the department of anaesthesia at the Rigshospitalet in Copenhagen, Denmark, in 1990. From 1992 to 1995 he was assistant professor of medicine at Texas Southwestern as well as director of the autonomic and exercise physiology laboratories of the Institute for Exercise and Environmental at Presbyterian Hospital in Dallas. Since 1995 Pawelczyk has been an assistant professor of physiology and kinesiology at Penn State.

Pawelczyk has published over 20 medical papers, and is the coeditor of the text, *Blood Loss and Shock* (1994).

As a coinvestigator for Neurolab experiments, as well as two flown on Shuttle-Mir missions, Pawelczyk became a payload specialist candidate in April 1996. He was selected to fly aboard STS-90 in May 1997.

Payton, Gary Eugene
1948–

Air Force manned spaceflight engineer Gary Payton became the first military astronaut when he served as payload specialist of Shuttle Mission 51-C in January 1985. Most NASA astronauts to that time had been active duty officers, but Payton was the first representative of an ongoing military program. Previous efforts such as the X-20 Dyna-Soar and Manned Orbiting Laboratory had been canceled before they could be flown.

During Mission 51-C Payton supervised the deployment of a classified signals intelligence satellite called Magnum, which was placed in geosynchronous orbit by an inertial upper stage. The 3-day flight of the orbiter Discovery was shortened by a day because of weather problems at its prime landing site, the NASA Kennedy Space Center in Florida.

Payton was born June 20, 1948, in Rock Island, Illinois. He attended Bradley University in Peoria for one year, then entered the Air Force Academy at Colorado Springs, graduating in 1971 with a B.S. in astronautical engineering. He went on to earn an M.S. in astronautical and aeronautical engineering from Purdue University in 1972.

After completing pilot training in 1973, Payton served as a flight instructor at Craig Air Force Base, Alabama. In 1976 he became a spacecraft test controller at Cape Canaveral and remained in that job until selected for the first group of manned spaceflight engineers in 1980.

Payton logged 1,080 hours of flying time in the T-37, T-38 and T-39 aircraft.

As one of the first 13 Department of Defense Shuttle payload specialists, Payton underwent a course of training that familiarized him with Shuttle systems, including use of the remote manipulator arm and underwater simulations of extravehicular activity. In May 1983 he was selected as the DOD payload specialist assigned to STS-10, then scheduled for launch in November of that year. But continuing problems with the Air Force inertial upper stage forced the postponement of Payton's secret payload.

Following his flight Payton trained as a flight director for Mission 62-A, the first manned Vandenberg Shuttle flight, originally scheduled for launch in the summer of 1986. The Challenger disaster in January 1986 forced the postponement, then the cancellation of 62-A. In 1987 Payton transferred to the Pentagon, where he became executive officer to Lieutenant General James Abrahamson, director of the Strategic Defense Initiative. Payton later worked as associate director, then director, for technology of SDIO and its successor, the Ballistic Missile Defense Organization. In this job he was one of the architects of the Delta Clipper reusable spacecraft program.

In January 1995 Payton abruptly retired from the Air Force in a public dispute with the head of BMDO, Army Lieutenant General Malcolm O'Neill, who had refused to detail Payton to NASA to head up the civilian agency's new reusable launch vehicle office.

Payton is currently director of reusable launch vehicles at NASA Headquarters, overseeing development of the X-33 prototype, scheduled for flight testing in 1999.

Peterson, Donald Herod
1933–

Don Peterson was a mission specialist on STS-6, the first flight of the orbiter Challenger, in April 1983. Peterson and three other astronauts conducted experiments in materials processing and deployed the first Tracking and Data Relay satellite using the Intertial Upper Stage. The IUS failed to operate as planned, though the TRDS eventually reached its intended orbit.

Peterson and astronaut Story Musgrave performed the first space walk of the Shuttle program, spending 4 hours and 15 minutes in the Challenger's payload bay.

Peterson was born October 22, 1933, in Winona, Mississippi, where he grew up. He earned an appointment to the Military Academy at West Point, graduating with a bachelor of science degree in 1955. He later earned an M.S. in nuclear engineering from the Air Force Institute of Technology (1962) and performed further work toward a Ph.D. at the University of Texas.

Peterson elected to serve in the Air Force and, after pilot training, served as an instructor with the Air Training Command until 1960. He was also a nuclear systems analyst with the Air Force Systems Command, a pilot with the Tactical Air Command, and a student at the Aerospace Research Pilot School at Edwards AFB, California.

He logged over 5,300 hours of flying time, including 5,000 hours in jets.

He was one of four pilots chosen for the USAF Manned Orbiting Laboratory program in June 1967. When MOL was canceled in June 1969, Peterson and six other pilots transferred to NASA as astronauts. Peterson served on the support crew for Apollo 16 in 1972, then was assigned to Space Shuttle development. He was named a mission specialist for STS-6 in March 1982.

Peterson retired from the Air Force with the rank of colonel in January 1980, though he remained at NASA in a civilian capacity. In 1985 he resigned from NASA to become an aerospace consultant in the Houston area.

Peterson, Forrest Silas
1922–1990

Forrest Peterson was the only Navy pilot to fly the X-15. Between September 1960 and January 1962 he made five flights in the rocket plane, ultimately reaching an altitude of 101,800 feet.

He went on to a distinguished career in naval aviation, including a tour as captain of the carrier *U.S.S. Enterprise* (1969–71). His last assignment was vice chief of naval operations for air at the Pentagon.

Peterson was born May 16, 1922, in Holdrege, Nebraska, but grew up in Gibbon, Nebraska, where he graduated from high school in 1939. After a year at the University of Nebraska, he entered the Naval Academy, graduating with a B.S. in electrical engineering in 1944. He later earned a B.S. in aeronautical engineering from the Naval Postgraduate School in 1952 and an M.S. in engineering from Princeton University in 1953.

Peterson served aboard the destroyer *U.S.S. Caperton* in the Pacific in 1945, then underwent pilot training at Pensacola, Florida, beginning in January 1946. He graduated in June 1947 and later flew combat missions in Korea. He attended the Naval Test Pilot School at Patuxent River, Maryland, graduating first in his class in 1956, then served as an instructor at the school prior to joining the X-15 program in August 1958.

After leaving the X-15 project in February 1962 Peterson became commander of two different naval air squadrons. In January 1963 he entered a training course in naval nuclear power plants administered by the Atomic Energy Commission. After completing the course in February 1964 he became executive officer of the *Enterprise*, which took part in combat operations in the South China Sea during the Vietnam War.

Peterson returned to the Pentagon in May 1966 as assistant to the director of naval program planning, and in November of that year was given command of his own ship, the oiler *U.S.S. Bexar*, which was deployed to

Southeast Asia. He was captain of the *Enterprise* from July 1969 to December 1971.

Peterson's subsequent posts included a tour in the Office of the Director for Defense Research and Engineering (1972–74) and command of the Sixth Fleet's Carrier Group Two (1974–75).

In August 1975 he returned to the Pentagon as vice chief of Naval Materiel. He served as vice chief of the Naval Air Systems Command from October 1976 until his retirement, with the rank of vice admiral, in May 1980.

He logged over 4,000 hours of flying time, including 2,600 hours in jets, in more than 40 types of aircraft.

He became vice-president of the Kaman Aircraft Company, then left to head his own aerospace consulting firm, Peterson-Baldwin Enterprises, based in Alexandria, Virginia.

Peterson died in Omaha, Nebraska, on December 8, 1990.

Petit, Donald Roy
1955–

Chemical engineer Don Petit is one of the 35 astronaut candidates selected by NASA on May 1, 1996. In August of that year he reported to the Johnson Space Center to begin a yearlong training and evaluation course that should qualify him as a Shuttle mission specialist and International Space Station crewmember.

Petit was born April 20, 1955, in Silverton, Oregon, where he graduated from high school in 1973. He attended Oregon State University, receiving a B.S. in chemical engineering in 1973, and later earned his Ph.D. from the University of Arizona, Tucson (1983).

From 1984 to 1996 Petit was a staff scientist at Los Alamos National Laboratory, Los Alamos, New Mexico, where his projects included flying materials processing experiments aboard the NASA KC-135 aircraft. He also studied cloud seeding with sounding rockets, performed gas sampling at active volcanoes, and studied the physics of weapons detonations.

In 1990–91 Petit was a member of the Synthesis Group, a study team headed by former astronaut Thomas

Stafford that proposed methods for returning Americans to the Moon and for the manned exploration of Mars.

Phillips. John Lynch

1951–

Former Navy pilot and space physicist John Phillips is one of the 35 astronaut candidates selected by NASA on May 1, 1996. In August of that year he reported to the Johnson Space Center to begin a training and evaluation course that should qualify him as a Shuttle mission specialist and International Space Station crewmember. He is currently assigned to the payloads/habitation branch of the astronaut office.

Phillips was born April 15, 1951, in Fort Belvoir, Virginia, but considers Scottsdale, Arizona, to be home, graduating from high school there in 1966. He attended the Naval Academy at Annapolis, receiving a B.S. in mathematics and Russian in 1972. He has earned an M.S. in aeronautical systems from the University of Florida (1974) as well as an M.S. (1984) and Ph.D. (1987) in geophysics and space physics from the University of California, Los Angeles (UCLA).

Commissioned in the Navy upon graduation from Annapolis, Phillips did graduate work, then qualified as a naval aviator in November 1974. He joined Attack Squadron 155 at Lemoore, California, as an A-7 Corsair pilot and made overseas deployments aboard the carriers *U.S.S. Oriskany* and *U.S.S. Roosevelt*. He later served as a Navy recruiting in Albany, New York, and as a CT-39 pilot based at North Island, Coronado, California.

Phillips left active duty in 1982 to enroll in graduate school at UCLA. While there he did research on the planet Venus using data from the Pioneer Venus spacecraft. He joined the Los Alamos National Laboratory, Los Alamos, New Mexico, as a J. Robert Oppenheimer Fellow in 1987, and became a permanent member of the staff two years later. His fields of research include the sun and the space environment. He has been principal investigator for the solar wind plasma experiment aboard the Ulysses spacecraft and is the author of 150 scientific papers.

Phillips has been a Navy reservist since 1982, commanding a merchant ship convoy unit and serving as a science and technology officer for the Office of Naval Research.

As a pilot he has logged over 4,000 hours of flying time and 250 carrier landings.

Phillips, Robert Ward

1929–

Veterinarian Robert Phillips served as backup payload specialist for the STS-40/Spacelab Life Sciences mission flown in June 1991. During the 10-day mission a crew of 7, including 3 physicians and a biochemist, performed 20 experiments studying the effects of weightlessness on humans, and on rats and jellyfish.

Phillips was originally assigned as one of the prime SLS payload specialists, but age and health problems caused his physical disqualification in 1989, two years prior to the long-delayed launch.

He later served in a support capacity for the second Spacelab Life Sciences mission, STS-58, in October 1993.

Phillips was born January 21, 1929, in Peoria, Illinois, graduating from high school there in 1946. He served in the U.S. Army for several years, then, upon leaving service, entered Colorado State University in Fort Collins. He received his B.S. in nutrition from Colorado State in 1959 and a doctorate of veterinary medicine there in 1961. He later earned a Ph.D. in physiology at the University of California at Davis (1964).

Phillips was a postdoctoral fellow at UC-Davis from 1961 to 1964. Since then he has been associated with Colorado State University as assistant professor (1964–67), associate professor (1967–71) and professor (from 1971) of physiology in its College of Veterinary Medicine and Biomedical Science.

He was selected as a Spacelab Life Sciences payload specialist in January 1984. A year later, he and Andrew Gaffney were chosen as prime payload specialists for the first SLS mission, then known as Shuttle Mission 61-D/Spacelab-4. That flight, originally scheduled for launch January 1986, was later canceled. A second SLS mission was postponed for several years because of the Challenger disaster.

Phillips is currently employed by the NASA Jet Propulsion Laboratory, after serving as a visiting scientist at NASA Headquarters for Space Station Freedom.

Pogue, William Reid

1930–

Air Force test pilot Bill Pogue was a member of the crew that made America's longest manned spaceflight prior to Shuttle-Mir, the 84-day Skylab 4 mission from November 1973 to February 1974. During that flight Pogue and fellow astronauts Gerald Carr and Edward Gibson conducted extensive observations of the sun in addition to experiments in space medicine and Earth resources.

The Skylab 4 astronauts also became notorious for staging the first "strike" in space. Tired and overworked in their sixth week aboard Skylab, they announced that they were taking some time off, and did. During their first days in space the crew had been reprimanded for covering up the fact that Pogue had become ill. From that point on, the relationship between the astronauts and mission control was often contentious, though engineers and scientists on the ground were later grateful for the astronauts' frankness.

Pogue was born January 23, 1930, in Okemah, Oklahoma. He attended Oklahoma Baptist University, receiving a B.S. in secondary education in 1951, and later earned an M.S. in mathematics from Oklahoma State University in 1960.

He joined the Air Force in 1951 and after earning his wings, he flew 43 combat missions in Korea as a member of the Fifth Air Force. From 1955 to 1957 he was a member of the Thunderbirds air demonstration team, and later was a mathematics instructor at the Air Force Academy. He also attended the Empire Test Pilot School in Farnborough, England, and was an instructor at the Air Froce Aerospace Research Pilot School at Edwards AFB, California, when chosen by NASA.

He logged over 5,000 hours of flying time, including 4,200 hours in jets.

Pogue was one of the 19 astronauts selected in April 1966. He served as a support crewman for the first manned Apollo flight, and later for Apollos 11, 13, and 14. He was training as a command module pilot for the planned Apollo 19 lunar landing mission when that flight was canceled. He transferred to the Skylab program and was named pilot of the third mission, Skylab 4, in January 1972.

MAKING ADJUSTMENTS

by William Pogue

[William Pogue was pilot of Skylab-4, the third crew to visit the Skylab space station, spending 84 days in orbit between November 1973 and February 1974, the longest U.S. manned mission until the start of Shuttle-Mir in 1995.]

The first thing you notice when you go into space is an absence of pressure on your body. You may feel light-headed or giddy. After half an hour or so, your face may feel flushed and you might feel a throbbing in your neck. As you move about, you will notice a strong sensation of spinning or tumbling every time you turn or nod your head. This makes some people uncomfortable or nauseated. You will also have a very "full feeling" or stuffiness in your head. You may get a bad headache after a few hours, and this too may make you feel sick to your stomach.

Most all of these symptoms will go away in a few days. The head congestion or stuffiness may bother you off and on during your entire time in space. Throughout the space-flight, you will feel a powerful sensation of tumbling or spinning every time you move your head too fast.

. . .

It takes the body about three days to become adjusted to weightlessness. You will become accustomed to working in space in a few hours, but you will be learning better ways to do things throughout the mission. Even though I got sick the first evening in space, the following day, which was our first full day in orbit, I worked fourteen hours.

We did, quite literally, develop bird legs. We called it bird legs because our legs became thinner and thinner as the weeks passed. The calves, in particular, became quite small. During the first few days in space, the legs become smaller because the muscles of the legs force blood and other fluids toward the upper part of the body, thus decreasing the girth measurement around the thighs and calves. In addition, muscle tissue is progressively lost due to insufficient exercise. These changes produce a "bird leg" effect.

We grew one and a half to two and a quarter inches taller. This height increase was due to spinal lengthening and straightening. The discs between the vertebrae expand and compress slightly, depending on the weight the back is supporting. Even on Earth an adult will be slightly taller (about one-half inch) in the morning than in the evening because the discs expand during sleep and compress as you walk or sit during the day. In weightlessness the discs expand, but they don't compress again, because there is never weight on the spine. Our space suits were custom-tailored on Earth to our height and posture; thus, they fit tighter in space because of the height increase. Also, my waist measurement decreased by almost three inches, due to an upward shift of the internal organs of the body, creating a "wasp waist" appearance.

. . .

Facial appearance changes quite a lot. I was really surprised, if not shocked, the first time I looked in the mirror: I didn't look like me anymore! Loose flesh on the face rises, or floats, on the bone structure, giving a high-cheekboned or "Oriental" appearance. The face also looks puffy, with bags under the eyes, especially during the first few days, and the veins in your forehead and neck appear swollen. After about three or four days, some of the facial puffiness (edema) and vein enlargement goes away, but your face still looks quite a bit different. . . .

[Returning to Earth] everything felt very heavy, including our own bodies. I picked up a three-pound camera just after splashdown, and it felt like it weighed fifteen or twenty pounds. When I rolled over on my side in the spacecraft couch to pick up the camera, it felt like one side of my rib cage was collapsing onto the other. These exaggerated impressions of heft and weight lasted only a few days, disappeared completely in less than a week.

We were able to walk, but were a bit unsteady at first. I involuntarily turned to the right even though I was looking straight ahead and trying to walk straight. I also drove off the right shoulder of the road twice during my first week back. It's as if I were watching someone else drive—a weird and confusing situation! One passenger suggested that NASA was putting something in our Tang. I was upset, because I didn't understand what was happening, and after I drove off the road a second time, I was very careful. This "right turn" tendency went away after the first week.

He resigned from NASA and retired from the Air Force on September 1, 1975, to become vice-president of the High Flight Foundation, a religious organization founded by fellow astronaut James Irwin and based in Colorado Springs, Colorado. He returned to NASA in 1976 and 1977 as a consultant on programs to study the Earth from space. He currently works in Springdale, Arkansas, as a privately-employed consultant to aerospace and energy corporations. (His partners in one venture are former Skylab astronauts Jack Lousma and Gerald Carr.)

Pogue is also the author of two nonfiction books, *How Do You Go to the Bathroom in Space?* and *Astronaut Primer*, both published in 1985. In collaboration with science fiction author and former *Omni* magazine editor Ben Bova, Pogue has written a novel, *The Trikon Deception* (1992).

Poindexter, Alan Goodwin

1961–

Navy test pilot Alan Poindexter is one of the 25 astronaut candidates selected by NASA in June 1998. In August of that year he reported to the Johnson Space Center to begin a training and evaluation course that should qualify him as a Shuttle pilot.

Poindexter was born November 5, 1961, in Pasadena, California, and graduated from high school in Coronado, California, in 1979. He attended the Georgia Institute of Technology, receiving a B.S. in aerospace engineering in 1986, and later earned an M.S. in aeronautical engineering from the Naval Postgraduate School (1995).

At the time of his selection by NASA, Poindexter was a naval aviator stationed in Virginia Beach, Virginia.

Polonsky, Mark Lewis

1956–

Former Air Force and NASA test pilot Mark Polonsky is one of the 35 astronaut candidates selected by the space agency on May 1, 1996. In August of that year he began a training and evaluation course that should qualify him as a Shuttle pilot.

Polonsky was born June 2, 1956, in Paterson, New Jersey, and grew up in Edison, where he graduated from John P. Stevens High School in 1974. He attended Purdue University, where he received a B.S. in aeronautical and astronautical engineering, and an M.S. in aeronautics and astronautics, both in 1978.

An Air Force ROTC student at Purdue, Polonsky went on active duty in 1978, and completed pilot training at Vance AFB, Oklahoma, in January 1980. He served for three years at Langley AFB, Virginia, as an F-15 pilot. In 1983 he made the transition to the F-5E, serving at Clark AFB, the Philippines, and at Nellis AFB, Nevada, as an Aggressor Pilot in training Air Force crews to defeat enemy tactics.

Polonsky attended the Air Force Test Pilot School at Edwards AFB, California, in 1986, then was assigned to Eglin AFB, Florida, to do weapons tests on the F-15, the F-15E, and the A-10. He left active duty in 1992 to join the aircraft operations division at the NASA Johnson Space Center, becoming an instructor in Shuttle landing techniques on the Shuttle Training Aircraft and on the NASA T-38.

He has logged over 5,000 hours of flying time in 30 different types of aircraft.

Prahl, Joseph Markel

1943–

Joseph Prahl was backup payload specialist for STS-50, the flight of the first U.S. Microgravity Laboratory. Launched on June 25, 1992, USML-1 was a 14-day Spacelab mission dedicated to research in space manufacturing and the effects of long-term flight on humans. Prahl supported the mission from the NASA Marshall Spaceflight Center.

Prahl was born March 30, 1943, in Beverly, Massachusetts. He attended Phillips Academy in Andover, then enrolled at Harvard College, receiving a B.A. (emphasis in engineering) in 1963. He went on to earn an M.S. and Ph.D. (1968) in mechanical engineering from Harvard University.

With the exception of a year as a visiting lecturer at Harvard (1974), Prahl's academic career has been spent at Case Western Reserve University in Cleveland, Ohio, originally as assistant professor of engineering in the department of fluid, thermal, and aerospace sciences (1968). Since 1985 he has been professor of engineeering in the department of mechanical and aerospace engineering.

Prahl's association with NASA's Lewis Research Center in Cleveland began in 1970, when he served as codirector of a summer faculty fellowship program there. Since 1980 he has worked with Lewis researchers on experiments in surface tension and combustion intended for flight aboard the Shuttle.

He holds two patents and has published over 20 technical papers. He also has been a consultant to numerous commercial firms such as Kennecott Copper, Republic Steel and Union Carbide.

Precourt, Charles Joseph
1955–

Air Force test pilot Charlie Precourt has made two dockings with the Russian Mir space station, and is scheduled to command a third.

Precourt was pilot of STS-71, the first Shuttle-Mir docking mission, flown in June 1995, and the first Russian-American linkup since Apollo-Soyuz 20 years earlier. STS-71 carried a crew of 7 to Mir, including Mir-18 cosmonauts Anatoly Solovyov and Nikolai Budarin, who remained aboard the Russian station, returning to Earth with eight, including Mir-17 cosmonauts Vladimir Dezhurov and Gennady Strekalov, and the first NASA-Mir crewmember, Norman Thagard. The orbiter Atlantis was also configured with a Spacelab module for medical tests of the "down" crew.

In May 1997 Precourt returned to Mir as commander of STS-84, which delivered NASA-Mir crewmember Michael Foale to the station while returning Jerry Linenger to Earth. This flight of Atlantis also transferred 4,000 pounds tons of food, water and technical equipment to the Mir crew.

Precourt is assigned as commander of STS-91, the ninth and last Shuttle-Mir docking, which was scheduled for launch in June 1998. STS-91 will return NASA Mir crewmember Andy Thomas to Earth.

Previously Precourt served as mission specialist in the crew of STS-55. This 10-day flight of the orbiter

Columbia in April–May 1993 carried the second German Spacelab and a crew of 7. Precourt, selected as a Shuttle pilot, served as the flight engineer in the crew.

Precourt was born June 29, 1955, in Waltham, Massachusetts, and grew up in Hudson, Massachusetts, where he graduated from high school in 1973. He attended the Air Force Academy, receiving a B.S. in aeronautical engineering in 1977, and later earned an M.S. in management from Golden Gate University (1988). In 1976 he was an exchange student at the French Air Force Academy. He has also attended the Naval War College (1990).

Precourt underwent pilot training at Reese AFB, Texas, in 1978, then for the next four years served as a a T-37 instructor, and a T-37 and T-38 maintenance test pilot. In 1982 he became an F-15 pilot based at Bitburg Air Base, Germany. Three years later he enrolled at the US Air Force Test Pilot School at Edwards AFB, California. Following graduation he remained at Edwards as a test pilot flying the F-15E, F-4, A-7, and A-37. In mid-1989 entered the Naval War College in Newport, Rhode Island.

He has logged over 6,500 hours of flying time in 45 different types of aircraft.

Precourt was one of the 23 astronaut candidates selected by NASA in January 1990. In July 1991 he completed a training program that qualified him as a Shuttle pilot. He has worked in the astronaut office operations development branch as a specialist in ascent, entry and abort issues, and from 1993 to 1994 was an ascent/entry, capcom in mission control.

From August 1995 to April 1996 he served as NASA's director of operations, Russia, based at the Gagarin Center. In the fall of 1997 he was acting assistant director (technical), Johnson Space Center.

Prinz, Dianne Kasnic
1938–

Physicist Dianne Prinz was the backup payload specialist to John-David Bartoe on the Spacelab-2/Mission 51-F shuttle flight in July 1985. She served as scientific capcom and provided mission support from the payload operations center at the NASA Marshall Spaceflight Center.

Until the Challenger disaster forced the delay or cancellation of many scientific Shuttle missions, Prinz was a candidate to fly as a crewmember on a future Spacelab mission.

Prinz was born Dianne Kasnic on September 29, 1938, in Economy, Pennsylvania. She received a B.S. in physics from the University of Pittsburgh in 1960 and a Ph.D. from Johns Hopkins University in 1967.

She became a research physicist with the Naval Research Laboratory in Washington, D.C., where she and Dr. Bartoe both designed optics and computer software for Spacelab 2 experiments. Both were chosen as candidate payload specialists in April 1978.

Puz, Craig Anton
1954–

Air Force engineer Craig Puz trained for five years as a payload specialist for a Shuttle/Spacelab mission dedicated to experiments for the Strategic Defense Initiative. The SDIO Spacelab, known as StarLab, was scheduled for launch on STS-50 in 1992, but became a sudden victim of budget cuts in September 1990, and was canceled. Puz had already left the program by that time, having transferred to the Pentagon in February 1990.

Puz was born June 24, 1954, in Pasadena, California, and grew up in nearby West Covina, where he graduated from Edgewood High School in 1972. He attended the Air Force Academy, receiving a B.S. in general studies (chemistry, behavioral science and management) in 1976. He later earned an M.B.A. from the University of Wyoming (1980) and an M.S. in space operations from the Air Force Institute of Technology (1982).

From August 1976 to May 1981 Puz served on a Minuteman III missile combat crew at F. W. Warren AFB, Wyoming. Following a year at Wright-Patterson AFB, Ohio, attending graduate school, he was selected for the Manned Spaceflight Engineer Program.

His initial assignment was working on the Talon Gold project, a system for tracking aircraft and missiles from space and a forerunner of the StarLab project. He was designated a StarLab payload specialist in November 1985.

On June 16, 1988, while training for StarLab in Boston, Puz and fellow payload specialist Maureen LaComb were seriously injured in an automobile accident. Both recovered.

Following StarLab's cancellation, Puz served with the Office of Space Systems at the Pentagon until retiring from the Air Force for medical reasons (he had been diagnosed with leukemia).

Puz is currently a civilian engineer with the Scitor Corporation in northern Virginia.

Reassy, William Francis
1952–

Former Navy aviator Bill Readdy commanded STS-79, the fourth Shuttle-Mir docking mission. This 10-day flight of the orbiter Atlantis, launched in September 1976 after a 6-week delay due to worries about the Shuttle's solid rocket motors, delivered John Blaha, the third NASA-Mir crewmember, to the Russian station, along with three tons of food, water, and other supplies. STS-79 also returned Shannon Lucid to Earth.

Readdy made two previous Shuttle flights, first as a mission specialist aboard STS-42 mission, the flight of the International Microgravity Laboratory. This 8-day Spacelab mission carried a crew of 7 who conducted 55 experiments in space manufacturing and life sciences for scientists from all over the world.

Readdy later flew as pilot for STS-51, a 1993 Shuttle mission that deployed the Advanced Communications Technology Satellite.

Readdy was born January 24, 1952, in Quonset Point, Rhode Island, and grew up in McLean, Virginia, where his father served as a Navy officer. He attended the Naval Academy at Annapolis, graduating in 1974 with a B.S. in aeronautical engineering.

Ready underwent pilot training at Beeville, Texas, earning his wings in September 1975, then qualified as an A-6 Intruder pilot at Oceana, Virginia. From 1976 to 1980 he flew with Attack Squadron 45 aboard the carrier U.S.S. Forrestal, serving in the North Atlantic and the Mediterranean. In 1980 he attended the Naval Test Pilot School at Patuxent River, Maryland, and upon completion of that course he became A-6 program manager and project pilot at the test center there. He later served as an instructor at the test pilot school. From 1984 to 1986 Readdy was strike operations officer aboard the carrier *U.S.S. Coral Sea*, flying A-6 and F/A-18 Hornet aircraft.

He is a captain in the U.S. Naval Reserve with over 6,500 hours of flying time in 60 different types of aircraft, including 550 carrier landings.

Readdy joined NASA in October 1986 as an aerospace engineer and instructor pilot in the aircraft operations division, where he served as program manager for the Shuttle Carrier Aircraft. He was selected as an astronaut candidate in June 1987, and qualified as a pilot astronaut in August 1988. His technical assignments have involved him in work on various Shuttle orbiter systems such as auxiliary power systems. He was assigned to STS-42 in December 1989. From July to October 1994 he was NASA's director of operations in Russia.

In January 1997, following STS-79, Readdy was assigned to the Shuttle program office at the Johnson Space Center. He remains an active astronaut.

Reightler, Kenneth Stanley, Jr.

1951–

Navy aviator Ken Reightler was pilot of the STS-48 mission, a 5-day flight of the orbiter Atlantis in September 1991. The crew of 5 deployed the Upper Atmosphere Research Satellite (UARS), designed to study ozone depletion in the upper atmosphere.

In February 1994 Reightler piloted STS-60, which carried the Wake Shield Facility.

Reightler was born March 24, 1951, in Patuxent River, Maryland, where his father was stationed as a Navy test pilot. He grew up in Virginia Beach, Virginia, where he graduated from Bayside High School in 1969. He went on to attend the Naval Academy, receiving a B.S. in aerospace engineering (1973). He later earned an M.S. in aeronautical engineering from the Naval Postgraduate School (1984), and in systems management from the University of Southern California (1984).

Upon graduation from Annapolis, Reightler entered flight school at Corpus Christi, Texas, and became a naval aviator in August 1974. His first assignment was as a P-3C pilot with Patrol Squadron Sixteen at Jacksonville, Florida, making deployments to Iceland and Sicily. In 1976 he was trained as a jet pilot, and the following year attended the Naval Test Pilot School. From 1978 to 1980 he was a Navy test pilot on programs involving the P-3, S-3, and T-39 airplanes. He then returned to the test pilot school as an instructor.

In 1981 and 1982 he made two overseas deployments aboard the carrier *U.S.S. Dwight D. Eisenhower*. Following postgraduate study in 1983 he was an F/A-18 pilot at NAS Lemoore, California. At the time of his selection by NASA he was again an instructor at the Naval Test Pilot School.

He logged over 4,000 hours of flying time in 60 different types of aircraft.

Reightler was one of the 15 astronaut candidates selected by NASA in June 1987. In August 1988 he qualified as a Shuttle pilot. His technical assignments have included serving as the weather coordinator for Shuttle launches and landings and as lead astronaut in the Shuttle Avionics Integration Lab (SAIL).

Reightler resigned from NASA and retired from the Navy in July 1995 to join the Lockheed Corporation. He is currently vice-president for science, engineering, analysis, and test at the Lockheed-Martin Houston office.

Reilly, James Francis II

1954–

Geoscientist James Reilly was a mission specialist in the crew of STS-89. This February 1998 flight of the orbiter Atlantis carried a SpaceHab module on the eighth Shuttle-Mir docking mission, delivering Andy Thomas, the last NASA-Mir crewmember, to the station, and returning David Wolf to Earth. STS-89 also transferred almost four tons of food, water, and technical supplies to the Mir crew.

In June 1997, while still training for STS-89, Reilly was assigned as an EVA mission specialist for International Space Station assembly mission 7A, scheduled for launch as STS-100 in the spring of 2000.

Reilly was born March 18, 1954, at Mountain Home Air Force Base, Idaho. He grew up in Texas, graduating from Lake Highlands High School in Dallas in 1972. He attended the University of Texas-Dallas, receiving a B.S. (1977), M.S. (1987) and Ph.D. (1995) in geosciences.

In 1977 and 1978, while working on his master's degree at Texas, Reilly took part in a scientific expedition to Marie Byrd Land in West Antarctica, studying the geochronology of the region. He joined Santa Fe Minerals, Inc., in Dallas, a year later, and in 1980 joined Enserch Exploration, also in Dallas. He has worked as an oil and gas exploration geologist, and has logged 22 days in deep submergence vehicles operated by the Harbor Branch Oceanographic Institution and the U.S. Navy.

Reilly was one of the 19 astronaut candidates selected by NASA on December 8, 1994. In May 1996 he qualified as a Shuttle mission specialist and prior to being named to the STS-89 crew worked in the astronaut office computer science branch.

Reisman, Garrett Erin
1968–

TRW aerospace engineer Garrett Reisman is one of the 25 astronaut candidates selected by NASA in June 1998. In August of that year he reported to the Johnson Space Center to begin a training and evaluation course that should qualify him as a Shuttle mission specialist and International Space Station crewmember.

Reisman was born February 10, 1968, in Morristown, New Jersey, graduating from high school in Parsippany in 1986. He attended the University of Pennsylvania, where he received a B.S. in mechanical engineering in 1991, then did graduate work at the California Institute of Technology, earning his M.S. (1992) and Ph.D. (1997).

At the time of his selection by NASA, Reisman was a spacecraft guidance, navigation and control engineer with TRW's space and technology division, Redondo Beach, California.

Resnik, Judith Arlene
1949–1986

Judith Resnik, the second American woman to go into space, was killed in the explosion of the Shuttle Challenger on January 28, 1986. The 7-person crew for the flight, known as Mission 51-L, included high school teacher Christa McAuliffe and was scheduled to last 6 days, during which Resnik would deploy and retrieve the Spartan scientific satellite for observations of Halley's Comet.

Resnik's first flight was aboard Mission 41-D, the maiden voyage of the orbiter Discovery. The first attempt to launch Discovery on June 26, 1984, ended in a launch-pad abort, with the Shuttle's main engines igniting, then shutting down just seconds before liftoff. The abort was caused by a hydrogen fuel leak near those main engines, and was corrected for a successful launch two months later, on August 30. In the next seven days Resnik and five fellow space travelers deployed three communications satellites and erected a 100-foot-long experimental solar panel in the Discovery payload bay.

Resnik was born April 5, 1949, in Akron, Ohio. She graduated from Firestone High School in Akron in 1966, then attended Carnegie-Mellon University in Pittsburgh, earning a B.S. in electrical engineering in 1970. She later earned a Ph.D. in electrical engineering from the University of Maryland in 1977.

After graduating from college, Resnik went to work as an engineer for RCA in Moorestown, New Jersey, and Springfield, Virginia, where her projects included designs for sophisticated radar systems and for telemetry from rockets. From 1974 to 1977 she was a biomedical engineer in the Laboratory of Neurophysiology at the National Institutes of Health in Bethesda, Maryland, and then spent a year as an engineer with the Xerox Corporation in El Segundo, California.

Resnik was one of the 35 astronauts selected by NASA in January 1978. In August 1979 she completed a training and evaluation course which qualified her as a mission specialist on Shuttle crews. She worked on the remote manipulator system (the Shuttle robot arm) and on Shuttle computer software until being named to a flight crew in February 1983.

A crater on the planet Venus and an asteroid have been named for her.

Richards, Paul William

1964–

NASA engineer Paul Richards is one of the 35 astronaut candidates selected by the space agency on May 1, 1996. In August of that year he reported to the Johnson Space Center to begin a training and evaluation course that should qualify him as a Shuttle mission specialist and International Space Station crewmember.

Richards was born May 20, 1964, in Scranton, Pennsylvania, and grew up in Dunmore, where he graduated from high school in 1982. He attended Drexel University, where he received a B.S. in mechanical engineering in 1987. He later earned an M.S. in mechanical engineering from the University of Maryland (1991).

While at Drexel from 1983 to 1987 Richards worked at the Naval Ship Systems Engineering Station. Upon graduation he joined NASA at the Goddard Space Flight Center in Beltville, Maryland, where he spent 9 years in the engineering directorate, working variously in the verification office, the electromechanical branch, the robotics branch and the guidance and controls branch. He was senior EVA tool development engineer for the Hubble Space Telescope servicing project, helping with the design, fabrication, and integration of EVA tools, sometimes testing them in mission simulations as a utility diver.

Richards, Richard Noel

1946–

Navy test pilot Dick Richards made four Shuttle flights, most recently as commander of STS-64. This August 1994 flight of the orbiter Atlantis carried the Lidar in Space Experiment and saw an EVA by crewmembers Mark Lee and Carl Walz, testing a rescue chestpack for future space walkers.

Previously Richards commanded STS-50, a 2-week mission launched June 25, 1992, the longest Shuttle flight to date. STS-50 carried the U.S. Microgravity Laboratory and a crew of 7, who performed experiments in space manufacturing.

He also commanded STS-41, a flight of the orbiter Discovery in October 1990 during which the European Space Agency's Ulysses solar polar space probe was deployed.

In August 1989 Richards served as pilot for the STS-28 mission, a classified Department of Defense mission during which an advanced Satellite Data System relay vehicle was deployed in Earth orbit.

Richards was born August 24, 1946, in Key West, Florida, and grew up in St. Louis, Missouri, where he graduated from Riverview Gardens High School in 1964. He attended the University of Missouri, receiving a B.S. in chemical engineering in 1969, and earned an M.S. in aeronautical systems from the University of West Florida in 1970.

He was commissioned in the Navy after graduation from Missouri and underwent pilot training, winning his wings in August 1969. From 1970 to 1973 he was an A-4 Skyhawk and F-4 Phantom pilot with Tactical Electronic Warfare Squadron 33 in Norfolk, Virginia, then served aboard the carriers *U.S.S. America* and *U.S.S. Saratoga* with Fighter Squadron 103. In March 1976 he entered the Naval Test Pilot School at Patuxent River, Maryland, and after graduation remained at Pax River as a test pilot until 1980, working on the first carrier catapults and landings of the F-18A Hornet. He was on his way to a new assignment with Fighter Squadron 33 in May 1980 when chosen by NASA.

As a pilot Richards accumulated over 4,400 hours of flying time in 16 different types of airplanes. He has also made more than 400 carrier landings.

Richards was one of the 19 astronauts selected by NASA in May 1980, qualifying as a Shuttle pilot in August 1981. He worked as deputy chief of aircraft operations and also managed the inflight refueling of the Shuttle carrier aircraft in addition to serving as a Shuttle capcom from April 1984 to September 1985.

He was scheduled to be pilot aboard Shuttle Mission 61-E, the Spacelab ASTRO 1 intended to observe Halley's Comet in March 1986. But 61-E was canceled following the explosion of the Shuttle Challenger during launch on January 28, 1986.

Richards retired from the Navy and left the astronaut office in July 1995. He is currently with the Shuttle program office at the Johnson Space Center and served as mission manager for STS-75 (February–March 1996) and STS-82 (February 1997).

Ride, Sally Kristen

1951–

Physicist Sally Ride became the first American woman space traveler on June 27, 1983, when she was one of 5 astronauts launched aboard the Shuttle Challenger on STS-7. During the 6-day STS-7 flight she served as flight engineer and took part in the deployment of two communications satellites and in the deployment and retrieval of the German built Shuttle Pallet Satellite (SPAS-01).

She went into space a second time aboard Shuttle Mission 41-G in October 1984. On this mission she deployed the Earth Radiation Budget Satellite and took part in scientific observations of the Earth made with the OSTA-3 pallet and the Large Format Camera. It was during 41-G that Kathryn Sullivan, who had attended the same first grade class as Ride, became the first American woman to walk in space.

Ride was born May 26, 1951, in Los Angeles, California. She attended Westlake High School in Los Angeles, where she was a nationally ranked tennis player, and graduated in 1968. She went on to attend Stanford University, earning a BA in English and a B.S. in physics in 1973, and an M.S. (1975) and Ph.D. (1978) in physics.

She was a teaching assistant and researcher in laser physics at Stanford when selected by NASA as an astronaut in January 1978. In August 1979 she qualified as a Shuttle mission specialist while assigned to the Shuttle Avionics Integration Laboratory. She served as capcom for STS-2 and STS-3 prior to being assigned to the STS-7 crew in April 1982.

Prior to the explosion of the Shuttle Challenger and the suspension of all Shuttle flights, Ride was training for her third mission, 61-M, scheduled for launch in the summer of 1986. Instead she served as the astronaut office representative to the presidential commission investigating the tragedy. Upon completion of the commission's report she was assigned as special assistant to the administrator for strategic planning at NASA Headquarters in Washington, D.C. In 1987 she coauthored a report on future options for the U.S. space program.

She resigned from NASA in August 1987 to join Stanford University as an arms control scholar. In June 1989 she left Stanford to become head of the Space Science Institute at the University of California at San Diego.

Ride is the coauthor of two books for children, *To Space and Back* (1986) and *Voyager: An Adventure to the End of the Solar System* (1992).

Rij, Jerry Jerome

1950–

Air Force engineer Jerry Rij was one of the 13 officers selected for the first cadre of Manned Spaceflight Engineers in January 1990. Members of the MSE cadre were to train as payload specialists for Department of Defense Shuttle missions. Though two MSEs eventually flew in space, Rij did not.

Rij was born February 23, 1950, in Elizabeth, New Jersey. He attended the Newark College of Engineering, graduating with a B.S. in electrical engineering in 1972.

Entering the Air Force through ROTC, Rij was first assigned as a systems engineer at the Rome Air Development Center, Griffiss AFB, New York. In 1976 Rij transferred to Los Angeles AFS as a program manager in Special Projects.

Rij left the MSE group in the summer of 1985 and transferred to the Pentagon, where he remained until 1990, when he transferred to the Consolidated Space Test Center at Onizuka AFB, California. He retired from the Air Force in 1995 and currently works in the aerospace business in northern Virginia.

Roberts, Katherine Eileen
1954–

Air Force engineer Kathy Roberts was assigned as a payload specialist for Shuttle Mission 62-B, the second polar orbiting manned spaceflight, originally scheduled for launch in January 1987. Following the Challenger disaster in January 1986, all polar Shuttle missions were canceled.

Roberts's payload, the $500-million Lacrosse imaging radar, was shifted to STS-27, and launched in December 1988. For a brief time she was considered as a candidate for that crew, but when NASA Administrator James Fletcher announced that no payload specialists would fly on the first five post-Challenger missions, she lost her opportunity.

Roberts was born Katherine Eileen Sparks on June 25, 1954, in Wichita, Kansas. She attended Indiana University, graduating in 1976 with a B.A. in physics. In 1981 she earned an M.S. in space physics and engineering from Johns Hopkins University.

A distinguished graduate of Air Force ROTC at Indiana, Roberts entered active duty in 1976 and spent three years at NORAD in Colorado Springs, Colorado, as an orbital analyst. In July 1979 she was assigned to the National Security Agency in Laurel, Maryland. It was while working at the NSA that she completed work for her master's degree.

Roberts transferred to Los Angeles Air Force Station in 1982, and was a satellite integration officer in Special Projects when selected for the Manned Spaceflight Engineer program in 1983. She was assigned as a payload specialist in November 1985.

From 1987 to 1992 Roberts was stationed at Lowry Air Force Base in Denver. Following a tour at the Pentagon in the technology office of the National Reconnaissance Office, she returned to Los Angeles, where she works at the Space and Missile Systems Center as manager for the low element of the Space-Based Infrared System (SBIRS).

Robinson, Stephen Kern
1955–

NASA engineer Steve Robinson was a mission specialist in the crew of STS-85. This July 1997 flight of the orbiter Discovery deployed and retrieved the Crista-SPAS payload, which studied changes in the Earth's atmosphere. The crew of 6 also tested a prototype Japanese-built robot arm for future use on the International Space Station.

He is assigned to the crew of STS-95, which will carry SpaceHab and Spartan payloads into space in October 1998, along with payload specialist John Glenn.

Robinson was born October 26, 1955, in Sacramento, California. He graduated from Campolindo High School in Moraga, California, in 1973, then attended the University of California at Davis, where he received a B.S. in mechanical/aeronautical engineering in 1978. He did graduate work at Stanford University, receiving an M.S. (1985) and Ph.D. (1991) in mechanical engineering.

In 1975, while still a student at UC-Davis, Robinson went to work at the NASA Ames Research Center. Following graduation in 1978 he became a full-time research scientist. He continued to work in fluid dynamics and experimental instrumentation while working on his graduate degrees at Stanford.

He became chief of the experimental flow physics branch at NASA Langley Research Center in 1990. In 1993 and 1994 Robinson was a visiting engineer at the Massachusetts Institute of Technology's Man Vehicle Laboratory, where he conducted research on space construction and EVA, and also took part in the second Spacelab Life Sciences Shuttle mission (STS-58). At the time of his selection as an astronaut Robinson was a research scientist in the fluid dynamics and acoustics division and leader of the aerodynamics and acoustics element of the General Aviation Technology Program.

Robinson is a privately licensed pilot with over 1,000 hours of flying time in a variety of aircraft.

He was one of the 19 astronaut candidates selected by the space agency on December 8, 1994. In May 1996 he qualified as a Shuttle mission specialist while working in the computer support branch of the astronaut office at the Shuttle Avionics Integration Laboratory (SAIL).

Rogers, Russell Lee
1928–1967

Russ Rogers was one of the 6 test pilots originally selected for the USAF X-20 Dyna-Soar program in April 1960. The Dyna-Soar was a Boeing-built spaceplane designed for launch aboard a Titan booster on either suborbital or orbital flights. Before launches could begin, however, it was canceled in December 1963.

Rogers himself was killed on September 13, 1967, while stationed at Kadena Air Force Base, Okinawa. He had been on a training flight to Ie Shima, a nearby gunnery range, when his F-105 suffered engine failure. Rogers bailed out, but did not survive.

Rogers was born April 12, 1928, in Lawrence, Kansas, and grew up in Phoenix, Arizona, where he graduated from North High in 1946. He joined the Navy, serving a 2-year tour, then returned to Phoenix. In 1949 he joined the Air Force, became a fighter pilot and flew combat missions in Korea. While still on active duty, he attended the University of Colorado, receiving a B.S. in electrical engineering in 1958. He later received an M.B.A. from the University of Southern California in 1966.

He attended the Air Force Test Pilot School at Edwards AFB, California, in 1958, and remained at Edwards as a test pilot until being assigned to the X-20.

Following the cancellation of Dyna-Soar he did further flight test work, then attended the University of Southern California. He was assigned to the 18th Fighter Wing at the time of his death.

Rominger, Kent Vernon
1956–

Former Navy test pilot Kent Rominger has been pilot on three different Shuttle crews, beginning with STS-73 in October 1995. This 16-day flight of the orbiter Columbia carried a crew of 7 and the second U.S. Micogravity Lab.

Rominger made a second flight aboard STS-80 in November 1996. The orbiter Columbia deployed the Wake Shield Facility and carried a payload of space manufacturing experiments. A pair of planned EVAs by crewmembers Tom Jones and Tammy Jernigan had to be canceled because of a faulty airlock hatch. At 18 days in duration, STS-80 is the longest Shuttle mission yet flown.

Rominger made a third flight aboard STS-85 in July 1997, having replaced pilot Jeff Ashby in the crew the previous February. STS-85 deployed and retrieved the Crista-SPAS astronomical satellite.

Rominger was born August 7, 1956, in Del Norte, Colorado, where he graduated from high school. He attended Colorado State University, receiving a B.S. in civil engineering in 1978. He earned an M.S. in aeronautical engineering from the Naval Postgraduate School in 1987.

Commissioned through ROTC in 1979, Rominger became a naval aviator in September 1980. From 1981 to 1985 he flew F-14 Tomcats with Fighter Squadron 2 aboard the carriers *U.S.S. Ranger* and *U.S.S. Kitty Hawk*. He also attended the Navy Fighter Weapons School, aka "Top Gun."

In 1986 and 1987 Rominger attended the Naval Postgraduate School/Test Pilot School cooperative program, and upon completion became F-14 project officer at the Naval Air Test Center, Patuxent River, Maryland. In September 1990 he joined Fighter Squadron 211 aboard the carrier *U.S.S. Nimitz*, and flew combat missions during Operation Desert Storm.

He has logged over 3,800 hours of flying time in 35 different types of aircraft, with 685 carrier landings.

Rominger was one of the 19 astronaut candidates selected by NASA in March 1992. In August 1993 he qualified as a Shuttle pilot while assigned to the operations development branch of the astronaut office.

Ronney, Paul David

1957–

Materials engineer Paul Ronney was alternate payload specialist for both flights of the Material Science Laboratory, flown aboard STS-83 and STS-94 in 1997, supporting the missions from the NASA Marshall Spaceflight Center.

Ronney was born May 1, 1957, in Los Angeles, California, and grew up in Newport Beach. He attended the University of California at Berkeley, receiving a B.S. in mechanical engineering (1978). He did graduate work at the California Institute of Technology, earning an M.S. in aeronautics (1980), and at the Massachusetts Institute of Technology, where he received his D.Sci. in aeronautics and astronautics (1983).

His first post doctoral position with NASA at the Lewis Research Center in Cleveland, Ohio. In 1985 and 1986 he was on the staff of the Naval Research Laboratory. He became assistant professor in the department of mechanical engineering at Princeton University. Since 1993 he has been an associate professor in the mechanical and aerospace engineering departments.

Ronney was the principal investigator for the SOF-BALL experiment aboard MSL-01.

Roosa, Stuart Allen

1933–1994

Air Force test pilot Stu Roosa was the command module pilot of Apollo 14, the first lunar landing mission to be flown after the near-disaster of Apollo 13. Roosa orbited the Moon in the command module Kitty Hawk while astronauts Alan Shepard and Edgar Mitchell spent over 33 hours on the surface in the lunar module Antares. Apollo 14 was launched on January 31, 1971 and splashed down on February 9.

Roosa was born August 16, 1933, in Durango, Colorado. He joined the Air Force in 1953 and later attended the University of Colorado through the Air Force Institute of Technology program, receiving a B.S. in aeronautical engineering in 1960. He later completed the advanced management course at Harvard University (1973).

After earning an Air Force commission in the Aviation Cadet Program, Roosa was an F-84F and F-100 pilot at Langley AFB in Virginia. Following college he served in Japan and in Pennsylvania. He graduated from the Air Force Aerospace Research Pilot School at Edwards AFB, California, in 1965, and was assigned to the flight test center there when selected by NASA.

He logged 5,500 hours of flying time, including 5,000 hours in jets.

Roosa was one of the 19 astronauts selected by NASA in April 1966. He served as a support crewman for Apollo 9 in 1969, then was named as command module pilot of Apollo 14. He later served as backup command module pilot for Apollo 16 and Apollo 17, and worked for several years on Space Shuttle development.

Roosa retired as an Air Force Colonel and resigned from NASA on February 1, 1976, to become vice-president for international affairs for the U.S. Industries Middle East Development Company in Athens, Greece. In 1977 he returned to the United States as president of Jet Industries in Austin, Texas. In 1981 he became president and owner of Gulf Coast Coors in Gulfport, Mississippi.

He died in Falls Church, Virginia, on December 12, 1994, of pancreatitis.

Ross, Jerry Lynn

1948–

Air Force test engineer Jerry Ross has made five Shuttle flights. On two of them he made four EVAs, logging over 21 hours.

As a mission specialist aboard STS-37, the April 1991 flight of the orbiter Atlantis, Ross and fellow EVA crewman Jay Apt took an unscheduled EVA to free a stuck antenna on the Gamma Ray Observatory. The massive astronomical satellite was in the process of being deployed when the problem occurred: Ross and Apt had been standing by for just such a contingency. "The Jay and Jerry Show," as capcom Marsha Ivins called it, went smoothly, as Ross moved up to the arm and tugged it free. He and Apt spent the rest of their 4-hour space walk practicing space station construction and maintenance techniques. Those same tests were the goal of the scheduled 6-hour EVA Ross and Apt took the next day.

During Shuttle Mission 61-B in November and December 1985, Ross had made two 6-hour space walks that also demonstrated space construction techniques. Along with astronaut Woody Spring, Ross erected and tore down two experimental structures called EASE and ACCESS while occasionally being moved from point to point by the Shuttle Atlantis's remote manipulator arm. Ross and Spring proved that a future space station could be assembled manually by astronauts from elements delivered to orbit in pieces.

Ross also went into space aboard STS-27 in December 1988. This flight of the Shuttle Atlantis carried a secret radar reconnaissance satellite named Lacrosse into orbit. Problems during the deployment of Lacrosse almost caused Ross and fellow EVA crewman William Shepherd to take a space walk to retrieve the satellite, but it proved unnecessary.

In March 1993 Ross served as payload commander for the second German Spacelab mission, STS-55, and in November 1995 flew aboard STS-74, the second Shuttle-Mir docking mission.

He is currently assigned as an EVA crewmember for STS-88, scheduled to be the first International Space Station assembly mission, in December of 1998.

Ross was born January 20, 1948 in Crown Point, Indiana, where he graduated from high school in 1966. He attended Purdue University and received a B.S. (1970) and M.S. (1972) in mechanical engineering.

Ross was an Air Force ROTC student at Purdue and was commissioned in 1970, though he did not enter active duty until 1972. His first assignment was at the Aero-Propulsion Laboratory at Wright-Patterson Air Force Base, Ohio, where he worked on ramjet engines and air-launched missiles. In 1975 he entered the Air Force Test Pilot School at Edwards AFB, California, and was named outstanding flight test engineer graduate. He remained at Edwards until 1979, serving as project engineer for the B-1 bomber. In February 1979 he was assigned to the payload operations division at the NASA Johnson Space Center.

He holds a private pilot's license and has flown 21 different types of aircraft, accumulating more than 2,800 hours of flying time.

Ross was one of 19 astronauts selected by NASA in May 1980 and in August 1981 qualified as a Shuttle mission specialist. He has worked on the remote manipulator arm, as a chase plane crewman, and as an EVA specialist. He served as support crewman for Shuttle missions 41-B, 41-C and 51-A, all of which involved extensive EVA work, and was capcom for those missions and flights 41-D and 51-D as well.

In November 1984 he was assigned to be a mission specialist for Mission 62-A, the first Shuttle flight to be launched from the West Coast of the United States. That mission was later canceled when the Air Force mothballed the Vandenberg Shuttle launch complex.

During the post-Challenger hiatus Ross was involved in planning for EVA assembly and maintenance for the proposed Space Station Freedom. He was assigned to STS-27 in September 1987.

From November 1993 to July 1994 Colonel Ross was acting deputy chief of the astronaut office. He later served as chief of the EVA/robotics branch.

Runco, Mario, Jr.

1952–

A former New Jersey state trooper, astronaut Mario Runco has been a mission specialist aboard three different Shuttle flights, including STS-77. This May 1996 flight of the orbiter Atlantis carried the fourth SpaceHab experiment module and accomplished four different rendezvous with satellites deployed during the mission.

Runco's first mission was STS-44 aboard the orbiter Atlantis in November 1991. The crew of STS-44 sent a Defense Support Program early warning satellite into geosynchronous orbit. Runco also took part in a number of observations of military targets from orbit with Terra Scout payload specialist Tom Hennen.

In January 1993 Runco made his second Shuttle flight, this time aboard STS-54, which deployed the fifth Tracking and Data Relay Satellite from the orbiter Endeavour.

Runco was born January 26, 1952, in Bronx, New York, though he considers Yonkers to be his hometown.

He received a B.S. in meteorology and physical oceanography from City College of New York in 1974, and an M.S. in meteorology from Rutgers University in 1976.

Following graduation from Rutgers Runco worked for the U.S. Geological Survey doing ground water surveys. In 1977 he joined the New Jersey State Police, and served as a state trooper until joining the Navy in June 1978.

After completing officer candidate school in September 1978, Runco was assigned to the Naval Environmental Prediction Research Facility in Monterey, California, as a research meteorologist. From April 1981 to December 1983 he served as geophysics officer aboard the *U.S.S. Nausau*, an amphibious assault vehicle. In 1984 and 1985 he served as an instructor in the Naval Geophysics Technical Readiness Laboratory at the Naval Postgraduate School in Monterey. In December 1985 he assumed command of Oceanographic Unit Four and embarked in the *Chauvenet*, a Naval Survey Vessel, on a survey of the Java Sea and Indian Ocean. At the time of his selection as an astronaut he was flight environmental services officer at the Nava Western Oceanography Center, Pearl Harbor, Hawaii.

Runco was one of the 17 astronaut candidates selected by NASA in June 1987. In August 1988 he qualified as a mission specialist while working in the astronaut office's operations development branch, where he worked on the Shuttle crew escape system. He later worked in the mission support branch, including a tour in SAIL, and in the astronaut support team at NASA Kennedy Space Center. In 1994 and 1995 Commander Runco was a capcom in mission control. From August 1996 to August 1997 he worked in the payload/habitation branch of the astronaut office, and is currently assigned to the astronaut support team at the Kennedy Space Center.

Rushworth, Robert Aitken
1924–1993

Air Force Major Bob Rushworth made 34 flights in the X-15 rocket plane, more than any other test pilot, and earned Air Force Astronaut Wings on June 27, 1963, when he flew X-15 #3 to an altitude of 285,000 feet, or 55 miles.

Rushworth was born October 9, 1924, in Madison, Maine, where he graduated from high school in 1942. He attended Hebron Academy for a year, and in June 1943 enlisted in the Army. He entered the aviation cadet program and became a pilot, winning his wings in September 1944.

Assigned to the 12th Combat Cargo Squadron in the China-Burma-India theater of operations, he flew C-47 Skytrain and C-46 Commando transports on combat missions, including many over the Himalayas. Returning to the States, he left active duty in January 1946 and entered the University of Maine, where he received a B.S. in mechanical engineering in 1951.

Recalled to active duty in the Air Force in February 1951, Rushworth became an F-80C Shooting Star pilot with the 132nd Fighter Interceptor Squadron, Dover AFB, Maine. In August 1953 he was enrolled in the Air Force Institute of Technology at Wright-Patterson AFB, Ohio, where he earned an M.S. in aeronautical engineering in 1954. He remained at Wright-Pat for two more years as an engineer, then was sent to Edwards AFB, California.

He graduated from the Experimental Test Pilot School there in January 1957 and for the next ten years flew aircraft and rocket planes at Edwards, including the F-101, TF-102, F-104, F-106, and X-15. He won a Distinguished Flying Cross for landing an X-15 safely after its landing gear extended prematurely.

Rushworth left Edwards in 1966 to attend the National War College, then became assistant deputy commander of the 17th Tactical Fighter Wing at Cam Ranh Bay, Vietnam, flying 189 combat missions in the F-4 Phantom. Returning to the United States in 1969, he served as director of several test programs at Wright-Pat (1969–73), inspector general for the Air Force Systems Command (1973–74), commander of the flight test center at Edwards (1974–75), commander of the test center at Kirtland AFB, New Mexico (1975–76), and vice-commander of the Aeronautical Systems Division at Wright-Pat (1976–81).

He logged over 6,900 hours of flying time in 50 different types of aircraft.

Rushworth died at Camarillo, California, on March 18, 1993.

Sacco, Albert, Jr.

1949–

Albert Sacco was a payload specialist aboard STS-73, the second U.S. Microgravity Spacelab (USML-2), flown in October 1995. This 16-day flight of the orbiter Columbia carried a crew of 7 who completed over 40 different experiments in fluid dynamics and crystal growth. They also demonstrated new systems to monitor and control such experiments from ground stations, an important tool for future International Space Station development.

In June 1992 Sacco served as a backup payload specialist for STS-50, the first U. S. Microgravity Laboratory. This 14-day mission of the orbiter Columbia was devoted to research in space manufacturing and the effects of long-term spaceflight on humans. Sacco supported the mission from the NASA Marshall Spaceflight Center.

Sacco was born May 3, 1949, in Boston, Massachusetts. He attended Northeastern University in Boston, graduating with a B.S. in chemical engineering in 1973. He later earned a Ph.D. from the Massachusetts Institute of Technology (1977).

He is currently a professor and head of the department of chemical engineering at Worcester Polytechnic University, Worcester, Massachusetts.

Sacco is also the author of over 25 technical papers.

He was selected as a payload specialist for USML in August 1990.

Schirra, Walter Marty, Jr.

1923–

Navy test pilot Wally Schirra was the only one of the original 7 American astronauts to go into space in Mercury, Gemini, and Apollo spacecraft.

On October 3, 1962, Schirra piloted Mercury-Atlas 8, which he had named Sigma 7, on a 6-orbit mission lasting 9 hours and 13 minutes, proving that an astronaut could carefully manage the limited amounts of electricity and maneuvering fuel necessary for longer, more complex flights. (The Mercury missions of Glenn and Carpenter, which preceded Schirra's, had been plagued by fuel and control problems.) Schirra had chosen the name Sigma because it symbolized engineering precision, and a precisely engineered flight was the result, ending with a splashdown just five miles from the carrier *U.S.S. Kearsarge* in the Pacific Ocean. True to his Navy background, Schirra elected to remain aboard the capsule until it was lifted to the deck of the carrier.

Schirra's second flight, as command pilot of Gemini 6, was intended to perform the first rendezvous and docking between different spacecraft, a vital prerequisite for missions to the Moon. But the unmanned Agena target for Gemini 6 failed to reach orbit on October 25, 1965. Gemini 6 was removed from the pad and replaced by Gemini 7, which was launched on December 4 on a planned 14-day flight. Eight days later Schirra and fellow astronaut Thomas Stafford were in their Gemini spacecraft atop the Titan booster when it ignited, then shut down after only two seconds. Schirra had the option at that point of ejecting himself and Stafford, but chose to remain in the spacecraft while technicians confirmed that the booster was not going to explode. Two days later Schirra and Stafford finally got off the ground, and less than 6 hours into the flight were "station keeping" just a few feet from astronauts Frank Borman and James Lovell in Gemini 7, 170 miles above the Mariana Islands.

A day later, after the astronauts made a Christmas "UFO" sighting (which ended with Schirra playing the harmonica and singing "Jingle Bells"), Schirra and Stafford were back on Earth.

In October 1968 Schirra and astronauts Donn Eisele and Walter Cunningham made the first manned flight of the Apollo spacecraft, spending an uncomfortable 11 days (the astronauts all developed head colds) qualifying the re-designed Apollo for future flights to the Moon after the tragic fire that killed astronauts Grissom, White, and Chaffee in January 1967.

Schirra was born March 12, 1923, in Hackensack, New Jersey, and graduated from Dwight Morrow High School in Englewood. His father was a World War I ace who later flew in air circuses. Schirra's mother did wing-walking stunts. Nevertheless, though he grew up around airplanes, Schirra didn't solo until Naval pilot training.

After high school he spent a year at the Newark College of Engineering, then attended the Naval Academy at Annapolis, earning a bachelor of science degree in 1945.

Schirra served in the surface navy for a year, then underwent pilot training at Pensacola, Florida, earning his wings in 1948. He was a carrier pilot for three years, then flew 90 combat missions in Korea as an exchange pilot with the Air Force, shooting down two MiGs. Returning to the United States, he helped develop the Sidewinder missile while stationed at the Naval Ordnance Training Station at China Lake, California. After a 3-year tour with the 124th Fighter Squadron aboard the carrier *U.S.S. Lexington,* Schirra attended the Naval Test Pilot School at Patuxent River, Maryland. He was a test pilot at Pax River when selected by NASA.

Schirra admitted later that he was reluctant to give up his Navy career for the space program, but nevertheless was one of the 7 astronauts chosen by NASA in April 1959. A precise pilot and engineer, Schirra also became notorious for his practical jokes.

In addition to his three spaceflights he served as backup to Scott Carpenter in 1962, and as backup command pilot for Gemini 3, the first manned Gemini mission, in 1965. He and his Apollo crew were originally assigned to the second manned Apollo flight, but were made backups to the Apollo 1 astronauts in November 1966.

He retired from the Navy as a captain and resigned from NASA on July 1, 1969, to become president of Regency Investors, a financial company based in Denver, Colorado. He later formed his own company, the Environment Control Corporation (ECCO), and from January 1975 to December 1977 was employed by the Johns-Manville Corporation. Since 1978 he has headed his own firm, Schirra Enterprises, and works as a consultant in San Diego and Hawaii.

Schirra was Walter Cronkite's partner during the television coverage of Apollo 11. For many years he was also a television commercial spokesman for Actifed cold remedy.

His autobiography, *Schirra's Space*, written with Richard N. Billings, was published in 1988.

Schmitt, Harrison Hagen "Jack," Jr.

1935–

Jack Schmitt became the first geologist to land on the Moon when he served as lunar module pilot of Apollo 17, the last Apollo lunar landing.

Schmitt, commander Eugene Cernan and command module pilot Ronald Evans were launched in the early morning hours of of December 7, 1972, the fiery climb of their Saturn 5 lighting up the Florida sky for hundreds of miles around. Reaching lunar orbit three days later Schmitt and Cernan left Evans in the command module America and boarded the lunar module Challenger to descend to a region of the Sea of Serenity, near the crater Littrow and the surrounding Taurus Mountains.

Over the next three days the astronauts set up scientific experiment packages and drove to the nearby mountains in a lunar rover, collecting soil and rock samples. During these excursions, while mission controllers operated a television camera mounted on the rover, geologist Schmitt gave detailed descriptions of the various craters, boulders, and soil found in the Taurus-Littrow Valley. At one point Schmitt and Cernan found orange-colored soil, which probably came from a lunar volcano, indicating that the Moon was far from a geologically "dead" body. The astronauts returned to Earth on December 19, 1972, with a record 249 pounds of lunar material, ending the first phase of man's exploration of the Moon.

Schmitt was born July 3, 1935, in Santa Rita, New Mexico, and graduated from Western High School in Silver City in 1953. His father was a geologist who studied the American Southwest. Schmitt attended the California Institute of Technology, receiving a B.S. in science in 1957, then studied at the University of Oslo in Norway as a Fulbright Fellow in 1957 and 1958. He received his Ph.D. in geology from Harvard University in 1964.

Between 1957 and 1961 Schmitt worked as a geologist, primarily with the U.S. Geological Survey, at sites in southeastern Alaska, western Norway, New Mexico and Montana. He taught a course in ore deposits at Harvard in 1961, then joined the U.S.G.S. Astrogeology Center at Flagstaff, Arizona, where he participating in photographic and telescopic mapping of the Moon. He was also one of the U.S.G.S. scientists who acted as instructors for NASA astronauts.

Schmitt was one of 6 scientist-astronauts selected in June 1965, the first Americans chosen for space training because of their scientific skills and not because of their flying abilities. Nevertheless, two of the new scientists were already qualified jet pilots, and the four who were not—including Schmitt—were required to complete flight training. Schmitt attended a 53-week flight school at Williams Air Force Base in Arizona. Eventually he would log over 2,100 hours of flying time, including 1,600 hours in jets.

In 1966 Schmitt began to train for a possible Apollo lunar flight while also assisting veteran astronauts, who would make up the first Apollo crews, in lunar navigation and geology. He also took part in the analysis of samples returned from the Moon.

In late 1969 Schmitt was assigned as backup lunar module pilot for Apollo 15, then planned for October 1970, which put him in line for Apollo 18. But the Apollo 13 accident in April 1970 and Congressional budget cuts delayed some missions and eliminated others, including Apollos 18, 19, and 20. As the first and only scientist-astronaut assigned to an Apollo crew, Schmitt had apparently lost his chance to go to the Moon. Director of flight crew operations Donald Slayton, holding to his long standing crew rotation system, submitted the Apollo 14 backup crew, Cernan, Evans and lunar module pilot Joe Engle, to NASA headquarters as candidates for Apollo 17. But headquarters overruled Slayton and replaced Engle with Schmitt.

In July 1973, following Apollo 17, Schmitt was named a Sherman Fairchild Distinguished Scholar at Cal Tech, an appointment that ran through July 1975. At the same time Schmitt served as chief of NASA scientist-astronauts (from February 1974) and, beginning in May 1974, as NASA assistant administrator for energy programs.

In August 1975 Schmitt resigned from NASA to return to his home state of New Mexico to enter the race for the U.S. Senate. On November 2, 1976, Schmitt, a Republican, was elected with 57 percent of the votes cast. He served in the Senate from January 1977 to January 1983 as a member of committees dealing with commerce, science and space, banking, urban affairs, and ethics. He was defeated in his campaign for reelection in November 1982.

Schmitt is an adjunct professor of engineering at the University of Wisconsin, Madison.

Schweickart, Russell Louis
1935–

Rusty Schweickart's only space-flight was Apollo 9, during which he took part in the first manned test of the Apollo lunar module and the first test of the pressure suit and backpack designed for walking on the Moon.

Schweickart's space walk on March 6, 1969, was originally scheduled to last over two hours, during which he would crawl from the front hatch of the lunar module Spider to the open hatch of the command module Gumdrop. But during the first three days of the mission Schweickart suffered from dizziness and nausea, what would later be called space adaptation syndrome (SAS). Mission controllers, worried about Schweickart's safety, should he become sick in his pressure suit, shortened the EVA and eliminated the transfer from one spacecraft to another. Schweickart spent 38 minutes on the front porch of Spider, confirming that the Apollo spacesuit and backpack worked well.

Two days later Schweickart and command pilot James McDivitt separated Spider from Gumdrop and flew off to a distance of 85 miles before returning.

Schweickart was born October 25, 1935, in Neptune, New Jersey, and graduated from high school in Manasquan in 1952. He attended the Massachusetts Institute of Technology, receiving a B.S. in aeronautical engineering in 1956. He later earned an M.S. in aeronautics and astronautics in 1963 from M.I.T. for a thesis concerning stratospheric radiance.

From 1956 to 1960 Schweickart was a pilot in the U.S. Air Force. He returned to M.I.T. in 1960 as a graduate student and researcher, though he was recalled to active duty for a year in 1961 and subsequently served with the Air National Guard. At the time of his selection by NASA he was a scientist at the Experimental Astronomy Laboratory at MIT, doing research in the physics of the upper atmosphere and in star tracking.

As a pilot Schweickart eventually logged over 4,200 hours of flying time, including 3,500 hours in jets.

He was one of the 14 astronauts selected by NASA in October 1963 and following preliminary training, worked on inflight scientific experiments for Gemini and Apollo missions. In January 1966 he was assigned as backup lunar module pilot for the first manned Apollo mission. Ultimately that crew, consisting of astronauts McDivitt, Scott, and Schweickart, was assigned to the third manned Apollo mission, Apollo 9.

In April 1969, following Apollo 9, Schweickart was assigned to the Skylab program, then known as Apollo Applications, and trained for a long-duration Earth orbit mission. He also served as a willing subject for NASA doctors studying space adaptation syndrome.

Schweickart served as backup commander for Skylab-2, the first mission to Skylab. When the SL-2 launch was delayed because of problems aboard Skylab itself, Schweickart spent many hours in EVA simulations developing and testing the tools that astronauts Conrad, Weitz, and Kerwin would use to repair the station. He also served as capcom for all three Skylab missions.

At the conclusion of the Skylab program in April 1974, Schweickart was transferred to NASA Headquarters in Washington, D.C., to serve as director of user affairs in the Office of Applications, where he was responsible for making NASA technology available to companies and individuals outside the space program. In November 1976 he returned to the Johnson Space Center to work on policies regarding Shuttle payloads, and the following summer took a leave to serve California governor Edmund G. "Jerry" Brown Jr. as assistant for science and technology.

Schweickart resigned from NASA in July 1979 to become Commissioner of Energy for the State of California. He served with the Energy Commission—including three years as chairman—for five and a half years. In 1987 and 1988 he chaired the U.S. Antarctic Program Safety Review Panel for the National Science Foundation.

He also founded the Association of Space Explorers (ASE), an international professional society of astronauts and cosmonauts which now numbers 155 members from 18 countries. He served as ASE president, and contributed the preface to ASE's first book, *The Home Planet* (1988).

More recently Schweickart served as president of NSR Communications, an international computer and communcations company. In August 1994 he joined CTA, Incorporated, in Rockville, Maryland, as executive vice president. He continues to be a frequent lecturer on space and the environment.

Scobee, Francis Richard
1939–1986

The commander of Shuttle Mission 51-L, Dick Scobee was killed along with 6 crewmembers in the explosion of the Challenger during launch on January 28, 1986. It was the worst disaster in the history of manned spaceflight and brought the American space program to a halt for almost three years.

Scobee, pilot Michael Smith, mission specialists Judith Resnik, Ronald McNair, and Ellison Onizuka, payload specialist Gregory Jarvis of Hughes Aircraft, and teacher Christa McAuliffe were to have spent 5 days in orbit. Among their tasks were the deployment of the TDRS-B communications satellite and observation of Halley's Comet with the Spartan satellite. McAuliffe, the first private citizen to be selected for a Shuttle flight, was to conduct two lessons to be televised live to schoolchildren all over America.

The launch of 51-L was delayed twice by technical and weather problems, and finally lifted off at 11:38 A.M., EDT, after a night in which temperatures at Cape Canaveral dropped below freezing, a night in which, unknown to the crew, engineers at Morton Thiokol (builders of the Shuttle's powerful solid rocket boosters) and the NASA Marshall Space Flight Center were engaged in a debate over the safety of a launch in such weather. Some engineers were concerned that the O-rings, the seals between segments of the huge boosters, would loose their flexibility in the cold, allowing superhot gases to escape from the SRB.

As analysis of films taken of the launch showed, a plume of smoke escaped from the right SRB at liftoff.

Moments later, unknown to the crew or NASA flight controllers in Houston, the smoke was replaced by a jet of flame with a temperature of over 6000 degrees F—a blowtorch aimed at the metal strut that joined the SRB to the huge external fuel tank. As the Challenger rocketed to an altitude of nine miles, to the point known as "max Q," where speed and aerodynamic pressure maximum stress on the vehicle, the attach point burned through and the aft wall of the tank blew open. A sudden and violent thrust forward, caused by fuel escaping from the ruptured tank, slammed the errant SRB into the right wing of the Challenger, shearing it off. An instant later the whole ET vaporized. The Challenger, initially thought to have been destroyed with the tank, broke apart due to the violent stress. The astronauts are believed to have died in first surge from the external tank or in the disintegration of the Challenger itself, in spite of the fact that the crew cabin emerged from the cloud of debris relatively intact, smashing into the Atlantic three minutes later.

The crew compartment, resting on the floor of the Atlantic at a depth of over 100 feet, was not discovered until early March, six weeks after the accident. Recovery of the astronaut remains from the site took several more weeks. Scobee was finally buried at Arlington National Cemetery.

Mission 51-L was to have been Scobee's second Shuttle flight. In April 1984 he served as pilot of Mission 41-C, maneuvering the Challenger into a rendezvous with the ailing Solar Max satellite, which was then retrieved, repaired, and redeployed.

Scobee was born May 19, 1939, in Cle Elum, Washington, and grew up in Auburn, where he graduated from high school in 1957. He enlisted in the Air Force in October 1957 and was trained as an aircraft mechanic. While stationed at Kelly Air Force Base in San Antonio, Texas, Scobee took classes in night school, eventually qualifying for the Airman's Education and Commissioning Program. In 1963 he was enrolled at the University of Arizona in Tucson, and graduated two years later with a B.S. in aerospace engineering.

Commissioned as a second lieutenant in September 1965, Scobee managed to avoid being sent back to aircraft maintenance by volunteering for flight school. He spent eleven months at Moody AFB in Valdosta, Georgia, qualifying as a pilot, then learned to fly transport and cargo planes in South Carolina and Oklahoma. In November 1967 he began a tour in Vietnam with the 535th Tactical Airlift Squadron, flying C-7A Caribou twin-engine cargo planes into and out of combat zones. Returning to the United States in 1969, he was a C-141 pilot at Charleston when he received a form letter soliciting his application for the Aerospace Research Pilot School at Edwards AFB.

The ARPS, as it was known, was originally an offshoot of the better-known Air Force Test Pilot School, serving as a postgraduate course in 1962 and 1963, until the two were merged. The ARPS name was adopted for both until the early 1970s, when it, too, reverted. Name aside, the school accepted only the best pilots, especially those who were young (under 30) with experience in high-performance fighter planes, and who had Academy backgrounds that put them on a fast career track. Scobee, in 1971, was already 32 years old, a cargo pilot (a "heavy" in Air Force slang), and a former enlisted man. He didn't think he had a chance, but applied. Unknown to him, the Air Force was changing the entrance requirements to allow pilots with more diverse backgrounds to enter the school. (Just two years later the requirements were changed again to allow flight engineers, such as Ellison Onizuka, to enroll.) And out of the hundreds who applied for the school, Scobee was one of the dozen chosen for Class 71-B. He arrived at Edwards in July 1971.

Following graduation the next summer, Scobee remained at Edwards as a test pilot. He flew the C-5, the E-4 (a specially modified Boeing 747), the F-111 and, beginning in 1975, the X-24B lifting body, a precursor to the Shuttle. When NASA announced that applications were being taken for a new group of astronauts, Scobee applied and was accepted.

As a pilot he logged over 6,500 hours of flying time in 45 different types of aircraft.

He was one of the 35 astronauts selected in January 1978 and in August 1979 completed a training and evaluation course. He served on the support crew for STS-1 and also flew the NASA/Boeing 747 shuttle carrier airplane. He was assigned to the STS-13 crew (later known as 41-C) in February 1983.

Scott, David Randolph
1932–

Air Force test pilot Dave Scott made 3 spaceflights between 1966 and 1972, taking part in the first docking in space, the first flight of the Apollo lunar module, and the first use of the lunar rover.

As pilot of Gemini 8, launched March 16, 1966, Scott and commander Neil Armstrong maneuvered their spacecraft to a linkup with an unmanned Agena 6.5 hours after launch, fulfilling one of the main goals of the Gemini program. Gemini 8 also became the first American spaceflight to be aborted when a steering thruster malfunctioned, causing the linked vehicles to revolve once a second. In order to control this dangerous spin, Armstrong was forced to use fuel reserved for reentry maneuvers. Mission rules dictated a return to Earth at the first opportunity, and Gemini 8 landed in the Pacific Ocean less than 11 hours after launch, cutting short a planned 3-day mission and cancelling Scott's 2-hour space walk.

Scott's second flight came in March 1969, as command module pilot for Apollo 9. During this 10-day mission, Scott piloted the command module Gumdrop while fellow astronauts James McDivitt and Russell Schweickart tested the lunar module Spider in free flight.

In July 1971 Scott commanded Apollo 15, the fourth lunar landing mission, becoming the seventh person to walk on the Moon. Scott and James Irwin, aboard the lunar module Falcon, used a four-wheeled electric car to explore an area of the lunar Apenines known as the Hadley Rille.

Scott was born June 6, 1932, in San Antonio, Texas. His father was an Air Force general. Scott attended the University of Michigan for one year, then was accepted at the U.S. Military Academy at West Point, graduating with a B.S. in 1954 and ranking fifth in a class of 633. He later did graduate work at the Massachusetts Institute of Technology, earning an M.S. in aeronautics and astronautics for a thesis concerning interplanetary navigation (1962).

After Air Force pilot training in Arizona Scott served with the 32nd Tactical Fighter Squadron, based in the Netherlands. He was at M.I.T from 1960 to 1962, then attended the USAF Experimental Test Pilot School at Edwards AFB, California. He did test flying after graduation in 1963, then was enrolled in the new Aerospace Research Pilot School, a special course designed to prepare Air Force officers for NASA and Department of Defense space programs. He was at ARPS when selected by NASA.

Scott came close to death in August 1963 when the NF-104 jet he was piloting crashed while simulating X-15 landings. Fellow ARPS student, and future MOL and X-15 pilot Michael Adams, riding in the back seat, ejected safely. Scott elected to stay with the aircraft, making a crash landing. Investigation later showed that both men would have been killed had they made any other choice.

As a pilot Scott eventually logged over 5,600 hours of flying time, most of it in jets.

He was one of the 14 astronauts chosen by NASA in October 1963, and during early training specialized in spacecraft guidance and navigation systems. He served as a capcom for Gemini 4 and, in September 1965, became the first of his group to be assigned to a flight crew when he was named to pilot Gemini 8.

Scott trained for much of 1966 as a member of the backup crew for the first manned Apollo. When Apollo assignments were shuffled, he found himself on the prime crew for the first flight involving a manned lunar module. He later served as backup commander for Apollo 12, and had was training as backup commander for Apollo 17 when he was removed in July 1972.

His removal was the result of an official reprimand directed at the entire crew of Apollo 15. Scott, Worden and Irwin had carried approximately 630 first day covers, specially printed and stamped envelopes, to the Moon in their personal kits. Eventually some of these envelopes were sold by stamp dealers to collectors. When NASA officials heard of the sales, they conducted an investigation and determined since the crew had carried a large number of unauthorized envelopes (some of the covers were authorized and other astronauts had carried similar covers on flights), a reprimand was in order. Scott was transferred to a desk job as technical assistant for the remaining Apollo missions while Worden left the astronaut group to take a job at the NASA Ames Research Center. Irwin resigned altogether.

By early 1973 Scott, who had met with Soviet cosmonauts on two different occasions, was assisting in the training of crew for the Apollo-Soyuz Test Project. He visited the Soviet Union in June of that year. In August 1973 he became deputy director of the NASA Dryden Flight Research Center at Edwards AFB. Following retirement from the USAF with the rank of colonel in March 1975 Scott was named director of Dryden, a job he held until resigning from NASA in October 1977.

Initially Scott founded Scott-Preyss Associates, a technical firm, and more recently has been president of Scott Science and Technology in Los Angeles and Lancaster, California. One of his company's projects is the development of an orbital transfer module for use with the Space Shuttle.

Scott also served as technical adviser to the Tom Hanks-Ron Howard film *Apollo 13* (1995) and the Home Box Office series *From the Earth to the Moon* (1998).

Scott, Winston Elliott

1950–

Navy captain Winston Scott was a mission specialist in the crew of STS-72. This January 1996 flight of the orbiter Endeavour retrieved the Japanese Space Flyer Unit while also deploying and retrieving a NASA Office of Astronautics and Space Technology (OAST) vehicle. Scott and fellow astronaut Leroy Chiao took a 6-hour EVA to test International Space Station construction techniques.

Scott went into space a second time in November 1997 aboard STS-87. This flight of the orbiter Endeavour carried a crew of 6 and the fourth U.S. Microgravity Payload and deployed the Spartan astronomical satellite. Because the Spartan failed to respond to commands, Scott and Japanese astronaut Takao Doi made an unscheduled EVA to manually retrieve it. They later performed a second EVA.

Scott was born August 6, 1950, in Miami, Florida. He graduated from high school in Coral Gables, Florida, then attended Florida State University, receiving a B.A. in music in 1972. He later earned an M.S. in aeronautical engineering from the Naval Posgraduate School.

Scott entered the Navy following graduation from Florida State; in August 1974 he became a naval aviator,

and for the next four years he flew the SH-2F Light Airborne Multi-Purpose System (LAMPS) helicopter with Anti-Submarine Light Squadron 33 at North Island, California. Following graduate work at the Naval Postgraduate School, Scott trained as an A-4 pilot, then did a 4-year tour with Fighter Squadron 84 at the Oceana, Virginia, Naval Air Station, flying F-14s.

In June 1986 Scott became an aerospace engineering duty officer, serving at the Jacksonville, Florida, Naval Air Station as production test pilot for the A-7 Corsair and F/A-18 Hornet. He also served as director of the product support department.

At the time of his selection by NASA Scott was deputy director for tactical air systems at the Naval Air Warfare Center, Warminster, Pennsylvania.

He has logged over 2,300 hours of flying time in 16 different types of aircraft, with 200 shipboard landings. Scott has also served as an instructor in electrical engineering at Florida A&M and Florida Community College in Jacksonville.

Scot was selected by NASA in March 1992 and in August 1993 qualified as a Shuttle mission specialist. His first technical assignment was in the mission support branch, serving with the astronaut support team at the Kennedy Space Center.

Scully-Power, Paul Desmond

1944–

Paul Scully-Power, a professional oceanographer, was a payload specialist aboard Shuttle Mission 41-G in October 1984.

During this 8-day flight, which was devoted to a number of different Earth-oriented experiments, Scully-Power was able to make observations of three-fourths of the world's oceans. "When you look down from this field of view you can easily see not just one eddy but a whole series of them," he said at one point in the mission.

Scully-Power's work was scientific in nature, but it also had some value to the Navy, which was concerned about its ability to hide submarines from the cameras of orbiting satellites. In March 1985 Admiral James D. Watkins admitted that Scully-Power had "found some fantasically important new phenomenology that will be vital to us in trying to understand the ocean depths."

Scully-Power was born May 28, 1944, in Sydney, Australia. He attended primary and secondary schools there and in London, England, and graduated with a B.S. degree (including honors in education and applied mathematics) from the University of Sydney in 1966. He received a postgraduate diploma in education in 1967, and later a doctorate in science in applied mathematics (1990) from the same institution.

After graduation from college Scully-Power was asked by the Royal Australian Navy to set up its first oceanographic group. He did so, earning an appointment at scientific officer in January 1967, and remaining with the group as its head until July 1972, when he went to the United States to serve as an exchange scientist with the Navy at its Underwater Systems Center in New London, Connecticut. During this time he assisted the Earth observations team on Skylab, and since then has taken part in briefings before and debriefings after each Shuttle flight.

In March 1974 Scully-Power returned to Australia, where he planned and executed project ANZUS EDDY, a combined Australian-New Zealand-American yearlong oceanographic study. He was a principal investigator on an experiment flown on the NASA Heat Capacity Mapping Mission satellite in 1976, and in October 1977 emigrated to the United States to take a permanent position with the Naval Underwater Systems Center.

He was added to the crew of Shuttle Mission 41-G in June 1984, just 4 months prior to its scheduled launch, when deletion of a satellite from the payload allowed NASA and the Navy space oceanographic committee to add another payload specialist to the crew, taking advantage of Mission 41-G's 57-degree inclination. (Most Shuttle missions are flown at a 28-degree inclination to the equator and thus "see" only half as much of the Earth's surface. The few Shuttle missions flown at 57 degrees are usually Spacelab missions, which already have crews of 7 or 8.)

Scully-Power has also taken part in 24 scientific cruises and is a qualified Navy diver. He has published over 60 scientific articles and served as an instructor in the astronaut office at the NASA Johnson Space Center, Houston.

Following his flight Scully-Power became chairman of Prime Solutions Pacific, Pty., Ltd., an oceanographic consulting firm based in Mystic, Connecticut, and McMahons Point, Australia.

Searfoss, Richard Alan
1956–

Air Force test pilot Rick Searfoss was pilot of STS-58, the Spacelab Life Sciences mission flown in October 1993. This 14-day flight of the orbiter Columbia carried a crew of 7 and was the longest ever devoted to medical research.

He later flew as pilot for STS-76, the third Shuttle-Mir docking mission, launched in April 1996. This 9-day long flight of Atlantis, delivered NASA-Mir researcher Shannon Lucid to the Russian station along with two tons of water, food, and scientific equipment. Two members of the STS-76 crew—Linda Godwin and Rich Clifford—also made the first American EVA at Mir.

Searfoss is currently assigned as commander of STS-90, scheduled to carry a crew of 7 and the Neurolab Spacelab, in the spring of 1998.

Searfoss was born June 5, 1956, in Mount Clemens, Michigan, though he considers Portsmouth, New Hampshire, to be his hometown. He attended the U.S. Air Force Academy, graduating in 1978 with a B.S. in aeronautical engineering. In 1979 he earned an M.S. in aeronautics from the California Institute of Technology via a National Science Foundation Fellowship.

Following undergraduate pilot training at Williams Air Force Base in 1980, Searfoss flew F-111s at RAF Lakenheath, England. From 1985 to 1987 he was an F-111 instructor pilot at Mountain Home AFB, Idaho. In 1988 he attended the U.S. Naval Test Pilot School as an Air Force exchange officer. When selected by NASA he was an instructor at the Air Force Test Pilot School, Edwards AFB, California.

He has logged 4,000 hours of flying time in 56 different types of aircraft.

Searfoss was one of the 23 astronaut candidates selected by NASA in January 1990 and in July 1991 qualified as a Shuttle pilot. He served with the astronaut support team at the Kennedy Space Center and in the Shuttle Avionics Integration Lab prior to being assigned to a flight crew. In 1996–97 he was chief of the astronaut office vehicle systems/operations branch.

Seddon, Margaret Rhea
1947–

Dr. Rhea Seddon took part in an improvised and unsuccessful satellite rescue as a member of the crew of Shuttle Mission 51-D in April 1985.

Seddon deployed a Hughes Navy communications satellite, Leasat IV-3, from the Shuttle Discovery on April 13, only to have it fail to activate. Astronauts aboard the Discovery, including U.S. senator Jake Garn, observed that an arming switch on the side of the Leasat had failed to close. Working with ground controllers, Seddon and the other astronauts built a makeshift "flyswatter," which was attached to the end of the Shuttle's robot arm by astronauts David Griggs and Jeffrey Hoffman. Seddon used the flyswatter to snag the arm on the Leasat, but the satellite remained adrift. (It was later retrieved, repaired, and redeployed during another Shuttle mission.)

In June 1991 Seddon made a second flight, this time aboard STS-40, a 9-day Spacelab Life Sciences mission. The SLS crew of 7, which included three medical doctors and a chemist, conducted the most extensive series of tests yet into how humans physically adapt to life in space.

Seddon made her third flight as payload commander of the second Spacelab Life Sciences mission, STS-58, flown in October 1993. The crew of 7 aboard the orbiter Columbia made the longest flight ever devoted to research in space medicine—16 days—and also served as subjects for some of the tests.

Seddon was born November 8, 1947, in Murfreesboro, Tennessee, and graduated from high school there in 1965. She attended the University of California at Berkeley, receiving a B.A. in physiology in 1970, and earned an M.D. degree from the University of Tennessee College of Medicine in 1973.

She completed a surgical internship and spent three years as a general surgical resident in Memphis, Tennessee. One of her areas of specialization was surgical nutrition; she also served as an emergency room physician. She continues to perform emergency room service in the Houston area.

Seddon was one of 35 astronauts selected by NASA in January 1978, qualifying as a Shuttle mission specialist in August 1979. Her first technical assignment was working on computer software at SAIL, and on the Shuttle medical kit. She served as support crewmember for STS-6 and also as technical assistant to the director of flight crew operations.

In August 1983 Seddon was assigned to a Shuttle crew scheduled to fly in July 1984. Because of various technical problems, she and her crewmates saw two different missions canceled prior to their launch on 51-D. In the meantime Seddon was assigned to Spacelab 4, a life sciences mission originally scheduled for launch in January 1986. That, too, was canceled.

During the post-Challenger hiatus Seddon served on the NASA Aerospace Medical Advisory Committee. She was assigned to STS-40 in February 1989.

In 1996 Seddon transferred to Vanderbilt University, Nashville, Tennessee, to coordinate medical experiments for the Neurolab Spacelab, launched in the spring of 1998 as STS-90. She resigned from NASA at the conclusion of STS-90.

Seddon is married to five-time Shuttle veteran Robert Gibson.

See, Elliott McKay, Jr.
1927–1966

Former civilian test pilot Elliott See was training as commander of Gemini 9 when he was killed in a plane crash at Lambert Field, St. Louis, Missouri, on February 28, 1966. Killed with him was astronaut Charles Bassett, scheduled to be the pilot of Gemini 9. See and Bassett were training for a 3-day rendezvous, docking, and EVA mission scheduled for launch in May 1966.

See was born July 23, 1927, in Dallas, Texas. He received a B.S. from the U.S. Merchant Marine Academy in 1949, then joined the General Electric Company, originally as a flight test engineer. From 1953 to 1956 he served on active duty as a Navy pilot, then returned to G.E. As a company test pilot he was involved in the initial flights of the F4H aircraft. He later earned an M.S. in engineering from the University of California at Los Angeles in 1962.

He logged over 3,900 hours of flying time, including 3,300 hours in jets.

See was one of 9 astronauts chosen by NASA in September 1962. He served as backup pilot for Gemini 5 prior to being named commander of Gemini 9 in September 1965.

Sefchek, Paul Andrew
1946–1997

Air Force major Paul Sefchek was a member of the first group of Department of Defense manned spaceflight engineers chosen in February 1980. He was a candidate for selection as a payload specialist on at least two Shuttle missions, but never flew in space.

Sefchek was born July 7, 1946, in Perth Amboy, New Jersey, and grew up in nearby Woodbridge. He attended Stevens Institute of Technology in Hoboken, earning a B.E. in astronautics (1968). In 1975 he received an M.B.A. in engineering management from the Wharton School of Business at the University of Pennsylvania in Philadelphia.

He entered the Air Force via ROTC in 1968 and spent four years at the Satellite Control Facility (now Onizuka AFB) in Sunnyvale, California. In 1975, following two years at graduate school, he was assigned to the Special Projects Office at Los Angeles AFS as a systems project officer. He joined the MSE program in 1980 and first served as chief systems engineer and deputy program manager for the CIRRIS sensor package, which flew on STS-4, the first DOD Shuttle mission, in June 1982. (Had CIRRIS flown on an "operational" Shuttle mission as opposed to a "flight test," Sefchek would have been the likely payload specialist.) A reflight of CIRRIS was scheduled for the first Vandenberg-launched Shuttle mission and Sefchek was again a candidate. Though he was ultimately not selected, he remained program manager for the payload.

When the Challenger disaster delayed the CIRRIS reflight Sefchek became chief of the carrier integration division of the Space Division's Space Test Program, overseeing all of that agency's projects whether scheduled for launch on Shuttle or expendable vehicles.

Sefchek retired from the Air Force in July 1989 to become senior director of the government systems group for Trident Data Systems in Los Angeles. He died of complications from cancer surgery on July 23, 1997.

Sega, Ronald Michael
1952–

Physicist Ron Sega, a former Air Force pilot, was a mission specialist in the crew of STS-60, a February 1994 flight of the orbiter Discovery that carried the SpaceHab-2 experiment module.

STS-60 also attempted to deploy the Wake Shield Facility, a space science and manufacturing pallet. Its failure was especially disappointing to Sega because he had helped to develop the WSF prior to becoming an astronaut.

Sega was later a mission specialist in the crew of STS-76. This flight of the orbiter Atlantis accomplished the third Shuttle-Mir docking in March 1996, delivering NASA-Mir crewmember Shannon Lucid to the station, along with 4,800 pounds of food, water, and scientific equipment.

Sega was born December 4, 1952, in Cleveland, Ohio, though he considers Northfield, Ohio, and Colorado Springs, Colorado, to be his hometowns. He attended the Air Force Academy, graduating in 1974 with a B.S. in mathematics and physics. He went on to earn an M.S. in physics from Ohio State (1975) and a Ph.D. in electrical engineering (1982) from the University of Colorado.

Following completion of his graduate work at Ohio State in 1975, Sega, then a second lieutenant in the Air Force, underwent pilot training at Williams AFB, Arizona, serving as an instructor pilot there until 1979. From 1979 to 1982 he was a member of the faculty of the Air Force Academy in the department of physics.

Sega left active duty in 1982 to join the University of Colorado at Colorado Springs as assistant professor in the department of electrical and computer engineering. He became associate professor in 1985, received tenure in 1988, and was promoted to full professor in 1990. He also served concurrently on the staff of the Frank J. Seiler Research Laboratory at the Air Force Academy. In 1989 he took a leave of absence from Colorado to do research at the University of Houston, where he became co-principal investigator of the Wake Shield Facility experiment. He remains an adjunct professor at Houston. He is also the author or coauthor of over 50 technical papers.

Sega holds the rank of colonel in the US Air Force Reserve, serving with the Air Force Space Command. As a pilot he has logged over 3,400 hours of flying time.

He was one of the 23 astronaut candidates selected by NASA in January 1990, qualifying as a Shuttle mission specialist in July 1991.

In addition to his flight and technical assignments, Sega served as NASA's director of operations, Russia, in 1994–95, while his then-wife, astronaut Bonnie Dunbar, was in that country training as backup for Norman Thagard in the Mir-18 crew, launched aboard Soyuz TM-21.

Sega resigned from NASA in the summer of 1996 to return to the University of Colorado.

Sellers, Piers John

1955–

Atmospheric scientist Piers Sellers is one of the 35 astronaut candidates selected by NASA on May 1, 1996. In August of that year he reported to the Johnson Space Center to begin a training and evaluation course that should qualify him as a Shuttle mission specialist and International Space Station crewmember. He is currently assigned to the computer support branch of the astronaut office.

Sellers was born April 11, 1955, in Crowborough, Sussex, England, and grew up in Cyprus and other countries where his father served with the British army. He graduated from Cranbook School, Cranbook, England, in 1973, then entered the University of Edinburgh, Scotland, were he received a B.S. in ecological science in 1976. He earned his Ph.D. in biometeorology from Leeds University In 1981.

After a year working for a software company in England, Sellers joined the staff of the NASA Goddard Space Flight Center in 1981. His research included computer modeling of the Earth's climatic system, remote sensing studies, and field work in the United States, Russia, Canada, Africa, and South America.

He is also a privately licensed pilot with over 1,100 hours of flying time.

Shaw, Brewster Hopkinson, Jr.

1945–

Air Force test pilot Brewster Shaw was aboard three Shuttle flights between 1983 and 1989, including America's first multinational mission, STS-9/Spacelab 1. Spacelab 1 was crewed by 6 astronauts, the largest to fly aboard a single spacecraft, and carried a variety of scientific experiments that were operated around the clock for 10 days in November and December 1983. Shaw served as pilot of the 6-man crew and leader of the blue team, which included mission specialist Robert Parker and German payload specialist Ulf Merbold.

Two years later Shaw was commander of Mission 61-B, a 6-day flight of the orbiter Challenger during which the Morelos and RCA SatCom communications satellites were deployed. Mission 61-B also saw the first demonstration of space construction techniques during two EVAs by astronauts Woody Spring and Jerry Ross.

In August 1989 Shaw commanded STS-28, a long-delayed flight of the orbiter Atlantis, during which a secret relay satellite for intelligence data was deployed. STS-28 ended after a 5-day mission.

Shaw was born May 16, 1945, in Cass City, Michigan, and graduated from high school there in 1963. He attended the University of Wisconsin at Madison, receiving B.S. and M.S. degrees in engineering mechanics in 1968 and 1969.

After graduation from Wisconsin, Shaw joined the Air Force and completed pilot training at Craig AFB, Alabama in 1970. He received advanced training as an F-100 pilot at Luke AFB, Arizona, then was assigned to the 352nd Tactical Fighter Squadron at Phan Rang Air Base in Vietnam. For most of the next two years Shaw flew combat missions in Vietnam and Thailand, earning two "Top Gun" awards. Returning to the United States, he served as an F-4 instructor pilot at George AFB, California, then attended the Air Force Test Pilot School at Edwards AFB. He served as a test pilot at Edwards, and in 1978 was an instructor at the school there when selected by NASA.

He logged over 5,000 hours of flying time, including 644 hours of combat, in over 30 different types of aircraft.

Shaw was one of 35 astronauts chosen by NASA in January 1978 and in August 1979 qualified as a Shuttle pilot. He served as capcom for STS-3 and STS-4, and in April 1982 he was named to the STS-9 crew.

In November 1985 Shaw was named to command Mission 61-N, a Department of Defense Shuttle mission then scheduled for launch in late 1986. The Challenger accident delayed the launch by three years, by which time 61-N had been renamed STS-28. During the hiatus Shaw served as a staff member of the Rogers Commission investigating the disaster.

In October 1989 Shaw left the astronaut office to become Shuttle director at the NASA Kennedy Space Center. In this job he made the final go/no go decision for each Shuttle launch. He served as director of Shuttle operations at NASA headquarters from 1993 to 1995. He resigned from NASA in August 1995 and in February 1996 was named director of major programs for Rockwell International in Seal Beach, California.

Shepard Alan Bartlett, Jr.
1923–1998

Navy test pilot Al Shepard became the first American in space on May 5, 1961, when he rode the Mercury-Redstone 3 spacecraft he had named Freedom 7 on a 15-minute flight, reaching an altitude of 116 miles and landing in the Atlantic 302 miles downrange from Cape Canaveral.

Shepard later commanded Apollo 14, the third manned lunar landing, in 1971, spending two days on the Moon. He and fellow astronaut Ed Mitchell used a two-wheel trolley to haul experiments and samples to sites near the crater Fra Mauro. Shepard also fulfilled a 10-year-old dream by becoming the first person to golf on the Moon.

He was the only one of the original 7 Mercury astronauts to make a flight to the Moon.

Shepard was born November 18, 1923, in East Derry, New Hampshire. His father was a career Army officer who had attended West Point. Following graduation from Pinkerton Academy in Derry, Shepard spent a year at Admiral Farragut Academy in New Jersey before attending the Naval Academy, where he earned a B.S. in 1944.

During the final year of World War II Shepard served aboard the destroyer *U.S.S. Cogswell* in the Pacific. Upon his return to the United States, he underwent pilot training at Corpus Christi, Texas, and Pensacola, Florida, receiving his wings in 1947. For the next three years he served with Fighter Squadron 42 at bases in Virginia and Florida, and aboard aircraft carriers in the Mediterranean. Between 1953 and 1956 he served as operations officer of Fighter Squadron 193, making two tours in the Pacific aboard the carrier *U.S.S. Oriskany*.

Shepard attended the Naval Test Pilot School at Patuxent River, Maryland, in 1950, and served as a test pilot and instructor at Pax River from 1951 to 1953, and from 1956 to 1958. During his second tour there he graduated from the Naval War College. When selected by NASA for the Mercury program in 1959 he was on the staff of the commander-in-chief of the Atlantic Fleet, preparing to become commander of his own carrier squadron.

He would eventually log over 8,000 hours of flying time, including 3,700 hours in jets.

As an astronaut, Shepard quickly established himself as a first-rate pilot and engineer, and in January 1961 was chosen by NASA officials and by a vote of his fellow astronauts to make the first Mercury flight. He served as capcom for the flights of Gus Grissom and John Glenn, and was backup to Gordon Cooper on the last Mercury flight.

Shepard and some NASA engineers lobbied for an additional Mercury flight, MA-10, a planned 3-day flight to take place late in 1963. But senior NASA officials decided that priority should go to the new Gemini program.

In July 1963 Shepard and astronaut Tom Stafford were named as prime crew for the first manned Gemini mission, but within weeks Shepard was diagnosed with Meniere's syndrome, an inner ear ailment that caused the

Navy to forbid him to fly solo in jet planes, and forced NASA to ground him. Shepard became chief of the astronaut office—in effect, boss of all the other astronauts, except Deke Slayton, who had already taken an administrative job.

According to astronaut memoirs, Shepard ran the office "like an admiral," with authority tempered occasionally by humor: Shepard's imitation of comedian Bill Dana's character "Jose Jimenez" became legendary. Unable to take part in active astronaut training, Shepard devoted his free time to investments, and by 1970 had become a millionaire.

In early 1968 Shepard underwent experimental surgery which corrected the inner ear problem; he was restored to full flight status in May 1969 and assigned to command Apollo 14 that August. (Slayton originally assigned Shepard to command Apollo 13, but was overruled by NASA Headquarters, which thought that Shepard needed more time to train.)

Promoted to the rank of rear admiral following Apollo 14, Shepard resumed his position as chief astronaut in June 1971 and remained there until his retirement from NASA and the Navy on August 1, 1974.

After leaving NASA Shepard became partner and chairman of the Marathon Construction Company in Houston, Texas, and for many years owned the Windward Coors Company in nearby Deer Park. He was also a commercial spokesman. He died July 21, 1998.

In 1971 Shepard served as a delegate to the 26th United Nations General Assembly.

He contributed to the book *We Seven* (1962) and *Moonshot* (1994), and is featured in the book and movie *The Right Stuff*.

Shepherd, William McMichael

1949–

Former Navy SEAL Bill Shepherd is scheduled to command the first incremental crew to inhabit the International Space Station during the first phase of its assembly. In early 2000 Shepherd and Russian cosmonauts Sergei Krikalev and Yuri Gidzenko will be launched to the ISS aboard a Soyuz

in a mission designated 2R. During a planned six months on orbit the crew will inhabit three modules—the Russian-built control and service Modules, linked to the U.S.-built Node 1. Two more modules will be added to the ISS during Shepherd's mission.

Shepherd is a veteran of three Shuttle missions, beginning with STS-27 (December 1988). This Department of Defense flight saw the deployment of the first Lacrosse radar reconnaissance satellite into low Earth orbit. Shepherd served as a standby EVA crewman for that flight.

In October 1990 he was a member of the STS-41 crew that successfully deployed the Ulysses space probe, sending it on its 4-year journey, via Jupiter, into orbit around the polar regions of the Sun.

Shepherd made a third flight aboard STS-52, which deployed the Lageos II satellite in October 1993.

Shepherd was born July 26, 1949, in Oak Ridge, Tennessee, and grew up in Phoenix, where he graduated from Arcadia High School in suburban Scottsdale in 1967. He attended the Naval Academy at Annapolis, graduating with a B.S. in aerospace engineering in 1971. He later earned the degree of ocean engineer and an M.S. in mechanical engineering from the Massachusetts Institute of Technology (1978).

Following graduation from Annapolis, Shepherd underwent Basic Underwater Demolition/SEAL training prior to being assigned as platoon commander for Underwater Demolition Team Eleven in San Diego. In 1973 he served as platoon commander for SEAL Team One during deployments to the Western Pacific and Alaska. From 1975 to 1978 he was a graduate student at M.I.T. He then became team operations officer for SEAL Team Two at the Naval Amphibious Base in Little Creek, Virginia, followed by a tour with the Naval Military Personnel Command in Washington, D.C. At the time of his selection by NASA he was the commanding officer of Special Boat Unit 20 at Little Creek.

Shepherd was one of the 17 astronauts selected by NASA in May 1984 and in June 1985 qualified as a Shuttle mission specialist while serving with the astronaut support team at the Kennedy Space Center.

Following his third flight, in November 1993, Shepherd was named NASA deputy manager for space station at the Johnson Space Center, serving in this job until January 1996, when he began training at JSC and at the Gagarin Center in Russia for his ISS mission.

Shriver, Loren James

1944–

Air Force pilot Loren Shriver commanded STS-31, the Shuttle mission that deployed the Hubble Space Telescope into Earth orbit. The $2 billion telescope, designed to detect objects 20 to 25 times fainter than the best Earth-based telescopes, had been awaiting launch for five years when the orbiter Discovery lifted off on April 24, 1990. Following the successful deployment at a record Shuttle altitude of 381 miles, ground controllers discovered a manufacturing flaw in the Hubble's wide field camera, the one designed to produce the sharpest pictures of the most distant objects in the universe. Although some Hubble instruments could continue to be used, the loss of the camera crippled the telescope for several years, until a spectacular repair mission in December 1993 allowed the Hubble to reach its potential.

Previously Shriver had been pilot of Mission 51-C in January 1985, the first Shuttle flight to be carried out in relative secrecy. Launch and landing times were not disclosed in advance, communications between the astronauts and mission control were encrypted, and no films or videotapes of activities aboard the Shuttle Challenger were ever released. The payload itself was classified, though press reports described it as a large National Security Agency electronic spy satellite code-named Magnum, which was placed in geosynchronous orbit.

In 1990 Shriver replaced fellow astronaut Robert Gibson, who was grounded for violations of NASA flying rules, as commander of STS-46. This 7-day flight of the orbiter Discovery, ultimately launched in July 1992, deployed the EURECA pallet. An attempt to deploy a Tethered Satellite System failed, however.

Shriver was born September 23, 1944, in Jefferson, Iowa, and grew up in Paton, Iowa, graduating from Consolidated High School there in 1962. A year later he entered the Air Force Academy, earning a B.S. in aeronautical engineering in 1967. In 1968 he earned an M.S. in astronautical engineering from Purdue.

Following pilot training, Shriver was stationed at Vance Air Force Base, Oklahoma, as a T-38 instructor until 1973. He completed F-4 combat training in Florida, then was stationed in Thailand until October 1974. Returning to the United States, he attended the Air Force Test Pilot School at Edwards AFB, California, remaining at Edwards as a test pilot until his selection by NASA.

He logged over 6,000 hours of flying time in 30 different types of aircraft, including multiengine craft and helicopters.

Shriver was one of 35 astronauts selected by NASA in January 1978, and in August 1979 qualified as a Shuttle pilot. He was a member of the support crew for STS-1 and STS-2. In September 1982 he was assigned to the crew scheduled to fly the first Department of Defense Shuttle mission in November 1983. The original mission, STS-10, was delayed several times before eventually flying as 51-C.

Following his flight Shriver was named to command Mission 61-M, scheduled for late summer 1986. That mission was canceled following the Challenger disaster. Shriver replaced John Young as commander of the Hubble Space Telescope mission in November 1988.

From September 1992 to May 1993 Shriver was deputy chief of the astronaut office. He resigned from the Air Force with the rank of colonel at that time and as a civilian NASA employee was reassigned to the Shuttle Program Office at the Kennedy Space Center.

Shriver is currently on the staff of the director, NASA Kennedy Space Center.

Simon, George Warren

1934–

Space scientist George Simon was a backup payload specialist for Spacelab 2, flown in July 1985. During the 8-day Shuttle Mission 51-F, which was dedicated to astronomical experiments, Simon served as a communicator for the Spacelab crew from the Payload Operations Center at the NASA Marshall Space Flight Center.

Simon was born April 22, 1934, in Frankfurt, Germany, but came to the United States in 1940 at the age of six. He graduated from Grinnell College in 1955 with a B.A. degree, and later earned an M.S. from the California Institute of Technology (1961), as well as his Ph.D. (1963). In 1976 he received an M.B.A. from the University of Utah.

Simon is a senior scientist at the Air Force Geophysics Laboratory and is stationed at the National Solar Observatory in Sunspot, New Mexico. He developed the Solar Optical Universe Polarimeter, one of the experiments flown aboard Spacelab 2. He was selected as one of the 4 payload specialist candidates in June 1978.

Skantze, Lawrence Albert
1928–

General Lawrence Skantze, commander of the U.S. Air Force Systems Command, was scheduled to serve as a Department of Defense payload specialist aboard a 1986 Space Shuttle mission. That mission was canceled following the Shuttle Challenger disaster, and Skantze never flew in space.

He was one of 2 senior Air Force officials—Air Force Undersecretary Edward Aldridge was the other—who in 1985 requested flights on the Shuttle in order to evaluate its uses for military missions. The Systems Command was the branch of the Air Force responsible for the development of advanced aircraft and spacecraft, and for the operation of space systems.

Skantze was born June 24, 1928, in Bronx, New York. He attended the Naval Academy at Annapolis, graduating with a B.S. in 1952. He later earned an M.S. from the Air Force Institute of Technology (1959).

Skantze joined the Navy at the age of 18 in 1946, and served as a seaman for two years until winning a competitive appointment to the Naval Academy. Commissioned as a second lieutenant in the Air Force, Skantze underwent flight training and served as a bomber pilot in Korea. From 1955 to 1969 he held a variety of engineering jobs in the Air Force, including two years working on the Manned Orbiting Laboratory.

His first command position was director of personnel for the Air Force Systems Command (1969–71). He went on to head the development programs for the Short

Range Attack Missile (1971–73) and the Airborne Warning and Command airplane (1973–77). He was also deputy chief of staff for systems development for the Systems Command (1977–79), commander of the Aeronautical Systems Division (1979–82), deputy Air Force chief of staff for research and development, (1982–83) and vice chief of staff (1983–85). He was promoted to the rank of general in 1983.

Retired in 1987, Skantze serves as a consultant.

Slayton, Donald Kent
1924–1993

Donald "Deke" Slayton was one of the original 7 Mercury astronauts chosen by NASA in 1959. Grounded because of a heart condition in 1962, he supervised the training and selection of all Gemini and Apollo astronaut crews until he was restored to flight status in 1972. He eventually went into space in the Apollo-Soyuz Test Project in July 1975.

During the two and a half years preceding the launch, Slayton and the other American astronauts assigned to the prime and backup crews studied Russian and trained for weeks at Star Town, the cosmonaut center near Moscow.

The flight of ASTP had worldwide attention at its launch on July 15, 1975. Two days later Apollo docked with Soyuz-19 over Europe. Slayton and fellow astronauts Stafford and Brand swapped places with cosmonauts Leonov and Kubasov during the two days the ships remained linked. After five more days, Apollo returned to Earth. A fuel leak during splashdown seared the astronauts' lungs, a fortuitous accident for Slayton, since the detailed medical examination that followed showed that he had an undetected lung tumor, which was then removed.

Slayton was born March 1, 1924, in Sparta, Wisconsin, and grew up on a farm there. At the age of 18 he enlisted in the Army Air Corps and earned his pilot's wings a year later. As a B-25 bomber pilot he flew 56 combat missions over Southern Europe and 7 over Japan. (In her 1966 book *If the Sun Dies*, Italian journalist Oriana Fallaci discovers, during her meeting with Slayton, that he was one of the pilots of Allied planes that bombed her village.)

Returning the United States, Slayton entered the University of Minnesota, receiving a B.S. in aeronautical engineering in 1949.

From 1949 to 1951 Slayton was an aeronautical engineer with the Boeing Company in Seattle, Washington. Recalled to active duty during the Korean War, he was first assigned to 12th Air Force Headquarters in Germany, then, in 1955, to the Air Force Test Pilot School at Edwards Air Force Base, California. From 1956 to 1959 Slayton was a test pilot there.

Selected as one of the original Mercury astronauts, Slayton was intended to be the first American to orbit the Earth. Astronauts Alan Shepard, Gus Grissom, and John Glenn were assigned to make suborbital flights, but following the flights of Shepard and Grissom, Glenn's was canceled. He was given the first orbital Mercury flight and Slayton, in November 1961, was assigned to the second.

In March 1962, however, just three weeks after Glenn's successful flight, NASA physicians grounded Slayton because of concerns over a long-standing heart condition. Slayton was replaced on the Mercury-Atlas 7 flight by Scott Carpenter.

Slayton remained with NASA as an astronaut, resigning his commission as a major in the USAF in November 1963, and taking on the additional duties of director, flight crew operations. In this job Slayton controlled astronaut selection and flight assignments, subject to approval by NASA headquarters. He was not overruled until he assigned fellow Mercury astronaut Shepard to command Apollo 13. Shepard had been grounded for physical reasons from 1963 to 1969 and Slayton's bosses decided that the first American in space needed more training. He was assigned to Apollo 14.

Slayton never gave up in his quest to return to flight status. He continued to attend training sessions in Gemini and Apollo, but it wasn't until 1972 that he was judged physically able to fly in space. Slayton won assignment to the Apollo-Soyuz Project in January 1973 and resigned as director of flight crew operations in February 1974.

As a pilot Slayton logged over 9,000 hours of flying time, most of it in jet aircraft. He also flew his own homebuilt craft in Formula One air races.

Following his spaceflight Slayton managed the Approach and Landing Tests of the Space Shuttle Enterprise, and the orbital flight test program for the first four Shuttle missions. He retired from NASA in February 1981 (though he served as a consultant to the space agency for another year) to become vice chairman of the board of Space Services, Inc., a Texas-based private space firm that successfully launched its Conestoga rocket in 1983, and which was the first organization to propose sending human ashes into permanent orbital repose. (The Celestis Company accomplished this with a Pegasus launch in 1996.) Later a division of the EER Corporation, SSI launched several other sounding rockets while failing in its attempt to launch an orbital version of Conestoga in 1995

Slayton was a contributor to *We Seven* (1962) and was profiled in Tom Wolfe's *The Right Stuff* (1979). Later works include *Moonshot*, with Alan Shepard, Howard Benedict, and Jay Barbaree (1994) and an autobiography, *Deke!*, with Michael Cassutt (1994).

He died of brain cancer on June 13, 1993.

Smith, Michael John
1945–1986

Navy test pilot Mike Smith was the pilot of the Shuttle Challenger for Mission 51-L, which exploded 74 seconds after launch on January 28, 1986, killing Smith and 6 other astronauts, including teacher Sharon Christa McAuliffe. Mission 51-L would have been Smith's first spaceflight.

Smith was born April 30, 1945, in Beaufort, North Carolina, where he graduated from high school in 1963. Always interested in aviation, he entered the Naval Academy, planning to become a navy pilot. He graduated in 1967 with a B.S in naval science, and a year later earned an M.S. in aeronautical engineering from the Naval Postgraduate School.

After completing pilot training at Kingsville, Texas, in May 1969, Smith was assigned to the Advanced Jet Training Command, where he served as an instructor until March 1971. During the next two years he piloted A-6 Intruders from the carrier *U.S.S. Kitty Hawk* on combat missions over Vietnam.

Returning to the United States in 1973, he attended the Naval Test Pilot School at Patuxent River, Maryland, then spent two years as a test pilot and another 18 months as an instructor at Pax River. He was then assigned as maintenance and operations officer of Attack Squadron 75 aboard the carrier *U.S.S. Saratoga.*

As a pilot Smith had logged over 4,500 hours of flying time, including over 4,200 hours in jets, in 28 different types of aircraft.

He was one of the 19 astronauts selected by NASA in May 1980. In August 1981 he qualified as a Shuttle pilot while serving in the Shuttle Avionics Integration Laboratory. He then served as chief of the aircraft operations division, technical assistant to the director of flight operations, and chase plane pilot for STS-5. Smith was originally assigned as pilot of Shuttle Mission 51-K, the Spacelab Earth Observation Mission 1, scheduled for the summer of 1985, but was transferred to Mission 51-L in January 1985 when EOM 1 was canceled.

At the time he was serving as an unofficial backup to Loren Shriver, the pilot of Mission 51-C. (Shriver's medical eligibility was under review.)

He is buried at Arlington National Cemetery.

Smith, Steven Lee

1958–

Former NASA flight controller Steve Smith was a mission specialist in the crew of STS-68, the second flight of the Shuttle Radar Laboratory. This 11-day mission of the orbiter Endeavour was delayed by a launch-pad abort on August 19. When launched successfully on September 30, its purpose was to make radar images of the Earth's surface in autumn, to complement those made by the SRL on its previous flight in the spring of 1994. During the mission the volcano Klyuchevskaya erupted on Russia's Kamchatka Penninsula, and there was a magnitude eight earthquake near the Japanese island of Hokkaido. Both events were observed by the SRL crew, which completed its mission successfully after 11 days in space.

Smith made his second flight on the second Hubble Space Telescope servicing mission, STS-82, launched in February 1997. On three different EVAS, totaling 19 hours, Smith and payload commander Mark Lee installed upgraded systems and performed repairs to the Hubble's thermal protection blankets.

Smith was born December 30, 1958, in Phoenix, Arizona, and graduated from Leland High School in San Jose, California. He attended Stanford University, receiving a B.S. and M.S. in electrical engineering in 1981 and 1982. He also earned an M.B.A. from Stanford in 1987.

From 1982 to 1985 Smith was employed by IBM's Large Scale Integration Technology Group in San Jose as a technical group lead in the field of semiconductor manufacturing. Following leave for graduate work, he returned to IBM in 1987 as a product manager at its Hardware and Systems Management Group in Santa Clara, California. He joined NASA in 1989 as a payload officer and worked on preflight integration and mission support for STS-37, STS-48 and STS-49. He also had assignments on STS-46 and STS-57.

Smith was one of 19 astronaut candidates in March 1992. In July 1993 he qualified as a Shuttle mission specialist. His first technical assignment was serving as astronaut office representative for Shuttle main engines, solid rocket motors, and external tank. He was assigned to STS-68 in October 1993, and in 1995-96 served with the astronaut support team at the NASA Kennedy Space Center.

Sponable, Jess Mitchell

1955–

Air Force engineer Jess Sponable was one of the 14 Manned Spaceflight Engineers selected by the Air Force in January 1983. He left the program in 1985 without flying in space, but has since become one of the most prominent military program managers for reusable space launch systems, including the Delta Clipper.

Sponable was born November 29, 1955, in Madrid, Spain. He attended the Air Force Academy, graduating in 1978 with a B.S. in physics. He later earned an M.S. in astronautical engineering from the Air Force Institute of Technology (1982).

As an MSE Sponable worked on the Navstar Global Positioning Satellite program. In 1987 he left the MSE group to transfer to Wright-Patterson AFB, Ohio, served as chief of the space applications branch of the National Aerospace Plane (NASP) project.

In 1992 Sponable joined the Strategic Defense Initiative Organization as head of its reusable launcher program, supervising the development of the Delta Clipper. With the crash of the Clipper in 1995, ending the program, Sponable went on a detached assignment to NASA as head of the X-33 program—under former MSE Gary Payton, the space agency's manager for reusable launch systems.

Since 1997 Sponable has been manager of the Space Maneuver Vehicle project, an unmanned reusable aerospace plane, at the Phillips Laboratory, Kirtland AFB, New Mexico.

Along with former MSE David Thompson, Sponable was named one of 25 "future space pioneers" by *Ad Astra* magazine in 1994.

Spring, Sherwood Clark
1944–

Army pilot Woody Spring took part in the two EVAs testing space construction techniques during Shuttle Mission 61-B in November and December 1985.

Spring and fellow mission specialist Jerry Ross, who billed themselves as the "Ace Construction Company," assembled and then disassembled a 45-foot triangular truss called ACCESS and a 12-foot tetrahedron called EASE while working in the payload bay of the Shuttle Atlantis. Both structures were prototypes for elements of future space station construction. The astronauts also practiced assembling the structures while perched at the end of the Shuttle's robot arm. Spring and Ross found that they were able to work quickly in microgravity, but also discovered after the EVAs that their hands got stiff and numb, and that they were extremely tired.

The crew of Mission 61-B also deployed three communications satellites and carried a McDonnell Douglas pharmaceutical experiment.

Spring was born September 3, 1944, in Hartford, Connecticut, but considers Harmony, Rhode Island, to be his hometown. He graduated from Ponagansett High School

in Chepachet, Rhode Island, in 1963, then attended the U.S. Military Academy at West Point, earning a B.S. in general engineering in 1967. He later earned an M.S. in aerospace engineering from the University of Arizona in 1974.

After spending a year at airborne, ranger and microwave communication schools, Spring did a tour of duty in Vietnam with the 101st Airborne Division. He returned to the United States in 1969 for training as a helicopter pilot at Fort Wolters, Texas, then went back to Vietnam for another tour with the 1st Air Cavalry.

After his second tour in Vietnam Spring received jet pilot training at Ft. Stewart, Georgia, and Ft. Rucker, Alabama, then attended the University of Arizona for two years. During the next five years he was stationed at the Army's flight test center at Edwards Air Force Base, California, and at the Naval Test Pilot School at Patuxent River, Maryland, as a student and test pilot. When selected by NASA in 1980 he was operations officer for the 19th Aviation Battalion in Pyontaek, Korea.

As a pilot Spring logged over 3,500 hours of flying time in 25 different types of airplanes and helicopters.

Spring was one of the 19 astronauts chosen by NASA in May 1980, qualifying as a Shuttle mission specialist in August 1981. His first technical assignment was in SAIL, and in the flight simulation laboratory.

Following his spaceflight Spring worked on advanced space suit designs in the space station branch of the astronaut office. He resigned from NASA in June 1988 to become director of space operations for the U.S. Army at the Pentagon.

He retired from the Army in 1994 and is currently a consultant with The Analytical Sciences Corporation, Fairfax, Virginia.

Springer, Robert Clyde
1942–

Marine test pilot Bob Springer was a mission specialist aboard two Shuttle flights. On STS-29 in March 1989 he took part in the deployment of a Tracking and Data Relay Satellite from the orbiter Discovery. The crew of STS-29 also took more than 4,000 photographs of the Earth using several different cameras, including the 70mm IMAX movie camera.

In November 1990 Springer was member of the STS-38 crew, the last secret Department of Defense Shuttle mission. STS-38 deployed a relay satellite for intelligence data into orbit.

Springer was born May 21, 1942, in St. Louis, Missouri, and grew up in Ashland, Ohio, where he graduated from high school in 1960. He attended the Naval Academy, where he received a B.S. in naval science in 1964. He later earned an M.S. in operations research and systems analysis from the Naval Postgraduate School in 1971.

Springer elected to serve in the Marine Corps and was commissioned upon graduation from Annapolis. He underwent basic training at Quantico, Virginia, then attended flight school at Pensacola, Florida, and Beeville, Texas, earning his wings in August 1966. He was stationed at Cherry Point, North Carolina, then transferred to Chu Lai, Vietnam, where he flew 300 combat missions in the F-4 Phantom. Beginning in June 1968 Springer served as an advisor to the marine corps of the Republic of Korea and flew 75 further combat missions in 01 Bird Dogs and UH1 Huey helicopters.

Returning to the United States, Springer attended the Naval Postgraduate School, then served in a variety of assignments at El Toro and Camp Pendleton, California; Okinawa; and Beaufort, South Carolina. He attended the Navy Fighter Weapons School (better known as "Top Gun") at Miramar, California, and, in 1975, the Naval Test Pilot School at Patuxent River, Maryland, remaining there as a helicopter test pilot until 1977. He later attended the Armed Forces Staff College, and at the time of his selection by NASA was serving as aide-de-camp to the Commanding General, Fleet Marine Force, Atlantic.

As a pilot Springer logged over 4,500 hours flying time, including 3,500 hours in jets.

Springer was one of the 19 astronauts selected by NASA in May 1980 and in June 1981 qualified as a Shuttle mission specialist. He was assigned to one Shuttle/Spacelab mission, 51-K, which was canceled before it could be flown. Prior to the Challenger accident in January 1986 he was assigned to Mission 61-H, scheduled for the summer of that year.

Among Springer's technical assignments were working on development studies for a Space Operations Cen-

ter (later known as the space station), the remote manipulator arm, Get-Away-Special payloads, and other satellites. From October 1984 to October 1985 he was a Shuttle capcom at mission control.

Springer resigned from NASA and retired from the Marine Corps (with the rank of colonel) in December 1990, to become manager for space station Freedom integration for Boeing Aerospace, Huntsville, Alabama. He is currently manager for man-tended capabilities for Boeing's International Space Station.

Stafford, Thomas Paten
1930–

Thomas Stafford made four spaceflights between 1965 and 1975, two in Gemini and two in Apollo, taking part in a number of space firsts, including the first rendezvous and the first international flight.

Stafford was pilot of the Gemini 6 mission launched December 15, 1965, after a series of delays, including the first launchpad abort of a manned spacecraft on December 13. Stafford and command pilot Walter Schirra were originally scheduled to go into space in October 1965 on a 3-day flight during which they would rendezvous with a previously launched Agena and dock with it. But the Agena failed to reach orbit, and Gemini 6 was taken off the pad and replaced by Gemini 7, launched December 4, 1965, on a 2-week endurance flight with astronauts Borman and Lovell. The first attempt to launch Stafford and Schirra for a rendezvous ended less than two seconds after ignition of the Titan II first stage, but by not ejecting the astronauts allowed the Titan, and Gemini 6, one more chance, and on December 16 they met up with Gemini 7 in orbit.

Stafford was command pilot of Gemini 9, launched just six months later. He was originally backup commander, but prime crew astronauts See and Bassett were killed and backups Stafford and Eugene Cernan took their places. Once again, Stafford's "Agena jinx" was working, as the Gemini 9 target Agena failed. This time NASA had an alternative, a smaller Augmented Target Docking Adaptor, which reached orbit but failed to shed its protective shroud, preventing a docking. The rendezvous was successful and Stafford later supervised Cernan's difficult and unsuccessful 2-hour space walk.

In May 1969 Stafford commanded Apollo 10, the final, full-scale dress rehearsal for a manned lunar landing. While John Young orbited the Moon in the command module Charlie Brown, Stafford and Cernan took the lunar module Snoopy to within 50,000 feet of the lunar surface to test the LM's propulsion and navigation systems. (That particular LM was too heavy to survive a lunar landing and liftoff, or Stafford might have become the first man to walk on the Moon.)

And in July 1975 Brigadier General Stafford, the first general to make a spaceflight, commanded the American half of the Apollo-Soyuz Test Project. In orbit over Europe, Stafford, Vance Brand, and Donald Slayton rendezvoused and docked their Apollo to Soyuz 19, crewed by Alexei Leonov and Valery Kubasov. Two days of joint activities followed, then each vehicle returned to Earth. During Apollo's splashdown a fuel leak caused problems for the astronauts.

Stafford was born September 17, 1930, in Weatherford, Oklahoma, where he grew up. He earned an appointment to the Naval Academy at Annapolis, graduating in 1952 with a bachelor of science degree.

Stafford elected to serve in the Air Force and underwent pilot training in Texas, earning his wings in 1953. From 1953 to 1958 he served as an interceptor pilot at Ellsworth AFB, South Dakota, and Hahn AFB, Germany. Returning to the U.S., he attended the USAF Experimental Flight Test Pilot School at Edwards AFB, California, and on graduation in April 1959 received the A. B. Honts award as outstanding student. He remained at Edwards as an instructor, coauthoring *The Pilot's Handbook for Performance Flight Testing* and *The Aerodynamics Handbook for Performance Flight Testing*.

He eventually logged over 7,100 flying hours in 110 different types of aircraft.

Stafford was one of the 9 astronauts selected by NASA in September 1962. He served as backup pilot for Gemini 3, the first manned Gemini flight, in 1965, and was variously backup command module pilot for Apollo 2, then backup commander for Apollo 7, in addition to his four spaceflights.

In June 1969 Stafford succeeded Alan Shepard as the chief of the astronaut office and played a major role in the selection of astronaut crews for Apollo and Skylab missions. In June 1971 he became deputy director of flight crew operations at the Manned Spacecraft Center until being named, in January 1973, to Apollo-Soyuz.

Major General Stafford left NASA in November 1975 to assume command of the Air Force Flight Test Center at Edwards AFB. Promoted to lieutenant general in March 1978, he became deputy chief of staff for research development and acquisition at Headquarters USAF in Washington. His tenure in Washington was notable for his promotion of Air Force use of the Space Shuttle, and for his successful opposition to President Jimmy Carter's plan to scrap the B-1 bomber. Stafford retired from the Air Force on November 1, 1979 and became vice-president of Gibraltar Exploration, Ltd., in Oklahoma City, Oklahoma. He is currently vice-chairman of Stafford, Burke and Hecker, an aerospace consulting firm based in northern Virginia, and serves on numerous corporate boards.

In 1990 Stafford was named chairman of the Lunar/Mars Synthesis Group, a NASA panel charged with studying innovative concepts for the future exploration of the Moon and Mars. Members of the panel included former Secretary of the Air Force Pete Aldridge and Shuttle director (and Strategic Defense chief) James Abrahamson. The group's report was delivered in April 1991.

Stafford continues to contribute to joint U.S.–Russian space programs, serving as adviser to NASA Administrator Dan Goldin on the International Space Station program, and also head of a joint American–Russian task force on the Shuttle-Mir program. Stafford conducted a safety review of Mir following the June 1997 collision between the station and a Progress supply ship.

Staib, David Paul, Jr.
1955–

Air Force engineer Dave Staib was one of the 5 third-cadre Manned Spaceflight Engineers selected in April 1986. Following a change in policy regarding the use of Department of Defense payload specialists in the wake of the Challenger accident, the MSE program was canceled in 1988. Staib never flew in space.

Staib was born June 20, 1955, in Ft. Campbell, Kentucky, and grew up in Williamsport, Pennsylvania. When he was in grade school he wanted to become an astronaut, but his eyesight wouldn't permit him to qualify as a pilot, so he decided to study engineering. He attended Penn State, where he received a B.S. in electrical engineering in 1977. He later earned an M.S. in systems management (1982) from the University of Southern California.

Commissioned in the Air Force through ROTC in August 1977, Staib's first station was Space and Missile Systems Division in Los Angeles, where he worked in the inertial upper stage (IUS) program office for four years. From October 1981 to September 1985 he was a launch controller, then IUS vehicle controller at Cape Canaveral Air Force Station in Florida. He was the lead Air Force representative for STS-6 cargo processing and Mission 51-C IUS processing. At the time of his selection for the MSE program he was with the 6595th Aerospace Test Group at Vandenberg AFB, California, as Shuttle test director.

Following the termination of the MSE program in 1988, Staib remained at Space Division working on the Space Test Program. In 1990 he was reassigned to the Pentagon to the Office of Space Systems. More recently he has served at Bolling AFB and is currently at Falcon AFS, Colorado Springs, Colorado, where he took part in evaluations of the safety of the Mir space station for a panel headed by former astronaut Thomas Stafford.

Stefanyshyn-Piper, Heidemarie Martha

1963–

Navy engineer Heide Piper is one of the 35 astronaut-candidates selected by NASA on May 1, 1996. In August of that year she reported to the Johnson Space Center to begin a training and evaluation course that should qualify her as a Shuttle mission specialist and International Space Station crewmember. Since February 1997 she has worked on ISS matters in the vehicle systems/operations branch of the astronaut office.

Stefanyshyn-Piper was born February 7, 1963, in St. Paul, Minnesota, where she graduated from Derham Hall High School in 1980. She attended the Massachusetts Institute of Technology, receiving a B.S. (1984) and an M.S. (1985) in mechanical engineering.

She entered the Navy through ROTC in June 1985, and was trained at the Naval Diving and Salvage Training Center, Panama City, Florida. Over the next 10 years she did several tours as an engineering duty officer doing ship maintenance and repair. Stefanyshyn-Piper is also an experienced salvage officer who took part in the salvage of the Peruvian submarine *Pachoca* and of the tanker *Exxon Houston*.

At the time of her selection by NASA Stefanyshyn-Piper was underwater ship husbandry officer for the supervisor of salvage and diving at the Naval Sea Systems Command.

Stevens (Tittle), Theresa Mary

1960–

Air Force engineer Terry Stevens was one of the 5 officers selected for the third cadre of Manned Spaceflight Engineers in April 1986. Members of this group became candidates for selection as Shuttle payload specialists supervising the deployment and operation of Department of Defense satellites and experiments. Two MSEs flew in space and several more were assigned to future missions prior to the Challenger accident, when all launches were halted. When they resumed, many DoD payloads had been shifted to unmanned expendable launch vehicles, and MSE payload specialist assignments were cancelled.

Stevens was born November 25, 1960, in Springfield, Massachusetts. She attended the U.S. Air Force Academy, graduating in 1982 with a B.S. in operations research.

Her first assignment was to the NASA Johnson Space Center, where she worked as a Shuttle flight controller.

With the termination of the MSE program in 1988, Stevens left Space Division, spending two years at Woomera Air Station in Australia. She was later assigned to the Pentagon.

Stevenson, Robert Everett

1921–

Robert Stevenson, the father of space oceanography, was selected in 1982 to be the first oceanographer in space. Just months before his scheduled assignment to Shuttle Mission 41-G, however, he withdrew from the consideration and was replaced by his colleague Paul Scully-Power. (Stevenson's wife was dying of cancer and he felt he could not devote any time to training.)

Beginning with the Gemini 12 crew of James Lovell and Edwin Aldrin in 1966, Stevenson (and later, Scully-Power) instructed every American astronaut crew in oceanography. When payload specialist flight opportunities became available in 1982, astronaut Richard Truly suggested that Stevenson and Scully-Power be included in the crews of STS-7 and STS-8, a suggestion that was quickly approved by astronaut chief George Abbey and Rear Admiral J. B. Mooney Jr. oceanographer of the Navy.

However, occurrences of space adaptation syndrome—so-called space sickness—on the first five Shuttle missions forced NASA to assess its impact on crew performance. Astronauts Norman Thagard and William Thornton, who were also medical doctors, were assigned to STS-7 and STS-8. Stevenson's assignment was postponed; he was tentatively assigned to the scheduled Department of Defense mission STS-10; then, in April 1984, to Mission 41-G. After withdrawing in favor of Scully-Power, Stevenson's assignment bounced from Mission 51-I to 61-B to 61-C to 51-L, and at the time of the Challenger disaster in January 1986, he was in the process of being assigned to Mission 61-K, the Spacelab Earth Observation Mission—"a perfect choice for me"—then scheduled for August 1986.

Stevenson was born January 15, 1921, in Fullerton, California, where he grew up, graduating from Fullerton High School in 1939. He attended Fullerton Junior College from 1939 to 1941, then went on to UCLA, earning his A.B. in oceanography in 1946, and his A.M. in 1948. He earned his Ph.D. in oceanography from the University of Southern California in 1954.

Stevenson's academic career was interrupted by World War II, in which he served as a navigator for the

Army Air Force on missions in Europe and the Pacific. In 1951 he was recalled to active duty by the Air Force and served as chief of photo interpretation research at Wright Air Development Center (later Wright-Patterson AFB), Dayton, Ohio, until 1953.

For the next eight years Dr. Stevenson did research at USC's Allan Hancock Foundation, where he was director of inshore research. He later worked at Texas A&M University, at Florida State University, and the Texas Bureau of Commercial Fisheries.

In 1970 he joined the Office of Naval Research, assigned to the Scripps Institution of Oceanography at La Jolla, California. He served as scientific officer and deputy director for space oceanography there until his retirement in 1988. He continues to consult for the astronaut office at the NASA Johnson Space Center.

Stewart, Robert Lee

1942–

Army test pilot Bob Stewart was one of the first astronauts to make an untethered space walk. As a member of the crew of Shuttle Mission 41-B in February 1984, Stewart took part in two test flights of the self-contained Manned Maneuvering Unit, the so-called Buck Rogers rocket pack, which allows astronauts to fly freely in space away from the Shuttle. Mission 41-B also launched two communications satellites. Both satellites suffered propulsion failures and were retrieved and returned to Earth in November 1984.

In October 1985 Stewart was a mission specialist aboard 51-J, the first flight of the orbiter Atlantis, which carried two Department of Defense communications satellites into space.

Stewart was born August 13, 1942, in Washington, D.C., and grew up in El Lago, Texas. He graduated from high school in Hattiesburg, Mississippi, in 1960, and attended the University of Southern Mississippi, earning a B.S. in mathematics in 1964. He later earned an M.S. in aerospace engineering from the University of Texas in 1972.

Stewart joined the Army in 1964 and served initially as an air defense artillery director at Gunter Air Force

Base, Alabama. He became a helicopter pilot in 1966 and logged over 1,000 hours in combat missions in Vietnam. Upon his return to the United States he was an instructor pilot, then attended the Naval Test Pilot School at Patuxent River, Maryland, graduating in 1974 and being assigned to the Army's helicopter test pilot group at Edwards Air Force Base, California.

He logged over 6,000 hours of flying time in 38 different types of military and civilian aircraft.

Selected as an astronaut candidate by NASA in January 1978, Stewart qualified as a Shuttle mission specialist in August 1979. He served as support crewman for STS-4 and capcom for STS-5. In September 1985 he was assigned as mission specialist aboard the Spacelab Earth Observation Mission scheduled for 1986. That mission was postponed for several years following the Challenger accident in January 1986. During the hiatus, in August 1986, the Army reassigned Stewart to the Strategic Defense Command at Redstone Arsenal, Huntsville, Alabama, where he served as deputy commander.

In November 1989 Brigadier General Stewart became the director of plans for the U.S. Space Command, and commander of the Army Element of U.S. Space Command, Peterson AFB, Colorado.

Stewart retired from the Army in 1995 and currently works as director of advanced programs for the Nichols Corporation, Colorado Springs.

Still, Susan Leigh
1961–

Navy test pilot Susan Still was pilot of STS-83, the April 1997 flight of the orbiter Columbia that carried a crew of 7 and the Materials Science Spacelab. Due to a faulty fuel cell, the planned 16-day MSL mission was shortened to three, a major disappointment to the scientists involved. MSL-1 was then reflown as STS-94 in July 1997, with the same crew, accomplishing a complete mission devoted to studies in space manufacturing processes.

Still was born October 24, 1961, in Augusta, Georgia, and graduated from Walnut Hill High School in Natick, Massachusetts, in 1979. She attended Embry-Riddle University, receiving a B.S. in aeronautical engineering in 1982. In 1985 she received an M.S. in aerospace engineering from the Georgia Institute of Technology.

Following graduation from Embry-Riddle in 1983 Still worked as a wind tunnel project officer for the Lockheed Corporation in Marietta, Georgia. When she earned her graduate degree three years later she was commissioned in the Navy, and in 1987 qualified as a naval aviator. Her first assignment was as an instructor pilot on the TA-4J Skyhawk, and later flew EA-6A Intruders with Tactical Electronic Warfare Squadron 33, based in Key West, Florida. She attended the Naval Test Pilot School in 1993, and was training as an F-14 Tomcat pilot with Fighter Squadron 101 at Oceana, Virginia, when selected by NASA.

Lieutenant Commander Still has logged 2,000 hours of flying time in 30 different types of aircraft.

Still was one of the 19 astronaut candidates selected on December 8, 1994. In May 1996 she qualified as a Shuttle pilot, and worked in the vehicle systems and operations branch of the astronaut office prior to being assigned to STS-83.

Sturckow, Frederick Wilford
1961–

Marine test pilot Rick Sturckow is assigned as pilot of STS-88. This flight of the orbiter Discovery will carry the first element—the Boeing-built Node One—of the International Space Station into Earth orbit. Originally scheduled for launch in December 1997, STS-88 is likely to slip to December 1998.

Sturckow was born August 11, 1961, in La Mesa, California, where he graduated from high school in 1978. He attended California Polytechnic University, receiving a B.S. in mechanical engineering in 1984.

He was commissioned in the Marine Corps in December 1984 and qualified as an aviator in April 1987. His first assignment was flying F/A-18s with Marine Air Squadron 333 at Beaufort, South Carolina. He made deployments to Japan, Korea and the Philippines, then, in March 1990, was selected to attend the Navy's Fighter Weapons School ("Top Gun").

Stationed at Shiek Isa Air Base in Bahrain beginning in August 1990, Sturckow flew 41 combat missions during Operation Desert Storm, serving as mission commander for airstrikes into Iraq and Kuwait involving 30 planes.

He returned to the United States in January 1992 to attend the Air Force Test Pilot School at Edwards AFB, California, then served as project pilot for the F/A-18 and several classified programs at the Naval Air Warfare Center at Patuxent River, Maryland.

Major Sturckow has logged over 2,500 hours of flying time in 40 different types of aircraft.

He was one of the 19 astronaut candidates selected by NASA on December 8, 1994. In May 1996 he qualified as a Shuttle pilot, and worked in the vehicle systems and operations branch of the astronaut office before being assigned to STS-88.

Sullivan, Kathryn Dwyer

1951–

Former oceanographer Kathryn Sullivan became the first American woman to walk in space when she spent 3.5 hours outside the orbiter Challenger on October 11, 1984. Sullivan and astronaut David Leestma successfully conducted a satellite refueling test. In addition, the 7 astronauts of Mission 41-G, the largest crew sent into space in a single spacecraft to that date, deployed the Earth Radiation Budget Satellite and conducted observations of the Earth's surface.

In April 1990 Sullivan was a mission specialist aboard STS-31, which deployed the Hubble Space Telescope. During this 5-day mission Sullivan took part in a series of unique Earth observations made possible by the record altitude of 380 miles reached by the orbiter Discovery.

Sullivan went into space a third time in March 1992, as mission specialist and payload commander in the crew of STS-45. This flight of the orbiter Atlantis carried the Spacelab ATLAS, a scientific package devoted to studies of the Earth's atmosphere.

Sullivan was born October 3, 1951, in Paterson, New Jersey, and grew up in Woodland Hills, California. She and future astronaut Sally Ride were briefly classmates in the same elementary school. Sullivan graduated from Taft

High School in Woodland Hills in 1969 and went on to attend the University of California at Santa Cruz, where she received a B.S. in Earth sciences in 1973. She later earned her Ph.D. in geology from Dalhousie University in Halifax, Nova Scotia, in 1978.

As a graduate student at Dalhousie Sullivan took part in a number of oceanographic expeditions by the U.S. Geological Survey, visiting the Mid-Atlantic Ridge, the Newfoundland Basin, and fault zones off the coast of Southern California. She also taught at Dalhousie and worked for Geological Survey of Canada. In 1985 Sullivan became an adjunct professor of Geology at Rice University in Houston, Texas.

Sullivan was one of the 35 astronauts selected by NASA in January 1978. In August 1979 she qualified as a mission specialist on future Shuttle crews, then worked on the support crews of STS-3 through STS-8. She also continued her research in geoscience by making high-altitude flights in the NASA WB-57F aircraft and being coinvestigator of the Shuttle Imaging Radar system flown on Mission 41-G.

She was assigned to the Hubble Space Telescope mission, then known as Mission 61-J, in April 1985. The flight was delayed five years by the Challenger disaster. During the hiatus Sullivan accepted an appointment by President Reagan to serve on the National Commission on Space, a yearlong study to determine goals for U.S. civilian space programs for the next 25 years. In 1988 she was appointed to the Chief of Naval Operations Executive Panel. (Sullivan was an oceanography officer in the Naval Reserve, with the rank of lieutenant commander.)

In October 1992 Sullivan became chief scientist for the National Oceanographic and Atmospheric Administration in Washington.

Since 1996 Sullivan has been director of the Ohio Center for Space Research in Columbus, Ohio.

Sundberg, Eric Edward
1945–

Air Force engineer Eric Sundberg was assigned as a payload specialist candidate in June 1982 for STS-15, a dedicated Department of Defense mission then scheduled for launch in 1984 and intended to carry the Teal Ruby satellite. Technical and political problems caused Teal Ruby to be shifted to a planned Vandenberg-launched Shuttle mission, and Sundberg lost his chance to fly in space.

Sundberg was born April 10, 1945, in Tonopah, Nevada. He attended the University of California at Santa Barbara, receiving a B.S. in physics in 1967. He later earned an M.S. in physics from the Air Force Institute of Technology (1976).

Entering active duty with the Air Force in 1967, Sundberg was trained as a weather officer. He was stationed in Vietnam during the conflict there. In December 1971 he was assigned to the Satellite Control Facility at Sunnyvale, California, as staff meteorologist. Following a year in graduate school he became a project officer at Los Angeles AFS, and was working in Special Projects when selected as one of the first 13 Manned Spaceflight Engineers in February 1980.

Following the cancellation of his Shuttle mission Sundberg left the MSE program and Los Angeles to become a training officer with the U.S. Space Command, Colorado Springs. He later held the Space Command chair at the Air War College, Maxwell AFB, Alabama, for four years. He is returned to Special Projects—actually the National Reconnaissance Office—as director for technology. He served as vice commander of that organization until his retirement from the Air Force in August 1997.

Sundberg is currently a civilian consultant to the NRO.

Swanson, Steven Roy
1960–

NASA flight engineer Steve Swanson is one of the 25 astronaut candidates selected in June 1998. In August of that year he began a training and evaluation course that should qualify him as a Shuttle mission specialist and International Space Station crewmember.

Swanson was born December 3, 1960, in Syracuse, New York. He graduated from high school in Steamboat Springs, Colorado, in 1979, then attended the University of Colorado at Boulder, where he received a B.S. in engineering physics in 1983. He later earned an M.A.S. in computer systems from Florida Atlantic University (1986) and a Ph.D. in computer science from Texas A&M University (1998).

At the time of his selection as an ASCAN, Swanson was a flight engineer on the Shuttle training aircraft with NASA's aircraft operations directorate, Johnson Space Center.

Swigert, John Leonard, Jr.
1931–1982

Test pilot Jack Swigert became the first astronaut to step into a flight crew on short notice when he replaced Thomas Mattingly as command module pilot of Apollo 13 on April 8, 1970, just three days before launch.

When Apollo 13 suffered an explosion that forced the cancellation of its lunar landing, Swigert joined James Lovell and Fred Haise in using the lunar module Aquarius as a "lifeboat"—a procedure, ironically, for which Swigert had written the manual.

For three harrowing days the astronauts improvised, using Aquarius's rockets to maneuver the huge command and service module complex, rigging makeshift air filters, and keeping close track of their limited supplies of oxygen, electricity, and water. They also tried to keep warm, since the temperature in the powerless command module Odyssey dropped to freezing. The astronauts returned to Earth on April 17, 1970, splashing down safely in the Pacific near the carrier *U.S.S. Iwo Jima*.

The unusual change occurred in the first place because all six prime and backup crewmen had been mistakenly exposed to German measles. Mattingly had never had the illness in childhood and NASA officials feared that should he become sick during the mission (he would be orbiting alone around the Moon for two days) he would be unable to function. Swigert was asked to step in, though he had to pass a grueling session in the flight simulator to prove to NASA officials that he was ready. (Because of the complexity of the lunar landing missions and the limited availability of simulators, backup crewmen were never trained as thoroughly as were members of the prime crew.) Swigert was ready to fly Apollo 13, but in the confusion of those three days he neglected one item of personal business: he forgot to file his income tax return and had to ask for an extension from space.

Swigert was born August 30, 1931, in Denver, Colorado, where he attended Regis and East High Schools, then went on to the University of Colorado, where he received a B.S. in mechanical engineering in 1953. He would later earn an M.S. in aerospace science from Rensselaer Polytechnic Institute in 1965 and an M.B.S. from the University of Hartford in 1967.

Swigert joined the Air Force upon graduation from Colorado and served as a jet fighter pilot in Japan and Korea until 1956. Leaving active duty, he flew with the Massachusetts Air National Guard until 1960, and with the Connecticut Air National Guard from 1960 to 1965. He became a pilot for Pratt and Whitney, builders of jet engines, and applied for the 1963 astronaut group. Rejected because of lack of test pilot experience or advanced schooling, Swigert enrolled at Rensselaer to work on a master's degree and also tested the inflatable Rogallo wing, a dart-shaped parasail that was intended to "fly" returning spacecraft to landing sites.

As a pilot Swigert would eventually log over 8,000 hours of flying time, including more than 6,500 hours in jets.

Swigert was one of the 19 astronauts selected by NASA in April 1966. He became a specialist in the Apollo command module and served on the support crew for Apollo 7, the first manned Apollo mission, and for Apollo 11, the first manned lunar landing. He was a capcom for Apollo 7 as well. In August 1969 he joined John Young and Charles Duke on the backup crew for Apollo 13.

Following Apollo 13 Swigert trained for the Apollo-Soyuz Test Project and had been informally assigned to the mission with Thomas Stafford and Donald Slayton when NASA began investigating the Apollo 15 envelope scandal. Other Apollo astronauts who had signed envelopes (which were later sold to collectors) were asked to disclose it. Swigert denied signing them, but later admitted that he had. His failure to make the disclosure when asked cost him the seat on ASTP.

Shortly thereafter, in April 1973, Swigert left the astronaut office to become executive director of the Committee on Science and Technology of the U.S. House of Representatives, a position he held until August 31, 1977.

Swigert had the option of returning the astronaut office as a Shuttle pilot in 1977 and considered it, but resigned instead to run for the U.S. Senate from Colorado. His 1978 campaign was unsuccessful. From 1979 to 1981 Swigert was vice president for technology development of the BDM Corporation in Denver, and in 1981 and 1982 served as vice president for financial and corporate affairs for International Gold and Minerals, Ltd.

In February 1982 Swigert announced his candidacy for the U.S. House of Representatives seat for the Colorado's Sixth Congressional District. On November 2, 1982, Swigert was elected Republican congressman with 64 percent of the popular vote.

During the campaign, however, it was learned that Swigert was suffering from bone cancer. He died in Washington, D.C., on December 27, 1982, just one week before he was to take his Congressional seat.

Tani, Daniel Michio
1961–

Aerospace engineer Dan Tani is one of the 35 astronaut candidates selected by NASA on May 1, 1996. In August of that year he reported to the Johnson Space Center to begin a training and evaluation course that should qualify him as a Shuttle mission specialist and International Space Station crewmember. Since February 1997 he has had a technical assignment in the payloads/habitation branch of the astronaut office.

Tani was born February 1, 1961, in Ridley Park, Pennsylvania, and grew up in Lombard, Illinois, where he graduated from Glenbard East High School in 1979. He attended the Massachusetts Institute of Technology, receiving a B.S. (1984) and an M.S. (1988) in mechanical engineering.

After graduating from M.I.T. in 1984, Tani worked for the Space and Communications Group of Hughes Aircraft

Corporation, El Segundo, California, as a design engineer. He returned to M.I.T. in 1986 to work on his master's degree, then joined Bolt, Beranek and Newman, Cambridge, Massachusetts, as an experimental psychologist.

Since 1988 Tani has worked for the Orbital Sciences Corporation, Dulles, Virginia, first as a structures engineer, than as mission operations manager for the transfer orbit stage (TOS), which carried the Advanced Communications Technology Satellite into geosynchronous orbit following its deployment from the orbiter Discovery (STS-51) in September 1993. He later served as launch operations manager for the Pegasus program.

Tanner, Joseph Richard
1950–

Former Navy and NASA jet pilot Joe Tanner took part in the second mission to service and repair the Hubble Space Telescope. STS-82, launched in February 1997 aboard the orbiter Discovery, carried a crew of 7, including 2 two-man EVA teams.

With Greg Harbaugh, Tanner made the second and fourth of what turned out to be five EVAs. On their first the two astronauts installed a new Fine Guidance Sensor and a data recorder while discovering several cracks in the Hubble's multilayer insulation. During their second EVA, Tanner and Harbaugh repaired some of those cracks while installing a drive mechanism for the ESA-built solar arrays.

Earlier Tanner was a mission specialist in the crew of STS-66. This November 1994 Shuttle mission carried the third Spacelab ATLAS, a set of experiments designed to study the sun and the Earth's atmosphere. The crew of the orbiter Atlantis also deployed and retrieved the CRISTA-SPAS satellite.

Tanner is currently assigned as an EVA crewmember for International Space Station assembly mission 4A, scheduled for launch aboard STS-97 in the spring of 2000.

Tanner was born January 21, 1950, in Danville, Illinois, where he graduated from high school. He attended the University of Illinois, receiving a B.S. in mechanical engineering in 1973.

Following graduation from Illinois Tanner joined the Navy, earning his wings in 1975. He became an A-7E pilot with Light Attack Squadron 94 (VA-94) aboard the carrier *U.S.S. Coral Sea*, and also served as an instructor at Pensacola, Florida.

Tanner left active duty in 1984 to join NASA as an aerospace engineer and research pilot, working as an instructor on the Shuttle Training Aircraft. He continues to fly A-7s with the Naval Reserve and has logged over 7,000 hours of flying time.

At the time of his selection as one of 19 astronaut candidates in March 1992, Tanner was deputy chief of aircraft operations at the NASA Johnson Space Center. In July 1993 he qualified as Shuttle mission while assigned to the mission support branch working in the Shuttle Avionics Integration Laboratory (SAIL). He was assigned to the STS-66 crew in August 1993.

Taylor, James Martin
1930–1970

Air Force test pilot James Taylor was one of the first 8 pilots chosen for the Manned Orbiting Laboratory Program in November 1985. He remained with MOL, training for proposed 30-day Earth orbital spaceflights, until the program was canceled in May 1969. According to program managers, Taylor was the leading candidate to command the first manned MOL mission.

Taylor became an instructor at the Air Force Aerospace Research Pilot School at Edwards AFB, and was killed in the crash of a T-38 jet there on September 4, 1970.

Taylor was born November 27, 1930, in Stamps, Arkansas. He received an associate of arts degree from Southern State University in 1950 and joined the Air Force as an enlisted man the next year. He became an aviation cadet in 1952 and earned his pilot's wings in 1953, then served with the Air Defense Command. He returned to school, earning a B.S. in electrical engineering from the University of Michigan in 1959.

After serving as a flight test engineer for bombers and cargo aircraft, Taylor entered the Air Force Test Pilot School at Edwards AFB in 1963. The next year he attended the Aerospace Research Pilot School. He was project pilot for the F-106 when selected for MOL.

Thagard, Norman Earl
1943–

Physician Norman Thagard made 5 spaceflights between 1983 and 1995, four aboard the Shuttle and one aboard the Russian space station Mir.

It was during the 112-day Mir mission, March-July 1995, that Thagard became the first of 7 Americans to live and work with Russian crewmembers. Thagard was launched aboard Soyuz TM-21 with commander Vladimir Dezhurov and Gennady Strekalov, forming the Mir-18 crew. For the next four months Thagard served as the crew's researcher, conducting medical tests and other studies. He also used equipment brought to Mir aboard the Spektr module.

Thagard showed no ill effects from his mission, but he reported later that he found himself isolated by language and culture. Even the food aboard Mir struck him as bland. Some Russian officials dismissed the complaints as "whining," but adjustments were made, and subsequent NASA-Mir crewmembers benefited.

Thagard, Dezhurov, and Strekalov returned to Earth aboard the orbiter Atlantis, which docked with Mir in late June 1995.

Previously Thagard was a mission specialist aboard four different Shuttle flights, beginning with STS-7 in June 1983. He was a late addition to the crew of 4 astronauts that included Sally Ride, America's first woman in space. Thagard's job was to study space adaptation syndrome (SAS), so-called "space sickness" that affected about half of all the astronauts who had flown on the Shuttle until then. During the 6-day STS-7 mission Thagard conducted physical tests and collected data on the crewmembers' adaptation to space. The astronauts also deployed two communications satellites and deployed and retrieved a third.

Thagard went into space a second time on Shuttle Mission 51-B carrying Spacelab 3, a mission dedicated to space manufacturing and medicine. In addition to its crew of 7, Spacelab 3 carried 24 experimental rats and a pair of squirrel monkeys. Caring for the monkeys, one of whom got sick, proved frustrating and time-consuming; nevertheless, 14 of the 15 scientific experiments carried on Spacelab 3 provided data to experimenters.

Thagard's third flight was the 4-day STS-30, which saw the deployment of the Magellan-Venus space probe. His fourth was STS-42. This January 1992 flight of the orbiter Discovery carried the International Microgravity Spacelab. The crew of 7 conducted 55 experiments in space manufacturing and life sciences studies. Thagard served as payload commander for the international scientific team that included German physicist Ulf Merbold and Canadian physician Roberta Bondar.

Thagard was born July 3, 1943, in Marianna, Florida, and grew up in Jacksonville, where he graduated from Paxon Senior High School in 1961. He attended Florida State University, receiving B.S. and M.S. degrees in engineering science in 1965 and 1966 while also taking courses in premed. He received his M.D. from the University of Texas Southwestern Medical School in 1977.

On active duty with the Marine Corps Reserve beginning in September 1966, Thagard underwent pilot training, earning his wings in 1968. He flew F-4 Phantoms at Beaufort, South Carolina, then was assigned to duty in Vietnam, flying 163 combat missions in 1969 and 1970. Returning to the United States, he was an aviation weapons division officer at Beaufort until leaving the service in 1971. He then resumed his medical education while also continuing to study electrical engineering. He also continued to fly, and logged over 2,200 hours of flying time, most of it in jet aircraft.

In 1977 Thagard was an intern at the Medical University of South Carolina when he learned NASA's search for new astronauts through his wife, Kirby, who saw the announcement, Thagard applied and in January 1978 was one of 35 new astronauts who were selected. In August 1979 he qualified as a Shuttle mission specialist, working in the Shuttle Avionics Integration Laboratory and also with the payloads for STS-7. He was already training for the Spacelab 3 mission in December 1982 when he was added to the STS-7 crew.

Following Spacelab 3 Thagard was assigned to the crew of Mission 61-H, scheduled for June 1986, then transferred to Mission 61-G upon the resignation of astronaut John Fabian, only to have the new mission canceled following the Challenger explosion. He was assigned to STS-30 in February 1988.

Beginning in 1992 Thagard underwent Russian language training, and in February 1994 was officially named as the first NASA-Mir crewmember.

Thagard retired from NASA in January 1996 to become professor of engineering at his alma mater, Florida State University.

Thomas, Andrew Sydney Withiel

1951–

Space scientist Andy Thomas was the seventh and last NASA-Mir crewmember, arriving at the Russian space station aboard STS-89 in January 1998. He returned to Earth in June 1998 aboard STS-91.

During his first days aboard Mir Thomas came into conflict with his Russian crewmates and ground controllers. In order formally to transfer from the STS-89 crew to the Mir-27 team of Solovyov and Vinogradov, Thomas had to fit a Sokol launch and entry space suit. Thomas's suit, which had been improperly sized on the ground, did not fit. Mir-25 commander Solovyov solved the problem by altering the suit himself, but not until Thomas was criticized by Russian flight controllers for "whining."

Another controversy soon followed, when Mir-26 commander Talgat Musabayev, who replaced Solovyov in early February 1998, derided Thomas's Russian language skills. Questioned by Russian reporters while onboard Mir, Thomas could only give answers in English.

In fairness to Thomas, he had originally been assigned as a backup for the NASA 7 position, only moving up when David Wolf took Wendy Lawrence's place as the NASA 6 crewmember in September 1997. Thomas had less time to train in Russia than any previous NASA-Mir crewmember.

In spite of his early problems, Thomas proved a valuable crewmember to Musabayev and flight engineer Nikolai Budarin during their first abortive EVA, when Budarin broke tools that would have opened the Mir's airlock.

THE VIEW FROM MIR

by Andy Thomas (Mir-24/25)

May 22, 1998

When you first look down on the Earth you see its obvious curvature, and the thin layer of atmosphere on the horizon, with the dark blackness of space above it. It is striking to see the abundance of clouds carpeting the planet. Very seldom do we see extended areas that are free from cloud cover, particularly in the tropics. We can see these clouds building to thunderstorms during the day, and then collapsing at night back down to Earth and spreading out in huge circles as if they had been poured down onto the planet.

As you continue to watch the Earth, you begin to recognize land forms and can see that some countries have broad features allowing them to be recognized at a glance; northern Africa has its desert regions, south America has its forested regions, and Australia its redness. Then there are the characteristic coastlines that we are so accustomed to seeing on a map that stand out very clearly from space; the boot shape of Italy, the Red Sea, the Mediterranean, the Florida peninsular, the gulf of California, and so on. Finally, there are readily identifiable geographic features that only occur in certain places: the huge expanse of Lake Baikal, the Namib desert, the Himalayas bounding the plains of Tibet and the fertile areas of India, and the Andes separating the rain forests from the western deserts of South America.

After even a short time in orbit, we learn to recognize these and can quickly know our approximate position above the Earth from a glance out the window.

Evidence of human habitation is visible from low Earth orbit. Cities can be seen, although, surprisingly, they do not stand out readily. But we can make out their grid-like patterns of streets. In remote areas, certain roads and railway lines can be seen as faint lines across the Earth, such as the road through the rain forests of Brazil, and the long straight railway line crossing south western Australia, but generally these are too small to make out clearly. The fencing off of farm land into individual fields can also be made out, particularly in the Midwest of the U.S. and Canada. There is even one area in South America where they alternate their growing cycles on adjacent fields, giving rise to a very obvious checkerboard pattern. Of course, national boundaries do not stand out by themselves as on a map, but some national boundaries can be seen where there are different land usage policies in effect on each side of a border, giving rise to different surface texture or color. In this way the southern border of Israel can be made out, as can part of the division between the U.S. and Canada. The stories about the Great Wall of China being visible from space may be true, but I have yet to see it.

One of the most readily visible signs of human presence, is the occurrence of contrails from aircraft in the upper atmosphere. These are crystals of ice formed from water, a byproduct of the combustion process in the aircraft engines, and which is collected into the wake vortices of the aircraft. They are very long lasting, and can be seen over virtually all parts of the world as white streaks across the sky. They can be striking around cities that are major air traffic hubs, and can often times be seen radiating out from these cities, like spokes in a wheel.

The view of the Earth at night is equally spectacular, and cities can be made out very clearly with all their street lights. Some areas stand out very noticeably such as Japan, where the high population density is given away by the abundance of night lights. In fact there are so many lights you can delineate the shape of the Japanese island chain with ease. The presence of myriad small points of light off shore, probably fishing boats, shows Japan's heavy reliance on seafood.

There are a host of natural phenomena that are spectacular at night. In the temperate zones, we can see vast thunderstorm fronts stretching for miles and being lit up by huge flashes of lightning. Occasionally I have seen lightning start at one point on a storm front and trigger a cascade of lightning flashes propagating along the storm front, like a falling row of dominoes.

Of course stars are visible at night, but without any atmospheric attenuation, so they can be seen clearly. They look much as they do when viewed from an isolated desert region away from city lights, but of course they do not twinkle. Perhaps one of the most sublime of all the cosmic sights I have seen to date is the Aurora Australis over the southern polar regions. Only visible at night, it is an eerie curtain of pale green phosphorescence that waves and twists above the Earth, stretching for hundreds of miles.

Meteors are visible from space too. However, we have the unique vantage of being able to look down on the Earth and see meteors streaking into the atmosphere way below us. Having that perspective is a compelling reminder that we are indeed flying in space.

Unfortunately, this orbital vantage also gives us a unique view of the deleterious effects of human habitation. As I write this, there are huge areas in Central America that are burning. A giant pall of smoke is blanketing the entire south western peninsular of the North American continent and is being carried in the winds over much of the United States and as far north as Canada. Indeed, at the northern extreme of one of our orbits, while crossing the Great Lakes, I could see the smoke haze coming up from the distant south and blanketing the land below us. This kind of perspective from space allows us to appreciate that all lands are connected into a common biosphere and that the environmental policies in one country have far reaching effects in other countries.

Earlier Thomas served as payload commander for STS-77, a flight of the orbiter Endeavour in May 1996. STS-77 carried the fourth SpaceHab experiment module, and also deployed and retrieved the Spartan platform, which tested an inflatable space antenna. A second satellite called PAMS was also deployed; it was designed to test the ability of a satellite to orient itself in relation to the Earth without a costly attitude control system.

Thomas was born December 18, 1951, in Adelaide, Australia. He graduated from Saint Peters College in Adelaide, then attended the University of Adelaide, where he received a B.E. and Ph.D. in mechanical engineering in 1972 and 1978.

Thomas joined the Lockheed Aeronautical Systems Company at Marietta, Georgia, in 1977, as a research scientist in the field of fluid dynamics and aerodynamics. In 1983 he became head of the advanced flight sciences department, and also managed the research laboratory, wind tunnels, and test facilities. In 1987 Thomas was named manager of Lockheed's flight sciences division, supporting advanced aerospace vehicles developed by the company for NASA and the USAF.

He joined the NASA Jet Propulsion Laboratory in 1989, becoming leader of J.P.L.'s program for microgravity materials processing in space.

Thomas was one of the 19 astronaut candidates selected by NASA in March 1992, qualifying as a Shuttle mission specialist in August 1993 while assigned to the astronaut support team at the Kennedy Space Center. He arrived at the Gagarin Center in January 1997 to begin Soyuz-Mir and International Space Station training.

Thomas, Donald Alan
1955–

Materials scientist Don Thomas has been a mission specialist in four Shuttle crews, beginning with STS-65, which carried the second International Microgravity Laboratory in July 1994. The crew of 7 conducted a number of experiments in life sciences and space manufacturing in what became—thanks to weather problems that forced a delay in landing — the longest Shuttle mission flown to that time, almost 15 days in duration.

In August 1995 Thomas flew a second time on STS-70, which deployed the sixth and last Tracking and Data Relay Satellite.

Thomas made his third and fourth spaceflights with the Materials Science Laboratory on STS-83 and STS-94 in April and July 1997. (STS-83 was cut short by a fuel cell problem aboard the orbiter Columbia and reflown three months later.) STS-94 completed the MSL experiments on a record 16-day mission.

Thomas was born May 6, 1955, in Cleveland, Ohio, where he graduated from Cleveland Heights High School in 1973. He attended Case Western University, where he received a B.S. in physics in 1977, and Cornell University, where he earned an M.S. (1980) and Ph.D. (1982) in materials science.

After graduation from Cornell in 1982 Thomas became a senior member of the technical staff at AT&T Bell Laboratories in Princeton, New Jersey. At the same time he

NASA Mission Crew Patches

GEMINI 5

Cooper and Conrad

GEMINI 6

Schirra and Stafford

GEMINI 7

Borman and Lovell

GEMINI 8

Armstrong and Scott

GEMINI 9

Stafford and Cernan

GEMINI 10

Young and Collins

GEMINI 11

Conrad and Gordon

GEMINI 12

Lovell and Aldrin

APOLLO 1
White, Grissom, and Chaffee

APOLLO 7
Schirra, Eisele, and Cunningham

APOLLO 8
Borman, Lovell, and Anders

APOLLO 9
McDivitt, Scott, and Schweickart

APOLLO 10
Stafford, Young, and Cernan

APOLLO 11
Armstrong, Collins, and Aldrin

APOLLO 12
Conrad, Gordon, and Bean

APOLLO 13
Lovell, Swigert, and Haise

APOLLO 14

Shepard, Roosa, and Mitchell

APOLLO 15

Scott, Worden, and Irwin

APOLLO 16

Young, Mattingly, and Duke

APOLLO 17

Cernan, Evans, and Schmitt

SKYLAB 1

Conrad, Kerwin, and Weitz

SKYLAB 2

Bean, Garriott, and Lousma

SKYLAB 3

Carr, Gibson, and Pogue

**ASTP (APOLLO-SOYUZ
[USSR] PROJECT)**

Stafford, Brand, and Slayton;
Leonov and Kubasov

STS-1

Young and Crippen

STS-2

Engle and Truly

STS-3

Lousma and Fullerton

STS-4

Mattingly and Hartsfield

STS-5

Allen, Brand, Overmeyer, and Lenoir

STS-7

Crippen, Fabian, Hauck, Ride,
and Thagard

STS-6

Peterson, Weitz, Bobko, and Musgrave

STS-8

Gardner, Bluford, Thornton, Truly,
and Brandenstein

STS-9

Merbold, Parker, Young, Shaw, Garriott, and Lichtenberg

41-B

Brand, Gibson, McCandless, McNair, and Stewart

41-C

Crippen, Scobee, Hart, Van Hoften, and Nelson

41-D

Mullane, Hawley, Resnik, Walker, Coats, and Hartsfield

41-G

Crippen, Sullivan, Leestma, Ride, McBride, Garneau, and Scully-Power

51-A

Allen, Fisher, Gardner, Hauck, and Walker

51-C

Mattingly, Shriver, Onizuka, Payton, and Buchli

51-D

Bobko, Williams, Seddon, Griggs, Hoffman, Walker, and Garn

51-B

Lind, Thagard, Overmeyer, Gregory,
Thornton, van den Berg, and Wang

51-G

Brandenstein, Creighton, Nagel, Lucid,
Fabian, Baudry, and Al-Saud

51-F

Fullerton, Bridges, Musgrave, England,
Henize, Acton, and Bartoe

51-I

Engle, Covey, Lounge, Fisher,
and Van Hoften

51-J

Pailes, Hilmers, Grabe, Bobko,
and Stewart

61-A

Hartsfield, Nagel, Dunbar, Bluford,
Buchli, Messerschmid, Ockels,
and Furrer

61-B

Walker, Neri, Shaw, O'Connor,
Cleave, Ross, and Spring

61-C

Gibson, Bolden, Nelson, Hawley,
Chang-Diaz, Cenker, and Nelson

51-L

McAuliffe, Jarvis, Scobee, Smith,
McNair, Onizuka, and Resnik

STS-26

Hauck, Covey, Lounge, Hilmers,
and Nelson

STS-27

Gibson, Mullane, Ross, Shephard,
and Gardner

STS-29

Bagian, Springer, Buchli, Coats,
and Blaha

STS-30

Walker, Grabe, Cleave, Lee,
and Thagard

STS-28

Adamson, Leestma, Brown, Shaw,
and Richards

STS-34

Lucid, Williams, McCulley, Baker, and
Chang-Diaz

STS-33

Gregory, Blaha, Carter, Musgrave,
and Thornton

STS-32

Dunbar, Ivins, Low, Brandenstein, and Wetherbee

STS-36

Casper, Creighton, Thuot, Hilmers, and Mullane

STS-31

Shriver, Bolden, Hawley, McCandless, and Sullivan

STS-41

Cabana, Akers, Shepherd, Melnick, and Richards

STS-38

Covey, Culbertson, Meade, Springer, and Gemar

STS-35

Brand, Lounge, Hoffman, Parker, Gardner, Durrance, and Parise

STS-37

Cameron, Ross, Apt, Godwin, and Nagel

STS-39

Harbaugh, Hieb, Veach, Bluford,
McMonagle, Coats, and Hammond

STS-40

O'Connor, Jernigan, Gutierrez, Seddon,
Gaffney, Hughes-Fulford, and Bagian

STS-43

Blaha, Baker, Lucid, Adamson,
and Low

STS-48

Reightler, Buchli, Gemar, Brown,
and Creighton

STS-44

Henricks, Gregory, Hennen, Runco,
Voss, and Musgrave

STS-42

Bondar, Readdy, Grabe, Oswald,
Merbold, Thagard, and Hilmers

STS-45

Lichtenberg, Frimout, Sullivan, Foale,
Bolden, Duffy, and Leestma

STS-49

Chilton, Brandenstein, Melnick, Thuot,
Hieb, Thornton, and Akers

STS-50

Baker, Meade, Delucas, Trinh, Dunbar,
Richards, and Bowersox

STS-46

Allen, Ivins, Malerba, Chang-Diaz,
Nicollier, Hoffman, and Shriver

STS-47

Gibson, Apt, Brown, Lee, Davis,
Jemison, and Mohri

STS-52

Veach, Shepherd, Wetherbee, Baker,
Jernigan, and MacLean

STS-53

Bluford, Voss, Clifford, Cabana,
and Walker

STS-54

Helms, Harbaugh, Runco, Casper,
and McMonagle

STS-55

Precourt, Nagel, Henricks, Schlegel,
Harris, Ross, and Walter

STS-56

Foale, Cameron, Oswald, Cockrell,
and Ochoa

STS-57

Sherlock, Voss, Grabe, Duffy, Low,
and Wisoff

STS-51

Walz, Culbertson, Readdy, Newman,
and Bursch

STS-58

Seddon, Lucid, Wolf, Fettman,
McArthur, Blaha, and Searfoss

STS-61

Musgrave, Covey, Bowersox, Akers,
Hoffman, Nicollier, and Thornton

STS-60

Bolden, Sega, Reightler, Chang-Díaz,
Davis, and Krikalev

STS-62

Thuot, Gemar, Ivins, Casper, and Allen

STS-59

Apt, Clifford, Gutierrez, Chilton,
Godwin, and Jones

STS-65

Cabana, Halsell, Walz, Hieb, Chiao,
Thomas, and Mukai

STS-64

Lee, Linenger, Helms, Meade, Richards,
and Hammond

STS-68

Baker, Wilcutt, Smith, Wisoff, Bursch,
and Jones

STS-66

Parazynski, Tanner, McMonagle,
Brown, Ochoa, and Clervoy

STS-63

Voss, Harris, Wetherbee, Collins, Foale,
and Titov

STS-67

Grunsfeld, Jernigan, Oswald, Gregory, Lawrence, Parise, and Durrance

STS-71

Dunbar, Harbaugh, Baker, Precourt, and Gibson; Solovyov, Budarin, Thagard, Strekalov, and Dezhurov

STS-70

Currie, Kregel, Henricks, Thomas, and Weber

STS-69

Walker, Cockrell, Newman, Gernhardt, and Voss

STS-73

Bowersox, Rominger, Thornton, Sacco, Lopez-Algeria, Leslie, and Coleman

STS-74

McArthur, Halsell, Cameron, Ross, and Hadfield

STS-72

Scott, Wakata, Duffy, Jett, Barry, and Chiao

STS-75

Allen, Horowitz, Hoffman, Cheli,
Chang-Diaz, and Guidoni

STS-76

Sega, Chilton, Searfoss, Lucid, Clifford,
and Godwin

STS-77

Casper, Brown, Thomas, Bursch,
Runco, and Garneau

STS-78

Favier, Linnehan, Thirsk, Brady,
Kregel, Henricks, and Helms

STS-79

Lucid, Blaha, Apt, Wilcutt, Readdy,
Akers, and Walz

STS-80

Jones, Jernigan, Musgrave, Rominger,
and Cockrell

STS-81

Baker, Jett, Ivins, Wisoff, Grunsfeld,
Blaha, and Linenger

STS-82

Bowersox, Horowitz, Hawley, Smith, Tanner, Lee, and Harbaugh

STS-83

Crouch, Gernhardt, Thomas, Voss, Halsell, Still, and Linteris

STS-84

Noriega, Clervoy, Foale, Precourt, Collins, Linenger, Kondakova, and Lu

STS-94

Crouch, Gernhardt, Thomas, Voss, Halsell, Still, and Linteris

STS-85

Tryggvasin, Davis, Brown, Rominger, Curbeam, and Robinson

STS-86

Wolf, Lawrence, Foale, Chretien, Bloomfield, Wetherbee, and Parazynski

STS-87

Kregel, Lindsey, Chawla, Scott, Doi, and Kadenyuk

STS-89

Sharipov, Wilcutt, Edwards, Anderson,
Dunbar, and Reilly

STS-91

Precourt, Chang-Diaz, Kavandi,
Thomas, Ryumin, Lawrence, and Gorie

STS-90

Williams, Pawelczyk, Buckey, Hire,
Linnehan, Searfoss, and Altman

STS-95

Glenn, Mukai, Duque, Brown, Lindsey,
Robinson, and Parazynski

STS-88

Ross, Newman, Krikalev, Cabana,
Sturchow, and Currie

became an adjunct professor of physics at Trenton State College, New Jersey. In 1987 he left AT&T to join Lockheed Engineering and Sciences Company in Houston, where he worked on Shuttle payloads. A year later he became an engineer at the NASA Johnson Space Center, reviewing materials planned for use on Space Station Freedom. He was also principal investigator for an experiment which flew on the STS-32 mission in January 1990.

Thomas is a privately licensed pilot with 250 hours of flying time in planes and gliders.

He was one of the 23 astronaut candidates selected by NASA in January 1990 and in July 1991 qualified as a Shuttle mission specialist. His first technical assignments were in the safety and operations development branches of the astronaut office. In 1992 he was capcom for STS-47, ST-52 and STS-53.

Thompson, Milton Orville
1926–1993
NASA test pilot Milt Thompson was one of the 6 pilots chosen in April 1960 to fly the Air Force X-20 Dyna-Soar spaceplane, which was ultimately never built. He later made 14 flights in the X-15 rocket plane.

He became the first person to fly a "lifting body" aircraft, a wingless vehicle that gets lift from its shape, when on August 16, 1963, he was pilot aboard the plywood, powerless M2-F1. Lifting body aircraft served as precursors to the Space Shuttle and all future aerospace planes.

Thompson was born May 4, 1926, in Crookston, Minnesota. He joined the Navy during World War II and served as a combat pilot in China and Japan. Returning to the States after the War, he enrolled at the University of Washington, where in 1953 he received a B.S. in engineering.

He joined NASA as an engineer in 1956, becoming a test pilot two years later. Among other assignments, he flew as F-104 chase pilot for X-15 flights (he was forced to eject during one of these flights) and tested a rudimentary "space kite," the Parasev, an abortive design to return early manned spacecraft on land rather than water by using a steerable, delta-shaped parachute. He was involved in tests of remotely piloted research vehicles.

Thompson became director of research projects at Dryden Flight Center in the fall of 1966 and later chief engineer for that facility. He is the author of *On the Edge*, a history of the X-15 program (1992).

He died August 6, 1993, in Lancaster, California.

Thompson, William David
1956–
Air Force engineer Dave Thompson was training as a payload specialist for the second Shuttle deployment of a Navstar Global Position System satellite at the time of the Challenger accident in January 1986. When Shuttle launches resumed, all Navstar payloads had been transferred to unmanned Delta II rockets for launch, and Thompson lost his chance to fly in space.

Thompson was born January 14, 1956, in Charleston, West Virginia. He attended the Air Force Academy, graduating with a B.S. in electrical engineering in 1978. In 1981 he received an M.S. in that field from Stanford University.

From 1978 to 1980 Thompson was a project officer at Space Division in Los Angeles. Following a year at Stanford, he returned to Space Division as a payload electronics engineer. He was one of the 14 officers selected for the second cadre of Manned Spaceflight Engineers in January 1983.

Thompson left the Air Force and the MSE program in 1987. He is currently president of Spectrum Astro, based in Gilbert, Arizona. Spectrum specializes in the construction of small satellites, including MSTI-3, which became a target for the test of the Army's MIRACL laser in 1997. *Ad Astra* magazine named Thompson one of its 25 "future space pioneers" in 1994.

Thorne, Stephen Douglas
1953–1986

Former Navy test pilot Steve Thorne was one of the 13 astronaut candidates selected by NASA in June 1985. In August of that year he began a training and evaluation course that would have qualified him as a Shuttle pilot.

However, on May 24, 1986, Thorne was killed in an off-duty accident. He was a passenger in a Pitts 2-A sports plane piloted by NASA flight controller Jim Simons when it went out of control and crashed in Arcadia, Texas, south of Houston.

Thorne was born February 11, 1953, in Frankfurt-on-Main, Germany, and graduated from T. L. Hanna High School in Anderson, South Carolina, in 1971. He attended the Naval Academy, receiving a B.S. in systems engineering in 1975.

Following graduation from Annapolis Thorne underwent pilot training, earning his wings in 1976. He flew F-4 Phantoms aboard the carrier *U.S.S. Ranger* in the Pacific, then, in 1981, attended the Naval Test Pilot School at Patuxent River, Maryland. He was a test pilot at Pax River until 1984, and was an F-18 pilot aboard the carrier *U.S.S. Coral Sea* when selected by NASA.

Thorne had logged over 2,500 hours of flying time, including 200 carrier landings, in 30 different types of aircraft.

Thornton, Kathryn Cordell Ryan
1952–

Kathy Thornton holds the record for space-walking by a woman astronaut. With fellow mission specialist Tom Akers, she made two 7-hour EVAs during the first Hubble Space Telescope repair mission in December 1993.

Earlier, in May 1992, she and Akers tested space station construction techniques and EVA rescue procedures aboard the orbiter Endeavour during STS-49. Thornton's 7-hour, 45-minute EVA was longer than the combined duration of the two previous woman space walkers, Kathryn Sullivan and Svetlana Savitskaya.

Earlier in the mission she took part in the successful retrieval and redeployment of the errant Intelsat VI communications satellite.

STS-49 was Thornton's second flight. In November and December 1989 she was a mission specialist aboard STS-33, a flight of the orbiter Discovery during which the National Security Agency electronic intelligence satellite Mentor was deployed into geosynchronous orbit. Thornton and fellow mission specialist Story Musgrave also conducted a number of experiments in space medicine during the 5-day mission.

Thornton made her fourth flight as payload commander for STS-73. This October-November 1995 flight of the orbiter Columbia carried a crew of 7 and the second U.S. Microgravity Laboratory.

Thornton was born Kathryn Cordell Ryan on August 17, 1952, in Montgomery, Alabama, where she grew up, graduating from Sidney Lanier High School there in 1970. She attended Auburn University, receiving a B.S. in physics in 1974, and earned her M.S. (1977) and Ph.D. (1979) in physics from the University of Virginia.

While a graduate student at Virginia, Thornton took part in nuclear research programs at Oak Ridge National Laboratory, Brookhaven National Laboratory, the Indiana University Cyclotron Facility, and the Space Radiation Effects Laboratory. In 1979 she was awarded a NATO post-doctoral fellowship which enabled her to study at the Max Planck Institute for Nuclear Physics in Heidelberg, West Germany. Returning to the United States in 1980, she went to work at the Army Foreign Science and Technology Center in Charlottesville, Virginia.

Thornton was one of the 17 astronaut candidates selected by NASA in May 1984. In July 1985 she qualified as a Shuttle mission specialist. Among her technical assignments was serving on an escape test crew, working in SAIL, and serving as capcom for several 1990 Shuttle missions.

She resigned from NASA in May 1996 to return to her alma mater, the University of Virginia, as professor of physics.

Thornton, William Edgar
1929–

Bill Thornton waited 16 years for his first spaceflight, STS-8 in August and September 1983, becoming, at age 54, the oldest person to fly in space at that time. Technically assigned as a mission specialist, Thornton, like astronaut Norman Thagard on STS-7, had been added to the crew just months prior to launch in order to make a firsthand study of space adaptation syndrome (SAS), the so-called space sickness that affects approximately half of all space travelers.

Thornton was well known as the astronaut office's resident SAS expert, and during the 6-day STS-8 flight he did get sick. By the time he returned to Earth he claimed he had moved "years ahead" in the study of SAS.

Thornton had further opportunity to study SAS when he served as mission specialist aboard Spacelab 3 in April 1985. Spacelab 3, Shuttle Mission 51-B, was dedicated to life sciences and in addition to the crew of 7 astronauts carried a crew of experimental rats and monkeys. Problems with the monkey cages caused Thornton and other astronauts to spend an unfortunate amount of time cleaning up after their passengers, but Thornton was still able to continue gathering data on his pet subject.

He was also able to use a special exercise treadmill he had originally designed for Skylab flights and that had become standard equipment aboard all Shuttle flights. Thornton used the treadmill for 90 minutes one day, the amount of time it takes a Shuttle to circle the Earth, in effect, taking a "walk around the world."

Thornton was born April 14, 1929, in Faison, North Carolina, where his father was a farmer. He attended schools in Faison and also ran a radio repair shop to support his family after the death of his father. He attended the University of North Carolina as an Air Force ROTC student, graduating in 1952 with a B.S. in physics. He earned his M.D. from North Carolina in 1963.

On active duty with the Air Force, Thornton served at the Flight Air Test Proving Ground at Eglin AFB, Florida, where he developed a scoring system for pilots delivering missiles and bombs to targets. Leaving the Air Force in 1956, Thornton worked as an electronics engineer, even-

tually becoming chief engineer of the electronics division of Del Mar Engineering Laboratories in Los Angeles. He also organized and headed Del Mar's avionics research division.

From 1959 to 1963 Thornton attended medical school at North Carolina. He completed his internship in 1964 at Wilford Hall Air Force Hospital at Lackland AFB, Texas, then returned to active duty. At the Aerospace Medical Division at Brooks AFB, Texas, Thornton became involved in the study of human adaptation to spaceflight. He worked on a program of exercise for the Manned Orbiting Laboratory with Dr. Kenneth Cooper, later known as the "father" of aerobic fitness.

Thornton was one of 11 scientist-astronauts selected by NASA in August 1967, at a time when NASA expected to make several Apollo flights a year both to the Moon and in Earth orbit well into the 1970s. Shortly after the new scientist-astronauts reported, however, NASA's budget was cut and it was soon apparent that most of the 1967 group would have to wait years for a flight, if they got one at all. They dubbed themselves the XS-11, "Excess Eleven." By 1972 four of them would leave NASA without going into space.

Thornton was one of those who stayed, completing Air Force flight training at Reese AFB, Texas, in 1968, to become, at 39, a jet pilot. He would eventually log over 2,500 hours of flying time.

He was involved in the development of the Skylab orbital workshop, joining astronauts Robert Crippen and Karol Bobko for the Skylab Medical Experiments Altitude Test (SMEAT), a 56-day simulation of a Skylab mission, in 1970. And he served as member of the support crew and capcom for all three Skylab missions in 1973-74.

After Skylab, in 1976, Thornton took a year's leave from NASA to study internal medicine at the University of Texas Medical School at Galveston, where he would eventually become a clinical instructor. Returning to the astronaut office, he took part in SMD III, a simulation of a Spacelab life sciences mission, and developed SAS experiments for STS-4, STS-5, STS-6 and STS-7.

In 1977 he applied as a candidate payload specialist for Spacelab 1, but was not selected.

Following his two Shuttle flights Thornton continued his research into exercise and SAS countermeasure equipment for extended duration Shuttle and space station missions. An inventor as well as a scientist and astronaut, Thornton holds 35 patents. He retired from NASA and the astronaut office on May 31, 1994.

Thornton continues to serve as a clinical assistant professor at the Department of Medicine, University of Texas-Galveston, as well as an adjunct professor at the University of Houston-Clear Lake.

Thuot, Pierre Joseph
1955–

Pierre Thuot took part in the riskiest satellite rescue in manned space history.

As mission specialist in the crew of STS-49, the maiden voyage of the orbiter Endeavour in May 1992, Thuot made a record three space walks, ultimately—with the help of fellow astronauts Rick Hieb and Tom Akers—retrieving the errant Intelsat VI satellite after two failed attempts.

Thuot and Hieb first attempted to latch on to Intelsat on day 4 of the STS-49 mission, only to learn that the 2-ton satellite was far more sensitive to motion than had previously been believed. Thuot merely touched a special capture bar to the satellite, which immediately began to rotate away from him. A second EVA on mission day 4 also ended in failure: Thuot appeared to have gently placed the capture bar in the proper position, only to have it float away when the latches were to fire.

The space walkers, members of a crew of 7, spent a day considering their options, then emerged on mission day 6 with a plan to capture the satellite by hand. Joining Thuot and Hieb was mission specialist Akers, who had been scheduled to take a different kind of space walk during the flight. As Endeavour commander Dan Brandenstein and pilot Kevin Chilton slowly brought the orbiter within a few feet of Intelsat, Thuot and his companions positioned themselves in the payload bay. On Thuot's signal, they reached out and literally grabbed the satellite with their gloves, slowing it to a stop. Once that was accomplished, Thuot was able to attach the balky capture bar, which allowed robot arm specialist Bruce Melnick to place Intelsat atop its new rocket motor. At the end of the record 8.5 hour space walk, Intelsat VI was sent spinning out of the payload

bay. A day later it was boosted into its intended geosynchronous orbit.

Thuot previously served as mission specialist aboard STS-36, a 4-day dedicated-Department of Defense Shuttle mission, in February and March 1990. During the flight he took part in the deployment of a 15-ton Crystal imaging reconnaissance satellite.

In March 1994 he made his third Shuttle flight in the crew of STS-62, which carried the U.S. Microgravity Payload, a set of experiments that were operated by the crew of 5 over 14 days.

The son of a Navy captain, Thuot was born May 19, 1955, in Groton, Connecticut, and graduated from high school in Fairfax, Virginia, in 1973. He attended the US Naval Academy, receiving a B.S. in physics in 1977, and later earned an M.S. in systems management from the University of Southern California in 1985.

After graduation from Annapolis, Thuot was trained as a naval flight officer. From 1978 through 1981 he flew aboard F-14s based on the carriers *U.S.S. John F. Kennedy* and *U.S.S. Independence* in the Mediterranean and Caribbean seas. He also attended the Naval Fighter Weapons School, better known as "Top Gun," and in 1982 graduated from the Naval Test Pilot School at Patuxent River, Maryland. He was an instructor at Pax River when chosen by NASA.

Thuot logged over 2,600 hours of flying time in 40 different aircraft, making over 270 carrier landings.

He was one of the 13 astronauts selected by NASA in June 1985 and in August 1986 qualified as a Shuttle mission specialist. His first technical assignment was in the mission development branch, working on EVA and RMS systems. His next assignment, in August 1987, was to the mission support branch, where he worked at the Shuttle Avionics Integration Laboratory (SAIL) and at mission control as a capcom (STS-26 through STS-30).

Captain Thuot left the astronaut office in the summer of 1995. He is currently an instructor at Annapolis.

Townsend Ronald Dean
1948–

Air Force meteorologist Ron Townsend was one of 2 alternate payload specialists chosen for the Air Force Weather Officer in Space Experiment (WOSE), originally scheduled for a Space Shuttle flight in late 1986. The Challenger disaster indefinitely postponed the WOSE mission.

Townsend was born June 19, 1948, in Concordia, Kansas, where he graduated from high school in 1966. He attended Bethany College and Kansas State University, receiving a B.S. (1970) and M.S. (1972) in mathematics. He would later receive a Ph.D. in atmospheric dynamics from the University of Wisconsin at Madison through the Air Force Institute of Technology in 1980.

Entering the Air Force via R.O.T.C., Townsend's first duty station was at Offutt AFB, Nebraska, where he was a weather forecaster and staff officer for Air Force Global Weather Central. Following graduate school, he was assigned to the Satellite Control Facility at Sunnyvale, California, as staff meteorologist. At the time of his selection for the WOSE program in 1985 he was commander of Detachment 8, 20th Weather Squadron, at Kadena AFB on Okinawa. From 1986 to 1990 he was stationed at Scott AFB, Illinois. He served with the Air Combat Command at Langely AFB, Virginia, until his retirement from the Air Force in 1995.

Trinh, Eugene Huu-Chau
1950–

Physicist Eugene Trinh was a payload specialist in the crew of STS-50, the first U.S. Microgravity Laboratory mission. Launched on June 25, 1992, USML-1 was a 14-day Spacelab mission during which two payload specialists and five astronauts conducted more than 30 experiments in space manufacturing and materials processing.

He previously served as backup payload specialist for Spacelab 3 (Mission 51-B) in April and May 1985,

supporting the scientific work aboard the lab from the payload operations center at the NASA Marshall Space Center.

Trinh was born September 14, 1950, in Saigon, South Vietnam. He came to the United States to attend school, earning a B.S. in engineering science from Columbia University in 1972, and, from Yale University, an M.S. (1974), M.Ph. (1976) and Ph.D. (1978) in applied physics.

After a year and a half as a postdoctoral fellow at Yale, Trinh joined the staff of the Jet Propulsion Laboratory in Pasadena, California, where his research involved fluid mechanics and acoustics. His work required dozens of flights aboard the NASA KC-135 aircraft flying "low-G" parabolas, simulating weightlessness for short periods of time. He also holds three patents and has published over 30 technical papers.

Trinh worked in a group headed by Dr. Taylor Wang preparing a Drop Dynamics Module experiment for Spacelab 3. When Wang was selected in June 1983 to fly aboard Spacelab 3, Trinh was chosen as his backup.

Following the Spacelab 3 mission he became a technical group leader at JPL. In 1988 he became been a project scientist for the modular containerless processing facility. Since August 1995 he has been supervisor of the advanced materials and fluid processing technology group.

Truly, Richard Harrison
1937–

Navy test pilot Dick Truly made two Space Shuttle flights, as pilot of STS-2 in November 1981, and as commander of STS-8 in August and September 1983. During STS-2 Truly and commander Joe Engle became the first astronauts to go into space aboard a "used" spacecraft, the Shuttle Columbia, which had made its first trip into orbit the previous April. Truly and Engle's flight, launched on November 12, 1981, Truly's forty-fourth birthday, was the first to test the Canadian-built Remote Manipulator System (RMS), the robot arm. The flight had to be cut from five days to two by a faulty fuel cell.

Truly later commanded STS-8, the first nighttime Shuttle launch and landing. The crew for this 6-day flight included America's first black astronaut, Guy Bluford, and 54-year-old physician William Thornton. The astronauts deployed a satellite for India and conducted tests of the ability of the RMS to move heavy payloads. Unknown at the time, one of the STS-8 solid rocket boosters came close to burning through its casing, which could have resulted in a catastrophe like that which would later destroy Challenger and claim the lives of the 7 crewmen of Mission 51-L.

In February 1986, following that disaster, Truly was named head of the entire Space Shuttle program.

Truly was born November 12, 1937, in Fayette, Mississippi, and attended schools in Fayette and Meridien, Mississippi. A Navy ROTC student, he graduated from the Georgia Institute of Technology with a B.S. in aeronautical engineering in 1959.

Truly completed flight training at Beeville, Texas, in 1960, then was assigned to Fighter Squadron 33, serving aboard the carriers *U.S.S. Intrepid* and *U.S.S. Enterprise*, making more than 300 carrier landings. In 1963 and 1964 he attended the Air Force Aerospace Research Pilot School at Edwards AFB, California, and upon graduation became an instructor there.

In November 1965 Lieutenant Truly was one of 8 astronauts selected for the Air Force Manned Orbiting Laboratory program. He remained with the MOL program until its termination, and in September 1969 was one of 7 MOL pilots who transferred to NASA as astronauts.

As a pilot Truly has logged almost 7,000 hours of flying time in many different types of aircraft.

At NASA Truly worked on the Skylab program, eventually serving on the support crew and as capcom for all three manned missions. He was also a capcom and member of the support crew for the Apollo-Soyuz Test Project.

At the end of 1975 Truly was teamed with Joe Engle as one of the astronaut crews for the Approach and Landing Test of the Shuttle Enterprise. Between June and October 1977 Truly and Engle took part in captive flights, in which the Enterprise remained attached to its Boeing 747 carrier, and in two of the five free flights, when the Enterprise was released from its carrier plane to glide to landing at Edwards AFB. In March 1978 Engle and Truly were chosen as backups for STS-1, and in April 1981 were named to fly STS-2.

In October 1983 Truly left NASA to head the US Navy Space Command at Dahlgren, Virginia. He returned to NASA in February 1986 as associate administrator for space transportation systems, assisting NASA Administrator James Fletcher with returning the Shuttle to flight. In January 1989 Truly, then a vice admiral, succeeded Fletcher as NASA Administrator. He served until February 1992, when he was fired by President George Bush, reportedly for failing to accept White House suggestions for reorganizing the space agency.

He became a professor at his alma mater, Georgia Tech, as well as director of the Georgia Tech Institute. Since early 1997 he has been head of the National Renewable Energy Laboratory in Golden, Colorado.

Van den Berg, Lodewijk
1932–

Chemical engineer Lodewijk van dan Berg was a payload specialist aboard the Shuttle Mission 51-B/Spacelab 3 flight in April and May 1985. During that flight van den Berg was one of four astronaut scientists who conducted experiments in space medicine and manufacturing.

Van den Berg was born March 24, 1932, in Sluiskil, the Netherlands. He received an M.S. in chemical engineering from Technical University at Delft in the Netherlands in 1961, and later earned an M.S. and Ph.D. in applied science from the University of Delaware in 1972 and 1975. From 1961 to 1971 he was employed as a chemical engineer.

Since receiving his doctorate van den Berg has been a scientist with the EG&G Corporation in Goleta, California, specializing in the growth of crystals for scientific and industrial uses. One of the results of this work has been the publication of over 15 articles in scientific journals.

He took part in the design and development of the Spacelab 3 vapor crystal growth system experiment and in June 1983 was selected to supervise its operation, and the operation of other space manufacturing experiments, on the flight of Spacelab 3.

Following Spacelab 3 he was a candidate for the first U.S. Microgravity Spacelab mission (STS-50), but was not selected.

Vangen, Scott Duane

1959–

NASA engineer Scott Vangen was the alternate payload specialist for STS-67, the second Spacelab ASTRO mission, flown in March 1995. This 14-day mission carried a crew of 7, including payload specialists Sam Durrance and Ron Parise, and three ultraviolet telescopes. Vangen supported the flight from the Payload Operations Center at the NASA Marshall Spaceflight Center.

Vangen was born December 12, 1959, in Granite Falls, Minnesota, and attended the South Dakota School of Mines and Technology, where he received a B.S. in electrical engineering in 1982. He also holds an M.S. in space technology from the Florida Institute of Technology (1986).

Since 1982 he has worked with the NASA payload directorate at the NASA Kennedy Space Center as an engineer in spacecraft checkout and avionics. In this capacity he worked in support of the first ASTRO mission, STS-35, launched in December 1990.

Vangen was also a finalist in the December 1994 and May 1996 astronaut candidate selections.

Van Hoften, James Dougal Adrianus

1944–

James van Hoften, better known to his fellow astronauts as "Ox" because of his size, took part in two different space walks repairing damaged satellites.

Van Hoften was a mission specialist aboard Shuttle Mission 41-C, launched April 6, 1984, and intended to retrieve, repair, and redeploy the ailing Solar Maximum Mission satellite, which had been in space for four years. The first attempt to grab the satellite, by astronaut George Nelson using the Manned Maneuvering Unit backpack, failed, but the next day astronaut Terry Hart succeeded, using the orbiter's remote manipulator arm to haul Solar Max into the payload bay of the Challenger. Van Hoften did the major repairs on the satellite during a 7-hour EVA.

On van Hoften's second flight, Mission 51-I in August and September 1985, he also had the chance to demonstrate his satellite repair skills. The Hughes Leasat 3, had failed to launch itself into a higher orbit after being deployed by the Mission 51-D astronauts in April. During a record-breaking 7-hour, 8-minute space walk on August 31, 1985, van Hoften grabbed the drum-shaped, 7.5 ton satellite and attached a specially designed capture bar to it, so it could be lowered to the orbiter Discovery's payload bay for repairs. The process was complicated by problems with the robot arm, which limited its movements, but was completed. Astronaut William Fisher did most of the repair work, "hot wiring" the satellite so its rockets would fire on command. During a second space walk on September 1, van Hoften, perched on the end of the robot arm, literally pushed the satellite into a 3 revolutions-per-minute spin, then shoved it into space.

By the end of October, Leasat 3 was on station in its geosynchronous orbit and operating as designed.

Van Hoften was born June 11, 1944, in Fresno, California, and grew up in Burlingame. He graduated from Mills High School in nearby Milbrae in 1962, then attended the University of California at Berkeley, where he received a B.S. in civil engineering in 1966. He went on to earn an M.S. and Ph.D. in hydraulic engineering from Colorado State University in 1968 and 1976.

After completing work on his master's van Hoften entered the Navy, completing jet pilot training in 1970. He was stationed at Miramar, California, then flew F-4 Phantoms on 60 combat missions from the carrier *U.S.S. Ranger* in Southeast Asia. He left the Navy in 1974 and resumed his academic studies. In September 1976 he became assistant professor of civil engineering at the University of Houston, teaching fluid mechanics and performing research on valves for artificial hearts.

After leaving active duty van Hoften continued to fly with the Naval Reserve (1978 to 1980) and the Texas Air National Guard (1980 to 1986) in addition to NASA. He logged over 3,300 hours of flying time, most of it in jet aircraft.

Van Hoften was one of the 35 astronauts selected by NASA in January 1978. At 6 feet 4 inches and 200 pounds he was at the upper limit of NASA's newly relaxed astronaut physical requirements, hence the nickname "Ox." He completed the training and evaluation course in August 1979, then worked at the Flight Systems Laboratory in Downey, California, on Shuttle computer software. He also led the astronaut support team at the Kennedy Space Center from 1981 to 1982, until being named to his first flight crew.

In July 1985 he was assigned to a third Shuttle mission scheduled for launch in 1986. When that mission was canceled in July 1986 following the Challenger disaster, van Hoften resigned from NASA to join Bechtel National, Inc., in San Francisco, where he is vice president and general manager of the Hong Kong Airport project.

Van Hoften one of five friends profiled in Larry Colton's memoir *Goat Brothers* (1995).

Veach, Charles Lacy

1944–1995

Former Air Force fighter pilot Lacy Veach served as a mission specialist in the crew of STS-39, a Department of Defense Shuttle flight of April and May 1991. During the 8-day mission a crew of 7 astronauts deployed and retrieved the Infrared Background Signature Survey satellite and operated a series of military experiments, including CIRRIS 1A, an infrared sensor designed to track hostile missiles in the upper atmosphere. Operation of CIRRIS and related experiments was Veach's job during one of the 12-hour working shifts.

Veach made a second flight aboard STS-52 in October 1992. This flight of the orbiter Columbia deployed the Lageos II satellite.

Veach was born September 18, 1944, in Chicago, and grew up in Honolulu. He graduated from Punahou School there in 1962, then entered the Air Force Academy in Colorado Springs, graduating with a B.S. in engineering management in 1966.

After earning his pilot's wings, Veach was assigned to duty in Vietnam, flying 275 combat missions in the F-100 aircraft. His next assignment was with USAF units in England flying the F-100 and F-111. Veach returned to Southeast Asia in 1973 for a tour flying F-105s with the 17th Wild Weasel Squadron. In 1974 he was stationed at Nellis

AFB, Nevada, as an F-105 instructor pilot and aide to the commander of the Tactical Fighter Weapons School.

From 1975 to 1977 Veach was member of the U.S. Air Force air demonstration team, the Thunderbirds. Following an assignment with Headquarters, Tactical Air Command at Langley AFB, Virginia, Veach left active duty in 1981. He continued to fly F-16s with the Texas Air National Guard, ultimately logging over 5,000 flying hours.

Veach joined NASA in January 1982 as an engineer and research pilot based at the Johnson Space Center, where he was an instructor pilot for the Shuttle Training Aircraft. He was one of the 17 astronauts selected by NASA in May 1984 and in August 1985 qualified as a Shuttle mission specialist. He served as a capcom for Shuttle Missions 61-B, 61-B and 61-C, and worked in the Shuttle Avionics Integration Laboratory (SAIL). He was assigned to STS-39 in May 1989.

In 1993 Veach was diagnosed with brain cancer. He died on October 2, 1995.

Vidrine, David Matthew

1943–

Navy engineer Dave Vidrine came within a single phone call of becoming first Manned Spaceflight Engineer to make a Shuttle flight. He was training as a payload specialist for Mission 41-C, the Shuttle flight that retrieved and repaired the ailing Solar Max satellite, in April 1984, when a last-minute decision took him off the crew. Vidrine left the MSE program, of which he was director, shortly thereafter.

Vidrine was born November 21, 1943, in Ville Platte, Louisiana. He moved with his family to Lafayette in 1955 and graduated from high school there in 1961. Growing up, Vidrine was interested in aviation, and following the launch of Sputnik in October 1957, in space exploration. He attended South West Louisiana University in Lafayette, intending to major in aeronautical engineering, but found that it wasn't offered and settled for mechanical engineering instead. He would later earn a B.S. in aeronautics (1973) and an M.S. in aeronautical engineering (1974) from the Naval Postgraduate School.

Vidrine joined the Navy aviation cadet program in February 1964 and entered pilot training. About two-thirds of the way through the program he switched to navigator training, a move he later regretted, in spite of the fact that he believed it saved him from being shot down over North Vietnam, as were many of his classmates.

Stationed at McGuire AFB, New Jersey, Vidrine did one tour in Southeast Asia, flying C-130 cargo planes. Returning to the United States, he was an instructor at Pensacola for two years, then a P-3 crewman at Jacksonville for another two years. He ultimately logged over 2,500 hours of flying time.

From 1972 to 1975 he was in Monterey, California, attending the Naval Postgraduate School.

Between 1975 and 1980 Vidrine was assigned to the Navy Space Project, first at Los Angeles Air Force Station, then in Washington, D.C. He was selected for the Manned Spaceflight Engineer program in February 1980, and commuted between Washington and Los Angeles for most of the year.

As an MSE, Vidrine became thoroughly familiar with Space Shuttle systems and operations, with a wide variety of military satellites and research payloads, and with NASA centers, including the Marshall Spaceflight Center in Alabama, where MSEs donned spacesuits and took part in EVA simulations in the huge water tank. In November 1983 Vidrine was named director of manned spaceflight, the head of the MSE program.

Upon leaving the program and retiring from the Navy Vidrine worked for TRW Space Systems in Los Angeles for six years. He is currently employed by Hughes Aircraft in Tucson, Arizona.

Vidrine has also published science fiction stories as "D. M. Vidrine."

Voss, James Shelton
1949–

Army flight test engineer Jim Voss is scheduled to command the second incremental crew to occupy the International Space Station during its assembly. Voss, NASA astronaut Susan Helms and Russian cosmonaut Yuri Usachev are scheduled to be delivered to the ISS by the orbiter Discovery (STS-101) in June 2000, commencing a 5-month mission.

Voss is a veteran of three previous Shuttle missions, beginning with STS-44, a flight of the orbiter Atlantis launched in November 1991. Voss oversaw the deployment of a DSP (Defense Support Program) early warning satellite into into geosynchronous orbit. In November 1992 he was aboard STS-53, which deployed a military data relay satellite. His third mission was STS-69, in September 1995. That mission deployed the Wake Shield Facility. Voss and fellow astronaut Michael Gernhardt also made a 6-hour EVA.

Since January 1996 Voss has been training at the Gagarin Cosmonaut Training Center as backup Shuttle-Mir crewmember for astronaut Michael Foale, who served aboard Mir from April to September 1997, and for the last Shuttle-Mir crewmember, Andrew Thomas.

Voss was born March 3, 1949, in Cordova, Alabama, though he grew up in Opelika, where he graduated from high school. He attended Auburn University, receiving a B.A. in aerospace engineering in 1972, and in 1974 earned an M.S. in aerospace engineering sciences from the University of Colorado.

Voss entered the Army as a second lieutenant upon graduation from Auburn. Following work on his master's at Colorado, he underwent Infantry, Airborne, and Ranger training, then served as platoon leader, intelligence staff officer, and company commander with the 2nd Battalion, 48th Infantry based in Germany. Returning to the United States in 1979 he became an instructor in mechanics at West Point. In 1982 he entered the Naval Test Pilot School at Patuxent River, Maryland, where he was named outstanding student in his class. He was then assigned to Army Aviation Engineering Flight Activity at Edwards AFB, California, as a flight test engineer.

In November 1984 he was detailed to the NASA Johnson Space Center as a vehicle integration test engineer, working on Shuttle missions 51-D, 51-F, 61-C, and 51-L. He was taking part in the 51-L accident investigation when selected for astronaut training in June 1987.

Voss qualified as a Shuttle mission specialist in August 1988. From May 1988 to July 1989 he worked as flight crew representative for Shuttle safety, then served as a capcom in mission control from STS-28 (August

1989) through STS-35 (December 1990). He was assigned to STS-44 in May 1990. In 1993 Voss served as training officer for astronaut candidates.

Voss, Janice Elaine
1957–

Janice Voss has been a mission specialist on four Shuttle missions. Her first was STS-57, a June 1993 flight of the orbiter Discovery that carried the first SpaceHab equipment and experiment module. She flew with another SpaceHab payload on STS-63. This February 1995 flight of the orbiter Atlantis also made the first American rendezvous with the Russian Mir space station.

Voss then served as payload commander for the Materials Science Laboratory, first launched as STS-83 in April 1997. When STS-83 had to be shortened because of a fuel cell problem, NASA officials elected to refly the crew and payload on the next opportunity, as STS-94 in July 1997. This MSL flight lasted a full 16 days, conducting over 33 experiments from 23 different nations in combustion, fluid dynamics, and other processes that will be used in manufacturing aboard the International Space Station.

Voss was born October 8, 1956, in South Bend, Indiana, but considers Rockford, Illinois, to be her hometown. She received a B.S. in engineering science from Purdue University in 1975, as well as an M.S. (1977) and Ph.D. (1987) in aeronautics/astronautics from the Massachusetts Institute of Technology. She has also studied at the University of Oklahoma and at Rice University.

Voss worked as a co-op at the NASA Johnson Space Center from 1973 to 1975 doing computer simulations. After a 2-year break doing graduate work at M.I.T., she returned to J.S.C. in 1977 and worked as a crew trainer in entry guidance and navigation. Following completion of her doctorate in 1987 Voss joined the Orbital Sciences Corporation to work on the Transfer Orbit Stage, an upper stage that deployed the Advanced Communications Technology Satellite on STS-51 in 1993.

She applied for the astronaut group four times before being accepted as one of 23 astronaut candidates selected by NASA in January 1990. In July 1991 she qualified as a Shuttle mission specialist while working in the mission development branch on Spacelab/SpaceHab. She is currently assigned to the robotics branch.

Walheim, Rex Joseph
1962–

Air Force engineer Rex Walheim is one of the 35 astronaut candidates selected by NASA on May 1, 1996. In August of that year he reported to the Johnson Space Center to begin a training and evaluation course that should qualify him as a Shuttle mission specialist and International Space Station crewmember. He is currently assigned to the vehicle systems/operations branch of the astronaut office.

Walheim was born October 10, 1962, in Redwood City, California, and grew up in San Carlos, where he graduated from high school in 1980. He attended the University of California at Berkeley, receiving a B.S. in mechanical engineering in 1984. He later earned an M.S. in industrial engineering from the University of Houston (1989).

Walheim entered the Air Force through R.O.T.C. in May 1984, and following basic training was assigned to Cavalier AFS, North Dakota, as a missile warning operations crew commander. He transferred to the NASA Johnson Space Center in October 1986, serving as a mechanical systems flight controller and as lead operations engineer for the Shuttle's landing gear, brakes, and emergency runway barrier.

In August 1989 Walheim became manager of a program upgrading missile warning radars at HQ USAF Space Command, Colorado Springs, Colorado. Two years later he attended the Air Force Test Pilot School at Edwards AFB, California, graduating as the outstanding flight test engineer of Class 92A. He was assigned to the F-16 Combined Test Force at Edwards as a project manager. At the time of his selection as an ASCAN he was an instructor at the Test Pilot School.

Walker, Charles David
1948–

Charles Walker became the first commercial (paying) space traveler when he served as payload specialist on Shuttle Mission 41-D in August and September 1984. An employee of the McDonnell Douglas Corporation, which paid NASA $80,000 to cover the costs of his training, Walker operated his company's electrophoresis unit, a machine designed to manufacture drugs in space. The unit flew on missions 51-D (April 1985) and 61-B (November–December 1985) in addition to 41-D.

There had been previous space travelers who were not career astronauts, such as STS-9 payload specialists Byron Lichtenberg and Ulf Merbold. But Lichtenberg and Merbold were career scientists with qualifications similar to those of professional astronauts who had undergone years of training prior to their flight. Walker's training, on the other hand, consisted of only 125 hours of workbook instruction, with some hands-on study.

The electrophoresis project, technically known as the Continuous Flow Electrophoresis System (CFES), was a joint venture of McDonnell Douglas and the Ortho Pharmaceutical Division of Johnson & Johnson that was designed to produce a medical hormone. Electrophoresis is a process in which an electric charge is used to separate biological materials. It works most efficiently in microgravity, where it is able to process 463 times as much material as it can on Earth.

Under an agreement between the companies and NASA, the CFES unit was intended to fly on the Shuttle without fee until the companies began to sell the hormone, at which time McDonnell Douglas would become a paying customer.

Earlier versions of CFES were flown on STS-4, STS-6, STS-7, and STS-8, and operated by astronauts, but a full-scale machine designed to run for an entire week required an onboard specialist. Walker, who had worked on CFES since 1978 and had trained the astronauts who used the earlier model, was the only candidate considered by McDonnell Douglas. His assignment to the crew of Mission 41-D, then known as STS-12, was made in June 1983.

As luck would have it, Walker had to perform on the spot repairs to the CFES unit during the first flight. The hormone had become contaminated. During the second flight, however, Walker reported that hardware and contamination problems had been overcome, and on the third flight Walker actually produced some of the hormone, paving the way for flights by a still more advanced machine called EOS. Following the Challenger disaster in 1986, however, the whole CFES/EOS project was shelved.

Walker was born August 29, 1948, in Bedford, Indiana, where he grew up and became interested in space-flight. he attended Purdue University, receiving a B.S. in aeronautical and astronautical engineering in 1971.

In 1972 he went to work for the Bendix Aerospace Company as a design engineer; he was later employed in the same capacity by the Naval Sea Systems Command Engineering Center in Crane, Indiana. Walker joined McDonnell Douglas in 1977. During that time he applied for the NASA astronaut group, but was not selected. Ironically, he flew in space before many who were selected.

Since his three flights Walker has served as special assistant for space station to the president of McDonnell Douglas. He is currently Senior Manager, space station Division, Space Programs Development at that company's office in Arlington, Virginia.

Walker is also president of the National Space Society.

Walker, David Mathiesen
1944–

Navy test pilot Dave Walker was commander of STS-30, a 5-day mission of the orbiter Discovery during which the Magellan Venus probe was deployed. Eight months after deployment in May 1989 Magellan successfully entered orbit around Venus and began to produce the most detailed images yet of the surface of that world.

In December 1992 Walker was commander of STS-53. This flight of Discovery deployed DOD-1, a classified Department of Defense payload later reported to be a relay satellite for intelligence data. Walker's third command was STS-69, which deployed and retrieved the

Wake Shield Facility and the Spartan 201 solar astronomy satellite, during an 11-day Endeavour mission in September 1995.

Walker previously served as pilot aboard Shuttle Mission 51-A in November 1984, during which astronauts Joseph Allen and Dale Gardner performed the first "space salvage" operation, collecting two malfunctioning satellites and stowing them in the payload bay of the orbiter Discovery for return to Earth. The 51-A crew also deployed two new satellites.

Walker was born May 20, 1944, in Columbus, Georgia, and grew up in Eustis, Florida, where he graduated from high school in 1962. He attended the Naval Academy at Annapolis, receiving a bachelor of science degree in 1966.

Walker underwent flight training in Florida, Mississippi and Texas, and after becoming a naval aviator in 1967, served two combat tours in Vietnam as an F-4 Phantom pilot flying from the carriers *U.S.S. Enterprise* and *U.S.S. America*. After returning to the United States in 1970 he attended the Air Force Aerospace Research Pilot School at Edwards AFB, California, then was assigned to the Navy's Air Test Center at Patuxent River, Maryland, as a test pilot. He later became an F-14 pilot aboard the *America* in the Mediterranean and was based at Oceana, Virginia, when chosen by NASA.

He logged over 7,000 hours of flying time, including 6,500 hours in jets.

Walker was one of the 35 astronauts selected by NASA in January 1978 and qualified as a Shuttle pilot in August 1979. He served as a chase plane pilot for STS-1 and has worked on Shuttle computer software at the Shuttle Avionics Integration Laboratory (SAIL). Other technical assignments include a tour as technical assistant to the director of flight crew operations (1981), mission support group leader (1982–83), and head of the astronaut support team at the Kennedy Space Center (1985). He was in training to command Shuttle Mission 61-G, scheduled for May 1986 when the Challenger accident forced NASA to suspend all Shuttle flights. Following STS-30 in 1989 he acted as head of the space station design and development branch of the astronaut office.

On May 5, 1989, while piloting a NASA T-38 to Washington, D.C., for ceremonies honoring the crew of STS-30, Walker had a near miss with an Airbus jetliner. That encounter and other infractions of NASA flying rules caused him to be grounded from July to September 1990, costing him the command of STS-44, to which he had been assigned in April 1990.

Walker's last technical assignments were chief of the station/exploration support office in the flight crew operations directorate and chairman of the JSC safety review board.

He retired from the Navy and resigned from NASA in April 1996 to become vice president for sales and marketing for NDC Voice Communications, San Diego, California.

Walker, Joseph Albert
1921–1966

Joe Walker, aside from Chuck Yeager, the best-known pilot of the rocket plane era at Edwards Air Force Base, made 25 flights in the X-15 between March 1960 and August 1963. He established a world speed record of 4,104 miles per hour in the X-15, and on three different occasions piloted the rocket plane to an altitude greater than 50 miles, including his final X-15 flight on August 22, 1963, which reached 354,300 feet, an altitude of almost 67 miles. In fact, two of Walker's X-15 flights exceeded 62 miles altitude and qualified as spaceflights to the International Aeronautical Federation (FAI).

Walker was killed in a midair collision between his F-104 Starfighter and the XB-70 on June 8, 1966.

Walker was born February 20, 1921, in Washington, Pennsylvania, and grew up on a farm there. He attended Washington and Jefferson College, graduating in 1942 with a B.A. in physics.

He enrolled in the civilian pilot training program in 1941 and, after graduation from college, entered the Army Air Corps. He flew P-38s in combat over North Africa and Italy during World War II. Returning to the States in 1945, he left the Army and went to work for the National Advisory Committee on Aeronautics (NACA) as a physicist at its Lewis Laboratory in Cleveland. NACA, the forerunner of NASA, soon transferred Walker to research flying, and in 1951 he moved to the NACA test facility at Edwards Air Force Base, California.

For the next 15 years Walker flew the hottest airplanes and rocket planes in the world, serving as project pilot on the D-558, X-1, X-3 (which he considered the worst plane he ever flew), X-4, and X-5. He also served as research pilot on the B-47, F-100, F-101, F-102, and F-104. In addition to becoming the prime NASA pilot for the X-15, Walker also helped develop the lunar landing training vehicle, the so-called flying bedstead, which his X-15 backup, Neil Armstrong, would later use to rehearse a landing on the Moon.

Like Yeager, who was famous for his "Aw, shucks" approach to test flying, Walker affected a casual, fatalistic attitude, claiming that for pilots in trouble, the only option was to "put yourself in the hands of a supernatural power." He was honored by his fellow test pilots with the Robert J. Collier Trophy, the Harmon International Trophy for Aviators, the Iven Kincheloe Award, and the Octave Chanute Award, all in 1961. He was a charter member of the Society of Experimental Test Pilots.

Walz, Carl Erwin

1955–

Air Force physicist Carl Walz is assigned as member of the fourth incremental crew scheduled to occupy the International Space Station during its assembly phase. Walz, with NASA astronaut Dan Bursch and Russian cosmonaut Yuri Onufriyenko, is to be delivered to the ISS by the orbiter Atlantis (STS-105) in early 2000.

Walz is a veteran of three previous Shuttle missions, beginning with STS-51 (September 1993). STS-51 deployed the Advanced Communications Technology Satellite (ACTS). In July 1994 Walz was a crewmember aboard the second International Microgravity Laboratory (STS-65), a 15-day mission during which the crew of 7 conducted over 80 experiments in life sciences. Walz's third mission was STS-79, the fourth Shuttle-Mir docking, in September 1996.

Walz was born September 6, 1955, in Cleveland, Ohio. He received a B.S. in physics from Kent State University in 1977, and an M.S. in solid state physics from John Carroll University, Ohio, in 1979.

Walz entered the Air Force upon graduation from Kent State in 1977, though he did not commence active duty until completion of his graduate work in 1979. His first Air Force assignment was as radiochemical project officer with the 1155th Technical Operations Squadron at McClellan AFB, California. In this job he was responsible for analysis of radioactive samples from the Atomic Energy Detection System.

In 1982 he enrolled as a flight engineer at the US Air Force Test Pilot School at Edwards AFB, California. From January 1983 to June 1987 he was a member of the F-16 Combined Test Force at Edwards. At the time of his selection by NASA he was flight test program manager at Detachment 3, Air Force Flight Test Center, better known as Area 51.

He was one of the 23 astronaut candidates selected by NASA in January 1990, and in July 1991 qualified as a Shuttle mission specialist. His technical assignments have included working on the flight data file for the mission support branch of the astronaut office, and as capcom.

Wang, Taylor Gun-Jin

1940–

Physicist Taylor Wang, a payload specialist aboard Spacelab 3, was one of the first scientists to go into space with a scientific experiment he had designed and built on Earth. During his spaceflight, Mission 51-B aboard the orbiter Challenger in April and May 1985, Wang also became the first scientist to repair his malfunctioning device.

Wang's Drop Dynamics Module, a machine in which drops of water, glycerine, and silicon oil can be manipulated and mixed by sound waves, was an experiment designed to demonstrate one of the basic elements of space manufacturing: "containerless processing." The DDM failed on its first day in space, forcing Wang and ground controllers to spend two days diagnosing the problem. Once they did that, Wang repaired the machine in three hours and exposed 15,000 feet of film before the DDM broke down permanently.

Wang and the six other astronauts, 2 squirrel monkeys, and 24 experimental rats aboard Spacelab 3 also conducted experiments in space medicine and atmospheric physics during the 8-day flight.

Wang was born in Shanghai, China, on June 16, 1940. His father was a businessman there who was forced to leave the country with his family when the Communist regime came to power in 1949. Wang grew up in Taiwan, then came to the United States, attending the University of California at Los Angeles, receiving his B.S. (1967), M.S. (1968), and Ph.D. (1971) in physics. He also became a U.S. citizen.

Wang joined the Jet Propulsion Laboratory at the California Institute of Technology in 1972 as a senior scientist. Eventually he became program manager for experiments devoted to materials processing in space. His experiments were flown on other Shuttle missions and on high-altitude aircraft and rocket flights. He holds ten patents.

Selected as a Spacelab 3 payload specialist in June 1983, Wang spent the next two years training at JPL and at NASA's Marshall Space Flight Center in Huntsville, Alabama.

Following his flight Wang left JPL and is currently Centennial Professor and Director of the Center for Microgravity Research and Applications at Vanderbilt University in Nashville, Tennessee.

Watterson, John Brett
1949–

Air Force engineer Brett Watterson was to have been one of two military payload specialists on the first Space Shuttle launched from Vandenberg Air Force Base, California.

That flight, originally designated Mission 62-A, was scheduled to carry the Teal Ruby satellite and the CIRRIS surveillance package, and was originally scheduled for launch in July 1986. Mission 62-A was first postponed by the explosion of the Shuttle Challenger in January 1986. It was later canceled altogether when the Air Force decided to mothball the $3-billion West Coast Shuttle launch facility before it could be used.

Watterson was born September 10, 1949, in Garden City, New York, and grew up in Littleton, Colorado, where he graduated from high school in 1967. He attended Virginia Military Institute, receiving a B.S. in physics in 1971. He later earned an M.S. in engineering physics (1976) from the Air Force Institute of Technology at Wright-Patterson AFB, Ohio.

Entering active duty with the Air Force, Watterson served at Korat Royal Thai AFB, Thailand, from 1972 to 1973, then spent three years with the Foreign Technology Division at Wright-Patterson. From 1976 to 1980 he was a systems engineer in the Secretary of the Air Force's Special Projects Office at Los Angeles AFS. In 1980 he became one of the first 13 DOD manned spaceflight engineers and after completing the initial training course worked in support of STS-4, the first DOD Shuttle mission.

In June 1982 he was assigned as a payload specialist for STS-16, a Shuttle mission scheduled to carry Teal Ruby into orbit in the summer of 1984. Problems with the Air Force's inertial upper stage, which surfaced during the STS-6 mission in April 1983, ultimately caused the cancellation of STS-16. Watterson was assigned to the Vandenberg mission in October 1984.

At the time of the Challenger disaster on January 28, 1986, Watterson was assigned to the payload specialist office at the NASA Johnson Space Center. In 1987, when it became clear that Mission 62-A was never going to fly, he transferred to Europe as director of a satellite downlink station.

He returned to the United States in 1990 and was assigned to a space policy position with the Office of Space Systems at the Pentagon. From 1993 until his retirement from the Air Force in September 1997 Watterson worked for the National Reconnaissance Office at Space and Missile Systems Center, Los Angeles AFB, California.

He currently works on commercial communications satellite systems for Hughes Space and Communications, El Segundo, California.

Weaver, Carol Lynn (Belt)
1953–

For four years Carol Weaver was a candidate to become the first meteorologist in space. A member of the Air Weather Service, she was selected in March 1988 as the prime payload specialist for the first

Weather Officer in Space Experiment, scheduled for a future Shuttle mission. During her mission she was to provide the first expert assessment of atmospheric conditions from a low-Earth orbit. The WOSE mission was canceled in 1992, however.

Weaver was born Carol Lynn Belt on January 30, 1953, in Red Oak, Iowa, where she grew up, graduating from high school in 1971. She attended Cottey College in Nevada, Missouri, receiving an A.A. degree (1973), followed by Texas A&M University, where she received a B.S. in meteorology (1975). She later earned an M.S. (1981) and Ph.D. (1984) in meteorology from St. Louis University.

Weaver entered the Air Force in October 1975, and after being commissioned in January 1976 served as a weather officer at Eielson AFB, Alaska. From 1978 to 1980 Weaver was an aerial reconnaissance weather officer at Andersen AFB, Guam, logging over 500 hours in the WC-130 Hercules aircraft that, among other tasks, flew through typhoons.

Following graduate work at St. Louis University, Weaver was assigned to Air Weather Service headquarters at Scott AFB, Illinois, where she served as assistant chief of the Projects Division in the Directorate of Special Projects. She was a semifinalist in the 1985 WOSE selection.

Following the cancellation of the WOSE mission, Weaver separated from the service. She is now a reserve officer.

Weber, Mary Ellen
1962–
Chemical engineer and sky-diver Mary Ellen Weber was a mission specialist in the crew of STS-70. This July 1995 flight of the orbiter Endeavour deployed the sixth and last Tracking and Data Relay Satellite.

Weber was born August 24, 1962, in Cleveland, Ohio, and graduated from high school in suburban Bedford. She attended Purdue University, receiving a B.S. in chemical engineering in 1984, then the University of California at Berkeley, where she received a Ph.D. in chemistry in 1988.

While an undergraduate Weber had internships with Ohio Edison, Delco Electronics and the 3M Corporation. After receiving her doctorate in 1988 she spent two years with Texas Instruments researching new techniques for microelectronic manufacturing. In 1990 she was assigned to the SEMATECH Division of Texas Instruments, Austin, Texas, where she worked as a materials engineer.

Weber was one of the 19 astronaut candidates selected by NASA on March 31, 1992 and in July 1993 qualified as a Shuttle mission specialist and space station crewmember. Her first technical assignment was with the astronaut support team at the Kennedy Space Center. She has also served a tour in SAIL and in the payload development branch.

Following her flight on STS-70 she was assigned to NASA Headquarters in Washington, D.C., to serve as a congressional liaison in the legislative affairs office.

Weber is not only an instrument-rated pilot, but a sky-diver with over 1,900 dives.

Weitz, Paul Jospeh
1932–
Paul "P.J." Weitz commanded STS-6, the first flight of the Space Shuttle Challenger, in April 1983. The Challenger, the second Shuttle in the NASA fleet, was scheduled to make its maiden voyage in January 1983, but engine problems kept it grounded for three more months. When it was finally launched on April 4, 1983, it performed flawlessly during five days in orbit. In addition to qualifying the Challenger for future flights, Weitz and fellow astronauts Karol Bobko, Donald Peterson, and Story Musgrave were to deploy the first Tracking and Data Relay Satellite, part of a planned system that would allow future Shuttle missions to remain in almost constant communication with mission control.

The Air Force Inertial Upper Stage (IUS), which was supposed to boost TDRS-A into its synchronous orbit 22,500 miles above the Earth, suffered a malfunction, placing the satellite in a useless, looping orbit. Ground controllers, firing tiny maneuvering rockets aboard TDRS, were eventually able to steer the satellite to its proper station, but only after weeks. The IUS problem forced the cancellation of at least three subsequent Shuttle missions.

STS-6 was Weitz's second spaceflight. Ten years earlier he was the pilot of Skylab 2, the first manned visit to America's orbiting laboratory. The SL-2 crew of Weitz, Charles Conrad, and Joseph Kerwin, almost had their flight canceled when Skylab was severely damaged during its ride to orbit on May 14, 1973. One of the station's two huge solar panels was torn off along with a vital sun shield, designed to wrap around the station, providing needed insulation and temperature control. Skylab appeared to be dead. But ground controllers postponed the SL-2 launch and quickly developed a makeshift sunshield that could be deployed by the astronaut crew.

SL-2 was launched on May 25, 1973, and made rendezvous with Skylab. As commander Charles Conrad maneuvered the Apollo-Skylab command and service module close to the huge station, Weitz leaned out the door of the CSM and tried to free the remaining solar panel, which was stuck in a closed position. Before Weitz could free the panel, however, darkness fell and he had to give up. The astronauts then docked with Skylab, after several harrowing attempts, and the next day entered the station, where the temperature was over 100 degrees F. Conrad and Kerwin managed to raise the makeshift sunshield—called the "parasol"—and freed the jammed solar panel during a space walk. Weitz later joined Conrad in another EVA. Eventually Skylab was restored to use and the astronauts completed the planned 28-day mission, a record at the time.

Weitz was born July 25, 1932, in Erie, Pennsylvania, and graduated from high school in nearby Harborcreek in 1950. He attended Pennsylvania State University as a Naval ROTC student, graduating with a B.S. in aeronautical engineering in 1954. He later earned an M.S. in aeronautical engineering from the Naval Postgraduate School in 1964.

Weitz entered active duty with the Navy in 1954 and served first in destroyers. He completed flight school in 1956 and was assigned to Jacksonville, Florida, as an instructor in tactics. In 1960 he was transferred to the Naval Weapons Center at China Lake, California, where he served as project officer for several different tests of air-to-ground delivery systems. Following further schooling at the Naval Postgraduate School, Weitz flew combat

missions in Vietnam. He was a detachment officer-in-charge at Whidbey Island, Washington, when selected by NASA.

Chosen as one of 19 astronauts in April 1966, Weitz specialized in the Apollo command and service module system. He served as capcom for Apollo 12 and had been informally selected as backup command module pilot for Apollo 17 (putting him in line for a flight to the Moon on Apollo 20) when congressional budget cuts eliminated that mission. In 1970 he began to work on the Apollo Applications Program Saturn Workshop, later known as Skylab, and was officially selected as pilot of Skylab 2 in January 1972.

On June 1, 1976, while working on Space Shuttle development, Captain Weitz retired from the Navy, though he remained with NASA as a civilian astronaut. He was assigned to command STS-6 in March 1982.

Following STS-6 Weitz served as deputy chief of the astronaut office, often flying the Shuttle Training Aircraft to check weather conditions just prior to Shuttle launches. In 1988 he became deputy director of the NASA Johnson Space Center and in 1993, acting director of JSC. He retired from NASA in April 1995.

Wetherbee, James Donald
1952–

Navy aviator James Wetherbee was commander of STS-63, the February 1995 flight of the orbiter Discovery that closed to within 30 feet of the Russian space station Mir. The planned rendezvous was designed to test mission control techniques and communications systems for a series of planned Shuttle-Mir dockings. Discovery's crew of 6 included Russian cosmonaut Vladimir Titov.

In September 1997 Wetherbee commanded STS-86, the sixth and most controversial of the Shuttle-Mir dockings. Final approval for the delivery of NASA-Mir crewmember Dave Wolf to the Russian station was not given until two days prior to launch. STS-86 did launch on schedule, delivering Wolf and three tons of water, food, and supplies to the beleaguered Russian station, and returned Michael Foale to earth.

Wetherbee also commanded STS-52, a November 1992 flight of the orbiter Columbia that deployed the LAGEOS-2 scientific satellite in earth orbit. While successful, the STS-52 mission was criticized as unnecessary because it used an expensive manned vehicle to deploy a relatively small satellite. It was later revealed that Wetherbee had carried the ashes of *Star Trek* creator Gene Roddenberry aboard Columbia.

Wetherbee had previously flown as pilot STS-32 in January 1990. This mission, one of the most complex attempted following the 1986 Challenger disaster, saw the successful deployment of the Syncom IV-5 communications satellite, and the retrieval and return to Earth of the Long Duration Exposure Facility.

Wetherbee was born November 27, 1952, in Flushing, New York, and graduated from Holy Family Diocesan High School in South Huntington, New York, in 1970. He attended Notre Dame, where he received a B.S. in aerospace engineering in 1974.

In 1975 Wetherbee joined the Navy, becoming a pilot in 1976. From 1977 to 1980 he served as an A-7E pilot aboard the carrier *U.S.S. John F. Kennedy*. He then attended the Naval Test Pilot School at Patuxent River, Maryland, and went on to spend three years as an F/A-18 test pilot. He was with Fighter Squadron 132 at the naval air station in Lemoore, California, when chosen by NASA.

He has logged over 4,200 hours of flying time in 20 different types of aircraft and has made 345 carrier landings.

Wetherbee was one of the 17 astronauts selected by NASA in May 1984. In June 1985 he qualified as a Shuttle pilot while serving as a capcom for Shuttle flights 51-G through 51-L. He has also been technical assistant to the director of flight crew operations.

From December 1989 to August 1990 Wetherbee was assigned as pilot of STS-46, until being promoted to commander of his own mission, STS-52. In 1993 he served at NASA Headquarters as a technical manager.

Since May 1995 Wetherbee has been deputy director of the Johnson Space Center, except for a year training for STS-86.

Wheelock, Douglas Harry

1960–

Army aviator Douglas Wheelock is one of the 25 astronaut candidates selected by NASA in June 1998. In August 1998 he began a training and evaluation course that should qualify him as a Shuttle mission specialist and International Space Station crewmember.

Wheelock was born May 5, 1960, in Binghamton, New York, graduating from Windsor (N.Y.) Central High School in 1978. He attended the U.S. Military Academy, receiving a B.S. in applied science in 1982, and later earned an M.S. in aerospace engineering from the Georgia Institute of Technology (1992).

At the time of his selection as an ASCAN, Major Wheelock was a space operations officer with the Army Space Command, assigned to the NASA Johnson Space Center.

White Alvin Swauger

1918–

Al White is the veteran corporate test pilot who was Scott Crossfield's backup for the X-15 rocket plane project. An employee of North American Aviation, White went through all the difficult training and physical conditioning that Crossfield did, but never flew the X-15. He did fly chase planes for many X-15 flights, however.

White was born December 9, 1918, in Berkeley, California, where he grew up. As a student at the University of California in 1940 he enrolled in the civilian pilot training program, which was designed to provide the military with a pool of pilots in the case of war. When World War II began, White joined the Army Air Corps, first as an instructor. He flew combat missions beginning in 1944.

Returning to the States in 1946, White left the Army and returned to Cal, where he received a B.S. in mechanical engineering in 1947. He tried the general contracting business for a while, but disliked it and rejoined the Air Force. He attended the Air Force Test Pilot School in 1951 and was a military test pilot until 1954.

In that year he went to work for North American Aviation in Los Angeles and was involved in the X-15 and in XB-70 Valkyrie supersonic bomber programs. On June 8, 1966, White was the pilot of an XB-70A when a chase plane piloted by former X-15 pilot Joe Walker collided with it. Walker was killed instantly. The huge XB-70, its vertical fins gone and its wings damaged, began to tumble out of the sky. White managed to eject; his copilot was killed.

White left North American shortly thereafter to become manager of flight operations research and development for TWA. In 1969 he formed Al White & Associates, an Irvine, California, aviation consulting firm.

Now retired, White lives in Tucson, Arizona.

White, Edward Higgins II
1930–1967

Air Force test pilot Ed White was the first American astronaut to take a walk in space. On June 3, 1965, White opened the hatch of the Gemini 4 spacecraft and, clad only in a special pressure suit and attached to the Gemini by a lifeline, floated free for 22 minutes, propelling himself with a small maneuvering gun that fired jets of gas while commander James McDivitt photographed him. Pictures of White floating in space became probably the most familiar of all space shots.

White and McDivitt returned to earth on June 7 after spending 4 days in space, an American record at the time.

In March 1966 White was chosen to be senior pilot of the first manned Apollo mission, scheduled for the first months of 1967. On January 27, 1967, White and astronauts Virgil Grissom and Roger Chaffee were killed on a flash fire inside their Apollo 1 spacecraft during testing on the launch pad at the Kennedy Space Center. White was buried at West Point.

White was born November 14, 1930, in San Antonio, Texas. His father was a pilot who later became an Air Force general. White attended the Military Academy at West Point, earning a bachelor of science degree in 1952. He later received a master of science degree in aeronautical engineering from the University of Michigan in 1959.

After graduation from West Point, White underwent Air Force pilot training in Florida and Texas, earning his wings in 1953. For almost four years he was an F-86 and

---

FIRST AMERICAN WALK IN SPACE

Ed White with Jim McDivitt

(On June 3, 1965, 4 hours and 18 minutes into the flight of Gemini 4, astronaut Ed White opened the spacecraft hatch and floated free, using a handheld, gas-powered gun to propel himself at the end of a tether, as commander Jim McDivitt observed.)

WHITE: The maneuvering unit is good. The only problem I have is that I haven't got enough fuel. I exhausted the fuel now and I was able to maneuver myself down to the bottom of the spacecraft, and I was right up on top of the adapter. . . . I'm looking right down and it looks like we're coming up on the coast of California. And I'm going in slow rotation to the right. There is absolutely no disorientation. . . .

McDIVITT (to Capcom): One thing about it, when Ed gets out there and starts whipping around—it sure makes it hard to control the spacecraft.

WHITE: O.K., I'm drifting down underneath the spacecraft. There's no difficult with recontacting the spacecraft . . . particularly as long as you move nice and slow. . . . Feel very grateful to be having the experience to be doing this.

(Fuel for the maneuvering gun ran out just four minutes in to the EVA, so White was forced to move around by tugging on his tether and pushing against the spacecraft.)

WHITE: The sun in space is not blinding, but it's quite nice. . . . I can sit out here and see the whole California coast.

McDIVITT: Hey, Ed, smile.

(Fully engaged in the novel experience, neither White nor McDivitt heard several calls from Gus Grissom,
the capcom, relaying concerns from flight director Christopher Kraft that White might be overdoing it.)

CAPCOM (Grissom): Gemini 4, Houston capcom.

McDIVITT: Gus, this is Jim, got any message for us?

CAPCOM (Grissom): The flight director says get back in.

. . .

McDIVITT (to White) They want you to get back in now.

WHITE (laughs): I'm not coming in. This is fun.

McDIVITT: Come on.

WHITE: Hate to come back to you, but I'm coming.

CAPCOM (GRISSOM): You've got about four minutes to
Bermuda.

WHITE: I'm trying to . . .

McDIVITT: Don't wear yourself out now. Just come on in. . . .
How you doing there?

WHITE: Whenever a piece of dirt or something goes by, it
always heads right for that door and goes on out.

McDIVITT: Okay, come in then.

WHITE: Aren't you going to hold my hand?

McDIVITT: No, come on in the . . . Ed, come on in here.

WHITE: All right, I'll open the door and come through
there. . . .

McDIVITT: Come on. Let's get back in here before it gets
dark.

WHITE: It's the saddest moment of my life.

McDIVITT: Well, you're going to find it sadder when we
have to come down with this thing.

CAPCOM (GRISSOM): Gemini 4. . . .

WHITE: I'm fixing to come in the house.

CAPCOM (GRISSOM): Gemini 4, get back in. . . . You getting
him back in?

McDIVITT: He's standing on the seat now and his legs are
below the instrument panel.

CAPCOM (GRISSOM): Okay, get him back in. You're going to
have Bermuda in about 20 seconds.

F-100 fighter pilot based in Germany, serving with future
astronaut colleagues Deke Slayton and Michael Collins.
He returned to the United States in 1958 to attend Michigan, and after completing his M.S. he entered the Air
Force Test Pilot School at Edwards AFB, California. After
graduating in 1960 he was assigned to Wright-Patterson
AFB, Ohio, as a test pilot.

At the time of his death he had logged over 4,200
hours of flying time, including 3,000 hours in jets.

White was one of the 9 astronauts selected by NASA
in September. In addition to assignments on Gemini 4 and
Apollo 1 he was backup commander for Gemini 7.

White, Robert Michael
1924–

Air Force test pilot Bob White
was the first person to pilot an
X-15 to an altitude greater
than 50 miles, thus winning Air
Force astronaut wings. On July
17, 1962, White flew X-15 number three to 314,750 feet, more
than 59 miles high, in the first unofficial "spaceflight" of
the X-15 program.

Several years later the Federation Aeronautique
International (FAI), the world aviation record-keeping
body, would define a spaceflight as any flight that
exceeded an altitude of 100 kilometers, or 62 miles.
White's flight, therefore, did not qualify (though two

other X-15 flights did); nevertheless, he was the first to pilot a winged rocket plane in near-space. The previous November he had also become the first pilot to fly six times the speed of sound. These accomplishments earned him a profile in *Life* magazine, which at that time was heavily involved in the promotion of the NASA Mercury astronauts. Tom Wolfe in *The Right Stuff* (1979) describes White as the epitome of the "blue suit" Air Force test pilot, unconcerned with and perhaps even uncooperative when it came to public relations, interested only in being the best pilot. During his nine years at Edwards, White was considered to be the best.

White was born July 6, 1924, in New York City, where he grew up. He joined the Army Air Corps in November 1942 at the age of 18, and became a pilot in February 1944.

During World War II he flew P-51s with the 355th Fighter Group in Europe. In February 1945, on his fifty-second combat mission, he was shot down over Germany, captured, and imprisoned until released that April. He returned to the States later that year and enrolled at New York University. He received a B.S. in electrical engineering from that institution in 1951.

He was recalled to active duty in May 1951 and served at Mitchell AFB, New York, and with the 40th Fighter Squadron based near Tokyo, Japan. He served as an engineer at the Rome Air Development Center in New York before going to Edwards AFB in California to enter the test pilot school in June 1954. He stayed at Edwards for 9 years.

Between October 1963 and May 1967 White served as an operations officer and squadron commander in Germany and attended George Washington University, where he earned an M.S. in business administration (1966). He also worked on the F-111 program at Wright-Patterson AFB, Ohio.

In 1967 and 1968 he did a tour of duty in Vietnam, flying 70 combat missions in the F-105. He returned to Wright-Patterson in June 1968, and two years later was named commander of the Flight Test Center at Edwards. While at Edwards he completed the Naval Test Parachutist course.

White left Edwards in November 1972 to become commandant of the ROTC at Maxwell AFB, Alabama, then chief of staff of the 4th Allied Tactical Air Force in Europe (1975). He retired on February 1, 1981.

Whitson, Paggy Annette
1960–

NASA scientist Peggy Whitson is one of the 35 astronaut candidates selected by the space agency on May 1, 1996. In August of that year she began a training and evaluation course that should qualify her as a Shuttle mission specialist and International Space Station crewmember.

Whitson was born February 9, 1960, in Mt. Ayr, Iowa, where she graduated from Mt. Ayr Community High School in 1978. She attended Iowa Wesleyan University, receiving a B. S. in biology/chemistry (1981). She later earned her Ph.D. in biochemistry from Rice University (1985).

While working on her doctorate at Rice Whitson was a Robert A. Welch Predoctoral Fellow. In 1986 she became a National Research Council Resident Associate at the NASA Johnson Space Center. Two years later she joined Krug International, a medical sciences firm that performed services for JSC as a contractor.

Whitson joined NASA in 1989 as a research biochemist in the biomedical operations and research branch. Her medical research payloads flew aboard STS-47 (Spacelab Japan) in 1992. That year she was named project scientist for the Shuttle-Mir program, working on STS-60, STS-63, STS-71, Mir-18, and Mir-19 while also serving as deputy chief of the medical sciences division at JSC.

Since 1991 Whitson has also been an adjunct professor in the department of internal medicine and the department of human biological chemistry and genetics, Unversity of Texas Medical Branch, Galveston.

Wilcutt, Terrence Wade
1949–

A former high school teacher, Marine test pilot Terry Wilcutt commanded STS-89, the eighth Shuttle-Mir docking mission, launched in January 1998. STS-89 delivered 6,000 pounds of cargo and water to the troubled Russian station, along with Andy Thomas, the last NASA-Mir crewmember, replacing astronaut Dave Wolf, who returned to Earth with Wilcutt's crew aboard the orbiter Endeavour.

Previously Wilcutt was pilot of STS-68, which carried the second Space Radar Laboratory into orbit on September 30, 1994. This 12-day flight of the orbiter Endeavour collected over 40,000 images of the Earth's autumnal surface, complementing the first Space Radar Lab mission (STS-59) flown in the spring of 1994. The crew of STS-68 suffered through an aborted launch on August 19, 1994.

Wilcutt's second mission was STS-79, the fourth Shuttle-Mir docking mission, launched September 16, 1996. During this 10-day flight the orbiter Atlantis spent three days docked with Mir, transferring thousands of pounds of supplies to the onboard crew, dropping off astronaut John Blaha and returning astronaut Shannon Lucid after 6 months aboard the station. Wilcutt also piloted the Atlantis's separation from Mir, flying the orbiter manually for 50 minutes to test handling techniques for future missions.

Wilcutt was born October 31, 1949, in Russellville, Kentucky. He attended Western Kentucky University, receiving a B.A. in math in 1974.

In 1976, following two years as a high school math teacher, Wilcutt entered the Marine Corps. He earned his wings in 1978 and became an F-4 Phantom pilot with VMFA-235. During the next four years he made two overseas deployments to Japan, Korea and the Philippines, and also attended the Naval Fighter Weapons School (better known as "Top Gun"). Following conversion training as an F/A-18 pilot in 1983, Wilcutt spent three years as an F/A-18 instructor at Lemoore NAS, California. In 1987 he attended the US Naval Test Pilot School at Patuxent River, Maryland, where he was named distinguished graduate. At the time of his selection by NASA he was assigned as a test pilot/project officer at the Naval Aircraft Test Center there.

He has logged over 3,000 hours of flying time in more than 30 different aircraft.

Wilcutt was one of the 23 astronaut candidates selected by NASA in January 1990. In July 1991 he qualified as a Shuttle pilot while serving as astronaut office contact for Space Shuttle Main Engine and External Tank matters. Later technical assignments include working on

the astronaut support team at the Kennedy Space Center (1992–93).

Williams, Bill Alvin
1942–

Physiologist Bill Williams trained for one year as a potential payload specialist for Mission 61-D/Spacelab 4 (later known as Spacelab Life Sciences) until resigning for personal reasons late in 1984. He had been a member of one of the investigating teams.

Williams was born February 9, 1942, in Oakland, California. He attended the University of California at Berkeley, receiving a B.A. in physiology (1963). He went on to do graduate study at the University of Illinois, Urbana-Champaign, receiving his M.S. (1965) and Ph.D. (1969) in the same field.

From 1969 to 1983 he served as a researcher and scientist for both the National Academy of Sciences and NASA at the Ames Research Center in Palo Alto, California. He is the author of over 88 scientific papers, many of them concerning the physiology of animals.

During his time at NASA Ames Williams took part in the ASSESS III Spacelab mission simulation (May 1977) and was a finalist in the 1980 astronaut selection. At the time he was named a Spacelab 4 payload specialist in January 1984 Williams was a scientist with the Environmental Protection Agency in Corvallis, Oregon.

Williams is currently president of an environmental research company in Corvallis.

Williams, Clifton Curtis, Jr.
1932–1967

Marine test pilot C. C. Williams was killed in the crash of his T-38 jet aircraft on October 5, 1967, at Miccosukee, Florida, just north of Tallahassee. At the time of his death he was training as the lunar module pilot of an Apollo crew commanded by Charles Conrad. Had he lived he would have been the fourth man to walk on the Moon.

Williams was born on September 26, 1932, in Mobile Alabama. He graduated from Murphy High School in Mobile in 1949 and attended Spring Hill College. He received his B.S. in mechanical engineering from Auburn in 1954, then joined the Marine Corps. After serving as a Marine aviator he attended the Naval Test Pilot School at Patuxent River, Maryland, and was stationed there as a test pilot for three years. Prior to becoming an astronaut he was a student at the Marine Corps Intermediate Staff and Command School at Quantico, Virginia.

As a pilot, he had logged 2,600 hours of flying time, 2,200 in jets.

Williams was one of 14 astronauts selected by NASA on October 14, 1963. He was a capcom for Gemini 4 and Gemini 11 and backup pilot for Gemini 10. The mission patch for Apollo 12, the lunar landing flight eventually made by Conrad's crew, contains four stars, the extra one as a tribute to Williams.

Williams, Donald Edward
1942–

In October 1989 Don Williams commanded STS-34, a 5-day Shuttle mission during which the controversial and oft-delayed Galileo space probe was deployed. Galileo, the most sophisticated and expensive ($1.5 billion) space probe ever launched, was originally to have arrived at the planet Jupiter in 1986. A number of technical delays, and the Challenger disaster, forced the NASA Jet Propulsion Laboratory, the probe's designers, to redesign the vehicle two different times. Galileo was finally propelled toward its December 1995 rendezvous with Jupiter on October 18, 1989.

Williams and his crew also had to overcome a legal obstacle to their mission. Antinuclear protesters claimed that the 48-pound plutonium power supply carried by Galileo might pose a health hazard to residents of Florida if the Atlantis should suffer a Challenger-type explosion during launch. On October 10, 1989, U.S. District Judge Oliver Gasch refused to grant a temporary restraining order blocking the launch.

Following 5 days of additional Earth resources studies and medical experiments, the crew of STS-34 landed

at Edwards AFB, California, on October 23, 1989, having shortened their mission by 3 hours because of concerns about high winds at the desert landing site.

Williams had previously served as pilot of Shuttle Mission 51-D in April 1985. The 7-astronaut crew of 51-D included United States senator Jake Garn of Utah, who was acting as a congressional observer and payload specialist. Williams and commander Karol Bobko performed an unscheduled re-rendezvous with the ailing Leasat 3 satellite, which had been deployed earlier in their mission, so that David Griggs and Jeffrey Hoffman could attempt to repair it in an unscheduled and unrehearsed EVA. Their attempt failed, but a later visit from the Mission 51-I astronauts in August successfully repaired Leasat 3, and by November 1985 it had reached its proper orbit.

Williams was born February 13, 1942, in Lafayette, Indiana, graduating from high school in nearby Otterbein in 1960. He attended Purdue University in Lafayette, receiving a B.S. in mechanical engineering in 1964.

A Navy ROTC student at Purdue, Williams entered the service after graduation. He underwent A-4 pilot training in Florida, Mississippi and Texas, earning his wings in 1966. Assigned to Attack Squadron 113, he made two combat deployments aboard the carrier U.S.S. Enterprise. Following a 2-year tour as an instructor, he made two more Vietnam deployments with the Enterprise as an A-7 pilot. Ultimately he flew a total of 330 combat missions.

In 1973 Williams attended the Armed Forces Staff College, then went to the Naval Test Pilot School at Patuxent River, Maryland, where he remained until 1977. At the time of his selection as an astronaut Williams was an A-7 pilot with Attack Squadron 94.

Williams logged over 6,000 hours of flying time, 5,700 hours in jets, including 745 carrier landings.

He was one of the 35 astronaut candidates chosen by NASA on January 15, 1978. In August 1979 he qualified as a Shuttle pilot, working in SAIL and at the Kennedy Space Center in orbiter test, checkout, launch, and landing operations. From September 1982 to July 1983 he was deputy manager for operations integration of the National Space Transportation System program office at the Johnson Space Center.

In September 1985 he was named to command a Shuttle mission originally scheduled for 1986, but ultimately canceled following the Challenger disaster. He served concurrently as the deputy chief of the aircraft operations division at JSC (July 1985 through August 1986), then as chief of the mission support branch of the astronaut office (September 1986 through December 1988). He was assigned as commander of STS-34 in August 1988.

Williams retired from NASA and the Navy on March 1, 1990, to join Science Applications International Corporation, Houston, Texas, where he currently works as a deputy division manager.

Williams, Jeffrey Nels

1958–

Army aviator Jeffrey Williams is one of the 35 astronaut candidates selected by NASA on May 1, 1996. In August of that year he reported to the Johnson Space Center to begin a training and evaluation course that should qualify him as a Shuttle mission specialist and space station crewmember. His current technical assignment is in the computer support branch of the astronaut office, working in SAIL.

Williams was born January 18, 1958, in Superior, Wisconsin, and grew up in Winter, where he graduated from high school in 1976. He attended the Military Academy at West Point, receiving a B.S. in applied science and engineering in 1980. He later earned an M.S. in aeronautical engineering and the degree of aeronautical engineer from the Naval Postgraduate School, Monterey, California (1987), and an M.A. in national security and strategic studies from the Naval War College (1996).

Commissioned in the Army following graduation from West Point, Williams qualified as an army aviator in September 1981. He spent three years with the aviation battalion of the 3rd Armored Division, Germany, serving as aeroscout platoon leader and operations officer. He returned to the United States in 1984 to do graduate work, then, in 1987, was assigned to the NASA Johnson Space Center.

During his first five years at JSC Williams worked as a Shuttle launch and landing operations engineer, a pilot in the Shuttle Avionics Integration Laboratory, and chief of

the operations development office in the flight crew operations directorate. In 1992 Williams attended the Naval Test Pilot School at Patuxent River, Maryland, then served as an experimental test pilot and flight test division chief with the Army's Aircraft Airworthiness Test Directorate at Edwards AFB, California. Williams was an Army exchange student at the Naval War College when selected as an ASCAN.

Lieutenant Colonel Williams has logged over 2,000 hours of flying time in 50 different types of aircraft.

Williams, Sunita Lyn

1965–

Navy engineer Sunita Williams is one of the 25 astronaut candidates selected by NASA in June 1998. In August of that year she reported to the Johnson Space Center to begin a training and evaluation course that should qualify her as a Shuttle mission specialist and International Space Station crewmember.

Williams was born Sunita Pandya in Euclid, Ohio, on September 19, 1965. She graduated from high school in Needham, Massachusetts, in 1983, then attended the U.S. Naval Academy, where she received a B.S. in physical science in 1987. She later earned an M.S. in engineering management from the Florida Institute of Technology (1995).

At the time of her selection by NASA, Lieutenant Commander Williams was an aircraft handler aboard the *U.S.S. Saipan.*

Wilson, Stephanie Diana

1966–

NASA engineer Stephanie Wilson is one of the 35 astronaut candidates selected by the space agency on May 1, 1996. In August of that year she reported to the Johnson Space Center to begin a training and evaluation course that should qualify her as a Shuttle mission specialist and International Space Station crewmember.

Wilson was born September 27, 1966, in Boston, Massachusetts, graduating from Taconic High School in Pittsfield in 1984. She attended Harvard University, receiving a B.S. in engineering science in 1988. She later earned an M.S. in aerospace engineering from the University of Texas (1992).

After graduation from Harvard Wilson spent two years with the Martin Marietta Astronautics Group in Denver, Colorado, as a loads and dynamics engineer on the Titan IV launch vehicle program. She then spent two years doing graduate work at Texas before joining the NASA Jet Propulsion Laboratory in Pasadena, California. At JPL she worked with a team of 100 engineers monitoring the performance of the Galileo space probe, recommending changes in software and flight operations as needed.

Wisoff, Peter Jeffrey Karl
1956–

Physicist Jeff Wisoff has been a mission specialist on three Shuttle flights, beginning with STS-57 in June 1993. During STS-57 Wisoff took part in the operations of the Spacehab module and also performed a 5 hour-50 minute EVA.

As a member of the crew of STS-68, Wisoff suffered through a launch abort on August 19, 1994. STS-68 was successfully launched five weeks later and carried the Shuttle Radar Laboratory, which allowed the crew to collect over 14,000 photographs of the Earth's surface and perform real-time environmental observations.

Wisoff made a third spaceflight aboard STS-81 in January 1997. This 10-day flight of the orbiter Atlantis made the fifth Shuttle-Mir docking, delivering astronaut Jerry Linenger to Mir and returning John Blaha to Earth. The crew also resupplied Mir with three tons of food, water, and other supplies.

In June 1997 Wisoff was assigned as an EVA crewmember for ISS assembly mission 3A, scheduled for launch as STS-92 in November 1999.

Wisoff was born August 16, 1958, in Norfolk, Virginia. He received a B.S. in physics (with highest distinction) from the University of Virginia in 1980, then went on to earn an M.S. (1982) and a Ph.D. (1986) in applied phyics at Stanford.

As a National Science Foundation Graduate Fellow, Wisoff did work at Stanford involving the development of short wavelength lasers. After completing his doctorate at Stanford he joined the faculty of Rice University in the electrical and computer engineering department. He also worked with Texas Medical Center researchers on medical applications of lasers.

Wisoff was one of the 23 astronaut candidates selected by NASA in January 1990, qualifying as a Shuttle mission specialist in July 1991. He served as a capcom in mission control until being assigned to STS-57 in February 1992. Later technical assignments include a tour in SAIL and working on EVA equipment and techniques for the International Space Station. Since March 1997 he has been head of the payloads/habitability branch of the astronaut office.

Wolf, David Alan
1956–

Physician Dave Wolf followed a torturous route to become the sixth NASA astronaut to serve a 4-month tour aboard the Russian space station Mir. Originally assigned as the seventh and last NASA-Mir crewmember, Wolf was asked to replace astronaut Wendy Lawrence in July 1997, a month after the collision between Mir and a Progress supply ship intensified a series of control and life support system failures, including a fire, computer guidance failures, and power loss, aboard the station. Mir's problems required that all crewmembers, including NASA astronauts, be qualified for EVA operations in the Russian Orlan suit. Unlike Lawrence, Wolf was qualified, both in size and because he had trained as backup to Michael Foale, the fifth NASA-Mir crewmember.

Assigned to the crew of STS-86, Wolf had to wait until September 24, 1997, two days prior to its scheduled launch, until two reviews of Mir's habitability cleared him for his mission. He reached Mir on September 29, replacing Foale and joining Mir-24 crewmembers Anatoly Solovyov and Pavel Vinogradov, who undertook a series of repair EVAs over the first few weeks of Wolf's mission. Wolf was also able to resume scientific work aboard the station that had been interrupted by the various accidents during the summer. His mission was relatively quiet, compared to that of predecessors Linenger and Foale, though Mir's onboard cooling system malfunctioned at one point, raising temperatures in the station and spewing coolant.

Wolf himself performed an EVA in January 1998 prior to returning to Earth aboard STS-89 in January 1998.

Previously Wolf was a mission specialist aboard STS-58. This 11-day flight of the orbiter Columbia carried the second Life Sciences Spacelab and a crew of 7.

Ordinarily Wolf would have been assigned to a second Shuttle crew within a year, but his career almost ended when, in early 1994, he inadvertently became part of an F.B.I. sting aimed at discovering kickbacks by employees of the Johnson Space Center. Wolf was approached by undercover officers during an evening at a nightclub and declined their overtures. The bad publicity reportedly caused JSC managers to tell Wolf he would not be assigned to another flight. He spent the next two years in the flight support branch of the astronaut office as a Shuttle capcom.

It was only the scarcity of volunteers among active astronauts for duty on the "Russian front" that allowed Wolf another opportunity. Unlike many other astronauts, he was willing to commit to a year of training and living in Russia for what was seen to be a slim chance of actually making a flight to Mir. His medical background was also a bonus. Wolf was officially assigned as NASA-Mir crewmember in December 1996.

Wolf was born August 23, 1956, in Indianapolis, Indiana. He attended Purdue University, graduating with a B.S. in electrical engineering in 1978, and received an M.D. from Indiana University in 1982. He did his medical internship at Methodist Hospital in Indianapolis, and also completed Air Force flight surgeon primary training at Brooks AFB, Texas.

From 1980 to 1983, while studying for his medical degree, Wolf worked as a research scientist at the Indianapolis Center for Advanced Research. His specialty was digital and ultrasonic medical imaging. In 1983 he joined the medical sciences division at the NASA Johnson Space Center, where his assignments included working on the development of the medical facility for space station Freedom.

Wolf serves as a flight surgeon in the Air National Guard and has logged 500 hours of flying time as an F-4 Phantom weapons systems officer. He is also an acrobatic pilot flying the Pitts Special Airplane.

Wolf was one of the 23 astronaut candidates selected by NASA in January 1990. In July 1991 he qualified as a Shuttle mission specialist while serving with the astronaut support team at the Kennedy Space Center. He was assigned to STS-58 that December.

Wood, James Wayne
1924–1990

James "Woody" Wood was the leader of the group of test pilots originally selected for the X-20 Dyna-Soar program in April 1960. Had flights of the Dyna-Soar taken place in 1966 as planned, he would almost certainly have become the first person to pilot a winged spacecraft. However, Dyna-Soar was canceled in December 1963.

Wood did go on to become the first military pilot to fly the F-111 swing-wing fighter bomber. He ultimately served as commander of test operations at Edwards Air Force Base.

Wood was born August 9, 1924, in Paragould, Arkansas, and grew up in Pueblo, Colorado. He joined the Army Air Corps in 1943 as an aviation cadet, and became a B-17 bomber pilot. He flew 10 missions over France and Germany during World War II.

He was retrained as a fighter pilot after the war, and flew 100 combat missions in the F-80 Shooting Star—the first operational American jet fighter—during the Korean conflict.

Returning to the United States, he served as a gunnery instructor, then attended the Air Force Institute of Technology at Wright-Patterson AFB, Ohio, where he received a B.S. in aeromechanical engineering in 1954.

He arrived at Edwards in August 1956 to attend the Test Pilot School, and after completion of that course remained at the center for the next nine years as a test pilot, working on the X-20, the F-111, F-102, F-104, and F-5 programs. In 1967 he attended the Air War College at Maxwell AFB, Alabama, and headed a test unit developing a guided bomb at Eglin AFB, Florida.

Wood flew 34 combat missions in Vietnam, his third war, from 1968 to 1969 as an F-4 Phantom pilot based in Thailand and Saigon. He returned to the United States for a 2-year tour planning test programs for the new F-15 Eagle fighter at Wright-Patterson, then was assigned again to Edwards, where he became commander for test operations, supervising over 1,200 military and civilian pilots, engineers, researchers and support personnel.

As a pilot Wood logged over 6,000 hours of flying time in 35 different types of aircraft.

Wood retired from the Air Force with the rank of colonel in 1978. He worked for several aircraft companies in Southern California as a pilot and consultant, including Flight Systems, Inc., and the Tracor Company.

Wood died on January 1, 1990, in Melbourne, Florida.

Wood, Robert Jackson
1957–

Robert Wood was assigned as an industrial payload specialist for Shuttle Mission 61-M, once scheduled for launch in July 1986. During that mission he was to have operated a space-manufacturing unit called EOS, built by the McDonnell Douglas Astronautics Company and Johnson & Johnson. The destruction of the Challenger in January 1986 forced the cancellation of the EOS flight, however, and Wood did not go into space.

An earlier version of EOS (Electrophoresis Operations in Space), a system that takes advantage of the space environment to separate and purify biological materials in the manufacture of unique drugs, was flown by Wood's fellow McDAC engineer Charles Walker on three Shuttle missions.

Wood was born June 26, 1957, in Fitchburg, Massachusetts, and graduated from high school in Wilton, New Hampshire, in 1975. He attended Ohio University, earning a B.S. in physics (summa cum laude) in 1978, and later earned an M.S. in physics from the Massachusetts Institute of Technology in 1980.

Wood has worked as a research assistant at M.I.T.'s Bates Linear Accelerator, and as a senior research scientist with the Fisher Scientific Company, developing automated laboratory instruments. In 1983 he went to work for McDonnell Douglas Astronautics in Houston, designing computer software for the EOS unit and supporting its previous flights from mission control. He was desig-

nated as the second industrial payload specialist in March 1985 and served as backup to Walker on Shuttle Mission 61-B in 1985.

Since 1986 Walker has worked for McDonnell Douglas on the Neutral Particle Beam Integrated Experiment and the National Aerospace Plane Program. He is currently a systems engineer for Joint Direct Attack Munitions.

Woodward, Neil Whitney III
1962–

Navy engineer Neil Woodward is one of the 25 astronaut candidate selected by NASA in June 1998. In August of that year he reported to the Johnson Space Center to begin a training and evaluation course that should qualify him as a Shuttle mission specialist and International Space Station crewmember.

Woodward was born July 26, 1962, in Chicago, Illinois, and graduated from Putnam City High School in Oklahoma City in 1980. He attended the Massachusetts Institute of Technology, receiving a B.S. in physics in 1984. He later earned an M.S. in physics from the University of Texas at Austin (1988).

At the time of his selection by NASA, Lieutenant Woodward was a project officer with the naval strike test squadron, Patuxent River, Maryland.

Worden, Alfred Merrill
1932–

Al Worden was the command module pilot of Apollo 15 and spent three days orbiting the Moon alone in the command module Endeavour while fellow astronauts David Scott and James Irwin explored the lunar surface. On the return voyage to earth, Worden performed the first "deep space" space walk, retrieving an experiment package attached to the Apollo service module.

Worden was born February 7, 1932, in Jackson, Michigan. He attended the Military Academy at West Point, graduating in 1955 with a bachelor of science, and in 1963 earned an M.S. in astronautical/aeronautical engineering and instrumentation from the University of Michigan.

Commissioned in the Air Force after his graduation from West Point, Worden completed flight training in

Texas and Florida, then served as a pilot and armament officer with the 95th Fighter Interceptor Squadron at Andrews AFB, Maryland. In 1965 he attended the Empire Test Pilot School in Farnborough, England and the Air Force Aerospace Research Pilot School at Edwards AFB, California. He was an instructor at the aerospace school when chosen by NASA.

Worden was one of the 19 astronauts selected by NASA in April 1966. He was a member of the Apollo 9 support crew, then backup command module pilot for Apollo 12. After his flight on Apollo 15 he served briefly as backup command module pilot for Apollo 17, until he and fellow astronauts Scott and Irwin were removed for disciplinary reasons because of improprieties involving the sale of Apollo 15 souvenir stamps. (In 1983, following a NASA decision to allow the sale of commemorative stamps carried aboard the Space Shuttle, Worden sued the agency and, in a settlement, won back the materials he had lost in 1972.)

In September 1972 Worden was assigned to NASA's Ames Research Center at Moffet Field, California, serving as senior aerospace scientist, then as chief of the systems studies division. He resigned from NASA and retired from the Air Force as a lieutenant colonel on September 1, 1975.

Beginning in 1975 Worden worked with High Flight, the Colorado-based ministry founded by fellow astronaut James Irwin, while serving as director of energy management for the Northwood Institute, Palm Beach, Florida. He then became president of his own firm, Alfred M. Worden, Inc., in Palm Beach Gardens, Florida, and in 1985, president of MW Aerospace, Vero Beach. He is currently staff vice-president of the B. F. Goodrich Company, Grand Rapids, Michigan.

He has also published a children's book, *A Flight to the Moon* (1974), and a book of poems, *Hello, Earth: Greetings from Endeavour* (1974).

Wright, Keith Charles
1947–

Air Force engineer Keith Wright served as backup payload specialist for Shuttle Mission 51-C in January 1985. During that flight a National Security Agency electronic intelligence satellite code-named Magnum was placed in geosynchronous orbit.

Wright was one of the first 13 officers selected for the Air Force manned spaceflight engineer program in February 1980, and was assigned as a shuttle payload specialist in June 1982.

Wright was born August 31, 1947, in St. Louis, Missouri. He attended the University of Maryland in College Park, graduating in 1969 with a B.S. in electrical engineering.

He entered the Air Force through ROTC and served as an orbital analyst at the North American Aerospace Command (NORAD) in Colorado Springs, Colorado, until August 1974, when he was assigned to Shemya AFB, Alaska, as a space surveillance officer. In 1975 he was transferred to the Special Projects Office at Los Angeles AFS as a project engineer.

Wright left the MSE group in May 1985 and was reassigned to the Satellite Control Facility (Onizuka AFB) in Sunnyvale, California, as director of operations for military Shuttle flights. He retired with the rank of lieutenant colonel in October 1993, and is now employed by the Sparta Corporation, El Segundo, California.

Yeakel, Glenn Scott
1956–

Air Force engineer Scott Yeakel was one of 14 Manned Spaceflight Engineers chosen in January 1983. On two occasions, in 1985 and 1987, he was a candidate payload specialist for Shuttle missions flying Department of Defense experiments such as MARC-DN and IBSS, but ultimately was not assigned to the missions.

Yeakel was born May 28, 1956, in Allentown, Pennsylvania. He attended the Air Force Academy, graduating in

1978 with a B.S. in aeronautical engineering. In 1981 he received an M.S. in astronautical engineering from the Air Force Institute of Technology.

Following graduation from the Air Force Academy, Yeakel spent two years at Wright-Patterson AFB, Ohio, as a project engineer, then attended A.F.I.T., which is located at Wright-Patt. He was assigned to Space Division in Los Angeles as a systems acquisition engineer when selected for the MSE program.

With the termination of the MSE program in 1988, Major Yeakel remained at Space Division assigned to support of the STS-39 mission. In 1990 he transferred to Washington, D.C., where he was stationed at the State Department. He is currently assigned to the National Reconnaissance Office.

Young, John Watts
1930–

John Young is the world's most experienced space traveler, having made six different flights involving four different types of manned vehicles. Among his accomplishments are two trips to the Moon and command of the first flight of the Space Shuttle, the world's first reusable spacecraft.

Young's first trip into space came on March 23, 1965, as pilot of Gemini 3. This 3-orbit mission was the first manned Gemini flight, the first 2-person American flight, and the first manned spacecraft to maneuver in orbit. It is also memorable as the flight in which Young, never a fan of astronaut food, smuggled a sandwich aboard, offering his surprised commander Gus Grissom a bite. That action also resulted in the first astronaut reprimand, which had little effect on Young's career.

He flew as commander on his second flight, Gemini 10 in July 1966. Young and pilot Michael Collins used their Gemini to rendezvous with two different Agena spacecraft and set a record by reaching an altitude of 475 miles.

In May 1969 Young served as command module pilot for Apollo 10, a full dress rehearsal for a manned lunar landing conducted in lunar orbit. Astronauts Thomas

Stafford and Eugene Cernan took the lunar module Snoopy to within 10 miles of the surface of the Moon while Young waited in the command module Charlie Brown.

The next time Young got close to the Moon, in April 1972, he landed on it. As commander of Apollo 16, he and Charles Duke set the lunar module Orion down in the highlands near the crater Descartes. For three days they remained on the Moon, setting up scientific experiments, collecting over 200 pounds of Moon rocks, and driving 17 miles in a lunar rover.

Young's fifth flight was STS-1, the first flight in the Space Shuttle program. On April 12, 1981, the twentieth anniversary of the flight of Yuri Gagarin, and following years of delay, the orbiter Columbia carrying Young and pilot Robert Crippen roared off Pad 39A at the Kennedy Space Center. It was the first time men had been launched with dangerous solid rocket boosters, indeed, the first time the Shuttle configuration had been tested at all. Columbia performed well during its 54.5-hour maiden voyage, and returned to Earth on April 14, gliding to a landing on the dry lakebed at Edwards Air Force Base, California, the first controlled landing ever by a manned spacecraft.

In November and December 1983 Young commanded a second Shuttle mission, STS-9, which carried a record crew of 6. STS-9 was the first flight of the European-built Spacelab, a scientific module crammed with experiments and carried in the orbiter Columbia's payload bay. During the 10-day mission the crew worked 12-hour shifts and reached all of its goals, performing more than 70 experiments in a variety of fields. Computer problems delayed the landing by several hours, but Columbia returned safely to Edwards.

Though STS-9 was widely thought to be his last mission, Young was named in September 1985 to command the Shuttle deployment of the Hubble Space Telescope. That flight, originally set for September 1986, had to be postponed following the explosion of the Shuttle Challenger and the deaths of 7 crewmembers. In March 1988, when the crew was reassigned to what was now known as STS-31, Young had been replaced as commander by Loren Shriver. The change was probably the result of a controversy centered on Young that followed the Challenger disaster.

Memos Young had written (before and after the accident) complaining of compromises in flight crew safety found their way to the press. During testimony before the presidential commission investigating the disaster, the chief astronaut admitted that he considered 1985, when 9 Shuttle missions were launched, "a good year for the Shuttle program," and did not see how 15 missions, the number scheduled for 1986, could have been accomplished safely. Some unnamed astronauts complained that Young himself had been ineffective in raising safety issues with NASA management. In any case, NASA management punished Young, removing him as chief of the astronaut office in May 1987 and giving him the job of special assistant to the director of the NASA Johnson Space Center for engineering, operations, and safety.

Young was born September 24, 1930, in San Francisco, California, and grew up in Orlando, Florida, where he graduated from high school. He attended the Georgia Institute of Technology, receiving a B.S. in aeronautical engineer (with the highest honors) in 1952.

A Navy ROTC student, Young began active duty after graduation from Georgia Tech. He served aboard the destroyer *U.S.S. Laws* for a year, then underwent pilot training. From 1955 to 1959 he served with Fighter Squadron 103.

He attended the Naval Test Pilot School at Patuxent River, Maryland, in 1959, then remained at the Naval Air Test Center for the next three years. In 1962 he set world time-to-climb records in the F4 Phantom. At the time of his selection by NASA he was maintenance officer with Fighter Squadron 143 at Miramar, California.

As a pilot he has logged over 11,500 hours of flying time.

Young was one of 9 astronauts chosen by NASA in October 1962. He became the first of that group, which included Charles Conrad, Frank Borman, and Neil Armstrong, to be assigned to a spaceflight when he was named pilot of Gemini-3 in April 1964. He was assigned to flight crews almost continuously for the next nine years: in addition to flights on Gemini 3, Gemini 10, Apollo 10, and Apollo 16, he was backup pilot for Gemini 6, backup command module pilot for Apollo 7, and backup commander for Apollo 13 and Apollo 17.

In January 1973 Young went to work on development of the Space Shuttle. A year later he was also made acting chief astronaut, and in January 1975, permanent chief. He stepped aside from March 1978 to April 1981 to concentrate training for STS-1.

Young, Laurence Retman
1935–

Laurence Young was one of the two alternate payload specialists for the second Spacelab Life Sciences mission, STS-58, flown in October 1993. The two-week-long SLS-02 mission carried a crew of 7 who operated 12 major experiments designed to study the effects of zero-G on human beings. Young supported the mission from the NASA Marshall Spaceflight Center.

Young was born December 19, 1935, in New York City. He attended Amherst College, receiving an A.B. in physics (1957). He was a French Government Fellow at the Sorbonne in 1958, earning a certificate in applied mathematics. He later earned bachelor's and master's degrees in electrical engineering, and a doctor of science degree in instrumentation, from M.I.T. (1957 to 1962).

Young joined the Sperry Gyroscope Corporation in 1957. From 1958 to 1962 he was a staff researcher at M.I.T., joining the M.I.T. faculty upon completion of his doctorate. He became professor of aeronautics and astronautics, and Director, Man-Vehicle Laboratory, at M.I.T.

He has served as a visiting professor at the ETH Federal Institute of Technology and the Zurich Kantonsspital in Switzerland (1972–73) and at the Conservatoire des arts et Metiers in Paris. In 1987–88 he was a visiting scientist at the NASA Ames Research Center. He has also served on several NASA advisory committees, and one of his experiments flew aboard the first Spacelab Life Sciences (1991).

Young is currently director of the National Space Biomedical Research Institute in Houston.

Zamka, George David

1962–

Marine test pilot George Zamka is one of the 25 astronaut candidates selected by NASA in June 1998. In August of that year he reported to the Johnson Space Center to begin a training and evaluation course that should qualify him as a Shuttle pilot.

Zamka was born June 29, 1962, in Jersey City, New Jersey, and graduated from Rochester (N.Y.) Adams High School in 1980. He attended the U.S. Naval Academy, where he received a B.S. in mathematics.

At the time of his selection by NASA, Zamka was a project officer with the strike aircraft test squadron, Patuxent River, Maryland.

RUSSIAN
COSMONAUTS
by Rex Hall

The idea of sending men into space was more acceptable in the Soviet Union than it was for many years in the United States. The pioneering theorist, Konstantin Tsiolkovsky, was honored by the young Soviet government, and early rocket experimenters, including a test pilot and engineer named Sergei Korolev, were given financial support. Shortly after World War II, Mikhail Tikhonravov, an engineer with NII–4, a research institute within the Academy of Artillery Sciences, proposed Project RD–90, in which a cabin containing two men would be propelled into space on a suborbital trajectory.

Nevertheless, the challenges of the Cold War kept Soviet rocket research focused on the development of ballistic missiles as weapons. The team led by Korolev concentrated on improvements to the captured German V–2, developing the R–1, R–2 and R–5 missiles. Suborbital flights aboard the R–5 missile from the Kapustin Yar range were considered in 1956. Three military medical specialists—Abram Genin, V. Sheryapin, and Ye. Yuganov—proposed themselves as candidates. But the resources of the Korolev bureau were devoted to the creation of the USSR's first intercontinental ballistic missile, and the manned suborbital program was seen as a drain on the limited resources of the bureau.

It was only with the success of the Soviet Union's first artificial Earth satellite, Sputnik, that serious work began on a manned spacecraft. In the spring of 1958 the section of the Korolev bureau headed by Konstantin Bushuyev devised a spherical vehicle called Vostok, which would be launched aboard a modified R–7 ICBM. Korolev was able to present Vostok to the Committee on Science and Technology in June 1958, as a combined manned orbital (Vostok–1K) and unmanned orbital reconnaissance platform (Vostok–2K). Only after Vostok was approved did selection of the cosmonauts take place.

In February 1959—just scant weeks before America's Mercury astronauts were introduced to the world, Mstislav Keldysh of the USSR Academy of Sciences chaired the first meeting to discuss the selection of space travelers.

Like the Americans, the Soviets also wondered where their space travelers—cosmonauts—would be found. Would they be engineers? Submarine crewmen, used to isolation and cramped quarters? Mountain climbers? Or pilots? The faction supporting the choice of pilots won out. Korolev said: "The fighter pilot is the all–arounder we require. He flies in the stratosphere in a single–seat, high–speed aircraft. He is a pilot, navigator and radio operator. . . ."

Beginning in August 1959, a recruiting team of military medical specialists headed by Lieutenant Colonel Yevgeny Karpov, 38, of the Central Aviation Research Hospital, began to visit air bases from the Urals to the Far East, interviewing young pilots for a program involving "aircraft of a completely new type." (The invitation process was limited to European Russia, since it was assumed that that pool of pilots was sufficient to produce the required candidates.) Upon hearing the presentation, one pilot with the Northern Fleet, 24–year–old Georgy Shonin, recalled:

> I immediately cooled off. A lot of pilots were then being transferred to helicopter units, and these did not at that time enjoy any great popularity among us. 'I'm a fighter pilot, I specially chose a flying school where I would be taught to fly jet fighters, and you—'
>
> 'No, no! You don't understand,' the older of the two reassured me, having guessed what I was worried about. 'What we're talking about are long–distance flights, flights on rockets, flights around the Earth.'[1]

Shonin reported that his "mouth dropped open in surprise." He volunteered for the new program, as did 3,000 other pilots. That number was quickly cut to 102 who not only passed the initial physical examinations, but demonstrated "a fundamental desire" to fly in space. These candidates underwent rigorous medical and psychological screening at the Central Aviation Research Hospital in the Moscow suburb of Sokolniki.

The 1st Enrollment: March 1960

The selection criteria for the first cosmonaut group required that candidates, in addition to being qualified fighter pilots holding a 3d class certificate:

- Be under thirty years of age
- Be fewer than 170 cm (5'7") tall
- Weigh less than 70 kg (154 lbs)

The first results of the medical screening produced an insufficient number of candidates, so the height and age requirements were relaxed somewhat. (When asked how many cosmonauts he thought necessary, Korolev had asked for "three times" the number of Mercury astronauts, or 21.)

On February 24, 1960, a credentials committee consisting of representatives from the Soviet air forces, its military medical service and political (Communist Party) administration, and others met to review 29 candidates: 20 were approved.

---

[1] *Our Gagarin*, Progress Publishers, 1981.
Known in Russian as the *mandat commissiya* or mandate commission.

Sr. Lieut. Ivan I. Anikeyev

Maj. Pavel I. Belyayev

Sr. Lieut. Valentin V. Bondarenko

Sr. Lieut. Valery F. Bykovsky

Sr. Lieut. Valentin I. Filatyev

Sr. Lieut. Yuri A. Gagarin

Sr. Lieut. Viktor V. Gorbatko

Capt. Anatoly Ya. Kartashov

Sr. Lieut. Yevgeny V. Khrunov

Eng.–Capt. Vladimir M. Komarov

Lieut. Alexei A. Leonov

Sr. Lieut. Grigori G. Nelyubov

Sr. Lieut. Andrian G. Nikolayev

Capt. Pavel R. Popovich

Sr. Lieut. Mars Z. Rafikov

Sr. Lieut. Georgy S. Shonin

Sr. Lieut. Gherman S. Titov

Sr. Lieut. Valentin S. Varlamov

Sr. Lieut. Boris V. Volynov

Sr. Lieut. Dmitri A. Zaikin

All finalists were military officers who had graduated from Higher Air Force Schools (the educational equivalent of American junior colleges). Two (Belyayev and Komarov) had graduated from air force academies as well. Fifteen were Party members and five belonged to the Komsomol, the Party youth organization.

Contrary to widespread belief, unlike America's Mercury astronauts none of the first cosmonauts was a test pilot, though Komarov had performed test–engineer work on new aircraft equipment. The most experienced pilot (Belyayev) had logged only 900 hours of flying time, while Gagarin, for example, had logged as little as 250. Again, the Mercury astronauts were required to have a minimum of 1,500 flying hours. Only one pilot, Popovich, had flown the high–performance MiG–19. The others had been limited to the older MiG–15 and MiG–17.

The cosmonaut–candidates were presented to Marshal Konstantin Vershinin, commander–in–chief of the Soviet air forces (VVS), on March 7, 1960, and one week later began training at a military barracks at Khodynka Airport in downtown Moscow. The senior officer in the "squad," Major Pavel Belyayev, was named its commander.

A military unit—Number 26566—was formed that would include the cosmonaut team and its training and medical support staff. Its first commander was Lieutenant Colonel Karpov.

Kamanin

The overall head of space programs for the Russian air forces was Lieutenant General Nikolai Kamanin, 52. Kamanin had received one of the first Hero of the Soviet Union medals as a young aviator in 1937, for taking part in the rescue by air of the *Chelyushin* arctic expedition. He had commanded units in the World War II, and in early 1960 was the chief of combat training for the staff of the air force high command. The volunteer defense forces, DOSAAF, reported to Kamanin, as did the Central Aviation Research Hospital.

During the early weeks of training the cosmonaut candidates spent three days in classroom study concentrating on aviation medicine and three days in physical training.

In contrast to the American astronauts, whose exploits were closely followed by their secret competitors in the Soviet Union, the cosmonauts' physical conditioning was extensive, planned, and monitored. (Medical control of the cosmonauts by space program doctors continues to this day.) The early candidates found the emphasis on physical training to be demoralizing, so Korolev, Kamanin, and Karpov added lectures on astronomy, aerospace medicine, and physics by a number of experts drawn from the staff of Korolev's design bureau, including rocket designer Tikhonravov and future cosmonauts Vitaly Sevastyanov and Oleg Makarov. The training program was also supported by a cadre of test pilots, including Heroes of the Soviet Union Ivan Dzyuba and Mark Gallai. As time went on the academic load increased with the addition of radio and electrical engineering, spacecraft telemetry, and guidance systems as subjects.

The candidates also had to undergo an intensive course of parachute training designed to make them experts in a matter of weeks. Most of the young pilots had made just five mandatory jumps early in their air force careers; now they found themselves making over 40 jumps in six weeks, each one of increasing complexity in a program directed by world record holder Lieutenant Colonel Nikolai Nikitin. (Parachute training was essential for the first cosmonauts, since that was how one returned

to Earth from a Vostok spacecraft. Space doctors also discovered that parachuting gave cosmonauts experience with weightlessness and also with stress, and such training continues today.)

By the end of May 1960 it was clear to Kamanin and Karpov that it was neither necessary nor possible to train 20 pilots for the first Vostok flight. Six candidates were selected for accelerated training in the new Vostok simulator, under the direction of Colonel Gallai. They were Gagarin, Kartashov, Nikolayev, Popovich, Titov, and Varlamov. This group, known jokingly among the other cosmonauts as the "lilies of the field," had the official designation "group of immediate readiness." The formation of such an advanced training group within the overall cosmonaut team is still used today.

In July 1960 the cosmonaut team moved from Khodynka to a new site near the village of Shchelkovo, 24 miles northeast of Moscow. (Shchelkovo was also the home of the Chkalov air base, location of the air force flight test center.) A training center for cosmonauts, including residences for their families and others involved in the manned program, was under construction. It eventually be known as *Zvezdni Gorodok*, literally "stellar village," more commonly called Star Town. The training center itself was known by its Russian language acronym—TsPK.

In early May the group had suffered its first casualty when Komarov was hospitalized for a hernia operation. Then Kartashov had a bad reaction to centrifuge testing, which began in early July. On July 24, 1960, Varlamov cracked a vertebrae in his neck while diving into a lake near Star Town and was hospitalized for a month. While Komarov eventually returned to cosmonaut training, Kartashov and Varlamov were permanently grounded, and were replaced in the "lilies" by Nelyubov and Bykovsky.

The six candidates for the first Vostok completed their training program in late February 1961, then underwent a two–day series of examinations. The results of these tests ranked Gagarin, Titov, and Nelyubov as the best candidates for the first Vostok flight. These three, and Bykovsky, Nikolayev, and Popovich, were then designated cosmonauts. Gagarin was soon selected by Kamanin as the prime pilot for Vostok, with Titov as his backup.

Most of the other members of the 1st Enrollment were designated as cosmonauts on April 8, 1961. Zaikin,

Filatyev, and Anikeyev's "promotions" were delayed until December of that year.

In September 1961 all of the remaining members of the March 1960 group, with the exceptions of Belyayev and Komarov, were enrolled at the Zhukovsky Military Engineering Academy in Moscow. Eleven would eventually graduate in February 1968.

In all, 12 of the first enrollment flew in space during the first 20 years of manned flight. A number took up senior positions in the Soviet air force, the Ministry of Defense, and the cosmonaut training center.

Expansion: Fall 1961

The driving force behind the manned space program was Sergei Pavlovich Korolev, whose imagination and ability put the program on its path to the stars. He headed Experimental Design Bureau #1 (OKB–1), the large enterprise that designed and built the rockets, the spacecraft, and the facilities that still, as the RKK Energiya, support the manned program today.

With Korolev's approval, the search for the first Soviet cosmonauts was limited to air force pilots, but it was in Korolev's mind that a time would come when civilians would fly—including himself. After all, he had been a glider test pilot in the 1930s.

It was a senior designer in Bushuyev's Department 9 who lobbied hardest for the right to fly in space. This was Konstantin Petrovich Feoktistov, a brilliant and independent–minded engineer who never really accepted Korolev's decision to limit candidates for spaceflight to military pilots. As soon as Titov's 1961 flight proved that it was possible for a person in ordinary good health to fly in space, Feoktistov asked to be examined by Kamanin's doctors at TsNIAG. He was refused, and as long as Soviet manned spacecraft had only a single seat, there was nothing Feoktistov or anyone else could do to break the military's monopoly on cosmonauts.

Women Cosmonaut Enrollment: March–April 1962

The publicity surrounding the daylong Vostok 2 flight of cosmonaut Titov in August 1961 encouraged hundreds of Soviet citizens, many of them women, to write to the Center asking to join the cosmonaut team. Kamanin seized on the idea of sending a woman into space, using these letters as a starting place in the eventual recruitment of five women. He hoped to find 100 candidates for medical testing, but had to settle for 58. The credentials committee meeting on February 28, 1962, produced five candidates:

Tatyana D. Kuznetsova

Valentina L. Ponomareva

Irina B. Solovyova

Valentina V. Tereshkova

Zhanna D. Yorkina

All five women were experienced parachutists, and they were instructed to tell their families they had been chosen to join a special parachuting team. (Solovyova was already a member of the Soviet national team.) Enlisted as privates in the Soviet air force, the new cosmonauts were given instruction to qualify them as passengers in MiG–15 trainers. (Ponomareva was already rated as a pilot, having learned to fly through a DOSAAF air club.)

Ponomareva, Solovyova, Tereshkova, and Yorkina were officially designated as cosmonauts in October 1962, following completion of state examinations. Kuznetsova had fallen behind the others in the training syllabus because of health problems and a later marriage, and did not officially complete training until January 1965.

Tereshkova was the only one to fly, becoming the first woman in space in June 1963. The other four were candidates for Voskhod and Soyuz missions, but without success, and were transferred out of the military cosmonaut team in October 1969.

The 2d Enrollment: January 11, 1963

The success of the first two Vostok flights by Gagarin and Titov encouraged the Soviet government to authorize a long–term manned space program using improved versions of the Vostok–3K spacecraft developed by the Korolev organization, as well as a whole new spacecraft, originally known as the Vostok–7K, later to be called Soyuz or Union. Air force space chief Kamanin won approval for the expansion of the TsPK staff from 250 to

800, with a larger cosmonaut team, from the current 17 members to as many as 80.

With that goal in mind, in March 1962, as the women cosmonauts began their training, Kamanin issued a call for more military cosmonauts. The new candidates were older on the average (the age limit was raised to 35) and included not only fighter pilots but also engineers and navigators. More significantly, all candidates were required to be graduates of a military academy or civilian university.

Only 65 officers were invited for medical testing. Kamanin and the credentials committee examined 25 new candidates on January 8, 1963. The committee recommended 21 candidates for enrollment, but VVS chief of staff Sergei Rudenko would allow Kamanin to select only 15. (Rudenko had authorized the TsPK to train 20 new cosmonauts in 1962 and 1963, and chose to include the five women in his headcount.) These reported to Star Town on January 11, 1963:

Eng.–Capt. Yuri P. Artyukhin

Sr. Eng.–Lieut. Eduard I. Buinovsky

Eng.–Lt. Col. Lev S. Demin

Maj. Georgy T. Dobrovolsky

Maj. Anatoly V. Filipchenko

Maj. Alexei A. Gubarev

Sr. Eng.–Lieut. Vladislav N. Gulyayev

Eng.–Capt. Pyotr I. Kolodin

Sr. Eng.–Lieut. Eduard P. Kugno

Maj. Anatoly P. Kuklin

Eng.–Capt. Alexandr N. Matinchenko

Maj. Vladimir A. Shatalov

Maj. Lev V. Vorobyov

Capt. Anatoly P. Voronov

Sr. Eng.–Lieut. Vitaly M. Zholobov

Shatalov, an air force inspector, was the senior pilot of the seven selected. Vorobyov, Gubarev, Dobrovolsky, Kuklin, Matinchenko, and Filipchenko were the others. The seven engineers included a researcher at the Ministry of Defense's NII–30 selected on his thirty–seventh birthday (Demin) and a member of the Zhukovsky AF Engineering Academy staff (Artyukhin). Buinovsky, Gulyayev, Kolo-

din, and Zholobov had served with the Strategic Rocket Forces at the Baikonur, Kapustin Yar, and Plesetsk launch ranges. Kugno was an aircraft engineer. The fifteenth man, Voronov, was a navigator who had taken part in H–bomb tests as a bomber crewman.

Seven members of the 2d Enrollment eventually flew in space.

The arrival of the second group caused some friction in the ranks. The young pilots of the 1st Enrollment largely worked as a collective, unconcerned with rank and title. With the addition of senior pilots and engineers the cosmonaut team took on the structure of an air force squadron.

Kamanin's vision of the TsPK called for several squadrons, in fact. He foresaw a system in which pilots would make training flights in space aboard single–seat Vostok vehicles, then move on to command multiseat Soyuz and military space station missions. He also hoped to use the young pilots of the 1st Enrollment as a cadre of future military space commanders, and gave them trials in positions of increasing responsibility as soon as he could. In December 1963, as the TsPK expanded, for example, Colonel Yuri Gagarin was made deputy director of the center in charge of air–space flight training. Lieutenant Colonel Andrian Nikolayev was named to replace him as commander of the cosmonaut detachment.

Senior Cosmonauts: January 17, 1964

In late 1963, as the 15 members of the 2d Enrollment were deep in training, Rudenko asked Kamanin to consider the creation of a small cadre of "senior" cosmonauts, who would fly missions immediately, then move into management positions at the expanding training center.

Three candidates were proposed, military test pilot and Hero of the Soviet Union Colonel Georgy Beregovy, an operational military pilot named Sidorenko, and a civilian space scientist and protege of Msistlav Keldysh named Georgy Katys.

All three passed the medical examinations in December 1963, but the credentials committee rejected the three candidates because of their age.

Nevertheless, Vershinin and Rudenko overruled the committee in Beregovoy's case, and on January 17, 1964,

Vershinin signed a special order enrolling Beregovoy in the air force cosmonaut team.

Beregovoy's training syllabus was shortened to allow him to graduate with the 2d Enrollment on January 25, 1965.

The Voskhod Program

On March 13, 1964, the Council of Ministers of the USSR authorized Korolev's OKB–1 to build a new version of the Vostok–3K spacecraft capable of carrying a crew of three. The Vostok–3KD program—soon called Voskhod or "Sunrise"— was created in response to an order by Soviet premier Khrushchev, who wanted to have three men in space at one time before the start of the two-man American Gemini missions. Three 3KD craft were to be built, with an unmanned launch in July to be followed by two manned missions, in August and November 1964.

It was obvious by this time that cosmonauts need not be extraordinary physical specimens, and the Soviet air force, which had fought plans to fly doctors or engineers in single–seat Vostok on the grounds that a spacecraft needed a pilot, could hardly argue that highly automated Voskhod required three or even two pilots. A number of organizations involved in the Soviet space effort wanted their own employees to become cosmonauts. These were the Academy of Sciences, the Ministry of Health, and the Ministry of Aviation Production. There were immediate problems:

"The flights already conducted have confirmed our initial assumptions: it is possible to engage in fruitful work in space. This, however, does not mean that we have achieved everything. Though up until now things have gone along rather smoothly, the perils of space still remain: danger lurks everywhere. There is much we still do not know and are only in the process of trying to discover.

. . .

"In order to obtain the maximum amount of information from each flight, the time has come to send into space researchers, scientists, physicians, engineers and journalists."

The audience laughed.

"Yes, I'm serious. Good journalists and other specialists capable of objectively and eloquently describing spaceflight."

"The doctors won't allow it." Someone in the audience spoke up.

"I think that the doctors will have to change their minds. We must utilize the knowledge of scientists and specialists, and how many of them are in perfect health?"

"We are against this proposal," a voice called out from the door.

Startled, Korolev looked up. He frowned across the table and said in a quiet voice: "Who is 'we,' may I ask?"

A heavy man rose from his seat." Our organization will not accept the risk," he announced categorically." We will not sign the document."[2]

The organization in question was the medical service of the Soviet Ministry of Defense, under Kamanin, who was nevertheless forced to develop plans to integrate employees of these organizations into the TsPK effort. He proposed to examine 30 "passengers" and 30 physicians, at the TsNIAG in April 1964, with six to be approved for cosmonaut training. He did this grudgingly: at the same time, he prepared his own group of nine military cosmonauts to fly both manned missions. (In fairness to Kamanin, he was not the only one to resist the idea: the military cosmonauts themselves were against it, too.)

In April and May 1964 36 candidates were selected from the Academy of Sciences and Ministry of Health with 14 passing the medical board. On May 27–28 a credentials committee met to examine the professional and political suitability of eight Ministry of Health physicians and two Academy of Sciences researchers, approving five candidates for training:

Major Vasily G. Lazarev	NII–7
Boris B. Yegorov	IMBP
Boris N. Polyakov	IMBP
Captain Alexei V. Sorokin	TsPK
Georgy P. Katys	Academy of Sciences

Korolev's OKB–1 was tardy in submitting its candidates, ultimately proposing a list of 14 on May 17, 1964. Eight of the engineer candidates qualified medically:

SOURCE: "A Leader Among Leaders," Nikolai Kuznetsov, from *Pioneers of Space*, Moscow: Progress Publishers, 1989.

Vladislav N. Volkov

Georgy M. Grechko

V. P. Zaitsev

Valery N. Kubasov

Oleg G. Makarov

A. M. Sidorov

Konstantin P. Feoktistov

Valery I. Yazdovsky

Only Feoktistov was approved for training on June 11, 1964, however, and then only due to a personal appeal by Korolev. Because of a spinal injury, Feoktistov was unable to undero parachute training, so Kamanin would only approve him for space missions lasting a single day. Worst of all, Feoktistov was not a member of the Communist Party or of the Komsomol.

But Feoktistov was the principal designer of the Vostok, and also of the unique braking system for Voskhod (a retrorocket mounted on the shroud lines of the parachute lowering the spherical spacecraft to the Earth), and Korolev felt that he should have the honor of testing it himself.

The initial pool of candidates for the three-man Voskhod flight, then, consisted of:

Pilots and engineers from the Soviet air force cosmonaut group: Bykovsky, Titov, Popovich, Komarov, Volynov, Leonov, Khrunov, Demin, Belyayev;

Vladimir N. Benderov, a test pilot from the Tupolev bureau of the Ministry of Aviation Production;

Physicians Lazarev, Yegorov, Polyakov, and Sorokin from the Ministry of Health, which included military medical specialists from NII–7 (TsNIAG) and from the TsPK itself, and civilians from the newly created Institute for Medical–Biological Problems.

Researcher Katys from the USSR Academy of Sciences, selected personally by Academy President Mstislav V. Keldysh;

Feotistov from the OKB–1.

Benderov and Polyakov were dropped from training in the first week because of their size and bad reactions to the centrifuge. (Benderov was later killed in the Tu–144 crash at the Paris Air Show in May 1973.) TsPK cosmonauts Shonin and Demin were also excluded, and through a dizzying series of combinations, from all military to all civilian, seven Voskhod candidates (Komarov,

Volynov, Katys, Feoktistov, Lazarev, Sorokin, and Yegorov) trained for four months, until the successful launch on October 12, 1964, of the first multimanned spacecraft, Voskhod, carrying a crew of Komarov, Feoktistov, and Yegorov.

The Voskhod "group" was not seen to be part of the permanent cosmonaut team; only the two civilians who flew in space (Feoktistov and Yegorov) and Katys, who was a candidate for later flights, were given the status of cosmonaut by the Soviet government.

Nevertheless, encouraged by his victory in the war with Kamanin, Korolev went ahead with plans for a civilian cosmonaut unit within the OKB–1. In August 1964 he identified 12 young engineers—including most of those who passed the Voskhod 1 medical examinations—for transfer to a new Department 90 under test pilot Sergei Anokhin. (The 12 were Vladimir Bugrov, Gennady Dolgopolov, Georgy Grechko, Valery Kubasov, Oleg Makarov, Nikolai Rukavishnikov, Vitaly Sevastyanov, Vladimir Timchenko, Vladislav Volkov, Valery Yazdovsky, and Alexei Yeliseyev in addition to Feoktistov. All but Timchenko, who became a group leader at the bureau and was involved in the Apollo–Soyuz Test Project, would eventually be enrolled as engineer–cosmonauts.)

Korolev also considered Anokhin a potential cosmonaut. Anokhin had tested the early MiG 15 and became head of the flight test department at Korolev's bureau. But he was in his mid–fifties and though proposed as an early Soyuz flight engineer, was never to receive medical approval for training.

Voskhod 2, the second in the series, was crewed by military cosmonauts Belyayev and Leonov, with Gorbatko, Zaikin, and Khrunov as backups.

In April 1965 Kamanin proposed researcher Georgy Katys for the crew of Voskhod 3, which was originally scheduled to carry a number of Academy of Sciences experiments.

A Voskhod flight devoted to medical studies was also considered, so on February 10, 1965, Kamanin returned Voskhod 1 physicians Lazarev and Sorokin to the TsPK, though he did not enroll them in the cosmonaut team at that time. The IMBP also designated four candidates for that program:

Yevgeny I. Ilyin

Alexei S. Senkevich

Alexandr S. Kissilev

Sergei Nikolayev

At the same time, Korolev also encouraged two noted space journalists, Yaroslav Golovanov and Yuri Letunov, to undergo medical testing. Neither one was able to pass, however.

None of the scientific, medical or journalistic Voskhod missions progressed beyond the planning stage. The potential cosmonauts from the IMBP took part in less than a week of actual training, and were never enrolled in the cosmonaut team.

The 3d Enrollment: October 28, 1965

In January 1965 the 13 remaining candidates of the 2d Enrollment, plus Beregovoy, were judged to have completed their training and qualified as air force cosmonauts. A new training selection and training cycle began in March and April.

Candidates for this 3d Enrollment were less experienced than the members of the first enrollment. Mindful of the external pressure that had resulted in the assignment of Feoktistov and Yegorov to Voskhod, Kamanin opened applications not only to air forces and rocket forces personnel, the navy (air and sea forces), and the army, but also to civilian design bureaus with ties to the military as well as personnel from the Academy of Sciences and Ministry of Health. Candidates were limited to those under the age of 30 to 32. The intent was to take a large number of men and train them specifically for cosmonaut careers. Given the number of active senior men, the new arrivals could not expect to make flights for five or six years, which would give them time to complete the two–year basic training course, to perform technical assignments such as serving as communications operators, and to attend test pilot schools or the Red Banner (later named for Yuri Gagarin) Military Academy.

Kamanin wanted to select 40 new cosmonaut–candidates, but was limited to half that number because of the lack of living space, instructors, and facilities. Scientists and civilian candidates were then excluded from the first phase of the selection process.

At least 3,000 military officers applied, with 284 undergoing medical testing. The credentials committee met five times between October 16 and 25, 1965, to examine 65 potential candidates. Twenty–one were chosen, reporting to the training center by December 1, 1965:

Maj. Vladimir A. Degtyarev

Lieut. Anatoly P. Fedorov

Sr. Eng.–Lieut. Yuri A. Glazkov

Lieut. Vitaly A. Grishchenko

Sr. Eng.–Lieut. Yevgeny N. Khludeyev

Lieut. Leonid D. Kizim

Lieut. Pyotr I. Klimuk

Eng.–Capt. Gennady M. Kolesnikov

Lieut. Alexandr Ya. Kramarenko

Eng.–Capt. Mikhail I. Lisun

Lieut. Alexandr Ya. Petrushenko

Sgt. Vladimir Ye. Preobrazhensky

Sr. Eng.–Lieut. Valery I. Rozhdestvensky

Lieut. Gennady V. Sarafanov

Lieut. Ansar I. Sharafutdinov

Lieut. Vasily D. Shcheglov

Lieut. Alexandr A. Skvortsov

Eng.–Capt. Eduard N. Stepanov

Lieut. Valery A. Voloshin

Lieut. Oleg D. Yakovlev

Lieut. Vyacheslav D. Zudov

The actual size of the 3d Enrollment was 22—at the last minute an engineer from the Strategic Rocket Forces, Major Boris N. Belousov, 35, was added at the personal request of OKB–1 Chief Designer Korolev and Academy of Sciences President Keldysh. (Belousov was one of the 6 candidates approved but not selected for the 2d Enrollment.)

The oldest pilot was just 25; the engineers were slightly older. Glazkov, Khludeyev, Kolesnikov, and Stepanov were air force engineers. Grishchenko was a navigator. Degtyarev was a physician. Lisun had been trained as a combat engineer. Preobrazhensky was a graduate of the Moscow Aviation Institute recently drafted into the military, hence his enlisted rank. Rozhdestvensky was a navy officer. The rest were young pilots.

Only six members of this group flew in space, though some trained for many years. Degtyarev withdrew almost immediately, and never, in fact, trained at all. Five members of the 3d Enrollment failed to complete the training course and were dismissed between December 1967 and February 1968—Grishchenko, Belousov, Skvortsov, Kolesnikov, and Sharafutdinov. (Skvortsov's son, also named Alexandr, would be selected as a cosmonaut candidate in 1997.)

When Degtyarev withdrew, his place was taken by Lieutenant Colonel Vasily Lazarev, 37, a pilot and physician from NII–7 who had served as a Voskhod backup in 1964, and had been returned to training at Kamanin's request. The special order authorizing Lazarev's enrollment was dated January 31, 1966.

TsPK Organization

The large number of candidates selected in the 3d Enrollment was based on overly optimistic projections by Soviet officials of the number of manned missions. In addition to flights in the Soyuz lunar program, in 1965 "space fighter" and reconnaissance versions of the 7K spacecraft were in development in addition to the Almaz military manned space station and Spiral spaceplane.

The air force cosmonaut team was divided into two "squads" in May 1966, the first squad headed by Nikolayev, with Leonov as deputy, to concentrate on the Soyuz and lunar programs. The second squad was headed by Titov, with Popovich as his deputy, for military programs such as Almaz and Spiral.

Gagarin continued to work as one of several deputy directors of the TsPK. Belyayev became chief of staff and Komarov head of the 1st Directorate.

The Civilian Cosmonaut Team

Kamanin failed in his attempt to exercise ironclad military control over all Soviet cosmonaut selection. For one thing, he found his own recommendations overruled or altered by his immediate superior on the High Command, General Rudenko. And he had to contend with powerful personalities in other organizations, including the Academy of Sciences, the Ministry of Health, the Ministry of Aviation Production, and most notably, the new Ministry of General Machine Building (MOM), created in late 1965 to oversee the development of space programs for the Soviet government. Each organization had its allies and enemies on the Central Committee, on the Council of Ministers, and on the Scientific–Technical Council (VPK), and its own agenda. The Academy of Sciences wanted scientific researchers in space crews. The Ministry of Health wanted doctors. Various aircraft bureaus wanted their test pilots to fly. Gagarin's diary reveals that in 1966, not long after Korolev's death, the cosmonaut spoke with Tikhonravov, who was apparently very enthusiastic about recruiting more test pilots into the cosmonaut team. Gagarin agreed that test pilots were a welcome addition, but wondered if officials were making full use of the cosmonauts already in the program.

Korolev died on January 13, 1966, and was succeeded as general designer of the TsKBEM (the designation for the OKB–1 under the new MOM) by his deputy, Vasily Mishin. Although Korolev had succeeded in getting Feoktistov into the first Voskhod crew, it fell to Mishin to establish the civilian cosmonaut team. Mishin and his allies were also able to get a decree passed at the ministerial level *requiring* each space crew to include an employee of the enterprise that built the space vehicle.

On May 23, 1966—five months after Korolev's death—Mishin created department 291 of the TsKBEM, under Sergei Anokhin, the so–called flight test department. There were eight "flight testers":

Sergei N. Anokhin
Vladimir Ye. Bugrov
Gennady A. Dolgopolov
Georgy M. Grechko
Valery N. Kubasov
Oleg G. Makarov
Vladislav N. Volkov
Alexei S. Yeliseyev

Mishin and Kamanin engaged in a bureaucratic struggle that lasted for several months. Kamanin resisted the selection of crewmembers who could not meet the physical standards—Feoktistov for one, and especially Anokhin, who was 56 years old. Mishin needlessly antagonized Kamanin and the air force by threatening to assign only civilian engineers to Soyuz crews, elminating military pilots altogether.

In late August 1966 the eight prospective TsKBEM engineer–cosmonauts underwent testing at the military hospital. Four passed and commenced Soyuz training on October 1, 1966: Yeliseyev, Kubasov, Volkov, and Grechko. Within two weeks Grechko had injured himself in a parachuting accident and been forced to drop out. He was replaced by Makarov.

None of these men had official status as cosmonauts. They were merely civilians who were being allowed to train at Kamanin's TsPK. Yeliseyev and Kubasov were only officially included in Soyuz crews on November 25, 1966, just prior to the first unmanned Soyuz test flights, in anticipation of a manned Soyuz mission in January 1967.

A second pair of TsKBEM engineers commenced training at the TsPK for the lunar orbital program at the end of January 1967:

Nikolai N. Rukavishnikov

Vitaly I. Sevastyanov

Both had been part of the TsKBEM team, but had not been available to undergo cosmonaut training due to other work.

The first manned Soyuz mission—ultimately launched as Soyuz 1 on April 23, 1967—ended with the death of Colonel Vladimir Komarov. All manned flights were suspended pending investigation.

The 4th Enrollment: April 1967

In April 1967, 12 new cosmonaut candidates, including nine who had passed the examinations for the 3d Enrollment two years earlier, but had been placed in reserve—arrived at the Center:

Eng.–Maj. Vladimir B. Alexeyev

Sr. Lieut. Valery Beloborodov

Eng.–Maj. Mikhail N. Burdayev

Capt. Sergei N. Gaidukov

Sr. Lieut. Vladimir T. Isakov

Sr. Eng.–Lt. Vladimir V. Kovalenok

Sr. Lieut. Vladimir S. Kozelsky

Sr. Lieut. Vladimir A. Lyakhov

Sr. Lieut. Yuri V. Malyshev

Sr. Lieut. Viktor M. Pisarev

Eng.–Maj. Nikolai N. Porvatkin

Capt. Mikhail V. Sologub

Alexeyev, Burdayev, and Porvatkin were military research scientists from the NII–2, the Institute for Air Defense. Gaidukov, Isakov, and Sologub were navigators. The others were pilots.

Three men—Beloborodov, Pisarev, and Sologub—failed to complete the candidate course. Gaidukov was injured in a parachute accident, leading to his medical disqualification in 1978. Alexeyev, Burdayev, Isakov, Kozelsky, and Porvatkin were transferred en masse to the flight control staff in April 1983, having, it was judged, "no chance to fly in space." Only Kovalenok, Lyakhov, and Malyshev ever did, again, like the 1965 group, largely because of the cutback in the Almaz program.

The Ministry of General–Machine Building Team: May 1968

By the spring of 1968, when manned Soyuz launches were ready to be resumed, Mishin and Kamanin had concluded a "peace" treaty concerning cosmonaut training and selection. The air force would remain the host organization for the training center, and all cosmonauts, military and civilian, would be trained there.

But civilian organizations would be allowed to propose their own candidates, whose medical examinations would be conducted at the civilian Insitute for Medical–Biological Problems. Like their military counterparts, the aspiring civilian cosmonaut–candidates would then have their moral and professional fitness examined by a credentials committee. The final step in the process was the Joint State Committee (GMVK), which approved or denied the applications of military and civilian candidates.

The first civilian "medical commmission" was conducted at the IMBP in November 1967, and produced three new aspiring cosmonaut–candidates:

Vladimir A. Fartushny

Viktor I. Patsayev

Vladimir P. Nikitsky

Fartushny was one of 2 staffers at the Paton Welding Institute in Kiev who were considered as early as December 1966 as potential Soyuz crewmembers. Patsayev and Nikitsky had been transferred by Mishin to Department 291 of the TsKBEM in June 1967. These three were submitted to the credentials committee, which Nikitsky failed to pass.

On May 23, 1968, the Ministry of General Machine–Building officially created a civilian cosmonaut team, certifying 10 candidates who had passed the medical commissions in 1966 and whose credentials had been certified:

Yeliseyev

Kubasov

Volkov

Grechko

Makarov

Patsayev

Rukavishnikov

Sevastyanov

Fartushny

Feoktistov

These men made up the first cosmonaut team not controlled by Kamanin and the air force.

Academy of Sciences Cosmonauts

The role of the scientist as a working cosmonaut is a sad story of missed opportunity. Through April 1998, no scientist was included in a Soviet flight crew.

In 1964, as part of the first Voskhod training group Georgy Katys, a staff member of the Academy, was selected. He served as backup to Feoktistov on the October 1964 three–man flight. He also trained for the Voskhod 3 mission in 1965 until being replaced by an air force cosmonaut, at which point he returned to his research.

Nevertheless, thanks to the prominence of Academy of Sciences President Keldysh, the Ministries of Defense and General Machine–Building encouraged the creation of a cadre of "scientist–cosmonauts."

Twenty–four candidates from the Academy's Moscow region centers were submitted to the military medical commission headed by Major–General Ivan Babichik in September 1966. Eighteen were judged healthy, and submitted to the credentials committee. In May 1967 four were approved:

Valentin Yershov

Rudolf Gulyayev

Ordinard Kolomitsev

Mars Fatkhullin

They joined Katys in forming a cosmonaut group within the Academy of Sciences. Yershov, a specialist in trajectories, was included in the general group of cosmonauts training for lunar orbit and landing missions at the TsPK: his position would have been navigator–flight engineer. Kolomitsev, Fatkhullin, and Gulyayev did little or no training. By May 1970 the scientist–cosmonaut group, with the exception of Yershov, was disbanded.

Several other members of Academy institutes went before the medical commission in the 1970s and 1980s, some passing, but none was approved by the credentials committee. (See the entry on Other Design Bureaus and Institutes, below.)

TsPK Reorganization: March 1969

Colonel Yuri Gagarin, deputy director of the TsPK for air–space training, was killed in a MiG–15 crash on March 28, 1968, along with Colonel Vladimir Seregin, commander of the TsPK's aircraft support squadron at nearby Chkalov Air Base. In June 1968 the TsPK was renamed in Gagarin's honor, and Colonel Andrian Nikolayev was named the new deputy director for air–space training. Colonel Valery Bykovsky succeeded Nikolayev as commander of the 1st squad of the cosmonaut detachment.

This was a time of transformation for the cosmonaut team and the TsPK. The Center had expanded between 1963 and 1966, but the the creation of the MOM, and of yet another organization within the Ministry of Defense for military space programs (TsUKOS), had siphoned resources and personnel. The replacement of air forces commander–in–chief Vershinin, a supporter of manned space programs, by Marshal Pavel Kutakhov, cost the Center its sponsor. The cancellation or stretchout of military manned programs, and the awareness that the expensive Soviet manned lunar program was about to be eclipsed by the American Apollo, forced a retrenchment and reorganization.

On March 28, 1969, the TsPK (Gagarin Center) was divided into departments for each of its manned programs, with the cosmonaut squads divided and dispersed as well:

- The spacecraft team, headed by Col. Vladimir Shatalov

- The Almaz team, headed by Col. Pavel Popovich

- The lunar team, headed by Col. Valery Bykovsky

- The Spiral team, headed by Col. Gherman Titov

A fifth department, for cosmonaut–candidates, was formed in late 1969, with Colonel Boris Volynov as head.

The 5th Enrollment: April 27, 1970

Even as the reorganization proceeded, Kamanin still wanted to reach his goal of a cosmonaut team of 80. The medical board and credentials committee produced another list of candidates for enrollment in April 1970:

Capt. Anatoly N. Berezovoy

Capt. Anatoly I. Dedkov

Capt. Vladimir A. Dzhanibekov

Sr. Eng.–Lt. Nikolai N. Fefelov

Eng.–Capt. Valery V. Illarionov

Capt. Yuri F. Isaulov

Sr. Lieut. Vladimir Kozlov

Sr. Lieut. Leonid I. Popov

Sr. Lieut. Yuri V. Romanenko

Following completion of the two–year candidate's course the pilot cosmonauts were assigned to the long–term orbital version of Salyut (DOS), the military Salyut (Almaz), or the Soyuz–T programs. Several were also enrolled in the Gagarin Air Force Academy.

Kozlov and Dedkov would leave the cosmonaut group without flying in space. Isaulov was medically disqualified in 1982. Fefelov and Illarionov remained active into the 1990s, but did not have an opportunity to fly.

Institute of Medical–Biological Problems

Medical doctors have always played a prominent role in the Soviet and Russian manned space program, developing the original criteria for the selection of cosmonauts, constantly monitoring training and inflight operations, and having a major voice in the selection of crews through the medical board. Korolev himself supported this involvement, planning Vostok–Voskhod missions in 1964 and 1965 with clear medical objectives.

The first doctor–cosmonaut, Boris Yegorov, was selected from the staff of the IMBP. Two of his Voskhod 1 backups, Alexei Sorokin and Vasily Lazarev, were military officers, Sorokin with the medical support staff at the TsPK, Lazarev with TsNIAG itself.

In 1965 three doctors from the Academy of Medical Sciences were encouraged to apply for training to take part in a 14–day biomedical Voskhod or Soyuz mission in the 1960s. These three men, Alexei Senkevich, Yevgeny Ilyin, and Alexandr Kissilev, only did a day of preliminary ground training and were never officially enrolled in any cosmonaut team.

The first doctor to be considered a permanent member of the cosmonaut team was Lazarev, who also happened to be an air force pilot. He was enrolled in the military cosmonaut team on January 31, 1966.

In the early 1970s, with the prospect of long duration space station missions, Soviet space officials concluded that the presence of doctors working in orbit would be an advantage. The Institute for Medical Biological Problems (a unit of the USSR Ministry of Health) founded by Dr. Oleg Gazenko, created its own cosmonaut candidate group in 1969.

Lev Smirenny had passed the medical examinations in May 1968. Valery Lobachek and German Machinsky passed in December 1969. Valery Polyakov and Voskhod candidate Yuri Senkevich passed in July 1970. These men formed the core of the IMBP cosmonaut team, but were still subject to final approval of the joint state commission.

On March 22, 1972, three IMBP staffers were approved:

German Machinsky

Valery Polyakov

Lev Smirenny

Polyakov was named director of the IMBP cosmonaut group, whose function was to be ready to render any kind of assistance in orbit, including surgery. Polyakov flew aboard Soyuz TM–5 in 1988 and Soyuz TM–16 in 1994. He still holds the record for longest spaceflight, 438 days aboard Mir from 1994 to 1995.

In 1976 the IMBP began to increase the size of its cosmonaut candidate unit, winning medical approval for Anatoly Bobrov, Alexandr Borodin, and Mikhail Potapov in June 1976; Leonid Bragin and Boris Morukov in October 1976; Boris Afonin in January 1977; and German Arzamazov in November of that year.

At the meeting of the joint state commission on December 1, 1978, these candidates were approved:

German S. Arzamazov

Alexandr V. Borodin

Mikhail G. Potapov

None of these men ever flew in space, though Arzamazov was backup to Polyakov for both of his flights.

Chelomei Bureau

Vladimir Nikolayevich Chelomei, head of the OKB–52 (later known as the TsKBM), was Korolev and Mishin's rival in the launch and spacecraft business. A canny politician as well as engineer, Chelomei prospered under the Khrushchev administration by, among other moves, hiring the Soviet premier's son, Sergei. Chelomei's organization was originally given responsibility for the Soviet manned lunar orbit program, LK–1, only to lose it to the Korolev–Mishin organization in 1966. Concentrating on military manned programs, Chelomei went ahead with the OPS program, consisting of the Almaz space station program and the TKS spacecraft. OPS was given ministerial approval in July 1967, and over the next year 4 of Chelomei's engineers were allowed to take part in preliminary crew training at the TsPK, in teams with military cosmonauts:

Oleg N. Berkovich

Valery G. Makrushin

Eduard D. Sukhanov

Viktor N. Yeremich

It soon became apparent that Chelomei's OPS station would be ready long before its TKS spacecraft, and the Ministries of General Machine and Defense chose to purchase several Soyuz (7K) spacecraft to carry cosmonauts to the OPS until TKS had been tested.

This postponed the need for crewmembers from Chelomei's organization. The first Almaz crews would consist of three military officers from the Gagarin Center team.

Berkovich passed the civilian medical commission on May 20, 1968, and the other three on October 16, 1968, but there was no cosmonaut team within the TsKBM as such until 1969, when Chelomei approved its creation with three initial candidates:

Alexei Grechanik

Valery Makrushin

Dmitri Yuyukov

At the time of the team's formation, the TsKBM was two years away from manned launches of its Almaz military space station. Military cosmonaut teams at the Gagarin Center were already in training.

But in the fall of 1969, with the collapse of the Soviet manned lunar effort, the Ministry of General Machine Building chose to create a civilian manned space station program—and ordered Chelomei's organization to transfer several Almaz vehicles to their hated rivals, the Korolev–Mishin team, for outfitting as Zarya, later Salyut stations.

This move delayed manned Almaz launches by at least another year. The Soyuz 11 accident in June 1971, which killed three cosmonauts and forced a redesign of the Soyuyz transport vehicle, eliminated the seat for the third Soyuz crewmember, who would have been a Chleomei engineer.

It was only in March 1972 that any of Chelomei's cosmonaut candidates were considered by the joint state commission, and only one—Makrushin—passed at this time. Yuyukov and Grechanik received medical approval in February 1971, but were not enrolled at this time. Yuyukov was finally approved a year later, in March 1973.

Still hoping to press forward with his TKS transport vehicle, Chelomei added three more candidates to his team in 1973:

Alexandr Gevorkyan

Alexandr Khatulev

Valery Romanov

Romanov passed the medical commission in July 1973, Gevorkyan in August 1977, Khatulev in November 1977. All three were approved by the joint state commission on December 1, 1978. Gevorkyan and Romanov took part—along with Makrushin and Yuyukov—in crew training at the Gagarin Center between 1979 and 1981. Khatulev withdrew almost immediately and did not train at all.

Chelomei doubled the size of his in–house team in 1978, adding six more candidates, including his son, Sergei, in the hopes they would be approved in the July 1980 selection.

Sergei Kondratyev

Boris Morozov

Lev Tararin

Sergei Chelomei

Anatoly Chekh

Sergei Chukhin

Tararin and Chekh were removed from consideration for political reasons. Chekh passed the medical board in July 1979, Morozov in October 1979, Chelomei and Chukhin in April 1981. None of the 4 were ever approved for training. The Almaz–TKS program for which they had been enrolled was officially cancelled in December 1981, though the Chelomei cosmonaut team was not dissolved until 1987.

More Civilian Cosmonauts: March 1972 and March 1973

Seven engineers and physicians passed medical boards in 1969, 1970, and 1971 and were approved by the joint state commission on March 22, 1972:

Boris D. Andreyev	TsKBEM (OKB–1)
Valentin V. Lebedev	TsKBEM (OKB–1)
German V. Machinsky	IMBP
Valery G. Makrushin	TsKBM (OKB–52)
Valery V. Polyakov	IMBP
Yuri A. Ponomarev	TsKBEM (OKB–1)
Lev N. Smirenny	IMBP

Of these seven, only Lebedev and Polyakov would fly in space, though all but Machinsky were named to crews at different times.

On March 27, 1973, the GMVK approved five more engineers:

Vladimir V. Aksenov	TsKBEM (OKB–1)
Alexandr S. Ivanchenkov	TsKBEM (OKB–1)
Valery V. Ryumin	TsKBEM (OKB–1)
Gennady M. Strekalov	TsKBEM (OKB–1)
Dmitri Yuyukov	TsKBM (OKB–52)

Aksenov had passed medical examinations as early as 1966, but had been asked to delay his entry into the cosmonaut group. Ivanchenkov, Ryumin, and Strekalov had passed in 1971, but had elected to wait because of involvement in other duties. Yuyukov was another of Chelomei's engineers. He was the only one of the 5 not to fly in space.

Reorganization: The Buran Program (1970s)

In 1974 the TsKBEM (former OKB–1) was reorganized upon orders of the Ministry of General Machine Building. Chief designer Vasily Mishin was fired and replaced by Valentin Glushko, head of his own Leningrad–based OKB—which was merged with the TsKBEM to form the Energiya Scientific Production Association, NPO Energiya.

Glushko's first task was cancellation of the lingering N1 rocket program, which was replaced by the Energiya superbooster and the Buran space shuttle. The Buran, then projected for manned operations in the early 1980s, could carry as many as 10 crewmembers, most of them engineers or researchers. Consequently NPO Energiya's flight–test deparment, #291, which was still directed by Sergei Anokhin, made plans for a new enrollment for continuing Soyuz–Salyut missions, and for Buran flights.

The Energiya recruitment began in late 1975 and early 1976 with medical screening of applicants. Twelve engineers were admitted as candidates in 1976: Alexandr Alexandrov, Alexandr Balandin, Valery Chervyakov, Gennady Isayev, Alexandr Kulik, Alexandr Laveikin, Musa Manarov, Viktor Petrenko, Nikolai Petrov, Viktor Savinykh, Alexandr Serebrov, and Vladimir Solovyov. Following two years of initial training and examinations under the direction of cosmonaut Valery Kubasov, seven of these men were enrolled in the cosmonaut team on December 1, 1978:

Alexandr P. Alexandrov

Alexandr N. Balandin

Alexandr I. Laveikin

Musa Kh. Manarov

Viktor P. Savinykh

Alexandr A. Serebrov

Vladimir A. Solovyov

Four of these engineers—Alexandrov, Savinykh, Serebrov, and Solovyov—were included in the Soyuz–Salyut training group. The three younger men (Balandin, Laveikin, and Manarov) were initially assigned to the new Buran program.

The overall group approved by the joint state commission on December 1, 1978, numbered 14—in addition the the seven from NPO Energiya, three cosmonauts from the Chelomei organization, and four from IMBP (see those sections, above, for details).

Women Cosmonauts: July 30, 1980

In spite of having sent the first women into space in 1963, Soviet officials disbanded the program six years later, ostensibly out of concern for the effect of cosmonaut training on women and their families. As late as 1980 cosmonaut chief Vladimir Shatalov insisted that "we just had no moral right to subjected the 'better half' of mankind to such [physical] loads."

Nevertheless, in 1979 the joint state commission, encouraged by Energiya chief Glushko, perhaps in response the selection of the first female American astro-

nauts, began to recruit a second group of women cosmonauts, to consist of employees of Energiya, the Academy of Sciences, the Institute for Medical–Biological Problems, and other aerospace organizations. To allay doubts about the women's ability to perform, a large group numbering more than a dozen was subject to medical testing (beginning in May 1979) and given several months of basic cosmonaut training (December 1979–June 1980) at the Gagarin Center before selection.

On July 30, 1980, nine women were approved for enrollment as cosmonaut–candidates:

Galina V. Amelkina	IMBP
Yelena I. Dobrokvashina	IMBP
Olga N. Klyushnikova	IMBP
Natalya D. Kuleshova	NPO Energiya
Irina D. Latysheva	IKI
Larisa G. Pozharskaya	IMBP
Irina R. Pronina	NPO Energiya
Svetlana Ye. Savitskaya	KB Yakovlev
Tamara Zakharova	IMBP

In spite of approval by the MVK, Klyushnikova was not enrolled in the IMBP cosmonaut team. Savitskaya was the only one to make spaceflights, aboard Soyuz T–7 (1982) and Soyuz T–12 (1984).

In its July 30, 1980, decision, the joint state commission also reviewed test pilot applicants from the civilian flight research institute (LII) who would fly Soyuz missions to qualify them for orbital Buran flights.

Oleg G. Kononenko

Anatoly S. Levchenko

Alexandr V. Shchukin

Rimantas A. Stankyavichus

Igor P. Volk

For full details on the civilian and military Buran test pilot group, see the article by Vis and Shkorking, page 321.

The 6th Enrollment: August 1976

The nine cosmonauts of the 5th Enrollment had reached the limit of 80 authorized by Vershinin for the Gagarin

Center in 1962. Although many of those selected between 1962 and 1970 were no longer on flight status, most were still included in the headcount. Further, program cancellations (such as the lunar orbit and landing effort) and stretchouts made it clear that a smaller team was all that was required. There were no enrollments for military cosmonauts from 1970 and for several years thereafter.

During this time some senior cosmonauts assumed the leadership of the manned space program: in the summer of 1971 Vladimir Shatalov succeeded Kamanin as the air force's staff official in charge of cosmonaut training. Georgy Beregovoy succeeded Nikolai Kuznetsov as director of the Gagarin Center in June 1972, with Andrian Nikolayev as first deputy director. Veteran cosmonauts Popovich, Shonin, Leonov, and Filipchenko also began serving as heads of directorates as the center expanded in the mid–1970s.

It was only with the creation of the Buran program that the air force won authorization to add to the Gagarin Center cosmonaut team. The candidates were to be operational pilots who could be trained as test pilots in order to fly Buran. Although it was hoped that a group of 20 could be found, only nine candidates qualified and were enrolled on August 23, 1976:

> Capt. Leonid G. Ivanov
>
> Capt. Leonid K. Kadenyuk
>
> Capt. Nikolai T. Moskalenko
>
> Capt. Sergei F. Protchenko
>
> Capt. Yevgeny V. Salei
>
> Sr. Lieut. Alexandr Ya. Solovoyov
>
> Capt. Vladimir V. Titov
>
> Sr. Lieut. Vladimir V. Vasyutin
>
> Capt. Alexandr A. Volkov

All nine were enrolled at the Chkalov test pilot school at Akhtubinsk for their first year of training. From 1977 to 1979 they underwent general space training at the Center under the guidance of Lev Demin and Vitaly Zholobov. They then returned to test flying, until recalled to the Center for assignment to a Soyuz–Salyut training group.

Ivanov was killed during a test flight on October 23, 1980. Moskalenko, Protchenko, and Salei were dismissed from the program before flying in space. So was Kadenyuk, but he later returned to active cosmonaut training as a

Buran pilot and ultimately flew in space as a Ukrainian payload specialist aboard the American Space Shuttle in 1997.

The 7th Enrollment: May 23, 1978

Since the air force had not been able to provide enough candidate cosmonauts to meet the authorization for the Buran program, the commission agreed to consider applicants from the naval air forces (VM–F) and the air defense forces (PVO). Only two candidates were found this time:

> Capt. Nikolai S. Grekov
>
> Capt. Alexandr S. Viktorenko

Their training was similar to that of the 6th Enrollment— a year at test pilot school followed by a two–year general course at Gagarin Center. Of the two, only Viktorenko flew in space. Grekov was medically disqualified in 1986 and joined the flight control team. He later became a department head at the training center.

Other Design Bureaus and Institutes

During the mid to late 1960s a number of other bureaus put forward candidates for training as potential cosmonauts. Vladimir Fartushny of the Paton Institute was the first, in May 1968.

The OKB Pilyugin, which specialized in automatic spacecraft control systems, put forward two candidates, one of whom, Anatoly P. Demyanenko, passed the medical board in October 1969 and underwent some general training. He was drowned in a training accident on the Black Sea in 1971 before winning approval from the joint state commission.

Yuri G. Petrov, a member of the staff of TsNIIMash, the central research institute for spaceflight based in Kaliningrad, passed the medical board in December 1969.

An oceanographer named Ziyatdin K. Abuzyarov of the Gidromettsentr (USSR Weather Service) passed the medicals in July 1970 at the same time as IMBP physicians Polyakov and Senkevich, and was given approval for cosmonaut training. He was never summoned, however, and was removed from the candidate reserve along with Yershov in 1974.

Geologist Gurgen A. Ivanyan of Leningrad State University, passed the medical board in February 1971 along with Chelomei engineers Grechanik and Yuyukov, but went no further in the selection process.

OKB Yangel, builders of Soviet intercontinental missiles, also submitted candidates for the Korolev group, but none was successful in receiving commission approval.

The 1979 decision to create a second selection of women cosmonauts opened the door for two candidates from organizations other than the military, NPO Energiya or the IMBP.

Svetlana Ye. Savitskaya, a civilian test pilot with the Yakovlev aircraft design bureau within the Ministry of Aviation Production, was given medical approval in May 1979 and officially enrolled as a cosmonaut candidate in the NPO Energiya team in July 1980. Savitskaya went on to make two spaceflights, aboard Soyuz T–7 (1982) and Soyuz T–12 (1984), and made the first EVA by a woman space traveler.

Irina D. Latysheva of the Institute for Space Research of the Academy of Sciences was also one of the 9 women candidates approved at that time. She also joined the Energiya team, but though she remained qualified for training for fifteen years, was never even submitted for basic cosmonaut training at the Gagarin Center.

A physician from the All–Union Cardiological Institute Oleg Yu. Atkov, was approved by the medical board in 1977 and the joint state commission in 1983. He made a spaceflight aboard Salyut–7 in 1984.

NPO Molniya, builders of the Buran shuttle, got one of its engineers, Vitaly S. Karlin, approved by the medical board in October 1979, but he was not given final approval.

A representative of the Ministry of Higher Education, Yekaterina Ivanova of the Leningrad Institute of Mechanics, was approved for training with Atkov in March 1983. Although in 1985 she trained as a member of the all–woman Soyuz crew, Ivanova did not fly in space.

In spite of the grim prospects for a flight, several scientists persisted in applying. An information specialist at the Institute of Natural Sciences and History of Technology in Leningrad, Arkady I. Melua, passed the medicals in April 1985; again, he was never approved for cosmonaut training. In July 1988, Sergei Ye. Fursov of the Academy of Medical Sciences went before the medical board and was approved, but, like most others, was never enrolled in a cosmonaut team. Two more medical specialists, Anatoly Yu. Murashov and Alexei V. Karateyev, passed in 1989, to no avail.

A commercial copilot from the Ministry of Civil Aviation (MGA), Talgat A. Musabayev, was medically approved in February 1989 and officially enrolled as a cosmonaut on May 11, 1990, as part of an effort to recruit an ethnic Kazakh into the cosmonaut team. Musabayev was given a commission in the Soviet air force and joined the Gagarin Center cosmonaut team, serving as a flight engineer for Soyuz TM–19 (1994) and commander of Soyuz TM–27 (1998).

In the same joint state commission session of May 11, 1990, engineer Vladimir G. Severin from the NPO Zvezda, a bureau that specializes in space suits and aircraft ejection seats, was approved. He was the son of NPO Zvezda general director Gay Severin.

KB Salyut

In 1977, as manned TKS–Almaz operations drew closer, officials of KB Salyut, the branch of the TsKBM (OKB–52) that actually built the spacecraft and modules, created its own cosmonaut team of six candidates: N. Gerasimov, V. Gevorkyan, V. Davydov, A. Medvedev, A. Mokin, and V. Khatulev. Gevorkyan and Khatulev were included in the group of Chelomei candidates submitted to the Joint State Commission and approved on December 1, 1978. The others received medical approvals at various stages, but never reached the status of cosmonaut–candidate.

In February 1996, however, Sergei Ivanovich Moshchenko, an employee of the KB Salyut—now reorganized as the Khrunichev Space Center, builders of Mir and of Russia's International Space Station components—was approved for cosmonaut training. Some of the failed aspiring cosmonauts of the late 1970s—Medvedev and Gerasimov in particular—had gained enough power and position to enable younger members of the organization to realize their dreams of personally flying in space.

Buran Test Pilots

From January 1979 to the summer of 1980 several military and civilian Soviet test pilots underwent the general course at the Gagarin Center. For details, see the accompanying "Buran Test-Pilot Cosmonauts," page 321.

Enrollments in the 1980s

From 1960 to the present, all Soviet (now Russian) cosmonauts, military and civilian, are trained at the Cosmonaut Training Center named for Gagarin, a complex of laboratories, classrooms, simulators, apartments, and office buildings 25 miles northeast of Moscow. The Center is part of a village known as Star Town, which has 3,500 inhabitants, most of them officials of the space program and their families. It is here that cosmonauts and former cosmonauts from the air force and now–disbanded military test pilot groups lived. Civilian cosmonauts retain residences in Moscow and reside in Star Town only when assigned to missions.

Unlike American astronauts, who are officially "loaned" to the space program by their parent service, and usually leave after several years, an assignment to the Center was considered permanent, even for cosmonauts who no longer worked in the space program, such as Shonin or Khrunov, or candidates who were cosmonauts only briefly, such as Beloborodov.

Academic and medical dropouts were usually employed elsewhere in the space program; the families of those who were killed in training or space–related accidents remained in the community of Star Town.

Many inactive cosmonauts assumed administrative jobs in the space program, as communications operators and controllers at the flight control center and engineers at RKK Energiya. Heads of directorates at the Gagarin Center in the 1970s and 1980s included Popovich, Shonin, Filipchenko, Dzhanibekov, and Romanenko. Nikolayev was first deputy director of the Center from 1970, with Leonov as deputy director for air–space training from 1976.

Colonel Boris Volynov succeeded Colonel Viktor Gorbatko as head of the cosmonaut team in September 1982. (Gorbatko had held the job for only nine months.)

To cope with the challenges of training cosmonaut candidates from different organizations for different programs, in 1981 Leonov reorganized the cosmonaut training program, resulting in a more standardized 18–month program resulting in the qualification of "test–cosmonauts," a title reserved for pilots and flight engineers. Physicians, scientists, and most other candidates would earn the title of "cosmonaut–researcher."

Test–cosmonaut certificates were awarded, most of them retroactive, on February 12, 1982, to 85 individuals, the 50 publicly known and honored cosmonauts who had flown (some awards were made posthumously) plus those such as Kolodin who had completed training and served on backup crews, but who had yet to fly in space, as well as military cosmonaut–candidates Grekov and Viktorenko, military test pilots Bachurin, Borodai, Mossolov, and Sokovykh, civilian test pilots Volk, Levchenko, Stankyavichus, and Shchukin, Energiya engineers Alexandrov, Serebrov, and Solovyov, and women cosmonauts Savitskaya and Pronina.

Some cosmonauts, notably Gherman Titov, Vladimir Kovalenok, and Georgy Shonin, left the Gagarin Center in the 1970s and 1980s to pursue careers in other branches of the armed forces.

Soyuz launch rates remained stable at an average of three per year, meaning that as few as six civilian flight engineers were needed in active training at any given time. Enrollments of the 1980s were therefore smaller, consisting of one or two new engineers. Both military and civilian candidates were considered at these meetings of the joint state commission:

March 9, 1983:

Oleg Yu. Atkov	Academy of Medical Sciences
Yekaterina Ivanova	Institute of Higher Education
Magomed O. Tolboyev	LII
Ural N. Sultanov	LII

Physician Atkov and engineer Ivanov underwent basic space training at the Center in 1983, qualyfing as cosmonaut–researchers, though only Atkov flew in space. Civilian Buran test pilots Sultanov and Tolboyev underwent the longer test–cosmonaut course in 1985–87.

February 2, 1984:

Alexandr Yu. Kaleri	NPO Energiya
Sergei A. Yemelyanov	NPO Energiya
Viktor V. Zabolotsky	LII

Kaleri and Yemlyanov underwent basic cosmonaut training from November 1985 to October 1986. Zabolotsky started at the same time, but completed training in November 1987. Kaleri was the only one to fly in space, in 1992 and 1996.

In 1984 three additional medical specialists from the Gagarin Center staff, not from the IMBP, were put forward as cosmonaut candidates: Robert Dyakonov, Anatoly Zhernovov, and Vladimir Bystrov. They did not complete general training and were not certified as cosmonaut–researchers.

September 2, 1985:

Sergei K. Krikalev	NPO Energiya
Andrei Ye. Zaitsev	NPO Energiya
Yuri N. Stepanov	IMBP
Sergei N. Tresvyatsky	LII
Yuri P. Sheffer	LII

Enerigya engineers Krikalev and Zaitsev, along with Kaleri and Yemelyanov from the February 1984 selection, began cosmonaut training in November 1985, completing it in October 1986. For the first phase of training the engineers joined by three civilian Buran test pilots selected in 1983 and 1984 (Sultanov, Tolboyev, and Zabolotsky) plus three new candidates for the military Buran test pilot team (Afanasyev, Artsebarsky, and Manakov) underwent the basic training course at the Gagarin Center from November 1985 to May 1987. Krikalev, Afanasyev, Artsebarsky, and Manakov made flights to Mir beginning in 1988.

The Buran program, originally scheduled for manned test flights in 1984, continued to be delayed. Nevertheless, with attrition in the Gagarin Center cosmonaut team, the Ministry of Defense finally authorized a new enrollment of five pilots.

March 26, 1987:

Capt. Vladimir N. Dezhurov
Capt. Yuri P. Gidzenko
Lieut. Col. Valery G. Korzun
Capt. Yuri I. Malenchenko
Lieut. Col. Vasily V. Tsibliyev

The Ministry of Defense order transferring these pilots was dated July 23, 1987.

Two NPO Energiya engineers also passed the medical board, but only one passed the technical examinations:

Sergei V. Adveyev   NPO Energiya

All six completed their candidate's course in July 1989, and all made Soyuz–Mir flights beginning in 1993.

The 9th Military Enrollment: January 8, 1988

Lieutenant General Vladimir Shatalov succeeded Georgy Beregovy as head of the Gagarin Center in January 1987. Shatalov's deputies included Major Generals Alexei Leonov, Yuri Glazkov, Pyotr Klimuk, and Vladimir Dzhanibekov. The head of the cosmonaut team until 1990 was Boris Volynov. Volynov was succeeded by Colonel Alexandr Volkov, with Alexandr Viktorenko as his deputy.

In the fall of 1987, seeing the continued delays in the Buran program, Shatalov proposed the transfer of several military test pilot candidates to the TsPK. The pilots themselves agreed:

Lt. Col. Viktor M. Afanasyev
Lt. Col. Anatoly A. Artsebarsky
Lt. Col. Gennady M. Manakov

Because they had already undergone basic space training from 1985 to 1987, these three pilots were eligible for immediate assignment to Soyuz–Mir training groups, ahead of the candidates of the 8th Enrollment.

This MVK screening produced another mixture of candidates from the military, Energiya and also from the flight research center.

February 9, 1989

Nikolai M. Budarin	NPO Energiya
Yelena V. Kondakova	NPO Energiya
Alexandr F. Poleshchuk	NPO Energiya
Yuri V. Usachev	NPO Energiya

The three male engineers commenced general space training in April 1989, completing it in January 1991. Kondakova's was delayed until 1990.

The military candidates were:

Lieut. Col. Sergei V. Krichevsky

Sr. Lieut. Yuri I. Onufriyenko

Capt. Gennady I. Padalka

Making up the 10th Enrollment, these three were officially transferred to the Gagarin Center by the Ministry of Defense on April 22, 1989. They completed their general training from July 1989 to January 1991. Onufriyenko made his first spaceflight aboard Soyuz TM–24 in the spring of 1996, and Padalka aboard Soyuz TM–28 in the summer of 1998. Krichevsky left the cosomonaut team in July 1997 without flying.

The Buran test pilot was:

Yuri V. Prikhodko   LII

Prikhodko joined the Energiya and Gagarin Center candidates in basic space training, 1989–1991.

Three other physicians were approved by the joint state commission at this time:

Vladimir V. Karashkin	IMBP
Vasily Yu. Lyukyanuk	IMBP
Boris V. Morukov	IMBP

The total number of IMBP staffers who underwent undergone cosmonaut training between 1964 and 1998 stands at 15, but only these three remain eligible for assignment to flight crews as of April 1998.

Three other names were approved by the joint state commission on this date. They were military test pilots from the GKNII, the military flight test center in the city of Akhtubinsk:

Lieut. Col. Anatoly B. Polonsky	GKNII
Col. Valery I. Tokarev	GKNII
Lieut. Col. Alexandr N. Yablontsev	GKNII

These three pilots, along with three others approved by the commission in May 1990, underwent basic space training as a group between July 1989 and January 1991. None flew in space, though Tokarev, who won a transfer to the Gagarin Center cosmonaut team in July 1987, remains a candidate for assignment to an International Space Station crew.

This enrollment was the largest and most diverse since the first Buran group of December 1, 1978. It included another group of military candidates, the 11th Enrollment:

May 11, 1990

Sr. Lieut. Salizhan S. Sharipov

Capt. Sergei Yu. Vozovikov

Sr. Lieut. Sergei V. Zaletin

These candidates were certified as test–cosmonauts in April 1992. Vozovikov was killed in a training accident in July 1993. Sharipov went into space for the first time aboard STS–89 in March 1998.

There were two researchers from other organizations:

Talgat A. Musabayev	LGA
Vladimir G. Severin	NPO Zvezda

There was also a group of six candidates for a USSR Journalist–in–Space program:

Lieut. Col. Alexandr S. Andryushkov

Lieut. Col. Valery V. Baberdin

Yuri Yu. Krikun

Pavel P. Mukhortov

Svetlana O. Omelchenko

Valery Yu. Sharov

As we have seen, Sergei Korolev had stated his desire to send a poet or journalist into space as early as 1965, when Yaroslav Golovanov and Yuri Letunov were submitted to the medical commission. Nothing came of those plans at the time, however. A third journalist, Lieutenant Colonel Mikhail Rebrov of the Ministry of Defense newspaper *Krasnaya Zvezda*, was a trained engineer and was briefly included in the group of cosmonauts preparing for manned Soviet lunar missions in late 1967 and early 1968. Again, he was never approved by the commission and was not considered to be a cosmonaut.

In 1989, largely in response to the outcry over the Soviet–Japanese Mir flight from Soviet journalists, notably Golovanov himself, NPO Energiya agreed to launch a Soviet journalist to coincide with the International Space Year, 1992.

After considerable public wrangling among the Soviet Writer's Union and the leadership of the Center, the six candidates passed the medical board and the joint state commission and were approved. (Golovanov and Rebrov were among the unsuccessful applicants.) They completed the cosmonaut–researcher course at the Gagarin Center in February 1992, by which time the Journalist–in–Space mission had lost its funding. Krikun was announced as researcher in a proposed all–Ukraine cosmonaut crew once suggested for launch in late 1992, but that mission never took place and none of the journalists went into space.

Kazakh researcher Musabayev later trained as a flight engineer and became a permanent resident at Star Town.

Finally, three more military test pilots from the Chkalov flight test center (GKNII) were approved:

Col. Valery Ye. Maximenko	GKNII
Col. Alexandr S. Puchkov	GKNII
Col. Nikolai A. Pushenko	GKNII

Maximenko, Puchkov, and Pushenko were already enrolled in the basic training course at the Gagarin Center at the time of their approval, completing it in January 1991. Maximenko returned to Chkalov at that time and did no further training for spaceflight. Puchkov and Pushenko were enrolled in the GKNII test pilot–cosmonaut team, but never flew in space.

Training for these groups of candidates was directed by Colonel Anatoly Berezovoy.

The Phantom Enrollment: August 1991

Screening for what would have become an August 28, 1991, meeting of the joint state commission began as expected in 1989, producing four candidates who were scheduled to be approved by the Joint State Commission. However, the abortive right–wing coup in late August caused the postponement of the meeting of the commission. The subsequent political disintegration of the Soviet Union in the next several months put a halt to the selection process that had existed for twenty–five years.

The four phantoms included Kazakh test pilot who had already been assigned to a Soyuz mission and did,

indeed, go into space without "approval." The other three were engineers from Enerigya.

Toktar O. Aubakirov	MAP
Alexandr I. Lazutkin	NPO Energiya
Sergei A. Treshchev	NPO Energiya
Pavel V. Vinogradov	NPO Energiya

They were finally approved when the joint state commission resumed its work on May 15, 1992. Aubakirov had gone into space aboard Soyuz TM–13 the previous October, having completed a four–month cosmonaut–researcher training program prior to that. Lazutkin, Treshchev, and Vinogradov underwent basic cosmonaut training from July 1992 to February 1994, at which point Lazutkin and Treshchev were designated test–cosmonauts. Vinogradov was forced to wait until a later meeting of the joint state commission.

The coup also had a profound effect on the Gagarin Center. Colonel General Yevgeny Shaposhnikov, the post–coup Minister of Defense, ordered the immediate retirement of all general officers over the age of 55. In mid–September 1991 Shatalov, who had been intending to retire in 1992, was replaced as Center director by Klimuk. Shortly thereafter Alexei Leonov retired as the deputy for air–space training and was replaced by Major General Yuri Glazkov.

Over the next several years the Gagarin Center struggled to redefine its mission. It continued to provide Russian crew commanders for Soyuz–Mir missions, and also expanded its training of astronauts from other countries—including NASA astronauts—in a time of radically shrunken budgets and diminished resources.

The number of active air force cosmonauts dropped from 48 in 1991 to less than half that by 1996. Volkov continued to serve as commander of the cosmonaut detachment, with branches or squads headed by Solovyov, Viktorenko, and Afanasyev.

April 15, 1994

Nadezhda V. Kuzhelnaya	NPO Energiya
Mikhail V. Tyurin	NPO Energiya

These two Energiya engineers underwent basic cosmonaut training from July 1994 to April 1996. Later that year both were assigned to the Gagarin Center training group for International Space Station missions.

The first plans for a unified cosmonaut team were made by the Russian Space Agency (RKA) in 1995, but little action was taken. The next meeting of the joint state commission in February 1996 approved six new candidates from a greater variety of organizations than it had for several years, but the candidates still were assigned to either the Gagarin Center team or the Energiya unit.

February 9, 1996:

Lieut. Colonel Yuri Shargin	RVSN
Capt. Oleg Kotov	TsPK
Konstantin Kozeyev	NPO Energiya
Sergei Revin	NPO Energiya
Oleg D. Kononenko	TsKB Progress
Sergei I. Moshchenko	Krunichev Space Center

All but Moshchenko reported to the Gagarin Center in May 1996 to begin basic space training, which was completed in March 1998. Shagin, Kozeyev, Revin, and Kononenko were candidate test–cosmonauts, while Kotov was classed as a cosmonaut–researcher.

Present Day

Unlike the United States, which has a single astronaut team within its civilian National Aeronautics and Space Administration, Russia has two separate cosmonaut teams, and a third cosmonaut group.

The oldest is military unit 26566, formed in 1960 and based at the RGNII TsPK imeni Gagarin—formally the Russian State Scientific and Test Institute, Center for Cosmonaut Training named for Yuri Gagarin, aka the Gagarin Center. The commander of the cosmonaut team is Colonel Alexandr Volkov, with branches headed by Colonel Anatoly Solovyov, Colonel Valery Korzun, and Major Oleg Kotov.

The other team is Department 291 of the RKK Energiya, the flight test department created in May 1966 within the former Korolev spacecraft design bureau (OKB–1, later TsKBEM). This is the department that selects and trains civilian flight engineers. Director of the department is former cosmonaut Alexandr Alexandrov, with Gennady Strekalov as his principal deputy.

The smaller cosmonaut group is that of the Institute for Medical and Biological Problems, consisting of three physician cosmonauts.

Other groups belonging to the flight research institute (LII, civilian Buran test pilots), the military flight research institute (GKNII, military Buran test pilots), the Academy of Sciences, and the Chelomei design bureau (TsKBM) have been disbanded.

The most recent meeting of the Joint State Committee (MVK) took place on July 25, 1997. In addition to approving new cosmonaut–candidates listed below, it also reaffirmed the status of the Russian cosmonaut teams.

There were 38 active Russian cosmonauts, 16 in the RGNII TsPK Gagarin Center team: Afanasyev, A. Volkov, Gidzenko, Dezhurov, Zaletin, Korzun, Malenchenko, Musabayev, Onufriyenko, Padalka, Sharipov, Solovyov, Titov, Tsibliyev, and now Tokarev, with candidate Kotov.

Three candidates from other organizations were assigned to the TsPK group for training: Shargin from the VKS (Military Space Forces), Kononenko (the Progress organization), and Moshchenko (Krunichev Space Center), bringing the Gagarin Center total to 19.

Fourteen civilian cosmonauts from RKK Energiya's flight–test department were certified: Avdeyev, Budarin, Vinogradov, Kaleri, Kondakova, Kuzhelnaya, Lazutkin, Revin, Treshchev, Tyurin, Usachev, and Revin (candidate). Candidate Kozeyev's medical status was under review, as is that of veteran cosmonaut Poleshchuk.

Though neither worked in Department 291, Energiya employees Krikalev and Ryumin were certified as eligible for assignment to flights—Krikalev to the first ISS crew, Ryumin to STS–91, bringing the Energiya total to 16.

Three IMBP doctors, Karashtin, Lukyanyuk, and Morukov, remain eligible for assignment to crews.

Two new civilian cosmonaut candidates were enrolled:

Fyodor N. Yurchikin	NPO Energiya
Oleg I. Skripockha	NPO Energiya

The transfer of military Buran test pilot Colonel Valery Tokarev to the Gagarin Center team was approved. Since he had undergone basic cosmonaut training in 1989–91, he was immediately eligible for assignment to an ISS crew.

And eight new pilots of the 12th Gagarin Center Enrollment were approved:

Capt. Dmitri Yu. Kondratyev

Maj. Yuri V. Lonchakov

Lt. Col. Oleg Yu. Moshkin

Capt. Roman Yu. Romanenko

Capt. Maxim V. Surayev

Maj. Alexandr A. Skvortsov

Sr. Lieut. Konstantin A. Valkov

Sr. Lieut. Sergei A. Volkov

What was most unusual about this group was the presence of two sons of well–known cosmonauts—Yuri Romanenko and Alexandr Volkov—as well as the son of cosmonaut candidate Alexandr Skvortsov.

The eight new military candidates, along with the two new candidates from Energiya, as well as the Krunichev Space Center's Moshchenko, commenced basic space training at the Center in January 1998. They are expected to complete it in the fall of 1999, when they will become eligible for assignment to International Space Station crews.

Shortly thereafter, in August 1997, the medical commission cleared Russian politician Yuri M. Baturin for advanced training as a cosmonaut–researcher. Baturin, a former engineer at Energiya, held the post of first deputy in the Ministry of Defense, and had convinced Russian President Boris Yeltsin to send him on a "fact–finding" visit to the Mir space station. By the time of the medical approval, Baturn had undergone several months of preliminary training, on a part–time basis. He ultimately completed the cosmonaut–researcher course in January 1998 and was officially assigned to the Soyuz TM–28 crew at that time.

On February 24, 1998, the joint state commission met again to approve Soyuz–Mir and ISS crews. It also certified Mikhail B. Korniyenko as a candidate–cosmonaut in the RKK Energiya team.

BURAN TEST-PILOT COSMONAUTS

By Bert Vis and Lida Shkorking

The Russian dream of a manned, reusable spacecraft that could land like an airplane led to tests of a small air–launched spaceplane called Spiral in the late 1960s and early 1970s. Spiral was conceived by Gleb Lozino–Lozinsky of the Mikoyan design bureau.

A training group was formed within the existing team at the military cosmonaut training center (later the Gagarin Center) in 1965 to assist in the development of Spiral. Because of the spaceplane's complexity, the cosmonauts were first required to undergo training as test pilots at the military test pilot school in Akhtubinsk (later Aktuba). Between 1965 and 1973, when the Spiral group was dissolved, eight cosmonauts were so trained:

Col. Gherman S. Titov (group leader)

Lieut. Col. Anatoly V. Filipchenko

Lieut. Col. Anatoly V. Kuklin

Capt. Leonid K. Kizim

Capt. Vladimir V. Kozelsky

Capt. Vladimir A. Lyakhov

Capt. Yuri V. Malyshev

Capt. Alexandr Ya. Petrushenko

Military engineer–cosmonauts such as Mikhail Burdayev, Nikolai Porvatkin, and Valery Illarionov also worked on Spiral through 1972, though in the role of design engineers, not as potential flight crewmembers.

In the 1970s and 1980s, more advanced versions of Spiral—now known as the BOR spaceplane, nicknamed *Lapot* (Sandal) for its appearance—were launched unmanned on hypersonic suborbital flights. Some were even dropped from carrier aircraft and flown by civilian and military test pilots. These men were not cosmonauts, though Volk would later become one.

The fourth version of BOR was flown on several unmanned orbital missions, beginning with Kosmos 1445 in 1982. No pilots were selected for that program.

Results of this research into hypersonic flight allowed the NPO Energiya, under the direction of chief designer Valentin Glushko and with the assistance of Lozino–Lozinsky, to begin development of a larger manned vehicle modelled on the U.S. Space Shuttle. The Soviet shuttle program was called *Buran* (Snowstorm), and was intended to be launched by the Energiya booster with a crew of up to 10. It was approved by the Ministry of General Machine-Building in 1976.

The Civilian Test Pilot Group

Soon after, in 1977, the Soviet Ministry of Aviation Production selected a group of five test pilots for Buran, officially known as vehicle 11F35.

Based at the Flight Research Institute (later named for M. M. Gromov) in the town of Zhukovsky, just outside Moscow, the Buran group consisted of

Igor P. Volk

Oleg G. Kononenko

Anatoly S. Levchenko

Rimantas A. Stankyavichus

Alexandr V. Shchukin

The group would eventually become known as the "Wolf Pack," after its commander, Volk, whose name means wolf in Russian. Its formal title was actually the Branch Complex (of the LII) for Test–Cosmonaut Training, OKPKI in its Russian language acronym.

Two years later these five pilots began the general course of spaceflight training at the Yuri Gagarin Cosmonaut Training Center in Star Town while still remaining active as test pilots at Zhukovsky. The pilots themselves considered 1979 to be the year of the birth of the Buran cosmonaut group, since that was when they were first assigned to the candidate program.

Although they completed the training course in November 1980, it was only on February 12, 1982, that four members of the group received their test cosmonaut certificates. The fifth, Kononenko, had been killed on September 8, 1980, while testing the Yak–38A VTOL aircraft on the carrier *Minsk* on the South China Sea.

In the meantime, in 1979 the MAP selection committee met again to consider additional pilots, since the original plans called for a group of 10. The personnel files were screened, and four more candidates emerged: Viktor V. Zabolotsky, Ural N. Sultanov, Vladimir Ye. Turovets, and Pyotr V. Gladkov.

Turovets was ultimately not selected and Gladkov, following discussion with officials of the MAP, declined the offer for the time being. Zabolotsky and Sultanov were not enrolled in the Buran team at that time, remaining at their other jobs.

In 1982 the committee met again, reviewing the earlier selection of Zabolotsky, Sultanov, and Gladkov. (Turovets was killed in the crash of an Mi–8 helicopter on February 8, 1982.) Two more candidates were considered, Magomed O. Tolboyev and Vladimir V. Biryukov.

From this group of five finalists three were approved for the Buran branch:

Ural N. Sultanov

Magomed O. Tolboyev

Viktor V. Zabolotsky

Sultanov and Tolboyev were approved by the joint state commission on March 9, 1983, and transferred to the Buran branch on April 25, 1983. Zabolotsky suffered a delay for medical reasons, finally winning approval from the joint state commission on February 2, 1984, transferring to the Buran branch on June 12.

On November 21, 1985, two more pilots were approved by the committee:

Sergei N. Tresvyatsky

Yuri P. Sheffer

They joined the 1983–84 trio, becoming the "Wolf Cubs"—that is, the junior members of the Wolf Pack—and underwent the general cosmonaut training course themselves from November 1985 to October 1987.

In 1988 two members of the Wolf Pack died—Anatoly Levchenko on August 6 of a brain tumor, and Alexandr Shchukin on August 18 in the crash of an Su–26 sport plane.

To replace Levchenko and Shchukin a new pilot was recruited. Yuri V. Prikhodko joined the Buran branch on March 22, 1989. He, too, underwent cosmonaut training, earning certification on March 28, 1991.

Tragically, there had by that time been a fourth fatality in the Wolf Pack ranks: Rimantas Stankyavichus was killed on September 9, 1990, when his Su–27 jet crashed during an air show in Treviso, Italy.

Ultimately 11 test pilots—one more than original planned—were selected and trained by the MAP for the Buran program, with two (Volk and Levchenko) flying in space as crewmembers aboard Soyuz.

The Air Force Test Pilot Group

The practice in Soviet military flight test was to have initial aircraft test flights conducted by civilian MAP pilots, with military test pilots conducting acceptance flights later in the program. Such was the case with Buran, with an initial MAP group selected in 1977. A year later, in 1978, the Soviet air force flight test center—the GKNII, or Chkalov flight test center—selected its own group of test pilots for Buran, hoping that they would form the core of a future test pilot cosmonaut team:

Col. Ivan I. Bachurin

Lieut. Col. Alexei S. Borodai

Lieut. Col. Viktor M. Chirkin

Lieut. Col. Vladimir Ye. Mosolov

Lieut. Col. Nail S. Sattarov

Lieut. Col. Anatoly M. Sokovykh

These men commenced the basic training course at the Gagarin Center in January 1979 in a group with the members of the Wolf Pack. All six of the military pilots completed the course in November 1980, but soon thereafter Sattarov and Chirkin left the program. The other four pilots—Bachurin, Borodai, Mosolov, and Sokovykh—were certified as test–cosmonauts on February 12, 1982, but were still not enrolled in any cosmonaut detachment.

In 1984 the GKNII took the first steps toward the creation of such a unit, and in September 1985, three new candidates for Buran were approved by a joint state commission:

Col. Viktor M. Afanasyev

Lt. Col. Anatoly P. Artsebarsky

Lt. Col. Gennady M. Manakov

They underwent basic cosmonaut training on a part–time basis at the Gagarin Center between November 1985 and October 1987 along with the MAP Wolf Cubs, Zabolotsky, Sultanov, Tolboyev, Tresvyatsky, and Sheffer.

In April 1987, Gagarin Center director Lieutenant General Vladimir Shatalov offered the military Buran test pilots the chance to transfer to the Soyuz–Mir cosmonaut team. By this time Sokovkyh had been dismissed from the program and Mossolov was also leaving. Bachurin and Borodai declined to leave Akhtubinsk, but the three new candidates—Afanasyev, Artsebarsky, and Manakov, who were still undergoing basic cosmonaut training—accepted the offer, transferring to the Gagarin Center in January 1988. All three commanded Soyuz–Mir missions in 1990 and 1991.

In September 1987, Bachurin and Borodai relocated to the Gagarin Center to be closer to the Zhukovsky civilian flight test center, where between October and March 1988 they took part in six approach and landing flights of a jet–powered version of Buran.

An unmanned Buran was readied for an orbital mission that autumn, and a manned docking between an unmanned Buran and a manned Soyuz was also proposed in which a Soyuz crew would work aboard the orbiter for several days.

With the Buran program thus gearing up, in October 1988 the GKNII won approval of its own test pilot–cosmonaut group, with Bachurin (commander) and Borodai as initial members, along with a third military test pilot, Colonel Leonid K. Kadenyuk, a former member of the Gagarin Center military cosmonaut team (1976–83).

While Bachurin, Borodai and Kadenyuk trained for the Soyuz–Buran mission, selections for additional candidates in the new GKNII team continued. Six test pilots were selected by the center:

Col. Valery Ye. Maximenko

Lt. Col. Anatoly B. Polonsky

Col. Alexandr S. Puchkov

Lt. Col. Nikolai A. Pushenko

Col. Valery I. Tokarev

Lt. Col. Alexandr N. Yablontsev

These six underwent general cosmonaut training at the Gagarin Center beginning in March 1989 with MAP test pilot Yuri Prikhodko. All were certified as test cosmonauts by April 4, 1991.

The Buran program, including the Soyuz–Buran mission, was a victim of the collapse of the Soviet Union in the fall of 1991. By early 1992 it was clear that further Buran missions, unmanned or manned, would not take place for years, if ever.

Nevertheless, Puchkov and Yablontsev were assigned as GKNII test pilot–cosmonauts on April 8, 1992, bringing the total number of pilots in the group to five.

Bachurin retired for medical reasons in December 1992, and was succeeded as commander of the team by Borodai in January 1993. At that time, Tokarev was also officially enrolled in the team. Tokarev became commander upon Borodai's retirement in December 1993, at which time Pushenko was officially enrolled.

Though he completed the cosmonaut training course and was designated a test cosmonaut, Maximenko declined to join the GKNII team and remained at the Chkalov flight test center's military test pilot school.

Polonsky transferred to the Gagarin Center in hopes of officially joining the GKNII team there, working at the GKNII branch at nearby Chkalov air base, but was not enrolled.

Between 1992 and 1996 the GKNII cosmonauts, while living at the Gagarin Center, remained military test pilots. They were also involved in potential aerospace programs such as MAKS.

Kadenyuk resigned in February 1996 to become an astronaut with the National Space Agency of Ukraine. The whole GKNII group was officially disbanded by order of Colonel–General Pyotr I. Deneikin, commander–in–chief of the Russian air forces, on September 30, 1996. Tokarev won a transfer to the Gagarin Center cosmonaut team while Polonsky, Puchkov, Pushenko, and Yablontsev went into civil aviation or returned to full–time military flight test work.

Atmospheric Test Flights

As NASA did with the Space shuttle, trial landings were made with a specially–modified Buran orbiter called the BTS—*Bolshoi Transportni Samolyot* or large transport aircraft—in an approach and landing test program. Both civilian and military members of the Buran test pilot groups took part in the flights, which occurred between November 1985 and April 1988. A taxi test and a number of ground runs were also part of the program.

A total of 24 approach and landing flights were flown. Stankyavichus made 13, two as commander; Volk made 12, 10 as commander; Shchukin made seven, two as commander; Bachurin and Borodai made six flights together in which each man acted as commander three times.

Levchenko flew four missions, all of them as commander. Zabolotsky piloted a single ground run made twenty months after the completion of the approach and landing series.

The NPO Energiya Group

The NPO Molniya, builder of the Buran space shuttle, was originally an element of the Energiya organization. As with other civilian Soviet spacecraft, flight engineers for

Buran crews were to come from the Energiya's cosmonaut group.

Beginning in 1979 a group of newly selected engineer cosmonauts—Alexandr Balandin, Alexandr Laveikin, and Musa Manarov—began working on Buran. They were joined by two–time space veteran Valentin Lebedev in the spring of 1983. Other senior cosmonauts who later worked on Buran include Alexandr Ivanchenkov and Gennady Strekalov, in addition to the engineer–researchers selected in 1984–85: Andrei Zaitsev, Alexandr Kaleri, Sergei Krikalev, and Yuri Stepanov.

All of these engineer–cosmonauts moved between the Soyuz–Mir and Buran programs as needed. At the time the program began to be severely cut back in 1992, the lead flight engineers were Ivanchenkov and Balandin.

Flight Assignments

Although all members of the Buran cosmonaut team completed the general training course at the Gagarin Center, qualifying them as test cosmonauts, through 1990 only five had actually trained for missions: Volk, Stankyavichus, Levchenko, Shchukin, and Zabolotsky.

Igor Volk and Rimas Stankyavichus began training in 1983 for what became Soyuz T–12, launched June 1984. In a crew that included commander Vladimir Dzhanibekov and flight engineer Svetlana Savitskaya, Volk spent 12 days in space aboard the Salyut 7 space station. (Originally Volk was assigned to the crew of Kizim–Solovyov, but the Soyuz launch abort on September 26, 1983, forced a postponement.)

Three years later, in December 1987, Anatoly Levchenko flew as cosmonaut–researcher of Soyuz TM–4, spending almost eight days in space. Levchenko's backup was Alexandr Shchukin, not Stankyavichus, who declined the assignment.

These two flights were sufficient to qualify Buran crews for the commencement of manned orbital fights, since each crew—Volk–Stankyavicius and Levchenko–Shchukin—was required to have one member who had flown in space.

But Levchenko's death in August 1988 necessitated a third mission. Stankyavichus was selected and assigned to

BURAN APPROACH AND LANDING TESTS

CREW (CDR/PILOT)	DATE	MISSION	DURATION
Volk/Stankyavichus	Dec. 29, 1984	taxi test	:05
Volk/Stankyavichus	Aug. 2, 1985	ground–run	:14
Volk/Stankyavichus	Oct. 5, 1985	ground–run	:12
Volk/Stankyavichus	Oct. 15, 1985	ground–run	:31
Volk/Stankyavichus	Nov. 5, 1985	ground–run	:12
Volk/Stankyavichus	Nov. 10, 1985	flight #1	:12
Volk/Stankyavichus	Jan. 3, 1986	flight #2	:36
Levchenko/Shchukin	Apr. 26, 1986	ground–run	:14
Volk/Stankyavichus	May 27, 1986	flight #3	:23
Volk/Stankyavichus	June 10, 1986	flight #4	:22
Levchenko/Shchukin	June 20, 1986	flight #5	:25
Levchenko/Shchukin	June 28, 1986	flight #6	:23
Volk/Stankyavichus	Dec. 10, 1986	flight #7	:24
Volk/Stankyavichus	Dec. 23, 1986	flight #8	:17
Levchenko/Shchukin	Dec. 29, 1986	flight #9	:17
Volk/Stankyavichus	Feb. 16, 1987	flight #10	:28
Shchukin/Levchenko	Mar. 25, 1987	ground–run	:02
Stankyavichus/Volk	Mar. 30, 1987	ground–run	:25
Levchenko/Shchukin	May 21, 1987	flight #11	:20
Stankyavichus/Volk	June 25, 1987	flight #12	:19
Shchukin/Volk	Oct. 5, 1987	flight #13	:21
Bachurin/Borodai	Oct. 15, 1987	flight #14	:19
Volk/Stankyavichus	Jan. 16, 1988	flight #15	:22
Bachurin/Borodai	Jan. 24, 1988	flight #16	:22
Bachurin/Borodai	Feb. 23, 1988	flight #17	:22
Volk/Stankyavichus	Mar. 4, 1988	flight #18	:32
Borodai/Bachurin	Mar. 12, 1988	flight #19	:21
Borodai/Bachurin	Mar. 23, 1988	flight #20	:21
Bachurin/Borodai	Mar. 28, 1988	flight #21	:22
Stankyavichus/Shchukin	Apr. 2, 1988	flight #22	:20
Shchukin/Stankyavichus	Apr. 8, 1988	flight #23	:21
Volk/Stankyavichus	Apr. 15, 1988	flight #24	:19
Stankyavichus/Zabolotsky	Dec. 28, 1989	ground–run	n.a.

the crew of Soyuz TM–9 (Viktorenko–Balandin), scheduled for launch to the Mir space station in April 1989. His backup was Viktor Zabolotsky.

Budget cuts forced a stand–down in Soyuz–Mir flights from April to August 1989; Stankyavichus's flight was canceled, since all other cosmonaut–researcher seats had been sold to commercial customers such as the Japanese television network TBS, who were paying much–needed hard currency.

In July 1990 Igor Volk revealed that the prime crew for Buran's first manned flight had indeed been Volk–Stankyavicius, and that Levchenko–Shchukin had been selected as backups. Following the deaths of Levchenko and Shchukin in 1988 the backup role was taken by GKNII test pilot–cosmonauts Bachurin and Borodai. In order to have a flight–qualified crewmember in the second crew, Bachurin or Borodai would have to make a Soyuz flight.

So, beginning in 1988, plans were made for a second unmanned orbital flight of Buran during which the Energiya–launched vehicle would automatically rendezvous and dock with a free–flying Soyuz TM. Three crews were formed, each consisting of an air force Buran test pilot and an air force engineer–navigator from the Gagarin Center:

Ivan Bachurin–Eduard Stepanov

Alexei Borodai–Nikolai Fefelov

Leonid Kadenyuk–Valery Illarionov.

This Buran–Soyuz mission, originally targeted for launch in December 1991, was postponed indefinitely by the Soviet Union's political and economic crisis.

The battle among the MAP, the air force, and the NPO Energiya over who would crew the first manned orbital flight of Buran was settled by August 1991: the crew would be commanded by Igor Volk, with veteran Energiya cosmonaut Alexandr Ivanchenkov as flight engineer–navigator. Ivanchenkov had replaced test pilot Magomed Tolboyev, who was the MAP choice.

But within two years, following the breakup of the Soviet Union into separate republics, which shattered central management and funding for manned spaceflights, the Buran program was canceled.

COSMONAUT BIOGRAPHIES

Afanasyev, Viktor Mikhailovich

1948–

Viktor Afanasyev has commanded two expeditions to the Mir space station, beginning with the eighth Mir residency, launched as Soyuz TM–11 on December 2, 1990. Afanasyev commanded a crew that included Soviet flight engineer Musa Manarov and Japanese journalist Toyohiro Akiyama. Akiyama returned to Earth after 10 days, but Afanasyev and Manarov remained aboard Mir.

The crew overcame one crisis: during the approach of the Progress M–7 supply ship to the Mir complex on March 21 the Kurs automatic guidance system failed, causing Progress to miss its target by over 500 yards. A second attempt 2 days later almost resulted in disaster, with Progress sailing past the complex at a distance of five yards, barely missing solar panels and aerials. A collision between Mir and Progress did occur in June 1997, with near–disastrous results.

Flight controllers studied the problem and concluded that the problem was in the Kurs system on the Kvant docking module, not in Progress. On March 26, Afanasyev and Manarov boarded their Soyuz TM–11 craft, backed away from the forward port and approached the Kvant or rear end of the complex. They quickly learned that an antenna aboard Kvant was malfunctioning. The cosmo-

nauts were able to dock successfully, and on March 28 Progress M–7 was linked to the station.

Afanasyev and Manarov took four space walks, repairing an EVA hatch damaged during a 1990 space walk, and moving several solar power panels.

Most of the working time of the eighth Mir residency was devoted to space manufacturing using the Krater V, Gallar, and Optizon furnaces. The cosmonauts also performed observations with the Roentgen observatory in the Kvant module in addition to Earth resources studies and observations of action during the United States–Iraq war.

In January 1994 Afanasyev commanded the 15th Mir residency, launched as Soyuz TM–18 with flight engineer Yuri Usachev and physician Valery Polyakov. The crew concentrated on X–ray astronomy studies and Earth resources photography in addition to medical studies. (Polyakov went on to spend 14 months aboard Mir.) They also fired an electron beam gun at the Swedish Freja satellite as part of a study of the Earth's magnetic field. The Mir–15 mission ended in July 1994, after 182 days.

Afanasyev was born December 31, 1948, in the city of Bryansk. He graduated from the Kacha Higher Air Force School (named for Myasnikov) in 1970, then served as a fighter pilot in the Soviet air force flying MiG–29s and MiG–31s. In 1980 he graduated from the Moscow Aviation Institute. He also attended the Chkalov Test Pilot School (1976–77).

Afanasyev has logged over 2,000 hours of flying time in 40 different types of aircraft.

He was serving as a test pilot at the Flight Research Center at Akhtubinsk, near Volgograd, in November 1985 when he became one of 3 pilots selected for training on the Buran space shuttle. In January 1988, when the initial manned orbital flight of Buran was delayed, Afanasyev was transferred to the Gagarin Center for training as a Soyuz–Mir cosmonaut.

He served as backup commander for the Soyuz TM–10 mission to the Mir space station in August 1990 and for Soyuz TM–27/Mir–25 in February 1997.

Aksenov, Vladimir Viktorovich

1935–

Vladimir Aksenov made two Soyuz flights, including the first manned flight of the new Soyuz T transport, Soyuz T–2, in June 1980. The Soyuz T carried a new onboard computer that unfortunately malfunctioned during rendezvous and docking with the Salyut 6 space station. Aksenov and commander Yuri Malyshev were able to dock manually with Salyut 6. They returned to Earth after 4 days.

In September 1976 Aksenov was flight engineer aboard Soyuz 22, an 8–day mission with commander Valery Bykovsky. The cosmonauts used the German–built MKF–6 multispectral camera to study of Earth resources from space.

Aksenov was born February 1, 1935, in the village of Giblitsy in the Ryazan Region of Russia. His father was killed in World War II, and his mother died in 1949, so Aksenov was raised by his grandparents.

After graduation from secondary school he attended the Kasimov Industrial School and the Mytishchi Engineering School, graduating in 1953. He was drafted into the military and sent to the Kremenchug Higher Air Force School for pilot training. Two years later he transferred to the Chuguyev school, but in January 1957 he left to become an engineer with the Korolev spacecraft design bureau (OKB–1), working on the first Sputnik.

In 1964 Aksenov applied to become one of the OKB's first civilian cosmonauts, but was told to wait until he had more experience. Nevertheless, he was transferred to the

new flight test department there, where he participated in weightless flights aboard aircraft, EVA training, and emergency splashdown exercises. This work put him in close contact with Soviet cosmonauts such as Valery Bykovsky, his future Soyuz 22 commander. Aksenov also continued his studies, attending the All–Union Polytechnic Institute, earning his degree in 1963. He was finally accepted as a candidate in March 1973 and was assigned to Soyuz 22 in January 1976.

Following his flight on Soyuz T–2 he helped train cosmonauts for the Soviet–French mission in 1982 and for the Soviet–Indian mission in 1984. He was involved in the design of the Mir space station and served as a crew instructor for the Soyuz TM–2 and Soyuz TM–3 missions in 1987.

He earned a candidate of technical sciences degree in 1981. He also published *The Hard Road* (1982), a biography of engineer–test pilot Sergei Anokhin, the first director of the civilian cosmonaut group.

Aksenov left the cosmonaut group at Energiya in October 1988 to become director of the State Central Scientific–Research Institute for Natural Resources.

Alexandrov, Alexandr Pavlovich

1943–

Alexandr Alexandrov took part in one of the most harrowing missions in Soviet space history. On June 27, 1983, Alexandrov and commander Vladimir Lyakhov were launched into space aboard Soyuz T–9 for a planned 4–month stay operating Salyut 7 and an FBG module called Kosmos 1443. They were replacements for the crew of Titov, Strekalov, and Serebrov, whose attempt 2 months earlier to reach the Salyut 7/Kosmos 1443 orbital complex had been aborted.

Alexandrov and Lyakhov docked successfully with the orbital complex on June 29. On July 25 the station was struck by a micrometeorite, which left a noticeable crater in one of the windows. More serious was an accident that occurred on September 9, when the complex was being refueled by the unmanned Progress cargo vessel: a fuel line burst, leaking fuel and damaging Salyut's control systems. Lyakhov and Alexandrov took refuge in their Soyuz until ground controllers could be sure the complex was still safe.

Salyut 7 was still habitable, but it was damaged. Soviet program managers developed repair procedures and trained cosmonauts Vladimir Titov and Gennady Strekalov to carry them out. Unfortunately, the attempt to launch Titov and Strekalov on September 26 was disastrous: a fire broke out at the base of their launch vehicle seconds before ignition and they were forced to escape from the pad. Alexandrov and Lyakhov were left in a difficult situation (some Western observers reported that the men were "marooned") because the Soyuz spacecraft had already been in orbit for more than 100 days, the limit for safe operations.

Nevertheless, a new cargo ship, Progress 18, was launched to the complex; it carried materials for repairing Salyut. Alexandrov performed two unrehearsed space walks on November 1 and 3, and he and Lyakhov returned safely to Earth 3 weeks later.

In 1987 Alexandrov served a 6–month shift aboard the Mir space station, replacing Alexandr Laveikin, who had been recalled to Earth because of concerns about his health. Alexandrov, who had been training for a Soyuz TM–3 mission lasting 10 days, was told about the change in plans only a month before launch. Alexandrov joined Mir commander Yuri Romanenko in completing a program of medical, Earth resources, and space manufacturing experiments, returning in December 1987.

Alexandrov was born February 20, 1943, in Moscow. His father was a military officer. As a boy Alexandrov grew interested in rockets and kept a scrapbook about GIRD, the early Soviet rocket study group. Alexandrov attended the same primary school as future cosmonaut Valery Ryumin.

After graduation from secondary school in 1961, Alexandrov hoped to become an air force pilot, but physical problems prevented it. Instead he enrolled at the Serpukhov Military–Technical school, and upon graduation served in the Strategic Rocket Forces at Poltava, Vitebsk region.

Demobilized in August 1964, Alexandrov joined the OKB–1, working under the direction of propulsion specialist Boris Raushenbakh on the Voskhod spacecraft. Alexandrov says that he found the March 1965 "space walk" of cosmonaut Alexei Leonov inspiring. He began to think of applying for the cosmonaut group himself.

Soviet chief designer Korolev had begun the process of recruiting young engineers from his design bureau into the cosmonaut team in 1964, and when a new opportunity arose in 1967, Alexandrov applied and went before the strict state medical commission. But Alexandrov's inability to tolerate high G–loads on the centrifuge prevented his selection.

Undaunted, Alexandrov continued his work at the design bureau in the training of cosmonaut teams, a job that required him to travel all over the USSR. He studied nights at the Bauman Technical School and obtained his degree in 1969. He also became a parachutist and pilot.

In December 1978 he was finally accepted as a cosmonaut at what was now known as NPO Energiya. While awaiting a flight opportunity he worked at the flight control center in Kaliningrad near Moscow as a Soyuz–Salyut ground controller. One of the missions he worked on was the 175–day Soyuz 32/Salyut 6 flight of Vladimir Lyakhov, his future space partner, and Valery Ryumin, his former schoolmate.

His first assignments were as backup flight engineer for Soyuz T–5 in 1982 and Soyuz T–8 in 1983. He has also been a backup for Soyuz T–13 and Soyuz T–14. From March 1987 to October 1993 Alexandrov was director of the manned spaceflight department (which includes flight controllers and engineer cosmonauts) at Energiya.

He returned to active training in 1991 as flight engineer (with commander Valery Korzun and researcher Toktar Aubakirov) for the proposed Soviet–Kazakh visit to Mir, Soyuz TM–14. That mission was canceled in July 1991.

In October 1993 Alexandrov retired as an active cosmonaut, though he remains head of Department 291, the unit within Energiya that includes the engineer–cosmonaut team.

Alexeyev, Vladimir Borisovich

1933–

Vladimir Alexeyev is a military engineer who was one of 12 air force candidates enrolled in the cosmonaut team in April 1967. He completed the course of cosmonaut training in August 1969 and remained active until April 1983 without ever going into space.

Alexeyev was born August 19, 1933, and raised in Moscow. When he finished secondary school at the age of 18 he hoped to enter Moscow State University to study either physics or chemistry, but wound up in the Soviet military, attending the Zhukovsky Air Force Engineering Academy. He graduated in 1957, then served with a fighter squadron for a year. When the squadron was disbanded, Alexeyev transferred to the staff of the Ministry of Defense's Research Institute for Air Defense (NII–2) in the city of Kalinin (now Tver). He was there when invited to apply for the cosmonaut group in 1967.

Before becoming a cosmonaut Alexeyev received a candidate of technical sciences degree (April 1968).

As a cosmonaut Alexeyev worked on the Salyut civilian space station program and also took part in crew training, specializing in survival techniques for emergency landings in deserts and the Arctic. (He had taken up mountaineering in 1953 and found that training to be useful.)

Beginning in 1973 Alexeyev served in the Kaliningrad flight control center as communications operator (capcom) for manned Soviet space missions. In 1988 he transferred to reserve status as a colonel, becoming a civilian research associate with NPO (now RKK) Energiya.

Amelkina, Galina Vasilyevna

1954–

Galina Amelkin was one of the women cosmonauts approved by the Joint State Commission on July 30, 1980. A physician on the staff of the Institute for Medical–Biological Problems, she underwent cosmonaut training at NPO Energiya in 1979 and at the Gagarin Center in 1981 and 1982, but was medically disqualified in May 1983.

Amelkina was born May 22, 1954, in Berlin, Germany, where her father was stationed with the Soviet military. She attended the Moscow Medical–Stomatological Institute named for N. A. Semashko, graduating in 1978.

After leaving the IMBP cosmonaut unit in 1983, Amelkina returned to the Semashko Institute, where she is currently assistant professor in the orthopedics faculty.

Andreyev, Boris Dmitryevich

1940–

Boris Andreyev was the backup flight engineer for several Soyuz missions, including the Soviet–American Soyuz–19 mission, between 1975 and 1981, without ever flying in space. His cosmonaut career ended in 1983 when a back injury suffered during a parachuting mishap medically disqualified him. He had been training for a long–duration flight aboard a Salyut space station.

Andreyev was born October 6, 1940, in Moscow. After completing secondary school he attended the Bauman Higher Technical School, graduating in 1965. He was known as a good athlete and was also active in the student scientific society.

After graduation Andreyev went to work at the Korolev spacecraft design bureau (OKB–1), at first as an engineer, later as head of a data–processing department involved with automatic spacecraft control systems. During this time he learned to speak English.

He became a cosmonaut in March 1972 and was first assigned to the training group for the Soyuz 13 mission. A year later he was named to one of the 4 cosmonaut crews training for the Apollo–Soyuz Test Project. During the 2–year course of training Andreyev made several trips to the United States.

Following ASTP he served as backup flight engineer for Soyuz 22 in 1976, and for Soyuz 35 (1980) and Soyuz T–4 (1981). He came closest to going into space on Soyuz 35.

Andreyev and commander Vyacheslav Zudov were backups to a crew of Leonid Popov and Valentin Lebedev for a planned 6–month mission aboard Salyut 6. In March

1980, a month prior to the scheduled launch, Lebedev was injured in a trampoline accident and medically disqualifed from the flight. His replacement was Valery Ryumin, who had just returned from the 6–month Soyuz 32 mission, and the Popov–Ryumin crew became the backups.

Flight controllers and instructors soon decided, however, that Zudov and Andreyev weren't as well trained as they should be. At the same time, Ryumin stepped forward and volunteered to fly a second 6–month mission. Soviet doctors found the idea intriguing; the team of Popov and Ryumin was judged to be better trained. So Zudov and Andreyev were relegated to the backup role.

They had another chance to fly aboard Soyuz T–4 in early 1981, but program managers wanted one of the crewmen to have experience aboard Salyut 6, which was nearing the end of its useful lifetime. The crew of Kovalenok (veteran of a 4–month stay aboard the station) and Savinykh flew instead.

Andreyev left the Energiya cosmonaut team in May 1983 to become a communications operator at the Kaliningrad flight control center, where he has worked in support of all Russian manned spaceflights to Salyut 7 and Mir. Previously he had been an operator for Soyuz 32 in 1979.

Andryushkov, Alexandr Stepanovich

1947–

Colonel Alexandr Andryushkov is one of the 6 Soviet journalists who underwent cosmonaut–researcher training from October 1990 to February 1992. It was planned that one of them would spend a week aboard the Mir space station in 1992 or 1993, but the mission was later canceled for budgetary reasons.

Andryushkov was born October 6, 1947, in the town of Luga, Leningrad (now St. Petersburg) Region, Russia. His father was in the military. Andryushkov grew up in the Kaluga Region, and upon finishing secondary school he moved to Lugansk, where he attended a trade school, graduating in 1965 as a lathe operator. While working at the factory he enrolled in a course at an aeroclub. At the age of 19 he qualified as a pilot on the Yak–18A, then entered the Armavir Higher Air Force School.

He became a Su–9 interceptor pilot in the Leningrad Military District (1970–75), then served with the 12th Detached Air Army in Turkestan. He eventually earned the rating of military pilot first class, logging 1,500 hours of flying time in 10 different types of fighter aircraft.

In 1979 he entered the Lenin Military–Political Academy, and following graduation in 1982 joined the editorial staff of *Krasnaya Zvezda—Red Star*—the newspaper published by the Soviet Ministry of Defense, where he continues to write on space and cosmonautics.

Andryushkov also took part in a 90–day simulated Mars mission called EKO–PSI, based at the Moscow Aviation Institute, from November 1995 to January 1996.

Anikeyev, Ivan Nikolayevich

1933–1992

Soviet air force pilot Ivan Anikeyev was one of the first 20 cosmonauts selected in March 1960, and was officially certified as a military cosmonaut on April 5, 1961. During training he was the first to test the centrifuge, and he also served as a communications operator for the Vostok 3/4 flights in August 1962.

His cosmonaut career ended in April 1963, however, following an incident at the Chkalovskaya train station, near Star Town, where Anikeyev and fellow cosmonauts Grigory Nelyubov and Valentin Filatyev got into a fight with officers from the militia. All three men, including Anikeyev, were summarily dismissed from the cosmonaut team.

Anikeyev was born February 12, 1933, in the city of Liski, Voronezh region, Russia. He attended the Stalin Naval Aviation School (later known as the 12th Naval Aviation School) from March 1952 to July 1956, then served as a fighter pilot with the 524th Air Fighter Regiment of the 107th Air Fighter Division, Northern Fleet.

After leaving the cosmonaut team, Anikeyev returned to the Northern Fleet, serving as a fighter pilot until 1965. He then spent 10 years as a controller and navigator until transferring to reserve status.

Anikeyev lived in the city of Bezhetsk, Kalinin district, Russia, until his death from cancer on August 8, 1992.

Anokhin, Sergei Nikolayevich

1910–1986

Sergei Anokhin was the first chief of the civilian engineer–cosmonaut group, selecting and training such cosmonauts as Alexei Yeliseyev, Valery Kubasov, and Georgy Grechko.

A veteran test pilot, Anokhin served as deputy to Sergei Korolev, the chief designer of Soviet manned spacecraft, who harbored a not–so–secret desire to fly in space himself. Like Anokhin, Korolev had originally been a glider test pilot. Korolev knew he was too old and physically frail to endure training, but he persisted in winning high–level approval for the inclusion of engineers from his bureau in space crews . . . something the Soviet air force resisted for years.

The breakthrough came in May 1964, when OKB Korolev engineer Konstantin Feoktistov was confirmed as a member of the crew of the first Voskhod. Korolev announced to his staff that a team of engineer–cosmonauts would be created, and was inundated with 500 applications. He turned the matter over to Anokhin, who included himself in the 13 selected. The state commission refused to allow any additional civilian engineers to begin cosmonaut training, however, and there the matter rested for 2 years.

It was only on May 23, 1966, 5 months after Korolev's death, and following a series of medical examinations, physical training and other evaluations, that a group of 8 civilian cosmonauts was officially formed, Department 291, with Anokhin as director.

Anokhin himself took part in the physical regime, hoping, somehow, to prove that at age 56 he was not too old to fly in space. His involvement had the blessing of chief designer Vasily Mishin and drew attention from Defense Minister Dmitri Ustinov, but the medical commission soon ended the experiment.

Anokhin continued to work with the engineer cosmonauts, serving as flight instructor for those who became pilots. He also became head of the International Astronautical Federation office in Moscow and remained "commissioner" of space records until 1984.

He died on April 15, 1986.

Anokhin was born March 19, 1910, in Moscow in the family of a tsarist civil servant. At the age of 17 he went to work on a railroad gang, but after 8 years entered a Higher Air Force School for glider pilots in the Crimea. He began to work as an airplane and glider test pilot and in 1940 set a series of records for glider altitude, distance and flight duration.

When the World War II began, Anokhin commanded a squadron in the Soviet air force. He saw action on the Byelorussian Front and fought in support of partisans.

In 1943 he became chief test pilot for projects that included the first Soviet jet plane. He continued to work as a pilot and test pilot for many years, until in 1964 chief spacecraft designer Korolev asked him to head the flight methods section of his construction bureau, training cosmonauts for flights on Voskhod, Soyuz and Salyut. He served as director of Department 291 until November 1978, then was deputy director until his death in 1986.

Cosmonaut Vladimir Aksenov published a biography of Anokhin, *The Hard Way*, in 1980.

Artsebarsky, Anatoly Pavolich

1956–

Anatoly Artsebarsky was commander of the Soyuz TM–12 mission, the ninth residency aboard the Mir space station complex, that began on May 18, 1991.

Joining Artsebarsky in the TM–12 crew were flight engineer Sergei Krikalev and British researcher Helen Sharman, who became the first woman to visit Mir. She returned to Earth with resident cosmonauts Afanasyev and Manarov on May 26, but not before suffering through an orbital press conference in which Artsebarsky complained about the extra problems caused by the inclusion of a woman in his crew.

Artsebarsky and Krikalev's main work was EVA construction, including the erection of a 50–foot–long girder called Sofora on the exterior of the Mir complex. Sofora was to be used as a mounting for a control module. Over the course of a month, between late June and late July 1991, Artsebarsky and Krikalev made six EVAs totaling over 33 hours in open space. During the last EVA—just as

Sofora had been completed—Artsebarsky's suit became overheated. His visor fogged over, making it impossible for him to see and stranding him at the top of the tower. Krikalev came to his rescue and towed him back to the safety of the Mir EVA hatch.

Artsebarsky and Krikalev also had the misfortune to be in orbit during the abortive Soviet coup in mid–August 1991. They suffered through a few anxious days wondering who, if anyone, was in command of the complex. They watched news reports of the disintegration of the Soviet Union, occasionally asking nervously if they and Mir were "for sale."

Artsebarsky returned to Earth on October 10, 1991, after almost 145 days in space.

Artsebarsky was born September 9, 1956, in the village of Prosyanaya, Pokrovskoye District, Dnepropetrovsk Region of the Ukraine. He attended the Kharkov Higher Air Force School, graduating in 1977, then served as a flight instructor. He also attended the Chkalov test pilot school at Akhtubinsk (1982–83).

Artsebarsky is a military pilot first class with over 1,400 hours of flying time in 35 different types of aircraft.

In November 1985 he was one of the 3 air force test pilots assigned to the Buran space shuttle program. He also did graduate work, earning a degree from the Moscow Aviation Institute in 1987.

Continuing delays in the start of manned Buran flights caused cosmonaut training chief Vladimir Shatalov to reassign Artsebarsky, Viktor Afanasyev, and Gennady Manakov to the Soyuz–Mir program in January 1988. Artsebarsky served as backup commander to Soyuz TM–11 in December 1990.

Following his mission aboard Mir Artsebarsky was medically disqualified from future missions. He left the cosmonaut unit at the Gagarin Center in September 1993 to join the Russian Academy of Sciences and NPO Energiya, working on the development of future space station structures.

Artyukhin, Yuri Petrovich

1930–1998

Communications engineer Yuri Artyukhin was a member of the first successful Soviet space station crew, spending 2 weeks aboard Salyut–3 in July 1974.

At that time there were two different Soviet manned space station programs operating under the Salyut name, a civilian long–term orbital station (DOS) developed by the Korolev bureau (OKB–1, later called the TsKBEM) and a military version conceived by Vladimir Chelomei (OKB–52, later the TsKBM) and originally named Almaz. Launched in April 1971, Salyut 1, the first DOS, had been occupied by the crew of Soyuz 11, who had been killed on return to Earth. The second DOS failed to reach orbit in June 1972. The first Almaz—called Salyut–2—suffered technical problems following its launch in April 1973 and was never occupied. A third DOS was launched in May 1973 as Kosmos 557, and it, too, failed.

Artyukhin and commander Pavel Popovich were launched aboard Soyuz 14 to Salyut 3 (the second Almaz) on July 3, 1974, docking with and boarding the station safely 2 days later. Their 2–week mission consisted of a number of medical experiments and Earth surface observations, many of them of a military nature. (Western observers quickly realized that Salyut 3 was a military mission when the crew used frequencies different from earlier Soviet manned flights, and also encrypted some communications with mission control in Yevpatoriya.) Artyukhin and Popovich returned to Earth on July 19, 1974.

Artyukhin was born June 22, 1930, in Pershutino, a village in the Moscow region. His father was an air force bomber pilot who died in the World War II when Artyukhin was eleven. Artyukhin himself applied for military service at 17, entering the Balashov Higher Air Force School in hopes of becoming a pilot like his father. Medical problems washed him out of flight school, but he remained in the service, graduating from the Serpukhov Air Force Technical School in December 1950. He became a specialist in military communications systems, serving with an Il–10 assault squadron in the 45th Air Army in the Trans–Baikal military district before entering the Zhukovsky Air Force Engineering Academy in 1952.

He completed the 5–year advanced engineering course at Zhukovsky in 1958 and remained on staff there as a senior engineer until joining the military cosmonaut group in January 1963. In April 1965, after completing his basic course of training, Artyukhin was assigned to a crew training for a planned 15–day Voskhod 3 mission with commander Vladimir Shatalov. A year later he transferred to the Soyuz program, and in 1967 was assigned to Program L–1 as crewmember for manned Soviet circumlunar missions. He served as a communications operator aboard the tracking ships *Kosmonavt Vladimir Komarov* and *Akademik Sergei Korolev* for the 5 Soyuz missions launched in 1969, and for Soyuz 9 (June 1970) and Soyuz 10 and 11 (1971) before joining the Almaz cosmonaut training group in December 1971.

Following his Salyut–3 Artyukhin became head of Almaz cosmonaut training within the First Directorate of the Gagarin Cosmonaut Training Center. For 2 years, in 1977–78, he trained as a crewmember for the fourth Almaz station, which was ultimately launched unmanned in 1987.

Artyukhin received his candidate of technical sciences degree in 1980, and left the cosmonaut team in January 1982 to become deputy director, First Directorate, for science, research and testing, a job he held for 5 years. He transferred to the military reserve in May 1988 and joined the staff of the NPO Molniya, builders of the Buran space shuttle.

Artyukhin died in Moscow on August 4, 1998.

Arzamazov, German Semenovich

1946–

German Arzamazov twice served as backup medical researcher–flight engineer for Valery Polyakov. The first time was the Soyuz TM–6 mission to the Mir space station in August 1988. Polyakov eventually spent 8 months in space, with Arzamazov serving as ground support. As Polyakov's backup, Arzamazov had to be prepared to fly in case Polyakov couldn't. In this case it meant undergoing a painful bone marrow extraction.

In 1993 Arzamazov was assigned again as Polyakov's backup, this time for Soyuz TM–18, which would carry Polyakov to the Mir space station for a planned 16–month visit. Resentful over his second tour as a backup without a flight, Arzamazov complained openly about Polyakov's unsuitability for the mission, and in early January 1994, weeks before the TM–18 launch, Arzamazov was removed from the backup position.

Arzamazov was born March 9, 1946 in the village of Shubino, Sharansk District, Gorky Region, Russia. Following secondary school he attended the Sanchursk medical school, becoming a medical assistant. He then served in the Soviet army. Following his military service he attended the Sechenov First Moscow Medical Institute. Upon graduation in 1974 Arzamazov went to work at the Institute for Medical–Biological Problems.

He joined the group of IMBP candidate doctor–cosmonauts in 1976 and was enrolled as a cosmonaut–researcher 2 years later.

Arzmazov is a sport parachutist with over 100 jumps to his credit.

He retired from the IMBP cosmonaut team in June 1994.

Atkov, Oleg Yuriyevich

1949–

Oleg Atkov was the third Soviet medical doctor assigned to a cosmonaut crew, but the first to spend more than 2 days in space. During 237 days in the unique environment of Salyut 7, Atkov had the unprecedented opportunity to study the effects of space travel on himself and fellow cosmonauts Leonid Kizim and Vladimir Solovyov. That mission, Soyuz T–10, lasted from February to to October 1984 and at that time was the longest manned spaceflight in history.

Atkov was born May 9, 1949, in the town of Khvorostyanka in the Kuybyshev Region of Russia. In 1973 he graduated from the Sechenov First Moscow Medical Institute, the same school that cosmonaut Boris Yegorov, the first doctor in space, attended. From 1973 to 1977 Atkov was an intern and student at the All–Union Cardiological Center of the USSR Academy of Medical Sciences specializing in ultrasound as a method of detecting heart disease. While at the Center he took part in preflight and postflight physical examinations of cosmonauts.

Atkov was selected as a cosmonaut candidate by the Academy of Medical Sciences in 1977, but not approved by the state commission until March 1983. While awaiting a flight opportunity he designed a portable ultrasound cardiograph for use on the Soyuz T–5 flight in 1982. His generic Soyuz–Salyut training commenced in June 1983, during which he logged 12 hours of flying time in an L–39 aircraft, made four zero–G flights in an Il–76K, and made two parachute jumps. In September he joined the "main crew" of Kizim and Solovyov.

Atkov works at the All–Union Cardiology Institute in Moscow.

Aubakirov, Toktar Ongarbayevich

1946–

Kazakh test pilot Toktar Aubakirov spent 8 days in space in October 1991 as the flight engineer for Soyuz TM–13. Aubakirov, commander Alexandr Volkov and Austrian researcher Franz Viehbock joined resident cosmonauts Artsebarsky and Krikalev aboard the Mir space station.

Aubakirov's mission was devoted to experiments designed by the Academy of Sciences of the Kazakh SSR. It was also fraught with political overtones, coming as it did during the breakup of the Soviet Union into different republics. When asked at a prelaunch press conference whether he represented Kazakhstan or the USSR, Aubakirov diplomatically replied, "I represent Kazakhstan in the USSR."

Aubakirov was the first Soviet citizen to go into space without having been officially certified as a cosmonaut. Under the unwieldy process of cosmonaut training and selection, in which different organizations select and submit candidates, some cosmonauts train and even join crews months or years before their "official" selection. Aubakirov was one. The State Commission meeting to certify him was to have taken place on August 28, 1991—

little more than a week after the abortive coup, which caused it to be postponed.

Aubakirov was born July 27, 1946, on the May 1st Collective Farm near Karakalinsk, Karaganda District of the Kazakh SSR. He was certified as a parachutist by the DOSAAF school in Karagalinsk, then entered the Armavir Higher Air Force School. Following graduation in 1969 he served as a Soviet air force pilot in the Far East.

Aubakirov left active duty in 1975 to enroll at the Ministry of Aviation Industry's test pilot school at Zhukovsky. Upon graduation in May 1976 he worked as a test pilot in Ulan–Ude; in August of that year he joined the Mikoyan design bureau in Moscow.

As a Mikoyan test pilot based at Zhukovsky, Aubakirov logged over 3,300 hours of flying time in 50 different types of aircraft. In 1988 he became the first pilot to fly a MiG–29 from an aircraft carrier—the *Tblisi* (since renamed the *Admiral Kuznetsov*). For this he was named a Hero of the Soviet Union.

At the time of his selection for cosmonaut training he was deputy chief test pilot for the Mikoyan design bureau working on the MiG–31 fighter. He also graduated from the Moscow Aviation Institute (1979).

Aubakirov was enrolled in the cosmonaut team in January 1991 at the personal request of Kazakh SSR President Nursultan Nuzarbayev, joining Kazakh pilot Talgat Musabayev, who had been selected the previous May.

Following his flight Aubakirov was appointed a major–general in the armed forces of the Kazakh Republic, serving as first deputy defense minister. From January 1993 to May 1994 he was the first chief of the Kazakh Space Agency and deputy minister of science and technology. He is currently a deputy in the parliament of the Supreme Kenges, the legislature of the Republic of Kazakhstan.

Avdeyev, Sergei Vasilyevich

1956–

Sergei Avdeyev was the flight engineer for the 12th Mir resident crew, launched aboard Soyuz TM–15 in July 1992. With Avdeyev were commander Anatoly Solovyov and French researcher Michel

Tognini. Tognini returned to Earth with the Mir–11 crew after 12 days in space, but Adveyev and Solovyov went on to complete a 189–day mission that included work on materials manufacturing and X–ray astronomy. In September they conducted four different EVAs to install a special engine block atop the Sofora tower on the Mir exterior. They also struck the last official Soviet flag, originally placed on the Sofora in 1991 by cosmonaut Anatoly Artsebarsky. The Mir–12 crew returned to Earth on February 1, 1993.

Avdeyev made a second mission to Mir in the crew of Soyuz TM–22 (Mir–20), launched September 3, 1995. Avdeyev and commander Yuri Gidzenko were accompanied by German researcher Thomas Reiter, representing the European Space Agency and its EuroMir–95 series of 47 experiments, most of them in the field of space medicine. Avdeyev made two EVAs during the mission, including one with Reiter. The crew also hosted the STS–74 mission, which delivered a special Shuttle docking module to the Russian station in November. Mir–20's planned 135–day duration was extended by over a month due to financial problems within the Russian Space Agency that delayed the Mir–21 relief mission, ultimately lasting 179 days.

Avdeyev was born January 1, 1956, in the city of Chapayevsk, Samarskaya (formerly Kuybyshev) Region, Russia. Following completion of secondary school in 1973 he was enrolled at the Moscow Institute of Physical Engineering (MIFI), where he majored in nuclear engineering. Since 1979 he has been employed by Energiya, though he also completed a postgraduate course at MIFI in 1986.

Avdeyev was enrolled in the cosmonaut team as a candidate in March 1987 and underwent the training course from December 1987 to July 1989. As a cosmonaut candidate he logged 30 hours of flying time on the L–39 trainer, and also made 35 parachute jumps.

In 1990 Avdeyev was assigned to the Mir training group with commander Alexandr Viktorenko and briefly served with him on the backup crew for Soyuz TM–13 (Mir–10) until plans for that mission were changed and Adveyev was replaced by Talgat Musabeyev. With Anatoly Solovyov and Reinhold Ewald, Avdeyev backed up Soyuz TM–12 (Mir–9), launched March 17, 1992, on a four–month stay aboard Mir. Avdeyev later served, with Gidzenko and Pedro Duque, as backups for Soyuz

TM–20/Mir, launched in October 1994, and with Gennady Padalka, for Soyuz TM–26/Mir–24 in August 1997.

Avdeyev is scheduled to make his third Mir mission with commander Padalka and Russian politician Yuri Baturin on the Mir–26 mission, Soyuz TM–28, beginning in August 1998.

Baberdin, Valery Vasilyevich
1948–

Russian military journalist Valery Baberdin was one of the 6 Soviet journalists who were trained as cosmonaut–researchers from October 1990 to February 1992. A Russian journalist was to have spent a week aboard the Mir space station, but the mission was canceled in 1992 for financial reasons.

Baberdin was born October 28, 1948, in a military family stationed in Sterlitamak, Bashkirian ASSR, Russia. He grew up in Noginsk, where he graduated from secondary school. In 1966 Baberdin enrolled at the Kuybyshev Military Engineering Academy in Moscow, studying electromechanics. Following graduation in 1971 he became a quality control officer at a military factory in Khabarovsk.

Four years later he joined the staff of the journal *Teknika i Vooryzheniya*, a military–technical publication. In 1980 he graduated from a journalism curriculum at Moscow State University, then, in 1983, joined *Krasnaya Zvezda (Red Star)*, the publication of the Soviet Ministry of Defense, as a writer on science, technology, and spaceflight. He is currently head of the science department at that paper, and lives at Star Town.

Bachurin, Ivan Ivanovich
1942–

Ivan Bachurin is a Soviet air force test pilot who trained to command orbital flights of the Buran II space shuttle. From 1991 to 1992 he also trained as a Soyuz TM commander for a planned docking of a manned Soyuz with an unmanned Buran in Earth orbit. That mission was canceled in 1992, however. Bachurin was medically disqualified and removed from flight status later the same year.

Bachurin was born January 23, 1942, in Berestovenka in the Kharkov Region of the Ukraine. He entered the Soviet air force in 1959, enrolling at the Orenburg Higher Air Force School. Following graduation in 1963, he served as an instructor pilot at Orenburg. He attended the Chkalov test pilot school in 1967 and 1968, then went to work as a test pilot.

He later graduated from the Moscow Aviation Institute (1973).

Selected as one of 6 military test pilots for the Buran program in December 1978, Bachurin and his colleagues underwent general cosmonaut training at the Gagarin Center in 1979 and 1980. With Alexei Borodai, Bachurin flew six approach and landing tests of the jet–powered version of Buran between October 1987 and March 1988, logging a total of 2 hours, seven minutes flying time.

In June 1989 Bachurin and Borodai accompanied the Buran orbiter to the Paris Air Show. A year later civilian Buran test pilot Igor Volk revealed that the Bachurin–Borodai team were backups for the first manned orbital Buran mission.

Bachurin retired from the Russian air force in 1993 and now works in commercial aviation.

Balandin, Alexandr Nikolayevich

1953–

Alexandr Balandin was the flight engineer of Soyuz TM–9, a 6–month mission aboard the Mir space station in 1990. Balandin and commander Anatoly Solovyov were charged with the difficult task of completing the world's first "profitable" spaceflight, producing manufacturing materials and data worth at least $25 million dollars, the stated cost of 6 months of Mir operations. According to Soviet reports, they returned at least half that amount.

But that success did not come easily. On February 11, 1990, the first day of their mission, Balandin and Solovyov's Soyuz TM spacecraft suffered a malfunction in which several vital insulation blankets tore lose from their pinnings, blocking sensors necessary for the eventual return to Earth and possibly exposing the spacecraft to undesirable extremes of temperature.

During March and April, while the cosmonauts adapted to life aboard Mir and began their manufacturing and Earth resources studies, flight controllers developed plans for repairing the Soyuz, constructing special ladders and tools that were delivered to Mir in the unmanned Progress 42 tanker in May.

On July 17, 1990, Balandin and Solovyov exited Mir to inspect and repair Soyuz. They managed to reattach the blankets and to reassure themselves that other damage had not occurred, but while attempting to reenter Mir's main airlock discovered that the outer door would not close. The EVA had already gone on two hours longer than its scheduled 5–hour duration, and the cosmonauts were in danger of running out of oxygen. They managed to use a secondary hatch into the Mir, and a week later performed another EVA, retrieving the special ladders and restoring the outer door.

The Soyuz TM–9 mission ended on August 9, 1990. Balandin has spent 177 days in space.

Balandin was born July 30, 1953, in Fryazino, a suburb of Moscow. As a child he was a reader of science fiction stories by authors such as Isaac Asimov, Ray Bradbury, Ivan Yefremov, and the Strugatsky brothers. He attended the Bauman Higher Technical School, graduating in 1976.

That same year Balandin went to work with the Korolev spacecraft design bureau, now known as the Energiya Scientific Production Association (NPO Energiya), at its Leningrad center, where he took part in tests of a prototype manned rocket plane like the American X–15. He applied for the cosmonaut group in 1976 and was enrolled in December 1978. From 1980 to 1987 he worked on the Buran space shuttle program.

In February 1989 Balandin was assigned to make a 6–month flight aboard the Mir space station with pilot–commander Alexandr Viktorenko. That mission, Soyuz TM–8, was canceled in April 1989 because technical problems continued to delay the launch of add–on modules for Mir. When Soyuz TM–8 was finally launched in September 1989, Balandin served as backup to Alexandr Serebrov.

Balandin left the Energiya cosmonaut team in October 1994, though he remains employed by that organization.

The Soyuz TM–9 mission of Balandin and Solovyov was the subject of an episode of the television series *Nova* in 1991.

Baturin, Yuri Mikhailovich
1949–

Russian politician Yuri Baturin, a deputy to President Boris Yeltsin, is scheduled to make a 10–day visit to the Mir space station in August 1998. Baturin will serve as cosmonaut researcher in the crew of Soyuz TM–28, the Mir–26 crew commanded by Gennady Padalka with flight engineer Sergei Avdeyev.

Baturin was born May 19, 1949, in Moscow, and attended the Moscow Physical–Technical Institute, majoring in astrophysics and space research, and studying under the famed spacecraft designer Boris Raushenbakh. Baturin began working part–time at NPO Energiya, builders of the Soyuz, Salyut and Mir spacecraft, while still an undergraduate, and became a full–time employee in the guidance department in 1975.

Baturin applied for enrollment in the Energiya cosmonaut group in the late 1970s, but was rejected because of his eyesight.

After leaving Energiya in 1980, Baturin entered law school, and upon graduation worked for the Soviet, then Russian government, ultimately becoming first deputy minister of defense. It was while serving in this post in 1997 that he convinced Russian President Boris Yelstin to send him on a fact–finding flight to Mir, and began part–time training at the Gagarin Center. Baturin was removed from that job in August of that year, but remained on Yeltsin's staff. He was officially approved as a cosmonaut candidate in September 1997.

Beloborodov, Valery Mikhailovich
1939–

Russian air force pilot Valery Beloborodov was one of the 12 candidates enrolled in the military cosmonaut team on April 24, 1967. He did not complete the initial training course, failing his final examinations for political reasons (refusing to join the Communist Party), and left the team on August 20, 1969.

Beloborodov was born October 26, 1939, in the village of Oloviyanna, Chita region, Russia. He attended the Chernigov Higher Air Force School, graduating in 1963, then served with Soviet air forces in East Germany. In March 1965 he was invited to apply for the military cosmonaut team, and in October was one of the 60 finalists examined. He was not selected at that time, however, but placed in reserve for another 18 months.

Following his dismissal, Beloborodov served as a fighter pilot in Byelorussia and at Kubinka air base, near Moscow. He later became a military transport pilot, serving in Afghanistan, and also flew for Aeroflot from Chkalov air base.

Beloborodov retired from the Soviet air force with the rank of major in 1987, and currently works as a dispatcher in a factory.

Belousov, Boris Nikolayevich
1930–1998

Boris Belousov was the senior officer of the 22 air force candidates enrolled in the cosmonaut team on October 30, 1965. In September 1966, while still completing his initial training course, Belousov was teamed with pilot Alexei Gubarev for a possible mission in the 7K–VI, a military manned reconnaissance vehicle. The program was canceled in 1967 before any manned missions could be flown.

Belousov also served as a communications operator (capcom) for the ill–fated Soyuz 1 flight of cosmonaut

Vladimir Komarov in April 1967. He was dismissed from the cosmonaut team on January 5, 1968 without ever flying in space, ostensibly for health reasons, but also for poor performance on the state examinations given the candidates of the Third Enrollment in December 1967.

Belousov was born July 24, 1930, in the city of Khotimsk, Mogilev District, Byelorussia. He attended a school for aircraft instrument technicians in Leningrad from 1946 to 1950, then worked in an aircraft factory there. In 1951 he entered the Soviet air force and studied at the Kazan technical school, graduating in 1953, then spent 2 years in the city of Bryansk as an aircraft technician. Belousov later graduated from the Mozhaisky Air Force Academy in Leningrad (1960).

From 1960 until his selection as a cosmonaut Belousov served as an engineer–researcher with the Strategic Rocket Forces and was stationed at the Baikonur Cosmodrome. He was selected for the Second Enrollment at the cosmonaut training center in January 1963, but was held back at the last moment.

After leaving the cosmonaut team in 1968 Belousov became a researcher at a branch of NII–4, the Central Scientific Research Institute of the USSR Ministry of Defense, in Bolshevo, Moscow region. In 1976 he became an editor at Voenizdat, the military–technical publishing house. Belousov died on June 27, 1998.

Belyayev, Pavel Ivanovich
1925–1970

Pavel Belyayev commanded the spaceflight during which fellow cosmonaut Alexei Leonov took the world's first walk in space. It was March 18, 1965, and Belyayev acted as live commentator to a Soviet television audience as his copilot floated free outside the Voskhod 2 spacecraft for 10 minutes. "Man has stepped out into open space!" Belyayev announced.

The Voskhod 2 flight lasted only a day. Because of a failure in the automatic guidance system, Belyayev was forced to make a manual reentry. He and Leonov landed far off course in the mountains near Perm and spent a cold night in the wilderness, chasing away wolves, before being reached by rescue teams and returned to Moscow for a triumphant welcome.

Belyayev was born June 26, 1925, in the village of Chelishchevo, Roslyatinsky district, Vologda region of Russia. He grew up in Kamensk–Uralsk, where he often had to ski to school. At the age of 16 he went to work in a pipe factory, then, at the age of 18, he entered the Sarapulsky Air Force School. In 1944 he transferred to the Stalin Naval Air School, graduating in 1945.

As a fighter pilot with the 19th Guards Air Regiment of the Pacific Fleet, Belyayev saw action against the Japanese during the last days of World War II. In 1948 he transferred to the 88th Guards Air Regiment of the 165th Air Division, Pacific Fleet, flying the La–11, Yak–9, and Yak–11 aircraft until August 1956, when he entered the Red Banner Air Force Academy in Moscow in 1956. He graduated in 1959 and was serving as a squadron commander of the 241st Guards Air Regiment in the 4th Air Division of the Northern Fleet when he was selected for the cosmonaut team in March 1960.

Major Belyayev was the oldest and most experienced pilot among the cosmonauts and he became the first commander of the group, though a variety of physical ailments prevented him from becoming one of the first to make a spaceflight. He suffered a badly broken ankle during a parachute jump in August 1961 and spent a year recuperating, then supervised the selection and training of a new group of pilot and engineer cosmonauts who came to the training center in January 1963.

In April 1964 he was chosen to command Voskhod 2, though physical problems almost got him dropped. (Personal appeals by cosmonauts Vladimir Komarov and Alexei Leonov helped the State Commission decide to keep Belyayev as commander.)

Following Voskhod 2 Belyayev hoped to return to space, training briefly for the first pair of manned Soyuz missions, and ultimately working on the Almaz military space station program. But health problems grounded him, and in May 1967 he became chief of staff of the Cosmonaut Training Center, supervising the training of the fourth candidate cosmonaut enrollment. When the center was reorganized in 1969, Belyayev was named head of its First Directorate.

Suspicious of the training center doctors who grounded him, Belyayev apparently concealed a stomach ailment until he had to be hospitalized in December 1969. During surgery for an ulcer he developed peritonitis, and died on January 10, 1970.

A crater on the Moon, an asteroid, and a Soviet space tracking ship are named for him.

Beregovoy, Georgy Timofeyevich

1921–1995

Georgy Beregovoy became the first Soviet test pilot to go into space when he served as commander of Soyuz 3 in October 1968, a mission that ended an 18–month hiatus in Soviet manned flights caused by the Soyuz 1 accident.

The 47–year–old Beregovoy, at that time also the oldest person to make a spaceflight, spent 4 days testing the redesigned vehicle and rendezvousing with the unmanned Soyuz 2. A planned docking failed due to pilot error.

Following his only flight, Beregovoy became the first cosmonaut promoted to the rank of major general. He gave up active space training in April 1969 to become deputy director of the Gagarin Cosmonaut Training Center, and in June 1972 was appointed director, a post he held until January 3, 1987.

In January 1969, during welcoming ceremonies in Moscow for the Soyuz 4/5 cosmonauts, a would–be assassin fired pistol shots at Beregovoy in a motorcade, mistaking the cosmonaut for Soviet President Leonid Brezhnev, whom he resembled. Beregovoy was not hurt.

Beregovoy was born April 15, 1921, in the village of Fyodorovka, Poltava Region, Ukraine. In 1922 Beregovoy's family moved to Yenyakiyevo in the Donbass area, a land of iron and coal mines and steel mills, and at age 17 Beregovoy took a job in a steel plant there.

But he had built model airplanes and become an amateur pilot through a local flying club, so in December 1938 he joined the air force, attending the Lugansk (later known as Voroshilovgrad) Air Force School. He graduated in June 1941, just in time for the World War II, and went from school directly to the front.

From 1941 to 1945 Beregovoy flew 185 combat missions against the Nazis with a number of units, including the 4th Air Assault Division, 5th Air Army, 2nd Ukrainian Front. This division was commanded by Major General Nikolai Kamanin, who would later become the first chief of cosmonaut training. Flown in the Il–2 attack plane, most of Beregovoy's missions were in support of infantry and tank assaults. He was shot down three times, but always managed to return to his own lines. In October 1944 he earned his first Hero of the Soviet Union medal.

After the war (1948) Beregovoy graduated from the Chkalov test pilot school in Shchelkovo, then served at the flight test center there, flying 63 different types of aircraft, logging 80 test flights and 2,500 flying hours. Among his accomplishments were the first service tests of an all–weather version of the MiG–15 fighter, and rocket–assisted takeoffs of the MiG–19. He attended the Red Banner Air Force Academy by correspondence from 1953 to 1956.

Beregovoy's selection as a cosmonaut was almost an accident. He was interested in flying in space but assumed that his age—he was 40 when Gagarin flew—prevented it. He was already an honored Hero of the Soviet Union, a full colonel, and over–qualified for the cosmonaut group. In November 1963, air force chief of staff Sergei Rudenko urged cosmonaut training chief Kamanin to create a small cadre of "senior" cosmonauts, including civilians, who would fly one mission, then move into space program management. The first set of candidates included Beregovoy, but Kamanin resisted, only to be overruled by air force commander–in–chief Vershinin, who signed a special order enrolling Beregovoy as a cosmonaut on January 17, 1964.

Training center director Nikolai Kuznetsov wanted Beregovoy to undergo accelerated training in order to command the first Voskhod mission, but Kamanin and Korolev—not to mention the cosmonauts selected in 1960 and 1963—felt others had priority. Beregovoy spent most of 1964 in a rigorous physical conditioning program, losing over 15 pounds and markedly improving his stamina.

In April 1965 Beregovoy and Lev Demin were assigned as the second crew for a planned 2–week Voskhod 3 mission, then scheduled for launch in early 1966. The crews were later shuffled, with Vladimir Shatalov replacing Demin as Beregovoy's crewmate. Following the death of chief designer Korolev in January 1966, however, the entire Voskhod program was reevaluated, and four of its six manned missions were canceled. In November 1966 Beregovoy joined the group of cosmonauts training for the first Soyuz flights.

When Vladimir Komarov was killed in the Soyuz 1 accident, Kamanin personally selected Beregovoy to return Soyuz to flight, replacing Yuri Gagarin (who had been Komarov's backup) and fighting off a challenge from Korolev bureau designer Konstantin Feoktistov, who thought he should make the test flight.

Beregovoy was almost replaced as Soyuz 3 commander when he did poorly on the final state examinations. A retest was hurriedly ordered, and he managed to qualify.

During his tenure as director of the Gagarin Center Beregovoy continued his academic studies (he earned his candidate of psychological sciences degree in 1975) and remained politically active as a member of the Supreme Soviet. He was promoted to lieutenant general in 1977.

Beregovoy published several books, including two autobiographies, *Angle of Attack* (1971) and *The Sky Begins on Earth* (1976), as well as *Earth—Stratosphere—Space* (1969), *Space for Earthlings* (1981), and *Three Altitudes* (1986). He is coauthor of *Space Academy* (1987).

Following his retirement he worked with the Lidar All–Union Information Service of the Soviet Academy of Sciences. He died following routine surgery on June 30, 1995.

Berezovoy, Anatoly Nikolayevich
1942–

Anatoly Berezovoy commanded the first flight to Salyut 7, the 7–month Soyuz T–5 mission. He and engineer Valentin Lebedev were launched May 13, 1982, planning to remain in space for 6 months, with a possible extension. After docking with Salyut 7 on May 14, they activated the station, a process that took several days, and deployed an amateur radio satellite called Iskra 2, before settling down to a routine of Earth surface observations and space manufactur-

ing. In June the expedition cosmonauts were host to three visitors, the crew of Soyuz T–6, which included French spationaut Jean–Loup Chretien. In August a second crew of 3 visited Salyut 7; this crew included Svetlana Savitskaya, the second woman in space.

By early December Berezovoy and Lebedev had taken over 20,000 pictures of the Earth's surface and had manufactured electronic crystals in a special factory.

Though Berezovoy and Lebedev had had moments of personal strain during the 7–month mission—it was later rumored that they were barely on speaking terms during its final weeks—they had survived in good physical condition as they prepared to return to Earth in Soyuz T–7, which had been left for their use by the August visitors.

Berezovoy and Lebedev's greatest challenge was the recovery following their landing in snowy Kazakhstan. They came down at night in unexpected fog and low clouds and rolled down a hillside. The first rescue helicopter attempting to reach them crash–landed and its commander had to "talk down" the second. Eventually the cosmonauts were rescued from their frigid spacecraft and given shelter in a rugged all–terrain vehicle. When they returned to the launch complex at Baikonur the next morning they were unable to walk without assistance. Within days, however, both men had recovered.

Berezovoy was born April 11, 1942, in the village of Enem, Oktyabr District, Adigei Autonomous Region, Russia. As a teenager he took a job as a lathe operator at the Neftemash factory in the city of Novocherkassk, but soon joined the army. From 1961 to 1965 he attended the Kacha Higher Air Force School near Volgograd, then spent 2 years there as a flight instructor. He later served with a fighter squadron in Moldavia.

Berezovoy was enrolled in the military cosmonaut group in May 1970 and completed the basic training course 2 years later. He commenced a 4–year course of study at the Yuri Gagarin Air Force Academy in 1973 and soon joined the Salyut–Almaz military space station training group. By the time of his thirty–third birthday, he later wrote, he was sure he would never fly in space. (He had been assigned as commander of a crew that was fourth in line for a series of two flights to Salyut–Almaz 5. The Almaz program was not the assignment of choice for Soviet cosmonauts, since its once ambitious program of missions had been seriously diminished over the years.)

The Soyuz 23 abort in October 1976 caused Soviet officials to make a third flight to Salyut–Almaz 5, Soyuz 24, and Berezovoy served as backup commander for this mission.

From 1978 to 1981 Berezovoy trained as commander of a 3–man Almaz crew that was intended to test the TKS manned spacecraft. TKS was a 4–ton Gemini–like vehicle attached to an Almaz station, with both being placed in orbit by a Proton launcher. The Almaz program received its final cancellation in 1981. As the senior commander in the program, Berezovoy was well placed to transfer to the Salyut 7 training group when one of that station's commanders, Yuri Isaulov, was medically disqualified in January 1982.

Following Soyuz T–5 Berezovoy served as backup commander for the Soviet–Indian Soyuz T–11 flight, launched in April 1984.

In 1986 Berezovoy was assigned to the Rescuer group of senior pilot–cosmonauts who stood by to fly solo missions in case of an emergency aboard the Mir complex. Rescuer pilots Vladimir Lyakhov and Berezovoy were assigned as commanders for the two Soviet–Afghan crews named rather hurriedly in February 1988 for a mission to be launched just 6 months later. Berezovoy served as backup commander for that mission. In July 1990, when cosmonauts Anatoly Solovyov and Alexandr Balandin performed an unplanned EVA in order to repair their Soyuz TM vehicle, Berezovoy stood by to fly a rescue Soyuz TM. It was not needed.

In addition to his duties in the Rescuer group, Colonel Berezovoy supervised the training of the 1989 and 1990 enrollments of candidate pilot–cosmonauts. He returned to active flight training in 1991 in a crew with Nikolai Budarin, but in August 1992 was medically disqualified, because of injuries received in a mugging.

He retired from the Russian air force with the rank of colonel in January 1993, but remains at the Gagarin Center as a civilian training official.

Bondarenko, Valentin Vasilyevich
1937–1961

Valentin Bondarenko, the youngest member of the first group of Soviet cosmonauts, was killed in a fire that engulfed a pressure chamber on March 23, 1961, just 3 weeks before the flight of Yuri Gagarin. He was the first space traveler to die in training.

Bondarenko was completing 10 days of experiments in the chamber, where, like others in the cosmonaut group, he had been subjected to isolation and silence. The atmospheric pressure inside the chamber was reduced, requiring a higher oxygen content. Following a medical examination, Bondarenko removed the sensors and cleaned himself with a piece of cotton dipped in alcohol. Unthinking, he tossed the cotton aside. It landed on a hot plate and ignited, quickly turning the oxygen–rich chamber into an inferno. Before the chamber could be opened, a process that took several minutes, Bondarenko had been burned over 90 percent of his body. He was taken to the Botkin Hospital not far away, where he died eight hours later.

According to one account, the cosmonaut who accompanied Bondarenko to the hospital was Gagarin. The next day, on March 24, Gagarin and the other cosmonauts left Moscow for their first visit to the Baikonur space center.

Bondarenko was born February 16, 1937 in the Ukrainian city of Kharkov. His father was a resistance fighter during the World War II and Bondarenko was said to have been very proud of his exploits.

Bondarenko attended the Armavir Higher Air Force School, graduating in 1957, then served as a fighter pilot with the Soviet air force in the Baltics. He was one of the 20 candidates enrolled in the cosmonaut team in March 1960.

News of the accident that killed Bondarenko was suppressed for 25 years, though rumors that a cosmonaut trainee had died just prior to Gagarin's flight existed almost from the beginning.

Borodin, Alexandr Viktorovich
1953–
Alexandr Borodin is a physician who was enrolled as a candidate cosmonaut–researcher in December 1978. He served as support flight engineer/researcher with commander Yuri Malyshev for the Soyuz TM–6 mission in August 1988.

Borodin was born March 3, 1953, in the city of Volgograd. He attended the Sechenov 1st Moscow Medical Institute, graduating in 1976, then joined the staff of the Institute for Medical–Biological Problems.

He left the IMBP cosmonaut team on March 10, 1993, though he remains on staff at the Institute.

Borodai, Alexei Sergeyevich
1947–
Alexei Borodai was one of the 6 Soviet air force test pilots selected to train for the Buran shuttle program in January 1979. He underwent cosmonaut training at the Gagarin Center in 1979 and 1980, then returned to the Chkalov Flight Test Center at Akhtubinsk. With Ivan Bachurin Borodai flew six test flights with the jet–powered version of Buran between October 1987 and March 1988.

In 1991, following delays to manned Buran flights, Borodai transferred to the Gagarin Center full–time, to train as commander for a proposed Soyuz–Buran docking mission. That mission was canceled in 1993.

Borodai was born July 28, 1947, in the village of Borodayevka, Volgograd Region, Russia. Following graduation from secondary school he went to work at a plant in Volgograd and also joined a flying club. In 1965 he enrolled at the Kacha Higher Air Force School in Volgograd, becoming a pilot in 1969.

He served for 3 years as a fighter pilot, then entered the Chkalov test pilot school, graduating in 1977. While based at the military flight test center in Akhtubinsk he flew several different types of aircraft, including transports and bombers. He also attended a local branch of the Moscow Aviation Institute, graduating in 1981.

Borodai served as commander of the test pilot cosmonaut team from January 1993 until his retirement that December. He was an airplane pilot until being injured in a crash in Italy in December 1996.

Budarin, Nikolai, Mikhailovich
1953–
Nikolai Budarin was flight engineer in the Mir–19 crew. He and commander Anatoly Solovyov were transported to the Mir space station by STS–71 in June 1995, and went on to serve a relatively short shift of 75 days. It was a busy mission nonetheless, marked by three demanding EVAs in a single week in late July, erecting new solar arrays and installing a French–Belgian spectrometer on the exterior of the Kristall module. They returned to Earth aboard Soyuz TM–21 in early September.

Budarin returned to Mir in January 1998. With commander Talgat Musabayev, he formed the 25th Mir crew, Soyuz TM–27. The two cosmonauts, working with French researcher Leopold Eyharts and NASA astronaut Andy Thomas, are scheduled to remain aboard the station until August 1998.

Budarin was born April 29, 1953, in Kira, Alatyr district, Chuvash ASSR. He entered the Moscow Aviation Institute in 1970, but saw his education interrupted for 2 years of service with Soviet military forces in Czechoslovakia. Demobilized, he returned to MAI, but also worked part–time at two spacecraft factories. In 1979, when he received his diploma from MAI, he joined NPO Energiya at its test–control station (KIS), becoming a section head there in 1986. Budarin also managed to complete a course at the University of Marxism–Leninism (1981).

Approved by the state medical commission for cosmonaut training in February 1986, Budarin was one of the 4 civilian engineers enrolled in the cosmonaut team as candidates in February 1989. He completed the general space training course in 1990 and in 1992 was assigned to a possible Mir crew with commander Anatoly Berezovoy. In April 1994 he was assigned with Solovyov to the Mir–18/STS–71 crew, serving first as backups to Mir–17/Soyuz TM–21.

Bugrov, Vladimir Yevgrafovich

1933–

Engineer Vladimir Bugrov was one of the 8 engineers selected for cosmonaut training by the OKB–1 in May 1966. OKB–1 chief designer Vasily Mishin wanted to fly Bugrov on the first pair of manned Soyuz missions, but could not get Bugrov approved by the military medical commission.

From August 1967 to July 1968 Bugrov was a candidate for Program L–1, the Soviet manned lunar orbit mission, and also worked on the Cheget lunar EVA space suit, but never trained in a crew. Without medical clearance, he gave up training in 1969.

Bugrov was born January 18, 1933, in Moscow, and attended the Moscow Aviation Institute, graduating in 1956 as a mechanical engineer.

Beginning in March 1956 Bugrov worked for the OKB Lavochkin, builders of early Soviet lunar and interplanetary probes. Wanting to become a cosmonaut, Bugrov transferred to the OKB–1 (Korolev) in November 1961, shortly after the flight of Gherman Titov. He continued to work on space probes for that organization while lobbying successfully for the creation of a civilian–engineer cosmonaut group within the OKB–1.

From 1968 to 1972 Bugrov worked as lead engineer for the Lunar Orbit Spacecraft (LOK), a version of the Soyuz designed to carry two cosmonauts to lunar orbit. He later served as a section head (1972–87), laboratory chief (1987–92), and finally senior scientific staffer (1992–95) at NPO Energiya. He is now retired.

Buinovsky, Eduard Ivanovich

1936–

Eduard Buinovsky was one of the 15 candidates enrolled in the cosmonaut team on January 11, 1963. Buinovsky failed a test on the centrifuge toward the end of his general space–training course and was dis-charged from the cosmonaut team on medical grounds on December 11, 1964. He never flew in space.

Buinovsky was born February 26, 1936, in Novocherkassk in the Rostov Region of Russia, and after completing secondary school entered the air force. He graduated from the Riga Higher Air Force Engineering School in 1958, and became a specialist in the construction, development, and launching of missiles and spacecraft. From September 1958 to January 1960 he was an R–7 launch crewmember at the Baikonur Cosmodrome and the Plesetsk missile base. He then became a representative of the Main Directorate for Missile Systems (GURVO) at the NII–885 organization under Nikolai Pilyugin, builders of missile control systems. This work frequently took him to the Baikonur Cosmodrome (where he supported Yuri Gagarin's mission).

After leaving the cosmonaut team he returned to work on space control systems as GURVO representative at NII–885. In 1970 he became an inspector with TsUKOS, the military space agency, ultimately joining the Energiya–Buran launch team. In July 1989, following the only successful Energiya–Buran mission (launched November 15, 1988), he transferred to reserve status with the rank of colonel. Buinovsky is currently a specialist in communications and control systems for the Ministry of Foreign Affairs.

Burdayev, Mikhail Nikolayevich

1932–

Mikhail Burdayev is an engineer who was one of 12 air force candidates enrolled in the cosmonaut team in April 1967. He left the cosmonaut team in 1983 without ever having had a chance to fly in space.

Burdayev was born August 27, 1932, in Feodosia in the Crimea, where his father was a test pilot. He attended the Mozhaisky Air Force Engineering Academy in Leningrad, earning a degree in mechanical engineering in 1956. In 1963 he earned a candidate of technical sciences degree, and in 1987 a doctor of science in space ballistics.

Burdayev served as a squadron engineer with the long range aviation branch of the Soviet air force from 1956 to 1959. He then joined the staff of the Research Institute for Air Defense of the USSR Ministry of Defense (NII–2) in the city of Kalinin (now Tver), where he remained until joining the cosmonaut team.

As a cosmonaut Burdayev completed the initial training course in August 1969. Like most of the air force engineers selected in 1965 and 1967, he was to have flown missions in the Salyut–Almaz military space station program or the "space fighter" version of Soyuz. But Salyut–Almaz and the military Soyuz were essentially replaced by unmanned systems, and by the civilian Salyut program. Beginning as early as 1968 Burdayev and his colleagues were assigned jobs in support of Soyuz missions at the flight control centers in Yevpatoryia, then at Kaliningrad near Moscow. This arrangement was formalized on April 20, 1983, when Burdayev and several other engineers left the cosmonaut team to join the staff of the flight control center. They had been classed as having "no prospects for flying in space."

During his long training as a cosmonaut Burdayev became a parachuting instructor (1972), a diver (1975), and flight test engineer (1982). He also published 80 technical papers and three books.

Colonel Burdayev left active duty in November 1989, though he remains employed at the Gagarin Center.

Bykovsky, Valery Fyodorovich

1934–

Valery Bykovsky set a manned space duration record by spending 5 days in orbit aboard Vostok 5 in June 1963. Bykovsky's flight, one of the most spectacular of the early manned missions, was somewhat overshadowed by that of Valentina Tereshkova, the first woman in space, which took place at the same time. Nevertheless, Bykovsky's flight remains the longest space mission ever flown by a single astronaut or cosmonaut.

A biography of Bykovsky published in 1989 gave new details of this pioneering mission, revealing that technical delays all too familiar to observers of the American space program had seen Bykovsky's launch canceled on June 12, and delayed several hours on June 14. The reentry was complicated by the failure of the instrument module to separate from the spherical Vostok. Like Yuri Gagarin, who had faced the same situation, Bykovsky went through reentry watching pieces of the instrument module burn and fail away.

With Nikolai Rukavishnikov as flight engineer, Bykovsky later trained as commander of a planned Soviet manned circumlunar mission scheduled for launch in March 1969. This Soyuz–Zond mission was canceled due to the successful Apollo 8 circumlunar flight in December 1968, and because of continuing technical problems.

Bykovsky would go on to command Soyuz 22, a scientific mission with flight engineer Vladimir Aksenov, in 1976 and Soyuz 31, an Interkosmos flight with German researcher Sigmund Jaehn, in 1978.

Bykovsky was born August 2, 1934, in Pavlovsky–Posad, a suburb of Moscow. While still in secondary school he joined a flying club and became a pilot. At the age of 18 he entered the Kacha Higher Air Force School, graduating in 1955, then served as an interceptor pilot and parachute instructor with the 23rd Air Squadron, 17th Air Division, Moscow military district. He became a cosmonaut in March 1960.

During the first months of cosmonaut training Bykovsky earned the Order of the Red Star for testing the isolation chamber. He was one of the finalists for the first manned flight flown by Gagarin in April 1961, and was backup to Andrian Nikolayev on the Vostok 3 flight in August 1962.

Following his record–breaking flight Bykovsky was designated a cosmonaut–instructor and supervised training for the first space walk, by Alexei Leonov in March 1965. In September 1966 he was named commander of the Soyuz 2 mission scheduled for launch on April 24, 1967. Bykovsky and fellow cosmonauts Alexei Yeliseyev and Yevgeny Khrunov were to rendezvous and dock with Soyuz 1, carrying Vladimir Komarov and launched a day earlier. Yeliseyev and Khrunov were to make a space walk to Soyuz 1 and return to Earth aboard that spacecraft. It was hoped that this demonstration of rendezvous and docking procedures and of a new space suit would give the Soviet space program experience required for manned lunar landings.

But Soyuz 1 developed technical problems during its first hours of flight. The launch of Soyuz 2 was canceled, and when Komarov was killed trying to land Soyuz 1, the whole manned program was suspended.

When Soyuz flights were ready to resume, Bykovsky was reassigned to the group of cosmonauts training for Program L, flights to the Moon.

In March 1969, the Gagarin Cosmonaut Training Center was also reorganized. Bykovsky, who had been one of 2 squad leaders within the cosmonaut detachment since July 1968, became head of Section 3 of the First Directorate, in charge of training for the lunar program, which included the Apollo–Soyuz crews from 1973 to 1975. He was assigned to Soyuz 22 in January 1976. His last assignment was as backup commander for Soyuz 37 in 1980.

Bykovsky left the cosmonaut team in January 1982, and retired from the Soviet air force in April 1988. For the next 3 years he lived in Berlin, where he ran the Soviet House of Science and Culture. He has since returned to Star Town.

A biography of Bykovsky, *Cosmonaut 5* by Grigory Reznichenko, was published in 1989.

Chirkin, Viktor Martinovich

1944–

Viktor Chirkin is a Soviet air force test pilot who trained for flights of the Buran space shuttle from 1979 to 1981. He also underwent a general cosmonaut training course at the Gagarin Center.

He resigned from the program in 1981 because he doubted it would ever fly.

Chirkin was born in 1944 and trained as a Soviet air force pilot.

Major General Chirkin is currently deputy director of the Chkalov military test pilot school at Akhtubinsk.

Dedkov, Anatoly Ivanovich

1944–

Pilot Anatoly Dedkov was one of the 9 candidates enrolled in the military cosmonaut team on April 27, 1970. He completed the training course in 1972 and was assigned to the Salyut space station program as a mission commander. From September 1975 to October 1977 he and flight engineer Yuri Ponomarev trained as a crew for Salyut 6, but were unable to pass the final examinations. Neither man ever flew in space.

Dedkov was born July 27, 1944, in the village of Luchin, Rogachovsky District of the Gomel Region, Byelorussia. He graduated from secondary school in Rogachev, then enrolled at the Kharkov Higher Air Force School. He graduated as a pilot in December 1966 and served with the 35th Air Regiment, 126th Air Division of the 24th Air Army.

While he was a member of the cosmonaut group Dedkov graduated from the Gagarin Air Force Academy (1976).

After failing to be assigned to Salyut 6, Dedkov remained in the Salyut training group, serving as a communications operator and flight controller at the Kaliningrad mission control center. On April 20, 1983, he left the cosmonaut team while continuing to work at Kaliningrad.

Since October 1994 Dedkov has been a civilian engineer–instructor in the 1st Directorate of the Gagarin Cosmonaut Training Center.

Degtyarev, Vladimir Alexandrovich

1932–

Vladimir Degtyarev was one of the 22 candidates enrolled in the military cosmonaut team on October 28, 1965. The only physician in a group that consisted of young pilots, engineers, and navigators, Degtyarev might have gone into space aboard one of the several proposed Voskhod missions devoted to medical studies. But he withdrew from the cosmonaut team on January 17, 1966, only 2 months after selection, without performing a single day of cosmonaut training. His place was taken by "reserve" doctor–cosmonaut Vasily Lazarev.

Degtyarev was born April 9, 1932, in the city of Voronezh, Russia. He attended the medical institute in that city from 1950 to 1951, then entered the S. M. Kirov Military Medical Academy in Leningrad. Following graduation in 1956 he served as chief of medical services for a paratroop battalion of the 105th Paratroop Division in the city of Kostroma. In September 1959 he transferred to the Soviet air force's Insititute of Aviation (now Aviation and Space) Medicine in Chkalovskaya, near Moscow. He was a senior scientist there when selected for cosmonaut training.

Degtyarev reportedly withdrew voluntarily from the cosmonaut team following a conversation with training chief General Nikolai Kamanin, who could not promise Degtyarev a flight in space.

Degtyarev returned to his medical institute, serving as a laboratory chief, deputy director of a department, and ultimately a department chief. He earned a candidate of medical sciences degree (1966) and a doctorate (1984). He also earned the rank of professor (1985) and published 162 medical papers.

He left the institute in 1987 and transferred to reserve status with the rank of colonel. For 2 years he was a civilian laboratory head at the Institute for Medical–Biological Problems in Moscow. Since 1989 he has directed his own scientific–technical research center. He also serves as general director of a Russian–American joint venture, and more recently as president of a company called Water, Ecology, Life.

Demin, Lev Stepanovich
1926–

Lev Demin was the flight engineer aboard the Soyuz 15 mission to Salyut–Almaz 3 in August 1974. He and commander Gennady Sarafanov were assigned to spend up to 25 days aboard the station continuing the military observations of cosmonauts Popovich and Artyukhin when the Igla automatic docking system aboard Soyuz failed. Their docking aborted, Demin and Sarafanov

were forced to make an early return to Earth, overcoming another failure, this one of the orientation system, as well as a thunderstorm in their darkened landing zone. Soyuz 15 was Demin's only flight.

Demin was born January 11, 1926, in Moscow. When World War II began he was a lathe operator in a drilling machine plant. He wanted to join a military school and was accepted, but only temporarily: his lack of proper mathematical training and the German advance on Moscow (which forced the school to relocated to Siberia) ended his schooling for the time being. Demin tried to join a flying club with the idea of becoming an air force pilot, but failed in this as well. He wound up working in a defense plant for the duration.

When the war ended he was finally able to complete ground training at the 1st Moscow Special Air Force School, where one of his classmates was future cosmonaut Vladimir Komarov. Demin no sooner got his certificate of proficiency than he saw his school disbanded. Undaunted, he applied to the Borisoglebsk Higher Air Force School, only to face another rejection, this time from the school's medical commission, for his nearsightedness.

Demin remained in the air force and was trained as an aircraft mechanic. After working briefly on Tu–2 bombers he enrolled at the 1st Moscow Air Force Signals School, where he specialized in communications technology. Following graduation he served as commander of the 131st Signals Squadron in the Moscow Military District. In 1949 he entered the Zhukovsky Air Force Engineering Academy, graduating in 1956.

From 1956 to 1958 Demin was a researcher at Zhukovsky. He then joined the staff of NII–30, a research institute of the USSR Ministry of Defense that specialized in radar and communications. Demin also remained an adjunct professor at Zhukovsky while pursuing his doctorate in systems analysis.

It was his old friend Vladimir Komarov, a member of the 1960 cosmonaut group, who encouraged Demin to apply for the second cosmonaut recruitment, which had begun in March 1962. Demin was hesitant at first: he was completing his doctoral thesis, he was older than Komarov and other cosmonauts, and the selection process was in its final phase. Nevertheless, Demin went before the medical commission and passed, and became one of the 15 candidates enrolled in January 1963. He finished his thesis that same month.

Demin's first training assignment was as a potential spacewalker for Voskhod 2, a job that ultimately went to Alexei Leonov. In 1965 Demin was teamed with commander Georgy Beregovoy in one of the crews training for a 15–day Voskhod mission, then scheduled for launch in 1966. When the series of additional Voskhod flights was ended following the death of chief designer Korolev in January 1966, Demin was reassigned to the Almaz space station program, then scheduled for launch in 1969. Political and technical problems delayed the first Almaz launch—known as Salyut 2— until April 1973.

Following the Soyuz 15 mission Demin served as deputy commander of the Almaz training group, then commander of the cosmonaut–candidate group enrolled in August 1976. In January 1978 he was named deputy director in the first directorate of the Gagarin Center.

He left the Russian air force and the Gagarin Center in August 1983 to work for Yuzhmorgeologiya, a company specializing in detecting resources beneath the sea, based in Gelendzhik on the Black Sea. He retired in 1989.

Dezhurov, Vladimir Nikolayevich

1962–

Vladimir Dezhurov commanded the eighteenth Mir residency, launched as Soyuz TM–21 in March 1995. Joining Dezhurov on his 4–month mission were flight engineer Gennady Strekalov and NASA astronaut Norman Thagard. Dezhurov and Strekalov supervised the docking of the Spektr module to the Mir complex in March 1995, and also conducted a pair of EVAs.

On July 1, 1995, the orbiter Atlantis docked with the Mir complex. It was Dezhurov who shook hands with Atlantis commander Robert "Hoot" Gibson at the docking module, commencing 5 days of joint activities involving 10 astronauts and cosmonauts.

The three Mir–18 crewmembers returned to Earth aboard Atlantis in July 1995.

In November 1997 Dezhurov was assigned to the third incremental crew for the International Space Station. With flight engineer Mikhail Tyurin and NASA mission commander Kenneth Bowersox, Dezhurov will launch to ISS aboard a Soyuz vehicle for a 2–month mission. The same crew will serve as backups to the first incremental crew of Shepherd, Gidzenko, and Krikalev, scheduled for launch in early 2000.

Dezhurov was born July 30, 1962, in the village of Yavas, Zubova Polyana District, Mordovsk Autonomous Republic of Russia. He attended the Kharkov Higher Air Force School, graduating in 1983, then served as a MiG-23 fighter pilot with the 684th Air Guards Regiment of the 119th Air Division in Tiraspol, then with the 161st Air Guards Regiment in Odessa.

He was one of 3 pilot candidates enrolled in the military cosmonaut team on October 6, 1987. From December 1987 to July 1989 he underwent the basic cosmonaut training course at the Gagarin Center, qualifying as a Soyuz TM commander. While awaiting assignment to a flight crew he attended the Moscow Institute of Cartography and Engineering Geodesy. He also served in the support crew for the Soyuz TM–19 mission (launched July 1994). He was named commander of Soyuz TM–21/Mir 18 in August of that year.

Dobrokvashina, Yelena Ivanova

1947–

Yelena Dobrokvashina is a physician who trained as the cosmonaut–researcher for an all–woman Soyuz crew in 1984. The other crewmembers were Svetlana Savitskaya (commander) and Yekaterina Ivanova (flight engineer). The three women were to have made an 8–day visit to the Salyut 7 space station in 1985, but when control problems cast Salyut 7 adrift (necessitating a special rescue mission in July 1985), their mission was canceled.

Dobrokvashina was born in Moscow on October 8, 1947. She graduated from the Sechenov First Moscow Medical Institute in 1979, then joined the staff of the Institute for Medical–Biological Problems (IMBP) in Moscow. She was enrolled as a cosmonaut candidate in July 1980 and completed training in 1984. She left the cosmonaut team in March 1993, but still works at the IMBP.

Dobrovolsky, Georgy Timofeyevich
1928–1971

Georgy Dobrovolsky commanded the first space station flight in history when he and two fellow cosmonauts spent 23 days aboard Salyut 1 in June 1971.

Dobrovolsky, Vladislav Volkov, and Viktor Patsayev were not even the intended crew for the planned 6–week mission. The first crew, commanded by Vladimir Shatalov, had been unable to enter the station after docking on April 24, and had had to return to Earth. The second crew of Alexei Leonov, Valery Kubasov and Pyotr Kolodin had been replaced just 2 days prior to launch because Kubasov had failed the final medical examinations.

Nevertheless, Dobrovolsky and his colleagues docked with and entered Salyut, setting up housekeeping and—since their exploits were televised nightly on Soviet state TV—becoming national celebrities. In addition to numerous tests to monitor their adaptation to space over time, the cosmonauts used a gamma ray detector and also conducted Earth resources photography as well as military observations of nighttime missile launches.

There were also problems. Early on there was tension between Dobrovolsky, who was on his first spaceflight, and Volkov, who was making his second. Volkov apparently declared himself "commander" of the mission until flight controllers intervened. Then, on June 17 a cable caught fire inside Salyut, forcing the cosmonauts to prepare Soyuz 11 for an emergency return to Earth. The fire went out and the return was postponed.

But during reentry on June 30, following the separation of the spherical orbital module, a valve opened prematurely on the crew module, venting the cabin's atmosphere. Patsayev struggled to block it, but failed, and the three cosmonauts were asphyxiated. Chief designer Vasily Mishin, recounting the tragedy years later, blamed the crew for failing to use a backup system that could have closed the valve. "Maybe they forgot, or didn't know. Maybe it had been omitted from their training."

Dobrovolsky was born June 1, 1928, in the Ukrainian Black Sea port city of Odessa. During the German occupation of Odessa he was arrested by the Nazis for illegal possession of firearms and sentenced to 25 years at hard labor, but escaped from jail.

As a boy Dobrovolsky dreamed of becoming a sailor, but failed to win admittance to a naval school, so he joined the air force and attended a prep school for pilots in 1945. In 1950 he graduated from the Chuguyev Higher Air Force School and became a naval aviator, first with the 32nd Air Army in Odessa, then with the 24th Air Army in East Germany. From October 1956 to January 1963 he served with the 30th Air Army, based in Valga, Estonia, becoming deputy squadron commander and political officer for the 43rd Air–Bomber Regiment there in 1961.

From September 1957 to July 1961 he took correspondence courses at the Red Banner Air Force Academy.

One of the 15 candidates enrolled in the military cosmonaut team on January 11, 1963, Dobrovolsky was popular in the group for playing Grandfather Winter at the cosmonaut New Year's celebration. Beginning in 1965 he worked in the Almaz training group followed by 5 years (1966–71) in the Soviet manned lunar program. From 1967 to 1969 he also served as a capcom for manned Soyuz missions, and as deputy commander of the cosmonaut team for political affairs. He was assigned to the Salyut program in January 1971.

A Soviet Academy of Sciences space tracking vessel was named for him in 1978, and he is the subject of a biography, *The Flight Continues* (1977).

Dolgopolov, Gennady Alexandrovich
1935–

Gennady Dolgopolov was one of the 8 engineers in the group of civilian cosmonauts enrolled in May 1966. According to one of his colleagues, he kept accepting jobs that took him away from the OKB Korolev cosmonaut office on the mistaken assumption that he would be called back for a flight assignment. He eventually left the group without flying in space.

Dolgopolov was born November 14, 1935, in the village of Krasnogorodsk, Pskov Region, Russia. He attended the Moscow Aviation Institute, graduating in 1959 as a mechanical engineer.

He joined the OKB–1 in April 1959 and worked as an engineer, then group head, until joining the flight–test department (#291) in May 1966. Chief designer Vasily Mishin wanted to include Dolgopolov in one of the early Soyuz crews, but could not get him approved by the military medical commission.

Dolgopolov left Department 291 in May 1967 to become a chief engineer, group chief, section chief, and ultimately department head at what is now known as the RKK Energiya, where he still works.

Dzhanobekov, Vladimir Alexandrovich

1942–

Vladimir Dzhanibekov was one of the most experienced and successful Soviet cosmonaut of the 1970s and 1980s, taking part in five different missions and participating in the dramatic repair of the Salyut 7 space station.

At a time when close to one out of four Soviet docking flights failed or suffered some difficulty, Dzhanibekov commanded five successes without a failure. It was his demonstrated skill at rendezvous that caused Soviet program managers to choose him to pilot Soyuz T–13 to a linkup with the dead Salyut 7 station in June 1985.

Salyut 7 had been in operation since its launch in April 1982, with seven cosmonaut crews spending as much as 9 months at a time aboard it. But the station suffered a fuel leak in 1983 which damaged it; repaired by one crew, it suffered repeated power shortages all through 1984. And by early 1985 it was adrift in space, cold, unresponsive to commands from the ground.

Sending a manned crew to repair a dead station was not an attractive idea. The highly automated Soyuz T docking procedures depend on range and radar data from the target station. Without that data, the cosmonaut crew is flying "by the seat of its pants." In March 1985 Dzhanibekov and flight engineer Viktor Savinykh were chosen to attempt this tricky maneuver.

Launched on June 6, 1985, Dzhanibekov and Savinykh spent 2 days chasing Salyut–7 around the Earth, eventually making a successful docking. Going aboard the station, they found it cold and almost lifeless. They were forced to rely on their Soyuz T–13 systems for support, even for radio contact with the ground. But within days they had made repairs to the Salyut 7 power systems, using the supplies they had brought and materials shipped to them aboard a Progress tanker. They performed a 5–hour space walk on August 2 to install new solar panels. By mid–September Salyut 7 was habitable again, and a new, long–term crew was launched to occupy it. Savinykh remained aboard while Dzhanibekov returned to Earth in the exchange Soyuz on September 27.

Dzhanibekov was born Vladimir Krysin on May 13, 1942, in the town of Iskander, Tashkent District, Uzbekistan. His original family name, "Krysin," unfortunately means "rat." Dzhanibekov adopted the Uzbek name of his wife's family at marriage.

Dzhanibekov intended to become a physicist and after graduation from secondary school attended Leningrad University for one year. But he had always wanted to fly—at LGU joined an aeroclub—and ultimately he decided to enlist in the air force. In 1961 he entered the Yeisk Higher Air Force School, graduating in October 1965, but remaining at the school as an instructor pilot for the next five years.

He was one of the 9 candidates enrolled in the cosmonaut team on April 27, 1970, and completed the basic training course 2 years later. In May 1973 Dzhanibekov—who is fluent in English—became one of 8 Soviet cosmonauts assigned to the training group for the Apollo–Soyuz Test Project, the joint Soviet–American spaceflight. During the next 2 years "Johnny" was a frequent visitor to NASA's Johnson Space Center in Houston and became well known to American astronauts. When the Soviet half of ASTP was launched in June 15, 1975, Dzhanibekov served as backup commander to Alexei Leonov.

Following ASTP Dzhanibekov was teamed with flight engineer Pyotr Kolodin in the group of cosmonauts training to fly the advanced Soyuz T spacecraft. Problems with the first missions to Salyut 6 in October 1977, however, necessitated a visiting flight. Dzhanibekov and Oleg Makarov were selected to fly the 8–day mission, Soyuz 27. They docked with Salyut–6 in January 1978 and performed the first exchange of space vehicles, returning to

Earth in Soyuz–26 and leaving Soyuz–27 for the use of expedition cosmonauts Yuri Romanenko and Georgy Grechko.

Dzhanibekov then trained for flights in the Interkosmos program, during which guest cosmonauts from Eastern European nations went into space. He was backup commander for the Soviet–Hungarian flight in 1980 and commanded the Soviet–Mongolian team in March 1981, when he spent another week aboard Salyut 6.

Later that year Dzhanibekov was finally assigned to an expedition crew, this time for a planned 8–month mission aboard Salyut 7, but again found himself called upon to fill in: Yuri Malyshev, commander of the Soviet–French team, had to be replaced for health reasons, and recommended Dzhanibekov as his replacement. In June 1982 Dzhanibekov commanded Soyuz T–6 and spent 8 more days in space with crewmates Alexandr Ivanchenkov and France's Jean–Loup Chretien. It was during Soyuz T–6 that Dzhanibekov had a chance to demonstrate his docking skills. The Soyuz rendezvous computer failed during final approach to Salyut and Dzhanibekov made the docking manually. Chretien was later to describe the situation as "serious," praising Dzhanibekov for his calm piloting.

Dzhanibekov's fourth spaceflight, unusual for a Soviet cosmonaut, came in July 1984, a two–week visit to Salyut–7 and its resident crew of Kizim, Solovyov, and Atkov with crewmates Svetlana Savitskaya and Igor Volk. Savitskaya and Dzhanibekov made a space walk in an attempt to repair Salyut 7's troubled power system, which would fail completely within a few months, bringing Dzhanibekov back to space for a fifth time.

Dzhanibekov was promoted to major general in June 1986 and deputy director of the 1st Directorate of the Gagarin Cosmonaut Training Center. From March 1988 to August 1997 he was head of that directorate.

In addition to his cosmonaut career Dzhanibekov has been a deputy in the Supreme Soviet of Uzbek SSR. He is also a painter whose work has appeared in several publications and exhibitions.

In late 1991 Dzhanibekov took a leave from the Gagarin Center to join an international crew attempting a round–the–world balloon trip in a craft called *Earthwinds*. The 20,000–mile trip was expected to take anywhere from 12 to 21 days. Finally launched from Reno, Nevada, after many delays, on November 19, 1992, the 300–foot–high balloon hit a mountain just five miles away, landing safely but far short of its goal.

Fartushny, Vladimir Grigoryevich
1938–

Vladimir Fartushny was one of the civilian cosmonauts approved by the State Commission in March 1968. For the next year he trained as a candidate researcher with commander Alexei Gubarev for a Soyuz flight that would have carried a special space welding experiment named Vulkan, designed by Fartushny.

The Vulkan experiment was ultimately assigned to the Soyuz 6 mission, and though Fartushny was a candidate to join the crew of Georgy Shonin and Valery Kubasov, concerns about the spacecraft weight eliminated the third crew seat, which would have been Fartushny's. A brief attempt to assign him as the flight engineer in place of Kubasov failed, since it would have violated a rule requiring that seat to be filled by a cosmonaut from the Korolev design bureau.

Fartushny's experiment was tested in space by cosmonauts Kubasov and Shonin in October 1969. He remained a cosmonaut for two more years, but was discharged from the civilian cosmonaut team for medical reasons following a 1971 auto accident. He never flew in space.

Fartushny was born February 3, 1938, in Ukraine, and at the time of his selection was employed at a research insitute in Kiev headed by Georgy Paton.

He is currently first deputy general director of the Paton Institute, now known as the NPO VISP.

Fatkullin, Mars Nurgaliyevich
1939–

Mars Fatkullin was one of the Academy of Sciences researchers enrolled in the cosmonaut team in May 1967. He trained as a Soyuz crewmember until May 1970, when the scientist–cosmonaut group was disbanded.

He was born May 14, 1939, in Starry Shaimurzin, Drozhavinsky Region, Tatarstan, and graduated from the Kazan State University named for V. I. Lenin in 1961. He does atmospheric studies at IZMIRAN, an institute of the Russian Academy of Sciences in the city of Troisk, Moscow region.

Fedorov, Anatoly, Pavlovich

1942–

Pilot Anatoly Fedorov was one of 22 candidates enrolled in the military cosmonaut team on October 28, 1965. In December 1967 he completed the initial training course and was assigned to the Almaz group of cosmonauts. He was teamed with flight engineer Lev Demin in 1972 for the first manned Almaz mission, but was ultimately replaced for medical reasons, leaving the cosmonaut team in May 1974. He never flew in space.

Fedorov was born April 14, 1942, in the village of Sestrenki, Kamishinsky District, Stalingrad (later Volgograd) Region, Russia. He graduated from secondary school in the town of Kamishin, then entered the Yeisk Higher Air Force School, graduating in October 1963.

From December 1963 to January 1964 Fedorov was a pilot with the 274th Air Fighter–Bombardier Regiment of the 9th Air Division, Moscow military district, based in Kubinka. At the time of his enrollment in the cosmonaut team he was with the 320th Air Guards Regiment there.

After leaving the cosmonaut team Fedorov became deputy director of the section in the 1st Directorate, Gagarin Center, for planning of cosmonaut training. In June 1982 he became head of the group of military cosmonauts who served as Salyut–Mir flight controllers, a post he held until transferred to reserve status in October 1992.

While working the 1st Directorate Fedorov did graduate work at the Bauman Higher Technical School, receiving a degree in 1977.

Fefelov, Nikolai Nikolayevich

1945–

Nikolai Fefelov was one of the 9 air force candidates selected for cosmonaut training in the Fifth Enrollment on April 27, 1970. He worked in support of Soyuz–Almaz and Soyuz–Salyut space station missions from 1972 to 1982 while simultaneously serving as deputy flight director for 10 visits to Salyut 6, Salyut 7 and Mir through 1989.

Fefelov also performed centrifuge tests for the VA (return vehicle) of the Almaz transport spacecraft (1981) and was a candidate for an orbital flight with the Pion–K system, ultimately launched as Kosmos–1686 in 1985.

He was assigned to the Buran cosmonaut branch at the Gagarin Center from 1985 to 1995, but never flew in space.

Fefelov was born May 20, 1945, in the village of Nuzhni Kuba, Chernushinski District, Perm Region, Russia. He attended the Perm Higher Air Force Engineering School, graduating in 1968, then served with the 656th Missile Squadron of the Strategic Rocket Forces near Kaluga, commanding an SS–8 unit.

Fefelov logged over 900 hours of flying time in the L–29 training as a cosmonaut, and also made 51 parachute jumps. Other test work included 200 hours in the Orlan EVA space suit and 120 hours of weightless flight in the Tu–154 laboratory aircraft.

On July 18, 1995, Fefelov was named acting commander of the Gagarin Center cosmonaut team, a post he held until his retirement from active duty on November 9 of that year. He is currently a civilian on the Gagarin Center staff.

Feoktistov, Konstantin Petrovich

1926–

Konstantin Feoktistov was a member of the world's first space crew, one of 3 cosmonauts sent into space for a single day aboard the first Voskhod on October 12, 1964. With Feoktistov were commander Vladimir Komarov and physician Boris Yegorov.

For Feoktistov, it was the culmination of a dream of many years. Then a 38–year–old senior engineer at Sergei Korolev's OKB–1, Feoktistov was the person most responsible for the design of the Vostok spacecraft in which Yuri Gagarin made the world's first manned flight in 1961.

Feoktistov was born February 7, 1926, in the city of Voronezh. At an early age he became interested in astronomy and spaceflight; by the age of ten he was making plans for the exploration of the Moon. But World War II forced him to postpone his dreams, and almost killed him. Feoktistov became a scout for a partisan unit when the Nazis occupied the Voronezh region. In 1942 the 16–year–old Feoktistov was captured by the Nazis, put before a firing squad and shot. Amazingly, he was only wounded. Left for dead, he waited until dark, then crawled away to safety.

The next year, after recuperating from his wounds, he entered the Bauman Higher Technical School in Moscow. He graduated in 1949, then worked as an industrial engineer at a weapons plant in Zlatoust.

In 1955 the USSR began a program aimed at the construction of long–range missiles and Earth satellites, and Feoktistov, who had recently completed graduate work for a candidate of technical sciences degree under rocket designer Mikhail Tikhonravov, followed his mentor to the Korolev design bureau. Feoktistov was involved in the Sputnik program and in all phases of the development of manned space vehicles. He served as a lecturer to the first group of air force cosmonauts, though he admitted he was jealous of them, wanting to fly in space himself. He became a tireless promoter of civilians in space, winning a seat on the first multiseat spacecraft through these efforts.

In May 1967, shortly after Vladimir Komarov was killed in the Soyuz 1 accident, Feoktistov visited the Paris Air Show, where he met American astronauts David Scott and Michael Collins. At that time Feoktistov was engaged in a political struggle with the Soviet air force and Lieutenant General Nikolai Kamanin, the cosmonaut training chief. Feoktistov felt that he, as one of the designers of the Soyuz spacecraft, was the most qualified person to pilot the requalification flight. Kamanin, who did not like Feoktistov and thought him medically unfit, gave the mission instead to test pilot Georgy Beregovoy.

Feoktistov returned to his work at the Korolev bureau (later known as NPO Energiya) and also completed his doctoral thesis. From 1967 on he was actively involved in the design of the Soyuz–T transport spacecraft, the Progress supply vehicle, and beginning in 1969, the civilian or "long term orbital station" version of Salyut. (Kamanin later removed Feoktistov from consideration for the first Salyut 1 crews, too.) Feoktistov was a flight director for Salyut missions in the summer of 1975.

In 1980, long after Kamanin's departure from the scene, Feoktistov was again included in a cosmonaut crew. He trained with pilot Leonid Kizim and engineer Oleg Makarov for the Soyuz T–3 mission to Salyut 6. But physical problems ultimately forced Feoktistov to step aside just days before launch.

The advent of glasnost allowed the fiercely independent Feoktistov to speak out publicly on issues such as the Buran shuttle program, which he termed a "colossal waste" of resources. This outspokenness put Feoktistov in direct opposition to Yuri Semenov, who became the general director of NPO Energiya upon the death of Valentin Glushko in 1989. Semenov happened to be the chief designer of the Buran. He forced Feoktistov's retirement from the NPO Energiya in 1990.

Feoktistov is the author of numerous technical works, and of two popular books, *On Spaceflight* (1982) and *Seven Steps to the Stars* (1984), in which he discusses manned missions to the planet Mars.

Filatyev, Valentin Ignatyevich
1930–1990

Pilot Valentin Filatyev was a member of the first cosmonaut group selected in March 1960. He was a friend and colleague of Pavel Belyayev, the senior member of the group in age and military service, but Filatyev's appearance made him look older, so he was dubbed "Ded" ("Gramps") by the other pilots.

Though he was designated a military cosmonaut on December 16, 1961, Filatyev never made a spaceflight. On the evening of March 27, 1963, he and fellow cosmonauts Grigori Nelyubov and Ivan Anikeyev were returning to Star Town from an evening out. They had been drinking, and at the Chkalovskaya railway station got into a fight with several officers in the militia, the Soviet police. The police offered to forget the incident if the cosmonauts apologized; Filatyev and Anikeyev were only too happy to comply. But Nelyubov refused. A report was filed, and the cosmonauts themselves voted to dismiss the offenders. (The vote was unanimous; the three men agreed that they had broken the rules.)

Filatyev was born January 21, 1930, in the village of Malinovka, Ishimsk District, Tyumen Region, Russia. He originally attended the Ishimsk Teacher's School, graduating in 1951, and then joined the Soviet air force. He attended the Stalingrad Higher Air Force School from 1951 to 1955.

He spent the next 4 years as a fighter pilot, and was serving with the 3rd Air Fighter Regiment, 15th Air Fighter Division of the Air Defense Forces when selected for cosmonaut training.

After leaving the cosmonaut team Filatyev returned to the Air Defense Forces as a pilot until transferring to reserve status in 1969. From 1970 to 1977 he worked for the Gipropribor State Institute in the city of Orel, and then taught civil defense courses for ten years.

He died of cancer on September 15, 1990.

Filipchenko, Anatoly Vasilyevich

1928–

Anatoly Filipchenko commanded Soyuz 7 in October 1969, one element in a Soviet manned "space fleet." Carrying 7 cosmonauts, 3 Soyuz spacecraft launched on successive days were in orbit at the same time. The goal of this "troika" mission wasn't clear for many years. Western observers judged it to be a poor man's space spectacular aimed at stealing a bit of thunder from the recent American landing on the Moon.

This was partly true: the Soyuz 6 flight could have been launched at any time, but Soviet cosmonauts needed additional rendezvous and docking experience in order to be able to carry out their own lunar landing program. Soyuz 7 (carrying Filipchenko, Vladislav Volkov, and Viktor Gorbatko) was intended to dock with Soyuz 8 (crewed by Vladimir Shatalov and Alexei Yeliseyev). The docking had to be canceled because of technical problems aboard Soyuz 8.

In December 1974 Filipchenko and engineer Nikolai Rukavishnikov made up the crew of Soyuz 16, a full–scale orbital dress rehearsal for the Apollo–Soyuz Test Project. The following summer they served as the crew of a second, stand–by Soyuz, to be launched if the American Apollo suffered a delay.

Filipchenko was born February 26, 1928, in the town of Davydovka, Voronezh District, Russia, and raised in the city of Ostrogozhsk. As a 15–year–old during the War Filipchenko worked as a lathe operator in a munitions factory, but he was interested in flying. He attended an air force preparatory school in Voronezh, then the Chuguyev Higher Air Force School, graduating in 1950.

Filipchenko's first assignment was flying MiG–15s with the 161st Fighter Air Regiment, 330rd Fighter Division of the 76th Air Army, Leningrad military district. In 1952 he was reassigned to the Southern Group, serving in Romania and other Eastern European countries for the next 6 years as a pilot, flight commander, deputy squadron commander, and instructor. Between 1957 and 1961 he studied at the Red Banner (later named for Yuri Gagarin) Air Force Academy via its correspondence course. At the time of his enrollment in the cosmonaut group he was an air force inspector for the 48th Air Army, Odessa military district.

He logged over 1,500 hours of flying time.

Filipchenko was one of 15 candidates enrolled in the team in January 1963. While completing the training course, Filipchenko served as a communications operator for the Voskhod missions. Assigned to the Spiral spaceplane program in early 1965, Filipchenko enrolled in the Chkalov test pilot school with fellow cosmonauts Gherman Titov and Anatoly Kuklin, earning a third–class rating in July 1967.

In June 1968 he joined the cosmonaut group training for Soyuz missions and was backup commander for Soyuz 4 and later for Soyuz 9. In 1970–71 Filipchenko trained for a Soyuz flight to test the Kontakt docking system with flight engineer Georgy Grechko, but the mission was canceled.

Before and after ASTP Filipchenko was deputy director of the Gagarin Center's 1st Directorate, for cosmonaut training. He was promoted to major general in January 1978 when he became head of that directorate. That same year he published his autobiography, *The Safe Orbit*. He also served as head of the Federation of Cosmonauts from 1978 to 1980.

Filipchenko left the cosmonaut team in January 1982 and the Gagarin Center in May 1988. He was deputy director of the Pilyugin Research Institute in Kharkov, Ukraine, until retiring in June 1993.

Gagarin, Yuri Alexeyevich
1934–1968

Yuri Gagarin became the first person to make a spaceflight when he rode a Vostok spacecraft on a single orbit of the Earth on the morning of Wednesday, April 12, 1961.

It was a cloudless spring day at the Baikonur launch center on the arid steppes of Kazakhstan when the 24 rocket engines of the first stage of the R–7 rocket ignited. *"Poyekhali!"* Gagarin said as the rocket rose. "Here we go!" Within minutes he was in space reporting that he felt fine, that the Vostok was functioning. "I can see the Earth's horizon," he said, describing sights no human had ever seen. "It has a very beautiful sort of halo, a rainbow. . . . " He passed over the Pacific Ocean and over America (and thought of Alan Shepard, who Gagarin had believed would be the first to go into space). Over Africa the Vostok retrorockets fired, nudging the spacecraft out of orbit. After the fiery reentry, made tricky by the failure of the retrorocket package to separate as commanded, Gagarin ejected as planned from Vostok and parachuted safely to a field on a collective farm near Saratov.

Gagarin's flight lasted 1 hour and 48 minutes.

Gagarin was born March 9, 1934, in the village of Klushino in the Smolensk Region west of Moscow. His father was a carpenter, and the Gagarin family lived under German occupation in the village of Gzhatsk for several years during World War II. After graduating from secondary school in 1949 Gagarin attended the Lyubertsy Agricultural Machinery School for 2 years followed by the Saratov Industrial Technical School. But while studying to become a factory worker Gagarin joined an amateur pilot's club and learned to fly. One of his instructors recommended him for air force duty and Gagarin entered the Orenburg Higher Air Force School in 1955.

After graduation in November 1957 Gagarin was offered the chance to be an instructor at Orenburg, but he opted instead for service with the Northern Fleet. For 2 years he was a pilot based at Zapolyarny, north of the Arctic Circle, until volunteering for the cosmonaut group in October 1959. The following March, after months of medical, psychological, and political testing, Gagarin was one

of 20 young pilots who reported to the Frunze Central Airport in Moscow to begin training for manned flights into space.

Gagarin quickly established himself as one of the candidates for the first flight and in late March 1961 was advised by Lieutenant General Nikolai Kamanin, the director of cosmonaut training, that he would be the pilot of the first Vostok. A meeting of the State Commission for Space Flight on April 8, 1961, confirmed the appointment.

Following his historic flight Gagarin spent many days and weeks making public appearances and trips, visiting Czechoslovakia, Britain, and Canada. He found it difficult to devote time to his career as an active pilot and cosmonaut and so found himself in administrative jobs. He was, in fact, named commander of the cosmonaut team on May 25, 1961, a post he held until December 1963, when he was made deputy director of the Cosmonaut Training Center. In these posts he directed the training of the first women cosmonauts (who arrived at the Center in March 1962) and acted as communications operator for the twin flights of Vostok 3 and Vostok 4, Voskhod 1, and Voskhod 2. He was also active politically as a delegate to Party Congresses in 1961 and 1966.

As of June 1964 Gagarin was also forbidden to fly and train actively, a restriction he found increasingly frustrating. He made repeated requests to General Kamanin to be allowed to train again, and in April 1966 Kamanin relented, allowing Gagarin to join the group of cosmonauts beginning to train for manned Soyuz flights.

The preliminary crew assignments for the proposed Soyuz 1/Soyuz 2 mission, made in September 1966, originally didn't include Gagarin. But he fought for inclusion, and was finally named as second or backup pilot to Komarov on Soyuz 1. He was expected to fly a weeklong Soyuz mission later in 1967.

But following launch on April 23, 1967, Komarov's Soyuz 1 developed severe technical problems: one solar panel failed to unfold, leaving the spacecraft short of power. There were also problems with the attitude control system. The scheduled Soyuz 2 launch was scrubbed, and Soyuz 1 was ordered to land.

Following reentry, however, the parachute on Komarov's spacecraft failed to open properly. The vehicle smashed into the ground and burst into flames, killing

Komarov and bringing the Soviet manned space program to a sudden halt. Gagarin took part in Komarov's memorial service, and hoped to involve himself in the investigation and return to flight. But 5 days after the accident General Kamanin again removed Gagarin from flight status.

Throughout 1967 Gagarin continued his studies at the Zhukovsky Air Force Engineering Academy (he would graduate in February 1968) and supervised training for not only the Earth orbit Soyuz, but also the Soyuz–Zond circumlunar missions.

On March 12, 1968, following completion of Gagarin's academic work, Kamanin was able to restore him to flight status. Gagarin immediately joined cosmonauts Shatalov, Volynov, Gorbatko, and others in weightless flights aboard the Tu–104, and set out to requalify himself as a jet pilot.

At 10:19 on the morning of March 27, 1968, Gagarin and flight instructor Vladimir Seregin took off from the Chkalov air base near the Center in a MiG–15. After one request from the pilots for a change of course, nothing further was heard. Ground controllers became alarmed. Search and rescue helicopters were ordered into the air.

POST–FLIGHT REPORT OF COMRADE YURI GAGARIN OF APRIL 13, 1961, TO THE MEETING OF THE STATE COMMISSION

Top Secret

The rocket got under way from its pad, smoothly, softly. I didn't even notice when it moved. Then I felt a small quiver through the vehicle. As for the vibrations, the frequency was high, but the amplitude was low.

I was ready to eject [if necessary]. I sat and observed the liftoff–process. I heard Sergei Pavlovich [Korolev] report that we had reached the 70 second mark. In the 70s the character of the vibrations changed smoothly. The frequency decreased but the amplitude grew, like a shaking. Then this shaking abated gradually, and by first stage burnout the vibration was the same as at ignition.

The overload grew smoothly, but was endurable, much like that of an aircraft, about 5 Gs. During the overload I was reporting in and able to converse the whole time, though it was rather difficult to talk because the muscles of my face had tightened. I strained myself slightly.

Then the overload began to grow, mounting to its peak. Then it began to decrease smoothly. Suddenly there was a sharp overload and I felt as if something had blown off the vehicle. I felt something like a bang. With that the sound ceased and it was if I had suddenly become weightless, though the load was still 1 G.

The overload resumed, pressing me to my seat, but the sound was significantly less. At the 150th second the nose cone separated with a jolt and a bang. . . .

At this moment the Earth was easily visible in the Vzor. There was not much cloudiness, so I could see marks on the ground of a mountainous area. Forests, rivers, and ravines were visible. I don't know exactly where I was looking, since the field of vision in Vzor was so small, but I believed it was the Ob or Irtush rivers—in any case, a large river with islands. . . .

[Following third stage cutoff] I saw a horizon, stars and sky. The sky was black, absolutely black, and against this black background stars could be clearly seen, as could the sense of speed from looking out the Vzor and the right porthole. A very beautiful horizon was visible, and so was the Earth's circumference. The horizon has a beautiful blue color. Near the very surface of the Earth is a bluish color which gradually becomes darker, then purple, then black.

. . .

I made reports according to the plan with telegraph and telephone. I took water and food. I didn't feel any physiological problems doing this. The feeling of weightlessness was rather unusual compared to being on the ground. I felt I was hanging on a belt in a horizontal position, probably because I was belted to my seat. I got accustomed to it; I did not feel bad.

I wrote in the spacecraft logbook and I worked with a telegraph key. When I took a bite of food and drank some water I set free my writing table, and with a pencil it "flew" in front of me. I retrieved the table, but the pencil had flown somewhere.

[At the 56 minute point] . . . I felt as the TDU (re–entry rocket) fired, feeling a little pitch and a sound through the vehicle hardware. I noted the time of the TDU firing, having set my stopwatch to zero. The TDU worked well, though its firing was harsh. The G–overload grew slightly, but then weightlessness returned abruptly. At this time the pointers of the self–actuating orientation system and of the TDU tank dropped to zero right away. The time of the TDU burn was 40 seconds exactly.

As soon as the TDU cut off a hard bump occurred and the craft began to revolve on its axis at a very high speed. In the Vzor the Earth passed from above, and from right to left, and down. The speed of rotation was about 30 degrees a second, no less. It was a "corps de ballet" turned inside–out, heads–feet, heads–feet, at a very high speed.

I saw Africa, then I saw a horizon, then I saw the sky. I only just had time to close my eyes before behind blinded by the Sun. I put my feet to the porthole, but didn't close the blinds, because it was all very interesting to me.

I waited for separation [of the retro module], but separation did not occur. I knew that it should have happened 10–12 seconds after the end of the TDU firing. I realized that enough time had passed, but there was still no separation. The Spusk–1 display was still lit and there was no "ready to eject" light. . . .

Two minutes had passed and there was still no separation.

I reported on the shortwave that the TDU had worked normally. I estimated that I would land normally, because I still had 6,000 km of the Soviet Union to cross and the Soviet Union is 8,000 km across, even as I traveled to the Far East. I didn't make a noise. I reported via telephone that separation had not occurred.

. . .

In the Vzor I saw the north coast of Africa and the Mediterranean. Everything was clearly visible, though the craft continued to rotate. Separation finally occurred at 10:35, not 10:25, that is, about ten minutes after retro fire.

I felt the separation sharply, hearing a bang, then feeling a bump as the craft continued to rotate. . . . I assumed the ejection attitude, sat and waited.

The rotation began to decrease on all three axes. The craft began to oscillate from right to left to almost 90 degrees. It was not a full revolution. There were similar oscillations, decelerating, on another axis. The blinds of the Vzor port closed. Suddenly a bright crimson light appeared around the border of the blinds. I saw the same crimson light through a small aperture in the right port-hole. I could feel the craft's oscillations, and the burning of the [thermal] coating. Something crackled, as if burning, a piece of the coating or some hardware, but very audible. It was clear to me that the temperature outside was very high.

Then the light in the Vzor faded. Overloads were small, about 1 to 1.5 G. Then they began to increase, smoothly. The ball's oscillations on its axis continued the whole time.

At the moment of separation the globe had stopped roughly in the middle of the Mediterranean, so everything was all right. I waited for ejection. At an altitude of 7,000 meters the cover of hatch #1 jettisoned. There was a bang, and the hatch cover went. I sat there, thinking, what about me? I slowly turned my head upwards, and at that moment the charge fired and I was ejected.

It occurred quickly and gently. I bumped nothing, bruised nothing, everything was normal. I flew out [of the spacecraft] with the seat. Then there was a cannon shot and the drag parachute opened.

I remained on my seat comfortably, as if sitting in a chair, feeling that I was turning to my right. At once I saw a large river and thought it was the Volga, since there are no large rivers other than the Volga in the landing zone. I saw a sort of town [on the river]. A large town was on one bank, a great town on the other bank. I thought I recognized them. . . . During parachute training we jumped above this very place.

Other air bases in the region were alerted. Hours passed without word. Finally wreckage was spotted in a forest little more than a mile from the village of Novoselovo. Kamanin himself flew to the site, wading through waist–deep snow to the crater, which had now filled with melted water. It was almost dusk and darkness made it impossible to tell what had happened. It wasn't until dawn the next day that Gagarin's remains were found.

An investigation and reconstruction of the accident 20 years later concluded that Gagarin and Seregin's MiG–15 had been caught in the vortex of another jet and thrown into a spin. The pilots recovered, but found themselves in a steep dive at an altitude of not much more than 1,000 feet. They were unable to pull out or eject.

Gagarin has been the subject of several biographies published around the world, including *Orbits of a Life* by Oleg Nudenko (1971), *My Brother Yuri* by Valentin Gagarin (1973), *It couldn't Have Been Otherwise* by Pavel Popovich and Vasily Lesnikov (1980), *108 Minutes and an Entire Life* by his wife, Valentina (1981), *Words About a Son* by his mother, Anna (1983), and *Gagarin* by V. Stepanov (1986). His autobiographies include *My Road to Space* (1961) and *Flame* (1968). Gagarin also coauthored several technical works, including *Survival in Space* (1969).

A crater on the far side of the Moon, a Soviet space tracking vessel, the Red Banner (Order of Kutuzov) Air Force Academy, the Cosmonaut Training Center, and his former hometown of Gzhatsk have all been named for Yuri Gagarin, the "first citizen" of space travel.

Gaidukov, Sergei Nikolayevich

1936–

Sergei Gaidukov was one of the 12 air force candidates enrolled in the cosmonaut team in May 1967. He completed the training course in 1969 and remained a flight engineer until December 1978, when health problems forced him to retire.

Gaidukov was born October 31, 1936, in the village of Zhuravka, Kantemirovsky District of the Voronezh Region, Russia. In 1956 he graduated from the Chelyabinsk Air Force Navigator School, then remained there as an instructor. (In 1960 Chelyabinsk was made a Higher Air Force School and Gaidukov had to take additional exams to qualify.) He also served as in aircraft crews prior to joining the cosmonaut team.

Upon completing the training course in August 1969 Gaidukov was assigned to the test group, supporting manned Soyuz and Salyut missions from various tracking posts: he was at the Khabarovsk site for Soyuz 9 (1970) and Salyut 1 (1970) and aboard the tracking ships *Kosmonavt Yuri Gagarin* and *Kosmonavt Vladimir Komarov* during Salyut 3 (1974). In 1975 he was enrolled at the Gagarin Air Force Academy.

But in December 1976 Gaidukov underwent hip surgery. Two years later he was forced to leave the cosmonaut group for medical reasons, and was unable to complete his degree at the air force academy. He has been on a medical disability pension since that time, and lives at Star Town.

Gevorkyan, Vladimir Mkrtyovich

1952–

Vladimir Gevorkyan was one of the 10 civilian engineers and researchers enrolled in the cosmonaut team in December 1978. Unlike most of the engineer–cosmonauts, who were employees of the NPO Energiya (the former OKB–1), Gevorkyan worked for NPO Salyut, a division of the larger Machinstroyeniye organization headed by Vladimir Chelomei. NPO–M, as it was called, designed and built the Proton launch vehicle, the Almaz military space station (which predated Salyut) and the TKS manned space transport.

At the time of his selection in 1978 a TKS/Almaz mission was still planned for launch in 1980. Four 3–man crews were formed, but before the mission could win government approval, it was canceled in 1981.

Gevorkyan was born May 28, 1952, in Ashtarak, Armenia, and attended the Bauman Higher Technical Institute, graduating in 1975.

He is currently general director of the scientific manufacturing firm "Terra."

Gidzenko, Yuri Pavolich

1962–

Yuri Gidzenko was commander of the twentieth resident crew aboard the Mir space station, launched as Soyuz TM–22 in September 1995. Joining Gidzenko were flight engineer Sergei Avdeyev and ESA astronaut Thomas Reiter.

Unlike other guest researchers, Reiter was scheduled to remain with Gidzenko–Avdeyev for the entire length of their mission, scheduled to last 135 days. Much of the crew's time was devoted to a package of European Space Agency experiments, notably the TITUS furnace for crystal growth. In addition to performing needed maintenance on Mir's gryodynes, the cosmonauts also hosted the STS–74 mission, which delivered a special Shuttle docking module to the Russian station in November. Mir–20's duration was extended by over a month due to financial problems within the Russian Space Agency, which delayed the Mir–21 relief mission, ultimately lasting 179 days.

In November 1996 Gidzenko replaced Anatoly Solovyov as Soyuz pilot in the first incremental International Space Station crew. Scheduled for launch in early 2000, Gidzenko, flight engineer Sergei Krikalev, and American mission commander William Shepherd are to spend 5 months aboard the Node One–Zaryg during its assembly phase.

Gidzenko was born March 26, 1962, in Yelanets, Nikolayev District, Ukraine. He graduated from the Kharkov Higher Air Force School in 1983, then served as a fighter pilot with the Soviet air force in Tiraspol.

He was one of the pilot candidates enrolled in the military cosmonaut team in March 1987. From December 1987 to July 1989 he underwent the training course at the Gagarin Center that qualified him as a Soyuz TM–Mir commander. He served as backup commander for Soyuz TM–20.

Glazkov, Yuri Nikolayevich
1939–

Yuri Glazkov spent 18 days in space aboard Soyuz 24 and the Salyut 5 (Almaz) space station in February 1977. He and commander Viktor Gorbatko were the first cosmonauts to undertake major repairs to an orbiting space station, replacing Salyut's entire air supply. The station's first occupants, cosmonauts Volynov and Zholobov, had been forced to cut short their mission because of impurities in that air supply. Glazkov and Gorbatko successfully completed a mission of military reconnaissance and Earth resources studies.

Glazkov was born in Moscow on October 2, 1939. He attended the Suvurov military prep school in Sevastopol, then went on to the Kharkov Higher Air Force Engineering School, graduating in 1962. He spent a year as a representative in a military factory, then served with the 2nd Main Directorate for Rocket Forces (2nd GURVO).

Glazkov was one of the 22 candidates enrolled in the cosmonaut team on October 28, 1965. He completed the training course in December 1967, ranking first in his group in the examinations, then underwent pilot training. He also became an expert parachutist, eventually earning an instructor's rating in parachuting.

Glazkov and the many young air force engineers and navigators selected with him in 1965 and 1967 were originally intended to serve as crewmen aboard the Almaz military manned space station, which was being designed and built by the OKB–Machinostroyeniye (Machine Building), the organization headed by Vladimir Chelomei.

Designed for launch aboard Chelomei's Proton rocket, Almaz was similar in size and shape to the later "civilian" Salyut, although it was originally intended to have a 3–man Gemini–like spacecraft called TKS (transport spacecraft) in place of the Soyuz docking module. TKS would ultimately never carry crews into space, though three unmanned launches were made and the program survived until 1981. TKS–Almaz was severely cut back in October 1969 and its resources—and spacecraft— diverted to the Salyut program.

This left military engineer–cosmonauts like Glazkov with little chance to fly in space, and many of them were assigned to jobs in support working at the flight control center and aboard tracking ships. Glazkov served as communications operator (capcom) for the Soyuz 6/7/8 missions in October 1969, for the Salyut–Almaz 3 flights in 1974 and the Salyut 4 flights in 1975.

He also did graduate work in aerospace engineering with emphasis on EVA, receiving his candidate of technical science degree in that subject in 1974.

During the Soyuz troika flight he became friends with pilot Viktor Gorbatko, and he and Gorbatko were teamed for Salyut–Almaz training in 1972. They were backups for Soyuz 23 in October 1976.

Following his flight on Soyuz 24, Glazkov trained for another Almaz mission with Anatoly Berezovoy and Valery Makrushin, but the program was canceled in 1981. Glazkov left the cosmonaut team on January 26, 1982, to become head of the Salyut training section within the 1st Directorate, supervising international space crews, notably those involving French, Indian, and English cosmonauts. From 1986 to 1988 he was deputy director of the operations department at the Gagarin Center, responsible for flight simulators and other training equipment. In 1989 he was appointed to succeed the retiring Pavel Popovich as deputy director of the Center for scientific support and testing. He was also promoted to major general. Since April 1992 he has been first deputy director of the Gagarin Center.

Glazkov has written a technical book on EVA titled *Outside Orbiting Spacecraft* (1977) and several general books on space exploration, including *The Earth Below Us* (1986) and *In Open Space* (1990). He has also published science fiction stories and mysteries.

Gorbatko, Viktor, Vasilyevich
1934–

A member of the first group of Soviet cosmonauts, Viktor Gorbatko overcame two medical disqualifications that threatened his career and eventually took part in three successful spaceflights, including an 18–day mission aboard Salyut 5 in 1977, and the joint Soviet–Vietnamese flight in 1980.

Gorbatko was born December 3, 1934 at the Ventsy–Zarya collective farm, Gulkevichsky District,

Krasnodar Territory of the Russia, and grew up in the Kuban Region, which was occupied by the Nazis during World War II. After completing secondary school he entered the Soviet army and was sent to a prep school for pilots in Pavlograd, Ukraine. From December 1953 to June 1956 he attended the Bataisk Higher Air Force School, where one of his classmates was future cosmonaut Yevgeny Khrunov. Following graduation, Gorbatko and Khrunov served together as jet pilots in the same unit, the 86th Air Guards Regiment, 199th Air Division, 48th Air Army in Moldavia. From 1961 to 1968 Gorbatko attended the Zhukovsky Air Force Engineering Academy.

As a member of the cosmonaut team, Gorbatko was assigned as backup commander for Pavel Belyayev on the Voskhod 2 flight in March 1965. Cosmonaut Alexei Leonov took man's first walk in space on that flight. But Gorbatko contracted tonsilitis; even worse, the related medical examination showed Gorbatko to have an irregular heartbeat and he was hospitalized for 6 weeks, losing his position on the crew.

Gorbatko trained as a backup to Khrunov for the canceled Soyuz 2 mission in April 1967, ultimately flown as Soyuz 4 in January 1969. Two months later, as he was preparing for his own Soyuz mission, Gorbatko broke his ankle during a parachute jump. He was afraid he would be dropped from the flight crew and the space program, but he recovered in time.

Gorbatko first went into space aboard Soyuz 7 on October 12, 1969. Soyuz 7 was the second of three manned Soyuz spacecraft launched in a period of 3 days for simultaneous maneuvers over the space of a week. Soyuz 7 was intended to dock with Soyuz 8, but technical problems prevented it.

After Soyuz 7 Gorbatko became deputy director of the Almaz cosmonaut group within the 1st Directorate of the Gagarin Center. He also served as a communications operator (capcom) for other manned flights such as Soyuz 9 (1970). In April 1974 he began to train for a Salyut 5 (Almaz) mission, serving as backup commander for Soyuz 23 (launched October 1976). He commanded Soyuz 24, launched in February 1997, with flight engineer Yuri Glazkov. During this flight the crew spent 17 days performing military Earth observations and medical experiments.

Later that year Gorbatko joined the group of Soviet commanders for Interkosmos missions, becoming backup commander for the Soviet–East German flight in 1978, and went into space for the third time with Vietnamese cosmonaut Pham Tuan in July 1980.

From January 1978 to January 1982 Gorbatko was also deputy director, 1st Directorate, for air–space training. He was then named commander of the cosmonaut detachment, holding that post from January to August 1982, when he was promoted to major general and left the cosmonaut team.

Gorbatko spent 5 years (1982–87) as first deputy director of the USSR Ministry of Defense sports committee, then became head of faculty at the Zhukovsky Air Force Engineering Academy in Moscow. He was also active politically, serving in the Congress of People's Deputies from April 1989 to December 1991.

Since leaving the Zhukovsky Academy in November 1992 Gorbatko has been general director of the commercial firm AA&AL.

Grechanik, Alexei Anatolyevich
1939–

Alexei Grechanik was one of the 10 civilian engineers enrolled in the cosmonaut team as candidates in December 1978. Three of the ten—Grechanik, Vladimir Gevorkyan, and Valery Romanov—were selected from the staff of the Machinostroyeniye organization headed by Vladimir Chelomei. OKB–M, as it was then called, designed and built the Almaz military space station and the TKS manned space transport vehicle.

From 1978 to 1981 Grechanik was assigned as flight engineer in a 3–man crew training for a TKS–Almaz mission. First Anatoly Berezovoy, then Vladimir Kozlesky, was the crew commander with Yuri Artyukhin as the researcher. Upon final cancellation of the manned portion of the TKS–Almaz program in 1981 Grechanik returned to his work at OKB–Machinstroyeniye.

Grechanik was born March 25, 1939, in Moscow. He attended the Moscow Aviation–Technology Institute named for K. E. Tsiolkovsky, graduating in 1967, prior to joining OKB–52.

He later retired, becoming senior engineer at the Science pavilion at the Exhibit of Science and Technical Achievements (VDNKh), Moscow.

Grechko, Georgy Mikhailovich

1931–

Georgy Grechko made three spaceflights, setting duration records on two of them, and was also the first Soviet cosmonaut to make a space walk to repair a manned spacecraft.

On December 20, 1977, flight engineer Grechko and mission commander Yuri Romanenko were in the second week of a planned 90–day mission aboard the Salyut 6 space station. They were not the intended crewmembers: the previous cosmonaut crew had accidentally rammed its Soyuz 25 vehicle into the Salyut 6 docking mechanism, preventing them from going aboard the station. Their replacements, launched aboard Soyuz 26 on December 10, 1977, docked their spacecraft at the aft or secondary adaptor and moved into the station.

But in order for Salyut 6 to be resupplied by unmanned Progress vehicles it was necessary for both docking adaptors to be functional. Grechko, in fact, was included in the crew specifically to inspect and repair the forward adaptor. In the course of the one hour, 28–minute space walk Grechko concluded that the Soyuz 25 accident had not damaged the adaptor, thus salvaging the billion–ruble station and clearing the way for a full 4 years of operation.

There was an almost comic footnote to the EVA, however. Romanenko, who had neglected to fasten his safety line, suddenly floated out of the Salyut 6 airlock. Acting quickly, Grechko grabbed the trailing line. Weeks later, in a postflight news conference, Grechko told the story with a joking comment that he had saved Romanenko's life. Romanenko had actually been tethered by another line, but the story was repeated for years—to Romanenko's annoyance.

Grechko and Romanenko spent 90 days aboard Salyut–6, shattering the 5–year–old record of 84 days held by America's Skylab 4 astronauts. They were host to two visiting crews, including one composed of Grechko's Soyuz 17 comrade Alexei Gubarev and the first of the Interkosmos pilots, Czech Vladimir Remek. (Grechko's father died during the mission, a fact that commander Romanenko withheld from him until their return to Earth.) The mission was a complete success.

Grechko's first flight was Soyuz 17, launched January 11, 1975. He and commander Gubarev made rendezvous and docked with the Salyut 4 station the next day, and spent 30 days in space performing medical experiments and a host of astronomical observations. It was the longest Soviet manned spaceflight to that date.

Grechko continued to work on the Salyut 6 missions in a support role, sometimes as communications operator during EVAs. He trained as backup flight engineer for the joint Soviet–Indian mission in 1984, and made his third spaceflight aboard Soyuz T–14 in September 1985, when he spent 8 days aboard the recently repaired Salyut–7, raising his total time in space to 134 days.

At the time of Soyuz T–14 Grechko was 54 years old, then the oldest person to fly a Soviet mission.

Grechko was born in Leningrad (St. Petersburg) on May 25, 1931, though he spent much of his teens in the Urals, where his family was evacuated during World War II. After the War, Grechko attended the Leningrad Institute of Mechanics, graduating with honors in 1955. His specialty was mathematics.

Grechko went immediately to work in Sergei Korolev's rocket and spacecraft design bureau, OKB–1, and was one of those engineers who calculated—often by hand—trajectories for the first Sputnik. By 1964 Grechko was head of his own team of spacecraft designers. He received the Lenin Prize for this work, which resulted in the Luna series of space probes. Luna 9 was the first unmanned spacecraft to softland on the Moon.

Grechko was one of the 14 OKB–1 engineers proposed for the first flight of Voskhod in May 1964. He passed the medical examinations and was briefly considered Feoktistov's engineer backup. But Grechko's cosmonaut career did not really begin until May 1966, when he was assigned to the new flight test department of the Korolev bureau. His cosmonaut career almost ended that October, when he broke his leg in a parachuting accident. He was sidelined for several months. Ultimately Grechko made 64 parachute jumps.

When he returned to active training he was included in the group of cosmonauts who were training for Soviet manned circumlunar and lunar landing flights. He was teamed with commanders Andrian Nikolayev and Pavel Popovich at times.

The circumlunar mission was canceled in March 1969 and Grechko shifted his attention to the Earth orbital Soyuz program, working in a support role for the Soyuz 6/7/8 missions launched in October 1969. A month later he was assigned as backup flight engineer for Soyuz 9. He later served in the same role for Soyuz 12 (1973).

In 1986 Grechko left the Korolev organization (then known as NPO Energiya) to become head of a laboratory in the Russian Academy of Sciences Institute of Atmospheric Sciences. He has earned a doctorate in physics and math (1984).

Grekov, Nikolai Sergeyevich
1950–

Pilot Nikolai Grekov was one of 2 candidates enrolled in the military cosmonaut team in May 1978. He attended the Chkalov test pilot school in 1978–79, and then completed the 2–year training course at the Gagarin Center, qualifying as a Soyuz commander. But he left the cosmonaut team in February 1986, before he could fly in space.

Grekov was born February 15, 1950, in Kalinin, Sokuluksky Region, Kirgiz SSR. He attended the Armavir Higher Air Force School, graduating in 1971, then served with Soviet Air Defense Forces in Byelorussia and in the city of Gorky.

As a pilot Grekov logged over 1,000 flying hours in 15 different types of aircraft.

As a cosmonaut, Grekov worked in the Salyut–Mir group until 1984, when he began a tour as a flight controller at Kaliningrad (now Korolev) mission control. He later returned to the Gagarin Center staff, serving as head of the section that trains cosmonauts for desert and Arctic survival.

He also attended the Gagarin Air Force Academy from 1984 to 1987.

Since 1996 Colonel Grekov has been director of the 3nd Directorate, Gagarin Center.

Grishchenko, Vitaly Andreyevich
1942–1992

Navigator Vitaly Grishchenko was one of the 22 candidates enrolled in the military cosmonaut team on October 29, 1965. He completed the training course and took the final examinations in December 1967, but was given poor grades and was dismissed from the team in February 1968.

Cosmonaut training director Nikolai Kamanin's diaries show that Grishchenko's dismissal, like those of several other cosmonaut candidates, was for political unreliability: the KGB discovered that Grishchenko's grandfather had been banished to Siberia in 1921 on suspicion of being a German agent. As a cosmonaut candidate, Grishchenko had also been placed under "medical control," reportedly to improve his "discipline."

Grishchenko was born April 26, 1942, in the village of Naifeld, Moskalensky District, Omsk Region, Russia. Grishchenko's family was German, although his ancestors had come to Russia at the time of Catherine the Great. Grishchenko attended the Chelyabinsk Higher Air Force Navigator School, graduating in 1963.

While still a cadet at Chelayabinsk in 1961, Grishchenko personnally wrote to Soviet Premier Nikita Khrushchev, asking to be admitted to the cosmonaut team. He received a rejection from the state commission in charge of selection, but 4 years later, while serving as an instructor at Chelyabinsk, Grishchenko was selected.

After leaving the cosmonaut team Grishchenko joined the staff of the Gagarin Air Force Academy in Monino. He also continued to fly, qualifying as a navigator first class. He transferred to reserve status in 1987, taking a job with an economic research institute within the Ministry of Aviation Production.

Grishchenko died in Moscow on May 4, 1992.

Gubarev, Alexei Alexandrovich

1931–

Alexei Gubarev commanded two successful space missions, including a monthlong stay aboard Salyut 4 (1975), and the world's first multi–national crew (1978).

Gubarev and flight engineer Georgy Grechko were launched January 11, 1975, aboard Soyuz 17, which docked with the orbiting Salyut 4 the next day. For the next 4 weeks they performed observations of the sun and medical experiments in what was, to that time, the Soviet Union's longest and most successful space mission.

In March 1978 Gubarev was commander of Soyuz 28. With him on that flight was Captain Vladimir Remek, a Czechoslovakian pilot and the first person to travel into space who was not Soviet or American. Gubarev and Remek docked with Salyut 6 during their 8–day mission.

Gubarev was born March 29, 1931, in the village of Gvardeitsy, Borsky District, Kuybyshev Region of Russia, though he grew up in the Moscow area. He entered the Soviet army in 1950, enrolling in the Perm Air Force Technical School, then transferred to the Nikolayev Torpedo School, graduating in 1952.

Gubarev was assigned to the the Naval Air Forces of the Pacific Fleet. Stationed in Vladivostok, in December 1952 he flew combat missions in Tu–2 and Il–28 bombers supporting Chinese and North Korean units. In 1957 Gubarev entered the Red Banner (later named for Yuri Gagarin) Air Force Academy, graduating in 1961. At the time of his selection has a cosmonaut he was commander of a naval air squadron with the 855th Mine–Torpedo Regiment of the Black Sea Fleet.

Gubarev became a cosmonaut in January 1963 and served in several support assignments, including communications operator (capcom) for Voskhod and Soyuz missions. In 1966 and 1967 he was assigned as a commander for a proposed Soyuz "space fighter" mission, a military interceptor verson of the Soyuz, which ultimately never flew in space. Following the cancellation of the Soyuz space fighter, Gubarev transferred to the Soyuz training group, teaming with flight engineer Vladimir Fartushny in a possible crew. He joined the long–duration space station

(DOS) group in 1970, and was assigned as commander of the second backup crew for Soyuz 11, with flight engineer Vitaly Sevastyanov and researcher Anatoly Voronov, in 1971. He was backup commander for Soyuz 12 in 1973.

In September 1981 Gubarev left the cosmonaut team and the Gagarin Center, returning to duty with the Soviet air force as deputy commandant of the military's Chkalov Flight Research Institute. He was promoted to major general in 1983 and earned a candidate of technical sciences degree in 1985. He has transferred to reserve status in June 1988, becoming deputy general director of Shchelkovavtotrans Assocation, a transport company based northeast of Moscow.

Gubarev is the author of *The Lure of Weightlessness* (1982) and *Orbits of a Life* (1990). With Vladimir Remek he wrote *Meeting in Orbit* (1983).

Gulyayev, Rudolf Alexeyevich

1934–

Rudolf Gulyayev was one of the 4 Academy of Sciences researchers enrolled in the cosmonaut team in May 1967. He trained briefly as a potential Soyuz crewmember, but left the program in 1968.

Gulyayev was born November 14, 1934, in Izhevsk, Moscow Region, and graduated from the physics faculty at Moscow State University in 1957. He became a researcher specializing in solar studies at IZMIRAN, (the Insitute for Terrestrial Magnetism, Ionosphere and Radio Wave Propagation of the Academy of Sciences) in the city of Troisk, Moscow Region. He is still on the staff there.

Gulyayev, Vladislav Ivanovich

1937–1990

Vladislav Gulyayev was one of the 15 candidates enrolled in the cosmonaut team in January 1963. He worked for several years on the Almaz space station and military 7K–VI programs. On July 15, 1967, he was injured in a car accident, which forced his retirement from the cosmonaut team on March 6, 1968.

Gulyayev was born May 31, 1938, in the Siberian city of Omsk. He attended the Kronstadt Higher Naval Engineering School in Leningrad, but his navy career was ended by a general cutback in Soviet naval forces that began in 1957. Following graduation he transferred to the new Strategic Rocket Forces. At the time of his enrollment as a cosmonaut–candidate he was serving at an SRF launch range.

Following his departure from the cosmonaut team, Colonel Gulyayev continued to work at the Gagarin Center. He died on April 19, 1990.

Illarioniv, Valery Vasilyevich
1939–

Radio engineer Valery Illarionov was one of the 9 candidates enrolled in the military cosmonaut team in April 1970. He completed the training course in June 1972, serving as an active cosmonaut in a variety of programs for the next 20 years, without ever flying in space.

Illarionov was born June 2, 1939, in Moscow, graduating from secondary school in the town of Kaunas, Latvia. He attended the Riga Industrial Technicum in 1956–57, then entered the Soviet military. He graduated from the Dvinsk Air Force Radiotechnical School in June 1960. Illarionov later attended the Zhukovsky Air Force Engineering Academy from 1962 to 1967.

Prior to entering the Zhukovsky Academy Illarionov spent 2 years as a Ministry of Defense representative at OKB–25. After earning his graduate degree, Illarionov worked in the Zhukovsky laboratories (1967–69), then served on the staff of the High Command of the Soviet air force (1969–70), working directly for cosmonaut training director Colonel–General Nikolai Kamanin. At the time of his selection for cosmonaut training Illarionov was a senior scientific researcher at the Gagarin Center.

As a cosmonaut, Illarionov first worked on the Apollo–Soyuz Test Project, originally as backup flight engineer with commander Yuri Romanenko, then on the support crew with Georgy Shonin. He served as Soviet capcom at the NASA Johnson Space Center for the flight in July 1975. From 1976 to 1979 he was a support crewmember for the Interkosmos missions, then worked on Salyut.

In January 1982 Illarionov was assigned to the Buran space shuttle program, working as an equipment tester and from 1990 to 1992 as a crewmember for a proposed Buran–Soyuz docking mission. At one point in his long career Illarionov complained to the press that he and fellow Gagarin Center engineers Eduard Stepanov and Nikolai Fefelov were being "wasted," and futilely called on center director Vladimir Shatalov to assign them as Soyuz commanders.

Illarionov transferred to reserve status in October 1992.

Isakov, Vladimir Timofeyevich
1940–

Vladimir Isakov was one of the 12 air force candidates enrolled in the cosmonaut team in April 1967. He completed preliminary training in 1969 and was assigned to flight support duties.

Cosmonaut training chief Nikolai Kamanin planned to team Isakov with commander Vladimir Kovalenok for a Soyuz mission in the early 1970s, but the flight never progressed beyond the planning stage. From 1975 to 1977 Isakov was in a proposed Soyuz–Almaz crew with commander Yuri Isaulov. Military flight engineers had few opportunities to fly in space, however, and in April 1983 Isakov transferred to a full–time position at the flight control center.

Isakov was born April 4, 1940, in the village of Zilaur, Zilaur District, Bashkir ASSR. He attended the Chelyabinsk Higher Air Force Navigator's School, graduating in 1963. He served in the long–range aviation branch of the Soviet air force, becoming a navigator first class and a parachute instructor.

As a cosmonaut Isakov trained on the Soyuz, Almaz, Salyut and Mir spacecraft. In 1975 he also served concurrently on the faculty of the Gagarin Air Force Academy, and 3 years later began to study the problems of surveying the world's oceans from orbital stations. For this work he received a candidate of technical sciences degree in oceanography.

Since 1989 he has been lead operator (capcom) for Soyuz–Mir missions at the Kaliningrad (now Korolev) mission control center.

Isaulov, Yuri Fyodorovich

1943–

Yuri Isaulov is a pilot–cosmonaut who trained as the commander of several different Soyuz crews between 1975 and 1981 without flying in space.

He was first teamed with air force engineer Vladimir Isakov for a proposed Soyuz T mission in 1975, which was never flown. In 1977 Isaulov was the original backup commander for Soyuz 28, the USSR–Czech mission, until changes in flight rules required each crew to include one veteran cosmonaut. Isaulov, who had been training with Czech pilot Oldrich Pelczak, was replaced by veteran cosmonaut Nikolai Rukavishnikov.

In 1980 Isaulov was commander of the backup crews for two Soyuz T missions, with Rukavishnikov and physician Mikhail Potapov. And in 1981 Isaulov trained with engineer Valentin Lebedev for both the Soyuz T–4 flight to Salyut 6, and for the first visit to Salyut 7. Medical problems forced Isaulov to withdraw from the mission in January 1982 before he could fly.

Isaulov was born August 31, 1943, in the city of Omsk. He left secondary school at the age of 16 to become a worker, but he had always wanted to be a pilot, and managed to enroll in a flying school, soloing in a Yak–18. Joining the air force in 1962, he attended the Armavir Higher Air Force School, graduating in 1966. He later graduated from the Gagarin Air Force Academy (1975) and has also earned a candidate of technical sciences degree (1979).

A fighter pilot with the Air Defense Forces in Krasnoyarsk Region at the time of his selection for cosmonaut training, Isaulov completed the training course 2 years later, when he was assigned to the Soyuz–T program. In 1982 he transferred from the cosmonaut team to the flight control team, and in 1990 was a flight director for the Soyuz TM–9 mission to the Mir space station. He retired from the air force in 1993 and is now in business.

Ivanchenkov, Alexandr Sergeyevich

1940–

Alexandr Ivanchenkov was flight engineer on two Soyuz flights, including a 140–day expedition aboard the Salyut 6 space station in 1978.

During that flight, Soyuz 29, he and commander Vladimir Kovalenok broke the previous record of 96 days in space established by the crew of Soyuz 26. They performed the usual experiments in space manufacturing and Earth resources observations but, more important, were able to establish health maintenance and exercise routines that were of great value to later Salyut crews. (Both men were able to walk away from their Soyuz upon landing on Earth, in contrast to the Soyuz 26 cosmonauts.) They also learned valuable lessons about the effectiveness of their ground training when it was put to use in weightlessness. (They found that the procedures they had rehearsed on the ground to unload the Progress robot tankers were useless in space.)

Ivanchenkov and Kovalenok also conducted a space walk lasting just over 2 hours on June 29, 1978.

In June 1982 Ivanchenkov visited Salyut 7 for a week as a member of the Soyuz T–6 crew, which included French spationaut Jean–Loup Chretien. Ivanchenkov has logged over 147 days in space.

Ivanchenkov was born September 28, 1940, in Ivanteyevka, near Moscow. He graduated from secondary school with a gold medal in 1958 and was admitted to the Moscow Aviation Institute, where he studied engineering and computer science. Upon graduation from MAI in 1964 he went to work at the Korolev design bureau. While he was working at the bureau he learned to fly; his teacher was Colonel Sergei Anokhin, director of training for the civilian cosmonaut group at OKB Korolev.

Ivanchenkov was one of the 5 civilian engineers enrolled in the cosmonaut group in March 1973. His first assignment was as a backup flight engineer for the Apollo–Soyuz Test Project. He made several trips to the United States for training and served on the backup crew for Soyuz 16, the ASTP dress rehearsal flown in December 1974.

Ivanchenkov and Yuri Romanenko trained as a Salyut main crew from late 1975 to October 1977, when they were reassigned in a shuffle of cosmonaut assignments following the Soyuz 25 abort. Ivanchenkov and Vladimir Kovalenok were backups for Soyuz 26 and Soyuz 27.

Following his second flight Ivanchenkov returned to the OKB Korolev—now known as the NPO Energiya—to work on the design and development of the Salyut 7 and Mir space stations and more recently as a flight engineer in the Buran space shuttle program. In 1991 he returned to active Soyuz–Mir training in a crew with Buran test pilot Ivan Bachurin. When their proposed Soyuz–Buran flight was canceled in 1993, he retired as an active cosmonaut.

Ivanov, Leonid Georgyevich
1950–1980

Pilot Leonid Ivanov was one of the 9 candidates enrolled in the military cosmonaut team in August 1976. He qualified as a military test pilot in 1977, then completed the 2–year basic cosmonaut training course at the Gagarin Center.

He was killed in a plane crash at the Chkalov flight test center at Aktubinsk (now Aktuba). He was making a tst flight in a MiG–23 when the aircraft went into a spin.

Ivanov was born June 25, 1950, in the town of Safonovo, Smolensk District. He attended the Kacha Higher Air Force School, graduating in 1971, then served with the Soviet air force in the town of Myzhachevo, Prikarpat military district.

Ivanova, Yekaterina Alexandrovna
1949–

Katya Ivanova is a scientist who trained as flight engineer in a proposed all–woman Soyuz crew, once scheduled for launch in the spring of 1986. The mission, to have been commanded by Svetlana Savitskaya, with cosmonaut researcher Yelena Dobrokvashina, would have visited the Salyut 7 space station. However, control problems aboard the station developed in the spring of 1985, necessitating a daring rescue mission by cosmonauts Dzhanibekov and Savinykh, and the all–woman flight was canceled.

Ivanova previously served as backup flight engineer for the Soyuz T–12 mission, launched in June 1984.

Ivanova was born October 3, 1949, in Leningrad (now St. Petersburg), where she attended the Mechanical Institute. Following graduation in 1973 she worked at the Command Instrument scientific–research institute for 2 years while doing graduate study. In 1975 she returned to the Mechanical Institute as a researcher, and also completed her candidate of technical sciences thesis.

She was one of the women cosmonaut candidates recruited in 1980, passing the state medical commission that November. She was approved for Soyuz–Salyut training by the joint station commission in March 1983, and qualified as a Soyuz flight engineer and EVA crewmember a year later.

In addition to the all–women Soyuz crew, Ivanova was also briefly assigned to a Soyuz visiting crew scheduled for launch in 1987. When her place on that mission was given to a cosmonaut from Afghanistan, Ivanova returned to the staff of the Leningrad Mechanical Institute (later known as the Baltic Higher Technical School). She remained medically qualified for a flight assignment for several years, but retired as a cosmonaut in October 1994 without flying.

Kaleri, Alexandr Yuriyevich
1956–

Aerospace engineer Alexandr Kaleri has made two tours aboard the Mir space station. The first was as a member of the Mir-11 crew commanded by Alexandr Viktorenko, launched March 17, 1992. With German researcher Klaus-Dietrich Flade, who returned to Earth after 8 days, Kaleri and Viktorenko relieved the Mir-10 crew of Alexandr Volkov and Sergei Krikalev. Kaleri and Viktorenko made an EVA during the mission, which lasted over 145 days.

Kaleri returned to Mir in August 1996 aboard Soyuz TM-24, with commander Valery Korzun and French researcher Claudie-Andre Deshays. Kaleri and Korzun were last-minute replacements for the original Mir-22 core crew of Pavel Vinogradov and Gennady Manakov, grounded because of Manakov's medical problems. The Mir-22 mission also included NASA-Mir researchers Shannon Lucid, John Blaha (who replaced Lucid in September 1996), and Jerry Linenger (who replaced Lucid in January 1997). Kaleri and Korzun made two EVAs, installing American-built solar arrays on the Mir exterior. They survived a fire in the Kvant module on February 23, 1997, and returned safely to Earth after 197 days.

Kaleri was born May 13, 1956, in Yurmala, Latvia, an ethnic Russian in spite of his Latvian surname. He entered the Moscow Physical-Technical Institute (MFTI) in 1973, graduating in 1979; he then joined the NPO Energiya. He remained a postgraduate fellow at MFTI through 1983, developing experiments flown on Salyut-7 and on Mir.

He wanted to become a cosmonaut as soon as he joined Energiya, but the organization's rules required 3 years of service. In December 1982 Kaleri passed the medical commission, and was approved for cosmonaut training by the joint state commission on April 13, 1984. He underwent the basic cosmonaut training course from November 1985 to October 1986, and in April 1987 was assigned to the Salyut cosmonaut training group in a reserve team with Vladimir Lyakhov. A month later he replaced Sergei Yemelyanov on the backup crew for the Soyuz TM-4 mission, launched December 1987.

Kaleri immediately went into training for the Soyuz TM-7 crew with commander Alexandr Volkov, but was replaced for medical reasons in March 1988 by Sergei Krikalev. He requalified for flight in October 1989, and returned to active training as backup for Soyuz TM-12, launched in May 1991. Kaleri and Volkov were assigned to Soyuz TM-13, but Volkov saw this assignment vanish, too, when Kazakh test pilot Toktar Aubakirov was given his place.

He is currently assigned as a backup for Soyuz TM-28, the Mir-26 mission, scheduled for launch in August 1998.

Karashtin, Vladimir Vladimirovich
1962–

Vladimir Karashtin is one of the 3 physicians selected as cosmonaut-candidates by the Institute for Medical-Biological Problems (IMBP) in January 1989. In October 1990 he was enrolled as a researcher at the Gagarin cosmonaut training center, and completed training in February 1992. He is awaiting assignment to an International Space Station crew.

Karashtin was born November 18, 1962, in Kaliningrad (now Korolev), Moscow Region. He graduated from the Pirogov 2nd Moscow Medical Institute in 1986, then joined the staff of the IMBP, where he works while awaiting a flight opportunity.

Kartashov, Anatoly Yakovlevich
1932–

Pilot Anatoly Kartashov was one of the first 20 Soviet cosmonauts who began training in March 1960. A highly regarded pilot, within 2 months of selection he had earned a place among the 6 early finalists for the first manned spaceflight. However, when centrifuge tests began in July 1960, Kartashov developed pinpoint hemorrhaging along his spine. The super cautious doctors grounded him in spite of a personal appeal by Yuri Gagarin, who said Kartashov "is the best among us. He will be the first man in space."

Kartashov was born August 25, 1932, in the Pervoy Sadovoye settlement, Sadovoye District, Voronez Region, Russia. He learned to fly at the Voronezh flying school, then attended the Chuguyev Higher Air Force School, graduating in 1954. For the next 6 years he was a fighter pilot in the Soviet air force, based in Petrozavodsk.

After leaving the cosmonaut team in April 1962 Kartashov served in the Soviet Far East and in Saratov. He later qualified as a test pilot, and worked for the Antonov aircraft bureau in the city of Kiev. He retired from the air force with the rank of colonel in 1985.

Katys, Georgy Petrovich
1926–

Georgy Katys was the backup cosmonaut to Konstantin Feoktistov for the daylong flight of the first Voskhod in October 1964. Feoktistov, Vladimir Komarov and Boris Yegorov made the first multiman spaceflight in history.

Katys was born August 31, 1926, in Moscow. He attended the Moscow Auto-Mechanical Institute, graduating in 1948, then went on to perform graduate work at the Bauman Higher Technical School, earning a doctor of technical sciences degree in 1953. For the next 11 years he was involved in space research at the USSR Academy of Sciences at its Institute of Automation and Telemechanics.

Katys was originally recruited as a possible "senior" cosmonaut in December 1963, only to have his application rejected by cosmonaut training director Nikolai Kamanin. When the Voskhod program was authorized shortly thereafter, Katys was still a natural candidate. With Boris Volynov and Boris Yegorov, Katys was originally chosen to be the "first" or prime crew, but Feoktistov's familiarity with Voskhod—a vehicle he had helped design—won him the mission in place of Katys.

Katys's selection was also damaged by the belated discovery that his father, Pyotr, an employee of the State Telegraph Office, had once been denounced as an enemy of the people and shot in 1931. Pyotr Katys was officially rehabilitated in 1957, after the death of Stalin, but the KGB also discovered that Katys had a much older brother and sister living in Paris—another political black mark.

Throughout much of 1965 Katys and commander Boris Volynov trained as the prime crew for a 15-day Voskhod 3 mission, then scheduled for launch as early as November of that year. The Soviet air force, however, caused Katys to be replaced first by Viktor Gorbatko, then by Georgy Shonin. In March 1966 Voskhod 3 was canceled before it could be flown.

Katys was also a member of an abortive scientist-cosmonaut group formed in May 1970, which disintegrated 2 months later due to opposition from the Soviet air force and the Korolev bureau.

In between flight assignments, and full-time from June 1970, Katys returned to research at the Academy of Sciences. Among his later accomplishments was involvement in designing the Lunokhod series of space probes.

Khatulev, Vladimir Alexandrovich
1947–

Vladimir Khatulev was one of the civilian engineers enrolled in the cosmonaut team in December 1978. Four of the engineers, including Khatulev, were employed by the NPO-Machinstroyeniye, builders of the Proton launch rocket, the Salyut-Almaz space stations, and a proposed Gemini-like manned spacecraft called the TKS.

Based in the Russian city of Mozhaisk at the time of selection, Khatulev could not find suitable lodging in the city of Moscow; when he also found that he was going to suffer a pay cut, he withdrew from the cosmonaut team after less than 5 months.

Khatulev was born February 26, 1947, in Tikhoretsk, Krasnodar District, Russia, and graduated from the Bauman Higher Technical School in 1973. He still lives and works in Mozhaisk for NPO Salyut.

Khludeyev, Yevegny Nikolayevich
1940–1995

Yevgeny Khludeyev was one of the 22 candidates enrolled in the military cosmonaut team on October 28, 1965. In December 1967 he completed the training course and qualifed as a cosmonaut, working for the next 14 years on the Almaz military space station program. He was an active cosmonaut for 23 years, but never flew in space.

Khludeyev was born September 10, 1940, in Moscow. In 1957 he entered the Soviet air force, enrolling at the Kiev Higher Air Force Engineering School for the Air Defense Forces to qualify as an aircraft technician. Following graduation in September 1962 he spent 3 years as an engineer with the Strategic Rocket Forces.

His first crew assignment came in November 1969, when he was assigned as a third crewman with Boris Volynov and Vitaly Zholobov for the first series of Almaz missions, eventually flown as Salyut 3 (1974). The death of the Soyuz 11 cosmonauts in 1971 forced a redesign of the Soyuz spacecraft, reducing crew size from three to two, and Khludeyev lost his chance to fly. In 1982 he was a candidate for a flight with a special Almaz-class module carrying the Pion-K sensor (flown as Kosmos-1686), but was not selected. From 1986 to 1988 he worked on the Buran space shuttle program.

During his cosmonaut career Khludeyev logged over 1,500 hours of flying time, including 200 hours of zero-G arcs in a special laboratory aircraft. He became a parachute instructor and a diver.

In 1975 Khludeyev earned his candidate of technical sciences degree. After leaving the cosmonaut team on October 11, 1988, he was a senior scientific researcher at the Gagarin Center heading a group of specialists who trained cosmonaut-candidates for emergencies such as winter landings. He left active duty in October 1992, though he continued to work at the Gagarin Center as a civilian. He died of a heart attack on September 19, 1995.

Khrunov, Yevegny Vasilyevich
1933–

Yevgeny Khrunov became the first person to transfer from one manned spacecraft to another when he took a walk in space from Soyuz 5 to Soyuz 4 on January 15, 1969. Khrunov and fellow cosmonaut Alexei Yeliseyev completed the historic transfer in one hour.

Following their daring transfer to Soyuz 4, piloted by Vladimir Shatalov, Khrunov and Yeliseyev returned to Earth aboard that spacecraft, having spent 48 hours in space.

Soviet publicity at the time claimed that Soyuz 4 and Soyuz 5 formed the first "experimental" manned space station, which was questionable. It was later revealed that Khrunov and Yeliseyev were testing pressure suits and transfer techniques for a Soviet manned lunar landing.

Khrunov was born September 10, 1933, in the village of Prudy, Volovsky District, Tula Region, south of Moscow. He attended the Kashirsky Agricultural-Technical school but a lifelong interest in flying caused him to join the Soviet air force in 1953. After graduation from the Serov Higher Air Force School in Bataisk in 1956, he served with

future cosmonaut Viktor Gorbatko (who was one of his Bataisk schoolmates as well) in the 86th Air Guards Regiment, 199th Air Division of the 48th Air Army in Moldavia.

Chosen as one of the first cosmonauts in March 1960, Khrunov was a communications operator (capcom) during the flight of Yuri Gagarin. In the fall of 1962 he began to train for the world's first space walk, which was performed by Alexei Leonov in March 1965. Khrunov was his backup.

Later in 1965 Khrunov joined the group of cosmonauts training for the first Soyuz missions, which were designed to demonstrate rendezvous, docking, and EVA crew transfer. In September 1966 Khrunov was confirmed as a member of the Soyuz 2 team with commander Valery Bykovsky and flight engineer Alexei Yeliseyev. The commander of Soyuz 1 was Vladimir Komarov.

Shortly after the launch of Soyuz 1 on April 23, 1967, however, it became apparent that the spacecraft was difficult to control. The Soyuz 2 launch was canceled. When Komarov was killed in a reentry accident, Khrunov and Yeliseyev realized how close they had come to joining him.

The Soyuz 1/2 mission was finally flown as Soyuz 4/5 almost 2 years later.

Following his spaceflight, Khrunov returned to the Zhukovsky Air Force Engineering Academy, which he attended from 1961 to 1968, to perform graduate work, eventually earning a candidate's degree (1971). In 1972 he also graduated from the Lenin Military-Political Academy.

In the spring of 1969, Khrunov was briefly assigned as backup commander for the Soyuz 6/7/8 missions, but was removed for disciplinary reasons, which kept him from future crew assignments for the next 11 years. He was a training director and communications operator for the Salyut-Almaz 3 flights in 1974.

In September 1979 Khrunov was named backup commander of the joint Soviet-Cuban mission, flown as Soyuz 38 mission in September 1980. Khrunov left the cosmonaut team that December.

From 1981 to 1983 Khrunov was a researcher on the staff of the NII-30, a military research institute based in Chkalovskaya. He then worked with the USSR State Commitee for Foreign-Economic Relations until leaving military service in October 1989.

Khrunov has published several books, including textbooks on astronautics such as *Man as an Operator in Open Space* (1974); a science fiction novel, *The Way to Mars*; and an autobiography, *The Conquest of Weightlessness* (1976). He is also the subject of a book, *Cosmonaut, Son of the Land of Tula* (1970).

Kizim, Leonid Dinsovich

1941–

Leonid Kizim commanded the record-setting Soyuz T-10 flight during which he and two fellow cosmonauts spent 237 days in space. Kizim and Vladimir Solovyov, a flight engineer, and Oleg Atkov, a cardiologist, were launched aboard Soyuz T-10 on February 8, 1984, and docked with the Salyut 7 station the next day. For the next 8 months they performed experiments in space medicine, made astronomical observations, took detailed photographs of the Earth's surface, and tested space manufacturing techniques. They were host to two teams of visiting cosmonauts, including the Soyuz T-11 crew, which included Indian pilot Rakesh Sharma.

Kizim and Solovyov performed a record 6 different space walks, most of them aimed at repairing the Salyut's main rocket engines, which had been badly damaged in a refueling accident the previous year.

The long spaceflight meant that Kizim was in space when his daughter Tatyana was born on May 24, 1984. When the Soyuz T-12 cosmonauts visited the space station in July, they brought Kizim videotapes of his new daughter. Sadly, Kizim's father, Denis, died while his son was in orbit.

The three cosmonauts returned to Earth on October 1, 1984, in frail physical condition. (Kizim had trouble walking for several days after landing.) But within 3 weeks they were back to normal and Soviet space doctors were predicting that manned flights lasting a year or longer were possible.

As a further step toward a permanent manned presence in space, Soviet program managers launched what was described as a "third generation" station, called "Mir" ("Peace"), on February 19, 1986. Mir outwardly resembled Salyut 7, but its interior had been redesigned to provide more comfortable accommodations for as many as 6 cosmonauts. Scientific and engineering experiments that occupied volume inside Salyut were moved to add-on vehicles, that could be attached to Mir's special five-port docking module.

In November 1985 Kizim and Solovyov were chosen for the difficult double task of activating the new station and continuing operations with the still-functioning Salyut 7.

The Soyuz T-15 launch on March 13, 1986, was, in a break with past Soviet practice, announced publicly in advance, and televised live. Two days later Kizim and Solovyov reached Mir and transferred to it.

Since Mir and Salyut 7 were in almost identical orbits, it was possible for the two cosmonauts, once their initial work aboard Mir was complete, to reboard Soyuz T-15, separate it, and transfer to Salyut 7. This, the first maneuver of its kind in space history, took place on May 5, 1986, and required 28 hours.

While aboard Salyut 7, Kizim and Solovyov took two additional space walks, constructing a 50-foot tower in addition to retrieving scientific experiments abandoned by the previous occupants, cosmonauts Vasyutin, Savinykh, and Volkov.

Kizim and Solovyov used Soyuz T-15 to return to Mir on June 25 and June 26, and landed back on Earth on July 16.

Soyuz T-15 was Leonid Kizim's third spaceflight. In addition to Soyuz T-10, in November and December 1980 he commanded a crew of 3 Soyuz T-3 cosmonauts who performed repairs on the Salyut-6 station, which at that time had been in operation for 3 years.

Kizim was born August 5, 1941, in the city of Krasny Liman in the Donestk Region of the Ukraine. At the age of 18 he was enrolled in the Chernigov Higher Air Force School and graduated as a pilot in 1963. For the next 2 years he served as an air force pilot in the Caucasus before being invited to join the cosmonaut team.

As a pilot Kizim eventually logged 1,500 hours of flying time and made 80 parachute jumps.

Kizim was one of 22 young pilots and flight engineers selected as military cosmonaut candidates on October 28, 1965. In December 1967 he completed the basic course and was assigned to the Chkalov test pilot school, ultimately flying 12 different types of aircraft and earning a Test Pilot 3rd Class rating. In October 1969 he was a support cosmonaut for the Soyuz 6, 7, and 8 missions. From 1971 to 1975 he attended the Yuri Gagarin Red Banner Air Force Academy.

In 1976 he joined a group of cosmonauts helping in the development of an advanced Soyuz spacecraft, eventually known as the Soyuz T (for Transport). He served as backup commander for Soyuz T-2, the first manned flight of the new vehicle. After his first spaceflight he served as backup commander for the Soviet-French Soyuz T-6 mission in 1982, and for the aborted Soyuz T-10-1 in September 1983.

As is traditional, following his third spaceflight, Kizim supervised the training of the next Mir crews, Titov-Serebrov and Romanenko-Laveikin, accompanying them to the Baikonur Cosmodrome. He was a TV commentator during the Soyuz TM-2 mission. In June 1987 Kizim left the cosmonaut team to attend the Voroshilov General Staff Academy. Upon graduation 2 years later he served on the general staff of the Soviet Ministry of Defense.

Since May 1995 Colonel-General Kizim has been director of the Mozhaisky Aerospace Engineering Academy in St. Petersburg.

He has published a book, *Mysteries of Islands in Space* (1987).

Klimuk, Pyotr Ilyich
1942–
Pyotr Klimuk commanded three manned spaceflights before he was 36, the age when many cosmonauts are making their first.

As commander of Soyuz 13 in December 1973, Klimuk and engineer Valentin Lebedev flew an 8-day astronomical mission using the Orion observatory (which had been developed for use in Salyut space stations) to observe the comet Kahoutek. Klimuk and Lebedev were originally the backup crew for the mission; a week prior to launch they replaced the prime crew of Vorobyov and Yazdovsky because the latter two were not getting along.

From May to July 1975, Klimuk and Vitaly Sevastyanov occupied the Salyut 4 space station. Their Soyuz 18 mission lasted a total of 63 days, a Soviet record. Most of the cosmonauts' time was devoted to studies of the

Earth's surface; they took over 2,000 photographs of suspected ore deposits and other features. They also used a special telescope to photograph the sun. The mission was not without its challenges: the Salyut environmental system allowed the station's internal humidity to rise to uncomfortable levels, fogging the windows and causing green mold to grow on the walls.

Klimuk's third flight came as commander of Soyuz 31 in July 1978. With him on that 8-day Interksomos mission, which docked with Salyut 6, was Polish researcher Miroslaw Hermaszewski.

Klimuk was born July 10, 1942, in the city of Komarovka, Brest Region, Byelorussia. At the age of 18 Klimuk entered the Kremenchug Higher Air Force School; when it was disbanded in January 1960, he transferred to the Chernigov Schhool, qualifying as a pilot in October 1964. He flew MiG-15s with the 57th Air Guards Regiment of the Air Defense Forces, Leningrad Military District, until enrolled in the cosmonaut team.

After completing the 2-year basic training course in December 1967, Klimuk was immediately assigned to the Soviet lunar orbit program, serving with Yuri Artyukhin in one of the 5 two-man crews. When lunar orbit missions were postponed in 1969, he trained for a manned orbital test of the lunar spacecraft docking system (Kontakt) until joining the Salyut group in October 1971.

While still an active cosmonaut Klimuk graduated from the Gagarin Red Banner Air Force Academy (1977). He later graduated from the Lenin Military-Political Academy (1983). He served as the cosmonaut team's political officer from March 1976 to January 1978, then became deputy director of the Gagarin Center for political matters, a job he held until September 1991. Klimuk was also a member of the Supreme Soviet, the Central Committee of the Communist Party, and, from 1989 to 1991, the Congress of People's Deputies. He published an autobiography, *Next to the Stars* (1979).

He succeeded Lieutenant General Vladimir Shatalov as director of the Gagarin Center in September 1991. In his first statement Klimuk pledged that his first goal would be to pursue "profitability" in space research. He successfully maintained the Center's independence in a time of shrinking Russian space budgets while also modernizing its facilities for training Shuttle-Mir and International Space Station crewmembers.

Kolesnikov, Gennady Mikhailovich

1936–

Engineer Gennady Kolesnikov was one of the 22 candidates enrolled in the military cosmonaut team on October 28, 1965. A military scientist by training, he left the team on December 16, 1967, without ever flying in space.

As a cosmonaut candidate in September 1966 he was assigned with commander Pavel Popovich for a military reconnaissance flight aboard a spacecraft called 7K-VI. A year later, with the approval of the larger, more capable Almaz military space station program, the 7K-VI program was downgraded. Kolesnikov protested this decision, among others affecting military engineer cosmonauts, and found himself sent to the Central Aviation and Space Medicine Institute, where he was diagnosed with "a dozen" medical ailments, including an ulcer, leading to his dismissal from the cosmonaut team on December 16, 1967. He was not allowed to take the exams that would have certified him as a military cosmonaut.

Kolesnikov was born October 7, 1936, in Dauriya, Borozinsky District, Chita Region, Russia. He attended the Riga Higher Air Force Engineering School, graduating in 1959, then served as an air force engineer in the Turkestan Military District. In 1964 Kolesnikov was admitted to the Zhukovsky Air Force Engineering Academy to do graduate work, and was in his second year of study when he enrolled in the cosmonaut team.

He returned to the academy in early 1968 to complete his interrupted studies, but was invited back to the Gagarin Center in the spring of 1969 by chief of staff Pavel Belyayev. Initially a section chief, he became a department head in 1977.

One of his projects was the Pion-K military sensor, to be mounted in a TKS-class module and launched to an Almaz or Salyut space station. From 1983 to 1985 Kolesnikov was a candidate to accompany the Pion-K to space; he had regained medical clearance for spaceflight, though he did not return to the cosmonaut team. Pion-K was ultimately flown as Kosmos 1686 in the fall of 1985.

Kolesnikov is the author of over 150 scientific papers and is credited with 40 inventions. He is a specialist in post-spaceflight adaptation and has conducted research in low-pressure chambers, zero-G aircraft, and parachute jumps. He himself has made over 1,550 jumps.

He transferred to military reserve status in 1996, joining the staff of the Gagarin Red Banner Air Force Academy as a civilian senior scientist.

Kolodin, Pytor Ivanovich

1930–

Pyotr Kolodin is the hard-luck Soviet cosmonaut who was assigned to 5 different flight crews between 1965 and 1978 without ever going into space.

He was the second backup to Alexei Leonov on Voskhod 2, the mission in which Leonov became the first person to "walk in space," and backup cosmonaut-researcher for Viktor Gorbatko on Soyuz 7 in 1969. Soyuz 7 was intended to dock with Soyuz 8, a plan that was canceled because of technical problems.

It was in 1971 that Kolodin came closest to going into space. With commander Leonov and flight engineer Valery Kubasov, he was assigned as the second main crew for the first series of Salyut missions. The initial crew of Shatalov, Yeliseyev, and Rukavishnikov failed to board the station on their April 19, 1971, attempt. As their backups, Leonov, Kubasov, and Kolodin were scheduled to make another attempt in June.

But the final preflight examinations before the strict medical commission discovered a spot on Kubasov's lung, disqualifying him from the mission. Soviet program managers such as chief designer Vasily Mishin, Gagarin Center director Nikolai Kuznetsov, and cosmonaut training chief Nikolai Kamanin weighed their options: replace Kubasov with his backup, Vladislav Volkov, or send the entire third crew (Georgy Dobrovolsky, Volkov, and Viktor Patsayev) instead. On June 4, 1971, 2 days before launch, the decision was made to send a new replacement crew.

According to Kuznetsov, Kolodin reacted badly to the decision, marching straight to Mishin to complain. Mishin told him the decision would stand, and the replacements were launched aboard Soyuz 11 on June 6. Neither Kolodin, Leonov, nor Kubasov was present at the traditional prelaunch press conference that always included the prime and backup crews. Their places were taken by Shatalov, Yeliseyev, and Rukavishnikov.

With tragic irony, the replacement team of Dobrovolsky, Volkov, and Patsayev was killed on their return to Earth 24 days later.

Kolodin was born September 23, 1930, in the village of Novovasilyevka, Novovasilyevsky District, Zaporozhye Region of Ukraine. He attended the Kharkov Artillery School (1946–1949), then the Second Leningrad Artillery School, graduating in June 1952. He spent 2 years stationed at an artillery range in the Tavrichesky Military District, then entered the Govorov Military Engineering and Radio-Technical Academy. After completing the academy's 5-year course, Kolodin served in the new Soviet Strategic Rocket Forces at the Baikonur and Plesetsk Cosmodromes. At the time of his selection as a cosmonaut, he was military representative at a missile plant in Kharkov.

Kolodin was one of 15 candidates enrolled in the cosmonaut detachment on January 11, 1963, having passed the medical commission in spite of the fact that he had lost a thumb in a 1950 accident. Chief Designer Sergei Korolev wanted Kolodin to become a cosmonaut, and offered to design a special spacecraft control panel, if necessary.

After completing the initial training course in January 1965, Kolodin was assigned as an EVA crewmember for Voskhod and Soyuz missions (1965–69), then to the Salyut program (1970–77). After the Salyut 1 affair, Kolodin worked in support of Salyut missions. In 1977 he was teamed with Vladimir Dzhanibekov for the proposed Soyuz 26 mission, which would test the new Salyut 6 anterior docking port and perform the first spacecraft swap.

This plan, too, changed. The Soyuz 25 team of Kovalenok and Ryumin failed to dock with Salyut 6. Crews were reshuffled at that point so that each included at least one space veteran. Replaced by veteran Oleg Makarov, space rookie Kolodin went on to support Salyut 6 and later Salyut 7 missions as a "Zarya" operator (capcom) at the Kaliningrad flight control center. He finally gave up his dream of flying in space in April 1983 when he was permanently transferred from the cosmonaut group to the flight control staff.

Kolodin is currently retired and lives at Star Town.

Kolomitsev, Ordinard Panteleymonovich
1939–

Ordinard Kolomitsev was one of the Academy of Sciences researchers enrolled in the cosmonaut team in May 1967. He was a candidate for inclusion in a Soyuz crew beginning in June 1968, and remained medically qualified for a flight assignment for several years thereafter although the scientist-cosmonaut group was disbanded by 1972.

Kolomitsev was born January 29, 1939, in Tula, Moscow Region, and graduated from the Saratov State University named for N. G. Chernishevsky in 1956. He joined the staff of IZMIRAN, an institute of the Russian Academy of Sciences located in Troisk, Moscow Region, as a researcher in ionospheric sciences. In the 1960s he made three research trips to the Soviet Antarctic research station Vostok, spending 4 years and 4 months studying the Earth's southern magnetic field.

Kolomitsev received his candidate of technical sciences degree in 1969, and his doctorate in 1992. He still works at IZMIRAN.

Komarov, Vladimir Mikhailovich
1927–1967

Vladimir Komarov was the first person to die in a spaceflight. The tragedy occurred on April 24, 1967, during the return to Earth of Soyuz 1, which had been launched the day before.

Komarov's Soyuz 1 had been intended to dock in space with Soyuz 2, crewed by cosmonauts Bykovsky, Yeliseyev, and Khrunov, at which time Khrunov and Yeliseyev would transfer from one vehicle to the other by space walk. The docking and the space walk were both part of the Soviet Program L mission profile.

Soyuz 1 was a highly ambitious mission, intended to be the first manned test of a brand-new spacecraft designed to take Soviet cosmonauts to the Moon. Each of the three unmanned Soyuz flights suffered some sort of system failure, but the State Commission and Chief

Designer Vasily Mishin went ahead with the launches anyway.

When soon as Soyuz 1 reached orbit one of the 2 solar panels aboard the spacecraft failed to deploy, depriving Soyuz 1 of much of its power, and there were communications problems. The boom for the Igla docking system also failed to deploy. Making a bad situation even worse, from orbits 7 through 12 Komarov was on his own in trying to solve the problems. (Soviet spacecraft at that time were out of range of tracking stations and ships for 8 out of every 24 hours.)

When contact between Soyuz 1 and the flight control center in Yevpatoriya was resumed, it was clear that the problems hadn't been solved. The Soyuz 2 launch was canceled and flight controllers tried to return Komarov safely to Earth, something that would normally occur on the sixteenth orbit.

Only on their third try—orbit 18—were controllers successful in getting Soyuz 1 into a proper orientation for reentry. But problems forced Komarov to use a "ballistic" reentry mode in which the spacecraft spins like a bullet. Fighting unusually high G-forces, with a damaged guidance system, Komarov was unable to stop Soyuz 1 from spinning, and when its parachutes deployed the lines fouled, preventing the chutes from opening properly.

For years it was claimed that American employees of the National Security Agency at a listening post in Norway had heard conversations between Soviet Premier Alexei Kosygin, Komarov's family, and the "doomed" cosmonaut, as well as Komarov's final struggles with the parachutes. Later disclosures by the Soviets themselves claim that Komarov was really had no idea that the lines were being fouled. In any case, Soyuz 1 crashed at several hundred miles an hour to the Orenburg steppe, 25 miles from the settlement of Novoorsk. The impact ignited the Soyuz's retrorocket system, causing a fire. Komarov was killed instantly and the Soviet manned space program came to a halt.

Komarov was born in Moscow on March 16, 1927. He enlisted in the army at the age of 18 and was sent to the 1st Moscow Air School, a prep school for potential air force officers. He received pilot training at the Chkalov Higher Air Force School in Borisoglebsk (1945–46) and Bataisk Higher Air Force School, from which he graduated in 1949.

For the next 3 years Komarov was a fighter pilot with the 382nd Air Regiment, 42nd Air Division, South Caucasus Military District, based in the city of Grozny. In 1952 he transferred to the 486th Air Regiment, 279th Air Division of the 57th Air Army. He entered the Zhukovsky Air Force Engineering Academy in August 1954, completing the 5-year course September 1959. He was assigned to the Chkalovskaya branch of the Main Air Force Research Institute of the USSR Ministry of Defense as a test engineer when invited to undergo examinations for enrollment in the first group of Soviet cosmonauts.

Selected in March 1960, Komarov quickly became known for his intelligence and piloting skills, and also for his bad luck. He had to undergo a hernia operation on May 15, 1960, which came close to ending his cosmonaut career before it really started. He spent 6 months recuperating and trying to keep up with his studies. In 1962, after being named as backup to cosmonaut Pavel Popovich for Vostok 4, a medical examination showed that Komarov had an irregular heartbeat, a condition very similar to the one that grounded American astronaut Donald Slayton for 10 years. Komarov had to submit to dozens of tests by a variety of cardiologists before he was allowed to continue his cosmonaut career.

But in April 1964, when chief designer Korolev needed a pilot for the world's first space "crew," it was Komarov who was selected, and on October 16, 1964, he went into space aboard Voskhod 1. With him were an engineer from the Korolev design bureau, Konstantin Feoktistov, and a young aerospace physician, Boris Yegorov. They returned safely to Earth after 24 hours.

Komarov served as the chief cosmonaut member of the Soyuz design team beginning in April 1965, and in October 1966 was named to command its maiden flight. He was the first Soviet cosmonaut to make two space-flights.

He was the subject of a biography, *Tester of Space-ships*, written by his close friend and fellow cosmonaut Vasily Lazarev (in collaboration with Mikhail Rebrov), published in 1976.

A Soviet space tracking vessel was later named for Komarov, as was the Yeisk Higher Air Force School.

Kondakova, Yelena Vladimirovna

1957–

Aerospace engineer Yelena Kondakova has made 2 space-flights to the Mir space station, once as a Soyuz-Mir crewmember—the first woman to make a long-duration flight—and then aboard the American Shuttle.

Launched October 4, 1994, aboard Soyuz TM-20 with commander Alexandr Viktorenko and ESA researcher Ulf Merbold, Kondakova became only the third Russian woman in space, 31 years after Valentina Tereshkova. This Mir-17 main crew joined cosmonauts Malenchenko, Musabayev, and Polyakov for 30 days of joint experiments. Kondakova and Viktorenko continued their mission with Polyakov, much of it devoted to medical studies, with a female subject and a long-stay physician on board. The crew also saw a rendezvous by the orbiter Discovery on STS-63, which approached to within 35 feet of the station to test techniques for future Shuttle-Mir dockings. Kondakova, Viktorenko, and Polyakov returned to Earth on March 21, 1995.

Kondakova returned to Mir as a mission specialist in the crew of STS-84. This May 1997 flight of the orbiter Atlantis made the sixth Shuttle-Mir docking, transferring several thousand pounds of food, water, and technical equipment to the Mir-22 crew of Vasily Tsibliyev and Alexandr Lazutkin. Atlantis also delivered NASA-Mir researcher Michael Foale to the station and returned Jerry Linenger to Earth.

Kondakova was born March 30, 1957, in the settlement of Rabochi, Pushkin District, Moscow Region, and attended the Bauman Higher Technical School. Following graduation as a mechanical engineer in 1980 she went to work at the NPO Energiya. She became a flight controller for the Mir space station.

One of 4 engineers enrolled in the cosmonaut team as candidates on January 25, 1989. She underwent a general training course at the Gagarin Center from October 1990 to March 1992, and was assigned, with Viktorenko, as backup to Soyuz TM-19 in February 1994.

Kondakova married former cosmonaut Valery Ryumin in 1985. It was Ryumin, in his post as deputy chief designer of NPO Energiya, who once signed an order forbidding women cosmonauts to be assigned to long-duration space missions.

Kondakova was assigned to Shuttle-Mir in October 1996 and moved to Houston, Texas, for training. Her husband, Russian director for Shuttle-Mir flights, returned to active cosmonaut training in 1997 and was assigned to STS-91.

Kondratyev, Dmitri Yuriyevich

1969–

Major Dmitri Kondratyev is one of the 8 Russian air force pilots selected for cosmonaut training in 1997. In the spring of 1999 he should qualify as a Soyuz commander and International Space Station crewmember.

Kondratyev was born May 26, 1969, in the city of Irkutsk. He graduated from the Kacha Higher Air Force School in Volgograd in 1990, and at the time of his selection for cosmonaut training served with the 76th Air Army in Petrozavodsk.

Kononenko, Oleg Dmitryevich

1964–

Space engineer Oleg Kononenko was one of the 5 candidates selected for cosmonaut training in February 1996. In March 1998 he completed the training course at the Gagarin Center and is qualified as a flight engineer for future International Space Station crews.

Kononenko was born June 21, 1964, in the city of Chardzhou, Turkmen SSR. After leaving secondary school he worked for a year at the Chardzhou airport, then enrolled at the Zhukovsky Aviation Institute in the city of Kharkov, Ukraine, graduating in 1988, as a specialist in aircraft engines.

He went to work at the Central Specialized Design Bureau (TsSKB) Progress in the city of Samara, manufacturer of the Soyuz launch vehicles.

Kononenko, Oleg Grigoryevich

1938–1980

Oleg Kononenko was one of the 5 civilian test pilots originally selected to fly the Soviet space shuttle Buran. For 3 years he took part in the initial development of that vehicle, and from 1979 to 1980 underwent cosmonaut training at the Gagarin Center. But on September 8, 1980, Kononenko was killed in a flying accident.

Kononenko was born August 16, 1938, in the village of Samarsku in the Rostov Region of Russia. In 1958 he graduated from the DOSAAF School in Saransk, then became a civilian instructor-pilot. He attended the helicopter course at the Ministry of Aviation Industry's civilian test pilot school in Zhukovsky (1966), and also attended evening classes at the Moscow Aviation Institute, graduating in 1975.

Beginning in 1966 Kononenko worked as a civilian test pilot at Zhukovsky. Among his projects was the Yak-38A vertical takeoff-landing aircraft. The fatal crash occurred during sea trials aboard the carrier *Minsk* in the South China Sea.

Korniyenko, Mikhail Borisovich

1960–

Mikhail Korniyenko is a cosmonaut-candidate approved by the joint state commission in February 1998. On March 23, 1998, he entered the basic training course at the Gagarin Center, hoping to qualify as an International Space Station crewmember in late 1999.

Korniyenko was born April 15, 1960, in Syzran, Kuybyshev Region (now Samara Region), Russia. After completing secondary school in 1977 he served in the Soviet Army for 2 years. He then entered the Moscow Aviation Institute, graduating in 1987 as a mechanical engineer.

From 1987 to 1991 Korniyenko was an engineer with the KB General Machine-Building (KBOM). He then spent 4 years as head of manufacturing for the Transvostok Enterprise before joining the RKK Energiya in April 1995, where he worked as a spacecraft engineer until his selection for cosmonaut training.

Korzun, Valery Grigoryevich

1953–

Valery Korzun commanded the Mir-22 mission, launched as Soyuz TM-24 on August 17, 1996, with flight engineer Alexandr Kaleri and French researcher Claudie Andre-Deshays. Until August 10 Korzun and Kaleri had been backups to the planned Mir-22 crew of Gennady Manakov and Pavel Vinogradov. Manakov was diagnosed with a heart ailment in early August, however, forcing the change.

The most pronounced effect of the crew change was on NASA-Mir crewmember John Blaha, who replaced Shannon Lucid aboard the station when the orbiter Atlantis (STS-79) docked on September 19. Blaha had only trained with Korzun and Kaleri for a few hours and found that it took the crew several weeks to feel comfortable with one another.

Among the usual tasks of Earth resources observations, medical studies, and materials processing, Korzun and Kaleri also made two EVAS to install new American-built solar arrays on the station exterior.

The Mir-22 crew was resupplied by a second Shuttle mission, STS-81, in January 1997, which brought NASA-Mir researcher Jerry Linenger to the station. On February 23, 1997 a fire broke out in the Kvant module. Smoke filled Mir's interior as flames spurted from a faulty oxygen "candle." Ultimately the fire burned itself out.

After a mission of 197 days, Korzun and Kaleri returned to Earth with German researcher Reinhold Ewald on March 2, 1997.

In February 1998 the joint state commission selected Korzun and Vinogradov as members of the fifth incremental International Space Station crew, scheduled to launch to I.S.S. in the summer of 2001.

Korzun was born March 5, 1953 (the day Josef Stalin died), in Krasny Sulin, Rostov Region, Russia. He attended the Kachinsk Higher Air Force School, graduating in 1974, becoming a MiG-21 pilot with the 899th Air Fighter Regiment, 1st Air Guards Division, 15th Air Army in Pribaltic.

In October 1976 Korzun was transferred to the Moscow Military District, flying with the 234th Air Guards

FIRE ABOARD MIR

by Valery Korzun with Bert Vis

On the evening of February 23, 1997, we were sitting at the table: Reinhold Ewald, myself, Sasha Kaleri, and Vasily Tsibliyev. Jerry Linenger was not there. He was in the next module. It was already after dinner. We had had tea already and we were talking.

Between 10:20 and 10:30 P.M., in the Kvant module, Aleksandr Lazutkin used the last of four oxygen-generating cartridges recommended to us. The principle is that the cartridge is placed in the solid fuel oxygen generator, or TDK. The TDK is equipped with a special filter and that filter caught fire. As soon as the fire broke out, Reinhold saw it and he exclaimed: "Fire!"

I rushed to Kvant and saw that there were smoke and flames. It was burning inside and there was kind of a transparent flame. Some substance was pushed out in drops and flying everywhere. We had to keep out of the way and could only position ourselves on the side. Lazutkin tried to take the filter away. He was in the smoke for a while so I asked him to move away from that section. It was evident that we couldn't cope with the fire without the help of special equipment.

We got out of Kvant and decided to put on oxygen masks and to use fire extinguishers. Once all of us had oxygen masks, I took an extinguisher and went back to the TDK.

The first extinguisher wasn't very effective. It seemed to me that it wasn't working. I turned back again and asked for another one. The guys—all of them. Vasily and Jerry from one place, Sasha from another place—brought extinguishers, which were located in different parts of the station.

We used foam and water extinguishers. Using the foam extinguisher was useless, since the foam disappeared immediately, because of the oxygen that was still being produced by the cartridges pushed away the foam. We then used the water extinguisher and managed to slow down the flow of oxygen. We then again used foam. Since we expected another stage of the fire, we stayed close by with the extinguisher.

We decided to prepare the station in case we would not succeed in putting out the fire, and thought about whether or not we could reach the two Soyuzes that were docked to Mir. The TDK is inclined in such a position relative to Kvant's hatch, about a 20 degree angle, that we could have gone underneath the fire. The hatches of both Soyuzes were open.

The crew started preparations to evacuate the station. Sasha Kaleri was near the computer. Vasha and Jerry were preparing a medical post in the airlock, a part of the station that was considered less filled with smoke. We found out that was very useful and at the time, we were trying to find out what kind of medical aids we could use in case of an emergency. So it was kind of an organizing job at that moment; for instance, we turned off the ventilators.

I don't know exactly how long it took us to put out the fire. I think it was around 10:30 P.M. The flames burned maybe for only three minutes.

One problem was to put out the fire and another was to purify the atmosphere. We used all purifying systems. Between the moment of the fire and our next voice communications period with the ground, we had approximately one hour. So the atmosphere was purified, but we reported to the ground that we didn't know if we could breathe the atmosphere after purifying. We didn't know if there was sufficient oxygen in the atmosphere or if there still was carbon monoxide. The filters on the oxygen masks wouldn't work for a long time and we didn't know the percentage of harmful particles. We realized that some of us might not feel well but still, the atmosphere was quickly purified. We took off the masks and found we didn't feel bad.

Our onboard doctor, Jerry Linenger, took care of the oxygen masks and had the medical aids ready as well. He was prepared for cardiac problems and such, and had syringes ready to be used. In case of such problems, we were to use the second set of oxygen masks.

Jerry examined our lungs and the level of oxygen in our blood. None of us had less than 90%. If you have less than 80%, it's not very good for your organism.

The fire happened in the zone where we had no voice communication with the flight control center. We were flying between southeastern Australia and the U.S. Since we could have communications with some amateurs in the U.S., Jerry tried to use his amateur radio to inform the amateurs that we had had a fire, and to send an SOS. Communications were not very successful though. They were garbled. We informed Earth but they didn't hear us. We already had communications for several minutes, but they didn't hear us. We still repeated all the information, but only about ten seconds before loss of signal, did the capcom report that they had understood us. Then voice communications ceased again. We had our next voice communications only at 04:00 A.M. We call those periods 'deaf orbits.'

The Americans have methods to analyze the atmosphere. They use these to detect harmful particles in the atmosphere. We carried out an experiment that night, and when we landed days later, we carried the results with us. We took air samples, samples of condensed water and samples of the air that were taken close to the location of the fire. The concentration was rather high, but didn't exceed safety limits. On Earth the samples were analyzed and they came to the same conclusion: that the atmosphere was normal.

Regiment, 9th Air Division, ultimately becoming a squadron commander.

He entered the Gagarin Red Banner Air Force Academy in 1984, graduating from its command faculty in June 1987.

As a pilot Korzun has logged over 1,500 hours of flying time. He is also a qualified parachute instructor, with 377 jumps.

Korzun was one of 5 air force pilots enrolled in the military cosmonaut team on June 23, 1987. He underwent the basic training course at the Gagarin Center from December 1987 to June 1989.

In March 1991 Korun began training to command Soyuz TM-14, a visit to the Mir space station scheduled for launch in November 1991. The TM-14 mission was canceled, however, and the crew—which included Kazakh test pilot Toktar Aubakirov—was reshuffled, with Aubakirov flying aboard Soyuz TM-13.

Korzun was then assigned, with flight engineer Alexandr Laveikin and French spationaut Jean-Pierre Haignere, as the backup crew for the third Russian-French mission, scheduled for launch in August 1992. In early 1992, however, Korzun was limited to assignment for short or visiting Mir missions only. (With a growing database from missions lasting 6 months or longer, Russian space doctors judged that after several weeks in orbit Korzun would be too tall for his seat in a Soyuz spacecraft.) Korzun spent 2 years in the Soyuz Rescue program without a flight prospect until engineers at NPO Energiya, responding to requests from Gagarin Center managers and Korzun's fellow cosmonauts, developed a special Soyuz seat that could accommodate him.

Kotov, Oleg Valeriyevich

1965–

Major Oleg Kotov of the medical service of the Russian Air Force is qualified as a cosmonaut-researcher on Mir and International Space Station crews. He was backup cosmonaut-researcher for the crew of Soyuz TM-28, launched to Mir in August 1998.

Kotov was born October 27, 1965, in Simferopol, USSR. He attended the Kirov Military Medical Academy, graduating in 1988. He has also studied at the Moscow Institute for Industrial Property and Innovation as a patent specialist.

Since 1988 Kotov has been serving as a military flight surgeon based at the Gagarin Cosmonaut Training Center. He won medical clearance for cosmonaut training in 1993 and began training prior to official approval from the State credentials committee on February 9, 1996. He completed basic cosmonaut training in March 1998.

Kovalenok, Vladimir Vasilyevich

1942–

Vladimir Kovalenok made three visits to the Salyut 6 space station between 1977 and 1981, two of them for long-duration missions.

He was commander of Soyuz 25, launched October 9, 1977, for a planned 90-day stay aboard Salyut 6, a mission that would have included activation of the station. But technical problems forced the docking to be canceled and Kovalenok and flight engineer Valery Ryumin returned to Earth after only 2 days.

The failure, the third involving an all-rookie crew, had repercussions on several cosmonaut careers. The State Commission managing Soviet spaceflights passed a law requiring all future Soviet crews to include at least one veteran cosmonaut. Presumably the veteran would have sufficient experience with space adaptation syndrome (SAS) to be able to function during the delicate rendezvous and docking process, which because of the limitations of the Soyuz spacecraft took place in the first 2 days of a mission.

The new rule meant that "rookie" cosmonauts such as Yuri Isaulov and Pyotr Kolodin lost missions because they were teamed with other rookies. It also caused Kovalenok and Ryumin to be assigned to different teams.

Kovalenok's next visit, as commander of Soyuz 29 with flight engineer Alexandr Ivanchenkov, was much more successful. The two cosmonauts occupied Salyut 6 from June 16, 1978, until November 2, 1978, spending over 139 days in space, a record at the time. During their mission they hosted visits from two Interkosmos crews and three Progress supply vehicles while carrying out space manufacturing and Earth resources work. Kovalenok and Ivanchenkov also performed an EVA of 2 hours and 5 minutes on June 29, 1978.

Following the repair of Salyut 6 by three other cosmonauts in late 1980, Kovalenok and flight engineer Viktor Savinykh were launched March 13, 1981, aboard Soyuz T4. During their 75 days in space they were visited by two more Interkosmos crews.

Kovalenok was born March 3, 1942, in the town of Beloye in the Krupsk District, near the city of Minsk in Byelorussia. He attended the Balashov Higher Air Force School from 1959 to 1963 and served as a crew commander flying An-24 transport planes in the Soviet air force, logging over 1,600 hours flying time. He also became a parachute instructor.

Kovalenok applied for the 1965 cosmonaut selection and was accepted, but placed in a reserve group. He was already involved with the space program, however: beginning with the unmanned Kosmos 33 in June 1964 Kovalenok flew search and recovery missions locating returning spacecraft. He would later fly rescue planes for the Voshkod 2 crew, who landed far off course, and for

Komarov's ill-fated Soyuz 1. Kovalenok became one of the 12 cosmonaut candidates enrolled in April 1967.

Kovalenok joined the Salyut training group in 1972 and was backup commander to Soyuz 18 in 1975. He was also backup commander to Soyuz 26, Soyuz 27 and Soyuz 35. At the same time he was actively training for Salyut missions he graduated from the Gagarin Red Banner Air Force Academy in 1976.

Kovalenok was also politically active as a deputy in the Supreme Soviet of the Byelorussian Soviet Socialist Republic. He attended the International Astronautical Federation congress in Munich in 1979.

Following the Soyuz T-4 mission Kovalenok supervised the training of the next crews of cosmonauts, those assigned to the first Salyut 7 mission, launched in May 1982. Later that year Kovalenok enrolled at the Voroshilov General Staff Academy, graduating with a candidate of military science degree in 1984. At that time he was promoted to major general.

From 1984 to 1986 Kovalenok was a deputy director of the Gagarin Center, in charge of crew training. He left the cosmonaut team in February 1986 and was assigned to duties with the Strategic Rocket Forces at the Baikonur Cosmodrome, during which time he also managed to take part in a series of Earth observation experiments called Kursk 85 and conducted by Dzhanibekov and Savinykh aboard Salyut 7.

In 1988, when the implementation of the SALT II arms control treaty caused the elimination of some Soviet missiles, Kovalenok became an instructor at the Voroshilov General Staff Academy. From January 1991 to 1994 he was director of the Ministry of Defense's Central Scientific Research Institute.

Now a colonel-general, Kovalenok is director of the Zhukovsky Air Force Engineering Academy. He has publicly critized Russia's involvement in the International Space Station program as a giveaway of homegrown technical capability.

Kozelsky, Vladimir Sergeyevich

1942–

Vladimir Kozelsky was one of the 12 air force candidates enrolled in the cosmonaut team in April 1967. He served as second backup commander for the Soyuz 23 mission in February 1977. Soyuz 23 cosmonauts Gorbatko and Glazkov spent 19 days aboard the Salyut 5, the second Salyut-Almaz military space station.

In 1979 and 1980 Kozelsky trained as commander of two different 3-man crews assigned to missions aboard the third Salyut-Almaz. But the program was canceled and Kozelsky lost his chance to fly in space.

Kozelsky was born January 12, 1942, in the Stavropol District of southern Russia. He attended the Kacha Higher Air Force School, graduating in 1963, then served as a pilot with the Soviet air force in Byelorussia. He graduated from the Gagarin Air Force Academy by correspondence in 1980.

Kozelsky's then-radical political views—he supported private ownership of property and a multiparty political system—led to his dismissal from the cosmonaut team in April 1983. The official reason given was "age"; he was 41 at the time.

He is currently a deputy Mir flight director and communications operator at the Kaliningrad flight control center.

Kozeyev, Konstantin Mirovich

1967–

Aerospace engineer Konstantin Kozeyev is a candidate for assignment to a future International Space Station crew. A meeting of the joint state commission in July 1997 pronounced Kozeyev technically qualified for crew assignment, but required a review of his medical status at a later date.

Kozeyev was born December 1, 1967, in Kaliningrad (now known as Korolev), the Moscow-region city that is home to the Russian spaceflight control center and to RKK Energiya. He attended the Tsiolkovsky Moscow Aviation-Technical Institute (MATI), graduating in 1992.

Even before graduation Kozeyev was working at the RKK Energiya. He was approved as a cosmonaut candidate by the State credentials committee on February 9, 1996.

Kozlov, Vladimir Ivanovich

1945–

Vladimir Kozlov was one of the 9 air force candidates enrolled in the cosmonaut team in April 1970. He completed the training course in 1972, but was dropped from the cosmonaut team the follow May without ever flying in space.

Kozlov was born October 2, 1945 in the Moscow region. He graduated from a higher air force school in 1968 and was serving with the Soviet air forces when selected for cosmonaut training.

After leaving the Gagarin Center Kozlov served in the Main Staff of the Soviet air forces until 1989. He transferred to reserve status and is currently director of flight support for the Zhukovsky Air Force Engineering Academy and works at its airfield in the town of Monino.

Kramarenko, Alexandr Yakovlevich

1942–

Alexandr Kramarenko was one of the 22 military candidates enrolled in the cosmonaut team on October 30, 1965. He completed the initial training program and was designated a cosmonaut on December 30, 1967, but left the team on April 20, 1969, for medical reasons, before ever flying in space.

Kramarenko was born November 8, 1942, in the settlement of Novaya Mayachka, Kherson Region, Ukraine. He entered the Soviet air force in August 1959, attending the Kirovograd Higher Air Force School. When that school was closed the following summer, he transferred to the Orenburg Higher Air Force School, graduating in October 1963. Until his enrollment as a cosmonaut candidate Kramarenko was an Il-28 fighter-bomber pilot with

the 143rd Air Fighter-Bomber Regiment of the 34th Air Army.

As a cosmonaut Kramarenko trained for flights in the Almaz military space station program. Following his departure from the cosmonaut team he remained with the Almaz program as a test engineer until the program's cancellation in January 1982. Since that time Kramarenko has served as head of the department at the Gagarin Center that trains cosmonauts to operate equipment on board orbital space stations.

Kramarenko did graduate work at the Bauman Higher Technical School, receiving an engineering degree in 1973. He also attended the Moscow Pedagogical Institute from November 1989 to December 1990.

Krichevsky, Sergei Vladimirovich

1955–

Russian air force pilot Sergei Krichevsky trained for 9 years to command a Soyuz mission to Mir, serving as commander of a crew with flight engineer Alexandr Kaleri in 1994 and 1995. But he retired from cosmonaut training in July 1998 without a mission.

Krichevsky was born July 9, 1955, in Lesozavodsk, Primorsky Region, Russia. He graduated from secondary school in Blagoveshchensk, Amur district, then enrolled at the Armavir Higher Air Force School. Following graduation in 1976 he became a military pilot first class with the air defense forces of the Soviet air force, serving in Kazakhstan and in Russia.

In 1982 he enrolled at the Zhukovsky Air Force Engineering Academy, graduating in 1986. He received a candidate of technical sciences degree in 1987. Krichevsky is the author of 30 technical papers.

Krichevsky was one of the 3 air force candidates enrolled in the cosmonaut team in June 1989. In January 1991 he completed the training necessary to qualify him as a Soyuz commander. From January 1992 to April 1994 he was one of 5 cosmonauts who underwent special instruction in Earth resources at Moscow State University.

He is currently doing graduate scientific study at the Institute for Space Research (IKI) in Moscow.

Krichevsky is the author of a book of poems and impressions, *The Earthly Soul* (1996).

Krikalev, Sergei Konstantinovich

1958–

Sergei Krikalev is one of the world's most experienced space travelers. In addition to having spent over a year in space aboard the Mir space station on two different missions, he has also flown aboard the U.S. Space Shuttle. He is currently assigned as a flight engineer in the first incremental crew for the International Space Station, scheduled for launch in early 2000.

Krikalev was a mission specialist aboard STS-60, an 8-day flight of the orbiter Discovery in February 1994 which carried the Wake Shield Facility and other experiments.

Previously Krikalev had served a 6-month shift aboard the Mir space station (1988–89) and a 9-month stay (1991–92). Krikalev's second visit coincided with the abortive Soviet coup of August 1991, and the disintegration of the Soviet Union in the months that followed, leading to the rumor that he had become a "man without a country" who had been left stranded in space.

Krikalev had been scheduled to return to Earth with his expedition commander, Anatoly Artsebarsky, and Austrian visitor Franz Viehbock in October 1991. Their replacement crew was to have been Alexandr Volkov and Alexandr Kaleri, who were to have hosted a short visiting mission in November of a crew including Kazakh researcher Toktar Aubakirov.

But a funding crunch led to the cancellation of the visiting mission in early July 1991. The crews for Soyuz TM-13 (Volkov-Kaleri-Viehbock) and TM-14 (Korzun-Laveikin-Aubakirov) were combined into a team of Volkov-Aubakirov-Viehbock. Only Volkov was qualified to serve a shift aboard Mir, so Krikalev was asked if he would extend his mission until the next scheduled visit in March 1992. He agreed.

The political and financial headlines easily overshadowed what was a routine, if unexpectedly lengthy, visit by Krikalev. His most notable activity was taking part in six different space construction EVAs with Artsebarsky, including one near-emergency in which he rescued an overheated and temporarily blinded Artsebarsky from the top of a space structure.

Krikalev's first visit to Mir began on November 16, 1988, when he and commander Alexandr Volkov were launched aboard Soyuz TM-7 along with French spationaut Jean-Loup Chretien for 3 weeks of joint operations. When Chretien returned to Earth along with the previous Mir occupants, Vladimir Titov and Musa Manarov, Krikalev, and Volkov remained aboard the station with physician Valery Polyakov.

During the mission Krikalev and Volkov were scheduled to perform an EVA and to attach a large habitation module to Mir. But technical difficulties delayed the launch of the Kvant-2 module, and the 3-man crew was forced to leave Mir unmanned for the first time in 2 years.

(Krikalev found that he was a wanted man during his first spaceflight. As a senior lieutenant in the Soviet air force reserve, he had been called for his yearly service commitment by his district draft center. Receiving no response to several letters to Krikalev's home, the center labeled him a draft dodger—until it was pointed out that Krikalev was at present in orbit and unable to receive the summons!)

Krikalev was born August 27, 1958, in Leningrad. As a young boy he decided he wanted to become a cosmonaut and with that in mind, entered the Leningrad Institute of Mechanics, graduating in 1981. While still a college student Krikalev became a sport pilot flying the Yak 18A, Yak 50, and other aerobatic aircraft. He earned a USSR Master of Sport title.

Even before he graduated from college, Krikalev was doing pre-diploma work at the NPO Energiya design bureau, assisting in the preparation of flight documentation. As soon as he earned his degree, Krikalev immediately applied for enrollment in the cosmonaut group, passing the medical commission at the IMBP in March 1983. While the long selection process took place he served as a trainer for the Salyut 7 "rescue" crew of Dzhanibekov and Savinykh in 1985. In September 1985 he was approved by the joint state commission and enrolled in the training program for cosmonaut candidates; he completed it in December 1987 while working on the Buran space shuttle program. He was assigned as flight engineer for the Soviet-French crew in March 1988.

Krikalev was assigned to Shuttle-Mir in November 1992 and spent 2 and a half years at the NASA Johnson Space Center in Houston, training for STS-60 and serving as backup to Vladimir Titov on STS-63.

Krikun, Yuri Yuriyevich
1963–

A writer-director with UkrTele-film in the Ukraine, Yuri Krikun was one of the 6 Soviet journalists enrolled as candidate researchers in the cosmonaut team in October 1990. But the USSR Journalist-in-Space mission never took place.

In November 1991, as the Soviet Union was breaking up, the new republic of Ukraine announced that it was planning an all-Ukraine Soyuz mission for late 1992. The goal was to study the effects of the Chernobyl disaster. Krikun was also a candidate for that crew. Again, the all-Ukraine mission was canceled.

Krikun was also considered for the astronaut team of the National Space Agency of Ukraine, formed in 1997, but was not selected.

Krikun was born June 3, 1963, in the city of Kiev, Ukraine. He graduated from the theater faculty of the I. K. Karpenko Institute of Theatrical Arts in that city. He also attended the journalist curriculum at the Higher Journalistic Institute.

He has written screenplays for and directed the films *The World Champion Bicycle Race Begins in Kiev* (1986) and *The Farmer* (1989). He is also the author of two books, including one on spaceflight titled *Steps to the Cosmodrome*.

Since 1984 he has been a regular contributor to such publications as *Pravda, Sovietskaya Ukraina, Komsomoslkoye Znamya, Ogonyok* and others. He was a member of the Journalist's Union of the USSR.

Kubasov, Valery Nikolayevich
1935–

Valery Kubasov became the world's first space construction worker when, as flight engineer of Soyuz 6 in October 1969, he operated a prototype welding unit that may one day be used in the assembly of orbiting space stations. The Vulkan unit, as it was called, remained in the orbital module of Soyuz 6 and was operated by remote control by Kubasov, who remained inside the reentry module with commander Georgy Shonin.

It was the single highlight of a spaceflight whose original goals remained secret for many years: the simultaneous flight of three manned Soyuz spacecraft, 6, 7, and 8, carrying seven cosmonauts, for one week. It is now known that Soyuz 7 and Soyuz 8 were to have docked, which was prevented by a failure in the Soyuz 8 range-finder. Soyuz 6 was to have photographed the docking.

Kubasov later served as flight engineer for the Soviet half of the Apollo-Soyuz Test Project. For 6 days Kubasov and commander Alexei Leonov orbited the Earth in Soyuz 19, remaining docked with the American Apollo spacecraft for 2 of those days. It was the culmination of a 2-year training and public relations program that involved astronauts and cosmonauts visiting other's space centers.

On his third spaceflight, Soyuz 36, Kubasov served as commander with Hungarian pilot Bertalan Farkas as cosmonaut-researcher. This Interkosmos mission lasted 8 days, during which Kubasov and Farkas visited cosmonauts Popov and Ryumin aboard the Salyut 6 space station. Altogether, Kubasov spent almost 19 days in space.

Kubasov was born January 7, 1935, in Vyazniki, Vladimir Region, northeast of Moscow. His aptitude for mathematics and excellent grades in secondary school earned him easy admittance to the Moscow Aviation Institute in 1952. After graduating as an aerospace engineer in 1958, Kubasov immediately went to work at the Korolev spacecraft design bureau.

Kubasov was first involved in ballistics, the calculation of spacecraft trajectories, but later worked on the Voskhod spacecraft under designer Mikhail Tikhonravov.

Kubasov was one of the young engineers who deluged chief designer Korolev with applications for cosmonaut training. Kubasov was accepted by Korolev in June 1964, but the formation of the civilian cosmonaut group was postponed. He finally began space training in May 1966 with seven others.

He was chosen as a backup crewman for the proposed dual flight of Soyuz 1 and Soyuz 2 scheduled for April 1967, working with Andrian Nikolayev and Viktor Gorbatko on Soyuz 2 on techniques for walking in space from one docked Soyuz to another. Soyuz 2 was not launched, however, due to problems that arose early in the Soyuz 1 mission, and the death of cosmonaut Vladimir Komarov at the end of that flight forced an 18-month suspension of Soviet manned launches.

When they resumed, Kubasov remained as backup to Alexei Yeliseyev, who performed an EVA transfer from Soyuz 5 to Soyuz 4 during the January 1969 mission.

Following Soyuz 6, Kubasov trained for the second in a series of missions aboard the new Salyut space station in 1971. But the first crew sent to Salyut failed to go aboard the station. Kubasov, commander Alexei Leonov, and researcher Pyotr Kolodin then prepared to fly the initial mission, scheduled to last 2 months. But on June 4, 1971, just 2 days prior to the launch, Kubasov was diagnosed with a lung ailment. He was immediately removed from flight status.

Kubasov's ailment was soon diagnosed as nothing more than an allergic reaction to pesticides being sprayed around the cosmodrome. Returned to flight status, he and Leonov trained as a 2-man team for Salyut missions in 1972 and 1973, which were not launched because of other problems.

Following the second abortive flight, in May 1973, they were assigned to Apollo-Soyuz. Neither of them spoke English but, as cosmonaut chief Vladimir Shatalov pointed out to them, they had more than 2 years in which to learn. However, during his encounters with American astronauts Kubasov rarely spoke, in marked contrast to the ebullient Leonov.

In 1975 Kubasov succeeded Sergei Anokhin as the director of the civilian cosmonaut department at the Korolev bureau, which was now being called the Energiya scientific-production enterprise (NPO). Kubasov super-

vised the selection of the 1978 group of candidate flight engineers and physician cosmonauts.

Kubasov became a civilian Soyuz commander in October 1977, when the Soyuz 25 docking failure caused the state commission in charge of manned spaceflights to issue an edict: no more rookie crews. All experienced Soyuz commanders were assigned elsewhere, so engineers Nikolai Rukavishnikov and Kubasov were given what turned out to be a unique opportunity. Replacing a rookie pilot, Kubasov served as backup commander for the Soviet-Polish Soyuz-30 in 1978.

In June 1987 Kubasov became deputy director of a department at NPO Energiya developing new life support systems for long-term missions. He retired as an active cosmonaut in October 1993.

He is the author of several technical papers and of a memoir, *To Touch Space* (1984).

Kugno, Eduard Pavlovich

1935–

Aviation engineer Eduard Kugno was enrolled in the Soviet cosmonaut group in January 1963. Without ever training for a spaceflight, he was dismissed from the group on June 17, 1964, for "inability to tolerate weightlessness."

The stated reason masked one of the earliest dismissals from the cosmonaut group for political unreliability: at a meeting in the spring of 1964 Kugno was rash enough to openly criticize the "new cult of personality" he saw forming around Soviet Premier Nikita Krushchev. He was supported in his views by Lev Vorobyov, another cosmonaut. Gagarin Center training officials—notably director Nikolai Kamanin—were outraged, and began the process of expelling both Kugno and Vorobyov.

Ultimately Vorobyov, who was a member of the Communist Party, was allowed to stay, but Kugno was transferred to a laboratory at the Yeisk Higher Air Force School in the Crimea.

But Kugno's involvement with the cosmonaut group didn't end there. Following Khrushchev's ouster in October 1964, Kugno applied directly to air force chief of staff

Marshal Konstantin Vershinin for reinstatement as a cosmonaut. Vershinin reportedly promised Kugno that given the new political circumstances, his banishment would be considered to be a "temporary reassignment," and that after a year he would be readmitted to the group. Kugno returned to Yeisk, where he was now an engineer with an air force squadron based there.

After a year at Yeisk, was summoned to Moscow. For 10 days he waited as his documents were scrutinized. Eventually he was told there were no present "openings" in the cosmonaut team, and that he was not going to be readmitted. Kugno realized he had better get on with his career, and made no further attempts to return to the cosmonaut team.

Kugno was born June 27, 1935, in Poltava, Ukraine. He attended the Kiev Higher Air Force Engineering School, graduating in 1958, then was assigned to a squadron in the Northern Fleet near Murmansk, where future cosmonauts Yuri Gagarin and Georgy Shonin were also serving.

In 1961 Kugno was transferred to Moscow, then to Leningrad. It was at this time that he wrote a letter to General Kamanin, the director of cosmonaut training, asking for admittance to the group. On January 11, 1963, following several months of medical and other tests, Kugno was one of the 15 candidates included in the second air force enrollment.

While at Yeisk in 1965 Kugno began graduate study for his candidate of technical sciences degree. He left Yeisk in 1968 and spent 2 years as a Soviet air force advisor in the Algerian People's Democratic Republic. He returned to the USSR in 1970 to work at the Riga Higher Air Force Engineering School, followed by assignments at similar institutions in Irkustk (1976–86) and Kiev (1986–90). He retired from the air force in 1990 with the rank of colonel.

Kugno eventually became a Party member, in 1967, only to leave it in 1991, to protest oppression by Soviet police forces in Lithuania.

He also became a Master of Sport, with 876 parachute jumps to his credit.

Kugno currently lives in Irkutsk.

Kuklin, Anatoly Petrovich
1932–

Pilot Anatoly Kuklin was a member of the second cosmonaut enrollment in January 1963. He trained as a potential Spiral spaceplane pilot, and also as a Soyuz commander, but ultimately never flew in space.

Kuklin was born January 3, 1932, in Satka, Chelyabinsk Region, Russia, and graduated from secondary school in Sverdlovsk. He attended a special military prep school there in 1949, then entered the Stalingrad (or Volgograd) Higher Air Force School.

Upon qualifying as a pilot in October 1952, Kuklin served for a year with 119th Air Regiment, 104th Air Division of the 22nd Air Army, Northern Military District. From 1953 to 1957 he was with the 770th Air Regiment, 16th Air Guards Division, 22nd Air Army with Soviet forces in Germany. He attended the Red Banner (later Yuri Gagarin) Air Force Academy from 1957 to 1961, and was a senior pilot with the 234th Air Regiment, 9th Air Division, Moscow military district when enrolled in the cosmonaut team.

Qualified as a cosmonaut in January 1965, Kuklin was assigned to the Spiral manned orbital spaceplane program. Along with Gherman Titov and Anatoly Filipchenko, Kuklin attended the Chkalov test pilot school from January to June 1967. A year later Kuklin transferred to the Soviet manned lunar orbit program, serving as a potential commander. From April to July 1969 he was backup commander for the Soyuz 6/7/8 missions, until he was removed for medical reasons. He was declared ineligible for assignment to spaceflights in 1971, but remained in the cosmonaut team for another 4 years.

After leaving the cosmonaut team in September 1975 Kuklin worked on the Main Staff of the Soviet air force. He left military service in 1980.

Kuleshova, Natalya Dmitryevna

1956–

Aerospace engineer Natalya Kuleshova was one of the 9 women candidates approved by the state commission for cosmonaut training on July 30, 1980. In the summer of 1982 Kuleshova, an engineer from NPO Energiya, was the first selection to be backup for Svetlana Savitskaya in the crew of Soyuz T-7, but was later disqualified. She subsequently trained as a potential flight engineer for a Mir space station crew, but, again, she was was not selected.

She left the Energiya cosmonaut team in April 1992.

Kuleshova was born March 14, 1955, in Novy Gorodok, Odintsovo District, Moscow Region. She attended the Moscow Aviation Institute, graduating in 1978, when she joined NPO Energiya.

Kuzhelnaya, Nadezdha Vasilyevna

1962–

Nadezhda Kuzhelnaya is an engineer with the RKK Energiya who enrolled as a cosmonaut candidate in April 1994. She completed the initial training course in the spring of 1996 and in September of that year was assigned to the cosmonaut group preparing for missions to the International Space Station.

In July 1997 she was named flight engineer for a Soyuz visit to I.S.S. scheduled for launch in the summer of 2000. She and commander Talgat Musabayev are to deliver a fresh Soyuz return vehicle to the second incremental crew (Yuri Usachev, James Voss, and Susan Helms).

Kuzhelnaya was born January 6, 1962, in the settlement of Alexeyevskaya, Alexeyevskaya District, Tatar Republic. When she was a year old her family moved to Ukraine, where Kuzhelnaya graduated from secondary school and entered an institute for the construction industry. At the insitute she also joined the airplane and parachuting club and realized she would rather work in the aviation business. In 1984 Kuzhelnaya transferred to the Moscow Aviation Institute, graduating in 1988.

From 1988 to 1994 Kuzhelnaya worked at RKK Energiya as a design engineer specializing in spacecraft flight control systems. She applied to join the cosmonaut team in 1991.

Kuznetsova (Pitskelauri), Tatyana Dmitryevna

1941–

Tanya Kuznetsova was one of the 5 women selected for cosmonaut training in March 1962. A 20-year-old parachutist at the time, she is the youngest person ever selected for spaceflight training.

Beginning in April 1965 she trained in the second crew of the proposed Voskhod 4 mission, scheduled for launch in 1966. Voskhod 4 was to have carried a crew of 2 women on a 10-day flight, during which one of them would have performed an EVA. The mission was canceled, however, in early 1966.

Kuznetsova was born July 14, 1941, in Gorky, where she became a member of a flying club and a parachutist. She moved to Moscow, continuing her parachuting and setting several world records.

While attending an air show at Tushino, a Moscow suburb, in September 1961 she heard about the formation of a group of women cosmonauts. She applied and was selected. Like others, she was enlisted in the Soviet air force as a private, though later commissioned a junior lieutenant.

Kuznetsova may have hurt her chances of making a flight when she married an air force officer named Pitskelauri while in training. Both air force space chief Nikolai Kamanin and chief designer Sergei Korolev had asked the women cosmonauts to remain single until they had a chance to fly in space. At any rate, Kuznetsova was not qualified as a cosmonaut in October 1962 along with her four colleagues, but in January 1965.

Kuznetsova also attended the Zhukovsky Air Force Engineering Academy from 1962 to 1969.

When the women's cosmonaut group was disbanded in October 1969, Kuznetsova joined the staff of the

Gagarin Cosmonaut Training Center. Most recently she has been head of a geophysical laboratory at the Center, training crews in the execution of geophysical experiments in space.

Latysheva, Irina Dmitryevna

1953–

Radio engineer Irina Latysheva was designated a cosmonaut-researcher in February 1982, and from 1982 to 1984 underwent training for a possible mission aboard the Salyut space station but ultimately was not assigned to a crew.

Latysheva was born July 9, 1953, in Moscow. She graduated from the Moscow Energy Institute in 1977, then joined the staff of the Moscow Institute of Radiotechnology and Electronics (MIRZ), a unit of the Academy of Sciences. Beginning in December 1979 Laytsheva underwent preliminary selection and training at the NPO Energiya for the proposed women cosmonaut unit, and upon being enrolled the following July 30, transferred from MIRZ to the Institute for Space Research (IKI), the Russian equivalent of the NASA Jet Propulsion Laboratory.

Latysheva was officially retired as an Academy of Sciences cosmonaut-researcher in 1994, but continues to work as a senior scientific staffer at the IKI.

Laveikin, Alexandr Ivanovich

1951–

Alexandr Laveikin was the flight engineer of Soyuz TM-2, the first expedition to the Mir space station. Two days after launch from the Baikonur center Laveikin and mission commander Yuri Romanenko reached Mir on February 7, 1987, for a scheduled 10-month mission.

Laveikin, like many astronauts and cosmonauts, was ill during his first days in orbit. Eventually, however, he and Romanenko set up housekeeping, receiving supplies from the Progress 27 and Progress 28 tankers in February and March, and overseeing the attachment of the first permanent "add-on" Mir module, the astrophysical observatory Kvant (Quantum).

Unknown problems prevented Kvant from docking with Mir during the first attempt on April 9. Three days later, with the massive module resting just a few feet from Mir, the cosmonauts performed an unplanned space walk during which Laveikin discovered a plastic bag blocking one of the latches in the docking module. (The bag had been stashed inside Progress 28 by the cosmonauts, but had floated out and become jammed in the adaptor.) Once the blockage was removed, Kvant was able to dock with Mir.

The stressful training and performance of the space walk, however, had an adverse affect on Laveikin. He apparently blamed himself for the obstruction, which nearly resulted in the loss of Kvant. And he had been complaining of difficulty in sleeping. Soviet doctors, monitoring Laveikin from the flight control center, also noted an irregularity in his heartbeat. Reluctantly, flight directors made plans to replace him on Mir with cosmonaut Alexandr Alexandrov, then training for the USSR-Syrian mission scheduled for launch on July 23. The decision was made in late June, but Laveikin himself was not told until a week before the swap. Predictably, he was depressed, but returned to Earth without incident on July 30 along with pilot Alexandr Viktorenko and Syrian researcher Mohammed Faris.

Laveikin was born April 21, 1951, in Moscow. His father was an air force pilot and Hero of the Soviet Union, Major General Ivan Pavlovich Laveikin, who died 2 months before his son's launch. The younger Laveikin attended the Bauman Higher Technical School, graduating in 1974, then went to work at the Energiya Scientific and Production Association (NPO), where he tested space structures.

Laveikin was enrolled as a candidate cosmonaut in December 1978, working on the Buran space shuttle and serving at the control center in Kaliningrad. During this time he also became a pilot, learning to fly the L-29 aircraft in which cosmonauts were able to simulate weightlessness.

In 1982 Laveikin trained with commander Yuri Malyshev for a visiting mission to Salyut 7 that was later canceled.

He was assigned to the Mir training group in 1984 and joined commander Yuri Romanenko in August 1985. The Romanenko-Laveikin team trained as backups to cosmonaut Titov and Serebrov for the first Mir mission, moving up to prime crew less than a month prior to launch when Serebrov failed the final preflight physicals.

Following his premature return to Earth Laveikin was recertified as fit for future spaceflights. In 1991 he was assigned as backup flight engineer for Soyuz TM-13, a planned Soviet-Austrian visit to Mir. Financial problems forced two missions to be combined and no flight engineer flew on Soyuz TM-13. Laveikin subsequently lost flight status and retired from the Energiya cosmonaut team in March 1994, and from Energiya itself the following month.

Lazarev, Vasily Grigoryevich
1928–1990

Vasily Lazarev was a test pilot and flight surgeon who had the bad luck to command the Soviet Union's first launch abort.

Lazarev and flight engineer Oleg Makarov were launched toward the orbiting Salyut 4 space station on April 5, 1975, for a planned 60-day mission. In September 1973 these same two cosmonauts had flown the 2-day Soyuz 12 mission, which requalified the Soviet spacecraft for manned flight following the Soyuz 11 disaster. This new, long-duration mission would set a Soviet space record and with the presence of a veteran aerospace physician, would provide new insights into human adaptability to weightlessness.

But just minutes after launch from the Baikonur Cosmodrome, at a height of about 90 miles—the point where the Soyuz launcher drops its second stage and continues to orbit using the single third stage engine—a malfunction occurred. The explosive bolts that should have separated the stages failed. The third stage engine ignited with the massive second stage still attached, and the whole vehicle began to tumble out of control. Ground controllers had to no choice but to separate the Soyuz from the errant rocket. Lazarev and Makarov endured a painful 18-G reentry that landed them on a mountainside near the Soviet-Chinese border. Their "flight" lasted just 21 minutes—the shortest in Soviet space history—was later known as the April 5th Anomaly, and finally as Soyuz 18-1.

It is thought that Lazarev, who was 47 at the time of Soyuz 18-1, suffered injuries during the reentry that made him ineligible for future missions, but in 1980, at the age of 52, he served as backup commander for the Soyuz T-3 mission to Salyut 6.

Lazarev was born February 23, 1928, in the village of Poroshino, Kytmanovsky District in the Altai Territory of Siberia. He grew up in the city of Sverdlovsk (later renamed Yekaterinburg) and attended the medical institute there from 1948 to 1951, intending to become a surgeon. During his final year he switched his field of study to aviation medicine and transferred to the Saratov Medical Institute, where he received his degree in 1952. Following several months as a flight surgeon in the 30th Air Army, he spent 2 years at the Chuguyev Higher Air Force School becoming a military pilot.

Lazarev served initially as an air force flight instructor at Chuguyev, but in January 1956 joined the flight test center in Chkalovskaya, outside of Moscow, where he served for 3 years. In August 1959, he joined the nearby Institute for Aviation Medicine (NII-7), where he tested new equipment for aircraft. He applied for admission to the cosmonaut team in 1959, like his fellow test engineer Vladimir Komarov, but was not selected. A second application in 1962 also failed. However, later that year Lazarev took part in a series of flights in Volga-class high-altitude balloons, during which test subjects wearing prototype pressure suits were carried to altitudes of 20 miles, from which they parachuted to Earth. This work brought Lazarev to the attention of the Soviet air force's deputy commander for space, Lieutenant General Nikolai Kamanin, who also headed the cosmonaut training program. In May 1964 Kamanin personally nominated Lazarev as a crewmember for the first Voskhod mission; Lazarev went through several flight simulations with other crewmembers before being replaced by Boris Yegorov, a civilian physician.

Kamanin recalled Lazarev to training in February 1965, for another proposed Voskhod mission, later canceled. When an opening occurred in the military cosmonaut team in January 1966, Lazarev was made a permanent member, officially completing training in December 1967.

Lazarev spent 2 years training for the Almaz military space station program. When Almaz was delayed, he joined the Soyuz training group as backup commander for Soyuz 9 in 1970 and as commander for the Kontakt program. He began training for Salyut flights in October 1971.

From March 1976 to January 1982, Lazarev headed the Salyut training group within the cosmonaut team, supervising the training of cosmonauts from Interkosmos countries. With flight engineer Gennady Strekalov and physician Valery Polyakov he trained throughout much of 1980 for a Soyuz T mission. In early 1981, however, he failed a physical and lost flight status, though he continued to command the group of military cosmonaut-researchers. He remained on staff at the Gagarin Center until November 1985, when he transferred to reserve status, becoming a civilian associate of the *Znaniye* organization.

Lazarev coauthored a biography of cosmonaut Vladimir Komarov, *Spacecraft Test Pilot* (1976), and an autobiography, *Runway* (1990).

He died in Moscow on December 31, 1990, after what was described as a "long illness" but was later confirmed to have been a case of alcohol poisoning. (Lazarev and another air force officer had been given a gift of what turned out to be wood alcohol during a visit to the city of Lvov. The other officer died almost instantly; Lazarev lingered for 10 days before succumbing.)

Lazutkin, Alexandr Ivanovich

1957–

Alexandr Lazutkin was flight engineer of the ill-starred Mir-23 crew, launched to the orbital space station in February 1997 aboard Soyuz TM-25. While still in the process of taking over the station from the Mir-22 crew of Korzun and Kaleri, Lazutkin and commander Vasily Tsibliyev were confronted with a serious fire in the station's Kvant module on the evening of February 23. It started when Lazutkin ignited a perchlorate "candle" to generate extra oxygen for the six crewmembers aboard Mir at the time. The faulty candle spewed smoke and flame for several minutes, forcing the crew to don gas masks and consider emergency evacuation procedures if the fire burned through the wall of Kvant. Fortunately the fire died out.

Within 2 weeks, the primary and secondary oxygen-generation systems aboard Mir both failed, forcing the crew to rely on the candles until repairs could be made.

Lazutkin and Tsibliyev resumed normal day-to-day operations in March and April, with NASA-Mir researcher Jerry Linenger, who was replaced by Michael Foale in May. Among their experiments the crew observed Comet Hale-Bopp with Mir's Glazar-2 ultraviolet telescope. There were other nagging problems with a failed toilet and a coolant leak.

The crisis began on June 25, when the Progress M-34 supply craft rammed the Spektr module during a routine redocking. As Spektr began to vent its atmosphere into space, Lazutkin and Foale scrambled to cut cables so the damaged module could be sealed off. They were successful, but at a price: for weeks Mir was forced to operate with reduced power.

Resupplied by Progress M-35 in early July, the crew began the fatiguing task of making repairs to systems, which kept failing, and planning an intravehicular space walk to examine Spektr. Sleeping badly, Tsibliyev began to suffer an irregular heartbeat, and mission doctors forbade him to take part in the IVA. On July 16, 1987, a fatigued Lazutkin inadvertently disconnected a cable, which caused Mir to drift out of control for several hours. Control was successfully reestablished, but the incident caused Mir controllers to assign the difficult IVA to the next crew, Solovyov and Vinogradov, who would have time to simulate the repairs in the Gagarin Center hydrobasin.

Returning to Earth on August 14, Lazutkin and Tsibliyev suffered a hard landing when the special braking rockets of their Soyuz fired at an altitude of several hundred feet rather than the usual six feet. Their reception by Gagarin Center and Energiya officials was also strained, with talk that the cosmonauts would lose all or most of their flight bonuses (a sum equivalent to $70,000) for purported mistakes made during the mission.

An investigative panel concluded that the fire, collision, and subsequent system failures could not be blamed on the cosmonauts, and they received their bonuses.

In spite of the experience, Lazutkin remains an active cosmonaut and is currently assigned as backup flight engineer for Soyuz TM-29, scheduled for launch in early 1999.

Lazutkin was born October 30, 1957, and attended the Moscow Aviation Institute, graduating in 1981. From 1981 to 1984 he was an instructor at MAI in aviation technology and parachuting. Since 1984 he has been employed at the RKK Energiya.

Lazutkin was one of 3 Energiya engineers approved for cosmonaut training on March 3, 1992, by the state credentials committee. (He had passed the medical examinations on September 14, 1989.) In March 1994 he completed the training course that qualified him as a Soyuz-Mir crewmember.

Lazutkin and fellow candidate Sergei Treshchev were teamed with pilot Sergei Vozovikov for survival training near the Black Sea in July 1993. It was during a break in training that Vozovikov went diving and was drowned.

Lebedev, Valentin Vitalyevich

1942–

Valentin Lebedev was flight engineer aboard the Soyuz-T-5 mission to Salyut 7 in 1982. Lebedev and commander Anatoly Berezovoy spent 7 months in space—a record at the time—performing a variety of technical and scientific work, deploying two student satellites, and playing host to visitors who included French spationaut Jean-Loup Chretien and the second woman space traveler, Svetlana Savistkaya.

In his diary, *211 Days in Space*, published after his return to Earth, Lebedev was frank about the experience of such a long mission, discussing the joy with which he and Berezovoy greeted the Soyuz T-7 crew (understandably, they weren't quite so relaxed about the Soyuz T-6 visit, which included a Westerner) and the nervousness they felt before a space walk.

He also wrote candidly that while he and Berezovoy both thought they knew each other well before the flight, in spite of the fact that they had only trained together for 5 months prior to launch, they found out that both were nitpickers and perfectionists. (Berezovoy had replaced Lebedev's original commander, Yuri Isaulov, when Isaulov failed a medical examination.)

It was later revealed that by the end of the mission the two cosmonauts were barely speaking to each other.

Lebedev and Berezovoy have since suggested that space teams should consist of people with opposite personality traits.

Lebedev was in an earlier space crew, Soyuz 13 in December 1973. He and Pyotr Klimuk spent 8 days in orbit using the Orion observatory to do astronomical studies of Comet Kahoutek.

Lebedev was born April 14, 1942, in Moscow. After completing secondary school in 1958, Lebedev, who was fascinated by aviation, attended the Orenburg Higher Air Force School, the same one that trained Yuri Gagarin to be a pilot, intending to qualify as an air force navigator. Unfortunately, Lebedev had completed only a year of training when the Orenburg school was closed. He was given the option of transferring to another air force school, or enrolling in a civilian university and completing his military service as a reservist. He chose the latter, entering the Moscow Aviation Institute, where one of his professors was Vasily Mishin, deputy to Sergei Korolev, the chief designer of Soviet manned spacecraft.

When a new group of air force cosmonaut candidates was recruited in the spring of 1965, Mishin suggested Lebedev as a candidate. Lebedev had high blood pressure and could not pass the physical, however. A second attempt in August of that year also failed.

By this time Lebedev was already working at the OKB Korolev, first as a test engineer on the N1 rocket, then in search-and-rescue teams. (He accompanied the Zond 5 Moon probe back from its landing site in the Indian Ocean in 1968.) He also served on tracking ships. In 1970 he became an instructor for the crews training for Soyuz 9 and the first Salyut.

Lebedev never stopped trying to become a cosmonaut. He took pilot instruction from Sergei Anokhin, head of the OKB Korolev engineer-cosmonaut department. (Ultimately he would log 300 hours of flying time in jets and helicopters.) Finally, in 1971, he passed the medical examinations.

He was one of the 7 engineers and physicians enrolled as cosmonaut candidates in March 1972. His first assignment was to the group training for the Soyuz 13 mission. Originally Lebedev had a supporting role behind a pair of two-man teams: Vorobyov-Yazdovsky and Klimuk-Ponomarev. But in 1973 he joined Klimuk, replacing Ponomarev, and in November of that year—a month before launch—the Klimuk-Lebedev team replaced the prime crew.

Returning from Soyuz 13 Lebedev completed work on a candidate of technical sciences degree (1975) and served as an advisor to a Moscow Aviation Institute team working on the Baikal-Amur railway. He had very little association with the cosmonaut team until October 1977, when Alexei Yeliseyev—the head of the Korolev/NPO Energiya manned space department—asked him to return to active training. Assigned with rookie commander Leonid Popov to one of the Soyuz 27 backup crews, Lebedev had to learn Salyut 6's systems in 6 weeks.

Lebedev and Popov later served as backups to Soyuz 28 (1978) and Soyuz 32 (1979). In March 1980, while preparing for the Soyuz 35 mission, Lebedev injured his knee while working out on a trampoline. (Lebedev was then chairman of the USSR Federation of Acrobatics.)

Forced to undergo surgery, he had to give up his place on the Soyuz 35 crew.

Returning from Soyuz T-5 Lebedev felt that he would not be assigned to another Soyuz-Salyut mission, so in April 1983 he joined the team of test pilots and engineers working on the Buran space shuttle. He was told that he would probably be the first flight engineer included in a Buran crew.

Three years later, however, the often outspoken Lebedev published an article in the newspaper *Izvestia* that angered NPO Energiya chief Valentin Glushko. Glushko summoned Lebedev to his office the following morning for a dressing down, then transferred him out of the Buran program.

Lebedev continued to work at Energiya until November 1989, when he accepted a position at the GeoInformation Institute of the USSR Academy of Sciences. In February 1991 he became director of the institute.

ROUGH DAYS

by Valentin Lebedev

(Valentin Lebedev, a 40-year-old civilian fight engineer, teamed with Soviet pilot cosmonaut Anatoly Berezovoy, also 40, for a mission aboard Salyut-7 that began in May 1982. Scheduled to last 6 months, the cosmonauts were offered the chance to remain in space for an additional month, breaking Ryumin and Popov's endurance record. At the same time, the strain was beginning to tell on the crew, as Lebedev recorded in his in-flight diary.)

September 14, 1982

The day for "signing" the working agreement to continue the flight. We also conducted geophysical experiments. At the same time we are making a video of the Earth. We want to follow Gagarin's orbit and see the Earth as he first saw it.

At 2 P.M. we were told officially that we could continue the flight for 40 days more than [the 175] scheduled. We agreed, but only on the condition that our goal is not just

setting a new record of over 200 days in space; the extension must be justified with additional experimental work. We also asked for more freedom in planning our days, and for another EVA. The flight control center promised to consult with scientists about a second EVA, and said it would try to arrange all our other requests.

Now we will fly 3 more months! This will be hard, but isn't it what I wanted before launch? The record? Everybody wants to set one to test his own abilities! After it's over, we'll be glad we did it. Our health is good and so is our mood.

The [Progress] re-supply ship will come soon. Our life will be better. I'm happy and confident that we will handle this. So, Valya, we'll see if you have the stomach for it. After the flight we will rest separately, as we agreed. We are tired of each other, cramped in here in this small station.

September 15, 1982
Now we will try to get the Korund furnace to work. Twice we turned it on, and both times after 2.5 hours the automatic signal went off, indicating overheating. We have to do something with it.

Flight control asked us to program the Delta computer with 325 six-digit number codes. I almost went blind entering those numbers! If I had made a mistake in a single one, the check sums wouldn't have matched and I would have had to repeat the whole process from scratch! A hell of a job.

I wish I could be sure that everything is all right. The other day I lost half a day because of two mistakes in a radiogram [from flight control]. When I told the shift director about it, he said that he knew about the mistakes, but decided not to worry us! What can I say to that? For the sake of good relations with TsUP I have to restrain myself. It's like enduring a long period of celibacy during a marriage—painful, but sometimes necessary.

I begin to collect data for my Ph.D. dissertation.

September 16, 1982
Today we must test the dynamic orientation of the station and work out methods of autonomous navigation. I made a table of astrophysical sources incorporating data from the AO-2 startracker and the C-2 sextant.

I remember the proposal I made about the Orion radio-telescope on my first flight [Soyuz 13, 1973]. The 3000-angstrom emissions from stars and other galaxies are completely absorbed by the atmosphere, and are impossible to register from the ground, even with high-tech equipment and large telescopes. A 1-meter telescope in space is the equivalent of a 6-meter one on the ground. I asked the shift director to to arrange such an experiment with scientists from the Sternberg State Astrophysical Institute. He promised to do it.

The station is silent. We don't turn on the music. Tolya and I don't talk to each other much, either. For some reason I don't sleep well any more. I wake up at 4 or 5 A.M. every day and I don't understand why. I'm probably filled with anxiety from the constant excitement during the day. Fatigue and anxiety from hard work press down on me. I fall asleep immediately, but eventually the anxiety overwhelms me, and wakes me up. I try to do more work during the day, to exhaust myself so I can get more sleep. I also try to get to bed later.

Now I am lying in my sleeping bag. I feel that something presses and oppresses me. I have a strange double feeling: my mind is heavy, but inside I feel a peace born of the assurance that one day everything will be over. Thinking of that, I imagine the depth of the world and myself, believing in the power that can calm the anxiety of mind. Suddenly I can feel the anxiety evaporate, and relaxation and peace come to me. I fall asleep immediately.

Leonov, Alexei Arkhipovich
1934–

Alexei Leonov became the first man to walk in space when he floated outside the spacecraft Voskhod 2 for 10 minutes on March 18, 1965.

It was during the second orbit of the Voskhod 2 flight, just as the spacecraft approached the Soviet Union, that Leonov, clad in a white pressure suit and wearing a backpack that would supply him with oxygen, crawled into a cylindrical airlock that had been inflated on the side of Voskhod. Commander Pavel Belyayev closed the inner hatch behind Leonov and, moments later, after the air had been bled out of the airlock, Leonov, secured by a safety line, opened the outer hatch and uncovered a movie camera. Then he pushed himself away from the spacecraft, stretching the lifeline to its 17.5-foot limit, and pulled himself back. Inside Voskhod, Belyayev heard scraping noises as Leonov's feet contacted the spacecraft.

Minutes later Leonov was back inside Voskhod 2, after a nervous moment when he discovered that his pressure suit was so rigid he could not bend enough to get inside the airlock. He quickly solved the problem by bleeding some of the air out of his suit.

Leonov and Belyayev were to experience further unplanned adventure. The next day, as ground controllers prepared to fire the Voskhod retrorockets and return the craft to Earth, the cosmonauts noticed that their ship was facing the wrong direction. Belyayev activated the manual control system and fired the retrorockets on the next orbit.

The delay, however, meant that Voskhod 2 did not land in the prime recovery area, but in the snowy Ural mountains near the city of Perm. Though they were able to make radio contact with rescue teams, the cosmonauts were forced to spend a cold night in the wilderness.

Leonov, a gifted athlete and pilot who had also trained himself to be a painter, was later chosen to command the Soviet crew for the Apollo-Soyuz Test Project. During this weeklong mission in July 1975, Leonov and flight engineer Valery Kubasov spent 2 days docked with three American astronauts aboard an Apollo spacecraft.

Leonov was born May 30, 1934, in the Siberian village of Listvyanka, Kemerovo Region, Russia. He came from a large family and decided to become a pilot after one of his older brothers became an air force mechanic. First he attended the Kremenchug Higher Air Force School (1953–55), then the Chuguyev Higher Air Force school in the Ukraine, graduating in 1957. He served as a fighter pilot with the 113th Air Regiment, 10th Air Guards Division of the 69th Air Army in the Kiev military district from 1957 to 1959. At the time of his selection for the cosmonaut team he was with the 294th Air Reconnaissance Regiment, 24th Air Army, with Soviet forces in East Germany.

Of the first twenty Soviet cosmonauts, who began training in March 1960, Leonov was the least senior in rank, a fact that subjected him to some good-natured teasing. But his quick wit and cheerful temperament won him many friends, and according to at least one published report he was an early candidate to make the world's first flight into space, until concern over the Vostok hatch and ejection seat encouraged program managers to choose cosmonauts Gagarin and Titov, who were several inches shorter than Leonov. Nevertheless, Leonov was actively involved in Gagarin's flight, acting as assistant communications operator.

In 1960 Leonov's space career and his life almost came to an end when his car skidded off an icy road near the entrance to Star Town and plunged into a lake. Leonov managed to pull his wife and his driver from the icy water. The lake has since been known as Lake Leonov.

Leonov was selected to train for the world's first walk in space in the fall of 1962. For the next 18 months he would make dozens of special "weightless" flights in aircraft and spend hundreds of hours running (logging 300 miles), bicycling (600 miles), and skiing (almost 200 miles) in order to prepare himself.

After Voskhod 2 Leonov was named deputy commander of the first squad (civilian programs) within the cosmonaut team, supervising EVA training for Soyuz-1/Soyuz-2 space walk and serving as communications operator for that ill-fated mission. He also completed studies at the Zhukovsky Academy (1968).

Beginning in November 1966, however, Leonov had a more challenging assignment: as commander of a crew training for manned circumlunar and lunar landing missions. Teamed with flight engineer Oleg Makarov, Leonov trained on the Soyuz-Zond spacecraft, made test "moon-walks" on a special lunar surface built at the training center, and even learned to pilot helicopters (just like American Apollo astronauts).

In the fall of 1968 the teams of Leonov-Makarov and Bykovsky-Rukavishnikov were ready to fly a Soyuz-Zond around the Moon in hopes of beating the American Apollo 8. But one of the necessary unmanned preliminary flights, Zond 6 in November, suffered a loss of cabin pressure during reentry. The cosmonauts felt that the problem could be solved, and were ready for flight, but the state commission decided otherwise. The manned circumlunar mission, known as L-1, was canceled.

Leonov and Makarov continued to train for a possible lunar landing until late in 1969, when that attempt was indefinitely postponed. Leonov transferred to the group of cosmonauts training for long-term Earth orbital missions aboard the Salyut space station.

In early June 1971 Leonov, flight engineer Valery Kubasov and researcher Pyotr Kolodin were preparing for a 40-day visit to the first Salyut Kubasov was diagnosed with a lung ailment. With launch less than 2 days away, the men in charge of crew assignments—Gagarin Center director Nikolai Kuznetsov, cosmonaut training director Nikolai Kamanin, chief designer Vasily Mishin, and state commission chairman Kerim Kerimov—elected to replace Kubasov with his backup, Vladislav Volkov.

Volkov joined Leonov and Kolodin in a simulation, which convinced Leonov that Volkov was not as well trained as he should be. Volkov, however, appealed to chief designer Mishin—his mentor—who then proposed to replace the entire prime crew with the backup crew. Kolodin protested angrily, but the decision stood. Soyuz 11 was launched with Dobrovolsky, Volkov, and Patsayev, who spent 24 days aboard Salyut 1, only to die on return to Earth.

When Kubasov recovered and returned to flight status, he and Leonov made up a 2-man Salyut crew. They saw two different Salyut stations fail—one because of a Proton launch failure in July 1972, the other because of a stuck steering rocket aboard Salyut in May 1973.

Following the second failure Leonov and Kubasov were assigned to the Apollo-Soyuz Test Project, becoming frequent visitors to the United States (where Leonov impressed American astronauts with his charm and humor) and hosting visits by their NASA counterparts.

Following Apollo-Soyuz Major General Leonov served as deputy director of the Gagarin Center for air-space training (March 1976 to January 1982), then as first deputy director of the center, in charge of crew training until his retirement in October 1991. He also received a candidate of technical sciences degree (1981).

In 1985 he and Kubasov traveled to the United States for the 10-year anniversary commemoration of the Apollo-Soyuz Test Project. A frequent traveler, Leonov is active in the Association of Space Explorers.

He is also well known as a painter, having published four art books, *Wait for Us, Stars* (1967), *Stellar Roads* (1977), *Life Among the Stars* (1981), and *Man and Universe* (1984), all in collaboration with artist Andrei Sokolov. He has written and illustrated a children's book, *I Walk in Space* (1980), and has also been involved in several motion pictures: *Star System, The Loop of Orion, and The Seven Acts of God.*

For many years Leonov was the editor and chief designer of the cosmonaut group newspaper *Neptune*, which is now called *Apogee*.

Leonov left military service in March 1992 and is now a principal in the investment fund Alfa-Kapital, Moscow.

Levchenko, Anatoly Semenovich
1941–1988

Anatoly Levchenko was the cosmonaut-researcher aboard Soyuz TM-4, launched December 21, 1987, to the Mir space station. Levchenko's crewmates, commander Vladimir Titov and flight engineer Musa Manarov, relieved the resident crew of Romanenko and Alexandrov. At that time, Romanenko had spent 325 days in space.

After 8 days of difficult work executing this first "handover" mission, Levchenko, Romanenko, and Alexandrov returned to Earth in Soyuz TM-3. Because Soviet doctors were concerned about Romanenko's health after his time in space, Levchenko served as standby spacecraft pilot.

Levchenko's work didn't end upon landing in Kazakhstain on December 28. He left the Soyuz spacecraft and went immediately to a nearby airport, where he took the controls of a Tu-154 aircraft and, under medical supervision, flew it to Moscow, then back to the Baikonur Cosmodrome, a flight of 5 hours. The head of the state commission for manned flight, Lieutenant General Kerim Kerimov, revealed prior to the TM-4 launch that Levchenko, like Soyuz T-12 cosmonaut Igor Volk, was flying in space at the request of the Soviet Ministry of Aviation Production, the organization charged with the development of the Buran space shuttle. Levchenko and Volk were veteran test pilots, and these spaceflights served to give doctors an idea of how each would function during the difficult piloted reentry of such a vehicle.

Levchenko was born May 21, 1941, in the city of Krasnokutsk, Kharkhov Region, Ukraine. Tolya grew up wanting to become a pilot, but upon joining the Soviet armed forces found himself enrolled in the Air Force Engineering School in Riga. He managed to get himself reassigned to the Kremenchug Higher·Air Force School, only to have it close a year later. Ultimately he completed pilot training at the Lenin Komsomol Higher Air Force School in Chernigov, where future cosmonaut Pyotr Klimuk was one of his classmates.

Following 5 years of active duty as a MiG-21 pilot in Turkmenistan, Levchenko left the air force to enroll in the USSR Ministry of Aviation Production's civilian test pilot school in Zhukovsky. Following graduation in 1971 he became a test pilot, logging over 3,500 hours of flying time in 87 different types of aircraft. He earned the titles Merited Pilot of the USSR and Test Pilot 1st Class.

In 1978 Levchenko was one of the 5 MAP test pilots selected to train for flights of the Buran. Led by Igor Volk, the group became known as the "Wolf Pack." In 1979 and 1980 the Wolf Pack underwent a general course of cosmonaut training at the Gagarin Center.

Between April 1986 and May 1987 Levchenko commanded five flights of the BTS (large atmospheric transport) version of the Buran, one ground run and four jet-powered approach and landing tests. His pilot was his Soyuz TM-4 backup, Alexandr Shchukin.

Levchenko and Shchukin had been tentatively assigned as the backup crew for the first manned orbital flight of Buran when Levchenko died suddenly on August 6, 1988, at the Nikolai Burdenko Neurosurgical Institute in Moscow. The cause of death was a previously undetected brain tumor. (Ironically, Shchukin died 12 days later in an unrelated airplane crash.)

Lisun, Mikhail Ivanovich
1935–

Mikhail Lisun is a cosmonaut who was backup flight engineer for the Soyuz 23 and Soyuz 24 missions to the Salyut 5 space station in 1976 and 1977. He never had the chance to actually fly in space.

Lisun was born September 5, 1935, in Bakhmach, Chernigov District, Ukraine. He joined the Soviet army and graduated from the Zhdanov Higher Engineering School in Kaliningrad in 1956, then spent 4 years stationed in Brovary, Ukraine, as a combat engineer. In 1960 he entered the Kuybyshev Engineering Academy in Moscow to do graduate study.

During his senior year, 1965, the head of the academy ordered him to write a request to be enrolled in the cosmonaut team. Lisun was stunned, but complied. He was assigned to the Ministry of Defense satellite command and control center in Monino as a shift engineer, then went before the state medical commission, which approved him for cosmonaut training on October 28, 1965.

Lisun completed his initial training in December 1967. At that time he went to work on the Soyuz "VI" program, a space fighter-satellite interceptor version of the Soyuz spacecraft that was ultimately never launched. He also became qualified as a pilot and completed work for his candidate of technical sciences degree in electrical engineering (1971).

Following cancellation of Soyuz VI in 1974, Lisun joined the group of cosmonauts training for the Salyut-Almaz program. He was assigned to a crew with commander Anatoly Berezovoy in December 1974 for the second manned Almaz, Salyut 5. He trained for a later proposed Almaz mission from 1979 to 1981, but the program was canceled before launches could be made.

During much of this time Lisun served as a flight director for Soyuz-Interkosmos missions, and as a flight controller for the Kvant 2 module.

Lisun retired from the air force and resigned from the cosmonaut team in October 1989. He is currently director of the Korolev Museum in Moscow.

Lonchavov, Yuri Valentinovich

1965–

Major Yuri Lonchakov is one of the 8 Russian air force pilots selected for cosmonaut training at the Gagarin Center in July 1997. In the spring of 1999 he should qualify as a Soyuz commander and International Space Station crewmember.

Lonchakov was born March 4, 1965, in Balkash, Kazakh SSR (now the Republic of Kazakstan). He graduated from the Orenburg Higher Air Force School in 1986, then served as a pilot. At the time of his selection for cosmonaut training he was a student at the Zhukovsky Air Force Engineering Academy.

Lukyanyuk, Vasily Yurievich

1958–

Vasily Lukyanyuk is one of the 3 physicians selected for cosmonaut training by the Institute for Medical-Biological Problems (IMBP) in January 1989. In October 1990 he was enrolled as a candidate researcher at the Gagarin Center, and in February 1992 completed training.

Lukyanyuk was born September 22, 1958, in Moscow, and educated at the Sechenov First Moscow Medical Institute. He graduated in 1981, joining the staff of the Institute for Medical-Biological Problems of the Ministry of Health. In 1984 he became a candidate of medical sciences.

Since June 1994 Lukyanyuk has served as director of the IMBP cosmonaut team, replacing German Arzamazov.

Lyakhov, Vladimir Afanaseyevich

1941–

Vladimir Lyakhov commanded three of the most difficult manned missions in Soviet space history.

On September 6, 1988, he and Afghan cosmonaut-researcher Ahmad Ahad found themselves in a genuine emergency aboard their Soyuz TM-6 spacecraft. The two had undocked from the orbiting Mir space station for return to Earth following a 10-day mission. They had discarded the large, spherical orbital module on the front of the Soyuz and were awaiting the firing of the retrorockets when an infrared sensor aboard Soyuz—designed to lock on to the Earth's horizon—locked on to the sun instead. A backup sensor had the same problem, so the computer controlling the spacecraft aborted the retrofire. Seven minutes later—while Soviet flight controllers in Kaliningrad failed to find an explanation for the failure—the sensors lost the sun, so the computer switched on the rockets. Lyakhov manually shut them down after 3 seconds, afraid that the delay would land Soyuz in China.

Soyuz made two further orbits while controllers reprogrammed the computer to ignore the faulty sensor. When a second attempt at a computer-controlled reentry was made, the engines fired for only 6 seconds. Lyakhov, knowing that a failure in this attempt meant reentry couldn't be attempted for another 24 hours, restarted the engine. But it only fired for 60 seconds instead of the planned 230.

Kaliningrad ordered Lyakhov to make no further attempt to start the engines. The cosmonauts would have to wait 16 orbits, until the path of the Soyuz took it over the recovery zones, while controllers figured out how to get the engines working properly.

All the cosmonauts could do was wait in the cramped confines of the Soyuz descent module, where the temperature was 45 degrees, food was almost nonexistent, the air supply was limited, in space suits with no sanitary facilities. They had the additional worry of knowing that another reentry failure could doom them to death by suffocation.

Fortunately, the problem was traced to an incorrect computer program. A fifth reentry attempt was made on September 7, and the cosmonauts landed safely.

Ironically, the actual vehicle flown as Soyuz TM-6 had also been used earlier, on Soyuz 33 in April 1979, when cosmonauts Nikolai Rukavishnikov and Bulgarian Georgy Ivanov nearly became stranded in space.

One of the witnesses to that earlier emergency was Lyakhov himself, then commander of the crew aboard the Salyut 6 space station.

On that earlier mission, Soyuz 32, launched in February 1979, Lyakhov and flight engineer Valery Ryumin performed experiments in radio astronomy, Earth resources, and space manufacturing on Salyut 6 while establishing a new endurance record of 175 days. According to a Ryumin's diary, the flight was especially difficult psychologically because the cosmonauts had no visitors. The first scheduled guest crew of Rukavishnikov and Ivanov had been forced to return to Earth before they could dock. A second flight planned for July was postponed.

Lyakhov's second long stay in space was equally challenging. He and flight engineer Alexandr Alexandrov docked their Soyuz T-9 spacecraft with the Salyut 7 space station on June 28, 1983, for a mission scheduled to last 3 months. A fuel leak aboard Salyut forced the cosmonauts to curtail many of their scientific studies, which lengthened the mission, and then on September 26 a manned resupply craft was forced to abort at launch. Lyakhov and Alexandrov were left aboard Salyut 7 with a Soyuz T-9 vehicle that was close to exceeding its safe design lifetime. Nevertheless, after performing repairs—including emergency EVAs—on the station, Lyakhov and Alexandrov returned safely to Earth on November 23, 1983.

Lyakhov was born July 20, 1941, in the village of Antratsit, Antratsit District, Lugansk (later Voroshilovgrad) Region, Ukraine. At the age of 19 he enrolled in the Chuguyev (renamed Kharkov soon after) Higher Air Force School, graduating in 1964, then served as an air force pilot with the 777th Air Regiment, 24th Air Division, 11th Air Army, based on Sakhalin Island in the Far East. In February 1966 he transferred to the 300th Air Regiment, 29th Air Division, 11th Air Army of the Air Defense Forces in Pereslavka, Khabarovsk region.

Lyakhov applied for the October 1965 cosmonaut group but was placed in reserve, finally enrolling with 11

other officers on May 7, 1967. He completed the initial training course in June 1969 and was assigned to the Spiral spaceplane program. In 1972–73 he attended the Chkalov test pilot school at Akhtubinsk, qualifying as a test pilot third class. He has logged over 1,300 hours of flying time in 14 different types of aircraft.

From 1973 to 1975 Lyakhov attended the Gagarin Red Banner Air Force Academy. While still studying at the Academy, in 1973, he was assigned with engineer Anatoly Voronov to the group of cosmonauts training for flights in the improved Soyuz T spacecraft. In 1977 he and Georgy Grechko served as second backups for the Soyuz 25 mission. All told Lyakhov had numerous assignments as backup commander in his career. The others were Soyuz 26, Soyuz 29 (1978), the Soviet-Mongolian Soyuz 39 flight (1980), Soyuz T-5 (1982), Soyuz T-8 (1983), and Soyuz TM-5 (1988). From October 1988 to April 1993 Lyakhov served as deputy director of the 1st Directorate of the Gagarin Center while remaining an active cosmonaut. He was commander of the cosmonaut team from April 1993 until leaving active military duty in August 1994.

Lyakhov is currently deputy general director of the Rossiya publishing house.

Machinksy, Georgy Vladimirovich

1937–

Physician Georgy Machinsky was one of the 7 cosmonaut candidates enrolled in March 1972. He trained for 2 years as a cosmonaut-researcher until injuries suffered in an auto accident forced him to withdraw from the group. At the time of his selection Machinsky was on the staff of the Institute for Medical-Biological Problems of the USSR Ministry of Health.

Machinsky was born October 11, 1937, in Moscow. He attended the 1st Moscow Medical Institute named for I. M. Sechenov, graduating in 1965.

He is currently a senior researcher at IMBP.

Makarov, Oleg Grigoryevich
1933–

Oleg Makarov was the flight engineer for 4 Soviet space-flights between 1973 and 1980, twice visiting the Salyut 6 station he had helped design.

Makarov's first flight was Soyuz 12 in September 1973, the first Soviet manned mission in the wake of the Soyuz 11 tragedy that killed three cosmonauts. Following the accident the Soyuz command module had been redesigned to allow two cosmonauts to wear pressure suits, if necessary, during launch and reentry. Weight and volume limitations had made it impossible for Soyuz to carry three cosmonauts with suits, so cosmonauts from Soyuz 1 through Soyuz 11 had not worn them.

Makarov and commander Vasily Lazarev, who had been training for a long duration mission aboard a Salyut station, only to see it postponed when their 1973 Salyut failed to reach orbit, returned safely to Earth after just 2 days.

On April 5, 1975, Makarov and Lazarev were launched aboard Soyuz 18 for a planned 60-day mission aboard Salyut 4, which had been occupied for 30 days by cosmonauts Alexei Gubarev and Georgy Grechko. But only minutes into the flight problems developed with the Soyuz booster. The Soyuz command module containing Makarov and Lazarev was separated from the booster and plunged back to Earth, eventually coming to rest on a Siberian mountainside near the Chinese border. The emergency reentry profile forced the cosmonauts to endure as many as 18 Gs, twice the normal load.

The abort also created a dispute between the cosmonauts and the state commission for manned spaceflight. Soviet cosmonauts are paid bonuses (usually a lump sum equivalent to a year's salary) for each space mission. Some officials didn't think the Lazarev-Makarov abort qualified. The dispute was eventually resolved by Soviet president Leonid Brezhnev himself, who agreed to label the flight a "test of the spacecraft escape system," and paid the cosmonauts their bonus.

Makarov flew two more times, with better luck. He was aboard Soyuz 27 in January 1978, a weeklong flight during which he and commander Vladimir Dzhanibekov

docked with the Salyut 6 station, swapping vehicles with the Soyuz 26 crew of Yuri Romanenko and Georgy Grechko, who were in the first month of a planned 3-month mission. It was a rehearsal for future operations that permitted cosmonauts to remain aboard Salyut and Mir stations for missions lasting one year.

In November 1980 Makarov returned to Salyut 6 as a member of the Soyuz T-3 crew. The 3-man crew of Makarov, Leonid Kizim, and Gennady Strekalov overhauled several systems inside Salyut 6 during their 13 days in space, permitting Salyut 6 to be occupied in early 1981 for another long-duration mission.

Makarov was born January 6, 1933, in Udomlya, Udomelsky District, Tver Region, Russia. As a boy he became interested in space travel rather than airplanes, and earned admittance to the Bauman Higher Technical School in Moscow, planning to become a rocket scientist. His timing was perfect: upon graduation in 1957 he immediately went to work in Sergei Korolev's OKB-1 spacecraft design bureau and was involved in the development of Vostok, the world's first manned spaceship. He also lectured to the cosmonaut group.

He played an important role in the preparations for Voskhod 1 during 1964. One of the Voskhod crewmen was Makarov's friend and boss, engineer Konstantin Feoktistov. As soon as Makarov learned that Feoktistov had been chosen to fly in space he applied himself, earning a place in Korolev's cosmonaut team—which only existed on paper. It was only 2 years later, during which he helped design the new Soyuz spacecraft, that Makarov was enrolled in the cosmonaut team.

Beginning in November 1966 Makarov worked on the Soviet manned lunar program. The crew of Makarov and commander Alexei Leonov, in fact, was prepared for a manned circumlunar Soyuz-Zond mission in December 1968. But a technical problem with the Zond 6 unmanned flight that December forced a delay. When the American Apollo 8 astronauts succeeded in circling the Moon, the Leonov-Makarov mission was canceled.

In 1971 Makarov began to train for a long-duration mission aboard the Salyut space station.

In addition to his four spaceflights, Makarov was a backup for Soyuz T-2 in 1980. Between active flight training he continued to work at the Korolev bureau, now known as NPO Energiya. He left the Energiya cosmonaut

team in 1987, but remains a senior engineer at the company. He has also been president of the Russian chapter of the Association of Space Explorers.

In 1980 Makarov earned his candidate of technical sciences degree. A year later he published a futuristic work, *The Sails of Stellar Brigantines*, written in collaboration with Grigory Nemetsky.

Makrushin, Valery Grigoryevich
1940–

Valery Makrushin was assigned to be a cosmonaut-researcher aboard the planned flight of the fourth Almaz military space station. This Almaz vehicle—which would have been designated Salyut 7—carried an imaging radar reconnaissance system, and was to have been launched in 1981. This would also have been the first manned flight of the TKS (transport spacecraft), a 3-man Gemini-type vehicle that had been in development since 1966.

Political and budgetary problems caused the cancellation of the Almaz-TKS program in 1981, however, and Makrushin, who had been training in a crew with commander Anatoly Berezovoy and flight engineer Yuri Glazkov, returned to his job at the NPO Machinostroyeniye, builders of the Almaz-TKS system.

Makrushin was born in 1940. He attended the Leningrad (now St. Petersburg) Institute of Aviation Instrumentation, graduating in 1964, then joined the Chelomei spacecraft design bureau. Though he underwent cosmonaut training beginning in 1968, he was officially enrolled as a candidate only in March 1972, the first of several Chelomei engineers to become cosmonauts.

He left the NPO-M in 1983.

Malenchenko, Yuri Ivanovich
1961–

Yuri Malenchenko was commander of the sixteenth Mir crew, launched as Soyuz TM-19 on July 1, 1994. Malenchenko and flight engineer Talgat Musabayev joined physician-cosmonaut Valeri Polyakov, who had been aboard Mir since January of that year, for a 4-month research flight that included two EVAs.

On September 2, 1994, at the beginning of the crew's third month aboard Mir, Malenchenko performed an emergency procedure that saved not only his mission, but several follow-ons as well. Progress M-25, an unmanned cargo vessel, failed to dock automatically to the Mir complex. Knowing that without its supplies, he and Musabayev would be forced to return to Earth, Malenchenko commanded the docking from Mir itself, working with the flight control center in Kaliningrad. Progress docked and the Mir expeditions continued.

Colonel Malenchenko is assigned as the Russian member of the sixth incremental International Space Station crew, scheduled for launch aboard a Shuttle mission late in the year 2001.

Malenchenko was born December 22, 1961, in Svetlovodsk, Kirovgrad Region, Ukraine. He attended the Kharkov Institute of Radio-Electronics in 1979, then enrolled at the Kharkov Higher Air Force School, graduating in 1983. For the next 4 years he served as a fighter pilot in Tiraspol, Odessa military district.

He was one of 5 candidate pilots enrolled in the cosmonaut team in June 1987. He qualified as a Soyuz-Mir commander in July 1989 and was assigned with flight engineer Andrei Zaitsev to a proposed 18-month Mir mission that was later canceled. Between 1991 and 1993 he was teamed in different crews with flight engineers Sergei Krikalev, Nikolai Budarin, and Gennady Strekalov. He served as backup commander for Soyuz TM-18 in January 1994.

From 1990 to 1993 Malenchenko also attended the Zhukovsky Air Force Engineering Academy.

In late 1994, following his return from Mir-16, Malenchenko was severely injured in an auto accident. He was medically ineligible for flight assignment for almost 2 years thereafter, though he did serve as the Gagarin Center's representative at the NASA Johnson Space Center in early 1997.

He has also been assigned to the crew of STS-96, ISS assembly mission 2A.1, scheduled to launch in the summer of 1999.

Malyshev, Yuri Vasilyevich

1941–

Yuri Malyshev commanded the first manned test flight of a redesigned Soyuz spacecraft, Soyuz T-2 in June 1980. Malyshev and flight engineer Vladimir Aksenov made a successful rendezvous and docking with the orbiting Salyut 6 space station in spite of the failure of the new Soyuz T guidance computer. They returned to Earth after 4 days.

Four years later Malyshev commanded his second flight, Soyuz T-11, which also carried engineer Gennady Strekalov and Indian pilot Rakesh Sharma into space. The three men spent a week aboard Salyut 7, visiting the crew of Kizim, Solovyov, and Atkov.

Malyshev was born August 27, 1941, in Nikolayevsk, a city near Volgograd, then known as Stalingrad.

Malyshev originally enrolled in the Kacha Higher Air Force School in Volgograd, but transferred to the Kharkov School, graduating in 1963. He served as a fighter-bomber pilot flying MiG-17s and MiG-21s until joining the cosmonaut group in April 1967.

Malyshev was one of several pilots originally screened and approved in October 1965, but whose enrollment in the space program was postponed for 18 months because only 20 could be trained at a time. He finally reported to the training center just days after the death of cosmonaut Vladimir Komarov in the Soyuz 1 accident, while Komarov's colleagues and friends, including Pavel Belyayev, Malyshev's new boss, were still in a state of shock. Training proceeded, however, and by August 1969 Malyshev had completed the basic course and was assigned to the group training for future manned lunar landings. When that program was cut back in 1970, he spent a year in the Almaz military space station group, then was sent to the Chkalov test pilot school, where he earned a test pilot third class rating in 1973. He then joined the Soyuz T group while also attending the Gagarin Air Force Academy, where he graduated in 1977.

In 1976 Malyshev served as backup commander to the Soyuz 22 Earth resources mission flown by Valery Bykovsky and Vladimir Aksenov. Malyshev and Aksenov worked together in the new Soyuz T program.

Following his first flight Malyshev was chosen to command Soyuz T-6, the Soviet-French mission, and trained with flight engineer Alexandr Ivanchenkov and French spationaut Jean-Loup Chretien for many months. In January 1982, 6 months prior to the scheduled launch, Soviet officials announced that Malyshev had been replaced by Vladimir Dzhanibekov because of health problems, but it was later learned that Malyshev and Chretien were not getting along. Malyshev then assumed command of the Soviet-Indian prime crew.

In 1985 Malyshev was a candidate for the Soyuz T-13 Salyut 7 "rescue" mission ultimately commanded by Vladimir Dzhanibekov. The success of that mission and the subsequent abbreviation of the followup flight aboard the station caused Soviet managers to create a cadre of Soyuz commanders who were ready to stand by in case a short replacement or repair mission was needed. In 1986 Malyshev was assigned to this group along with Anatoly Berezovoy.

Malyshev later served as deputy director of the Gagarin Center political department.

He retired from the Russian air force with the rank of colonel in January 1993, and remains a civilian training official at the Gagarin Center.

Manakov, Gennady Mikhailovich

1950–

Veteran test pilot Gennady Manakov commanded two expeditions to the Mir space station, the seventh (September–December 1990) and the thirteenth (January–July 1993).

During the 1990 visit, Soyuz TM-10, Manakov and his flight engineer, Gennady Strekalov, performed a space walk intended to repair a broken hatch and conducted materials processing experiments with the Gallar and Krater V installations. They also took part in astrophysicial observations with the Buket and Mariya instruments.

During their final week aboard Mir in December 1990 they were joined by a new crew that included Japanese journalist Toyohiro Akiyama, with whom they returned to Earth.

On Manakov's second visit his flight engineer was Alexandr Poleshchuk. Their Soyuz TM-16 spacecraft was a different model of Soyuz, known as Machine #101, which carried the special APAS-89 docking adaptor originally intended for use on the canceled Soyuz-Buran docking mission. Manakov's manually piloted Machine #101 to a successful docking on the Kristall module of Mir.

During their first weeks aboard the station Manakov and Poleshchuk deployed a Progress vehicle with a solar sail experiment called *Znamya* or Banner. The crew also did considerable maintenance on Mir's sytems, as resupplied by three more Progress vehicles. They conducted two EVAs in addition to medical, manufacturing, and astronomical tasks.

Manakov was assigned to command a third Mir mission, scheduled for launch as Soyuz TM-24 in August 1996, but was replaced in the last 10 days of training when he developed heart problems. Unable to win clearance to return to flight status, he left the cosmonaut team in December 1997 to become a training official at the Gagarin Center.

Manakov was born June 1, 1950, in the village of Yefimovka in the Andreyevsky District, Orenburg Region, Russia. He attended the Armavir Higher Air Force School, graduating in 1973. In 1985 he earned a degree from the Moscow Aviation Institute.

Manakov's career as a pilot saw him spend 2 years as a MiG-17 instructor at Armavir followed by service the with air defense forces in Kamchatka and the Moscow military district. He became a parachutist, making 248 jumps, and also served as a *zampolit* (political officer).

In 1979, fulfilling a lifelong dream, he was allowed to enroll in the military test pilot at the Chkalov test pilot school at Akhtubinsk, near Volgograd. Upon graduation in 1980 he became a fighter test pilot while concurrently studying at Moscow Aviation Institute.

This academic achievement combined with his experience as a test pilot—he has flown over 1,620 hours in 42 different types of aircraft—made Manakov a candidate for advanced flight test projects such as the Buran shuttle program. He was one of 3 pilots selected in November 1985 for the planned military Buran test pilot-cosmonaut group at Chkalov, and commenced the basic cosmonaut training course at the Gagarin Center, completing it in May 1987. When manned flights of Buran continued to be delayed, Manakov and colleagues Viktor Afanasyev and Anatoly Artsebarsky were transferred to the Gagarin Center in January 1988 to be trained as Soyuz TM-Mir cosmonauts.

Manakov was assigned to the Mir main crew training group in 1988, and selected as backup commander for Soyuz TM-9 in September 1989. He later served as backup commander for Soyuz TM-15 (1992).

Manarov, Musa Khiramanovich
1951–

Musa Manarov is one of the most experienced space travelers in the world, having spent 541 days in orbit during two residencies aboard the Mir space station.

The first began in 1987, when Manarov served as flight engineer of Soyuz TM-4, the first yearlong manned spaceflight. With commander Vladimir Titov and researcher Anatoly Levchenko, Manarov was launched from Baikonur on December 21, 1987, to relieve the crew of Yuri Romanenko (who had spent 324 days aboard Mir himself at that point) and Alexandr Alexandrov. On December 29, with Levchenko acting as reserve pilot, Soyuz TM-3 returned to Earth with Romanenko and Alexandrov, leaving Manarov and Titov on Mir for a planned 1-year residency.

During their 365 days aboard Mir Manarov and Titov performed hundreds of hours of scientific, industrial, and medical experiments while also hosting two visiting international cosmonaut crews. They took three space walks, two of which repaired the Roentgen observatory aboard the Kvant module. During the last third of their mission they were joined by physician-cosmonaut Valery Polyakov, who monitored their physical condition, which was generally good.

The cosmonaut's psychological condition was also judged to be good, though prior to Polyakov's arrival the cosmonauts had one serious disagreement that resulted in their not speaking to each other for 3 days.

On December 2, 1990, Manarov returned to space as the flight engineer of the Soyuz TM-11 mission. His commander was Viktor Afanasyev; the cosmonaut-researcher was Japanese journalist Toyohiro Akiyama, who returned to Earth after 10 days with the resident crew of Manakov and Strekalov.

Manarov and Afanasyev's residency was limited to 6 months by design. They devoted their time to space manufacturing, astrophysical and Earth resources observations, and, increasingly, maintenance of the Mir complex, which by early 1991 consisted of the Mir core, the Kvant observatory module, the Kvant-2 docking and EVA module, and the Kristall space manufacturing module. A Progress supply ship and a Soyuz TM vehicle were also docked to the complex during crew residencies. Some of this maintenance took the form of EVAs: the crew conducted 4 of them, logging over 20 hours outside the station.

Manarov and Afanasyev survived one crisis when the Progress M-7 supply ship failed to dock on March 21, 1991. A second attempt 2 days later also failed, and almost resulted in a collision between Progress and Mir. The cosmonauts boarded their Soyuz TM-11 craft and moved it from the front docking port to the rear, allowing Progress to link up.

They returned to Earth on May 26, 1991, with British researcher Helen Sharman.

Manarov was born in March 22, 1951, in the city of Baku, Azerbaijan. His father was in the Soviet army and Manarov lived in many different cities while growing up. He is a Lakets by nationality, one of the many ethnic groups that made up the former Soviet Union, and his first name was originally Musakhi. Manarov attended the Moscow Aviation Institute from 1969 to 1974, then went to work at the NPO Energiya (formerly the OKB Korolev) as tester of space equipment and experiment analyst.

He became a cosmonaut in December 1978 after 2 years of examinations, though did not begin actual training for spaceflight until 1983. In the interim he served as a Mir flight controller and shift flight director at the Kaliningrad control center. He began training with Yuri Romanenko in 1984, then was teamed with Vladimir Titov in early 1987.

Between his visits to Mir Manarov underwent training on the Buran space shuttle. In 1990 he served as backup flight engineer for the Soyuz TM-10 mission.

Manarov left NPO Energiya and the cosmonaut team in April 1992. He is currently vice president of a space manufacturing firm in Russia called Small Sat.

Matinchenko, Alexandr Nikolayevich
1927–

Alexandr Matinchenko was one of the 15 members of the second cosmonaut enrollment in January 1963. He completed the initial training course in January 1965 and was one of the first 6 cosmonauts assigned to the Soyuz program.

In spite of the fact that he was a pilot, Matinchenko trained as a Soyuz flight engineer, and the addition of civilian engineers to the cosmonaut team in early 1966 cost him a chance to fly on Soyuz. He then worked on the development of the Salyut-Almaz military space station for several years, ultimately leaving the cosmonaut team in November 1972 without having flown in space.

Matinchenko was born September 4, 1927, in the village of Verkhny Mamon, Pavlovsky District (now Verkhny-Mamon District), Voronezh Region, Russia. In 1943, at the age of 18, he entered military service and was trained at the Leningrad Naval Training School, then evacuated to the city of Kuybyshev. He completed the course in 1945 and served for 3 years as a radio operator with the 73rd Air Division of the Long Range Air Forces in the city of Ostafevo. In 1948 Matinchenko entered the Balashov Higher Air Force School, qualifying as a pilot on the Yak-19, UTB-2 and Li-2 in December 1950.

For the next 4 years he was a second pilot flying Li-2 and Il-14 transports with the 89th Air Transport Regiment, 73rd Air Division, Long Range Air Forces. In April 1954 he became an aircraft commander with the same unit.

Matinchenko took part in tests of Soviet air defense missiles at the Vladimirovka test range in 1955, flying 3 missions in American C-47s in which he aimed the craft at missile batteries, set the autopilot, then bailed out.

In November 1956 he flew 26 missions for Soviet forces invading Hungary.

From 1957 to 1962 Matinchenko was a student at the Zhukovsky Air Force Engineering Academy. It was during his final year at Zhukovsky that he was ordered to undergo medical testing for the cosmonaut team. By the time the selection process was completed in late 1962, Matinchenko was working as a flight test engineer at the military flight test center in Chkalovskaya.

Following his departure from the cosmonaut group he worked at the NII-30 research institute in Chkalovskaya as editor of technical publications. He transferred to reserve air force status in 1973 and joined the 11th Main Directorate of the Ministry of Aviation Production, where he worked as an inspector and crash investigator. In February 1992 he retired.

Maximenko, Valery Yevgenyevich

1950–

Soviet air force test pilot Valery Maximenko was selected in 1988 to join the cosmonaut unit of the Chkalov military flight test center, the GNIKI, as a crewmember for manned orbital flights of the Buran space shuttle. Approved by the joint state commission as well in January 1989, he underwent the basic cosmonaut training course at the Gagarin Center from May 1990 to April 1991.

At that time, however, he returned to the Chkalov center to resume his test pilot career. The Buran program was canceled in April 1993.

Maximenko was born July 16, 1950, in Tyumen, Tyumen District, Russia. Following graduation from a secondary school in 1967 he entered the Soviet air force, attending the Kharkov Higher Air Force School. From 1971 to 1977 he was an instructor at Kharkov.

He graduated from the Chkalov test pilot school in 1978, remaining at the center as a pilot. In 1982 he graduated from the Akthubinsk branch of the Moscow Aviation Institute.

Colonel Maximenko is currently a deputy commander of the Chkalov test pilot school.

Morukov, Boris Vladimirovich

1950–

Boris Morukov is one of the 3 physicians enrolled in the cosmonaut team of the Institute for Medical-Biological Problems (IMBP) in January 1989. From October 1990 to March 1992 he underwent Soyuz-Mir training at the Gagarin Center, qualifying as a cosmonaut-researcher.

He was the second backup for physican-cosmonaut Valery Polyakov on his record-setting 438-day mission to Mir (January 1994 to March 1995). And in July 1987 he was one of 3 candidates to be the Russian crewmember of the STS-89 crew, but lost the assignment to military pilot Salizhan Sharipov.

Morukov was born January 10, 1950, and attended the Pigorov 2nd Moscow Medical Institute, graduating in 1973. He joined the staff of IMBP as a researcher, and successfully passed the medical examinations for the IMBP cosmonaut team in 1976. He was not one of the physician-cosmonauts selected in December 1978, however, and remained in reserve until 1989.

While awaiting a flight opportunity Morukov serves as an office chief at the IMBP.

Moshchenko, Sergei Ivanovich

1954–

Engineer Sergei Moshchenko is currently a cosmonaut-candidate undergoing training at the Gagarin Center. In July 1999 he should qualify as a flight engineer for future International Space Station crews.

Moshchenko was born in 1954. He is employed by the Krunichev Space Center in the Moscow suburb of Fili, builders of the Proton launch vehicle and Mir and the I.S.S. control and service modules. He was approved by the joint state commission on February 9, 1996, but did not start cosmonaut training until January 1998.

He is qualified as a pilot on the Yak-12, Yak-18, and Yak-52, with 138 flying hours. He has also made 96 parachute jumps.

Moshkin, Oleg Yuriyevich

1964–

Major Oleg Moshkin is one of the 8 Russian air force pilots approved as a cosmonaut-candidate on July 28, 1997. In the fall of 1999 he should qualify as a Soyuz commander and International Space Station crewmember.

Moshkin was born April 23, 1964, in Barabash, Khasan District, Primorsky Region, Russia. He attended the

Suvurov military secondary school in Ussuriysk, graduating in 1981, then entered the Armavir Higher Air Force School (named for Kutakhov). Following qualification as a pilot in 1985, he served with the Russian military air forces. He later attended the Gagarin Air Force Academy.

At the time of his selection for cosmonaut training Moshkin was a flight commmander with the 70th Detached Air Wing (Special Destination). This wing, named for the late Vladimir Seregin, is the aircraft support unit for the Gagarin Center and is located at nearby Chkalovskaya air base.

Moskalenko, Nikolai Tikhonovich

1949–

Nikolai Moskalenko was one of the 9 candidate pilots enrolled in the Gagarin Center cosmonaut team on August 23, 1976. In 1984–85 he served as second backup cosmonaut researcher for the Soyuz T-14 mission to Salyut 7. He left the cosmonaut team in June 1986.

Moskalenko was born January 1, 1949, in the village of Goragorsky, Nadterechnovo District, Chechen-Ingush SSR, Russia. From 1966 to 1970 he attended the Yeisk Higher Air Force School, then served for 6 years as a fighter bomber pilot with the 523rd Air Regiment, 303rd Air Division of the 1st Air Army.

From September 1976 to July 1977, as part of his cosmonaut training, he completed a course at the Chkalov test pilot school at Akhtubinsk. After a year of parachute training and basic cosmonaut training, Moskalenko was designated a Gagarin Center cosmonaut on January 30, 1979. While awaiting a Soyuz-Salyut flight opportunity, he spent the next 3 years doing flight test work at Akhtubinsk. He began full-time space training at the Gagarin Center in 1982, and was teamed with commander Anatoly Solovyov and engineer Alexandr Serebrov in a crew in 1984.

Upon leaving the cosmonaut team Moskalenko transferred to the Chkalov Center as an air force test pilot. On February 5, 1990, while flying a MiG-27, he was involved in a midair collision with another MiG. Both pilots survived, but Moskaleno was downgraded from military pilot first class to second class as a result.

Mossolov, Vladimir Yemelyanovich

1944–

Vladimir Mossolov was one of the 6 Soviet air force test pilots selected in 1979 to train for the Buran space shuttle program. He underwent a course of basic cosmonaut training at the Gagarin Center between January 1979 and November 1980, and was designated a test-cosmonaut on February 12, 1982. He left the Buran test pilot-cosmonaut group in August 1987 to return to full-time military flight test work.

Mossolov was born February 22, 1944, in Kaliningrad, Moscow District. He graduated from secondary school in 1960, then worked as an operator of milling machines prior to entering the Soviet air force.

He attended the Tambov Higher Air Force School, graduating in 1967, then served with the long range aviation (bomber and transport) branch of the Soviet air force, flying Tu-16 and Tu-22 bombers. In 1976 he graduated from the Chkalov military test pilot school at Akhtubinsk, remaining at the flight test center there and ultimately flying over 40 different types of aircraft. He did further study at the Moscow Aviation Institute, graduating in 1981.

In 1989, while still at Akhtubinsk, Mossolov set 9 world records in the Tu-95MS bomber. In 1990 he transferred to the Main Staff of the Soviet air force, as director of the test pilot group. He left the service in June 1995.

Mossolov is currently flying Tu-134 aircraft for the civil aviation company AlRosAviya.

Mukhortov, Pavel Petrovich

1966–

Pavel Mukhortov is one of the 6 Soviet journalists selected as cosmonaut candidates in February 1990. In October of that year he was enrolled at the Gagarin Center, completing the basic training course in February 1992. By that time, however, the journalist visit to Mir had been canceled for lack of funds.

Mukhortov was born March 11, 1966, at Ognennoy Loshchadi on the Kamchatka Penninsula. He attended secondary school in the city of Kuybyshev, since renamed Samara. He dreamed of a career in flying or cosmonautics, but was unable to pass the air force medical examinations. Instead he enrolled at the Lvov Higher Military-Political School, intending to become a military journalist.

Upon graduation in 1987 he was commissioned as a lieutenant and assigned to a military newspaper in Kazakhstan. He left the service 2 years later, settling in Riga, Latvia, where he became a reporter for the magazine, *Sovietskaya Molodezh* (Soviet Youth).

He has been a member of both the Journalist's Unions of the USSR and of Latvia, and still works as a reporter in Riga.

Musabayev, Talgat Amangeldyevich
1951–

Talgat Musabayev is the first commercial airline pilot to fly in space, and first citizen of a foreign nation to command a Russian space mission.

Though he is a colonel in the Russian air force, Musabayev is also a citizen of the recently independent nation of Kazakhstan, and currently serves as commander of the Mir-25 crew, launched as Soyuz TM-27 on January 31, 1998. Musabayev and flight engineer Nikolai Budarin are scheduled to remain aboard the station until September 1998.

Previously Musabayev served as flight engineer in the crew of Soyuz TM-19—the sixteenth Mir residency—launched July 1, 1994. He and commander Yuri Malenchenko spent over 3 months aboard Mir, working with long-duration physician-researcher Valery Polyakov on medical studies while completing their own work in materials manufacturing, Earth studies, and astronomical observations.

The cosmonauts also accomplished a manual docking on September 2 with an errant Progress resupply craft. Had the cosmonauts been unable to link up, they would have had to abandon Mir for lack of consumables.

Later that month the two cosmonauts also performed two EVAs inspecting the Mir exterior.

Musabayev was backup cosmonaut-researcher to fellow Kazakh Toktar Aubakirov for Soyuz TM-13, an 8-day mission to Mir flown in October 1991. Musabayev and Aubakirov had been originally selected as representatives of the Kazakhstan SSR, one of the republics that made up the former USSR.

Following the TM-13 flight, Musabayev, unlike other cosmonaut-researchers, was admitted to the cosmonaut team on a permanent basis and commissioned a major in the Russian air force. This move deflected public criticism at the time of the Soyuz TM-19 launch about the flight of a Kazakh citizen aboard a Russian spacecraft. Musabayev had was an active duty lieutenant colonel by then.

Musabayev was born January 7, 1951, in Kargama, Dzhambul District, Kazakhstan. He attended the Red Banner School for Civil Aeronautics Engineers in Riga, graduating in 1974, then served at the Burundai Air Center in the city of Alma Ata.

Between 1975 and 1987 Musabayev was a Komsomol and Communist Party official in the Kazakh Department of Civil Aeronautics. Since 1987 he has been a copilot flying An-2 and Tu-134 aircraft. He holds a master of sport for aerobatic flying.

Musabayev was selected for cosmonaut training in May 1990, when a search of the Soviet air forces failed to turn up a suitable military candidate. In October of that year Musabayev arrived at the Gagarin Center. He was joined in January 1991 by Aubakirov.

Nelyubov, Grigori Grigoryevich
1934–1966

Grigori Nelyubov came close to being the first man in space. One of the original group of 20 Soviet cosmonauts selected in March 1960, he quickly established himself as perhaps the most talented pilot among them and earned a place among the 6 men selected for concentrated training by July 1960.

In addition to his flying skills, Nelyubov was unusually dynamic, described by fellow cosmonaut Georgy Shonin as a "real Hussar," witty, charming, athletic, and outspoken. He was quite competitive, attempting to set an endurance record in the thermal chamber and openly admitting he wanted to be the first man in space. Boris Raushenbakh, one of the senior officials in the Soviet manned space program, thought these traits made Nelyubov his choice to be the first pilot of the Vostok.

But Nelyubov's personality won him some powerful enemies, notably Lieutenant General Nikolai Kamanin, the chief of the cosmonaut training. Nelyubov also managed to embarrass chief designer Korolev during their first encounter, when he criticized the cosmonaut training program for its emphasis on physical conditioning at the expense of flying.

Nevertheless, Nelyubov served as second backup to Gagarin on the first Vostok mission. Classic films of the Gagarin's ride to the launchpad show Nelyubov blithely popping a candy into Gagarin's mouth.

He should then have served as backup to Titov for the Vostok 2 flight in August 1961, but Kamanin thought him ill-suited to such a long flight, and replaced him with the more placid Andrian Nikolayev. Kamanin also scratched Nelyubov from consideration for the Vostok 3/4 missions in August 1962, relegating him to the role of communications operator. Nevertheless, he would certainly have flown in space eventually, except for an incident that occurred on March 27, 1963.

Nelyubov and fellow cosmonauts Ivan Anikeyev and Valentin Filatyev were returning to Star Town one evening after a dinner in Moscow. They had been drinking and got into an altercation with several offices of the militia at a railway depot. Nelyubov arrogantly threatened to go over the head of the arresting officers if they dared to make a report. The police, obviously wishing to avoid a scandal, offered to forget the whole matter if the cosmonauts would apologize. Anikeyev and Filatyev were ready, but Nelyubov refused.

When General Mikhail Odintsev, the new head of the training center, received a report of the misconduct he allowed the cosmonaut group itself to determine the punishment: the unanimous vote was to expel Nelyubov, Anikeyev, and Filatyev. Interestingly enough, the vote was unanimous: the three guilty men agreed that they had let their comrades down.

Nelyubov was born April 9, 1934, in the city of Porfiryevka, Yevpatoriya District, Crimea Region, Ukraine. He attended the Stalin Naval Air School (later renamed the 12th Naval Air School), graduating in 1957, then served as a MiG-19 pilot with the 49th and 127th Air Divisions of Black Sea Fleet of the Soviet navy.

During his first months of cosmonaut training Nelyubov made no secret of his desire to return, ultimately, to flying jets, saying that he wanted to fly in space once. Following his dismissal in May 1963, he was assigned to the 303rd Air Division of the 1st Far East Air Army.

It was apparently very difficult for Nelyubov to watch not only his comrades from the "first 6" going into space, such as Bykovsky, but also others like Komarov and Belyayev, who had not rated as highly as he. He would tell people that he had been a cosmonaut, a backup to the famous Gagarin, no less, but was not often believed. On February 18, 1966, while drunk, he was hit by a train and killed on a railroad bridge at Ippolitovka in the Far East. The official report suggested that Nelyubov had gone through "a crisis of the soul" and hinted that his death might have been a suicide.

Nikolayev, Andrian Grigoryevich

1929–

Andrian Nikolayev set endurance records on both of his flights into space. He was the pilot of Vostok 3 in August 1962, spending 4 days in space when the American record for all flights totaled 9 hours. In 1970 Nikolayev commanded the Soyuz 9 mission; he and flight engineer Vitaly Sevastyanov spent almost 18 days in space. It was a difficult flight: upon landing the two cosmonauts had to be carried from their spacecraft.

Nikolayev was a logical choice for these early space marathons because of his incredible stamina. During the diabolical medical testing before and after joining the cosmonaut group he consistently surprised Soviet doctors with his ability to endure silence, isolation, and temperature extremes. Yuri Gagarin said of Nikolayev, "He is the most unflappable man in a crisis I know."

Nikolayev was born September 5, 1929 in the village of Shorshely, Marinsky-Posad District, Chuvash Autonomous Republic of the former USSR. His father was a farmer and his older brother a lumberjack, so Nikolayev followed the family tradition, attending the Marinsky-Posad Forestry Institute. From December 1947 until he was drafted into the army in 1950 he was a lumberjack and the foreman of a logging operation, the Derevyanski Timber Industrial Farm in Karelia.

Joining the Soviet military in April 1950, Nikolayev was first trained as an aircraft gunner at the Kirovobad Higher Air Force school and served on Tu-2 bomber crews in for several months. Then he earned a chance to become a pilot, entering the Chernigov Higher Air Force School in April 1951, later transferring the Frunze Higher Air Force School, graduating in December 1954. For 5 years he served as MiG-15 pilot with the 401st Air Regiment, Air Defense Forces, Moscow military district.

Nikolayev became a cosmonaut in March 1960 and was backup to Gherman Titov on Vostok 2 in 1961. Between his flights in 1962 and 1970 he served as commander of the 1st squad (civilian programs) of the cosmonaut team (1966–68) and graduated from the Zhukovsky Air Force Engineering Academy (1968). Following Yuri Gagarin's death in an air crash in March 1968, Nikolayev became deputy director of the cosmonaut training center for air-space training.

His involvement with Soyuz began in the summer of 1965, when he was one of the first 4 pilots assigned to the program. Chief Designer Korolev told cosmonaut training chief Kamanin that Nikolayev or Bykovsky should be assigned to the first manned circumlunar mission. Nikolayev served as backup commander to the canceled Soyuz 2 mission in 1967; had the Soyuz 1-Soyuz 2 docking and EVA crew transfer gone as scheduled, he might very well have made a circumlunar flight in 1968.

He and Vitaly Sevastyanov were selected as the Soyuz 8 crew in April 1969, but failed their technical examinations early in training, and wound up serving as backups to Shatalov and Yeliseyev.

Nikolayev was promoted to major general in 1970; in April 1974 he became first deputy director of the Gagarin Center, a position he held until leaving active military service in August 1992. From 1991 to 1993 he was a deputy in the Great Soviet of the Russian Federation.

He visited the United States in 1970 and met several American astronauts. He has also authored several books, including the autobiographies *Meeting in Orbit* (1966)

and *Space, a Road Without End* (1974, 1979). Nikolayev is currently a deputy to former cosmonaut and Soyuz 9 crewmember Vitaly Sevastyanov, a member of the Russian State Duma.

He was married to Valentina Tereshkova, the first woman in space, from 1963 to 1982.

Omelchenko, Svetlana Oktyabrevna

1951–

Svetlana Omelchenko is one of the 6 Soviet journalists selected as cosmonaut candidates in February 1990. From October 1990 to February 1992 she underwent the basic cosmonaut training course at the Gagarin Center, qualifying as a Soyuz-Mir cosmonaut-researcher. By that time, however, the Soviet Journalist-in-Space mission had been canceled for lack of funds.

Omelchenko was born Svetlana Yeremeyeva on August 20, 1951, to a military family living in Sleptsovsk, Chechen-Ingush ASSR, Russia. When her father left the service, the family moved to the nearby Stavropol region. Omelchenko graduated from secondary school in Livnom, Stavropol, in 1968, and began working at a local newspaper, *Primanycheski Stepi*. A year later she moved to Moscow to study at a technical school. She also attended the journalism faculty at Moscow State University, graduating in 1975.

For the next 3 years she worked at the newspaper *Vozdushny Reys* (*Air Travel*), then at *Vozdushny Transport* (*Air Transport*), specializing in stories about air safety. She is currently on the staff of the newspaper *Delovoy Mir* (*Business World*).

Onufriyenko, Yuri Ivanovich

1961–

Yuri Onufriyenko was commander of the 21st resident crew aboard the Mir space station. Joining Onufriyenko on this 5-month mission, launched in January 1996 as Soyuz TM-23, were flight engineer Yuri Usachev and NASA-Mir researcher Shannon Lucid, who arrived at Mir that March. Onufriyenko and Usachev conducted 4 different EVAs, and also supervised the addition of the Priroda module to Mir in April, completing the station 10 years after its initial launch.

The Mir-21 crew returned to Earth in early September after 192 days.

In July 1997 Colonel Onufriyenko was assigned as commander of the fourth incremental International Space Station crew, scheduled for launch aboard the Shuttle in the winter of 2000-2001. Joining Onufriyenko for a 4-month mission will be American astronauts Daniel Bursch and Carl Walz.

Onufriyenko was born February 6, 1961, in the village of Ryasnoye, Zolochevsky District, Kharkov Region, Ukraine. He attended the Yeisk Higher Air Force School, graduating in 1982, then served with the 229th Air Figher-Bombardier Regiment in the Far East Military District. He was later stationed in Khabarovsk Territory.

One of 3 pilots approved as cosmonaut candidates in January 1989, Onufriyenko completed the training course in January 1991 that qualified him as a Soyuz TM-Mir commander.

While awaiting a flight assignment Onufriyenko completed a graduate degree in environmental sciences at Moscow State University (April 1994). He joined the Mir training group that same month, serving with Usachev as backup crew for Mir-18, whose prime crewmembers (Anatoly Solovyov and Nikolai Budarin) were delivered to Mir by the Space Shuttle Atlantis (STS-71) in July 1995.

Padalka, Gennady Ivanovich

1958–

Pilot Gennady Padalka is currently training as commander for the Soyuz TM-28 crew. Padalka and flight engineer Sergei Avdeyev, along with Russian politician Yuri Baturin, was launched to Mir in early August 1998 for a planned six-month mission, one of the last Mir visits.

Padalka was born June 21, 1958, in the city of Krasnodar, Russia. He attended the Yeisk Higher Air Force School, graduating in 1979, then served as a fighter pilot in the Soviet air force.

He was one of the 3 candidates enrolled in the air force cosmonaut team in January 1989. He completed the basic Soyuz-Mir training course in January 1991 and while awaiting a flight opportunity completed a graduate degree in environmental science at Moscow State University (February 1992–February 1994).

Padalka was teamed with flight engineer Alexandr Poleshchuk in a Soyuz crew in the spring of 1994. The team was originally assigned as backups for the Soyuz TM-23 mission, but when Poleshchuk was removed from flight status for medical reasons, Padalka was assigned as backup commander for a different mission, Soyuz TM-26, with flight engineer Sergei Avdeyev. Launched in August 1997, Soyuz TM-26 carried the Mir-24 crew of Anatoly Solovyov and Pavel Vinogradrov, who had been trained to perform Mir repairs following the disastrous collision between the station and a Progress supply craft.

Patsayev, Viktor Ivanovich

1933–1971

Viktor Patsayev was a member of the cosmonaut crew that became the first in history to board an orbiting station, Salyut 1, spending a record 24 days in space.

Soyuz 11 carrying cosmonauts Georgy Dobrovolsky, Vladislav Volkov and Patsayev was launched on June 6, 1971, and docked with Salyut a day later. The previous Soyuz-Salyut crew had reached this point, but had been unable to transfer into the station because of a problem in their Soyuz orbital module. The problem had been corrected: Patsayev, who had helped in the design and construction of Salyut, was the first to float into the station.

The cosmonauts spent several days setting up communications and life support systems in addition to monitoring their own health. By June 11 they were beginning to use scientific instruments designed to observe the Earth and its atmosphere. Within the week they were also conducting military observations of nighttime missile launches and confronting the challenges of long-term missions in space, notably unsatisfactory food and inadequate hygienic facilities. Cosmonaut training chief Nikolai Kamanin likened the first mission to a marathon that kills the runner.

On June 17 a small fire broke out aboard the station, and the crew had to prepare for a sudden return to Earth. The fire was brought under control and the return was postponed, but the emergency caused some tension between rookie commander Dobrovolsky and veteran flight engineer Volkov that was only resolved by ground controllers.

A week later the crew began preparations for return to Earth. On June 30 they separated Soyuz 11 from the station and 4 hours later fired the braking rockets that would slow Soyuz so it would reenter the atmosphere. At this point the engine module and spherical orbital module were separated, and tragedy struck.

An air valve aboard Soyuz 11—designed to let fresh air into the craft once it reached the lower atmosphere—opened prematurely. The cosmonauts were not wearing pressure suits. Patsayev unbuckled from his couch and struggled to close the valve or block it, but he failed. Soyuz 11's parachutes opened as planned and the spacecraft landed safely, but when rescuers opened the hatch they found the cosmonauts dead.

A national state of mourning was declared. The cosmonauts were buried in the Kremlin Wall. And Soyuz was redesigned so that cosmonaut crews could wear pressure suits during launch and reentry.

Patsayev was born June 19, 1933, in the city of Aktyubinsk in Kazakhstan. His father was killed in October 1941 in the defense of Moscow. He grew up with his mother and sister in Aktyubinsk and, after 1946, Kaliningrad.

Always interested in science and space, Patsayev attended the Penza Industrial Institute, graduating in 1955. For the next few years he worked at the Central Aerological Observatory on studies of the atmosphere. Following the first Sputnik launches in 1957–58, he sought a job in the Korolev spacecraft design bureau (OKB-1).

As an engineer at the bureau, Patsayev became close friends with future cosmonaut Vladislav Volkov. Both of them were members of a flying club, and both were members of the recovery teams for manned spaceflights. Volkov was admitted to the cosmonaut team in 1966, but Patsayev had to wait 2 more years, finally enrolling in May 1968. He was assigned to a Soyuz crew with commander Lev Vorobyov prior to joining the Salyut group in the spring of 1970.

Patsayev earned his candidate's degree in 1971.

In 1974 his widow, Vera, published a book, *Salyut in Orbit*, dealing with her husband's space mission.

Petrushenko, Alexandr Yakovlevich
1942–1992

Alexandr Petrushenko was one of 22 military candidates enrolled in the Gagarin Center cosmonaut team in October 1965. He left the cosmonaut team in June 1973 without ever flying in space.

As a cosmonaut Petrushenko served as a capcom for Vladimir Komarov's ill-fated Soyuz 1 flight in April 1967. He was also assigned to the Spiral spaceplane program, and attended the Chkalov test pilot school from 1969 to 1970.

In late 1972, with manned Spiral flights indefinitely postponed, Petrushenko moved to the Salyut space station program, where he trained as a backup to Vladimir Kovalenok until leaving the cosmonaut team.

He remained at the Gagarin Center until May 1975, working in the Spiral program office and completing a degree at the Gagarin Air Force Academy. Upon graduation he became an instructor in astronautics at the Academy. He later worked at the military satellite command and control center (KIK) of the Military Space Units in the Moscow suburb of Monino.

Petrushenko was born January 1, 1942, in Martovy, Kharkov Region, Ukraine. He attended the Chernigov Higher Air Force School, and following graduation in 1964 served with the Air Defense Forces (PVO) in the Leningrad Military District.

He died of cancer on November 11, 1992.

Pisarev, Viktor Mikhailovich
1941–

Viktor Pisarev was one of the 12 candidates enrolled in the cosmonaut group in April 1967. He left the group in May 1968, having failed to complete the initial training course.

Pisarev was born August 15, 1941, and trained as an air force pilot. He returned to operational flying with the 7th Military Transport Aviation Division in the city of Melitopol, and ultimately attained the rank of lieutenant colonel. He is now in the reserve.

Poleshchuk, Alexandr Fedorovich
1953–

Alexandr Poleshchuk spent 6 months aboard the Mir station between January and July 1993. Launched with commander Gennady Manakov aboard Soyuz TM-16, he took part in a manual docking test of the APAS 89 system, originally intended for use with the Buran space shuttle.

In addition to a program of manufacturing, medical tests, Earth studies, and astronomical observations, Poleshchuk and Manakov performed a number of upgrades and repairs to Mir's systems, with components delivered by a series of Progress supply vehicles. They also conducted to EVAs, and deployed the *Znamya* or Banner solar sail experiment.

In the spring of 1994 Poleshchuk returned to active crew training and later that year was assigned to the backup crew for Mir-18 (Solovyov-Budarin) with commander Yuri Onufriyenko, which was to be delivered to the Russian space station by the Space Shuttle Atlantis in June 1995. While undergoing Shuttle-Mir training, in April 1995, Poleshchuk was medically disqualified, and removed from training.

Poleshchuk was born October 30, 1953, in Cheremkhovo, Irkutsk Region, Angara District, Russia. Following graduation from secondary school in 1971 he entered the Moscow Aviation Institute, earning his degree in 1977. He went to work at the NPO Energiya, where he became an expert in EVA and space construction, making over 150 flights in the zero-G training aircraft and logging 600 hours in the neutral buoyancy simulator.

Poleshchuk was one of the civilian engineers enrolled as cosmonaut candidates in February 1989. He completed his training as a flight engineer in 1991 and in December of that year was assigned, with commander Gennady Manakov, to the backup crew for Soyuz TM-15.

With his medical status still under review, Poleshchuk serves as a training officer in the Enerigya cosmonaut department.

Polonsky, Anatoly Borisovich
1956–

Anatoly Polonsky is a Soviet air force test pilot who was selected in October 1988 to join the new cosmonaut team of the Chkalov military flight research institute (GKNII), to train for manned orbital flights of the space shuttle Buran. A year later he commenced general cosmonaut training at the Gagarin Center, earning his certificate as a test-cosmonaut in April 1991.

In May 1992 he relocated to the Gagarin Center as a candidate commander for a proposed Soyuz-Buran orbital mission, replacing Ivan Bachurin, only to see the mission canceled later that year. While doing flight test work at the nearby Chkalovskaya branch of the GKNII, Polonsky applied for admission to the Gagarin Center's military team, but was not accepted.

Polonsky was born January 1, 1956, in the village of Pogranichnik, Taldy-Kurgan District, Kazakhstan. He graduated from secondary school in 1973, then entered the Polbin Higher Air Force School in Orenburg. From 1977 to 1985 he served as a pilot in the Soviet air force. He attended the Chkalov test pilot school at Akhtubinsk in 1985–86, ultimately earning a test pilot second class rating.

He is currently a test pilot based in Chkalovskaya.

Polyakov, Valery Vladimirovich

1942–

Valery Polyakov is the world's space endurance champion, an especially appropriate title for an aerospace physician. From January 1994 to March 1995 he lived aboard the Mir space station on a 14-month marathon that is the longest spaceflight likely to be attempted for decades. During Polyakov's mission he worked with 3 different Mir main crews in addition to researchers from the European Space Agency and NASA.

Polyakov proposed the lengthy stay over the objections of his wife, Nelya, who is also a physician, in order to prove that humans could survive a round-trip free-fall flight to Mars. He performed more than 1,000 different tests in 50 medical experiments, learning, for example, that he lost 15 percent of his bone density in weightlessness (most of it was recovered within a few months on Earth) in spite of a strict regimen of two hours of exercise each day. The soles of his feet softened, since he did no walking. He also suffered a loss of his oxygen-bearing red blood cells during the first weeks of the mission, until adjustments were made in the Mir's environment.

Polyakov concluded that the greatest barriers to long-duration flight were psychological. He had a brief conflict with Mir-17 flight engineer Yelena Kondakova, who felt that Polyakov wasn't paying attention to her unique medical needs.

In 1988–89 Polyakov had a prior 8-month shift aboard Mir. He was the flight engineer of Soyuz TM-6, launched from Baikonur on August 29, 1988, along with fellow cosmonaut Vladimir Lyakhov and Afghan pilot Ahmad Ahad. The TM-6 crew conducted a week of joint experiments with Mir expedition crewmen Vladimir Titov and Musa Manarov, then in the ninth month of their mission. On September 9 Lyakhov and Ahad returned to Earth, leaving Polyakov aboard the station to study firsthand the effects of long-duration spaceflight on the expedition crew, and upon their replacements, cosmonauts Alexandr Volkov and Sergei Krikalev.

As an example of the special preparation for this mission, Polyakov and his backup, German Arzamazov, had

bone marrow removed from their hips prior to launch so that it could be compared with a sample taken at the end of the mission.

Polyakov's first residency aboard Mir ended in April 1989 after a mission lasting 241 days. Thanks in part to the rigorous attention he paid to his program of exercise—often exceeding the required 1–2 hours on a treadmill and stationary bicycle—Polyakov suffered no negative long-term effects. Aside from a loss of calcium and muscle, which was expected, he recovered quickly, and 3 days after returning to Earth was able to run.

Polyakov was born April 27, 1942, in the city of Tula. As a child he wanted to be a pilot, but later grew interested in aviation medicine. He attended the Sechenov First Moscow Medical Institute, and graduated in 1965. Polyakov also holds a candidate of medical sciences degree (1976).

When cosmonaut Yuri Gagarin made his triumphant appearance in Moscow's Red Square on April 13, 1961, the day after his historic first manned spaceflight, 18-year-old Valery Polyakov was among the thousands in the crowd. Further inspired by Boris Yegorov's flight as the first doctor in space in October 1964, Polyakov decided to devote himself to space medicine. But upon his graduation in 1965 the commission at the medical institute placed him instead at the Institute of Medical Parasitology and Tropical Medicine. Two years later he joined the space medicine branch of the USSR Ministry of Health as an inspector, and also worked in emergency medicine. Polyakov refused to abandon his dream: in 1968 he applied for cosmonaut training and began to undergo medical tests, passing them in July 1970.

In October 1971 Polyakov enrolled in the graduate school of the Institute for Medical and Biological Problems of the USSR Ministry of Health. Here he studied under Dr. Nikolai Gurovsky, one of the USSR's space medicine experts. From the time of its formation in 1963 the IMBP had planned to create its own cadre of physician-cosmonauts, and Polyakov was one of the first selected in March 1972. In the succeeding years he completed the basic cosmonaut training course while serving as medical support for Soyuz and Salyut missions, including the Apollo-Soyuz Test Program in the mid-1970s. He served as backup cosmonaut-researcher for Gennady Strekalov on the Soyuz T-3 mission to Salyut 6 in November–December

1980, and to a fellow physician-cosmonaut, Soyuz T-10's Oleg Atkov, who spent 9 months aboard Salyut 7 in 1984. In February 1988 he was assigned to the Soyuz TM-6 crew.

Following his flight Polyakov served as chief crew physician for the Soyuz TM-9 mission, which lasted from September 1989 to February 1990.

Though he retired as a cosmonaut in June 1995, Polyakov continues to serve as a deputy director of the IMBP.

Polyakov is said to be an expert not only in conventional medicine, but in folk remedies and acupuncture as well.

Ponomarev, Yuri Anatolyevich

1932–

Yuri Ponomarev was the backup flight engineer for Soyuz 18, a 63-day mission aboard the Salyut 4 space station by cosmonauts Klimuk and Sevastyanov. During the flight Ponomarev and backup commander Vladimir Kovalenok served as communications operators in addition to performing other mission support activities.

Ponomarev later trained for 2 years with commander Anatoly Dedkov for the first mission to Salyut 6, but they were replaced by the crew of Kovalenok and Ryumin in 1977.

Ponomarev was born March 24, 1932, in Kadaya, a gold mining area in the Merchensky District, Chita Region of Russia. He attended the Moscow Aviation Institute, graduating in 1957, then went to work for the Korolev spacecraft design bureau.

Enrolled in the cosmonaut team as a flight engineer in March 1972, Ponomarev's first assignment was as a backup flight engineer for the Soyuz 13 mission. He joined the Salyut 4 training group in 1974. He remained active as a cosmonaut until 1983, when he returned to full-time work at the NPO Energiya (the former Korolev design bureau) supervising the training of the new group of women cosmonauts. He is currently on the staff of TsNII-Mash, the independent Russian research institute for spaceflight.

Ponomarev was married to Valentina Ponomareva, one of the first women cosmonauts.

Ponomareva, Valentina Leonidovna

1933–

Valentina Ponomareva was one of the first 5 Soviet women cosmonauts selected in March 1962. She trained for a Vostok mission for 16 months, ultimately serving as the second backup for Valentina Tereshkova, the first woman in space, for her 3-day Vostok 6 mission in June 1963.

In 1965 she was selected as commander of the planned Voskhod 4 mission, then scheduled for launch in the spring of 1966. Ponomareva and Irina Solovyova were to make a 10-day flight during which Solovyova would perform a space walk. Voskhod 4 was one of several Voskhod missions canceled in March 1966.

Ponomareva was born Valentina Kovalevskaya on September 18, 1933, in Moscow, and developed a fascination for airplanes as a young girl, often attending the annual Tushino Air Show with her father and her brothers. She enrolled at the Moscow Aviation Institute because it had an aero club that would allow her to become a pilot and parachutist through its DOSAAF program. Valentina graduated from MAI in 1959 and went to work at the USSR Academy of Sciences in the Institute of Applied Mathematics, headed by Mstislav Keldysh, who encouraged her to apply for the cosmonaut team. After passing the medical examinations, Ponomareva arrived at the cosmonaut training center on April 12, 1962, the first anniversary of Gagarin's flight in space.

From the beginning, Ponomareva was set apart from her colleagues Tereshkova, Solovyova, Yorkina, and Kuznetsova, who had arrived several weeks before her and were already in training. All of the others were single, while Ponomareva was already married (to fellow MAI student and future cosmonaut Yuri Ponomarev) and a mother. Most importantly, Ponomareva was already a qualified pilot and aeronautical engineer; the others were students or workers who had become sport parachutists. She has written that they were united only in their "fanaticism" to be the first woman in space, a prize that ultimately went to Tereshkova.

Chief Designer Vasily Mishin claimed that the final choice of the first woman in space was made by Soviet

Premier Nikita Khrushchev himself, who, reviewing the biographies of the 3 finalists, chose the one—Tereshkova—who came from a worker's family.

Following Vostok 6 Ponomareva enrolled in a graduate course at the Zhukovsky Air Force Engineering Academy, earning a candidate of technical sciences in 1969. The women cosmonaut group was disbanded that same year, and Ponomareva transferred to the training staff of the Gagarin Center where she became an instructor in spaceflight dynamics and control systems.

She retired from the Center and from the Soviet air force (with the rank of colonel) in September 1988 and is currently a senior research fellow at the Institute of the History of Natural Science and Technology of the Russian Academy of Sciences.

Popov, Leonid Ivanovich

1945–

Leonid Popov commanded 3 Soyuz missions, including a record 185-day aboard the Salyut 6 space station in 1980. During these 6 months in space, Popov and flight engineer Valery Ryumin hosted 4 different visiting crews, including cosmonauts from Hungary, Vietnam, and Cuba, in addition to carrying out extensive observations of the Earth, materials processing, and medical experiments.

Popov later commanded Soyuz 40, during which he and Rumanian cosmonaut Dumitru Prunariu visited Salyut 6, and Soyuz T-7, whose crew included woman cosmonaut Svetlana Savitskaya. During this third flight, launched August 19, 1982, Popov visited Salyut 7.

Popov was born August 31, 1945, in the city of Alexandria in the Kirovogradsky Region, Ukraine. At the age of 15 he left school to work as an industrial electrician, but 2 years later joined the Soviet air force. He attended the Chernigov Lenin Komsomol Higher Air Force School, graduating as a pilot in November 1968. For the next 2 years he served as a MiG-19 pilot with the 627th Air Guards Regiment, 15th Air Corps of the Air Defense Forces at a base in Azerbaijan.

By the time of his selection for the cosmonaut team he had logged 1,200 hours of flying time.

Popov was one of the 9 candidates enrolled in the cosmonaut group in April 1970. He completed the basic training course 2 years later, then went to work in a group preparing for flights in the Soyuz T spacecraft. He also attended the Gagarin Air Force Academy, receiving his diploma in 1976.

In January of that year Popov was assigned to his first flight crew, serving as backup commander for the Soyuz 22 mission with flight engineer Boris Andreyev. He joined the Salyut 6 training group in 1977 and became backup commander for Soyuz 32 in 1979.

He almost missed his chance to command Soyuz 35. His flight engineer, Valentin Lebedev, broke his knee during a trampoline accident just a month before launch, effectively promoting the second crew in training—Zudov and Andreyev—to the first position. But engineer Valery Ryumin, who had just returned from 6 months aboard Salyut 6, volunteered to join Popov as a crew. It was Ryumin who suggested that it might be an interesting medical experiment to send him into space again so soon, and who pointed out that he and Popov were better trained than their backups. The state commission agreed and appointed Popov and Ryumin to the mission.

Following his third flight in August 1982 Popov became a deputy to the Supreme Soviet, serving until 1986. He was also backup commander for the daring Soyuz T-13 mission which repaired and rescued the Salyut 7 space station in 1985.

In July 1987 he left to attend the Voroshilov General Staff Academy. Upon graduation in 1990 he joined the staff of the air forces of the Black Sea Fleet.

Major General Popov is currently head of a directorate of the Main Staff of the Russian air force that provides aviation support in response to natural disasters.

Popovich, Pavel Romanovich

1930–

Pavel Popovich took part in the world's first "group" spaceflight when his Vostok 4 spacecraft was launched into orbit on August 12, 1962, one day after Vostok 3 carrying cosmonaut Andrian Nikolayev. Popovich and Nikolayev passed within five miles of each other during their joint mission. The twin missions set duration records at the time, Nikolayev spending 4 days in space, Popovich three. Popovich's might have been extended but for a communications slip by the cosmonaut, who mistakenly used the phrase "observing thunderstorms from orbit," a code for space sickness. Even though Popovich tried to correct, mission controllers insisted on his return, as planned, on the 49th orbit.

He made a second spaceflight in July 1974 as commander of Soyuz 14, which docked with the Salyut 3 orbiting space station. Salyut 3 was actually the first Almaz military space station and was developed by the organization headed by Vladimir Chelomei, designer of the Proton launch vehicle. Popovich and flight engineer Yuri Artyukhin spent 16 days in space performing observations of intelligence targets on Earth, and doing medical experiments.

Popovich was born October 5, 1930, in Uzin, a town near Kiev in the Ukraine. He worked in a factory while completing his schooling, then earned entry to the Magnitogorsk Industrial Polytechnic, where he overcame a language barrier (Popovich grew up speaking Ukrainian, not Russian) and graduated as a building technician.

But while at trade school he had also joined an aero-club, becoming a pilot in September 1951, and his new-found love for flying caused him to join the air force. He attended the Stalingrad Higher Air Force School from 1951 to 1952, then the Kacha Higher Air Force School, graduating in December 1954.

Popovich spent 3 years as a MiG-15, MiG-17 and MiG-19 pilot with the 265th Air Regiment, 336th Air Division, 22nd Air Army of the Southern military district. In 1958 he transferred too the 234th Air Regiment, 9th Air Division at Kubinka air base, near Moscow.

Popovich was the first young pilot to join the cosmonaut group in March 1960, and served as unofficial greeter and quartermaster for the other arrivals. His outgoing personality and love of singing made him popular. He also earned selection as one of the finalists for the first manned flight ultimately made by Gagarin. It was Popovich who was communications operator (capcom) for Gagarin's launch.

After his Vostok 4 flight, Popovich became deputy commander of the cosmonaut detachment (August 1964 to June 1966), then deputy commander of the 2nd squad

(military programs) within the expanded cosmonaut team. In this position he head of the group training for the 7K-VI and Soyuz-VI programs. When those programs faced delay (and ultimately, cancellation), Popovich was transferred to the L-3 lunar orbit program, and from November 1966 to the spring of 1969 trained as a crew commander for a possible flight around the Moon with first Vitaly Sevastyanov, then Georgy Grechko. While involved in Program L Popovich graduated from the Zhukovsky Air Force Engineering Academy (1968).

When Program L was cut back, Popovich returned to military programs as leader of the group of cosmonauts training for flights in Chelomei's Almaz space station. In September 1972 Popovich was assigned to command the first Soyuz-Almaz, Salyut 2. Launched in April 1973, Salyut 2 suffered a propulsion failure before crews could be launched.

Beginning in December 1972 Popovich was head of the 1st Directorate at the Gagarin Center, in charge of Salyut and Almaz missions. He completed work on his candidate of technical sciences (1977), and in January 1978 became deputy director of the Gagarin Cosmonaut Training Center in charge of scientific support and testing, a position he held until December 1989. He also played a role in the development of the Soviet space shuttle Buran.

Major General Popovich left the Center in 1990 to become director of the All-Union Science and Research Center "AIUSagroresource," Moscow. (The center is currently known as the Russian Institute for Monitoring the Earth, the RosINS.)

He has also written several books, including an autobiography titled *Takeoff in the Morning* (1974); a biography of Yuri Gagarin, *It Couldn't Have Been Otherwise* (1980); *Testing in Space and on Earth* (1982) and *The Endless Roads to Space* (1985). He was active in Ukrainian politics as a deputy to the Supreme Soviet of that republic.

Porvatkin, Nikolai Stepanovich

1932–

Engineer Nikolai Porvatkin was one of 12 candidates enrolled in the military cosmonaut team in April 1967. He and fellow enrollees Vladimir Alexeyev and Mikhail Burdayev formed a subgroup within that selection: all were military scientists from NII-2, a research institute for the Air Defense Forces, who were expected to make spaceflights on the 7K-VI reconnaissance spacecraft as well as the Zvezda and Almaz military space stations.

Porvatkin completed the basic cosmonaut training course in August 1969 and joined the Almaz group. At the same time he worked in the flight control team.

In 1976 Porvatkin was assigned to an Almaz crew with commander Gennady Sarafanov, but never flew in space. He was transferred to full-time duties at the flight control center in April 1983.

Porvatkin was born April 15, 1932, in the village of Vozdvizhenka, Krasavsky District, Saratov Region, Russia. He attended the Serpuhov Higher Air Force Technical School, graduating in 1952, then served for 3 years as an engineer with the Air Defense Forces.

In 1955 he entered the Zhukovsky Air Force Engineering Academy, and upon graduating in 1960 served with an air defense squadron. He joined the staff of NII-2 in Kalinin (now Tver), Moscow Region, in 1962. He earned his candidate of technical sciences degree in 1968 for work performed at NII-2.

Porvatkin became a reserve officer in 1988, joining the spacecraft guidance department of the NPO Energiya. He currently works in the flight control center.

Potapov, Mikhail Gregoryevich

1951–

Mikhail Potapov is a physician-cosmonaut who served as the second backup for the flight of Oleg Atkov on Soyuz T-10 in 1984. He had previously trained as a second backup for

Soyuz T-3 in 1980. Potapov left the cosmonaut team in 1985 without having a chance to fly in space.

Potapov was born October 20, 1951, in the village of Babeyev, Noginsk District, Moscow Region. He attended the 1st Moscow Medical Institute named for I. M. Sechenov, graduating in 1976. He is currently a researcher at the Institute for Medical-Biological Problems in Moscow.

Pozharskaya, Larisa Grigoryevna

1947–

Larisa Pozharskaya was one of the physicians enrolled in the cosmonaut team of the Institute for Medical-Biological Problems (IMBP) in July 1980. Though she did not fly in space, she remained active in the cosmonaut team until March 1993.

Pozharskaya was born March 15, 1947, in Zaraisky, Moscow Region. She graduated from the Sechenov First Moscow Medical Institute in 1973, then worked at the institute for an additional 2 years. At the time of her selection for the cosmonaut team she was on the staff of the M. F. Vladimirovsky Clinic.

Preobrazhensky, Vladimir Yevgenyevich

1939–1993

Vladimir Preobrazhensky served as the second backup flight engineer for the flight of Soyuz 24. Launched February 5, 1977, Soyuz 24 cosmonauts Gorbatko and Glazkov reached the Alyut 5 space station and went on to complete a 19-day mission devoted to military reconnaissance. (Salyut 5 was the fourth in the Almaz series of orbital reconnaissance stations.)

Two years later Preobrazhensky was assigned to a 3-man crew training for a fifth Almaz mission—this one using the TKS manned space ferry. However, Almaz-TKS was canceled in the spring of 1981 before missions could be flown. Preobrazhensky had left the cosmonaut team for medical reasons in November 1980.

Preobrazhensky was born February 3, 1939, in Leningrad (now St. Petersburg). His father Yevgeny was a naval aviator who became a Hero of the Soviet Union for leading the first two bombing raids on Berlin in August 1941, and who later commanded Soviet naval aviation forces from 1950 to 1962.

The younger Preobrazhensky enrolled at the Moscow Aviation Institute, graduating in 1963. He entered the military, working as a sergeant at Main Directorate for Naval Aviation. In February 1965 he became an engineer at a bureau for special naval aviation technology; later that year he was commissioned as a junior engineer-lieutenant. He was one of the 22 candidates enrolled in the cosmonaut team on October 28, 1965, and completed the preliminary training in December 1967.

Preobrazhensky joined the group of cosmonauts training for Almaz military space station missions, working there for the next 12 years.

Upon leaving the cosmonaut team he served as a crew instructor. In 1986 he took part in cleanup efforts at the nuclear power facility in Chernobyl, Ukraine. He also attended the Voroshilov Military-Political Academy (1987-89), then transitioned to reserve status with the rank of lieutenant colonel in April 1989.

On October 25, 1993, Preobrazhensky was struck while crossing a street in the Moscow suburb of Monino. He died of his injuries.

Prikhodko, Yuri Viktorovich
1953–
Yuri Prikhodko was a member of the civilian test pilot-cosmonaut team at the Gromov flight research center for 5 years, training to fly manned orbital flights of the Soviet space shuttle Buran II. The program was canceled before any manned launches could be made.

Prikhodko was born November 15, 1953, in Dushanbe, the capital of the Tadjikistan ASSR.

At the age of 17 Prikhodko graduated from secondary school in the town of Gubkin, Belgorod Region, Russia, and began working as a lab assistant in a research institute there. The next year, in 1971, he joined the armed forces, entering the Kacha Higher Air Force School. One

of his classmates at Kacha that year was future Buran test pilot Sergei Tresvyatsky.

Following graduation Prikhodko spent the next 10 years at Kacha as an instructor. He left the air force in 1985 and enrolled at the civilian test pilot school. Following graduation in 1986 he became a test pilot at the Gromov flight research center in Zhukovsky.

He has logged over 2,800 hours of flying time. He has also earned a degree from the Moscow Aviation Insitute (1989).

Prikhodko was selected in 1988 as a replacement for Buran test pilots Levchenko and Shchukin, who had died within 2 weeks of each other in August of that year. He reported to the group on March 22, 1989, at which time he commenced the general cosmonaut training course at the Gagarin Center. He was certified as a cosmonaut-researcher in March 1991.

Following the cancellation of the Buran program, Prikhodko moved to the United States to work for Graystone Technology. He currently lives in San Diego, California, and hopes to join NASA as a Shuttle astronaut or test pilot.

Pronina, Irina Rudolfovna
1953–
Engineer Irina Pronina served as backup cosmonaut-researcher for the flight of Soyuz T-7 in August 1982. During that flight, Svetlana Savitskaya became the second woman to go into space, spending a week aboard the Salyut 7 space station. Pronina supported the flight from the control center in Kaliningrad.

Following her backup assignment for Soyuz T-7 Pronina trained as the cosmonaut-researcher for an 8-month residency aboard the Salyut 7 space station in 1983. But she was replaced on the mission, Soyuz T-8, a month before its scheduled launch, because of changing mission requirements. She was never assigned to another space crew.

Pronina was born April 14, 1953, in Moscow, and attended the Bauman Higher Technical School. Following graduation she went to work at the NPO Energiya. It was her father Rudolf, an engineer at the Baikonur Cosmodrome, who told her in 1979 that a new group of women cosmonauts was being recruited. She applied, passed the medical tests, and in July 1980 was enrolled in the cosmonaut team.

She remained an active member of the cosmonaut group until her retirement in April 1992. She still works for Energiya at the flight control center.

Protchenko, Sergei Filippovich

1947–

Sergei Protchenko was one of the 9 pilot candidates enrolled in the cosmonaut group in August 1976. He attended the Chkalov test pilot school, graduating in 1977, and was near the end of the 2-year Soyuz-Salyut training schedule when he was forced to leave the cosmonaut team for medical reasons.

Protchenko was born January 3, 1947, in the village of Senitsky, Pogarsky District, Byransk Region, Russia. He was trained as a pilot in the Soviet air force.

Since leaving the cosmonaut team in April 1979 he has worked as a test pilot for the Soviet Ministry of Radio Industry testing aviation radio systems. He is a lieutenant colonel in the reserve.

Puchkov, Alexandr Sergeyevich

1948–

Soviet air force test pilot Alexandr Puchkov was one of the 6 candidates selected for the military flight test center Buran cosmonaut group in October 1988, though his selection was not approved by the state commission until May 1990. Nevertheless, Puchkov commenced basic cosmonaut training at the Gagarin Center in February 1989 and in April 1991 was designated a test-cosmonaut.

Following his basic cosmonaut training Puchkov returned to active test flying at the flight test center branch in Chkalovskaya. He joined the military Buran team in April 1992.

Puchkov was born October 15, 1948, in Medyn, Kaluga District, Russia. In 1966 he joined the Soviet air force, enrolling at the Kacha Higher Air Force School. His classmates at Kacha included two future Buran Shuttle test pilots, Alexandr Shchukin and Yuri Sheffer. Puchkov and Sheffer remained at Kacha as flight instructors following graduation in 1970.

Puchkov was admitted to the Chkalov test pilot school in 1976, graduating the next year. While working as a test pilot he also attended the Moscow Aviation Institute, earning a degree in 1981.

When the military Buran cosmonaut team was dissolved in September 1996, Puchkov left the air force and retired.

Pushenko, Nikolai, Alexeyevixh

1952–

Nikolai Pushenko is a Soviet air force test pilot who was selected in November 1988 to train for manned orbital flights of the space shuttle Buran as a member of the cosmonaut unit of the military flight test center. He arrived at the Gagarin Center in 1989 to undergo general cosmonaut training, and in April 1991 was designated a test-cosmonaut, and moved permanently to the center in April 1992.

Pushenko was born August 10, 1952, in the village of Povalikha, Altai Territory, Russia. He graduated from secondary school in the town of Barnaul, then joined the Soviet air force, attending the Barnaul Higher Air Force School.

Following graduation in 1974 he served as a pilot until 1982, when he was admitted to the Chkalov test pilot school.

When the military Buran cosmonaut team was dissolved in September 1996, Pushenko returned to full-time flight test.

Rafikov, Mars Zakirovich

1933–

Mars Rafikov was one of the first Soviet cosmonauts whose training began in March 1960. When the members of that first group were asked for a "peer rating," a written evaluation of each member to select the one who should be sent into space first, Rafikov named himself: "I should be sent, although I know that they will not send me. But my first name is 'cosmic' and this would sound good."

He was dismissed from the cosmonaut team in March 1962, officially for being absent without leave. Cosmonaut training director Nikolai Kamanin and political officer Nikolai Nikeryasov reportedly found Rafikov politically unreliable.

Rafikov was born September 30, 1933, in Dzhalal-Abad, Kirghizia. He is a Tatar by nationality. He attended Air Force School No. 151 in Syzran, Kuybyshev Region, then entered the Chuguyev Higher Air Force School, graduating in 1954. He served as a fighter pilot in the same Soviet air regiment as future cosmonaut Valentin Varlamov, flying MiG-17s.

After leaving the space program Rafikov served as a fighter pilot in Trans-Caucacus air regiment with young pilots named Leonid Kizim and Yuri Malyshev, and was able to help them become cosmonauts.

Rafikov later served in Afghanistan and Prikarpatye. He left flying in 1979 and the air force altogether in 1982. He currently lives in Almaty (formerly Alma Ata), where he is employed by a housing collective and for many years still trained pilots through the DOSAAF program.

Revin, Sergei Nikolayevich
1966–

Engineer Sergei Revin is currently assigned as backup flight engineer for a 2000 Soyuz mission to the International Space Station. This visit, to be flown by Talgat Musabayev and Nadezhda Kuzhelnaya, will supply the incremental crew aboard the station with a fresh Soyuz rescue vehicle.

Revin was born June 12, 1966, in Moscow. He attended the Moscow Institute of Instrument Technology, specializing in automation and electronics. Following graduation in 1989 he worked for 4 years at the NPO Instrument Technology. Since 1993 he has worked at the RKK Energiya.

He was approved by the joint state commission as a cosmonaut-candidate on February 9, 1996, and underwent the basic training course at the Gagarin Center from May 1996 to March 1998.

Romanenko, Roman Yuriyevich
1970–

Captain Roman Romanenko is one of the 8 Russian air force pilots selected for cosmonaut training at the Gagarin Center in July 1997. In the spring of 1999 he should qualify as a Soyuz commander and International Space Station crew-member.

Romanenko was born August 9, 1971, in the town of Shchelkovo, Moscow region. His father, cosmonaut Yuri Romanenko, was a candidate at the Gagarin Center at that time. Like his father, young Romanenko graduated from the Chernigov Higher Air Force School (1992).

At the time of his selection for cosmonaut training Romanenko was a deputy aircraft commander with the 70th Detached Air Wing (Special Destination). This unit, named for the late Vladimir Seregin, is the aircraft support group for the Gagarin Center.

Romanenko, Yuri Viktorovich
1944–

Yuri Romanenko is one of the most experienced cosmonauts in the world, having spent almost 431 days in orbit on 3 different missions, including one 11-month marathon aboard the Mir space station in 1987.

Already the veteran of one 3-month mission, Romanenko was not even scheduled to fly Soyuz TM-2. He and rookie flight engineer Alexandr Laveikin were originally the backup crew for Vladimir Titov and Alexandr Serebrov, who were medically disqualified just days before the planned launch on February 5, 1987.

The Mir station had already been activated by cosmonauts Leonid Kizim and Vladimir Solovyov in the first half of 1986, but Romanenko and Laveikin's job was to make the station operational and to prepare it for expansion. The first add-on module, the astrophysical observatory Kvant, reached Mir on April 5, 1987, but failed to dock. Six days later Romanenko and Laveikin had to take an unplanned space walk to clear an obstruction (later revealed to be a garbage bag) from the docking module.

The next several weeks of the mission were taken up with activating Kvant and, during two EVAs, installing new solar power arrays on the exterior of the Soyuz TM-Mir-Kvant complex.

The strain of this work began to tell on Laveikin, whose cardiograms began to show irregularities. In June flight controllers decided to return him to Earth at the next opportunity. During the visit of Syrian cosmonaut Mohammed Faris in late July Laveikin was replaced by the Soyuz TM-3 flight engineer, Alexandr Alexandrov.

It was Romanenko and Alexandrov who conducted the first extensive observations with Kvant, and continued a series of Earth-sensing experiments.

By October, however, 6 months into the mission, Romanenko was able to work no more than 6 hours a day. He took up writing poetry and songs.

In December he and Alexandrov were relieved by Vladimir Titov and Musa Manarov. With the new expedition crew was Soviet shuttle test pilot Anatoly Levchenko, who would serve as "relief" for Romanenko during reentry.

By this time the stress had also begun to show on Romanenko. While Soyuz TM-3 was being loaded with equipment for return to Earth, Romanenko exploded at ground controllers, demanding that all "superfluous personnel" be removed from the control center and complaining that the cosmonauts were being distracted with "unnecessary talk."

Back on Earth after 326 days, Romanenko was revealed to be in relatively good physical condition. Three hours after landing he was walking on his own. A day later he was jogging. He said that he felt better after the eleven month mission than he had after the one lasting 3 months. He was tested regularly for the next 2 months, when his muscle volume and calcium levels—always depleted by long-term stays in space—appeared to have returned to normal.

Romanenko's previous marathon was the then record-breaking Soyuz 26/Salyut 6 mission in 1977 and 1978. He and flight engineer Georgy Grechko activated the Salyut 6 station and lived aboard it for 96 days, eclipsing the previous American record of 84 days, set by the third Skylab crew in 1974.

Their flight did more than just break an American a record—it demonstrated a new and more flexible Soviet approach to manned spaceflight. For example, 2-man cosmonaut teams for long duration missions are carefully screened and monitored during months of training to ensure that they are compatible and comfortable with each other's working habits. Romanenko and Grechko were thrown together just 6 weeks before launch, because suspected technical problems with the main Salyut docking port had prevented the original 90-day expedition crew (Kovalenok and Ryumin) from reaching the station. Grechko, a Salyut engineer as well as a cosmonaut, was a specialist in that docking system, so he was plucked from another crew and teamed with Romanenko, whom he barely knew.

The two cosmonauts got along quite well in spite of this. Early in the mission Romanenko was told by ground controllers that Grechko's father had died. His choice was to tell Grechko now, a third of the way through the mission, when the effect of the news would be unpredictable, or to wait. Romanenko waited until they returned to Earth.

During the last 2 weeks of the mission Grechko nursed Romanenko through a painful toothache that threatened to cut short the mission.

Romanenko and Grechko were the first cosmonauts to be resupplied by unmanned supply spacecraft and were host to two visiting cosmonaut crews, including Czech cosmonaut Vladimir Remek. Their flight was successful even though both cosmonauts skimped on their exercise program and found their readaptation to Earth's gravity to be more prolonged and painful as a result.

Romanenko later commanded Soyuz 38, an 8-day Interkosmos mission during which he and Cuban cosmonaut Arnaldo Tamayo-Mendez visited Salyut 6.

Romanenko was born August 1, 1944, in the Koltubanovsky settlement in the Orenburg Region of Russia. His father was a ship's captain in the Soviet navy, so Romanenko grew up in seaports.

As a secondary school student he became interested in math and physics, and built model airplanes. After spending a year working in construction he joined the Soviet air force, attending the Chernigov Lenin Komsomol Higher Air Force School. He graduated as a pilot-engineer in 1966 and spent the next 4 years at Chernigov as a flight instructor, eventually logging 1,100 hours of flying time in his career.

Romanenko was one of the 9 candidates enrolled in the cosmonaut team in May 1970. Upon completion of the basic training course, Romanenko and Vladimir Dzhanibekov were assigned as backup commanders for the Apollo-Soyuz Test Project. From May 1973 to July 1975 they made several trips to the United States and, in turn, played host to American astronauts who visited Star Town. Romanenko had to learn English as well. Teamed with flight engineer Alexandr Ivanchenkov, Romaneko served as backup commander for Soyuz 16, the ASTP dress rehearsal flown in December 1974.

In August 1975 Romanenko and Ivanchenkov began training for a long-duration Salyut 6 mission together. They were backups to Kovalenok and Ryumin for Soyuz 25, and found themselves reassigned to different crews in the subsequent shuffle.

Romanenko later served as backup commander for Soyuz 33, the flight of Bulgarian cosmonaut Georgy Ivanov in April 1979 and in the same capacity for the flight of Rumanian cosmonaut Dumitru Prunariu in May 1981. In late 1981 and 1982 he trained for a Salyut 7 mission as the backup commander for Soyuz T-7, but health problems forced him to step aside. He worked at Kaliningrad mission control for 2 years before returning to flight training.

He attended the Gagarin Air Force Academy from 1975 to 1980.

In 1988, after completing his mission to Mir, Romanenko moved into an administrative job at the Gagarin Center, ultimately becoming head of the 3rd Directorate for the Buran space shuttle.

Romanenko retired from the air force and the training center in December 1995. His son, Roman, was selected as a cosmonaut-candidate in 1997.

Romanov, Valery Alexandrovich

1946–

Valery Romanov is an engineer from the NPO Machinostroyeniye who was enrolled as a cosmonaut candidate in December 1978. For the next 2 years he trained as flight engineer of a 3-man crew intended for the TKS-Almaz program.

TKS was a 4-ton Gemini-style manned spacecraft designed and built by the NPO-M (originally known as the Chelomei design bureau, OKB-52) and designed to be used with the Almaz military space station.

Two manned Almaz vehicles (Salyut 3 and Salyut 5) were flown in space, though they were modified for use with Soyuz transports. And five TKS vehicles were tested in the unmanned mode (the return capsules from the two Salyuts plus Kosmos 929, 1271, and 1443). The TKS-Almaz program was canceled in 1981.

Romanov was born August 18, 1946, in Chernyakhovsk, Kaliningrad Region, Russia, and attended the Bauman Higher Technical School. He joined NPO-M upon graduation in 1970.

Romanov now works at the KB Salyut, builders of the Mir modules such as Kvant.

Rozhdestvensky, Valery Ilyich

1939–

Valery Rozhdestvensky took part in one of the most dangerous landings in space history. On October 24, 1976, he was flight engineer aboard Soyuz 23 when he and commander Vyacheslav Zudov made the first splashdown of a Soviet manned spacecraft, coming down by accident in the middle of the saltwater lake Tengiz during a nighttime snowstorm.

Rozhdestvensky and Zudov had been launched on October 23, 1976, for a planned 2-month military reconnaissance mission aboard Salyut-Almaz 5. During their approach to the space station, however, the Igla guidance system failed and the docking was called off. Mission rules dictated a swift return to Earth. The Soyuz braking engines were fired and a routine reentry took place.

The primary spacecraft recovery zone is an area of desert steppe almost 200 miles in diameter, bordered on the east by the city of Arkalyk and on the west by Tselinograd in Kazakhstan. Roughly halfway between these two cities lies Lake Tengiz, and Soyuz 23 had the bad luck to splash down about a mile from its southern shore.

Although cosmonauts train for water landings, the Soyuz makes a bad boat. The parachutes filled with water and capsized the spacecraft, allowing water to leak in via air vents.

Rescue craft were able to reach Soyuz 23 and divers attached a flotation collar to the craft, but it could not be towed to shore until dawn, many hours later. The cosmonauts spent almost 11 hours curled up inside the freezing, bobbing spacecraft.

Ironically, Rozhdestvensky had once commanded a team of deep-sea divers in the Soviet navy. As the only sailor in the cosmonaut team, he had the nickname "The Admiral," and had joked prior to liftoff that he might find his diving experience useful. He was speaking, however, about a possible space walk.

Rozhdestvensky was born on February 13, 1939, in Leningrad (St. Petersburg) and graduated from the F. E. Dzherzhinsky Higher Naval Engineering School in 1961. He served in the navy, first with the 446th Air-Sea Rescue Division of the Baltic Fleet, then as commander of an air-sea rescue group based in Liepaja, Latvia.

Rozhdestvensky was one of the 22 candidates enrolled in the cosmonaut team on October 28, 1965. In November 1967 he began to train as a potential crewmember for the Almaz military space station, then in development. He was assigned to an Almaz crew in the summer of 1971, and served as a backup flight engineer for Salyut 3 (the second Almaz) in 1974 and Salyut 5 (the third Almaz) in 1976.

Following Soyuz 23 Rozhdestvensky trained as a potential flight engineer for at least one other Almaz mission, originally scheduled for launch in 1980. The program was canceled, however, and Rozhdestvensky formed a group of cosmonaut-capcoms at the Kaliningrad mission control center, serving as lead capcom during the Salyut 6 missions from 1977 to 1981. During Salyut 7 missions he has worked as a flight controller.

He left the cosmonaut team in June 1986 to become head of the section at the Gagarin Center that designs and maintains spacecraft simulators. He was appointed deputy director, 2nd Directorate in July 1988, and served as head of that directorate from March 1989 to October 1992, when he became a reserve.

Rozhdestvensky currently works for the company Megapolis Industry.

Rukavishnikov, Nikolai Nikolayevich

1932–

Nikolai Rukavishnikov is the hard-luck engineer-cosmonaut whose three attempts to complete a flight aboard a Salyut space station all failed.

Rukavishnikov was the cosmonaut-researcher of the Soyuz 10 crew, launched April 23, 1971, for a planned 24-day mission aboard the first Salyut. It would have been the world's first space station mission, but though Soyuz 10 and its three cosmonauts were able to dock with the station, technical problems prevented them from going aboard, and they were forced to make an emergency return to Earth.

Rukavishnikov's second encounter with Salyut was even more dangerous. On April 10, 1979, he and Bulgarian cosmonaut Georgy Ivanov were launched aboard Soyuz 33 for an 8-day stay aboard Salyut 6. But during their final approach to the station on April 12 their main maneuvering engines failed, threatening to strand them in space. The cosmonauts were forced to use backup equipment to get home, landing in darkness after enduring unusually high G-loads during reentry.

By October 1982, when Rukavishnikov began to train as part of a USSR-Indian team for a Salyut 7 flight, the other cosmonauts were joking that each Salyut was equipped with an "anti-Rukavishnikov" device. (He had also been assigned to a Salyut crew in 1973, but Salyut itself had failed to reach orbit.) Sure enough, in March 1984, just weeks before launch, Rukavishnikov caught a bad cold that forced him off the flight crew.

Rukavishnikov did make one very successful flight aboard Soyuz 16 in December 1984. This 6-day mission was a full-scale dress rehearsal for the Apollo-Soyuz mission in 1975.

Rukavishnikov was born September 18, 1932 in the city of Tomsk in western Siberia. As a child he traveled all over the Soviet Union with his parents, who were both surveying and building new railways. He attended the Moscow Institute of Physics and Engineering, graduating in 1957, and immediately went to work in the Korolev spacecraft design bureau. His early field of work was in automatic controls for spacecraft. Later he headed a team of scientists who developed Earth and solar physics experiments.

Rukavishnikov was selected for cosmonaut training in January 1967. For the next 2 years he was involved in the Soviet manned lunar landing program. In 1968 he and commander Valery Bykovsky were prime candidates to fly a manned circumlunar Soyuz-Zond mission. But technical problems delayed the scheduled December 6, 1968, launch, and 3 weeks later the American Apollo 8 circled the Moon. The Soyuz-Zond mission was canceled, and Rukavishnikov began to train for an Earth orbital flight.

He and Anatoly Filipchenko were teamed in late 1971 for a planned flight to the Salyut space station. But a launch failure in the summer of 1972 and an in-orbit failure the following May left them without a spacecraft, and made them eligible for assignment to ASTP.

In 1977 Rukavishnikov became the first civilian assigned to command a Soviet space crew, serving as backup commander for Soyuz 28. (He had replaced rookie air force pilot Yuri Isaulov when mission rules were changed to require a veteran cosmonaut in every crew. Ironically, Rukavishnikov would later serve with Isaulov in the backup crew for Soyuz T-2 and Soyuz T-3.)

Rukavishnikov took part in the design of the Mir space station. He retired from the cosmonaut team in 1987, but still works at the RKK Energiya.

Ryumin, Valery Viktorovich
1939–

Between February 1979 and October 1980 Valery Ryumin spent almost one year in space during two visits to the Salyut 6 space station.

But where early Soviet candidates for long duration spaceflights were selected for their unusual endurance, Ryumin's record was set by accident. As flight engineer of Soyuz 25, launched October 9, 1977, Ryumin was trained for a planned 90-day mission that would involve activation of the newly launched Salyut 6 station, medical experiments, and tests of new systems that would allow a

Salyut to be refueled and resupplied by unmanned Progress supply tanker vehicles.

But Soyuz 25 failed to link up with Salyut 6 because of a mechanical failure in its docking mechanism and just 48 hours after launch Ryumin and commander Vladimir Kovalenok were back on Earth.

To make matters worse, early indications were that the docking failure might have been crew error: they were the first cosmonauts not named Heroes of the Soviet Union after a flight. The state commission in charge of manned flights also passed a new rule requiring each crew to include at least one veteran, theorizing that difficulties adapting to microgravity made it difficult for crews to respond to emergencies that occurred early in flight. (NASA applied similar rules in selecting Space Shuttle crews beginning in 1982.)

In the ensuing shuffle Kovalenok was assigned to one new Salyut 6 crew and Ryumin to another. On February 25, 1979, Ryumin and pilot Vladimir Lyakhov were sent into space aboard Soyuz 32. By this time cosmonauts had made successful "expeditions" aboard Salyut 6 of 96 days and 139 days, increasing the duration of their stays by about a month with each mission. Ryumin and Lyakhov were to attempt to spend 6 months in a living space approximately 25 feet long and 10 feet wide.

Ryumin, who would later publish frank diaries of his two long visits to Salyut 6, thought of a quote from the American writer O. Henry: "If you want to encourage the craft of murder, all you have to do is lock up two men for 2 months in an 18 by 20 foot room." But he and Lyakhov got along well during their months of confinement. They were kept busy with astronomical observations using a radio-telescope, with space manufacturing, and with repairs to equipment aboard Salyut 6, which had outlived its original 18-month design life.

One major disappointment for the cosmonauts was the lack of visitors. On April 12, 1979, as Ryumin and Lyakhov watched from Salyut, the first guests, Soviet commander Nikolai Rukavishnikov and Bulgarian researcher Georgy Ivanov, suffered a major engine failure aboard their Soyuz 33 craft and were forced to make an emergency return to Earth without going aboard the station. Ryumin knew that the subsequent investigation would postpone the Soviet-Hungarian flight scheduled for July.

On August 15, near the end of the mission, Ryumin made a daring space walk to cut away the radio-telescope, which had snagged as it was jettisoned from the outside of Salyut-6. Four days later, after 175 days in space, the cosmonauts were back on Earth. Their physical condition was better than expected, but not as good as it would have been if Ryumin had fully carried out his exercise program, something he would correct on his next flight.

Ryumin went on leave, then, in early 1980, took up his new job, supervising the training of the next Salyut 6 expedition crew, pilot Leonid Popov and engineer Valentin Lebedev, who had been backups to Lyakhov and Ryumin. But just weeks before the planned launch in April Lebedev broke his knee while working out on a trampoline. Soviet flight director and former cosmonaut Alexei Yeliseyev, head of the manned space department at NPO Energiya, wanted to replace the Popov-Lebedev crew with their backups, Zudov and Andreyev. He asked Ryumin to join Popov in the thankless and time-consuming backup role. When it became obvious that Zudov and Andreyev weren't as well trained as they should have been, Ryumin suggested instead that he and Popov be sent in their place. Popov was the best-trained commander, and Ryumin was already more familiar with Salyut 6 than Andreyev could be. There might also be some medical value in having him fly again.

After consulting with doctors, Yeliseyev agreed, and on April 9, 1980, Ryumin and Popov were launched aboard Soyuz 35.

Ryumin's second expedition went more smoothly. He was able to adapt to life aboard Salyut 6 more quickly, and his experience helped Popov, who was on his first flight, to be more productive. The cosmonauts were more faithful to their exercise regime than earlier crews, which made their eventual readaptation to Earth shorter and easier. The psychological burden of isolation wasn't nearly as great, since Ryumin and Popov were visited by four different crews, including guest cosmonauts from Hungary, Vietnam, and Cuba. The mission ended on October 11, 1980.

After a hiatus of 17 years, Ryumin returned to active flight training in the fall of 1997, as a mission specialist in the crew of STS-91. This flight of the orbiter Endeavour is scheduled to make the ninth and last Shuttle-Mir docking mission in the summer of 1999. Ryumin, the Russian director of Shuttle-Mir, fought for the chance to make a personal inspection of the station.

Ryumin was born August 16, 1939, in Komsomolsk-na-Amur in far-eastern Siberia. His father was a construction worker on the railroad being built there. Intending to become a metallurgical engineer, Ryumin attended a technical school in Kaliningrad, then was drafted into the army, where he became a tank commander in the Transcaucasus military district. Demobilized in 1961, he enrolled in the Moscow Forestry Institute's department of computer science, graduating in June 1966.

For the next 4 years Ryumin was an engineer in the Korolev spacecraft design bureau working on the 7K-L1 (Soyuz Zond) program. In 1970 he moved to the new Salyut space station, and played a major role in its development.

In March 1973, when Salyut specialists were recruited into the cosmonaut group, Ryumin was one of those accepted, in spite of the fact that he was too tall for the cramped quarters of most spacecraft and required a specially designed couch.

During the Salyut 4 and Apollo-Soyuz flights of 1975 Ryumin was a communications operator based aboard the tracking ship *Academician Sergei Korolev*. In September 1975 he was he was named to the first Salyut 6 crew with Vladimir Kovalenok.

After his third spaceflight Ryumin served as assistant flight director for Soyuz T-4, the last expedition to Salyut 6, which was commanded by Kovalenok. He was involved in the design of the new Salyut 7 station, and in January 1982 succeeded Alexei Yeliseyev as lead flight director and head of NPO Energiya's manned space department, a job that made him one of the more visible spokesmen for the Soviet space program.

His space diary was published as *A Year Without Earth* (1987).

Ryumin served as lead flight director until 1987, then was named deputy chief designer of NPO Energiya. Among his responsibilities there was the Buran space shuttle. He became head of Shuttle-Mir operations in 1994.

He is married to cosmonaut Yelena Kondakova, veteran of two spaceflights, including one aboard the American Space Shuttle in 1997.

ONE DAY OF ONE YEAR IN SPACE

by Valery Ryumin

(Valery Ryumin spent 6 months in space aboard Salyut-6 in 1979, only to return to the station in early 1980 for another 6 months. Like many Russian space station crewmembers, he kept an in-flight journal. Here he talks about the mundane joys of life aboard a space station, a routine that has come to be the standard aboard Mir, and very likely aboard the International Space Station.)

May 15, 1979

The days fly by and we have adjusted ourselves to our daily routine. We get up at eight every morning, awakened by the unpleasant sound of the siren. Then we do our morning exercises for 30 to 40 minutes, mainly with chest expanders, after which we make our toilet and have breakfast.

We shave with an electric shaver with a stub-collecting insert. We clean our teeth with a battery-powered toothbrush with no toothpaste. We moisten our faces and hands with napkins saturated with a special lotion.

Breakfast, as a rule, consists of canned meat, cottage cheese in tubes, bread, a choice of tea or coffee, pastries or biscuits. The food is heated before consumption. Canned meat is aplenty, including pork, beef, steaks, tongue, bacon, sausage, chicken, turkey and goose liver pate. The pate and sausage are our preferred dishes. Breakfast takes ten to fifteen minutes. I put the food into the heater upon awakening, and after we finish our physical exercises, it's ready for consumption.

Both tea and coffee are instant and we only have to pour hot water into a special container with powder. We get hot water mainly from the system which regenerates water from the condensate, a mixture of air and water formed by our sweat, and by moisture settling on the cold pipes of the thermal regulating system. This system provides about 0.85 liters of water per man each day. The rest is supplied to us by our [Progress] transport spacecraft. The quality of the condensate is largely dependent on the intensity of our physical exercises and how much sweating we do.

. . .

At about 9:30 A.M. we begin our programmed activities, which we follow for 2.5 to 3 hours, following which we resume our physical exercises for one hour. One of us works out on the stationary bicycle while the other uses the treadmill. . . . The treadmill is for running or walking. Volodya [Lyakhov] just runs at a slow pace while I prefer fast walking and fast running. Before embarking on the exercises we don our sports suits and put towels nearby to remove the sweat. After about ten to fifteen minutes our faces and open body parts are covered with drops of sweat. In weightlessness these drops, which have a spherical shape, do not roll down the body or coalesce with each other. These "water peas" can only be removed with a towel. Toward the end of our exercises our sports suits are soaked with sweat. We dry them on an exhaust fan.

The exercises are followed by dinner, which consists of a soup-in-a-tube first course followed by some canned meat, mashed potatoes, different juices, and then a choice of tea, coffee or milk. On Sundays we have garden strawberries with sugar for dessert. The first and second courses and bread are heated. At dinner we also have onions and garlic. For seasoning we prefer mustard and horseradish as well as fruit and applesauce.

After dinner we have about forty minutes of free time, which we can use to our liking, but which, as a rule, we devote to preparations for the next planned activity.

We then work for another two to four hours, and sometimes more, if an assignment cannot be interrupted. This is again followed by hour-long physical exercises. If I had exercised on the bicycle in the morning, after dinner I would take my turn on the treadmill.

(We don't do exercises because we want to. They may be a pleasant past-time on Earth, but in orbit you have to force yourself to do them. They are hard work that is also monotonous.)

. . .

Supper ordinarily consists of powdered mashed potatoes, meat and cottage cheese, followed by coffee or tea with pastries and biscuits. We have many sweets, such as candies, on board, but we eat little of them. We crave salty things, but they are in short supply.

Supper is followed by free time, which we use for going over tomorrow's program and checking with the ground team. At the same time we make small repairs. I would also make entries in my diary.

[Volodya and I] are both taciturn people. We rarely discuss abstract things unconnected with the mission. The only exceptions are the days when we have communications sessions with our families. With our souls harrowed by loneliness and memories, we long to recount our reminiscences to each other. We hear the latest news, including sports. Sometimes [flight control] feeds television programs to us, mainly variety shows and sports. On Saturdays the psychological support team organizes meetings with artists and performers.

We are supposed to go to bed at 11 P.M., but as a rule we don't until an hour later. We observe the Earth, take pictures with manual cameras, talk to the flight control team, and listen to music.

. . .

In general, we work as we do on Earth—with 2 days off, 1 for cleaning, either the station or ourselves! A space bath takes up an entire day, including heating the water and removing all the equipment following the bath. Have you ever watched a dog fuss around after a bath? In our celluloid "shower," we're like dogs fussing around, shaking water off ourselves instead of dust.

Still, it feels good.

Salei, Yevgeny Vladimirovich
1950–

Yevgeny Salei was the backup cosmonaut-researcher for Alexandr Volkov on Soyuz T-14. During that mission, cosmonauts Vasyutin, Grechko, and Volkov docked their Soyuz with the Salyut 7 space station, then occupied by Vladimir Dzhanibekov and Viktor Savinykh. Vasyutin, Savinykh, and Volkov went on to spend 75 days aboard the station before ending their mission prematurely due to Vasyutin's illness. Salei supported the flight from mission control in Kaliningrad, near Moscow.

Salei was born in Tavda, Sverdlovsk district, Russia, on January 1, 1950. He joined the air force in 1967 and spent 4 years at the Kacha Higher Air Force School near Volgograd.

Upon graduation in 1971 he served as a flight instructor at Kacha, then did tours as an operational pilot in Poland, and as a deputy squadron leader in Uzbekistan. In

1975 he applied for admission to the Gagarin Air Force Academy, only to find himself ordered to undergo physical examinations for the cosmonaut team. He passed, and was enrolled as a candidate in August 1976.

Salei and the other 8 pilots in his group were immediately enrolled in the Chkalov test pilot school, from which they graduated in 1977, before commencing the 2-year course of training on Soyuz and Salyut systems. He did further test pilot work in 1980, earning a rating of test pilot second class. In November 1984 he was assigned to the crews training for a long-duration mission aboard Salyut 7.

He would have undoubtedly flown as commander of a later Soyuz-Mir mission, but physical problems caused him to be dismissed from the cosmonaut team in July 1987.

Salei is currently an officer in the air force reserve and works as deputy director of the Chkalov Central Flying Club in Moscow.

Sarafanov, Gennady Vasilyevich

1942–

Gennady Sarafanov's only spaceflight was the aborted Soyuz 15 in August 1974. Sarafanov and flight engineer Lev Demin were launched into space on the evening of August 26, 1974, for a scheduled 25-day reconnaissance mission aboard an Almaz-class military space station called Salyut 3. But during the final approach to the space station the next morning a failure in the Igla guidance system forced the cosmonauts to abort the docking. They landed at night in a thunderstorm.

Sarafanov and Demin returned to Earth after just 2 days in space; their postflight criticisms of the Soyuz were not well received by Chief Designer Valentin Glushko, and the crew was officially blamed for the docking failure.

Sarafanov was born January 1, 1942, in the village of Sinenkiye near Saratov. At the age of 17 he joined the Soviet air force and commenced flight school at Kamenka, hoping to become a fighter pilot. A year later, as part of a general cutback in the Soviet military,

Sarafanov transferred to the Balashov Higher Air Force School. Following graduation in 1964, he served with the Long Range Aviation branch of the Soviet air force in the Baltic military district (Lithuania). In October 1965 he became one of the 22 air force candidates enrolled in the cosmonaut group.

After completing his basic cosmonaut training in December 1967, Sarafanov joined the training group for the Almaz military space station program. He was assigned to an Almaz flight crew in 1972.

Even though Sarafanov was effectively blackballed by Energiya Chief Designer Glushko following Soyuz 14, he was still accepted as a potential crew commander by Almaz Chief Designer Vladimir Chelomei. From 1976 to 1980 Sarafanov trained in a number of Almaz crews with flight engineers Nikolai Porvatkin and Vladimir Preobrazhensky. At the same time he attended the Gagarin Air Force Academy, graduating in 1980. He later earned a candidate of technical sciences degree.

Sarafanov remained a training official at the Gagarin Center until resigning on July 7, 1987. As a civilian he has been deputy chairman of the *Znaniye* (Knowledge) Society, an organization that became infamous for its *glasnost* magazine *Argumenti i Fakti*, and also a senior instructor on the staff of the Industrial Association Automation, Science, Technology (AO-ANT). More recently he has worked for Start, an aircraft transport company based in Moscow.

Sattarov, Nail Sharpovich

1941–

Nail Sattarov was one of the 6 Soviet air force test pilots selected in January 1979 to perform military flight tests—including orbital missions—in the Buran space shuttle program. In 1980 these 6 pilots underwent the general cosmonaut training course at the Gagarin Center.

That same year Sattarov was dismissed from the program because of "violations of testing discipline." While piloting a Tu-134 aircraft he did a barrel roll, a common piece of stunt flying that was nevertheless forbidden for the transport plane.

Sattarov was born December 23, 1941, and graduated from the Orenburg air force school and the Chkalov test pilot school. He was serving as a military test pilot at the flight research center in Akhtubinsk at the time of his involvement in the Buran program.

He later left military service to become a civilian test pilot with the Tupolev Aviation Scientific-Technical Complex (ANTK Tupolev), formerly the Tupolev design bureau. In December 1997 he was awarded the title Merited Test Pilot of the Russian Federation for his work there.

Savinykh, Viktor Petrovich
1940–

Viktor Savinykh took part in one of the most daring Soviet spaceflights ever, the rescue of the Salyut 7 space station in the summer of 1985.

Salyut 7 had been launched in April 1982 and designed to operate for 2 years as home to 3 long-duration crews of cosmonauts, who would successively spend 7, 8, and 9 months in orbit. Since this station's predecessor, Salyut 6, had doubled its intended lifetime, allowing for several "bonus" missions, Soviet planners were optimistic that Salyut 7 would, in fact, operate for 3 to 4 years, until the new Mir station was ready.

But a fuel leak in August 1983, which occurred when cosmonauts Lyakhov and Alexandrov were onboard, severely damaged the station. The 1984 main crew of Kizim, Solovyov, and Atkov were able to repair the damage done by the leak in a series of space walks, but just weeks after they left Salyut 7 in November 1984 the station suffered a massive electrical failure that allowed it to drift out of control, its solar panels useless.

Savinykh had been training as flight engineer for the crew of the 1985 residence. When contact with Salyut 7 was lost in the closing days of 1984, Soviet space officials devised a clever plan to rendezvous with the dead vehicle (a difficult task for the Soviet Soyuz-T spacecraft, which depends on response from its target for accurate maneuvering), go aboard it, and restore it to life. Savinykh was chosen to join 4-time space veteran Vladimir Dzhanibekov as the rescue team, and they were launched aboard Soyuz T-13 on June 6, 1985. Two days later, taking extra care on their approach to Salyut 7, they docked.

When the 2 cosmonauts opened the connecting hatch they found a dead space station. Dzhanibekov wrote later, "There was complete silence in the docking chamber. We remained in semi-darkness, the portholes half-covered with blinds. Only the rays of the flashlight picked out specks of dust hanging motionless in the air." Moving inside the station, to the central workstation, they found complete darkness (the shades were drawn) and a smell like that of a "stagnant machine shop." It was also cold; the windows had a layer of frost on the inside.

Savinykh and Dzhanibekov went to work trying to connect the solar panels to the batteries they normally charged. Within 2 days they had succeeded in bypassing the ruined circuit panel (which was the source of the original failure) and began to charge up the batteries. The cosmonauts' exhaled carbon dioxide built up, since the station's air circulating system had shut down, giving them headaches and making the repairs even more difficult. (Salyut 7 was so dead that the cosmonauts had to communicate with Kaliningrad flight control through the radios on their Soyuz.) But within 2 weeks they were ready to receive a supply of spare parts and fuel from a Progress robot tanker, which arrived on June 23. Progress was followed on July 21 by the Kosmos 1669 supply ship, which carried new EVA space suits to replace those ruined by the freezing temperatures aboard the station. On August 2 Savinykh and Dzhanibekov conducted a 5-hour EVA to install a third solar panel and dusty collectors designed by French scientists for the study of Halley's Comet.

On September 18, Soyuz T-14 arrived, crewed by cosmonauts Vladimir Vasyutin, Georgy Grechko, and Alexandr Volkov. Vasyutin and Volkov had been members of the original 1985 residency crew with Savinykh. Seven days later, Dzhanibekov and Grechko left Salyut 7 in the Soyuz T-13 spacecraft, having taken part in the first "handover" of space teams in history.

Savinykh, Vasyutin, and Volkov settled down for a winter of work with the Kosmos 1686 laboratory module, which was docked to the station on October 2, and for observations of Halley's Comet. But by mid-November Vasyutin had developed an infection that resisted treatment. Reluctantly the crew abandoned Salyut 7, landing on Earth on November 21.

Soyuz T-13 was Savinykh's second trip into space. In 1981 he and Vladimir Kovalenok spent 74 days aboard

Salyut 6, where they were visited by cosmonauts from Mongolia and Rumania.

In June 1988 he was flight engineer aboard Soyuz TM-5, the second Soviet-Bulgarian mission, a 10-day flight that included a week aboard the Mir space station.

Savinykh was born March 7, 1940, in the village of Berezkiny, Kirov Region, Russia. After completing secondary school he attended the Perm Institute of Railroads and was working on the Sverdlovsk railway when he was drafted. From 1961 to 1963 he served in the Soviet army as a topographer. When he was demobilized he went to Moscow to attend the Institute of Geodetic Engineering, Aerial Photogaphy and Cartography, where he specialized in the design of optical geodetic equipment.

In 1969 he joined the Korolev spacecraft design bureau, originally working on optical instruments for Soyuz, Progress, and Salyut spacecraft. Eventually he became a flight controller and planner, working with future space partner Kovalenok on Salyut 4 in 1975.

Later that year Savinykh applied for admittance to the cosmonaut team. He was enrolled as a candidate in December 1978 and assigned to the group of cosmonauts training for flights in the advanced Soyuz T transport. He served as backup cosmonaut-researcher for Soyuz T-3 in late 1980. Between flights he served as backup flight engineer for Soyuz T-7, Soyuz T-10, Soyuz T-12, and Soyuz TM-3.

Savinykh left the cosmonaut team and the NPO Energiya in the fall of 1988 to become rector of his alma mater, the Moscow Institute of Geodetic Engineering, Aerial Photography and Cartography.

He is the author of the memoir *The Earth Waits and Hopes* (1983).

Savitskaya, Svetlana Yevgenyevna

1948–

In August 1982, 19 years after Valentina Tereshkova's pioneering flight, Svetlana Savitskaya became the second woman to fly in space. She and fellow cosmonauts Leonid Popov and Alexandr Serebrov were sent into space in Soyuz T-7 and joined two other cosmonauts aboard the Salyut 7 space station.

Savitskaya made a second spaceflight in July 1984, another visit to Salyut 7, this time with commander Vladimir Dzhanibekov and Buran test pilot Igor Volk. During this 12-day mission Savitskay became the first woman to walk in space, testing space construction tools with Dzhanibekov outside Salyut 7.

Savitskaya was born August 8, 1948, in Moscow. Her father is Marshal of the Soviet Union Yevgeny Savitsky, former deputy chief the Air Defense Forces. While attending the DOSAAF Central Aerotechnical School as a teenager, Savitskaya became a parachutist and a pilot. She then attended the Moscow Aviation Institute from 1966 to 1972, graduating with a degree in aeronautical engineering.

From 1966 to 1974 Savitskaya was technically employed as a flight instructor at the flying club associated with the DOSAAF School. Her primary activity was sport flying, traveling in 1972 to Great Britain for the 6th World Aerobatics Championship and returning to the USSR as the world champion in all-around flying. She also earned a master of sport rating with 500 parachute jumps.

In 1974 Savitskaya enrolled at the Ministry of Aviation Production's civilian test pilot school in Zhukovsky, where one of her final examiners was future cosmonaut Igor Volk. She then went to work with the Yakovlev aircraft design bureau and established many speed records for Soviet planes.

Savitskaya was one of 9 women selected for enrollment in the cosmonaut team in July 1980.

Following the Soyuz T-12 flight Savitskaya was assigned as commander of an all-woman cosmonaut crew, including flight engineer Yekaterina Ivanova and researcher Yelena Dobrokvashina. They were to have made an 8-day visit to the Salyut 7 space station in early 1986. Problems with control of Salyut 7, which necessitated a special rescue mission, and then with the health of its resident crew, forced cancellation of the mission.

Savitskaya remained an active cosmonaut until October 1993. She now serves as deputy to Yuri Semenov, general designer of the NPO Energiya.

She is the author of a book, *Yesterday and Always* (1988), and in April 1989 was elected to the Congress of People's Deputies.

Serebrov, Alexandr Alexandrovich

1944–

Alexandr Serebrov was the first cosmonaut to fly a manned maneuvering unit during a walk in space. The 5-hour test on February 1, 1990, saw Serebrov donning the bulky Ikarus backpack and, firing its maneuvering jets, move as much as a hundred feet from the Kvant 2 airlock on the Mir space station. During the Ikarus flight Serebrov, unlike American astronauts who have used similar units, remained attached to the Kvant with a tether. Ikarus will allow future crews to better perform EVA maintenance on the International Space Station.

Serebrov and commander Alexandr Viktorenko completed four other EVAs, installing and removing scientific experiment packages on Mir's exterior and testing a new space suit. Viktorenko also flew the Ikarus on February 5.

The main goal of the Serebrov-Viktorenko residency aboard Mir was to supervise the addition of the Kvant 2 (also known as the "D" or equipment module), which had been at the Baikonur Cosmodrome awaiting launch since June 1988. Problems with yet another module, Kristall (the "T" or technology module) had forced the delay: worried about the problems of controlling an asymmetrical space complex, Soviet flight controllers didn't want to the huge D module to Mir without adding the T soon after.

Following launch on September 6, 1989, Serebrov and Viktorenko docked with the Mir complex after a momentary problem was overcome. They reactivated the station, which had been unoccuped since April, and settled down to await Kvant 2. Unfortunately, on October 6 it was announced that Kvant 2 was to be delayed yet again, until late November. Since the module carried the EVA equipment the cosmonauts were to use, they were forced to scramble in rearranging their work schedule.

Kvant 2 was finally launched on November 26, and after problems with a solar power panel that refused to unfold, and computer problems on both Mir and Kvant, was docked to the complex on December 6.

Serebrov and Viktorenko handed over Mir operations to cosmonauts Solovyov and Balandin in February, returning to Earth after a mission that had lasted 166 days.

Serebrov returned to Mir in July 1993 with commander Vasily Tsibliyev. During this residency, which ended in January 1994, Serebrov made five additional EVAs totalling 25 hours. The cosmonauts survived a collision between their Soyuz and Mir as they performed a fly-around just after undocking for their return home.

Previously Serebrov had flown in space on two successive missions: as flight engineer on Soyuz T-7 in August 1982, Serebrov was part of the crew that included cosmonaut Svetlana Savitskaya, the second woman to go into space. Serebrov, Savitskaya, and commander Leonid Popov rendezvoused and docked with the Salyut 7 space station and spent a week as guests of cosmonauts Berezovoy and Lebedev.

Serebrov's primary training involved "add-on" free-flying modules to the Salyut, and it was for a planned 8-month mission aboard a combined Salyut 7/Module complex that he was sent into space on Soyuz T-8 with commander Vladimir Titov and flight engineer Gennady Strekalov. But Soyuz T-8 suffered the loss of its rendezvous radar during its first day in space and was forced to return to Earth without reaching the space complex.

Serebrov was born February 15, 1944, in Moscow, and attended the Moscow Physical-Technical Institute, earning his degree in 1967. He remained at the Institute as a graduate student and researcher until earning his candidate of technical sciences degree in physics in 1976. Prior to that he had gone to work in the Petrov section of the NPO Energiya spacecraft design organization.

Serebrov became a candidate engineer cosmonaut in December 1978 and initially worked on the Soyuz T spacecraft. His first crew assignment came in 1982, when he replaced woman researcher Irina Pronina on the Soyuz T-8 crew.

Between 1983 and 1989 Serebrov was in constant crew training, serving as backup flight engineer for Soyuz T-14, Soyuz TM-2 (he was originally the prime engineer for this mission), Soyuz TM-5 and Soyuz TM-7. He kept slipping from one crew to another in 1988–89 because of delays in the Kvant 2/Ikarus launch. Like American astronaut Bruce McCandless, he was the manned maneuvering unit specialist for the cosmonaut team.

Serebrov currently works at RKK Energiya, and also serves as a space consultant to Russian President Boris Yeltsin.

Sevastyanov, Vitaly Ivanovich

1935–

Vitaly Sevastyanov is an engineer-cosmonaut who took part in two different long-duration space missions.

During the first, in June 1970 he spent a record 18 days in space aboard Soyuz 9, a difficult experience that left Sevastyanov and commander Andrian Nikolayev so weak at its end that they had to be carried from their spacecraft.

By the time Sevastyanov made his second flight, Soyuz 18 in May 1975, a new program of exercise and medical supervision and the roomier quarters aboard Salyut 4 allowed the cosmonauts to endure 63 days in space with happier results. Sevastyanov and commander Pyotr Klimuk were able to walk away from Soyuz 18 on landing. They had carried out a number of scientific experiments, including observing the sun with a solar telescope, while struggling with the space station's troubled environmental system, which raised the humidity inside Salyut 4 to the point where mold was starting to form on the walls.

Sevastyanov was born July 8, 1935, in Krasno-Uralsk, a village near the city of Sverdlovsk, and grew up in Sochi, a resort on the Black Sea, where during school holidays he worked as a deckhand on boats. He attended the Moscow Aviation Institute, studying to become an aeronautical engineer, and on graduation in 1959 went to work in Korolev's spacecraft design bureau.

At the OKB Korolev Sevastyanov was a member of the team that created the Vostok spacecraft. He was also a lecturer to the cosmonauts and sat on the review board that approved cosmonauts for spaceflight assignments. He did graduate work at MAI, receiving his candidate's degree in 1965.

Sevastyanov was enrolled in the cosmonaut team in January 1967. He had been the OKB Korolev engineer responsible for developing the training schedule for the manned lunar landing program—Program L—and it was here that he went to work. He was assigned, first with commander Valery Bykovsky, then with Pavel Popovich, to train for the Soyuz-Zond circumlunar mission. When

that was canceled in early 1969, Sevastyanov joined Andrian Nikolayev on the Soyuz 8 crew, a planned rendezvous and docking mission. The team was unable to qualify as prime crew, however, and served as backups for Soyuz 7 and Soyuz 8.

Following Soyuz 9 Sevastyanov joined commander Alexei Gubarev and researcher Anatoly Voronov in a Salyut crew. They were assigned as backups for a Soyuz 12 mission in June 1971 when the Soyuz 11 cosmonauts were killed in a freak landing accident.

The subsequent redesign of the Soyuz eliminated the researcher seat, and the 3-man crews were rearranged in 2-man configurations. Sevastyanov was teamed with commander Pyotr Klimuk at the end of 1971.

Between 1977 and 1979 he worked as a Salyut 6 flight controller at Kaliningrad. He also headed his own group at the OKB Korolev, now known as NPO Energiya.

He returned to active cosmonaut training in 1986 in a team with Alexandr Viktorenko. Physical problems cost him a flight on Soyuz TM-3 (July 1987). He earned his way back to flight status again in 1988 and served on a crew with Viktor Afanasyev. But in June 1990 physicians again removed Sevasthanov, restricting him only to missions up to 30 days in duration. He later trained for a flight aboard the Buran space shuttle, but in December 1993 retired from the cosmonaut team to work full-time on politics. He was elected to the Russian Parliament and still serves there as a member of the Communist Party.

Sevastyanov was president of the Soviet Chess Federation (during Soyuz 9 he played a game from orbit with fellow cosmonaut Viktor Gorbatko, who was at flight control), a member of the journalist's union of the USSR and also served as the host of a popular television series, *Man, the Earth and the Universe*. He has traveled to many foreign countries and has made two visits to the United States.

Severin, Vladimir Gayevich
1956–

Engineer Vladimir Severin was one of the civilian candidates approved for cosmonaut training by the joint state commission on May 11, 1990. In October of that year he arrived at the Gagarin Center to begin the general cosmonaut training course, which he completed in March 1992, qualifying as a cosmonaut-researcher for Soyuz-Mir missions.

He was not assigned to a flight however, and since he is not a member of either the Energiya or Gagarin Center cosmonaut teams, he is not considered a candidate for International Space Station missions.

Severin was born November 20, 1956, in Moscow. He attended the Moscow Aviation Institute, graduating in 1979, then joined the NPO Zvezda, builders of space suits, ejection seats, and the Ikarus manned maneuvering unit.

The general designer of NPO Zvezda is Gay Severin, the cosmonaut's father.

Sharafutdinov, Ansar Ilgamovich
1939–

Ansar Sharafutdinov was one of the 22 candidates enrolled in the cosmonaut training program in October 1965. He completed the initial training course in November 1967, but left the team in January 1968 because of a medical problem.

Sharafutdinov was born June 26, 1939, in the Chelyabinsk region of the Urals in Russia. He attended the Kacha Higher Air Force School, graduating in 1963, then served as a fighter pilot with Soviet air defense forces in Poland prior to his enrollment in the cosmonaut team.

While still a student at Kacha he corresponded with Yuri Gagarin, asking how he could become a cosmonaut.

Upon leaving the cosmonaut team Sharafutdinov became an An-12 transport pilot stationed in Ivanova. Requalified as a fighter pilot in 1969, he served for the next 11 years in a variety of posts, including Berlin.

Grounded permanently in January 1980, he became an air traffic controller at Tselinograd in Kazkahstan.

He left the air force in 1985 and is currently a military instructor in a secondary school in the village of Shchelkovo, near the Gagarin Center.

Shargin, Yuri Georgiyevich
1960–

Lieutenant Colonel Yuri Shargin of the Military Space Forces (VKS) is assigned to the backup crew for the Soyuz TM-28 mission to Mir, scheduled for launch in August 1998. Shargin is serving as backup to Russian politician Yuri Baturin, who is scheduled to spend a week aboard the Mir.

Shargin was born March 26, 1960 at a military encampment near the town of Engels, Saratov Region, in the family of a cadet. He attended the Mozhaisky Air Force Engineering Academy in Leningrad, graduating in 1982, and was commissioned in UNKS, the Space Units of the Soviet military, later renamed the VKS.

He served for 3 years at the Area 31 launch complex at the Baikonur Cosmodrome, working on vehicles of the Soyuz and Molniya type. He was a member of the Soyuz launch team in September 1983, the time of the spectacular launchpad fire and abort involving cosmonauts Titov and Strekalov.

In 1985 Shargin transferred to Kaliningrad facility of the NPO Energiya, the prime contractors for the Soyuz spacecraft and Mir space station, where he served as an acceptance officer.

He was officially approved as a cosmonaut candidate by the joint state commission on February 9, 1996, the first member of the VKS selected for the cosmonaut team, and completed the basic cosmonaut training course at the Gagarin Center in March 1998.

Sharipov, Salizhan Shakirovich
1964–

Russian air force pilot Salizhan "Sally" Sharipov was a mission specialist in the crew of STS-89. This January 1998 flight of the orbiter Atlantis made the eighth Shuttle-Mir docking mission delivering NASA-Mir researcher Andy Thomas to the Russian station and returning Dave Wolf to Earth. The crew of 6 also delivered badly needed equipment, including a new onboard computer and a new air conditioner, plus 200 pounds of water, to the resident crew.

Sharipov is scheduled to serve as a backup commander for one of the 1999 Mir missions, the last to the station.

Sharipov was born August 24, 1964, in the city of Uzgen, Osh Region, Kirghizia. He is Uzbek by nationality.

He was a student at the Kharkov Higher Air Force School from 1983 to 1987, then served as a flight instructor at the Frunze military-technical school. He has logged 950 hours of flying time in the L-39 and MiG-21.

Sharipov is one of the 3 pilot candidates enrolled in the Gagarin Center cosmonaut team in May 1990. In March 1992 he completed a training course that qualified him as a future Soyuz TM-Mir commander. While awaiting a flight assignment he completed a degree in cartography and Earth science at Moscow State University (April 1994). He was assigned as a Shuttle mission specialist in July 1997.

Sharov, Valery Yuriyevich
1953–

Valery Sharov is one of the 6 Soviet journalists enrolled in the cosmonaut team in October 1990 as candidates for a planned 1993 flight to Mir. By the time the journalists completed their training in February 1992, however, the Journalist-in-Space mission had been canceled.

Sharov was born December 26, 1953, in Moscow. He attended the State University in Gorky (now Nizhni-Nov-gorod), graduating in 1976 with a degree in physiology and biology.

From 1976 to 1980 he was a researcher at several medical institutes, then began working as a correspondent for the newspaper *Moskovski Universitet*. In 1982 he graduated from the journalism faculty at Moscow State University.

While working as a researcher and journalist Sharov was also a semiprofessional athlete, winning a silver medal in the 400-meter relay in the 1982 USSR national championships. He is a master of sport.

Since 1984 Sharov has been on the staff of the *Literaturnaya Gazeta (Literary Gazette)*, first as its science correspondent, and since 1987 as its Far East correspondent. His articles have dealt with criticism of local Communist Party leaders, Russian-Japanese relations, and population problems.

He is the coauthor of a book, *The Demographic Problem in the USSR*, published in 1990.

Shatalov, Vladimir Alexandrovich
1927–

Vladimir Shatalov commanded three Soyuz flights between 1969 and 1971, including the first rendezvous and docking between Soviet manned spacecraft, and went on to become chief of the cosmonaut training program.

Shatalov's first spaceflight began on January 14, 1969, when he was launched alone aboard Soyuz 4. The next day cosmonauts Boris Volynov, Alexei Yeliseyev, and Yevgeny Khrunov were put into space aboard Soyuz 5. Shatalov gave chase, and on January 16 made a successful rendezvous and docking with the 3-man vehicle. Yeliseyev and Khrunov donned pressure suits and made a space walk from Soyuz 5 to Soyuz 4, returning to Earth with Shatalov on January 17.

In October of that same year Shatalov and Yeliseyev stepped in late in training to replace the team of Nikolayev and Sevastyanov, who had failed a preflight training examination, as the crew of Soyuz 8, the "flagship" of a trio of Soyuz vehicles that were launched on successive days. Soyuz 8 was the last of the three sent into space; its mission was to rendezvous and dock with Soyuz 7 and its 3-man crew, but technical problems only allowed the two craft to close to within a few hundred feet of each other.

Shatalov's third flight, the most ambitious, was also troubled. On April 23, 1971, Shatalov, Yeliseyev, and research-engineer Nikolai Rukavishnikov were sent into orbit aboard Soyuz 10 intending to dock with the Salyut 1 space station for a 30-day mission. When they linked up with Salyut on April 25 the cosmonauts were unable to open the hatch between the two vehicles. They backed away from the station after only 5.5 hours and returned to Earth.

Shatalov was born December 8, 1927, in the city of Petropavlovsk in Kazakhstan, but moved to Leningrad (St. Petersburg) with his family at the age of 2. His father was a railroad engineer. Evacuated with his family to Kazakhstan during the War, young Vladimir decided that he wanted to become a heroic pilot. He attended prep schools for military pilots in Karaganda and Lipetsk until 1946, then the Kacha Higher Air Force School, graduating in September 1949.

He remained at Kacha for the next 4 years, serving as a flight instructor with its 706th and 707th Air Training Regiments. In August 1953 he entered the Red Banner (later named for Yuri Gagarin) Air Force Academy, graduating in November 1956.

Over the next 5 years Shatalov advanced from deputy squadron commander to squadron commander, then deputy air regiment commander with air force units. He was senior inspector pilot with the 48th Air Army, Odessa military district, in March 1962, when he learned that a new cosmonaut group was being selected, one whose members were required to be Academy graduates with command experience. Shatalov applied, was accepted, and reported to the training center on January 11, 1963.

Some cosmonaut memoirs report a certain amount of tension between the two groups. By the summer of 1963 the original group of 20 pilots had lost 6 men for a variety of medical and academic reasons, and 11 of the remaining 14 (including space veterans Gagarin, Titov, Nikolayev and Popovich) had been sent to the Zhukovsky Air Force Engineering Academy for further study. The younger men viewed the new arrivals with suspicion, fearing that they were being replaced and that their chances of ever going into space were disappearing. One sign of the dif-

ference between the two groups was that the younger pilots were forbidden to fly jets without instructors. This rule, when applied to the 1963 men, was quickly discarded, since men like Shatalov had already served as instructors, logging hundreds of hours of flying time.

It was Yuri Gagarin, the commander of the cosmonaut team, who acted as peacemaker between the two groups, reassuring the younger men that they would eventually fly in space, while making it clear that the senior pilots and engineers were going to play an important role in the next few years. Shatalov, the obvious leader of the second enrollment, served as a communications operator for the flights of the first Voskhod (1964) and Voskhod 2 (1965).

In May 1965 Shatalov and a late addition to the 1963 group, 44-year-old test pilot Georgy Beregovoy, were chosen as one of 2 cosmonaut teams training for a weeklong Voskhod 3 mission. At the same time work was proceeding on an entirely new spacecraft called Soyuz, which was designed to take Soviet cosmonauts to the Moon. Following the death of chief designer Sergei Korolev, who was the principal supporter of the Voskhod missions, in January 1966, the program was canceled as an unnecessary diversion of resources from the Soyuz program.

Shatalov and Beregovoy immediately moved over to the Soyuz program, where Shatalov served as communications operator for Soyuz 1, and had the difficult task of talking to the doomed Vladimir Komarov during his final, horrifying plunge to Earth.

When manned flights resumed with Soyuz 3 in October 1968, Shatalov served as Beregovoy's backup.

In June 1971, at the time of the Soyuz 11 mission, Shatalov was promoted to major-general and named to replace Colonel-General Nikolai Kamanin as director of cosmonaut training for the High Command of the Soviet air force.

In 1972 Shatalov earned a candidate of technical sciences degree. He traveled to the United States several times between 1973 and 1975 with the Apollo-Soyuz cosmonauts. (He revealed to American astronauts that he came close to assigning himself to the flight with Yeliseyev.) In 1975 he was promoted to lieutenant general. Active in Party politics, from 1976 to 1984 he was deputy of the Supreme Soviet.

Shatalov succeeded Georgy Beregovoy as director of the Gagarin Cosmonaut Training Center in January 1987, becoming responsible for its 4,000 employees and dependents. During his tenure as director of the Center Shatalov reshaped and opened up the cosmonaut selection process, and was quite outspoken about the lack of planning that hampered Soviet space efforts.

He was fired as Gagarin Center director in September 1991, following the abortive Soviet coup.

Shatalov authored and coauthored several books on spaceflight, notably *Man and Space* (1979) and an autobiography, *The Hard Road to Space* (1977).

Shcheglov, Vasily Dmitryevich

1940–1973

Vasily Shcheglov was one of the 22 candidates enrolled in the Gagarin Center cosmonaut team on October 28, 1965. He completed the training course and was officially designated a military cosmonaut on December 30, 1967. Shcheglov was assigned to the Almaz program and trained for 4 years as a potential crew commander. But on December 30, 1972, he was retired from the cosmonaut team because of ill health. He died of cancer on July 16, 1973, without having had a chance to fly in space.

Shcheglov was born April 9, 1940, in the town of Melovashka, Kremensky District, Lugansk Region, Ukraine. He graduated from the Yeisk Higher Air Force School in October 1963, then served as a fighter bomber pilot with the 940th Air Regiment, 1st Guards Air Division of the 26th Air Army.

Shchukin, Alexandr Vladimirovich

1946–1988

Alexandr Shchukin served as backup cosmonaut researcher for Anatoly Levchenko on the flight of Soyuz TM-4 in December 1987. The Soyuz TM-4 main crew of Vladimir Titov and Musa Manarov relieved the team of Romanenko and Alexandrov, who had been aboard Mir for months. When Romanenko and Alexandrov returned to Earth, Levchenko came with them, serving as relief pilot because of concerns about Romanenko's health after 326 days in space.

Levchenko was included in the TM-4 crew at the request of the USSR Ministry of Aviation Production, which was the agency responsible for the Buran space shuttle program. MAP wanted two or more Buran pilots to have experience with orbital flight before manned flights of the winged spacecraft began. Shchukin and Levchenko were tentatively chosen as the backup crew to Volk and Stankyavichus.

Unfortunately, both backup cosmonauts died within 2 weeks of each other in August 1988: Levchenko succumbed to an undetected brain tumor on August 6; 12 days later Shchukin died in the crash of a Su-26M sport plane at the Zhukovsky flight research center. He had been rehearsing for an appearance at an airshow.

Ironically, Buran pilot Stankyavichus was later killed in an airshow accident in September 1990.

Shchukin was born January 19, 1946, in Vienna, Austria, where his father was serving with the Soviet military. He is the first cosmonaut to have been born outside the USSR. In 1966 he enrolled at the Kacha Higher Air Force School, graduating in 1970, and served as a fighter pilot with Soviet air forces in Germany for the next 5 years. He reached the rank of major.

From December 1975 to May 1977 he attended the civilian test pilot school, and following graduation took part in the testing of several different types of aircraft at the Zhukovsky flight research institute. He also did graduate work at the Moscow Aviation Institute.

Shchukin was one of the 5 civilian test pilots selected for the Buran program in 1978 and approved by the joint state commission in July 1980. In 1979 and 1980 he underwent the cosmonaut training course at the Gagarin Center.

Between June 1986 and May 1987 the team of Levchenko-Shchukin made four approach and landing flights in a jet-powered version of Buran. With Igor Volk or Rimas Stankyavichus, Shchukin made three other such flights, one in October 1987, and two more in April 1988.

Sheffer, Yuri Petrovich
1947–

Yuri Sheffer is a civilian test pilot who trained for manned orbital flights on the Buran space shuttle. He was selected for the Buran program in April 1985, and also underwent Soyuz-Mir cosmonaut training at the Gagarin Center from 1985 to 1987.

Sheffer was born June 30, 1947, in Chelyabinsk, Russia. He attended the Kacha Higher Air Force School, graduating in 1970 with future Buran test pilot Alexandr Shchukin, then served as an instructor pilot and fighter pilot at the school, where another future Buran test pilot, Sergei Tresvyatsky, was one of his students.

Leaving active duty in December 1975, he enrolled at the Ministry of Aviation Production's civilian test pilot school at Zhukovsky, graduating in May 1977. He became a test pilot at the Zhukovsky flight research institute (since named for its founder, Mikhail Gromov). He also completed a graduate degree at the Moscow Aviation Institute (1980).

During the November 1988 orbital flight of an unmanned Buran, Sheffer was present at the Baikonur Cosmodrome as part of the chase team.

Sheffer has logged over 5,000 hours of flying time in 50 different types of aircraft. He still performs test work at the Gromov flight research center on commercial programs.

Shonin, Georgy Stepanovich
1935–1997

Georgy Shonin commanded the Soyuz-6 flight in October 1969, when three Soviet manned spacecraft were in orbit at the same time. Aboard Shonin's vehicle cosmonaut Valery Kubasov performed the first demonstration of welding in a vacuum, a necessary step for the future construction of space stations. Shonin returned to Earth after spending 6 days in space. It was his only flight.

Shonin was born August 3, 1935 in the city of Rovenki, in the Voroshilovgrad Region of the Ukraine. He attended the same Odessa air force prep school as fellow cosmonaut Georgy Dobrovolsky, then entered the Krasnodar Military Flight-Technical School for 3 years. He transferred to the Leningrad Naval Air School for a year, then qualified as a pilot in February 1957 after graduating from the Stalin Naval Air School.

As a naval air pilot, Shonin first served with the Baltic Fleet, then with the 768th Air Regiment, 122nd Air Division, Northern Fleet, the same unit as future cosmonaut Yuri Gagarin.

Shonin was a member of the first cosmonaut group that began training in March 1960. He was the original choice to be backup to Pavel Popovich for Vostok 4 in 1962, but was replaced when he developed an intolerance for high-G loads on the centrifuge. From 1964 to 1966 he trained for a 15-day Voskhod 3 mission, which was canceled before it could be flown. He served as backup commander for Soyuz-5 in January 1969.

Following Soyuz 6 Shonin was named commander of the first crew scheduled to inhabit the first Salyut space station. But in February 1971 he was removed from command for violations of training discipline. Shonin then became head of the Gagarin Center department overseeing training of cosmonauts for military manned space programs, and in April 1973 became an instructor-cosmonaut for the Apollo-Soyuz Test Project. He left active cosmonaut training in April 1974, and in January 1976 was named head of a new Gagarin Center directorate developing simulators and facilities for the new Buran space shuttle program. This work helped him earn his candidate of technical sciences degree (1978).

Promoted to major general in April 1979, Shonin left the Gagarin Center, serving for 4 years as deputy commander of the 5th Air Army. In 1983 he became head of a directorate within the Soviet air force for acquisition, and in 1998 was named director of NII-30, a scientific research institute of the Ministry of Defense, located in Shchelkovo, near Moscow. He retired in November 1990 with the rank of lieutenant general.

Shonin was the author of one of the earliest "uncensored" cosmonaut memoirs, *The Very First* (1977). He died on April 6, 1997.

Skripochka, Oleg Ivanovich

1969–

RKK Energiya engineer Oleg Skripochka is a cosmonaut-candidate who has been undergoing training at the Gagarin Center since January 1998. In the spring of 1999 he should qualify as an ISS crewmember.

Srkipochka was born December 24, 1969.

He was approved for cosmonaut training by the Joint State Commission on July 28, 1997.

Skvortsov, Alexandr Alexandrovich

1942–

Alexandr Skvortsov was one of the 22 candidates in the Third Enrollment of the air force cosmonaut team on October 28, 1965. He completed the 2-year training course, but left the team for medical reasons in January 1968 without having had the chance to fly in space.

Skvortsov was born June 8, 1942, in the city of Tambov, Russia. At the age of 17 he learned to fly at an air club in Voronezh, and the following year he entered the Armavir Higher Air Force School. Upon graduation in 1964 he served as a MiG-17 and Su-9 pilot with the 941st Interceptor Regiment, 4th Air Army of the Air Defense Forces (PVO).

After leaving the cosmonaut team Skvortsov became a senior pilot, sniper pilot, and political officer with the 153rd Air Regiment of the Moscow Military District Air Defense Forces, flying interceptor and ground attack aircraft until transferring to reserve status with the rank of lieutenant colonel in December 1987. He is retired and lives in Odessa.

Skvortsov's oldest son, also named Alexandr, born during the time he lived at the Cosmonaut Training Center, was selected as a cosmonaut candidate in 1997.

Skvortsov, Alexandr Alexandrovich

1966–

Major Alexandr Skvortsov is one of the 8 Russian air force pilots selected for cosmonaut training at the Gagarin Center in May 1997. In the spring of 1999 he should qualify as a Soyuz commander and International Space Station crewmember.

Skvortsov was born May 6, 1966, in Zelenyi Gorodok, soon to be named Zvezdny Gorodok or Star Town. His father Alexandr was a candidate cosmonaut at the training center at that time. Young Skvortsov attended the Stavropol Higher Air Force Engineering School (named for Sudets), graduating in 1989.

At the time of his selection for cosmonaut training Skvortsov was a student at the Academy of Air Defense in the city of Tver (formerly Kalinin).

Smirenny, Lev Nikolayevich

1932–

Lev Smirenny is a physicist who was enrolled in the cosmonaut detachment as a candidate-researcher in March 1972. Smirenny, who was a specialist in the effects of radiation on living organisms, and physicians Valery Polyakov and Georgy Machinsky, were the first employees of the Institute of Medical-Biological Problems to be enrolled in the cosmonaut team. (Ultimately the IMBP would have its own cadre of physician-cosmonauts and specialists.)

Smirenny passed the physical examinations for cosmonaut training in July 1965 when the controlling body was the military medical service. He passed the first civilian medical commission in May 1968, and in 1969 served as a crewman in a ground simulation of a lunar landing mission.

He left the cosmonaut detachment in November 1986 without ever flying in space. He is currently a laboratory head at the IMBP.

Smirenny was born October 25, 1932, in Ivanovo-Voznesensk, Ivanovsky District, Russia. He graduated from the Moscow Engineering-Physics Institute (MIFI) in 1956.

Sokovykh, Anatoly, Mikhailovich

1944–

Anatoly Sokovykh is one of 6 Soviet air force test pilots selected in January 1979 to perform military flight tests—including orbital missions—in the Buran space shuttle program. In 1980–81 these pilots underwent the general cosmonaut training course at the Gagarin Center. Sokovykh was designated a "test-cosmonaut" on February 12, 1982, returning to full-time work at the military flight test center in Akhtubinsk while waiting for the beginning of Buran appraoch and landing tests.

In 1986 he was forced to leave the Buran program because of a flying accident for which he was judged to be at fault. He left active duty in 1994 and is currently retired, living in Akhtubinsk (now Aktuba).

Sokovykh was born in 1944. He graduated from a higher air force school and from the Chkalov test pilot school.

Sologub, Mikhail Vladimirovich

1936–1996

Mikhail Sologub was one of the 12 air force candidates enrolled in the Russian air force cosmonaut team on May 7, 1967. In May 1968 Sologub volunteered for a series of medical tests on the 10-meter centrifuge at the Gagarin Center. Unfortunately, he suffered an extreme reaction to the tests, and was subsequently removed from training for medical reasons. He left the team in August.

Sologub was born November 6, 1936, in the town of Buguruslan, Orenburg District, Russia. He attended the 2nd Chkalov Air Force Navigator School, graduating in 1957, then served with the Russian air forces. He graduated from the Red Banner Air Force Academy (1964), then became an instructor at the Chelyabinsk Higher Air Force Navigator School.

Like fellow Chelyabinsk navigator Sergei Gaidukov, Sologub became a candidate for the cosmonaut team in 1965, but was not immediately selected. During the 2 year interval before the next round of admissions, he transferred to the Lugansk military navigator school.

After leaving the cosmonaut training center Sologub returned to Lugansk. In 1970 he joined the staff of the Gagarin Air Force Academy, where he served as a researcher until his retirement in 1990. He died August 4, 1996.

Solovyov, Anatoly Yakovlevich

1948–

The world's EVA champion, with over 78 hours of space suit work on 16 different occasions, Anatoly Solovyov made 5 visits to the Mir space station between 1988 and 1998, a career that spanned almost the entire life of the station. He has spent over 440 days aboard her.

Solovyov's first mission was Soyuz TM-5 in June 1988, a 10-day visit to Mir with flight engineer Viktor Savinykh and Bulgarian researcher Alexandr Alexandrov during Mir's second year of operation.

On February 9, 1990, Solovyov and flight engineer Alexandr Balandin were launched as the sixth Mir residency on what was billed as the world's first "profitable" spaceflight. The space manufacturing to have been performed by the cosmonauts with the new Kristall module was to have earned $25 million more than the estimated cost of the mission.

But the April 1990 launch of Kristall was delayed. Complicating matters, Solovyov and Balandin's Soyuz TM spacecraft suffered an accident during launch that caused several vital insulation blankets to detach. In July the cosmonauts made 2 space walks to repair the blankets, and they returned safely to Earth on August 9.

The story of Solovyov and Balandin's Mir mission was recounted in an episode of the TV series *Nova* in 1991. Soviet space officials later declared that the mission had indeed made a profit of $13 million.

Solovyov's third mission was as commander of the twelfth Mir residency, Soyuz TM-15, launched July 27, 1992, with Sergei Avdeyev as flight engineer and French spationaut Michel Tognini as researcher. Solovyov and Avdeyev conducted 4 EVAs erecting the Sofora crane on the Mir exterior. They also struck the last official flag of the USSR, placed on Mir by a 1991 crew. The Mir-12 mission lasted until February 1, 1993.

Solovyov's fourth trip to the Mir was via the American Space Shuttle Atlantis(STS-71) in June 1995. The Mir-19 crew of Solovyov and Budarin relieved cosmonauts Dezhurov and Strekalov, and the first NASA-Mir crewmember, Norman Thagard, who took their places for the return to Earth. Mir-19 was shorter than most Mir visits, lasting just 2 and a half months, long enough for Solovyov and Budarin to erect new solar arrays on the Mir exterior while resuming materials processing experiments.

When Solovyov reached Mir for the fifth time, as commander of Soyuz TM-26 or Mir-24, the station was suffering a series of system failures resulting from the June 25 collision with an errant Progress supply ship that cost the station half of its power. The first task of Solovyov and flight engineer Pavel Vinogradov was to conduct an internal space walk into the damaged Spektr module to try to locate a hole in its structure. They didn't find it. Later space walks and searches on the Mir exterior, in which Solovyov cut away pieces of the Spektr's insulation, also failed to show the hole. Flight controllers concluded it must be at the base of the Spektr solar array.

The Mir-24 crew was resupplied by the orbiter Atlantis on STS-86, which delivered Dave Wolf to the station along with several tons of needed equipment, including a new onboard computer. Solovyov and Vinogradov returned to Earth themselves in February 1998.

Solovyov was born January 16, 1948, in Riga, Latvia. He worked in a factory before joining the air force. After graduating from the Chernigov Higher Air Force School in 1972 he served with the Soviet air force in the Far East, eventually logging over 1,400 hours of flying time in 10 different types of aircraft. He is also a parachute instructor with over 140 jumps.

He was on of 9 candidates enrolled in the Gagarin Center cosmonaut team in August 1976. As a potential Buran shuttle commander, Solovyov was first trained at the Chkalov military test pilot school at Akhtubinsk until May 1977. He then returned to the Gagarin Center for Soyuz training, and was certified as a test-cosmonaut in January 1979.

He has served as backup commander for Soyuz TM-3 (1987), Soyuz TM-8 (1989), Soyuz TM-14 (1992), and Soyuz TM-12 (1995). Solovyov has also commanded a squad within the cosmonaut team since April 1990. He was assigned to the Shuttle-Mir program in April 1994 and during training served as coordinator for Russian Shuttle-Mir cosmonauts.

In 1996, after returning from the Mir-19 mission, Solovyov was selected to be the Russian commander for the first incremental crew aboard the International Space Station. But when it became clear that as the Russian Soyuz commander he would still be subordinate to an American astronaut, in this case William Shepherd, Solovyov withdrew from the assignment in favor of a fifth Mir flight.

Solovyov, Vladimir Alexandrovich

1946–

Vladimir Solovyov was flight engineer aboard a record-setting 10-month spaceflight, Soyuz T-10/Salyut 7, which lasted from February 8 to October 1, 1984.

With Solovyov and commander Leonid Kizim was a cardiologist, Oleg Atkov, the first medical specialist to make a long-duration flight in a Soviet spacecraft. Consequently many of the experiments aboard Salyut 7 dealt with the effects of weightlessness on human beings. Solovyov also performed numerous experiments in space manufacturing and made detailed observations of the Earth and stars.

His most interesting task was to act as an orbital repairman for Salyut 7's main rocket engines, which were badly damaged in a September 1983 accident. In six space walks totaling about 22 hours, Solovyov and Kizim, working in bulky pressure suits, replaced fuel lines in the delicate engine chamber, restoring it to use. (Ironically, Solovyov had helped design the Salyut propulsion system.) They also erected new solar panels on the outside of Salyut 7.

In March 1986, Solovyov went into space a second time, as flight engineer of Soyuz T-15. He and commander Kizim activated the new Mir space station, then, on May 5, transferred to the still-operating Salyut 7, where they retrieved experiments left by the previous cosmonaut crew and performed two more space walks, this time testing space construction techniques. Solovyov and Kizim returned to Mir on June 26, and landed back on Earth on July 16.

Solovyov was born November 11, 1946, in Moscow, and attended the Bauman Higher Technical School from 1964 to 1970, graduating as an aerospace engineer. He immediately went to work at the Korolev spacecraft design bureau, becoming an expert on space propulsion systems. He was a flight controller at Soviet mission control at Kaliningrad during Salyut 6 missions.

Solovyov joined the cosmonaut team with a group of engineer and physician candidates in December 1978. After training in Soyuz-T and Salyut systems, he was assigned to the backup crew of the Soviet-French Soyuz T-6 mission in 1981. He later served as backup for Soyuz T-8 and Soyuz T-10-1 (the September 1983 aborted launch).

Since his record flight, Solovyov has served as the lead flight director at the Russian flight control center for Salyut, supervising the difficult repairs to the derelict Salyut 7 in the summer of 1985, and becoming a familiar face to Western television audiences during the many crises aboard the Mir space station in the summer of 1997.

He retired as a cosmonaut in February 1994.

Solovyova, Irina Bayanovna
1937–

Irina Solovyova was the number-one backup to Valentina Tereshkova, who became the first woman in space when she spent 3 days aboard Vostok 6 in June 1963.

In 1965 Solovyova was assigned to perform a space walk during a planned 10-day Voskhod 4 mission. Voskhod 4 was canceled in March 1966.

Solovyova was born September 6, 1937, in the town of Kireyevsk, Tula District, Russia.

She attended the Ural Polytechnic Institute in Sverdlovsk, graduating in 1957, then went to work for the Uralenergomontazh Trust (the Ural Energy organization).

While a student at the polytechnic institute Solovyova joined an air club, becoming a parachutist. With future space program tester Pyotr Dolgov she was a member of the Soviet National Team in the 1957 world championships. She set several new records, and in 1960 was awarded the title master of sport. She would ultimately make over 2,200 parachute jumps.

Solovyova was one of the women parachutists recruited by cosmonaut training chief Nikolai Kamanin in late 1961. After several weeks of tests, she was enrolled in the military cosmonaut team as a candidate on March 12, 1962, completing her training in October.

All 5 women cosmonaut candidates were enlisted in the Soviet air force as privates. Ultimately Solovyova was commissioned, and reached the rank of colonel.

While still a member of the cosmonaut team Solovyova attended the Zhukovsky Air Force Engineering Academy, graduating in 1969. She then worked as a scientist at the Gagarin Center, a job she still holds. In the 1970s she received a candidate of psychological sciences degree.

In February 1988 Solovyova took a leave from the Center to join an expedition of women to Antarctica, serving as psychologist and Communist Party leader for the group.

Sorokin, Alexei Vasilyevich
1931–1976

Alexei Sorokin was one of the first medical doctors selected for a manned spaceflight. He and Boris Yegorov were chosen in June 1964 by Drs. Oleg Gazenko and Nikolai Gurovsky, the chief cosmonaut medical specialists, to be candidates for a flight aboard the first Voskhod spacecraft. Both men had worked in support of the Vostok missions.

Initially, Sorokin's experience made him the leading candidate. But when a third man, air force flight surgeon and test pilot Vasily Lazarev, was added to the group by Kamanin, Sorokin's chances of flight diminished. He was one of 2 backups for Yegorov on the mission.

Even though he was recalled to cosmonaut training by Lieutenant General Nikolai Kamanin in February 1965 for a later Voskhod mission, Sorokin was never enrolled in the military cosmonaut team.

Sorokin was born March 30, 1931, in the village of Dobroye, Solntsevsky District, Kursk Region, Russia. He attened a medical institute from 1951 to 1955, then, like his future associate Lazarev, entered the Saratov Medical Institute, a school for flight surgeons, graduating in September 1957.

From October 1957 to May 1963 Sorokin was a hospital director in the support battalion of the 724th Air Regiment, 26th Air Army. He then joined the medical staff of the cosmonaut training, where he served until his death on January 23, 1976.

Stankyavichus, Rimantas Antanas-Antano

1944–1990

Rimas Stankyavichus was one of the original 5 civilian test pilots recruited for the Buran space shuttle program in late 1977. On November 10, 1985, he was copilot (with Igor Volk) of the first approach and landing flight of a jet-powered version of Buran. He flew 12 other flights through April 1988, the longest lasting 32 minutes, including a completely automatic landing in December 1986.

Stankyavichus was assigned as copilot for the first manned orbital flight of the second Buran flight vehicle, scheduled for launch in 1992, but on September 9, 1990, he was killed in the crash of a Su-27 during the Salveda air show near Treviso, Italy. A security guard also died in the crash and eight bystanders among the crowd of 40,000 were injured.

An autopsy later showed that Stankyavichus had an .04 level of alcohol in his blood at the time of the crash.

Stankyavichus was born July 26, 1944, in the city of Mariyampole (formerly known as Kapsukas), Lithuania. At the age of 14 he took up parachuting at a local flying club, and 3 years later enrolled at the Chernigov Higher Air Force School.

After graduation from Chernigov in 1965 Stankyavichus served as a pilot in Poland, Soviet Central Asia, and Egypt, flying combat missions during the 1973 Arab-Israeli War. The next year Major Stankyavichus left active duty to attend the civilian test pilot school of the USSR Ministry of Aviation Production. He graduated cum laude

in 1975 and went to work at the Zhukovsky flight research institute.

Stankyavichus logged over over 4,000 hours of flying time in 57 different types of aircraft, including helicopters.

In 1977 he was one of 5 MAP test pilots recruited for the new Buran shuttle program. Preliminary flight training began the following year, and in 1979 and 1980 Stankyavichus and his four colleagues underwent cosmonaut training at the Gagarin Center. He was certified as a pilot-cosmonaut on February 12, 1982.

Most of his training, of course, was for the Buran shuttle program. He logged over 3,200 hours of simulator time and by the time of the first Buran free flight had spent 60 hours in the shuttle cockpit.

Stankyavichus was an alternate for Igor Volk on his flight aboard Soyuz T-12 in 1984, and second backup to Anatoly Levchenko on his flight aboard Soyuz TM-4 in 1987. In 1989 Stankyavichus was included in a crew with commander Viktor Afanasyev and flight engineer Vitaly Sevastyanov for a planned Soyuz TM-9 mission then scheduled for launch to the Mir space station in July of that year. Problems with Mir forced a suspension of manned operations from April to September 1989, and Stankyavichus lost his chance to fly in space.

Stepanov, Eduard Nikolayevich

1937–

Eduard Stepanov was one of the 22 cosmonaut candidates enrolled at the Gagarin Center on October 28, 1965. He completed the initial training course in December 1967 and was assigned to the Almaz military space station program, working there for the next 12 years in the hopes of a flight assignment. While working on Almaz he received his candidate of technical sciences degree (1974).

In 1979 he was assigned as researcher in one of the crews training for flights of the TKS spacecraft to the Almaz station, but the entire Almaz program was soon canceled.

Stepanov moved to the Buran program in January 1982, working as a potential crewmember and from 1990 to 1992 was assigned to the Soyuz rescue group training for a Soyuz-Buran test docking. That mission was also canceled.

Stepanov was born April 14, 1937, in the village of Verkhopeniye, Ultyansky District, Kursk Region, Russia. He graduated from the Kiev Higher Air Force School in 1959, then served with the Strategic Rocket Forces. In 1962 he spent several months as director of a radio-technical test range at the Kharkov Higher Air Force Engineering School. At the time of his selection as a cosmonaut he was a test-engineer at the military flight test center at Akhtubinsk.

He retired from the cosmonaut team in October 1992, never having flown in space.

Stepanov, Yuri Nikolayevich
1936–

Yuri Stepanov is a medical engineer who was selected for cosmonaut training in 1983 by the Institute for Medical Biological Problems, the organization within the USSR Ministry of Health that provides physician-cosmonauts for the Soviet space program.

Two years later, together with a pair of younger aerospace engineers from the NPO Energiya, he commenced the basic course at the Gagarin Cosmonaut Training Center. In February 1987 he was certified as a research-cosmonaut.

At the time of Stepanov's selection Soviet space managers planned to fly researchers in the third seat of Soyuz missions to the Mir space station. However, in the late 1980s and early 1990s most of those seats were sold to commercial customers such as the Japanese television network TBS or the governments of France and Germany. This situation combined with the cancellation of the Buran space shuttle—for which Stepanov was also selected—doomed Stepanov's chances of flying in space. In April 1994 he was transferred from the IMBP cosmonaut team to a smaller unit associated with the Russian Academy of Sciences, where he continues to work on the development of equipment and methods for the use of applied space physics aboard the Mir space station.

Stepanov was born September 27, 1936, in the city of Kiev, the son of an officer in the Soviet army who later became a general. The family was evacuated to Orenburg District in 1941, then moved to Moscow in 1943. Stepanov graduated from secondary school in 1954, then, following a year at a preparatory school, enrolled at the Moscow Auto-Mechanical Institute. He graduated in 1960, then went to work in a research institute under the Academy of Sciences.

Two years later Stepanov enrolled at the Moscow Institute of Physical Engineering, graduating from that school in 1967 as a specialist in medical technology. For the next 4 years he was employed by Experimental Design Bureau No. 300 (OKB-300), working on nuclear medical equipment. He joined the staff of the new Institute for Medical-Biological Problems in 1971.

Stepanov qualified as a pilot at the Zhukovsky air club prior to becoming a cosmonaut, learning to fly L-39 and Yak-52 aircraft at the civilian flight research institute in Zhukovsky. He is also the author of 22 scientific papers.

Strekalov, Gennady Mikhailovich
1940–

Gennady Strekalov served as flight engineer aboard 6 Soyuz missions, including the world's first launchpad abort.

Strekalov and commander Vladimir Titov were scheduled to be launched on September 27, 1983, docking their Soyuz T-10 spacecraft with the Salyut 7 station occupied by cosmonauts Lyakhov and Alexandrov, who had been aboard it since late June. During a 4-month mission Titov and Strekalov were to perform several space walks to add solar power cells to the already existing panels on the station.

But ninety seconds before launch a fire broke out at the base of the Soyuz T-10 rocket and quickly spread up the side of the vehicle. Horrified flight controllers activated the escape rocket mounted on the nose of the spacecraft, pulling the the Soyuz T away from the booster before it exploded. Soyuz T-10 reached an altitude of several thousand feet, then dropped safely to the ground by emergency parachute.

The abort was a disappointment for Strekalov and Titov, an especially bitter one since just 5 months earlier they had been involved in another failed mission.

With Alexandr Serebrov, Strekalov and Titov were launched April 20, 1983, aboard Soyuz T-8 for a planned 8-month mission aboard Salyut 7. But shortly after launch the cosmonauts discovered that their Soyuz rendezvous radar had failed. (Investigators later determined that the radar antenna had been torn off when a shroud separated from Soyuz during launch.) Flight controllers at Kaliningrad gave the crew permission to attempt a docking using ground radar data and optical sights, but the final approach—made in darkness—was too fast. The crew aborted the docking and sailed past Salyut 7 at a high speed, returning to Earth after just 2 days.

Strekalov's luck improved. In March 1984 he replaced the ailing Nikolai Rukavishnikov as flight engineer of Soyuz T-11, a Soviet-Indian mission, and spent 8 days in space, most of aboard Salyut 7, the next month.

In 1990, at the age of 50, Strekalov finally achieved his dream of a long-term mission in space, serving as flight engineer of Soyuz TM-10. Between August and December 1990 Strekalov and commander Gennady Manakov spent 4 months aboard Mir. Their primary goals were putting the Kristall module (docked to the station in June) into full operation and performing EVAs to repair a hatch damaged by an earlier crew, then to move solar power panels from Kristall to a new position on the Kvant module.

The first EVA had to be postponed several days because Strekalov was nursing a cold. When it took place, the cosmonauts found that the damaged hatch had been "shredded." Their tools weren't adequate for repairing such extensive damage, so the second EVA was canceled. Strekalov and Manakov handed over Mir operations to the crew of Afanasyev and Manarov in December.

In March 1995 Strekalov returned to Mir with Russian commander Vladimir Dezhurov and NASA astronaut Norman Thagard. This mission, launched as Soyuz TM-21 but generally known as Mir-18, lasted until July 1995, when Strekalov and his two colleagues returned to Earth aboard the Shuttle Atlantis (STS-71). Strekalov and Dezhurov devoted much of their time to moving several of the Mir modules to different docking ports, preparing for the arrival of the Spektr module in April as well as the

Atlantis in June. They also conducted five EVAs, moving Mir solar panels, among other tasks. The draining work eventually caused the cosmonauts to balk at additional work, causing a conflict with flight controllers.

On his first flight, Soyuz T-3 in November and December 1980, Strekalov joined Leonid Kizim and Oleg Makarov in forming the first 3-man Soviet space crew to fly in 9 years. They visited the Salyut 6 space station, which had been in operation at that time for almost twice its design life, in order to perform needed repairs to its control systems. The flight lasted approximately 13 days.

Strekalov was born October 28, 1940, in the Moscow suburb of Mytischi. After completing secondary school he worked as an apprentice coppersmith in the factory where Sputnik 1 was built, and in 1959 enrolled in the Bauman Higher Technical School to study aerospace engineering. He graduated in 1965 and immediately went to work at the Korolev spacecraft design bureau, taking part in the design and development of Soyuz.

Strekalov was enrolled as a cosmonaut engineer candidate in March 1973 and spent several years working as a ground controller at Kaliningrad flight control. He was also a member of the Soyuz T training group. In 1976 he was one of the backup flight engineers for Soyuz 22, and in 1980 was a last-minute addition to the Soyuz T-3 crew when veteran engineer Konstantin Feoktistov suffered a medical disqualification.

He later served as backup flight engineer for Soyuz T-14 (1985) and Soyuz TM-9 (1990).

In the 5-year gap between crew assignments Strekalov took part in the design and development of the Mir space station. He also served as chief of the NPO Energiya cosmonaut team from January 1985.

Strekalov retired as an Energiya cosmonaut in January 1995—2 months before the launch of Soyuz TM-21! (He flew the mission on a special contract with Energiya.)

Sultanov, Ural Nazibovich
1948–

Ural Sultanov is a civilian test pilot-cosmonaut who trained to fly the Soviet space shuttle Buran. In November 1988 he served as chase pilot for the first unmanned flight of Buran.

He was later assigned as copilot, with Viktor Zabolotsky, of the backup crew for the first manned orbital Buran mission, then scheduled for launch in early 1992. Funding and political problems first postponed Buran flights, then led in May 1993 to the program's cancellation.

Sultanov was born November 18, 1948, in Bashkiria. He is a Bashkir by nationality.

As a teenager he attended the Suvurov military prep school in Kazan, then joined the air force. From 1967 to 1971 he was a student at the Kharkov Higher Air Force School. Following graduation he remained at Kharkov as an instructor until 1977.

Sultanov left the air force in 1977 to attend the USSR Ministry of Aviation Production's civilian test pilot school at Zhukovsky. He also enrolled at the Moscow Aviation Institute, graduating in 1981.

Beginning in 1978 he was a test pilot at the Gromov flight research institute in Zhukovsky, earning the rank of test pilot first class. In April 1983 he joined the group of pilots training to fly Buran and from 1985 to 1987 he underwent Soyuz-Mir training at the Gagarin Center.

Sultanov is currently an instructor at the civilian test pilot school.

Surayev, Maxim Viktorovich
1972–
Senior Lieutenant Maxim Surayev is one of the 8 Russian air force pilots selected for cosmonaut training at the Gagarin Center in May 1997. In the spring of 1999 he should qualify as a Soyuz commander and International Space Station crewmember.

Surayev was born May 2, 1972, in Chelyabinsk, Russia. He graduated from the Kacha Higher Air Force School in Volgograd in 1994. He was a student at the Zhukovsky Air Force Engineering Academy when selected for cosmonaut training.

Tereshkova, Valentina, Vladimirovna
1937–
Valentina Tereshkova was the first woman in space. On June 16, 1963, the 26-year-old Tereshkova was launched into orbit aboard Vostok 6 and in the next 3 days circled the Earth 48 times, more than the 6 American astronauts combined.

During her flight Tereshkova, using the call sign *Chaika* (Seagull), made television broadcasts to viewers in the Soviet Union, and also maintained regular radio contact with fellow cosmonaut Valery Bykovsky, whose Vostok 5 spacecraft was in orbit at the same time. The two spacecraft once passed within three miles of each other, and both returned to Earth on June 19, 1963.

Famed as a heroine of the women's movement in Soviet society, Tereshkova eventually went on to a career in politics. She married cosmonaut Andrian Nikolayev in a lavish state wedding in November 1963, in which Soviet leader Nikita Khrushchev gave away the bride. (Tereshkova and Nikolayev were divorced in 1982.)

Tereshkova was born March 6, 1937, in the village of Masslenikovo, Yaroslavl Region of Russia. At the age of 18 she joined her mother and sister, who had jobs at the Red Canal textile mill. While working at the mill Tereshkova took a correspondence course from an industrial school and, more significantly, joined a club for parachutists, eventually making over 120 jumps.

In September 1961, shortly after the flight of cosmonaut Gherman Titov, Tereshkova, like hundreds of other young Soviet men and women, wrote a letter to the space center asking to join the cosmonaut team. Unknown to her, cosmonaut training chief Nikolai Kamanin, had begun to consider the selection of a group of women parachutists for cosmonaut training.

Invited to Moscow for an interview and medical examinations in December 1961, Tereshkova passed, and in March reported with four other women to the training center. Valentina's mother and sister were told she had been selected for a special skydiving team.

Most cosmonaut memoirs claim that the women were welcomed "like brothers" by the pilots, but other sources state that some of the men were not pleased by the new recruits, who apparently had little or no flying experience. Years later Tereshkova confided to an American in the Apollo-Soyuz project that the other cosmonauts avoided her "because I have invaded their little playground and because I am a woman."

Nevertheless, Tereshkova and the others were subjected to the same centrifuge rides and zero-G flights as the male cosmonauts. Because the Soviet air force was still jealously guarding its role as sole provider of cosmonauts, the women were also enlisted as privates in the Soviet air force. (They were later commissioned as junior lieutenants.)

One of the women, Valentina Ponomareva, was a pilot, but Tereshkova and the others were not, so they were given basic flight training.

In the spring of 1963 Tereshkova, Ponomareva and Irina Solovyova were chosen to train for specifically for the Vostok 6 flight.

Sergei Korolev's deputy, Vasily Mishin, claimed years later that the final choice concerning which of the women would fly in space was made by Krushchev himself, who glanced over their biographies and chose the one— Tereshkova—from a worker's family.

The flight itself seems to have disappointed Korolev, who felt that Tereshkova hadn't completed her schedule of experiments. She had further worried ground controllers by falling asleep so soundly she could not be wakened.

Nevertheless, Vostok 6 was successful enough that its scheduled single-day duration was extended after launch.

In the years following Vostok 6 Tereshkova made many public appearances and trips to other countries. She and Nikolayev had a daugther, Yelena. Tereshkova and the other women cosmonauts attended the Zhukovsky Air Force Engineering Academy, graduating in 1969.

In 1965 and 1966 some of the women cosmonauts trained for a possible Voskhod and later a Soyuz flight, but neither plan received final approval. The group was disbanded in October 1969 and new women cosmonauts were not selected again until 1980.

Tereshkova later earned a candidate of technical sciences degree (1976) and was eventually promoted to the rank of major-general, retiring in March 1997.

Tereshkova had been a Komsomol organizer at the textile mill and joined the Communist Party in 1962. She became a member of the Supreme Soviet in 1966 and, in 1974, a member of the Central Committee. She was elected to the Congress of People's Deputies in April 1989, and still works for the Russian government in the field of international relations.

She has been the subject of two biographies, *This is "Seagull!"* by Mitchell Sharpe (1975) and *Valentina: First Woman in Space*, by Antonella Lothian (1993).

Titov, Gherman, Stepanovich
1935–

Gherman Titov became the second human being to make an orbital spaceflight when he spent a record 24 hours in orbit aboard Vostok 2 in August 1961. With 5 weeks to go until his twenty-sixth birthday, Titov remains the youngest person to go into space.

Titov's flight, following, as it did, a single orbit by Yuri Gagarin and two suborbital flights by Americans Shepard and Grissom, was an electrifying world event, with the progress of the Vostok 2 reported hourly as it passed over the globe. Using his exuberant call sign—"*Ya Orel!*" or "This is Eagle!"—Titov was seen and heard on television, giving viewers a tour of his spacecraft and describing the sights he saw through his window.

What was not revealed at the time was that Titov was the first human to suffer from space adaptation syndrome—space sickness. He was hospitalized for a time following his flight and never made another spaceflight.

Titov was born on September 11, 1935, in the village of Verkhneye Zhilino, Kosikhinsky District, Altai Territory, Russia. His father was a schoolteacher and gave his son the name Gherman (Herman, unusual for a Russian) to honor his favorite Pushkin character. Young Gherman decided he wanted to become a pilot when his uncle, an aviator and war hero, paid the village a visit.

Titov entered the 9th Military Air School in Kustanai, Kazakhstan, in July 1953, transferring to the Stalingrad Higher Air Force School 2 years later. Following qualificaiton as a pilot in September 1957 he was a pilot in two different Air Guards regiments of the 41st Air Division, Leningrad military district.

One of the first 20 Soviet cosmonauts selected in March 1960, Titov came close to washing out, most notably when he rebelled at what he called "silly questions" during psychological testing. In March 1961, after a year of training, Titov was one of 6 finalists for the first manned flight.

On the morning of April 12, 1961, Senior Lieutenant Titov, dressed in his orange pressure suit and space helmet, accompanied Yuri Gagarin to the launchpad at the Baikonur cosmodrome. Gagarin went aboard the Vostok spacecraft and Titov, his standby, returned to the cosmonaut quarters to wait for the launch. Shortly after Gagarin returned to Earth, Titov learned that he had been selected to make the next Soviet spaceflight, then planned to be three orbits. The proposed duration was later lengthened to 17 orbits, or a full day.

Following his flight Titov attended the Zhukovsky Air Force Engineering Academy with other cosmonauts, graduating in 1968, and joined the editorial board of *Aviatsiya i Kosmonavtika* (*Aviation and Spaceflight*). For many years in the late 1960s he was the most visible of the Soviet cosmonauts, frequently interviewed by Western journalists and contributor to many Soviet and Western publications.

In 1967 Titov attended the Chkalov test pilot school under the instruction of aviator Vladimir Ilyushin. At the time Titov had logged 800 hours of flying time. He received a rating of test pilot third class and did some test piloting at the Chkalov military flight test center in addition to his work at the cosmonaut training center on the Spiral spaceplane program.

The death of Yuri Gagarin in March 1968 caused the cautious heads of the cosmonaut training center to ground Titov. Frustrated by his inability to serve as an active pilot, Titov left the cosmonaut team in July 1970 to attend the K. E. Voroshilov Military Staff Academy. He graduated with a candidate of military sciences degree in 1972.

He joined the Main Office for Space Facilities (GUKOS) of Soviet Ministry of Defense, serving as deputy director of that organization's command and control center (KIK) in Monino. At KIK Titov was involved in the ground control of the military's Salyut 3

mission in 1974. From 1973 to 1979 he was deputy commander of GUKOS for research and development, directing the development and construction of several spacecraft systems, including launch vehicles. He was promoted to lieutenant general in 1979, and named first deputy director of GUKOS, later UNKS. He received a candidate of technical sciences degree in 1981 and also served as a member of the committee for the 1980 Moscow Olympics.

Colonel General Titov retired in October 1991 to become president of the Kosmoflot Scientific-Technical Center. He later served as vice president of the Russian Center for the Conversation of Aerospace Complexes. In May 1995 he was elected to the Russian parliament from the city of Kolommna, near Moscow.

He is the author of several books, including *A Million Miles in Orbit* (1961), *My Blue Planet* (1977), *Conversations with Cosmonauts of the USSR* (1983), and *On Starry and Earthly Orbits* (1987). In addition, his autobiography, as told to journalists Wilfred Burchett and Anthony Purdy and written by Martin Caidin, was published as *I Am Eagle!* (1962).

Titov, Vladimir Georgyevich
1947–

Vladimir Titov commanded the first yearlong flight in space history.

On December 21, 1987, Titov, flight engineer Musa Manarov and Buran shuttle test pilot Anatoly Levchenko were launched into space aboard Soyuz TM-4. Two days later they docked with the Mir complex, where cosmonaut Yuri Romanenko was close to completing a record 326 days in orbit. Romanenko, Alexandr Alexandrov and Levchenko returned to Earth on December 29, leaving Titov and Manarov to soldier on.

For the next 12 months they took part in a wide variety of experiments and tests. They conducted three space walks: the first, on February 26, 1988, was designed to install new solar panels on Mir, and succeeded; the second, on June 30, to repair the Roentgen X-ray telescope on the Kvant module, failed; a second repair attempt, made on October 30, succeeded.

Using the MKF-6M multispectral camera the cosmonauts took part in numerous Earth resources experiments, including Caribe-Interkosmos-88, a multinational study of the region around Cuba, and Tien Shan-Interkosmos-88, a study of the Tajikistan and Kirghizian Republics of the USSR.

These were in addition to astronomical observations and the manufacture of new semiconductor materials.

The cosmonauts also learned to manage the increasingly unwieldy Mir complex, which at most times consisted of the basic Mir core module, the Kvant 1 module, a Soyuz TM spacecraft and a Progress tanker spacecraft. (By 1988 Mir was to have seen the addition of several more specialist modules, but these had been delayed by technical and budgetary problems.)

They also tested the endurance of interpersonal relationships, sometimes informally: Titov and Manarov had one serious argument which resulted in 3 days of silence between them and was only resolved with a bit of help from ground controllers, and the cosmonauts' families—who were brought to the flight control center to help!

The formal medical program was also quite extensive, requiring each cosmonaut to exercise for two hours each day. But at the same point—9 months into the mission—where Yuri Romanenko had shown signs of fatigue, Titov and Manarov were judged to be doing quite well. From August through December they were joined by cosmonaut-doctor Valery Polyakov, who arrived in August as part of the Soviet-Afghan Soyuz TM-6 visiting mission. (There had been a previous visiting mission, Soyuz TM-5, with Bulgarian cosmonaut Alexandr Alexandrov, in June.)

Titov, who speaks fluent English, developed a relationship with a ham radio operator in Orange County, California, with whom he spoke several times during the mission.

Titov, Manarov, and Polyakov welcomed a third visiting crew—Alexandr Volkov, Sergei Krikalev, and French spationaut Jean-Loup Chretien—on November 28. Three weeks later, on December 21, Titov, Manarov, and Chretien landed in the main recovery zone, two orbits later than planned because of a computer malfunction. The Soyuz TM-4 mission had lasted 365 days, 22 hours, and 39 minutes.

Within 3 hours of returning to Earth Titov was able to walk with assistance. Two days later he could walk by himself. He and Manarov seemed to have survived their record-breaking mission, but Soviet doctors have since concluded that the optimum length of a Mir mission is 4 to 6 months. The record of the Soyuz TM-4 crew is likely to stand for several years.

Prior to his yearlong mission, Titov had not always been so lucky.

Titov was the commander of Soyuz T-8, launched April 20, 1983, with a crew of 3 cosmonauts on a planned 8-month mission aboard the Salyut 7 space station. But a failure in the Soyuz-T rendezvous radar forced Titov to attempt a tricky manual docking with the station, an attempt that did not succeed. He and fellow cosmonauts Gennady Strekalov and Alexandr Serebrov returned to Earth. Titov later wrote an unusually candid account of the flight for the Soviet military newspaper *Red Star*.

Five months later, late in the evening of September 26, 1983, Titov and Strekalov were ready for launch on another mission to Salyut 7, this time to relieve the crew of Vladimir Lyakhov and Alexandr Alexandrov, who had been aboard the station for 64 days. Just seconds before engine ignition a fire broke out at the base of the Soyuz launch vehicle. Ground controllers activated the abort system and Titov and Strekalov's Soyuz-T module was separated from the launcher by escape rockets. As the launch vehicle exploded, the module containing Titov and Strekalov landed safely three miles away. The cosmonauts were quickly rescued and described as "safe but unhappy."

Titov and flight engineer Alexandr Serebrov then began working on the Mir space station program in 1984 and were assigned as the prime crew for the first long-term mission scheduled for launch in February 1987, but in December they were disqualified (some reports say Serebrov failed the medical exams, others say Titov) and replaced by Romanenko and Laveikin. In April 1987 the team was broken up and Titov was joined by Musa Manarov. Soviet doctors were concerned that this string of apparent failures would affect Titov's work, but it obviously did not.

In February 1995 Titov made his fourth spaceflight, this time aboard the orbiter Discovery on mission STS-63, which made rendezvous with the Mir space station.

He returned to space a fifth time, with the crew of STS-86. This flight of the orbiter Atlantis made the seventh

Shuttle-Mir docking, delivering NASA-Mir researcher Dave Wolf to the troubled station, along with several tons of supplies and repair equipment. Titov and NASA astronaut Scott Parazynski also conducted an EVA at Mir.

Titov was born January 1, 1947, in the city of Stretensk in the Chita Region of Russia. He originally wanted to become a radio technician, but failed the entrance exams to the Kiev Institute of Civil Engineering in 1965. He returned home for a year, working on an oil rig, then joined the Soviet air force. In 1970 he graduated from the Chernigov Higher Air Force School. He remained at Chernigov until 1974 as a flight instructor, then was stationed in Moscow. At the time of his selection as a cosmonaut he had logged 1,300 hours of flying time.

Titov was one of 9 pilots enrolled as candidates in the cosmonaut team in August 1976. Since these pilots were expected to one day fly the Buran space shuttle, they were enrolled at the Chkalov test pilot school in Akthubinsk, graduating as test pilots third class in 1977. Two years of instruction in Soyuz and Salyut systems at the Gagarin Training Center followed before Titov was designated a pilot-cosmonaut.

In September 1981 Titov was teamed with Gennady Strekalov as one of the backup crews for the first Salyut 7 mission.

Following his yearlong mission Colonel Titov served in the Rescuer group of cosmonauts—senior pilot-cosmonauts who stand by in case an emergency Soyuz flight is needed. In December 1988 he left the cosmonaut team to head a training unit at the Gagarin Center, returning to flight status in November 1992, when he was one of 2 Russian cosmonauts selected for training as Shuttle mission specialists.

Colonel Titov serves as head of the 3rd Directorate (biomedical training) of the Gagarin Center.

crew of Musabayev and Kuzhelnaya will provide the ISS incremental crew of Usachev, Voss and Helms with a rescue vehicle.

Tokarev was born October 29, 1952, in the village of Kapustin Yar, Astrakhan District. Kapustin Yar was the first Soviet missile launch center.

Following graduation from secondary school in the city of Rostov, Tokarev enrolled at the Stavropol Higher Air Force School. He served as a pilot in the Soviet air force from 1973 to 1981, when he entered the Chkalov test pilot school.

As a flight test pilot, Tokarev worked on programs for the Soviet Naval Air Forces, including the vertical takeoff Yak-38A. He applied for the Chkalov Center's Buran test pilot-cosmonaut group in 1986, passed the medical examinations in 1988, and was officially enrolled on January 25, 1989.

From February 1989 to April 1991 he underwent basic cosmonaut training at the Gagarin Center, then returned to Chkalov. Following the cancellation of the Buran program in May 1993, Tokarev and the other members of the military Buran group transferred to the Gagarin Center full-time. In 1995 Tokarev became commander of the unit upon the retirement of test pilot-cosmonaut Alexei Borodai, only to see the unit dissolved in September 1996 by order of General Pyotr Deneikin, head of the Soviet air force.

Colonel Tokarev worked on several proposed Russian aerospace programs while trying to earn enrollment in the Gagarin Center's Soyuz-Mir cosmonaut team. He succeeded in winning official approval in July 1997, and immediately commenced ISS training. He was originally assigned to the fourth incremental ISS crew with astronauts Dan Bursch and Carl Walz, but was transferred to his current mission in November 1997.

Tokarev, Valery Ivanovich

1952–

Valery Tokarev is a Soviet air force test pilot who is assigned as backup pilot for a Soyuz resupply mission to the International Space Station. Scheduled for launch in the summer of 2000, this Soyuz and its

Tolboyev, Magomed Omarovich

1951–

Magomed Tolboyev is a civilian test pilot-cosmonaut who trained for several years as a potential Buran space shuttle pilot. At one point he had even been designated as copilot for the first manned flight of the second Buran orbiter. As originally planned, Tolboyev and commander Igor Volk were to spend at least 2 days in orbit. However, later financial and political problems forced the Russian Space Agency to cancel the Buran program.

Tolboyev himself left the Buran test pilot-cosmonaut team in January 1994 following his election to the lower house of the Russian legistlature. He represents his native region of Dagestan.

Tolboyev was born January 20, 1951, in the village of Sogratl in the Dagestan ASSR. He is an Avar by nationality.

He attended the Komarov Higher Air Force School in Yeisk, graduating in 1973, then served as a Sukhoi and MiG fighter pilot in the Odessa Military District, and in East Germany. He has flown 37 different types of aircraft, including helicopters.

Tolboyev left the air force in 1980 to enroll at the Moscow Aviation Institute (he graduated in 1984) and at the civilian test pilot school at the Gromov flight research institute in Zhukovsky. He joined the group of Buran test pilots based there in April 1983 and participated in drop tests of early models of the orbiter. In November 1988 was lead chase pilot for the first unmanned flight of Buran.

Tolboyev applied for the 1976 and 1978 cosmonaut selections, but was twice rejected because he was still recovering from two recent air accidents. Between 1983 and 1986 he also trained for flights on Soyuz and Mir.

Treshchev, Sergei Vladimirovich
1958–

RKK Energiya engineer Sergei Treshchev is currently assigned as flight engineer for the Soyuz TM-29 mission, scheduled for launch in January 1999. Treshchev and commander Viktor Afanasyev will form the Mir-27 crew, which will begin the process of disassembling the Russian station for eventual de-orbit.

Treshchev was born August 18, 1958, in Russia, and attended the Moscow Electronics Insitute, graduating in 1982. For the next 2 years he served as an officer in the Soviet army. He then joined the NPO Energiya at its fac-

tory facility. In 1986 he transferred to the flight-test department as an instructor.

He was one of the 3 Energiya engineers approved for cosmonaut training enrolled in the cosmonaut team in March 1992. From September 1992 to March 1994 he underwent the basic cosmonaut training course at the Gagarin Center, and in April 1994 was assigned to the Soyuz-Mir group in a crew with pilot Gennady Manakov. In February 1995 he was replaced for failing several technical examinations, and spent a year working on International Space Station development.

He returned to flight training in April 1996, and with Afanasyev served as the backup crew for Soyuz TM-27, launched in January 1998.

In July 1993 Treshchev and fellow Energiya engineer Alexandr Lazutkin were teamed with pilot Sergei Vozovikov for survival training near the Black Sea. During a break in training Vozovikov went diving and, in spite of Treshchev's attempts to rescue him, drowned.

Tresvyatsky, Sergei Nikolayevich
1954–

Sergei Tresvyatsky was one of the civilian test pilot-cosmonauts who trained for manned orbital flights of the Buran space shuttle from 1985 until the program's cancellation in 1994. From 1985 to 1987 he underwent general cosmonaut training at the Gagarin Center.

Tresvyatsky was born May 6, 1954, in the town of Nizhnoidinsk, Irkustk Region, Russia, where his father was serving in the military. He grew up in Novospaskoye in the Ulyanovsk Region, where he graduated from secondary school. He entered the Soviet armed forces, attending the Kacha Higher Air Force School and was taught to fly by Yuri Sheffer—who years later would become his colleague in the Buran program.

After graduating from Kacha in 1975 Tresvyatsky served as a fighter pilot with units in what was then East Germany, then in the Soviet Far East. He left the service in 1981 to attend the civilian test pilot school at the Gromov flight research institute in Zhukovsky, and also the Moscow Aviation Institute. Since 1983 he has been a test pilot at Gromov. He has logged over 2,000 hours of flying time.

Tresvyatsky graduated from MAI in 1985 and in April of that year was selected for the Buran program.

He currently serves as a civilian test pilot at the Gromov Flight Research Center in Zhukovsky. In July 1993 he was involved in a spectacular midair collision at the Bristol, England, Air Show, but managed to eject safely.

Tsibliyev, Vasily Vasilyevich
1954–

"I hope that everything that went wrong here is leaving with us." That was the forlorn final message from Vasily Tsibliyev, commander of the ill-starred Mir-23 crew, as he and flight engineer Alexandr Lazutkin departed the Russian space station on August 14, 1997, heading back to a safe landing on Earth.

Tsibliyev and Lazutkin's 6-month stay aboard Mir began with the docking of their Soyuz TM-25 spacecraft on February 12, 1997, with their cosmonaut researcher, German astronaut Reinhold Ewald, joining NASA astronaut J. M. Linenger, who had been aboard Mir since January, and the Mir-22 crew of Korzun and Kaleri. On February 23, midway through Ewald's mission, Mir suffered its first crisis when a defective oxygen-generating "candle" exploded, causing a 14-minute fire that filled the station with smoke.

Troubleshooting the fire put strain on Tsibliyev: psychology support staff at the Russian mission control in Korolev (formerly Kaliningrad) noticed that he was waking up in the middle of the night, obsessing over minor problems.

On June 25, 1997, Tsibliyev was remotely piloting the Progress M-34 resupply spacecraft, which had been undocked from Mir. As Tsibliyev attempted to redock Progress he noticed that it was not responding properly to controls. He tried to guide it past the station, but the Progress collided with the Spektr module, punching a hole in it, then bounced into one of the Spektr's vital solar arrays before flying off into space.

Mir's atmosphere began to whistle out into space as Tsibliyev, Lazutkin, and Foale quickly cut all the instrument and power cables leading from the Mir core into Spektr, sealing off the crippled module. The problem was

that in doing so they isolated Foale's scientific gear and deprived Mir of at least half of its power supply.

With Spektr sealed off, the cosmonauts were forced to manage on Mir's diminished power supply. A crew error on July 17 caused the station to drift.

The landing was not trouble free, either: the Soyuz soft-landing rockets failed. The cosmonauts were fortunately not injured.

Three days after landing, Tsibliyev and Lazutkin faced critics at a press conference, insisting that they had followed mission rules, and blamed the problems on poorly designed equipment and training procedures. After several months, an investigative panel agreed with the cosmonauts' assessment, and paid them their full bonuses.

Mir-23 was Tsibliyev's second flight aboard Mir. With flight engineer Alexandr Serebrov, he spent 5 months aboard the station from July 1993 to January 1994.

Launched as the crew of Soyuz TM-17, Tsibliyev and Serebrov were accompanied by French researcher Jean-Pierre Haignere for the first 3 weeks of their mission, which was devoted to medical studies with long-duration crewmember Valery Polyakov, and five EVAs, two of them dedicated to the construction of the Rapan girder on Mir's exterior.

On January 14, 1994, during Tsibliyev and Serebrov's departure from Mir aboard Soyuz TM-17, a stuck switch caused the Soyuz control thrusters to malfunction, and the spacecraft struck the Kristall module. The impact, while frightening to the Soyuz and Mir crews, did no damage.

Tsibliyev was born February 20, 1954, in the Crimean village of Orekhovka, Kirov District, Russia. He attended the Kharkov Higher Air Force School, graduating in 1975, then served as a Soviet air force pilot in Germany and in the Odessa military district. He has logged over 1,500 hours of flying time in 6 different types of fighter aircraft, and has also made 100 parachute jumps.

He graduated from the Yuri Gagarin Air Force Academy in 1987 prior to joining the cosmonaut team.

Tsibliyev was one of the 5 pilot candidates enrolled in the military cosmonaut team in March 1987. From December 1987 to July 1989 he completed the preliminary training program, qualifying as a Soyuz TM commander.

His first assignment was in a crew with flight engineer Sergei Avdeyev in 1989: they trained for a planned 18-month long visit to Mir. But eventually Soviet space managers decided against increasingly longer visits to Mir, preferring cosmonauts to fly "shifts" of 4 to 6 months. Cosmonaut training chief Vladimir Shatalov said that once a cosmonaut had spent a year in space on a single mission, he was "used up."

In early 1991 Tsibliyev was assigned as backup commander—with flight engineer Alexandr Laveikin and Kazkah researcher Talgat Musabayev—for a short-term visit to the Mir space station scheduled for launch in November of that year. That mission was canceled in July 1991.

From July 1991 to January 1993 he Tsibliyev trained as a Soyuz crew commander, first with Alexandr Balandin, then with Yuri Usachev. Tsibliyev and Usachev were backups for Soyuz TM-16.

Since December 1997 Tsibliyev has had an administrative job at the Gagarin Center.

Tyurin, Mikhail Vladislavovich

1960–

Energiya engineer Mikhail Tyurin is assigned to the third incremental International Space Station crew, scheduled for launch aboard a Soyuz spacecraft in the fall of 2000. Tyurin, Soyuz pilot Yuri Dezhurov and American commander Ken Bowersox will spend 2 months aboard the ISS during its early assembly phase.

The same crew is scheduled to serve as backups to Shephard, Gidzenko, and Krikalev, the first incremental ISS crew, scheduled for launch in February 2000.

Tyurin was born March 2, 1960, and prior to his selection worked at the RKK Energiya. He was one of the 2 civilian candidates approved for cosmonaut training in April 1994. In April 1996 he completed the basic cosmonaut training course at the Gagarin Center.

Usachev, Yuri Vladimirovich

1957–

Yuri Usachev was the flight engineer of Soyuz TM-18, a cosmonaut crew launched to the Mir space station in January 1994. Usachev, commander Viktor Afanasyev and physician Valery Polyakov made up the Mir-15 crew, which concentrated on Polyakov's medical experiments (the physician went on to spend 14 months aboard Mir) as well as X-ray astronomical observations and space manufacturing. The crew also fired an electron beam gun at the Swedish Freja satellite as part of a study of the Earth's magnetic field. The Mir-15 mission ended in July 1994, after 182 days.

Usachev returned to Mir in February 1996 with commander Yuri Onufriyenko aboard Soyuz TM-23. The two cosmonauts, who formed the Mir-21 crew, were joined a month later by NASA-Mir researcher Shannon Lucid, who arrrived aboard STS-76. Usachev and Onufriyenko configured Mir for the addition of its final module, the Priroda, which arrived in early June. They also conducted five EVAs between May 13 and June 20, moving solar arrays, conducting repairs, and videotaped a Pepsi commercial. Usachev and Onufriyenko returned to Earth on September 2, 1996, with French researcher Claudie Andre-Deshays, after 193 days in space.

In July 1997 the joint state commission assigned Usachev as commander for the second incremental International Space Station crew, scheduled for launch aboard STS-104 in the summer of 1999. Usachev will join astronauts James Voss and Susan Helms on a 4-month mission.

Usachev was born October 9, 1957, in Donetsk, Rostov region, Russia, and attended the Moscow Aviation Institute, graduating in 1985. He joined the NPO Energiya and in February 1989 became one of 4 Energiya engineers enrolled in the cosmonaut team. He completed the basic training course in January 1991, and in March 1992 was assigned to a Soyuz-Mir crew with commander Anatoly Artsebarsky. He later served on the backup crews for Soyuz TM-16 and Soyuz TM-17.

Valkov, Konstantin Anatolyevich

1971–

Senior Lieutenant Konstantin Valkov is one of the 8 Russian air force pilots selected for cosmonaut training at the Gagarin Center in May 1997. In the spring of 1999 he should qualify as a Soyuz commander and International Space Station crewmember.

Valkov was born November 11, 1971, in Kamensk-Uralsky, Sverdlovsk (now Yekaterinberg) Region, Russia. He graduated from the Barnaul Higher Air Force School in 1994, and at the time of his selection for cosmonaut training served with the 76th Air Army at St. Petersburg.

Varlamov, Valentin Stepanovich

1934–1980

Valentin Varlamov was one of the most promising members of the first class of Soviet cosmonauts selected in March 1960. All through the first weeks of academic training, Varlamov was the best at mastering the intricacies of physics and astronavigation. By May 1960 he had been designated as one of the 6 finalists who were to undergo accelerated training for the first manned Vostok flight.

On July 24, 1960, however, Varlamov dislocated a vertabra in his neck while diving into a lake near Star Town. Hospitalized for a month, he was not allowed to continue training for spaceflight for medical reasons, and in April 1961 was the first to received a medical dismissal from the cosmonaut team.

Varlamov was born August 15, 1934, in the Penza region of Russia. He attended the Kacha Higher Air Force School at Volgograd, graduating in 1954, then served as a fighter pilot in the Soviet air force. In one regiment he flew with future cosmonaut Valentin Filatyev.

Varlamov remained with the space program, however, serving in the control center during the launch of Gagarin on April 12, 1961, and later assisting in the training of Pavel Belyayev and Alexei Leonov for the Voskhod 2 mis-

sion in 1964 and 1965. He eventually became an instructor in astronavigation at the training center, and stayed close friends with members of the cosmonaut group.

He died October 2, 1980 of a cerebral hemorrhage.

Vasyutin, Vladimir Vladimirovich

1952–

Vladimir Vasyutin was the commander of the Soyuz T-14 mission to Salyut 7 in September 1985. He had the bad luck to become the first space traveler to become so ill during a mission that the flight was cut short.

Vasyutin, flight engineer Georgy Grechko and researcher Alexandr Volkov were launched on September 17, 1985, and docked with Salyut 7 the next day. Already aboard the station were cosmonauts Vladimir Dzhanibekov and Viktor Savinykh, who had just completed a dramatic repair of a station that had been adrift and out of control. Savinykh had trained with Vasyutin for many years and the two of them, with Volkov, made up the original 1985 Salyut 7 expedition crew, so he remained on board when Grechko returned to Earth with Dzhanibekov on September 25.

For the next 3 weeks operations aboard the station went smoothly. The cargo and laboratory module Kosmos 1686 docked with the Salyut 7/Soyuz T-14 complex on October 2, carrying materials the cosmonauts would need during their "winter" mission, which would include observations of Halley's Comet in March 1986.

But in mid-October Vasyutin developed an infection that resisted treatment by antibiotics. By early November he was fighting a temperature that rose to 104 degrees F. Eventually there was no choice for Soviet space officials: the cosmonauts had to return to Earth, and they did, on November 21. Vasyutin was hospitalized for almost a month.

It was later learned the Vasyutin had actually been ill before launch with prostatitis, but had managed to conceal it from doctors. As a result, in 1986 the already stringent medical standards applied to members of the cosmonaut team were made even more stringent, resulting in the dismissal of pilots Yevgeny Salei and Nikolai Grekov.

Vasyutin was born March 8, 1952, in the city of Kharkhov in the Ukraine. In 1970 he entered the Kharkov Higher Air Force School, graduating in 1974, then served as an instructor pilot there until he was admitted to the cosmonaut team in August 1976.

Following graduation from the Chkalov test pilot school (1977) and completion of the 2-year basic cosmonaut training course, Vasyutin was assigned as commander of a three-man crew preparing for a Salyut-Almaz mission. The Salyut-Almaz series of manned military reconnaissance missions was canceled in 1981, however, and Vasyutin then joined the Salyut 7 training group.

In September 1982 he was backup commander for Soyuz T-7, replacing Yuri Romanenko, who had failed a physical exam. He then served as backup commander for Soyuz T-9, Soyuz T-10, and Soyuz T-12 before making his first flight.

Vasyutin left the cosmonaut team in February 1986 to attend the Gagarin Air Force Academy. He graduated in 1988, becoming an instructor at the Academy. Now a lieutenant general, he is deputy director of the school.

Viktorenko, Alexandr Stepanovich

1947–

Alexandr Viktorenko commanded 4 Soyuz missions to the Mir space station between 1987 and 1995, beginning with Soyuz TM-3 in July 1987. The crew for this visiting mission to Mir included flight engineer Alexandr Alexandrov and Syrian researcher Muhammed Faris. After 8 days of joint experiments, Viktorenko and Faris returned to Earth with cosmonaut Alexander Laveikin, who had spent 7 months aboard Mir, leaving cosmonaut Alexandr Alexandrov in his place.

From September 1989 to February 1990 Viktorenko commanded the fifth Mir resident crew, launched as Soyuz TM-8. During the 6-month mission, Viktorenko and flight engineer Alexandr Serebrov activated the Kvant-2 "technology" module, which was added to the Mir-Kvant-Soyuz TM complex in December. In addition, Viktorenko and Serebrov performed the first tests of the Ikarus manned maneuvering unit. On February 5, 1990, Vik-

torenko piloted Ikarus during a 3-hour, 45-minute EVA. He and Serebrov performed a total of five EVAs, logging almost 20 hours outside Mir.

Viktorenko's third visit was Mir-14, launched as Soyuz TM-14 in March 1992. Joining Viktorenko for this 5-month mission were flight engineer Alexandr Kaleri and German researcher Klaus-Dietrich Flade.

Most recently Viktorenko commanded Mir-17, launched as Soyuz TM-20 in October 1994. His crewmates on that flight were flight engineer Yelena Kondakova and ESA astronaut Ulf Merbold. The crew also included long-duration physician-cosmonaut Valery Polyakov, who returned to Earth with Viktorenko and Kondakova in March 1995.

Viktorenko was born March 29, 1947, in the village of Oglinka in the Sergeyevsky District of North Kazakhstan. He attended the Polbin Higher Air Force School in Orenburg, graduating in 1969, then served with the Baltic fleet as an Il-28 pilot. He has logged over 2,000 hours of flying time and made 150 parachute jumps.

One of the 2 candidates selected for the cosmonaut team in February 1978, Viktorenko first spent a year at the Chkalov test pilot school, qualifying as a test pilot third class. In 1979, while undergoing basic training on the Soyuz and Salyut spacecraft, Viktorenko was badly burned in an accident in an isolation chamber. His injuries were serious enough to cause him to be dropped from the cosmonaut team, but he persevered and was eventually restored to flight status. Official accounts refer to his "very long and difficult course of training." He was designated a cosmonaut in 1982 and served as backup commander for Soyuz T-14 and Soyuz T-15.

Following his first spaceflight he joined the Rescuer group of veteran Soyuz commanders who stand by to fly emergency missions. He also served as backup commander for the second Soviet-French mission, Soyuz TM-7 (1988), and for Soyuz TM-13 (1991).

Viktorenko left the air force and the cosmonaut team in July 1997. He works at the Gagarin Center as a civilian training officer.

Vinogradov, Pavel Vladimirovich

1953–

Engineer Pavel Vinogradov joined veteran commander Anatoly Solovyov in the difficult Mir-24 mission, launched August 13, 1997, as Soyuz TM-26. The cosmonauts were to relieve the beleaguered crew of Tsibliyev and Lazutkin who, with NASA research Michael Foale, had struggled with a staggering number of system failures—guidance, computer, environmental—aboard the station following a collision with a Progress supply vehicle on June 25.

Within days of arriving at Mir, Vinogradov and Solovyov's first job was to perform an internal EVA to the damaged Spektr module, in a vain search for the leak caused by the collision. They made another search of Mir's exterior, also in vain, forcing program managers to conclude that the leak was at the point where the boom of Spektr's solar array entered the module.

Vinogradov and Solovyov spent much of their mission installing new equipment shipped to the station by Progress, and by the STS-86 Shuttle mission, which arrived in late September. They returned to Earth themselves in early February, leaving Mir functioning again.

Before he had even returned to Earth, in February 1998, Vinogradov was assigned to the fifth incremental International Space Station crew. He and commander Valery Korzun will be launched by Soyuz to the I.S.S. in the spring of the year 2001, along with a NASA astronaut still to be named.

Vinogradov was born August 31, 1953, in the city of Magadan, Magadan Oblast, Russia, and grew up in Anadyr. He attended the Moscow Aviation Institute, graduating in 1977. For the next 6 years he worked in one of MAI's laboratories as a researcher and senior engineer. When one of his projects was selected for use on the Buran space shuttle, Vinogradov tried to become a cosmonaut himself and even passed the medical commission at the IMBP in February 1983.

Since he was not employed by either the NPO Energiya, which had the largest civilian cosmonaut team, or IMBP, with its smaller group, Vinogradov could not be selected. He wrote directly to NPO Energiya chief Valentin Glushko in search of a job, and was hired at Energiya, where he worked on manned spacecraft systems, including the androgynous docking unit intended for use by the Buran space shuttle.

Vinogradov passed the technical exams for cosmonaut candidates at Energiya employed in 1984, along with Sergei Krikalev and Alexandr Poleshchuk, but could still not be enrolled because he had not worked for the organization for the minimum 3 years.

Once he met that qualification, he went before the medical commission again, passing for a second time in August 1988. This time he was failed by the joint state commission itself on other grounds. It was only after the fall of the Soviet Union in 1991 and the subsequent reorganization of the joint state commission that Vinogradov was able to qualify. He became one of 3 Energiya engineers enrolled in the team in May 1992. In March 1994 he completed the basic training intended to qualify him as a future Mir crewmember. However, he was unable to pass the final medical examinations and was forced to wait until late in 1994 before being certified as a test-cosmonaut.

He was backup flight engineer for Soyuz TM-22, the twentieth Mir residency, launched in September 1995. He then trained for almost a year in the prime crew for Soyuz TM-24, only to be removed from the flight in August 1996, a week prior to launch, when his commander, Gennady Manakov, was medically disqualified.

Volk, Igor Petrovich

1937–

Igor Volk is a test pilot and cosmonaut who was for many years scheduled to command the first orbital flight of the Soviet space shuttle Buran sometime in 1992 or 1993.

Soviet manned spaceflights of Vostok and Soyuz craft always depended on automatic guidance and control systems, using pilots as backup systems. Buran, however, required its pilots to be capable of landing the vehicle. As preparation for this assignment, Volk served as cosmonaut-researcher aboard the Soyuz T-12 mission to Salyut 7 in July 1984. During his 12 days in space, Volk was subjected to a series of medical experiments designed to test his reactions to weightlessness. But more was to come.

Immediately upon landing Volk was transferred — trouserless and shoeless, he later reported—to a helicopter, which flew from the touchdown site to the city of Dzhezhkazgan. In the city he took the controls of a Tu-154 airplane and did a simulated Buran approach to the landing strip at the Baikonur Cosmodrome. As if that weren't enough, while the Tu-154 was taxiing to a stop, Volk was ordered back into his space suit. He was then put into the cockpit of a MiG-25 jet, which he flew to an altitude of 2.1 kilometers and down to a deadstick landing.

Volk revealed that he had found flying an aircraft to be more difficult after spending days in orbit.

The Buran program was ultimately canceled in the spring of 1993 before manned missions could be launched.

Volk was born April 12, 1937, in the city of Gotvald in the Kharkov Region of the Ukraine. He grew interested in becoming a pilot while he was still in grade school, but enrolled in the Govorov Artillery and Radiotechnical Academy to please his parents. Eventually, however, he transferred to the Kirovograd Higher Air Force School, where he became a bomber pilot. During his military service he was stationed in Baku, Azerbaijan, in the antiaircraft forces of the Transcaucausus Military District, where he flew Tu-16 and Il-28 bombers.

While in the air force he applied for admission to the All-Union Correspondence School of Machine Building, hoping to learn more about aircraft construction. He was told that the school did not accept military personnel as students. When he was discharged from the service 1962, Volk enrolled instead at the Moscow Aviation Institute, from which he graduated in 1969.

At the time of his enrollment at MAI Volk also underwent test pilot training at the civilian school in Zhukovsky.

Working with the Mikoyan aircraft design bureau, he was involved in attempts to set speed records in the MiG-21. Interestingly, he and Aviard Fastovets made unpowered test flights in a prototype Soviet rocketplane (Project 50-50) similar to the American X-20. In the mid-1960s Volk also flew a specially modified delta-wing MiG-25 in order to test the design of the Soviet supersonic airliner, the Tu-144. He later became an instructor test pilot. (In 1975, while chairing an examination board judging student test pilots, he gave a passing grade to Svetlana Savtiskaya, whom he would later accompany into space.)

Volk logged over 6,000 hours of flying time, 4,000 as a test pilot, in 80 different types of aircraft. He is qualified as a test pilot first class and an honored test pilot of the USSR.

In 1977 the Zhukovsky Flight Research Institute was instructed by the USSR Ministry of Aviation Production to select and train pilots for its new space shuttle program. Volk became the leader of the group of 5 pilots chosen the next year from over 500 applicants. They became known as the "Wolf Pack," after their leader ("volk" means "wolf," in Russian).

In 1979 and 1980 Volk and his four colleagues underwent training on the Soyuz and Salyut spacecraft at the TsPK. Having qualified as a cosmonaut, Volk was assigned to a flight crew in 1982 with Kizim and Solovyov. Changes in the Soyuz-Salyut launch schedule saw him transferred to a crew with Dzhanibekov and Savitskaya in late 1983.

Returning to work on Buran following the Soyuz T-12 mission, Volk and copilot Rimantas Stankyavichus prepared for a series of approach and landing tests of a jet-powered version of the Buran orbiter. The first, lasting 12 minutes, took place on November 10, 1985. Volk ultimately piloted 12 such flights (out of the total of 24) through April 1988.

In 1989 Volk visited the United States, including an unscheduled stop at the NASA Johnson Space Center, where he toured a Shuttle simulator.

Volk has also served as a spokesman for a group of Russian rocket engineers developing *Burlak*, a system for launch small satellites from a transport airplane.

Volkov, Alexandr Alexandrovich

1948–

Alexandr Volkov is a veteran of three long-duration space missions aboard two different Soviet stations.

The first was the Soyuz T-14 residency aboard Salyut 7, which began September 17, 1985. As researcher in a crew that included commander Vladimir Vasyutin and flight engineer Viktor Savinykh, Volkov supervised the operations of Kosmos-1686, a module equipped with the Pion military observation system. During the course of the planned 6-month mission, however, Vasyutin became ill. When he failed to respond to treatment, Soviet program managers cut short the mission. The cosmonauts returned to Earth on November 21, 1985.

Volkov was commander of Soyuz TM-7, the third Mir resident mission, launched November 26, 1988. Joining Volkov were flight engineer Sergei Krikalev and French researcher Jean-Loup Chretien. One of the goals of the

Mir-3 mission was group medical experiments with the resident crew of Titov, Manarov, and Polyakov.

Volkov and Chretien performed a 6-hour EVA on December 9, 1988, erecting a prototype space antenna called ERA. When ERA failed to deploy as planned, Volkov solved the problem by kicking its container, freeing the device.

Titov, Manarov and Chretien left the station on December 21, 1988, leaving physician Polyakov with Volkov and Krikalev.

In the spring of 1989 the Soviet manned space program began to suffer from Kremlin budget cutting. As a result, the remainder of the Mir-3 residency became frustrating for the cosmonauts. Two EVAs by Volkov and Krikalev, designed to erect new solar panels on the Mir exterior, were canceled, as was the launch of the Kvant 2 module. The scheduled handover to the Mir-4 crew of Viktorenko and Balandin was also canceled, and it was decided that Mir would be unoccupied for 4 months.

The cosmonauts continued with a series of astrophysical observations using the first Kvant observatory, and with a number of materials-processing experiments. The Mir-3 mission ended after 151 days.

On October 2, 1991, Volkov went into space for a third time, as commander of Soyuz TM-13. In his crew were Kazkah researcher Toktar Aubakirov and Austrian researcher Franz Viehbock. Volkov joined his former Mir-3 crewmate Sergei Krikalev, who had already spent over 5 months aboard Mir by that time, in completing the tenth Mir residency.

Volkov was born April 27, 1948, in Gorlovka, Donetsk Region, Ukraine. He attended the Kharkov Higher Air Force School from 1966 to 1970, then served for 6 years as an instructor there.

He was one of the 9 pilots enrolled as candidates in the Gagarin Center cosmonaut team in August 1976. Since it was assumed these pilots would ultimately fly the Buran space shuttle in addition to Soyuz, they were sent to the Chkalov military test pilot school at Akhtubinsk to qualify as test pilots. From 1977 to January 1979 Volkov underwent Soyuz training.

While awaiting a flight opportunity Volkov served as a test pilot. He has logged over 2,100 hours of flying time in 20 different types of aircraft, and has also made 119 parachute jumps.

Volkov served as backup commander for Soyuz TM-4 (1987) and Soyuz TM-12 (1991).

In addition to his crew assignments, Volkov has graduated (by correspondence) from the Lenin Military-Political Academy (1991). He served as deputy director of the Gagarin Center cosmonaut unit for political affairs from July 1988 to January 1991, when he succeeded Boris Volynov as chief of the cosmonaut team, a position he still holds.

Among those under Volkov's command are his son, Sergei, who was enrolled as a military cosmonaut candidate in May 1997.

Volkov, Sregei Alexandrovich
1973–

Senior Lieutenant Sergei Volkov is one of the 8 Russian air force pilots selected for cosmonaut-candidate training in May 1997. In the spring of 1999 he should qualify as a Soyuz commander and International Space Station crewmember.

Volkov was born April 1, 1973, in Chuguyev, Kharkov Region, Ukrainian SSR (now Ukraine), where his father, future cosmonaut Alexandr Volkov, was a flight instructor. Young Volkov attended the Tambov Higher Air Force School (named for Raskova), graduating in 1995.

At the time of his selection Volkov was a deputy aircraft commander with the 8th Air Division (Special Destination) at Chkalov Air Base, Moscow Region.

Volkov, Vladislav Nikolayevich
1935–1971

Vladislav Volkov was flight engineer of the Soyuz 11 crew, the first cosmonauts to occupy an orbiting Salyut station.

Volkov, commander Georgy Dobrovolsky and researcher Viktor Patsayev were launched on June 6, 1971, just 2 days after the state commission had approved them as the prime Soyuz 11 crew. The original crew of Leonov, Kubasov, and Kolodin had been disqualified en masse because Kubasov could not pass the final medical examinations. A brief attempt to replace Kubasov with Volkov had failed when Volkov and Leonov had a disagreement.

Upon reaching Salyut, the cosmonauts moved aboard, something the previous crew had been unable to do, and after 3 days testing communications, life support, and medical systems, they got down to work.

The program of experiments for what was scheduled to be a 24-day mission was ambitious: there was the Orion-1 telescope, the Anna-3 and gamma ray observatory called Anna-3, the Oazis hydroponic farm, in addition to other systems for making Earth observations and conducting medical tests.

A personality conflict developed during the first 2 weeks. According to chief designer Vasily Mishin, Volkov "declared himself commander" of the mission, probably reasoning that as the lone spaceflight veteran in the crew he had more experience in adapting to the rigors of the new environment. Making matters worse, under the cumbersome structure of the Soviet manned space program—in which different areas of the same mission were the responsibility of completely different organizations— Volkov and Patsayev, as employees of the OKB Korolev, had worked in the design and development of Salyut and were proteges of Mishin himself, who had the role of lead flight director. Dobrovolsky, an air force lieutenant colonel, had been assigned as their commander rather late in the training process.

According to Mishin, several conversations between the flight control center and Salyut fixed that problem. Then, on June 17, a fire broke out inside the station. The cosmonauts hurriedly boarded their Soyuz, intending to abandon Salyut. The fire went out and the mission could continue, but the incident did nothing to lessen the tension aboard the station.

A week later the cosmonauts were given permission to prepare for return to Earth. Although plagued by difficulties, they had still set a new space endurance record.

Tragically, during reentry a valve in the Soyuz opened prematurely, venting the spacecraft atmosphere and killing the cosmonauts, who were not wearing space suits. The accident was a serious blow to the Soviet manned space effort, resulting in a yearlong hiatus and a redesign of the Soyuz command module.

Earlier, in October 1969, Volkov served as flight engineer aboard Soyuz 7, one of 3 manned Soyuz craft which were in orbit at the same time. Soyuz 7 was to have been a passive docking target for Soyuz 8, but technical problems kept the two craft several hundred yards apart.

Volkov was born November 23, 1935, in Moscow. His father was a designer for the bureau headed by Vladimir Myasishchev (builder of the Bison bomber) and Vladislav grew up near the Tushino airfield. Since his mother also worked in an aircraft factory, and an uncle was a pilot and War hero, naturally Volkov wanted to become a pilot. He enrolled in a local flying club and took lessons. His family, however, suggested that rather than join the air force he should first study aeronautical engineering. Volkov took the advice and attended the Moscow Aviation Institute, graduating in 1959.

Volkov immediately went to work at the Korolev spacecraft design bureau, becoming a member of a group of young engineers known as the "kindergarten" under Korolev's chief assistant, Konstantin Feoktistov, designer of the Vostok and Voskhod spacecraft. In May 1964 Volkov and the others learned that their boss, Feoktistov, was going into space aboard the first Voskhod. When chief designer Sergei Korolev announced that engineers from the bureau would be included in future space crews, he was swamped with applications, one of them from Volkov. Two years later, in May 1966, Volkov was one of 8 civilian engineers admitted to the bureau's cosmonaut team.

During his cosmonaut training Volkov became an expert parachutist and also qualified as a jet pilot. He was not one of the first engineers to be chosen for a Soyuz crew, something he found frustrating, but he was patient, and earned an assignment of his own in 1968. In addition to two flights in space, he also served as backup flight engineer for Soyuz 10.

Shortly before his death Volkov completed an autobiography titled *Stepping into the Sky*, published in 1971.

Voloshin, Valery Abramovich

1942–

Valery Voloshin was one of the 22 candidates selected for the military cosmonaut team on October 28, November 1965. He left the group in April 1969 without having flown in space, though he trained for more than 2 years for a manned flight around the Moon.

Voloshin was born April 24, 1942, in Yangiyul in the Tashkent region of Uzbekistan. He attended the Chernigov Higher Air Force School, and served as a pilot in the Soviet air force prior to becoming a cosmonaut.

In November 1966, even before completion of the basic training course, Voloshin was assigned to Program L, and for the next 2 and a half years trained for both circumlunar flights and lunar landings. At one point his flight engineer was Vitaly Sevastyanov, but during most of the time he was teamed with Yuri Artyukhin.

Voloshin left the cosmonaut team in April 1969 for health reasons, returning to his previous duty station at Kubinka Air Base. He went on to attend the Gagarin Air Force Academy. He then served on the staff of the Kirov Military Medical Academy in St. Petersburg (formerly Leningrad).

Volynov, Boris Valentinovich

1934–

Boris Volynov commanded one of first manned spacecraft to dock in space.

Volynov was the pilot of the 3-man Soyuz 5, launched January 15, 1969, which made a successful rendezvous and docking with Soyuz 4, piloted by Vladimir Shatalov, the next day. Volynov's two comrades, Yevgeny Khrunov and Alexei Yeliseyev, then donned space suits and made a walk in space to Soyuz 4. Volynov returned to Earth alone on January 17.

He later commanded a 49-day military reconnaissance flight aboard the Salyut-Almaz 5 space station in July and August 1976. Volynov and flight engineer Vitaly

Zholobov used special cameras aboard the station to observed military targets on Earth, sometimes in conjunction with Soviet ground exercises. It was a stressful mission: later medical data showed that the cosmonauts were working 16-hour days, twice the recommended amount, and were skimping on their required exercise. Volynov reportedly fell ill.

To make matters worse, an unknown problem in the station's air supply began giving off an acrid odor. The cosmonauts tolerated it as long as they could, but were finally forced to cut short the mission (it was scheduled to last approximately 60 days) and return home.

Volynov was born December 18, 1934, in Irkutsk, Siberia. He was interested in the exploits of Soviet aviators as a child and joined the air force as soon as he was of age. He attended the Stalingrad Higher Air Force School, graduating in November 1955.

For the next 4 years Volynov served as a fighter pilot in the 133rd Air Division of the Air Defense Forces in the city of Yaroslav, becoming one of the first 20 Soviet cosmonauts selected in March 1960.

Volynov's cosmonaut career was an exercise in patience: he was a backup for 2 of the early Vostok flights, to Pavel Popovich on Vostok 4 in 1962, and to Valery Bykovsky on Vostok 5 in 1963. He was assigned as commander of one of 2 teams training for the first flight of a space crew, Voskhod 1 in 1964, but found himself relegated to a nominal backup role when the compressed training schedule (4 months from crew selection to planned launch) caused the 2 crews to be combined.

With a succession of partners—scientist Georgy Katys, pilot Viktor Gorbatko, and pilot Georgy Shonin—Volynov then trained for almost a year as commander of the planned Voskhod 3 mission. Voskhod 3 was scheduled to last up to 15 days and included an experiment in artificial gravity. But in March 1966, following the death of chief designer Sergei Korolev, the remaining four of the original six Voskhod missions were canceled.

Transferred to the Soyuz group, he was a backup for a fourth time (Soyuz 3) before finally making his first spaceflight. During this time he also graduated from the Zhukovsky Air Force Engineering Academy (February 1968).

After Soyuz 5 he was assigned to the group of cosmonauts training for flights to the Almaz military space station, becoming backup commander for the Soyuz 14 flight to the first Almaz, Salyut 3, in 1973. He also directed the training of the May 1970 cosmonaut group.

He has also worked as a Salyut 6 and Salyut 7 flight controller, and performed graduate work for a candidate of technical sciences degree awarded in 1980.

From November 1982 to March 1990 he was commander of the military cosmonaut team. He has since retired.

Vorobyov, Lev Vasilyevich
1931–

Lev Vorobyov was a pilot cosmonaut who should have commanded the Soyuz 13 mission in December 1973. (He had already chosen the callsign "Atlant.") But growing personal incompatibility between Vorobyov and flight engineer Valery Yazdovsky caused the two prime crewmen to be replaced by backups Pyotr Klimuk and Valentin Lebedev a week before launch.

Vorobyov was born February 24, 1931, in Borovichi, a city midway between Moscow and Leningrad. His father, who died when Vorobyov was very young, was a commissar in the Russian Revolution of 1917. Vorobyov was inspired to become a pilot by his older brother Viktor, who was killed in the Great Patriotic War in 1943.

After graduating from the Kiev air force prep school in 1949, Vorobyov entered the Serov Higher Air Force School at Bataisk, becoming a pilot in 1952. He spent 5 years as a MiG-15 pilot with the 101st Air Division, Ural Army of the Air Defense Forces, then enrolled at the Red Banner (later named for Gagarin) Air Force Academy. He graduated in 1961.

At the time of his selection as a cosmonaut in January 1963 he was a pilot-navigator in the 24th Air Division, 110th Army of the Air Defense Forces, based on Sakhalin Island in the Soviet Far East.

Vorobyov completed the candidate course in January 1965 and joined the group of cosmonauts training for flights in the Almaz military space station program. His space career almost came to an abrupt end in March 1964 when he and fellow cosmonaut Eduard Kugno criticized the policies of Soviet Premier Nikita Khrushchev during a Communist Party meeting. Kugno

was expelled from the team; Vorobyov was saved by his Party membership.

In 1969 Vorobyov moved over to the Soyuz program, training in crews with Nikolai Rukavishnikov and, later, Viktor Patsayev. He was teamed with Yazdovsky in 1972 for the Soyuz 13 program, and for several months in early 1974 was joined by Valery Ryumin in the first crew for the Salyut 4 program.

But continuing political problems led to Vorobyov's dismissal in June 1974. He worked on life support and rescue systems in the 2nd Directorate of the Gagarin Center until leaving military service in November 1986. He is now retired.

Voronov, Anatoly Feodorovich
1930–1993

Anatoly Voronov was a Soviet cosmonaut for 16 years who trained for flights in the lunar program and aboard the Salyut space station without going into space.

Voronov was born June 11, 1930, in the village of Klyuchevka, Sok-Karamalinsky District, Chkalovsky (now Orenburg) Region, Russia. He attended the Bugulminsk Teacher's School from 1948 to 1950, then entered the military.

After graduation from the Chelyabinsk Air Force Navigator's School in 1953, Voronov served on active duty with the 43rd Air Army, Long Range Aviation, in Poltova as a crewman on Tu-4 and T-16 aircraft. In May 1955 he transferred to the 13th Air Guards Regiment based at the nuclear test range in Semipalatinsk, taking part in seven different nuclear bomb tests.

From 1957 to 1960 he was a student at the Red Banner (later named for Gagarin) Air Force Academy, and at the time of his selection for the cosmonaut team was a flight test navigator with the 1st Air Test Squadron at the military flight research center's branch at Chkalovskaya. He logged over 6,000 hours of flying time in 24 different types of aircraft, including helicopters.

Voronov was one of the 15 pilots and engineers selected from 150 candidates for cosmonaut training in January 1963. After completing the candidate course in

January 1965, he trained as a crewman on the early Soyuz missions. From 1967 to 1970 he was involved in the Soviet manned lunar landing program, L-1, training for a flight around the Moon. When that effort was canceled, he began to train for a mission to Salyut 1.

In June 1971, with Alexei Gubarev and Vitaly Sevastyanov, Voronov was assigned to the backup crew for a planned two-month Soyuz 12 mission. But the deaths of cosmonauts Dobrovolsky, Volkov, and Patsayev aboard Soyuz 11 forced a cancellation of the followup mission. And when the subsequent redesign of the Soyuz spacecraft eliminated the seat for a third cosmonaut, Voronov was reassigned to the team developing a new Soyuz spacecraft called Soyuz-T. He trained with Vladimir Lyakhov for a test flight until April 1979, when he left the cosmonaut team.

For the next 14 years he worked at the Priroda State Center in Moscow, where he was involved in the study of Earth resources from space.

He died after a long illness on October 31, 1993.

Vozovikov, Sergei Yuriyevich
1958–1993

Major Sergei Vozovikov was one of the 3 pilots enrolled as military cosmonaut candidates in May 1990. In March 1992 he completed the training course that qualified him as a Soyuz TM-Mir commander.

Tragically, Vozovikov drowned in the Black Sea on July 11, 1993, while on a survival training assignment with cosmonaut candidates Alexandr Lazutkin and Sergei Treshchev.

Vozovikov was born April 17, 1958, in Almaty (then Alma-Ata), Kazakhstan. He attended the Armavir Higher Air Force School, graduating in 1979, then served as a fighter pilot with the Air Defense Forces (PVO) of the Soviet military. He logged over 1,200 hours of flying time in the L-29, MiG-23 and MiG-29 aircraft.

While awaiting a flight assignment Vozovikov was performing graduate work in environmental science at Moscow State University.

Yablontsev, Alexandr Nikolayevich
1955–

Test pilot Alexandr Yablontsev was selected as a candidate for flights of the Buran space shuttle in 1987. He was approved for cosmonaut training by the joint state commission on January 25, 1989, and from 1989 to April 1991 underwent the basic course at the Gagarin Center while still doing flight test work at the Chkalov flight test center in Akhtubinsk.

He transferred to the Gagarin Center in April 1992 to work on the Soyuz-Buran program. The Buran program was finally canceled in 1994 and the military test pilot group dissolved in September 1996.

Yablontsev was born April 3, 1955, in Warsaw, Poland, where his father was serving with Soviet forces. In 1972 he entered the Armavir Higher Air Force School, graduating in 1976, then served with units of the Soviet air force. He entered the Chkalov school in 1984 and following graduation in 1985 began to work as a test pilot.

In 1989 he also graduated from the Moscow Aviation Institute.

Yablontsev retired from the air force in 1997.

Yakovlev, Oleg Anatolyevich
1940–1990

Oleg Yakovlev was one of the 22 air force candidates enrolled in the cosmonaut team on October 28, 1965. From January 1968 to April 1969 he worked on the Almaz military space station program as a crew commander. He then transferred to the civilian Salyut space station program, but in May 1973, before he could be assigned to a crew, suffered a medical disqualification and lost his chance to fly in space.

Yakovlev was born December 31, 1940, in Leningrad. In 1959 he entered the Soviet air force and enrolled at the Chernigov Higher Air Force School. A year later he transferred to the Kharkov School, graduating in 1963. He spent the next 2 years as a fighter pilot with the 27th Air Guards Regiment of the 6th Air Army, Air Defense Forces, in the Leningrad military district.

After leaving the cosmonaut team Yakovlev enrolled at the Gagarin Air Force Academy. He graduated in 1976, then worked there as an instructor until 1980. In 1982 he received a candidate of military science degree.

Yakovlev later joined the staff of the Central Scientific Research Institute of the USSR Ministry of Defense, becoming a senior scientist in 1989 and serving as deputy chief of administration. He also published several scientific papers.

Colonel Yakovlev died of a heart attack on May 2, 1990.

Yazdovsky, Valery Alexandrovich

1930–

Valery Yazdovsky was the original flight engineer scheduled to spend 8 days in space aboard Soyuz 13 in December 1973. Designed to carry the Orion observatory during the Comet Kahoutek's encounter with Earth, this mission was developed by the Soviet Academy of Sciences.

Yazdovsky played a prominent role in the development of the mission's scientific program, but he and prime crew commander Lev Vorobyov were relegated to the backup role less than a month prior to launch. Their places were taken by a pair of 31-year-old rookie cosmonauts, Pyotr Klimuk and Valentin Lebedev.

It wasn't until 1989 that the reason for such a switch was revealed: Yazdovsky and Vorobyov were unable to get along. At one point during training they even refused to sit at the same lunch table. Viktor Blagov, a Soviet flight control director, had worked with Yazdovsky on a tracking ship and found him to be a capable scientist, but a poor choice for cosmonaut because he lacked a sense of teamwork.

Yazdovsky had previously served as flight engineer with Vasily Lazarev on one of the Soyuz 9 backup crews.

Yazdovsky was born July 8, 1930, in the town of Yenyakievo in the Donestk Region of the Ukraine. His father was a mining engineer and the family lived in sev-

eral places: the Don River basin, the Urals, and in Soviet Central Asia.

At a young age Yazdovsky worked as a miner near the city of Tula, eventually escaping from the mines to become a draftsman at the Institute of Coal Industry in Pushino, near Moscow. This led to his enrollment at the Moscow Aviation Institute, from which he graduated in March 1954. He also qualified as a pilot through that school's flying club.

Following graduation from MAI Yazodvsky went to work at the Korolev design bureau. In 1957 he was named a designer, becoming the first person to join the staff of Mikhail Tikhonravov, one of Korolev's senior officials. (Others who soon joined this same staff included future cosmonauts Konstantin Feoktistov and Oleg Makarov.) Yazdovsky took part in the design of the Vostok, Voskhod and Soyuz spacecraft prior to enrolling in the cosmonaut team in 1969.

He left the cosmonaut team in 1983, to return to full-time work at the OKB Korolev (later known as NPO Energiya). He has since retired.

Yegorov, Boris Borisovich

1937–1994

Boris Yegorov was the first medical doctor to make a spaceflight, as a member of the crew of the first Voskhod in October 1964. During this 1-day flight Yegorov observed his and his fellow cosmonauts' reactions to microgravity and drew blood samples.

Yegorov was born in Moscow November 26, 1937. His father, a noted brain surgeon, was a member of the USSR Academy of Medical Sciences. At a young age Boris decided to become a medical researcher specializing in aerospace medicine, enrolling at the Sechenov First Moscow Medical Institute in 1955.

During his last 2 years of study Yegorov took a part-time job at the Central Institute for Aviation Medicine, the organization which was conducting medical and psychological testing of military pilots who were candidate cosmonauts. (The first subject Yegorov met was his future commander, Vladimir Komarov.) Upon graduation from

Sechenov in 1961 Yegorov went to work full-time at the Institute in a group headed by Dr. Nikolai N. Gurovsky.

While working on the cosmonaut medical team Yegorov oversaw sessions in the so-called soundproof chamber by cosmonauts Titov, Leonov, and Popovich. Since he had become an amateur parachutist, Yegorov was assigned to one of the recovery teams for Vostok 1, the first manned spaceflight, in April 1961. Shortly thereafter Yegorov applied to Gurovsky for permission to join the cosmonaut group himself, but was rejected for nearsightedness. Two years later, however, following the approval of the 3-man Voskhod program, Yegorov became one of the candidates.

In order to win support from the Ministry of Health for the selection of Konstantin Feoktistov in the Voskhod crew, Korolev offered to support the civilian doctor (Yegorov) over the military physicians (Sorokin and Lazarev). And just weeks before launch a composite crew of Komarov, Feoktisov and Yegorov was formed.

After his Voskhod flight Yegorov was involved in the 22-day flight of two dogs aboard Kosmos 110 in 1966, and in the Soyuz 9 and Salyut 1 long duration missions.

He also did graduate study in medicine, earning a doctor of medicine degree (1965) and a candidate of medical sciences degree (1967) from Humbolt University in Berlin. He later earned an additional candidate of medical sciences degree (1979).

Yegorov later became a professor and head of a biomedical research institute under the USSR Ministry of Health. He died of a heart attack in Moscow on September 19, 1994.

Yeliseyev, Alexei Stanislavovich

1934–

Engineer-cosmonaut Alexei Yeliseyev took part in the world's first crew transfer in January 1969. He and fellow Soyuz 5 crewman Yevgeny Khrunov donned space suits and performed an hour-long EVA, moving from Soyuz 5 to Soyuz 4. The two spacecraft were docked nose-to-nose at the time.

The transfer tested procedures for a planned Soviet manned lunar landing mission. During such a flight it was necessary for a single pilot cosmonaut to transfer by EVA from a Soyuz-Zond command module to a docked lunar landing vehicle. Following a brief landing mission, the procedure had to be repeated. The lunar landing mission never took place, however.

In October of 1969 Yeliseyev served as flight engineer of Soyuz 8, a 6-day mission that saw three manned Soyuz spacecraft in orbit at the same time. This mission was also intended to rehearse techniques for the lunar landing program. Yeliseyev and commander Vladimir Shatalov were to have docked Soyuz 8 with Soyuz 7 and its three cosmonauts, but technical problems with the Soyuz 8 range-finding system prevented it.

In April 1971 Yeliseyev's third flight, intended to be a 24-day mission aboard the first Salyut space station, ended prematurely when the cosmonaut crew, after successfully docking Soyuz 10 with the station, could not open the hatch and enter the station. They were forced to return to Earth after just 2 days.

Yeliseyev was born Alexei Kuraytis on July 13, 1934, in the village of Zhizdra in the Kaluga Region of Russia. His Lithuanian father, Stanislav, was arrested in 1939 on a charge of anti-Soviet agitation and sentenced to 5 years in the GULAG, so Yeliseyev adopted his mother's Russian family name. She was a chemist and Yeliseyev grew up with an interest in science and mathematics. He won admittance to the elite Bauman Higher Technical School in Moscow, where he was not only an outstanding student but twice USSR champion in fencing. Following graduation in 1957 he went to work in the Korolev design bureau as an engineer.

Yeliseyev applied for the cosmonaut team in June 1964, as soon as he heard the engineers might be accepted, and finally began to train in May 1966. He was part of the Soyuz 2 crew, scheduled for launch in April 1967 on a docking and space walk mission. But Soyuz 1, the target ship, developed problems and then crashed on return to Earth, killing cosmonaut Vladimir Komarov. Soyuz 2 was never launched; 2 years later its mission was accomplished by Soyuz 4 and Soyuz 5.

After Soyuz 10 in 1971 Yeliseyev completed his doctor of science degree (1972), then became a flight director at the Kaliningrad flight control center in 1973. Later named deputy general designer of NPO Energiya, as the Korolev bureau was now known, he was in charge of all Soviet manned flights between 1973 and 1981.

The series of manned and unmanned Soyuz and Soyuz-T flights flown to the Salyut 6 space station between 1977 and 1981 inaugurated a new era in Soviet spaceflight.

Originally planned to last 2 years at most, Salyut 6 was in operation for almost 4 years, at the end of which the USSR held all manned space duration records. It was a major technical achievement and also a miracle in management terms, demonstrating a new flexibility and ability to work around problems that had until now eluded Soviet space officials. Much of the success was due to Yeliseyev.

In January 1986 Yeliseyev left Energiya to become rector of the Bauman Higher Technical School. He retired in 1991.

Yemelyanov, Segrei Alexandrovich
1951–1992

Sergei Yemelyanov was one of the 2 Energiya engineer candidates enrolled in the cosmonaut team in February 1984. He was trained as a Soyuz TM flight engineer and also worked on the Buran space shuttle program.

In early 1988 he was assigned as the flight engineer for the forthcoming Soyuz TM-7, the second Soviet-French space mission. But the rigors of training caused him to be medically disqualified, and he was replaced by Sergei Krikalev.

Yemelyanov was born March 3, 1951, in Kamensk-Uralsk, Sverdlovsk Region, Russia. He attended the Moscow Aviation Institute, graduating in 1974, then joined the NPO Energiya.

He left the Energiya cosmonaut team in April 1992, and died of a heart attack in Moscow on December 5 of that year.

Yershov, Valentin Gavrilovich
1928–1998

Valentin Yershov was one of the 5 scientists enrolled in the cosmonaut team in May 1967. Like Voskhod scientist candidate Georgy Katys, Yershov was a protégé—"nephew" in Russian slang—of Academy of Sciences President Msistlav V. Keldysh, one of the major powers in the Soviet space program of the 1960s.

Yershov took part in training for the Soviet manned lunar program for 2 years. He was a candidate to be a flight-engineer navigator. When Program L was canceled Yershov trained as a flight engineer in a possible Salyut crew. But in August 1974 he was dismissed from cosmonaut training, reportedly after refusing to join the Communist Party, and returned to the Academy of Sciences.

Yershov was born June 21, 1928, in Moscow.

Yershov attended the Moscow Aviation Institute, graduating in 1953. He joined the NKVD's aircraft design construction bureau headed by Sergei Beria. After a year he moved to Pavel Grishin's design bureau, working on surface-to-air missiles. In 1956 he joined the Institute of Applied Mathematics, working under Keldysh himself, in the field of spacecraft navigation.

From 1974 to his death on February 15, 1998, Yershov was a senior scientist at the same institute.

Yorkina (Sergeichik), Zhanna Dmitryevna
1939–

Zhanna Yorkina was one of the first Soviet women cosmonauts, selected in March 1962. Like the other members of her group, she worked in support of Valentina Tereshkova on Vostok 6 in June 1963, and also on Voskhod 2 in March 1965.

Beginning in April 1965 she trained as a member of the second or backup crew for the Voskhod 4 mission. Scheduled for launch in 1966, this would have been a 10-

day mission by two women cosmonauts during which one of them would have performed an EVA. Yorkina also trained for a later Soyuz mission.

Yorkina was born in Ryazan on May 6, 1939. She attended the Pedagogical Institute there, graduating as a teacher of English. While a student she became a sport parachutist through the DOSAAF program. It was through DOSAAF that she applied to join the cosmonaut team following Gagarin's flight in April 1961.

Between 1962 and 1969 Yorkina was also a student at the Zhukovsky Air Force Engineering Academy, graduating in 1969. In October of that year the women's cosmonaut group was disbanded. Yorkina joined the flight simulation staff at the Gagarin Center, where she still works.

Yurchikin, Fyodor Nikolayevich

1959–

RKK Energiya engineer Fyodor Yurchikin is a cosmonaut-candidate currently undergoing training at the Gagarin Center. In the fall of 1999 he should qualify as an International Space Station crewmember.

Yurchikin was born January 3, 1959. He was approved as a cosmonaut-candidate by the Joint State Commission on July 28, 1997.

Yuyukov, Dmitri Alexeyevich

1941–

Dmitri Yuyukov was one of the 5 civilian engineers enrolled as cosmonaut candidates in March 1973. The other four were from the Korolev design bureau; Yuyukov was employed by the NPO-Machinostroyeniye, builders of the Proton launcher and the Almaz military space station.

From 1978 to 1980 Yuyukov trained with commander Gennady Sarafanov and researcher Vladimir Preobrazhensky for a flight aboard an Almaz station using the TKS manned space transport. However, the TKS-Almaz program was canceled before the flight took place.

Yuyukov was born February 26, 1941, in Moscow, and attended the Moscow Aviation Institute, graduating in

1965. He then joined the Chelomei spacecraft design bureau, which later became known as NPO-M.

Yuyukov is currently a section leader at NPO-M.

Zabolotsky, Viktor Vasilyevich

1946–

Viktor Zabolotsky was one of the civilian test pilot-cosmonauts who trained for manned orbital flights on the Buran space shuttle. In December 1990 he was assigned as backup commander for the first Buran mission, then scheduled for launch in early 1992. Political and economic turmoil in the former Soviet Union caused the Buran flights to be postponed, then ultimately canceled.

Zabolotsky was born April 19, 1946, in Moscow. After completing secondary school he entered a vocational school. At this time he also joined the First Moscow Flying Club. From 1967 to 1969 he was a student at the DOSAAF Central Aerotechnical School, and following graduation he worked in the city of Kaluga as a DOSAAF pilot-instructor flying MiG-15 and MiG-17s.

In 1973 Zabolotsky entered the civilian test pilot school in Zhukovsky, graduating the following year. Since 1974 he has been a test pilot at Zhukovsky, logging over 4,500 hours of flying time in many different types of aircraft, including ultralights. He is rated a merited test pilot of the USSR (1989).

While working at Zhukovsky he received a degree (by correspondence) from the Civil Aviation Academy in Leningrad.

Zabolotsky was approved for cosmonaut training by the joint state commission on June 12, 1984, and from 1985 to 1987 underwent the general course at the Gagarin Center. Two years later he trained as backup cosmonaut-research to fellow Buran pilot Rimas Stankyavichus for Soyuz TM-9, then scheduled for launch in April of that year. The mission was postponed for several months, however, and Stankyavichus was taken off the crew.

Earlier Zabolotsky had trained as a chase pilot for the unmanned maiden voyage of Buran in November 1988. The death of Buran test pilot Alexandr Shchukin in August of that year caused Zabolotsky to be relieved of the chase assignment: he served on the board investigating Shchukin's accident.

Zabolotsky currently works on light aircraft programs at the civilian flight test center in Zhukovsky.

Zaikin, Dmitri Alexeyevich
1932–

Dmitri Zaikin was one of the first Soviet cosmonauts selected in March 1960. He served as backup commander to Pavel Belyayev on Voskhod 2 in 1965, replacing Viktor Gorbatko, who had to step aside for medical reasons. In April 1968 he was training to command an Almaz military space station mission when a medical exam revealed that he had an ulcer, medically disqualifying him. He left the cosmonaut team in October 1969.

Zaikin was born April 29, 1932, in the town of Yekaterinovka near Salsk, Rostov oblast, Russia. He attended the Rostov special air force school, then the Armavir Higher Air Force School. He was transferred to the Frunze Higher Air Force School in Chernigov, graduating in 1954 with future cosmonaut Andrian Nikolayev. For the next 5 years he served as a fighter pilot in Belorussia.

While still in the cosmonaut group Zaikin graduated from the Zhukovsky Air Force Engineering Academy (1968).

After his disqualification Zaikin served as deputy director of the cosmonaut-candidate group, supervising the training of the 9 pilots and engineers enrolled in May 1970. From 1972 to 1987 he was a senior engineer at the Gagarin Center working on flight simulators and onboard equipment. He currently works in a laboratory at the center.

Zaitsev, Andrei Yevgenyevich
1957–

Andrei Zaitsev served temporarily as the backup flight engineer for the second Soviet-Bulgarian space mission, Soyuz TM-5, in 1988. Shortly after Zaitsev won the assignment in December 1987, a medical check turned up an undisclosed problem which forced him off the active list. Veteran cosmonaut Alexandr Serebrov—who had himself been on and off crews because of recurring health problems—replaced Zaitsev prior to the launch of Soyuz TM-5 with cosmonauts Solovyov, Savinykh and Alexandrov on June 10, 1988.

Zaitsev later returned to active cosmonaut training and was to have been assigned with commander Anatoly Solovyov to the second backup team for Soyuz TM-13 in 1991. But instead he was dropped from the active cosmonaut list.

Zaitsev was born August 5, 1957, in Tula, a city south of Moscow. Like many engineer-cosmonauts, he attended the Bauman Higher Technical School in Moscow, graduating in 1980.

Zaitsev was enrolled in the cosmonaut group in September 1985 and retired in April 1994. He still works at the RKK Energiya.

Zakharova, Tamara Sergeyevich
1952–

Tamara Zakharova is a physician-cosmonaut employed at the Institute for Medical-Biological Problems in Moscow. She was eligible for assignment to a Soyuz TM-Mir crew for 15 years, but never flew in space.

Zakharova was born April 22, 1952, in Moscow. She attended the Sechenov First Moscow Medical Institute, graduating in 1976. She worked as a medical researcher until being recruited for the cosmonaut team in 1979. After preliminary training, she passed the medical commission in August 1980 and was officially enrolled as a cosmonaut researcher. She retired as a cosmonaut in October 1995.

Zaletin, Sergei Viktorovich
1962–

Pilot Sergei Zaletin is assigned as backup commander for Soyuz TM-28, scheduled for launch to the Mir space station in August 1998. The TM-28 crew will be the 26th Mir resident crew, staying aboard until early 1999. If Mir continues to operate as planned, Zaletin and flight engineer Alexandr Kaleri will be the last scheduled visitors in the summer of 1999.

Zaletin was born April 21, 1962, in the city of Shchekino, Tula Region, Russia. He attended the

Borisoglebsk Higher Air Force School, graduating in 1983, then served as a fighter pilot with the Soviet air force for 7 years.

He was one of 3 pilots enrolled as candidates in the military cosmonaut team on May 11, 1990. In March 1992 he completed the basic training course at the Gagarin Center, qualifying as a Soyuz-Mir commander. He spent the next 2 years doing graduate work in Earth resources at Moscow State University. He was assigned to the Soyuz-Mir group in 1996.

Zholobov, Vitaly Mikhailovich

1937–

Vitaly Zholobov was flight engineer aboard the Soyuz 21 long-duration mission in 1976. He and commander Boris Volynov were launched on July 6 of that year to a rendezvous with the Salyut 5 space station for a planned 60 days in space. Among their subjects for study were the effects of weightlessness on plants and animals.

Since Salyut 5 was actually the third in a series of manned military space laboratories called Almaz, a large portion of their time was also taken up with reconnaissance tasks. The mission ended after only 48 days because the cosmonauts seemed to be suffering from psychological problems caused by isolation; Salyut 5 had also suffered malfunctions in its air purification system.

One unconfirmed story is that the cosmonauts actually had a fistfight. In any case, Zholobov and Volynov returned safely to Earth on August 24, 1976.

Zholobov was born June 18, 1937, in the village of Zburyevka in the Kherson region of the Ukraine. His family moved to Azerbaijan when he was young, where his father became a ship's captain on the Caspian Sea. Zholobov attempted to emulate him by joining the Soviet navy at age 17. He was rejected because he was too small.

Zholobov attended the Azerbaijan Petrochemical Institute, graduating in 1959, and then joined the Soviet military, serving as a test engineer with the Strategic Rocket Forces at the Kapustin Yar launch center.

He was one of the 15 pilots and engineers enrolled as cosmonaut candidates in January 1963. After completing

the basic training course in January 1965 he became part of the Almaz program office at the Chelomei design bureau, specializing in flight dynamics. He also worked on Earth resources experiments. Assigned to the Salyut/Almaz training group in 1968, he served as backup flight engineer to Artyukhin on Soyuz 14 and Demin on Soyuz 15. In 1974 Zholobov received a degree from the Lenin Military-Political Academy.

Following his only spaceflight, Zholobov served as capcom for Soyuz-23 in February 1977. He then became deputy director of the candidate cosmonaut group, a post he held until January 1981, when he resigned from the cosmonaut team and retired from the air force.

He became director of an aerospace geological survey group at the Tyumen Geophysical Association in the city of Noyabrsk, Tyumen Region, Russia, then chief administrator of the Kherson Region, Ukraine.

Zudov, Vycheslav Dmitryevich

1942–

Vyacheslav Zudov commanded the ill-fated Soyuz 23 mission in October 1976. Zudov and flight engineer Valery Rozhdestvensky were to have linked up with the orbiting Salyut 5 space station for a 2-week mission, but technical problems prevented the docking and the cosmonauts were forced to make an emergency return to Earth after only 2 days in space.

They landed in Lake Tengiz, one of the few lakes in the primary spacecraft landing zone, late at night in the middle of a blizzard. It was the first and so far only splashdown by a Soviet manned spacecraft. Zudov and Rozhdestvensky were not rescued until the next morning, having spent over 10 hours huddled and freezing in the unseaworthy Soyuz command module.

Zudov was born January 8, 1942, in the village of Bor in the Gorky Region of Russia, and grew up in the Moscow area. He joined the Soviet air force and attended the Balashov Higher Air Force School, graduating in 1963, in the same class with future cosmonaut Gennady Sarafanov. Zudov flew An-12s with the 12th Military Air Transport Division based in Chkalovskaya, eventually logging 1,200 hours of flying time. The 12th VTAD performed spacecraft recovery flights.

One of the 22 military candidates enrolled in the cosmonaut team on October 28, 1965, Zudov learned to fly high performance jets and also became an expert parachutist. He served as capcom for Soyuz flights from 1967 to 1969 while also training for flights in the Almaz-Salyut military space station. Zudov served as backup to Sarafanov on Soyuz 15 in 1974, and to Boris Volynov on Soyuz 21 in 1976.

Following his spaceflight Zudov graduated from the Gagarin Air Force Academy (1979) and joined the Salyut 6 training group. He was backup commander to Soyuz 35 in 1980 and should have commanded the Soyuz T-4 flight in 1981, but he and flight engineer Boris Andreyev failed to pass the examinations.

From January 1982 to October 1986 Zudov served as a squad leader for Almaz within the cosmonaut team. He then became deputy to Pyotr Klimuk as head of the political department of the Gagarin Center. He has also studied at the Central Committee's Academy of Political Science.

He left military service in June 1992.

INTERNATIONAL
ASTRONAUTS

In the 37-year history of manned spaceflight, only the former Soviet Union and the United States have demonstrated the ability to put human beings into space. However, beginning in the mid-1970s, following the joint Soviet-American Apollo-Soyuz Test Project, both spacefaring nations began to provide citizens of other countries with the chance to go into space as guests. Through May 1998, 51 of the 378 world space travelers—approximately 13 percent—were international astronauts.

The 1st Interkosmos Selection: December 1976

In September 1976, the Soviet Union announced that it was recruiting pilots and engineers from countries who were members of Interkosmos, the international space organization formed in April 1967, for flights aboard Soyuz and Salyut spacecraft. Two guest cosmonauts were to be chosen from each member nation.

The first selections were from the Czechoslovakian, Polish, and German Democratic Republics.

Selections in Czechoslovakia began in the early summer of 1976, in anticipation of the public announcement, with a screening of service records. One hundred possible cosmonauts candidates were identified and given medical examinations, with 20 selected for further medical and psychological exams at the Czech Military Aviation Institute in July 1976. Eight finalists were sent to the Gagarin Center in November, and 2 men—

Engineer-Major Oldrich Pelczak and Captain Vladimir Remek—were selected. They began training on December 6, 1976.

A similar process took place in Poland, with 5 candidates being sent to the Gagarin Center in November 1976:

Major Andrei Bulgala
Major Henrik Halka
Major Miroslaw Hermaszewski
Major Zenon Jankowski
Captain Tadeusz Kuziora

Hermaszewski and Jankowski were the selectees.

East Germany, under the direction of Lieutenant-General Wolfgang Reinhold, asked for volunteers from qualified pilots in the GDR air force. Thirty candidates underwent testing, and four were submitted to the Gagarin Center in November:

Lieutenant Colonel Rolf Berger
Lieutenant Colonel Eberhard Golbs
Lieutenant Colonel Sigmund Jaehn
Lieutenant Colonel Eberhard Kohllner

Jaehn and Kohllner were selected.

All of the first Interkosmos cosmonauts were military officers and many had already studied in the Soviet Union.

The 2nd Interkosmos Selection: April 1978

A second wave of Interkosmos selection began in 1977, initially involving five countries: Bulgaria, Cuba, Hungary, Mongolia, and Rumania. A sixth, Vietnam, joined the process in 1979.

Bulgaria sent 6 candidates to the Gagarin Center:

Senior Lieutenant Alexandr Alexandrov

Captain Chavdar Djurov

Major Georgy Lovchev

Major Georgy Kakalov (Ivanov)

Captain Ivan Nakov

Lieutenant Colonel Kyril Radev

Djurov was the son of the Bulgarian Minister of National Defense. Kakalov and Alexandrov were the cosmonauts, with Kakalov finding his name changed to Ivanov because Kakalov sounded obscene in Russian!

The failure of Bulgaria's 1979 flight to reach the Salyut space station (see the entry on Georgy Ivanov) made a second joint mission possible, though this one did not take place under Interkosmos. A joint agreement between Glavkosmos and the Bulgarian Academy of Sciences was signed in August 1986. Cosmonaut selection began that November. Alexandrov and Ivanov reapplied. Alexandrov and a new pilot, Senior Lieutenant Krasimir Stoyanov, were selected on January 5, 1987, and left for the Gagarin Center 2 days later. Alexandrov went into space aboard Soyuz TM-5 in the summer of 1988.

Cuba selected nine candidates and sent four to the Gagarin Center in January 1978. Lieutenant Colonel Arnaldo Tamayo-Mendez and Captain Jose Lopez Falcon were the cosmonauts selected.

Hungary selected 20 candidate pilots in September 1977, with 4 finalists being sent to the Gagarin Center:

Captain Imre Buczko

Captain Laszlo Elek

Captain Bertalan Farkas

Captain Bela Magyari

Farkas and Magyari became cosmonauts.

Little is known of Mongolia's selection process. Two candidates were selected in January 1978, Captain Jugderdimdyn Gurracgha, and a civilian engineer, Maidarjavin Ganzorig. Ganzorig was commissioned in the Mongolian People's Army upon selection.

Rumania had approximately 100 candidates, from which 3 engineers were sent to the Gagarin Center in December 1977:

Major Dumitru Dediu

Christian Guran

Dumitru Prunariu

Prunariu and Dediu were selected as finalists. Because Prunariu was a civilian, he was commissioned in the Romanian Air Force.

Vietnam joined Interkosmos in May 1979. A month earlier 4 cosmonaut candidates had been sent to the Gagarin Center. Only 3 names are known:

Captain Bui Thanh Liem

Colonel Nguyen van Quoc

Lieutenant Colonel Pham Tuan

Tuan and Liem were selected and began training that July.

Additional Guests

In 1980 the guest cosmonaut program was expanded to allow flights by citizens of nations other than those involved in Interkosmos.

The idea of a flight to Salyut by a French cosmonaut arose during a visit to the Soviet Union by French president Valery Giscard d'Estaing in April 1979. Following negotiations between the Soviet government and the French space agency CNES, selections began in September of that year. CNES received 413 applications; 193 candidates were invited for medical examinations, which reduced the number to 72. A second phase of examinations in December 1979 and January 1980 reduced the number of candidates to 7, including 2 women. Another set of examinations reduced this even further, until 5 remained:

Major Patrick Baudry

Lieutenant Colonel Jean-Loup Chretien

Gerard Juin

Major Jean-Pierre Joban

Francoise Varnier

The single female candidate, Varnier, was eliminated from the competition because of a parachuting accident. The other 4 finalists were sent to the Gagarin Center in March 1980 for Russian language study. On June 12 Baudry and Chretien were selected as candidates for the Soviet-French mission, and they began their training at the Center on September 7.

Following Chretien's weeklong flight to Salyut 7 in 1982, French scientists lobbied for a second space station mission, this one of longer duration. An agreement was reached in October 1985 for mission lasting up to 2 months. In July 1986 four CNES candidates were sent to the Gagarin Center for testing:

Colonel Jean-Loup Chretien

Major Michel Tognini

Major Jean-Pierre Haignere

Lieutenant Commander Antoine Covette

Tognini and Haignere were new members of the CNES spationaut team, a group of career space travelers recruited in 1985 for flights on the American Shuttle, Soviet Soyuz, and European Hermes vehicles. (See details below.) Covette had been a finalist for the spationaut group. Chretien was selected as the prime candidate for the long mission to Mir, with Tognini as his backup, in August 1986. They took up residence at the Gagarin Center on November 15.

The day before Chretien's launch aboard Soyuz TM-7 in November 1988, CNES and Glavkosmos reached tentative agreement for a third flight, to take place in 1992. This was later made part of a series of five more flights, to take place on a biannual basis through the end of the century.

Six candidates were submitted to the Gagarin Center in July 1990:

Major Leopold Eyharts

Major Jean-Marc Gasparini

Lieutenant Colonel Jean-Pierre Haignere

Major Phillipe Perrin

Major Benoit Silve

Lieutenant Colonel Michel Tognini

The 4 new pilots were the second group of career spationauts, whose selection had begun in February 1990. Tognini and Haignere were announced as the prime and backup candidates for the 1992 mission in August 1990.

In late 1991 three spationauts underwent preliminary weightless training at the Gagarin Center in anticipation of future missions in the series:

Jean-Francois Clervoy

Claudie Andre-Deshays

Major Leopold Eyharts

For details on the later French-Mir missions, see below.

Agreement between India and the USSR for a joint manned space mission was announced by Prime Minister Indira Gandhi in March 1981. There were 240 applications, eventually reduced to 10 semifinalists, all of them officers in the Indian Air Force. Four candidates were submitted to the Gagarin Center for final testing, and two were announced in September 1982:

Major Ravish Malhotra

Major Rakesh Sharma

Sharma served as cosmonaut-researcher in the crew of Soyuz T-11, launched to dock with Salyut-7 in April 1984.

Syria and the USSR reached a similar agreement in late 1985. No details of the selection process have been released. Two Syrian Air Force pilots arrived at the Gagarin Center in October 1985:

Major Munir Habib

Major Muhammed Faris

Faris was the cosmonaut-researcher selected for the flight, Soyuz TM-3 in July 1987.

Commercial Guest Cosmonauts

In 1985 the Soviet Union created an organization called Glavkosmos, which was originally envisioned as a Soviet

NASA—a central organization that would coordinate spaceflight research and launches. Until that time responsibility for program development and management had been spread over a number of different ministries, such as Defense, Aviation Production, and General Machine-Building.

Glavkosmos never truly fulfilled its goals, but under director Alexandr Dunayev, it did take the lead in making commercial agreements between the Soviet Union and other nations for the sale of launch services, including manned flights aboard Soviet spacecraft.

For example, in September 1987 Afghanistan and Glavkosmos reached tentative agreement for a flight to Mir, then scheduled for early 1989. The selection process began that November, with 457 applications. These were ultimately reduced to 8 finalists, who were sent to the Gagarin Center for examinations in January 1988:

Captain Abdul Ahad Mohmand

Colonel Mohammed Dauran

Colonel Akar Jan

Mohammed Jahid

Amer Khan

Kyal Mohammed

Syra-Juden

Major Shere Zamin

Changes in the political relationship between the USSR and Afghanistan—Soviet troops were pulling out—forced the flight to be moved forward by a year. The final agreement for the mission was signed on February 11, 1988, and cosmonauts Abdul Ahad Mohmand and Mohammed Dauran were announced the next day. They began training immediately, with Mohmand selected as the primary crewmember in April, flying aboard Soyuz TM-6 in August 1988.

Glavkosmos and the Austrian Ministry of Science agreed in October 1988 for the flight of an Austrian researcher to Mir in 1991 under the name "AustroMir." Austria was to pay $10 million for the mission. Selection for the Austrian guest cosmonaut began in late 1988, with 200 applicants. Seven candidates were ultimately submitted to the Soviets:

Elke Greidel

Gertraud Vieh

Manfred Eitler

Peter Friedrich

Lieutenant Colonel Robert Haas

Clemens Lothaller

Franz Viehbock

Lothaller and Viehbock were selected, arriving at the Gagarin Center in January 1990. Viehbock served as researcher aboard Soyuz TM-13 in October 1991.

In its most controversial agreement, on March 27, 1989, Glavkosmos contracted with the Japanese television network TBS for the flight of a journalist to the Mir space station in 1991. The fee was a reported $11 million.

Over 100 TBS employees applied for selection, and by August 17, 1989, 7 had been given conditional medical approval:

Toyohiro Akiyama

Naoko Goto

Ryoko Kikuchi

Toshio Koiki

Atsuyoshi Murakami

Kouichi Okada

Nobuhiro Yamamori

Candidates Toyohiro Akiyama and Rioko Kikuchi arrived at the Gagarin Center in October 1989. Akiyama's flight eventually took place aboard Soyuz TM-11 in December 1990.

Glavkosmos also got involved in an ill-starred deal with the British company Antequera, Ltd., for the flight of a British citizen to Mir in 1991. Four candidates were selected from over 13,000 applicants who responded to advertisements that said, "Astronaut Wanted—No Experience Necessary":

Lieutenant Commander Gordon J. Brooks

Major Timothy K. Mace

Helen P. Sharman

Clive P. G. Smith

The selection of Mace and Sharman was announced on November 25, 1989. Within days they had arrived at the Gagarin Center. During their training, however, Antequerra lost much of its funding, and the $11 million Glavkosmos expected to receive was reduced to less than $2 million. Sharman's flight took place nonetheless in May 1991.

By 1990 Glavkosmos had been supplanted as the Soviet agency of record by NPO Energiya, which announced an agreement with CNES for 5 Soviet-French flights on a biannual basis through the year 2000. The first candidates, Tognini and Lieutenant Colonel Jean-Pierre Haignere, arrived at Gagarin Center in October 1990 to fly the "Antares" mission, scheduled for launch in 1992.

The Energiya organization also reached agreement in May 1990 with the new German Space Agency (DLR) for the flight of a German astronaut to Mir in 1992. Candidates Reinhold Ewald and Klaus Flade arrived at Gagarin Center in November 1990, with Flade launching to Mir aboard Soyuz TM-17 in March 1992.

The need for Energiya and Glavkosmos to make commercial missions led to two other agreements.

In December 1990 Space Travel Services of Houston, Texas, announced plans to conduct a telephone lottery with the winner to spend a week aboard Mir in late 1992. (Unfortunately the Dream Flight program, as it was called, ran afoul of Texas state laws banning lotteries, and did not take place.)

In April 1991 Aerospace Ambassadors announced a plan to select an American teacher for a flight to Mir in 1993. That plan also failed to proceed much beyond a public announcement.

In 1988 American singer John Denver, having failed to convince NASA to let him fly aboard the Shuttle, waged his own campaign to become a commercial visitor to the Mir space station. The Soviets responded that they were willing to fly him provided he learn Russian, spend a year in training, and pay a fee of $11 million. Denver declined.

Slovak Republic

In the summer of 1997, under the direction of General Stefan Gombik (a finalist in the 1976 Czech Interkosmos group), the Slovak Republic began the process of selecting a candidate for a flight to Mir, to take place in early 1999. The mission, valued at $20 million, was seen as a way of erasing a debt owed by the former Soviet Union to the Slovaks.

Thirty military pilots were screened, and in February 1998 4 finalists were identified:

Colonel Martin Babiak
Lieutenant Colonel Mihal Fulier
Major Ivan Bella
Captain Miroslaw Groshaft

In March 1998 Fulier and Bella were selected to undergo flight training, though a formal agreement for the mission was still to be signed.

International Shuttle Payload Specialists

The first international space travelers on American spacecraft were selected by the European Space Agency for flights on Spacelab originally scheduled to begin in 1980. Following an announcement of opportunity on March 28, 1977, over 2,000 scientists and engineers applied to ESA. On December 22, 1977, 4 semifinalists were chosen:

Franco Malerba (Italy)
Ulf Merbold (West Germany)
Claude Nicollier (Switzerland)
Wubbo Ockels (The Netherlands)

The 3 finalists, Merbold, Nicollier, and Ockels, were announced in May 1978. Merbold and Ockels eventually flew as European Shuttle payload specialists, in 1983 and 1985. Malerba flew as a payload specialist with the Italian Tethered Satellite System in 1992.

Ockels and Nicollier underwent NASA astronaut training in 1980-81, allowing Nicollier to be assigned as a mission specialist on Shuttle missions. These three formed the core of a cadre of European career astronauts (see below).

In December 1982, West Germany selected two scientists to train for the German Spacelab, D-1:

Reinhard Furrer

Ernst W. Messerschmid

Both flew aboard Shuttle Mission 61-A in November 1985, with ESA astronaut Ockels. ESA astronaut Merbold served as their backup.

Five more German payload specialists were announced in September 1987. (See National Astronaut Teams, below.)

As Shuttle launches became more frequent, NASA liberalized its criteria for payload specialist opportunities. Prior to 1982, only customers (nations or companies) buying half of a Shuttle payload, or who were flying an experiment that required the presence of a particular scientist or engineer, were allowed to provide a payload specialist. Beginning in 1984, NASA said, all major Shuttle customers could, for a fee (usually $80,000 to cover 100 hours of training) send someone into space with a payload.

With these criteria, international payload specialists were selected by a number of countries.

In March 1984 Great Britain selected 4 candidates for a pair of planned deployments of Skynet communications satellites:

Major Tony Boyle, Royal Army

Christopher J. Holmes

Commander Peter H. Longhurst, Royal Navy

Major Nigel R. Wood, Royal Air Force

(Boyle would drop out in June 1984, to be replaced by Major Richard Farrimond.) Wood was assigned as payload specialist on Shuttle Mission 61-H (June 1986), with Farrimond as his backup, while Longhurst was assigned to Mission 71-C (February 1987), with Holmes as backup. Neither Wood nor Longhurst flew in space, as the Skynet launches were moved to expendable launch vehicles following the Challenger disaster.

In April 1984 CNES assigned its two Interkosmos veterans, Chretien and Baudry, as Shuttle payload specialists. Baudry flew aboard Mission 51-G in June 1985.

In April 1985 Saudi Arabia selected 2 payload specialists for its deployment of the Arabsat communications satellite:

Major Abdul al-Bassam

Prince Sultan Salman al-Saud

Salman flew aboard Mission 51-G in June 1985.

Mexico selected payload specialists for the Morelos satellite deployment in June 1985:

Rodolfo Neri Vela

Ricardo Peralta y Fabi

Neri flew aboard Mission 61-B in November 1985.

In October 1985, Indonesia submitted 4 candidates for payload specialist for the scheduled 1986 deployment of its Palapa satellite:

Taufik Akbar

Captain M. K. Jusuf

Bambang Narymurti

Pratiwi Sudarmono

Akbar and Sudarmono were selected, and reported to the NASA Johnson Space Center for preliminary training, but never flew.

The same fate awaited India's Insat payload specialist candidates, selected in November 1985:

P. Radhakrishnan Nair

N. C. Bhat

In addition, prior to the Challenger disaster Brazil and Australia were invited to select a Shuttle payload specialists. There were also tentative discussions between the Reagan administration and the People's Republic of China as well as between NASA and Israel, but no actual astronaut candidates were ever announced.

Following Challenger, NASA's policy on international Shuttle payload specialists was much more restrictive, allowing them only on Spacelab missions or on missions where the primary scientific payload required a trained specialist.

Canada's Roberta Bondar and ESA's Ulf Merbold flew aboard the first International Microgravity Laboratory (IML-01) on STS-42, January 1992. Ken Money (Canada) and Roger Crouch (NASA) were alternates.

Belgium's Dirk Frimout was a payload specialist aboard STS-45, the ATLAS-01 Spacelab (March 1992), replacing American PS Michael Lampton.

Franco Malerba flew with Italy's Tethered Satellite System on STS-46 in August 1992. Umberto Guidoni was ate, and flew with TSS himself on STS-75 in February 1996.

Japan's Mamoru Mohri was a payload specialist for Spacelab-Japan, launched on STS-47 in August 1992. Takao Doi and Chiaki Naito-Mukai were his alternates.

Steve MacLean of Canada flew with the Space Vision System aboard STS-52 in October 1992. Bjarni Tryggvason was his alternate.

Germany's Hans Schlegel and Ulrich Walter were payload specialists on Spacelab D-2, STS-55 (April 1993), with Gerhard Thiele and Renate Brummer as alternates.

NASA began to accept international astronauts for mission specialist training on a regular basis beginning in 1992, but several scientific payload specialist positions remained:

Japan's Chiaki Mukai was a payload specialist for the second International Microgravity Laboratory, launched aboard STS-65 in July 1994. Jean-Jacques Favier of CNES was her alternate.

Favier and Canada's Robert Thirsk flew with the Life and Microgravity Spacelab (LMS-01) on its 17-day mission aboard STS-78, July 1996. Their backups were Luca Urbani (Italian Space Agency) and Pedro Duque (ESA).

Bjarni Tryggvason of Canada flew aboard STS-85 in July 1985.

Mukai of Japan served as alternate payload specialist for the last Spacelab mission, Neurolab, flown aboard STS-90 in April 1998. She is assigned to fly with a series of medical experiments aboard STS-95 in October 1995 as the last international Shuttle payload specialist.

National Astronaut Teams: Canada

With the increased opportunities for flight aboard the Shuttle, Soviet spacecraft, and the proposed French Hermes and European Columbus, several nations selected teams of career astronauts who became employees of various national space agencies.

Canada became the first. Its National Research Council in Ottawa received over 4,400 applications for "Space Team Canada" beginning in June 1983. Eventually this number was reduced to 19, who were given medical and psychological examinations at the National Defence Medical Center in October and November of

that year. Six astronauts were announced on December 5, 1983:

Roberta K. Bondar

Commander Marc Garneau, Royal Canadian Navy

Steven G. MacLean

Ken Money

Robert K. Thirsk

Bjarni Tryggvason

Five members of the team eventually made spaceflights, beginning with Garneau aboard Shuttle Mission 41-G in October 1984. Bondar followed in January 1992 (STS-42), then Maclean (STS-52, October 1993), Thirsk (STS-78, July 1996), and Tryggvason (STS-85, July 1997).

With the contracts of its original 6 astronauts expiring, the CSA started a new selection process in 1991, hoping to recruit 6 new candidates. From over 5,300 applicants, 53 were chosen in October 1991 to undergo medical testing. Four new astronauts were announced on June 8, 1992:

Major Chris Hadfield

Julie Payette

Robert Stewart

Daffyd R. Williams

Almost immediately the composition of the group changed when Stewart withdrew following the announcement. He was replaced by the next alternate, Canadian Forces captain Michael McKay.

At the same time Garneau and Hadfield were included in NASA's fourteenth group of astronaut candidates, and following a year of training were qualified as Shuttle mission specialists. Hadfield went into space aboard STS-74, the second Shuttle-Mir docking mission, in November 1995 and will make a second flight with the 6th International Space Station assembly mission in 2000.

CSA astronaut Daffyd Williams was included in NASA's fifteenth group of astronaut candidates in January 1995 and made his first spaceflight with the Neurolab Spacelaboad aboard STS-90 in April 1998.

CSA astronauts Steve MacLean and Julie Payette were selected for training with the sixteenth group in August 1996.

France

Beginning in November 1984, 2 years after the successful flight of Jean-Loup Chretien to Salyut 7, the French space agency CNES sought to create its own cadre of what it called "spationauts." Candidates had to be French citizens between the ages of 25 and 35, with either engineering, scientific or medical degrees, and appropriate professional experience. Over 700 applicants responded to the announcement of opportunity.

The seven spationauts were announced on September 9, 1985. Three were "ingenieurs du board" (flight engineers) and 3 were "experimentateurs" (scientists).

Jean-Francois Clervoy	FE
Claudie Deshays	S
Jean-Jaques Favier	S
Major Jean-Pierre Haignere	FE
Frederic Patat	S
Major Michel Tognini	FE
Michel Viso	S

Five years later, in February 1990, CNES announced that it would add to the cadre, announcing its plans to select up to 8 pilots. This selection process was conducted in relative secrecy, but in July 1990 4 names were released when the new pilots were submitted as candidates for the 1992 Soviet-French mission: Eyharts, Gasparini, Perrin, and Silve. Even though selected and subjected to medical testing, all 4 remained with their military posts until specifically assigned to a mission: Eyharts to the Pegasus project in 1992 and Perrin to NASA in 1996. Gasparini performed test work for ESA and CNES and Silve remained an operational pilot with the French navy.

Clervoy left the CNES team to join the ESA astronaut group in May 1992 (see below).

Favier served as backup payload specialist for STS-65, the International Microgravity Spacelab, in July 1994. In February 1995 he left the CNES team to work full-time at the NASA Marshall Spaceflight Center, where he became a payload specialist in the crew of STS-78, the Life and Microgravity Spacelab, launched in August 1996.

Andre-Deshays was assigned as researcher for the Cassiopeia mission, launched to Mir as Soyuz TM-23 in August 1996. Eyharts was her backup.

Eyharts and Viso were the original prime candidates for a proposed 1997 Mir mission, but when training commenced at the Gagarin Center in January 1997, the candidates were Eyharts and Haignere. Eyharts was assigned to the crew of Soyuz TM-26, scheduled for launch in September 1997, but was removed because of that summer's crisis aboard Mir, caused by the collision between the station and a Progress supply vehicle in June. Eyhart's mission was postponed to Soyuz TM-28 and launched successfully in February 1998.

CNES astronaut Phillip Perrin, meanwhile, was included in the 1996 NASA astronaut candidate group.

Italy

In 1984 Italy selected three candidate payload specialists for the Shuttle flight of its Tethered Satellite System:

Cristiana Cosmovici

Andrea Lorenzoni

Franco Rossito

The Challenger disaster in January 1986 put the TSS flight on hold. During the Shuttle launch hiatus, Italy formed the Agenzia Spaziale Italiana (ASI, the Italian Space Agency), and in February 1989 announced plans to form its own astronaut cadre—not only for the TSS mission, but also for European Spacelab flights.

Ten candidates were identified, and 4 were submitted to NASA for the TSS mission in May 1989: Malerba, Cosmovici, Rossitto, and Umberto Guidoni. Malerba and Rossitto were chosen TSS payload specialists that September, but Rossitto withdrew to take a job with ESA in Cologne, Germany. He was replaced by Guidoni. Malerba flew with the TSS aboard STS-46 in August 1992.

In September 1994 Guidoni was named prime payload specialist for the TSS reflight, STS-75, which flew in February 1996. Following the mission Guidoni was included in the 1996 NASA astronaut candidate group, becoming a candidate for assignment to future International Space Station crews.

Japan

The National Space Development Agency of Japan (NASDA) chose 3 scientists from 533 applicants in August 1985 to train for dedicated Japanese Spacelab missions and other Shuttle flights:

Takao Doi

Mamoru Mohri

Chiaki Naito (later Mukai)

Mohri was later assigned as the prime payload specialist for Spacelab J and flew aboard STS-47 in September 1992. Naito-Mukai was assigned as a payload specialist for the second International Microgravity Spacelab missions, and went into space aboard STS-65 in July 1995. She later served as backup PS for the Neurolab mission, STS-90 (April 1998), then made a second flight aboard STS-95 in October 1998.

In July 1991, while Spacelab J was still awaiting launch, NASDA began the process of selecting two more Japanese astronauts, to be announced in May 1992. Applicants had to be under 35 years of age, with a bachelor of science degree and 3 years's experience. Only one candidate was found, engineer Koichi Wakata, who joined astronauts from Europe and Canada in becoming a member of the fourteenth NASA astronaut group announced March 1992. Wakata went into space aboard STS-72, which in January 1996 retrieved the SFU spacecraft launched by Japan earlier that year. He has since been assigned to STS-92, International Space Station assembly mission 3A.

NASDA payload specialist Takao Doi was included in the December 1994 NASA astronaut candidate group and went into space aboard STS-87 in November 1997.

In 1996 NASDA conducted another recruitment, selecting engineer Soichi Noguchi in July 1996. Along with STS-47/Spacelab-Japan veteran Mamoru Mohri, Noguchi was trained as a Shuttle and International Space Station crewmember with the fifteenth group of NASA astronaut candidates (August 1996).

West Germany

West Germany's Federal Aerospace Research Establishment (DFVLR) was in the final stages of selection for six science astronauts at the time of the Shuttle Challenger disaster in January 1986. The announcement of the finalists and the start of their training was postponed until August 3, 1987, when the number was reduced to 5:

Renate L. Brummer

Hans W. Schlegel

Gerhard P. J. Thiele

Heike Walpot

Ulrich Walter

These science astronauts were to serve as prime and backup payload specialists for the Spacelab D-2 mission. Walter and Schlegl flew aboard STS-55 in April 1993.

The German reunification in 1989 and subsequent changes in that nation's relations with the Soviet Union made a Soyuz-Mir mission also possible. On April 18, 1990, an agreement was signed between DLR (the German Aerospace Establishment) and the NPO Energiya, for such a flight. Since all of the astronauts selected in 1987 were already involved in D-2 training, 2 more German astronauts—Reinhold Ewald and Major Klaus-Dietrich Flade—were chosen in October 1990. They came from the list of semifinalists for the August 1988 group. Flade went into space aboard Soyuz TM-16 in March 1992.

The DLR astronaut unit was disbanded in November 1993. However, DLR and the Russian Space Agency negotiated a second Mir mission. Heike Walpot and Ulrich Walter commenced Russian language lessons in the spring of 1995 in anticipation of assignment as candidate researchers. Ultimately it was Ewald and Schlegel who were selected for training, and Ewald was aboard Soyuz TM-24/Mir-22 in February 1997.

In the summer of 1997 Schlegel resumed Soyuz-Mir training for a possible mission to the Russian space station in 1999.

Gerhard Thiele was included in the 1996 NASA astronaut candidate group.

European Space Agency

In June 1989 ESA began the long-delayed selection of a new group of astronauts for flights on the Shuttle, Soyuz-Mir-Buran, and Hermes-Columbus. Between 1994 and 1997 2 Shuttle Spacelab missions—E1 and E2—were scheduled, in addition to a second flight of the EURECA platform

The 13 ESA member states, plus Canada, were invited to submit 3-5 candidates each by April 30, 1991. Sixty applications were screened by the ESA committee beginning in May, with comprehensive physical and psychological tests and interviews to follow. ESA Director General Jean-Marie Luton was to make the final selection of ten, from a list of semifinalists.

Among the candidates submitted by ESA members were several who had already trained as international space travelers: Lothaller and Viehbock of Austria; Flade, Schlegel, Thiele, and Walter of Germany; Sharman and Mace of Great Britain. All 6 French candidates—Clervoy, Deshays, Eyharts, Favier, Perrin, and Tognini—were from that nation's spationaut cadre.

Original plans called for the ESA astronauts to be designated as laboratory specialists (for Spacelab, Mir, Space Station Freedom, and Columbus flights) or Spaceplane Specialists. Four laboratory specialists were to begin training in early 1992 with the remaining 6 ESA astronauts, 2 laboratory specialists and 4 spaceplane specialists, to commence training in late 1992.

However, during the last weeks of the selection process ESA scaled back its requirements, and on May 15, 1992, only 6 new astronauts were named:

Maurizio Cheli (Italy)

Jean-Francois Clervoy (France)

Pedro Duque (Spain)

A. Christer Fuglesang (Sweden)

Marianne Merchez (Belgium)

Thomas Reiter (Germany)

Cheli and Clervoy were included in the fourteenth group of NASA astronauts announced in May 1992. They qualified as Shuttle mission specialists a year later, and in November 1994 Clervoy flew in that capacity aboard STS-66 (November 1994), Cheli in the crew of STS-75 (February 1996).

In May 1993 four ESA astronauts were assigned as candidates for 2 different planned flights aboard the Mir space station. Two-time Shuttle veteran Ulf Merbold and ESA Duque were named as candidates for the first, EuroMir 94. This 30-day mission was launched October 3, 1994, with Merbold as cosmonaut-researcher.

Astronauts Fuglesang and Reiter trained for EuroMir 95. In March 1995 Reiter was named the prime crewmember for this 135-day mission to be launched in September of that year.

EuroMir 94 backup Duque immediately became a candidate for payload specialist aboard STS-78, the planned Life and Microgravity Spacelab, scheduled for launch in August 1996. When Duque was selected as a backup, however, the European Space Agency withdrew him from that program.

Duque and Fuglesang were candidates for a proposed EuroMir-97 mission considered by ESA and the Russian Space Agency. When negotiations stalled, both men were included in NASA's fifteenth astronaut group on August 12, 1996, along with 7 other international astronauts: Duque and Fuglesang from ESA, Guidoni from Italy (ASI), MacLean and Payette from Canada (CSA), Mohri and Shoguchi from Japan (NASDA), Perrin from France (CNES), and Thiele from Germany (DLR).

With the retirement of Merbold and Ockels and the resignation of Cheli and Merchez (1996), ESA realized it needed additional astronauts. In April 1998 it announced the formation of a unified European astronat team to be based at the ESA center in Cologne, Germany. The core of the new team would be the five ESA astronauts then in the team plus two European astronauts then assigned to NASA as future International Space Station crewmembers: Clervoy, Duque, Fuglesang, Nicollier, and Reiter plus Guidoni (ASI), and Thiele (DLR).

Between July and October 1998 7 new ESA astronauts were selected, 3 from existing national astronaut teams (Haignere and Eyharts from CNES, Schlegel from DLR) with 4 new candidates: Paula Nespoli and Major Robert Vittori (Italy), Andre Kuipers (Netherlands), and Major Frank DeWinne (Belgium).

Ukraine

When Ukraine, formerly a republic within the Soviet Union, became independent in 1992, it was home to several design bureaus, including the famous Mikhail Yangel (NPO Yuzhnoe) organization, as well as tracking facilities and other space-related enterprises.

Financial problems kept Ukraine from developing a vigorous space program of its own, but nevertheless, in November 1994 President Leonid Kuchma and U.S. president Bill Clinton concluded an agreement to fly a series of scientific experiments developed by the Ukraine Academy of Sciences. A Ukrainian astronaut would fly on the Shuttle with the experiments, and four candidates were selected from 30 applicants in September 1996:

Nadezhda I. Adamchuk

Leonid K. Kadenyuk

Vyacheslav G. Meytarchan

Yaroslav I. Pustovyi

Kadenyuk was an experienced test pilot and former Soviet cosmonaut who had resigned from the Russian air force to return to Ukraine. He and Pustovyi were selected as payload specialists in May 1997, with Kadenyuk flying aboard STS-87 that November.

All 4 candidates remain in the astronaut office of the National Space Agency of Ukraine, however, in hopes of future ISS flights.

China

The People's Republic of China became the fifth nation, after the United States, Soviet Union, France, and Japan, to launch its own unmanned spacecraft. On April 24, 1970, China's Long March 1 booster sent a satellite called The East Is Red into Earth orbit. Five years later, China launched a satellite that later reentered and was recovered, a test of spy satellite technology that could also be applied to a future manned spacecraft.

Although Western reporters circulated rumors in 1978 that China was considering a manned space flight—even publishing photos of purported Chinese astronauts—active development of a manned vehicle began only in 1992, with the code name Project 921.

Scheduled for its first manned flight possibly as early as October 1999, the fiftieth anniversary of the creation of the People's Republic, the Project 921 spacecraft is said to be similar in design to the Russian Soyuz-TM. Thanks to a joint technology exchange agreement between the Russian Space Agency and China signed in Beijing on April 25, 1996, Project 921 may use some of the same equipment.

Prior to that, in June and July 1993, 5 medical specialists from the Chinese Institute of Space Medicine spent a month at the Gagarin Center in order to study cosmonaut selection and training. And from November 1996 to November 1997, two Chinese "instructor-cosmonauts" underwent training at the center:

Wu Ji Li

Li Quinlong

Wu Ji Li and Li Quinlong revealed that upon their return to China they would serve as the senior members of a Chinese astronaut team, size and other members still unknown.

If successful, Project 921 would make China the world's third independent spacefaring nation.

INTERNATIONAL ASTRONAUT BIOGRAPHIES

Afghanistan

Dauran Ghulam Masum, Mohammed

1954–

Mohammed Dauran served as backup cosmonaut researcher to fellow Afghan pilot Abdul Mohmand on the flight of Soyuz TM-6 in August 1988. Mohmand and two Soviet cosmonauts docked their spacecraft with the orbiting Mir space station for a 10-day flight marred by reentry problems that delayed their return to Earth. Dauran was present at the the control center at Kaliningrad (now Korolev) during the mission.

Dauran was born January 20, 1954, in the Nidgrab District of Kapsy Province, Afghanistan, and is a member of the Tajik tribe. He attended a military prep school as a teenager, then joined the Afghan armed forces in 1972. Following training in the Soviet Union, he served as a MiG-21 pilot and deputy squadron commander in the Afghan war. He has logged over 1,400 hours of flying time.

Dauran and Mohmand arrived at the Gagarin Center in February 1988. The usual 18-month basic Soyuz-Mir training schedule was cut in half because the Soviet Union was planning to withdraw its forces from Afghanistan later in 1988. Because they were military pilots already fluent in Russian, Dauran and Mohmand

were judged to be capable of accelerated training. Nevertheless, certain items were omitted from the training. Dauran also contracted appendicitis and had to undergo an operation.

Following the mission Dauran returned to Afghanistan. He is currently a major general in the air defense forces.

Mohmand, Abdul Ahad

1959–

Abdul Mohmand was the first citizen of Afghanistan to go into space. He served as cosmonaut-researcher aboard Soyuz TM-6, which docked with the orbiting Mir space station on August 31, 1988, 2 days after launch from Baikonur. Mohmand, mission commander Vladimir Lyakhov, and flight engineer Valery Polyakov conducted a week of experiments with Vladimir Titov and Musa Manarov, then in the ninth month of their stay aboard Mir. Among the experiments were observations of Afghanistan.

Leaving Polyakov aboard Mir, Mohmand and Lyakhov entered Titov and Manarov's Soyuz TM-5 spacecraft and undocked from Mir in the early hours of September 6, 1988, planning to fire retrorockets and land in Kazakhstan within a few hours. But their first attempt at reentry was aborted by a failure in guidance sensing. A second attempt one orbit later was manually aborted by Lyakhov

EMERGENCY!

Abdul Ahad Mohmand (Soyuz TM-6) with Bert Vis

(On September 6, 1998, 8 days after launch from Earth, 6 days after arriving on the Mir space station, Afghan cosmonaut-researcher Abdul Ahad Mohmand and Russian commander Vladimir Lykahov jettisoned the spherical orbit module and prepared to fire their Soyuz retrorockets and return to Earth. A solar sensor failed, however, and the moment of retrofire passed without ignition. Seven minutes later, while the cosmonauts were trying to discover the cause of the failure, the solar sensor located the sun, and fired the engines. Lyakhov manually shut them down after only three seconds. He also had to abort a second try a revolution later.)

After the engine stopped, I said that we should first try to find out what was going on, because at the time we didn't have contact with TsUP. I told Lyakhov once, twice, three times. Later, on Earth, I heard that we had had only twenty seconds before the engine would have exploded . . . the second time, we even had less . . . only 2 seconds. I did all that.

(Because of the limited number of Soyuz landing zones, permitting safe landing only on two revolutions per day, Mohmand and Lyakhov were forced to wait in the cramped Soyuz descent module until their orbital path again took them over the landing zones.)

It was a difficult situation! TsUP ordered us to remove our space suits. I told them, "No, we won't do that! It's better if we keep them on." I wasn't sure we would be able to land the next day. If we would have taken the suits off, and would have had to put them on again the next day, they would have to be tested again, to see if they were airtight. I believed it would be better if we would keep them on. Oxygen was a valuable thing and we should be saving it, just in case we would have to wait another day. So I told them we wouldn't do it. All I did was talk with Lyakhov. And sleep.

All the food and drink was in the orbital module. All the food and drink—and also the toilet!

I had taken my sleeping bag with me from the Mir station. When we had to wait for 24 hours without a toilet, we took some plastic bags that were part of my sleeping bag. Lyakhov used them, I didn't. I said I would wait.

When you are in a truly dangerous situation, you forget about fear. Three times, I asked TsUP to play some music for me. I feel that when you are afraid, you can't function properly. Before the launch, you are a little bit afraid . . . no, afraid isn't the correct word, you are a little . . . tense.

I had felt at home in space. Right after I arrived in the station, I read part of the Koran. I also photographed the entire area of Afghanistan. That was of interest to our delegation. They wanted to map the country's resources. Water, for instance, is very important for Afghanistan. And oil, gas. . . . And for the first time, we could make an atlas of Afghanistan. Until then, there was no atlas of Afghanistan. (I have heard that after my research, one has been produced. The chief of this firm has said that he would send me the first copy, but I haven't received it. . . . The Mujahedin came and I don't know whether or not it was ever sent to me.)

There were two parts in my experiment program. A national one, from Afghanistan, and an international one. A major part consisted of taking photographs of Afghanistan from the station, with different cameras: Nikon, Hasselblad, the MKF-100 spectral camera. Whenever the station flew over Afghanistan, I would be prepared to begin taking photographs. Every time, I was being assisted by one or more of the Soviet cosmonauts, so that we could take photographs of the same area at the same time with different cameras. For instance, Lyakhov would use the spectral camera, I would work with the MKF-100 and Polyakov with a Hasselblad. Also the second, international, part of the experiment program, the medical experiments, wasn't conducted just by me. Here too, the Soviet cosmonauts helped. Some of them couldn't even be done by me alone. I would need help to attach instruments, for example.

These experiments originated from our delegation. But we didn't have the possibility to make the necessary hardware. We had to use Soviet hardware and cameras. But the program, what to study and photograph, came from Afghanistan.

When I was on board Mir, Vladimir Titov told me that he almost had the idea that I was there already for 6 months, instead of a newcomer.

(After an agonizing wait, and following new instructions radioed to them by the flight control center, Mohmand and Lyakhov successfully fired their Soyuz retros on September 7, landing safely in the primary zone.)

I was happy my mission was over and that I had done a good job. Of course, I was also happy that we had made it. But in particular, I was happy, because before the flight, many people in Afghanistan had thought that it had been a wrong choice that I had become a cosmonaut and that [backup Afghan Mohammed] Dauran would have done a better job. But I had performed well, had made a good flight and had overcome difficulties. I had assisted my commander during the difficulties. So after the landing, I was happy.

6 seconds into a planned 180-second burn when he noted other irregularities.

While mission controllers attempted to solve the problem, the two cosmonauts were forced to remain in space in the cramped Soyuz TM command module (the larger orbital module containing the docking unit had been jettisoned prior to retrofire) for the better part of a day, without food, water, or sanitary facilities. Mohmand and Lyakhov finally landed safely at 0540 Moscow Time on September 7.

Mohmand was born January 1, 1959, in the village of Sardah, Shangar District, Ghazni Province, Afghanistan. He is Pashtoon by birth. At the age of 17 he moved to the capital city of Kabul to attend the Polytechnic University there.

The following year Mohmand was drafted and sent to the USSR for pilot training, first at the Krasnodar Higher Air Force School, then at the Kiev Higher Air Force Engineering School. He returned to his homeland in 1981 and served in the air force, then was sent back to the USSR for further education, graduating from the Yuri Gagarin Air Force Academy in 1987. He later flew combat missions and served as the deputy commander of an air regiment. He has logged 600 hours of flying time.

Mohmand and Colonel Mohammed Dauran arrived at the Gagarin Center in February 1988 to begin training for a mission then scheduled for launch in August 1989. Newly announced Soviet plans to withdraw its troops from Afghanistan before that date made it prudent to fly the mission a year earlier, resulting in an abbreviated training schedule. Soviet space officials noted that unlike other guest cosmonauts, Mohmand and Dauran were fluent speakers of Russian, making them easier to train. Evidence suggests, however, that the crew was not as prepared as it should have been.

Mohmand spent the 2 years following his mission as a student at the Voroshilov General Staff Academy in Moscow, then returned to Afghanistan. When the Mujhaddin forces took control of the country following the collapse of the Soviet Union in 1991, he fled to Russia. He currently lives in Stuttgart, Germany.

Austria

Lothaller, Clemens

1963–

Austrian physician Clemens Lothaller was the backup cosmonaut-researcher for the Soyuz TM-13 mission in October 1991. That mission, called "AustroMir," called for an 8-day mission during which cosmonaut-researcher Franz Viehbock performed a total of 15 major experiments prepared by Austrian universities and industrial research institutes. AustroMir was supervised by the Austrian Ministry of Science and Research, which paid Glavkosmos, the Soviet space agency, an $11-million fee for the mission.

Lothaller and Viehbock were selected from approximately two dozen applicants, in October 1989. They reported to the Gagarin Center near Moscow the following January.

Lothaller was born May 8, 1963, in Vienna, where he grew up. After graduation from gymnasium in 1981 he attended the University of Vienna while working part-time as a ski instructor. He earned his doctorate in anathesiology in 1987.

He served a tour in the Austrian army, and later worked in the surgery department of a Vienna clinic. He is currently in medical practice in Vienna.

Viehbock, Franz

1960–

Franz Viehbock was the Austrian cosmonaut-researcher in the crew of Soyuz TM-13, launched October 2, 1991. Viehbock, Soviet commander Alexandr Volkov, and Soviet-Kazakh researcher Toktar Aubakirov, docked with the Mir space station complex a day later.

During the 8-day mission the AustroMir cosmonaut-researcher was responsible for 15 principal experiments devised by Austrian universities and industrial insitutes. Viehbock returned to Earth aboard Soyuz TM-12 with Aubakirov and Soviet commander Anatoly Artsebarsky.

Austria's Ministry of Science and Research paid the Soviet space agency Glavkosmos a fee of $11-million for the mission. Approximately two dozen Austrian citizens applied to be their nation's first space traveler; 7 finalists were announced in July 1989, with Viehbock and Dr. Clemens Lothaller chosen in October. They reported to the Gagarin Cosmonaut Training Center near Moscow in January 1990.

Viehbock was born August 24, 1960, in Vienna, and grew up there, attending the Realgymnasium until he was 18. He studied electronics at the Studium der Electrotechnik, earning an electrical engineering degree.

He has worked at the Siemens Company, and as an assistant at the University of Vienna. Following his Soyuz flight he emigrated to the United States, joining the staff of Rockwell International (now Boeing) Space Systems Division, builders of the Space Shuttle, in Downey, California.

Belgium

Frimout, Dirk Dries David Damiaan

1941–

Belgian physicist Dirk Frimout was a payload specialist in the crew of STS-45, the Spacelab ATLAS mission launched in March 1992. The 9-day ATLAS mission was devoted to studies of the Earth's atmosphere. Among other experiments, Frimout and his fellow crewmen used an electron beam gun to create artificial auroras over the southern hemisphere. The gun was one of 13 principal ATLAS experiments.

Frimout was originally assigned as backup payload specialist, but moved to the prime position in September 1991 when Michael Lampton was medically disqualified.

Frimout was born March 21, 1941, in Poperinge, Belgium. He attended the University of Gent in Belgium, earning a degree as an electrotechnical engineer in 1963, and later received his Ph.D. in applied physics from that institution in 1970. He has done postdoctoral study at the University of Colorado.

From 1965 to 1978 Frimout worked at the Belgian Institute for Space Aeronomy, studying the upper atmosphere with instruments launched on balloons and rockets. He went to work for the new European Space Agency at its SPICE installation in 1978 as the crew activities coordinator responsible for training the Spacelab 1 astronauts.

He was one of a dozen semifinalists for selection as an ESA payload specialist for Spacelab 1 in 1978. His selection as backup payload specialist for the EOM mission came in December 1985. EOM 1 was then scheduled for launch the following August, but the Challenger disaster caused it to be postponed for almost 6 years.

From 1984 to 1989 Frimout was principal engineer in the microgravity division of ESA's European Space Technology Center (ESTEC) in Noordwijk, the Netherlands. For the next 5 years he served as senior engineer in the payload utilization department of the Columbus program office there and also held a post in the Space Policy Office

of the Belgian government. In April 1994 he joined Belgacom, the operator of public telecommunications in Belgium, as research manager.

Brazil

Pontes, Marcos Cesar

1963–

Brazilian air force test pilot Carlos Pontes is one of the 6 international astronaut candidates selected by NASA in 1998. In August of that year he began a training and evaluation course that should qualify him as a Shuttle mission specialist and International Space Station crewmember in 1999.

He is the first astronaut selected by the Brazilian Space Agency.

Pontes was born in 1963 in Baura, Brazil, and received a degree in aeronautical engineering from the Instituto Technologico de Aeronautica University. Most recently he was a student at the U.S. Naval Postgraduate School in Monterey, California.

A captain in the Brazilian air force, Pontes has logged over 1,700 hours of flying time and is qualified as a test pilot.

Bulgaria

Alexandrov, Alexandr Panayatov

1951–

Bulgarian air force pilot Alexandr Alexandrov was the cosmonaut-researcher for Soyuz TM-5, the second Soviet-Bulgarian space mission, flown in June 1988. With commander Anatoly Solovyov and engineer Viktor Savinykh, Alexandrov spent 8 days aboard the Mir space station carrying out a number of scientific experiments—including some developed by Alexandrov himself. The Soyuz TM-5 mission lasted a total of 10 days.

Nine years earlier, in April 1979, Alexandrov served as backup to countryman Georgy Ivanov for Soyuz 33, the first Soviet-Bulgarian flight. That mission, intended to last 8 days, had to be aborted because of an engine failure aboard Soyuz 33 which prevented docking with the Salyut 6 space station.

Alexandrov was born December 1, 1951, in Omourtag, in northern Bulgaria. He attended the Georgy Benkovsky Higher Air Force School near Dolna. Injured in a parachuting accident while at school, he spent several months recuperating, but nevertheless managed to keep up with his studies and graduated with his class in 1974.

Alexandrov served as a fighter bomber pilot in the air defense arm of the Bulgarian air force for 4 years until his selection as one of the 2 Bulgarian Interkosmos candidates. He and Ivanov reported to te Gagarin Center in April 1978.

Following the Soyuz 33 mission Alexandrov did postgraduate work at the Space Research Institute (IKI) of the USSR Academy of Sciences. He received a candidate of technical sciences degree in 1983, then returned to Bulgaria, where he became deputy director of Bulgaria's Central Space Research Laboratory (later renamed the Space Research Institute). He also did additional graduate work at the Rakovsky Military Academy.

In 1986, following a new agreement between the Soviet and Bulgarian governments for a second joint manned spaceflight, Alexandrov was one of the 2 candidates selected, arriving with Krasimir Stoyanov at the Gagarin Center in January 1987. (Alexandrov's younger brother Plamen, an air force pilot, was also one of the 4 semifinalists.)

Alexandrov has returned to the Bulgarian Space Research Institute, where he is a senior research scientist.

Ivanov, Georgy Ivanov
1940–

Georgy Ivanov became the first Bulgarian in space when he served as cosmonaut-researcher of Soyuz 33. Ivanov's flight, however, unlike those of the other Interkosmos cosmonauts, was aborted after 2 days when an engine failure aboard Soyuz prevented docking with the Salyut 6 space station.

By its seventeenth orbit of the Earth on April 11, Soyuz 33 was less than half a mile from Salyut 6—visible to cosmonauts Lyakhov and Ryumin, who were the resident crew—when its main engine shut down three seconds into a planned 6-second burn. Lyakhov and Ryumin saw the engine firing, and noted an ominous lateral plume from the engine module as well.

The docking was called off while the problem was studied. Flight controllers were afraid the errant plume not only meant that the main engine had failed, but that the backup engine was also damaged, effectively stranding the cosmonauts in space. Soyuz 33's orbit would decay naturally after about 10 days, but the cosmonauts only carried about 5 days' supply. (A rescue from the Salyut 6 crew was not possible.)

Eventually controllers decided to attempt a reentry at the next best opportunity, orbit 34 on April 12. The ideal engine burn time for reentry was 188 seconds: anything less than this would strand the cosmonauts, much more and Soyuz would be destroyed by excess heat.

When the backup engine ignited, it fired past the 188 second point, forcing Rukavishnikov to shut it down manually 33 seconds later. As a result, Soyuz 33 reentered the atmosphere on an unusually steep trajectory, subjecting the cosmonauts to 8-10 Gs, twice the normal load, and falling well short of the target landing site. The cosmonauts landed safely, however.

Ivanov was born Georgy Kakalov July 2, 1940, in Lovech, Bulgaria. He attended a technical secondary school, where he joined the DOSO, a junior civil defense organization, in which he became a parachutist and light aircraft pilot. He tried to join the air force, but failed the physical. A year later he was accepted, and enrolled in the Georgy Benkovsky air force college, graduating in 1964.

His lifelong dream was to be a fighter pilot and he found his first assignment after leaving school—teaching other students—frustrating. He persevered, however, and ultimately became a flight leader, then a squadron commander, with the air defense units of the Bulgarian air force, ultimately logging over 1,900 hours of flying time.

In 1976 the Interkosmos organization announced plans to fly citizens of member nations aboard Soviet spacecraft. Ivanov applied, and he and another pilot, Alexandr Alexandrov, were selected as Bulgaria's representatives. At that point though Ivanov's original name—

Kakalov—was changed by Russian authorities. Ivanov and Alexandrov reported to the Gagarin Center in April 1978.

Following his mission Ivanov returned to duty with the Bulgarian air force, though he was originally forbidden to fly aircraft. (Pilot Chavdar Djurov, a cosmonaut-candidate and the son of the Bulgarian minister of defense, had recently been killed in a crash.) Ivanov eventually got the minister to change his mind and resumed flying MiG-21s as an inspector in the Bulgarian air force.

Ivanov also earned a candidate's degree (1984) and published a book, *Flights*. In 1986 he applied for the second Soviet-Bulgarian mission, but was not among the finalists.

Major General Ivanov later served as a deputy in the Great People's Assembly of the Republic of Bulgaria.

Stoyanov, Krasimir Mikhailov

1961–

Bulgarian air force pilot Krasimir Stoyanov served as the backup cosmonaut-researcher to countryman Alexandr Alexandrov during the Soyuz TM-5 mission in June 1988. Alexandrov spent 8 days conducting scientific experiments aboard the Mir space station during his 10-day flight, which Stoyanov supported from the flight control center in Kaliningrad (now Korolev).

Stoyanov was born January 24, 1961, in the city of Varna, Bulgaria. Following graduation from secondary school Stoyanov enrolled at a vocational shipbuilding school. His interest in flying led him to join an air club in Varna, becoming a glider pilot. In the fall of 1979 he was admitted to the Georgy Benkovsky Higher Air Force School.

From the spring of 1984 to 1986 Stoyanov served as a fighter pilot in the Bulgarian air force. He was selected as a candidate for the second Soviet-Bulgarian spaceflight that year, and arrived at the Gagarin Center with Alexandr Alexandrov in January 1987.

Canada

Bondar, Roberta Lynn

1945–

Canadian physician Roberta Bondar was a payload specialist in the crew of STS-42, the 8-day flight of the International Microgravity Laboratory in January 1992. The IML mission was devoted to space manufacturing and studies in life sciences. Ultimately over 50 experiments were performed. They had been developed by 200 scientists in 13 different countries, especially Canada, which contributed a suite of experiments in space physiology.

Bondar was born December 4, 1945, in Sault Ste. Marie, Ontario, where she attended primary and secondary schools. She earned several university degrees: a B.S. in zoology and agriculture from the University of Guelph (1968), M.S. in experimental pathology from the University of Western Ontario (1971), Ph.D. in neurobiology from the University of Toronto (1974), and M.D. degree from McMaster University in 1977. She has been a Fellow of the Royal College of Physicians and Surgeons of Canada since 1981.

While still an undergraduate, Bondar began working for the Canadian Fisheries and Forestry Department, an association that lasted for 6 years. She also completed medical training at Toronto General Hospital and at Tufts New England Medical Center in Boston. Her specialization is neuro-ophthalmology. In 1982 she became assistant professor of medicine at McMaster University while also serving as director of the Multiple Sclerosis Clinic for the Hamilton-Wentworth Region. After joining the Canadian space program she also served as a part-time lecturer at the University of Ottawa and taught at Ottawa General Hospital.

Bondar was one of the 6 astronauts of Space Team Canada selected in December 1983. In 1984 and 1985 she trained as a backup payload specialist to Robert Thirsk for a Shuttle mission then scheduled for launch in 1987. She also headed the Life Sciences Subcommittee for Canada's participation in the NASA Freedom Space Station.

She was named an IML candidate payload specialist in 1989 and selected as one of the 2 prime PS in March 1990. In August 1992 she resigned from the Canadian astronaut program to return to full-time medical work at McMaster University, and lecturing on her experiences as an astronaut.

She is currently distinguished professor at the Centre for Advanced Technology Education (CATE), Ryerson Polytechnic University in Toronto and also serves as a visiting professor/scientist with the University of Western Ontario, the University of New Mexico, and the Universities Space Research Assocation at the NASA Johnson Space Center.

CANADA FROM SPACE

by Roberta Bondar

[Canadian physician Roberta Bondar spent 10 days in space in January 1992 aboard the orbiter Discovery, as part of the STS-42 crew working with the experiments of the first International Microgravity Laboratory. During this Spacelab mission Bondar took time to look back at planet Earth.]

The view from Spacelab is incredible. Its window is closer to the Earth than any other Shuttle window, with the orbiter tail facing the planet. Unfortunately, all the 70-mm cameras are located up on the flight deck, leaving me with only a 35-mm camera, which I know will not capture the Earth as clearly. I'll have to let my eyes and brain capture the colours below.

The rich blues of the ocean, the exquisite turquoise of the Great Barrier Reef, and the soft white snows of winter are soothing to eyes that have been engrossed in demanding scientific studies. Greens and browns predominate on the landscape except when we fly over deserts. These provide the greatest visual contrast—green vegetation against beige sand, dried salt pans against iron-laden red sand. The wide range of individual shades that I have come to expect from walking through a greenhouse, or even looking in my mid-deck locker for a brightly coloured polo shirt (the upper-body apparel of the Shuttle astronaut) are absent.

In space flight, the only sounds I hear are scientific exchanges, instrument noise, crewmember chatter, and music from tapes selected pre-launch for off-duty enjoyment. Before my mission, I carefully chose music and sounds that would remember of my youthful dream of becoming a space explorer. "One Moment in Time" and the theme song from Return of the Jedi fill my pre-sleep hours. For Earth viewing, I picked out a selection of emotional melodies—"Nothing like the Freedom" and "From a Distance"—and for special interest passes, "Oh Canada" and "The Star Spangled Banner"—musical renditions played by my aunt on the organ and piano, and vocal renditions performed in a deep, stirring voice by a policeman from my hometown. If that doesn't test tear-duct secretions in weightlessness, I can play pre-taped messages from my family and friends, music from a variety of Canadian artists and a high school band, and Girl Guide songs.

It is very easy to become so involved in the technical and scientific aspects of this Spacelab flight that I overlook something that I love most about living on our planet: the sounds of Earth itself. Looking at the blue-and-white world that fills my heart, I cannot hear what is beyond the windows. The Earth is silent. I cannot hear the plaintive cry of a Swainson's thrush, the piercing echoes of a blue jay, or even the conversational barking of a dog. In fact, the planet seems devoid of anything that might be able to communicate with me.

. . .

I now perceive home and myself, though, in a different way. On the ground, visual imagery bombards me daily, assuring me that I am the superior life form on Earth. But I wonder. The great distance above the ground in which I am floating changes my Earth-bound mind-set. The Rockies become rows of crisply defined mounds, and the Himalayas, a chaotic collection of small stalagmites. In one pass, it is difficult to pinpoint the great one, Mount Everest, in the vast sea of over ice-covered peaks. On Earth, we climb these mountains to answer an inner challenge, "because it's there." "Conquering" Everest demonstrates our courage and our ability to persevere against all odds. Such feats become high-profile events when they haven't been done before, if they require great physical or mental stamina, or if they set us "against" a naturally occurring phenomena. Interesting, the Earth perception. From out here, I don't attach the same importance to what now appears to be a remote event on a tiny part of the Earth's crust. In space, I feel like a pretty small, fragile lifeform. The huge physical presence that I see below will endure long after I and my kind are gone.

Garneau, (Joseph Jean-Pierre) Marc

1949–

Marc Garneau became the first citizen of Canada to make a spaceflight when he was a payload specialist aboard Shuttle Mission 41-G in October 1984. During his 8 days aboard the orbiter Challenger Garneau worked on 10 different experiments designed by Canadian scientists, including medical tests devoted to discovering the causes of space adaptation syndrome (SAS).

In August 1992 Garneau moved to the NASA Johnson Space Center in Houston, Texas, and a year later qualified as a Shuttle mission specialist. He served in that capacity aboard STS-77, a flight of the orbiter Endeavour in May 1996. STS-77 carried the fourth SpaceHab experiment module and also accomplished 4 different rendezvous with previously deployed satellites. Garneau was the operator of the Shuttle's Canadian-built remote manipulator arm for the retrieval.

Garneau was born February 23, 1949, in Quebec City, Quebec. He attended primary and secondary schools there and in London, England. In 1970 he received a bachelor of engineering physics degree from the Royal Military College of Canada at Kingston. He went on to earn a doctorate in electrical engineering from the Imperial College of Science and Technology, London, in 1973.

From 1974 until joining Space Team Canada in December 1983 Garneau served in the Canadian Navy in a number of posts. He was a combat systems engineer aboard HMCS Algonquin from 1974 to 1976, and the following year worked as an instructor at the Candian Forces Fleet School. He later served as a project engineer in naval weapons systems in Ottawa and Halifax.

In July 1983, while on vacation, Garneau saw a newspaper ad soliciting applicants for a team of Canadian astronauts. He applied and was selected, and in March 1984 was assigned to a Space Shuttle crew.

He retired from the Canadian Navy in 1989 with the rank of captain.

A candidate for assignment to future International Space Station crews, Garneau serves in the flight support branch of the astronaut office as a mission control capcom.

Hadfield, Chris Austin

1959–

Canadian test pilot Chris Hadfield was a mission specialist in the crew of STS-74. This November 1995 flight of the orbiter Atlantis made the second Shuttle-Mir docking mission, attaching a Russian-built docking module to the station. The crew of 5 also transferred over a ton of food, water, and other supplies to the Mir crew of Gidzenko, Avdeyev, and Reiter.

He is currently assigned to the crew of International Space Station assembly mission 6A, scheduled for launch as STS-99 in the summer of 2000. Hadfield will perform several ISS construction EVAs during that mission, which will also carry the second incremental ISS crew.

Hadfield was born August 29, 1959, in Sarnia, Ontario, Canada, and educated at the Royal Military College of Canada, where he received a bachelor's degree in mechanical engineering in 1982. He also earned an M.S. in aviation systems from the University of Tennessee in 1992.

Following graduation from the Royal Military College, Hadfield underwent flight training, becoming a CF-18 pilot with the Canadian Armed Forces at Bagotville, Quebec. He also attended the Air Force Test Pilot School at Edwards Air Force Base, California, where he received the Liethen-Tittle Award as outstanding graduate in his class in 1988. He then became an exchange officer with the strike test directorate, Naval Air Test Center, Patuxent River, Maryland.

He has logged over 2,500 hours of flying time in 50 different types of aircraft.

Hadfield was one of the 4 astronauts selected by the Canadian Space Agency in June 1992. In August of that year he reported to the NASA Johnson Space Center, to join the Group 14 astronaut candidates, qualifying as a Shuttle mission specialist in August 1993. His first technical assignment was in the operations development branch, and he also served with the astronaut support team at the Kennedy Space Center.

Hadfield is currently assigned to the flight support branch of the astronaut office.

McKay, Michael John

1963–

Armed forces captain Michael McKay is one of the 4 astronauts selected by the Canadian Space Agency in June 1992. He was active within that program until 1995, when a medical problem disqualified him from astronaut training.

McKay was born May 10, 1963, and entered the Royal Military College of Canada in 1981. He graduated with a bachelor of engineering physics degree 4 years later. In 1991 he received a master's of electrical engineering and computer engineering degree from the same institution.

Following training as an aeronautical engineer, McKay served from 1986 to 1989 as an aircraft maintenance officer at the Canadian Forces Base at Cold Lake. In 1989 he returned to the Royal Military College for graduate work, and at the time of his selection was a lecturer in computer science and applied physics at the College Militaire Royal de St. Jean.

McKay is also a glider pilot and instructor with 250 hours of flying time.

He currently works for the Canadian Space Agency at its office in Quebec.

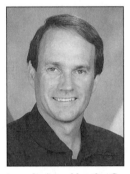

MacLean, Steven Glenwood

1954–

Physicist Steve MacLean was a payload specialist aboard STS-52, a 7-day flight of the orbiter Atlantis flown in October 1992. Among other scientific and medical experiments, MacLean operated the space vision system designed by the Canadian National Research Council. The SVS, one of 5 Canadian experiments to fly with MacLean, was designed to test improvements in the use of the Shuttle's remote manipulator arm (also built in Canada).

In June 1996 MacLean was selected by the Canadian Space Agency to undergo astronaut candidate training. He qualified as a Shuttle mission specialist in April 1998, and is currently working in the robotics branch of the astronaut office while awaiting assignment to a future crew.

MacLean was born December 14, 1954, in Ottawa, Canada, where he grew up. He attended York University, receiving a B.S. in honors physics in 1977, and a Ph.D. in astrophysics in 1983.

While still an undergraduate at York University in 1974-76, MacLean worked in sports administration and public relations. In 1976 and 1977 he was a member of the Canadian National Gymnastics Team. He taught at York while working on his doctorate, and also did research in laser physics at Stanford University in California.

MacLean was one of the first 6 Canadian astronauts selected in December 1983. Two years later he was named as payload specialist for the CANEX-2 flight, then scheduled for launch in early 1987. When CANEX-2 was delayed due to the Challenger disaster, MacLean worked as astronaut adviser to the Strategic Technologies in Automation and Robotics Program (STEAR), and as program manager for the Advanced Space Vision System.

Following his flight aboard STS-52, MacLean became an adjunct professor at the University of Toronto Institute for Advanced Space Studies, and from April 1994 to August 1996 was acting director general of the Canadian Astronaut Program.

Money, Kenneth Eric

1935–

Ken Money, a physiologist and pilot, served as backup to fellow Canadian Roberta Bondar for the STS-42 mission. The 8-day flight, which carried the International Microgravity Laboratory, was devoted to experiments in space manufacturing and life sciences. Money supported the mission from the Payload Operations Control Center at the NASA Marshall Spaceflight Center.

Money was born January 4, 1935, in Toronto, Ontario. He attended primary and secondary schools in Toronto and Noranda, Quebec, then attended the University of Toronto, where he received a B.S. in phsyiology and biochemistry (1958), an M.S. in physiology (1959), and a Ph.D. in physiology (1961).

While he was still a college undergraduate Money earned Royal Canadian Air Force pilot's wings at the Advanced Flying School in Portage La Prairie, Manitoba, in 1957. He eventually logged over 4,000 hours of flying time in T-33, F-86, C-45 and Otter aircraft as a member of the Canadian Forces Air Reserve. In 1972 he attended the National Defence College.

He also found time to represent Canada as a high jumper in the 1956 Olympic Games in Melbourne, Australia, and in the 1958 British Empire and Commonwealth Games in Cardif, Wales.

In 1961 Money became a scientist at the Defence and Civil Institute of Environmental Medicine, Department of National Defence in Toronto. His main area of research was motion sickness and its effects on pilots. He has published over 80 scientific papers, and, as a result of a long association with NASA, has seen his experiments concerning motion sickness selected for several Spacelab missions.

He was one of the 6 members of Space Team Canada selected in December 1983. He was assigned to the IML mission in 1989.

In August 1992 he retired from the Canadian astronaut program, but continues his medical work with St. Michael's Hospital, Toronto, and with the University of Toronto.

Payette, Julie

1963–

Canadian engineer Julie Payette qualified as a Shuttle mission specialist in April 1998, one of 9 international MS candidates selected by NASA almost 2 years earlier. She is currently working in the robotics branch of the astronaut office while awaiting a flight assignment.

Payette was born October 20, 1963, in Montreal, Canada, and attended McGill University in Toronto, where she received a B.S. in electrical engineering in 1986. In 1990 she received an M.S. in applied science from the University of Toronto.

Following graduation from McGill Payette worked for the IBM Corporation in Canada. From 1988 to 1990 she was an assistant in computer engineering at the University of Toronto, then joined Bell-Northern Research in Montreal, where she investigated new methods of making computers respond to human voice commands.

Payette was one of the 4 astronauts selected by the Canadian Space Agency in June 1992. Following initial training she worked as project manager for human-computer interaction research. She also studied Russian and logged over 120 hours of reduced gravity flying time as an experimenter and test subject in various parabolic aircraft.

In the fall of 1995 she underwent military jet pilot training at the Moose Jaw, Saskatchewan, Canadian Air Force Base. She has now logged almost 150 hours of flying time on the CT-114 Tutor jet trainer.

Thirsk, Robert Brent

1953–

Dr. Bob Thirsk, a physician, was a payload specialist in the crew of STS-78, the flight of the Life and Microgravity Spacelab. The LMS mission carried 41 different experiments, including many from Canadian and European researchers, in the fields of space medicine and manufacturing. With its duration of 17 days—longest so far in the Shuttle program—it served as a rehearsal for future International Space Station missions.

Thirsk was born August 17, 1953, in New Westminster, British Columbia, attending primary and secondary schools there and in Alberta. He graduated from John Taylor Collegiate in Winnipeg, then received a a B.S. in mechanical engineering from the University of Calgary (1976), an M.S. in mechanical engineering from the Massachusetts Institute of Technology (1978), and a doctor of medicine degree from McGrill University (1982).

Thirsk was chief resident in family medicine at Queen Elizabeth Hospital in Montreal when chosen for the Canadian astronaut group in December 1983. He had also done research in biomedical engineering.

In 1984 Thirsk was backup payload specialist to Commander Marc Garneau, who became the first Canadian in space aboard Shuttle Mission 41-G in October of that year.

While awaiting a flight opportunity Thirsk continued his research into the effects of weightlessness on the human body, designing an experimental "antigravity" suit to help space travelers readjust to gravity, and taking part in numerous parabolic flights aboard NASA's KC-135 aircraft. In the early 1990s Thirsk was the leading candidate to be a Canadian cosmonaut research aboard the Mir space station, but the program did not proceed beyond discussions. Nevertheless, from September 1994 to March 1995 Thirsk underwent specialized medical and Russian language training at the University of Victoria, British Columbia. He remains an adjunct professor there.

In 1993–94 Thirsk served as chief of the Canadian astronaut office. In February 1994 he was crew commander for CAPSULS, a 7-day ground simulation of a space mission. He was assigned as an LMS payload specialist in May 1995.

Tryggavson, Bjarni Vladimir

1945–

Canadian aerospace engineer Bjarni Tryggvason was a payload specialist in the crew of STS-85. This August 1997 flight of the orbiter Discovery carried a new Japanese-designed remote manipulator arm for possible future use on the International Space Station and also deployed and retrieved the Crista-SPAS payload. Among other duties, Tryggvason tested Canada's space vision system (SVS) in conjunction with the new remote manipulator and Crisa-SPAS operations.

Tryggvason previously served as backup to fellow Canadian payload specialist Steve MacLean for the STS-52 mission, launched in November 1992. STS-52 carried the CANEX-2 series of Canadian scientific and technical experiments, including the SVS.

Tryggvason was born September 21, 1945, in Reykjavik, Iceland, but grew up in Nova Scotia and British Columbia. He attended the University of British Columbia, receiving a B.S. in physics in 1972. He received a Ph.D. in engineering (aerodynamics and applied mathematics) from the University of Western Ontario in 1984.

Beginning in 1972 Tryggvason worked as a meteorologist at the Atmospheric Environment Service in Toronto. Two years later he became a research associate at the University of Western Ontario, performing studies of the effects of wind on structures such as the Sears Tower in Chicago. He later did research at Kyoto University in Japan, at James Cook University of North Queensland in Australia, finally joining the National Research Council in 1982.

He was one of the 6 members of Space Team Canada selected in December 1983, and was assigned to CANEX-2 in 1985. While serving as a payload specialist he also lectured part-time at the University of Ottawa and at Carleton University, and served as Canadian Space Agency representative to the NASA Microgravity Measurement Working Group.

Tryggvason is also a pilot and instructor with over 3,500 hours of flying time.

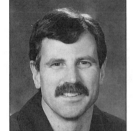

Williams, Daffyd Rhys

1954–

Canadian physician Daffyd (David) Williams was a mission specialist in the crew of STS-90, which carried the Neurolab Spacelab. Flown in April 1998, STS-90 carried a crew of 7, including 2 veterinarians, and over 2,000 experimental animals, ranging from pregnant mice to swordtail fish and crickets. Williams and his medical crewmates performed investigations into the functioning of such basic processes of DNA replication, cell division, and migration in microgravity. They also performed the first surgeries on living creatures in microgravity.

The experiments were marred by a death rate among the rats that was much higher than expected, sparking protests from animal rights groups. The crew also had to repair a faulty environmental control system that threatened to shorten the mission, which ultimately ran to its full 16-day duration.

Williams was born May 16, 1954, in Saskatoon, Saskatchewan, Canada. He attended McGill University in Montreal, receiving a B.S. in biology in 1976. He earned his M.D. and master of surgery degrees from McGill University in 1983. He has served as a staff emergency physician at the Sunnybrook Health Science Center in Toronto,

and also as lecturer in the department of surgery at the University of Toronto.

He also holds a private pilot's license.

Williams was one of the 4 astronaut candidates selected by the Canadian Space Agency in June 1992. During his training he served as a crewmember for a weeklong flight simulation called CAPSUL (February 1994).

In January 1995 he was also selected by NASA as a mission specialist candidate, qualifying in May 1996 while assigned to the payloads/habitability branch of the astronaut office.

China

Quinlong, Li

n.a.

Li Quinlong is one of 2 Chinese astronauts who underwent Soyuz-Mir training at the Gagarin Center between November 1996 and December 1997. Quinlong and his colleague Wu Ji Li have since returned to China, where they are said to be candidates for the first manned Chinese space launch, scheduled to take place in late 1999.

Li, Wu Ji

n.a.

Wu Ji Li is one of 2 Chinese astronauts who underwent Soyuz-Mir training at the Gagarin Center between November 1996 and December 1997. Li and his colleague Li Quinlong have returned to China and are said to be candidates for the first manned Chinese space launch, scheduled to take place in late 1999.

Cuba

Lopez-Falcon, Jose Armando

1950–

Jose Lopez-Falcon was the backup cosmonaut-researcher for fellow Cuban Arnaldo Tamayo-Mendez during the Soyuz 38 flight in September 1980.

Lopez-Falcon was born February 8, 1950, in Havana, and was a captain in the Cuban air force when he began cosmonaut training in April 1978.

Tamayo-Mendez, Atnaldo

1942–

Arnaldo Tamayo-Mendez, a pilot in the Cuban air force, became the first Latin and the first black in space when he served as cosmonaut-researcher aboard Soyuz 38 in September 1980. He and Soviet commander Yuri Romanenko spent 8 days in space, 7 of them visiting cosmonauts Popov and Ryumin aboard the Salyut 6 space station.

Tamayo-Mendez was born January 29, 1942, in Guantanamo, Cuba. He was orphaned as a child and by the age of 13 was working as a shoeshine boy. He later worked as an apprentice carpenter, then became an anti-Batista activist and rebel. After the Cuban Revolution in 1959, Tamayo-Mendez, now a soldier, was enrolled in the Rebeldi Technical Institute where he was first trained as an aviation technician prior to becoming a pilot.

He was sent to the Soviet Union in April 1961 to attend the Yeisk Higher Air Force School for a year. He returned to Cuba in May 1962 to serve in the Playa Giron Brigade as a flight instructor. He was later based in Cuba's central region as a squadron leader and deputy wing commander. He became a member of Cuba's Communist Party in 1967, and also studied at the General Maximo Gomez Basic College of Revolutionary Armed Forces (1969–71).

Tamayo-Mendez logged 1,400 hours of flying time and was a staff officer with a fighter brigade when selected as a candidate for cosmonaut training on 1976. He arrived at the Gagarin Center with countryman Jose Lopez-Falcon in April 1978.

More recently Colonel Tamayo-Mendez has served as director of Cuba's civil defense organization.

Czechoslovakia

Pelczak, Oldrich

1943–

Oldrich Pelczak was the backup cosmonaut-researcher for Vladimir Remek, the first citizen of a nation other than the Soviet Union or the United States to make a spaceflight.

Remek, from Czechoslovakia, was launched into space aboard Soyuz 28 in March 1978. He and Soviet commander Alexei Gubarev joined two other Soviet cosmonauts aboard the Salyut 6 space station as they broke the American-held space enduruance record of 84 days. Pelczak supported his countryman's 8-day flight from Soviet mission control at Kaliningrad (now Korolev), near Moscow.

Pelczak was born November 2, 1943, in the city of Gottwaldow, Czechoslovakia. In 1962 he graduated from the Ugerske-Gradiste junior engineering college, then entered the Kosice Higher Air Force College. From 1965 to 1972 he was an air defense fighter pilot in the Czech air force. He then spent 4 years in the Soviet Union as a student at the Yuri Gagarin (Red Banner) Air Force Academy. Shortly after his graduation he and his countryman Remek began training for spaceflight (December 1976).

Remek, Vladimir

1948–

Vladimir Remek was the first citizen of a nation other than the United States or the USSR to go into space. A pilot in the Czechoslovakian air force, the 29-year-old Remek served as cosmonaut-researcher aboard Soyuz 28 in March 1978. He and Soviet commander Alexei Gubarev spent 8 days in space, most of it aboard the Salyut 6 space station as visitors to cosmonauts Romanenko and Grechko. During the flight Remek supervised the operation of several Czech-designed scientific experiments.

Remek was born September 26, 1948, in Ceske-Budejovice, Czechoslovakia. His father, Josef, is a pilot who became a lieutenant general in the Czech air force. Remek finished secondary school (majoring in physics and mathematics) in 1966 and enrolled in the Kosice air force college, graduating in 1970.

Beginning in 1970 he served as a jet pilot with the Zvolensky unit of the Czech air force. In September 1972 he was sent to the USSR to attend the Gagarin Air Force Academy and had just completed that program in 1976 when he was selected for Interkosmos training.

After leaving the Gagarin Cosmonaut Training Center in 1978 Remek returned to Czechoslovakia, where he worked in the military's Institute of Aviation, a scientific-research organization based in Prague. He was briefly deputy commander of fighter bomber squadron in 1986, then attended the Voroshilov General Staff Academy in Moscow, graduating in 1988. He also published two books, *Above Our Planet Earth* and, with Gubarev, *Meeting in Orbit*.

Remek served as deputy commander of an air division in the Czechoslovakian air defense forces until 1990, when he went to work on the establishment of an aviation and space museum in the city of Prague.

He retired from the military in June 1995 and currently lives in Strakonitse, Czech Republic, where he serves as a representative of the Moscow firm Che-Zet.

European Space Agency

Cheli, Maurizio

1959–

Italian test pilot Maurizio Cheli was a mission specialist in the crew of STS-75, the February 1996 mission of the orbiter Columbia, which carried the third U.S. Microgravity Payload. STS-75 also made the second attempt to deploy Italy's Tethered Satellite System, this time succeeding in reeling the TSS to a distance of more than 12 miles, less than a mile short of its planned length, when the tether broke, forcing the crew to take evasive action. Nevertheless, the experiment proved that electricity could be generated by passing a long tether through the Earth's magnetic field.

Cheli served as the flight engineer for ascent and entry and as a member of the red team with commander Andy Allen, pilot Doc Horowitz, and payload specialist Umberto Guidoni, for USMP operations.

Cheli was born May 4, 1959, in Modena, Italy, and studied physics at the University of Rome. After entering the Italian air force and becoming a pilot, he attended the Empire Test Pilot School in Great Britain.

He has logged over 2,000 hours of flying time.

Cheli was one of the 6 astronauts selected by ESA in May 1992. Between August 1992 and July 1993 he underwent Shuttle mission specialist training at the NASA Johnson Space Center. His first technical assignment was in the Shuttle Avionics Integration Lab.

Following STS-75, in June 1996, Cheli resigned from ESA and left the NASA astronaut office to return to active duty with the Italian Air Force.

He is married to former ESA astronaut Marianne Merchez.

Clervoy, Jean François André

1958–

Jean-Francois Clervoy has made two flights as a mission specialist aboard the U.S. Space Shuttle. His first was STS-66, the November 1994 flight of the orbiter Atlantis, which carried the third Spacelab ATLAS. ATLAS-03 was an experiment package designed to study the Earth's atmosphere during the 11-year solar cycle. As operator of the orbiter's remote manipulator arm, Clervoy also deployed and retrieved the Crista-SPAS satellite.

Clervoy returned to space as a mission specialist in the crew of STS-84, the Shuttle-Mir docking, flown in May 1997. This flight of Atlantis delivered NASA-Mir crewmember Michael Foale to the Russian space station, while returning Jerry Linenger to Earth. The crew also transferred almost 3,000 pounds of food, water, and equipment to the Mir crew.

Clervoy was one of the 6 astronaut candidates selected by the European Space Agency in May 1992. In August 1992 he arrived at the NASA Johnson Space Center to qualify as a Shuttle mission specialist, working in the mission development branch of the astronaut office on robotics until assigned to STS-66 in January 1994.

Previously Clervoy was one of 7 French spationauts selected in September 1985. In April 1986 he joined French space veteran Jean-Loup Chretien and pilot Michel Tognini in preliminary tests and training at the Gagarin Center for the 3-week mission to Mir ultimately flown by Chretien in late 1988. He underwent further Soyuz-Mir training in 1991.

Clervoy was born November 19, 1958, at Longueville, France. He attended the Polytechnic Academy in Palaiseau, France, where he studied avionics, then earned a degree from the National Higher School for Aeronautics and Space in 1983.

A private pilot who has also made over 155 parachute jumps, Clervoy was an engineer employed by CNES in Toulouse at the time of his original selection.

De Winne, Frank

1961–

Belgian test pilot Frank De Winne was selected as an ESA atsronaut in October 1998. In the summer of 2000 he will begin astronaut training at the NASA Johnson Space Center to qualify him as a Shuttle mission specialist and International Space Station crewmember.

De Winne was born April 25, 1961, in Ghent, Belgium. He graduated from the Royal School of Cadets in Lier in 1979, then entered the Royal Military Academy in Brussels. He received a master's degree in telecommunications and civil engineering in 1984.

Following flight training De Winne served from 1986 to 1989 as a Mirage V pilot with the Belgian air force. He was then detailed to the SAGEM Company in Paris to work on safety improvement programs for the Mirage.

De Winne attended the Empire Test Pilot School at Boscombe Down, England, in 1992, and was assigned to the test and evaluation branch of the Belgian air force. For the next two years he worked on the CARAPACE F-16 electronic warfare program at Eglin AFB, Florida, and on a protection program for the C-130 aircraft, as well as serving as an acceptance pilot.

He was flight safety officer for the 1st Fighter Wing of the Belgian air force at Beauvechain from January 1994 to April 1995, then returned to flight test work, first with the European Participating Air Forces program at Edwards AFB, California, then as senior test pilot in the Belgian air force.

De Winne has logged over 2,300 hours of flying time in several different types of aircraft, including the Mirage, the F-16, the Jaguar, and the Tornado. At the time of his selection by ESA, De Winne was commander of the 349th Fighter Squadron, Kleine Brogel Airbase, Belgium.

Duque, Pedro Francisco

1963–

Spanish engineer Pedro Duque was backup ESA crewmember for Soyuz TM-20, a 32-day mission to the Mir space station by fellow ESA astronaut Ulf Merbold in September–October 1994. Duque served as primary crew interface coordinator for that mission, providing a link between Merbold on Mir and the EuroMir 94 payload operations control centre in Toulouse, France.

From April 1995 to July 1996 Duque was alternate ESA payload specialist for STS-78, which carried the Life and Microgravity Spacelab.

In July 1996 Duque was selected by ESA for astronaut candidate training. Since August of that year he has been at the Johnson Space Center, qualifying as a Shuttle mission specialist and International Space Station crewmember. He is currently assigned to the crew of STS-95, scheduled for launch in October 1998.

Duque was born March 14, 1963, in Madrid, Spain. He attended the Polytechnic University there, receiving a degree in aeronautical engineering.

While still an undergraduate Duque worked for the polytechnic's laboratory of flight mechanics, and also on a European Space Agency research contract. Following graduation he spent a year with GMV (Grupo Mecanica del Vuelo) as technical leader on a project simulating helicopter rotors. In December 1986 he joined the staff of the European Space Agency's space operations center at Darmstadt, Germany, where he became a member of the flight control team for the ERS-1 and EURECA satellites.

He was one of the 6 European astronaut candidates selected by ESA in May 1992 and in October-November 1992 underwent a preliminary Soyuz-Mir training course at the Gagarin Cosmonaut Training Center. His basic ESA astronaut training took place in Cologne, Germany, from January to July 1993. Duque and Merbold were named candidates for EuroMir 94 in August 1993.

Eyharts, Leopold
1957–

Franch test pilot Leopold Eyharts visited the Mir space station in February 1998. With commander Talgat Musabayev and flight engineer Nikolai Budarin, Eyharts was part of the Mir-25 main crew, launched aboard Soyuz TM-27.

Eyharts's 3-week mission was devoted to the Pegasus series of expetiments developed by CNES, the French space agency. Eyharts and Pegasus were originally sched-

uled to be launched to Mir in August 1997, but that mission was postponed for several months due to problems aboard the station.

With conditions aboard Mir stabilized, Eyharts was able successfully to complete studies in space medicine. He returned to Earth with Mir-24 cosmonauts Anatoly Solovyov and Pavel Vinogradov.

Eyharts previously served as backup cosmonaut-researcher for the August 1996 Russian-French Cassiopeia mission to Mir. French physician Claudie Andre-Dushays spent two weeks aboard Mir while Eyharts provided ground support.

Eyharts was born April 28, 1957, In Biarritz, France. He enrolled at the French Air Academy at Salon-de-Provence in 1977 and received a diploma of engineer in 1979.

Beginning in 1980 he served as a Jaguar pilot at Tours and at Istres, and also as a squadron commander at Saint-Dizier, taking part in operations in Africa and exercises in the United States. He attended the French test pilot school at Bretigny-sur-Orge.

He has logged over 3,500 hours of flying time in 50 types of aircraft, including 20 parachute jumps.

Eyharts was originally selected for spationaut training by CNES in January 1990. In July of 1990 he was one of 6 candidates submitted by CNES to the Soviet space agency Glavkosmos as a potential cosmonaut-researcher for a 1992 mission to Mir. In 1991 and 1993 he did advanced training at the Gagarin Center in preparation for a future flight to Mir and was named a candidate for the Cassiopeia mission in July 1994.

Following his flight Eyharts became an international astronaut candidate at the NASA Johnson Space Center.

Fuglesang, Arne Christer
1957–

Swedish physicist Christer Fuglesang was the backup cosmonaut researcher for fellow ESA astronaut Thomas Reither, who spent 179 days aboard the Mir space station between September 1995 and February 1996. During the mission Fuglesang served at the Russian mission control center as the prime crew interface coordinator between the Mir crew and the EuroMir mission control at Oberpfaffenhofen, Germany.

In July 1996 Fuglesang was selected by ESA to undergo astronaut candidate training. In August of that year he reported to the NASA Johnson Space Center to train as a Shuttle mission specialist and International Space Station crewmember. He is currently assigned to the computer support branch of the astronaut office.

Fuglesang was born March 18, 1957, in Nacka, Sweden. He attended the Royal Institute of Technology in Stockholm, receiving an M.S. in physics, mathematics, and engineering. He earned a Ph.D. in experimental physics from Stockholm University.

In 1988 Fuglesang joined CERN, the European Organization for Nuclear Research, in Geneva, working as a project leader. He later became a research assistant with the Manne Siegbahn Institute in Stockholm, working on the Large Hadron Collider project.

Fuglesang was one of the 6 astronaut candidates selected by the European Space Agency in May 1992. In October–November 1992 he underwent a preliminary Soyuz-Mir training course at the Gagarin Center, and basic ESA astronaut training at Cologne, Germany, from January to July 1993. He was selected, along with Thomas Reiter, as a candidate for EuroMir 95 in March 1994, and returned to the Gagarin Center that August to begin mission training.

Kuipers, Andre

1958–

Durch physician Andre Kuipers was selected as an ESA in October 1998. Beginning in the summer of 2000 he will undergo training at the NASA Johnson Space Center to qualify him as a Shuttle mission specialist and International Space Station crewmember.

Kuipers was born October 5, 1958, in Amsterdam, Netherlands, where he graduated from the van der Waals Lyceum in 1977. He received a medical doctor degree from the University of Amsterdam in 1987. While studying for his degree he worked at the Academic Medical Centre in Amsterdam.

In 1987 and 1988 Kuipers served as an officer in the Royal Netherlands Air Force Medical Corps. He then joined the Netherlands Aerospace Medical Centre in Soesterberg, where his research subjects included space adaptation syndrome. Sine 1991 he has worked with ESA, with medical experiments flying on the Spacelab D-2 mission (STS-55, 1993), aboard Mir (1995), and the Life and Microgravity Spacelab (STS-78, 1998). Future experiments are scheduled to fly aboard STS-107 (2000) and aboard ISS. Kuipers also served as experiment operator, test subject, and flight surgeon for ESA's parabolic flight program.

Merbold, Ulf Dietrich

1941–

German scientist Ulf Merbold was the first non-American to join a U.S. astronaut crew. He served as payload specialist on Spacelab 1/STS-9, launched November 28, 1983. As a member of the crew of 6, Merbold operated experiments in a variety of disciplines aboard the European-built Spacelab. The orbiter Columbia returned to Earth at Edwards Air Force Base, California, on December 8, 1983.

In 1985 Merbold served as backup payload specialist for Spacelab D-1, the German Spacelab, launched aboard Shuttle Mission 61-A.

He made his second spaceflight as payload specialist aboard STS-42, the International Microgravity Spacelab, in January 1992. This 8-day mission by a crew of 7, including Canadian physician Roberta Bondar, performed over 50 experiments in life sciences and space manufacturing developed by scientists in 13 different countries.

In October 1994 Merbold began his third flight, this time as cosmonaut-researcher aboard Soyuz TM-20. Merbold, commander Alexandr Vitorenko, and flight engineer Yelena Kondakova made up the Mir-17 crew. Over the next month Merbold conducted the EuroMir-94 set of experiments, most of them aimed at the study of human response to microgravity.

Merbold was born in Greiz, Germany, on 20 June 1941. His father was killed in World War II, and Merbold grew up in Soviet East Germany until he fled to the West at the age of 19. His mother still lives in the eastern sector of the now-united Germany.

Following a year at Falk-Schule Berlin in 1961, Merbold attended Stuttgart University, receiving a diploma in physics in 1968. While still a student he began working at the Max-Planck Institute in Stuttgart and later became a staff member there. One of his projects studied the irradiation damage inflicted on iron and vanadium by fast neutrons. This research led to Merbold's doctorate in natural science from Stuttgart University in 1976.

Merbold was a researcher at Max-Planck in 1977 when the European Space Agency selected him as a finalist for payload specialist aboard the Spacelab 1 mission, then planned for 1981. From 1984 to 1986 he worked in support of Spacelab D-1, then was assigned to the European Space Agency's European Space Technology Center at Noordwijk in the Netherlands to assist in the development of the Columbus space platform. On September 1, 1987, Merbold was named head of the DLR (German Space Agency) Astronaut Office while remaining on the staff of ESA. He was selected as IML payload specialist in December 1988.

He is a private pilot with over 2,000 hours of flying time in light aircraft and gliders. He is also the author of two books, *Flight into Space* (1986) and *D-1, Our Way into Space* (1985).

Since returning from the EuroMir-94 mission Merbold has been chief of the ESA astronaut team.

Merchez, Marianne

1960–

Belgian physician and pilot Marianne Merchez was one of the 6 astronaut candidates selected by the European Space Agency in May 1992. In October and November 1992 she underwent a preliminary Soyuz-Mir training course at the Gagarin Center, but withdrew from consideration for the 1994 and 1995 ESA-Mir missions in order to join her husband, ESA astronaut Maurizio Cheli, at the NASA Johnson Space Center.

In early 1995, having failed to be assigned as a mission specialist candidate for the International Space Station program, Merchez left the ESA astronaut team.

Merchez was born October 25, 1960, in Uccle, Belgium. She received an M.D. degree from Catholic University of Louvain, Belgium, where she also took courses in aerospace medicine. Since 1985 she has been a general practitioner.

She also qualified as an airline pilot through the Civil Aviation School in Belgium, eventually logging over 1,200 hours of flying time as co-pilot in the Falcon 20 and Boeing 737.

Nespoli, Paolo

1957–

European Space Agency engineer Paolo Nespoli is one of the 6 international astronauts who reported to the NASA Johnson Space Center in August 1998 to begin a training and evaluation course that should qualify him as a Shuttle mission specialist and International Space Station crewmember in 1999.

Nespoli was born April 6, 1957, In Milan, Italy. He graduated in 1977 from the Liceo Scientifico Paolo Frisi of Desio in that city and later received a B.S. in aeronautical engineering (1988), followed by an M.S. in aeronautics/astronautics (1989) from Polytechnic University, New York.

Drafted into the Italian army in 1977 when he was 20, Nespoli served as a noncommissioned officer and parachute instructor at the military school in Pisa. Beginning in 1982 he was stationed in Beirut, Lebanon, with the Italian contingent of the Multinational Peacekeeping Force, eventually earning a promotion to lieutenant.

After leaving military service he went to college in the United States, returning to Italy in 1989 to become a design engineer for Proel Technologie, Florence, working on components for Italy's Tethered Satellite in Space vehicle.

In 1991 Nespoli joined the European Space Agency's astronaut training division in Cologne, Germany, and four years later moved to the ESTEC Center in Noordwijk, Netherlands, to support the EuroMir missions.

At the time of his selection by ESA and the Italian Space Agency (ASI) in July 1998, Nespoli was already working with the spaceflight training division at the NASA Johnson Space Center on the International Space Station.

Nicollier, Claude
1944–

Claude Nicollier is a European Space Agency astronaut who was a mission specialist in the crew of STS-46, flown in July–August 1992. This 8-day flight of the orbiter Atlantis carried ESA's EURECA scientific platform and the Italian Space Agency's Tethered Satellite System. The EURECA deployment succeeded, but the TSS experiment had to be abandoned when the satellite failed to unreel to its intended 12-mile length.

Nicollier later served as mission specialist aboard STS-61. This December 1993 flight of the orbiter Endeavour accomplished the dramatic repair of the Hubble Space Telescope with 5 EVAs by two teams of astronauts. Nicollier served as operator of the remote manipulator system for the mission.

He made his third flight on STS-75, launched in February 1996. This mission carried the third U.S. Microgravity Payload as well as the TSS, which was deployed to a distance of 12 miles, just short of its planned 13 miles, when it broke.

Nicollier was born September 2, 1944, in Vevey, Switzerland. He graduated from Gymnase de Lausanne (secondary school) in 1962, then received a B.S. in physics from the University of Lausanne in 1970. He later earned his M.S. in astrophysics from the University of Geneva in 1975.

Nicollier worked as a scientist with the Institute of Astronomy at Lausanne University and at the Geneva Observatory while also attending the Swiss Air Transport School and piloting DC-9s for Swissair. In 1976 he accepted a fellowship at the ESA Space Science Department at Noordwijk, the Netherlands, where he took part in the ASSESS-II Spacelab mission simulation. In July 1978 he was selected by ESA as one of 3 ESA Spacelab 1 payload specialists.

Under a special agreement between ESA and NASA, Nicollier and Wubbo Ockels joined the May 1980 group of astronaut candidates for training that qualified them as Shuttle mission specialists in July 1981. Nicollier was eventually assigned as an astronaut on Mission 61-K, the Spacelab Earth Observation Mission, originally scheduled for launch in the summer of 1986, but postponed because of the Shuttle Challenger disaster.

Nicollier is a captain in the Swiss Air Force and has logged over 5,400 hours of flying time, including 3,800 hours in jets.

During the hiatus caused by the Challenger accident Nicollier attended the Empire Test Pilot School at Boscombe Down, England, graduating in December 1988. He was assigned to STS-46 in September 1989.

Nicollier is currently chief of the robotics branch of the NASA astronaut office.

Ockels, Wubbo, Johannes
1946–

Wubbo Ockels was a payload specialist aboard the Spacelab D-1 (Deutschland 1), Space Shuttle Mission 61-A in October and November 1985. He and seven other astronauts performed experiments in life sciences and materials processing that were designed and controlled by the Federal German Aerospace Research Establishment (DFVLR).

The eight astronauts aboard Spacelab D-1 were divided into two 3-astronaut teams working in 12-hour shifts. Ockels and mission commander Henry Hartsfield "floated" between shifts, working where and as much as each wanted, and during the flight Ockels had to be reminded by German mission control to make sure he got some sleep.

Ockels was born March 28, 1946, in Almelo, The Netherlands, though he grew up in Groningen. He received his doctorate in physics and mathematics from the University of Groningen in 1973 and finished his thesis in 1978.

From 1973 to 1978 Ockels was a researcher at the Nuclear Physics Accelerator Institute (KVI) at Groningen, involved in designing computer software and detection devices for the particle accelerator there. He also taught.

In 1978 Ockels was chosen by the European Space Agency as one of 3 finalists for the Spacelab 1 mission. When Spacelab 1 was launched in November 1983 Ockels was the backup payload specialist for Ulf

Merbold, and supported the flight from the mission control center at NASA's Marshall Space Center in Huntsville, Alabama.

In May 1980, under an agreement between NASA and the ESA, Ockels and fellow Spacelab payload specialist Claude Nicollier began astronaut training with 19 NASA candidates, successfully completing this course in August 1981.

Following his flight aboard Mission 61-A Ockels worked at ESA's European Space Technology Center (ESTEC) in Noordwijk, the Netherlands, while remaining an active ESA astronaut. He was a candidate payload specialist for two International Microgravity Spacelab missions, STS-42 and STS-65, but was not selected.

In May 1993 he was appointed to the ESTEC Professional Chair in the faculty of aerospace engineering at the Technical University at Delft in the Netherlands.

Reiter, Thomas
1958–
German test pilot Thomas Reiter spent 179 days aboard the space station Mir from September 1995 through February 1996, becoming the most experienced European space traveler.

Reiter was part of the Mir-20 crew, which included Russian cosmonauts Yuri Gidzenko and Sergei Avdeyev. The crew hosted the visiting Shuttle crew of STS-74 during its docking in November 1995, and performed 3 EVAs—2 of them by Reiter.

Originally launched on a planned 135-day mission, the crew's stay was extended because of financial problems suffered by the Russian Space Agency. Reiter used the extra time to perform additional work on a suite of European Space Agency experiments.

Reiter was born May 23, 1958, in Frankfurt-am-Main, Germany. He attended the University of the Armed Forces in Munich, receiving an engineering diploma, then underwent pilot training. At the time of his selection he was a student at the Empire Test Pilot School in Great Britain. He has logged 1,500 hours of flying time.

Reiter was one of the 6 astronaut candidates selected by the European Space Agency in May 1992. In December 1992 and January 1993 he underwent a preliminary Soyuz-Mir training course at the Gagarin Center, and in May 1993 was named as a candidate for the EuroMir-95 mission.

Following EuroMir-95 Reiter remained at the Gagarin Center for a year and a half, long enough to complete an additional 600 hours of training on Soyuz, qualifying as a rescue/return Soyuz pilot.

Reiter is currently on temporary duty with the German air force and still eligible for assignment to future ESA missions.

Schlegel, Hans Wilhelm
1951–
Physicist Hans Schlegel spent 9 days in space aboard the orbiter Columbia during STS-55, the second German Spacelab mission. Launched in April 1993—after the crew endured a launchpad abort on March 22—Spacelab D-2 featured experiments in space manufacturing and medicine as well as the German-built Rotex robotic arm, and Holop, a telepresence system that allowed ground-based scientists to take an active part in onboard activities. Schlegel was part of the red team with mission specialists Charles Precourt and Bernard Harris, working a 12-hour shift throughout the mission.

In September 1995 Schlegel began training at the Gagarin Center as backup to fellow German researcher Reinhold Ewald, who spent three weeks aboard Mir in February 1997, then became a candidate for the third German-Mir visit, which was canceled.

Schlegel was born August 3, 1951, in Oberlingen, Germany. He graduated from secondary school in Cologne after spending a year as an exchange student in Council Bluffs, Iowa. From 1972 to 1979 he attended Aachen University, receiving a diploma in physics.

Schlegel served as a second lieutenant in the German Federal armed forces between secondary school and college. After graduating from Aachen he worked as a scientist in the Physics Institute there. In 1986 he joined the research and development staff at the Institute Dr. Forster GmbH & Co.

He is the holder of a private pilot's license.

Schlegel became an ESA astronaut in July 1998.

Vittori, Roberto

1964–

Italian air force test pilot Roberto Vittori is one of 4 astronauts selected by the European Space Agency in July 1998. In August of that year he reported to the NASA Johnson Space Center to begin a training and evaluation course that should qualify him as a Shuttle mission specialist and International Space Station crewmember in 1999.

Vittori was born October 15, 1964, in Viterbo, Italy, and attended the Italian Air Force Academy, graduating with a degree in 1989. He has done graduate work in physics at the University of Perugia.

From 1991 to 1994 Vittorio was a Tornado GR1 pilot with the Italian air force. He then attended the U.S. Naval Test Pilot School at Patuxent River, Maryland, and following graduation served as project test pilot for the EuroFighter 2000 program at the test center for the Italian air force. In 1996 he joined the team developing the Beyond Visual Range Air-to-Air Missile (BVRAAM) for the EF2000.

A major in the Italian air force, Vittori has logged over 1,500 hours of flying time in 40 different types of aircraft, including glides and helicopters.

He was one of 4 new astronauts selected jointly by ESA and the Italian Space Agency (ASI) in July 1998.

France

Andre-Deshays, Claudie

1957–

French physician Claudie Andre-Deshays spent 16 days in space, most of it aboard the Russian space station Mir, in August and September 1996. With commander Valery Korzun and flight engineer Alexandr Kaleri, Andre-Deshays formed the Mir-22 crew, launched aboard Soyuz TM-24. (Andre-Deshays had trained for months with Gennady Manakov and Pavel Vinogradov, only to see them removed from the mission a week prior to launch.) The crew joined the current Mir residents of Yuri Onufriyenko, Yuri Usachev, and Shannon Lucid.

Andre-Deshays's set of experiments, known as Cassiopeia, concentrated on medical studies, notably with the Physiolab, a system for measuring blood pressure and cardiac frequency, and Cognilab, a means of testing human perceptions (visual, aural, and muscular) in microgravity.

Andre-Deshays was born Claudie Andre on May 13, 1957, in Creusot, Burgundy region, France. She earned her doctorate in medicine (with honors) in 1981 from Dijon University, specializing in biology and sports medicine. She performed further study in aviation medicine in 1983 while also serving as professor of rheumatics at Cochin Hospital in Paris.

Andre-Deshays was one of the 7 French spationauts selected in September 1985 to train for flights aboard the Soviet Mir space station, the American Space Shuttle, and the French Hermes spacecraft in the 1990s. She also helped develop space medical experiments for CNES and worked on the staff of the Laboratoire de Physiiologie Neurosensorielle in Paris.

In 1991 Andre-Deshays took part in advanced weightless training at the Gagarin Center near Moscow, in preparation for assignment to a future Soyuz-Mir mission. In December 1992 she was named backup to French researcher Jean-Pierre Haignere for the Soyuz TM-17 mission, launched in July 1993. She then coordinated experiments for the EuroMir-94 flight of Ulf Merbold, and was assigned to the Cassiopeia mission in July 1994.

Andre-Deshays still lives at Star Town and is currently training as backup researcher for a 1999 mission to Mir by French spationaut Jean-Pierre Haignere.

Baudry, Patrick Pierre Roger

1946–

Test pilot Patrick Baudry was the first French spationaut to fly aboard the American Space Shuttle, serving as payload specialist of Mission 51-G in May 1985. During that flight of the orbiter Discovery, Baudry operated a specially designed French echocardiograph similar to the one flown aboard the Soviet Salyut 7 space station in 1982.

Baudry was born March 6, 1946, in Douala, United Repulic of Cameroon. In 1967 he entered the Ecole de l'Air (the French Air Force Academy), graduating 2 years later with a master's degree in aeronautical engineering.

He underwent pilot training at Salon-de-Provence and Tours in France, receiving his wings in 1970. For the next 8 years he served as a fighter pilot with Squadron 1/11 "Roussillon," flying F-100s and Jaguars on missions in France and Africa. He entered the Empire Test Pilot School at Boscombe Down, England, in 1978, and won the Patuxent River Trophy as the highest-ranking student. In 1979 he was assigned to the flight test center at Bretigny-sur-Orge in France.

As a pilot he has logged over 4,000 hours of flying time, including 3,300 hours in jets, in over 100 different types of aircraft.

In June 1980 Baudry was one of 2 French Air Force pilots chosen by CNES, the French space agency, as "spationauts." For the next 2 years he trained at the CNES center in Toulouse and at the Gagarin Center near Moscow for a Soyuz/Salyut mission, serving as backup cosmonaut-researcher to Chretien at the launch in 1982. In April 1984 Baudry was chosen to be prime French payload specialist for an American Shuttle flight and came to the United States for training.

In 1986, following his Shuttle mission, Baudry left the French air force to join the company Aerospatiale, becoming chief test pilot for the proposed Hermes spaceplane. Hermes was ultimately canceled, however, and since 1995 Baudry has worked as a test pilot for Airbus.

Chretien, Jean-Loup Jacques Marie

1938–

French test pilot Jean-Loup Chretien became the first Westerner to go into space aboard a Soviet spacecraft when he served as the Soyuz T-6 cosmonaut-researcher in June and July 1982. Chretien and Soviet cosmonauts Vladimir Dzhanibekov and Alexandr Ivanchenkov spent 8

days in space, 7 of them with cosmonauts Berezovoy and Lebedev aboard the Salyut 7 space station. During the mission Chretien supervised the operations of a French-built echocardiograph, a heart-monitoring system designed for use in space.

In November 1988 Chretien scored another first, becoming the first non-Soviet, non-American to take a walk in space. He was a member of the crew of Soyuz TM-7, launched November 26 for a 3-week stay aboard the Mir space station. On December 9 Chretien and commander Alexandr Volkov exited the Mir complex to erect an experimental space structure developed by French engineers. The container for the structure, called ERA, proved balky, but Volkov kicked it open and the spacewalk proceeded.

The remainder of Chretien's mission was devoted to French medical and scientific experiments and to preparing cosmonauts Titov and Manarov—who were concluding a year in space—for return to Earth.

Chretien went into space a third time aboard the American Shuttle Atlantis, on mission STS-86 in September 1997. During this 11-day mission Chretien returned to Mir to take part in a logistics and crew transfer.

Chretien was born August 20, 1938, in La Rochelle, France, and attended the Ecole de l'Air (the French Air Force Academy), graduating in 1961. He later earned a master's degree in aeronautical engineering.

Chretien underwent flight training and earned his wings in 1962. For the next 7 years he was a Mirage III fighter pilot with the 5th Fighter Squadron based in Orange, France. In 1970 he entered the test pilot school at Istres, becoming the chief test pilot for the Mirage F1. At the time of his selection to be a French space traveler he was deputy chief of the South Air Defense Division.

He has logged over 6,000 hours of flying time.

In June 1980 Chretien and Patrick Baudry, another French Air Force pilot, were chosen by CNES, the French space agency, to train for a flight on the Soviet Soyuz and Salyut spacecraft. In October 1980 they arrived at the Gagarin Cosmonaut Training Center at Star Town, outside Moscow, where they lived and worked for the next 18 months.

Though training went smoothly, there were problems: the French spationauts found themselves eating lunch in a section of the center's cafeteria that had been cordoned off. And the original Soviet commander, Yuri Malyshev, was replaced in early 1982, apparently because he insisted on treating veteran test pilot Chretien as nothing more than a passenger.

In 1984 and 1985 Chretien served as backup to Baudry during training for an American Shuttle flight, eventually flown as Mission 51-G in May 1985. The French pilots also had some problems with the American system, beginning on their first day at the Johnson Space Center, when they were left waiting at the entrance for hours.

Following the Shuttle mission Chretien became head of the manned spaceflight division of CNES and leader of the Hermes test pilot group, positions he held until returning the Gagarin Center in November 1986.

Chretien returned to JSC in the spring of 1995, along with Michel Tognini, to undergo Shuttle mission specialist training while also serving as a consultant to NASA's Phase One (Shuttle-Mir) program.

General Chretien is currently director of the CNES spationaut group.

Favier, Jean-Jacques
1949–

Physicist Jean-Jacques Favier was a payload specialist aboard STS-78, the flight of the Life and Microgravity Spacelab (LMS) launched June 20, 1996. The LMS mission carried a suite of 41 different experiments in a variety of fields, from aerospace medicine to fluid physics and space manufacturing. STS-78 lasted 17 days, the longest Shuttle mission flown so far, and served as a forerunner of operations for the upcoming International Space Station.

Favier was born April 13, 1949, in Kehl, France. After completing secondary school in 1968 he entered the Grenoble Polytechnical Institute to study electrical engineering. He earned a degree in physics in 1972, a doctor of engineering in 1976 and a doctor of science in 1977.

While working on his doctorate Favier joined the Nuclear Research Center in Grenoble, eventually becoming head of the physics group there. He later became adviser to the director of the Material Science Research Center (CEREM) of the French Atomic Energy Commis-

sion (CEA). He has also been a visiting professor at the University of Alabama, Huntsville (1994–95).

In September 1985 Favier was selected as one of 7 French spationauts for flights aboard Soviet, American, and European spacecraft in the 1990s. He was one of 4 "experimenters" (scientists) in the group.

In 1992 Favier was named backup payload specialist for STS-65, the second International Microgravity Space-lab mission. During the flight of IML-02 in July 1995 he served as crew interface coordinator at the NASA Marshall Payload Operations Center in Huntsville, Alabama.

Gasparini, Jean-Marc Michel Daniel
1963–

Jean-Marc Gasparini is a French air force pilot selected for spationaut training by CNES in January 1990. In July 1990 he was one of 6 candidates submitted by CNES to the Soviet space agency Glavkosmos as a potential cosmonaut-researcher for a 1992 mission to Mir.

Although he is a French spationaut, he remains on active duty with the air force and is not employed by CNES.

Gasparini was born January 22, 1963, in Marseilles, France. He attended the French Polytechnic School, graduating in 1985, then entered the French Air Force. From 1985 to 1989 he served as a fighter pilot flying the Mirage F1 and Alpha Jet, then as a flight commander in the Mirage 2000. He graduated from the French test pilot school at Istres, France, in 1992, then served at the Bretigny Test Base on several programs.

He has logged over 1,500 hours of flying time.

Gasparini is currently chief test pilot of the French Flight Test Center (CEV), Bretigny, flying, among other aircraft, a specially modified Caravelle transport used to train European astronauts in zero-G environments.

Haignere, Jean-Pierre

1948–

French test pilot Jean-Pierre Haignere was cosmonaut-researcher in the crew of Soyuz TM-17, launched to the Mir space station in July 1993. During his 3-week mission Haignere and Russian cosmonauts Vasily Tsibliyev and Alexandr Serebrov operated the Altair series of French scientific experiments. Two of the major Altair experiments, Nausica and Eceq, designed to study different radiation dosages, had actually been in place since the visit to Mir by Haignere's predecessor, Michel Tognini, in the summer of 1992. Others experiments dealt with medical subjects.

In 1992 Haignere was backup to Tognini on the Soyuz TM-15 flight. More recently he served as backup for French spationaut Leopold Eyharts, who spent 3 weeks aboard Mir in February 1998, after seeing his mission delayed from August 1997 because of problems aboard the Russian station.

He remains the leading candidate for the last French mission to Mir, this one of 4 months' duration, and scheduled for launch in 1999.

Haignere was born May 19, 1948, in Paris. He entered the French Air Academy in 1969 and earned a diploma in engineering in 1971. He served as a fighter pilot and squadron leader in the French air force, then attended the Empire Test Pilot School at Boscombe Down, England, graduating in 1982.

He was one of the 7 spationauts selected in September 1985 to train for flights aboard Soviet, American and French spacecraft. At the time of his selection by CNES, the French space agency, he was chief test pilot at the flight test center in Bretigny, France, with over 3,000 hours of flying time.

In 1990 he was one of the 6 pilot candidates who underwent preliminary testing at the Gagarin for the 1992 Soviet-French Antares mission. He was designated backup cosmonaut-researcher to Michel Tognini in August 1990.

In addition to training for Antares, Haignere served as chief of the manned spaceflight division of CNES, and has taken part in the development of the Hermes spaceplane.

Patat, Frederic

1958–

Frederic Patat was one of the 4 "experimenters" (scientists) chosen with three "onboard engineers" as French spationauts in September 1985. For several years he was a candidate for possible spaceflights aboard the Russian Mir space station and the American Space Shuttle until being medically disqualified in 1989.

Patat was born June 24, 1958, in the city of Lyons, France. He attended a polytechnical school, and in 1980 earned a degree in engineering from the Ecole Polytechnique (1980) and a doctorate in acoustic physics from the University of Paris (1984).

At the time of his selection he was a biophysicist at the Faculty of Medicine in Tours, France, where he worked on the development of the echocardiograph experiment that was flown on the Soviet Salyut 7 space station and on the American Space Shuttle Discovery.

Patat became a medical doctor in 1991 and is currently a teacher on the medical faculty of Tours University.

Perrin, Phillipe

1963–

French air force test pilot Phillipe Perrin was selected in June 1996 as an international astronaut candidate by CNES, the French national space agency. He is currently training at the NASA Johnson Space Center to qualify as a Shuttle mission specialist and International Space Station crewmember.

Perrin was born January 6, 1963 in the city of Meknes, Morocco, though he considers Avignon, Provence, to be his hometown. He graduated from the Polytechnic Academy in Palaiseau in 1985, then entered the French Air Force. After flight training at Tours in 1985-86 he served as a formation leader with the 33rd Reconnaissance Wing flying the Mirage F1. In 1991 he flew 26 combat missions in Operation Desert Shield over Iraq and Kuwait.

In June 1990, while assigned to the 33rd Reconnaissance Wing, Perrin was selected by CNES as a spationaut candidate. In July 1990 he was one of 6 French astronauts submitted by CNES to the Soviet space agency Glavkosmos as a potential cosmonaut-researcher for a 1992 mission to Mir. In November–December of that year he underwent preliminary Soyuz-Mir training at the Gagarin Center.

Perrin attended the Ecole du Personnel navigant d'Essais et de Reception (EPNER, the French test pilot school) at Istres, France, in 1991-92. Following his temporary training at the Gagarin Center, he became senior operations officer with the 2nd Air Defense Wing based at Dijon Air Force Base, flying missions in Operation Southern Watch.

In 1995 he became chief deputy pilot on the Mirage 2000-5 program at the flight test center at Bretigny, France.

Lieutenant Colonel Perrin has logged over 2,000 hours of flying time in 30 different types of aircraft.

Silve, Benoit

1959–

Benoit Silve is a French navy pilot selected for spationaut training by CNES in January 1990. In July 1990 he was one of 6 candidates submitted by CNES to the Soviet space agency Glavkosmos as a potential cosmonaut-researcher for a 1992 mission to Mir.

Silve was born in 1959 and trained as a fighter pilot in the French air force. Most recently he was stationed aboard the carrier *Foch*.

Tognini, Michel Ange Charles

1949–

French test pilot Michel Tognini spent 14 days aboard the Mir space station in July and August 1992. Launched with Russian cosmonauts Anatoly Solovyov and Sergei Avdeyev aboard Soyuz TM-15, Tognini initiated a series of 10 French experiments named Antares. Most of the experiments, such as an inflight echocardiograph, designed to measure the functioning of a human heart,

were medical, while others were aimed at the space environment, measuring radiation inside and outside Mir. Tognini returned to Earth with cosmonauts Manakov and Poleshchuk.

Tognini previously served as backup cosmonaut-researcher to fellow spationaut Jean-Loup Chretien for the Soyuz TM-7 (Aragatz) mission in 1988.

In the spring of 1995 Tognini was assigned by CNES to the NASA Johnson Space Center to serve as a consultant for Shuttle-Mir missions. He qualified as a Shuttle mission specialist in May 1996, and in September 1997 was assigned to the crew of STS-93, scheduled to deploy the AXAF astrophysical observatory in early 1999.

Tognini was born September 30, 1949, in Vincennes, France. He graduated from the French Air Force Academy in 1973 with an engineering degree, then became a fighter pilot the following year. After serving in the air force, he attended the Empire Test Pilot School at Boscombe Down, England, graduating in 1982.

At the time of his selection by CNES, the French space agency, in September 1985, he was chief test pilot at the Cazaux air base, with over 3,700 hours of flying time in 80 different types of aircraft.

In July 1986 Tognini, Chretien, and Jean-Francois Clervoy were tested as semi-finalists for the 1988 Soviet-French mission. Tognini and Chretien were selected, and reported to the Gagarin Center for training that November. Tognini returned to the Gagarin Center in August 1990 to train as cosmonaut-researcher for the third Soviet-French manned mission.

Tognini attended the French Institute for High Studies of National Defense (IHEDN) from 1993 to 1994 before moving to the United States.

Viso, Michel

1951–

Michel Viso, a veterinary surgeon and engineer, was one of the 7 French spationauts chosen in September 1985. Viso, like the 3 other "experimenters" (scientists) and three "onboard engineers" chosen with him, was a candidate for flights into space on the American Space Shuttle, the Soviet Mir space station, and the French Hermes spaceplane. In November-December 1992 he underwent preliminary Soyuz-Mir cosmonaut training at the Gagarin Center, but was not assigned to a mission at that time.

He was also a candidate for a medical Spacelab mission once planned by the European Space Agency for launch in the late 1990s.

Viso was born June 16, 1951, in Mauvezin, France. From 1971 to 1975 he attended the Maison Alfort Veterinary School, then practiced for 3 years. He taught from 1978 to 1980, when he joined the National Institute for Agronomical Studies, where he studied immunology and became a researcher in the pathology of viruses.

He remains an active spationaut with CNES, the French space agency, while continuing his association with the Maison Alfort Veterinary School.

Germany

Brummer, Renate Louise
1955–
Meteorologist Renate Brummer was alternate payload specialist for STS-55, the second German Spacelab mission (Spacelab D-2). The 9-day flight of the orbiter Columbia was launched in April 1993 with a crew of 7, including German payload specialists Ulrich Walter and Hans Wilhelm Schlegel.

Brummer was born May 4, 1955, in St. Gallen, Switzerland. She attended Max Born Gymnasium in Germering, Germany, graduating in 1975, then was a student of math and physics at the University of Munich, qualifying as a secondary schoolteacher in 1981.

From 1981 to 1986 she was a doctoral student in meteorology, receiving her Ph.D. in 1986 from the University of Miami, Florida. During her doctoral research she took part in investigating the effects of mountains on weather and studied the prediction of tornadoes in the central United States. At the time of her selection as a German astronaut in August 1987 she was a research associate at the University of Colorado in Boulder. She is the holder of a private pilot's license.

When the German astronaut team was disbanded in 1993, Brummer returned to the United States, where she works for the National Oceanographic and Atmospheric Administration at its Boulder, Colorado, office.

Ewald, Reinhold
1956–
German physicist Reinhold Ewald was cosmonaut-researcher in the crew of Soyuz TM-25. Launched in February 1997 as the twenty-third main Mir crew, Ewald, commander Vasily Tsibliyev and flight engineer Alexandr Lazutkin joined cosmonauts Valery Korzun and Alexandr Kaleri and NASA-Mir researcher Jerry Linenger for 3 weeks of planned joint operations. The first 11 days of Ewald's mission went smoothly, concentrating on a set of 27 investigations, most of them medical, as well as technology demonstrations for the future International Space Station.

On February 23, however, a fire broke out in the Mir core module, forcing the crew of 6 to don gas masks and prepare for evacuation. That proved not to be necessary, but the cleanup efforts prevented Ewald from completing his program as planned. He returned to Earth with Korzun and Kaleri as scheduled on March 2.

Previously Ewald served as backup cosmonaut researcher to Klaus-Deitrich Flade for Soyuz TM-14, the Russian-German "Mir '92" mission launched March 17, 1992. Ewald supported the 8-day mission from the flight control center in Kaliningrad (now Korolev).

Ewald was born December 18, 1956, in Munchengladbach, where he grew up. He studied at the University of Cologne, majoring in experimental physics. From 1983 to 1986 he worked on his thesis in spectroscopy of interstellar matter. He also worked with the three-meter radiotelescope at Cologne.

In 1987 Ewald joined the German Establishment of Air and Space Flight (DLR) in Cologne-Porz. His most recent assignment was as coordinator for space activities. He was selected as a candidate for the Mir '92 mission in September 1990. Two months later he and Flade arrived at the Gagarin Center to begin their training.

Flade, Klaus-Dietrich

1952–

German test pilot Klaus-Dietrich Flade was the cosmonaut-researcher for Soyuz TM-14, a Russian-German visit to the Mir space station launched March 17, 1992. Launched with Russian commander Alexandr Viktorenko and flight engineer Alexandr Kaleri, Flade spent 8 days operating 14 different experiments in space manufacturing and medicine for German researchers. He returned to Earth with the crew of Alexandr Volkov and Sergei Krikalev aboard Soyuz TM-13.

Flade was born August 23, 1952, in Budesheim. In 1974 he became an aircraft mechanic and officer candidate with the Federal German Air Force. In 1976 he enrolled in the University of the German Armed Forced in Munich, graduating in 1980 with a degree in engineering and a diploma in chemistry.

He became a pilot for fighter and transport aircraft with the German Air Force. In 1988 and 1989 he attended test pilot school at Manching, and the Empire Test Pilot School at Boscombe Down, England. He has flown the F-104 Starfighter, the Tornado, and the Alpha-Jet, in addition to transports and helicopters.

Flade applied for the first group of West German astronauts selected in 1987, becoming one of the 13 semifinalists. He and Reinhold Ewald, another unsuccessful candidate, got a second chance to become space travelers when the Soviet Union and West Germany agreed in 1988 for a commercial German mission to Mir.

In November 1990 Flade and Ewald arrived at the Gagarin Center to being their cosmonaut training. Flade was announced as a member of the first or prime crew in August 1991.

Following his mission Flade worked with the German Space Agency for 2 years. He retired from the German Air Force in 1995 to join Airbus as a test pilot.

Furrer, Reinhard Alfred

1940–1995

Reinhard Furrer was a payload specialist aboard the Spacelab D-1 (Deustchland 1), Space Shuttle Mission 61-A flight in October and November 1985. During this weeklong flight Furrer and seven other astronauts performed 76 experiments, many of them involving the manufacturing of new metals in a weightless environment, and the study of human reactions to spaceflight.

The experiments aboard Spacelab D-1 were controlled by the Federal German Aerospace Research Establishment (DFVLR), not NASA, as had been the case in three previous Spacelab missions.

Furrer was born in Worgl, Austria, on November 25, 1940. He attended secondary school at Kempten/Allgau, then studied physics at the Universities of Kiel and Berlin. He received a diploma in physics in 1969 and a doctorate in physics in 1972.

Prior to his selection for D-1 training in December 1982 Furrer was a researcher at the University of Stuttgart and at the Free University of Berlin, and a visiting scientist at the University of Chicago's Argonne National Laboratory. After his mission he continued his association with the German Space Agency (DLR) while remaining on the faculty of the Free University in Berlin.

Holder of a commercial pilot license, Furrer was killed in the crash of a vintage Me-108 on September 9, 1995, at an air show in the Berlin suburb of Johannisthal.

Jaehn, Sigmund

1937–

Sigmund Jaehn became the first German in space when he served as cosmonaut-researcher aboard Soyuz 31 during an 8-day flight in August and September 1978. He and Soviet commander Valery Bykovsky visited cosmonauts Kovalenok and Ivanchenkov aboard Salyut 6, returning to Earth in their Soyuz 29 vehicle.

Jaehn was born February 13, 1937, in Rautenkranz in what later became East Germany (the German Democratic Republic). He grew up in a war-torn land in difficult circumstances, going to work as a printer at the age of 13. Five years later he joined the army, enrolling at the Franz Mering Air Force School, from which he graduated in 1958.

He served as a pilot, instructor, and squadron commander until 1966, when his worked earned him an appointment to the Gagarin Air Force Academy in the Soviet Union. Returning to Germany, he became an inspector for the general staff of the German air force. At the time of his selection for cosmonaut training in December 1976 he had logged over 1,200 hours of flying time.

Returning to the GDR after Soyuz 31, Jaehn was promoted to major general and became deputy chief of the main political control department of the air force (1980). He published a book, *Experiencing Space* (1983).

In the summer of 1990, following the reunification of the two Germanies, Jaehn described himself to one Soviet reporter as an "unemployed general." He became a consultant to the German Space Agency, serving as training advisor and interpreter for German Mir cosmonauts Flade and Ewald for their 1992 and 1997 space missions.

Kohllner, Eberhard
1939–

Eberhard Kohllner served as backup cosmonaut-researcher for Sigmund Jaehn, the first German in space. During the 8-day Soyuz 31 flight of Jaehn and Soviet cosmonaut Valery Bykovsky, Kohllner served as communications operator and support crewman from mission control at Kalinin, near Moscow.

Kohllner was born September 29, 1939, in Strassfurt, Germany. In 1961 he graduated from the Franz Mering Air Force School in Kamenz, and served as a pilot, logging over 1,000 hours of flying time in jets. He spent several years in the Soviet Union as a student at the Yuri Gagarin (Red Banner) Air Force Academy, graduating in 1970. In April 1978 he and Jaehn were selected for cosmonaut training.

After returning to Germany Kollner became director of the Mering Air Force School. He is now retired.

Messerschmid, Ernst Willi
1945–

Ernst Messerschmid was a payload specialist aboard Spacelab D-1 (Deustchland 1), Space Shuttle Mission 61-A, the first spaceflight to be controlled by a country other than the United States or the USSR.

For 7 days Messerschmid and 7 fellow astronauts (D-1 had a crew of 8, the largest sent into space in one vehicle) performed 76 different experiments, most of them concerning materials processing and life sciences. The flight was unique because the scientific payloads were directed from the mission control center of the DFVLR (Federal German Aerospace Research Establishment) at Oberpfaffenhoffen, near Munich, West Germany. The German control center was known as "D-Eins Munchen" during the flight, for which the DFVLR had paid NASA $75 million.

Messerschmid himself suffered mild symptoms of space adaptation syndrome, one of the subjects he was sent into space to study. He also kept tabs on the adaptation to spaceflight of a fruit fly—named "Willi"—who escaped from one of the experiments.

Messerschmid was born May 21, 1945, in the city of Reutlingen, Germany. He passed the entrance examinations for the Technisches Gymnasium in Stuttgart in 1965, but was drafted and spent 2 years in the army. He studied physics at Tubingen and Bonn Universities, receiving his diploma in 1972 and his doctorate in 1976.

Messerschmid has been a scientist at the CERN high energy physics institute in Geneva and at the Brookhaven National Laboratory in New York. From 1978 to 1987 he was a full-time employee of the DFVLR. He was selected as a D-1 payload specialist in December 1982.

Since 1987 Messerschmid has been a professor and director of the Institute for Space Science at Stuttgart University.

Thiele, Gerhard Paul Julius

1953–

German physicist Gerhard Thiele was a backup payload specialist for STS-55, the Spacelab D-2 mission launched aboard the orbiter Columbia in April 1993. Thiele and fellow backup Renate Brummer supported the 10-day mission from the Germany flight control center at Oberpfaffenhoffen, near Munich.

In July 1996 Thiele was selected by DARA, the German Space Agency, and DLR, the German Aerospace Research Establishment, to train as an international NASA astronaut candidate. In the summer of 1998 he qualified as a Shuttle mission specialist and International Space Station crewmember. He is currently assigned to the computer support branch of the astronaut office.

Thiele was born September 2, 1953, in Heidenheim-Brenz, Germany, though he considers Bruhl, Nordrhein-Westfalen, to be his hometown. He graduated from secondary school in Ludwigsburg, then served as a patrol boat crewman in the Federal German Navy from 1972 to 1976.

He entered the Ludwig Maximilians University in Munich after leaving the service, studying physics there for 2 years. From 1978 to 1982 he was at the Ruprecht Karls University in Heidelberg. He received a diploma in physics in 1980 from the Max Planck Institute and in July 1985 a doctorate from the Institute for Environmental Physics at Heidelberg University.

After receiving his doctorate Thiele was a visiting scientist at Princeton University. He was selected as a German astronaut in August 1987 and began training at the DLR in 1988. He was assigned to the Spacelab D-2 program in 1990.

Following the D-2 mission Thiele served with the DLR on its strategic planning group, and also as a member of the International Academy of Astronautics subcommittee on lunar development. In 1995 he was named as head of the DLR's crew training center at Cologne, Germany.

Walpot, Heike

1960–

Physician Heike Walpot is a member of the German astronaut team of the German Space Research Institute (DLR). Originally selected in 1987, she underwent astronaut training for a year, then worked as a German crew representative to the Hermes spaceplane program. In 1992 to she was assigned to serve as a crew interface coordinator for the Spacelab D-2 mission, launched as STS-55 in April 1993.

With D-2 veteran Ulrich Walter, Walpot began Russian language lessons in April 1995 for a possible flight to Mir, but Schlegel was the one selected to serve as backup to Reinhold Ewald on the Mir-23 crew (February–March 1997).

Walpot was born June 19, 1960, in Dusseldorf. She attended St. Leonard secondary school in Aachen, then became a medical student at Aachen University. She received her medical degree in 1987.

Between 1980 and 1983 Walpot worked at St. Franciscus Hospital in Aachen, then became a student assistant in the pathology department of the university clinic. Since 1987 she has been a resident in the anaesthesiology department of Aachen University.

Walpot was for many years a member of the German national swimming team, competing in the 1976 Olympics.

In August 1987 Walpot was one of 5 German astronauts team selected as possible Shuttle payload specialist for the Spacelab D-2 mission. The group was dissolved in November 1993 and its members redeployed to other areas of the German space research establishment. Walpot, holder of a commercial pilot's license, became a pilot with Lufthansa Airlines.

Walter, Ulrich

1954–

Physicist Ulrich Walter was a payload specialist in the crew of STS-55, the Spacelab D-2 mission, launched aboard the orbiter Columbia in April 1993 following a delay caused by an aborted launch attempt on March 22. Spacelab D-2 featured experiments in space manufacturing and medicine as well as tests of a German robotic arm called Rotex and a new system to involve ground-based scientists in onboard experiments (Halop). Walter was part of the blue team with commander Steve Nagel, pilot Tom Henricks, and mission specialist Jerry Ross, working 12-hour shifts throughout the mission.

Walter was born February 9, 1954, in Iserlohn, where he graduated from Markisches Gymnasium in 1972. Following 2 years as a volunteer with the Federal German Armed Forces, he enrolled at the University of Cologne. He received his diploma in solid-state physics in 1980 and his doctorate in 1985.

After receiving his doctorate Walter held a position at the Argonne National Laboratory in Chicago, Illinois (1985–86) and a fellowship at the University of California, Berkeley (1986-87). He was selected as a German astronaut in August 1987.

He is holder of a private pilot's license.

Following the disbanding of the German astronaut office in November 1993 Walter remained with the DLR its remote sensing division at Oberpfaffenhofen, Germany. He was briefly a candidate in 1995 for a later German Spacelab.

He left the DLR in 1998 to join IBM.

Great Britain

Boyle, Anthony Hugh

1941–

Royal Signals officer Tony Boyle was named in March 1984 as one of 4 British payload specialist training for the deployment of Skynet satellites on Space Shuttle missions. But a security breach in his former command in West Germany forced him to drop out of the space program in 1985.

Boyle was born January 18, 1941, in Kidderminster. He attended the Army's Welbeck College and St. Catharine's College, Cambridge, where he earned a B.A. in mechanical sciences in 1965. He later added an M.A.

He served as a military communications officer in the Far East and in Germany, and also held a position in the Ministry of Defense. He was commander of the 20th Armored Brigade Headquarters and Signals Squadron in West Germany prior to becoming an instructor at the Royal Military College of Science in Shrivenham, his post at the time he was chosen for space training.

Boyle was later promoted to the rank of major general, and became director-general for command, control, communications, and information as well as Army Signal Officer-in-Chief, Ministry of Defense, London.

Farrimond, Richard Alfred

1947–

Royal Signals officer Richard Farrimond was assigned as backup to fellow British payload specialist Nigel Wood for Shuttle Mission 61-H. Originally scheduled for launch in the summer of 1986, Mission 61-H was to have deployed the first Skynet 4 communications satellite. However, Mission 61-H was canceled following the Challenger disaster.

Farrimond was added to the group of four previously selected British Shuttle payload specialists in June 1984 when Lieutenant Colonel Tony Boyle, also of Signals, was recalled to other duties.

Farrimond was born September 15, 1947, in Birkenhead, Cheshire. He was educated at Clifton College in Bristol, and at Welbeck College, then entered the Sandhurst military college, graduating in 1967.

From 1968 to 1982 he served at a variety of signals posts in Germany, Northern Ireland, and Canada, and also did further study in telecommunications engineering at King's College, Cambridge, and the Royal Military College of Science at Shrivenham. At the time of his selection as a British astronaut, Farrimond was commander of the 8th Infantry Brigade Headquarters and Signals Squadron in Northern Ireland.

After the cancellation of Mission 61-H Farrimond retired from military service. He worked for British Aerospace, and currently works for Matra Marconi.

Holmes, Christopher John Nicholas

1950–

Physicist Christopher Holmes was assigned as the backup payload specialist for Shuttle Mission 71-C, originally scheduled for launch in 1987. The British Skynet 4B communications satellite was to have been deployed from the orbiter Columbia during that mission. But the Challenger disaster in January 1986 forced the British government to launch Skynet 4B on an Ariane expendable rocket instead.

Holmes was born July 10, 1950, in London and attended Queen Mary College there, earning an honors degree in physics in 1972. He joined the Ministry of Defense at that time, as a procurement executive and satellite specialist in the field of military telecommunications. When selected for space training in 1984 he was deputy project manager for Skynet 4.

More recently Holmes has worked for the British National Space Centre in London.

Longhurst, Peter Hervey

1943–

Royal Navy engineer Peter Longhurst was assigned as the prime payload specialist for the deployment of the Skynet 4B satellite on a Shuttle mission originally scheduled for launch in early 1987. That mission was canceled in the spring of 1986 following the Challenger disaster.

Longhurst was born March 8, 1943, in Staines, Middlesex, though he spent much of his youth in Devon. He attended Ardling School and Dartmouth, then spent a year at sea as a midshipman. He graduated from the Royal Naval Engineering College at Manadon, earning a B.S. in electrical engineering. He then served in a series of Navy berths as a weapons engineer specialist on frigates and as a teacher. He joined the Skynet program in 1981 as the Ministry of Defense director of naval operational requirements.

It was widely rumored in London newspapers in 1983 that Longhurst, a specialist in the Skynet satellite, had already been chosen to be the first British astronaut. The publication of those rumors apparently roused the competing services to action. When the Ministry of Defense announced its astronauts in early 1984, there were four: one from each of the services, and one civilian.

Longhurst has since retired from the Royal Navy and is a cattle farmer in Somerset, England.

Mace, Timothy Kristian Charles

1955–

Royal Air Force pilot Tim Mace was the backup cosmonaut researcher to Helen Sharman, who became the first Briton in space in May 1991. Sharman was a member of the crew of Soyuz TM-12 and spent 8 days aboard the Mir space station. Mace supported the mission from the flight control center at Kaliningrad (now Korolev).

Mace was born November 20, 1955, in Catterick, Yorkshire, England. Mace attended the Lancaster Royal Grammar School, leaving in 1974.

While at school Mace had received a scholarship from the Royal Navy. This allowed him to qualify as a pilot at the age of 17—3 years before he received his driver's license.

In 1974 Mace joined the Army Air Corps and was enrolled at the Military University at Shrivenham. He graduated in 1977 with a B.S. in aeronautical engineering. He then underwent training as a reconnaissance and helicopter pilot, earning his wings in October 1979. For the next 7 years he served on classified assignments in "all theatres of operation except the Far East." From 1986 to 1989 he was a flying instructor.

Mace has logged over 2,800 hours of flying time, most of it in the Lynx and Gazelle helicopters, and hundreds of parachute jumps, including 2,600 freefalls. (He was a member of the British National Parachuting Team from 1985 to 1989.)

He applied for the Juno program soon after its announcement by Antequera, Ltd., and Glavkosmos in June 1989. In November 1989 he was selected as one of 4 finalists.

Mace was later a finalist for the 1992 ESA astronaut group, but was not selected.

Married to Yelena Zholobova, daughter of Russian cosmonaut Vitaly Zholobov, Mace now lives in South Africa, where he serves as a helicopter pilot for South African President Nelson Mandela.

Sharman, Helen Patricia
1963–

Chemist Helen Sharman became the first Briton in space when she served as cosmonaut researcher aboard Soyuz TM-12 in May 1991.

Along with Soviet commander Anatoly Artsebarsky and flight engineer Sergei Krikalev, Sharman joined the Mir resident crew of Viktor Afanasyev and Musa Manarov. The docking was piloted manually by Artsebarsky after a guidance failure.

During her 7 days aboard Mir Sharman conducted medical and Earth observation experiments for British scientists while also contacting schoolchildren by radio during the mission. One awkward moment arose when commander Artsebarsky was quoted during the mission as saying, "Women have no business being in space." Sharman graciously ignored the remark, which was later reported to have been a "misquotation."

Sharman was born May 30, 1963, in Sheffield, England. Following graduation from the Jordanthorpe Comprehensive School there in 1981 she entered the University of Sheffield, receiving a B.S. in chemistry in 1984.

In July 1984 she went to work for MOV, a division of General Electric, in Hammersmith, London, as an electronics engineer. She also did further study toward a Ph.D. at Birbeck College.

She left MOV in August 1987 to join the Mars candy company in Slough, where she did research into the chemical and physical properties of chocolate.

When the British company Antequara, Ltd., announced in July 1989 that it had reached agreement with the Soviet space organization Glavkosmos to send a British citizen into space, Sharman applied. In November of that year she was selected as one of the 4 finalists. Early in 1990 she and Major Timothy Mace enrolled at the Gagarin cosmonaut training center near Moscow.

In 1994 Sharman published an account of her Mir mission, *Seize the Moment*.

Since her flight she has worked as a television commentator and public speaker on spaceflight.

RESEARCH IN SPACE

by Helen Sharman

(British chemist Helen Sharman, employed by the Mars candy company, spent 8 days in space aboard Mir in May 1991. Among her tasks was the supervision of a package of twelve different scientific experiments, several of which she describes here.)

It was my job, as a scientifically qualified cosmonaut, to oversee a number of experiments during my short stay on Mir. I carried out a range of them while I was there, from medical tests to physical and chemical research.

I conducted the medical tests on myself, starting with the wearing of electrodes on my heart for a continuous 24-hour period. This measured the way my heart was beating in comparison with my pre-flight and post-flight recordings.

Also of interest to medical researchers is the way mental coordination and reaction speed might vary before, during and after spaceflight. An experiment called "Prognos" allowed me to monitor this through measured reactions to a series of randomized lights. These appeared in different patterns and combinations. I would memorize the pattern; when future patterns appeared I would have to remember the first and how it differed from what had just appeared, or be able to spot it when it appeared again. The instrument recorded whether I was right and how long I took.

I also took samples of my own blood by pricking the end of my finger. I had to take about twelve samples a day, so you can imagine that by the time I returned to Earth my fingers bore an uncanny resemblance to pin-cushions!

An incidental point to these medical experiments was the fact that I was only in space for a total of 8 days. Most of the Soviet cosmonauts go up for extended periods, usually several months, so they now have many test results on long-stay subjects, but not on shorter-term people. My work was intended to help fill this gap.

One of the minor problems associated with spacecraft is that in "weightless" conditions dust does not settle. Because of the constant human activity aboard Mir, the movement of so many objects around the station, so much food being consumed, hair and whiskers being snipped off, epidermal flaking and so on, the air becomes pretty dusty. Cosmonauts tend to sneeze a lot: I found myself sneezing an average of about twenty to thirty times an hour.* The researchers were interested in the amount of dust found throughout the station and what was in it. I took samples of air at various in the station, collected the filter papers and brought them back.

As part of the biological experiments I grew some what seedlings, researching into the possibility one day of growing food in space. By the time I was able to set up this experiment the seedlings had been "weightless" and in the dark for 2 days, so their roots and shoots were all over the place. I put them by a light, and when I went back twenty-four hours later to water them, all the shoots were growing towards the light, while the roots remained chaotic. For similar reasons I took some potato roots up to the station, trying to learn about early growth phases in these. (I have since found out that potatoes have been grown from the tissue culture I brought back.)

---

* On Mir the air is constantly moved, filtered and cooled by the ventilating fans, but much dust remains. A similar situation exists on the American Shuttles.

Another aspect of being in space is that although you may remain within the Earth's normal magnetic field, the altitude does introduce experimentally significant differences. I had other seeds that I grew in a non-uniform magnetic field, placing magnets around them at certain positions. I first had to start the seeds growing in water, then I halted the growth in a fixating medium, so I knew exactly how long they had been growing and what the orientation of the magnetic field had been.

Although I did no actual work with them, I took some snails up with me, kept them in a part of the station that was subject to a minimum of vibrations, then brought them back.

We took up a tiny lemon tree, so small as to almost be a bonsai. The idea of this was to see if higher plants can actually be kept alive in space. This will be important in the future if we want to be self-sufficient in space, such as during a long journey to Mars or one of the other planets. We know we can grow seeds, but producing fruit or flowers inside a spacecraft is still a largely unknown quantity.

Wood, Nigel Richard
1949–

British test pilot Nigel Wood, Royal Air Force, was scheduled to become Great Britain's first astronaut in the summer of 1986, supervising the deployment of a British satellite during Shuttle Mission 61-H. The Challenger disaster in January of that year forced the British government to find another launch vehicle for the satellite, Skynet 4A.

Wood and his backup, Richard Farrimond, reported to the NASA Johnson Space Center in early February 1986, just one week after the explosion of the Shuttle Challenger. They completed stand-alone payload specialist training.

Wood was born July 21, 1949, in York and educated at Brockenhurst Grammar School and Bristol University, where he received a B.S. with first-class honors in aeronautical engineering. He joined the RAF in 1968 at the same time he entered Bristol, and earned his wings at RAF Cranwell in 1972.

From 1974 to 1976 Wood was based at RAH Gutersloh in Germany, where in addition to regular duties as a Lightning pilot, he was part of the "Cobra Five" air demonstration team. He was then chosen for test pilot training and served at the French Istres center near Marseille (1977–78), the RAF center in Farnborough (1978–80), and the Air Force Test Pilot School at Edwards AFB, California (1980–83). At Edwards he observed at 6 Shuttle landings.

At the time of his selection as a Shuttle payload specialist in March 1984, Wood was based at RAF Binbrook in Lincolnshire.

From 1986 to 1988 Wood served with the RAF press team, then attended the Bracknell staff college. Following 2 years at Ministry of Defense headquarters in London, Group Captain Wood was assigned to the Experimental Test Pilot Center at Boscombe Down, where he is currently chief test pilot.

Hungary

Farkas, Bertalan

1949–

Bertalan Farkas was the cosmonaut-researcher aboard Soyuz 36 in May 1980, becoming the first citizen of Hungary to make a spaceflight. He and Soviet commander Valery Kubasov docked with the Salyut 6 space station, visiting cosmonauts Popov and Ryumin, during their 8-day flight. Kubasov and Farkas were originally to have flown in July of 1979, but the Soyuz 33 abort that April suspended new manned Soyuz launches for several months.

Farkas was born August 2, 1949, in Gyulahaza, Hungary. As a secondary school student he joined the Hungarian Defense Union, a junior civil defense organization, where he learned to parachute jump, and eventually became a light plane pilot. Upon graduation from school in 1967 he joined the air force, enrolling in the Gyorgy Kilian Aeronautical College in Szolnok.

Following 2 years of instruction at the Kilian school and 3 more years in the Soviet Union, Farkas became an air force pilot. From 1972 to 1978 he served as a fighter pilot and instructor.

Farkas and his close friend Bela Magyari were chosen as Hungary's Interkosmos pilots in 1977, and reported to the Gagarin Cosmonaut Training Center near Moscow the following April.

Upon his return to Hungary Farkas became a researcher at the Polytechnical University in Budapest. With cosmonaut Vladimir Kovalenok he took part in "Kursk 85," a series of Earth resources studies conducted by the Salyut 7 crew of Dzhanibekov and Savinykh. Farkas later earned his candidate of technical sciences degree.

Colonel Farkas is currently the air attache at the Hungarian embassy in Washington, D.C.

Magyari, Bela

1949–

Bela Magyari is the Hungarian air force pilot who served as backup to Bertalan Farkas, the cosmonaut-researcher of Soyuz 36 in May 1980. During the 8-day mission Magyari served as communications operator at the flight control center in Kaliningrad (now Korolev).

Magyari was born August 8, 1949, in Kiskunfelegyhaza, Hungary. He graduated from the Gyorgy Kilian Aeronautical College in 1969 and, following 3 years of additional instruction in the Soviet Union, served as a fighter pilot with the Hungarian air force.

Magyari and Bertalan Farkas, who had been close friends since 1965, were the two candidates chosen as Hungary's representatives in the Interkosmos program in 1977. They reported to the Gagarin Center in April 1978.

When he returned to Hungary in 1980, Magyari, like Farkas, enrolled at the Polytechnical University in Budapest. He graduated as a mechanical engineer in 1987 and is currently involved in aerospace research.

India

Bhat, Nagpathi, Chidambar "N.C."

1948–

Indian space scientist N. C. Bhat was selected as a Shuttle payload specialist candidate in November 1985 for the future deployment of the Insat 1-C communications satellite. Then scheduled for Shuttle Mission 61-I in September 1986, the Insat deployment was first postponed, then canceled following the Challenger disaster in January of that year. Neither Bhat nor fellow Insat PS candidate Rad Nair flew in space.

Bhat was born January 1, 1948, in North Kanara, Karnataka State, India. He earned a B.S. from Arts & Science College in Sirsi, and a B.E. in mechanical engineering from Engineering College in Gulbarga (1970). He did graduate work in mechanical engineering at the Indian Institute of Science in Bangalore, receiving an M.S. in 1972.

After working for a year as an engineer with Jyoti, Ltd., Bhat joined ISRO, the Indian Space Agency, in July 1973. He was a satellite engineer on the Aryabhata and Bhaskara programs when selected as an Insat payload specialist.

Bhat later became head of a design and development section at the ISRO Satellite Center, Bangalore.

Malhotra, Ravish

1943–

Squadron Leader Ravish Malhotra of the Indian air force served as backup cosmonaut-researcher for Soyuz T-11 in April 1984, during which fellow pilot Rakesh Sharma became the first Indian in space.

Malhotra was born December 25, 1943, in Lahore, India, but grew up in Calcutta. He joined the Indian air force, enrolling as a cadet at the National Defense Academy in Khadakvasala. Following graduation in 1963 he became a fighter pilot, serving in the India-Pakistan conflicts in 1964 and 1971.

In 1974 Malhotra attended the U.S. Air Force Test Pilot School at Edwards AFB, California.

At the time of his selection as a cosmonaut in September 1982, Malhotra was commandant of the Bangalore test pilot school. He had logged 3,400 hours of flying time. Upon his return to India he was stationed again at Bangalore test center.

Nair, P. Radhakrishnan

1942–

Indian space scientist Rad Nair was selected in November 1985 as a payload specialist candidate for the deployment of the Insat 1-C communications satellite from the U.S. Shuttle. The Insat deployment, originally scheduled for Shutte Mission 61-I in September 1986, was postponed, then canceled because of the Challenger

disaster in January of that year. Nair and fellow Insat payload specialist N. C. Bhat never flew in space.

Paramaswaren Radhakrishnan Nair was born October 2, 1943, in Trivandrum, Kerala State, India, and attended University College in that city, receiving a B.S. in physics and mathematics (1963) and an M.S. in physics (1965).

In April 1966 Rad joined ISRO, the Indian Space Research Organization, where he worked as an engineer for several Indian satellite programs, including Rohini, Aryabhata, and Apple. He later became head of test and evaluation for launch vehicles and other projects at the Vikram Sarabhai Space Center in Trivandrum. More recently he has been deputy project director for the GSLV launch vehicle there.

Sharma, Rakesh

1949–

Rakesh Sharma became the first citizen of India in space when he joined Soviet cosmonauts Yuri Malyshev and Gennady Strekalov in the crew of Soyuz T-11 in April 1984. Sharma, who acted as cosmonaut-researcher, spent 8 days in space performing scientific experiments devised by Indian scientists. The T-11 cosmonauts worked with the Salyut 7 resident crew, cosmonauts Kizim, Solovyov, and Atkov, launched in February.

Sharma was born January 13, 1949, in Patiala, India. At the age of 15 he qualified for the Kharakvasla National Defense Academy while an undergraduate at the Nizam College in Hyderabad. Commissioned in 1970, he flew 21 combat missions in MiG-21s during the 1971 India-Pakistan conflict. He later attended the Bangalore test pilot school.

For several years prior to becoming a cosmonaut Sharma served as a test pilot at Bangalore. He has logged over 1,600 hours of flying time a number of different aircraft, including several types of MiG fighters, Hunter, Kiron, Ajeet, and Marut.

Sharma and fellow Indian pilot Ravish Malhotra arrived at the Gagarin Center to begin cosmonaut training in September 1982. Following his flight Sharma returned to India and resumed his military test pilot career. In 1988 he was injured while ejecting from an aircraft, but recovered. He is currently a senior test pilot with Hindustan Aeronautics in the city of Bombay.

Indonesia

Akbar, Taufik

1951–

Indonesian telecommunications engineer Taufik Akbar was selected in October 1985 as alternate payload specialist for Shuttle Mission 61-M. Then scheduled for launch in the fall of 1986, Mission 61-M was to have deployed Indonesia's Palapa communications satellite under the supervision of payload specialist Pratiwi Sudarmono.

The mission was canceled following the January 1986 Challenger disaster, however.

Akbar was born January 8, 1951, in Medan, Indonesia. He studied at the Bandung Institute of Technology, graduating with a telecommunications degree in 1975. He later studied at Hughes Aircraft in El Segundo, California, and at the University of Concordia in Montreal, Quebec, Canada.

He is currently employed by Peruntel, the Indonesian government's telecommunications company.

Sudarmono, Pratiwi

1952–

Indonesian microbiologist Pratiwi Sudarmono was assigned in October 1985 as prime payload specialist for Shuttle Mission 61-M. Then scheduled for launch in the fall of 1986, Mission 61-M was to have deployed Indonesia's Palapa communications satellite. But the Challenger disaster in January 1986 forced a postponement, and finally a cancellation, of the Palapa Shuttle deployment and Sudarmono's flight with it. The Indonesian satellite was eventually launched aboard a Delta II launch vehicle.

Sudarmono was born July 31, 1952, in Sanduko, Indonesia. She graduated from high school in Jakarta in 1971, then attended the University of Indonesia, receiving a medical degree in 1976 and a microbiology degree in 1980. She earned her Ph.D. in genetic engineering and biotechnology from the University of Osaka, Japan, in 1984.

At the time of her selection as a payload specialist candidate, Sudarmono was a lecturer in microbiology at the University of Indonesia. She is currently a researcher there, as well as a consultant to the Bandung Institute of Technology.

Israel

Mayo, Itzhak

1954–

Israeli Air Force test pilot Itzhak Mayo is assigned as a backup payload specialist for the flight of a multispectral camera that will study deserts, including those of his homeland, on a 1999 Shuttle mission. Mayo began PS training at the NASA Johnson Space Center with fellow Israeli test pilot Ilon Ramon in July 1998.

Mayo was born September 14, 1954, in the village of Kfar Hittim, Israel. Following graduation from high school in 1972, he was drafted into the Israel Defense Forces. From 1979 to 1988 he attended Ben Gurion University in Beer Sheva where he received a B.S. in 1986 and an M.S. in 1988 in physics. His special areas of study were spectroscopy and chemical lasers.

On his first tour of military duty in the early 1970s, Mayo was a weapons system operator and navigator on F-4 aircraft. In 1988–99 he qualified as an F-16D pilot, then joined the IAF Flight Test Center as head of its avionics section.

Lieutenant Colonel Mayo has logged over 3,200 hours of flying time. He was selected as a payload specialist by the Israel Ministry of Defense in April 1997.

Ramon, Ilon

1954–

Israeli Air Force test pilot Ilon Ramon is scheduled to serve as a payload specialist on a 1999 flight of the Space Shuttle. In July 1998 Ramon and his backup, Itzhak Mayo, arrived at the NASA Johnson Space Center to begin training for a flight with a multispectral camera designed to record desert aerosol.

Ramon was born June 20, 1954, In Tel Aviv, Israel, where he graduated form high school. From 1983 to 1987 he attended the University of Tel Aviv where he received a B.S. in electronics and computer in engineering in 1987.

Serving with the Israeli Air Force after graduation from high school, Ramon qualified as an A-4 pilot in 1974 and spent 2 years flying the aircraft in an operational squadron. In 1976 he cross-trained to the Mirage III and flew that aircraft until 1980, when he became a member of the IAF's F-16 establishment team, qualifying on that aircraft at Hill Air Force Base, Utah. From 1981 to 1983 Ramon was deputy commander for the F-16 Squadron.

Following 4 years at Tel Aviv University, Ramon returned to operational flying in 1988 with the IAF's F-14 Phantom Squadron, then commanded the F-16 Squadron from 1990 to 1992. Since that time he has held posts in the IAF's Flight Test Center, most recently as head of operational requirements for weapons testing and acquisition.

Ramon was selected by the Israel Ministry of Defense as payload specialist candidates in April 1997.

Italy

Guidoni, Umberto

1954–

Umberto Guidoni was a payload specialist aboard STS-75, the February 1996 flight of the orbiter Columbia that made the second attempt to deploy Italy's Tethered Satellite System. The TSS experiment was designed to demonstrate the ability of an extremely long tether to produce electricity as it passes through the Earth's magnetic field. The first attempt, aboard STS-46 in July–August 1992, failed. (Guidoni was the alternate PS for that mission.)

During the STS-75 attempt the tethered satellite was reeled out to 12 miles, less than a mile short of its full 12.8 mile length. It generated almost 3 times as much energy as scientists had predicted, then suddenly broke, causing

the crew of the Columbia some nervous moments as they maneuvered the orbiter away from the tether and its satellite. The failure was later traced to a break in the insulation of the tether cable.

In July 1996 Guidoni was selected by the Italian Space Agency to undergo astronaut training. He reported to the Johnson Space Center that August, and in April 1998 qualified as a Shuttle mission specialist.

Guidoni was born August 18, 1954, in Rome, where he graduated from secondary school in 1973. He received a B.S. and Ph.D. in astrophysics from the University of Rome in 1978.

In 1979-80 Guidoni won a postdoctoral fellowship from CNEN, the Italian Nuclear Energy Commission, then went on to work at the solar energy division of the National Committee for Renewable Energy. In 1984 he joined the staff of the Space Physics Institute, part of Italy's Center for National Research, and designed ground support and data processing equipment for experiments to be flown aboard the Tethered Satellite. In 1988 he became project scientist for the RETE experiment.

He was named an Italian Space Agency Shuttle astronaut candidate in May 1989 and designated alternate payload specialist for STS-46 in September 1991. His assignment as prime PS was announced in October 1993.

Guidoni is currently working in the robotics branch of the NASA astronaut office while awaiting a flight assignment.

Malerba, Franco

1946–

Franco Malerba was the Italian Space Agency payload specialist for STS-46, the flight of the Tethered Satellite System in July–August 1992. The TSS was a half-ton ball intended to be reeled out from the Shuttle to a distance of 12 miles. The process would, among other goals, demonstrate a new space-based power system. But the TSS deployment went awry and was returned to the orbiter Atlantis after reaching a distance of only 300 yards.

Malerba was born October 10, 1946, in Busalla, Italy. He received an engineering degree in 1970 from Genoa

University, and a doctor of physics from the same institution in 1974.

During his academic career he held research fellowships at the Italian National Research Council (CNR) and at the NATO Saclant Research Center in La Spezia, Italy.

In 1974 and 1975 Malerba was a visiting scientist at the National Institutes of Health in Bethesda, Maryland, performing research in neurophysiology. He joined the Digital Equipment Company in France in 1975, transferring a year later to DEC's special computer systems group in Milan.

From 1978 to 1982 he was Italy's candidate payload specialist for the Spacelab 1 mission while remaining an employee of DEC. He joined the ASI astronaut team in February 1989.

Following his flight aboard STS-46, Malerba was elected as an Italian representative to the European Parliament, based in Brussels.

Urbani, Luca

1957–

Luca Urbani, a lieutenant colonel in the medical corps of the Italian Air Force, was an alternate payload specialist for the Life and Microgravity Spacelab mission, launched on STS-78 in June 1996. This flight of the orbiter Columbia carried a crew of 7, which conducted over 40 studies in space medicine and lasted a record 17 days, serving as a forerunner for future International Space Station missions.

Urbani was born May 11, 1957, in Rome, Italy, and educated at the medical school of the University of Rome. He received his M.D. in 1981, then served a 3-year residency at the university. From 1984 to 1989 he was a resident at the University of Naples.

Beginning in 1983 Urbani served as a medical officer in the Italian military, first in the army (1983–84), then in the air force. He has been stationed at the Vigna di Vallo and Pratica di Mare air bases in Rome. In 1989 Urbani completed the aerospace medical course at the USAF School of Aerospace Medicine, Brooks AFB, San Antonio, Texas.

Urbani has been a glider pilot since the age of 18, logging over 2,500 hours in glider aircraft and winning several international medals. He is also an airplane pilot with 250 hours of flying time.

He was a candidate for the 1992 ESA astronaut selection, and has served as a test crewman for several of ESA's ground-based long duration spaceflight simulations, including the Experimental Campaign for European Manned Space Infrastructure (EXEMSI) in July–November 1992, the Human Behavior during Extended Spaceflight program (HUBES) in 1994, and the Columbus Utilization Simulation in February 1994.

Japan

Akiyama, Toyohiro

1942–

TV newsman Toyohiro Akiyama become the first journalist and the first citizen of Japan to go into space when he served as cosmonaut-researcher aboard the Soyuz TM-11 mission to the Mir space station in December 1990.

Since Akiyama's seat had been purchased for a reported $12 million by the Japanese television network TBS, he was the first commercial passenger to fly aboard a Soviet spacecraft. (Several American commercial payload specialists had flown aboard the Shuttle as early as 1984.)

The project began in the spring of 1989 when TBS, searching for a way to celebrate its fortieth anniversary, hit upon the idea of sending one of its employees into space to broadcast a weeklong series of special reports. Following the conclusion of negotiations with Glavkosmos, the Soviet space agency, medical examinations were begun. At first not one of the 163 candidates passed; the rules were relaxed, and seven TBS staffers were sent to the Gagarin Cosmonaut Training Center for further testing.

In December 1990 Akiyama and camera operator Rioko Kikuchi were chosen in spite of the fact that

Akiyama had a four-pack a day cigarette habit, and Kikuchi still had her appendix.

In August 1990 Akiyama was designated the prime candidate and teamed with Soviet commander Viktor Afanasyev and flight engineer Musa Manarov. With logos of TBS corporate sponsors such as American Express Japan, Sony, and Minolta blazoned on the side of the Soyuz launcher, the mission began on December 2, 1990. Two days later Soyuz TM-11 docked with the Mir complex, where cosmonauts Gennady Manakov and Gennady Strekalov were completing a 4-month mission.

TBS's national ratings soared during the first days of Akiyama's flight, even though his broadcasts emphasized the unpleasantness of his situation: he craved a cigarette, he had forgotten to pack enough underwear, and he was suffering from space adaptation syndrome. He described the latter as just like having a hangover. However, he was also able to describe the view of Mt. Fuji from orbit, and went on to describe the islands of Japan as looking "moss-covered" from that altitude.

Halfway through the mission TBS's ratings slipped back to their preflight levels. Akiyama returned to Earth on December 10, 1990, in the Soyuz TM-10 spacecraft with Manakov and Strekalov. His first words back on Earth were "I'm hungry."

Toyohiro Akiyama was born July 22, 1942, in the Setagaya Ward of the city of Tokyo. He was educated at International Christian University's Department of Social Science before going to work as a journalist.

At TBS Akiyama has been a news director for specials and for foreign reports. At the time of his selection in 1989 he was Washington, D.C., bureau chief for TBS. He volunteered to give up his smoking habit for the chance to make a spaceflight.

Doi, Takao
1954–

Japanese aerospace engineer Takao Doi was a mission specialist in the crew of STS-87. This November 1997 flight of the orbiter Columbia carried the fourth U.S. Microgravity Payload and a crew of 6. Doi took part in a pair of EVAs, one of them an unscheduled retrieval of the errant Spartan 201 free-flying payload, which had been improperly deployed by the crew. STS-87 lasted a total of 16 days.

Previously Doi served as a backup payload specialist for STS-47, the Japanese Spacelab mission flown in September 1992. During this 8-day flight of the orbiter Endeavour a crew of 7, including Japanese payload specialist Mamoru Mohri, performed 43 experiments in space manufacturing and life sciences.

Doi was born September 18, 1954, in Minamitama-Gun, Tokyo, and attended the University of Tokyo, where he received his B.S. (1978), M.S. (1980) and Ph.D. (1983) in aeronautical engineering.

From 1983 to 1985 he served as a research associate with the Japanese Institute of Space and Astronautical Science. He then joined the NASA Lewis Research Center in Cleveland, Ohio, as a propulsion engineer. He was at Lewis in August 1985 when he was first selected as a Spacelab J payload specialist candidate. Following the STS-47 flight Doi returned to the JISAS.

In 1992 he was a candidate for assignment to the second International Microgravity Spacelab mission, which ultimately went to Chiaki Naito. In January 1995 Doi was selected as an international astronaut candidate by NASA, qualifying as a a Shuttle mission specialist in the spring of 1996. He served in the vehicle systems/operations branch of the astronaut office until selected for the crew of STS-87 in November 1996.

Kikuchi, Ryoko
1964–

TV camera operator Ryoko Kikuchi was the backup to Toyohiro Akiyama, the first Japanese space traveler. Akiyama was cosmonaut-researcher in the crew of Soyuz TM-12, launched on December 2, 1990, and spent a week aboard the space station Mir.

Akiyama and Kikuchi were both employees of the Japanese television network TBS, which paid for the flight as part of a promotion to celebrate its fortieth anniversary.

Kikuchi was born September 15, 1964, in Zama City, Kanagawa Prefecture, Japan. She attended the Tokyo University of Foreign Studies, graduating from its Department of Chinese Studies. She went to work in the news division of TBS (Tokyo Broadcasting System), becoming the only female camera operator in the company. In addition to an assignment in China, she also worked on the coverage of the 1988 Seoul Olympics.

Following the signing of an agreement between TBS and Glavkosmos, the Soviet space agency, in March 1989, 163 employees of TBS and its affiliated companies applied to become a cosmonaut. Eventually 7 candidates were able to pass the medical screenings. Kikuchi and Akiyama were named the finalists on September 18, 1989, and arrived at the Gagarin Center for training on October 1.

On November 26, 1990, less than a week before the TM-12 launch, Kikuchi underwent an operation to remove her appendix. Fortunately she had already been designated as backup to Akiyama. Nevertheless, she was present at the Baikonur Cosmodrome for the TM-12 launch.

Kikuchi still works in television production for TBS.

Mohri, Mamoru Mark
1948–

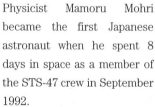

Physicist Mamoru Mohri became the first Japanese astronaut when he spent 8 days in space as a member of the STS-47 crew in September 1992.

Journalist Toyohiro Akiyama was the first citizen of Japan to make a spaceflight, aboard the Soviet Soyuz TM-11 in 1990, but he was strictly a passenger. Mohri was the scientific payload specialist in a crew of 7 that conducted 43 experiments in space manufacturing and life sciences.

The Spacelab J mission, known to its sponsor, the National Space Development Agency of Japan, as "Fuwatto 92" ("Floating 92"), had originally been scheduled for launch in 1988 and was delayed for four years by the Challenger disaster and recovery.

Mohri took part in the operation of a special furnace that forged glass using sound waves, and also observed several biological tests, including the fertilization of frog eggs in weightlessness.

In July 1996 Mohri was selected by NASDA as an astronaut candidate. He reported to the Johnson Space Center in August of that year and in the summer of 1998 qualified as a Shuttle mission specialist and International Space Station crewmember.

Mohri was born January 29, 1948, in Yoichi-Machi, Hokkaido, and educated at Hokkaido University, where he received his B.S. in 1970 and M.S. in 1972 in chemistry. He earned his Ph.D. in chemistry from Flinders University in Australia (1976).

In 1975 Mohri joined the faculty of the Hokkaidu University, conducting research in high energy physics and nuclear fusion. He was associate professor of nuclear engineering in 1985 when he spotted a newspaper ad headed "Wanted: Astronaut." He applied and became one of 3 Spacelab J payload specialist candidates selected from 533 applicants in August of that year.

Following STS-47, in October 1992, Mohri became the first general manager of the NASDA astronaut office at Tsukuba Science City, Japan.

Mukai, Chiaki Naito
1952–

Japanese surgeon Chiaki Mukai was a payload specialist in the crew of STS-65. This July 1994 flight of the orbiter Columbia carried the second International Microgravity Payload and a crew of 7. During this 16-day mission, Mukai took part in 82 different investigations in the field of life sciences and microgravity research.

Mukai will continue her space medical research as a payload specialist in the crew of STS-95. This flight of the orbiter Columbia, scheduled for launch in October 1998, carried a crew of 7, including 77-year-old former astronaut John Glenn.

Mukai has served as alternate payload specialist for two Shuttle-Spacelab missions, beginning with STS-47, the Spacelab-Japan mission flown in September 1947. This 8-day mission by a crew of 7, including Japanese payload specialist Mamoru Mohri, conducted over 40 experiments in life sciences and space manufacturing.

In April 1998 Mukai was alternate payload specialist for STS-90, the 16-day Neurolab research mission.

Mukai was born Chiaki Naito on May 6, 1952, in Tatebayashi City, Gumma Prefecture, Tokyo. She attended Keio University, receiving her M.D. in 1977, then worked for two years as a resident in general surgery at Keio University Hospital. From 1979 to 1985 she was an instructor in the department of cardiovascular surgery at that institution. She has since earned a Ph.D. in physiology from Keio University.

Mukai was selected as a payload specialist candidate by Japan's National Space Development Agency (NASDA) in August 1985. While awaiting the launch of STS-47/Spacelab J she served as a visiting scientist at the Space Biomedical Institute at the NASA Johnson Space Center (1987-88) and still serves as a research instructor in the Baylor College of Medicine, Houston, Texas. Her primary job, in addition to being a NASDA science astronaut, is as a visiting associate professor in the department of surgery, Keio University.

Noguchi, Soichi

1965–

Aviation engineer Soichi Noguchi was selected as a Japanese astronaut by NASDA on May 27, 1996. In August of that year he and fellow NASDA astronaut Mamoru Mohri arrived at the NASA Johnson Space Center to begin a training and evaluation course that should qualify them as Shuttle mission specialists and International Space Station crewmembers.

Noguchi was born April 15, 1965, in Yokahama, Japan, but considers Chigasaki to be his hometown. He graduated from Chigasaki-Hokuryo High School in 1984, then attended the University of Tokyo, where he received a B.E. (1989) and M.E. (1991) in aeronautical engineering.

In April 1991 Noguchi joined Ishikawajima-Harima Heavy Industries (IHI), where he became a design engineer in that company's aerodynamics group.

In June 1996 he was selected by NASDA from 572 candidates to undergo astronaut candidate training.

Wakata, Koichi

1963–

Japanese engineer Koichi Wakata was a mission specialist in the crew of STS-72. This January 1996 flight of the orbiter Discovery deployed the Spartan 201 and retrieved the Japanese Space Flyer Unit, launched aboard an H-2 rocket the previous April.

Wakata is assigned to the crew of STS-92, the third International Space Station assembly mission (3A), scheduled for launch in December 1999.

Wakata was born August 1, 1963, in Omiya, Saitama, Japan. He attended Kyushu University, receiving a B.S. in aeronautical engineering in 1987, and an M.S. in applied mechanics in 1989.

In 1989 Wakata went to work for Japan Airlines, first spending 3 months training in aircraft maintenance. For the next 2 years he worked at the Narita Maintenance Center of JAL. Beginning in 1991 he was employed by the Airframe Group of the JAL Engineering Department.

In April 1992 Wakata was selected by NASDA as a Japanese astronaut, joining the March 1992 group of NASA astronaut candidates. He qualified as a Shuttle mission specialist training in August 1993, and worked in the computer support branch of the astronaut office prior to his assignment to STS-72. From 1996 to 1998 he worked in the EVA/robotics branch.

Mexico

Neri Vela, Rudolfo

1952–

Communications engineer Rudolfo Neri became the first Mexican citizen in space when he served as payload specialist in the crew of Shuttle Mission 61-B. This November 1985 launch of the orbiter Atlantis carried a crew of 7 and deployed Mexico's Morelos-B communications satellite. In addition to monitoring the Morelos deployment, Neri conducted several scientific experiments and served as a medical test subject during his weeklong mission.

Neri was born February 19, 1952, in Chilpancingo, Guerrero, Mexico. He attended the National University of Mexico, where he received a B.S. in mechanical and electronic engineering in 1975. He did graduate work in telecommunications science at the University of Essex, England, receiving an M.S. in 1976, and at the University of Birmingham, where he received a Ph.D. in electromagnetic radiation in 1979.

He joined the staff of the Institute of Electrical Research in Mexico, specializing in satellite communications systems, becoming head of the Morelos satellite program for the Mexicon Ministry of Communication and Transportation. When selected as Morelos payload specialist in July 1985 he was also a lecturer and researcher at the National University of Mexico.

Following his Shuttle flight Neri published a memoir, *The Blue Planet* (1987) and worked at the European Space Technology Center (ESTEC) in Noordwijk, the Netherlands, (1989–90).

He is currently on the faculty of the National University of Mexico.

Peralta Y Fabi, Ricardo
1950–
Satellite engineer Ricardo Peralta was backup payload specialist to Rudolfo Neri for Shuttle Mission 61-B. This flight of the orbiter Atlantis in November 1985 successfully deployed Mexico's Morelos-B communications satellite. Peralta supported the mission from the NASA Johnson Space Center.

Peralta was born Augsut 15, 1950, in Mexico City. He attended the University of Illinois, Chicago, where he receved a B.S. in aerospace engineering in 1973. He later earned an M.S. (1975) and a Ph.D. (1977) in mechanical engineering from McGill University in Toronto, Canada.

In 1979, following a year with the Mexican Petroleum Institute, Peralta jointed the faculty of the National University of Mexico, where he is currently a professor and researcher in the department of engineering. Prior to his selection as a Morelos payload specialist in July 1985 he developed several small, inexpensive experiments that flew on the U.S. Space Shuttle as Get-Away Specials.

Mongolia

Ganzorig, Maidarzhavin
1949–
Maidarzhavin Ganzorig was the backup cosmonaut-researcher for the Soviet-Mongolian Interkosmos mission, Soyuz 39, in March 1981. While his countryman Jugderdemidin Gurragcha and Soviet commander Vladimir Dzhanibekov spent a week aboard the Salyut-6 space station, Ganzorig worked in Kaliningrad (now Korolev) mission control center.

Ganzorig was born Maidarzhavin Gankhyuhag on February 5, 1949, in the village of Tsetserleg in the Khangai region of Mongolia. (His name was changed by Soviet authorities when he was selected for cosmonaut training.) In 1969 he was sent to the Soviet Union to attend the Order of Lenin Polytechnical Institute in Kiev, graduating in February 1975 as an engineer specializing in thermodynamics. For the next 2 years he worked as a surveyor in the capital city of Ulan-Bator.

In 1977 and 1978 he completed further studies at the Mongolian Institute of Physics and Technology. Upon being selected as one of 2 Mongolian cosmonaut-researchers in April 1978, he entered the Mongolian people's army.

Ganzorig spent the next three years at the Gagarin Cosmonaut Training Center near Moscow. Following the Soyuz 39 mission he did postgraduate work at the Space Research Institute of the USSR Academy of Sciences, receiving a candidate of technical sciences degree in 1984.

He later became manager of a laboratory at the Mongolian Institute of Physics and Technology.

Gurragcha, Jugderdemidin
1947–

Judgermidin Gurragcha became the first Mongolian in space when he served as cosmonaut-researcher aboard Soyuz-39 in March 1981. Gurragcha and Soviet commander Vladimir Dzhanibekov spent 8 days in space, 7 of them with cosmonauts Kovalenok and Ivanchekov aboard Salyut-6.

Gurragcha was born December 5, 1947, in the settlement of Gurvan-Bulak in the Bulgan province of Mongolia. He attended the Ulan-Bator Agricultural Institute from 1966 to 1968, then was drafted into the army, where he served as a radio operator.

In 1971 Gurragcha was sent to an aviation engineering school in the Soviet Union, where he qualified as a mechanic for helicopter communications systems. From 1973 to 1977 he attended the Zhukovsky Air Force Engineering Academy. He returned to Mongolia, where, following brief service in an air force squadron, he was selected for cosmonaut training.

Upon returning to Mongolia in 1981 Gurragcha was named deputy manager of the administrative office of the Mongolian Peoples Party's central council. He has also published a book, *To a Friendly World* (1988).

He is currently head of a research institute in the city of Ulan-Bator.

Poland

Hermaszewski, Miroslaw
1941–

Miroslaw Hermaszewski was the first citizen of Poland to make a spaceflight. In June 1978 he was cosmonaut-researcher aboard the Soyuz 30 spacecraft; he and Soviet commander Pyotr Klimuk spent 8 days in space, most of them with cosmonauts Kovalenok and Ivanchenkov aboard the Salyut 6 space station. During his flight Hermaszewski operated several experiments created by Polish scientists.

Hermaszewski was born September 15, 1941, in Lipniki, Poland. He grew interested in space and aviation at an early age, and by the time he was 16 he had enrolled in a flying club. In 1961 he was admitted to Officer's Flying School at Deblin, graduating in 1964.

He served as a fighter pilot and flight instructor in the air defense branch of the Polish air force for several years, then attended the Karol Swierczewsky Military Staff Academy in Warsaw, graduating in 1971. He was commander of a regiment of flight instructors when selected for cosmonaut training in December 1976.

Following his spaceflight Hermaszewski remained in the Soviet Union as a student at the Voroshilov General Staff Academy, graduating in 1982. He was promoted to the rank of brigadier general.

The previous December he had been one of 20 officers named to the Military Committee for National Salvation, formed when martial law was imposed on Poland.

He later served as commandant of the Deblin Flying School and as deputy director of the political department of the Polish armed forces.

Jankowski, Zenon
1937–

Zenon Jankowski was the backup cosmonaut-researcher for Miroslaw Hermaszewski, who became the first citizen of Poland in space in June 1978. During the 8-day Soyuz 30 flight Hermaszewski and Soviet cosmonaut Pyotr Klimuk spent a week aboard the Salyut 6 space station. Jankowski supported the flight from mission control at Kaliningrad, near Moscow.

Jankowski was born November 22, 1937, in Poznan, Poland, and entered the Polish Air Force in 1956. He attended the Officer's Flying School at Deblin, graduating in 1960, then served as a fighter pilot. In 1966 he enrolled at the Karol Swierczewski General Staff Academy.

Between 1969 and 1976 Jankowski served with the Polish air force, ultimately logging over 2,000 hours of flying time. At the time of his selection for cosmonaut training in December 1976 he was leader of a squadron of variable geometry (swing-wing) fighters.

Jankowski later became commandant of the Deblin Flying School. He is now retired in Poznan.

Romania

Dediu, Dumitru
1942–

Dumitru Dediu served as backup cosmonaut-researcher to fellow Romanian Dumitru Prunariu for the Soyuz 40 mission to the Salyut 6 station in May 1981.

Dediu was born May 12, 1942, in the city of Galati. He attended the Vasily Alexandri school, where he excelled in mathematics and physics, then studied electronics at a military academy. He served as an engineer with the Romanian air force and, like Prunariu, was selected for cosmonaut training in April 1978.

Colonel Dediu serves with the Romanian military and lives in Bucharest.

Prunariu, Dumitru Dorin
1952–

Dumitru Prunariu became the first citizen of Romania to go into space when he served as cosmonaut-researcher aboard Soyuz 40 in May 1981. Prunariu and Soviet commander Leonid Popov spent 8 days in space, joining cosmonauts Kovalenok and Savinykh aboard the Salyut 6 space station for a week of scientific and space manufacturing experiments.

Prunariu was born September 27, 1952, in Brashov, Romania, and grew up there. As a teenager he built award-winning model airplanes and rockets. He attended the Bucharest Polytechnical Institute, graduating in 1976, and went to work as an aviation engineer at the Brasov aircraft factory.

Prunariu took flying lessons from a pilot in the Romanian air force reserve who encouraged him to join the service, and in September 1977 the young engineer enrolled in a school for air force officers. Shortly after graduation he was chosen as a candidate to become Romania's Interkosmos space traveler. Prunariu and fellow air force engineer Dumitru Dediu reported to the Gagarin Center in April 1978.

Returning to Romania in 1981, Prunariu published a book about his experiences but, reportedly out of favor with dictator Nikolai Ceausescu, found himself assigned as an air force inspector. Following Ceausescu's overthrow in December 1989, Prunariu became director of his country's civil aviation program.

Saudi Arabia

Al-Bassam, Abdulmohsen
1948–

Saudi air force pilot Abdulmohsen Hamad al-Bassam was the backup payload specialist for Shuttle Mission 51-G (June 17–24, 1985) during which Prince Sultan al-Saud became the first Arab in space.

During the weeklong flight Al-Bassam provided ground support from the Johnson Space Center, acting occasionally as capcom for his colleague in orbit.

Al-Bassam was born December 12, 1948, in the city of Onaizah, Saudi Arabia. He graduated from high school in Damman in 1968 and then attended the King Faisal Air Academy in Riyadh, graduating with a bachelor of air science degree. He attended schools for military pilots at Randolph Air Force Base, Texas, and Williams Air Force Base, Arizona, while serving in the Saudi air force.

He has logged more than 2,600 hours of flying time, including over 1,000 hours as an instructor pilot.

Lieutenant Colonel Albassam is currently air attache at the Saudi Embassy in London.

Al-Saud, Sultan bin Salman bin

1956–

Prince Sultan al-Saud was the first Arab to go into space, spending one week in orbit aboard the orbiter Discovery (Mission 51-G) in June 1985.

Sultan's launch date of June 17, 1985, coincided with the last day of Ramadan and gave the astronaut the opportunity to be the first Muslim to see the setting of the Moon, which, according to Islamic law, would signal the end of the holy month. Sultan did not see the Moon set that day, however. Nevertheless, he was able to successfully complete his primary tasks: performing scientific experiments designed by his country's University of Petroleum and Minerals in Dharan and observing the launch of the Arabsat 1-B communications satellite.

During his week in space Sultan was able to take his countrymen on a televised tour of the Discovery, remarking that the Shuttle was being "guided through the stars, just like our Bedouins used to navigate in the desert." Sultan carried with him an astrolabe, the ancient Arab instrument of celestial navigation.

Sultan bin Salman bin Abdulaziz al-Saud was born June 27, 1956, in Riyadh, Saudi Arabia. His parents are His Royal Highness Prince Salman bin Abdul Aziz (the governor of Riyadh) and Sultana Al-Sudairy.

Sultan completed his elementary and secondary schooling in Saudi Arabia, then attended the University of Denver in Colorado, where he studied mass communications. He became a commercial pilot and logged over 1,000 hours in jet aircraft and helicopters. He was employed as a researcher in the Saudi Ministry of Information from 1982-84, and also was Deputy Director in the Saudi Arabian Olympic Information Committee during the 1984 Olympiad in Los Angeles.

At the time of his selection to fly aboard the Shuttle in 1985 Sultan was acting Director of the Saudi Arabian Television Commercial Department.

Following his spaceflight Sultan served in the Saudi Royal Air Force in Riyadh.

Slovakia

Bella, Ivan

1964–

Major Ivan Bella, a pilot in the armed forces of the Slovak Republic, was selected in March 1998 as a candidate for a Soyuz mission to Mir in the spring of 1999.

Bella was born May 21, 1964, in the town of Brezno, Czechoslovakia. He graduated from the Kosice Air Force Academy in 1987, then served as a fighter pilot with the Czech air force.

He has logged 800 hours of flying time and 88 parachute jumps.

Fulier, Mihal Mihal

1955–

Lieutenant Colonel Mikhal Fulier, a pilot in the armed forces of the Slovak Republic, was selected in March 1998 as a candidate for a spring 1999 visit to the Russian Mir space station. The Slovak Republic negotiated this flight as payment for Russian debts to that country. It will last approximately 10 days.

Fulier was born February 20, 1955, in the town of Skalitsa, North Moravia. He attended the Kosice Air Force Academy, graduating in 1973, then served as a fighter pilot in the Czech air force.

He has logged over 2,000 hours of flying time and 65 parachute jumps.

Syria

Faris, Muhammed Ahmed

1951–

Syrian air force pilot Muhammed Faris served as cosmonaut researcher aboard Soyuz
TM-3 in July 1987. During this
8-day mission Faris and Soviet
cosmonauts Alexandr Vik-
torenko and Alexandr Alexan-
drov joined the resident crew of Yuri Romanenko and
Alexandr Laveikin aboard the Mir space station. Faris
took part in conducting a number of experiments in
medicine and space manufacturing developed by Syrian
and Soviet researchers. He and Viktorenko returned to
Earth with Laveikin; worries about his health had
caused him to be replaced in the Mir resident crew by
Alexandrov.

Faris was born May 26, 1951, in Aleppo, Syria. He
attended the air force school in Aleppo from 1969 to 1973.

For the next 12 years Faris served as a fighter pilot
and instructor in the Syrian air force. At one time he was
in the same squadron as future cosmonaut-researcher
Munir Habib.

Faris and Habib arrived at the Gagarin Center in October 1985 to begin training for a Soyuz TM flight to Mir.

Following his flight he returned to duty with Syrian
air force and lives in Aleppo.

Habib, Munir Habib

1953–

Syrian air force pilot Munir
Habib served as backup to
countryman Mohammed Faris
during the flight of Soyuz TM-
3. During the 8-day flight Faris
performed a number of scientific experiments aboard the
Mir space station. Habib supported the mission from the
flight control center at Kaliningrad.

Habib was born September 3, 1953, in the town of
Zhablya, Syria. After completing secondary school he
entered a university to study English, and then joined the
Syrian air force. He attended the air force school in
Aleppo, graduating in 1973.

For the next 12 years Habib served as a fighter pilot
and instructor in the Syrian air force. (He and Faris were
in the same squadron at one point.) He logged over 3,400
hours of flying time.

Habib and Faris arrived at the Gagarin Center in October 1985 to train as Soyuz cosmonaut-researchers.

Ukraine

Adamchuk, Nadiya Ivanyvna

1970–

Botanist Nadiya Adamchuk is one of the 4 astronaut candidates selected by the National Space Agency of Ukraine
in September 1996. As one of the principal investigators
of the Collaborative Ukrainian Experiment she was a candidate to be payload specialist aboard STS-87, though
Leonid Kadenyuk was ultimately selected. She remains a
candidate for future flights to the International Space
Station.

Adamchuk was born October 4, 1970, in Kyiv (Kiev),
Ukraine, where she graduated from high school in 1987.
She studied to be a teacher at the Dragomanov National
Pedagogical University, receiving a degree in biology and
geography in 1992. She later received a candidate's
degree (Ph.D.) in biology (botany) from the Hryshko
Central Botanical Garden in Kyiv.

Since 1992 Adamchuk has been a researcher at the
Kholodnyi Institute of Botany of the National Academy of
Sciences of Ukraine. One of her fields of study is how pho-
tosynthesis changes in microgravity.

Kadenyuk, Leonid Konstantinovich

1951–

Leonid Kadenyuk is a former
Russian cosmonaut and test
pilot who became an astronaut
with the National Space
Agency of Ukraine, then
served as payload specialist in
the crew of STS-87. This 16-day flight of the orbiter
Columbia, launched in November 1997, carried the fourth

U.S. Microgravity Payload in addition to a set of scientific experiments developed by NSAU, the Collaborative Ukrainian Experiment (CUE).

Kadenyuk's road to space was an unusually long one, with 21 years elapsing between his selection for the military cosmonaut team based at the Gagarin Center and his eventual flight on the American Shuttle.

Kadenyuk was born January 28, 1951, in the village of Klishovsky in the Chornovtsky Region, Ukraine. Kadenyuk attended the Chernigov (now Chernihiv) Higher Air Force School from 1967 to 1971, then served at the school as an instructor, training 15 pilots.

He was one of the 9 air force candidates enrolled in the cosmonaut team in August 1976. He spent the next year at the military test pilot school at the Chkalov flight test center, earning his test pilot third class rating, then underwent general cosmonaut training at the Gagarin Center. After qualifying as a test-cosmonaut in 1979 Kadenyuk continued to perform flight test work at Chkalov, working on the development of the Buran space shuttle and flying several different models of aircraft, including transports.

Kadenyuk returned to the Gagarin Center in March 1982 to join the Soyuz-Salyut training group, but was dismissed a year later. He spent a year at the Lipetsk flight center, then was assigned again to Chkalov. In addition to work on three state flight test programs—the Su-27, Su-27UB and MiG-25—he served as chairman of the state committee on the Su-27M cockpit.

In October 1988 he was selected to join the group of military Buran test pilot-cosmonauts training for orbital test flights. He trained for the Soyuz-Buran docking mission, as commander of a proposed all-Ukraine Soyuz crew and as a Soyuz-Rescue commander, but was not assigned to a mission.

With the cancellation of Buran in 1994, and the formation of the NSAU in 1985, Kadenyuk left the Russian air force and joined the staff of the Institute of Botany, National Academy of Sciences, Ukraine.

Kadenyuk has logged over 2,400 flying hours in over 54 types of aircraft. Since 1986 he has held the rating of test pilot first class.

Shortly after his return to Ukraine in February 1998 following STS-87, Kadenyk was promoted to major general.

Meytarchan, Vyacheslav Georgiovych
1965–

Aerospace engineer Vyacheslav Meytarchan is one of the 4 astronauts selected by the National Space Agency of Ukraine in September 1996. He was a candidate for Ukrainian payload specialist on STS-87, ultimately flown by Leonid Kadenyuk, and hopes to fly a mission to the International Space Station.

Meytarchan was born December 7, 1965, in Slobudka, Brest Region, Belarus, but grew up in the city of Brovary, Kiev Region, Ukraine, where he graduated from high school in 1983. He attended the Polytechnic Institute in Kiev (now Kyiv), graduating in 1989, and later received his candidate of technical sciences degree in aerospace systems from the National Technical Institute of Ukraine.

Beginning in 1989 Meytarchan worked for the Ritm Special Design Bureau in association with NPO Energiya, developing computer models for the construction of large space components, testing flight equipment and serving as a spacecraft ground controller. After finishing his candidate's degree in 1994 he joined the National Technical Institute of Ukraine, working on personal computer communication systems.

Meytarchan has also been a member of the Young Ukrainian National Parachute Team, making over 1,300 freefall jumps. He is now with NASA.

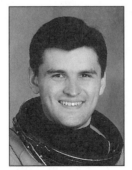

Pustovyi, Yaroslav Ihorovych
1970–

Physicist Yaroslav "Yarko" Pustovyi was alternate payload specialist for the STS-87 mission. This November 1987 flight of the orbiter Columbia carried the Collaborative Ukrainian Experiment, a suite of 11 experiments in plant growth and pollination in microgravity operated by astronaut Leonid Kadenyuk of the National Space Agency of Ukraine.

Pustovyi was born December 29, 1970, in the city of Kostroma, Russia. After completing secondary school in 1988 he entered the Mozhaisky Aerospace Engineering Academy in Leningrad (now St. Petersburg), receiving a master's degree in radio electronics engineering in 1993.

He did a year of graduate work at Mozhaisky from 1993 to 1994, then entered Kharkiv State University, Ukraine, where he received a candidate of science (Ph.D.) in physics and mathematics in June 1996.

Beginning in January 1995 Pustovyi was a researcher at the Ukrainian Academy of Sciences Institute of Magnetism. He was a member of the first group of NSAU astronauts selected in September 1996.

Vietnam

Liem Bui Thanh
1949–1980

Bui Thanh Liem served as backup to Pham Tuan, the first Vietnamese space traveler, during the Soyuz 37 mission in July 1980. While Tuan and Soviet commander Viktor Gorbatko spent a week aboard Salyut 6, Liem provided ground support from mission control in Kaliningrad (now Korolev).

Liem was born June 30, 1949, in Hanoi, Vietnam. He would have been exempt from military service, but enlisted in the Vietnamese air force in February 1966. He was sent to the USSR for pilot training, returning in 1970, when he became a fighter pilot with the "Red Star" regiment.

During the Vietnam War Liem served as an interceptor pilot and was credited with shooting down two American planes.

In 1974 Liem was sent back to the Soviet Union to attend the Gagarin Air Force Academy, graduating in 1978. He was a staff officer in the Vietnamese Air Force when selected for cosmonaut training along with Pham Tuan in July 1979.

Major Bui Thanh Liem returned to Vietnam and operational flying in 1980. On September 30, 1981, he was killed in a plane crash.

Tuan, Pham
1947–

Vietnamese air force pilot Pham Tuan became the first Asian in space when he served as cosmonaut-researcher aboard Soyuz 37 in July 1980. Tuan and Soviet commander Viktor Gorbatko spent 8 days in space, seven of them aboard the Salyut 6 space station with cosmonauts Popov and Lebedev. Tuan also carried out Earth observations for scientists in his country.

Pham Tuan was born February 14, 1947, in the village of Quoc Tuan, Thai Binh province. He studied to be an engineer, but when the Vietnam War began he was drafted into the North Vietnamese army. He was sent to the Soviet Union for flight school, graduating in May 1968.

Tuan flew air defense missions over North Vietnam with the Red Star Regiment. It is reported that on December 27, 1972, he shot down a U.S. Air Force B-52 bomber over Hanoi. (The USAF denies that any bomber was shot down by a fighter during the war.) He later served as a regimental commander, and in 1977 was sent to the Soviet Union again to attend the Gagarin Air Force Academy. He was a student there when selected for cosmonaut training in April 1979, and following the conclusion of his cosmonaut career, graduated from the Academy (1982).

Major General Tuan later became head of the political department of the Vietnamese Armed Forces.

MANNED SPACEFLIGHTS, 1961–98

MISSION refers to the official designation given to a particular space flight. As there are obvious numerical and sequential anomalies, some explanation is in order:

1. Unmanned test flights of Soviet Vostok and Voskhod spacecraft were identified as Kosmos satellites, eliminating any gaps in numbering. But several Soyuz missions have been flown unmanned: Soyuz 2 (1968), Soyuz 20 (1975), Soyuz 34 (1979), Soyuz T (1979), and Soyuz TM (1986).

2. Unmanned test flights in American manned space programs were usually included in the numerical sequence: Mercury-Redstone 3 (Alan Shepard) was preceded by 2 unmanned launches, Mercury-Atlas 6 (John Glenn) by 5, Gemini-Titan 3 (Grissom and Young) by 2.

3. Apollo missions were originally intended to have *two* designations. The first, a 3-digit number such as Apollo-Saturn 202 or Apollo-Saturn 504, would identify a specific mission—manned or unmanned. (The 200 series referred to vehicles launched by Saturn 1B rockets, the 500 series to those launched by Saturn 5s.) Only manned Apollo flights would be designation Apollo 1, Apollo 2, etc. That's why the ill-fated Apollo 1, in which astronauts Grissom, White, and Chaffee were killed, is officially known as Apollo-Saturn 204—the fourth Apollo spacecraft launched aboard a Saturn 1B. (In fact, Apollo-Saturn 204 *was* launched in 1968. It carried the first unmanned lunar module and was designated Apollo 5. See below.)

   When Apollo launches were resumed in November 1967 NASA jettisoned its original system and designated Apollo-Saturn 501, the first unmanned test of the Saturn 5 booster, as Apollo 4, the fourth flight of Apollo hardware after Apollo-Saturns 201, 202 and 203, which could be known as Apollos 1, 2, and 3 only retrospectively. The Apollo-Saturn 204 mentioned above became Apollo 5 and Apollo-Saturn 502 was Apollo 6. The first manned Apollo mission, number 205, was Apollo 7.

4. Although the three manned Skylab mission were officially known as Skylabs 2-4 (Skylab 1 was the unmanned station itself), some NASA documents—including the crew mission patches—called them Skylab 1, 2, and 3.

5. The American spacecraft used in the Apollo-Soyuz Test Project has been variously known as "ASTP," "Apollo 18," or simply "Apollo." The mission designation was "ASTP"; the call sign was simply "Apollo."

6. The first four Shuttle missions—later known as STS (Space Transportation System) 1 through 4—were originally to have been designated OFT (Orbital Flight Tests) 1-4.

7. In 1983, following the cancellation of STS-10, which produced a Shuttle flight manifest predicting a sequence of STS-11, STS-13, STS-12, STS-14, NASA adopted a new designation system which consisted of three elements: fiscal year (4, 5, 6, etc., for 1984, 1985, 1986); launch site (1 for Kennedy Space Center, 2 for Vandenberg AFB); and sequence within a fiscal year (A, B, C, etc.), transforming STS-11 in Mission 41-B, STS-13 into Mission 41-C, and so on.

   Although later NASA documents subsequently referred to, for example, Mission 51-A as STS 51-A, the designation in use at the time was the word Mission followed by the 3-way combination.

In 1986, following the Challenger disaster, NASA reverted to the original system—the 26th Shuttle mission became STS-26—and by the third launch was out of sequence.

LAUNCH DATA are that given by the agency responsible, with times based on mission control center. Former Soviet launch times are based on Moscow Time, later known as Decreed Moscow Time; actual launch time at the Baikonur Cosmodrome is plus 2-hours. Early NASA launch times were given in Eastern Time, since mission control was based at Cape Canaveral in Florida until Gemini 4 in June 1965. Later times are given in Central Time, the zone in which NASA mission control is located.

It is interesting to note that very few reported launch sites, Soviet or American, are accurate. The complex known as the Baikonur Cosmodrome is located 200 miles from the city of Baikonyr in what is now the indepededent nation of Kazakhstan; its actual location, near the small town of Tyuratam (later known as Leninsk), was fictionalized by the USSR for reasons of secrecy. The official name for the launch center within the Soviet government was NIIP-5, Scientific Research Institute and Range Number 5.

In addition, of American launches, only Mercury and Gemini flights were launched from Cape Canaveral—and from 1963 to 1973 Cape Canaveral was renamed Cape Kennedy. Apollo and Shuttle launches are actually launched from the NASA John F. Kennedy Space Center on Merritt Island, Florida—which is not part of Cape Canaveral.

CREWS are given in the order used in original launch announcements, with these abbreviations for functions:

CDR . . Commander; command pilot (Gemini)
PLT . . . . Pilot
PLT2 . . . . Second pilot
SCI . . . . Scientist (Voskhod 1)
DR . . . . Doctor (Voskhod 1)
FE . . . . Flight engineer
RE . . . . Research engineer
TE . . . . Test engineer
CR . . . . Cosmonaut-researcher
CMP . . . . Command module pilot
LMP . . . . Lunar module pilot
DMP . . . . Docking module pilot
SP . . . . Science pilot
MS . . . . Mission specialist
PS . . . . Payload specialist
SR PLT . . . . Senior pilot (Apollo 204)

CALL SIGNS refer to the spacecraft names used in communications beteen ground controllers and cosmonauts or astronauts during their missions.

LANDING DATA are that given by official announcements, with all distances converted to statute miles.

DURATION is the time from liftoff to splashdown (American missions from Mercury through ASTP); liftoff to touchdown (Soviet missions); or liftoff through main landing gear touchdown (STS). Apparent discrepancies are due to rounding.

REMARKS are significant mission events, records, unusual orbits, or inclinations, and so forth.

FLIGHT	VOSTOK	MERCURY-REDSTONE 4
LAUNCH DATA	April 12, 1961 0907 MT Baikonur 1	July 21, 1961 0720 EDT Cape Canaveral 5/6
CREW	Gagarin	Grissom
CALL SIGN	Kedr (Cedar)	Liberty Bell 7
LANDING DATA	April 12, 1961 1055 MT Near Smelovka, Saratov region	July 21, 1961 0736 EDT 302 miles downrange, recovered by *U.S.S. Randolph*
DURATION	1 hour, 48 minutes	16 minutes
REMARKS	The world's first manned spaceflight. The only orbit ranged from 112 to 203 miles in altitude. Following reentry, Gagarin ejected at 22,000 feet, as planned, landing in a pasture.	Grissom made the second U.S. suborbital flight, reaching an altitude of 126 miles. The Liberty Bell 7 capsule sank before it could be recovered, though Grissom was rescued.

FLIGHT	MERCURY-REDSTONE 3	VOSTOK 2
LAUNCH DATA	May 5, 1961 0934 EDT Cape Canaveral 5/6	August 6, 1961 0900 MT Baikonur 1
CREW	Shepard	Titov
CALL SIGN	Freedom 7	Orel (Eagle)
LANDING DATA	May 5, 1961 0949 EDT 303 miles downrange, recovered by *U.S.S. Lake Champlain*	August 7, 1961 1018 MT Saratov
DURATION	15 minutes	25 hours, 18 minutes
REMARKS	Shepard became the first American in space, 3 weeks after Gagarin's flight, rocketing to an altitude of 125 miles.	Titov became the first to spend an entire day in space. His orbit ranged from 113 to 151 miles.

FLIGHT	MERCURY-ATLAS 6	VOSTOK 3
LAUNCH DATA	February 20, 1962 0948 EST Cape Canaveral 14	August 11, 1962 1130 MT Baikonur 1
CREW	Glenn	Nikolayev
CALL SIGN	Friendship 7	Sokol (Falcon)
LANDING DATA	February 20, 1962 1443 EST Atlantic Ocean, 40 miles from the *U.S.S. Noa*	August 15, 1962 0955 MT Kazakhstan
DURATION	4 hours, 55 minutes	3 days, 22 hours, 22 minutes
REMARKS	Glenn accomplished the United States' first manned orbital flight, circling the Earth 3 times in an orbit ranging from 100 to 162 miles at an inclination of 28 degrees.	First 4-day flight and the first "group" flight with Vostok 4 carrying Popovich, launched a day later. Orbit: 112 to 145 miles.

FLIGHT	MERCURY-ATLAS 7	VOSTOK 4
LAUNCH DATA	May 24, 1962 0745 EDT Cape Canaveral 14	August 12, 1962 1102 MT Baikonur 1
CREW	Carpenter	Popovich
CALL SIGN	Aurora 7	Berkut (Golden Eagle)
LANDING DATA	May 24, 1962 1241 EDT Atlantic Ocean, 260 miles from the *U.S.S. Intrepid*	August 15, 1962 0959 MT Kazkahstan
DURATION	4 hours, 56 minutes	2 days, 22 hours, 57 minutes
REMARKS	Carpenter flew the second American manned orbital flight, completing 3 orbits. Attitude control problems caused Aurora 7 to overshoot its landing target by 260 miles and Carpenter and his spacecraft spent an hour in the water before being rescued.	The other half of the first space "group" flight. Vostok 4 closed to within 5 miles of Vostok 3. Popovich landed just 6 minutes after Nikolayev, but 190 miles away. Orbit: 111 to 147 miles.

FLIGHT	**MERCURY-ATLAS 8**	**VOSTOK 5**
LAUNCH DATA	October 3, 1962 0715 EDT Cape Canaveral 14	June 14, 1963 1500 MT Baikonur 1
CREW	Schirra	Bykovsky
CALL SIGN	Sigma 7	Yastreb (Hawk)
LANDING DATA	October 3, 1962 1628 EDT Pacific Ocean, 4.5 miles from the *U.S.S. Kearsarge*	June 19, 1963 1406 MT Kazakhstan
DURATION	9 hours, 13 minutes	4 days, 23 hours, 6 minutes
REMARKS	Schirra piloted a "textbook" engineering flight, doubling the duration for which Mercury was intended to operate.	Bykovsky set an endurance record, 5 days in space, that would last for 2 years. This was also the second group flight. Orbit: 99 to 146 miles, too low to permit the originally-hoped-for 8-day duration.

FLIGHT	**MERCURY-ATLAS 9**	**VOSTOK 6**
LAUNCH DATA	May 15, 1963 0804 EDT Cape Canaveral 14	June 16, 1963 1230 MT Baikonur 1
CREW	Cooper	Tereshkova
CALL SIGN	Faith 7	Chaika (Seagull)
LANDING DATA	May 16, 1963 1824 EDT Pacific Ocean, 4 miles from the *U.S.S. Kearsarge*	June 19, 1963 1120 MT Kazakhstan
DURATION	34 hours, 20 minutes	2 days, 22 hours, 50 minutes
REMARKS	Cooper piloted the longest, most difficult, and last Mercury mission, spending a day and a half in orbit.	First spaceflight by a woman and second group flight, though Vostok 6 did not get as close to Vostok 5 as did Vostok 3/Vostok 4. Orbit: 108 to 143 miles.

FLIGHT	VOSKHOD	GEMINI-TITAN 3
LAUNCH DATA	October 12, 1964 1030 MT Baikonur 1	March 23, 1965 0924 EST Cape Kennedy 19
CREW	Komarov (CDR), Feoktistov (SCI), Yegorov (DR)	Grissom (CDR), Young (PLT)
CALL SIGN	Rubin (Ruby)	Molly Brown
LANDING DATA	October 13, 1964 1047 MT Kazakhstan	March 23, 1965 1417 EST Atlantic Ocean, 50 miles from the *U.S.S. Intrepid*
DURATION	1 day, 17 minutes	4 hours, 53 minutes
REMARKS	First space crew, consisting of a pilot and two passengers. It was later disclosed that all three suffered from space sickness during their single day in space. They were the first space travelers to do without space suits and the first cosmonauts to land inside their spacecraft. Orbit: 111 to 254 miles.	Gemini was the first true spaceship, carrying a computer for guidance and powered by rocket that enabled it to maneuver in space. From an initial orbit of 161 by 224 miles, Grissom and Young lowered Molly Brown to a 158 by 169 mile orbit, a vital step toward the eventual rendezvous and docking of vehicles in space.

FLIGHT	VOSKHOD 2	GEMINI-TITAN 4
LAUNCH DATA	March 18, 1965 1000 MT Baikonur 1	June 3, 1965 0916 CDT Cape Kennedy 19
CREW	Belyayev (CDR), Leonov (PLT2)	McDivitt (CDR), White (PLT)
CALL SIGN	Almaz (Diamond)	Gemini 4
LANDING DATA	March 19, 1965 1202 MT Perm region	June 7, 1965 1112 CDT Atlantic Ocean, 40 miles from the *U.S.S. Wasp*
DURATION	1 day, 2 hours, 2 minutes	4 days, 1 hour, 56 minutes
REMARKS	Leonov became the first space walker, floating outside Voskhod 2 for 12 minutes. Belyayev also became the first Soviet cosmonaut to control his spacecraft, manually firing the retrorockets on the seventeenth orbit after the autopilot had failed. The delay forced the cosmonauts to land far from the prime recovery zone. Orbit: 107 by 308, a record altitude at the time.	McDivitt and White set an American space endurance record during their 4 days aboard Gemini 4. They failed to "station keep" with their Titan 2 booster, but White later made America's first space walk. First mission to be controlled from the Manned Spacecraft Center in Houston.

FLIGHT	GEMINI-TITAN 5	GEMINI-TITAN 6-A
LAUNCH DATA	August 21, 1965 0800 CDT Cape Kennedy 19	December 15, 1965 0737 CST Cape Kennedy 19
CREW	Cooper (CDR), Conrad (PLT)	Schirra (CDR), Stafford (PLT)
CALL SIGN	Gemini 5	Gemini 6
LANDING DATA	August 29, 1965 0655 CDT Atlantic Ocean, 104 miles from the *U.S.S. Lake Champlain*	December 16, 1965 0928 CST Atlantic Ocean, 8 miles from the *U.S.S. Wasp*
DURATION	7 days, 22 hours, 55 minutes	1 day, 1 hour, 51 minutes
REMARKS	Cooper and Conrad endured 8 days, many of them drifting, in the cramped Gemini 5 spacecraft, giving America the world space endurance record for the first time, and proving that humans could survive in space long enough to travel to the Moon and back.	Schirra and Stafford, frustrated in previous attempts to accomplish the first rendezvous and docking in space, guided Gemini 6 to within a few feet of Gemini 7 during their single day in space.

FLIGHT	GEMINI-TITAN 7	GEMINI-TITAN 8
LAUNCH DATA	December 4, 1965 1330 CST Cape Kennedy 19	March 16, 1966 1041 CST Cape Kennedy 19
CREW	Borman (CDR), Lovell (PLT)	Armstrong (CDR), Scott (PLT)
CALL SIGN	Gemini 7	Gemini 8
LANDING DATA	December 18, 1965 0805 CST Atlantic Ocean, 7 miles from the *U.S.S. Wasp*	March 16, 1966 2122 CST Pacific Ocean, 600 miles east of Japan, recovered by *U.S.S. Mason*
DURATION	13 days, 18 hours, 35 minutes	10 hours, 41 minutes
REMARKS	Borman and Lovell set a new space endurance record aboard Gemini 7 and participated in the first rendezvous between two manned spacecraft when visited by Gemini 6, carrying Schirra and Stafford, on December 15.	Armstrong and Scott guided Gemini 8 to the first docking with another spacecraft, an Agena, before being forced to abort the mission because of a stuck thruster on their Gemini. They made an emergency landing in the Pacific.

FLIGHT	GEMINI-TITAN 9-A	GEMINI-TITAN 11
LAUNCH DATA	June 3, 1966 0740 CDT Cape Kennedy 19	September 12, 1966 0842 CDT Cape Kennedy 19
CREW	Stafford (CDR), Cernan (PLT)	Conrad (CDR), Gordon (PLT)
CALL SIGN	Gemini 9	Gemini 11
LANDING DATA	June 6, 1966 0800 CDT Atlantic Ocean, a half-mile from the *U.S.S. Wasp*	September 15, 1966 0659 CDT Atlantic Ocean, 3 miles from the *U.S.S. Guam*
DURATION	3 days, 20 minutes	2 days, 23 hours, 17 minutes
REMARKS	Stafford and Cernan made rendezvous with the unmanned Augmented Target Docking Adaptor, but were unable to dock with the vehicle. Cernan's planned 2-hour space walk using a maneuvering backpack was unsuccessful.	Conrad and Gordon made rendezvous and docking with a target Agena, using it to raise their orbit to a new record altitude of 850 miles. Gordon made 2 space walks. The reentry and landing were flown on autopilot, another American first.

FLIGHT	GEMINI-TITAN 10	GEMINI-TITAN 12
LAUNCH DATA	July 18, 1966 1620 CDT Cape Kennedy 19	November 11, 1966 1447 CST Cape Kennedy 19
CREW	Young (CDR), Collins (PLT)	Lovell (CDR), Aldrin (PLT)
CALL SIGN	Gemini 10	Gemini 12
LANDING DATA	July 21, 1966 1507 EDT Atlantic Ocean, 4 miles from the *U.S.S. Guadalcanal*	November 16, 1966 1321 CST Atlantic Ocean, 3 miles from the *U.S.S. Wasp*
DURATION	2 days, 22 hours, 17 minutes	3 days, 22 hours, 34 minutes
REMARKS	Young and Collins piloted Gemini 10 to rendezvous and docking with 2 different Agena targets, one of them left over from Gemini 8, and reached a record altitude of 468 miles. Collins performed 2 space walks.	Lovell and Aldrin again demonstrated rendezvous and docking techniques, including a final approach to the Agena using manual systems. Aldrin also completed three space walks totalling 5.5 hours, the most successful so far. Last Gemini flight.

FLIGHT	APOLLO-SATURN 204	APOLLO-SATURN 7
LAUNCH DATA	— — —	October 11, 1968 1003 CDT Kennedy Space Center 34
CREW	Grissom (CDR), White (SR PLT), Chaffee (PLT)	Schirra (CDR), Eisele (CMP), Cunningham (LMP)
CALL SIGN	Apollo 1	Apollo 7
LANDING DATA	— — —	October 22, 1968 0612 CDT Atlantic Ocean, recovered by *U.S.S. Essex*
DURATION	—	10 days, 20 hours, 9 minutes
REMARKS	At 1830 EST on January 27, 1967, while training for a 14-day mission scheduled for launch on February 21, 1967, astronauts Grissom, White, and Chaffee were killed in a fire aboard their Apollo spacecraft at launch complex 34.	Schirra, Eisele, and Cunningham piloted Apollo on its maiden voyage, the first American manned flight since the Apollo 1 fire. They performed rendezvous exercises with the upper stage of their Saturn IB launch vehicle during their 11 days in space.

FLIGHT	SOYUZ 1	SOYUZ 3
LAUNCH DATA	April 23, 1967 0325 MT Baikonur 1	October 26, 1968 1134 MT Baikonur 1
CREW	Komarov	Beregovoy
CALL SIGN	Rubin	Argon
LANDING DATA	April 24, 1967 0613 MT Orenburg region, 40 miles E of Orsk	October 30, 1968 1025 MT Kazakhstan
DURATION	1 day, 2 hours, 48 minutes	3 days, 22 hours, 51 minutes
REMARKS	Komarov was launched alone in this new spacecraft, to be joined on April 24 by Soyuz 2 and cosmonauts Bykovsky, Yeliseyev, and Khrunov, with the latter two performing a space walk to Soyuz 1. Technical problems with Soyuz 1 canceled the second launch and forced Komarov to attempt a re-entry on the 18th orbit. Soyuz 1 crashed, killing Komarov. Initial orbit: 124 to 139 miles with a new inclination, 51.7 degrees.	First manned flight of the redesigned Soyuz. Beregovoy made a rendezvous with the unmanned Soyuz 2, launched October 25, but failed to dock. Initial orbit: 109 to 127 at 51.7 inclination.

FLIGHT	**APOLLO-SATURN 8**	**SOYUZ 5**
LAUNCH DATA	December 21, 1968 0651 CST Kennedy Space Center 39A	January 15, 1969 1014 MT Baikonur 1
CREW	Borman (CDR), Lovell (CMP), Anders (LMP)	Volynov (CDR), Yeliseyev (FE), Khrunov (RE)
CALL SIGN	Apollo 8	Baikal
LANDING DATA	December 28, 1968 0951 CST Pacific Ocean, recovered by *U.S.S. Yorktown*	January 18, 1969 1108 MT Kazakhstan
DURATION	6 days, 3 hours	3 days, 54 minutes
REMARKS	Borman, Lovell, and Anders were launched aboard the Saturn 5, the most powerful rocket ever used in manned flight, and became the first humans to reach the Moon. They made 10 orbits of the Moon on December 24 and December 25, 1968.	Soyuz 5 served as the passive docking target for Soyuz 4. Khrunov and Yeliseyev transferred to the other spacecraft (total EVA time, 37 minutes) and Volynov returned to Earth alone. Initial orbit: 124 by 131.

FLIGHT	**SOYUZ 4**	**APOLLO-SATURN 9**
LAUNCH DATA	January 14, 1969 1039 MT Baikonur 1	March 3, 1969 1000 CST Kennedy Space Center 39A
CREW	Shatalov	McDivitt (CDR), Scott (CMP), Schweickart (LMP)
CALL SIGN	Amur	Apollo 9, Gumdrop, and Spider
LANDING DATA	January 17, 1969 1000 MT Kazakhstan	March 13, 1969 1101 CST Atlantic Ocean, recovered by *U.S.S. Guadalcanal*
DURATION	2 days, 23 hours, 21 minutes	10 days, 1 hour, 1 minute
REMARKS	Shatalov on Soyuz 4 was joined in orbit on January 15 by Soyuz 5 and cosmonauts Volynov, Yeliseyev, and Khrunov. Shatalov piloted the rendezvous and docking on January 16. The latter 2 performed a space walk to Soyuz 4 and returned to Earth in that vehicle. Initial orbit: 131 to 139 miles.	McDivitt and Schweickart made the first manned test of the lunar module Spider while Scott remained aboard the command module Gumdrop. Schweickart also made a space walk testing the Apollo lunar space suit.

FLIGHT	APOLLO-SATURN 10	SOYUZ 6
LAUNCH DATA	May 18, 1969 1149 CDT Kennedy Space Center 39B	October 11, 1969 1410 MT Baikonur 1
CREW	Stafford (CDR), Young (CMP), Cernan (LMP)	Shonin (CDR), Kubasov (FE)
CALL SIGN	Apollo 10, Charlie Brown, and Snoopy	Antei (Anteus)
LANDING DATA	May 26, 1969 1152 CDT Pacific Ocean, recovered by *U.S.S. Princeton*	October 16, 1969 1253 MT Kazakhstan
DURATION	8 days, 3 minutes	4 days, 22 hours, 43 minutes
REMARKS	Stafford, Young, and Cernan completed a full dress rehearsal for a lunar landing. Stafford and Cernan, aboard the LM Snoopy, came to within 10 miles of the surface of the Moon.	Soyuz 6 was the first of three Soviet manned vehicles launched on successive days, forming the first "space squadron." Kubasov performed the first space welding experiment.

FLIGHT	APOLLO-SATURN 11	SOYUZ 8
LAUNCH DATA	July 16, 1969 0832 CDT Kennedy Space Center 39A	October 13, 1969 1329 MT Baikonur 1
CREW	Armstrong (CDR), Collins (CMP), Aldrin (LMP)	Shatalov (CDR), Yeliseyev (FE)
CALL SIGN	Apollo 11, Columbia, and Eagle	Granit (Granite)
LANDING DATA	July 24, 1969 1150 CDT Pacific Ocean, recovered by *U.S.S. Hornet*	October 18, 1969 1220 MT Kazakhstan
DURATION	8 days, 3 hours, 18 minutes	4 days, 22 hours, 51 minutes
REMARKS	Armstrong and Aldrin made the historic first manned landing on the Moon in the LM Eagle on July 20, 1969. Collins remained in lunar orbit in the CM Columbia. Armstrong and Aldrin remained on the lunar surface for 20 hours and took a 2-hour Moon walk.	Shatalov and Yeliseyev made their second flights in 10 months. Intended to dock with Soyuz 7, due to failure of the rendezvous radar, Soyuz 8 merely made rendezvous on October 15. Initial orbit: 128 to 139 miles.

FLIGHT	**APOLLO-SATURN 12**	**SOYUZ 9**
LAUNCH DATA	November 14, 1969 1022 CST Kennedy Space Center 39A	June 1, 1970 2200 MT Baikonur 1
CREW	Conrad (CDR), Gordon (CMP), Bean (LMP)	Nikolayev (CDR), Sevastyanov (FE)
CALL SIGN	Apollo 12, Yankee Clipper, and Intrepid	Sokol
LANDING DATA	November 24, 1969 1458 CST Pacific Ocean, recovered by *U.S.S. Hornet*	June 19, 1970 1501 MT Kazakhstan
DURATION	10 days, 4 hours, 36 minutes	17 days, 16 hours, 59 minutes
REMARKS	Conrad and Bean landed on the Moon's Ocean of Storms on November 18 just 300 yards from the unmanned Surveyor 3. The 2 astronauts took 2 Moon walks totaling 7.5 hours.	Nikolayev and Sevastyanov's 18-day flight set a new endurance record. However, the cosmonauts had to be carried from their spacecraft after landing.

FLIGHT	**APOLLO-SATURN 13**	**APOLLO-SATURN 14**
LAUNCH DATA	April 11, 1970 1313 CDT Kennedy Space Center 39A	January 31, 1971 1503 CST Kennedy Space Center 39A
CREW	Lovell (CDR), Swigert (CMP), Haise (LMP	Shepard (CDR), Roosa (CMP), Mitchell (LMP)
CALL SIGN	Apollo 13, Odyssey, and Aquarius	Apollo 14, Kitty Hawk, and Antares
LANDING DATA	April 17, 1970 1118 CDT Pacific Ocean, recovered by *U.S.S. Iwo Jima*	February 9, 1971 1545 CST Pacific Ocean, recovered by *U.S.S. New Orleans*
DURATION	5 days, 22 hours, 55 minutes	9 days, 42 minutes
REMARKS	A planned third manned lunar landing (by Lovell and Haise near the crater Fra Mauro) was aborted by an explosion aboard the command module Odyssey on April 13. Lovell, Swigert, and Haise used the lunar module Aquarius as a lifeboat during a loop around the Moon and a safe return to Earth.	Shepard and Mitchell landed the lunar module Antares at Fra Mauro on February 5 and performed 2 Moon walks totaling 9 hours.

FLIGHT	SOYUZ 10	APOLLO-SATURN 15
LAUNCH DATA	April 23, 1971 0254 MT Baikonur 1	July 26, 1971 0834 CDT Kennedy Space Center 39A
CREW	Shatalov (CDR), Yeliseyev (FE), Rukavish-nikov (TE)	Scott (CDR), Worden (CMP), Irwin (LMP)
CALL SIGN	Granit	Apollo 15, Endeavour, and Falcon
LANDING DATA	April 25, 1971 0250 MT Kazakhstan	August 7, 1971 1546 CDT Pacific Ocean, recovered by *U.S.S. Okinawa*
DURATION	1 day, 23 hours, 46 minutes	12 days, 7 hours, 12 minutes
REMARKS	Soyuz 10 was launched 4 days after Salyut, the first Soviet space station. Cosmonauts Shatalov, Yeliseyev, and Rukavishnikov docked their spacecraft to the station on April 24, but were unable to enter. After 5.5 hours the two craft separated and the cosmonauts returned to Earth, aborting a planned 24 days in space. Initial orbit: 131 to 155 miles.	Scott and Irwin spent 3 days on the lunar surface near Hadley Rille, including almost 21 hours in Moon walks and excursions with the lunar rover. On the return to Earth, Worden took a space walk to recover materials from an experiment bay on the Endeavour's service module.

FLIGHT	SOYUZ 11	APOLLO-SATURN 16
LAUNCH DATA	June 6, 1971 0755 MT Baikonur 1	April 16, 1972 1154 CDT Kennedy Space Center 39A
CREW	Dobrovolsky (CDR), Volkov (FE), Patsayev (TE)	Young (CDR), Mattingly (CMP), Duke (LMP)
CALL SIGN	Yantar (Amber)	Apollo 16, Casper, and Orion
LANDING DATA	June 30, 1971 0217 MT Kazakhstan	April 27, 1972 1345 CDT Pacific Ocean, recovered by *U.S.S. Ticon-deroga*
DURATION	23 days, 18 hours, 22 minutes	11 days, 1 hour, 51 minutes
REMARKS	The Soyuz 11 cosmonauts succeeded in docking with Salyut on June 7 and spent 23 days aboard the station. During their return to Earth on June 30, however, a valve in their Soyuz opened by mistake, causing their spacecraft to depressurize and killing all three cosmonauts. Orbit at docking: 116 to 136 miles.	Young and Duke landed the LM Orion near the crater Descartes for 3 days of exploration using a lunar rover. Problems with the main engine of the CM Casper delayed the lunar landing, and shortened the flight by one day.

FLIGHT	**APOLLO-SATURN 17**	**SKYLAB SL-3**
LAUNCH DATA	December 6, 1972 2333 CST Kennedy Space Center 39A	July 28, 1973 0611 CDT Kennedy Space Center 39B
CREW	Cernan (CDR), Evans (CMP), Schmitt (LMP)	Bean (CDR), Garriott (SP), Lousma (PLT)
CALL SIGN	Apollo 17, Challenger, and America	Skylab
LANDING DATA	December 19, 1972 1324 CST Pacific Ocean, recovered by *U.S.S. Ticonderoga*	September 25, 1973 1719 CDT Pacific Ocean, recovered by *U.S.S. New Orleans*
DURATION	12 days, 13 hours, 51 minutes	59 days, 11 hours, 9 minutes
REMARKS	Following the first nighttime launch in the U.S. space program, Cernan and geologist Schmitt landed the LM America near the Taurus mountains, spending the next 3 days exploring the lunar surface.	Bean, Garriott, and Lousma made further repairs to Skylab and completed a 2-month mission aboard the station.

FLIGHT	**SKYLAB SL-2**	**SOYUZ 12**
LAUNCH DATA	May 25, 1973 0800 CDT Kennedy Space Center 39B	September 27, 1973 1518 MT Baikonur 1
CREW	Conrad (CDR), Kerwin (SP), Weitz (PLT)	Lazarev (CDR), Makarov (FE)
CALL SIGN	Skylab	Urali (Urals)
LANDING DATA	June 22, 1973 0850 CDT Pacific Ocean, recovered by *U.S.S Ticonderoga*	September 29, 1973 1434 MT Kazakhstan
DURATION	28 days, 50 minutes	1 day, 23 hours, 16 minutes
REMARKS	Conrad, Kerwin, and Weitz boarded Skylab, America's first space station on May 26, and following repairs to the station (which had been damaged during launch on May 14), completed a successful 28-day mission.	Following the Soyuz 11 accident, the Soyuz spacecraft was redesigned. Lazarev and Makarov tested its systems on a 2-day mission, becoming the first cosmonauts since 1965 to wear space suits in flight.

FLIGHT	SKYLAB SL-4	SOYUZ 14
LAUNCH DATA	November 15, 1973 0801 CST Kennedy Space Center 39B	July 3, 1974 2151 MT Baikonur 1
CREW	Carr (CDR), Gibson (SP), Pogue (PLT)	Popovich (CDR), Artyukhin (FE)
CALL SIGN	Skylab	Berkut
LANDING DATA	February 8, 1974 0916 CST Pacific Ocean, recovered by *U.S.S. New Orleans*	July 19, 1974 1521 MT 88 miles SE of Dzhezkagan, Kazakhstan
DURATION	84 days, 1 hour, 15 minutes	15 days, 17 hours, 30 minutes
REMARKS	Carr, Gibson, and Pogue set a world space endurance record by spending 84 days aboard Skylab in the most scientifically productive mission in the program.	Popovich and Artyukhin conducted the USSR's first successful space-station mission, spending almost 14 days aboard Salyut 3 in a low Earth orbit performing medical studies and military reconnaissance. Orbit at docking on July 5 was 159 by 173 miles.

FLIGHT	SOYUZ 13	SOYUZ 15
LAUNCH DATA	December 18, 1973 1455 MT Baikonur 1	August 26, 1974 2258 MT Baikonur 1
CREW	Klimuk (CDR), Lebedev (FE)	Sarafanov (CDR), Demin (FE)
CALL SIGN	Kavkaz (Caucasus)	Dunai (Danube)
LANDING DATA	December 26, 1973 1150 MT Kazakhstan	August 28, 1974 2310 MT 30 miles NE of Tselinograd, Kazakh.
DURATION	7 days, 20 hours, 55 minutes	2 days, 12 minutes
REMARKS	Soyuz 13 carried the Orion astrophysical observatory originally intended to be flown on Salyut space stations, but a series of Salyut failures prevented that. Klimuk and Lebedev observed Comet Kahoutek as did the Skylab astronauts. It was the first time that Soviet and American space travelers were in orbit simultaneously.	Sarafanov and Demin were scheduled to spend 2 weeks aboard Salyut 3 but a failure in the Igla guidance system of Soyuz 15 forced them to call off their docking on August 28 and return to Earth.

FLIGHT	SOYUZ 16	SOYUZ 18-1
LAUNCH DATA	December 2, 1974 1240 MT Baikonur 1	April 5, 1975 1402 MT Baikonur 1
CREW	Filipchenko (CDR), Rukavishnikov (FE)	Lazarev (CDR), Makarov (FE)
CALL SIGN	Buran	Urali
LANDING DATA	December 8, 1974 1104 MT 188 miles N of Dzhezkazgan, Kazakh	April 5, 1975 1423 MT Near Gorno-Altaisk, Siberia
DURATION	5 days, 22 hours, 24 minutes	21 minutes
REMARKS	Apollo-Soyuz backups Filipchenko and Rukavishnikov conducted a 6-day dress rehearsal for the Soviet-American flight scheduled for the following July. NASA ground stations tracked Soyuz 16 after launch was announced.	Lazarev and Makarov were to have spent 2 months aboard Salyut 4, but saw the mission aborted when 2 stages of their booster rocket failed to separate. Soyuz reached an altitude of approximately 90 miles, then reentered without reaching orbit.

FLIGHT	SOYUZ 17	SOYUZ 18
LAUNCH DATA	January 11, 1975 0043 MT Baikonur 1	May 24, 1975 1758 MT Baikonur 1
CREW	Gubarev (CDR), Grechko (FE)	Klimuk (CDR), Sevastyanov (FE)
CALL SIGN	Zenit (Zenith)	Kavkaz
LANDING DATA	February 9, 1975 1403 MT 69 miles NE of Tselinograd, Kazakh	July 26, 1975 1718 MT 35 miles NE of Arkalyk, Kazakh
DURATION	29 days, 13 hours, 20 minutes	62 days, 23 hours, 20 minutes
REMARKS	Gubarev and Grechko conducted scientific experiments aboard Salyut 4, launched December 29, 1974. Docking took place on January 13 with Soyuz 17 in a corrected orbit of 183 by 221 miles.	Klimuk and Sevastyanov, backups for Lazarev and Makarov, docked with Salyut 4 on May 26 and spent the next 61 days performing scientific experiments and making Earth observations. Soyuz 18 was in orbit during Apollo-Soyuz.

FLIGHT	APOLLO-SOYUZ TEST PROJECT (ASTP)	SOYUZ 21
LAUNCH DATA	July 15, 1975 1450 CDT Kennedy Space Center 39B	July 6, 1976 1509 MT Baikonur 1
CREW	Stafford (CDR), Brand (CMP), Slayton (DMP)	Volynov (CDR), Zholobov (FE)
CALL SIGN	Apollo	Baikal
LANDING DATA	July 24, 1975 1618 CDT Pacific Ocean, recovered by *U.S.S. New Orleans*	August 24, 1976 2133 MT 125 miles SW of Kokchetav, Kazakh
DURATION	9 days, 1 hour, 28 minutes	49 days, 6 hours, 23 minutes
REMARKS	American astronauts Stafford, Brand, and Slayton linked up with Soviet Soyuz 19 and cosmonauts Leonov and Kubasov on July 17, spending 2 days in joint activities. The remainder of the mission was devoted to Earth observations and scientific experiments. A fuel leak during splashdown caused one of the astronauts to black out, but all were recovered safely.	On July 7, Volynov and Zholobov linked up with Salyut 5, launched June 22, for a mission devoted to military reconnaissance. The cosmonauts returned to Earth 3 weeks early because of physical and psychological problems.

FLIGHT	SOYUZ 19	SOYUZ 22
LAUNCH DATA	July 15, 1975 1520 MT Baikonur 1	September 15, 1976 1458 MT Baikonur 1
CREW	Leonov (CDR), Kubasov (FE)	Bykovsky (CDR), Aksenov (FE)
CALL SIGN	Soyuz	Yastreb
LANDING DATA	July 21, 1975 1351 MT 34 miles NW of Arkalyk, Kazakh	September 23, 1976 1042 MT 94 miles NW of Tselinograd
DURATION	5 days, 22 hours, 31 minutes	7 days, 21 hours, 52 minutes
REMARKS	On July 17 cosmonauts Leonov and Kubasov docked with an American Apollo crewed by astronauts Stafford, Brand, and Slayton. The spacecraft remained linked for 2 days, during which crewmen performed scientific experiments and made television broadcasts commemorating this first international spaceflight. Soyuz 19 inaugurated a new mission control center in Kaliningrad.	Bykovsky and Aksenov flew the backup Apollo-Soyuz spacecraft on a mission devoted to observations of the Earth's surface with the East German-built MKF-6 camera. Soyuz 22 was the first Soviet manned flight since 1965 to have an orbital inclination of 65 degrees.

FLIGHT	SOYUZ 23	SOYUZ 25
LAUNCH DATA	October 14, 1976 2040 MT Baikonur 1	October 9, 1977 0540 MT Baikonur 1
CREW	Zudov (CDR), Rozhdestvensky (FE)	Kovalenok (CDR), Ryumin (FE)
CALL SIGN	Rodon	Foton (Photon)
LANDING DATA	October 16, 1976 2047 MT Lake Tengiz, 122 miles SW of Tselinograd, Kazakh	October 11, 1977 0626 MT 116 miles NW of Tselinograd, Kazakh
DURATION	2 days, 7 minutes	2 days, 46 minutes
REMARKS	Zudov and Rozhdestvensky were to have spent at least 20 days aboard Salyut 5, but Soyuz guidance problems again canceled the docking. The cosmonauts made the Soviet Union's first "splashdown" on their return.	Kovalenok and Ryumin were to have boarded Salyut 6, launched September 29, for a planned 90-day mission, the most ambitious Soviet spaceflight ever attempted, involving a visit by a second cosmonaut team and resupply by an unmanned Progress supply ship. But a mechanical failure in the Salyut docking mechanism on October 11 prevented the cosmonauts from boarding the station and they returned to Earth that day.

FLIGHT	SOYUZ 24	SOYUZ 26
LAUNCH DATA	February 7, 1977 1912 MT Baikonur 1	December 10, 1977 0419 MT Baikonur 1
CREW	Gorbatko (CDR), Glazkov (FE)	Romanenko (CDR), Grechko (FE)
CALL SIGN	Terek	Taimyr
LANDING DATA	February 25, 1977 1238 MT 23 miles NE of Arkalyk, Kazakh	March 16, 1978 1419 MT 166 miles W of Tselinograd, Kazakh
DURATION	17 days, 17 hours, 26 minutes	96 days, 10 hours
REMARKS	Gorbatko and Glazkov, backups for Soyuz 23, docked with Salyut 5 on February 8 for a relatively short mission to complete experiments begun by the Soyuz 21 cosmonauts and to transfer military photographs to the Salyut-Almaz reentry module.	Romanenko and Grechko set a space endurance record aboard Salyut 6, which they boarded on December 11. In addition to scientific and medical work, they performed the Soviet Union's first EVA since 1969 and were visited by two teams of cosmonauts. They were also resupplied by the Progress unmanned craft. The cosmonauts returned to Earth in Soyuz 27.

FLIGHT	SOYUZ 27	SOYUZ 29
LAUNCH DATA	January 10, 1978 1526 MT Baikonur 1	June 15, 1978 2317 MT Baikonur 1
CREW	Dzhanibekov (CDR), Makarov (FE)	Kovalenok (CDR), Ivanchenkov (FE)
CALL SIGN	Pamir	Foton
LANDING DATA	January 16, 1978 1425 MT 194 miles W of Tselinograd, Kazakh	November 2, 1978 1405 MT 113 miles SE of Dzhezkazgan
DURATION	5 days, 22 hours, 59 minutes	139 days, 14 hours, 48 minutes
REMARKS	Dzhanibekov and Makarov docked with Salyut 6, joining cosmonauts Romanenko and Grechko, on January 11. They swapped spacecraft with the expedition crew and returned to Earth in Soyuz 26.	The second Salyut 6 resident crew, Kovalenok and Ivanchenkov set a new endurance record. They were visited by two teams of guest cosmonauts and resupplied by 3 Progress tankers. The cosmonauts returned to Earth aboard Soyuz 31.

FLIGHT	SOYUZ 28	SOYUZ 30
LAUNCH DATA	March 2, 1978 1828 MT Baikonur 1	June 27, 1978 1827 MT Baikonur 1
CREW	Gubarev (CDR), Remek [Czechoslovakia] (CR)	Klimuk (CDR), Hermaszewski [Poland] (CR)
CALL SIGN	Zenit	Kavkaz
LANDING DATA	March 10, 1978 1624 MT 194 miles W of Tselinograd	July 5, 1978 1630 MT 188 miles W of Tselinograd
DURATION	7 days, 22 hours, 16 minutes	7 days, 22 hours, 03 minutes
REMARKS	Remek, the first non-Soviet, non-American space traveler, and Gubarev joined Romanenko and Grechko aboard Salyut 6 on March 3 for a week of experiments.	Hermaszewski, the first Polish cosmonaut, and Klimuk spent a week with Kovalenok and Ivanchenkov aboard Salyut 6 beginning June 28.

FLIGHT	SOYUZ 31	SOYUZ 33
LAUNCH DATA	August 26, 1978 1751 MT Baikonur 1	April 10, 1979 2024 MT Baikonur 1
CREW	Bykovsky (CDR), Jaehn [German Dem. Rep.] (CR)	Rukavishnikov (CDR), Ivanov [Bulgaria] (CR)
CALL SIGN	Yastreb	Saturn
LANDING DATA	September 3, 1978 1440 MT near Dzhezkazgan	April 12, 1979 1935 MT 200 miles SE of Dzhezkazgan
DURATION	7 days, 20 hours, 49 minutes	1 day, 23 hours, 1 minute
REMARKS	Jaehn, the first German space traveler, and commander Bykovsky joined Kovalenok and Ivanchenkov aboard Salyut 6 beginning August 27. The visitors returned to Earth aboard Soyuz 29.	Soyuz 33 suffered a major engine failure during final approach to Salyut 6 on April 12. Cosmonauts Rukavishnikov and Ivanov were forced to use a backup engine to return to Earth.

FLIGHT	SOYUZ 32	SOYUZ 35
LAUNCH DATA	February 25, 1979 1454 MT Baikonur 1	April 9, 1980 1638 MT Baikonur 1
CREW	Lyakhov (CDR), Ryumin (FE)	Popov (CDR), Ryumin (FE)
CALL SIGN	Proton	Dnepr (Dniepr)
LANDING DATA	August 19, 1979 1530 MT 106 miles SE of Dzhezhkagan	October 11, 1980 1250 MT 113 miles SE of Dzhezkazgan
DURATION	175 days, 36 minutes	184 days, 20 hours, 12 minutes
REMARKS	Lyakhov and Ryumin, the third Salyut 6 resident crew, set another endurance record of almost 6 months in space. Their work included astronomical observations with the KT-10 radiotelescope and they also performed an unscheduled EVA. The cosmonauts did not have visitors during their mission, returning to Earth aboard Soyuz 34, which had been launched unmanned.	The fourth expedition to Salyut 6 included Ryumin, a last-minute replacement. He and Popov were resupplied by 4 Progress tankers and visited by 4 different teams of cosmonauts during their 6 months. The cosmonauts returned to Earth in Soyuz 37.

FLIGHT	SOYUZ 36	SOYUZ 37
LAUNCH DATA	May 26, 1980 2121 MT Baikonur 1	July 23, 1980 2133 MT Baikonur 1
CREW	Kubasov (CDR), Farkas [Hungary] (CR)	Gorbatko (CDR), Pham Tuan [Vietnam] (CR)
CALL SIGN	Orion	Terek
LANDING DATA	June 3, 1980 1807 MT 88 miles SE of Dzhezkazgan	July 31, 1980 1815 MT 112 miles SE of Dzhezkazgan
DURATION	7 days, 20 hours, 46 minutes	7 days, 20 hours, 42 minutes
REMARKS	Hungarian pilot Farkas and Soviet commander Kubasov joined Popov and Ryumin aboard Salyut 6 on May 27. The visitors returned to Earth a week later in Soyuz 35.	Vietnamese pilot Tuan and Soviet commander Gorbatko docked with Salyut 6 on July 24. Among their tasks was a commemoration of the 1980 Moscow Summer Olympics. They returned to Earth aboard Soyuz 36.

FLIGHT	SOYUZ T-2	SOYUZ 38
LAUNCH DATA	June 5, 1980 1719 MT Baikonur 1	September 18, 1980 2211 MT Baikonur 1
CREW	Malyshev (CDR), Aksenov (FE)	Romanenko (CDR), Tamayo Mendez [Cuba] (CR)
CALL SIGN	Yupiter (Jupiter)	Taimyr
LANDING DATA	June 9, 1980 1539 MT 124 miles SE of Dzhezkazgan	September 26, 1980 1854 MT 109 miles SE of Dzhezkazgan
DURATION	3 days, 22 hours, 19 minutes	7 days, 20 hours, 43 minutes
REMARKS	Malyshev and Aksenov made the first manned test flight of an improved Soyuz. The new guidance system failed on approach to Salyut 6, though the cosmonauts were able to dock manually. They spent 3 days with Popov and Ryumin before returning to Earth.	Cuban pilot Tamayo Mendez and Soviet commander Romanenko joined expedition cosmonauts Popov and Ryumin for a week aboard Salyut 6.

FLIGHT	SOYUZ T-3	SOYUZ 39
LAUNCH DATA	November 27, 1980 1718 MT Baikonur 1	March 22, 1981 1759 MT Baikonur 1
CREW	Kizim (CDR), Makarov (FE), Strekalov (CR)	Dzhanibekov (CDR), Gurragcha [Mongolia] (CR)
CALL SIGN	Mayak (Beacon)	Pamir
LANDING DATA	December 10, 1980 1226 MT 81 miles E of Dzhezkazgan	March 30, 1981 1442 MT 106 miles SE of Dzhezkazgan
DURATION	12 days, 19 hours, 08 minutes	7 days, 20 hours, 43 minutes
REMARKS	The first 3-man Soviet space crew since 1971 docked with the unoccupied Salyut 6 on November 28. For the next 12 days they performed repairs on the station to prepare it for a fifth resident crew.	Mongolian engineer Gurragcha and Soviet commander Dzhanibekov joined Kovalenok and Savinykh aboard Salyut 6 beginning on March 23.

FLIGHT	SOYUZ T-4	STS-1
LAUNCH DATA	March 12, 1981 2200 MT Baikonur 1	April 12, 1981 0600 CST Kennedy Space Center 39A
CREW	Kovalenok (CDR), Savinykh (FE)	Young (CDR), Crippen (PLT)
CALL SIGN	Foton	Columbia
LANDING DATA	May 26, 1981 1638 MT 78 miles E of Dzhezkazgan	April 14, 1981 1221 CST Edwards AFB, Runway 23
DURATION	74 days, 18 hours, 38 minutes	2 days, 6 hours, 21 minutes
REMARKS	Kovalenok and Savinykh conducted a "bonus" mission aboard Salyut 6, which had already exceeded its designed lifetime. The cosmonauts were visited by 2 guest crews.	Young and Crippen were launched on the 20th anniversary of Gagarin's flight aboard the first winged, reusable spacecraft, landing 2 days later on the lakebed at Edwards AFB.

FLIGHT	SOYUZ 40	STS-3
LAUNCH DATA	May 14, 1981 2117 MT Baikonur 1	March 22, 1982 1000 CST Kennedy Space Center 39A
CREW	Popov (CDR), Prunariu [Rumania] (CR)	Lousma (CDR), Fullerton (PLT)
CALL SIGN	Dnepr	Columbia
LANDING DATA	May 22, 1981 1758 MT 141 miles SE of Dzhezkazgan	March 30, 1982 1005 CST Northrup Strip, Runway 17, White Sands, New Mexico
DURATION	7 days, 20 hours, 41 minutes	8 days, 5 minutes
REMARKS	Rumanian pilot Prunariu and Soviet commander Popov spent 7 days aboard Salyut 6 beginning May 15.	Lousma and Fullerton made the third Shuttle orbital flight test aboard Columbia, which carried an experiment package called OSS-1. The mission was extended by one day and landing was switched to backup site in New Mexico because of rains at Edwards AFB.

FLIGHT	STS-2	SOYUZ T-5
LAUNCH DATA	November 12, 1981 0910 CST Kennedy Space Center 39A	May 13, 1982 1358 MT Baikonur 1
CREW	Engle (CDR), Truly (PLT)	Berezovoy (CDR), Lebedev (FE)
CALL SIGN	Columbia	Elbrus (Mt. Elbrus)
LANDING DATA	November 14, 1981 1523 CST Edwards AFB, Runway 23	December 10, 1982 2203 MT 119 miles E of Dzhezkazgan
DURATION	2 days, 6 hours, 13 minutes	211 days, 8 hours, 05 minutes
REMARKS	After several delays, Engle and Truly made the second flight aboard the reusable Shuttle Columbia, though technical problems shortened the mission from 5 to 2 days.	On May 14 Berezovoy and Lebedev docked Soyuz T-5 to the new Salyut 7, which had been launched April 19, for a mission scheduled to last 4 months, with possible extensions. Ultimately they spent seven months in space, hosting 2 teams of visiting cosmonauts, deploying a scientific satellite, performing space walks, in addition to other medical, engineering, and scientific work. They returned to Earth in the middle of a raging blizzard aboard Soyuz T-7.

FLIGHT	SOYUZ T-6	SOYUZ T-7
LAUNCH DATA	June 24, 1982 2029 MT Baikonur 1	August 19, 1982 2112 MT Baikonur 1
CREW	Dzhanibekov (CDR), Ivanchenkov (FE), Chretien [CNES] (CR)	Popov (CDR), Serebrov (FE), Savitskaya (CR)
CALL SIGN	Pamir	Dnepr
LANDING DATA	July 2, 1982 1821 MT 41 miles SE of Arkalyk	August 27, 1982 1904 MT 44 miles SE of Arkalyk
DURATION	7 days, 21 hours, 52 minutes	7 days, 21 hours, 52 minutes
REMARKS	French test pilot Chretien became the first Westerner to go into space aboard a Soviet vehicle. He and fellow cosmonauts Dzhanibekov and Ivanchenkov spent a week with Berezovoy and Lebedev on Salyut 7 beginning June 25.	Savitskaya, a test and sport pilot, became the second woman in space. She and Popov and Serebrov joined cosmonauts Berezovoy and Lebedev for a week aboard Salyut 7, then returned to Earth aboard Soyuz T-5.

FLIGHT	STS-4	STS-5
LAUNCH DATA	June 27, 1982 1000 CDT Kennedy Space Center 39A	Nov. 11, 1982 0619 CST Kennedy Space Center 39A
CREW	Mattingly (CDR), Hartsfield (PLT)	Brand (CDR), Overmyer (PLT), Allen (MS1), Lenoir (MS2)
CALL SIGN	Columbia	Columbia
LANDING DATA	July 4, 1982 1109 CDT Edwards AFB, Runway 22	Nov. 16, 1982 0833 CST Edwards AFB, Runway 22
DURATION	7 days, 1 hour, 10 minutes	5 days, 2 hours, 14 minutes
REMARKS	Mattingly and Hartsfield completed the fourth and final Shuttle orbital flight test, landing on the concrete runway at Edwards AFB. Columbia carried a Department of Defense payload and the first commercial experiment.	First operational flight of the Space Shuttle, and the first manned spacecraft to carry 4 crewmembers. The astronauts deployed 2 commercial communications satellites.

FLIGHT	STS-6	STS-7
LAUNCH DATA	April 4, 1983 1230 CST Kennedy Space Center 39A	June 18, 1983 0633 CDT Kennedy Space Center 39A
CREW CALL SIGN	Weitz (CDR), Bobko (PLT), Musgrave (MS1), Peterson (MS2) Challenger	Crippen (CDR), Hauck (PLT), Fabian (MS1), Ride (MS2), Thagard (MS3) Challenger
LANDING DATA	April 9, 1983 1254 CST Edwards AFB, Runway 22	June 24, 1983 0857 CDT Edwards AFB, Runway 15
DURATION	5 days, 25 minutes	6 days, 2 hours, 24 minutes
REMARKS	First flight of the Shuttle Challenger. Musgrave and Peterson performed the first space walk in the Shuttle program, and the astronauts deployed the first TDRS communications satellite.	Ride became the first American woman to make a spaceflight as a member of this 5-person crew that deployed 2 communications satellites as well as a retrievable satellite. A landing at Kennedy Space Center was canceled because of weather at the site.

FLIGHT	SOYUZ T-8	SOYUZ T-9
LAUNCH DATA	April 20, 1983 1711 MT Baikonur 1	June 27, 1983 1312 MT Baikonur 1
CREW	VTitov (CDR), Strekalov (FE), Serebrov (CR)	Lyakhov (CDR), Alexandrov (FE)
CALL SIGN	Okean (Ocean)	Proton
LANDING DATA	April 22, 1983 1729 MT 38 miles SE of Arkalyk	November 23, 1983 2258 MT 100 miles E of Dzhezkazgan
	2 days, 18 minutes	149 days, 9 hours, 46 minutes
DURATION REMARKS	A planned 8-month mission aboard the Salyut 7/Kosmos 1443 complex by cosmonauts Titov, Strekalov, and Serebrov had to be aborted because of failed rendezvous radar on Soyuz T-8.	Lyakhov and Alexandrov docked their Soyuz T-9 to the Salyut 7/Kosmos 1443 complex on June 28. During their 5-month mission they operated the Kosmos 1443 module and were resupplied by several Progress tankers. Salyut 7 suffered a massive fuel leak in August that almost disabled the station, forcing the cosmonauts to make 2 space walks to make repairs.

FLIGHT	STS-8	STS-9
LAUNCH DATA	August 30, 1983 0130 CDT Kennedy Space Center 39A	November 28, 1983 1000 CST Kennedy Space Center 39A
CREW	Truly (CDR), Brandenstein (PLT), Bluford (MS1), Gardner (MS2), Thornton (MS3)	Young (CDR), Shaw (PLT), Garriott (MS1), Parker (MS2), Lichtenberg (PS1), Merbold [ESA] (PS2)
CALL SIGN	Challenger	Columbia, Spacelab
LANDING DATA	September 5, 1983 0240 CDT Edwards AFB, Runway 22	December 8, 1983 1747 CST Edwards AFB, Runway 17
DURATION	6 days, 1 hour, 9 minutes	10 days, 7 hours, 47 minutes
REMARKS	First nighttime launch and landing in the Shuttle program. The astronauts deployed an Indian communications satellite. Bluford became the first African American in space.	First flight of the European Space Agency's Spacelab, after many delays. The 4 scientists in the crew conducted 72 different investigations in round-the-clock operations. The flight was extended by one day.

FLIGHT	SOYUZ T-10-1	41-B
LAUNCH DATA	September 26, 1983 2338 MT Baikonur 1	February 3, 1984 0700 CST Kennedy Space Center 39A
CREW	VTitov (CDR), Strekalov (FE)	Brand (CDR), Gibson (PLT), McNair (MS1), Stewart (MS2), McCandless (MS3)
CALL SIGN	Okean	Challenger
LANDING DATA	Launch pad abort	February 11, 1984 0617 CST Kennedy Space Center, Runway 15
DURATION		7 days, 23 hours, 17 minutes
REMARKS	Cosmonauts Titov and Strekalov were to have replaced Lyakhov and Alexandrov aboard Salyut 7 and performed repair EVAs to the station. A fire broke out in their launch vehicle shortly before ignition; the Soyuz T capsule separated and the cosmonauts landed safely several miles away.	McCandless made the first untethered space walk in history using the manned maneuvering unit (MMU). Two communications satellites deployed by the crew went into improper orbits, and were later recovered on Mission 51-A. The astronauts were the first to land at their launching site.

FLIGHT	SOYUZ T-10	41-C
LAUNCH DATA	February 8, 1984 1507 MT Baikonur 1	April 6, 1984 0758 CST Kennedy Space Center 39A
CREW	Kizim (CDR), Solovyov (FE), Atkov (CR)	Crippen (CDR), Scobee (PLT), Hart (MS1), van Hoften (MS2), Nelson (MS3)
CALL SIGN	Mayak	Challenger
LANDING DATA	October 2, 1984 1357 MT 91 miles SE of Dzhezkazgan	April 13, 1984 0738 CST Edwards AFB, Runway 17
DURATION	236 days, 22 hours, 50 minutes	6 days, 23 hours, 40 minutes
REMARKS	Kizim, Solovyov and Atkov set a new space endurance record during their 8 months aboard Salyut 7. Medical studies supervised by cardiologist Atkov occupied most of their time—87 working days. Kizim and Solovyov also made 6 EVAs. The crew was visited by 2 other cosmonaut teams and resupplied by 5 Progress tankers and logged over 3,400 orbits, traveling almost 100 million miles.	Nelson and van Hoften conducted the first capture, repair, and redeployment of a satellite using MMUs. The astronauts also deployed the long-duration exposure facility (LDEF).

FLIGHT	SOYUZ T-11	SOYUZ T-12
LAUNCH DATA	April 3, 1984 1709 MT Baikonur 1	July 17, 1984 2141 MT Baikonur 1
CREW	Malyshev (CDR), Strekalov (FE), Sharma [India] (CR)	Dzhanibekov (CDR), Savitskaya (FE), Volk (CR)
CALL SIGN		Pamir
LANDING DATA	April 11, 1984 1450 MT 35 miles E of Arkalyk	July 29, 1984 1655 MT 88 miles NE of Dhzezkazgan
DURATION	7 days, 21 hours, 41 minutes	11 days, 19 hours, 14 minutes
REMARKS	Sharma became the first citizen of India to make a spaceflight, spending a week aboard Salyut 7 with crewmates Malyshev and Strekalov visiting Kizim, Solovyov, and Atkov. They returned to Earth in the Soyuz T-10 spacecraft.	Dzhanibekov, Savitskaya and Volk rendezvoused with Salyut 7 and Kizim, Soloyov, and Atkov on July 13. Savitskaya became the first woman to make a space walk when, on July 25, she and Dzhanibekov spent 3.5 hours outside Salyut 7 testing space welding equipment. This was an unusually long (13 days instead of 8) resupply mission.

FLIGHT	41-D	51-A
LAUNCH DATA	August 30, 1984 0741 CDT Kennedy Space Center 39A	November 8, 1984 0615 CST Kennedy Space Center 39A
CREW	Hartsfield (CDR), Coats (PLT), Mullane (MS1), Hawley (MS2), Resnik (MS3), CWalker (PS)	Hauck (CDR), DWalker (PLT), Allen (MS1), Fisher (MS2), Gardner (MS3)
CALL SIGN	Discovery	Discovery
LANDING DATA	September 5, 1984 0837 CDT Edwards AFB, Runway 17	November 16, 1984 0600 CST Kennedy Space Center, Runway 15
DURATION	6 days, 56 minutes	7 days, 23 hours, 45 minutes
REMARKS	First flight of the Shuttle Discovery, following many delays, including a launchpad abort on June 26. The crew included industrial payload specialist Charles Walker, who operated the Continuous Flow Electrophoresis Experiment. The astronauts deployed 3 communications satellites.	In the most spectacular of the early Shuttle flights, astronauts Allen and Gardner used MMUs to retrieve 2 errant communications satellites, which were then returned to Earth. The crewmembers also launched 2 new satellites.

FLIGHT	41-G	51-C
LAUNCH DATA	October 5, 1984 0603 CDT Kennedy Space Center 39A	January 24, 1985 1350 CST Kennedy Space Center 39A
CREW	Crippen (CDR), McBride (PLT), Sullivan (MS1), Ride (MS2), Leesmta (MS3), Scully-Power [US Navy] (PS1), Garneau [CSA] (PS2)	Mattingly (CDR), Shriver (PLT), Onizuka (MS1), Buchli (MS2), Payton (PS)
CALL SIGN	Challenger	Discovery
LANDING DATA	October 13, 1984 1126 CDT Kennedy Space Center, Runway 33	January 27, 1985 1523 EST Kennedy Space Center, Runway 15
DURATION	8 days, 5 hours, 23 minutes	3 days, 1 hour, 33 minutes
REMARKS	First crew of 7. The astronauts deployed the Earth Radiation Budget Satellite and conducted an EVA satellite refueling test, making Sullivan the first American woman to walk in space.	The first classified U.S. Department of Defense Shuttle mission, 51-C reportedly deployed an electronic intelligence satellite called Magnum. The mission was shortened by 1 day because of weather problems at KSC.

FLIGHT	51-D	SOYUZ T-13
LAUNCH DATA	April 12, 1985 0759 CST Kennedy Space Center 39A	June 6, 1985 1040 MT Baikonur 1
CREW	Bobko (CDR), Williams (PLT), Seddon (MS1), Griggs (MS2), Hoffman (MS3), Walker (PS1), Garn (PS2)	Dzhanibekov (CDR), Savinykh (FE)
CALL SIGN	Discovery	Pamir
LANDING DATA	April 19, 1985 0755 EST Kennedy Space Center, Runway 33	September 26, 1985 1352 MT 138 miles NE of Dzhezkazgan
DURATION	6 days, 23 hours, 55 minutes	112 days, 3 hours, 12 minutes (Dzhanibekov) 168 days, 3 hours, 51 minutes (Savinykh)
REMARKS	This oft-delayed flight successfully deployed one communications satellite but suffered failure with a second, which astronauts Hoffman, Griggs, and Seddon attempted to repair, but could not.	Veteran commander Dzhanibekov and flight engineer Savinykh docked with the dead Salyut 7 on June 8 and in days following performed repairs, restoring it to usefulness. They were resupplied Progress 24 and by Kosmos 1669 until the arrival of Soyuz T-14 and cosmonauts Vasyutin, Grechko, and Volkov on September 18. Dzhanibekov returned to Earth in Soyuz T-13 with Grechko.

FLIGHT	51-B	51-G
LAUNCH DATA	April 29, 1985 1102 CST Kennedy Space Center 39A	June 17, 1985 0633 CDT Kennedy Space Center 39A
CREW	Overmyer (CDR), Gregory (PLT), Lind (MS1), Thagard (MS2), Thornton (MS3), Wang (PS1), van den Berg (PS2)	Brandenstein (CDR), Creighton (PLT), Fabian (MS1), Nagel (MS2), Lucid (MS3), Baudry [CNES] (PS1), Al-Saud [Saudi Arabia] (PS2)
CALL SIGN	Challenger, Spacelab	Discovery
LANDING DATA	May 6, 1985 0811 CDT Edwards AFB, Runway 17	June 24, 1985 0812 CDT Edwards AFB, Runway 23
DURATION	7 days, 8 minutes	7 days, 1 hour, 39 minutes
REMARKS	Spacelab 3, the first dedicated life sciences and space manufacturing Spacelab mission, carried 5 scientists who successfully operated 14 of 15 planned experiments.	The first trinational space crew deployed 3 communications satellites. Nagel became the one hundredth American in space.

FLIGHT	51-F	SOYUZ T-14
LAUNCH DATA	July 29, 1985 1600 CDT Kennedy Space Center 39A	September 17, 1985 1639 MT Baikonur 1
CREW	Fullerton (CDR), Bridges (PLT), Henize (MS1), Musgrave (MS2), England (MS3), Acton (PS1), Bartoe (PS2)	Vasyutin (CDR), Grechko (FE), AVolkov (CR)
CALL SIGN	Challenger, Spacelab	Cheget (Russian mountain peak)
LANDING DATA	August 6, 1985 1445 CDT Edwards AFB, Runway 23	November 21, 1985 1331 MT 113 miles SE of Dzhezkazgan
DURATION	7 days, 22 hours, 45 minutes	64 days, 21 hours, 52 minutes (Vasyutin/Volkov); 8 days, 21 hours, 13 minutes (Grechko)
REMARKS	Spacelab 2 carried experiments in life sciences, plasma physics, astronomy, and solar physics, operated by 5 scientists, including 58-year-old Henize, the oldest person yet to make a spaceflight.	Following the repair of Salyut 7 by Dzhanibekov and Savinykh, resident cosmonauts Vasyutin and Volkov with veteran flight engineer Grechko arrived at the station on September 18, performing the first "relief" mission in space history. Vasyutin, Savinykh, and Volkov were to have remained aboard Salyut 7 through March 1986, but had to return on November 21 because of Vasyutin's illness. They used the Kosmos 1686 laboratory module during the mission.

FLIGHT	51-I	51-J
LAUNCH DATA	August 27, 1985 0558 CDT Kennedy Space Center 39A	October 3, 1985 1015 CDT Kennedy Space Center 39A
CREW	Engle (CDR), Covey (PLT), van Hoften (MS1), Lounge (MS2), W. Fisher (MS3)	Bobko (CDR), Grabe (PLT), Hilmers (MS1), Stewart (MS2), Pailes (PS)
CALL SIGN	Discovery	Atlantis
LANDING DATA	September 3, 1985 0816 CDT Edwards AFB, Runway 23	October 7, 1985 1201 CDT Edwards AFB, Runway 23
DURATION	7 days, 2 hours, 18 minutes	4 days, 1 hour, 46 minutes
REMARKS	The astronauts successfully deployed two communications satellites, then retrieved and repaired the ailing Leasat 3 (launched earlier aboard Mission 51-D) in space walks by van Hoften and Fisher.	The first flight of the Shuttle Atlantis was the second classified Department of Defense Shuttle mission, deploying a pair of DSCS III military communications satellites and setting a Shuttle altitude record of 320 nautical miles.

FLIGHT	61-A	61-C
LAUNCH DATA	October 30, 1985 1100 CST Kennedy Space Center 39A	January 12, 1986 0555 CST Kennedy Space Center 39A
CREW	Hartsfield (CDR), Nagel (PLT), Dunbar (MS1), Buchli (MS2), Bluford (MS3), Furrer [West Germany] (PS1), Messerschmid [West Germany] (PS2), Ockels [ESA] (PS3)	Gibson (CDR), Bolden (PLT), Nelson (MS1), Hawley (MS2), Chang-Diaz (MS3), Cenker (PS1), BNelson (PS2)
CALL SIGN	Challenger, Spacelab D1	Columbia
LANDING DATA	November 6, 1985 1145 CST Edwards AFB, Runway 17	January 18, 1986 0759 CST Edwards AFB, Runway 22
DURATION	7 days, 45 minutes	6 days, 2 hours, 4 minutes
REMARKS	This Spacelab flight, D1, was controlled by the West German Federal Aerospace Research Establishment (DFVLR) and carried experiments devoted to materials processing, communications, and microgravity. It also carried the largest space crew in history.	Its launch delayed by weather and technical problems 7 times, Mission 61-C suffered nagging failures throughout its duration, which was extended by 1 day to ensure a return to KSC. Weather problems still forced an Edwards landing.

FLIGHT	61-B	51-L
LAUNCH DATA	November 26, 1985 1829 CST Kennedy Space Center 39A	January 28, 1986 1038 CST Kennedy Space Center 39B
CREW	Shaw (CDR), O'Connor (PLT), Ross (MS1), Cleave (MS2), Spring (MS3), Walker (PS1), Neri [Mexico] (PS2)	Scobee (CDR), Smith (PLT), Onizuka (MS1), Resnik (MS2), McNair (MS3), Jarvis (PS1), McAuliffe (PS2)
CALL SIGN	Atlantis	Challenger
LANDING DATA	December 3, 1985 1533 CST Edwards AFB, Runway 22	— — —
DURATION	6 days, 21 hours, 4 minutes	—
REMARKS	The crew of Mission 61-B deployed 3 communications satellites and also conducted space walks (by Ross and Spring) testing space construction techniques.	This scheduled 5-day Shuttle mission carrying teacher McAuliffe, the first citizen in space, ended in tragedy when the Challenger disintegrated 75 seconds after launch, killing all 7 crewmembers.

FLIGHT	**SOYUZ T-15**	**SOYUZ TM-3**
LAUNCH DATA	March 13, 1986 1533 MT Baikonur 1	July 22, 1987 0559 MT Baikonur 1
CREW	Kizim (CDR), Solovyov (FE)	Viktorenko (CDR), Alexandrov (FE), Faris [Syria] (CR)
CALL SIGN	Mayak	Vityaz (Knight)
LANDING DATA	July 16, 1986 1634 MT 33 miles NE of Arkalyk	July 30, 1987 0505 MT 85 miles NE of Arkalyk
DURATION	125 days, 1 minute	7 days, 23 hours, 5 minutes (Viktorenko/Faris) 160 days, 7 hours, 17 minutes (Alexandrov)
REMARKS	Space endurance record holders Kizim and Solovyov were launched in the last Soyuz T vehicle to perform a difficult dual mission: to activate the new Mir space station, launched February 20, and to retrieve vital scientific experiments from Salyut 7. Kizim and Solovyov docked with Mir on March 15 and remained aboard until May 5, when they used Soyuz T-15 to transfer to Salyut 7. Aboard Salyut 7 they performed 2 space walks (May 28 and May 31), then returned to Mir on June 25 to complete their mission.	The twelfth Soviet international mission with a Syrian cosmonaut turned into a crew swap, with TM-3 engineer Alexandrov remaining aboard Mir, replacing resident engineer Laveikin, who returned with Viktorenko and Faris.

FLIGHT	**SOYUZ TM-2**	**SOYUZ TM-4**
LAUNCH DATA	February 6, 1987 0038 MT Baikonur 1	December 21, 1987 1518 MT Baikonur 1
CREW	Romanenko (CDR), Laveikin (FE)	VTitov (CDR), Manarov (FE), Levchenko (CR)
CALL SIGN	Taimyr	Okean
LANDING DATA	December 29, 1987 1316 MT 56 miles from Arkalyk	December 21, 1988 1257 MT 108 mi SE of Dzhezhkazgan
DURATION	326 days, 11 hours, 8 minutes (Romanenko) 174 days, 3 hours, 26 minutes (Laveikin)	365 days, 22 hours, 9 minutes (Titov/Manarov) 7 days, 21 hours, 58 minutes (Levchenko)
REMARKS	The second resident Mir crew, Romanenko and Laveikin were assigned to complete 11 months aboard the station, supervising the addition of the Kvant module to the complex. Lavekin was forced to return to Earth in July and was replaced by Alexandrov (Soyuz TM-3). Romanenko returned in December.	The Mir-3 resident crew, Titov and Manarov accomplished the world's first yearlong space mission. In addition to space manufacturing and astronomical experiments, they also performed 3 EVAs. Levchenko was a Buran shuttle test pilot who returned to Earth with Romanenko and Alexandrov.

FLIGHT	**SOYUZ TM-5**	**STS-26**
LAUNCH DATA	June 7, 1988 1803 MT Baikonur 1	September 29, 1988 1037 CDT Kennedy Space Center 39B
CREW	ASolovyov (CDR), Savinykh (FE), Alexandrov [Bulgaria] (CR)	Hauck (CDR), Covey (PLT), Lounge (MS1), Hilmers (MS2), Nelson (MS3)
CALL SIGN	Rodnik (Spring)	Discovery
LANDING DATA	June 17, 1988 1413 MT 121 miles SE of Dzhezhkazgan	October 3, 1988 1038 CDT Edwards AFB, Runway 17
DURATION	9 days, 20 hours, 10 minutes	4 days, 1 hour, 1 minute
REMARKS	Bulgarian pilot Alexandrov spent a week aboard Mir performing research developed by scientists and engineers in his country. The crew returned to Earth in Soyuz TM-4.	The Shuttle program's "return to flight" after the Challenger disaster saw the successful deployment of the third Tracking and Data Relay Satellite.

FLIGHT	**SOYUZ TM-6**	**SOYUZ TM-7**
LAUNCH DATA	August 29, 1988 0823 MT Baikonur 1	November 26, 1988 1850 MT Baikonur 1
CREW	Lyakhov (CDR), Polyakov (FE), Mohmand [Afghanistan] (CR)	Volkov (CDR), Krikalev (FE), Chretien [France] (CR)
CALL SIGN	Proton	Donbass
LANDING DATA	September 7, 1988 0450 MT 96 miles SE of Dzhezkazgan	April 26, 1989 1989 MT 84 mi NE of Dzhezkazgan
DURATION	8 days, 20 hours, 27 minutes	150 days, 12 hours, 9 minutes (Volkov/Krikalev); 24 days, 18 hours, 7 minutes (Chretien)
REMARKS	This visiting mission allowed Afhgan researcher Ahad to spend a week aboard the Mir complex. Polyakov remained aboard Mir to monitor the health of resident crewmen Titov and Manarov. Lyakhov and Ahad faced an emergency during their return: faulty guidance forced them to delay landing for a day.	The Mir-4 crew included France's Chretien, on his second space mission. He and Volkov performed the first international EVA on Dec. 9. Volkov and Krikalev were joined by physician Polyakov, aboard Mir since August, for their stay.

FLIGHT	STS-27	STS-30
LAUNCH DATA	December 2, 1988 0831 CST Kennedy Space Center 39B	May 4, 1989 1347 CDT Kennedy Space Center 39B
CREW	Gibson (CDR), GGardner (PLT), Mullane (MS1), Ross (MS2), Shepherd (MS3)	DWalker (CDR), Grabe (PLT), Thagard (MS1), Cleave (MS2), Lee (MS3)
CALL SIGN	Atlantis	Atlantis
LANDING DATA	December 6, 1988 1736 CST Edwards AFB, Runway 17	May 8, 1989 1445 CDT Edwards AFB, Runway 22
DURATION	4 days, 9 hours, 5 minutes	4 days, 0 hours, 58 minutes
REMARKS	This classified Department of Defense Shuttle mission deployed the Lacrosse radar imaging reconnaissance satellite into a 57-degree low Earth orbit.	Deployed the radar mapping space probe Magellan, sending it on a 9-month voyage to the planet Venus.

FLIGHT	STS-29	STS-28
LAUNCH DATA	March 13, 1989 0857 CST Kennedy Space Center 39B	August 8, 1989 0737 CDT Kennedy Space Center 39B
CREW	Coats (CDR), Blaha (PLT), Buchli (MS1), Springer (MS2), Bagian (MS3)	Shaw (CDR), Richards (PLT), Leestma (MS1), Adamson (MS2), Brown (MS3)
CALL SIGN	Discovery	Columbia
LANDING DATA	March 18, 1989 0836 CST Edwards AFB, Runway 22	August 13, 1989 0838 CDT Edwards AFB, Runway 22
DURATION	4 days, 23 hours, 40 minutes	5 days, 1 hour, 1 minute
REMARKS	Deployed TDRS-D, the fourth tracking and data relay satellite, into geosynchronous orbit.	This classified Department of Defense Shuttle mission deployed an advanced Satellite Data Systems intelligence relay satellite into lower Earth orbit.

FLIGHT	**SOYUZ TM-8**	**STS-33**
LAUNCH DATA	September 6, 1989 0138 MT Baikonur 1	November 22, 1989 1823 CST Kennedy Space Center 39B
CREW	Viktorenko (CDR), Serebrov (FE)	Gregory (CDR), Blaha (PLT), Carter (MS1), Musgrave (MS2), KThornton (MS3)
CALL SIGN	Vityaz	Discovery
LANDING DATA	February 19, 1990 0736 MT 34 miles NE of Arkalyk	November 27, 1989 1831 CST Edwards AFB, Runway 4
DURATION	166 days, 5 hours, 58 minutes	5 days, 8 minutes
REMARKS	The Mir-5 crew added the Kvant 2 module to the Mir complex while also conducting the first tests of the Soviet manned maneuvering unit on 2 of the crew's 5 EVAs.	This classified Department of Defense Shuttle mission deployed the National Security Agency's Mentor signals intelligence satellite into geosynchronous orbit.

FLIGHT	**STS-34**	**STS-32**
LAUNCH DATA	October 18, 1989 1153 CST Kennedy Space Center 39B	January 9, 1990 0635 CST Kennedy Space Center 39A
CREW	Williams (CDR), McCulley (PLT), Lucid (MS1), Chang-Diaz (MS2), Baker (MS3)	Brandenstein (CDR), Wetherbee (PLT), Dunbar (MS1), Ivins (MS2), Low (MS3)
CALL SIGN	Atlantis	Columbia
LANDING DATA	October 23, 1989 1132 CST Edwards AFB, Runway 23	January 20, 1990 0336 CST Edwards AFB, Runway 22
DURATION	4 days, 23 hours, 41 minutes	10 days, 21 hours, 1 minute
REMARKS	Deployed the space probe Galileo, sending it on its 5-year mission to Jupiter.	The longest and most complex Shuttle mission to date deployed the Syncom IV-5 (Leasat), then retrieved and returned the Long Duration Explosure Facility to Earth.

FLIGHT	SOYUZ TM-9	STS-31
LAUNCH DATA	February 11, 1990 0916 MT Baikonur 1	April 24, 1990 0634 CDT Kennedy Space Center 39B
CREW	A. Solovyov (CDR), Balandin (FE)	Shriver (CDR), Bolden (PLT), McCandless (MS1), Hawley (MS2), Sullivan (MS3)
CALL SIGN	Rodnik	Discovery
LANDING DATA	August 9, 1990 0735 MST Near Arkalyk, Kazakhstan	April 29, 1990 0849 CST Edwards AFB, Runway 22
DURATION	178 days, 21 hours, 19 minutes	5 days, 2 hours, 15 minutes
REMARKS	Solovyov and Balandin, the Mir-6 crew, added the long-delayed Kristall module to the complex on June 10. They also performed 2 EVAs.	Deployed the long-delayed Hubble Space Telescope at a record Shuttle altitude of 323 miles.

FLIGHT	STS-36	SOYUZ TM-10
LAUNCH DATA	February 28, 1990 0150 CST Kennedy Space Center 39A	August 1, 1990 0932 MT Baikonur 1
CREW	Creighton (CDR), Casper (PLT), Hilmers (MS1), Mullane (MS2), Thuot (MS3)	Manakov (CDR), Strekalov (FE)
CALL SIGN	Atlantis	Vulkan (Vulcan)
LANDING DATA	March 4, 1990 1109 CST Edwards AFB, Runway 23	December 10, 1990 0908 MT 41 miles NW of Arkalyk
DURATION	4 days, 10 hours, 19 minutes	131 days, 0 hours, 36 minutes
REMARKS	This classified Department of Defense Shuttle mission deployed an advanced National Reconaissance Office KH-11 imaging satellite in a 62-degree low Earth orbit.	The Mir-7 crew continued operations aboard the orbital complex, performing an unsuccessful EVA on Oct. 29 to repair a docking hatch.

FLIGHT	STS-41	STS-35
LAUNCH DATA	October 6, 1990 0647 CDT Kennedy Space Center 39B	December 2, 1990 0049 CST Kennedy Space Center 39B
CREW	Richards (CDR), Cabana (PLT), Melnick (MS1), Shepherd (MS2), Akers (MS3)	Brand (CDR), GGardner (PLT), Hoffman (MS1), Lounge (MS2), Parker (MS3), Durrance (PS1), Parise (PS2)
CALL SIGN	Discovery	Columbia, Spacelab
LANDING DATA	October 10, 1990 0857 CDT Edwards AFB, Runway 22	December 10, 1990 2354 CST Edwards AFB, Runway 22
DURATION	4 days, 2 hours, 10 minutes	8 days, 23 hours, 5 minutes
REMARKS	Deployed the Ulysses space probe, sending it on a journey around the poles of the sun.	The first post-Challenger Spacelab mission with payload specialists. The crew of 7 performed astronomical experiments with the ASTRO 1 Spacelab. Mission was shortened a day because of weather problems at Edwards.

FLIGHT	STS-38	SOYUZ TM-11
LAUNCH DATA	November 15, 1990 1748 CST Kennedy Space Center 39A	December 2, 1990 1113 MT Baikonur 1
CREW	Covey (CDR), Culbertson (PLT), Springer (MS1), Meade (MS2), Gemar (MS3)	Afanasyev (CDR), Manarov (FE), Akiyama [Japan] CR)
CALL SIGN	Atlantis	Derbent
LANDING DATA	November 20, 1990 1543 CST Kennedy Space Center, Runway 33	May 26, 1991 1305 MT 41 miles SE of Dzhezkazgan
DURATION	4 days, 21 hours, 55 minutes	175 days, 2 hours, 52 minutes (Afanasyev/Manarov); 7 days, 21 hours, 55 minutes (Akiyama)
REMARKS	This Department of Defense Shuttle mission deployed an advanced Satellite Data System intelligence relay satellite into geosynchronous orbit. It was also the first post-Challenger mission to land at the Kennedy Space Center, diverted there by bad weather at Edwards AFB.	First Soviet flight of a commercial passenger, Japanese newsman Akiyama, who returned with expedition crewmen Manakov and Strekalov. Afanasyev and Manarov went on to perform 4 EVAs in addition to Mir repairs during the eighth main crew residency.

FLIGHT	STS-37	SOYUZ TM-12
LAUNCH DATA	April 5, 1991 0823 CST Kennedy Space Center 39B	May 18, 1991 1553 MT Baikonur 1
CREW	Nagel (CDR), Cameron (PLT), Godwin (MS1), Ross (MS2), Apt (MS3)	Artsebarsky (CDR), Krikalev (FE), Sharman [Britain] (CR)
CALL SIGN	Atlantis	"Ozon"
LANDING DATA	April 11, 1991 0855 CST Edwards AFB, Runway 33	October 10, 1991 0712 MT 41 miles SE of Arkalyk
DURATION	6 days, 32 minutes	144 days, 15 hours, 22 minutes (Artsebarsky) 311 days, 20 hours, 1 minute (Krikalev) 7 days, 21 hours, 12 minutes (Sharman)
REMARKS	Deployed the Gamma Ray Observatory, second in the NASA program of Great Observatories. Ross and Apt performed 2 EVAs—1 planned, 1 added to assist in GRO deployment.	First flight of a British citizen, Sharman, who spent 6 days aboard the Mir complex, returning to Earth with Afanasyev and Manarov. Artsebarsky and Krikalev, the Mir-9 crew, performed 6 different EVAs, including 1 on July 27 that required Krikalev to rescue Artsebarsky.

FLIGHT	STS-39	STS-40
LAUNCH DATA	April 28, 1991 0633 CDT Kennedy Space Center 39B	June 5, 1991 0825 CDT Kennedy Space Center 39B
CREW	Coats (CDR), Hammond (PLT), Harbaugh (MS1), McMonagle (MS2), Bluford (MS3), Veach (MS4), Hieb (MS5)	O'Connor (CDR), Gutierrez (PLT), Bagian (MS1), Jernigan (MS2), Seddon (MS3), Gaffney (PS1), Hughes-Fulford (PS2)
CALL SIGN	Discovery	Columbia, Spacelab
LANDING DATA	May 6, 1991 1355 CDT Kennedy Space Center, Runway 15	June 14, 1991 1039 CDT Edwards AFB, Runway 22
DURATION	8 days, 7 hours, 22 minutes	9 days, 2 hours, 14 minutes
REMARKS	This unclassified Department of Defense Shuttle mission was devoted to military scientific experiments, most of them of sensor technology. The crew of 7 astronauts also deployed and retrieved the Infrared Background Signature Survey satellite.	The second post-Challenger Spacelab mission was devoted to life sciences. The crew of 7 included 3 medical doctors and a chemist.

FLIGHT	STS-43	SOYUZ TM-13
LAUNCH DATA	August 2, 1991 1002 CDT Kennedy Space Center 39A	October 2, 1991 0759 MT Baikonur 1
CREW	Blaha (CDR), MBaker (PLT), Lucid (MS1), Low (MS2), Adamson (MS3)	AVolkov (CDR), Aubakirov (CR), Viehbock [Austria] (CR)
CALL SIGN	Atlantis	Donbass
LANDING DATA	August 11, 1991 0723 CDT Kennedy Space Center, Runway 15	March 25, 1992 1151 MT 40 miles NE of Arkalyk
DURATION	8 days, 21 hours, 21 minutes	175 days, 3 hours, 52 minutes (AVolkov) 7 days, 23 hours, 13 minutes (Aubakirov/Viehbock)
REMARKS	The crew of 5 deployed the fifth Tracking and Data Relay Satellite into geosynchronous orbit, then went on to perform experiments for the Freedom Space Station and extended-duration orbiter programs.	First flight of Austrian citizen (Viehbock) and representative of Kazakh SSR (Aubakirov), who spent 7 days aboard the Mir complex. Volkov remained aboard Mir with Krikalev, forming the Mir-10 crew.

FLIGHT	STS-48	STS-44
LAUNCH DATA	September 12, 1991 1811 CDT Kennedy Space Center 39B	November 24, 1991 1744 CST Kennedy Space Center 39A
CREW	Creighton (CDR), Reightler (PLT), Gemar (MS1), Buchli (MS2), Brown (MS3)	Gregory (CDR), Henricks (PLT), Voss (MS1), Musgrave (MS2), Runco (MS3), Hennen (PS1)
CALL SIGN	Discovery	Atlantis
LANDING DATA	September 18, 1991 0238 CDT Edwards AFB, Runway 5	December 1, 1991 1635 CST Edwards AFB, Runway 5
DURATION	5 days, 8 hours, 27 minutes	6 days, 22 hours, 50 minutes
REMARKS	The crew of 5 deployed the Upper Atmosphere Research Satellite (UARS). Landing was diverted from KSC to Edwards because of weather.	This unclassified Department of Defense Shuttle mission deployed the DSP-16 early warning satellite Liberty into geosynchronous orbit. The crew then went on to perform military Earth observations. The mission was cut short by 3 days because of the failure of a guidance unit.

FLIGHT	STS-42	STS-45
LAUNCH DATA	January 22, 1992 0853 CST Kennedy Space Center 39A	March 24, 1992 0714 CST Kennedy Space Center 39A
CREW	Grabe (CDR), Oswald (PLT), Thagard (MS1), Readdy (MS2), Hilmers (MS3), Bondar [CSA] (PS1), Merbold [ESA] (PS2)	Bolden (CDR), Duffy (PLT), Sullivan (MS1), Leestma (MS2), Foale (MS3), Frimout [Belgium] (PS1), Lichtenberg (PS2)
CALL SIGN	Discovery, Spacelab	Atlantis
LANDING DATA	January 30, 1992 1007 CST Edwards AFB, Runway 22	April 2, 1992 0523 CDT Kennedy Space Center, Runway 15
DURATION	8 days, 1 hour, 14 minutes	8 days, 22 hours, 10 minutes
REMARKS	Discovery carried the first International Microgravity Lab, a Spacelab mission devoted to experiments in space medicine and manufacturing.	Atlantis carried ATLAS, the Atmospheric Laboratory for Applications and Science, on a Spacelab mission devoted to studies of the Earth's atmosphere.

FLIGHT	SOYUZ TM-14	STS-49
LAUNCH DATA	March 17, 1992 1354 MT Baikonur 1	May 7, 1992 1840 CDT Kennedy Space Center 39B
CREW	Viktorenko (CDR), Kaleri (FE), Flade [Germany] (CR)	Brandenstein (CDR), Chilton (PLT), Hieb (MS1), Melnick (MS2), Thuot (MS3), Thornton (MS4), Akers (MS5)
CALL SIGN	Vityaz	Endeavour
LANDING DATA	August 10, 1992 0505 MT 85 miles E of Dzhezkazgan	May 16, 1992 1557 CDT Edwards AFB, Runway 22
DURATION	145 days, 15 hours, 11 minutes (Viktorenko/Kaleri); 7 days, 21 hours, 57 minutes (Flade)	8 days, 21 hours, 18 minutes
REMARKS	The Mir-11 resident crew (Viktorenko/Kaleri) relieved Volkov and extended Mir crewmember Krikalev. The mission was devoted to Earth resources, some for new Russian commercial firms.	This first flight of the orbiter Endeavour captured, repaired and redeployed the errant Intelsat VI-3 satellite in EVAs by Thuot, Hieb, and Akers. Akers and Thornton also did an EVA to test Space Station construction.

FLIGHT	STS-50	STS-46
LAUNCH DATA	June 25, 1992 1112 CDT Kennedy Space Center 39A	July 31, 1992 0856 CDT Kennedy Space Center 39B
CREW	Richards (CDR), Bowersox (PLT), Dunbar (MS1), Baker (MS2), Meade (MS3), DeLucas (PS1), Trinh (PS2)	Shriver (CDR), Allen (PLT), Nicollier [ESA] (MS1), Ivins (MS2), Hoffman (MS3), Chang-Diaz (MS4), Malerba [Italy] (PS1)
CALL SIGN	Columbia	Atlantis
LANDING DATA	July 9, 1992 0642 CDT Kennedy Space Center, Runway 15	August 8, 1992 0714 CDT Kennedy Space Center, Runway 15
DURATION	13 days, 19 hours, 30 minutes	7 days, 23 hours, 11 minutes
REMARKS	Columbia carried the first U.S. Micogravity Lab, a Spacelab mission devoted to space manufacturing, on the longest U.S. manned mission since Skylab 4.	This international crew deployed the European Space Agency's EURECA platform in orbit, and attempted to unreel the 12-mile-long Italian Tethered Satellite. The TSS experiment had to be abandoned.

FLIGHT	SOYUZ TM-15	STS-47
LAUNCH DATA	July 27, 1992 0908 MT Baikonur 1	September 12, 1992 0923 CDT Kennedy Space Center 39B
CREW	A. Solovyov (CDR), Avdeyev (FE), Tognini (CR)	Gibson (CDR), CBrown (PLT), Lee (MS1/PC), Apt (MS2), Davis (MS3), Jemison (MS4), Mohri [NASDA] (PS1)
CALL SIGN	Rodnik	Endeavour
LANDING DATA	February 1, 1993 1852 MT 62 miles NW of Arkalyk	September 20, 1992 0754 CDT Kennedy Space Center, Runway 33
DURATION	188 days, 21 hours, 49 mintues (Solovyov/Avdeyev); 13 days, 19 hours, 57 minutes (Tognini)	7 days, 22 hours, 30 minutes
REMARKS	The twelfth Mir resident crew relieved Viktorenko/Kaleri. Solovyov/Avdeyev made 4 EVAs mounting the Sofora propulsion module on the Mir complex.	Carried Spacelab-J, sponsored by the National Space Development Agency of Japan.

FLIGHT	STS-52	STS-54
LAUNCH DATA	October 22, 1992 1209 CDT Kennedy Space Center 39B	January 13, 1993 0900 CST Kennedy Space Center 39B
CREW	Wetherbee (CDR), Baker (PLT), Veach (MS1), Shepherd (MS2), Jernigan (MS3), MacLean [CSA] (PS1)	Casper (CDR), McMonagle (PLT), Harbaugh (MS1), Runco (MS2), Helms (MS3)
CALL SIGN	Columbia	Endeavour
LANDING DATA	November 1, 1992 0806 CST Kennedy Space Center, Runway 33	January 19, 1993 0738 CST Kennedy Space Center, Runway 33
DURATION	9 days, 20 hours, 56 minutes	5 days, 23 hours, 38 minutes
REMARKS	Deployed the Italian-built LAGEOS II geophysical satellite and operated the first U.S. Microgravity Payload; also carried ashes of late *Star Trek* creator Gene Roddenberry.	Deployed sixth and last Tracking and Data Relay Satellite. Harbaugh and Runco performed an EVA.

FLIGHT	STS-53	SOYUZ TM-16
LAUNCH DATA	December 2, 1992 0724 CST Kennedy Space Center 39A	January 24, 1993 0858 MT Baikonur 1
CREW	Walker (CDR), Cabana (PLT), Bluford (MS1), Voss (MS2), Clifford (MS3)	Manakov (CDR), Poleshchuk (FE)
CALL SIGN	Discovery	Vulkan
LANDING DATA	December 9, 1992 1443 CST Edwards AFB, Runway 22	July 22, 1993 0942 MST 87 miles E of Dzhezhkazgan
DURATION	7 days, 7 hours, 19 minutes	179 days, 00 hours, 44 minutes
REMARKS	The last classified Shuttle mission, deployed the third advanced Satellite Data Systems intelligence relay satellite (DOD-1) into Earth orbit.	Manakov/Poleshchuk, the Mir-13 crew, relieved Solovyov and Avdeyev using Soyuz TM No. 101, equipped with a special docking adaptor originally intended for use with the Buran shuttle. Manakov/Avdeyev also deployed Znamya experiment, and performed 2 EVAs.

FLIGHT	STS-56	STS-57
LAUNCH DATA	April 7, 1993 1129 CDT Kennedy Space Center 39B	June 21, 1993 0807 CDT Kennedy Space Center 39B
CREW	Cameron (CDR), Oswald (PLT), Foale (MS1/PC), Cockrell (MS2), Ochoa (MS3)	Grabe (CDR), Duffy (PLT), Low (MS1/PC), Sherlock (MS2), Wisoff (MS3), JE Voss (MS4)
CALL SIGN	Discovery	Endeavour
LANDING DATA	April 17, 1993 0637 CDT Kennedy Space Center, Runway 33	July 1, 1993 0752 CDT Kennedy Space Center, Runway 33
DURATION	9 days, 6 hours, 9 minutes	9 days, 23 hours, 45 minutes
REMARKS	Carried the second ATLAS Spacelab.	Carried the first SpaceHab payload module. Deployed and retrieved the EURECA satellite. Low and Wisoff performed a 5-hour, 50-minute EVA.

FLIGHT	STS-55	SOYUZ TM-17
LAUNCH DATA	April 26, 1993 0950 CDT Kennedy Space Center 39A	July 1, 1993 1733 MST Baikonur 1
CREW	Nagel (CDR), Henricks (PLT), Ross (MS1/PC), Precourt (MS2), Harris (MS3), Walter [DLR] (PS1), Schlegel [DLR] (PS2)	Tsibliyev (CDR), Serebrov (FE), Haignere [CNES] (CR)
CALL SIGN	Columbia	Sirius
LANDING DATA	May 6, 1993 0930 Edwards AFB, Runway 22	January 14, 1994 1218 MT 126 mi W of Karaganda
DURATION	9 days, 23 hours, 40 minutes	197 days, 17 hours, 45 minutes (Tsibliyev/Serebrov); 20 days, 16 hours, 9 minutes (Haignere)
REMARKS	Carried the second German Spacelab.	The Mir-14 crew of Tsibliyev/Serebrov launched with CNES researcher Haignere to relieve Solovyov/Avdeyev on 6-month mission. Crew conducted 6 EVAs, erecting Rapan structure on Mir exterior. Their departure from Mir on January 14, 1994, marred by a brief collision.

FLIGHT	STS-51	STS-61
LAUNCH DATA	September 12, 1993 0645 CDT Kennedy Space Center 39B	December 2, 1993 0327 CST Kennedy Space Center 39B
CREW	Culbertson (CDR), Readdy (PLT), Newman (MS1), Bursch (MS2), Walz (MS3)	Covey (CDR), Bowersox (PLT), Thornton (MS1), Nicollier (MS2), Hoffman (MS3), Musgrave (MS4/PC), Akers (MS5)
CALL SIGN	Discovery	Endeavour
LANDING DATA	September 22, 1993 0256 CDT Kennedy Space Center, Runway 15	December 12, 1993 2326 CST Kennedy Space Center, Runway 33
DURATION	9 days, 20 hours, 11 minutes	10 days, 18 hours, 59 minutes
REMARKS	Deployed the Advanced Communications Technology Satellite; deployed, then retrieved the SPAS. Walz and Newman made a 7-hour EVA.	Performed the first, very successful Hubble Space Telescope repair and refurbishment mission. Two teams of astronauts made 5 EVAs totalling 35 hours.

FLIGHT	STS-58	SOYUZ TM-18
LAUNCH DATA	October 18, 1993 0953 CST Kennedy Space Center 39B	January 8, 1994 1306 MT Baikonur 1
CREW	Blaha (CDR), Searfoss (PLT), Seddon (MS1/PC), McArthur (MS2), Lucid (MS3), Wolf (MS4), Fettman (PS1)	Afanasyev (CDR), Usachev (PLT), Polyakov (CR)
CALL SIGN	Columbia	Derbent
LANDING DATA	November 1, 1993 0906 CST Edwards AFB, Runway 22	July 09, 1994 1333 MT 68 mi W of Arkalyk
DURATION	14 days, 8 hours, 13 minutes	182 days, 00 hours, 27 minutes (Afanasyev/Usachev); 438 days, 17 hours, 58 minutes (Polyakov)
REMARKS	Carried the second Spacelab Life Sciences mission.	The Mir-15 main crew of Afanasyev and Usachev relieved Tsibliyev and Serebrov on a 6-month mission. Physician Polyakov commenced planned 16-month endurance test.

FLIGHT	**STS-60**	**STS-59**
LAUNCH DATA	February 3, 1994 0610 CST Kennedy Space Center 39A	April 9, 1994 0605 CST Kennedy Space Center 39A
CREW CALL SIGN	Bolden (CDR), Reightler (PLT), Davis (MS1), Sega (MS2), Chang-Diaz (MS3), Krikalev [RKA] (MS4)	Gutierrez (CDR), Chilton (PLT), Apt (MS1), Clifford (MS2), Godwin (MS3/PC), Jones (MS4)
LANDING DATA	Discovery February 11, 1994 1319 CST Kennedy Space Center, Runway 33	Endeavour April 20, 1994 1154 CST Edwards AFB, Runway 22
DURATION	8 days, 7 hours, 9 minutes	11 days, 5 hours, 49 minutes
REMARKS	Carried the second SpaceHab and also attempted to deploy the Wake Shield Facility. The crew of 6 included Krikalev, the first Russian cosmonaut to fly as a mission specialist.	First flight of the $366-million dollar Shuttle Radar Lab, an environmental imaging system that surveyed 25 million square miles of the Earth's surface, returning enough data to fill 20,000 encyclopedia volumes.

FLIGHT	**STS-62**	**SOYUZ TM-19**
LAUNCH DATA	March 4, 1994 0753 CST Kennedy Space Center 39B	July 1, 1994 1525 MST Baikonur 1
CREW CALL SIGN	Casper (CDR), Allen (PLT), Thuot (MS1), Gemar (MS2), Ivins (MS3)	Malenchenko (CDR), Musabayev (FE) Agat
LANDING DATA	Columbia March 18, 1994 0810 CST Kennedy Space Center, Runway 33	November 4, 1994 1418 MT 49 miles NE of Arkalyk
DURATION	13 days, 23 hours, 17 minutes	125 days, 22 hours, 54 minutes
REMARKS	Carried the second U.S. Microgravity Payload. The crew also tested equipment for a new Shuttle remote manipulator arm.	The Mir-16 crew performed 2 EVAs during its 4.5-month mission while continuing medical studies with long-duration physician Polyakov.

FLIGHT	STS-65	STS-68
LAUNCH DATA	July 8, 1994 1143 CDT Kennedy Space Center 39A	September 30, 1998 0616 CDT Kennedy Space Center 39A
CREW	Cabana (CDR), Halsell (PLT), Hieb (MS1/PC), Walz (MS2), Thomas (MS3), Chiao (MS4), Mukai [NASDA] (PS1)	Baker (CDR), Wilcutt (PLT), Smith (MS1), Bursch (MS2), Wisoff (MS3), Jones (MS4/PC)
CALL SIGN	Columbia	Endeavour
LANDING DATA	July 23, 1994 0538 CDT Kennedy Space Center, Runway 33	October 11, 1994 1202 CDT Edwards AFB, Runway 22
DURATION	14 days, 17 hours, 56 minutes	11 days, 5 hours, 46 minutes
REMARKS	Carried the second International Microgravity Laboratory.	Mission delayed following an August 18, 1994, on-pad abort. Second flight of the Shuttle Radar Lab.

FLIGHT	STS-64	SOYUZ TM-20
LAUNCH DATA	September 9, 1994 1723 CDT Kennedy Space Center 39B	October 4, 1994 0141 MT Baikonur 1
CREW	Richards (CDR), Hammond (PLT), Linenger (MS1), Helms (MS2), Meade (MS3), Lee (MS4/PC)	Viktorenko (CDR), Kondakova (FE), Merbold [ESA] (CR)
CALL SIGN	Columbia	Vityaz
LANDING DATA	September 20, 1994 1613 CDT Edwards AFB, Runway 4	March 22, 1995 0704 MT 34 miles NE of Arkalyk
DURATION	10 days, 23 hours, 50 minutes	169 days, 08 hours, 22 minutes (Viktorenko/Kondakova); 31 days, 22 hours, 36 minutes (Merbold)
REMARKS	Carried the Lidar-in-Space Technology Experiment. Lee and Meade also performed an EVA to test the SAFER backpack.	The Mir-17 crew included the first long-duration Russian female crewmember, Kondakova, relieving crew of Malenchenko and Musabayev. Highlight of 5-month mission was first visit (rendezvous) by Shuttle Discovery (STS-63) on February 6, 1995. Also continued medical studies with long-duration crewmember Polyakov, who returned to Earth with Viktorenko and Kondakova.

FLIGHT	STS-66	STS-67
LAUNCH DATA	November 3, 1994 1100 CST Kennedy Space Center 39B	March 2, 1995 1238 CST Kennedy Space Center 39A
CREW	McMonagle (CDR), CBrown (PLT), Ochoa (MS1/PC), Tanner (MS2), Clervoy [ESA] (MS3), Parazynski (MS4)	Oswald (CDR), WGregory (PLT), Grunsfeld (MS1), Lawrence (MS2), Jernigan (MS3), Durrance (PS1), Parise (PS2)
CALL SIGN	Atlantis	Endeavour
LANDING DATA	November 14, 1994 0934 CST Edwards AFB, Runway 22	March 18, 1995 1548 CST Edwards AFB, Runway 22
DURATION	10 days, 22 hours, 34 minutes	16 days, 15 hours, 10 minutes
REMARKS	Third and final Spacelab ATLAS mission.	Carried the second Spacelab ASTRO payload.

FLIGHT	STS-63	SOYUZ TM-21
LAUNCH DATA	February 2, 1995 1122 CST Kennedy Space Center 39B	March 14, 1995 0911 MT Baikonur 1
CREW	Wetherbee (CDR), Collins (PLT), Harris (MS1/PC), Foale (MS2), JE Voss-Ford (MS3), Titov (MS4)	Dezhurov (CDR), Strekalov (FE), Thagard [NASA] (CR)
CALL SIGN	Discovery	Uragan (Hurricane)
LANDING DATA	February 11, 1995 0550 CST Kennedy Space Center, Runway 15	September 11, 1995* 0943 MT* 67 miles N of Arkalyk*
DURATION	8 days, 6 hours, 28 minutes	122 days, 8 hours, 43 minutes
REMARKS	Carried the third SpaceHab module on the first Shuttle-Mir rendezvous, closing to within 30 feet of the Russian station. Harris and Foale performed EVA to test thermal values of space suit.	First Soyuz crew to include a NASA astronaut (Thagard). The Mir-18 crew completed 5 EVAs and also reconfigured Mir modules. Crew returned to Earth aboard Shuttle Atlantis (STS-71). Landing time and place (*) are for Soyuz TM-21 vehicle with Mir-19 crew.

FLIGHT	STS-71	SOYUZ TM-22
LAUNCH DATA	June 27, 1995 1432 CDT Kennedy Space Center 39A	September 3, 1995 1200 MT Baikonur 1
CREW	Gibson (CDR), Precourt (PLT), E Baker (MS1/PC), Harbaugh (MS2), Dunbar (MS3), Solovyov (Mir-19 CDR UP), Budarin (Mir-19 FE UP)	Gidzenko (CDR), Avdeyev (FE), Reiter [ESA] (FE2)
CALL SIGN	Atlantis	Uran (Uranus)
LANDING DATA	July 7, 1995 0954 CDT Kennedy Space Center Runway 15	February 29, 1996 1342 MT 65 miles NE of Dzhezhkazgan
DURATION	9 days, 19 hours, 22 minutes (STS-71 crew); 75 days, 11 hours, 20 minutes (Solovyov/Budarin)	179 days, 1 hour, 42 minutes
REMARKS	First of 9 Shuttle-Mir dockings, accomplished 20 years after Apollo-Soyuz. Crew delivered supplies and new Mir crewmembers Solovyov and Budarin to the station, returning Dezhurov, Strekalov and Thagard to Earth after performing medical checks in Spacelab.	The Mir-20 crew included the first long-duration ESA astronaut (Reiter) and accomplished 3 EVAs during a mission that was extended by 45 days because of booster unavailability. Visited by second Shuttle-Mir mission, STS-74.

FLIGHT	STS-70	STS-69
LAUNCH DATA	July 13, 1995 0842 CDT Kennedy Space Center 39B	September 7, 1995 1008 CDT Kennedy Space Center 39A
CREW	Henricks (CDR), Kregel (PLT), D Thomas (MS1), Currie (MS2), Weber (MS3)	Walker (CDR), Cockrell (PLT), Voss (MS1/PC), Newman (MS2), Gernhardt (MS3)
CALL SIGN	Discovery	Endeavour
LANDING DATA	July 22, 1995 0702 CDT Kennedy Space Center, Runway 33	September 18, 1995 0638 CDT Kennedy Space Center, Runway 33
DURATION	8 days, 22 hours, 20 minutes	10 days, 20 hours, 30 minutes
REMARKS	Delayed for weeks because of woodpecker damage to external tank, STS-70 deployed the fifth Tracking and Data Relay Satellite. First use of a new mission control center since Gemini 4 in 1965.	Second deployment and retrieval of the Wake Shield Facility. Crew also deployed and retrieved Spartan 201. Voss and Gernhard made an EVA testing International Space Station techniques.

FLIGHT	STS-73	STS-72
LAUNCH DATA	October 20, 1995 0853 CDT Kennedy Space Center 39B	January 11, 1996 0341 CST Kennedy Space Center 39B
CREW	Bowersox (CDR), Rominger (PLT), Coleman (MS1), Lopez-Alegria (MS2), K Thornton (MS3/PC), Leslie (PS1), Sacco (PS2)	Duffy (CDR), Jett (PLT), Chiao (MS1/PC), Scott (MS2), Wakata [NASDA] (MS3), Barry (MS4)
CALL SIGN	Columbia	Endeavour
LANDING DATA	November 5, 1995 0545 CST Kennedy Space Center, Runway 33	January 20, 1996 0642 CST Kennedy Space Center, Runway 15
DURATION	15 days, 21 hours, 52 minutes	8 days, 23 hours, 1 minute
REMARKS	Flight of the Columbia carried the second U.S. Microgravity Laboratory Spacelab. Crew operated in 2 shifts: red (Bowersox, Rominger, Thornton, Sacco) and blue (Lopez-Alegria, Coleman, Leslie).	Retrieved NASDA's Space Flyer Unit, launched 10 months earlier by H-2 rocket. Deployed and retrieved the OAST Spartan 206 flyer. Crew performed 2 EVAs to test ISS suits and techniques, Chiao/Barry and Chiao/Scott.

FLIGHT	STS-74	SOYUZ TM-23
LAUNCH DATA	November 12, 1995 0631 CST Kennedy Space Center 39A	February 23, 1996 1534 MT Baikonur 1
CREW	Cameron (CDR), Halsell (PLT), Hadfield [CSA] (MS1), Ross (MS2), McArthur (MS3)	Onufriyenko (CDR), Usachev (FE)
CALL SIGN	Atlantis	Skif
LANDING DATA	November 20, 1995 1101 CST Kennedy Space Center, Runway 33	September 2, 1996 1041 MST 62 miles SW of Akmola (formerly Tselinograd)
DURATION	8 days, 04 hours, 31 minutes	192 days, 04 hours, 10 minutes
REMARKS	Second Shuttle-Mir mission delivered the Russian-built Docking Module, to provide greater clearance for later planned Shuttle-Mir dockings.	The Mir-21 crew of Onufriyenko and Usachev was joined by FE2 Lucid on March 24, 1996, delivered by STS-76. Crew added the Priroda module to Mir (April 27) and carried out 4 EVAs.

FLIGHT	STS-75	STS-77
LAUNCH DATA	February 22, 1996 0218 CST Kennedy Space Center 39B	May 19, 1996 0530 CDT Kennedy Space Center 39B
CREW	Allen (CDR), Horowitz (PLT), Hoffman (MS1), Cheli [ESA] (MS2), Nicollier [ESA] (MS3), Chang-Diaz (MS4/PC), Guidoni [ASI] (PS1)	Casper (CDR), Brown (PLT), A Thomas (MS1/PC), Bursch (MS2), Runco (MS3), Garneau [CSA] (MS4)
CALL SIGN	Columbia	Endeavour
LANDING DATA	March 9, 1996 0759 CST Kennedy Space Center, Runway 33	May 29, 1996 0609 CDT Kennedy Space Center Runway 33
DURATION	15 days, 17 hours, 41 minutes	10 days, 00 hours, 39 minutes
REMARKS	Second attempt to deploy Italy's Tethered Satellite System, ultimately reaching almost 13 miles from orbiter before the tether broke.	Carried the fourth SpaceHab; deployed and retrieved Spartan 207. The crew also made 3 separate rendezvous with the PAMS.

FLIGHT	STS-76	STS-78
LAUNCH DATA	March 22, 1996 0213 CST Kennedy Space Center 39A	June 20, 1996 0949 CDT Kennedy Space Center 39B
CREW	Chilton (CDR), Searfoss (PLT), Sega (MS1/PC), Clifford (MS2), Godwin (MS3), Lucid (MS4 UP)	Henricks (CDR), Kregel (PLT), Linnehan (MS1), Helms (MS2/PC), Brady (MS3), Favier [CNES] (PS1), Thirsk [CSA] (PS2)
CALL SIGN	Atlantis	Columbia
LANDING DATA	March 31, 1996 0729 CST Edwards AFB, Runway 22	July 7, 1996 0737 CDT Kennedy Space Center, Runway
DURATION	9 days, 5 hours, 16 minutes (STS-76 core crew) 188 days, 4 hours, 0 minutes (Lucid)	16 days, 21 hours, 48 minutes
REMARKS	Carried SpaceHab with Mir supplies on third Shuttle-Mir docking. Also delivered NASA-Mir researcher Shannon Lucid to station. Godwin and Clifford performed first Shuttle EVA at Mir.	Carried the Life and Microgravity Laboratory.

FLIGHT	SOYUZ TM-24	STS-80
LAUNCH DATA	August 17, 1996 1618 MST Baikonur 1	November 19, 1996 0155 CST Kennedy Space Center 39B
CREW	Korzun (CDR), Kaleri (FE), Andre-Deshays [CNES] (CR)	Cockrell (CDR), Rominger (PLT), Jernigan (MS1), Jones (MS2), Musgrave (MS3)
CALL SIGN	Fregat (Frigate)	Columbia
LANDING DATA	March 2, 1997 0944 MT 80 miles SE of Dzhezhkazgan	December 7, 1996 0549 CST Kennedy Space Center, Runway
DURATION	196 days, 16 hours, 36 minutes (Korzun/Kaleri); 15 days, 18 hours, 23 minutes (Andre-Deshays)	17 days, 15 hours, 54 minutes
REMARKS	Korzun and Kaleri, the Mir-22 team, replaced prime crew of Manakov and Vinogradov a week prior to launch. FE2s included Lucid (to September), Blaha (September–January), and Linenger. Crew performed 2 EVAs and had to fight a fire aboard station on February 23, 1997.	Longest Shuttle mission to date, with 60-year-old veteran Musgrave on sixth flight. Deployed and retrieved Orfeus-SPAS and the Wake Shield Facility. EVA by Jernigan and Jones canceled because of hatch problems.

FLIGHT	STS-79	STS-81
LAUNCH DATA	September 16, 1996 0354 CDT Kennedy Space Center 39A	January 12, 1997 0327 CST Kennedy Space Center 39B
CREW	Readdy (CDR), Wilcutt (PLT), Apt (MS1), Akers (MS2), Walz (MS3), Blaha (MS4 UP), Lucid (MS4 DOWN)	Baker (CDR), Jett (PLT), Wisoff (MS1), Grunsfeld (MS2), Ivins (MS3), Linenger (MS4 UP), Blaha (MS4 DOWN)
CALL SIGN	Atlantis	Atlantis
LANDING DATA	September 26, 1996 0713 CDT Kennedy Space Center, Runway 15	January 22, 1997 0823 CST Kennedy Space Center Runway 33
DURATION	10 days, 3 hours, 18 minutes (STS-79 core crew); 128 days, 5 hours, 28 minutes (Blaha)	10 days, 5 hours, 36 minutes (STS-81 core crew); 132 days, 4 hours, 0 minutes (Linenger)
REMARKS	Carried a SpaceHab module on the fourth Shuttle-Mir docking mission, and docked with Russian station for 5 days. Returned Lucid to Earth while delivering Blaha.	Carried SpaceHab module on the fifth Shuttle-Mir docking, remaining linked with Russian station for 5 days. Delivered Linenger to Mir while returning Blaha to Earth.

FLIGHT	SOYUZ TM-25	STS-83
LAUNCH DATA	February 10, 1997 1710 MT Baikonur 1	April 4, 1997 1320 CST Kennedy Space Center 39A
CREW	Tsibliyev (CDR), Lazutkin (FE), Ewald [DARA] (CR)	Halsell (CDR), Still (PLT), JE Voss (MS1/PC), Gernhard (MS2), D Thomas (MS3), Crouch (PS1), Linteris (PS2)
CALL SIGN	Sirius	Columbia
LANDING DATA	August 14, 1997 1517 MST 104 miles SE of Dzhezhkazgan	April 8, 1997 1333 CDT Kennedy Space Center, Runway 33
DURATION	185 days, 1 hour, 42 minutes (Tsibliyev/Lazutkin); 19 days, 16 hours, 35 minutes (Ewald)	4 days, 0 hours, 13 minutes
REMARKS	Ill-starred crew, which included FE2s Linenger (February to May 1997), then Foale, suffered a fire aboard Mir on February 23, then nearly disastrous collision between Progress M-34 and Spektr module on June 25. August 14 return was marred by failure of Soyuz soft-landing rockets, though crew was not injured.	Planned 16-day flight of Columbia with Materials Science Laboratory was drastically shortened because of fuel cell problem aboard the orbiter. Reflown as STS-94 (see below).

FLIGHT	STS-82	STS-84
LAUNCH DATA	February 11, 1997 0255 CST Kennedy Space Center 39A	May 15, 1997 0308 CDT Kennedy Space Center 39A
CREW	Bowersox (CDR), Horowitz (PLT), Tanner (MS1), Hawley (MS2), Harbaugh (MS3), Lee (MS4/PC), Smith (MS5)	Precourt (CDR), Collins (PLT), Clervoy [ESA] (MS1), Noriega (MS2), Lu (MS3), Kondakova [RKA] (MS4), Foale (MS5 UP), Linenger (MS5 DOWN)
CALL SIGN	Discovery	Atlantis
LANDING DATA	February 21, 1997 0232 CST Kennedy Space Center, Runway 15	May 24, 1997 0828 CDT Kennedy Space Center, Runway 33
DURATION	9 days, 23 hours, 37 minutes	9 days, 18 hours, 50 minutes (STS-84 core crew); 144 days, 13 hours, 47 minutes (Foale)
REMARKS	Highly successful second Hubble Space Telescope retrieval and repair mission. Teams of Lee/Smith and Harbaugh/Tanner installed systems upgrades and made repairs during 5 EVAS totaling 33 hours.	Carried a SpaceHab supply module on the sixth Shuttle-Mir docking. UP crew of 7 included Russian cosmonaut Kondakova and NASA-Mir researcher Foale, who replaced Linenger.

FLIGHT	STS-94	STS-85
LAUNCH DATA	July 1, 1997 1302 CDT Kennedy Space Center 39A	August 7, 1997 0941 CDT Kennedy Space Center 39A
CREW	Halsell (CDR), Still (PLT), JE Voss (MS1/PC), Gernhardt (MS2), D Thomas (MS3), Crouch (PS1), Linteris (PS2)	Brown (CDR), Rominger (PLT), Davis (MS1/PC), Curbeam (MS2), Robinson (MS3), Tryggvason [CSA] (PS1)
CALL SIGN	Columbia	Discovery
LANDING DATA	July 17, 1997 0547 CDT Kennedy Space Center Runway 33	August 19, 1997 0608 CDT Kennedy Space Center, Runway 33
DURATION	15 days, 17 hours, 45 minutes	10 days, 20 hours, 27 minutes
REMARKS	Successful reflight of the STS-83 crew and Materials Science Laboratory payload.	Deployed and retrieved the Crista-SPAS.

FLIGHT	SOYUZ TM-26	STS-86
LAUNCH DATA	August 5, 1997 1836 MST Baikonur 1	September 25, 1997 2134 CDT Kennedy Space Center 39A
CREW	A Solovyov (CDR), Vinogradov (FE)	Wetherbee (CDR), Bloomfield (PLT), Titov [RKA] (MS1), Parazynski (MS2), Chretien [CNES] (MS3), Lawrence (MS4), Wolf (MS5 UP), Foale (MS5 DOWN)
CALL SIGN	Rodnik	Atlantis
LANDING DATA	February 19, 1998 1211 NT near Arkalyk	October 6, 1997 0455 CDT Kennedy Space Center, Runway 15
DURATION	197 days, 17 hours, 35 minutes	10 days, 19 hours, 21 minutes (STS-86 core crew); 127 days, 20 hours, 1 minute (Wolf)
REMARKS	The Mir-24 crew had its mission changed because of problems aboard the station following the Progress collision. CNES researcher Eyharts was removed from crew while Solovyov and Vinogradov trained for inspection and repair EVAs, ultimately performing 7 IVAs and EVAs totaling almost 40 hours. FE2s were Foale (August–September) and Wolf (September–January).	Seventh Shuttle-Mir docking carried SpaceHab and cargo. International crew included Russian cosmonaut Titov and French spationaut Chretien. Titov and Parazynski did EVA at Mir. MS4 Lawrence was supposed to be NASA-Mir researcher, but was replaced by Wolf. Foale returned to Earth.

FLIGHT	**STS-87**	**SOYUZ TM-27**
LAUNCH DATA	November 19, 1997 1346 CST Kennedy Space Center 39B	January 29, 1998 1933 MT Baikonur 1
CREW	Kregel (CDR), Lindsey (PLT), Chawla (MS1), Scott (MS2), Doi [NASDA] (MS3), Kadenyuk [NSAU] (PS1)	Musabayev (CDR), Budarin (FE), Eyharts [CNES] (CR)
CALL SIGN	Columbia	Kristall
LANDING DATA	December 5, 1997 0620 CST Kennedy Space Center, Runway 33	— — —
DURATION	15 days, 16 hours, 34 minutes	in progress (Musabayev/Budarin) 20 days, 19 hours, 37 minutes (Eyharts)
REMARKS	Carried the fourth U.S. Microgravity Payload and experiments from Ukraine, operated by Kadenyuk. Spartan deploy failed due to crew error, retrieved by Scott/Doi EVA. Duo also did an EVA to test ISS procedures.	The Mir-25 crew returned to normal, though limited, operations following intensive repairs by Mir-24 team. FE2 for the mission was NASA astronaut Thomas.

FLIGHT	**STS-89**	**STS-90**
LAUNCH DATA	January 22, 1998 2048 CST Kennedy Space Center 39A	April 17, 1998 1319 CDT Kennedy Space Center 39B
CREW	Wilcutt (CDR), Edwards (PLT), Reilly (MS1), Anderson (MS2), Dunbar (MS3/PC), Sharipov [RKA] (MS4), A. Thomas (MS5 UP), Wolf (MS5 DOWN)	Searfoss (CDR), Altman (PLT), Linnehan (MS1/PC), Hire (MS2), Williams [CSA] (MS3), Buckey (PS1), Pawelczyk (PS2)
CALL SIGN	Endeavour	Columbia
LANDING DATA	January 31, 1998 1635 CST Kennedy Space Center, Runway 15	May 3, 1998 1109 CDT Kennedy Space Center, Runway 33
DURATION	8 days, 20 hours, 47 minutes (STS-89 core crew); 140 days, 15 hours, 12 minutes (Thomas)	15 days, 21 hours, 50 minutes
REMARKS	Eighth Shuttle-Mir docking carried a SpaceHab cargo module. Crew included Russian cosmonaut Sharipov. The last NASA-Mir researcher, Thomas, delivered to Mir and Wolf returned.	Last scheduled Spacelab mission, this one called Neurolab and dedicated to medical studies of humans and experimental animals.

FLIGHT	**STS-91**
LAUNCH DATA	June 2, 1998 1706 CDT Kennedy Space Center 39A
CREW	Precourt (CDR), Gorie (PLT), Kavandi (MS1), Lawrence (MS2), Chang-Diaz (MS3), Ryumin [RKA] (MS4), A Thomas (MS5 DOWN)
CALL SIGN	Discovery
LANDING DATA	June 12, 1998 1300 CDT Kennedy Space Center, Runway 15
DURATION	9 days, 19 hours, 54 minutes (STS-91 core crew); 140 days, 15, hours, 12 minutes (Thomas)
REMARKS	This ninth and last Shuttle-Mir docking carried a SpaceHab supply module, delivering 2.5 tons of supplies to the Mir-25 crew. RKK Energiya deputy director, former Salyut-6 cosmonaut Ryumin made an inspection visit. Thomas, the seventh NASA-Mir researcher, returned to Earth.

SHUTTLE APPROACH AND LANDING TESTS

CREW (CDR/PLT)	DATE	MISSION	DURATION
none	Feb. 18, 1977	captive*	2:05
none	Feb. 22, 1977	captive	3:13
none	Feb. 25, 1977	captive	2:28
none	Feb. 28, 1977	captive	2:11
none	Mar. 2, 1977	captive	1:39
Haise/Fullerton	June 18, 1977	captive	:56
Engle/Truly	June 28, 1977	captive	1:02
Haise/Fullerton	July 26, 1977	captive	1:00
Haise/Fullerton	Aug. 12, 1977	free-flight**	:05
Engle/Truly	Sept. 13, 1977	free-flight	:05
Haise/Fullerton	Sept. 23, 1977	free-flight	:06
Engle/Truly	Oct. 12, 1977	free-flight	:03
Haise/Fullerton	Oct. 26, 1977	free-flight	:02

* Orbiter Enterprise mounted on 747 carrier aircraft.
** Orbiter Enterprise released from carrier aircraft, lands at Edwards AFB.

SPACE TRAVELERS, APRIL 1961–APRIL 1998

NOTE: This log does not include Mission 51-L crewmembers Michael J. Smith, Gregory K. Jarvis, or Christa McAuliffe, who died before reaching space, nor does it include X-15 rocketplane pilots who reached altitudes greater than 50 miles. For the latter, see the entry on X-15 Pilots.

1. Yuri Gagarin (USSR)	Vostok (1961)	
2. Alan B. Shepard (USA)	MR-3 (1961)	
3. Virgil I. Grissom (USA)	MR-4 (1961)	
4. Gherman Titov (USSR)	Vostok 2 (1961)	
5. John H. Glenn, Jr. (USA)	MA-6 (1962)	
6. M. Scott Carpenter (USA)	MA-7 (1962)	
7. Andrian Nikolayev (USSR)	Vostok 3 (1962)	
8. Pavel Popovich (USSR)	Vostok 4 (1962)	
9. Walter M. Schirra, Jr. (USA)	MA-8 (1962)	
10. L. Gordon Cooper, Jr. (USA)	MA-9 (1963)	
11. Valery Bykovsky (USSR)	Vostok 5 (1963)	
12. Valentina Tereshkova (USSR)	Vostok 6 (1963)	
13. Vladimir Komarov (USSR)	Voskhod (1964)	
Konstantin Feoktistov (USSR)	Voskhod (1964)	
Boris Yegorov (USSR)	Voskhod (1964)	
16. Pavel Belyayev (USSR)	Voskhod 2 (1965)	
Alexei Leonov (USSR)	Voskhod 2 (1965)	
18. John W. Young (USA)	Gemini 3 (1965)	
19. James A. McDivitt (USA)	Gemini 4 (1965)	
Edward H. White II (USA)	Gemini 4 (1965)	
21. Charles Conrad, Jr. (USA)	Gemini 5 (1965)	
22. Frank Borman (USA)	Gemini 7 (1965)	
James A. Lovell, Jr. (USA)	Gemini 7 (1965)	
24. Thomas P. Stafford (USA)	Gemini 6A (1965)	
25. Neil A. Armstrong (USA)	Gemini 8 (1966)	
David R. Scott (USA)	Gemini 8 (1966)	
27. Eugene A. Cernan (USA)	Gemini 9A (1966)	
28. Michael Collins (USA)	Gemini 10 (1966)	
29. Richard F. Gordon, Jr. (USA)	Gemini 11 (1966)	
30. Edwin E. Aldrin, Jr. (USA)	Gemini 12 (1966)	
31. Donn F. Eisele (USA)	Apollo 7 (1968)	
R. Walter Cunningham (USA)	Apollo 7 (1968)	
33. Georgy Beregovoy (USSR)	Soyuz 3 (1968)	
34. William A. Anders (USA)	Apollo 8 (1968)	
35. Vladimir Shatalov (USSR)	Soyuz 4 (1969)	
36. Boris Volynov (USSR)	Soyuz 5 (1969)	
Alexei Yeliseyev (USSR)	Soyuz 5 (1969)	
Yevgeny Khrunov (USSR)	Soyuz 5 (1969)	
39. Russell L. Schweickart (USA)	Apollo 9 (1969)	
40. Georgy Shonin (USSR)	Soyuz 6 (1969)	
Valery Kubasov (USSR)	Soyuz 6 (1969)	
42. Anatoly Filipchenko (USSR)	Soyuz 7 (1969)	

	Vladislav Volkov (USSR)	Soyuz 7 (1969)
	Viktor Gorbatko (USSR)	Soyuz 7 (1969)
45.	Alan L. Bean (USA)	Apollo 12 (1969)
46.	John L. Swigert, Jr. (USA)	Apollo 13 (1970)
	Fred W. Haise, Jr. (USA)	Apollo 13 (1970)
48.	Vitaly Sevastyanov (USSR)	Soyuz 9 (1970)
49.	Stuart A. Roosa (USA)	Apollo 14 (1971)
	Edgar D. Mitchell (USA)	Apollo 14 (1971)
51.	Nikolai Rukavishnikov (USSR)	Soyuz 10 (1971)
52.	Georgy Dobrovolsky (USSR)	Soyuz 11 (1971)
	Viktor Patsayev (USSR)	Soyuz 11 (1971)
54.	Alfred M. Worden (USA)	Apollo 15 (1971)
	James B. Irwin (USA)	Apollo 15 (1971)
56.	Thomas K. Mattingly II (USA)	Apollo 16 (1972)
	Charles M. Duke, Jr. (USA)	Apollo 16 (1972)
58.	Ronald E. Evans, Jr. (USA)	Apollo 17 (1972)
	Harrison H. Schmitt (USA)	Apollo 17 (1972)
60.	Joseph P. Kerwin (USA)	Skylab 2 (1973)
	Paul J. Weitz (USA)	Skylab 2 (1973)
62.	Owen K. Garriott (USA)	Skylab 3 (1973)
	Jack R. Lousma (USA)	Skylab 3 (1973)
64.	Vasily Lazarev (USSR)	Soyuz 12 (1973)
	Oleg Makarov (USSR)	Soyuz 12 (1973)
66.	Gerald P. Carr (USA)	Skylab 4 (1973–4)
	Edward G. Gibson (USA)	Skylab 4 (1973–4)
	William R. Pogue (USA)	Skylab 4 (1973–4)
69.	Pyotr Klimuk (USSR)	Soyuz 13 (1973)
	Valentin Lebedev (USSR)	Soyuz 13 (1973)
71.	Yuri Artyukhin (USSR)	Soyuz 14 (1974)
72.	Gennady Sarafanov (USSR)	Soyuz 15 (1974)
	Lev Demin (USSR)	Soyuz 15 (1974)
74.	Alexei Gubarev (USSR)	Soyuz 17 (1975)
	Georgy Grechko (USSR)	Soyuz 17 (1975)
76.	Vance D. Brand (USA)	ASTP (1975)
	Donald K. Slayton (USA)	ASTP (1975)
78.	Vitaly Zholobov (USSR)	Soyuz 21 (1976)
79.	Vladimir Aksenov (USSR)	Soyuz 22 (1976)
80.	Vyacheslav Zudov (USSR)	Soyuz 23 (1976)
	Valery Rozhdestvensky (USSR)	Soyuz 23 (1976)
82.	Yuri Glazkov (USSR)	Soyuz 24 (1977)
83.	Vladimir Kovalenok (USSR)	Soyuz 25 (1977)
	Valery Ryumin (USSR)	Soyuz 25 (1977)
85.	Yuri Romanenko (USSR)	Soyuz 26 (1977)
86.	Vladimir Dzhanibekov (USSR)	Soyuz 27 (1978)
87.	Vladimir Remek (Czechoslovakia)	Soyuz 28 (1978)
88.	Alexandr Ivanchenkov (USSR)	Soyuz 29 (1978)
89.	Miroslaw Hermaszewski (Poland)	Soyuz 30 (1978)
90.	Sigmund Jaehn (GDR)	Soyuz 31 (1978)
91.	Vladimir Lyakhov (USSR)	Soyuz 32 (1979)
92.	Georgy Ivanov (Bulgaria)	Soyuz 33 (1979)
93.	Leonid Popov (USSR)	Soyuz 35 (1980)
94.	Bertalan Farkas (Hungary)	Soyuz 36 (1980)
95.	Yuri Malyshev (USSR)	Soyuz T-2 (1980)
96.	Pham Tuan (Vietnam)	Soyuz 37 (1980)
97.	Arnaldo Tamayo-Mendez (Cuba)	Soyuz 38 (1980)
98.	Leonid Kizim (USSR)	Soyuz T-3 (1980)
99.	Gennady Strekalov (USSR)	Soyuz T-3 (1980)
100.	Viktor P. Savinykh (USSR)	Soyuz T-4 (1981)
101.	J. Gurragcha (Mongolia)	Soyuz 39 (1981)
102.	Robert L. Crippen (USA)	STS-1 (1981)
103.	Dumitru Prunariu (Rumania)	Soyuz 40 (1981)
104.	Joe H. Engle (USA)	STS-2 (1981)
	Richard H. Truly (USA)	STS-2 (1981)
106.	C. Gordon Fullerton (USA)	STS-3 (1982)
107.	Anatoly Berezovoy (USSR)	Soyuz T-5 (1982)
108.	Henry Hartsfield, Jr. (USA)	STS-4 (1982)
109.	Jean-Loup Chretien (France)	Soyuz T-6 (1982)
110.	Alexandr Serebrov (USSR)	Soyuz T-7 (1982)
	Svetlana Savitskaya (USSR)	Soyuz T-7 (1982)
112.	Robert F. Overmyer (USA)	STS-5 (1982)
	Joseph P. Allen IV (USA)	STS-5 (1982)
	William B. Lenoir (USA)	STS-5 (1982)
115.	Karol J. Bobko (USA)	STS-6 (1983)
	Donald H. Peterson (USA)	STS-6 (1983)
	F. Story Musgrave (USA)	STS-6 (1983)
118.	Vladimir Titov (USSR)	Soyuz T-8 (1983)
119.	Frederick C. Hauck (USA)	STS-7 (1983)
	John M. Fabian (USA)	STS-7 (1983)
	Sally K. Ride (USA)	STS-7 (1983)
	Norman E. Thagard (USA)	STS-7 (1983)
123.	Alexandr Alexandrov (USSR)	Soyuz T-9 (1983)
124.	Daniel C. Brandenstein (USA)	STS-8 (1983)
	Dale A. Gardner (USA)	STS-8 (1983)

	Guion S. Bluford, Jr. (USA)	STS-8 (1983)
	William E. Thornton (USA)	STS-8 (1983)
128.	Brewster H. Shaw, Jr. (USA)	STS-9 (1983)
	Robert A. R. Parker (USA)	STS-9 (1983)
	Byron K. Lichtenberg (USA)	STS-9 (1983)
	Ulf Merbold (ESA/FRG)	STS-9 (1983)
132.	Robert L. Gibson (USA)	41-B (1984)
	Bruce McCandless II (USA)	41-B (1984)
	Ronald E. McNair (USA)	41-B (1984)
	Robert L. Stewart (USA)	41-B (1984)
136.	Vladimir Solovyov (USSR)	Soyuz T-10 (1984)
	Oleg Atkov (USSR)	Soyuz T-10 (1984)
138.	Rakesh Sharma (India)	Soyuz T-11 (1984)
139.	Francis R. Scobee (USA)	41-C (1984)
	Terry J. Hart (USA)	41-C (1984)
	George D. Nelson (USA)	41-C (1984)
	James D. A. van Hoften (USA)	41-C (1984)
143.	Igor Volk (USSR)	Soyuz T-12 (1984)
144.	Michael L. Coats (USA)	41-D (1984)
	Steven A. Hawley (USA)	41-D (1984)
	Richard M. Mullane (USA)	41-D (1984)
	Judith A. Resnik (USA)	41-D (1984)
	Charles D. Walker (USA)	41-D (1984)
149.	Jon A. McBride (USA)	41-G (1984)
	David C. Leesmta (USA)	41-G (1984)
	Kathryn D. Sullivan (USA)	41-G (1984)
	Paul D. Scully-Power (USA)	41-G (1984)
	Marc Garneau (Canada)	41-G (1984)
154.	David M. Walker (USA)	51-A (1984)
	Anna L. Fisher (USA)	51-A (1984)
156.	Loren J. Shriver (USA)	51-C (1985)
	James F. Buchli (USA)	51-C (1985)
	Ellison S. Onizuka (USA)	51-C (1985)
	Gary E. Payton (USA)	51-C (1985)
160.	Donald E. Williams (USA)	51-D (1985)
	M. Rhea Seddon (USA)	51-D (1985)
	S. David Griggs (USA)	51-D (1985)
	Jeffrey A. Hoffman (USA)	51-D (1985)
	Jake Garn (USA)	51-D (1985)
165.	Frederick D. Gregory (USA)	51-B (1985)
	Don L. Lind (USA)	51-B (1985)
	Lodewijk van den Berg (USA)	51-B (1985)

	Taylor G. Wang (USA)	51-B (1985)
169.	John O. Creighton (USA)	51-G (1985)
	Shannon W. Lucid (USA)	51-G (1985)
	Steven R. Nagel (USA)	51-G (1985)
	Patrick Baudry (France)	51-G (1985)
	Sultan Al-Saud (Saudi Arabia)	51-G (1985)
174.	Roy D. Bridges (USA)	51-F (1985)
	Anthony W. England (USA)	51-F (1985)
	Karl G. Henize (USA)	51-F (1985)
	Loren W. Acton (USA)	51-F (1985)
	John-David F. Bartoe (USA)	51-F (1985)
179.	Richard O. Covey (USA)	51-I (1985)
	John M. Lounge (USA)	51-I (1985)
	William F. Fisher (USA)	51-I (1985)
182.	Vladimir Vasyutin (USSR)	Soyuz T-14 (1985)
	Alexandr Volkov (USSR)	Soyuz T-14 (1985)
184.	Ronald J. Grabe (USA)	51-J (1985)
	David C. Hilmers (USA)	51-J (1985)
	William A. Pailes (USA)	51-J (1985)
187.	Bonnie J. Dunbar (USA)	61-A (1985)
	Rheinhard Furrer (FRG)	61-A (1985)
	Ernst W. Messerschmid (FRG)	61-A (1985)
	Wubbo J. Ockels (ESA/Netherlands)	61-A (1985)
191.	Bryan D. O'Connor (USA)	61-B (1985)
	Jerry L. Ross (USA)	61-B (1985)
	Mary L. Cleave (USA)	61-B (1985)
	Sherwood C. Spring (USA)	61-B (1985)
	Rudolfo Neri Vela (Mexico)	61-B (1985)
196.	Charles F. Bolden, Jr. (USA)	61-C (1986)
	Franklin Chang-Diaz (USA)	61-C (1986)
	Robert J. Cenker (USA)	61-C (1986)
	Bill Nelson (USA)	61-C (1986)
200.	Alexandr Laveikin (USSR)	Soyuz TM-2 (1987)
201.	Alexandr Viktorenko (USSR)	Soyuz TM-3 (1987)
	Mohammed Faris (Syria)	Soyuz TM-3 (1987)
203.	Musa Manarov (USSR)	Soyuz TM-4 (1987)
	Anatoly Levchenko (USSR)	Soyuz TM-4 (1987)
205.	Anatoly Solovyov (USSR)	Soyuz TM-5 (1988)
	Alexandr Alexandrov (Bulgaria)	Soyuz TM-5 (1988)
207.	Valery Polyakov (USSR)	Soyuz TM-6 (1988)
	Ahmad Ahad (Afghanistan)	Soyuz TM-6 (1988)

209. Sergei Krikalev (USSR)	Soyuz TM-7 (1988)	Helen P. Sharman (Britain)	Soyuz TM-12 (1991)
210. Guy S. Gardner (USA)	STS-27 (1988)	250. F. Andrew Gaffney (USA)	STS-40 (1991)
William M. Shepherd (USA)	STS-27 (1988)	Sidney M. Gutierrez (USA)	STS-40 (1991)
212. James P. Bagian (USA)	STS-29 (1989)	Millie Hughes-Fulford (USA)	STS-40 (1991)
John E. Blaha (USA)	STS-29 (1989)	Tamara E. Jernigan (USA)	STS-40 (1991)
Robert C. Springer (USA)	STS-29 (1989)	254. Michael A. Baker (USA)	STS-43 (1991)
215. Mark C. Lee (USA)	STS-30 (1989)	255. Kenneth L. Reightler, Jr. (USA)	STS-48 (1991)
216. James C. Adamson (USA)	STS-28 (1989)	256. Toktar Aubakirov (USSR)	Soyuz TM-13 (1991)
Mark N. Brown (USA)	STS-28 (1989)	Franz Viehbock (Austria)	Soyuz TM-13 (1991)
Richard N. Richards (USA)	STS-28 (1989)	258. Thomas J. Hennen (USA)	STS-44 (1991)
219. Ellen S. Baker (USA)	STS-34 (1989)	Terence T. Henricks (USA)	STS-44 (1991)
Michael J. McCulley (USA)	STS-34 (1989)	Mario Runco, Jr. (USA)	STS-44 (1991)
221. Manley L. Carter (USA)	STS-33 (1989)	James S. Voss (USA)	STS-44 (1991)
Kathryn C. Thornton (USA)	STS-33 (1989)	262. Roberta K. Bondar (Canada)	STS-42 (1992)
223. Marsha S. Ivins (USA)	STS-32 (1990)	Stephen S. Oswald (USA)	STS-42 (1992)
G. David Low (USA)	STS-32 (1990)	William F. Readdy (USA)	STS-42 (1992)
James D. Wetherbee (USA)	STS-32 (1990)	265. Klaus-Dietrich Flade (Germany)	Soyuz TM-14 (1992)
226. Alexandr Balandin (USSR)	Soyuz TM-9 (1990)	Alexandr Yu. Kaleri (Russia)	Soyuz TM-14 (1992)
227. John H. Casper (USA)	STS-36 (1990)	267. Bryan Duffy (USA)	STS-45 (1992)
Pierre J. Thuot (USA)	STS-36 (1990)	Michael Foale (USA)	STS-45 (1992)
229. Gennady Manakov (USSR)	Soyuz TM-10 (1990)	Dirk D. Frimout (Belgium)	STS-45 (1992)
230. Thomas D. Akers (USA)	STS-41 (1990)	270. Kevin P. Chilton (USA)	STS-49 (1992)
Robert D. Cabana (USA)	STS-41 (1990)	271. Kenneth D. Bowersox (USA)	STS-50 (1992)
Bruce E. Melnick (USA)	STS-41 (1990)	Lawrence J. DeLucas (USA)	STS-50 (1992)
233. Frank L. Culbertson (USA)	STS-38 (1990)	Eugene H. Trinh (USA)	STS-50 (1992)
Charles D. Gemar (USA)	STS-38 (1990)	274. Sergei V. Adveyev (Russia)	Soyuz TM-15 (1992)
Carl J. Meade (USA)	STS-38 (1990)	Michel Tognini (France)	Soyuz TM-15 (1992)
236. Samuel T. Durrance (USA)	STS-35 (1990)	276. Andrew M. Allen (USA)	STS-46 (1992)
Ronald A. Parise (USA)	STS-35 (1990)	Franco Malerba (Italy)	STS-46 (1992)
238. Viktor Afanasyev (USSR)	Soyuz TM-11 (1990–1)	Claude Nicollier (ESA/Switzerland)	STS-46 (1992)
Toyohiro Akiyama (Japan)	Soyuz TM-11 (1990)	279. Curtis L. Brown, Jr. (USA)	STS-47 (1992)
240. Jay Apt (USA)	STS-37 (1991)	N. Jan Davis (USA)	STS-47 (1992)
Kenneth D. Cameron (USA)	STS-37 (1991)	Mae C. Jemison (USA)	STS-47 (1992)
Linda M. Godwin (USA)	STS-37 (1991)	Mamoru M. Mohri (Japan)	STS-47 (1992)
243. L. Blaine Hammond (USA)	STS-39 (1991)	283. Steven G. MacLean (Canada)	STS-52 (1992)
Gregory J. Harbaugh (USA)	STS-39 (1991)	284. Michael R. U. Clifford (USA)	STS-53 (1992)
Richard J. Hieb (USA)	STS-39 (1991)	285. Susan J. Helms (USA)	STS-54 (1993)
Donald R. McMonagle (USA)	STS-39 (1991)	286. Alexandr F. Poleshchuk (Russia)	Soyuz TM-17 (1993)
C. Lacy Veach (USA)	STS-39 (1991)	287. Kenneth D. Cockrell (USA)	STS-56 (1993)
248. Anatoly Artsebarsky (USSR)	Soyuz TM-12 (1991)	Ellen Ochoa (USA)	STS-56 (1993)

289.	Bernard A. Harris (USA)	STS-55 (1993)
	Charles J. Precourt (USA)	STS-55 (1993)
	Hans Wilhelm Schlegel (Germany)	STS-55 (1993)
	Ulrich Walter (Germany)	STS-55 (1993)
293.	Nancy J. Sherlock (USA)	STS-57 (1993)
	Janice E. Voss (USA)	STS-57 (1993)
	Peter J. K. Wisoff (USA)	STS-57 (1993)
296.	Jean-Pierre Haignere (France)	Soyuz TM-17 (1993)
297.	Vasily V. Tsibliyev (Russia)	Soyuz TM-17 (1993)
298.	Daniel W. Bursch (USA)	STS-51 (1993)
	James H. Newman (USA)	STS-51 (1993)
300.	Carl E. Walz (USA)	STS-51 (1993)
301.	Martin J. Fettman (USA)	STS-58 (1993)
	William S. MacArthur (USA)	STS-58 (1993)
	Richard A. Searfoss (USA)	STS-58 (1993)
	David A. Wolf (USA)	STS-58 (1993)
305.	Yuri V. Usachev (Russia)	Soyuz TM-18 (1994)
306.	Ronald M. Sega (USA)	STS-60 (1994)
307.	Thomas D. Jones (USA)	STS-59 (1994)
308.	Yuri N. Malenchenko (Russia)	Soyuz TM-19 (1994)
	Talgat A. Musbayev (Kazakhstan)	Soyuz TM-19 (1994)
310.	Leroy Chiao (USA)	STS-65 (1994)
	James D. Halsell (USA)	STS-65 (1994)
	Chiaki Naito-Mukai (Japan)	STS-65 (1994)
	Donald A. Thomas (USA)	STS-65 (1994)
314.	Jerry M. Linenger (USA)	STS-64 (1994)
315.	Steven L. Smith (USA)	STS-68 (1994)
	Terrence W. Wilcutt (USA)	STS-68 (1994)
317.	Yelena Kondakova (Russia)	Soyuz TM-20 (1994)
318.	Jean-Francois Clervoy (France)	STS-66 (1994)
	Scott L. Parazynski (USA)	STS-66 (1994)
	Joseph R. Tanner (USA)	STS-66 (1994)
321.	Eileen M. Collins (USA)	STS-63 (1995)
322.	William G. Gregory (USA)	STS-67 (1995)
	John M. Grunsfeld (USA)	STS-67 (1995)
	Wendy B. Lawrence (USA)	STS-67 (1995)
325.	Vladimir N. Dezhurov (Russia)	Soyuz TM-21 (1995)
326.	Nikolai N. Budarin (Russia)	STS-71 (1995)
327.	Yuri P. Gidzenko (Russia)	Soyuz TM-22 (1995)

	Thomas Reiter (Germany)	Soyuz TM-22 (1995)
329.	Kevin R. Kregel (USA)	STS-70 (1995)
	Mary Ellen Weber (USA)	STS-70 (1995)
331.	Michael L. Gernhardt (USA)	STS-69 (1995)
332.	Catherine G. Coleman (USA)	STS-73 (1995)
	Fred W. Leslie, Jr. (USA)	STS-73 (1995)
	Michael E. Lopez-Alegria (USA)	STS-73 (1995)
	Kent V. Rominger (USA)	STS-73 (1995)
	Albert Sacco, Jr. (USA)	STS-73 (1995)
337.	Chris A. Hadfield (Canada)	STS-74 (1995)
338.	Daniel T. Barry (USA)	STS-72 (1996)
	Brent W. Jett, Jr. (USA)	STS-72 (1996)
	Winston E. Scott (USA)	STS-72 (1996)
	Koichi Wakata (Japan)	STS-72 (1996)
342.	Maurizio Cheli (Italy/ESA)	STS-75 (1996)
	Umberto Guidoni (Italy)	STS-75 (1996)
	Scott J. Horowitz (USA)	STS-75 (1996)
345.	Yuri I. Onufriyenko (Russia)	Soyuz TM-23 (1996)
346.	Andrew S. W. Thomas (USA)	STS-77 (1996)
347.	Charles E. Brady (USA)	STS-78 (1996)
	Jean-Jacques Favier (France)	STS-78 (1996)
	Richard M. Linnehan (USA)	STS-78 (1996)
350.	Robert B. Thirsk (Canada)	STS-78 (1996)
351.	Valery G. Korzun (Russia)	Soyuz TM-24 (1996)
352.	Claudie Andre-Deshays (France)	Soyuz TM-24 (1996)
353.	Reinhold Ewald (Germany)	Soyuz TM-25 (1997)
354.	Alexandr I. Lazutkin (Russia)	Soyuz TM-25 (1997)
355.	Roger K. Crouch (USA)	STS-83 (1997)
	Gregory T. Linteris (USA)	STS-83 (1997)
	Susan L. Still (USA)	STS-83 (1997)
358.	Edward T. Lu (USA)	STS-84 (1997)
	Carlos I. Noriega (USA)	STS-84 (1997)
360.	Pavel V. Vinogradov (Russia)	Soyuz TM-26 (1997)
361.	Robert L. Curbeam, Jr. (USA)	STS-85 (1997)
	Stephen K. Robinson (USA)	STS-85 (1997)
	Bjarni V. Tryggvason (Canada)	STS-85 (1997)
364.	Michael J. Bloomfield (USA)	STS-86 (1997)
365.	Kalpana Chawla (USA)	STS-87 (1997)
	Takao Doi (Japan)	STS-87 (1997)
	Leonid K. Kadenyuk (Ukraine)	STS-87 (1997)
368.	Steven W. Lindsey (USA)	STS-87 (1997)

369.	Michael P. Anderson (USA)	STS-89 (1998)	374. Scott D. Altman (USA)	STS-90 (1998)
	Joe F. Edwards, Jr. (USA)	STS-89 (1998)	Jay C. Buckey (USA)	STS-90 (1998)
	James F. Reilly II (USA)	STS-89 (1998)	Kay P. Hire (USA)	STS-90 (1998)
372.	Salizhan Sh. Sharipov (Russia)	STS-89 (1998)	James A. Pawelczyk (USA)	STS-90 (1998)
373.	Leopold Eyharts (France)	Soyuz TM-27 (1998)	378. Daffyd R. Williams (Canada)	STS-90 (1998)

DURATION LOG, APRIL 12, 1961–JUNE 12, 1998

NAME	COUNTRY	FLTS	TIME IN SPACE
Valery Polyakov	USSR/Rus.	2	16,312:34
Anatoly Solovyov	USSR/Rus.	5	15,624:13
Musa Manarov	USSR	2	12,985:32
Alexandr Viktorenko	USSR/Rus.	4	11,741:46
Sergei Krikalev	USSR/Rus.	3	11,295:37
Yuri Romanenko	USSR	3	10,238:21
Vladimir Titov	USSR/Rus.	4	9,288:47
Alexandr Volkov	USSR	3	9,373:52
Vasily Tsibliyev	Russia	2	9,187:47
Alexandr Serebrov	USSR/Rus.	4	9,011:53
Leonid Kizim	USSR	3	8,993:59
Yuri Usachev	Russia	2	8,980:37
Valery Ryumin	USSR/Rus.	4	8,921:28
Sergei Avdeyev	Russia	2	8,831:31
Vladimir Solovyov	USSR	2	8,686:51
Viktor Afanasyev	USSR/Rus.	2	8,571:19
Alexandr Kaleri	Russia	2	8,215:47
Vladimir Lyakhov	USSR	3	7,998:49
Gennady Manakov	USSR/Rus.	2	7,437:20
Alexandr Alexandrov	USSR	2	7,433:03

NAME	COUNTRY	FLTS	TIME IN SPACE
Gennady Strekalov	USSR/Rus.	5	6,622:26
Viktor Savinykh	USSR	3	6,066:39
Oleg Atkov	USSR	1	5,686:50
Shannon W. Lucid	USA	5	5,362:34
Valentin Lebedev	USSR	2	5,262:00
Vladimir Kovalenok	USSR	3	5,194:12
Anatoly Berezovoy	USSR	1	5,073:05
Leonid Popov	USSR	3	4,814:55
Valery G. Korzun	Russia	1	4,720:36
Yuri I. Onufriyenko	Russia	1	4,612:10
Alexandr Lazutkin	Russia	1	4,441:42
Yelena Kondakova	Russia	2	4,299:12
Yuri P. Gidzenko	Russia	1	4,297:42
Thomas Reiter	Germany	1	4,297:42
Alexandr Balandin	USSR	1	4,297:18
Alexandr Poleshchuk	Russia	1	4,296:44
Alexandr Laveikin	USSR	1	4,179:26
C. Michael Foale	USA	4	4,104:33
John E. Blaha	USA	5	3,874:49
Andrew S. W. Thomas	USA	2	3,615:51
Alexandr Ivanchenkov	USSR	2	3,540:39
Vladimir Dzhanibekov	USSR	5	3,495:59
Anatoly Artsebarsky	USSR	1	3,471:22
Norman E. Thagard	USA	5	3,541:28
Jerry M. Linenger	USA	2	3,435:50
David A. Wolf	USA	2	3,412:34
Georgy Grechko	USSR	3	3,236:33
Yuri Malenchenko	Russia	1	3,022:54
Talgat Musabayev	Rus./Kaz.	1 [1]	3,022:54
Vladimir N. Dezhurov	Russia	1	2,936:43
Gerald P. Carr	USA	1	2,017:16
Edward G. Gibson	USA	1	2,017:16
William R. Pogue	USA	1	2,017:16
Vitaly Sevastyanov	USSR	2	1,936:19

NAME	COUNTRY	FLTS	TIME IN SPACE
Pyotr Klimuk	USSR	3	1,890:19
Nikolai V. Budarin	Russia	1[2]	1,811:20
Owen K. Garriott	USA	2	1,674:56
Alan L. Bean	USA	2	1,671:45
Jack R. Lousma	USA	2	1,619:14
Vladimir Vasyutin	USSR	1	1,557:52
F. Story Musgrave	USA	6	1,280:50
Tamara E. Jernigan	USA	4	1,278:15
Franklin R. Chang-Diaz	USA	6	1,267:48
Boris Volynov	USSR	2	1,255:20
Kenneth D. Bowersox	USA	4	1,211:58
Jeffrey A. Hoffman	USA	5	1,210:51
Bonnie J. Dunbar	USA	5	1,209:24
Ulf Merbold	Germany	3	1,207:37
Vitaly Zholobov	USSR	1	1,182:24
Charles Conrad, Jr.	USA	4	1,179:39
Kent V. Rominger	USA	3	1,066:13
Jean-Loup Chretien	France	3	1,043:19
Donald A. Thomas	USA	4	1,042:14
Marsha S. Ivins	USA	4	1,033:05
Thomas T. Henricks	USA	4	1,026:40
James D. Halsell, Jr.	USA	4	1,023:25
Kevin R. Kregel	USA	3	995:42
Kathryn C. Thornton	USA	4	973:27
Michael A. Baker	USA	4	965:40
Thomas D. Jones	USA	3	962:32
James D. Wetherbee	USA	4	955:46
Curtis L. Brown, Jr.	USA	4	954:00
Richard A. Searfoss	USA	3	947:19
Charles J. Precourt	USA	4	945:46
Janice E. Voss	USA	4	912:11
Kenneth D. Cockrell	USA	3	906:33
Andrew M. Allen	USA	3	904:05
Alexei Gubarev	USSR	2	899:37

NAME	COUNTRY	FLTS	TIME IN SPACE
Wendy B. Lawrence	USA	3	894:25
Robert L. Gibson	USA	5	868:18
Jerry L. Ross	USA	5	849:54
Jay Apt	USA	4	847:10
John W. Young	USA	6	835:42
Carl E. Walz	USA	3	833:25
Claude Nicollier	Switz.	3	827:51
Stephen S. Oswald	USA	3	814:33
Richard N. Richards	USA	4	814:30
Thomas D. Akers	USA	4	813:45
John H. Casper	USA	4	805:32
Gregory J. Harbaugh	USA	4	797:40
Paul J. Weitz	USA	2	793:14
Susan J. Helms	USA	3	792:56
Mark C. Lee	USA	4	790:55
Daniel C. Brandenstein	USA	4	789:07
Richard M. Linnehan	USA	2	787:38
Richard J. Hieb	USA	3	766:37
Peter J. K. Wisoff	USA	3	755:07
Daniel W. Bursch	USA	3	746:36
Vance D. Brand	USA	4	746:04
Michael L. Gernhardt	USA	3	734:28
Viktor Gorbatko	USSR	3	732:46
Margaret R. Seddon	USA	3	730:23
Terrence W. Wilcutt	USA	3	725:51
David M. Walker	USA	4	724:32
Steven R. Nagel	USA	4	721:36
James A. Lovell, Jr.	USA	4	715:05
G. David Low	USA	3	714:08
Carl J. Meade	USA	3	713:14
Kevin P. Chilton	USA	3	704:20
Vladislav Volkov	USSR	2	689:03
Ellen S. Baker	USA	3	687:31
Charles F. Bolden	USA	4	680:30

NAME	COUNTRY	FLTS	TIME IN SPACE
Joseph P. Kerwin	USA	1	672:50
William F. Readdy	USA	3	672:43
Guy Bluford	USA	4	688:35
Bryan Duffy	USA	3	668:55
Michael R. U. Clifford	USA	3	666:21
Pierre J. Thuot	USA	3	654:45
John M. Grunsfeld	USA	2	654:46
N. Jan Davis	USA	3	650:16
Steven A. Hawley	USA	4	648:54
Richard O. Covey	USA	4	644:11
Linda M. Godwin	USA	3	634:35
Ronald J. Grabe	USA	4	627:42
Robert D. Cabana	USA	3	627:25
Scott J. Horowitz	USA	2	617:18
Samuel T. Durrance	USA	2	614:15
Ronald A. Parise	USA	2	614:15
James S. Voss	USA	3	602:41
Winston E. Scott	USA	2	591:35
Donald R. McMonagle	USA	3	585:15
Charles D. Gemar	USA	3	581:39
Georgy Dobrovolsky	USSR	1	570:22
Viktor Patsayev	USSR	1	570:22
Leroy Chiao	USA	2	568:57
Eugene A. Cernan	USA	3	566:16
Robert L. Crippen	USA	4	565:48
William S. McArthur	USA	2	565:29
Kenneth L. Cameron	USA	3	562:13
David R. Scott	USA	3	546:54
Brewster H. Shaw, Jr.	USA	3	533:53
Kathryn D. Sullivan	USA	3	532:49
David C. Leestma	USA	3	532:33
Mario Runco, Jr.	USA	3	530:49
Scott L. Parazynski	USA	2	521:55
Andrian Nikolayev	USSR	2	519:24

NAME	COUNTRY	FLTS	TIME IN SPACE
Stephen L. Smith	USA	2	509:23
Thomas K. Mattingly II	USA	3	508:34
Thomas P. Stafford	USA	4	507:44
Joseph R. Tanner	USA	2	502:11
Leopold Eyharts	France	1	499:37
Valery Bykovsky	USSR	3	497:49
Oleg Makarov	USSR	4	497:43
Jean-Francois Clervoy	France	2	497:24
James H. Newman	USA	2	496:41
Jean-Pierre Haignere	France	1	496:09
David C. Hilmers	USA	4	494:17
James F. Buchli	USA	4	490:25
Sidney M. Gutierrez	USA	2	488:01
Ellen Ochoa	USA	2	484:43
Henry W. Hartsfield, Jr.	USA	3	482:51
John M. Lounge	USA	3	482:23
Charles D. Walker	USA	3	477:56
Frank Borman	USA	2	477:36
Roger K. Crouch	USA	2	473:58
Gregory T. Linteris	USA	2	473:58
Susan L. Still	USA	2	473:58
Svetlana Savitskaya	USSR	2	473:06
Reinhold Ewald	Germany	1	472:35
Michael L. Coats	USA	3	463:59
L. Blaine Hammond	USA	2	463:13
Robert A. R. Parker	USA	2	462:52
Byron K. Lichtenberg	USA	2	461:56
Brent W. Jett, Jr.	USA	2	460:37
Frederick D. Gregory	USA	3	455:08
Nancy [Sherlock] Currie	USA	2	454:05
Valery Kubasov	USSR	3	449:59
Pavel Popovich	USSR	2	448:29
William M. Shepherd	USA	3	440:12
Bernard A. Harris, Jr.	USA	2	438:08

NAME	COUNTRY	FLTS	TIME IN SPACE
Marc Garneau	Canada	2	438:03
Charles L. Veach	USA	2	436:19
Frederick H. Hauck	USA	3	434:09
Eileen M. Collins	USA	2	433:18
Yuri Glazkov	USSR	1	425:23
Ronald M. Sega	USA	2	420:35
George D. Nelson	USA	3	407:54
Charles E. Brady, Jr.	USA	1	405:48
Jean-Jacques Favier	France	1	405:48
Robert Brent Thirsk	Canada	1	405:48
John O. Creighton	USA	3	404:25
William Gregory	USA	1	399:10
Karol J. Bobko	USA	3	386:04
Loren J. Shriver	USA	3	386:00
Bryan D. O'Connor	USA	2	383:19
Charles G. Fullerton	USA	2	382:51
Catherine G. Coleman	USA	1	381:52
Michael E. Lopez-Alegria	USA	1	381:52
Fred W. Leslie	USA	1	381:52
Albert Sacco, Jr.	USA	1	381:52
Scott D. Altman	USA	1	381:50
Jay C. Buckey	USA	1	381:50
Kathryn P. Hire	USA	1	381:50
James A. Pawelczyk	USA	1	381:50
Dafyd R. Williams	Canada	1	381:50
Maurizio Cheli	Italy	1	377:41
Umberto Guidoni	Italy	1	377:41
Yuri Artyukhin	USSR	1	377:30
Kalpana Chawla	USA	1	376:34
Takao Doi	Japan	1	376:34
Leonid Kadenyuk	Ukraine	1	376:34
Steven W. Lindsey	USA	1	376:34
Richard M. Mullane	USA	3	356:21
Frank L. Culbertson, Jr.	USA	2	354:05

NAME	COUNTRY	FLTS	TIME IN SPACE
Chiaki Naito-Mukai	Japan	1	353:56
Martin J. Fettman	USA	1	344:13
Sally K. Ride	USA	2	343:48
James A. McDivitt	USA	2	338:57
James D. A. van Hoften	USA	2	337:58
James P. Bagian	USA	2	337:54
Dale A. Gardner	USA	2	336:54
James C. Adamson	USA	2	334:22
Michel Tognini	France	1	331:57
Lawrence J. DeLucas	USA	1	331:30
Eugene H. Trinh	USA	1	331:30
Kenneth S. Reightler, Jr.	USA	2	327:47
Guy S. Gardner, Jr.	USA	2	320:11
John M. Fabian	USA	2	316:03
Richard F. Gordon, Jr.	USA	2	315:53
Joseph P. Allen IV	USA	2	313:59
William E. Thornton	USA	2	313:18
Bruce McCandless II	USA	2	312:32
Bruce Melnick	USA	2	311:28
Ronald E. Evans, Jr.	USA	1	301:52
Harrison H. Schmitt	USA	1	301:52
Walter M. Schirra, Jr.	USA	3	295:13
James B. Irwin	USA	1	295:12
Alfred M. Worden, Jr.	USA	1	295:12
Robert F. Overmyer	USA	2	290:23
Eugene "Buzz" Aldrin	USA	2	289:54
Robert L. Stewart	USA	2	289:01
Donald E. Williams	USA	2	288:34
Vladimir Aksenov	USSR	2	284:15
Yuri Malyshev	USSR	2	284:02
Igor Volk	USSR	1	283:14
Claudie Andre-Deshays	France	1	278:23
Michael Collins	USA	2	266:06
Charles M. Duke, Jr.	USA	1	265:51

NAME	COUNTRY	FLTS	TIME IN SPACE
Mary L. Cleave	USA	2	262:02
Anatoly Filipchenko	USSR	2	261:05
Robert L. Curbeam, Jr.	USA	1	260:27
Stephen K. Robinson	USA	1	260:27
Bjarni V. Tryggvason	Canada	1	260:27
R. Walter Cunningham	USA	1	260:09
Donn F. Eisele	USA	1	260:09
Michael J. Bloomfield	USA	1	259:21
Mark N. Brown	USA	2	249:28
Russell L. Schweickart	USA	1	241:01
Hans W. Schlegl	Germany	1	239:40
Ulrich Walter	Germany	1	239:40
Vladimir Shatalov	USSR	'3	237:59
Robert C. Springer	USA	2	237:33
Nikolai Rukavishnikov	USSR	3	237:11
Steven G. MacLean	Canada	1	236:56
Alexandr Alexandrov	Bulgaria	1	236:10
Dominic L. Gorie	USA	1	235:54
Janet L. Kavandi	USA	1	235:54
Edward Tsang Lu	USA	1	234:50
Carlos I. Noriega	USA	1	234:50
L. Gordon Cooper, Jr.	USA	2	225:15
Joe H. Engle	USA	2	224:31
Millie Hughes-Fulford	USA	1	218:15
F. Andrew Gaffney	USA	1	218:15
Donald K. Slayton	USA	1	217:28
Alan B. Shepard, Jr.	USA	2	216:17
Edgar D. Mitchell	USA	1	216:02
Stuart A. Roosa	USA	1	216:02
Alexei Yeliseyev	USSR	3	214:25
Mary Ellen Weber	USA	1	214:20
Dirk D. Frimout	Belgium	1	214:09
Daniel T. Barry	USA	1	215:01
Koichi Wakata	Japan	1	215:01

NAME	COUNTRY	FLTS	TIME IN SPACE
Michael P. Anderson	USA	1	212:47
Joe Frank Edwards, Jr.	USA	1	212:47
James F. Reilly II	USA	1	212:47
Salizhan Sh. Sharipov	Russia	1	212:47
Ahmad Ahad Mohmand	Afghan.	1	212:27
Neil A. Armstrong	USA	2	206:00
Richard H. Truly	USA	2	199:22
Jon A. McBride	USA	1	197:24
Paul D. Scully-Power	USA	1	197:24
Chris Hadfield	Canada	1	196:31
Roberta K. Bondar	Canada	1	193:14
Anna L. Fisher	USA	1	191:45
Ronald E. McNair	USA	1	191:16
Franco Malerba	Italy	1	191:11
Mohammed Faris	Syria	1	191:05
Loren J. Acton	USA	1	190:46
John-David F. Bartoe	USA	1	190:46
Roy D. Bridges	USA	1	190:46
Anthony W. England	USA	1	190:46
Karl G. Henize	USA	1	190:46
Mae C. Jemison	USA	1	190:30
Mamoru M. Mohri	Japan	1	190:30
Vladimir Remek	Czech.	1	190:17
Toktar Aubakirov	USSR	1	190:13
Franz Viehbock	Austria	1	190:13
Miroslaw Hermaszewski	Poland	1	190:04
Anatoly Levchenko	USSR	1	189:58
Klaus-Dietrich Flade	Germany	1	189:57
Toyohiro Akiyama	Japan	1	189:55
Rakesh Sharma	India	1	189:41
Helen P. Sharman	Britain	1	189:14
Sigmund Jaehn	Germany	1	188:49
Bertalan Farkas	Hungary	1	188:46
Arnaldo Tamayo Mendez	Cuba	1	188:43

NAME	COUNTRY	FLTS	TIME IN SPACE
Pham Tuan	Vietnam	1	188:42
Dumitru Prunariu	Romania	1	188:41
M. Gurragcha	Mongolia	1	186:43
William F. Fisher	USA	1	170:18
Sultan Salman al-Saud	S. Arabia	1	169:39
Patrick Baudry	France	1	169:39
Wubbo Ockels	Neth.	1	168:44
Rheinhard Furrer	Germany	1	168:44
Ernst Messerschmid	Germany	1	168:44
Alexei Leonov	USSR	2	168:33
Don L. Lind	USA	1	168:09
Lodewijk van den Berg	USA	1	168:09
Taylor G. Wang	USA	1	168:09
S. David Griggs	USA	1	167:55
Jake Garn	USA	1	167:55
Terry J. Hart	USA	1	167:40
F. Richard Scobee	USA	1	167:40
Thomas J. Hennen	USA	1	166:52
Rudolfo Neri Vela	Mexico	1	165:04
Sherwood C. Spring	USA	1	165:04
William A. Anders	USA	1	147:01
Judith A. Resnik	USA	1	144:57
Robert J. Cenker	USA	1	143:04
Bill Nelson	USA	1	143:04
Fred W. Haise, Jr.	USA	1	142:55
John L. Swigert, Jr.	USA	1	142:55
William B. Lenoir	USA	1	122:14
Michael J. McCulley	USA	1	120:39
Donald H. Peterson	USA	1	120:24
Manley L. Carter, Jr.	USA	1	120:07
Georgy Shonin	USSR	1	118:42
Edward H. White II	USA	1	97:56
William A. Pailes	USA	1	97:45
Georgy Beregovoy	USSR	1	94:51

NAME	COUNTRY	FLTS	TIME IN SPACE
Ellison S. Onizuka	USA	1	78:33 ·
Gary E. Payton	USA	1	78:33
Valentina Tereshkova	USSR	1	70:50
Vladimir Komarov	USSR	1	50:54
Lev Demin	USSR	1	48:12
Gennady Sarafanov	USSR	1	48:12
Valery Rozhdestvensky	USSR	1	48:06
Vyacheslav Zudov	USSR	1	48:06
Yevgeny Khrunov	USSR	1	47:49
Vasily Lazarev	USSR	2	47:36
Georgy Ivanov	Bulgaria	1	47:01
Pavel Belyayev	USSR	1	26:02
Gherman Titov	USSR	1	25:18
Konstantin Feoktistov	USSR	1	24:17
Boris Yegorov	USSR	1	24:17
Virgil I. Grissom	USA	2	5:09
M. Scott Carpenter	USA	1	4:56
John H. Glenn, Jr.	USA	1	4:55
Yuri Gagarin	USSR	1	1:49

Top Ten USA

NAME	COUNTRY	FLTS	TIME IN SPACE
Shannon W. Lucid	USA	5	5,351:84
John E. Blaha	USA	5	4,007:50
Jerry M. Linenger	USA	2	3,454:51
Norman E. Thagard	USA	5	3,373:27
David A. Wolf	USA	2	3,403:14
C. Michael Foale	USA	4	3,113:45
Gerald P. Carr	USA	1	2,017:16
Edward G. Gibson	USA	1	2,017:16
William R. Pogue	USA	1	2,017:16
Owen K. Garriott	USA	2	1,674:56
Alan L. Bean	USA	2	1,671:45

Top Ten Shuttle (Not Updated)

NAME	COUNTRY	FLTS	TIME IN SPACE
F. Story Musgrave	USA	6	1,280:00
Tamara E. Jernigan	USA	4	1,278:15
Kenneth D. Bowersox	USA	4	1,211:59
Jeffrey A. Hoffman	USA	5	1,211:58
Bonnie J. Dunbar	USA	5	1,209:24
John E. Blaha	USA	5	1,039:21
Marsha S. Ivins	USA	4	1,034:57
Franklin R. Chang-Diaz	USA	5	1,033:53
Kathryn C. Thornton	USA	4	974:28
Michael A. Baker	USA	4	965:41

Top Five International

NAME	COUNTRY	FLTS	TIME IN SPACE
Thomas Reiter	Germany	1	4,297:42
Ulf Merbold	Germany	3	1,237:37
Claude Nicollier	Switz.	3	827:51
Jean-Loup Chretien	France	2	783:58

WORLD EVA LOG, MARCH 1965–APRIL 1998

EVA#	DATE	DURATION	MISSION	CREW	NOTES
1	Mar. 18, 1965	:12	Voskhod 2	Leonov	First EVA. Leonov had difficulty returning to airlock due to suit ballooning.
2	June 3, 1965	:21	Gemini 4	White	First American EVA. White used handheld "zip gun" to test mobility.
3	June 5, 1966	2:10	Gemini 9A	Cernan	Cernan attempted to don free-flying AMU but failed due to heating problems with suit.
4	July 19, 1966	:39	Gemini 10	Collins	Standup EVA to photograph stellar background. Cut short due to impurities in air system.
5	July 20, 1966	:50	Gemini 10	Collins	Used HHMU to remove experiment package from Agena 8; lost stills camera in orbit.
6	Sept. 13, 1966	:33	Gemini 11	Gordon	"Space Cowboy" Gordon straddled Agena target vehicle to attach 100-ft. tether.
7	Sept. 14, 1966	2:08	Gemini 11	Gordon	Standup EVA to photograph stellar background in ultraviolet.
8	Nov. 12, 1966	2:29	Gemini 12	Aldrin	Standup EVA to take astronomical photos and prepare equipment for later EVAs.
9	Nov. 13, 1966	2:09	Gemini 12	Aldrin	Aldrin evaluated EVA restraints and tethers while completing work-task tests.
10	Nov. 14, 1966	:59	Gemini 12	Aldrin	Final Gemini EVA; further astronomical photo tests.
11	Jan. 16, 1969	:37	Soyuz 5/4	Khrunov/Yeliseyev	First EVA crew transfer between two spacecraft. Test for USSR lunar program.
12	Mar. 6, 1969	1:07	Apollo 9	Schweickart/Scott	First EVA test of Apollo lunar suit in Earth orbit. Scott did standup EVA in CM hatch to photograph Schweickart and retrieve samples.
13	July 20, 1969	2:32	Apollo 11	Armstrong/Aldrin	First men to walk on the Moon. "Small step" at Tranquility Base was the most televised EVA of all.
14	Nov. 19, 1969	3:56	Apollo 12	Conrad/Bean	Second lunar surface EVA, set up first ALSEP and took geological samples.
15	Nov. 20, 1969	3:49	Apollo 12	Conrad/Bean	Retrieved parts from unmanned Surveyor 3. Conducted further geological sampling.
16	Feb. 5, 1971	4:48	Apollo 14	Shepard/Mitchell	Third lunar landing crew; deployed ALSEP and explored Fra Mauro site.

EVA#	DATE	DURATION	MISSION	CREW	NOTES
17	Feb. 6, 1971	4:35	Apollo 14	Shepard/Mitchell	Walked to Cone Crater with aid of MET; collected samples.
18	July 30, 1971	:27	Apollo 15	Scott	Standup EVA from top hatch of LM, surveying Hadley Rille landing site.
19	July 31, 1971	6:33	Apollo 15	Scott/Irwin	Deployed ALSEP and completed 7-mile traverse using first lunar roving vehicle.
20	Aug. 1, 1971	7:12	Apollo 15	Scott/Irwin	Second LRV traverse, 7-mile round trip to Hadely-Appenine Front.
21	Aug. 2, 1971	4:50	Apollo 15	Scott/Irwin	Third LRV traverse, a 3-mile trip to Hadley Rille.
22	Aug. 5, 1971	:39	Apollo 15	Worden/Irwin	First deep-space EVA; Worden retrieved film cassettes from SIM bay while Irwin did standup EVA.
23	Apr. 21, 1972	7:11	Apollo 16	Young/Duke	Deployed ALSEP and drove LRV-2 in 3-mile traverse to Flag Crater.
24	Apr. 22, 1972	7:23	Apollo 16	Young/Duke	Second LRV traverse, 7-mile trip to Stone Mountain.
25	Apr. 23, 1972	5:40	Apollo 16	Young/Duke	Third LRV traverse, 7-mile trip featuring so-called House Rock, largest boulder visited by Apollo crew.
26	Apr. 25, 1972	1:24	Apollo 16	Mattingly/Duke	Deep space EVA to retrieve SIM bay cassettes; Duke assisted from CM hatch.
27	Dec. 11, 1972	7:12	Apollo 17	Cernan/Schmitt	Sixth lunar landing crew, deployed ALSEP and made short traverse with LRV-3.
28	Dec. 12, 1972	7:37	Apollo 17	Cernan/Schmitt	Made 12-mile traverse for geological samples, finding "orange soil."
29	Dec. 13, 1972	7:15	Apollo 17	Cernan/Schmitt	Last lunar surface EVA, covered 7 miles collecting samples and performing ceremony.
30	Dec. 17, 1972	1:06	Apollo 17	Evans/Schmitt	Third and last deep-space EVA; Evans retrieved SIM bay cassettes.
31	May 25, 1973	:37	Skylab 2	Weitz	Standup EVA from command module hatch, attempt to deploy stuck solar panel.
32	June 7, 1973	3:25	Skylab 2	Conrad/Kerwin	Successful attempt to free solar panel, rescuing Skylab. Conrad catapulted into space by motion of solar array.
33	June 19, 1973	1:44	Skylab 2	Conrad/Weitz	Retrieved and replaced film from ATM; also examined solar array and parasol shade deployed earlier.
34	Aug. 6, 1973	6:31	Skylab 3	Garriott/Lousma	Second Skylab crew erected a twin pole sunshade to improve protection of Skylab.
35	Aug. 24, 1973	4:30	Skylab 3	Garriott/Lousma	ATM film retrieval and replacement.
36	Sept. 22, 1973	2:45	Skylab 3	Bean/Garriott	ATM film retrieval and replacement.
37	Nov. 22, 1973	6:33	Skylab 4	Gibson/Pogue	ATM film exchange; routine repair tasks and scientific observations.
38	Dec. 25, 1973	7:01	Skylab 4	Carr/Pogue	First Christmas EVA; exchange ATM film and observed Comet Kahoutek.
39	Dec. 29, 1973	3:28	Skylab 4	Carr/Gibson	Further observations of Kahoutek and replacement of ATM film.
40	Feb. 3, 1974	5:19	Skylab 4	Carr/Gibson	Retrieve ATM film and experiment packages from Skylab exterior.
41	Dec. 20, 1977	1:28	Soyuz 26	Grechko/Romanenko	Standup EVA to examine forward docking unit, believed to have been damaged during Soyuz 25 attempt.
42	July 29, 1978	2:05	Soyuz 29	Ivanchenkov/ Kovalenok	Removed samples from Salyut 6's exterior and replaced with new panels. Kovalenok did standup EVA.

EVA#	DATE	DURATION	MISSION	CREW	NOTES
43	Aug. 15, 1979	1:23	Soyuz 32	Ryumin/Lyakhov	Unscheduled EVA, freed KRT-10 telescope from from Salyut 6 aft docking port.
44	July 30, 1982	2:33	Soyuz T-5	Lebedev/Berezovoy	First EVA from Salyut 7; collected and replaced samples on station exterior.
45	Apr. 7, 1983	4:17	STS-6	Musgrave/Peterson	First demonstration EVA from Shuttle, testing new suits and restraint systems.
46	Nov. 1, 1983	2:50	Soyuz T-9	Alexandrov/Lyakhov	Added new solar array to central solar power panel on station; first of a series.
47	Nov. 3, 1983	2:55	Soyuz T-9	Alexandrov/Lyakhov	Added second new solar array to central power panel.
48	Feb. 7, 1984	5:55	41-B	McCandless/Stewart	First untethered EVA; McCandless tested MMU, flying to distance of 300 feet from orbiter Challenger. Stewart, too.
49	Feb. 9, 1984	6:17	41-B	McCandless/Stewart	Further MMU flights; also tested procedures for future satellite repairs.
50	Apr. 8, 1984	2:57	41-C	Nelson/van Hoften	Attempt by Nelson to retrieve Solar Max satellite with MMU was unsuccessful; later captured by Challenger's RMS.
51	Apr. 11, 1984	6:16	41-C	van Hoften/Nelson	Crew repaired Solar Max in payload bay; redeployed satellite. Van Hoften flew MMU.
52	Apr. 23, 1984	4:15	Soyuz T-10	Solovyov/Kizim	First of six EVAs; this one included transport of a 15-foot ladder, tools, and preparation of work area.
53	Apr. 26, 1984	4:56	Soyuz T-10	Solovyov/Kizim	Crew cut into station skin to install new propellant valve.
54	Apr. 29, 1984	2:45	Soyuz T-10	Solovyov/Kizim	Crew installed new conduit and replaced station thermal covering.
55	May 3, 1984	2:45	Soyuz T-10	Solovyov/Kizim	Second conduit installed and verified; fuel leak pinpointed.
56	May 18, 1984	3:05	Soyuz T-10	Solovyov/Kizim	Crew installed second set of solar power arrays.
58	July 25, 1984	3:35	Soyuz T-12	Savitskaya/ Dzhanibekov	First woman to walk in space; Savitskaya tested multipurpose welding gun.
58	Aug. 8, 1984	5:00	Soyuz T-10	Solovyov/Kizim	Sealed leaking pipe, then removed samples from solar arrays for return to Earth.
59	Oct. 11, 1984	3:27	41-G	Leestma/Sullivan	Conducted satellite refueling test in Shuttle payload bay. Sullivan first U.S. woman to walk in space.
60	Nov. 12, 1984	6:00	51-A	Allen/Gardner	Capture of rogue Palapa comsat using MMU.
61	Nov. 14, 1984	5:42	51-A	Gardner/Allen	Capture of rogue Westar comsat using MMU.
62	Apr. 16, 1985	3:00	51-D	Hoffman/Griggs	First unscheduled American EVA; crew attached "fly swatter" to RMS in attempt to activate Leasat.
63	Aug. 2, 1985	5:00	Soyuz T-13	Savinykh/ Dzhanibekov	Attached third set of new solar arrays to station's main panels; also tested new suits.
64	Aug. 31, 1985	7:08	51-I	van Hoften/W. Fisher	Captured by hand faulty Leasat deployed on 51-D; began repair in payload bay.
65	Sept. 1, 1985	4:26	51-I	van Hoften/W Fisher	Completed Leasat repairs and redeployed satellite by pushing it away from orbiter.
66	Nov. 29, 1985	5:30	61-B	Spring/Ross	Completed space construction tests EASE and ACCESS.
67	Dec. 1, 1985	6:30	61-B	Spring/Ross	More EASE/ACCESS tests for future Space Station construction techniques.
68	May 28, 1986	3:50	Soyuz T-15	Solovyov/Kizim	Crew tested a beam builder for future space construction; also collected experiments from Salyut 7 exterior.

EVA#	DATE	DURATION	MISSION	CREW	NOTES
69	May 31, 1986	5:00	Soyuz T-15	Solovyov/Kizim	Additional space construction tests; used improved URI welding gun.
70	Apr. 11, 1987	3:40	Soyuz TM-2	Laveikin/Romanenko	Unscheduled EVA to remove foreign object from Mir docking port; object had prevented docking of Kvant module.
71	June 12, 1987	1:53	Soyuz TM-2	Laveikin/Romanenko	Crew erected an extra set of solar power panels on Mir exterior.
72	June 16, 1987	3:15	Soyuz TM-2	Laveikin/Romanenko	Crew added a second new set of panels to Mir.
73	Feb. 26, 1988	4:25	Soyuz TM-4	Manarov/VTitov	Crew replaced elements of solar power panels erected by Laveikin-Romanenko.
74	June 30, 1988	5:10	Soyuz TM-4	Manarov/VTitov	Crew attempted to repair X-ray telescope on Kvant module; repair halted due to broken wrench.
75	Oct. 20, 1988	4:12	Soyuz TM-4	Manarov/VTitov	Completed repair of TTM telescope on Kvant.
76	Dec. 9, 1988	5:57	Soyuz TM-7	Chretien/AVolkov	First non-Soviet, non-American EVA; crew erected ERA structure—by kicking balky container—and deployed French experiments.
77	Jan. 8, 1990	2:56	Soyuz TM-8	Serebrov/Viktorenko	Crew deployed two star sensors on exterior of Kvant module.
78	Jan. 11, 1990	2:54	Soyuz TM-8	Serebrov/Viktorenko	Deployed new experiments and retrieved French sensors left by Chretien in Dec. 1988.
79	Jan. 26, 1990	3:02	Soyuz TM-8	Serebrov/Viktorenko	Installed docking device for use with Ikarus MMU; removed Kurs antenna; installed new TV system; tested new suits.
80	Feb. 1, 1990	4:59	Soyuz TM-8	Serebrov/Viktorenko	First flight of Ikarus MMU; Serebrov flew up to 100 ft. from station while tethered.
81	Feb. 5, 1990	3:45	Soyuz TM-8	Viktorenko/Serebrov	Viktorenko flew Ikarus 150 ft. from station; did a "victory roll."
82	July 17, 1990	7:00	Soyuz TM-9	Balandin/ASolovyov	Crew attempted to repair thermal blankets on Soyuz TM; damaged outer Kvant-2 hatch and were forced to use backup means to reenter Mir.
83	July 26, 1990	3:31	Soyuz TM-9	Balandin/ASolovyov	Stowed exterior ladders for future use; made temporary repairs to damaged Kvant-2 hatch.
84	Oct. 30, 1990	3:45	Soyuz TM-10	Strekalov/Manakov	Attempted to repair Kvant-2 hatch was only partly successful.
85	Jan. 7, 1991	5:18	Soyuz TM-11	Manarov/Afanasyev	Crew completed repairs to Kvant-2 hatch; also set up support structure for crane to move solar arrays from Kristall to Kvant modules.
86	Jan. 23, 1991	5:33	Soyuz TM-11	Manarov/Afanasyev	Set up first crane jib on Mir near multiple docking adaptor.
87	Jan. 26, 1991	6:20	Soyuz TM-11	Manarov/Afanasyev	Erected second crane jib on Kvant for future transfer of solar power arrays.
88	Apr. 7, 1991	4:38	STS-37	Ross/Apt	Unscheduled Shuttle EVA to deploy Gamma Ray Observatory's stuck high-gain antenna.
89	Apr. 8, 1991	6:11	STS-37	Ross/Apt	Crew conducted CETA mobility tests and other experiments for future Space Station construction.
90	Apr. 25, 1991	3:34	Soyuz TM-11	Manarov/Afanasyev	Inspected faulty Kurs docking antenna and found dish missing; replaced exterior TV camera.
91	June 25, 1991	4:58	Soyuz TM-12	Krikalev/Artsebarsky	Replaced damaged Kurs antenna.
92	June 28, 1991	3:24	Soyuz TM-12	Krikalev/Artsebarsky	Installed US cosmic ray detector experiment on Mir exterior.
93	July 15, 1991	5:55	Soyuz TM-12	Krikalev/Artsebarsky	Began construction of 50-ft. Sofora girder on exterior of Kvant module.
94	July 19, 1991	6:20	Soyuz TM-12	Krikalev/Artsebarsky	Additional construction on Sofora.

EVA#	DATE	DURATION	MISSION	CREW	NOTES
95	July 23, 1991	5:34	Soyuz TM-12	Krikalev/Artsebarsky	Additional construction on Sofora.
96	July 27, 1991	6:49	Soyuz TM-12	Krikalev/Artsebarsky	During completion of Sofora construction Artsebarsky's suit overheats; blinded by perspiration, he is rescued by Krikalev.
97	Feb. 20, 1992	4:12	Soyuz TM-13	Krikalev/Volkov	Installed new equipment on Kvant-2. Problems with Volkov's suit cut short EVA.
98	May 10, 1992	3:43	STS-49	Thuot/Hieb	Attempt to capture Intelsat VI satellite; fails.
99	May 11, 1992	5:30	STS-49	Thuot/Hieb	Second attempt to capture Intelsat VI satellite; also a failure.
100	May 13, 1992	8:29	STS-49	Thuot/Hieb/Akers	First 3-person EVA. Astronauts capture Intelsat VI by hand, attach new motor, and redeploy. Longest EVA in history.
101	May 14, 1992	7:45	STS-49	Thornton/Akers	Tests of Space Station Freedom construction techniques and rescue procedures. Thornton sets record for EVA by a woman.
102	July 8, 1992	2:05	Soyuz TM-14	Kaleri/Viktorenko	External repairs to D Module of the Mir complex.
103	Sept. 3, 1992	3:56	Soyuz TM-15	Avdeyev/Solovyov	Beginning of attempt to attach a new propulsion unit to the Sofora girder.
104	Sept. 7, 1992	5:08	Soyuz TM-15	Avdeyev/Solovyov	Continuing process of attaching new propulsion unit to Sofora. Lowered USSR flag from Mir exterior.
105	Sept. 11, 1992	5:44	Soyuz TM-15	Avdeyev/Solovyov	Continuing propulsion unit move.
106	Sept. 15, 1992	3:33	Soyuz TM-15	Avdeyev/Solovyov	Attached antenna to Module T (Kristall) to aid Buran/US Shuttle docking radar.
107	Jan. 17, 1993	4:28	STS-54	Harbaugh/Runco	Tested Space Station Freedom and Hubble Telescope construction and repair techniques.
108	Apr. 19, 1993	5:25	Soyuz TM-16	Poleshchuk/	Began process of transferring exterior Mir solar panels.
109	June 18, 1993	4:18	Soyuz TM-16	Poleshchuk/Manakov	Manakov configured Mir exterior for series of EVAs by next main crew.
110	June 25, 1993	5:50	STS-57	Low/Wisoff	Attached EURECA antennas; tested Space Station Freedom and Hubble repair methods.
111	Sept. 16, 1993	4:18	Soyuz TM-17	Serebrov/Tsibliyev	First of three EVAs to erect new Rapana mast on Mir exterior. Check for Perseid damage.
112	Sept. 16, 1993	7:05	STS-51	Walz/Newman	Tested Hubble Telescope repair tools and techniques.
113	Sept. 20, 1993	3:13	Soyuz TM-17	Serebrov/Tsibliyev	Continued deployment of Rapana mast, installing sample packages for later retrieval.
114	Sept. 28 1993	1:52	Soyuz TM-17	Serebrov/Tsibliyev	Planned EVA to complete Rapana and film Mir exterior shortened when Tsibliyev's suit overheated.
115	Oct. 22, 1993	:38	Soyuz TM-17	Serebrov/Tsibliyev	Installed new instrument block on Kvant-2 and completed Mir exterior filming.
116	Oct. 29, 1993	4:12	Soyuz TM-17	Serebrov/Tsibliyev	Inspected solar panels and exterior antenna; checked Sofora mount; retrieved materials samples to determine future Mir lifetime.
117	Dec. 4, 1993	7:54	STS-61	Hoffman/Musgrave	First Hubble Telescope repair EVA: replaced malfunctioning gyroscopes.
118	Dec. 5, 1993	6:36	STS-61	Thornton/Akers	Second HST repair EVA: installed new solar power panels.
119	Dec. 6, 1993	6:47	STS-61	Hoffman/Musgrave	Third HST repair EVA: installed new camera in HST.
120	Dec. 7, 1993	6:50	STS-61	Thornton/Akers	Fourth HST repair EVA: installed COSTAR and new computer; cut loose solar panel.

EVA#	DATE	DURATION	MISSION	CREW	NOTES
121	Dec. 8, 1993	7:21	STS-61	Hoffman/Musgrave	Fifth HST repair EVA: installed control systems for new solar panels, etc.
122	Sept. 9, 1994	5:06	Soyuz TM-19	Musabayev/ Malenchenko	Inspect Mir exterior for possible damage from Jan. 1994 collision; attach new solar panels configure Mir for planned Shuttle docking.
123	Sept. 13, 1994	6:01	Soyuz TM-19	Musabayev/ Malenchenko	Retrieve samples from Rapana; carry out maintenance on Sofora truss; maintenance on Kvant-2 exterior and solar panels.
124	Sept. 16, 1994	6:51	STS-64	Lee/Meade	Test SAFER, free-flying astronaut rescue jetpack.
125	Feb. 9, 1995	4:39	STS-63	Harris/Foale	Test astronaut ability to translate large objects in future Alpha EVA (EDFT-01); test of cold-temp EVA gloves is unsuccessful.
126	May 12, 1995	6:15	Soyuz TM-21	Strekalov/Dezhurov	Prepare exterior of Mir for transfer of solar panels to allow Shuttle docking.
127	May 17, 1995	6:30	Soyuz TM-21	Strekalov/Dezhurov	Begin moving solar panels; fail to finish initial move.
128	May 22, 1995	5:15	Soyuz TM-21	Strekalov/Dezhurov	Complete solar panel move from EVA-2.
129	May 28, 1995	:21	Soyuz TM-21	Strekalov/Dezhurov	Move docking cone to allow Spektr module to dock with Mir on June 1.
130	June 1, 1995	:24	Soyuz TM-21	Strekalov/Dezhurov	Return docking cone to pre-May 28 position.
131	July 14, 1995	5:34	Mir-19	Budarin/Solovyov	Inspect leaky docking collar and move two solar arrays to permit Kristall transfer.
132	July 19, 1995	3:08	Mir-19	Budarin/Solovyov	Solovyov remains inside adaptor because of EVA suit problem; Budarin begins installation of MIRAS infrared spectrometer.
133	July 21, 1995	5:50	Mir-19	Budarin/Solovyov	Completion of MIRAS installation.
134	Sept. 15, 1995	6:46	STS-69	Voss/Gernhardt	Test EVA thermal gear; practice Alpha techniques (EDFT-02).
135	Oct. 20, 1995	5:16	Mir-20/TM-22	Avdeyev/Reiter	ESA flight engineer Reiter erects European experiment on Mir exterior.
136	Dec. 8, 1995	:29	Mir-20/TM-22	Adveyev/Gidzenko	Transfer -Z docking cone to +Z for Priroda docking.
137	Jan. 15, 1996	6:09	STS-72	Chiao/Barry	Third EVA Development Flight Test (EDFT-03) of Space Station hardware: umbilical lines, utility boxes, work platforms.
138	Jan. 17, 1996	6:54	STS-72	Chiao/Scott	Continuation of EDFT-03, with added test of EMU thermal properties by Scott in a 30-min. "cold soak."
139	Feb. 8, 1996	3:06	Mir 20/TM-22	Reiter/Gidzenko	Retrieval of ESEF exposure facility mounted on EVA-1. Also move Ikarus MMU to exterior. Work on Kristall joint canceled.
140	Mar. 15, 1996	5:51	Mir-21/TM-23	Usachev/Onufriyenko	Install second Strela crane on base block; set cables for new solar panels on Kvant.
141	Mar. 27, 1996	6:02	STS-76	Godwin/Clifford	First Shuttle-Mir EVA. Astronauts attach MEEP dust collectors to Mir exterior.
142	May 20, 1996	5:20	Mir-21/TM-23	Usachev/Onufriyenko	Move solar battery from Mir docking module to exterior of Kvant-1.
143	May 24-5, 1996	5:43	Mir-21/TM-23	Usachev/Onufriyenko	Install Russian-American solar panel on exterior of Kvant-1.
144	May 30, 1996	4:20	Mir-21/TM-23	Usachev/Onufriyenko	Install MOMS-2 camera and EVA handrail on Mir exterior.
145	June 6, 1996	3:34	Mir-21/TM-23	Usachev/Onufriyenko	Replace KOMZA experiment and install SKK-11 experiment on Mir exterior. Film part one of Pepsi commercial.

EVA#	DATE	DURATION	MISSION	CREW	NOTES
146	June 13, 1996	5:46	Mir-21/TM-23	Usachev/Onufriyenko	Install and deploy Ferma-3 girder and repair Travers antenna. Complete filming of Pepsi commercial.
***	Nov. 28, 1996	****	STS-80	Jones/Jernigan	Failed attempt to exit orbiter Columbia for EVA due to stuck hatch. Crew in vacuum for :48.
147	Dec. 2, 1996	5:57	Mir-22/TM-24	Kaleri/Korzun	Link power cable from solar battery to Mir main bus.
148	Dec. 9, 1996	6:36	Mir-22/TM-24	Kaleri/Korzun	Complete linkage of power cable.
149	Feb. 13, 1997	6:42	STS-82	Lee/Smith	First Hubble Space Telescope servicing EVA. Astronauts replace older High Resolution Spectrograph and Faint Object Spectrograph with new Space Telescope Imaging Spectrgraph (STIS) and Near Infrared Camera and Multi-Object Spectrometer (NICMOS).
150	Feb. 14, 1997	7:27	STS-82	Harbaugh/Tanner	Second HST service EVA. Replace Far Guidance System (FGS) and out-of-date recorders. Install Optical Control Electronics Enhancement Kit (OCE-EK). Note insulation damage.
151	Feb. 15, 1997	7:11	STS-82	Lee/Smith	Third HST service EVA. Replace Data Interface Unit (DIU) and install new solid-state data recorder.
152	Feb. 16, 1997	6:34	STS-82	Harbaugh/Tannner	Fourth scheduled HST service EVA. Replace Solar Array Drive Electronics (SADE), install covers for magnetometers. Commence insulation repair.
153	Feb. 17, 1997	5:17	STS-82	Lee/Smith	Added HST service EVA. Attach thermal insulation blankets to HST exterior.
154	Apr. 29, 1997	4:58	Mir-23/TM-25	Linenger/Tsibleyev	Retrieved experiment package from Mir exterior. Linenger becomes first American to use Russian Orlan-M EVA suit.
155	Aug. 22, 1997	3:16	Mir-24/TM-26	Vinogradov/Solovyov	IVA to connect power cables from damaged Spektr module to Mir base block.
156	Spt. 6, 1997	6:00	Mir-24/TM-26	Solovyov/Foale	Searched for punctures on Spektr exterior but found none. Manually realigned solar panels.
157	Oct. 1, 1997	5:01	STS-86	Parazynski/Titov	Shuttle EVA, retrieved MEEP from Mir exterior.
158	Oct. 20, 1997	6:38	Mir-24/TM-26	Vinogradov/Solovyov	IVA to complete Spektr power cable connection.
159	Nov. 3, 1997	6:04	Mir-24/TM-26	Vinogradov/Solovyov	Launched mini Sputnik 1, disconnected old Kvant solar panel and replaced it.
160	Nov. 6, 1997	6:17	Mir-24/TM-26	Vinogradov/Solovyov	Installed cap for possible Spektr leak repair; transferred solar panel. Crew closeout delayed by hatch leak.
161	Nov. 24, 1997	7:43	STS-87	Scott/Doi	Unplanned Spartan retrieval. Tests of EVA hardware for ISS.
162	Dec. 3, 1997	4:59	STS-87	Scott/Doi	Continuation of originally planned EVA hardware/procedures tests.
163	Jan. 8, 1998	4:04	Mir-24/TM-26	Vinogradov/Solovyov	Attempt to repair leaking airlock hatch.
164	Jan. 14, 1998	6:38	Mir-24/TM-26	Solovyov/Wolf	Inspect Mir interior and examine faulty EVA hatch.
***	Mar. 3, 1998	****	Mir-25/TM-27	Budarin/Musabayev	Failed attempt at EVA; Budarin broke tool trying to open hatch.
165	April 1, 1998	6:40	Mir-25/TM-27	Budarin/Musabayev	Install handrails on Mir exterior for planned repairs to Spektr solar array mount.

EVA#	DATE	DURATION	MISSION	CREW	NOTES
166	April 6, 1998	4:23	Mir-25/TM-27	Budarin/Musabayev	Strengthened Spektr solar array mount; EVA shortened by ground control error regarding Mir orientation system.
167	April 11, 1998	6:25	Mir-25/TM-27	Budarin/Musabayev	Dismantle and discard VDU (exterior control engine).
168	April 17, 1998	6:32	Mir-25/TM-27	Budarin/Musabayev	Dismantle Strela boom and truss #3; began installation of new VDU.
169	April 22, 1998	6:21	Mir-25/TM-27	Budarin/Musabayev	Complete installtion of new VDU atop tower on Mir exterior.

U.S. FLIGHT CREWS

KEY: Crews are those given as of launch date, with the most notable last-minute changes footnoted. Flown missions are in Roman; planned but canceled missions for which crews were announced are in italics.

MISSION	PRIME PILOT	BACKUP PILOT
MR-3	Shepard	Glenn
MR-4	Grissom	Glenn
MA-6	Glenn	Carpenter
MA-7	Carpenter[1]	Schirra
MA-8	Schirra	Cooper
MA-9	Cooper	Shepard

MISSION	PRIME CREW	BACKUP CREW
GT-3	Grissom-Young	Schirra-Stafford
GT-4	McDivitt-White	Borman-Lovell
GT-5	Cooper-Conrad	Armstrong-See
GT-7	Borman-Lovell	White-Collins
GT-6A	Schirra-Stafford	Grissom-Young
GT-8	Armstrong-Scott	Conrad-Gordon
GT-9A	Stafford-Cernan[2]	Lovell-Aldrin
GT-10	Young-Collins	Bean-Williams
GT-11	Conrad-Gordon	Armstrong-Anders
GT-12	Lovell-Aldrin	Cooper-Cernan

[1] Carpenter replaced Slayton in March 1962.

[2] Stafford and Cernan were originally backups to See and Bassett, who died in a plane crash prior to launch.

MISSION	PRIME CREW	BACKUP CREW
Apollo 1	*Grissom-White-Chaffee*	*Schirra-Eisele-Cunningham* [3]
Apollo 2	*McDivitt-Scott-Schweickart* [4]	*Stafford-Young-Cernan*
Apollo 3	*Borman-Collins-Anders*	*Conrad-Gordon-Williams*
Apollo 7	Schirra-Eisele-Cunningham	Stafford-Young-Cernan
Apollo 8	Borman-Lovell-Anders[5]	Armstrong-Aldrin-Haise
Apollo 9	McDivitt-Scott-Schweickart	Conrad-Gordon-Bean
Apollo 10	Stafford-Young-Cernan	Cooper-Eisele-Mitchell
Apollo 11	Armstrong-Collins-Aldrin	Lovell-Anders-Haise
Apollo 12	Conrad-Gordon-Bean	Scott-Worden-Irwin
Apollo 13	Lovell-Swigert-Haise[6]	Young-none-Duke
Apollo 14	Shepard-Roosa-Mitchell	Cernan-Evans-Engle
Apollo 15	Scott-Worden-Irwin	Gordon-Brand-Schmitt
Apollo 16	Young-Mattingly-Duke	Haise-Roosa-Mitchell
Apollo 17	Cernan-Evans-Schmitt	Young-Roosa-Duke[7]
Skylab 2	Conrad-Kerwin-Weitz	Schweickart-Musgrave-McCandless
Skylab 3	Bean-Garriott-Lousma	Brand-Lenoir-Lind
Skylab 4	Carr-Gibson-Pogue	Brand-Lenoir-Lind
ASTP	Stafford-Brand-Slayton	Bean-Evans-Lousma
ALT	Haise-Fullerton	Engle-Truly
STS-1	Young-Crippen	Engle-Truly
STS-2	Engle-Truly	Mattingly-Hartsfield
STS-3	Lousma-Fullerton	Mattingly-Hartsfield
STS-4	Mattingly-Hartsfield	none

[Effective STS-4, NASA no longer trained or announced backup Shuttle pilots and mission specialists. Crew replacements, if needed, would come from the pool of qualified astronauts. Most payload specialists did have backups, however.]

MISSION	FLIGHT CREW	PS BACKUPS
STS-5	Brand-Overmyer-Lenoir-Allen	
STS-6	Weitz-Bobko-Musgrave-Peterson	
STS-7	Crippen-Hauck-Fabian-Ride-Thagard	

---

[3] Original backup crew was McDivitt-Scott-Schweickart, who rotated to "new" Apollo 2 (firsy manned lunar module) upon cancellation of CM-only Apollo 2 in December 1966.

[4] Original prime crew was Schirra-Eisele-Cunningham with backups Borman-Stafford-Collins, announced September 1966.

[5] Lovell replaced Collins prior to launch.

[6] Backup crewman Swigert replaced Mattingly 2 days prior to launch.

[7] Original backup crew was Scott-Worden-Irwin, replaced for disciplinary reasons in training.

MISSION	PRIME CREW	BACKUP CREW
STS-8	Truly-Brandenstein-Bluford-Gardner Thornton	
STS-9	Young-Shaw-Garriott-Parker Lichtenberg (Spacelab 1) Merbold (Spacelab 1)	Lampton Ockels
STS-10	*Mattingly-Shriver-Onizuka-Buchli*	
41-B	Brand-Gibson-McNair-Stewart-McCandless	
41-C	Crippen-Scobee-Hart-van Hoften-Nelson	
41-D	Hartsfield-Coats-Mullane-Hawley-Resnik CWalker (McDAC)	none
41-E	*Mattingly-Shriver-Onizuka-Buchli*	
41-F	*Bobko-Williams-Seddon-Griggs-Hoffman*	
41-G	Crippen-McBride-Sullivan-Ride-Leestma Scully-Power (U.S. Navy) Garneau (Canada)	none Thirsk
41-H	*Hauck-D. Walker-Allen-A. Fisher-D. Gardner-2 of Watterson-Sundberg-Detroye (Teal Ruby)*	
51-A	Hauck-D. Walker-Allen-A. Fisher-D. Gardner	
51-C	Mattingly-Shriver-Onizuka-Buchli Payton (DOD)	Wright
51-D	Bobko-Williams-Seddon-Griggs-Hoffman C. Walker (McDAC) Garn (U.S. Senate)	none none
51-B	Overmyer-Gregory-Lind-Thagard-Thornton Wang (Spacelab 3) van den Berg (Spacelab 3)	Trinh Johnston
51-G	Brandenstein-Creighton-Fabian-Nagel-Lucid Baudry (CNES) Salman (Arabsat)	Chretien al-Bassam
51-F	Fullerton-Bridges-Henize-Musgrave-England[8] Acton (Spacelab 2) Bartoe (Spacelab 2)	Simon Prinz
51-I	Engle-Covey-van Hoften-Lounge-W. Fisher[9]	
51-J	Bobko-Grabe-Hilmers-Stewart[10] Pailes (DOD)	Booen
61-A	Hartsfield-Nagel-Dunbar-Buchli-Bluford Furrer (Spacelab D-1) Messerschmid (D-1) Ockels (D-1)	Merbold
61-B	Shaw-O'Connor-Ross-Cleave-Spring C. Walker (McDAC) Neri Vela (Morelos)	RWood Peralta
61-C	Gibson-Bolden-Nelson-Hawley-Chang Diaz Cenker (RCA) B. Nelson (U.S. House)	Magilton none

---

[8] Griggs was originally announced as a pilot, replaced by Bridges when delays in launching an earlier mission led to schedule conflicts.

[9] Buchli was originally announced as a mission specialist; he was replaced by van Hoften because of schedule conflicts.

[10] Originally announced as the "DOD Standby" crew, with Mullane as the third mission specialist.

MISSION	PRIME CREW	BACKUP CREW
51-L	Scobee-Smith-Onizuka-Resnik-McNair Jarvis (Hughes) McAuliffe (Teacher-in-Space)	 Butterworth Morgan
61-E	*McBride-Richards-Leesmta-Parker-Hoffman* *Durrance (Spacelab Astro)* *Parise (Astro)*	 *Nordsieck*
61-F	*Hauck-Bridges-Hilmers-Lounge*	
61-G	*D. Walker-Grabe-Thagard-van Hoften*	
61-H	*Coats-Blaha-Buchli-Springer-A. Fisher* *Sudarmono (Palapa)* *N. Wood (Skynet)*	 *Akbar* *Farrimond*
62-A	*Crippen-G. Gardner-Ross-D. Gardner-Mullane* *Aldridge (DOD)* *Watterson (DOD)*	 *none* *Odle*
61-M	*Shriver-O'Connor-Ride-W. Fisher-Lee* *RWood (EOS)*	 *C. Walker*
61-K	*Brand-Griggs-Garriott-Stewart-Nicollier* *Lichtenberg (EOM)* *Lampton (EOM)* *Stevenson (U.S. Navy)*	 *Chappell* *Frimout*
61-I	*Williams-Smith-Bagian-Dunbar-Carter* *INSAT JOURNALIST-IN-SPACE*	
61-N	*Shaw-McCulley-Leestma-Adamson-Brown* *Casserino (DOD)* *Skantze (DOD)*	 *Joseph (DOD)* *none*
61-J	*Young-Bolden-McCandless-Hawley-Nelson*	
STS-26	Hauck-Covey-Lounge-Hilmers-Nelson	
STS-27	Gibson-G. Gardner-Mullane-Ross-Shepherd	
STS-29	Coats-Blaha-Buchli-Springer-Bagian	
STS-30	D. Walker-Grabe-Thagard-Cleave-Lee	
STS-28	Shaw-Richards-Leestma-Adamson-M. Brown	
STS-34	Williams-McCulley-Lucid-Chang Diaz-E. Baker	
STS-33	Gregory-Blaha-Carter-Musgrave-K. Thornton[11]	
STS-32	Brandenstein-Wetherbee-Dunbar-Ivins-Low	
STS-36	Creighton-Casper-Hilmers-Mullane-Thuot	
STS-31	Shriver-Bolden-McCandless-Hawley-Sullivan	
STS-41	Richards-Cabana-Melnick-Shepherd-Akers	
STS-38	Covey-Culbertson-Springer-Meade-Gemar	
STS-35	Brand-G. Gardner-Hoffman-Lounge-Parker Durrance (ASTRO) Parise (ASTRO)	 Nordsieck

---

[11] Griggs was originally assigned as PLT, but was killed in an off-duty plane crash and replaced by Blaha.

MISSION	PRIME CREW	BACKUP CREW
STS-37	Nagel-Cameron-Godwin-Ross-Apt	
STS-39	Coats-Hammond-Harbaugh-McMonagle-Veach-Hieb-Bluford	Crombie[12]
STS-40	O'Connor-Gutierrez-Bagian-Jernigan-Seddon[13] Gaffney (SLS) Hughes-Fulford (SLS)	Phillips Phillips
STS-43	Blaha-M. Baker-Lucid-Low-Adamson	
STS-48	Creighton-Reightler-Gemar-Buchli-Brown	
STS-44	Gregory-Henricks-Voss-Musgrave-Runco Hennen (TERRA SCOUT)	Belt
STS-42	Grabe-Oswald-Thagard-Readdy-Hilmers[14] Bondar (IML) Merbold (IML)	Money Crouch
STS-45	Bolden-Duffy-Sullivan-Leestma-Foale Lichtenberg (ATLAS) Frimout (ATLAS)	Chappell Lampton
STS-49	Brandenstein-Chilton-Thuot-K. Thornton-Hieb-Akers-Melnick	
STS-50	Richards-Bowersox-Dunbar-Meade-E. Baker DeLucas (USML) Trinh (USML)	Prahl Sacco
STS-46	Shriver-Allen-Hoffman-Chang-Diaz-Ivins-Nicollier Malerba (TSS)	Guidoni
STS-47	Gibson-C. Brown-Lee-Davis-Apt-Jemison Mohri (SLJ)	Doi Naito
STS-52	Wetherbee-M. Baker-Shepherd-Jernigan-Veach MacLean (CANEX)	Tryggvason
STS-53	D. Walker-Cabana-Bluford-Voss-Clifford	
STS-54	Casper-McMonagle-Harbaugh-Runco-Helms	
STS-56	Cameron-Oswald-Foale-Cockrell-Ochoa	
STS-55	Nagel-Henricks-Precourt-Harris-Ross Schlegel (D-2) Walter (D-2)	Brummer Thiele
STS-57	Grabe-Duffy-Low-J. E. Voss-Sherlock-Wisoff	
STS-51	Culbertson-Readdy-Bursch-Newman-Walz	
STS-58	Blaha-Searfoss-McArthur-Seddon-Wolf-Lucid Fettman (SLS-2)	Buckey, Young
STS-61	Covey-Bowersox-Nicollier-Musgrave-Akers-Thornton-Hoffman	Harbaugh
STS-60	Bolden-Reightler-Chang-Diaz-Davis-Sega-Krikalev	VTitov
STS-62	Casper-Allen-Thuot-Ivins-Gemar	

[12] DOD Payload specialist Crombie was a generic backup to mission specialists Veach, Bluford, and Hieb.

[13] Blaha was originally announced as PLT; replaced by Gutierrez when Blaha was reassigned to STS-33.

[14] Carter, who had replaced Cleve, was originally assigned as MS, but was killed in an off-duty plane crash and replaced by Hilmers.

MISSION	PRIME CREW	BACKUP CREW
STS-59	Gutierrez-Chilton-Apt-Godwin-Jones-Clifford	
STS-65	Cabana-Halsell-Hieb-Chiao-D. Thomas Mukai (IML-2)	Favier
STS-64	Richards-Hammond-Linenger-Helms-Meade-Lee	
STS-68	Baker-Wilcutt-Jones-Bursch-Smith-Wisoff	
STS-66	McMonagle-C. Brown-Ochoa-Tanner-Clervoy-Parazynski	
STS-63	Wetherbee-E. Collins-Harris-Foale-J. E. Voss-Ford V. Titov	Krikalev
STS-67	Oswald-W. Gregory-Jernigan-Lawrence-Grunsfeld Durrance (ASTRO-02) Parise (ASTRO-02)	Vangen Vangen
STS-71	Gibson-Precourt-E. Baker-Harbaugh-Dunbar Solovyov (Mir-19 UP) Budarin (Mir-19 UP) Dezhurov-Strekalov-Thagard (Mir-18 DOWN)	Onufriyenko Usachev
STS-70	Henricks-Kregel-Currie-D. Thomas-Weber	
STS-69	D. Walker-Cockrell-Voss-Gernhardt-Newman	
STS-73	Bowersox-Rominger-Coleman-Lopez-Alegria-K. Thornton Sacco (USML-02) Leslie (USML-02)	Holt Matthiesen
STS-74	Cameron-Halsell-Ross-McArthur-Hadfield	
STS-72	Duffy-Jett-Chiao-Scott-Barry-Wakata	
STS-75	Allen-Horowitz-Chang-Diaz-Hoffman-Nicollier Guidoni (TSS-1R)	none
STS-76	Chilton-Searfoss-Godwin-Sega-Clifford Lucid (NASA-Mir)	Blaha
STS-77	Casper-C. Brown-A. Thomas-Bursch-Runco-Garneau	
STS-78	Henricks-Kregel-Helms-Brady-Linnehan Favier (LMS) Thirsk (LMS)	Urbani Duque
STS-79	Readdy-Wilcutt-Akers-Apt-Walz Blaha (NASA-Mir)	Lawrence
STS-80	Cockrell-Rominger-Jones-Jernigan-Musgrave	
STS-81	M. Baker-Jett-Grunsfeld-Ivins-Wisoff Linenger (NASA-Mir)	Voss
STS-82	Bowersox-Horowitz-Hawley-Lee-Smith-Tanner- Harbaugh	
STS-83	Halsell-Still-J. E. Voss-D. Thomas-Gernhardt Crouch (MSL) Linteris (MSL)	Coleman[15] Ronney Ronney
STS-84	Precourt-E. Collins-Clervoy-Lu-Noriega-Kondakova Foale (NASA-Mir)	Lawrence

[15] Coleman assigned as backup for Thomas for several weeks in early 1997 due to Thomas' broken leg.

MISSION	PRIME CREW	BACKUP CREW
STS-94	Halsell-Still-J. E. Voss-D. Thomas-Gernhardt[16]	
	Crouch (MSL)	Ronney
	Linteris (MSL)	Ronney
STS-85	C. Brown-Rominger-Davis-Robinson-Curbeam	
	Tryggvason [CSA]	none
STS-86	Wetherbee-Bloomfield-Parazynski-V. Titov-	
	Chretien-Lawrence[17]	
	Wolf (NASA Mir DOWN)	Voss
STS-87	Kregel-Lindsey-Scott-Chawla-Doi	
	Kadenyuk [Ukraine]	Pustovyi
STS-89	Wilcutt-Edwards-Dunbar-Anderson-Reilly-Sharipov	
	A. Thomas [NASA-Mir UP]	Voss
STS-90	Searfoss-Altman-Linnehan-Hire-Williams	
	Buckey (Neurolab)	Mukai
	Pawelczyk (Neurolab)	Dunlap
STS-91	Precourt-Gorie-Kavandi-Lawrence-Ryumin	
	A. Thomas [NASA-Mir DOWN]	
STS-95	Brown-Lindsey-Duque-Parzynski-Robinson	
	Mukai [NASDA]	none
	Glenn	none
STS-88	Cabana-Sturckow-Ross-Currie-Newman-Krikalev	
STS-93	Collins-Ashby-Coleman-Hawley-Tognini	
STS-96	Rominger-Husband-Ochoa-Barry-Jernigan-Payette-Malenchenko	
STS-101	Halsell-Horowitz-Weber-J. Williams-Lu	
STS-99	Kregel-Goria-J. E. Voss-Kavandi-Mohri-Thiele	
STS-92	Duffy-Melroy-Chiao-Lopez-Alegria-McArthur-Wisoff-Wakata	
STS-97	Jett-Bloomfield-Garneau-Tanner-Noriega	
STS-98	Cockrell-Polansky-Ivins-Lee-Jones	
STS-100	Curbeam-Hadfield	
STS-101	Gernhardt-Reilly	

---

[16] Mission reflown with same flight crew because STS-83 had to be cut short due to fuel cell problem.

[17] Lawrence, the original NASA Mir crew member, replaced by Wolf because she was not qualified for Mir EVA. Crew expanded.

Appendix 7

RUSSIAN AND SOVIET FLIGHT CREWS

KEY: Crews are those given as of launch date, with the most notable last-minute changes footnoted. Flown missions are in Roman; canceled missions are only given if crews were approved for training by the Joint State Commission (italics). Second backups are in parentheses.

MISSION	PRIME PILOT	BACKUP
Vostok	Gagarin	Titov (Nelyubov)
Vostok 2	Titov	Nikolayev
Vostok 3	Nikolayev	Bykovsky
Vostok 4	Popovich	Komarov/Volynov
Vostok 5	Bykovsky	Volynov
Vostok 6	Tereshkova	Solovyova (Ponomareva)
Voskhod	Komarov-Feoktistov-Yegorov	Volynov-Katys-Lazarev
Voskhod 2	Belyayev-Leonov	Zaikin-Khrunov
Voskhod 3	*Volynov-Shonin*	*Beregovoy-Shatalov*
Soyuz 1	Komarov	Gagarin
Soyuz 2	*Bykovsky-Yeliseyev-Khrunov*	*Nikolayev-Kubasov-Gorbatko*
Soyuz 3	Beregovoy	Shatalov (Volynov)
Soyuz 4	Shatalov	Shonin
Soyuz 5	Volynov-Yeliseyev-Khrunov	Filipchenko-Kubasov-Gorbatko
Soyuz Zond	*Leonov-Makarov*	*Bykovsky-Rukavishnikov*
Soyuz 6	Shonin-Kubasov	Shatalov-Yeliseyev[1]

---

[1] Replaced crew of Kuklin-Grechko.

MISSION	PRIME PILOT	BACKUP
Soyuz 7	Filipchenko-Volkov-Gorbatko	Shatalov-Yeliseyev-Kolodin
Soyuz 8	Shatalov-Yeliseyev	Nikolayev-Sevastyanov
Soyuz 9	Nikolayev-Sevastyanov	Filipchenko-Grechko (Lazarev-Yazdovsky)
Soyuz Almaz	*Popovich-Demin-Zholobov*	*Volynov-Rozhdestvensky-Khludeyev*
Soyuz 10	Shatalov-Yeliseyev-Rukavishnikov	Leonov-Kubasov-Kolodin
Soyuz 11	Dobrovolsky-Volkov-Patsayev[2]	Shatalov-Yeliseyev-Rukavishnikov
Soyuz DOS 2	*Leonov-Rukavishnikov-Kolodin*	*Gubarev-Sevastyanov-Voronov*
Soyuz Almaz 2	*Popovich-Artyukhin*	*Sarafanov-Demin*
Soyuz Almaz 2	*Sarafanov-Demin*	*Volynov-Zholobov*
Soyuz DOS 3	*Leonov-Kubasov*	*Lazarev-Makarov*
Soyuz 12	Lazarev-Makarov	Gubarev-Grechko
Soyuz 13	Klimuk-Lebedev	Vorobyov-Yazdovsky
Soyuz 14	Popovich-Artyukhin	Sarafanov-Demin
Soyuz 15	Sarafanov-Demin	Volynov-Zholobov
Soyuz 16	Filipchenko-Rukavishnikov	Romanenko-Ivanchenkov
Soyuz 17	Gubarev-Grechko	Lazarev-Makarov
Soyuz 18-1	Lazarev-Makarov	Klimuk-Sevastyanov
Soyuz 18	Klimuk-Sevastyanov	Kovalenok-Ponomarev
Soyuz 19	Leonov-Kubasov	Dzhanibekov-Andreyev
Soyuz 21	Volynov-Zholobov	Zudov-Rozhdestvensky
Soyuz 22	Bykovsky-Aksenov	Malyshev-Strekalov (Popov-Andreyev)
Soyuz 23	Zudov-Rozhdestvensky	Gorbatko-Glazkov
Soyuz 24	Gorbatko-Glazkov	Berezovoy-Lisun (Kozelsky-Preobrazhensky)
Soyuz 25	Kovalenok-Ryumin	Romanenko-Ivanchenkov (Lyakhov-Grechko)
Soyuz 26	*Dzhanibekov-Kolodin*	
Soyuz 26	Romanenko-Grechko	Kovalenok-Ivanchenkov
Soyuz 27	Dzhanibekov-Makarov	Kovalenok-Ivanchenkov
Soyuz 28	Gubarev-Remek	Rukavishnikov-Pelczak
Soyuz 29	Kovalenok-Ivanchenkov	Lyakhov-Ryumin
Soyuz 30	Klimuk-Hermaszewski	Kubasov-Jankowski
Soyuz 31	Bykovsky-Jaehn	Gorbatko-Koehllner
Soyuz 32	Lyakov-Ryumin	Popov-Lebedev

---

[2] Replaced crew of Leonov-Kubasov-Kolodin two days before launch.

MISSION	PRIME PILOT	BACKUP
Soyuz 33	Rukavishnikov-Ivanov	Romanenko-Alexandrov
Soyuz 35	Popov-Ryumin[3]	Zudov-Andreyev
Soyuz 36	Kubasov-Farkas	Dzhanibekov-Magyari
Soyuz T-2	Malyshev-Aksenov	Kizim-Makarov
Soyuz 37	Gorbatko-Pham Tuan	Bykovsky-Bui Thanh Liem
Soyuz 38	Romanenko-Tamayo Mendez	Khrunov-Lopez Falcon
Soyuz T-3	Kizim-Makarov-Strekalov[4]	Lazarev-Savinykh-Polyakov
Soyuz T-4	Kovalenok-Savinykh	Zudov-Andreyev
Soyuz 39	Dzhanibekov-Gurragcha	Lyakhov-Ganzorig
Soyuz 40	Popov-Prunariu	Romanenko-Dediu
TKS-1	*Berezovoy-Glazkov-Makrushin*	*Kozelsky-Artyukhin-Romanov*
TKS-2	*Kozelsky-Artyukhin-Romanov*	*Sarafanov-Preobrazhensky-Yuyukov*
TKS-3	*Sarafanov-Preobrazhensky-Yuyukov*	*Vasyutin-Rozhdestvensky-Grechanik*
Soyuz T-5	Berezovoy-Lebedev	Titov-Strekalov (Lyakhov-Alexandrov)
Soyuz T-6	Dzhanibekov-Ivanchenkov-Chretien	Kizim-Solovyov-Baudry
Soyuz T-7	Popov-Serebrov-Savitskaya	Vasyutin-Savinykh-Pronina
Soyuz T-8	Titov-Strekalov-Serebrov	Lyakhov-Alexandrov-Savinykh
Soyuz T-9	Kizim-Solovyov-Volk	Vasyutin-Savinykh-Stankyavichus
Soyuz T-9	Lyakhov-Alexandrov	Titov-Strekalov (Kizim-Solovyov)
Soyuz T-10-1	Titov-Strekalov	Kizim-Solovyov
Soyuz T-10	Kizim-Solovyov-Atkov	Vasyutin-Savinykh-Polyakov
Soyuz T-11	Malyshev-Strekalov-Sharma[5]	Berezovoy-Grechko-Malhotra
Soyuz T-12	Dzhanibekov-Savitskaya-Volk	Vasyutin-Savinykh-Ivanova
Soyuz T-13	*Vasyutin-Savinykh*	*Viktorenko-Alexandrov*
Soyuz T-14	*Savitskaya-Ivanova-Dobrokvashina*	*Viktorenko-Alexandrov-Solovyov*
Soyuz T-13	Dzhanibekov-Savinykh	Popov-Alexandrov
Soyuz T-14	Vasyutin-Grechko-A Volkov	Viktorenko-Strekalov-Salei
Soyuz T-15	Kizim-Solovyov	Viktorenko-Sevastyanov/Alexandrov
Soyuz TM-2	Romanenko-Laveikin	Titov-Serebrov
Soyuz TM-3	Viktorenko-Alexandrov-Faris	ASolovyov-Savinykh-Habib
Soyuz TM-4	Titov-Manarov-Levchenko	AVolkov-Kaleri-Shchukin
Soyuz TM-5	A Solovyov-Savinykh-Alexandrov	Lyakhov-Zaitsev/Serebrov-Stoyanov
Soyuz TM-6	Lyakhov-Polyakov-Ahad	Berezovoy-Arzamazov-Dauran
Soyuz TM-7	A Volkov-Krikalev-Chretien	Viktorenko-Serebrov-Tognini
Soyuz TM-8	*Viktorenko-Balandin*	*A Solovyov-Serebrov*

[3] Ryumin replaced Lebedev one month before launch.

[4] Strekalov replaced Feoktistov prior to launch.

[5] Strekalov replaced Rukavishnikov prior to launch.

MISSION	PRIME PILOT	BACKUP
Soyuz TM-8	Viktorenko-Serebrov	A Solvoyov-Balandin
Soyuz TM-9	A. Solovyov-Balandin	Manakov-Strekalov
Soyuz TM-10	Manakov-Strekalov	Afanasyev-Sevastyanov/Manarov
Soyuz TM-11	Afanasyev-Manarov-Akiyama	Arstebarsky-Krikalev-Kikuchi
Soyuz TM-12	Artsebarsky-Krikalev-Sharman	Volkov-Kaleri-Mace
Soyuz TM-13	*Volkov-Kaleri-Viehbock*	*Viktorenko-Avdeyev-Lothaller*
Soyuz TM-14	*Korzun-Alexandrov-Aubakirov*	*Tsibliyev-Laveikin-Musabayev*
Soyuz TM-13	Volkov-Aubakirov-Viehbock	Viktorenko-Musabayev-Lothaller
Soyuz TM-14	Viktorenko-Kaleri-Flade	A. Solovyov-Adveyev-Ewald
Soyuz TM-15	A. Solovyov-Adveyev-Tognini	Manakov-Polshchuk-Haignere (Korzun-Laveikin)
Soyuz TM-16	Manakov-Polishchuk	Tsibliyev-Usachev
Soyuz Buran	*Bachurin-Ivanchenkov*	*Borodai-Balandin*
Soyuz TM-17	Tsibliyev-Serebrov	Afanasyev-Usachev (Malenchenko-Strekalov)
Soyuz TM-18	Afanasyev-Usachev-Polyakov	Malenchenko-Strekalov-Arzamazov (Viktorenko-Kondakova-Morukov)
Soyuz TM-19	Malenchenko-Musabayev	Viktorenko-Kondakova (Dezhurov-Strekalov)
Soyuz TM-20	Viktorenko-Kondakova-Merbold	Gidzenko-Avdeyev-Duque
Soyuz TM-21	Dezhurov-Strekalov-Thagard	A. Solovyov-Budarin-Dunbar (Onufriyenko-Poleshchuk)
STS-71	A. Solovyov-Budarin	Onufriyenko-Usachev [6]
Soyuz TM-22	Gidzenko-Avdeyev-Fuglesang	Manakov-Vinogradov-Reiter
Soyuz TM-23	Onufriyenko-Usachev	Tsibliyev-Lazutkin
Soyuz TM-24	Korzun-Kaleri-Andre Deshays	Manakov-Vinogradov-Eyharts [7]
Soyuz TM-25	Tsibliyev-Lazutkin	Musabayev-Budarin
Soyuz TM-26	A. Solovyov-Vinogradov	Padalka-Avdeyev
Soyuz TM-27	Musabayev-Budarin-Eyharts	Afanasyev-Treshchev-Haignere
Soyuz TM-28	Padalka-Avdeyev-Baturin	Zaletin-Kaleri-Kotov
Soyuz TM-29	Afanasyev-Haignere-Bela	Sharipov-Andre-Deshays-Fulier
Soyuz TM-30	Gidzenko-Krikalev-Shepherd	Dezhurov-Tyurin-Bowersox
Soyuz TM-31	Musabayev-Kuzhelnaya	Tokarev-Revin
Soyuz TM-32	Dezhurov-Tyurin-Bowersox	Korzun-Vinogradov-NASA

[6] Usachev replaced Poleshchuk.

[7] Korzun-Kaleri replaced Manakov-Vinogradov a week prior to launch.

INTERNATIONAL SPACE STATION MISSIONS AND CREWS

Assembly and habitation missions are given here, based on Revision D of the International Space Station launch manifest (June 1998). Only habitation crews—known as increments—are given here.

Each increment consists of three crewmembers. Increments launched aboard Soyuz will consist of two Russian crewmembers (a Soyuz commander and a flight engineer) and a NASA mission commander. (All NASA mission commanders for Soyuz-launched increments will be veteran astronauts who have commanded Shuttle missions.)

Increments launched aboard the Shuttle will consist of two astronauts assigned by NASA and one from the RKA, with the Russian astronaut (also a flight veteran) serving as the mission commander.

INCREMENT	DATES	LAUNCHER	PRIME CREW	BACKUPS
1st	June–Dec. 1999	Soyuz	Shepherd, Gidzenko, Krikalev	Bowersox, Dezhurov, Tyurin
2nd	Dec. 1999–May 2000	STS-99	Usachev, Voss, Helms	Onufriyenko, Walz, Bursch
3rd	May 2000–	Soyuz	Bowersox, Dezhurov, Tyurin	NASA, Korzun, Vinogradov
4th	Aug. 2000	STS-104	Onufriyenko, Walz, Bursch	Malenchenko, NASA, NASA
5th	Nov. 2000	Soyuz	NASA, Korzun, Vinogradov	NASA, RKA, RKA
6th	Apr. 2001	STS-111	Malenchenko, NASA, NASA	RKA, NASA, NASA

Phase 2 Assembly Sequence

NOTE: This schedule does not include all planned Progress resupply missions or X-38 flight tests, and omits several possible H-2 (Japan) transfer vehicle and Ariane (ESA) automated transfer vehicle launches. Only the first six crew increments are noted, but habitation is to be continuous beginning with mission 2R in July 1999.

FLIGHT	LAUNCH	MISSION	PAYLOAD/CREW
1A/R	Nov. 1998	Proton	Zarya control module (FGB)
2A	Dec. 1998	STS-88	Unity Node, PMA 1/2
1R	Apr. 1999	Proton	Service module
2A.1	May 1999	STS-96	SpaceHab Double Cargo Module
3A	June 1999	STS-92	Z1 truss, PMA3
2R	July 1999	Soyuz TM-31	First increment: Shepherd 204
4A	Aug. 1999	STS-97	Integrated Truss Structure P6, 2 photovoltaic modules (panels)
5A	Oct. 1999	STS-98	U.S. Lab Module
—	Nov. 1999	Soyuz TM-32 No. 201	Soyuz ACRV rotation
6A	Dec. 1999	STS-99	Second Increment, Usachev, MPLM (lab outfitting), UHF antenna; Space Station RMS
7A	Jan. 2000	STS-101	Joint Airlock, High Pressure Gas Assembly

Phase 3

FLIGHT	LAUNCH	MISSION	PAYLOAD/CREW
—	Feb. 2000	Soyuz TM-33	Third Increment: Bowersox No. 211
4R	Mar. 2000	Soyuz	Docking Compartment Module-1
7A.1	Mar. 2000	STS-102	MPLM
UF1	Apr. 2000	STS-104	Fourth Increment: Onufriyenko MPLM, PV Module batteries, spares pallet
8A	June 2000	STS-105	Integrated Truss Structure, Mobile Transporter
UF2	Aug. 2000	STS-106	MPLM plus Mobile Base System
9A	Oct. 2000	STS-108	Starboard truss segment (ITS S1) plus crew radiators and CETA-A
—	Nov. 2000	Soyuz TM	Fifth Increment: Malenchenko
9A.1	Jan. 2001	STS-109	Russian Solar Power Platform plus four power arrays
11A	Feb. 2001	STS-110	First port truss segment (P1) attached to central truss segment; CETA-B
3R	Apr. 2001	Proton	Universal Docking Module
12A	May 2001	STS-111	Sixth increment: NASA Second port truss segment (ITS P3/P4) plus solar array and batteries
5R	May 2001	Soyuz	Docking compartment 2
12A.1	June 2001	STS-112	Third port truss segment (ITS P5) plus solar array set
13A	June 2001	STS-113	Second starboard truss segment (ITS S3/S4) plus solar array set and batteries
10A	Spt. 2001	STS-114	Node 2
1J/A	Oct. 2001	STS-115	Japanese Experiment Module (JEM) plus science power platform solar arrays

FLIGHT	LAUNCH	MISSION	PAYLOAD/CREW
1J	Jan. 2002	STS-116	RMS for JEM
9R	Feb. 2002	Proton	Docking and stowage module (DSM)
UF3	Feb. 2002	STS-117	MPLM Express Pallet
UF4	May 2002	STS-118	Spacelab Express Pallet plus AMS and "Canada Hand"
2J/A	June 2002	STS-119	JEM solar array, batteries
14A	Aug. 2002	STS-120	Cupola science power platform (SPP) plus service module micrometeorite shields
8R	Aug. 2002	Soyuz	Research module 1
UF5	Spt. 2002	STS-121	MPLM Express Pallet
20A	Oct. 2002	STS-122	Node 3
10R	Nov. 2002	Soyuz	Research module 2
17A	Nov. 2002	STS-123	Racks for Node 3, U.S. Lab
1E	Feb. 2003	STS-124	ESA Columbus laboratory
18A	Mar. 2003	STS-125	U.S. crew return vehicle
19A	Jun. 2003	STS-127	MPLM
15A	Jul. 2003	STS-128	Photovoltaic module S6
UF6	Spt. 2003	STS-129	MPLM batteries
UF7	Nov. 2003	STS-130	Centrifuge accommodation module
16A	Jan. 2004	STS-131	U.S. Habitation module

Appendix 9

TEACHER-IN-SPACE CANDIDATES

Announced May 3, 1985. Selections were conducted by the Council of Chief State School Officers, Dr. William Pierce, Executive Director. There were 10,463 applicants from the 50 states, U.S. territories, Department of State and Defense overseas dependent schools, and the Bureau of Indian Affairs.

(*) Indicates finalists announced July 1, 1985.

STATE	NOMINEE NAME	SCHOOL	CITY
Alabama	Sophia Ann Clifford	Erwin High	Birmingham
	Pamela Sue Grayson	Minor High	Birmingham
Alaska	Mildred J. Heinrich	Robert Service High	Anchorage
	Richard C. Houghton	Napaaqtugmiut High	Noatak
Arizona	Robert Carpenter	Secrist Middle	Tucson
	Robin Kline	Tonalea Elementary	Scottsdale
Arkansas	William A. Dempsey	Arksansa Senior	Texarkana
	Mary Beth Greenway	Parkview High	Little Rock
Bureau Of Indian Affairs	—		
California	William M. Dillon, Jr.	Peninsula High	San Bruno
	Gloria M. McMillan	La Jolla High	La Jolla
Colorado	Kim Natala	Pomona High	Arvada
	Robert Stack	Shawsheen High	Greeley
Connecticut	Robert Mellette	Conte Arts Magnet	New Haven
	David Warner	Westminster	Simsbury

STATE	NOMINEE NAME	SCHOOL	CITY
Delaware	Henry E. W. Bouchelle	Pilot	Wilmington
	Stephanie Gerjovich-Wright	Stanton Middle	Wilmington
Department Of Defense	Mary Smothers	Kaiserslauten Am. High	APO New York
	Kenneth VanLew	Frankfurt High	APO New York
Department Of State	Donald Jonasson	Jakarta International	Jakarta Selatan
	Bruce Wixted	American of Kuwait	Hawalli
District Of Columbia	William A. Barwick, Jr.	Woodrow Wilson High	D.C.
	Nancy J. Cooksy	Eastern High	D.C.
Florida	Susan W. Forte	Georgestone Vocational	Pensaloca
	Michael D. Reynolds	Duncan U. Fletcher Sr.	Neptune Beach
Georgia	Thomas Phillip Garmon	Benjamin E. Mays High	Atlanta
	Carol G. Hickson	Fernback Science Center	Atlanta
Guam	Daniel J. Jenkins	St. John's	Tumon Bay
	M. Bernadette McCorkle	Vocational High	Barrigada
Hawaii	Joseph Ciotti	St. Louis High	Honolulu
	Arthur Kimura	McKinley High	Honolulu
Idaho	*David M. Marquart	Boise High	Boise
	*Barbara R. Morgan	McCall-Donnelly Elem.	McCall
Illinois	John D. Baird	Quincy Senior High	Quincy
	Lynne M. Haeffele	Bloomington High	Bloomington
Indiana	*Robert S. Foerster	Cumberland Elementary	W. Lafayette
	Stephen L. Tucker	West Vigo High	W. Terre Haute
Iowa	A. John Cazanas	Rockford Senior High	Rockford
	Lori M. Goetsch	Mt. Pleasant Jr. High	Mount Pleasant
Kansas	Wendell G. Mohling	Shawnee Mission NW High	Shawnee Mission
	Barry L. Schartz	Goddard High	Goddard
Kentucky	Sue Ellen W. Darnell	North Marshall Jr. High	Calvert City
	Judy A. White	L. C. Curry Elementary	Bowling Green
Louisiana	Debra Harris	Rusheon Junior High	Bossier City
	Denise Van Bigger	Alexandria Country	Alexandria

STATE	NOMINEE NAME	SCHOOL	CITY
Maine	Gordon L. Corbett	Yarmouth Intermediate	Yarmouth
	William C. Townsend	Sumner Memorial High	East Sullivan
Maryland	*Kathleen Beres	Kenwood High	Baltimore
	David R. Zahren	G. Gardner Shugard Mid.	Hillcrest Hts.
Massachusetts	*Richard Methia	New Bedford High	New Bedford
	Charles Sposato	Farley Middle	Framingham
Michigan	Derrick Fries	Seaholm High	Birmingham
	Sharon Newman	West Hills Middle	West Bloomfield
Minnesota	Steve L. Brehmer	Wanamingo Public	Wanamingo
	Katherine Koch-Laveen	Apple Valley High	Apple Valley
Mississippi	Connie Moore	Oak Grove High	Hattiesburg
	Joann Reid	Weir Attendance Center	Weir
Missouri	Christopher W. Brown	McCluer N. Senior High	Florissant
	Richard K. Kavanaugh	Park Hill R-5	Kansas City
Montana	Paul Dorrance	Helena High	Helena
	Patricia Johnson	Capital High	Helena
Nebraska	Roger Ray	Northwest High	Omaha
	James R. Schaeffer	Lincoln East High	Lincoln
Nevada	Ericka J. Turner	Chaparral High	Las Vegas
	Joan C. Turner	Las Vegas High	Las Vegas
New Hampshire	*Christa McAuliffe	Concord High	Concord
	Robert Veilleux	Central High	Manchester
New Jersey	Jeannine M. Duane	Black River Middle	Chester
	Binnie J. Thom	Walter C. Black	Hightstown
New Mexico	—		
New York	Susan A. Agruso	East Islip High	Islip Terrace
	Edwad F. Duncanson	Crispell Middle	Pine Bush
North Carolina	Ernest W. Morgan	Morganton Jr. High	Morganton
	Cynthia B. Zeger	Salisbury High	Salisbury

STATE	NOMINEE NAME	SCHOOL	CITY
North Dakota	Sherry L. Hanson	A. L. Hagen Jr. High	Dickinson
	Donald L. Hoff	Velva High	Velva
Ohio	Gail B. Klink	Newark High	Newark
	James B. Rowley	Centerville High	Centerville
Oklahoma	Freda D. Deskin	Pauls Valley Middle	Pauls Valley
	Frank E. Marcum	Booker T. Washington H.	Tulsa
Oregon	Stephen Boyarski	Medford High	Medford
	Michael Fitzgibbons	Forest Grove High	Forest Grove
Pennsylvania	Patricia Plazzolo	Clairton High	Clairton
	Charles Tremer	Southern Lehigh	Center Valley
Puerto Rico	Nancy M. Lee	Roosevelt Roads Middle	Ceiba
	John G. Wells	Roosevelt Roads Middle	Ceiba
Rhode Island	Ronald Reynolds	Barrington High	Barrington
	Leisa Sadwin	Halliwell	North Smithfield
South Carolina	Michael H. Farmer	Riverside High	Greer
	Myra J. Halpin	Goose Creek High	Goose Creek
South Dakota	Kevin J. Falon	Lincoln Senior High	Souix Falls
	Ferald E. Loomer	Rapid City Central High	Rapid City
Tennessee	Carolyn H. Dobbins	McMurray Middle	Nashville
	Bonnie D. Fakes	Lebanon High	Lebanon
Texas	*Peggy Lathlaen	Westwood Elementary	Friendswood
	Stephen A. Warren	Stephen F. Austin High	Austin
Utah	John W. Barainca	Brighton High	Salt Lake City
	Linda J. Preston	Park City High	Park City
Vermont	Gail Breslauer	Fayston Elementary	Waitsfield
	*Michael Metcalf	Hazen Union	Hardwick
Virginia	Ronald C. Fortunato	Norfolk Tech. Voc. Cntr.	Norfolk
	*Judith M. Garcia	Jefferson School for Science & Technology	Alexandria

STATE	NOMINEE NAME	SCHOOL	CITY
Virgin Islands	Carol Eby	Peace Corps Elementary	St. Thomas
	Rosa Hampson	Elena Christian Jr. High	Christiansted
Washington	Frances B. Call	Islander Middle	Mercer Island
	Michael R. Jones	Kellogg Middle	Seattle
West Virginia	*Niki M. Wenger	Vandevender Jr. High	Parkersburg
	Melanie B. Vickers	St. Albans Jr. High	St. Albans
Wisconsin	Ellen Baerman	Wisconsin Hills Elem.	Brookfield
	Larry Scheckel	Tomah Senior High	Tomah
Wyoming	Julie M. Gess	Evanston High	Evanston
	Michael G. Pearson	McCormick Jr. High	Cheyenne

JOURNALIST-IN-SPACE CANDIDATES

Selections were made by the Association of Schools of Journalism and Mass Communication, administered by the College of Journalism at the University of South Carolina, Columbia SC. Dean Emeritus Albert T. Scroggins was the chief program officer.

There were 1703 applicants, from which the following 100 regional semifinalists were chosen and announced in April 1986.

On May 14, 1986, the list was reduced to 40, indicated (*).

STATE	NAME	CITY	AFFILIATION
Arkansas	*Michael Masterston	Little Rock	WEHCO Media
California	*A. Blaine Baggett	Los Angeles	KCET-TV
	Marcida Dodson	Irvine	*Los Angeles Times*
	Susan Farrell	San Diego	KGTV-TV
	*Timothy Ferris	Hollywood	freelance
	Willard (Gene) Gleeson	Los Angeles	KABC-TV
	*Michael Gold	San Rafael	*Science 86* Magazine
	*Richard Hart	San Francisco	KPIX-TV
	Michael Hegedus	San Rafael	KPIX-TV
	Patricia Klein	Chatsworth	*Los Angeles Times*
	Martin Kimball Livingston	San Francisco	*San Francisco Chronicle*
	*Thomas (Jay) Mathews	Pasadena	*Washington Post*
	*Lee McEachern, Jr.	Greenbrae	KGO-TV
	Michael Parfit	Santa Barbara	freelance

STATE	NAME	CITY	AFFILIATION
	*Charles Petit	San Francisco	*San Francisco Chronicle*
	John Popejoy	Los Angeles	KCOP-TV
	Michael Rogers	Oakland	*Newsweek*
	Jim Schefter	Playa del Rey	freelance
	Douglas Struck	San Francisco	*Baltimore Sun*
Colorado	*Frederic (Ted) Conover	Denver	freelance
	*Diane Eicher	Lakewood	*Denver Post*
	John Meyer	Lakewood	*Rocky Mtn. News*
Connecticut	Burton Bernstein	Bridgewater	*The New Yorker*
	*Morton Dean	Ridgefield	INN
	Gayle Young	Westport	UPI
District Of Columbia	Warren Corbett	D.C.	BIZNET
	Richard Gore	D.C.	*National Geographic*
	*Anne (Kathy) Sawyer	D.C.	*Washington Post*
	Marty E. Thornton	D.C.	*Washington Post*
	*James Wooten	D.C.	ABC News
	*Storer Rowley	D.C.	*Chicago Tribune*
Florida	*Jay Barbaree	Cocoa Beach	freelance
	Thomas Fiedler	Miami	*Miami Herald*
	*Robert Navias	Coral Gables	UPI
	Mark Prendergast	Boca Raton	*Ft. Lauderdale News & Sun-Sentinel*
Georgia	Thomas Mintier, Jr.	Atlanta	CNN
Illinois	*John Hockenberry	Chicago	National Public Radio
	*Theresa (Terry) Anzur	Chicago	NBC News
	Linda Yu (Baer)	Chicago	WLS-TV
	Dennis Breo	Chicago	*American Medical News*
	*Joan Esposito	Chicago	WLS-TV
	Ronald Kotulak	Chicago	*Chicago Tribune*
	Donn Pearlman	Chicago	WBBM-TV and Radio
	Steven Vogel	Bloomington	WJBC-WBNQ Radio
Indiana	*Hal Higdon	Michigan City	freelance
	Thomas Tuley	Newburgh	*Evansville Press*
Iowa	Mary Murray	Iowa City	*Des Moines Register*
	Robert Shaw	Des Moines	*Des Moines Register*

STATE	NAME	CITY	AFFILIATION
Kansas	Mark Chamberlin	Wichita	KAKE-TV
	Larry Hatteburg	Wichita	KAKE-TV
Maryland	Jon Franklin	Glen Burnie	freelance
	James (Jim) Hartz	Chevy Chase	WNET-TV
	Malcolm McConnell	Queenstown	*Reader's Digest*
	Boyce Rensburger	Frederick	*Washington Post*
	James Reston, Jr.	Bethesda	*Newsweek*
	*Alexander Rossiter, Jr.	Columbia	UPI
Massachusetts	David Arnold	North Quincy	*Boston Globe*
	J. Kelly Beatty	Chelmsford	*Sky & Telescope*
	*Stanley Grossfield	Squantum	*Boston Globe*
	*Caroline (Terry) Marotta	Winchester	freelance
Michigan	Dinah Eng	Troy	*Detroit News*
	*Barbara Stanton	Detroit	*Detroit Free-Press*
Minnesota	Millard L. (Lew) Cope	Bloomington	*Minneapolis Star-Trib.*
	*Jim Klobuchar	Minnetonka	*Minneapolis Star-Trib.*
	Thomas Garrison	Minneapolis	KSTP-TV
	Linda Kohl	St. Paul	*St. Paul Pioneer Press*
Missouri	Diane Ackerman	St. Louis	*Parade* Magazine
	*Robert White II	Mexico	*Mexico Ledger*
	Al Wilman	St. Louis	KMOX-TV
New York	Robert Bazell	New York	NBC News
	*William Blakemore	New York	ABC News
	*Walter Cronkite	New York	CBS News
	*Jerry Flint	New York	*Forbes* Magazine
	Geraldo Rivera	New York	freelance
	*Roger Rosenblatt	New York	*Time* Magazine
	Peter Saigo	New York	WCBS-TV
	*Lynn Sherr	New York	ABC News
	Lindsy E. Van Gelder	New York	*Ms.* Magazine
	*John Noble Wilford	New York	*New York Times*
North Carolina	Frank Tursi	Clemmons	*Winston-Salem Journal*
Oklahoma	Charles Sasser	Gore	freelance
Pennsylvania	Mark Bowden	Philadelphia	*Philadelphia Inquirer*
	Maximo Gomez	Philadelphia	KYW-TV
	Dorothy Storck	Philadelphia	*Philadelphia Inquirer*

STATE	NAME	CITY	AFFILIATION
Rhode Island	Mark Patinkin	Providence	*Providence Journal*
Texas	*Paul Recer	Houston	Associated Press
	Steven Gauvain	Houston	KTRK-TV
	*James Asker	Houston	*Houston Post*
	Chris Rene Marrou	Boerne	KENS-TV
	Robert (Chip) Moody II	Houston	KHOU-TV
	Alcestis Oberg	Dickinson	freelance
	Daniel O'Rourke	Houston	KPRC-TV
	Scott Pelley	Dallas	WFAA-TV
	*Colice Kathryn (Katie) Sherrod	Fort Worth	*Fort Worth Star Telegram*
Virginia	*Marcia Bartusiak	Norfolk	freelance
	*Barry Serafin	Fairfax	ABC News
	*James Snyder (Jim Slade)	McLean	MBS
Washington	Steven Goldsmith	Seattle	*Seattle Post-Intel.*
	*Peter Rinearson	Seattle	*Seattle Times*
Wisconsin	*Paul Hayes	Milwaukee	*Milwaukee Journal*

INDEX

Note: page numbers in **bold** indicate main topics.

Yuri Gagarin Air Force Academy. *See*
Gagarin Air Force Academy
Yuri Gagarin Cosmonaut Training
Center. *See* Gagarin Center
Yuyukov, Dmitri Alexeyevich, 309, 310,
313, **464**

Z

Zabolotsky, Viktor Vasilyevich, 135,
314–15, 322, 323, 324, 325, 326,
443, **464–65**

Zaikin, Dmitri Alexeyevich, 298,
299–300, 303, **465**
Zaitsev, Andrei Yevgenyevich, 303, 315,
324, 400, **465**
Zakharova, Tamara Sergeyevich, 311, **465**
Zaletin, Sergei Viktorovich, 316, 318,
465–66
Zamin, Shere, 472
Zamka, George David, 17, **296**
Zegrahm Space Voyages, 39
Zhernovov, Anatoly, 315

Zholobov, Vitaly Mikhailovich, 301, 312,
360, 369, 458, **466**, 513
Zholobova, Yelena, 513
Zhukovsky Air Force Engineering
Academy, 300, 301, 356, 361, 434,
445, 446
Zircon (intelligence platform), 515
Zubrin, Robert, 38, 40
Zudov, Vycheslav Dmitryevich, 304, 330,
331, 414, 421, 424, **466–67**
Zvedzni Gorodok (Star Town). *See* TsPK